Strategic Management

Planning for Domestic & Global Competition

D1295535

Strategic Management

Planning for Domestic & Global Competition

Fourteenth Edition

John A. Pearce II
Villanova School of Business
Villanova University

Richard B. Robinson, Jr.
Darla Moore School of Business
University of South Carolina

Mc
Graw
Hill
Education

STRATEGIC MANAGEMENT: PLANNING FOR DOMESTIC & GLOBAL COMPETITION,
FOURTEENTH EDITION
International Edition 2015

Published by McGraw-Hill Education, 2 Penn Plaza, New York, NY 10121. Copyright © 2015 by
McGraw-Hill Education. All rights reserved. Previous editions © 2013, 2011 and 2009. No part of this
publication may be reproduced or distributed in any form or by any means, or stored in a database or
retrieval system, without the prior written consent of McGraw-Hill Education, including, but not limited to,
in any network or other electronic storage or transmission, or broadcast for distance learning.

Some ancillaries, including electronic and print components, may not be available to customers outside the
United States.

This book cannot be re-exported from the country to which it is sold by McGraw-Hill. This International
Edition is not to be sold or purchased in North America and contains content that is different from its North
American version.

10 09 08 07 06 05 04 03
20 15
CTP   SLP

All credits appearing on page or at the end of the book are considered to be extension of the copyright page.

When ordering this title, use ISBN 978-981-4577-37-3 or MHID 981-4577-37-5

The Internet addresses listed in the text were accurate at the time of publication. The inclusion of a website
does not indicate an endorsement by the authors or McGraw-Hill Education, and McGraw-Hill Education
does not guarantee the accuracy of the information presented at these sites.

Printed in Singapore

www.mhhe.com

To Susan McCartney Pearce, David Donham Pearce, Mark McCartney Pearce, John Braden Robinson, and Katherine Robinson Ast—for the love, joy, and vitality that they give to our lives.

About the Authors

John A. Pearce II   *Villanova University*

John A. Pearce II, Ph.D., holds the Villanova School of Business Endowed Chair in Strategic Management and Entrepreneurship at Villanova University. In 2009, he received the Fulbright Senior Specialist Award for work at Simon Fraser University's Segal Graduate School of Business in Vancouver, Canada. In 2004, he was the Distinguished Visiting Professor at ITAM in Mexico City. Previously, Professor Pearce was the Eakin Endowed Chair in Strategic Management at George Mason University and a State of Virginia Eminent Scholar. He received the 1994 Fulbright U.S. Professional Award, which he served at INTAN in Malaysia. Dr. Pearce has taught at Penn State University, West Virginia University, the University of Malta as the Fulbright Senior Professor in International Management, and at the University of South Carolina where he was Director of Ph.D. Programs in Strategic Management. He received a Ph.D. degree in Business Administration and Strategic Management from the Pennsylvania State University.

Professor Pearce is coauthor of 40 books and has authored more than 250 articles and refereed professional papers. The articles have appeared in journals that include *Academy of Management Executive, Academy of Management Journal, Academy of Management Review, Business Horizons, California Management Review, Entrepreneurship Theory and Practice, Journal of Applied Psychology, Journal of Business Venturing, Long-Range Planning, Organizational Dynamics, MIT-Sloan Management Review,* and *Strategic Management Journal.* Several of these publications have resulted from Professor Pearce's work as a principal on research projects funded for more than $2 million.

Professor Pearce is the recipient of several awards in recognition of his accomplishments in teaching, research, scholarship, and professional service, including three Outstanding Paper Awards from the Academy of Management and the 2003 Villanova University Outstanding Faculty Research Award. A frequent leader of executive development programs and an active consultant to business and industry, Dr. Pearce's client list includes domestic and multinational firms engaged in manufacturing and service industries.

Richard B. Robinson, Jr.   *University of South Carolina*

Richard B. Robinson, Jr., Ph.D., is a Distinguished Professor Emeritus at the Darla Moore School of Business, University of South Carolina. He also serves as Director Emeritus of the Faber Entrepreneurship Center at USC. Dr. Robinson received his Ph.D. in Business Administration from the University of Georgia. He graduated from Georgia Tech in Industrial Management.

Professor Robinson has authored or coauthored numerous books, articles, professional papers, and case studies addressing strategic management and entrepreneurship issues that students and managers use worldwide. His research has been published in major journals including the *Academy of Management Journal, Academy of Management Review, Strategic Management Journal, Entrepreneurship Theory and Practice, Business Horizons, Academy of Entrepreneurship Journal,* and the *Journal of Business Venturing.*

Dr. Robinson has previously held executive positions with companies in the pulp and paper, hazardous waste, building products, lodging, and restaurant industries. He currently serves as a director or adviser to entrepreneurial companies that are global leaders in niche markets in the animation and visualization software industries. Dr. Robinson teaches in USC's top-ranked international program with students that undertake field consulting projects and internships with entrepreneurial companies worldwide.

Preface

This fourteenth edition of *Strategic Management* builds upon the timely change we made in the previous edition—to increase our emphasis on planning for domestic and global competition in a global economy that is integral to strategic decision making in even the smallest business or organization on Main Street in any town worldwide every day. We have focused on the needs of strategy students to engage constructively in strategy development and execution in an exciting, fast-changing twenty-first century where they and the success of the organizations they join or create is shaped by an ability to instantly connect with over 6 billion people around the globe. Whether focused on domestic success or success in global markets, any firm or organization today is globally engaged. Strategic decisions must reflect that reality, and we have made that reality a central concern in this edition's coverage of all aspects of strategic management. IBM's catchy advertisements that have the catch phrase "let's build a smarter planet" reflect the mindset we took in working on this fourteenth edition—let's connect our chapters, examples, and cases with the reality and excitement of our global economy, which provides unprecedented opportunity for students better prepared to think strategically and act swiftly with confidence in their ideas.

These are exciting times, with economies rebounding, and opportunities worldwide literally at every student's fingertips. That reality is reflected in this book. There is much we have done to prepare students for strategic decisions in the increasingly fast-paced global business arena. It includes NEW or revised chapter material, 28 NEW globally engaged cases, 50 NEW Global Strategy in Action modules throughout the text material, and dozens of NEW illustrations examining:

- Globalization as the reality defining the strategic management challenge for any and every business worldwide.

- A separate chapter providing a new framework for examining and assessing a company's global business environment.

- Innovation and entrepreneurship frameworks to guide strategic decisions that accelerate growth and innovative opportunities for existing and newly created business organizations.

- Award-winning models for enabling business ethics and corporate social responsibility activities that make a difference in a globally sensitive marketplace.

- Networked, virtual, and adaptive organizational structures that accommodate an interconnected planet and drive success, which is dependent more than ever on diverse teams, peers, and partners residing anywhere.

- Simple, powerful new models for assessing a firm's capabilities for building true competitive advantage; for leading so as to leverage diversity; and for rethinking how culture can drive strategy execution.

- Global supply chains, and how to more effectively adapt them to ensure not only quality but soundness of strategy execution along with timely strategic control.

- The increased contribution and importance of women and minorities in leadership roles in top global companies, and in creating new companies that are quickly recreating core parts of the unfolding global economy.

Acting on our commitment to have mostly NEW in this revision, the fourteenth edition offers:

- 56 Global Strategy in Action boxes detailing how a diverse set of businesses large and small have designed and executed strategies and tactics enabling them to successfully compete in the twenty-first century.

- 8 new, short cases that address one or two strategic issues in well-recognized companies.
- 20 new, comprehensive cases covering business situations from around the world in both large and small companies.
- More than 50 total Strategy in Action boxes illustrating key concepts and leadership examples; and literally hundreds of new, contemporary examples woven into each of our new 14 chapters.

This fourteenth edition, while the majority of it is new, remains divided into 14 chapters. Reviewers and adopters say this organization works well to provide an overarching framework to explore strategic management. The text continues a solid academic connection, but students will find the text material practical, skills oriented, and relevant to their jobs and career aspirations.

All of the material in this edition is based on a proven model-based treatment of strategic management that allows for self-study and an easy-to-understand presentation. We have also significantly reduced the page length in this edition, providing a very focused presentation that is also the most cost-effective offering from McGraw-Hill Education for students and instructors of strategic management.

AN OVERVIEW OF OUR TEXT MATERIAL

The fourteenth edition uses a model of the strategic management process as the basis for the organization of the text material. Adopters have identified this model as a key distinctive competence for our text because it offers a logical flow, distinct elements, and an easy-to-understand guide to strategic management. The model reflects strategic analysis at different organizational levels as well as the importance of innovation in the strategic management process. The model and parallel chapter organization provides a student-friendly approach to the study of strategic management.

Chapters

The first chapter provides an overview of the strategic management process and explains what students will find as they use this book. The remaining 13 chapters cover each part of the strategic management process and techniques that aid strategic analysis, decision making, implementation, control, and renewal. The fourteenth edition includes several upgrades designed to incorporate major developments from both these sources. These cutting-edge concepts add to our emphasis on straightforward and logical presentation so that students can grasp these new ideas without additional reading.

Global Strategy in Action Modules and Strategy in Action Modules

Each chapter provides Global Strategy in Action modules and Strategy in Action modules, a key pedagogical feature. We have drawn on the work of prestigious business magazine field correspondents worldwide to fill more than 50 new modules with short, hard-hitting current illustrations of key chapter topics. They add excitement, interest, and practical illustration value to the essential cutting-edge theory that provides the foundation of this text.

Some of our modules also tell the personal story of a company or industry leader whose behavior, practices, or actions illustrate a key concept in the strategic management process. These boxes help personalize the lessons in the chapter through a vignette about a recognized expert.

CASES IN THE FOURTEENTH EDITION

Our cases offer a diverse set of 30 very contemporary business situations drawn from companies worldwide, written by some of the world's best case writers, and reflecting the breadth of structural change underway in the global economy today. We have a balance of case situations that call for sound analytical analysis, along with cases that call for behavioral considerations too. We have brought back the inclusion of both "short" cases, and traditional comprehensive cases. We have added an interesting case based on an actual consulting setting that allows instructors to provide their students with an interactive refamiliarization with basic financial and ratio analysis as they embark on a semester of in-depth strategic analysis of cases and company projects.

We have a good mixture of global and domestically focused companies. The cases involve service, retail, manufacturing, technology, and diversified activities. We explore companies in the United States, Europe, Asia, and Middle East economies.

OUR WEB SITE

A substantial Web site is designed to aid your use of this book. It includes areas accessible only to instructors and areas specifically designed to assist students. The instructor section includes supplement files, which include detailed teaching notes, PowerPoint slides, and case teaching notes for all the case studies, which keep your work area less cluttered and let you quickly obtain information. Students are provided company and related business periodical Web site linkages to aid and expedite their case research and preparation efforts. Practice quizzes are provided to help students prepare for tests on the text material and attempt to lower their anxiety in that regard. We expect students will find the Web site useful and interesting. Please visit us at www.mhhe.com/pearce14e.

SUPPLEMENTS

Components of our teaching package include a comprehensive instructor's manual, Power-Point presentations, and a computerized test bank. These are all available to qualified adopters of the text.

Acknowledgments

We have benefited from the help of many people in the evolution of this project over fourteen editions. Students, adopters, colleagues, reviewers, and business contacts have provided hundreds of insightful comments, suggestions, and contributions that have progressively enhanced this book and its supplements. We are indebted to the researchers and practicing managers who have accelerated the development of the literature on strategic management.

We are particularly indebted to the talented case researchers who have produced the cases used in this book, as well as to case researchers dedicated to the revitalization of case research as an important academic endeavor. First-class case research is a major avenue through which top strategic management scholars should be recognized.

Several reviewers provided constructive suggestions and feedback, which helped facilitate useful revisions, the addition of numerous current examples throughout the text, and a new case selection we find compelling. We extend particular thanks to the following who offered exceptionally comprehensive coverage:

Thomas D. Ashman
Eckerd College

Samuel H. Clovis Jr.
Morningside College

Matt C. Dwyer
Olivet Nazarene University

Phyllis Flott
Tennessee State University

Donald Grunewald
Iona College

Michael Harvey
Washington College

Nabil Ibrahim
Augusta State University

Donald J. Kopka Jr.
Towson University

Steven G. Morrissette, PhD
University of St. Francis

Jeffrey R. Nystrom
University of Colorado Denver

Dr. Michael D. Santonino III
Bethune-Cookman University

Greg Schultz
Carroll University

Sally Sledge
Norfolk State University

We are affiliated with two separate universities, both of which provide environments that deserve thanks. As the Villanova School of Business Endowed Chair at Villanova University, Jack is able to combine his scholarly and teaching activities with his coauthorship of this text. He is grateful to Villanova University and his colleagues for the support and encouragement they provide.

Richard is grateful for the encouragement and support at the University of South Carolina and its Darla Moore School of Business, particularly Harris Pastides, Michael Amiritis, Brian Klaas, Kendall Roth, Andrey Korsgaard, Joel Stevenson, DJ Schepker, and Sandra Bringley.

We want to acknowledge and thank Dr. Ram Subramanian, Montclair State University, for two key contributions he has made to this exciting 14th edition. First, he has authored or co-authored five new cases which are included in this edition. Second, his outstanding work on the instructor's manual and the ancillaries add much value to this fourteenth edition. His dedication and attention to detail make this a better book.

Leaders at McGraw-Hill Education deserve our utmost thanks and appreciation. Gerald Saykes, John Black, John Biernat, and Craig Beytein contributed to our early success. The editorial leadership of Michael Ablassmeir helps to assure that it will continue in this fourteenth edition. Development Editor Andrea Heirendt provided exceptional, practical leadership and support helping us stay on schedule, arrange permissions, and tirelessly and professionally enable us to produce a much improved book. The McGraw-Hill Education field organization deserves particular recognition and thanks for their ongoing worldwide adoption results for this text. We particularly wish to express appreciation to and acknowledge the hard work and excellent support provided to us by Sandy Wolbers, Kathleen Sutterlin, Stacey Flowerree, Brooke Briggs, Nick Miggans, Kevin Eichelberger, Colin Kelley, Steve Tomlin, Bryan Sullivan, Clark White, Meghan Manders, Lori Ziegenfuss, Jessica King, Rosalie Skears, Lisa Huinker, Bob Noel, Adam Rooke, John Wiese, Carlin Robinson, Courtney Kieffer, Rosario Valenti, Anni Lundgren, Deborah Judge-Watt, Nate Kehoe, David Wulff, Kim Freund, Joni Thompson, Mary Park, Colin Kelley, Ali Brown, Wendy Goldstein, Melissa Holt, Kim Hames, Mandy Jellerichs, Bryant Karnes, Robert Smith, Taina McCarren, Joni Thompson, Jeremy Jackson, Corey Specter, Rebecca Pillsbury, Jody McLaughlin, Tracy Ward, Brad Powers, Matt McLaughlin, and Michael Ginther. Their professionalism and dedication to the professors and instructors they serve during a time of strategic change at McGraw-Hill sets a standard we have worked very hard to match by making the fourteenth edition a text deserving of their representation.

We hope that you will find our book and ancillaries all that you expect. We welcome your ideas and recommendations about our material, and we wish you the utmost success in teaching and studying strategic management.

Dr. John A. Pearce II
Villanova School of Business
Villanova University
Villanova, PA 19085–1678

Dr. Richard Robinson
Darla Moore School of Business
University of South Carolina
Columbia, SC 29208

Brief Contents

Table of Contents

Overview of Strategic Management

The first chapter of this book introduces strategic management, the set of decisions and actions that result in the design and activation of strategies to achieve the objectives of an organization. The chapter provides an overview of the nature, benefits, and terminology of and the need for strategic management. Subsequent chapters provide greater detail.

The first major section of Chapter 1, "The Nature and Value of Strategic Management," emphasizes the practical value and benefits of strategic management for a firm. It also distinguishes between a firm's strategic decisions and its other planning tasks.

The section stresses the key point that strategic management activities are undertaken at three levels: corporate, business, and functional. The distinctive characteristics of strategic decision making at each of these levels affect the impact of activities at these levels on company operations. Other topics dealt with in this section are the value of formality in strategic management and the alignment of strategy makers in strategy formulation and implementation. The section concludes with a review of the planning research on business, which demonstrates that the use of strategic management processes yields financial and behavioral benefits that justify their costs.

The second major section of Chapter 1 presents a model of the strategic management process. The model, which will serve as an outline for the remainder of the text, describes approaches currently used by strategic planners. Its individual components are carefully defined and explained, as is the process for integrating them into the strategic management process. The section ends with a discussion of the model's practical limitations and the advisability of tailoring the recommendations made to actual business situations.

Strategic Management

After reading and studying this chapter, you should be able to

1. Explain the concept of strategic management.

2. Describe how strategic decisions differ from other decisions that managers make.

3. Name the benefits and risks of a participative approach to strategic decision making.

4. Understand the types of strategic decisions for which managers at different levels of the company are responsible.

5. Describe a comprehensive model of strategic decision making.

6. Appreciate the importance of strategic management as a process.

7. Give examples of strategic decisions that companies have recently made.

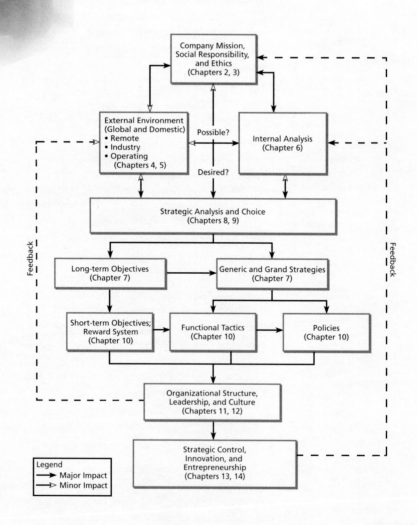

Company Mission, Social Responsibility, and Ethics (Chapters 2, 3)

External Environment (Global and Domestic)
• Remote
• Industry
• Operating
(Chapters 4, 5)

Possible?

Internal Analysis (Chapter 6)

Desired?

Strategic Analysis and Choice (Chapters 8, 9)

Long-term Objectives (Chapter 7)

Generic and Grand Strategies (Chapter 7)

Short-term Objectives; Reward System (Chapter 10)

Functional Tactics (Chapter 10)

Policies (Chapter 10)

Organizational Structure, Leadership, and Culture (Chapters 11, 12)

Strategic Control, Innovation, and Entrepreneurship (Chapters 13, 14)

Feedback

Feedback

Legend
→ Major Impact
⇢ Minor Impact

THE NATURE AND VALUE OF STRATEGIC MANAGEMENT

Managing activities internal to the firm is only part of the modern executive's responsibilities. The modern executive also must respond to the challenges posed by the firm's immediate and remote external environments. The immediate external environment includes competitors, suppliers, increasingly scarce resources, government agencies and their ever more numerous regulations, and customers whose preferences often shift inexplicably. The remote external environment comprises economic and social conditions, political priorities, and technological developments, all of which must be anticipated, monitored, assessed, and incorporated into the executive's decision making. However, the executive often is compelled to subordinate the demands of the firm's internal activities and external environment to the multiple and often inconsistent requirements of its stakeholders: owners, top managers, employees, communities, customers, and country.

To deal effectively with everything that affects the growth and profitability of a firm, executives practice strategic management. They develop and execute plans that they feel will position it optimally in its competitive environment by maximizing the anticipation of environmental changes and of unexpected internal and competitive demands.

To earn profits, firms need to perfect processes that respond to increases in the size and number of competing businesses; to the expanded role of government as a buyer, seller, regulator, and competitor in the free enterprise system; and to greater business involvement in international trade. Perhaps the most significant improvement in these management processes came when "long-range planning," "planning, programming, budgeting," and "business policy" were blended with increased emphasis on environmental forecasting and external considerations in formulating and implementing plans. This all-encompassing approach is known as strategic management.

strategic management
The set of decisions and actions that result in the formulation and implementation of plans designed to achieve a company's objectives.

Strategic management is defined as the set of decisions and actions that result in the formulation and implementation of plans designed to achieve a company's objectives. It comprises nine critical tasks:

1. Formulate the company's mission, including broad statements about its purpose, philosophy, and goals.
2. Conduct an analysis that reflects the company's internal conditions and capabilities.
3. Assess the company's external environment, including both the competitive and the general contextual factors.
4. Analyze the company's options by matching its resources with the external environment.
5. Identify the most desirable options by evaluating each option in light of the company's mission.
6. Select a set of long-term objectives and grand strategies that will achieve the most desirable options.
7. Develop annual objectives and short-term strategies that are compatible with the selected set of long-term objectives and grand strategies.
8. Implement the strategic choices by means of budgeted resource allocations in which the matching of tasks, people, structures, technologies, and reward systems is emphasized.
9. Evaluate the success of the strategic process as an input for future decision making.

strategy
Large-scale, future-oriented plans for interacting with the competitive environment to achieve company objectives.

As these nine tasks indicate, strategic management involves the planning, directing, organizing, and controlling of a company's strategy-related decisions and actions. By **strategy,** managers mean their large-scale, future-oriented plans for interacting with the competitive environment to achieve company objectives. A strategy is a company's game

Foot Locker, Inc. Announces Updated Strategic Plan and Elevated Long-Term Financial Objectives

Ken C. Hicks, Chairman and Chief Executive Officer of Foot Locker, Inc., the New York-based specialty athletic retailer, and other senior members of the management team announced an updated strategic plan and set of operating initiatives intended to further elevate the Company's long-term financial performance for the period 2012 through 2016. Specifically, the Company's new strategic priorities are:

- Create a clear customer focus to drive performance in its core athletic banners
- Make its stores and Internet sites more exciting, relevant places to shop and buy
- Deliver exceptional growth in high-potential business segments
- Aggressively pursue brand expansion opportunities

- Increase the productivity of all of its assets
- Build on its Industry-Leading Retail Team

The Company also substantially raised the financial objectives it expects to achieve over the next five years:

- Sales of $7.5 billion
- Sales per gross square foot of $500
- EBIT margin of 11 percent
- Net income margin of 7 percent
- Return on invested capital of 14 percent
- Inventory turnover of 3+ times

Source: Excerpted from "Foot Locker, Inc. Announces Updated Strategic Plan and Elevated Long-Term Financial Objectives," New York, March 6, 2012, *PR Newswire*, New York.

plan. Although that plan does not precisely detail all future deployment of people, finances, material, and information, it does provide a framework for managerial decisions. A strategy reflects a company's awareness of how, when, and where it should compete; against whom it should compete; and for what purposes it should compete. Strategic plans are typically very lengthy, with their length and level of detail correlated with the size and complexity of the company. However, most stock investors and analysts of the company want to read executive abstracts of the firm's objectives and strategic priorities. Strategy in Action, Exhibit 1.1, provides a great example from a public announcement by Foot Locker, Inc.

Dimensions of Strategic Decisions

What decisions facing a business are strategic and therefore deserve strategic management attention? Typically, strategic issues have the following dimensions.

Strategic Issues Require Top-Management Team Decisions   Because strategic decisions over-arch several areas of a firm's operations, they require top-management team involvement. Usually only top management has the perspective needed to understand the broad implications of such decisions and the power to authorize the necessary resource allocations.

Strategic Issues Require Large Amounts of the Firm's Resources   Strategic decisions involve substantial allocations of people, physical assets, or moneys that either must be redirected from internal sources or secured from outside the firm. They also commit the firm to actions over an extended period. For these reasons, they require substantial resources. Whirlpool Corporation's "Quality Express" product delivery program exemplified a strategy that required a strong financial and personnel commitment from the company. The plan was to deliver products to customers when, where, and how they wanted them. This proprietary service uses contract logistics strategy to deliver Whirlpool, Kitchen Aid, Roper, and Estate brand appliances to 90 percent of the company's dealer and builder customers within 24 hours and to the other 10 percent within 48 hours. In highly competitive service-oriented businesses, achieving and maintaining customer satisfaction frequently involve a commitment from every facet of the organization.

Strategic Issues Often Affect the Firm's Long-Term Prosperity Strategic decisions ostensibly commit the firm for a long time, typically five years; however, the impact of such decisions often lasts much longer. Once a firm has committed itself to a particular strategy, its image and competitive advantages usually are tied to that strategy. Firms become known in certain markets, for certain products, with certain technologies. They would jeopardize their previous gains if they shifted from these markets, products, or technologies by adopting a radically different strategy. Thus, strategic decisions have enduring effects on firms— for better or worse. For example, Commerce One created an alliance with SAP to improve its position in the e-marketplace for business to business (B2B) sales. After taking three years to ready its e-portals, Commerce One and SAP were ready to take on the market. Unfortunately, the market changed. The "foolproof strategy" got to the market too late and the alliance failed.

Strategic Issues Are Future Oriented Strategic decisions are based on what managers forecast, rather than on what they know. In such decisions, emphasis is placed on the development of projections that will enable the firm to select the most promising strategic options. In the turbulent and competitive free enterprise environment, a firm will succeed only if it takes a proactive (anticipatory) stance toward change.

Strategic Issues Usually Have Multifunctional or Multibusiness Consequences Strategic decisions have complex implications for most areas of the firm. Decisions about such matters as customer mix, competitive emphasis, or organizational structure necessarily involve a number of the firm's strategic business units (SBUs), divisions, or program units. All of these areas will be affected by allocations or reallocations of responsibilities and resources that result from these decisions.

Strategic Issues Require Considering the Firm's External Environment All businesses exist in an open system. They affect and are affected by external conditions that are largely beyond their control. Therefore, to successfully position a firm in competitive situations, its strategic managers must look beyond its operations. They must consider what relevant others are likely to do, including competitors, customers, suppliers, creditors, government, and labor.

Levels of Strategy

Exhibit 1.2 depicts the levels of strategic management as structured in practice. In alternative 2, the firm is engaged in only one business and the strategic responsibilities are concentrated in a single group of directors, officers, and managers. This is the organizational format of most small businesses. Alternative 1, the classic corporate structure, is composed of the corporate level, the business level, and the functional level.

The decision-making hierarchy of a large corporation typically contains three levels. At the top of this hierarchy is the corporate level, composed principally of a board of directors and the chief executive and administrative officers. They are responsible for the firm's financial performance and for the achievement of nonfinancial goals, such as enhancing the firm's image and fulfilling its social responsibilities. To a large extent, attitudes at the corporate level reflect the concerns of stockholders and society at large. In a multibusiness firm, corporate-level executives determine the businesses in which the firm should be involved. They also set objectives and formulate strategies that span the activities and functional areas of these businesses. Corporate-level strategic managers attempt to exploit their firm's distinctive competencies by adopting a portfolio approach to the management of its businesses and by developing long-term plans, typically for a three- to five-year period. A key corporate strategy of Airborne Express's operations involved direct sale to high-volume corporate accounts and developing an expansive network in the international arena. Instead of setting up operations overseas, Airborne's long-term strategy was to form

EXHIBIT 1.2
Alternative Strategic
Management
Structures

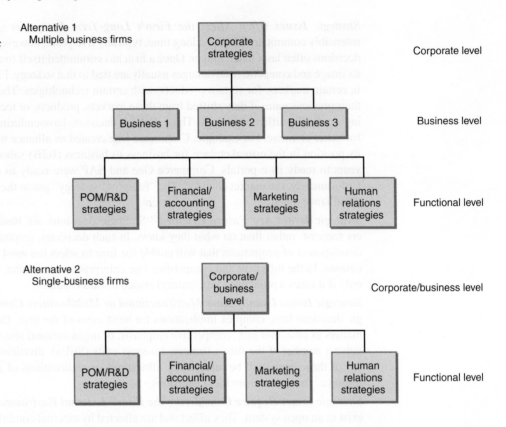

Alternative 1
Multiple business firms

Corporate level

Business level

Functional level

Alternative 2
Single-business firms

Corporate/business level

Functional level

direct associations with national companies within foreign countries to expand and diversify their operations.

Another example of the portfolio approach involved a plan by state-owned Saudi Arabian Oil to spend $1.4 billion to build and operate an oil refinery in Korea with its partner, Ssangyong. To implement their program, the Saudis embarked on a new "cut-out-the-middleman" strategy to reduce the role of international oil companies in the processing and selling of Saudi crude oil.

In the middle of the decision-making hierarchy is the business level, composed principally of business and corporate managers. These managers must translate the statements of direction and intent generated at the corporate level into concrete objectives and strategies for individual business divisions, or SBUs. A business, which by definition is a profit center that focuses on a specific combination of products, markets, and technologies, is also known as a strategic business unit ("SBU"). An SBU can operate as an independent company or as a semiautonomous strategic unit or division of its parent corporation. The study of business strategy is the study of SBU strategy. Throughout this book and in all business literature, the two terms are used interchangeably.

In essence, business-level strategic managers determine how the firm will compete in the selected product-market arena. They strive to identify and secure the most promising market segment within that arena. This segment is the piece of the total market that the firm can claim and defend because of its competitive advantages.

At the bottom of the decision-making hierarchy is the functional level, composed principally of managers of product, geographic, and functional areas. They develop annual objectives and short-term strategies in such areas as production, operations, research and development, finance and accounting, marketing, and human relations. However, their principal responsibility is to implement or execute the firm's strategic plans. Whereas corporate- and business-level managers center their attention on "doing the right things," managers at the functional level center their attention on "doing things right." Thus, they address such issues as the efficiency and effectiveness of production and marketing systems, the quality of customer service, and the success of particular products and services in increasing the firm's market shares.

Many people have a wrong impression about small businesses in the United States. They think that small refers to businesses with nine employees or fewer. Technically, this label is true, but it is even more accurate to refer to them as microbusinesses. For strategy purposes, small businesses are formally defined as having 10–500 employees and these companies often compete with larger, complex, well-financed, and globally competitive corporations. As is shown in Strategy in Action, Exhibit 1.3, these small businesses are employment dynamos and operate in almost every industry of the United States and globally. Strategic planning for small businesses is just as critical to economic and competitive success as it is for the larger companies in their industries, and the majority of models and recommendation that are offered in this book apply equally well to strategic planners in firms either large or small.

Characteristics of Strategic Management Decisions

The characteristics of strategic management decisions vary with the level of strategic activity considered. As shown in Exhibit 1.4, decisions at the corporate level tend to be more value oriented, more conceptual, and less concrete than decisions at the business or functional level. Corporate-level decisions are often characterized by greater risk, cost, and profit potential; greater need for flexibility; and longer time horizons. Such decisions include the choice of businesses, dividend policies, sources of long-term financing, and priorities for growth.

Functional-level decisions implement the overall strategy formulated at the corporate and business levels. They involve action-oriented operational issues and are relatively short range and low risk. Functional-level decisions incur only modest costs, because they depend on available resources. They usually are adaptable to ongoing activities and, therefore, can be implemented with minimal cooperation. For example, the corporate headquarters of Sears Holding Company spent $60 million to automate 6,900 clerical jobs by installing 28,000 computerized cash registers at its 868 stores in the United States. Although this move eliminated many functional-level jobs, top management believed that reducing annual operating expenses by at least $50 million was crucial to competitive survival.

Because functional-level decisions are relatively concrete and quantifiable, they receive critical attention and analysis even though their comparative profit potential is low. Common functional-level decisions include decisions on generic versus brand-name labeling, basic versus applied research and development (R&D), high versus low inventory levels, general-purpose versus specific-purpose production equipment, and close versus loose supervision.

Business-level decisions help bridge decisions at the corporate and functional levels.Such decisions are less costly, risky, and potentially profitable than corporate-level decisions, but they are more costly, risky, and potentially profitable than functional-level decisions. Common business-level decisions include decisions on plant location, marketing segmentation and geographic coverage, and distribution channels.

formality
The degree to which participation, responsibility, authority, and discretion in decision making are specified in strategic management.

Formality in Strategic Management

The formality of strategic management systems varies widely among companies. **Formality** refers to the degree to which participants, responsibilities, authority, and discretion in

The U.S. Small-Business Growth Engine

Small businesses, defined as companies with fewer than 500 employees, account for almost two-thirds of all net new job creation. They also contribute disproportionately to innovation, generating 13 times as many patents, per employee, as large companies do. While the small-business universe is vast, its real economic impact comes disproportionately from a much smaller subset of high-growth firms. These firms more or less double their revenues and employment every four years. And they are everywhere, in every industry sector and in many geographic areas.

It is really a subset of young businesses—those less than five years old—that want to grow that create the majority of jobs: 40 million over the last 25 years. This represents 20 percent of total gross job creation and total net new job creation in the United States over this time period. A subset of small businesses—high-growth ones—creates the vast majority of new jobs. Seventy-six percent of these high-growth firms are less than five years old. The 1 percent of all firms that are growing most quickly (fewer than 60,000 in all) account for 40 percent of economy-wide net new job creation. To provide a sense of magnitude, high-growth firms add an average of 88 employees a year, while the average non-high-growth company only adds 2 to 3.

Conventional wisdom suggests looking for high-growth firms in areas like Silicon Valley or the Route 128 corridor outside Boston, where many well-known ones have emerged. However, all industries have high-growth firms. While sectors do vary somewhat, in no industry do high-growth firms account for even 5 percent of the total number of firms in the industry, and there are very few industries where less than 1 percent of firms are growing quickly. In the United States, high-growth firms are found in every metropolitan statistical area, and no region has a disproportionate number of them. Conversely, Silicon Valley has many firms that struggle to grow and never become breakout stars, as well as many smaller companies that have no desire to grow quickly.

Source: Excerpted from John Horn and Darren Pleasance. November 2012. "Restarting the U.S. Small Business Growth Engine." *Strategy Practice*, McKinsey & Company.

High-growth U.S. companies as share of all U.S. companies, by selected industry, 2006[1].

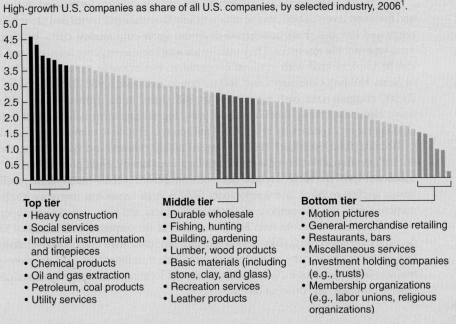

Top tier
- Heavy construction
- Social services
- Industrial instrumentation and timepieces
- Chemical products
- Oil and gas extraction
- Petroleum, coal products
- Utility services

Middle tier
- Durable wholesale
- Fishing, hunting
- Building, gardening
- Lumber, wood products
- Basic materials (including stone, clay, and glass)
- Recreation services
- Leather products

Bottom tier
- Motion pictures
- General-merchandise retailing
- Restaurants, bars
- Miscellaneous services
- Investment holding companies (e.g., trusts)
- Membership organizations (e.g., labor unions, religious organizations)

[1] Latest available data.

Source: Zoltan J. Acs, William Parsons, and Spencer Tracy, *High-Impact Firms: Gazettes Revisited*, Office of Advocacy, United States Small Business Administration, June 2008.

EXHIBIT 1.4   Hierarchy of Objectives and Strategies

Ends (What is to be achieved?)	Means (How is it to be achieved?)	Strategic Decision Makers			
		Board of Directors	Corporate Managers	Business Managers	Functional Managers
Mission, including goals and philosophy		✓✓	✓✓	✓	
Long-term objectives	Grand strategy	✓	✓✓	✓✓	
Annual objectives	Short-term strategies and policies		✓	✓✓	✓✓

Note: ✓✓ indicate a principal responsibility; ✓ indicates a secondary responsibility.

entrepreneurial mode
The informal, intuitive, and limited approach to strategic management associated with owner-managers of smaller firms.

planning mode
The strategic formality associated with large firms that operate under a comprehensive, formal planning system.

adaptive mode
The strategic formal-ity associated with medium-sized firms that emphasize the in-cremental modification of existing competitive approaches.

decision making are specified. It is an important consideration in the study of strategic management, because greater formality is usually positively correlated with the cost, comprehensiveness, accuracy, and success of planning.

A number of forces determine how much formality is needed in strategic management. The size of the organization, its predominant management styles, the complexity of its environment, its production process, its problems, and the purpose of its planning system all play a part in determining the appropriate degree of formality.

In particular, formality is associated with the size of the firm and with its stage of development. Some firms, especially smaller ones, follow an **entrepreneurial mode.** They are basically under the control of a single individual, and they produce a limited number of products or services. In such firms, strategic evaluation is informal, intuitive, and limited. Very large firms, on the other hand, make strategic evaluation part of a comprehensive, formal planning system, an approach that is called the **planning mode.** A third approach, labeled the **adaptive mode,** is associated with medium-sized firms in relatively stable environments. For firms that follow the adaptive mode, the identification and evaluation of alternative strategies are closely related to existing strategy. It is not unusual to find different modes within the same organization. For example, ExxonMobil might follow an entrepreneurial mode in developing and evaluating the strategy of its solar subsidiary but follow a planning mode in the rest of the company.

The Strategy Makers

The ideal strategic management planning process includes decision makers from all three company levels (the corporate, business, and functional)—for example, the chief executive officer (CEO), the product managers, and the heads of functional areas. In addition, the team obtains input from company planning staffs, when they exist, and from lower-level managers and supervisors. The latter provide data for strategic decision making and then implement strategies.

Because strategic decisions have a tremendous impact on a company and require large commitments of company resources, top managers must give final approval for strategic action. Exhibit 1.4 aligns levels of strategic decision makers with the kinds of objectives and strategies for which they are typically responsible.

Planning departments, often headed by a corporate vice president for planning, are common in large corporations. Medium-sized firms often employ at least one full-time staff member to spearhead strategic data-collection efforts. Even in small firms or less progressive larger firms, strategic planning often is spearheaded by an officer or by a group of officers designated as a planning committee.

Precisely what are managers' responsibilities in the strategic planning process at the corporate and business levels? Top management shoulders broad responsibility for all the major elements of strategic planning and management. They develop the major portions of the strategic plan and reviews, and they evaluate and counsel on all other portions. General managers at the business level typically have principal responsibilities for developing environmental analysis and forecasting, establishing business objectives, and developing business plans prepared by staff groups.

A firm's president or CEO characteristically plays a prominent role in the strategic planning process. In many ways, this situation is desirable. The CEO's principal duty often is defined as giving long-term direction to the firm, and the CEO is ultimately held responsible for oversight of the design and implementation of the firm's strategy and, therefore, for the success of its strategy.

However, when the CEO is very autocratic, the effectiveness of the firm's strategic planning and management processes is likely to be diminished. For this reason, establishing a strategic management system implies that the CEO will allow managers at all levels to participate in the strategic posture of the company.

In implementing a company's strategy, the CEO must have an appreciation for the power and responsibility of the board, while retaining the power to lead the company with the guidance of informed directors. The interaction between the CEO and board is key to any corporation's strategy. For example, IBM replaced its 92-year-old executive board structure with three newly created management teams: strategy, operations, and technology. Each team combined top executives, managers, and engineers going down six levels in some cases. This new team structure was responsible for guiding the creation of IBM's strategy and for helping to implement the strategies once they were authorized.

Benefits of a Participative Approach to Strategic Management

Using the strategic management approach, managers at all levels of the firm interact in planning and implementing. As a result, the behavioral consequences of strategic management are similar to those of participative decision making. Therefore, an accurate assessment of the impact of strategy formulation on organizational performance requires not only financial evaluation criteria but also nonfinancial evaluation criteria—measures of behavior-based effects. In fact, promoting positive behavioral consequences also enables the firm to achieve its financial goals. However, regardless of the profitability of strategic plans, several behavioral effects of strategic management improve the firm's welfare:

1. Strategy formulation activities enhance the firm's ability to prevent problems. Managers who encourage subordinates' attention to planning are aided in their monitoring and forecasting responsibilities by subordinates who are aware of the needs of strategic planning.

2. Group-based strategic decisions are likely to be drawn from the best available alternatives. The strategic management process results in better decisions because group interaction generates a greater variety of strategies and because forecasts based on the specialized perspectives of group members improve the screening of options.

3. The involvement of employees in strategy formulation improves their understanding of the productivity-reward relationship in every strategic plan and, thus, heightens their motivation.

4. Gaps and overlaps in activities among individuals and groups are reduced as participation in strategy formulation clarifies differences in roles.

5. Resistance to change is reduced. Though the participants in strategy formulation may be no more pleased with their own decisions than they would be with authoritarian

decisions, their greater awareness of the parameters that limit the available options makes them more likely to accept those decisions.

THE STRATEGIC MANAGEMENT PROCESS

Businesses vary in the processes they use to formulate and direct their strategic management activities. Sophisticated planners, such as General Electric, Procter & Gamble, and IBM, have developed more detailed processes than less formal planners of similar size. Small businesses that rely on the strategy formulation skills and limited time of an entrepreneur typically exhibit more basic planning concerns than those of larger firms in their industries. Understandably, firms with multiple products, markets, or technologies tend to use more complex strategic management systems. However, despite differences in detail and the degree of formalization, the basic components of the models used to analyze strategic management operations are very similar.

Because of the similarity among the general models of the strategic management process, it is possible to develop an eclectic model representative of the foremost thought in the strategic management area. This model is shown in Exhibit 1.5. It serves three major

EXHIBIT 1.5
Strategic
Management Model

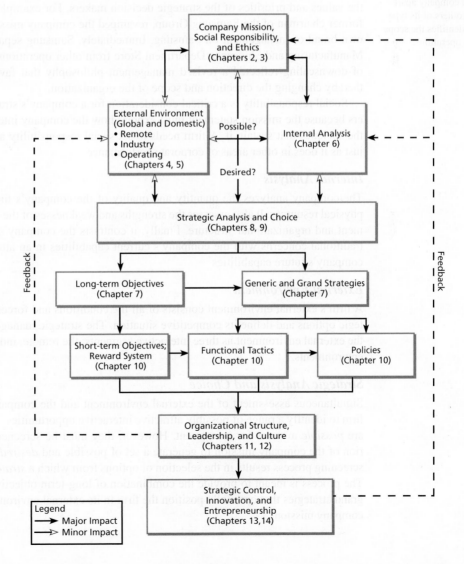

functions: (1) It depicts the sequence and the relationships of the major components of the strategic management process. (2) It is the outline for this book. This chapter provides a general overview of the strategic management process, and the major components of the model will be the principal theme of subsequent chapters. Notice that the chapters of the text that discuss each of the strategic management process components are shown in each block. (3) The model offers one approach for analyzing the case studies in this text and thus helps the analyst develop strategy formulation skills.

Components of the Strategic Management Model

This section will define and briefly describe the key components of the strategic management model. Each of these components will receive much greater attention in a later chapter. The intention here is simply to introduce them.

Company Mission

company mission
The unique purpose that sets a company apart from others of its type and identifies the scope of its operations.

The mission of a company is the unique purpose that sets it apart from other companies of its type and identifies the scope of its operations. In short, the **company mission** describes the company's product, market, and technological areas of emphasis in a way that reflects the values and priorities of the strategic decision makers. For example, Lee Kun-Hee, the former chairman of the Samsung Group, revamped the company mission by stamping his own brand of management on Samsung. Immediately, Samsung separated Chonju Paper Manufacturing and Shinsegae Department Store from other operations. This corporate act of downscaling reflected a revised management philosophy that favored specialization, thereby changing the direction and scope of the organization.

Social responsibility is a critical consideration for a company's strategic decision makers because the mission statement must express how the company intends to contribute to the societies that sustain it. A firm needs to set social responsibility aspirations for itself, just as it does in other areas of corporate performance.

Internal Analysis

The company analyzes the quantity and quality of the company's financial, human, and physical resources. It also assesses the strengths and weaknesses of the company's management and organizational structure. Finally, it contrasts the company's past successes and traditional concerns with the company's current capabilities in an attempt to identify the company's future capabilities.

External Environment

A firm's external environment consists of all the conditions and forces that affect its strategic options and define its competitive situation. The strategic management model shows the external environment as three interactive segments: the remote, industry, and operating environments.

Strategic Analysis and Choice

Simultaneous assessment of the external environment and the company profile enables a firm to identify a range of possibly attractive interactive opportunities. These opportunities are *possible* avenues for investment. However, they must be screened through the criterion of the company mission to generate a set of possible and *desired* opportunities. This screening process results in the selection of options from which a *strategic choice* is made. The process is meant to provide the combination of long-term objectives and generic and grand strategies that optimally position the firm in its external environment to achieve the company mission.

Strategic analysis and choice in single or dominant product/service businesses center around identifying strategies that are most effective at building sustainable competitive advantage based on key value chain activities and capabilities—core competencies of the firm. Multibusiness companies find their managers focused on the question of which combination of businesses maximizes shareholder value as the guiding theme during their strategic analysis and choice.

Long-Term Objectives

long-term objectives
The results that an organization seeks to achieve over a multiyear period.

The results that an organization seeks over a multiyear period are its **long-term objectives.** Such objectives typically involve some or all of the following areas: profitability, return on investment, competitive position, technological leadership, productivity, employee relations, public responsibility, and employee development.

Generic and Grand Strategies

generic strategies
Fundamental philosophical options for the design of strategies.

grand strategies
The means by which objectives are achieved.

Many businesses explicitly and all implicitly adopt one or more **generic strategies** characterizing their competitive orientation in the marketplace. Low cost, differentiation, or focus strategies define the three fundamental options. Enlightened managers seek to create ways their firm possesses both low cost and differentiation competitive advantages as part of their overall generic strategy. They usually combine these capabilities with a comprehensive, general plan of major actions through which their firm intends to achieve its long-term objectives in a dynamic environment. Called the **grand strategy,** this statement of means indicates how the objectives are to be achieved. Although every grand strategy is, in fact, a unique package of long-term strategies, 15 basic approaches can be identified: concentration, market development, product development, innovation, horizontal integration, vertical integration, joint venture, strategic alliances, consortia, concentric diversification, conglomerate diversification, turnaround, divestiture, bankruptcy, and liquidation.

Each of these grand strategies will be covered in detail in Chapter 7.

Short-Term Objectives

short-term objectives
Desired results that provide specific guidance for action during a period of one year or less.

Short-term objectives are the desired results that a company seeks over a period of one year or less. They are logically consistent with the firm's long-term objectives. Companies typically have many **short-term objectives** to provide guidance for their functional and operational activities. Thus, there are short-term marketing activity, raw material usage, employee turnover, and sales objectives, to name just four.

Action Plans

Action plans translate generic and grand strategies into "action" by incorporating four elements. First, they identify specific actions to be undertaken in the next year or less as part of the business's effort to build competitive advantage. Second, they establish a clear time frame for completion of each action. Third, action plans create accountability by identifying who is responsible for each "action" in the plan. Fourth, each "action" has one or more specific, immediate objectives that the action should achieve. Philips Healthcare describes its action plans for its supply chain in the event of a recession in Exhibit 1.6, Global Strategy in Action.

Functional Tactics

functional tactics
Short-term, narrow scoped plans that detail the "means" or activities that a company will use to achieve short-term objectives.

Within the general framework created by the business's generic and grand strategies, each business function needs to undertake activities that help build a sustainable competitive advantage. These short-term, limited-scope plans are called **functional tactics**. A radio ad campaign, an inventory reduction, and an introductory loan rate are examples of tactics.

Philips Healthcare: Keeping the Supply Chain Recession-Ready

Philips Healthcare (PHC), a leading supplier of diagnostic imaging systems and patient monitoring and cardiac devices, has implemented several supply chain practices to minimize the impact of recessions while maintaining high product quality.

"We use supplier-managed and -owned inventory programs that combine vendor-owned inventories and CPFR," says Steve Saunders, PHC's supply chain programs manager. "Philips shares its forecast information with its suppliers and provides visibility into its inventory and production schedules. We allow the suppliers to store supplier-owned inventory in a Philips warehouse. Philips takes ownership of the material only when it is pulled to the manufacturing line."

PHC also negotiates risk management contracts with suppliers to avoid having to make so many long-term, non-cancellable commitments. The company also actively monitors its suppliers' financial health. If the risks seem to be growing beyond what is acceptable, PHC is ready with risk mitigation plans such as alternate sourcing or temporary inventory increases. At the same time, the company runs a significant customer service organization that supports its installed base of equipment.

This service business generally remains stable regardless of economic conditions.

The company also ensures that its cost structure is flexible. Explains Saunders: "We try to minimize fixed overhead and have a variable cost structure. While we still perform most final assembly and test, we procure virtually all major materials, such as circuit boards, plastics and sheet metal. In addition, we outsource a wide variety of supply chain support functions such as warehousing, security and building maintenance. And by using a contingent workforce in most production operations, we have upside and downside flexibility as demand fluctuates."

Those approaches helped PHC expand sales 4–8 percent a year between 2005 and 2009, while earnings before interest, taxes, and amortization expenses have grown to more than 13 percent of revenue. In 2009, PHC commanded more than 22 percent of the global market for such healthcare equipment.

Source: Excerpted from Bruce Arntzen, "How to Recession-Proof Your Supply Chain," *Supply Chain Management Review* 13, no. 3 (April 2009), p. 12.

Managers in each business function develop tactics that delineate the functional activities undertaken in their part of the business and usually include them as a core part of their action plan. Functional tactics are detailed statements of the "means" or activities that will be used to achieve short-term objectives and establish competitive advantage.

Policies That Empower Action

Speed is a critical necessity for success in today's competitive, global marketplace. One way to enhance speed and responsiveness is to force/allow decisions to be made whenever possible at the lowest level in organizations. **Policies** are broad, precedent-setting decisions that guide or substitute for repetitive or time-sensitive managerial decision making. Creating policies that guide and "preauthorize" the thinking, decisions, and actions of operating managers and their subordinates in implementing the business's strategy is essential for establishing and controlling the ongoing operating process of the firm in a manner consistent with the firm's strategic objectives. Policies often increase managerial effectiveness by standardizing routine decisions and empowering or expanding the discretion of managers and subordinates in implementing business strategies.

policies
Predetermined decisions that substitute for managerial discretion in repetitive decision making.

The following are examples of the nature and diversity of company policies:

- A requirement that managers have purchase requests for items costing more than $5,000 cosigned by the controller.
- The minimum equity position required for all new McDonald's franchises.
- The standard formula used to calculate return on investment for the six strategic business units of General Electric.

- A decision that Sears service and repair employees have the right to waive repair charges to appliance customers they feel have been poorly served by their Sears appliance.

Restructuring, Reengineering, and Refocusing the Organization

Until this point in the strategic management process, managers have maintained a decidedly market-oriented focus as they formulate strategies and begin implementation through action plans and functional tactics. Now the process takes an internal focus—getting the work of the business done efficiently and effectively so as to make the strategy successful. What is the best way to organize ourselves to accomplish the mission? Where should leadership come from? What values should guide our daily activities—what should the organization and its people be like? How can we shape rewards to encourage appropriate action? The intense competition in the global marketplace has made this traditionally "internally focused" set of questions—how the activities within their business are conducted—recast themselves with unprecedented attentiveness to the marketplace. *Downsizing, restructuring,* and *reengineering* are terms that reflect the critical stage in strategy implementation wherein managers attempt to recast their organization. The company's structure, leadership, culture, and reward systems may all be changed to ensure cost competitiveness and quality demanded by unique requirements of its strategies.

The elements of the strategic management process are evident in the turnaround activities at Ford Motor Company. In 2008, Ford undertook to create a strategy to lower costs, increase efficiency, improve designs, and increase brand appeal. These improvements were needed to keep cash flows up to cover rising pension costs. For Ford to accomplish this new strategy it had to improve operations. New executives were brought in to lead product development and financial controls. To break down the bureaucratic boundaries, a committee was created that included employees from the major functional areas, and it was given the assignment to reduce the time needed to develop a new-concept vehicle.

Strategic Control and Continuous Improvement

strategic control
Tracking a strategy as it is being implemented, detecting problems or changes in its underlying premises, and making necessary adjustments.

Strategic control is concerned with tracking a strategy as it is being implemented, detecting problems or changes in its underlying premises, and making necessary adjustments. In contrast to postaction control, strategic control seeks to guide action on behalf of the generic and grand strategies as they are taking place and when the end results are still several years away. The rapid, accelerating change of the global marketplace of the last 10 years has made continuous improvement another aspect of strategic control in many organizations. **Continuous improvement** provides a way for managers to provide a form of strategic control that allows their organization to respond more proactively and timely to rapid developments in hundreds of areas that influence a business's success.

continuous improvement
A form of strategic control in which managers are encouraged to be proactive in improving all operations of the firm.

Continuous improvement includes preparing for contingencies. An extended period of economic decline brought on by a recession is an example. Exhibit 1.7, Strategy in Action provides guidelines for improvements that a company can make on an ongoing basis to recession-proof its supply chain.

Strategic Management as a Process

process
The flow of information through interrelated stages of analysis toward the achievement of an aim.

A **process** is the flow of information through interrelated stages of analysis toward the achievement of an aim. Thus, the strategic management model in Exhibit 1.5 depicts a process. In the strategic management process, the flow of information involves historical, current, and forecast data on the operations and environment of the business. Managers evaluate these data in light of the values and priorities of influential individuals and

Continuous Improvement to Recession-Proof Your Supply Chain

When a recession hits, customers can reduce your revenues and stop your outbound product flow faster than you can trim expenses and halt your inbound flow of raw materials. Working capital becomes stressed as your materials pipeline backs up and profits take a hit. To reduce the severity of these problems, here are six steps to take to improve operations in preparation for a downturn.

CHALLENGE 1: CUSTOMERS CANCEL ORDERS AND FINISHED GOODS INVENTORY BUILDS UP

Build a robust CPFR program. A healthy, ongoing CPFR program will encourage customers to discuss their plans with you, collaborate on risk-taking and work with you during the hard times.

Forge risk-aware contracts with customers. Too often in expansionary times, managers don't imagine how contentious material supply contracts can become if the customer stops buying. All contracts with customers should spell out very clearly what will happen to the material flow and cash flow if their forecasts turn out to be significantly in error.

Use demand-driven, lean manufacturing. By using build-to-order and "pull" manufacturing techniques with small lot sizes and just-in-time (JIT) replenishment, it is much easier to prevent supply from overshooting demand.

CHALLENGE 2: CUSTOMERS SLOW DOWN BILL PAYMENT, STRETCH OUT PAYABLES

Don't give away terms blithely. Control the sales teams' ability to give away terms. Whatever terms you do give will likely be stretched out during a recession. Focusing management on the cash-to-cash cycle time is a great way to call attention to the terms issue. After all, a dollar of accounts receivable counts as much toward working capital as a dollar of inventory.

Provide payment options through financing. It's smart to persuade customers to agree to attractive flexible financing and payment options during good times so a formal financing mechanism is in place when recession hits. The financing arms of organizations such as GMAC and GE Capital offer an array of payment options. The customer can choose the number of months to pay off the purchase and must agree to the interest rate. Later, if money is tight, they cannot unilaterally stretch payments, as they could during a "conventional" sale transaction.

CHALLENGE 3: RAW INVENTORY BUILDS UP AS MATERIAL KEEPS ARRIVING

Rely on VOI or VMI. The best situation, if you can do it, is to set up nearby stocking with vendor-owned (VOI) or vendor-managed (VMI) inventory programs that provide JIT delivery to your site.

---

stakeholders
Influential people who are vitally interested in the actions of the business.

groups—often called **stakeholders**—that are vitally interested in the actions of the business. The interrelated stages of the process are the 11 components discussed in the previous section. Finally, the aim of the process is the formulation and implementation of strategies that work, achieving the company's long-term mission and near-term objectives.

Viewing strategic management as a process has several important implications. First, a change in any component will affect several or all of the other components. Most of the arrows in the model point two ways, suggesting that the flow of information usually is reciprocal. For example, forces in the external environment may influence the nature of a company's mission, and the company may in turn affect the external environment and heighten competition in its realm of operation. A specific example is a power company that is persuaded, in part by governmental incentives, to include a commitment to the development of energy alternatives in its mission statement. The company then might promise to extend its research and development (R&D) efforts in the area of coal liquefaction. The external environment has affected the company's mission, and the revised mission signals a competitive condition in the environment.

A second implication of viewing strategic management as a process is that strategy formulation and implementation are sequential. The process begins with development or reevaluation of the company mission. This step is associated with, but essentially followed

Exhibit 1.7   continued

Place cancellable orders. All contracts need to have a reasonable "way out," yet many do not. Standard contracts are almost always heavily biased in favor of the large company and provide no risk-sharing and no reasonable exit for the smaller partner.

Establish CPFR systems with your suppliers. Giving suppliers as much forewarning as possible helps them react faster to your need to stem the inbound flow of raw materials.

CHALLENGE 4: PARTS SHORTAGES BECOME CRITICAL WHEN A SUPPLIER COLLAPSES

A detailed review of the supplier's financial health should be part of the quarterly business analysis discussed with each supplier. You can further reduce the risk of supply-chain disruption by using more industry-standard parts, thereby making it easier to find alternate sources.

Keep extra inventory on hand. In a push to create lean supply chains, many companies depend on rapid resupply from suppliers. But recessions make even dependable suppliers undependable, and parts we take for granted in good times may become critical-path if supplies are interrupted. Keeping some extra inventory of critical parts is a smart insurance policy.

CHALLENGE 5: DIRECT LABOR SPENDING STAYS HIGH

Move to a variable cost structure. Outsource operations based on a cost per piece. This approach could be used, for example, with contract manufacturing, common carriers, third-party logistics providers, and contract repair centers. Many of these providers are much more practiced at ramping up and down and shifting resources around than are typical large OEMs.

Deploy a more flexible workforce. Rethink your labor resources so they can more easily scale up and down based on need. Arrange this flexibility with workers during good times when the issue is less contentious so it will be in place when you need it.

CHALLENGE 6: OVERHEAD SPENDING STAYS HIGH

Implement a variable cost structure. Employees with flexible hours will enjoy overtime during good years and provide cost relief during lean years. In addition, call centers and a host of back-office functions can be outsourced as variable costs.

Install firm purchasing controls. Central control of spending and approved supplier lists are needed to enforce policies consistently to modulate spending in hard times. Employees must be required to get spending approved by someone accountable for the budget.

Source: Excerpted from Bruce Arntzen, "How to Recession-Proof Your Supply Chain," *Supply Chain Management Review* 13, no. 3 (April 2009), p. 12. http://proquest.umi.com/pqdweb?did=1737280001&Fmt=3&clientId =3260&RQT=309&VName=PQD

by, development of a company profile and assessment of the external environment. Then follow, in order, strategic choice, definition of long-term objectives, design of the grand strategy, definition of short-term objectives, design of operating strategies, institutionalization of the strategy, and review and evaluation.

The apparent rigidity of the process, however, must be qualified.

First, a firm's strategic posture may have to be reevaluated in response to changes in any of the principal factors that determine or affect its performance. Entry by a major new competitor, the death of a prominent board member, replacement of the chief executive officer, and a downturn in market responsiveness are among the thousands of changes that can prompt reassessment of a firm's strategic plan. However, no matter where the need for a reassessment originates, the strategic management process begins with the mission statement.

Second, not every component of the strategic management process deserves equal attention each time planning activity takes place. Firms in an extremely stable environment may find that an in-depth assessment is not required every year. Companies often are satisfied with their original mission statements even after a decade of operation and spend only a minimal amount of time addressing this subject.

A third implication of viewing strategic management as a process is the necessity of feedback from institutionalization, review, and evaluation to the early stages of the process.

Sorin Group: 2012–2017 Strategic Plan

On September 20, 2012, Sorin S.p.A.'s Board of Directors approved unanimously the 2012–2017 Strategic Plan. Sorin Group's Plan focuses on the implementation of the Company's medium-long term strategy.

The revenue targets in the 2012–2017 period by business units are the following:

- Expected revenue growth for the Cardiopulmonary Business Unit of 2–4% CAGR, also thanks to the full operational recovery of the Mirandola plant following the earthquakes.
- Expected revenue growth for the Cardiac Rhythm Management Business Unit of 2–4% CAGR, in light of challenging market conditions.
- Expected revenue growth for the Heart Valves Business Unit of 7–9% CAGR.

In addition to its base business, the Company has also identified the following additional growth opportunities:

- Investment into two new growth platforms addressing heart failure and mitral valve regurgitation.

Potential additional revenues from these new ventures could amount to EUR 100–150 million in 2017.

- Accelerated geographic expansion initiatives in emerging markets and primarily in the BRIC region. Potential additional revenues from local manufacturing and R&D investments in these regions could amount to EUR 30–40 million in 2017.
- Revenue-generating acquisitions aimed at increasing the Company's critical mass in markets in which it is already present or in adjacent business segments.

Including the additional growth opportunities, the Sorin Group expected consolidated revenues to grow 5–7% CAGR during the 2011–2015 period, despite challenging market conditions, then accelerating to 8–10% CAGR in the 2015–2017 period. EBITDA margin was expected to increase by an average of approximately 100 basis points per year during the period and reach 20% in 2015.

Source: Excerpted from "Sorin Group: 2012–2017 Strategic Plan," September 24, 2012. *Business Wire*, New York.

---

feedback
The analysis of postimplementation results that can be used to enhance future decision making.

dynamic
The term that characterizes the constantly changing conditions that affect interrelated and interdependent strategic activities.

Feedback can be defined as the analysis of postimplementation results that can be used to enhance future decision making. Therefore, as indicated in Exhibit 1.5, strategic managers should assess the impact of implemented strategies on external environments. Thus, future planning can reflect any changes precipitated by strategic actions. Strategic managers also should analyze the impact of strategies on the possible need for modifications in the company mission.

A fourth implication of viewing strategic management as a process is the need to regard it as a dynamic system. The term **dynamic** characterizes the constantly changing conditions that affect interrelated and interdependent strategic activities. Managers should recognize that the components of the strategic process are constantly evolving but that formal planning artificially freezes those components, much as an action photograph freezes the movement of a swimmer. Since change is continuous, the dynamic strategic planning process must be monitored constantly for significant shifts in any of its components as a precaution against implementing an obsolete strategy.

A final example of a strategic plan executive summary is provided in Global Strategy in Action, Exhibit 1.8. It presents an overview of the Sorin Group's 2012–2017 Strategic Plan. Having read this chapter, some qualities of the exhibit may be more evident. First, the plan was prepared by top management and approved by the company's board of directors. Second, it specifies quantifiable objectives for the firm, including the target year for their attainment. Third, it is clearly future oriented and provides a general guide to the company's overall strategy.

Summary

Strategic management is the set of decisions and actions that result in the formulation and implementation of plans designed to achieve a company's objectives. Because it involves long-term, future-oriented, complex decision making and requires considerable resources, top-management participation is essential.

Strategic management is a three-tier process involving corporate-, business-, and functional-level planners, and support personnel. At each progressively lower level, strategic activities were shown to be more specific, narrow, short-term, and action oriented, with lower risks but fewer opportunities for dramatic impact.

The strategic management model presented in this chapter will serve as the structure for understanding and integrating all the major phases of strategy formulation and implementation. The chapter provided a summary account of these phases, each of which is given extensive individual attention in subsequent chapters.

The chapter stressed that the strategic management process centers on the belief that a firm's mission can be best achieved through a systematic and comprehensive assessment of both its internal capabilities and its external environment. Subsequent evaluation of the firm's opportunities leads, in turn, to the choice of long-term objectives and grand strategies and, ultimately, to annual objectives and operating strategies, which must be implemented, monitored, and controlled.

Key Terms

adaptive mode, *p. 9*
company mission, *p. 12*
continuous improvement, *p. 15*
dynamic, *p. 18*
entrepreneurial mode, *p. 9*
feedback, *p. 18*
formality, *p. 7*

functional tactics, *p. 13*
generic strategies, *p. 13*
grand strategies, *p. 13*
long-term objectives, *p. 13*
planning mode, *p. 9*
policies, *p. 14*
process, *p. 15*

short-term objectives, *p. 13*
stakeholders, *p. 16*
strategic control, *p. 15*
strategic management, *p. 3*
strategy, *p. 3*

Questions for Discussion

1. Read an article in the business press about a major action taken by a corporation. Be prepared to briefly describe this action to your professor and to name the key strategic management terms that the author used in the article.
2. In what ways do you think the subject matter in this strategic management–business policy course will differ from that of previous courses you have taken?
3. After graduation, you are not likely to move directly to a top-level management position. In fact, few members of your class will ever reach the top-management level. Why, then, is it important for all business majors to study the field of strategic management?
4. Do you expect outstanding performance in this course to require a great deal of memorization? Why or why not?
5. You undoubtedly have read about individuals who seemingly have given single-handed direction to their corporations. Is a participative strategic management approach likely to stifle or suppress the contributions of such individuals?
6. Think about the courses you have taken in functional areas, such as marketing, finance, production, personnel, and accounting. What is the importance of each of these areas to the strategic planning process?
7. Discuss with practicing business managers the strategic management models used in their firms. What are the similarities and differences between these models and the one in the text?
8. In what ways do you believe the strategic planning approach of not-for-profit organizations would differ from that of profit-oriented organizations?
9. How do you explain the success of firms that do not use a formal strategic planning process?
10. Think about your postgraduation job search as a strategic decision. How would the strategic management model be helpful to you in identifying and securing the most promising position?

Strategy Formulation

Strategy formulation guides executives in defining the business their firm is in, the ends it seeks, and the means it will use to accomplish those ends. The approach of strategy formulation is an improvement over that of traditional long-range planning. As discussed in the next eight chapters—about developing a firm's competitive plan of action—strategy formulation combines a future-oriented perspective with concern for the firm's internal and external environments.

The strategy formulation process begins with definition of the company mission, as discussed in Chapter 2, which defines the purpose of its business and values. In Chapter 3 social responsibility is discussed as a critical consideration for a company's strategic decision makers because the mission statement must express how the company intends to contribute to the societies that sustain it. Central to the idea that companies should be operated in socially responsible ways is the belief that managers will behave in an ethical manner. Management ethics are discussed in this chapter with special attention to the utilitarian, moral rights, and social justice approaches.

Chapter 4 deals with the principal factors in a firm's external environment that strategic managers must assess so they can anticipate and take advantage of future business conditions. It emphasizes the importance to a firm's planning activities of factors in the firm's remote, industry, and operating environments.

Chapter 5 describes the key differences in strategic planning among domestic, multinational, and global firms. It gives special attention to the new vision that a firm must communicate when it multinationalizes.

Chapter 6 shows how firms evaluate their company's strengths and weaknesses to produce an internal analysis. Strategic managers use such profiles to target competitive advantages they can emphasize and competitive disadvantages they should correct or minimize.

Chapter 7 examines the types of long-range objectives strategic managers set and specifies the qualities these objectives must have to provide a basis for direction and evaluation. The chapter also examines the generic and grand strategies that firms use to achieve long-range objectives.

Comprehensive approaches to the evaluation of strategic opportunities and to the final strategic decision are the focus of Chapter 8. The chapter shows how a firm's strategic options can be compared in a way that allows selection of the best available option. It also discusses how a company can create competitive advantages for each of its businesses.

Chapter 9 extends the attention on strategic analysis and choice by showing how managers can build value in multibusiness companies.

Chapter **Two**

Company Mission

After reading and studying this chapter, you should be able to

1. Describe a company mission and explain its value.

2. Explain why it is important for the mission statement to include the company's basic product or service, its primary markets, and its principal technology.

3. Explain which goal of a company is most important: survival, profitability, or growth.

4. Discuss the importance of company philosophy, public image, and company self-concept to stockholders.

5. Give examples of the newest trends in mission statement components: customer emphasis, quality, and company vision.

6. Describe the role of a company's board of directors.

7. Explain agency theory and its value in helping a board of directors improve corporate governance.

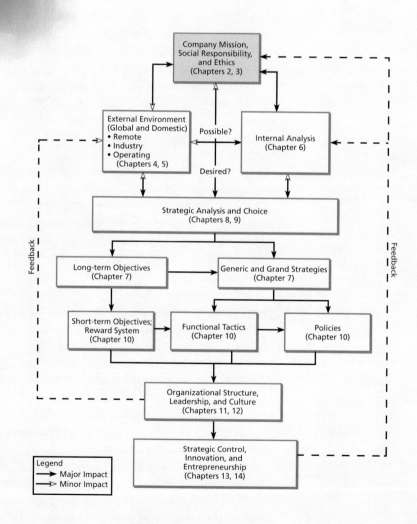

Mission Statement of Nicor Inc.

PREAMBLE

We, the management of Nicor Inc., here set forth our belief as to the purpose for which the company is established and the principles under which it should operate. We pledge our effort to the accomplishment of these purposes within these principles.

BASIC PURPOSE

The basic purpose of Nicor Inc. is to perpetuate an investor-owned company engaging in various phases of the energy business, striving for balance among those phases so as to render needed satisfactory products and services and earn optimum, long-range profits.

WHAT WE DO

The principal business of the company, through its utility subsidiary, is the provision of energy through a pipe system to meet the needs of ultimate consumers. To accomplish its basic purpose, and to ensure its strength, the company will engage in other energy-related activities, directly or through subsidiaries or in participation with other persons, corporations, firms, or entities.

All activities of the company shall be consistent with its responsibilities to investors, customers, employees, and the public and its concern for the optimum development and utilization of natural resources and for environmental needs.

WHERE WE DO IT

The company's operations shall be primarily in the United States, but no self-imposed or regulatory geographical limitations are placed upon the acquisition, development, processing, transportation, or storage of energy resources, or upon other energy-related ventures in which the company may engage. The company will engage in such activities in any location where, after careful review, it has determined that such activity is in the best interest of its stockholders.

Utility service will be offered in the territory of the company's utility subsidiary to the best of its ability, in accordance with the requirements of regulatory agencies and pursuant to the subsidiary's purposes and principles.

Source: Nicor Inc., http://www.nicor.com/

WHAT IS A COMPANY MISSION?

company mission
The unique purpose that sets a company apart from others of its type and identifies the scope of its operations in product, market, and technology terms.

Whether a firm is developing a new business or reformulating direction for an ongoing business, it must determine the basic goals and philosophies that will shape its strategic posture. This fundamental purpose that sets a firm apart from other firms of its type and identifies the scope of its operations in product and market terms is defined as the company mission. As discussed in Chapter 1, the **company mission** is a broadly framed but enduring statement of a firm's intent. It embodies the business philosophy of the firm's strategic decision makers, implies the image the firm seeks to project, reflects the firm's self-concept, and indicates the firm's principal product or service areas and the primary customer needs the firm will attempt to satisfy. In short, it describes the firm's product, market, and technological areas of emphasis, and it does so in a way that reflects the values and priorities of the firm's strategic decision makers. An excellent example is the company mission statement of Nicor Inc., shown in Exhibit 2.1, Strategy in Action.

The Need for an Explicit Mission

No external body requires that the company mission be defined, and the process of defining it is time-consuming and tedious. Moreover, it contains broadly outlined or implied objectives and strategies rather than specific directives. Characteristically, it is a statement, not of measurable targets but of attitude, outlook, and orientation.

The mission statement is a message designed to be inclusive of the expectations of all stakeholders for the company's performance over the long run. The executives and board who prepare the mission statement attempt to provide a unifying purpose for the company that will provide a basis for strategic objective setting and decision making. In general terms, the mission statement addresses the following questions:

Why is this firm in business?

What are our economic goals?

What is our operating philosophy in terms of quality, company image, and self-concept?

What are our core competencies and competitive advantages?

What customers do and can we serve?

How do we view our responsibilities to stockholders, employees, communities, environment, social issues, and competitors?

FORMULATING A MISSION

The process of defining the company mission for a specific business can perhaps be best understood by thinking about the business at its inception. The typical business begins with the beliefs, desires, and aspirations of a single entrepreneur. Such an owner-manager's sense of mission usually is based on the following fundamental beliefs:

1. The product or service of the business can provide benefits at least equal to its price.

2. The product or service can satisfy a customer need of specific market segments that is currently not being met adequately.

3. The technology that is to be used in production will provide a cost- and quality-competitive product or service.

4. With hard work and the support of others, the business can not only survive but also grow and be profitable.

5. The management philosophy of the business will result in a favorable public image and will provide financial and psychological rewards for those who are willing to invest their labor and money in helping the business to succeed.

6. The entrepreneur's self-concept of the business can be communicated to and adopted by employees and stockholders.

As the business grows or is forced by competitive pressures to alter its product, market, or technology, redefining the company mission may be necessary. If so, the revised mission statement will contain the same components as the original. It will state the basic type of product or service to be offered, the primary markets or customer groups to be served; the technology to be used in production or delivery; the firm's fundamental concern for survival through growth and profitability; the firm's managerial philosophy; the public image the firm seeks; the self-concept those affiliated with the firm should have of it. The company's attention to customers; and its commitment to product and service quality. This chapter will discuss in detail these components. The examples shown in Exhibit 2.2, Strategy in Action, provide insights into how some major corporations handle them.

Basic Product or Service: Primary Market; Principal Technology

Three indispensable components of the mission statement are specification of the basic product or service, specification of the primary market, and specification of the principal technology for production or delivery. These components are discussed under one heading because only in combination do they describe the company's business activity. A good example of the three components is to be found in the business plan of ITT Barton, a division

Identifying Mission Statement Components: A Compilation of Excerpts from Actual Corporate Mission Statements

1. Customer-market	We believe our first responsibility is to the doctors, nurses, and patients, to mothers and all others who use our products and services. (Johnson & Johnson)
	To anticipate and meet market needs of farmers, ranchers, and rural communities within North America. (CENEX)
2. Product-service	AMAX's principal products are molybdenum, coal, iron ore, copper, lead, zinc, petroleum and natural gas, potash, phosphates, nickel, tungsten, silver, gold, and magnesium. (AMAX)
3. Geographic domain	We are dedicated to total success of Corning Glass Works as a worldwide competitor. (Corning Glass)
4. Technology	Control Data is in the business of applying microelectronics and computer technology in two general areas: computer-related hardware and computing-enhancing services, which include computation, information, education, and finance. (Control Data)
	The common technology in these areas relates to discrete particle coatings. (NASHUA)
5. Concern for survival	In this respect, the company will conduct its operation prudently, and will provide the profits and growth which will assure Hoover's ultimate success. (Hoover Universal)
6. Philosophy	We are committed to improve health care throughout the world. (Baxter Travenol)
	We believe human development to be the worthiest of the goals of civilization and independence to be the superior condition for nurturing growth in the capabilities of people. (Sun Company)
7. Self-concept	Hoover Universal is a diversified, multi-industry corporation with strong manufacturing capabilities, entrepreneurial policies, and individual business unit autonomy. (Hoover Universal)
8. Concern for public image	We are responsible to the communities in which we live and work and to the world community as well. (Johnson & Johnson)
	Also, we must be responsive to the broader concerns of the public, including especially the general desire for improvement in the quality of life, equal opportunity for all, and the constructive use of natural resources. (Sun Company)
9. Consumers	Our core purpose is to create value for customers to earn their lifetime loyalty. (Tesco)
10. Quality	We will provide branded products and services of superior quality and value that improve the lives of the world's consumers. (Procter & Gamble)

of ITT. Under the heading of business mission and area served, the following information is presented:

The unit's mission is to serve industry and government with quality instruments used for the primary measurement, analysis, and local control of fluid flow, level, pressure, temperature, and fluid properties. This instrumentation includes flow meters, electronic readouts, indicators, recorders, switches, liquid level systems, analytical instruments such as titrators, integrators, controllers, transmitters, and various instruments for the measurement of fluid properties (density, viscosity, gravity) used for processing variable sensing, data collecting, control, and transmission. The unit's mission includes fundamental loop-closing control and display devices, when economically justified, but excludes broadline central control room instrumentation, systems design, and turnkey responsibility.

Markets served include instrumentation for oil and gas production, gas transportation, chemical and petrochemical processing, cryogenics, power generation, aerospace, government, and marine, as well as other instrument and equipment manufacturers.

In only 129 words, this segment of the mission statement clearly indicates to all readers—from company employees to casual observers—the basic products, primary markets, and principal technologies of ITT Barton.

Often the most referenced public statement of a company's selected products and markets appears in "silver bullet" form in the mission statement; for example, "Dayton-Hudson Corporation is a diversified retailing company whose business is to serve the American consumer through the retailing of fashion-oriented quality merchandise." Such an abstract of company direction is particularly helpful to outsiders who value condensed overviews.

Company Goals: Survival; Growth; Profitability

Three economic goals guide the strategic direction of almost every business organization. Whether or not the mission statement explicitly states these goals, it reflects the firm's intention to secure *survival* through *growth* and *profitability*.

A firm that is unable to survive will be incapable of satisfying the aims of any of its stakeholders. Unfortunately, the goal of survival, like the goals of growth and profitability, often is taken for granted to such an extent that it is neglected as a principal criterion in strategic decision making. When this happens, the firm may focus on short-term aims at the expense of the long run. Concerns for expediency, a quick fix, or a bargain may displace the assessment of long-term impact. Too often, the result is near-term economic failure owing to a lack of resource synergy and sound business practice. For example, Consolidated Foods, maker of Shasta soft drinks and L'eggs hosiery, sought growth through the acquisition of bargain businesses. However, the erratic sales patterns of its diverse holdings forced it to divest itself of more than four dozen companies. This process cost Consolidated Foods millions of dollars and hampered its growth.

Profitability is the mainstay goal of a business organization. No matter how profit is measured or defined, profit over the long term is the clearest indication of a firm's ability to satisfy the principal claims and desires of employees and stockholders. The key phrase here is "over the long term." Obviously, basing decisions on a short-term concern for profitability would lead to a strategic myopia. Overlooking the enduring concerns of customers, suppliers, creditors, ecologists, and regulatory agents may produce profit in the short term, but, over time, the financial consequences are likely to be detrimental.

The following excerpt from the Hewlett-Packard statement of mission ably expresses the importance of an orientation toward long-term profit:

> To achieve sufficient profit to finance our company growth and to provide the resources we need to achieve our other corporate objectives.
>
> In our economic system, the profit we generate from our operation is the ultimate source of the funds we need to prosper and grow. It is the one absolutely essential measure of our corporate performance over the long term. Only if we continue to meet our profit objective can we achieve our other corporate objectives.

A firm's growth is tied inextricably to its survival and profitability. In this context, the meaning of growth must be broadly defined. Although product impact market studies (PIMS) have shown that growth in market share is correlated with profitability, other important forms of growth do exist. Growth in the number of markets served, in the variety of products offered, and in the technologies that are used to provide goods or services frequently lead to improvements in a firm's competitive ability. Growth means change, and proactive change is essential in a dynamic business environment.

Hewlett-Packard's mission statement provides another excellent example of corporate regard for growth:

Objective: To let our growth be limited only by our profits and our ability to develop and produce technical products that satisfy real customer needs.

We do not believe that large size is important for its own sake; however, for at least two basic reasons, continuous growth is essential for us to achieve our other objectives.

In the first place, we serve a rapidly growing and expanding segment of our technological society. To remain static would be to lose ground. We cannot maintain a position of strength and leadership in our field without growth.

In the second place, growth is important in order to attract and hold high-caliber people. These individuals will align their future only with a company that offers them considerable opportunity for personal progress. Opportunities are greater and more challenging in a growing company.

The issue of growth raises a concern about the definition of the company mission. How can a firm's product, market, and technology be specified sufficiently to provide direction without precluding the exercise of unanticipated strategic options? How can a firm so define its mission that it can consider opportunistic diversification while maintaining the parameters that guide its growth decision? Perhaps such questions are best addressed when a firm's mission statement outlines the conditions under which the firm might depart from ongoing operations. General Electric Company's extensive global mission provided the foundation for its GE Appliances (GEA) in Louisville, Kentucky. GEA did not see consumer preferences in the world market becoming Americanized. Instead, its expansion goals allowed for flexibility in examining the unique characteristics of individual foreign markets and tailoring strategies to fit them.

The growth philosophy of Dayton-Hudson also embodies this approach:

The stability and quality of the corporation's financial performance will be developed through the profitable execution of our existing businesses, as well as through the acquisition or development of new businesses. Our growth priorities, in order, are as follows:

1. Development of the profitable market preeminence of existing companies in existing markets through new store development or new strategies within existing stores.
2. Expansion of our companies to feasible new markets.
3. Acquisition of other retailing companies that are strategically and financially compatible with Dayton-Hudson.
4. Internal development of new retailing strategies.

Capital allocations to fund the expansion of existing Dayton-Hudson operating companies will be based on each company's return on investment (ROI), in relationship to its ROI objective and its consistency in earnings growth and on the ability of its management to perform up to the forecasts contained in its capital requests. Expansion via acquisition or new venture will occur when the opportunity promises an acceptable rate of long-term growth and profitability, an acceptable degree of risk, and compatibility with Dayton-Hudson's long-term strategy.

Company Philosophy

company creed
A company's statement of its philosophy.

The statement of a company's philosophy, often called the **company creed**, usually accompanies or appears within the mission statement. It reflects or specifies the basic beliefs, values, aspirations, and philosophical priorities to which strategic decision makers are committed in managing the company. Fortunately, the philosophies vary little from one firm to another. Owners and managers implicitly accept a general, unwritten, yet pervasive code of behavior that governs business actions and permits them to be largely self-regulated. Unfortunately,

Growth Philosophy at AIM Private Asset Management Inc.

AIM's growth philosophy focuses on earnings—a tangible measure of a company's growth. Because stock prices can gyrate widely on rumors, we use earnings to weed out "high-flying" speculative stocks.

In selecting investments, we look for:
- Quality earnings growth—because we believe earnings drive stock prices.
- Positive earnings momentum—stocks with greater positive momentum will rise above the crowd.

Our growth philosophy adheres to four basic rules:
- Remain fully invested.
- Focus on individual companies rather than industries, sectors or countries.
- Strive to find the best earnings growth.
- Maintain a strong sell discipline.

Why growth philosophy?
- Investment decisions are based on facts, not guesses or big-picture economic forecasts.
- Earnings—not emotions—dictate when we should buy and sell.
- AIM's investment managers have followed the same earnings-driven philosophy for decades.
- This approach has proven itself in domestic and foreign markets.

Source: AIM Private Asset Management Inc.,
http://sma.aiminvestments.com/

statements of company philosophy are often so similar and so platitudinous that they read more like public relations handouts than the commitment to values they are meant to be.

Company executives attempt more than ever to provide a distinctive and accurate picture of the firm's managerial outlook. One such statement of company philosophy is that of AIM Private Asset Management, Inc. As Exhibit 2.3, Strategy in Action, shows, AIM's board of directors and executives have established especially clear directions for company decision making and action based on growth.

As seen in Exhibit 2.4, Global Strategy in Action, the philosophy of Nissan Motor Manufacturing is expressed by the company's People Principles and Key Corporate Principles. These principles form the basis of the way the company operates on a daily basis. They address the principal concepts used in meeting the company's established goals. Nissan focuses on the distinction between the role of the individual and the corporation. In this way, employees can link their productivity and success to the productivity and success of the company. Given these principles, the company is able to concentrate on the issues most important to its survival, growth, and profitability.

Exhibit 2.5, Strategy in Action, provides an example of how General Motors uses a statement of company philosophy to clarify its environmental principles.

Public Image

Both present and potential customers attribute certain qualities to particular businesses. Gerber and Johnson & Johnson make safe products; Cross Pen makes high-quality writing instruments; Étienne Aigner makes stylish but affordable leather products; Corvettes are power machines; and Izod Lacoste stands for the preppy look. Thus, mission statements should reflect the public's expectations, because this makes achievement of the firm's goals more likely. Gerber's mission statement should not open the possibility for diversification into pesticides, and Cross Pen's should not open the possibility for diversification into $0.59 brand-name disposables.

On the other hand, a negative public image often prompts firms to reemphasize the beneficial aspects of their mission. For example, in response to what it saw as a disturbing trend in public opinion, Dow Chemical undertook an aggressive promotional campaign to fortify

	People Principles **(All other objectives can only be achieved by people)**
Selection	Hire the highest caliber people; look for technical capabilities and emphasize attitude.
Responsibility	Maximize the responsibility; staff by devolving decision making.
Teamwork	Recognize and encourage individual contributions, with everyone working toward the same objectives.
Flexibility	Expand the role of the individual: multiskilled, no job description, generic job titles.
Kaizen	Continuously seek 100.1 percent improvements; give "ownership of change."
Communications	"Every day, face to face."
Training	Establish individual "continuous development programs."
Supervisors	Regard as "the professionals at managing the production process"; give them much responsibility normally assumed by individual departments; make them the genuine leaders of their teams.
Single status	Treat everyone as a "first class" citizen; eliminate all illogical differences.
Trade unionism	Establish single union agreement with AEU emphasizing the common objective for a successful enterprise.
	Key Corporate Principles
Quality	Building profitably the highest quality car sold in Europe.
Customer	Achieve target of no. 1 customer satisfaction in Europe.
Volume	Always achieve required volume.
New products	Deliver on time, at required quality, within cost.
Suppliers	Establish long-term relationship with single-source suppliers; aim for zero defects and just-in-time delivery; apply Nissan principles to suppliers.
Production	Use "most appropriate" technology; develop predictable "best method" of doing job; build in quality.
Engineering	Design "quality" and "ease of working" into the product and facilities; establish "simultaneous engineering" to reduce development time.

Source: Nissan Motor Co. Ltd., http://www.nissanmotors.com/

its credibility, particularly among "employees and those who live and work in [their] plant communities." Dow described its approach in its annual report:

> All around the world today, Dow people are speaking up. People who care deeply about their company, what it stands for, and how it is viewed by others. People who are immensely proud of their company's performance, yet realistic enough to realize it is the public's perception of that performance that counts in the long run.

Firms seldom address the question of their public image in an intermittent fashion. Although public agitation often stimulates greater attention to this question, firms are concerned about their public image even in the absence of such agitation. The following excerpt from the mission statement of Intel Corporation is an example of this attitude:

> We are sensitive to our *image with our customers and the business community*. Commitments to customers are considered sacred, and we are upset with ourselves when we do not meet our commitments. We strive to demonstrate to the business world on a continuing basis that

General Motors Environmental Principles

As a responsible corporate citizen, General Motors is dedicated to protecting human health, natural resources, and the global environment. This dedication reaches further than compliance with the law to encompass the integration of sound environmental practices into our business decisions.

The following environmental principles provide guidance to General Motors personnel worldwide in the conduct of their daily business practices:

1. We are committed to actions to restore and preserve the environment.

2. We are committed to reducing waste and pollutants, conserving resources, and recycling materials at every stage of the product life cycle.

3. We will continue to participate actively in educating the public regarding environmental conservation.

4. We will continue to pursue vigorously the development and implementation of technologies for minimizing pollutant emissions.

5. We will continue to work with all governmental entities for the development of technically sound and financially responsible environmental laws and regulations.

6. We will continually assess the impact of our plants and products on the environment and the communities in which we live and operate with a goal of continuous improvement.

Source: General Motors Corporation, http://www.gm.com/

we are credible in describing the state of the corporation, and that we are well organized and in complete control of all things that determine the numbers.

Exhibit 2.6, Strategy in Action, presents a marketing translation of the essence of the mission statements of six high-end shoe companies. The impressive feature of the exhibit is that it shows dramatically how closely competing firms can incorporate subtle, yet meaningful, differences into their mission statements.

Company Self-Concept

A major determinant of a firm's success is the extent to which the firm can relate functionally to its external environment. To achieve its proper place in a competitive situation, the firm realistically must evaluate its competitive strengths and weaknesses. This idea—that the firm must know itself—is the essence of the company self-concept. The idea is not commonly integrated into theories of strategic management; its importance for individuals has been recognized since ancient times.

Both individuals and firms have a crucial need to know themselves. The ability of either to survive in a dynamic and highly competitive environment would be severely limited if they did not understand their impact on others or of others on them.

In some senses, then, firms take on personalities of their own. Much behavior in firms is organizationally based; that is, a firm acts on its members in other ways than their individual interactions. Thus, firms are entities whose personality transcends the personalities of their members. As such, they can set decision-making parameters based on aims different and distinct from the aims of their members. These organizational considerations have pervasive effects.

Ordinarily, descriptions of the company self-concept per se do not appear in mission statements. Yet such statements often provide strong impressions of the company self-concept. For example, ARCO's environment, health, and safety (EHS) managers were adamant about emphasizing the company's position on safety and environmental performance as a part of the mission statement. The challenges facing the ARCO EHS managers included dealing with concerned environmental groups and a public that has become environmentally

Mission Statements for the High-End Shoe Industry

ALLEN-EDMONDS

Allen-Edmonds provides high-quality shoes for the affluent consumer who appreciates a well-made, finely crafted, stylish dress shoe.

BALLY

Bally shoes set you apart. They are the perfect shoe to complement your lifestyle. Bally shoes project an image of European style and elegance that ensures one is not just dressed, but well dressed.

BOSTONIAN

Bostonian shoes are for those successful individuals who are well-traveled, on the "go" and want a stylish dress shoe that can keep up with their variety of needs and activities. With Bostonian, you know you will always be well dressed whatever the situation.

COLE HAAN

Cole Haan offers a line of contemporary shoes for the man who wants to go his own way. They are shoes for the urban, upscale, stylish man who wants to project an image of being one step ahead.

FLORSHEIM

Florsheim shoes are the affordable classic men's dress shoes for those who want to experience the comfort and style of a solid dress shoe.

JOHNSTON & MURPHY

Johnston & Murphy is the quintessential business shoe for those affluent individuals who know and demand the best.

Source: "Thinking on Your Feet, the Johnston & Murphy Guerrilla Marketing Competition" (Johnston & Murphy, a GENESCO Company).

aware. They hoped to motivate employees toward safer behavior while reducing emissions and waste. They saw this as a reflection of the company's positive self-image.

The following excerpts from the Intel Corporation mission statement describe the corporate persona that its top management seeks to foster:

Management is self-critical. The leaders must be capable of recognizing and accepting their mistakes and learning from them.

Open (constructive) confrontation is encouraged at all levels of the corporation and is viewed as a method of problem solving and conflict resolution.

Decision by consensus is the rule. Decisions once made are supported. Position in the organization is not the basis for quality of ideas.

A highly communicative, open management is part of the style.

Management must be ethical. Managing by telling the truth and treating all employees equitably has established credibility that is ethical.

We strive to provide an opportunity for rapid development.

Intel is a results-oriented company. The focus is on substance versus form, quality versus quantity.

We believe in the principle that hard work, high productivity is something to be proud of.

The concept of assumed responsibility is accepted. (If a task needs to be done, assume you have the responsibility to get it done.)

Commitments are long term. If career problems occur at some point, reassignment is a better alternative than termination.

We desire to have all employees involved and participative in their relationship with Intel.

Newest Trends in Mission Components

Three issues have become so prominent in the strategic planning for organizations that they are now integral parts in the development and revisions of mission statements: sensitivity to consumer wants, concern for quality, and statements of company vision.

Mission Statements Express Attention to Customer Needs

The following excerpts from corporate mission statements express the companies' concern for satisfying the needs of their customers.

Bank of Montreal—"Our first responsibility is to our customers."

Bank of Nova Scotia—"Our core purpose is to be the best at helping customers become financially better off. This guides all our decisions."

BT (British Telecommunications)—"Our vision is to be dedicated to helping customers thrive in a changing world. The world we live in and the way we communicate are changing, and we believe in progress, growth and possibility. We want to help all our customers make their lives and businesses better with products and services that are tailored to their needs and easy to use."

Sun Life Financial—"Our mission is to help customers achieve lifetime financial security. Our vision is to be an international leader in protection and wealth management."

Customers

"The customer is our top priority" is a slogan that would be claimed by the majority of businesses in the United States and abroad. For companies including Caterpillar Tractor, General Electric, and Johnson & Johnson this means analyzing consumer needs before as well as after a sale. The bonus plan at Xerox allows for a 40 percent annual bonus, based on high customer reviews of the service that they receive, and a 20 percent penalty if the feedback is especially bad. For these firms and many others, the overriding concern for the company has become consumer satisfaction.

In addition many U.S. firms maintain extensive product safety programs to help ensure consumer satisfaction. GE, Sears, and 3M boast of such programs. Other firms including Calgon Corporation, Amoco, Mobil Oil, Whirlpool, and Zenith provide toll-free telephone lines to answer customer concerns and complaints.

A focus on customer satisfaction causes managers to realize the importance of providing quality customer service. Strong customer service initiatives have led some firms to gain competitive advantages in the marketplace. Hence, many corporations have made the customer service initiative a key component of their corporate mission. Strategy in Action Exhibit 2.7 provides clear examples. It shows excerpts from four corporations that specifically state their commitment to satisfying their customers' needs.

Quality

"Quality is job one!" is a rallying point not only for Ford Motor Corporation but for many resurging U.S. businesses as well. Two U.S. management experts fostered a worldwide emphasis on quality in manufacturing. W. Edwards Deming and J. M. Juran's messages were first embraced by Japanese managers, whose quality consciousness led to global dominance in several industries including automobile, TV, audio equipment, and electronic components manufacturing. Deming summarizes his approach in 14 now well-known points:

1. Create constancy of purpose.
2. Adopt the new philosophy.
3. Cease dependence on mass inspection to achieve quality.
4. End the practice of awarding business on price tag alone. Instead, minimize total cost, often accomplished by working with a single supplier.

Commitment to Quality

CADILLAC

The Mission of the Cadillac Motor Company is to engineer, produce, and market the world's finest automobiles known for uncompromised levels of distinctiveness, comfort, convenience, and refined performance. Through its people, who are its strength, Cadillac will continuously improve the quality of its products and services to meet or exceed customer expectations and succeed as a profitable business.

MOTOROLA

Dedication to quality is a way of life at our company, so much so that it goes far beyond rhetorical slogans. Our ongoing program is one of continued improvement reaching out for change, refinement, and even revolution in our pursuit of quality excellence.

It is the objective of Motorola Inc. to produce and provide products and services of the highest quality. In its activities, Motorola will pursue goals aimed at the achievement of quality excellence. These results will be derived from the dedicated efforts of each employee in conjunction with supportive participation from management at all levels of the corporation.

VERIZON COMMUNICATIONS

Verizon's commitment to top quality service is well known. Verizon is the preeminent service provider in the industry. Our legacy of customer service—bolstered by the nation's largest and most reliable network—is unparalleled. And, we continue to make strong progress in delivering on our promise to be the nation's best provider of quality local, data and long distance services.

ZYTEC

Zytec is a company that competes on value; is market driven; provides superior quality and service; builds strong relationship with its customers; and provides technical excellence in its products.

5. Improve constantly the system of production and service.
6. Institute training on the job.
7. Institute leadership.
8. Drive out fear.
9. Break down barriers between departments.
10. Eliminate slogans, exhortations, and numerical targets.
11. Eliminate work standards (quotas) and management by objective.
12. Remove barriers that rob workers, engineers, and managers of their right to pride of workmanship.
13. Institute a vigorous program of education and self-improvement.
14. Put everyone in the company to work to accomplish the transformation.

Firms in the United States responded aggressively. The new philosophy is that quality should be the norm. For example, Motorola's production goal is 60 or fewer defects per every billion components that it manufactures.

Exhibit 2.8, Strategy in Action, presents the integration of the quality initiative into the mission statements of three corporations. The emphasis on quality has received added emphasis in many corporate philosophies since Congress created the Malcolm Baldrige Quality Award. Each year up to two Baldrige Awards can be given in three categories of a company's operations: manufacturing, services, and small businesses.

vision statement
A statement that presents a firm's strategic intent designed to focus the energies and resources of the company on achieving a desirable future.

Vision Statement

Whereas the mission statement expresses an answer to the question "What business are we in?" a company **vision statement** is sometimes developed to express the aspirations of the executive leadership. A vision statement presents the firm's strategic intent that focuses the

Examples of Vision Statements

ALLIANCE CORPORATE VISION

Alliance is the most innovative and feature rich ACH processing platform available to client originators today and will remain on the cutting edge for electronic funds transfer services.

AMD CORPORATE VISION

A connected global population.

CUTCO CORPORATE VISION

To become the largest, most respected and widely recognized cutlery company in the world.

FEDERAL EXPRESS CORPORATE VISION

Our vision is to change the way we all connect with each other in the New Network Economy.

FIRSTENERGY CORPORATE VISION

FirstEnergy will be a leading regional energy provider, recognized for operational excellence and service; the choice for long-term growth, investment, value and financial strength; and a company committed to safety and driven by the leadership, skills, diversity, and character of its employees.

FORD MOTOR COMPANY CORPORATE VISION

Ford Motor Company's vision is to become the world's leading consumer company for automotive products and services.

GENERAL ELECTRIC CORPORATE VISION

We bring good things to life.

MAGNA CORPORATE VISION

Magna's corporate vision is to provide world class services that help maximize the customer's ROI (Return on Investment) and promote teamwork and creativity. The company strongly believes in the corporate philosophy of fulfilling its commitments to its customers.

MICROSOFT CORPORATE VISION

Microsoft's vision is to enable people and businesses throughout the world to realize their full potential.

---

energies and resources of the company on achieving a desirable future. However, in actual practice, the mission and vision statement are frequently combined into a single statement. When they are separated, the vision statement is often a single sentence, designed to be memorable. For examples, see Exhibit 2.9, Strategy in Action.

Vision statements can also be used to refocus the attention of investors and the public. In 2011, following a series of car recalls that damaged Toyota's reputation for quality, the company issued a vision statement to assure car buyers that the company had recognized its shortcomings and was committed to superior future performance, as explained in Exhibit 2.10, Global Strategy in Action.

An Exemplary Mission Statement

When BB&T merged with Southern Bank, the board of directors and officers undertook the creation of a comprehensive mission statement that was designed to include most of the topics that we discussed in this chapter. The company updated its statement and mailed the resulting booklet to its shareholders and other interested parties. The foreword to the document expresses the greatest values of such a public pronouncement and was signed by BB&T's chairman and CEO, John A. Allison:

> In a rapidly changing and unpredictable world, individuals and organizations need a clear set of fundamental principles to guide their actions. At BB&T we know the content of our business will, and should, experience constant change. Change is necessary for progress. However, the context, our fundamental principles, is unchanging because these principles are based on basic truths.

After Recall Debacle, Toyota Outlines a New Global Vision

Toyota Motor Corp. is aiming for an auto industry first by reaching annual sales of 10 million vehicles by 2015 even as it acknowledges that overly rapid growth was at the root of its recall fiasco. Toyota President Akio Toyoda gave the 10 million figure while outlining the company's "global vision" in his first major strategy announcement since the recall crisis that hit a year and a half ago.

The Japanese automaker reported worldwide sales of 8.42 million vehicles in 2010—30,000 more than General Motors Co.'s 8.39 million. Toyota dethroned GM as the world's No. 1 automaker by vehicle sales in 2008—a position GM held for 76 years.

Speaking at a Tokyo hotel, Toyoda said the carmaker wants to make millions of customers happy, and even denied he was giving a numerical sales target. He repeatedly emphasized goals like quality controls, customer satisfaction and solid profits.

Toyota, which makes the Prius hybrid and Lexus luxury models, hopes to achieve an annual operating profit of 1 trillion yen ($12 billion) "as soon as possible," even if the yen remains strong and vehicle sales drop by 20 percent, Toyoda said.

Analyst Jesse Toprak, vice president of Industry Trends and Insights at TrueCar.com, said the vision was too short on specifics such as model plans and marketing strategies. "It was a little bit too wishy-washy. We need to see more concrete examples of what needs to be done," he said in a telephone interview. "There was a lot of wishful thinking."

Since late 2009, Toyota has announced recall after recall, covering a wide range of defects, including faulty floor mats, sticky gas pedals and glitches in braking software, ballooning to more than 14 million vehicles globally. The company paid the U.S. government a record $48.8 million in fines for its handling of three recalls. Toyota faces dozens of lawsuits from owners in the United States, including fatalities allegedly linked to defects. The company has said quality problems emerged as it went through a period of rapid growth.

Toyoda said the automaker's board of directors will be reduced to 11 from 27, but the number of executives overseas will be boosted to 15 from 13, to make for quicker decision making and to be more responsive to regional needs.

Toyota will also empower its regions, including North America, which will center around development and production of the Camry sedan, to better cater to their needs, he said. The automaker will also focus more on emerging markets for new growth, aiming for 50 percent of its sales from those nations, up from the current 40 percent. It said green vehicles are another pillar for the future, planning to launch 10 more hybrid models by 2015.

Another big change from past visions, where the numbers game was big, was that the latest was written in English, which Toyoda said was the world's international language. Toyoda often switched into English during the presentation, using phrases like "smiles from customers around the world," and "our commitment to quality and constant innovation." "This vision is about what kind of company we are, our values and the road to what kind of company we want to be," Toyoda said.

Source: Excerpted from Yuri Kageyama, "After Recall Debacle, Toyota Outlines a New Global Vision," *The Associated Press*, March 9, 2011.

BB&T is a mission-driven organization with a clearly defined set of values. We encourage our employees to have a strong sense of purpose, a high level of self-esteem and the capacity to think clearly and logically.

We believe that competitive advantage is largely in the minds of our employees as represented by their capacity to turn rational ideas into action towards the accomplishment of our mission.

The Chapter 2 Appendix presents BB&T's vision, mission, and purpose statement in its entirety. It also includes detailed expressions of the company's values and views on the role of emotions, management style, the management concept, attributes of an outstanding employee, the importance of positive attitude, obligations to its employees, virtues of an outstanding credit culture, achieving the company goal, the nature of a "world standard" revenue-driven sales organization, the nature of a "world standard" client service community bank, the company's commitment to education and learning, and its passions.

BOARDS OF DIRECTORS

board of directors
The group of stockholder representatives and strategic managers responsible for overseeing the creation and accomplishment of the company mission.

Who is responsible for determining the firm's mission? Who is responsible for acquiring and allocating resources so the firm can thoughtfully develop and implement a strategic plan? Who is responsible for monitoring the firm's success in the competitive marketplace to determine whether that plan was well designed and activated? The answer to all of these questions is strategic decision makers. Most organizations have multiple levels of strategic decision makers; typically, the larger the firm, the more levels it will have. The strategic managers at the highest level are responsible for decisions that affect the entire firm, commit the firm and its resources for the longest periods, and declare the firm's sense of values. In other words, this group of strategic managers is responsible for overseeing the creation and accomplishment of the company mission. The term that describes the group is **board of directors.**

In overseeing the management of a firm, the board of directors operates as the representatives of the firm's stockholders. Elected by the stockholders, the board has these major responsibilities:

1. To establish and update the company mission.
2. To elect the company's top officers, the foremost of whom is the CEO.
3. To establish the compensation levels of the top officers, including their salaries and bonuses.
4. To determine the amount and timing of the dividends paid to stockholders.
5. To set broad company policy on such matters as labor–management relations, product or service lines of business, and employee benefit packages.
6. To set company objectives and to authorize managers to implement the long-term strategies that the top officers and the board have found agreeable.
7. To mandate company compliance with legal and ethical dictates.

In the current business environment, boards of directors are accepting the challenge of shareholders and other stakeholders to become active in establishing the strategic initiatives of the companies that they serve. For example, a more involved role for the BP board of directors was necessitated by the Deepwater Horizon oil spill, more often called the BP oil disaster. An oil spill in the Gulf of Mexico that lasted from April–July, 2010, it was the largest accidental marine oil spill in the history of the petroleum industry. The spill resulted from an offshore explosion that killed 11 men working on a platform. It released about 4.9 million barrels of crude oil into the Gulf, which caused extensive damage to marine and wildlife habitats as well as the Gulf's fishing and tourism industries. The U.S. government named BP as the responsible party and holds the company accountable for all cleanup costs and damage. To clarify its values, the duties of its board of directors, and its position on corporate governance and risk management, BP releases an annual Sustainability Review. A key excerpt from the 2012 review appears as Exhibit 2.11, Global Strategy in Action.

This chapter considers the board of directors because the board's greatest impact on the behavior of a firm results from its determination of the company mission. The philosophy espoused in the mission statement sets the tone by which the firm and all of its employees will be judged. As logical extensions of the mission statement, the firm's objectives and strategies embody the board's view of proper business demeanor. Through its appointment

BP's Sustainability Report on Its Corporate Governance and Risk Management[1]

MANAGING RISK FROM OPERATIONS TO THE BOARD

Our risk management system focuses on three levels of activity:

- Day-to-day risk identification and management occurs in the group's operations and functions, with the approach varying according to the types of risks faced. The aim is to address each different type of risk as well as we can—promoting safe, compliant and reliable operations.
- Periodic review of risks and risk management plans happens at the business and functional levels. Risk management activities are assessed and any further improvements are planned.
- Oversight and governance occurs at board, executive and function levels to help foster effective group-wide oversight, business planning and resource allocation, intervention and knowledge sharing.

THE BOARD

BP's board governance principles delegate management authority to the group chief executive within defined limits. These include a requirement that the group chief executive will not engage in any activity without regard to health, safety and environmental consequence. The board reviews key group risks and how they are managed as part of its planning process. On 1 January 2013 the board was composed of the chairman, four executive directors and 10 non-executive directors. BP recognizes the importance of diversity, including gender, at all levels of the company, including the board.

SAFETY, ETHICS AND ENVIRONMENT ASSURANCE COMMITTEE

The safety, ethics and environment assurance committee (SEA) monitors the management of non-financial risk. In 2012, the committee received specific reports on the company's management of risks in shipping, wells, pipelines, explosion or release at facilities containing hydrocarbons, contractor management and non-operated joint ventures. The committee reviewed these risks, and their management and mitigation, in detail with the relevant executive management.

BP'S MANAGEMENT OF SUSTAINABILITY RISKS AND ISSUES

BP Board
Direction and oversight of BP on behalf of the shareholders for all aspects of BP's business. Comprised of the chairman, four executive and 10 non-executive directors.

Safety, Ethics and Environment Assurance Committee	Gulf of Mexico Committee
Reviews BP's processes to identify and mitigate significant nonfinancial risks and receives assurances that they are appropriate in design and effective in implementation.	Oversees the Gulf Coast Restoration Organization and various other matters related to the Deepwater Horizon incident.

Executive Team
Supports the group chief executive in his accountability to the board for BP's overall business, including sustainability performance. Comprised of the group chief executive and the heads of businesses and certain functions including safety and operational risk.

Group Operations Risk Committee	Group Ethics and Compliance Committe	Group People Committee
Reviews comany safety and risk management.	Provides information and assurance on the ethics and compliance programme.	Has overall responsibility for policy decisions relating to employees.

Group Functions	Local Operations
Functions, such as safety and operational risk, define and support implementation of group-wide standards.	Specialists and line management identify risks and implement our group-wide operating managment system and other standards.

MANAGING OPERATIONAL RISK

Our safety and operational risk (S&OR) function supports the business in delivering safe, reliable and compliant operations across the business. S&OR:

- Sets clear requirements.
- Maintains an independent view of operating risk.
- Provides deep technical support to the operating businesses.
- Intervenes and escalates as appropriate to cause corrective action.

S&OR consists of a central team and teams deployed in BP's businesses. All teams report to the group chief executive via the head of S&OR, independently of the business line. S&OR includes some of BP's top engineers and safety specialists, several of whom have prior experience in industries where major hazards have to be managed, including the military, nuclear energy and space exploration.

[1] Source: The content in this exhibit was excerpted from the *BP Sustainability Review 2012*, pp. 24–24. bp.com/sustainability

of top executives and its decisions about their compensation, the board reveals its priorities for organizational achievement.

AGENCY THEORY

agency theory
A set of ideas on organizational control based on the belief that the separation of the ownership from management creates the potential for the wishes of owners to be ignored.

Whenever there is a separation of the owners (principals) and the managers (agents) of a firm, the potential exists for the wishes of the owners to be ignored. This fact, and the recognition that agents are expensive, established the basis for a set of complex but helpful ideas known as **agency theory.** Whenever owners (or managers) delegate decision-making authority to others, an agency relationship exists between the two parties. Agency relationships, such as those between stockholders and managers, can be very effective as long as managers make investment decisions in ways that are consistent with stockholders' interests. However, when the interests of managers diverge from those of owners, then managers' decisions are more likely to reflect the managers' preferences than the owners' preferences.

In general, owners seek stock value maximization. When managers hold important blocks of company stock, they too prefer strategies that result in stock appreciation. However, when managers better resemble "hired hands" than owner-partners, they often prefer strategies that increase their personal payoffs rather than those of shareholders. Such behavior can result in decreased stock performance (as when high executive bonuses reduce corporate earnings) and in strategic decisions that point the firm in the direction of outcomes that are suboptimal from a stockholder's perspective.

agency costs
The cost of agency problems and the cost of actions taken to minimize them.

If, as agency theory argues, self-interested managers act in ways that increase their own welfare at the expense of the gain of corporate stockholders, then owners who delegate decision-making authority to their agents will incur both the loss of potential gain that would have resulted from owner-optimal strategies and/or the costs of monitoring and control systems that are designed to minimize the consequences of such self-centered management decisions. In combination, the cost of agency problems and the cost of actions taken to minimize agency problems are called **agency costs.** These costs can often be identified by their direct benefit for the agents and their negative present value. Agency costs are found when there are differing self-interests between shareholders and managers, superiors and subordinates, or managers of competing departments or branch offices.

How Agency Problems Occur

moral hazard problem
An agency problem that occurs because owners have limited access to company information, making executives free to pursue their own interests.

Because owners have access to only a relatively small portion of the information that is available to executives about the performance of the firm and cannot afford to monitor every executive decision or action, executives are often free to pursue their own interests. This condition is known as the **moral hazard problem.** It is also called shirking to suggest "self-interest combined with smile."

As a result of moral hazards, executives may design strategies that provide the greatest possible benefits for themselves, with the welfare of the organization being given only secondary consideration. For example, executives may presell products at year-end to trigger their annual bonuses even though the deep discounts that they must offer will threaten the price stability of their products for the upcoming year. Similarly, unchecked executives may advance their own self-interests by slacking on the job; altering forecasts to maximize their performance bonuses; unrealistically assessing acquisition targets' outlooks in order to increase the probability of increasing organizational size through their acquisition; or manipulating personnel records to keep or acquire key company personnel.

adverse selection
An agency problem caused by the limited ability of stockholders to precisely determine the competencies and priorities of executives at the time they are hired.

The second major reason that agency costs are incurred is known as **adverse selection.** This refers to the limited ability that stockholders have to precisely determine the competencies and priorities of executives at the time that they are hired. Because principals cannot initially verify an executive's appropriateness as an agent of the owners, unanticipated problems of nonoverlapping priorities between owners and agents are likely to occur.

The most popular solution to moral dilemma and adverse selection problems is for owners to attempt to more closely align their own best interests with those of their agents through the use of executive bonus plans. Foremost among these approaches are stock option plans, which enable executives to benefit directly from the appreciation of the company's stock just as other stockholders do. In most instances, executive bonus plans are unabashed attempts to align the interests of owners and executives and to thereby induce executives to support strategies that increase stockholder wealth. While such schemes are unlikely to eliminate self-interest as a major criterion in executive decision making, they help to reduce the costs associated with moral dilemmas and adverse selections.

Problems That Can Result from Agency

From a strategic management perspective there are five different kinds of problems that can arise because of the agency relationship between corporate stockholders and their company's executives:

1. Executives pursue growth in company size rather than in earnings. Shareholders generally want to maximize earnings, because earnings growth yields stock appreciation. However, because managers are typically more heavily compensated for increases in firm size than for earnings growth, they may recommend strategies that yield company growth such as mergers and acquisitions.

In addition, managers' stature in the business community is commonly associated with company size. Managers gain prominence by directing the growth of an organization, and they benefit in the forms of career advancement and job mobility that are associated with increases in company size.

Finally, executives need an enlarging set of advancement opportunities for subordinates whom they wish to motivate with nonfinancial inducements. Acquisitions can provide the needed positions.

2. Executives attempt to diversify their corporate risk. Whereas stockholders can vary their investment risks through management of their individual stock portfolios, managers' careers and stock incentives are tied to the performance of a single corporation, albeit the one that employs them. Consequently, executives are tempted to diversify their corporation's operation, businesses, and product lines to moderate the risk incurred in any single venture. While this approach serves the executives' personal agendas, it compromises the "pure play" quality of their firm as an investment. In other words, diversifying a corporation reduces the beta associated with the firm's return, which is an undesirable outcome for many stockholders.

3. Executives avoid risk. Even when, or perhaps especially when, executives are willing to restrict the diversification of their companies, they are tempted to minimize the risk that they face. Executives are often fired for failure, but rarely for mediocre corporate performance. Therefore, executives may avoid desirable levels of risk if they anticipate little reward and opt for conservative strategies that minimize the risk of company failure. If they do, executives will rarely support plans for innovation, diversification, and rapid growth.

However, from an investor's perspective, risk taking is desirable when it is systematic. In other words, when investors can reasonably expect that their company will generate higher long-term returns from assuming greater risk, they may wish to pursue the greater payoff, especially when the company is positioned to perform better than its competitors that face the same nominal risks. Obviously, the agency relationship creates a problem—should executives prioritize their job security or the company's financial returns to stockholders?

4. Managers act to optimize their personal payoffs. If executives can gain more from an annual performance bonus by achieving objective 1 than from stock appreciation resulting from the achievement of objective 2, then owners must anticipate that the executives will target objective 1 as their priority, even though objective 2 is clearly in the best interest of the shareholders. Similarly, executives may pursue a range of expensive perquisites that have a net negative effect on shareholder returns. Elegant corner offices, corporate jets, large staffs, golf club memberships, extravagant retirement programs, and limousines for executive benefit are rarely good investments for stockholders.

5. Executives act to protect their status. When their companies expand, executives want to ensure that their knowledge, experience, and skills remain relevant and central to the strategic direction of the corporation. They favor doing more of what they already do well. In contrast, investors may prefer revolutionary advancement to incremental improvement. For example, when confronted with Amazon.com, competitor Barnes & Noble initiated a joint venture Web site with Bertelsmann. In addition, Barnes & Noble used vertical integration with the nation's largest book distributor, which supplies 60 percent of Amazon's books. This type of revolutionary strategy is most likely to occur when executives are given assurances that they will not make themselves obsolete within the changing company that they create.

Solutions to the Agency Problem

In addition to defining an agent's responsibilities in a contract and including elements like bonus incentives that help align executives' and owners' interests, principals can take several other actions to minimize agency problems. The first is for the owners to pay executives a premium for their service. This premium helps executives to see their loyalty to the stockholders as the key to achieving their personal financial targets.

A second solution to agency problems is for executives to receive backloaded compensation. This means that executives are paid a handsome premium for superior future performance. Strategic actions taken in year one, which are to have an impact in year three, become the basis for executive bonuses in year three. This lag time between action and bonus more realistically rewards executives for the consequences of their decision making, ties the executive to the company for the long term, and properly focuses strategic management activities on the future.

Finally, creating teams of executives across different units of a corporation can help to focus performance measures on organizational rather than personal goals. Through the use of executive teams, owner interests often receive the priority that they deserve.

Summary

Defining the company mission is the critical first step in strategic management. Emphasizing the operational aspects of long-range management activities comes much more easily for most executives. But the foundational role of the mission statement repeatedly is demonstrated by failing firms whose short-run actions have been at odds with their long-run purposes.

The principal value of the mission statement is its specification of the firm's ultimate aims. A firm gains a heightened sense of purpose when its board of directors and its top executives address these issues: "What business are we in?" "What customers do we serve?"

"Why does this organization exist?" However, the potential contribution of the company mission can be undermined if platitudes or ambiguous generalizations are accepted in response to these questions. It is not enough to say that Lever Brothers is in the business of "making anything that cleans anything" or that Polaroid is committed to businesses that deal with "the interaction of light and matter." Only when a firm clearly articulates its long-term intentions can its goals serve as a basis for shared expectations, planning, and performance evaluation.

A mission statement that is developed from this perspective provides managers with a unity of direction transcending individual, parochial, and temporary needs. It promotes a sense of shared expectations among all levels and generations of employees. It consolidates values over time and across individuals and interest groups. It projects a sense of worth and intent that can be identified and assimilated by outside stakeholders, that is, customers, suppliers, competitors, local committees, and the general public. Finally, it asserts the firm's commitment to responsible action in symbiosis with the preservation and protection of the essential claims of insider stakeholders' survival, growth, and profitability.

Key Terms

adverse selection, *p.* 39
agency costs, *p.* 38
agency theory, *p.* 38

board of directors, *p.* 36
company creed, *p.* 27
company mission, *p.* 23

moral hazard problem, *p.* 38
vision statement, *p.* 33

Questions for Discussion

1. Reread Nicor Inc.'s mission statement in Exhibit 2.1, Strategy in Action. List five insights into Nicor that you feel you gained from knowing its mission.
2. Locate the mission statement of a company not mentioned in the chapter. Where did you find it? Was it presented as a consolidated statement, or were you forced to assemble it yourself from various publications of the firm? How many of the mission statement elements outlined in this chapter were discussed or revealed in the statement you found?
3. Prepare a two-page typewritten mission statement for your school of business or for a firm selected by your instructor.
4. List five potentially vulnerable areas of a firm without a stated company mission.
5. Mission statements are often criticized for being lists of platitudes. What can strategic managers do to prevent their statements from appearing to be simple statements of obvious truths?
6. What evidence do you see that mission statements are valuable?
7. How can a mission statement be an enduring statement of values and simultaneously provide a basis of competitive advantage?
8. If the goal of survival refers to ability to maintain a specific legal form, what are the comparative advantages of sole proprietorships, partnerships, and corporations?
9. In the 1990s many Nasdaq firms favored growth over profitability; in the 2012s the goal of profitability is displacing growth. How might each preference be explained?
10. Do you agree that a mission statement provides substantive guidance while a vision statement provides inspirational guidance? Explain.

Chapter 2 Appendix

BB&T Vision, Mission, and Purpose

BB&T Vision

To create the best financial institution possible: *"The Best of The Best."*

BB&T Mission

To make the world a better place to live by: helping our clients achieve economic success and financial security; creating a place where our employees can learn, grow and be fulfilled in their work; making the communities in which we work better places to be; and thereby: optimizing the long-term return to our shareholders, while providing a safe and sound investment.

BB&T Purpose

Our ultimate purpose is to create superior long-term economic rewards for our shareholders.

This purpose is defined by the free market and is as it should be. Our shareholders provide the capital that is necessary to make our business possible. They take the risk if the business is unsuccessful. They have the right to receive economic rewards for the risk which they have undertaken.

However, our purpose, to create superior long-term economic rewards for our shareholders, can only be accomplished by providing excellent service to our clients, as our clients are our source of revenues.

To have excellent client relations, we must have outstanding employees to serve our clients. To attract and retain outstanding employees, we must reward them financially and create an environment where they can learn and grow.

Our economic results are significantly impacted by the success of our communities. The community's "quality of life" impacts its ability to attract industry for growth.

Therefore, we manage our business in a long-term context, as an integrated whole, with the ultimate objective of rewarding the shareholders for their investment, while realizing that the cause of this result is quality client service. Excellent service will be delivered by motivated employees working as an integrated team. These results will be impacted by our capacity to contribute to the growth and well-being of the communities we serve.

Values

"Excellence is an art won by training and habituation. We are what we repeatedly do. Excellence then is not an act, but a habit."—Aristotle

The great Greek philosophers saw values as guides to excellence in thinking and action. In this context, values are standards which we strive to achieve. Values are practical habits that enable us as individuals to live, be successful and achieve happiness. For BB&T, our values enable us to achieve our mission and corporate purpose.

To be useful, values must be consciously held and be consistent (noncontradictory). Many people have conflicting values which prevent them from acting with clarity and self-confidence.

There are 10 primary values at BB&T. These values are consistent with one another and are integrated. To fully act on one of these values, you must also act consistently with the other values. Our focus on values grows from our belief that ideas matter and that an individual's character is of critical significance.

Values are important at BB&T!

1. Reality (Fact-Based)

What is, is. If we want to be better, we must act within the context of reality (the facts). Businesses and individuals often make serious mistakes by making decisions based on what they "wish was so," or based on theories which are disconnected from reality. The foundation for quality decision making is a careful understanding of the facts.

There is a fundamental difference between the laws of nature (reality), which are immutable, and the man-made. The law of gravity is the law of gravity. The existence of the law of gravity does not mean man cannot create an airplane. However, an airplane must be created within the context of the law of gravity. At BB&T, we believe in being "reality grounded."

2. Reason (Objectivity)

Mankind has a specific means of survival, which is his ability to think, i.e., his capacity to reason logically from the facts of reality as presented to his five senses. A lion has claws to hunt. A deer has swiftness to avoid the hunter. Man has his ability to think. There is only one "natural resource"—the human mind.

Clear thinking is not automatic. It requires intellectual discipline and begins with sound premises based on observed facts. You must be able to draw general conclusions in a rational manner from specific examples (induction) and be able to apply general principles to the solution of specific problems (deduction). You must be able to think in an integrated way, thereby avoiding logical contradictions.

We cannot all be geniuses, but each of us can develop the mental habits which ensure that when making decisions we carefully examine the facts and think logically without contradiction in deriving a conclusion. We must learn to think in terms of what is essential, i.e., about what is important. Our goal is to objectively make the best decision to accomplish our purpose.

Rational thinking is a learned skill which requires mental focus and a fundamental commitment to consistently improving the clarity of our mental processes. At BB&T, we are looking for people who are committed to constantly improving their ability to reason.

3. Independent Thinking

All employees are challenged to use their individual minds to their optimum to make rational decisions. In this context, each of us is *responsible* for what we do and who we are. In addition, creativity is strongly encouraged and only possible with independent thought.

We learn a great deal from each other. Teamwork is important at BB&T (as will be discussed later). However, each of us thinks alone. Our minds are not physically connected. In this regard, each of us must be willing to make an independent judgment of the facts based on our capacity to think logically. Just because the "crowd" says it is so, does not make it so.

In this context, each of us is responsible for our own actions. Each of us is responsible for our personal success or failure; that is, it is not the bank's fault if someone does not achieve his objectives.

All human progress by definition is based on creativity, because creativity is the source of positive change. Creativity is only possible to an independent thinker. Creativity is not about just doing something different. It is about doing something better. To be better, the new method/process must be judged by its impact on the whole organization, and as to whether it contributes to the accomplishment of our mission.

There is an infinite opportunity for each of us to do whatever we do better. A significant aspect of the self-fulfillment which work can provide comes from creative thought and action.

4. Productivity

We are committed to being producers of wealth and well-being by taking the actions necessary to accomplish our mission. The tangible evidence of our productivity is that we have rationally allocated capital through our lending and investment process, and that we have provided needed services to our clients in an efficient manner resulting in superior profitability.

Profitability is a measure of the differences in the economic value of the products/services we produce and the cost of producing these products/services. In a long-term context and in a free market, the bigger the profit, the better. This is true not only from our shareholders' perspective (which would be enough justification), but also in terms of the impact of our work on society as a whole. Healthy profits represent productive work. At BB&T we are looking for people who want to create, to produce, and who are thereby committed to turning their thoughts into actions that improve economic well-being.

5. Honesty

Being honest is simply being consistent with reality. To be dishonest is to be in conflict with reality, which is therefore self-defeating. A primary reason that individuals fail is because they become disconnected from reality, pretending that facts are other than they are.

To be honest does not require that we know everything. Knowledge is always contextual and man is not omniscient. However, we must be responsible for saying what we mean and meaning what we say.

6. Integrity

Because we have developed our principles logically, based on reality, we will always act consistently with our principles. Regardless of the short-term benefits, acting inconsistently with our principles is to our long-term detriment. We do not, therefore, believe in compromising our principles in any situation.

Principles provide carefully thought-out concepts which will lead to our long-term success and happiness. Violating our principles will always lead to failure. BB&T is an organization of the highest integrity.

7. Justice (Fairness)

Individuals should be evaluated and rewarded objectively (for better or worse) based on their contributions toward accomplishing our mission and adherence to our values. Those who contribute the most should receive the most.

The single most significant way in which employees evaluate their managers is in determining whether the manager is just. Employees become extremely unhappy (and rightly so) when they perceive that a person who is not contributing is overrewarded or a strong contributor is underrewarded.

If we do not reward those who contribute the most, they will leave and our organization will be less successful. Even more important, if there is no reward for superior performance, the average person will not be motivated to maximize his productivity.

We must evaluate whether the food we eat is healthy, the clothes we wear attractive, the car we drive functional, etc., and we must also evaluate whether relationships with other people are good for us or not.

In evaluating other people, it is critical that we judge based on essentials. At BB&T we do not discriminate based on nonessentials such as race, sex, nationality, etc. We do discriminate based on competency, performance and character. We consciously reject egalitarianism and collectivism. Individuals must be judged individually based on their personal merits, not their membership in any group.

8. Pride

Pride is the psychological reward we earn from living by our values, that is, from being just, honest, having integrity, being an independent thinker, being productive and rational.

Aristotle believed that "earned" pride (not arrogance) was the highest of virtues, because it presupposed all the others. Striving for earned pride simply reinforces the importance of having high moral values.

Each of us must perform our work in a manner as to be able to be justly proud of what we have accomplished. BB&T must be the kind of organization with which each employee and client can be proud to be associated.

9. Self-Esteem (Self-Motivation)

We expect our employees to earn positive self-esteem from doing their work well. We expect and want our employees to act in their rational, long-term self-interest. We want employees who have strong personal goals and who expect to be able to accomplish their goals within the context of our mission.

A necessary attribute for self-esteem is self-motivation. We have a strong work ethic. We believe that you receive from your work in proportion to how much you contribute. If you do not want to work hard, work somewhere else.

While there are many trade-offs in the content of life, you need to be clear that BB&T is the best place, all things considered, for you to work to accomplish your long-term goals. When you know this, you can be more productive and happy.

10. Teamwork/Mutual Supportiveness

While independent thought and strong personal goals are critically important, our work is accomplished within teams. Each of us must consistently act to achieve the agreed-upon objectives of the team, with respect for our fellow employees, while acting in a mutually supportive manner.

Our work at BB&T is so complex that it requires an integrated effort among many people to accomplish important tasks. While we are looking for self-motivated and independent thinking individuals, these individuals must recognize that almost nothing at BB&T can be accomplished without the help of their team members. One of the responsibilities of leadership in our organization is to ensure that each individual is rewarded based on their contribution to the success of the total team. We need outstanding individuals working together to create an outstanding team.

Our values are held consciously and are logically consistent. To fully execute on any one value, you must act consistently with all 10 values. At BB&T values are practical and important.

The Role of Emotions

Often people believe that making logical decisions means that we should be unemotional and that emotions are thereby unimportant. In fact, emotions are important. However, the real issue is how rational are our emotions. Emotions are mental habits which are often developed as children. Emotions give us automatic responses to people and events; these responses can either be very useful or destructive indicators. Emotions as such are not means of decision or of knowledge; the issue is: How were your emotions formed? The real question is,

Are we happy when we should be happy, and unhappy when we should be unhappy, or are we unhappy when we should be happy?

Emotions are learned behaviors. The goal is to "train up" our emotions so that our emotions objectively reinforce the best decisions and behaviors toward our long-term success and happiness. Just because someone is unemotional does not mean that they are logical.

Concepts That Describe BB&T

1. Client-Driven

"World class" client service organization.

Our clients are our partners.

Our goal is to create win/win relationships.

"You can tell we want your business."

"It is easy to do business with BB&T."

"Respect the individual, value the relationship."

We will absolutely never, ever, take advantage of anyone, nor do we want to do business with those who would take advantage of us. Our clients are long-term partners and should be treated accordingly. One of the attributes of partnerships is that both partners must keep their agreements. We keep our agreements. When our partners fail to keep their agreements, they are terminating the partnership.

There are an infinite number of opportunities where we can get better together, where we can help our clients achieve their financial goals and where our client will enable us to make a profit in doing so.

2. Quality Oriented

Quality must be built into the process.

In every aspect of our business we want to execute and deliver quality. It is easier and less expensive to do things correctly than to fix what has been done incorrectly.

3. Efficient

"Waste not, want not."

Design efficiency into the system.

4. Growing Both Our Business and Our People

Grow or die.

Life requires constant, focused thought and actions towards one's goals.

5. Continuous Improvement

Everything can be done better.

Fundamental commitment to innovation.

Every employee should constantly use their reasoning ability to do whatever they do better every day. All managers of systems/processes should constantly search for better methods to solve problems and serve the client.

6. Objective Decision Making

Fact-based and rational.

BB&T Management Style

Participative

Team Oriented

Fact-Based

Rational

Objective

Our management process, by intention, is designed to be participative and team oriented. We work hard to create consensus. When people are involved in the decision process, better information is available to make decisions. The participant's understanding of the decision is greater and, therefore, execution is better.

However, there is a risk in participative decision making: the decision process can become a popularity contest. Therefore, our decision process is disciplined. Our decisions will be made based on the facts using reason. The best objective decision will be the one which is enacted.

Therefore, it does not matter whom you know, who your friends are, etc.; it matters whether you can offer the best objective solution to accomplishing the goal or solving the problem at hand.

BB&T Management Concept

Hire excellent people

Train them well

Give them an appropriate level of authority and responsibility

Expect a high level of achievement

Reward their performance

Our concept is to operate a highly autonomous, entrepreneurial organization. In order to execute this concept, we must have extremely competent individuals who are "masters" of BB&T's philosophy and who are "masters" in their field of technical expertise.

By having individuals who are "masters" in their field, we can afford to have less costly control systems and be more responsive in meeting the needs of our clients.

Attributes of an Outstanding BB&T Employee

Purpose

Rationality

Self-esteem

Consistent with our values, successful individuals at BB&T have a sense of purpose for their lives; that is, they believe that their lives matter and that they can accomplish something meaningful through their work. We are looking for people who are rational and have a high level of personal self-esteem. People with a strong personal self-esteem get along better with others, because they are at peace with themselves.

BB&T Positive Attitude

Since we build on the facts of reality and our ability to reason, we are capable of achieving both success and happiness.

We do not believe that "realism" means pessimism. On the contrary, precisely because our goals are based on and consistent with reality, we fully expect to accomplish them.

BB&T'S Obligations to Its Employees

We will do our best to:

Compensate employees fairly in relation to internal equity and market-comparable pay practices—performance-based compensation.

Provide a comprehensive and market-competitive benefit program.

Create a place where employees can learn and grow—to become more productive workers and better people.

Train employees so they are competent to do the work asked of them. (Never ask anyone to do anything they are not trained to do.)

Evaluate and recognize performance objectively, fairly and consistently based on the individual's contribution to the accomplishment of our mission and adherence to our values.

Treat each employee as an individual with dignity and respect.

Virtues of an Outstanding Credit Culture

Just as individuals need a set of values (virtues) to guide their actions, systems should be designed to have a set of attributes which optimize their performance towards our goals. In this regard, our credit culture has seven fundamental virtues:

1. Provides fundamental insight to help clients achieve their economic goals and solve their financial problems: We are in the high-quality financial advice business.
2. Responsive: The client deserves an answer as quickly as possible, even when the answer is no.
3. Flexible (Creative): We are committed to finding better ways to meet the client's financial needs.
4. Reliable: Our clients are selected as long-term partners and treated accordingly. BB&T must continue to earn the right to be known as the most reliable bank.
5. Manages risk within agreed-upon limits: Clients do not want to fail financially, and the bank does not want a bad loan.
6. Ensures an appropriate economic return to the bank for risk taken: The higher the risk, the higher the return. The lower the risk, the lower the return. This is an expression of justice.
7. Creates a "premium" for service delivery: The concept is to provide superior value to the client through outstanding service quality. A rational client will fairly compensate us when we provide sound financial advice, are

responsive, creative and reliable, because these attributes are of economic value to the client.

Strategic Objectives

Create a high performance financial institution that can survive and prosper in a rapidly changing, highly competitive, globally integrated environment.

Achieving Our Goal

The key to maximizing our probability of being both independent and prosperous over the long term is to create a superior earnings per share (EPS) growth rate without sacrificing the fundamental quality and long-term competitiveness of our business and without taking unreasonable risk.

While being fundamentally efficient is critical, the "easy" way to rapid EPS growth is to artificially cut cost. However, not investing for the future is long-term suicide, as it destroys our capability to compete.

The intelligent process to achieve superior EPS growth is to grow revenues by providing (and selling) superior quality service while systematically enhancing our margins, improving our efficiency, expanding our profitable product offerings and creating more effective distribution channels.

The "World Standard" Revenue-Driven Sales Organization

At BB&T, selling is about identifying our clients' legitimate financial needs and finding a way to help the client achieve economic goals by providing the right products and services.

Effective selling requires a disciplined approach in which the BB&T employee asks the client about financial goals and problems and has a complete understanding of how our products can help the client achieve objectives and solve financial problems.

It also requires exceptional execution by support staffs and product managers, since service and sales are fundamentally connected and creativity is required in product design and development.

"World Standard" Client Service Community Banks

BB&T operates as a series of "Community Banks." The "Community Bank" concept is the foundation for local decision making and the basis for responsive, reliable and empathetic client service.

By putting decision making closer to the client, all local factors can be considered, and we can ensure that the client is being treated as an individual.

To operate in this decentralized decision-making fashion, we must have highly trained employees who understand BB&T's philosophy and are "masters" of their areas of responsibility.

Commitment to Education/Learning

Competitive advantage is in the minds of our employees. We are committed to making substantial investments in employee education to create a "knowledge-based learning organization" founded on the premise that knowledge (understanding), properly applied, is the source of superior performance.

We believe in systematized learning founded on Aristotle's concept that "excellence is an art won by training and habituation." We attempt to train our employees with the best knowledge/methods in their fields and to habituate those behaviors through consistent management reinforcement. The goal is for each employee to be a "master" of his or her role, whether it be a computer operator, teller, lender, financial consultant or any other job responsibility.

Our Passions

To create the best financial institution possible.

To consistently provide the client with better value through rational innovation and productivity improvement.

At BB&T we have two powerful passions. Our fundamental passion is our Vision: To Create the Best Financial Institution Possible—The "World Standard"—The "Best of the Best." We believe that the best can be objectively evaluated by rational performance standards in relation to the accomplishment of our mission.

To be the best of the best, we must constantly find ways to deliver better value to our clients in a highly profitable manner. This requires us to keep our minds focused at all times on innovative ways to enhance our productivity.

Chapter **Three**

Corporate Social Responsibility and Business Ethics

After reading and studying this chapter, you should be able to

1. Understand the importance of the stakeholder approach to social responsibility.

2. Explain the continuum of social responsibility and the effect of various options on company profitability.

3. Describe a social audit and explain its importance.

4. Discuss the effect of the Sarbanes-Oxley Act on the ethical conduct of business.

5. Compare the advantages of collaborative social initiatives with alternative approaches to CSR.

6. Explain the five principles of collaborative social initiatives.

7. Compare the merits of different approaches to business ethics.

8. Explain the relevance of business ethics to strategic management practice.

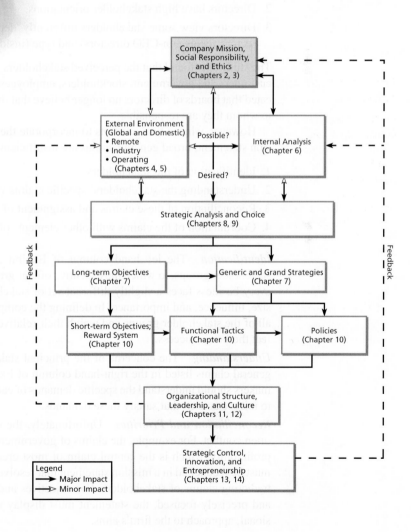

Company Mission, Social Responsibility, and Ethics (Chapters 2, 3)

External Environment (Global and Domestic)
• Remote
• Industry
• Operating
(Chapters 4, 5)

Possible?

Desired?

Internal Analysis (Chapter 6)

Strategic Analysis and Choice (Chapters 8, 9)

Long-term Objectives (Chapter 7)

Generic and Grand Strategies (Chapter 7)

Short-term Objectives; Reward System (Chapter 10)

Functional Tactics (Chapter 10)

Policies (Chapter 10)

Organizational Structure, Leadership, and Culture (Chapters 11, 12)

Strategic Control, Innovation, and Entrepreneurship (Chapters 13, 14)

Feedback

Feedback

Legend
→ Major Impact
⇾ Minor Impact

THE STAKEHOLDER APPROACH TO SOCIAL RESPONSIBILITY

In defining or redefining the company mission, strategic managers must recognize the legitimate rights of the firm's claimants. These include not only stockholders and employees but also outsiders affected by the firm's actions, sometimes referred to as stakeholders. Such outsiders commonly include customers, suppliers, governments, unions, competitors, local communities, and the general public. Each of these interest groups has justifiable reasons for expecting (and often for demanding) that the firm satisfy their claims in a responsible manner. In general, stockholders claim appropriate returns on their investment; employees seek broadly defined job satisfactions; customers want what they pay for; suppliers seek dependable buyers; governments want adherence to legislation; unions seek benefits for their members; competitors want fair competition; local communities want the firm to be a responsible citizen; and the general public expects the firm's existence to improve the quality of life.

According to a survey of 2,361 directors in 291 of the largest southeastern U.S. companies,

1. Directors perceived the existence of distinct stakeholder groups.
2. Directors have high stakeholder orientations.
3. Directors view some stakeholders differently, depending on their occupation (CEO directors versus non-CEO directors) and type (inside versus outside directors).

The study also found that the perceived stakeholders were, in the order of their importance, customers and government, stockholders, employees, and society. The results clearly indicated that boards of directors no longer believe that the stockholder is the only constituency to whom they are responsible.

However, when a firm attempts to incorporate the interests of these groups into its mission statement, broad generalizations are insufficient. These steps need to be taken:

1. Identification of the stakeholders.
2. Understanding the stakeholders' specific claims vis-à-vis the firm.
3. Reconciliation of these claims and assignment of priorities to them.
4. Coordination of the claims with other elements of the company mission.

Identification The left-hand column of Exhibit 3.1 lists the commonly encountered stakeholder groups, to which the executive officer group often is added. Obviously, though, every business faces a slightly different set of stakeholder groups, which vary in number, size, influence, and importance. In defining the company, strategic managers must identify all of the stakeholder groups and weigh their relative rights and their relative ability to affect the firm's success.

Understanding The concerns of the principal stakeholder groups tend to center on the general claims listed in the right-hand column of Exhibit 3.1. However, strategic decision makers should understand the specific demands of each group. They then will be better able to initiate actions that satisfy these demands.

Reconciliation and Priorities Unfortunately, the claims of various stakeholder groups often conflict. For example, the claims of governments and the general public tend to limit profitability, which is the central claim of most creditors and stockholders. Thus, claims must be reconciled in a mission statement that resolves the competing, conflicting, and contradicting claims of stakeholders. For objectives and strategies to be internally consistent and precisely focused, the statement must display a single-minded, though multidimensional, approach to the firm's aims.

EXHIBIT 3.1
A Stakeholder
View of Company
Responsibility

Stakeholder	Nature of the Claim
Stockholders	Participation in distribution of profits, additional stock offerings, assets on liquidation; vote of stock; inspection of company books; transfer of stock; election of board of directors; and such additional rights as have been established in the contract with the corporation.
Creditors	Legal proportion of interest payments due and return of principal from the investment. Security of pledged assets; relative priority in event of liquidation. Management and owner prerogatives if certain conditions exist with the company (such as default of interest payments).
Employees	Economic, social, and psychological satisfaction in the place of employment. Freedom from arbitrary and capricious behavior on the part of company officials. Share in fringe benefits, freedom to join union and participate in collective bargaining, individual freedom in offering up their services through an employment contract. Adequate working conditions.
Customers	Service provided with the product; technical data to use the product; suitable warranties; spare parts to support the product during use; R&D leading to product improvement; facilitation of credit.
Suppliers	Continuing source of business; timely consummation of trade credit obligations; professional relationship in contracting for, purchasing, and receiving goods and services.
Governments	Taxes (income, property, and so on); adherence to the letter and intent of public policy dealing with the requirements of fair and free competition; discharge of legal obligations of businesspeople (and business organizations); adherence to antitrust laws.
Unions	Recognition as the negotiating agent for employees. Opportunity to perpetuate the union as a participant in the business organization.
Competitors	Observation of the norms for competitive conduct established by society and the industry. Business statesmanship on the part of peers.
Local communities	Place of productive and healthful employment in the community. Participation of company officials in community affairs, provision of regular employment, fair play, reasonable portion of purchases made in the local community, interest in and support of local government, support of cultural and charitable projects.
The general public	Participation in and contribution to society as a whole; creative communications between governmental and business units designed for reciprocal understanding; assumption of fair proportion of the burden of government and society. Fair price for products and advancement of the state-of-the-art technology that the product line involves.

Source: William R. King and David I. Cleland, *Strategic Planning and Policy,* © 1978 Litton Educational Publishing, Inc., p. 153.

There are hundreds, if not thousands, of claims on any firm—high wages, pure air, job security, product quality, community service, taxes, occupational health and safety regulations, equal employment opportunity regulations, product variety, wide markets, career opportunities, company growth, investment security, high ROI, and many, many more. Although most, perhaps all, of these claims may be desirable ends, they cannot be pursued with equal emphasis. They must be assigned priorities in accordance with the relative emphasis that the firm will give them. That emphasis is reflected in the criteria that the firm uses in its strategic decision making; in the firm's allocation of its human, financial, and physical resources; and in the firm's long-term objectives and strategies.

Coordination with Other Elements   The demands of stakeholder groups constitute only one principal set of inputs to the company mission. The other principal sets are the managerial operating philosophy and the determinants of the product-market offering. Those determinants constitute a reality test that the accepted claims must pass. The key question is, How can the firm satisfy its claimants and at the same time optimize its economic success in the marketplace?

The Dynamics of Social Responsibility

As indicated in Exhibit 3.2, the various stakeholders of a firm can be divided into inside stakeholders and outside stakeholders. The insiders are the individuals or groups that are stockholders or employees of the firm. The outsiders are all the other individuals or groups that the firm's actions affect. The extremely large and often amorphous set of outsiders makes the general claim that the firm be socially responsible.

Perhaps the thorniest issues faced in defining a company mission are those that pertain to social responsibility. Corporate social responsibility is the idea that a business has a duty to serve society in general as well as the financial interests of its stockholders. The stakeholder approach offers the clearest perspective on such issues. Broadly stated, outsiders often demand that insiders' claims be subordinated to the greater good of the society; that is, to the greater good of outsiders. They believe that such issues as pollution, the disposal of solid and liquid wastes, and the conservation of natural resources should be principal considerations in strategic decision making. Also broadly stated, insiders tend to believe that the competing claims of outsiders should be balanced against one another in a way that protects the company mission. For example, they tend to believe that the need of consumers for a product should be balanced against the water pollution resulting from its production if the firm cannot eliminate that pollution entirely and still remain profitable. Some insiders also argue that the claims of society, as expressed in government regulation, provide tax money that can be used to eliminate water pollution and the like if the general public wants this to be done.

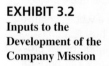

EXHIBIT 3.2
Inputs to the
Development of the
Company Mission

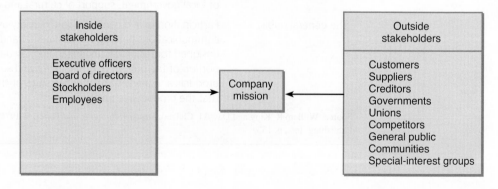

Inside stakeholders		Outside stakeholders
Executive officers Board of directors Stockholders Employees	Company mission	Customers Suppliers Creditors Governments Unions Competitors General public Communities Special-interest groups

The issues are numerous, complex, and contingent on specific situations. Thus, rigid rules of business conduct cannot deal with them. Each firm *regardless of size* must decide how to meet its perceived social responsibility. While large, well-capitalized companies may have easy access to environmental consultants, this is not an affordable strategy for smaller companies. However, the experience of many small businesses demonstrates that it is feasible to accomplish significant pollution prevention and waste reduction without big expenditures and without hiring consultants. Once a problem area has been identified, a company's line employees frequently can develop a solution. Other important pollution prevention strategies include changing the materials used or redesigning how operations are bid out. Making pollution prevention a social responsibility can be beneficial to smaller companies. Publicly traded firms also can benefit directly from socially responsible strategies.

Different approaches adopted by different firms reflect differences in competitive position, industry, country, environmental and ecological pressures, and a host of other factors. In other words, they will reflect both situational factors and differing priorities in the acknowledgment of claims. Obviously, winning the loyalty of the growing legions of consumers will require new strategies and new alliances in the twenty-first century. Exhibit 3.3, Global Strategy in Action, discusses a wide range of socially responsible actions in which corporations are currently engaged.

Occidental Petroleum faces issues of corporate social responsibility in addressing the needs of the many stakeholders involved in the firm's oil exploration in developing countries. Many parties have the potential to be affected by the company's endeavors, including local inhabitants and government, environmental groups, and institutional investors.

Despite differences in their approaches, most American firms now try to assure outsiders that they attempt to conduct business in a socially responsible manner. Many firms, including Abt Associates, Dow Chemical, Eastern Gas and Fuel Associates, ExxonMobil, and the Bank of America, conduct and publish annual social audits. Such audits attempt to evaluate a firm from the perspective of social responsibility. Private consultants often conduct them for the firm and offer minimally biased evaluations on what are inherently highly subjective issues.

TYPES OF SOCIAL RESPONSIBILITY

To better understand the nature and range of social responsibilities for which they must plan, strategic managers can consider four types of social commitment: economic, legal, ethical, and discretionary social responsibilities.

economic responsibilities
The duty of managers, as agents of the company owners, to maximize stockholder wealth.

Economic responsibilities are the most basic social responsibilities of business. As we have noted, some economists see these as the only legitimate social responsibility of business. Living up to their economic responsibilities requires managers to maximize profits whenever possible. The essential responsibility of business is assumed to be providing goods and services to society at a reasonable cost. In discharging that economic responsibility, the company also emerges as socially responsible by providing productive jobs for its workforce, and tax payments for its local, state, and federal governments.

legal responsibilities
The firm's obligations to comply with the laws that regulate business activities.

Legal responsibilities reflect the firm's obligations to comply with the laws that regulate business activities. The consumer and environmental movements focused increased public attention on the need for social responsibility in business by lobbying for laws that govern business in the areas of pollution control and consumer safety. The intent of consumer legislation has been to correct the "balance of power" between buyers and sellers in the marketplace. Among the most important laws are the Federal Fair

Who's Doing Well by Doing Good

Automobiles

Toyota	The maker of the top-selling Prius hybrid leads in developing efficient gas-electric vehicles.
Volkswagen	A market leader in small cars and clean diesel technologies.

Computers and Peripherals

Toshiba	At forefront of developing eco-efficient products, such as fuel cells for notebook PC batteries.
Dell	Among the first U.S. PC makers to take hardware back from consumers and recycle it for free.

Health Care

Fresenius Medical Care	Discloses costs of its patient treatment in terms of energy and water use and waste generated.
Quest Diagnostics	Diversity program promotes businesses owned by minorities, women, and veterans.

Oil and Gas

Norsk Hydro	Cut greenhouse gas emissions 32 percent since 1990; strong in assessing social, environmental impact.
Suncor Energy	Ties with aboriginals help it deal with social and ecological issues in Canada's far north.

Retail

Marks & Spencer	Buys local product to cut transit costs and fuel use; good wages and benefits help retain staff.
Aeon	Environmental accounting has saved $5.6 million; good employee policies in China and Southeast Asia.

Communications Equipment

Nokia	Makes phones for handicapped and low-income consumers; a leader in phasing out toxic materials.
Ericsson	Eco-friendly initiatives include wind- and fuel-cell-powered telecom systems in Nigerian villages.

Financial Services

ABN Amro	Involved in carbon-emissions trading; finances everything from micro-enterprises to biomass fuels.
ING	Weighs sustainability in project finance; helps developing nations improve financial institutions.

Household Durables

Philips Electronics	Top innovator of energy-saving appliances, lighting, and medical gear and goods for developing world.
Matsushita Electric	State-of-the-art green products; eliminated 96 percent of the most toxic substances in its global operations.

Pharmaceuticals

Novo Nordisk	Spearheads efforts in leprosy and bird flu and is a leading player in lower-cost generics.
Glaxo-SmithKline	Devotes R&D to malaria and TB; first to offer AIDS drugs at cost.

Utilities

FPL	Largest U.S. solar generator.
Scottish & Southern	Aggressively discloses environmental risk, including air pollution and climate change.

Source: From "Beyond the Green Corporation," by Pete Engardino. Reprinted from January 29, 2007 issue of *BusinessWeek* by special permission. Copyright © 2007 by The McGraw-Hill Companies, Inc.

Packaging and Labeling Act that regulates labeling procedures for business, the Truth in Lending Act that regulates the extension of credit to individuals, and the Consumer Product Safety Act that protects consumers against unreasonable risks of injury in the use of consumer products.

The environmental movement has had a similar effect on the regulation of business. This movement achieved stricter enforcement of existing environmental protections and it spurred the passage of new, more comprehensive laws such as the National Environmental Policy Act, which is devoted to preserving the United States' ecological balance and making environmental protection a federal policy goal. It requires environmental impact studies whenever new construction may threaten an existing ecosystem, and it established the Council on Environmental Quality to guide business development. Another product of the environmental movement was the creation of the federal Environmental Protection Agency, which interprets and administers the environmental protection policies of the U.S. government.

Clearly, these legal responsibilities are supplemental to the requirement that businesses and their employees comply fully with the general civil and criminal laws that apply to all individuals and institutions in the country. Yet, strangely, individual failures to adhere to the law have recently produced some of the greatest scandals in the history of American free enterprise. Probably the most disgraceful of these high-profile cases involved the Enron Corporation, an American company with headquarters in Houston, Texas. Enron was one of the world's largest electricity, natural gas, pulp and paper, and communication companies, before its bankruptcy in 2001. It had been named "America's Most Innovative Company" for six consecutive years and "100 Best Companies to Work For in America" by *Fortune* magazine. Its revenue in 2000 was $101 billion, making it the seventh largest corporation in the United States.

Enron's bankruptcy was caused by willful and creatively planned accounting fraud masterminded by three Enron executives. Kenneth Lay (founder, former chairman, and CEO), Jeffrey Skilling (former president, CEO, and chief operating officer [COO]), and Andrew Fastow (former chief financial officer [CFO]) received lengthy prison sentences for crimes including conspiracy, securities fraud, false statements, and insider trading.

It was revealed in court hearings that the majority of Enron's profits and revenue came from deals with special-purpose entities, while the majority of Enron's debts and losses were not reported in its financial statements. As the scandal was exposed to the general public, Enron's blue chip stock plummeted from more than $90 to pennies per share. Enron's accounting firm, Arthur Andersen, was found guilty of obstruction of justice for destroying documents related to Enron, was forced to stop auditing public companies, and suffered irreparable damage to its reputation. In 2007, Enron changed its name to Enron Creditors Recovery Corporation to reflect the reorganization and liquidation of remaining operations and assets of the company.

Strategy in Action, Exhibit 3.4, presents a retrospective on the lessons that strategic managers learned from the corporate scandals of 2002. Massive violations by Arthur Andersen Global, ImClone, WorldCom, Xerox and others led directly to major changes in U.S. governance laws and financial markets regulations.

ethical responsibilities
The strategic managers' notion of right and proper business behavior.

Ethical responsibilities reflect the company's notion of right and proper business behavior. Ethical responsibilities are obligations that transcend legal requirements. Firms are expected, but not required, to behave ethically. Some actions that are legal might be considered unethical. For example, the manufacture and distribution of cigarettes is legal. But in light of the often-lethal consequences of smoking, many consider the continued sale of cigarettes to be unethical. The topic of management ethics receives additional attention later in this chapter.

Exhibit 3.4

What We Learned from the U.S. Corporate Scandals of 2002

The year 2002 won't be missed by many. Shell-shocked investors withdrew from the markets to nurse wounded feelings of loss and betrayal. A stunned corporate elite retreated to ponder the plunge in respect it suffered from a wave of business scandals.

The lessons are sobering, and should motivate us to complete the job of restoring the checks and balances of our capitalist system—in corporate governance, accounting, Wall Street, and government regulation—that so failed us. The stakes are high. Risk-taking is a quintessentially American trait and plays a large role in its economic success.

Lesson No. 1: The problems revealed by the scandals were systemic, not the result of a few bad apples. While only a few CEOs may go to jail for breaking the law, the breakdown was endemic to both the corporate and financial systems. Most CEOs, not just a few, were overcompensated for success and protected from failure. Many, not just a few, accountants, analysts, attorneys, regulators, and legislators failed, to one degree or another, in ensuring the accuracy of financial statements and the free flow of honest data in the markets.

Lesson No. 2: Regulation matters. The failure to set rules in new markets cost investors and consumers billions of dollars. The absence of virtually any regulation in Internet energy-trading markets led to false shortages, fake trades, huge profits, and enormous financial and economic losses in California. Deregulation should not mean anarchy, deceit, and greed hiding behind a twisted interpretation of Chicago School economic theory. Markets need clear rules and policing to be open, transparent, and fair.

Lesson No. 3: On Wall Street, conflicts of interest are not synergy, as Jack Grubman would have it. Analysts who sit in on board meetings, go on road shows, mislead individual investors, and feign objectivity on CNBC but get paid for generating investment banking business are not being synergistic. They are being corrupt. Separation of financial activities, solid Chinese Walls and, above all, serious managing of conflicts of interest are crucial to the honest operation of capital raising and investment in the economy.

Lesson No. 4: Boards count. The most important check on CEO behavior is the board of directors. The failure of boards to do their job as shareholder representatives—and advocates—was a major cause of corporate scandal in 2002. Many boards condoned outlandish CEO demands for millions of options, personal loans, repricing of underwater options, loose accounting, and, in the case of Enron Corp., deliberately abandoning the corporate code of ethics. Independent board members heading audit and compensation committees are essential to the proper functioning of companies. Separating the function of CEO and chairman, who oversees the CEO, may also be needed at some companies.

Lesson No. 5: CEO pay is too high. Execs weren't entitled to become super-rich in the roaring '90s and are certainly not today. In the past decade, companies that granted 90% of all options to CEOs and a few top managers performed worse than those that distributed options more evenly and fairly among employees. There is no justification for increasing the compensation of CEOs from 40 times that of the average employee in the '60s to nearly 600 times today. Stock prices have come down since the bubble burst, investors have lost billions, people have been laid off, retirement funds have been cut, and profit projections have been trimmed. Yet CEO pay remains sky-high. This is untenable.

Lesson No. 6: We know a lot less than we think we know about economic policy. Supply-siders and deficit hawks battle over tax cuts, deficits, interest rates, and growth, but neither side has the economic theory or data to prove it's right. The failure of economy theory to decide key economic issues makes policy-making extremely ideological and partisan.

Lesson No. 7: Deflation is the new enemy. Our grandparents knew this from the '30s, but we're only discovering it now. Technology, higher productivity, greater competition and globalization (meaning huge imports from China), plus inflation-fighting monetary policies, have combined to send many prices lower, perhaps too low. Companies have difficulty generating profits partly because they can't raise prices. Without officially saying so, the Fed has gone into deflation-fighting mode, flooding the economy with money, cutting interest rates, and allowing the dollar to fall 5% on a trade-weighted basis this year.

Source: Excerpted from: What We Learned in 2002. *Bloomberg Businessweek Magazine*, December 29, 2002. http://www .businessweek.com/stories/2002-12-29/what-we-learned-in-2002

Swiss Re and Roche Team Up in China to Save Cancer Patients

Roche Holding found a way to sell its cancer drugs to millions of Chinese who could not otherwise afford them: First sell them insurance. The world's biggest maker of cancer medicines collaborated with Swiss Re, the world's second-largest reinsurer, to sell policies that brought in 10 million clients in 2012. The two Swiss companies dreamed up the program in 2010 as a way to skirt Chinese regulations that prevent foreign firms from selling retail insurance in China. The rules did not let foreign firms sell reinsurance, so in 2010 Roche and Swiss Re began trying to convince Chinese insurers to offer coverage for cancer treatment and drugs. The idea was to help the Chinese firms lessen the risk of covering cancer patients.

Roche provided the Chinese insurers and Swiss Re with statistical data on various types of cancer, including how treatable they were. Swiss Re used that data to calculate the risk and cost of treatment. The reinsurer designed and priced the policies for the Chinese insurers and then provided reinsurance so local firms did not assume the full risk. Roche had no financial arrangement with Swiss Re to share in revenues from the insurance policies. Roche and Swiss Re were working with six Chinese insurers, including China Life Insurance, the nation's biggest insurer. Their goal was to have 12 million people—nearly 1 percent of China's population—enrolled by the end of 2013.

About two million people die from cancer each year in China, accounting for about 25 percent of all deaths there. That rate is expected to rise for the next 10 to 25 years. A full course of some cancer medicines can cost 10 times the average Chinese worker's annual income, which despite nearly quadrupling over the past decade, was only 41,799 yuan ($6,681) in 2011. The prices of the new insurance policies ranged from about $50 a year to several thousand dollars, according to Swiss Re, far less than the drugs' cost. Basic government coverage provides for roughly 70 percent of hospital expenses, but not costly drugs or cancer treatments.

Source: Excerpted from Daryl Loo and Naomi Kresge. November 21, 2012. "Swiss Re and Roche Team Up in China." *Bloomberg Businessweek*.

---

discretionary responsibilities
Responsibilities voluntarily assumed by a business, such as public relations, good citizenship, and full corporate responsibility.

Discretionary responsibilities are those that are voluntarily assumed by a business organization. They include public relations activities, good citizenship, and full corporate social responsibility. Through public relations activities, managers attempt to enhance the image of their companies, products, and services by supporting worthy causes. This form of discretionary responsibility has a self-serving dimension. Companies that adopt the good citizenship approach actively support ongoing charities, public service advertising campaigns, or issues in the public interest. A commitment to full corporate responsibility requires strategic managers to attack social problems with the same zeal with which they attack business problems. For example, teams in the National Football League provide time off for players and other employees afflicted with drug or alcohol addictions who agree to enter rehabilitation programs.

In a striking example of corporate social responsibility (CSR), Swiss Re and Roche collaborated in China to provide assistance to cancer patients. Taking a unique approach that enabled poor Chinese to buy extremely low-cost medical insurance, the companies provided the poor Chinese subscribers with expensive cancer treatment that otherwise would have been far beyond their ability to afford. For the details of this innovative strategy to serve others, read Global Strategy in Action, Exhibit 3.5.

It is important to remember that the categories on the continuum of social responsibility overlap, creating gray areas where societal expectations of organizational behavior are difficult to categorize. In considering the overlaps among various demands for social responsibility, however, managers should keep in mind that in the view of the general public, economic and legal responsibilities are required, ethical responsibility is expected, and discretionary responsibility is desired.

Corporate Social Responsibility and Profitability
CSR and the Bottom Line

corporate social responsibility (CSR)
The idea that business has a duty to serve society in general as well as the financial interest of stockholders.

The goal of every firm is to maintain viability through long-run profitability. Until all costs and benefits are accounted for, however, profits may not be claimed. In the case of **corporate social responsibility (CSR),** costs and benefits are both economic and social. While economic costs and benefits are easily quantifiable, social costs and benefits are not. Managers therefore risk subordinating social consequences to other performance results that can be more straightforwardly measured.

The dynamic between CSR and success (profit) is complex. While one concept is clearly not mutually exclusive of the other, it is also clear that neither is a prerequisite for the other. Rather than viewing these two concepts as competing, it may be better to view CSR as a component in the decision-making process of business that must determine, among other objectives, how to maximize profits.

Attempts to undertake a cost-benefit analysis of CSR have not been very successful. The process is complicated by several factors. First, some CSR activities incur no dollar costs at all. For example, Second Harvest, the largest nongovernment, charitable food distributor in the nation, accepts donations from food manufacturers and food retailers of surplus food that would otherwise be thrown out due to overruns, warehouse damage, or labeling errors. In 10 years, Second Harvest has distributed more than 2 billion pounds of food. Gifts in Kind America is an organization that enables companies to reduce unsold or obsolete inventory by matching a corporation's donated products with a charity's or other nonprofit organization's needs. In addition, a tax break is realized by the company. In the past, corporate donations have included 130,000 pairs of shoes from Nike, 10,000 pairs of gloves from Aris Isotoner, and 480 computer systems from Apple Computer.

In addition, philanthropic activities of a corporation, which have been a traditional mainstay of CSR, are undertaken at a discounted cost to the firm since they are often tax deductible. The benefits of corporate philanthropy can be enormous as is shown by the many national social welfare causes that have been spurred by corporate giving. While such acts of benevolence often help establish a general perception of the involved companies within society, some philanthropic acts bring specific credit to the firm.

Second, socially responsible behavior does not come at a prohibitive cost. One needs only to look at the problems of A. H. Robbins Company (Dalkon Shield), Beech-Nut Corporation (apple juice), Drexel Burnham (insider trading), and Exxon (*Valdez*) for stark answers on the "cost" of social responsibility (or its absence) in the business environment.

Third, socially responsible practices may create savings and, as a result, increase profits. SET Laboratories uses popcorn to ship software rather than polystyrene peanuts. It is environmentally safer and costs 60 percent less to use. Corporations that offer part-time and adjustable work schedules have realized that this can lead to reduced absenteeism, greater productivity and increased morale. DuPont opted for more flexible schedules for its employees after a survey revealed 50 percent of women and 25 percent of men considered working for another employer with more flexibility for family concerns.

Proponents argue that CSR costs are more than offset in the long run by an improved company image and increased community goodwill. These intangible assets can prove valuable in a crisis, as Johnson & Johnson discovered with the Tylenol cyanide scare in 1982. Because it had established a solid reputation as a socially responsible company before the incident, the public readily accepted the company's assurances of public safety. Consequently, financial damage to Johnson & Johnson was minimized, despite the company's $100 million voluntary recall of potentially tainted capsules. CSR may also head off new regulation, preventing increased compliance costs. It may even attract investors

Mission Statement: Johnson & Johnson

"We believe our first responsibility is to the doctors, nurses and patients, to mothers and fathers and all others who use our products and services. In meeting their needs everything we do must be of high quality. We must constantly strive to reduce our costs in order to maintain reasonable prices. Customers' orders must be serviced promptly and accurately. Our suppliers and distributors must have an opportunity to make a fair profit.

We are responsible to our employees, the men and women who work with us throughout the world. Everyone must be considered as an individual. We must respect their dignity and recognize their merit. They must have a sense of security in their jobs. Compensation must be fair and adequate, and working conditions clean, orderly and safe. Employees must feel free to make suggestions and complaints. There must be equal opportunity for employment, development and advancement for those qualified. We must provide competent management, and their actions must be just and ethical.

We are responsible to the communities in which we live and work and to the world community as well. We must be good citizens—support good works and charities and bear our fair share of taxes. We must encourage civic improvements and better health and education. We must maintain in good order the property we are privileged to use, protecting the environment and natural resources.

Our final responsibility is to our stockholders. Business must make a sound profit. We must experiment with new ideas. Research must be carried on, innovative programs developed and mistakes paid for. New equipment must be purchased, new facilities provided and new products launched. Reserves must be created to provide for adverse times. When we operate according to these principles, the stockholders should realize a fair return."

Source: Johnson & Johnson, http://www.jnj.com

who are themselves socially responsible. Proponents believe that for these reasons, socially responsible behavior increases the financial value of the firm in the long run. The mission statement of Johnson & Johnson is provided as Exhibit 3.6, Strategy in Action.

Performance To explore the relationship between socially responsible behavior and financial performance, an important question must first be answered: How do managers measure the financial effect of corporate social performance?

Critics of CSR believe that companies that behave in a socially responsible manner, and portfolios comprising these companies' securities, should perform more poorly financially than those that do not. The costs of CSR outweigh the benefits for individual firms, they suggest. In addition, traditional portfolio theory holds that investors minimize risk and maximize return by being able to choose from an infinite universe of investment opportunities. Portfolios based on social criteria should suffer, critics argue, because they are by definition restrictive in nature. This restriction should increase portfolio risk and reduce portfolio return.

CSR Today

CSR is a priority with American business. In addition to a commonsense belief that companies should be able to "do well by doing good," at least three broad trends are driving businesses to adopt CSR frameworks: the resurgence of environmentalism, increasing buyer power, and the globalization of business.

Sustainability and the Resurgence of Environmentalism

In March 1989, the Exxon *Valdez* ran aground in Prince William Sound, spilling 11 million gallons of oil, polluting miles of ocean and shore, and helping to revive worldwide concern for the ecological environment. Six months after the *Valdez* incident, the Coalition for

Heinz Stresses CSR

Bill Johnson, the CEO of Heinz Corp, and his management team established a very aggressive strategic plan encompassing eight major global sustainability goals:

Greenhouse gas	Emissions	Decrease by 20%
Energy use in manufacturing	Usage	Decrease by 20%
Water use in manufacturing	Water consumption	Decrease by 20%
Solid waste	Waste from Heinz operations	Decrease by 20%
Packaging	Total packaging	Decrease by 15%
Transportation	Fossil fuel consumption	Decrease by 10%
Renewable energy	Renewable energy resources	Increase by 15%
Sustainable agriculture	Carbon footprint	Decrease by 15%
	Water usage	Decrease by 15%
	Field yield	Increase by 5%

These environmental goals were viewed by Johnson as an extension of the original vision of Henry J. Heinz, who believed that food safety regulations made a significant contribution to society.

The overarching theme of Johnson's corporate social responsibility plan was a 20 percent reduction of greenhouse gas emissions by the year 2015. He stated, "To achieve these goals we are executing numerous global initiatives to reduce non-value-added packaging, increase the use of recycled materials, lower energy consumption, conserve water, and increase our use of renewable energy sources at some of our largest plants."* Examples of successes in achieving his plan included a European plastics consumption reduction of 340 tons and a solid waste reduction in an Ohio plant of 800,000 pounds.

*H.J. Heinz Corp. Web site, 2011, http://www.heinz.com/sustainability/environment.aspx (released once every four years).

Environmentally Responsible Economies (CERES) was formed to establish new goals for environmentally responsible corporate behavior. The group drafted the CERES Principles to "establish an environmental ethic with criteria by which investors and others can assess the environmental performance of companies. Companies that sign these Principles pledge to go voluntarily beyond the requirements of the law."

The most prevalent forms of environmentalism are efforts to preserve natural resources and eliminating environmental pollution, often referred to as the concern for "greening." The Heinz Corporation is a company that is praised for its strong green stance. Some details of its aggressive sustainability program are provided in Strategy in Action, Exhibit 3.7.

The concern for the impact of business on the environment led to the term *sustainable business*. A sustainable business is one that takes a long-term approach to minimizing its negative impacts on the ecology, the society, and the economy. Its performance is judged by the triple bottom line of people, planet, and profit. Sustainable businesses, which are sometimes referred to as green businesses, manage all stages of their supply chains to be environmentally sensitive. They design their products and processes to minimize negative impacts on the environment, in part by incorporating renewable resources.

A distinctive priority of sustainable businesses is to minimize harm to the environment caused by the production and consumption of their products. The impact is commonly

Global Strategy in Action   Exhibit 3.8

WBCSD'S 10 Messages by Which to Achieve Sustainability

1. Business is good for sustainable development and sustainable development is good for business.

2. Business cannot succeed in societies that fail.

3. Poverty is a key enemy to stable societies. Poverty creates political and economic instability, a big threat to business and sustainable development. By contrast, businesses can lift living standards and eradicate poverty.

4. Access to markets for all supports sustainable development. Sustainable development is best achieved through open, transparent and competitive global markets.

5. Good governance is needed to make business a part of the solution. Supportive frameworks and regulations are needed for business to contribute fully to sustainable development.

6. Business has to earn its license to operate, innovate and grow. Accountability, ethics, transparency, social and environmental responsibility and trust are basic prerequisites for successful business and sustainable development.

7. Innovation and technology development are crucial to sustainable development. Business has always been, and will continue to be, the main contributor to technological development.

8. Eco-efficiency—doing more with less—is at the core of the business case for sustainable development.

9. Ecosystems in balance—a prerequisite for business. Business cannot function if ecosystems and the services they deliver, such as water, biodiversity, food, fiber and climate, are degraded.

10. Cooperation beats confrontation. Sustainable development challenges are huge and require contributions from all parties—governments, business, civil societies and international bodies.

Source: Copyright © World Business Council for Sustainable Development. All rights reserved. http://www.wbcsd.org/newsroom/key-messages.aspx. Retrieved July 11, 2013.

determined by the carbon footprint of the product, which is determined by the volume of greenhouse gases generated in its production, use, and disposal. Measured in units of carbon dioxide, the carbon footprint is derived from ecological footprint analysis, which examines the ecological capacity required to support the product over its useful life.

The World Business Council for Sustainable Development provides 10 recommendations by which to achieve sustainability, as presented in Global Strategy in Action, Exhibit 3.8.

A compatible perspective states that business sustainability requires firms to adhere to the principles of sustainable development. According to the World Council for Economic Development, for industrial development to be sustainable, it must address important issues at the macro level, involving economic efficiency, social equity, and environmental accountability. A number of best practices foster business sustainability. Four of these practices are described in Global Strategy in Action, Exhibit 3.9, and involve stakeholder engagement, environmental management systems, reporting and disclosure, and life cycle analysis.

Increasing Buyer Power   The rise of the consumer movement has meant that buyers—consumers and investors—are increasingly flexing their economic muscle. Consumers are becoming more interested in buying products from socially responsible companies. Organizations such as the Council on Economic Priorities (CEP) help consumers make more informed buying decisions through such publications as *Shopping for a Better World,* which provides social performance information on 191 companies making more than 2,000 consumer products. CEP also sponsors the annual Corporate Conscience Awards, which recognize socially responsible companies. One example of consumer power at work is the effective outcry over the deaths of dolphins in tuna fishermen's nets.

Investors represent a second type of influential consumer. There has been a dramatic increase in the number of people interested in supporting socially responsible companies

Business Sustainability

Business sustainability is often defined as managing the triple bottom line—a process by which companies manage their financial, social and environmental risks, obligations and opportunities. These three impacts are sometimes referred to as profits, people and planet. Additionally, business sustainability requires resiliency over time—businesses that can survive shocks because they are intimately connected to healthy economic, social and environmental systems. These businesses create economic value and contribute to healthy ecosystems and strong communities.

Business sustainability requires firms to adhere to the principles of sustainable development. According to the World Council for Economic Development, sustainable development is development that "meets the needs of the present without compromising the ability of future generations to meet their own needs." So, for industrial development to be sustainable, it must address important issues at the macro level, such as: economic efficiency (innovation, prosperity, productivity), social equity (poverty, community, health and wellness, human rights) and environmental accountability (climate change, land use, biodiversity).

There are a number of best practices that foster business sustainability. These practices include:

- Stakeholder engagement: Organizations can learn from customers, employees and their surrounding community. Engagement is not only about pushing out messages, but understanding opposition, finding common ground and involving stakeholders in joint decision making.

- Environmental management systems: These systems provide the structures and processes that help embed environmental efficiency into a firm's culture and mitigate risks. The most widely recognized standard worldwide is ISO 14001, but numerous other industry-specific and country-specific standards exist.

- Reporting and disclosure: Measurement and control are at the heart of instituting sustainable practices. Not only can organizations collect and collate the information, they can also be entirely transparent with outsiders. The Global Reporting Initiative is one of many examples of well-recognized reporting standards.

- Life-cycle analysis: Those organizations wanting to take a large leap forward should systematically analyze the environmental and social impact of the products they use and produce through life-cycle analysis, which measures more accurately impacts.

Source: Excerpted from "Sustainability." *Financial Times*, http://lexicon.ft.com/Term?term = business-sustainability. Retrieved July 12, 2013.

through their investments. Membership in the Social Investment Forum, a trade association serving social investing professionals, has been growing at a rate of about 50 percent annually. As baby boomers achieve their own financial success, the social investing movement has continued its rapid growth.

While social investing wields relatively low power as an individual private act (selling one's shares of ExxonMobil does not affect the company), it can be very powerful as a collective public act. When investors vote their shares on behalf of pro-CSR issues, companies may be pressured to change their social behavior. The South African divestiture movement is one example of how effective this pressure can be.

The Vermont National Bank has added a Socially Responsible Banking Fund to its product line. Investors can designate any of their interest-bearing accounts with a $500 minimum balance to be used by the fund. This fund then lends these monies for purposes such as low-income housing, the environment, education, farming, or small business development. Although it has had a "humble" beginning of approximately 800 people investing about $11 million, the bank has attracted out-of-state depositors and is growing faster than expected.

Social investors comprise both individuals and institutions. Much of the impetus for social investing originated with religious organizations that wanted their investments to mirror their beliefs. At present, the ranks of social investors have expanded to include educational institutions and large pension funds.

Large-scale social investing can be broken down into the two broad areas of guideline portfolio investing and shareholder activism. Guideline portfolio investing is the largest and fastest-growing segment of social investing. Individual and institutional guideline portfolio investors use ethical guidelines as screens to identify possible investments in stocks, bonds, and mutual funds. The investment instruments that survive the social screens are then layered over the investor's financial screens to create the investor's universe of possible investments.

Screens may be negative (e.g., excluding all tobacco companies) or they may combine negative and positive elements (e.g., eliminating companies with bad labor records while seeking companies with good ones). Most investors rely on screens created by investment firms such as Kinder, Lydenberg Domini & Co. or by industry groups such as the Council on Economic Priorities. In addition to ecology, employee relations, and community development, corporations may be screened on their association with "sin" products (alcohol, tobacco, gambling), defense/weapons production, and nuclear power.

In contrast to guideline portfolio investors, who passively indicate their approval or disapproval of a company's social behavior by simply including or excluding it from their portfolios, shareholder activists seek to directly influence corporate social behavior. Shareholder activists invest in a corporation hoping to improve specific aspects of the company's social performance, typically by seeking a dialogue with upper management. If this and successive actions fail to achieve the desired results, shareholder activists may introduce proxy resolutions to be voted upon at the corporation's annual meeting. The goal of these resolutions is to achieve change by gaining public exposure for the issue at hand. While the number of shareholder activists is relatively small, they are by no means small in achievement: shareholder activists, led by such groups as the Interfaith Center on Corporate Responsibility, were the driving force behind the South African divestiture movement. Currently, there are more than 35 socially screened mutual funds available in the United States alone.

Before leaving the topic of corporate sustainability it is important to note that objective evaluations of progress are decidedly mixed. A study by CRD Analytics, a sustainable investment research firm, and consulting firm Brandlogic found that stakeholders' perception of the sustainability efforts slipped in 2011, even though the companies the survey mentioned had reported major improvements. A survey by public relations and marketing agency Cone Communications may have uncovered a partial explanation. Cone found that 86 percent of survey respondents felt that stating a purpose for CSR efforts is no longer sufficient. "Proving purpose" is necessary.

Perhaps most disappointing are the findings of Rivel Research Group, which measures investor motivations and perceptions.[1] Rivel put together a list of 11 social responsibility and sustainability insight and benchmarking tools and surveyed 115 institutional investors. The Rivel 2012 survey found that few of the social responsibility and sustainability benchmarks were used by buy-side analysts and even fewer are commonly used in the investment decision-making process. The benchmarking tools included in the study were the Dow Jones Sustainability Index, the Carbon Disclosure Project, FTSE4Good Index, Goldman Sachs Sustain, Ceres, and the Global Reporting Initiative. The study reported that as few as 4 percent had ever used any of the eight top benchmarking tools, while less than half were even aware of them, raising serious questions about whether the sustainability reports are having any real impact on investment decision making.

---

[1]Louis Thompson Jr. 2012. "Getting the Word Out on Sustainability Progress." *Compliance Week*, 9 (107): 54–55.

The Mixed Potential of Global CSR

Many researchers and senior executives agree that under the right conditions, corporate social responsibility initiatives can simultaneously create value for society while also producing valuable rewards for companies. But can corporations capitalize on their corporate social responsibility investments when they expand overseas? Or are social initiatives simply a costly distraction for companies seeking to generate returns from their international ventures?

Cyril Bouquet, Andrew Crane, and Yuval Deutsch conducted research to investigate these questions. They looked at both social performance ratings and accounting and financial data for more than 800 U.S. public companies. Their analysis produced some intriguing results. Companies with low or high levels of social performance achieved far greater degrees of international success than those with moderate levels. In other words, the relationship between social responsibility and profitable sales in foreign markets is U-shaped. Companies with a low commitment to corporate social responsibility can reap cost benefits, while those with highly developed corporate social responsibility programs can build a strong reputation for good citizenship that makes a difference in international markets. However, companies with intermediate social performance struggle to reap the benefits of their corporate social responsibility investments overseas. When a company is "stuck in the middle" in its social performance, it is committing resources to corporate social responsibility and achieving some limited recognition for its efforts at home but is unable to translate that domestic recognition into a competitive advantage in foreign markets.

There are several reasons why such a scenario can have a negative impact on overseas performance. Unexceptional reputations may not transfer successfully across borders. Overseas stakeholders may lack the certainty that a company's social engagement is real and meaningful; a midrange corporate social responsibility profile will be more readily dismissed by overseas stakeholders as corporate "greenwash."

One implication of these findings for managers of multinationals is that investments in corporate social responsibility may lead to competitive disadvantages internationally unless a high level of social performance can be achieved and sustained. It is rare to find managers who do not talk proudly of their company's efforts to improve the rights of workers, to help local communities surmount poverty and to safeguard the environment—for example, by recycling office stationery. While these approaches are presumably important, they are also so common that they seldom represent a source of distinctive advantage in foreign markets. Executives will need to more finely attune corporate social responsibility initiatives both to their core business and to the needs and expectations of international stakeholders.

Source: Excerpted from Cyril Bouquet, Andrew Crane, and Yuval Deutsch, "The Trouble with Being Average," *MIT Sloan Management Review* 50, no. 3 (2009), pp. 79–80.

The Globalization of Business Management issues, including CSR, have become more complex as companies increasingly transcend national borders: It is difficult enough to come to a consensus on what constitutes socially responsible behavior within one culture, let alone determine common ethical values across cultures. In addition to different cultural views, the high barriers facing international CSR include differing corporate disclosure practices, inconsistent financial data and reporting methods, and the lack of CSR research organizations within countries. Despite these problems, CSR is growing abroad. The United Kingdom has 30 ethical mutual funds and Canada offers six socially responsible funds.

One of the most contentious social responsibility issues confronting multinational firms pertains to human rights. For example, many U.S. firms reduce their costs either by relying on foreign manufactured goods or by outsourcing their manufacturing to foreign manufacturers. These foreign manufacturers, often Chinese, offer low pricing because they pay very low wages by U.S. standards, even though they are extremely competitive by Chinese pay rates.

While Chinese workers are happy to earn manufacturer wages and U.S. customers are pleased by the lower prices charged for foreign manufactured goods, others are unhappy. They believe that such U.S. firms are failing to satisfy their social responsibilities. Some

U.S. workers and their unions argue that jobs in the United States are being eliminated or devalued by foreign competition. Some human rights advocates argue that the working conditions and living standards of foreign workers are so substandard when compared with U.S. standards that they verge on inhumane. A troubling twist on American corporations' role in the human rights debate about conditions in China arises from the sale of software to the Chinese government. Developed by Cisco, Oracle, and other U.S. companies, the software is used by China's police to monitor the activities of individuals that the Chinese government labels as criminals and dissidents.

As a result of the extreme pluses and minuses of global CSR, strategic planners have the difficult task of deciding the extent to which their companies should be involved in overseas efforts to benefit a host community beyond the normal consequences of commerce. Exhibit 3.10, Global Strategy in Action provides a research report that helps to clarify the issues.

SARBANES-OXLEY ACT OF 2002

Sarbanes-Oxley Act of 2002
Law that revised and strengthened auditing and accounting standards.

Following a string of wrongdoings by corporate executives in 2000 to 2002, and the subsequent failures of their firms, Washington lawmakers proposed more than 50 policies to reassure investors. None of the resulting bills were able to pass both houses of Congress until the Banking Committee chairman, Paul Sarbanes (D–MD), proposed legislation to establish new auditing and accounting standards. The bill was called the Public Company Accounting Reform and Investor Protection Act of 2002. Later the name was changed to the **Sarbanes-Oxley Act of 2002.**

On July 30, 2002, President George Bush signed the Sarbanes-Oxley Act into law. This revolutionary act applies to public companies with securities registered under Section 12 of the Securities Act of 1934 and those required to file reports under Section 15(d) of the Exchange Act. Sarbanes-Oxley includes required certifications for financial statements, new corporate regulations, disclosure requirements, and penalties for failure to comply. More details on the act are provided in Exhibit 3.11, Strategy in Action.

The Sarbanes-Oxley Act states that the CEO and CFO must certify every report containing the company's financial statements. The certification acknowledges that the CEO or CFO (chief financial officer) has reviewed the report. As part of the review, the officer must attest that the information does not include untrue statements or omit necessary information. Furthermore, based on the officer's knowledge, the report is a reliable source of the company's financial condition and result of operations for the period represented. The certification also makes the officers responsible for establishing and maintaining internal controls such that they are aware of any material information relating to the company. The officers must also evaluate the effectiveness of the internal controls within 90 days of the release of the report and present their conclusions of the effectiveness of the controls. Also, the officers must disclose any fraudulent material, deficiencies in the reporting of the financial reports, or problems with the internal control to the company's auditors and auditing committee. Finally, the officers must indicate any changes to the internal controls or factors that could affect them.

The Sarbanes-Oxley Act includes provisions restricting the corporate control of executives, accounting firms, auditing committees, and attorneys. With regard to executives, the act bans personal loans. A company can no longer directly or indirectly issue, extend, or maintain a personal loan to any director or executive officer. Executive officers and directors are not permitted to purchase, sell, acquire, or transfer any equity security during any pension fund blackout period. Executives are required to notify fund participants of any

Sarbanes-Oxley Act of 2002

The following outline presents the major elements of the Sarbanes-Oxley Act of 2002.

CORPORATE RESPONSIBILITY

- The CEO and CFO of each company are required to submit a report, based on their knowledge, to the SEC certifying the company's financial statements are fair representations of the financial condition without false statements or omissions.

- The CEO and CFO must reimburse the company for any bonuses or equity-based incentives received for the last 12-month period if the company is required to restate its financial statements due to material noncompliance with any financial reporting requirement that resulted from misconduct.

- Directors and executive officers are prohibited from trading a company's 401(k) plan, profit sharing plan, or retirement plan during any blackout period. The plan administrators are required to notify the plan participants and beneficiaries with notice of all blackout periods, reasons for the blackout period, and a statement that the participant or beneficiary should evaluate their investment even though they are unable to direct or diversify their accounts during the blackout.

- No company may make, extend, modify, or renew any personal loans to its executives or directors. Limited exceptions are for loans made in the course of the company's business, on market terms, for home improvement and home loans, consumer credit, or extension of credit.

INCREASED DISCLOSURE

- Each annual and quarterly financial report filed with the SEC must disclose all material off-balance-sheet transactions, arrangements, and obligations that may affect the current or future financial condition of the company or its operations.

- Companies must present pro forma financial information with the SEC in a manner that is not misleading and must be reconciled with the company's financial condition and with generally accepted accounting principles (GAAP).

- Each company is required to disclose whether they have adopted a code of ethics for its senior financial officers. If not, the company must explain the reasons. Any change or waiver of the code of ethics must be disclosed.

- Each annual report must contain a statement of management's responsibility for establishing and maintaining an internal control structure and procedures for financial reporting. The report must also include an assessment of the effectiveness of the internal control procedures.

- The Form 4 will be provided within two business days after the execution date of the trading of a company's securities by directors and executive officers. The SEC may extend this deadline if it determines the two-day period is not feasible.

- The company must disclose information concerning changes in financial conditions or operations "on a rapid and current basis," in plain English.

The SEC must review the financial statements of each reporting company no less than once every three years.

AUDIT COMMITTEES

- The audit committee must be composed entirely of independent directors. Committee members are not permitted to accept any fees from the company, cannot control 5 percent or more of the voting of the

blackout period and the reasons for the blackout period. The SEC will provide the company's executives with a code of ethics for the company to adopt. Failure to meet the code must be disclosed to the SEC.

The act limits some and issues new duties of the registered public accounting firms that conduct the audits of the financial statements. Accounting firms are prohibited from performing bookkeeping or other accounting services related to the financial statements, designing or implementing financial systems, appraising, internal auditing, brokering banking services, or providing legal services unrelated to the audit. All critical accounting policies and alternative treatments of financial information within generally accepted

Exhibit 3.11   continued

company, nor be an officer, director, partner, or employee of the company.
- The audit committee must have the authority to engage the outside auditing firm.
- The audit committee must establish procedures for the treatment of complaints regarding accounting controls or auditing matters. They are responsible for employee complaints concerning questionable accounting and auditing.
- The audit committee must disclose whether at least one of the committee members is a "financial expert." If not, the committee must explain why not.

NEW CRIMES AND INCREASED CRIMINAL PENALTIES
- Tampering with records with intent to impede or influence any federal investigation or bankruptcy will be punishable by a fine and/or prison sentence up to 20 years.
- Failure by an accountant to maintain all auditing papers for five years after the end of the fiscal period will be punishable by a fine and/or up to 10-year prison sentence.
- Knowingly executing, or attempting to execute, a scheme to defraud investors will be punishable by a fine and/or prison sentence of up to 25 years.
- Willfully certifying a report that does not comply with the law can be punishable with a fine up to $5,000,000 and/or a prison sentence up to 20 years.

NEW CIVIL CAUSE OF ACTION AND INCREASED ENFORCEMENT POWERS
- Protection will be provided to whistle-blowers who provide information or assist in an investigation by law enforcement, congressional committee, or employee supervisor.
- Bankruptcy cannot be used to avoid liability from securities laws violations.
- Investors are able to file a civil action for fraud up to two years after discovery of the facts and five years after the occurrence of fraud.
- The SEC can receive a restraining order prohibiting payments to insiders during an investigation.
- The SEC can prevent individuals from holding an officer's or director's position in a public company as a result of violation of the securities law.

AUDITOR INDEPENDENCE
- All audit services must be preapproved by the audit committee and must be disclosed to investors.
- The lead audit or reviewing audit partner from the auditing accounting firm must change at least once every five fiscal years.
- The registered accounting firms must report to the audit committee all accounting policies and practices used, alternative uses of the financial information within GAAP that has been discussed with management, and written communications between the accounting firm and management.
- An auditing firm is prohibited from auditing a company if the company's CEO or CFO was employed by the auditing firm within the past year.

A Public Company Accounting Oversight Board is established by the SEC to oversee the audits of public companies. The board will register public accounting firms, establish audit standards, inspect registered accounting firms, and discipline violators of the rules. No person can take part in an audit if not employed by a registered public accounting firm.

accounting principles (GAAP), and written communication between the accounting firm and the company's management must be reported to the audit committee.

The act defines the composition of the audit committee and specifies its responsibilities. The members of the audit committee must be members of the company's board of directors. At least one member of the committee should be classified as a "financial expert." The audit committee is directly responsible for the work of any accounting firm employed by the company, and the accounting firm must report directly to the audit committee. The audit committee must create procedures for employee complaints or concerns over accounting or auditing matters. Upon discovery of unlawful acts by the company, the audit committee must report and be supervised in its investigation by a Public Company Accounting Oversight Board.

The act includes rules for attorney conduct. If a company's attorneys find evidence of securities violations, they are required to report the matter to the chief legal counsel or CEO. If there is not an appropriate response, the attorneys must report the information to the audit committee or the board of directors.

Other sections of the Sarbanes-Oxley Act stipulate disclosure periods for financial operations and reporting. Relevant information relating to changes in the financial condition or operations of a company must be immediately reported in plain English. Off-balance-sheet transactions, correcting adjustments, and pro-forma information must be presented in the annual and quarterly financial reports. The information must not contain any untrue statements, must not omit material facts, and must meet GAAP standards.

Stricter penalties have been issued for violations of the Sarbanes-Oxley Act. If a company must restate its financial statements due to noncompliance, the CEO and CFO must relinquish any bonus or incentive-based compensation or realized profits from the sale of securities during the 12-month period following the filing with the SEC. Other securities fraud, such as destruction or falsification of records, results in fines and prison sentences up to 25 years.

The New Corporate Governance Structure

A major consequence of the 2000–2002 accounting scandals was the Sarbanes-Oxley Act of 2002, and a major consequence of Sarbanes-Oxley has been the restructuring of the governance structure of American corporations. The most significant change in the restructuring is the heightened role of corporate internal auditors, as depicted in Exhibit 3.12, Strategy in Action. Auditors have traditionally been viewed as performing a necessary but perfunctory function, namely to probe corporate financial records for unintentional or illicit misrepresentations. Although a majority of U.S. corporations have longstanding traditions of reporting that their auditors operated independently of CFO approval and that they had direct access to the board, in practice, the auditors' work usually traveled through the organization's hierarchical chain of command.

In the past, internal auditors reviewed financial reports generated by other corporate accountants. The auditors considered professional accounting and financial practices, as well as relevant aspects of corporate law, and then presented their findings to the chief financial officer (CFO). Historically, the CFO reviewed the audits and determined the financial data and information that was to be presented to top management, directors, and investors of the company.

However, because Sarbanes-Oxley requires that CEOs and audit committees sign off on financial results, auditors now routinely deal directly with top corporate officials, as shown in the new structure in Exhibit 3.12, Strategy in Action. Approximately 75 percent of senior corporate auditors now report directly to the board of directors' audit committee. Additionally, to eliminate the potential for accounting problems, companies are establishing direct lines of communication between top managers and the board and auditors that inform the CFO but that are not dependent on CFO approval or authorization.

The new structure also provides the CEO information provided directly by the company's chief compliance and chief accounting officers. Consequently, the CFO, who is responsible for ultimately approving all company payments, is not empowered to be the sole provider of data for financial evaluations by the CEO and board.

CSR's Effect on the Mission Statement

The mission statement not only identifies what product or service a company produces, how it produces it, and what market it serves, it also embodies what the company believes.

The New Corporate Governance Structure

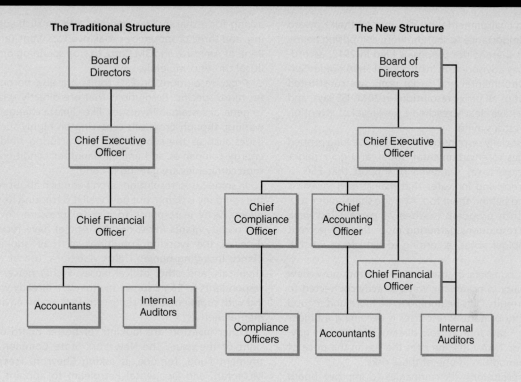

The Traditional Structure

- Board of Directors
  - Chief Executive Officer
    - Chief Financial Officer
      - Accountants
      - Internal Auditors

The New Structure

- Board of Directors
  - Chief Executive Officer
    - Chief Compliance Officer
      - Compliance Officers
    - Chief Accounting Officer
      - Accountants
    - Chief Financial Officer
      - Internal Auditors

As such, it is essential that the mission statement recognize the legitimate claims of its external stakeholders, which may include creditors, customers, suppliers, government, unions, competitors, local communities, and elements of the general public. This stakeholder approach has become widely accepted by U.S. business. For example, a survey of directors in 291 of the largest southeastern U.S. companies found that directors had high stakeholder orientations. Customers, government, stockholders, employees, and society, in that order, were the stakeholders these directors perceived as most important.

In developing mission statements, managers must identify all stakeholder groups and weigh their relative rights and abilities to affect the firm's success. Some companies are proactive in their approach to CSR, making it an integral part of their raison d'être (e.g., Ben & Jerry's ice cream); others are reactive, adopting socially responsible behavior only when they must (e.g., Exxon after the *Valdez* incident).

Social Audit

social audit
An attempt to measure a company's actual social performance against its social objectives.

A **social audit** attempts to measure a company's actual social performance against the social objectives it has set for itself. A social audit may be conducted by the company itself. However, one conducted by an outside consultant who will impose minimal biases may prove more beneficial to the firm. As with a financial audit, an outside auditor brings credibility to the evaluation. This credibility is essential if management is to take the results seriously and if the general public is to believe the company's public relations pronouncements.

Sustainability Grows on the Shareholder Agenda

Social and environmental issues continue their upward march in importance to shareholders, comprising nearly half of all shareholder proposals filed in 2012, according to proxy advisory firm Institutional Shareholder Services. Environmental and social proposals constituted 40 percent of all proxy resolutions in 2011, ISS says, and the topics have clearly reached a new level of attention to the investor's mind.

While socially responsible investors have long pushed for changes to environmental, social, and governance policies, experts say the levels of support that ESG issues are receiving indicates that mainstream investors are getting behind them too. Average shareholder support for such proposals reached 21 percent last year, with five resolutions garnering more than 50 percent of shareholder votes, according to data from Ernst & Young.

Larger numbers of traditional investors now view sustainability in pragmatic ways, directly connected to financial results. "It's beginning to be more understood that scarcity of natural resources is becoming a bigger risk factor," says John Wilson, director of corporate governance for TIAA-CREF; he cites the rise in the price of many commodities as one of those risks.

Most resolutions ask companies to improve board oversight of their lobbying and political giving practices and to provide better data on their contributions in the form of regular reports. Several proposals, however, are asking for a shareholder advisory vote on such spending, and three proposed by social investors want Target, Bank of America, and 3M Corp. to stop spending on political causes completely.

Proxy resolutions on ESG topics are also becoming far more specific. Resolutions that are directly related to general sustainability issues, like climate change, are waning, though proposals centering on highly specific issues such as the composition of fracturing fluids at energy companies and animal slaughter conditions at food companies are gaining ground.

In some cases, resolutions aren't as much about what the company is doing, but how well it is tracking its suppliers. Partly in response to investor pressure, several technology giants (most notably Apple) have recently detailed the working conditions at their suppliers' plants, including human rights violations, use of toxic chemicals, and other ethical lapses. Eighty percent of respondents to E&Y's survey say they are already working with suppliers to get reports from them on environmental metrics.

Other investors are looking for better board oversight of the issue. The New York State Common Retirement Fund, for one, is asking Chevron, Freeport McMoran, and Occidental Petroleum to appoint one board member each with environmental expertise.

Source: Excerpted from Alix Stuart. 2012. "Sustainability Grows on the Shareholder Agenda." *Compliance Week*, 9 (101): 44–45, 62.

Careful, accurate monitoring and evaluation of a company's CSR actions are important not only because the company wants to be sure it is implementing CSR policy as planned but also because CSR actions by their nature are open to intense public scrutiny. To make sure it is making good on its CSR promises, a company may conduct a social audit of its performance.

Once the social audit is complete, it may be distributed internally or both internally and externally, depending on the firm's goals and situation. Some firms include a section in their annual report devoted to social responsibility activities; others publish a separate periodic report on their social responsiveness. Companies publishing separate social audits include General Motors, Bank of America, Atlantic Richfield, Control Data, and Aetna Life and Casualty Company. Nearly all *Fortune* 500 corporations disclose social performance information in their annual reports.

Shareholders are increasingly asking executives of large corporations to report on their sustainability progress. As discussed in Strategy in Action, Exhibit 3.13, social and environmental issues comprised nearly half of all shareholder proposals filed in 2012. Experts say the increasing levels of support that environmental, social, and governance policies (ESG) issues are receiving indicates that mainstream investors are getting concerned. They are asking for improved oversight of lobbying and political giving practices by corporate boards of directors and for better data on the companies' charitable contributions.

Large firms are not the only companies employing the social audit. Boutique ice cream maker Ben & Jerry's, a CSR pioneer, publishes a social audit in its annual report. The audit, conducted by an outside consultant, scores company performance in such areas as employee benefits, plant safety, ecology, community involvement, and customer service. The report is published unedited.

The social audit may be used for more than simply monitoring and evaluating firm social performance. Managers also use social audits to scan the external environment, determine firm vulnerabilities, and institutionalize CSR within the firm. In addition, companies themselves are not the only ones who conduct social audits; public interest groups and the media watch companies who claim to be socially responsible very closely to see if they practice what they preach. These organizations include consumer groups and socially responsible investing firms that construct their own guidelines for evaluating companies.

The Body Shop learned what can happen when a company's behavior falls short of its espoused mission and objectives. The 20-year-old manufacturer and retailer of naturally based hair and skin products had cultivated a socially responsible corporate image based on a reputation for socially responsible behavior. However, *Business Ethics* magazine published an exposé claiming that the company did not "walk the talk." It accused The Body Shop of using nonrenewable petrochemicals in its products, recycling far less than it claimed, using ingredients tested on animals, and making threats against investigative journalists. The Body Shop's contradictions were noteworthy because Anita Roddick, the company's founder, made CSR a centerpiece of the company's strategy.[2]

SATISFYING CORPORATE SOCIAL RESPONSIBILITY[3]

William Ford Jr. angered Ford Motor Co. executives and investors when he wrote that "there are very real conflicts between Ford's current business practices, consumer choices, and emerging views of (environmental) sustainability." In his company's citizenship report, the grandson of Henry Ford, then the automaker's nonexecutive chairman, even appeared to endorse a Sierra Club statement declaring that "the gas-guzzling SUV is a rolling monument to environmental destruction."

Bill Ford moderated his strongest environmental beliefs since assuming the company's CEO position. Nevertheless, while he strives to improve Ford's financial performance and restore trust among its diverse stakeholders, he remains strongly committed to corporate responsibility and environmental protection. In his words, "A good company delivers excellent products and services, and a great company does all that and strives to make the world a better place."[4] Today, Ford is a leader in producing vehicles that run on alternative sources of fuel, and it is performing as well as or better than its major North American rivals, all of whom are involved in intense global competition. The company is successfully pursuing a strategy that is showing improved financial performance, increased confidence in the brand, and clear evidence that the car company is committed to contributing more broadly to society. Among Ford's more notable outreach efforts are an innovative HIV/AIDS initiative in South Africa that is now expanding to India, China, and Thailand; a partnership with the U.S. National Parks Foundation to provide environmentally friendly transportation for park visitors; and significant support for the Clean Air Initiative for Asian Cities.

[2]Jon Entine, "Shattered Image," *Business Ethics* 8, no. 5 (September/October 1994), pp. 23–28.

[3]This section was excerpted from J. A. Pearce II and J. Doh, "Enhancing Corporate Responsibility through Skillful Collaboration," *Sloan Management Review* 46, no. 3 (2005), pp. 30–39.

[4]"Ford Motor Company Encourages Elementary School Students to Support America's National Parks," http://www.theautochannel.com/news/2003/04/17/159567.html

Ford's actions are emblematic of the corporate social responsibility initiatives of many leading companies. Corporate-supported social initiatives are now a given. Many *Fortune* 500 corporations have senior manager titles dedicated to helping their organizations "give back" more effectively. CSR is now almost universally embraced by top managers as an integral component of their executive roles, whether motivated by self-interest, altruism, strategic advantage, or political gain. Their outreach is usually plain to see on the companies' corporate Web sites. CSR is high on the agenda at major executive gatherings such as the World Economic Forum. It is very much in evidence during times of tragedy and it is the subject of many conferences, workshops, newsletters, and more. "Consultancies have sprung up to advise companies on how to do corporate social responsibility and how to let it be known that they are doing it," noted *The Economist* in a survey on CSR.

Executives face conflicting pressures to contribute to social responsibility while honoring their duties to maximize shareholder value. They face many belligerent critics who challenge the idea of a single-minded focus on profits—witness the often violent antiglobalization protests in recent years. They also face skeptics who contend that CSR initiatives are chiefly a convenient marketing gloss. However, the reality is that most executives are eager to improve their CSR effectiveness. The issue is not whether companies will engage in socially responsible activities, but how. For most companies, the challenge is how best to achieve the maximum social benefit from a given amount of resources available for social projects.

Studies of dozens of social responsibility initiatives at major corporations show that senior managers struggle to find the right balance between "low-engagement" solutions such as charitable gift-giving and "high-commitment" solutions that run the risk of diverting attention from the company's core mission. In this section, we will see that collaborative social initiatives (CSIs)—a form of engagement in which companies provide ongoing and sustained commitments to a social project or issue—provide the best combination of social and strategic impact.

The Core of the CSR Debate

The proper role of CSR—the actions of a company to benefit society beyond the requirement of the law and the direct interests of shareholders—has generated a century's worth of philosophically and economically intriguing debates. Since steel baron Andrew Carnegie published *The Gospel of Wealth* in 1899, the argument that businesses are the trustees of societal property that should be managed for the public good has been seen as one end of a continuum with, at the other end, the belief that profit maximization is management's only legitimate goal. The CSR debates were largely confined to the background for most of the twentieth century, making the news after an oil spill or when a consumer product caused harm, or when ethics scandals reopened the question of business's fundamental purpose.

The debates surfaced in more positive ways in the last 30 years as new businesses set up shop with altruism very much in mind and on display. Firms such as ice cream maker Ben & Jerry's argued that CSR and profits do not clash; their stance was that doing good leads to making good money. That line of thinking has gained popularity as more executives have come to understand the value of their companies' reputations with customers—and with investors and employees. But only recently have business leaders begun to get a clearer understanding of the appropriate role of CSR and its effect on financial performance.

In the past, research on the financial effect of CSR produced inconsistent findings, with some studies reporting a positive relationship, others a negative one, and others no relationship at all. Since the mid-1990s, improvements in theory, research designs, data, and

EXHIBIT 3.14
Continuum of Corporate Social Responsibility Commitments

analysis have produced empirical research with more consistent results.[5] Importantly, a recent meta-analysis (a methodological technique that aggregates findings of multiple studies) of more than 10 studies found that on balance, positive relationships can be expected from CSR initiatives but that the primary vehicle for achieving superior financial performance from social responsibility is via reputation effects.[6]

There is no shortage of options with which businesses can advance their CSR goals. The greater challenge is finding the right balance. Philanthropy without active engagement—cash donations, for instance—has been criticized as narrow, self-serving, and often motivated to improve the corporation's reputation and keep nongovernmental organization (NGO) critics and other naysayers at bay.[7] However, redirecting the company toward a socially responsible mission, while seemingly attractive, may have the unintended consequences of diverting both managers and employees from their core mission. Exhibit 3.14 presents a simple illustration of the range of options available to corporations as they consider their CSR commitments.

What managers need is a model that they can use to guide them in selecting social initiatives and through which they can exploit their companies' core competencies for the maximum positive impact. As a starting point, research confirms that a business must determine the social causes that it will support and why and then decide how its support should be organized.[8] According to one perspective, businesses have three basic support options: donations of cash or material, usually to a nongovernmental or nonprofit agency; creation of a functional operation within the company to assist external charitable efforts; and development of a collaboration approach, whereby a company joins with an organization that has particular expertise in managing the way benefits are derived from corporate support.[9]

Mutual Advantages of Collaborative Social Initiatives

The term *social initiative* describes initiatives that take a collaborative approach. Research on alliances and networks among companies in competitive commercial environments tells us that each partner benefits when the other brings resources, capabilities, or other assets that it cannot easily attain on its own. These *combinative capabilities* allow the company to

---

[5]J. J. Griffin and J. F. Mahon, "The Corporate Social Performance and Corporate Financial Performance Debate: Twenty-Five Years of Incomparable Research," *Business and Society* 36 (1997), pp. 5–31; R. M. Roman, S. Hayibor, and B. R. Agle, "The Relationship between Social and Financial Performance: Repainting a Portrait," *Business and Society* 38 (1999), pp. 109–125; and J. D. Margolis and J. P. Walsh, "Misery Loves Companies: Rethinking Social Initiatives by Business," *Administrative Science Quarterly* 48 (2003), pp. 268–305.

[6]M. Orlitzky, F. L. Schmidt, and S. L. Rynes, "Corporate Social and Financial Performance: A Meta-Analysis," *Organization Studies* 24, no. 3 (2003), pp. 403–441.

[7]B. Husted, "Governance Choices for Corporate Social Responsibility: To Contribute, Collaborate or Internalize?" *Long Range Planning* 36, no. 5 (2003), pp. 481–498.

[8]N. C. Smith. "Corporate Social Responsibility: Whether or How?" *California Management Review* 45, no. 4 (2003), pp. 52–76.

[9]Husted, "Governance Choices for Corporate Social Responsibility."

acquire and synthesize resources and build new applications from those resources, generating innovative responses to rapidly evolving environments.

The same is true with collaborative social initiatives. While neither companies nor nonprofits are well equipped to handle escalating social or environmental problems, each participant has the potential to contribute valuable material resources, services, or individuals' voluntary time, talents, energies, and organizational knowledge. Those cumulative offerings are vastly superior to cash-only donations, which are a minimalist solution to the challenges of social responsibility. Social initiatives involve ongoing information and operational exchanges among participants and are especially attractive because of their potential benefits for both the corporate and not-for-profit partners.

There is strong evidence to show that CSR activities increasingly confer benefits beyond enhanced reputation. For some participants, they can be a tool to attract, retain, and develop managerial talent. The PricewaterhouseCoopers (PwC) Project Ulysses is a leadership development program that sends small teams of PwC partners to developing countries to apply their expertise to complex social and economic challenges. The cross-cultural PwC teams collaborate with nongovernmental organizations (NGOs), community-based organizations, and intergovernmental agencies, working pro bono in eight-week assignments in communities struggling with the effects of poverty, conflict, and environmental degradation. The Ulysses program was designed in part to respond to a growing challenge confronting professional services companies: identifying and training up-and-coming leaders who can find nontraditional answers to intractable problems.

All 24 Ulysses graduates still work at PwC; most say they have a stronger commitment to the firm because of the commitment it made to them and because they now have a different view of PwC's values. For PwC, the Ulysses program provides a tangible message to its primary stakeholders that the company is committed to making a difference in the world. According to Brian McCann, the first U.S.-based partner to participate in Ulysses, "This is a real differentiator—not just in relation to our competitors, but to all global organizations."

Five Principles of Successful Collaborative Social Initiatives

Corporate social responsibility has become a vital part of the business conversation. The issue is not whether companies will engage in socially responsible activities, but how. For most companies, the challenge is how best to achieve the maximum social benefit from a given amount of resources available for social projects. Research points to five principles that facilitate better outcomes for society and for corporate participants, as shown in Exhibit 3.15, Strategy in Action. When CSR initiatives include most or all of these elements, companies can indeed maximize the effects of their social contributions while advancing broader strategic goals. While most CSIs will not achieve complete success with all five elements, some progress with each is requisite for success. Here are the five principles, along with examples of companies that have adhered to them well:

1. Identify a Long-Term Durable Mission

Companies make the greatest social contribution when they identify an important, long-standing policy challenge and they participate in its solution over the long term. Veteran *Wall Street Journal* reporter and author Ron Alsop argues that companies that are interested in contributing to corporate responsibility and thus burnishing their reputations should "own the issue."[10] Companies that step up to tackle problems that are clearly important to

---

[10]R. Alsop, *The 18 Immutable Laws of Corporate Reputation* (New York: Free Press, 2004).

Five Principles of Successful Corporate Social Responsibility Collaboration

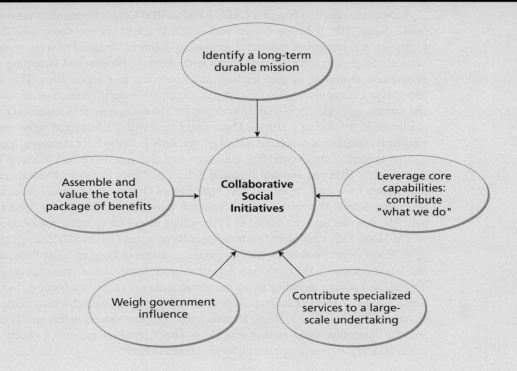

society's welfare and that require substantial resources are signaling to internal and external constituencies that the initiative is deserving of the company's investment.

Among the more obvious examples of social challenges that will demand attention for years to come are hunger, inadequate housing, ill health, substandard education, and degradation of the environment. While a company's long-term commitment to any one of those problems embeds that issue in the fabric of the company, it is more important that the company can develop competencies that allow it to become better at its social activities yet be able to keep investing in those outputs. It is also important to identify limited-scope projects and shorter-term milestones that can be accomplished through direct contributions by the company. Solving global hunger is a worthy goal, but it is too large for any individual company to make much of a dent.

Avon Products Inc., the seller of beauty and related products, offers a fine example of a long-term commitment to a pervasive and longstanding problem. In 1992, the company's Avon Foundation—a public charity established in 1955 to improve the lives of women and their families—launched its Breast Cancer Crusade in the United Kingdom. The program has expanded to 50 countries. Funds are raised through a variety of programs, product sales, and special events, including the Avon Walk for Breast Cancer series. The company distinguishes itself from other corporations that fund a single institution or scientific investigator because it operates as part of a collaborative, supporting a national network of research, medical, social service, and community-based organizations, each of which makes its own unique contribution to helping patients or advancing breast cancer research. The

Crusade has awarded more than $300 million to breast cancer research and care organizations worldwide. In its first 10 years, the Avon Walks program raised more than $250 million for research, awareness, detection, and treatment.

Another example of a powerful CSI is found in IBM Corp.'s Reinventing Education initiative. Since 1994, IBM has worked with nonprofit school partners throughout the world to develop and implement innovative technology solutions designed to solve some of education's toughest problems: from coping with shrinking budgets and increasing parental involvement to moving to team teaching and developing new lesson plans. This initiative responds to a nearly universal agreement that education—especially education of young girls and women—provides the essential foundation for addressing a range of social and economic challenges in developing countries. Overcoming the existing educational deficit requires a long-term commitment to achieve school reform, such as methods for measuring learning.

One element of the Reinventing Education initiative is a Web-based "Change Toolkit" developed by IBM and Harvard Business School professor Rosabeth Moss Kanter, with sponsorship from the Council of Chief State School Officers, the National Association of Secondary School Principals, and the National Association of Elementary School Principals. The program has been lauded as a compelling model for systemic school reform.

The Home Depot has identified housing as its principal CSI. In 2002, the company set up its Home Depot Foundation with the primary mission of building "affordable, efficient, and healthy homes." Thirty million Americans face some sort of challenge in securing dependable housing, including living in substandard or overcrowded housing; lacking hot water, electricity, toilet, or bathtub/shower; or simply paying too high a percentage of their income on housing. Hence, Home Depot's long-term commitment in this area is unassailable. Its foundation works closely with Home Depot suppliers and with a variety of nonprofits, placing a strong emphasis on local volunteer efforts.

2. Contribute "What We Do"

Companies maximize the benefits of their corporate contributions when they leverage core capabilities and contribute products and services that are based on expertise used in or generated by their normal operations. Such contributions create a mutually beneficial relationship between the partners; the social-purpose initiatives receive the maximum gains while the company minimizes costs and diversions. It is not essential that these services be synonymous with those of the company's business, but they should build upon some aspect of its strategic competencies.

The issue was aired at the recent World Economic Forum gathering in Davos, Switzerland. "We see corporate social responsibility as part and parcel of doing business, part of our core skills," said Antony Burgmans, chairman of consumer-products giant Unilever NV. "The major value for Unilever is the corporate reputation it helps create."

The thinking is similar at IBM, where, as part of its Reinventing Education initiative, the company contributes financial resources, researchers, educational consultants, and technology to each site to find new ways for technology to spur and support fundamental school restructuring and broad-based systemic change to raise student achievement. In effect, IBM leverages its technological and systems expertise, and its experience providing systems solutions to educational clients, to meet a broader educational challenge. Says Stanley Litow, vice president of Corporate Community Relations at IBM: "IBM believes that a strong community is a key to a company's success . . . To this end, a key focus of our work has been on raising the quality of public education and bridging the digital divide."[11] IBM

[11]"Reinventing Education," www.ibm.com/ibm/ibmgives/grant/education/programs/reinventing/re_school_reform.shtml

gains significant goodwill and brand identity with important target markets, in some ways repeating Apple Computer Inc.'s successful strategy in the 1980s under which it donated computers to schools as a way to gain recognition.

There are many comparable initiatives on the procurement side. Retailers such as Starbucks Coffee Company now source much of their bean supply directly from producers, thereby ensuring that those farmers receive fair compensation without being exploited by powerful middlemen. Many retail supermarkets have followed with their own versions of the "fair trade" model.

3. Contribute Specialized Services to a Large-Scale Undertaking

Companies have the greatest social impact when they make specialized contributions to large-scale cooperative efforts. Those that contribute to initiatives in which other private, public, or nonprofit organizations are also active have an effect that goes beyond their limited contributions. Although it is tempting for a company to identify a specific cause that will be associated only with its own contributions, such a strategy is likely to be viewed as a "pet project" and not as a contribution to a larger problem where a range of players have important interests.

A good example is the AES Corp.'s carbon offset program. AES, headquartered in Arlington, Virginia, is one of the world's largest independent power producers, with 30,000 employees and generation and distribution businesses in 27 countries. Some years ago, the company recognized that it could make a contribution to the battle against global warming—a significant environmental threat with serious consequences such as habitat and species depletion, drought, and water scarcity. AES developed a program that offsets carbon emissions, creating carbon "sinks," a practical and effective means of combating this global problem.

Researchers have concluded that planting and preserving trees (technically "forest enhancement") provides the most practical and effective way to address the CO_2 emissions problem. Trees absorb CO_2 as they grow and convert it to carbon that is locked up (sequestered) in biomass as long as they live. AES leaders believed that if their company could contribute to increasing the standing stock of trees, the additional trees might be able to absorb enough CO_2 to offset the emissions from an AES cogeneration plant. This approach became one of the many mitigation measures now accepted in the global climate change treaty—the Kyoto Protocol—as a means of achieving legally binding emissions reduction targets.

For its part, packaged-foods giant ConAgra Foods Inc. helps to fight hunger in partnership with America's Second Harvest, an organization that leads the food recovery effort in the United States. Set up as the nationwide clearinghouse for handling the donations of prepared and perishable foods, ConAgra's coordination efforts enable smaller, local programs to share resources, making the food donation and distribution process more effective. In October 1999, ConAgra joined with food bank network America's Second Harvest in a specific initiative, the Feeding Children Better program, distributing food to 50,000 local charitable agencies, which, in turn, operate more than 94,000 food programs.

4. Weigh Government's Influence

Government support for corporate participation in CSIs—or at least its willingness to remove barriers—can have an important positive influence. Tax incentives, liability protection, and other forms of direct and indirect support for businesses all help to foster business participation and contribute to the success of CSIs.

For instance, in the United States, ConAgra's food recovery initiatives can deduct the cost (but not market value) of the donated products plus one half of the product's profit margin; the value of this deduction is capped at twice the cost of the product. To encourage further participation of businesses in such food recovery programs, America's Second Harvest generated a series of recommendations for the U.S. government. The recommendations seek to improve the tax benefits associated with food donation, including a proposal that tax deductions be set at the fair market value of donations. Tax deductions provide economic enticement for companies to consider participation, as Boston Market, KFC, and Kraft Foods have publicly acknowledged. Donating food also allows companies to identify the amount of food wasted because it is tracked for tax purposes.

Similar efforts are being applied to reforms that will ease businesses' concerns about their liability from contributing to social enterprises. The Bill Emerson Good Samaritan Food Donation Act, enacted in 1996, protects businesses from liability for food donations except in the case of gross negligence. Building on this federal U.S. act, all 50 states and the District of Columbia have enacted "good Samaritan" laws to protect donors except in cases evidencing negligence. Many companies and nonprofits would like to see more comprehensive tort reform to support their efforts.

Government endorsements are invaluable too. The Home Depot's partnership with Habitat for Humanity is actively supported by the U.S. Department of Housing and Urban Development (HUD). This support takes the form of formal endorsement, logistical facilitation, and implicit acknowledgement that the partnership's initiatives complement HUD's own efforts. Home Depot is assured that the agency will not burden the program with red tape. In the case of AES's efforts in the area of global warming, organizations such as the World Bank, the Global Environmental Facility, and the U.N. Environment and Development Program endorse and encourage offsets via grants, loans, and scientific research.

5. Assemble and Value the Total Package of Benefits

Companies gain the greatest benefits from their social contributions when they put a price on the total benefit package. The valuation should include both the social contributions delivered and the reputation effects that solidify or enhance the company's position among its constituencies. Positive reputation—by consumers, suppliers, employees, regulators, interest groups, and other stakeholders—is driven by genuine commitment rather than episodic or sporadic interest; consumers and other stakeholders see through nominal commitments designed simply to garner short-term positive goodwill. "The public can smell if [a CSR effort] is not legitimate," said Shelly Lazarus, chairman and CEO of advertising agency Ogilvy & Mather USA. Hence, social initiatives that reflect the five principles discussed here can generate significant reputation benefits for participating companies.

AES's commitment to carbon offsets has won it several awards and generates favorable consideration from international financial institutions such as the World Bank, International Finance Corporation, and Inter-American Development Bank, as well as from governments, insurers, and NGOs. In the consumer products sector, Avon receives extensive media recognition from the advertising and marketing of cancer walks, nationwide special events including a gala fund-raising concert, and an awards ceremony. Avon has become so closely associated with the breast cancer cause that many consumers now identify the company's commitment—and the trademark pink ribbon—as easily as its traditional door-to-door marketing and distribution systems.

While difficult to quantify precisely, the potential value of the pink ribbon campaign, and the brand awareness associated with it, generates economic benefits for Avon in the form of goodwill and overall reputation. Avon's strategy of focusing on a cause that women care about, leveraging its contributions, and partnering with respected NGOs has enabled it to gain trust and credibility in the marketplace. "There needs to be a correlation between the cause and the company," said Susan Heany, director for corporate social responsibility at Avon. "The linkage between corporate giving and the corporate product creates brand recognition. Both buyers and sellers want to achieve the same goal: improving women's health care worldwide."[12]

Assembling the Components

A range of corporate initiatives lend themselves to the CSI model because they share most of the five key attributes we have described here: they have long-term objectives, they are sufficiently large to allow a company to specialize in its contributions, they provide many opportunities for the company to contribute from its current activities or products, they enjoy government support, and they provide a package of benefits that adds value to the company. Exhibit 3.16, Strategy in Action, summarizes five very successful CSI programs and their performance against each of the five principles.

Of the five principles, the most important by far is the second one. Companies must apply what they do best in their normal commercial operations to their social responsibility undertakings. This tenet is consistent with research that argues that social activities most closely related to the company's core mission are most efficiently administered through internalization or collaboration. It is applicable far beyond the examples in this chapter; to waste management companies and recycling programs, for instance, or to publishing companies and after-school educational initiatives, or pharmaceutical companies and local immunization and health education programs.

The Limits of CSR Strategies

Some companies such as Ben & Jerry's have embedded social responsibility and sustainability commitments deeply in their core strategies. Research suggests that such single-minded devotion to CSR may be unrealistic for larger, more established corporations. For example, some analysts have suggested that the intense focus on social responsibility goals by the management team at Levi Strauss & Co. may have diverted the company from its core operational challenges, accelerating the company's closure of all of its North American manufacturing operations.

Larger companies must move beyond the easy options of charitable donations but also steer clear of overreaching commitments. This is not to suggest that companies should not think big—research shows that projects can be broad in scale and scope and still succeed. Rather, it suggests that companies need to view their commitments to corporate responsibility as one important part of their overall strategy but not let the commitment obscure their broad strategic business goals. By starting with a well-defined CSR strategy and developing the collaborative initiatives that support that strategy by meeting the five criteria we have identified, companies and their leaders can make important contributions to the common good while advancing their broader financial and market objectives.

CSR strategies can also run afoul of the skeptics, and the speed with which information can be disseminated via the Web—and accumulated in Web logs—makes this an issue with serious ramifications for reputation management. Nike has been a lightning rod for CSR activists for its alleged tolerance of hostile and dangerous working conditions in its many factories and subcontractors around the world. Despite the considerable efforts the company has made to respond to its critics, it has consistently been on the defensive in trying to redeem its reputation.

[12]"Corporate Social Responsibility in Practice Casebook," *The Catalyst Consortium*, July 2002, p. 8. Available at www.rhcatalyst.org

Strategy in Action

Exhibit 3.16

Five Successful Collaborative Social Initiatives

Program	Pursue a Long-Term, Durable Mission	Contribute "What We Do"	Contribute Specialized Resources to a Large-Scale Undertaking	Weigh Government Influence	Assemble and Value Total Package of Benefits
ConAgra Foods' Feeding Children Better	Individuals needing food from charity in the United States grew to more than 23 million in 2001. In the United Kingdom, the total was 4 million people in 2003.	ConAgra uses its electronic inventory control systems and refrigerated trucks to assist America's Second Harvest's food rescue programs.	ConAgra fights child hunger in America by assembling a powerful partnership with America's Second Harvest, Brandeis University's Center on Hunger and Poverty, and the Ad Council.	The Bill Emerson Good Samaritan Food Donation Act protects businesses from liability for food donations.	ConAgra's brand-sponsored support of food rescue programs sustains its image as provider of "the largest corporate initiative dedicated solely to fighting child hunger in America."
Avon's Breast Cancer Crusade	Breast cancer is the second-leading cause of death in women in the United States and the most common cancer among women.	Avon's commitment to being "the company for women" is shown by their 550,000 sales representatives who sell Crusade "pink ribbon" items.	Avon distinguishes itself by supporting a national network of research, medical, social service, and local organizations to advance cancer research.	Government agencies often match individual contributions; local governments provide logistical support for fundraising walks.	Avon receives media recognition from the advertising and marketing of cancer walks and nationwide special events, including a gala fundraising concert and awards ceremony.
IBM's Reinventing Education	Education in developing countries requires a long-term commitment to school reform, such as methods for measuring learning.	IBM uses its leading researchers, educational consultants, and technology to spur and support fundamental school restructuring.	IBM monitors the program with rigorous, independent evaluations from the Center for Children & Technology in conjunction with the Harvard Business School.	IBM teams with the U.S. Department of Education and the U.K. Department of Education and Employment on many reinvention projects.	IBM views a commitment to education as a strategic business investment. By investing in its future workforce and its customers, IBM feels that it promotes its own success.
Home Depot's In Your Community	30 million Americans face housing problems, such as overcrowding, no hot water, no electricity, and no toilet, bathtub, or shower.	Home Depot offers help with the construction of homes, plus donations and volunteers to help provide affordable housing for low-income families.	More than 1,500 Home Depot stores have Team Depot volunteer programs to support Habitat for Humanity, Rebuilding Together, and KaBOOM with the help of its 315,000 company associates.	Home Depot's partnership with Habitat for Humanity is actively supported by the U.S. Department of Housing and Urban Development.	Home Depot's volunteer programs and "how-to" clinics "invite the community into their stores." Hundreds of thousands of potential customers participate each year.
AES's Carbon Offsets Program	Global warming is an environmental threat. Carbon offsets or "sinks" are one proven, effective means of combating this problem.	AES is a leading international power producer with extensive knowledge of developing countries and their resources, including the dangers from cogeneration plants.	AES has teamed with the World Resources Institute, Nature Conservancy, and CARE to find and evaluate appropriate forestry-based offset projects.	The Environmental Protection Agency, European environmental organizations, U.N. Development Program, and other agencies support carbon offsets.	AES has committed $12 million to carbon offset projects to offset 67 million tons of carbon emitted over the next 40 years—the equivalent of the emissions from a 1,000-MW coal facility over its lifetime.

Touching on this issue at the World Economic Forum, Unilever chief Antony Burgmans noted the importance of "making people who matter in society aware of what you do." His point was amplified by Starbucks CEO Orin Smith, who invited the authors of an NGO report critical of Starbucks' sourcing strategies to the company's offices and showed them the books. "In many instances we ended up partnering with them," he said.

The Future of CSR

CSR is firmly and irreversibly part of the corporate fabric. Managed properly, CSR programs can confer significant benefits to participants in terms of corporate reputation; in terms of hiring, motivation, and retention; and as a means of building and cementing valuable partnerships. And of course, the benefits extend well beyond the boundaries of the participating organizations, enriching the lives of many disadvantaged communities and individuals and pushing back on problems that threaten future generations, other species, and precious natural resources.

That is the positive perspective. The more prickly aspect of CSR is that for all of their resources and capabilities, corporations will face growing demands for social responsibility contributions far beyond simple cash or in-kind donations. Aggressive protesters will keep the issues hot, employees will continue to have their say, and shareholders will pass judgment with their investments—and their votes.

The challenge for management, then, is to know how to meet the company's obligations to all stakeholders without compromising the basic need to earn a fair return for its owners. As research shows, a collaborative approach is the foundation for the most effective CSR initiatives. By then adhering to the five key principles outlined in this section, business leaders can maintain ongoing commitments to carefully chosen initiatives that can have positive and tangible effects on social problems while meeting their obligations to shareholders, employees, and the broader communities in which they operate.

MANAGEMENT ETHICS

The Nature of Ethics in Business

Central to the belief that companies should be operated in a socially responsive way for the benefit of all stakeholders is the belief that managers will behave in an ethical manner. The term **ethics** refers to the moral principles that reflect society's beliefs about the actions of an individual or a group that are right and wrong. Of course, the values of one individual, group, or society may be at odds with the values of another individual, group, or society. Ethical standards, therefore, reflect not a universally accepted code, but rather the end product of a process of defining and clarifying the nature and content of human interaction.

ethics
The moral principles that reflect society's beliefs about the actions of an individual or group that are right and wrong.

Unfortunately, the public's perception of the ethics of corporate executives in America is near its all-time low. A major cause is a spate of corporate scandals prompted by self-serving, and often criminal, executive action that resulted in the loss of stakeholder investments and employee jobs. The goal of every company is to avoid scandal through a combination of high moral and ethical standards and careful monitoring to assure that those standards are maintained. However, when problems arise, the management task of restoring the credibility of the company becomes paramount.

Even when groups agree on what constitutes human welfare in a given case, the means they choose to achieve this welfare may differ. Therefore, ethics also involve acting to attain human goals. For example, many people would agree that health is a value worth seeking—that is, health enhances human welfare. But what if the means deemed necessary to attain this value for some include the denial or risk of health for others, as is commonly an issue faced by pharmaceutical manufacturers? During production of some drugs, employees are

Toyota Recalls: Solidifying the Company's Business Ethics

Toyota's announcement of a technical fix for its sticky gas pedals—which can lead to sudden acceleration problems—is not likely to bring a quick end to the company's current recall nightmare. Having already halted sales and production of eight of its top-selling cars in the United States—and recalled more than 9 million cars worldwide, in two separate recalls—Toyota faces the prospect of billions of dollars in charges and operating losses. The Toyota brand, once almost synonymous with top quality, has taken a heavy hit.

It is clear that Toyota's crisis did not emerge full-blown overnight. Fixing the problem and ensuring that something like it does not happen again will require an all-out effort, from assembly line to the boardroom. Even then, there are no guarantees. Maintaining a good corporate reputation in the 21st century is tricky business indeed.

Toyota's case offers a number of valuable lessons for other business people and companies to consider. Here, for starters, are two:

ACCEPT RESPONSIBILITY

This is one area where Toyota seems to be doing a good job, albeit maybe a year or more too late. Toyota seems to be avoiding the appearance of passing the buck. When pressed by the *New York Times* about problems that might have been caused by supplier CTS, for example, Toyota spokesman Mike Michels said: "I don't want to get into any kind of a disagreement with CTS. Our position on suppliers has always been that Toyota is responsible for the cars."

Accountability matters enormously. Johnson & Johnson's 1982 recall of its painkiller Tylenol, following the deaths of seven people in the Chicago area, has earned it a permanent place in the annals of crisis management. But that recall stemmed from the deadly act of an outsider, not any problem with the product itself, as is the case with Toyota.

TAKE THE LONG VIEW

The three leading factors burnishing corporate reputation these days are "quality products and services, a company I can trust and transparency of business practices," writes public relations executive Richard Edelman, who authors an annual corporate "Trust Barometer."

That is unfortunate news for Toyota. But the company does not have much choice. By one estimate, auto industry recalls conservatively cost an average of $100 per car—suggesting that Toyota might be on the hook for at least a one billion dollar charge. That does not include lost revenue to Toyota and its dealers from the production shutdown. And competitors are already trying to woo customers away and capitalize on Toyota's misfortune.

Reputation can be easily lost—and Toyota's reputation is indeed threatened—but it is highly unlikely the company will collapse completely. And that may be one of the biggest lessons for other companies as they study how Toyota emerges from this recall crisis. The reality is that Toyota is positioned for recovery about as well as it could be—owing, in large measure, to the reputation for quality products and corporate responsibility it has developed over the last two decades. That reputation is a valuable asset, and one that Toyota will undoubtedly be citing and calling upon, in the weeks and months ahead.

Source: Excerpted from Michael Connor, "Toyota Recall: Five Critical Lessons," *Business Ethics*, January 31, 2010.

---

sometimes subjected to great risk of personal injury and infection. For example, if contacted or inhaled, the mercury used in making thermometers and blood pressure equipment can cause heavy metal poisoning. If inhaled, ethylene oxide used to sterilize medical equipment before it is shipped to doctors can cause fetal abnormalities and miscarriages. Even penicillin, if inhaled during its manufacturing process, can cause acute anaphylaxis or shock. Thus, although the goal of customer health might be widely accepted, the means (involving jeopardy to production employees) may not be.

Although McDonald's faced a great deal of public criticism for the presumed poor nutritional balance of its food products that could contribute to poor consumer health, the law did not require the company or any of its competitors to disclose the exact nutritional contents of its products. However, in 2005, McDonald's broke ranks with its competitors and voluntarily provided the information on its labels.

Toyota is also concerned about the business ethics that it projects. Exhibit 3.17, Global Strategy in Action discusses five powerful lessons that the company learned after suffering serious damage to its reputation for automotive design and manufacturing, and the actions that it took to reestablish its business ethics.

The spotlight on business ethics is a widespread phenomenon. For example, a survey by the Institute of Business Ethics helps to clarify how companies use their codes of ethics.[13] It found that more than 90 percent of Financial Times Stock Exchange (FTSE) companies in the United Kingdom have an explicit commitment to doing business ethically in the form of a code of ethical conduct. The respondents also reported that 26 percent of boards of directors are taking direct responsibility for the ethical programs of companies. The main reasons for having a code of ethics were to provide guidance to staff (38 percent) and to reduce legal liability (33 percent). Many of the managers (41 percent) also reported that they had used their code in disciplinary procedures in the last three years, usually on safety, security, and environmental ethical issues.

Approaches to Questions of Ethics

Managers report that the most critical quality of ethical decision making is consistency. Thus, they often try to adopt a philosophical approach that can provide the basis for the consistency they seek. There are three fundamental ethical approaches for executives to consider: the utilitarian approach, the moral rights approach, and the social justice approach.

utilitarian approach
Judging the appropriateness of a particular action based on a goal to provide the greatest good for the greatest number of people.

Managers who adopt the **utilitarian approach** judge the effects of a particular action on the people directly involved, in terms of what provides the greatest good for the greatest number of people. The utilitarian approach focuses on actions, rather than on the motives behind the actions. Potentially positive results are weighed against potentially negative results. If the former outweigh the latter, the manager taking the utilitarian approach is likely to proceed with the action. That some people might be adversely affected by the action is accepted as inevitable. For example, the Council on Environmental Quality conducts cost-benefit analyses when selecting air pollution standards under the Clean Air Act, thereby acknowledging that some pollution must be accepted.

moral rights approach
Judging the appropriateness of a particular action based on a goal to maintain the fundamental rights and privileges of individuals and groups.

Managers who subscribe to the **moral rights approach** judge whether decisions and actions are in keeping with the maintenance of fundamental individual and group rights and privileges. The moral rights approach (also referred to as deontology) includes the rights of human beings to life and safety, a standard of truthfulness, privacy, freedom to express one's conscience, freedom of speech, and private property.

social justice approach
Judging the appropriateness of a particular action based on equity, fairness, and impartiality in the distribution of rewards and costs among individuals and groups.

Managers who take the **social justice approach** judge how consistent actions are with equity, fairness, and impartiality in the distribution of rewards and costs among individuals and groups. These ideas stem from two principles known as the liberty principle and the difference principle. The *liberty principle* states that individuals have certain basic liberties compatible with similar liberties of other people. The *difference principle* holds that social and economic inequities must be addressed to achieve a more equitable distribution of goods and services.

In addition to these defining principles, three implementing principles are essential to the social justice approach. According to the *distributive-justice principle,* individuals should not be treated differently on the basis of arbitrary characteristics, such as race, sex, religion or national origin. This familiar principle is embodied in the Civil Rights Act. The *fairness principle* means that employees must be expected to engage in cooperative activities according to the rules of the company, assuming that the company rules are deemed fair. The most obvious example is that, in order to further the mutual interests of the company, themselves, and other workers, employees must accept limits on their freedom to be

[13]Accessed in 2005 from http://www.ibe.org.uk/ExecSumm.pdf

Global Strategy in Action

Exhibit 3.18

Nike, Inc. Code of Conduct

At Nike, we believe that although there is no finish line, there is a clear starting line.

Understanding that our work with contract factories is always evolving, this Code of Conduct clarifies and elevates the expectations we have of our factory suppliers and lays out the minimum standards we expect each factory to meet.

It is our intention to use these standards as an integral component to how we approach NIKE, Inc. sourcing strategies, how we evaluate factory performance, and how we determine with which factories Nike will continue to engage and grow our business.

As we evolve our business model in sourcing and manufacturing, we intend to work with factories who understand that meeting these minimum standards is a critical baseline from which manufacturing leadership, continuous improvement and self-governance must evolve.

Beyond the Code, Nike is committed to collaborating with our contract factories to help build a leaner, greener, more empowered and equitable supply chain. And we will continue to engage with civil society, governments, and the private sector to affect systemic change to labor and environmental conditions in countries where we operate.

We expect our contract factories to share Nike's commitment to the goals of reducing waste, using resources responsibly, supporting workers' rights, and advancing the welfare of workers and communities. We believe that partnerships based on transparency, collaboration and mutual respect are integral to making this happen.

Our Code of Conduct binds our contract factories to the following specific minimum standards that we believe are essential to meeting these goals.

EMPLOYMENT IS VOLUNTARY

The contractor does not use forced labor, including prison labor, indentured labor, bonded labor or other forms of forced labor. The contractor is responsible for employment eligibility fees of foreign workers, including recruitment fees.

EMPLOYEES ARE AGE 16 OR OLDER

Contractor's employees are at least age 16 or over the age for completion of compulsory education or country legal working age, whichever is higher. Employees under 18 are not employed in hazardous conditions.

CONTRACTOR DOES NOT DISCRIMINATE

Contractor's employees are not subject to discrimination in employment, including hiring, compensation, promotion or discipline, on the basis of gender, race, religion, age, disability, sexual orientation, pregnancy, marital status, nationality, political opinion, trade union affiliation, social or ethnic origin or any other status protected by country law.

FREEDOM OF ASSOCIATION AND COLLECTIVE BARGAINING ARE RESPECTED

To the extent permitted by the laws of the manufacturing country, the contractor respects the right of its employees to freedom of association and collective bargaining. This includes the right to form and join

---

absent from work. The *natural-duty principle* points up a number of general obligations, including the duty to help others who are in need or danger, the duty not to cause unnecessary suffering, and the duty to comply with the just rules of an institution.

CODES OF BUSINESS ETHICS

To help ensure consistency in the application of ethical standards, an increasing number of professional associations and businesses are establishing codes of ethical conduct. Associations of chemists, funeral directors, law enforcement agents, migration agents, hockey players, Internet providers, librarians, military arms sellers, philatelists, physicians, and psychologists all have such codes. So do companies such as Amazon.com, Colgate, Honeywell, New York Times, Nokia, PricewaterhouseCoopers, Sony Group, and Riggs Bank.

Nike faces the problems of a large global corporation in enforcing a code of conduct. Nike's products are manufactured in factories owned and operated by other companies. Nike's supply chain includes more than 660,000 contract manufacturing workers in more than 900 factories in more than 50 countries, including the United States. The workers are predominantly

Exhibit 3.18   continued

trade unions and other worker organizations of their own choosing without harassment, interference or retaliation.

COMPENSATION IS TIMELY PAID

Contractor's employees are timely paid at least the minimum wage required by country law and provided legally mandated benefits, including holidays and leaves, and statutory severance when employment ends. There are no disciplinary deductions from pay.

HARASSMENT AND ABUSE ARE NOT TOLERATED

Contractor's employees are treated with respect and dignity. Employees are not subject to physical, sexual, psychological or verbal harassment or abuse.

WORKING HOURS ARE NOT EXCESSIVE

Contractor's employees do not work in excess of 60 hours per week, or the regular and overtime hours allowed by the laws of the manufacturing country, whichever is less. Any overtime hours are consensual and compensated at a premium rate. Employees are allowed at least 24 consecutive hours rest in every seven-day period.

REGULAR EMPLOYMENT IS PROVIDED

Work is performed on the basis of a recognized employment relationship established through country law and practice. The contractor does not use any form of home working arrangement for the production of Nike-branded or affiliate product.

THE WORKPLACE IS HEALTHY AND SAFE

The contractor provides a safe, hygienic and healthy workplace setting and takes necessary steps to prevent accidents and injury arising out of, linked with or occurring in the course of work or as a result of the operation of contractor's facilities. The contractor has systems to detect, avoid and respond to potential risks to the safety and health of all employees.

ENVIRONMENTAL IMPACT IS MINIMIZED

The contractor protects human health and the environment by meeting applicable regulatory requirements including air emissions, solid/hazardous waste and water discharge. The contractor adopts reasonable measures to mitigate negative operational impacts on the environmental and strives to continuously improve environmental performance.

THE CODE IS FULLY IMPLEMENTED

As a condition of doing business with Nike, the contractor shall implement and integrate this Code and accompanying Code Leadership Standards and applicable laws into its business and submit to verification and monitoring. The contractor shall post this Code, in the language(s) of its employees, in all major workspaces, train employees on their rights and obligations as defined by this Code and applicable country law; and ensure the compliance of any sub-contractors producing Nike branded or affiliate products.

Source: Nike Biz, www.nike.com; retrieved July 15, 2013.

women, ages 19 to 25. The geographic dispersion of its manufacturing facilities is driven by many factors including pricing, quality, factory capacity, and quota allocations.

With such cultural, societal, and economic diversity, the ethics challenge for Nike is to "do business with contract factories that consistently demonstrate compliance with standards we set and that operate in an ethical and lawful manner." To help in this process, Nike has developed its own code of ethics, which it calls a Code of Conduct. It is a set of ethical principles intended to guide management decision making. Nike's code is presented in Exhibit 3.18, Global Strategy in Action.

Major Trends in Codes of Ethics

The increased interest in codifying business ethics has led to both the proliferation of formal statements by companies and to their prominence among business documents. Not long ago, codes of ethics that existed were usually found solely in employee handbooks. The new trend is for them to also be prominently displayed on corporate Web sites, in annual reports, and next to Title VII posters on bulletin boards.

Business Ethics Self-Assessment: What Are the Ethics of Your Company?

Do you know what values you are establishing for your company? Does your business possess honesty and integrity? Does it respect and do well by its employees, customers, and the world at large? If you would like to find out how your business' ethics stack up, complete the following survey that was developed for business owners and managers.

Answer the questions below by circling A for Agree or D for Disagree. When you have finished, the professor will provide the answers and explanations.

1.   A   D   You receive a duplicate payment from a customer who does not realize he made a double payment. You cash the second check thinking he probably will not notice. If he asks for the money back, you will just feign ignorance and issue a refund.

2.   A   D   Your product prices are going up January 1. You purposely schedule a customer's automatic shipment for January 1 that should have been in December just so you can charge the higher rates.

3.   A   D   Due to unforeseen circumstances, customer orders become backlogged and customers are demanding their products. You explain to the customers the reason for the backlog, what you are doing to rectify the problem and when the products will be available. You offer customers a full refund if they cannot wait until the products are available.

4.   A   D   A customer complains about a service provided by one of your agents. This customer is a tiny account and the monies received negligible. When the customer complains a second time and cancels her account, you do not apologize or care because you do not need her money anyway.

5.   A   D   The same priority is given to customers' needs after you have gotten "the sale" as before.

6.   A   D   You are about to close a big sale. The potential customer asks you a question, and if you do not fib, you know you will lose the sale. You tell the fib and save the sale.

7.   A   D   You pretend to have a prior relationship with a potential client in order to get your foot in the door. What they do not remember will not hurt them.

8.   A   D   Business is suffering, and employees are leaving your sinking ship. You hold a meeting with existing employees and assure them that business is fine and their jobs are secure even though they are not. You certainly do not want to lose anyone else while you are still struggling to stay afloat.

9.   A   D   You have not gotten around to removing some discontinued products on your shopping cart. Customers are charging their credit cards for these discontinued items, and you take your time letting them know the products are discontinued. You suggest the monies already charged can be used for other product items on your shopping cart.

Source: This survey was excerpted from Patricia Schaefer. 2008. "Business Ethics Survey: How Ethical Are You?" Attard Communications, Inc.

A second trend is that companies are adding enforcement measures to their codes, including policies that are designed to guide employees on what to do if they see violations occur and sanctions that will be applied, including consequences on their employment and civil and criminal charges. As a consequence, businesses are increasingly requiring all employees to sign the ethics statement as a way to acknowledge that they have read and understood their obligations. In part this requirement reflects the impact of the Sarbanes-Oxley rule that CEOs and CFOs certify the accuracy of company financials. Executives want employees at all levels to recognize their own obligations to pass accurate information up the chain of command.

The third trend is increased attention by companies in improving employees' training in understanding their obligations under the company's code of ethics. The objective is to emphasize the consideration of ethics during the decision-making process. Training, and subsequent monitoring of actual work behavior, is also aided by computer software that identifies possible code violations, which managers can then investigate in detail.

BUSINESS ETHICS SELF-ASSESSMENT

Do you know what values you are establishing for your company? Does your business possess honesty and integrity? Does it respect and do well by its employees, customers, and the world at large? If you would like to find out how your business' ethics stack up, complete the survey in Strategy in Action, Exhibit 3.19, which was developed for business owners and managers.

Summary

Given the amount of time that people spend working, it is reasonable that they should try to shape the organizations in which they work. Inanimate organizations are often blamed for setting the legal, ethical, and moral tones in the workplace when, in reality, people determine how people behave. Just as individuals try to shape their neighborhoods, schools, political and social organizations, and religious institutions, employees need to help determine the major issues of corporate social responsibility and business ethics.

Strategic decisions, indeed all decisions, involve trade-offs. We choose one thing over another. We pursue one goal while subordinating another. On the topic of corporate social responsibility, individual employees must work to achieve the outcomes that they want. By volunteering for certain community welfare options they choose to improve that option's chances of being beneficial. Business ethics present a parallel opportunity. By choosing proper behaviors, employees help to build an organization that can be respected and economically viable in the long run.

Often, the concern is expressed that business activities tend to be illegal or unethical and that the failure of individuals to follow the pattern will leave them at a competitive disadvantage. Such claims, often prompted by high-profile examples, are absurd. Rare but much publicized criminal activities mask the meaningful reality that business conduct is as honest and honorable as any other activity in our lives. The people who are involved are the same, with the same values, ideals, and aspirations.

In this chapter, we have studied corporate social responsibility to understand it and to learn how our businesses can occasionally use some of their resources to make differential, positive impacts on our society. We also looked at business ethics to gain an appreciation for the importance of maintaining and promoting social values in the workplace.

Key Terms

corporate social responsibility (CSR), *p. 56*
discretionary responsibilities, *p. 55*
economic responsibilities, *p. 51*

ethical responsibilities, *p. 53*
ethics, *p. 79*
legal responsibilities, *p. 51*
moral rights approach, *p. 81*
Sarbanes-Oxley Act of 2002, *p. 63*

social audit, *p. 67*
social justice approach, *p. 81*
utilitarian approach, *p. 81*

Questions for Discussion

1. Define the term *social responsibility*. Find an example of a company action that was legal but not socially responsible. Defend your example on the basis of your definition.
2. Name five potentially valuable indicators of a firm's social responsibility and describe how company performance in each could be measured.
3. Do you think a business organization in today's society benefits by defining a socially responsible role for itself? Why or why not?

4. Which of the three basic philosophies of social responsibility would you find most appealing as the chief executive of a large corporation? Explain.

5. Do you think society's expectations for corporate social responsibility will change in the next decade? Explain.

6. How much should social responsibility be considered in evaluating an organization's overall performance?

7. Is it necessary that an action be voluntary to be termed socially responsible? Explain.

8. Do you think an organization should adhere to different philosophies of corporate responsibility when confronted with different issues, or should its philosophy always remain the same? Explain.

9. Describe yourself as a stakeholder in a company. What kind of stakeholder role do you play now? What kind of stakeholder roles do you expect to play in the future?

10. What sets the affirmative philosophy apart from the stakeholder philosophy of social responsibility? In what areas do the two philosophies overlap?

11. Cite examples of both ethical and unethical behavior drawn from your knowledge of current business events.

12. How would you describe the contemporary state of business ethics?

13. How can business self-interest also serve social interests?

The External Environment

After reading and studying this chapter, you should be able to

1. Describe the three tiers of environmental factors that affect the performance of a firm.

2. List and explain the five factors in the remote environment.

3. Give examples of the economic, social, political, technological, and ecological influences on a business.

4. Explain the five forces model of industry analysis and give examples of each force.

5. Give examples of the influences of entry barriers, supplier power, buyer power, substitute availability, and competitive rivalry on a business.

6. List and explain the five factors in the operating environment.

7. Give examples of the influences of competitors, creditors, customers, labor, and direct suppliers on a business.

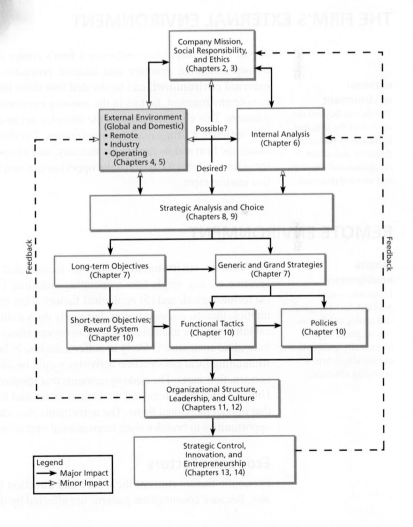

Legend
→ Major Impact
⇾ Minor Impact

EXHIBIT 4.1
The Firm's External Environment

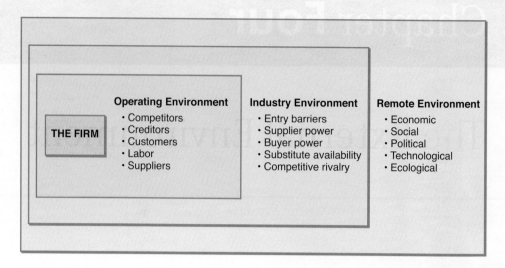

Operating Environment
- Competitors
- Creditors
- Customers
- Labor
- Suppliers

THE FIRM

Industry Environment
- Entry barriers
- Supplier power
- Buyer power
- Substitute availability
- Competitive rivalry

Remote Environment
- Economic
- Social
- Political
- Technological
- Ecological

THE FIRM'S EXTERNAL ENVIRONMENT

external environment
The factors beyond the control of the firm that influence its choice of direction and action, organizational structure, and internal processes.

A host of external factors influence a firm's choice of direction and action and, ultimately, its organizational structure and internal processes. These factors, which constitute the **external environment,** can be divided into three interrelated subcategories: factors in the remote environment, factors in the industry environment, and factors in the operating environment. This chapter describes the complex necessities involved in formulating strategies that optimize a firm's market opportunities. Exhibit 4.1 suggests the interrelationship between the firm and its remote, its industry, and its operating environments. In combination, these factors form the basis of the opportunities and threats that a firm faces in its competitive environment.

REMOTE ENVIRONMENT

remote environment
Economic, social, political, technological, and ecological factors that originate beyond, and usually irrespective of, any single firm's operating situation.

The **remote environment** comprises factors that originate beyond, and usually irrespective of, any single firm's operating situation: (1) economic, (2) social, (3) political, (4) technological, and (5) ecological factors. That environment presents firms with opportunities, threats, and constraints, but rarely does a single firm exert any meaningful reciprocal influence. For example, when the economy slows and construction starts to decrease, an individual contractor is likely to suffer a decline in business, but that contractor's efforts in stimulating local construction activities would be unable to reverse the overall decrease in construction starts. The trade agreements that resulted from improved relations between the United States and China and the United States and Russia are examples of political factors that impact individual firms. The agreements provided individual U.S. manufacturers with opportunities to broaden their international operations.

Economic Factors

Economic factors concern the nature and direction of the economy in which a firm operates. Because consumption patterns are affected by the relative affluence of various market

Where Wal-Mart Isn't: Four Countries the Retailer Can't Conquer

Wal-Mart (WMT) is the biggest retailer in the world, with sales of $135 billion in 26 countries outside the U.S. But it doesn't have stores in some of the world's biggest markets. Not in Germany, not in South Korea, not in Russia. And, not in India, either.

In 2013, Walmart announced that it is breaking up with its Indian partner, Bharti Enterprises, which means the American company's ambitious plans to open hundreds of supercenters around India won't be realized soon. In the official statement, Scott Price, head of Walmart Asia, referred obliquely to "investment conditions" as part of the problem. He had been more direct in an Associated Press interview two days earlier at the Asia-Pacific Economic Cooperation summit. Price said that the Indian government's requirement that foreign retailers source 30 percent of the products they sell from small and medium-sized Indian businesses is the "critical stumbling block." Walmart does have a wholesale business in India, which it is keeping.

Price didn't mention that the Indian government is investigating allegations that Walmart violated rules governing foreign investment in the retail industry, or that Walmart is conducting an internal probe on possible violations of U.S. anti-corruption laws.

Walmart has not figured out a way to enter Russia, either. For nearly six years, it looked to buy a local company that could ease potential cultural and bureaucratic misunderstandings. Walmart lost a bid for a promising partner, a discount chain called Kopeyka, in 2010. Walmart later closed its Moscow office after saying disagreements on price had thwarted its acquisition plans.

Then there's Germany and South Korea. After opening stores in both countries, Walmart closed them in 2006. Germans didn't like Walmart employees handling their groceries at the check-out line. Male customers thought the smiling clerks were flirting. And many Europeans prefer to shop daily at local markets. In South Korea, Walmart also stuck to its American marketing strategies, concentrating on everything from electronics to clothing and not what South Koreans go to big markets for: food and beverages.

However, Walmart's global ambitions remain strong. In 2013, the company was rumored to be interested in purchasing the Hong Kong chain, ParknShop (13:HK).

Source: Excerpted from: Susan Berfield. Where Wal-Mart Isn't: Four Countries the Retailer Can't Conquer. *Bloomberg Businessweek Magazine*, October 10, 2013. http://www.businessweek.com/articles/2013-10-10/where-walmart-isnt-four-countries-the-retailer-cant-conquer

segments, each firm must consider economic trends in the segments that affect its industry. On both the national and international level, managers must consider the general availability of credit, the level of disposable income, and the propensity of people to spend. Prime interest rates, inflation rates, and trends in the growth of the gross national product are other economic factors they should monitor.

Changes in economic factors can be difficult to interpret. Walmart has sales of $135 billion in 26 countries outside the U.S. But it has failed in attempts to understand the consumer shopping patterns and pricing preferences of several of the world's biggest markets, including Germany, South Korea, Russia, and India. As discussed in Strategy in Action, Exhibit 4.2, initial missteps halted Walmart's plans in 2013 to open hundreds of supercenters in India.

For example, in 2003, the depressed economy hit Crown Cork & Seal Co. especially hard because it had $2 billion in debt due in the year and no way to raise the money to pay it. The down market had caused its stock price to be too low to raise cash as it normally would. Therefore, Crown Cork managers turned to issuing bonds to refinance its debt. With the slow market, investors were taking advantage of such bonds because they could safely gain higher returns over stocks. Not only were investors getting a deal, but Crown Cork and other companies were seeing the lowest interest rates on bonds in years and by issuing bonds could reorganize their balance sheets.

The emergence of new international power brokers has changed the focus of economic environmental forecasting. Among the most prominent of these power brokers are the European Economic Community (EEC, or Common Market), the Organization of Petroleum Exporting Countries (OPEC), and coalitions of developing countries.

The EEC, whose members include most of the West European countries, eliminated quotas and established a tariff-free trade area for industrial products among its members. By fostering intra-European economic cooperation, it has helped its member countries compete more effectively in non-European international markets.

Social Factors

The social factors that affect a firm involve the beliefs, values, attitudes, opinions, and life-styles of persons in the firm's external environment, as developed from cultural, ecological, demographic, religious, educational, and ethnic conditioning. As social attitudes change, so too does the demand for various types of clothing, books, leisure activities, and so on. Like other forces in the remote external environment, social forces are dynamic, with constant change resulting from the efforts of individuals to satisfy their desires and needs by controlling and adapting to environmental factors. Teresa Iglesias-Solomon hopes to benefit from social changes with *Niños*, a children's catalog written in both English and Spanish. The catalog features books, videos, and Spanish cultural offerings for English-speaking children who want to learn Spanish and for Spanish-speaking children who want to learn English. *Niños'* target market includes middle- to upper-income Hispanic parents, consumers, educators, bilingual schools, libraries, and purchasing agents. Iglesias-Solomon has reason to be optimistic about the future of *Niños*, because the Hispanic population is growing five times faster than the general U.S. population and ranks as the nation's largest minority.

Another form of social change occurs in a nation when it is exposed to major business changes. One recent example is the phenomenal growth in the popularity of franchises in India. As discussed in Global Strategy in Action, Exhibit 4.3, this growth in 2012 was shown by its 1,200 franchise ventures, 300 international franchisors, sales of U.S. $7 billion, and growth in the range of 30–35 percent per year. The growth of franchising has been increasing so fast that India's legal infrastructure lags in providing specific rules to govern its operation. However, as detailed in the exhibit, there are numerous laws governing various aspects of franchising for strategic managers in India to obey.

One of the most profound social changes in recent years has been the entry of large numbers of women into the labor market. This has not only affected the hiring and compensation policies and the resource capabilities of their employers; it has also created or greatly expanded the demand for a wide range of products and services necessitated by their absence from the home. Firms that anticipated or reacted quickly to this social change offered such products and services as convenience foods, microwave ovens, and day care centers.

A second profound social change has been the accelerating interest of consumers and employees in quality-of-life issues. Evidence of this change is seen in recent contract negotiations. In addition to the traditional demand for increased salaries, workers demand such benefits as sabbaticals, flexible hours or four-day workweeks, lump-sum vacation plans, and opportunities for advanced training.

A third profound social change has been the shift in the age distribution of the population. Changing social values and a growing acceptance of improved birth control methods are

Franchising Laws in India

In the past two decades, India has witnessed a sea change in its foreign investment. Globalization, liberalization, and growing brand awareness have resulted in India becoming one of the largest and tastiest emerging markets. Being geographically vast and culturally diverse, India offered a favorable franchising environment with a huge consumer market. The popularity of franchising as a business model in India in 2012 was shown by its 1,200 franchise ventures, 300 international franchisors, sales of U.S. $7 billion, and growth in the range of 30–35 percent per annum.

Although India did not have franchise-specific legislation or regulation, there are numerous laws governing various aspects of franchising. The following are five of the most important laws for franchisors in India to consider:

- Contract Act. The contractual relationship between the franchisor and the franchisee would be governed by the Indian Contract Act, 1872. A franchise agreement would be enforceable under Indian law as it would meet the criteria of a valid contract. However, care would have to be taken that the agreement does not contain any provision which makes it void or voidable.

- Consumer Protection and Product Liability. The Consumer Protection Act, 1986, provides for remedies to consumers in case of defects in products or deficiency in services making the manufacturers and service providers liable for the same.

- Competition Law. In view of the globalization and liberalization of its economy, the focus has shifted from curbing monopolies to promoting healthy competition in India. Accordingly, the Competition Act, 2002, was enacted and is now in force in its entirety. The relevant provisions from the franchising perspective are those with respect to anticompetitive agreements and abuse of dominant position.

- Intellectual Property Rights Trademark Protection: India's IPR laws include the Trademark Act, 1999, the Designs Act, 2000, the Copyright Act, 1957, the Patent Act, 1970, which provide for protection of the IPR of the franchisor and enforcement mechanism against infringement of the same.

- Foreign Exchange Regulations. The Foreign Exchange Management Act, 1999, and the rules/regulations framed thereunder, govern payments in foreign exchange. A franchise arrangement would normally involve payments such as franchise fee, royalty for use of trademarks and system, training expenses, advertisement contributions, and so on and can be remitted to the foreign franchisor without any approvals. Issue of guarantees in favor of a foreign franchisor would require approval of the Reserve Bank of India.

Source: Preeti Mehta. 2012. "Franchising in India." *Franchising World*, 44 (7): 55–56.

expected to raise the mean age of the U.S. population, which was 27.9 in 1970, and 34.9 in the year 2000 to 43.7 years by 2030. This trend will have an increasingly unfavorable effect on most producers of predominantly youth-oriented goods and will necessitate a shift in their long-range marketing strategies. Producers of hair and skin care preparations already have begun to adjust their research and development to reflect anticipated changes in demand.

At times, the social preferences of a nation seem unique or at least uniquely intense. Such a case is presented in Global Strategy in Action, Exhibit 4.4. In 2013, "Pura Raza Espanola" or Pure Spanish Breed horses were being slaughtered and turned into horse meat for export. They were victims of a devastating economic recession that made extravagances difficult to maintain and socially inappropriate when more than a quarter of the Spanish population was unemployed. The anguish of the business decision about how to dispose of the highly valued horses was extremely hard on the Spanish society.

A consequence of the changing age distribution of the population has been a sharp increase in the demands made by a growing number of senior citizens. Constrained by fixed incomes, these citizens have demanded that arbitrary and rigid policies on retirement age be modified and have successfully lobbied for tax exemptions and increases in Social

Legendary Horses Victim of Spain's Economic Bust

In 2013, "Pura Raza Espanola" or Pure Spanish Breed [horses] were being slaughtered and turned into horse meat for export. They were victims of a wrenching economic downturn that has wiped out fortunes, turned housing developments into ghost towns, and left more than a quarter of the population out of work. The southern Spanish region of Andalusia, famed for flamenco and Moorish castles, is also home to a legendary breed of horses that carried conquistadors into battle in the Americas, featured in Hollywood epics and more recently became trophy acquisitions for Spaniards during a giddy economic boom.

The Pura Raza Espanola breed has always been popular in Spain but took off just after the start of the country's biggest ever economic boom in the late 1990s. They had already won fame as war horses and gifts exchanged between European nobility, and have been featured in Hollywood films such as *Gladiator* and *Braveheart*. The spike in demand over the last decade triggered a breeding frenzy in which the number of horses in Spain rose by the hundreds of thousands, nearly half of them purebreds like Pura Raza Espanola. Spain's newly minted affluent classes couldn't get enough of them.

Then came the bust of Spain's property bubble in 2008. First demand for the horses dried up. In 2013, as the financial crisis deepens with no end in sight, there was a new dilemma: Horse owners are increasingly unable to pay for an animal's upkeep of approximately $500 a month. It all means that they face slaughter if owners can't find anybody to take the animals off their hands. Until 2012, Spanish law even dictated that rejected horses must be sent to the slaughterhouse. That's no longer the case but most still are turned into meat because there's little alternative if nobody else is willing to take the horses in. Owners who simply abandon horses face steep fines.

The number of horses sent to slaughter in Spain by owners and breeders hit 70,000 in 2012, more than double the 30,000 recorded killed by the country's Agriculture Ministry in 2008. The Agriculture Ministry horse census counted 660,889 horses in Spain in 2013, down from a high of 748,622 in 2011—but the number is still much higher than the 435,598 counted in 2007 just before Spain's economic boom imploded. Veterinarians and horse experts warn that the high number of horses being killed in Spain could continue for years.

Source: Excerpted from Alan Clendenning. April 8, 2013. "Legendary Horses Latest Victim of Spain's Bust." *The Miami Herald*.

Security benefits. Such changes have significantly altered the opportunity-risk equations of many firms—often to the benefit of firms that anticipated the changes.

Cutting across these issues is concern for individual health. The fast-food industry has been the target of a great deal of public concern. A great deal of popular press attention has been directed toward Americans' concern over the relationship between obesity and health. As documented by the hit movie *Supersize Me*, McDonald's was caught in the middle of this new social concern because its menu consisted principally of high-calorie, artery-clogging foods. Health experts blamed the fast-food industry for the rise in obesity, claiming that companies like McDonald's created an environment that encouraged overeating and discouraged physical activity. Specifically, McDonald's was charged with taking advantage of the fact that kids and adults were watching more TV, by targeting certain program slots to increase sales.

McDonald's responded aggressively and successfully. The company's strategists soon established McDonald's Corp. as an innovator in healthy food options. By 2005, the world's largest fast-food chain launched a new promotional campaign touting healthy lifestyles, including fruit and milk in Happy Meals, activity programs in schools, and a new partnership with the International Olympic Committee. At the time of the announcement, McDonald's was enjoying its longest ever period of same-store sales growth in 25 years, with 24 consecutive months of improved global sales resulting from new healthy menu options, later hours, and better customer service, such as cashless payment options. McDonald's healthy options included a fruit and walnut salad, Paul Newman's brand lowfat Italian dressing, and premium chicken sandwiches in the United States and chicken flatbread and fruit smoothies in Europe.

U.S. Union Warns Obama on Trade Talk Tactics

The largest U.S. labor union has warned the Obama administration and the European Commission not to use fresh transatlantic trade negotiations to "tear down" regulatory standards, but rather to bolster workers' rights—a sign that support from the American left for any deal is far from guaranteed.

In an interview with the *Financial Times*, Celeste Drake, a trade and globalization policy specialist at the AFL-CIO, the largest federation of U.S. labor unions, said, "We are very concerned—as are our European brothers and sisters—that the agreement not be used as a way to tear down standards in areas such as food safety rules, or consumer right-to-know laws, or environmental protections."

U.S. labor unions are a critical part of President Barack Obama's Democratic base—and have often been opposed to trade liberalization policies under both Republican and Democratic administrations.

The unions could be a thorn in the side of the White House as it tries to build political support for the negotiations. As well as their worries about a race-to-the-bottom on regulatory standards, U.S. unions will have some demands of their own, in the hope of bringing in some European-style workers' rights to America, such as union representation on corporate boards,

transnational workers' councils, or greater barriers to redundancies.

"I'm not trying to imply that the U.S. is going to become a more democratic socialist nation but what I am saying is it does provide negotiators the opportunity to look deeply at their labor market policies to see if there are places where they could cooperate to harmonize upward instead of doing the traditional harmonizing downward," Ms. Drake said.

The AFL-CIO's views are distinctly at odds with the way that many U.S. business groups are eyeing the trade talks with the EU. Since tariffs are already low, the focus of the negotiations will be on ways to remove obstacles to trade across a broad range of sectors.

Such regulatory convergence—if successful—could be used by the U.S. and the EU as a global standard that would boost their competitiveness amid growing competition from emerging markets such as China, India, Brazil and others. Corporate America would be sorely disappointed if the negotiations did not achieve that goal.

Source: Politi, James. 2013. "U.S. Union Warns Obama on Trade Talk Tactics." *http://www.ft.com/intl/cms/s/0/46aed1b8-7928-11e2 -930b-00144feabdc0.html*, February 17.

Translating social change into forecasts of business effects is a difficult process, at best. Nevertheless, informed estimates of the impact of such alterations as geographic shifts in populations and changing work values, ethical standards, and religious orientation can only help a strategizing firm in its attempts to prosper.

Political Factors

The direction and stability of political factors are a major consideration for managers on formulating company strategy. Political factors define the legal and regulatory parameters within which firms must operate. Political constraints are placed on firms through fair-trade decisions, antitrust laws, tax programs, minimum wage legislation, pollution and pricing policies, administrative jawboning, and many other actions aimed at protecting employees, consumers, the general public, and the environment. Because such laws and regulations are most commonly restrictive, they tend to reduce the potential profits of firms. However, some political actions are designed to benefit and protect firms. Such actions include patent laws, government subsidies, and product research grants. Often, different stakeholders take different sides on important issues that affect business operations. They then work to influence legislators to vote for the position that they favor. The attempt of labor unions to influence President Barack Obama as payback for their support at the polls is a well-publicized example, as described in Exhibit 4.5, Strategy in Action.

Political factors either may limit or benefit the firms they influence. For example, in a pair of surprising decisions, the Federal Communications Commission (FCC) ruled that local phone companies had to continue to lease their lines to the long-distance carriers at what the locals said was below cost. At the same time, the FCC ruled that the local companies were not required to lease their broadband lines to the national carriers. These decisions were good and bad for the local companies because, although they would lose money by leasing to the long-distance carriers, they could regain some of that loss with their broadband services that did not have to be leased.

The decisions did not mean that the local carriers had to remove existing lines and replace them with broadband lines. Instead, the local carriers would have to run two networks to areas where they want to incorporate broadband because the long-distance carriers had a right to the conventional lines as ruled in the decision. These regulations caused the local carriers to alter their strategies. For example, they often chose to reduce capital investments on new broadband lines because they had to maintain old lines as well. The reduction in capital investments was used to offset the losses they incurred in subsidizing their current lines to the long-distance carriers.

There are many political factors that profoundly affect the nature and potential of business operations in a country, including government policy with regard to industry cooperation, antitrust activities, foreign trade, depreciation, environmental protection, deregulation, and foreign trade barriers. However, executives often point to a nation's corporate tax structure as the most important consideration in their deliberation about international expansion. Exhibit 4.6, Global Strategy in Action describes how Google's international tax maneuvering shelters billions of dollars of income annually.

The direction and stability of political factors are a major consideration when evaluating the remote environment. Consider piracy. Microsoft's performance in the Chinese market is greatly affected by the lack of legal enforcement of piracy and also by the policies of the Chinese government. Likewise, the government's actions in support of its competitor, Linux, have limited Microsoft's ability to penetrate the Chinese market.

Political activity also has a significant impact on two governmental functions that influence the remote environment of firms: the supplier function and the customer function.

Supplier Function

Government decisions regarding the accessibility of private businesses to government-owned natural resources and national stockpiles of agricultural products will affect profoundly the viability of the strategies of some firms.

Customer Function

Government demand for products and services can create, sustain, enhance, or eliminate many market opportunities. For example, the Kennedy administration's emphasis on landing a man on the moon spawned a demand for thousands of new products; the Carter administration's emphasis on developing synthetic fuels created a demand for new skills, technologies, and products; the Reagan administration's strategic defense initiative (the "Star Wars" defense) sharply accelerated the development of laser technologies; Clinton's federal block grants to the states for welfare reform led to office rental and lease opportunities; and the war against terrorism during the Bush administration created enormous investment in aviation.

Technological Factors

The fourth set of factors in the remote environment involves technological change. To avoid obsolescence and promote innovation, a firm must be aware of technological changes that might influence its industry. Creative technological adaptations can suggest possibilities for new products or for improvements in existing products or in manufacturing and marketing techniques.

"Dutch Sandwich" Saves Google Billions in Taxes

The heart of Google's international operations is a silvery glass office building in central Dublin, a block from the city's Grand Canal. In 2009, the office was credited with 88 percent of the search juggernaut's $12.5 billion in sales outside the U.S. Most of the profits, however, went to the tax haven of Bermuda.

To reduce its overseas tax bill, Google uses a complicated legal structure that has saved it $3.1 billion in 2007–2009 and boosted 2009's overall earnings by 26 percent. Google has managed to lower its overseas tax rate more than its peers in the technology sector. Its rate since 2007 has been 2.4 percent.

According to company disclosures, Apple, Oracle, Microsoft and IBM—which together with Google make up the top five technology companies by market capitalization—reported tax rates between 4.5 percent and 25.8 percent on their overseas earnings from 2007 to 2009.

"It's remarkable that Google's effective rate is that low," says Martin A. Sullivan, a tax economist who formerly worked for the U.S. Treasury Department. "This company operates throughout the world mostly in high-tax countries where the average corporate rate is well over 20 percent."

In Bermuda there's no corporate income tax at all. Google's profits travel to the island's white sands via a convoluted route known to tax lawyers as the "Dutch Sandwich." In Google's case, it generally works like this: When a company in Europe, the Middle East or Africa purchases a search ad through Google, it sends the money to Google Ireland. The Irish government taxes corporate profits at 12.5 percent, but Google mostly escapes that tax because its earnings don't stay in the Dublin office, which reported a pretax profit of less than 1 percent of revenues in 2008.

Irish law makes it difficult for Google to send the money directly to Bermuda without incurring a large tax hit, so the payment makes a brief detour through the Netherlands, since Ireland doesn't tax certain payments to companies in other European Union states. Once the money is in the Netherlands, Google can take advantage of generous Dutch tax laws. Its subsidiary there, Google Netherlands Holdings, is just a shell (it has no employees) and passes on about 99.8 percent of what it collects to Bermuda.

All of these arrangements are legal. Google Ireland licenses its search and advertising technology from Google headquarters in Mountain View, CA. The licensing agreement allows Google to attribute its overseas profits to its Irish operations instead of the U.S., where most of the technology was developed. The subsidiary is supposed to pay an "arm's length" price for the rights, or the same amount an unrelated company would. Yet because licensing fees from the Irish subsidiary generate income that is taxed at 35 percent, one of the highest corporate rates in the world, Google has an incentive to set the licensing price as low as possible. The effect is to shift some of its profits overseas in an arrangement known as "transfer pricing."

This, too, is legal. In 2006 the IRS approved Google's transfer pricing arrangements, which began in 2003. Transfer pricing arrangements are popular with technology and pharmaceutical companies in particular because they rely on intellectual property, which is easily transportable across borders.

Source: Excerpted from Jesse Drucker, "'Dutch Sandwich' Saves Google Billions in Taxes," *Bloomburg Businessweek*, Msnbc.com, October 22, 2010. http://www.msnbc.msn.com/id/39784907

A technological breakthrough can have a sudden and dramatic effect on a firm's environment. It may spawn sophisticated new markets and products or significantly shorten the anticipated life of a manufacturing facility. Thus, all firms, and most particularly those in turbulent growth industries, must strive for an understanding both of the existing technological advances and the probable future advances that can affect their products and services. This quasi-science of attempting to foresee advancements and estimate their impact on an organization's operations is known as **technological forecasting.**

technological forecasting
The quasi-science of anticipating environmental and competitive changes and estimating their importance to an organization's operations.

Technological forecasting can help protect and improve the profitability of firms in growing industries. It alerts strategic managers to both impending challenges and promising opportunities. As examples: (1) advances in xerography were a key to Xerox's success but caused major difficulties for carbon paper manufacturers, and (2) the perfection of transistors changed the nature of competition in the radio and television industry, helping

In China, Food Self-sufficiency vs. Industrial Growth

China faces a clash between a policy of food self-sufficiency and the industrial growth that has made it the world's No. 2 economy. "With rising living standards and more consumption of meat, eggs, and dairy, grain consumption is inevitably on the rise."

Growing cities, expanding deserts from years of overgrazing, and a reforestation effort have helped shrink China's farmland by 8.3 million hectares in the past 12 years, the government says. With less land under cultivation, Chinese farmers are unable to boost production of corn and wheat fast enough to cool surging domestic prices, so the country is importing more. "China's increased demand for agricultural commodities will mean an increase in prices for the entire world,"

says David Stroud, chief executive officer of New York hedge fund TS Capital Partners.

Making up for a 5 percent shortfall in China's grain harvest could consume 20 percent of current global grain exports, says Abah Ofon, a Singapore-based commodities analyst at Standard Chartered Bank. "As China continues to grow, demand and supply will struggle to keep up," Ofon says. "For China, the world's biggest consumer and producer, a small deficit can result in huge demand for imports."

Source: Excerpted from: Luzi-Ann Javier and Michael Forsythe. In China, Factories vs. Farms. *Bloomberg Businessweek Magazine*, April 28, 2011. http://www.businessweek.com/magazine /content/11_19/b4227009958677.htm

such giants as RCA while seriously weakening smaller firms whose resource commitments required that they continue to base their products on vacuum tubes.

The key to beneficial forecasting of technological advancement lies in accurately predicting future technological capabilities and their probable impacts. A comprehensive analysis of the effect of technological change involves study of the expected effect of new technologies on the remote environment, on the competitive business situation, and on the business-society interface. In recent years, forecasting in the last area has warranted particular attention. For example, as a consequence of increased concern over the environment, firms must carefully investigate the probable effect of technological advances on quality-of-life factors, such as ecology and public safety.

For example, by combining the powers of Internet technologies with the capability of downloading music in a digital format, Bertelsmann has found a creative technological adaptation for distributing music online to millions of consumers whenever or wherever they might be. Bertelsmann, AOL Time Warner, and EMI formed a joint venture called Musicnet. The ease and wide availability of Internet technologies is increasing the marketplace for online e-tailers. Bertelsmann's response to the shifts in technological factors enables it to distribute music more rapidly through Musicnet to a growing consumer base.

ecology
The relationships among human beings and other living things and the air, soil, and water that supports them.

pollution
Threats to life-supporting ecology caused principally by human activities in an industrial society.

Ecological Factors

The most prominent factor in the remote environment is often the reciprocal relationship between business and the ecology. The term **ecology** refers to the relationships among human beings and other living things and the air, soil, and water that support them. Threats to our life-supporting ecology caused principally by human activities in an industrial society are commonly referred to as **pollution.** Specific concerns include global warming, loss of habitat and biodiversity, as well as air, water, and land pollution.

Economic growth can contribute to ecological damage. For example, as described in Global Strategy in Action, Exhibit 4.7, China's extraordinary economic growth has led to rapidly competing demands for land, while threatening the national policy of food self-sufficiency.

The global climate has been changing for ages; however, it is now evident that humanity's activities are accelerating this tremendously. A change in atmospheric radiation, due in part to ozone depletion, causes global warming. Solar radiation that is normally absorbed into the atmosphere reaches the earth's surface, heating the soil, water, and air.

Another area of great importance is the loss of habitat and biodiversity. Ecologists agree that the extinction of important flora and fauna is occurring at a rapid rate and, if this pace is continued, could constitute a global extinction on the scale of those found in fossil records. The earth's life-forms depend on a well-functioning ecosystem. In addition, immeasurable advances in disease treatment can be attributed to research involving substances found in plants. As species become extinct, the life support system is irreparably harmed. The primary cause of extinction on this scale is a disturbance of natural habitat. For example, current data suggest that the earth's primary tropical forests, a prime source of oxygen and potential plant "cure," could be destroyed in only five decades.

Air pollution is created by dust particles and gaseous discharges that contaminate the air. Acid rain, or rain contaminated by sulfur dioxide, which can destroy aquatic and plant life, is believed to result from coal-burning factories in 70 percent of all cases. A health-threatening "thermal blanket" is created when the atmosphere traps carbon dioxide emitted from smokestacks in factories burning fossil fuels. This "greenhouse effect" can have disastrous consequences, making the climate unpredictable and raising temperatures.

Water pollution occurs principally when industrial toxic wastes are dumped or leak into the nation's waterways. Because fewer than 50 percent of all municipal sewer systems are in compliance with Environmental Protection Agency requirements for water safety, contaminated waters represent a substantial present threat to public welfare. Efforts to keep from contaminating the water supply are a major challenge to even the most conscientious of manufacturing firms.

Land pollution is caused by the need to dispose of ever-increasing amounts of waste. Routine, everyday packaging is a major contributor to this problem. Land pollution is more dauntingly caused by the disposal of industrial toxic wastes in underground sites. With approximately 90 percent of the annual U.S. output of 500 million metric tons of hazardous industrial wastes being placed in underground dumps, it is evident that land pollution and its resulting endangerment of the ecology have become a major item on the political agenda.

As a major contributor to ecological pollution, business now is being held responsible for eliminating the toxic by-products of its current manufacturing processes and for cleaning up the environmental damage that it did previously. Increasingly, managers are being required by the government or are being expected by the public to incorporate ecological concerns into their decision making. For example, between 1975 and 1992, 3M cut its pollution in half by reformulating products, modifying processes, redesigning production equipment, and recycling by-products. Similarly, steel companies and public utilities have invested billions of dollars in costlier but cleaner-burning fuels and pollution control equipment. The automobile industry has been required to install expensive emission controls in cars. The gasoline industry has been forced to formulate new low-lead and no-lead products. And thousands of companies have found it necessary to direct their R&D resources into the search for ecologically superior products, such as Sears's phosphate-free laundry detergent and Pepsi-Cola's biodegradable plastic soft-drink bottle.

Environmental legislation impacts corporate strategies worldwide. Many companies fear the consequences of highly restrictive and costly environmental regulations. However, some manufacturers view these new controls as an opportunity, capturing markets with products that help customers satisfy their own regulatory standards. Other manufacturers contend that the costs of environmental spending inhibit the growth and productivity of their operations.

Despite cleanup efforts to date, the job of protecting the ecology will continue to be a top strategic priority—usually because corporate stockholders and executives choose it, increasingly because the public and the government require it. As evidenced by Exhibit 4.8,

EXHIBIT 4.8
Federal Ecological Legislation

National Environmental Policy Act, 1969 Established Environmental Protection Agency; consolidated federal environmental activities under it. Established Council on Environmental Quality to advise president on environmental policy and to review environmental impact statements.

Air Pollution:

Clean Air Act, 1963 Authorized assistance to state and local governments in formulating control programs. Authorized limited federal action in correcting specific pollution problems.

Clean Air Act, Amendments (Motor Vehicle Air Pollution Control Act), 1965 Authorized federal standards for auto exhaust emission. Standards first set for 1968 models.

Air Quality Act, 1967 Authorized federal government to establish air quality control regions and to set maximum permissible pollution levels. Required states and localities to carry out approved control programs or else give way to federal controls.

Clean Air Act Amendments, 1970 Authorized EPA to establish nationwide air pollution standards and to limit the discharge of six principal pollutants into the lower atmosphere. Authorized citizens to take legal action to require EPA to implement its standards against undiscovered offenders.

Clean Air Act Amendments, 1977 Postponed auto emission requirements. Required use of scrubbers in new coal-fired power plants. Directed EPA to establish a system to prevent deterioration of air quality in clean areas.

Solid Waste Pollution:

Solid Waste Disposal Act, 1965 Authorized research and assistance to state and local control programs.

Resource Recovery Act, 1970 Subsidized construction of pilot recycling plants; authorized development of nationwide control programs.

Resource Conservation and Recovery Act, 1976 Directed EPA to regulate hazardous waste management, from generation through disposal.

Surface Mining and Reclamation Act, 1976 Controlled strip mining and restoration of reclaimed land.

Water Pollution:

Refuse Act, 1899 Prohibited dumping of debris into navigable waters without a permit. Extended by court decision to industrial discharges.

Federal Water Pollution Control Act, 1956 Authorized grants to states for water pollution control. Gave federal government limited authority to correct specific pollution problems.

Water Quality Act, 1965 Provided for adoption of water quality standards by states, subject to federal approval.

Water Quality Improvement Act, 1970 Provided for federal cleanup of oil spills. Strengthened federal authority over water pollution control.

Federal Water Pollution Control Act Amendments, 1972 Authorized EPA to set water quality and effluent standards; provided for enforcement and research.

Safe Drinking Water Act, 1974 Set standards for drinking water quality.

Clean Water Act, 1977 Ordered control of toxic pollutants by 1984 with best available technology economically feasible.

the government has made numerous interventions into the conduct of business for the purpose of bettering the ecology.

Benefits of Eco-Efficiency

Many of the world's largest corporations are realizing that business activities must no longer ignore environmental concerns. Every activity is linked to thousands of other transactions and their environmental impact; therefore, corporate environmental responsibility must be taken seriously and environmental policy must be implemented to ensure a comprehensive organizational strategy. Because of increases in government regulations and consumer environmental concerns, the implementation of environmental policy has become a point of competitive advantage. Therefore, the rational goal of business should be to limit its impact on the environment, thus ensuring long-run benefits to both the firm and society. To neglect this responsibility is to ensure the demise of both the firm and our ecosystem.

Responding to this need, General Electric unveiled plans to double its research funds for technologies that reduce energy use, pollution, and emissions tied to global warming. GE said it would focus even more on solar and wind power as well as other environmental technologies it is involved with, such as diesel-electric locomotives, lower emission aircraft engines, more efficient lighting, and water purification. The company's "ecomagination" plans for 2010 include investing $1.5 billion annually in cleaner technologies research; and doubling revenues to $20 billion from environmentally friendly products and services.

eco-efficiency
Company actions that produce more useful goods and services while continuously reducing resource consumption and pollution.

Stephen Schmidheiny, chairman of the Business Council for Sustainable Development, has coined the term **eco-efficiency** to describe corporations that produce more-useful goods and services while continuously reducing resource consumption and pollution. He cites a number of reasons for corporations to implement environmental policy: customers demand cleaner products, environmental regulations are increasingly more stringent, employees prefer to work for environmentally conscious firms, and financing is more readily available for eco-efficient firms. In addition, the government provides incentives for environmentally responsible companies.

Setting priorities, developing corporate standards, controlling property acquisition and use to preserve habitats, implementing energy-conserving activities, and redesigning products (e.g., minimizing packaging) are a number of measures the firm can implement to enhance an eco-efficient strategy. One of the most important steps a firm can take in achieving a competitive position with regard to the eco-efficient strategy is to fully capitalize on technological developments as a method of gaining efficiency.

There are four key characteristics of eco-efficient corporations:

- Eco-efficient firms are proactive, not reactive. Policy is initiated and promoted by business because it is in their own interests and the interest of their customers, not because it is imposed by one or more external forces.
- Eco-efficiency is designed in, not added on. This characteristic implies that the optimization of eco-efficiency requires every business effort regarding the product and process to internalize the strategy.
- Flexibility is imperative for eco-efficient strategy implementation. Continuous attention must be paid to technological innovation and market evolution.
- Eco-efficiency is encompassing, not insular. In the modern global business environment, efforts must cross not only industrial sectors but national and cultural boundaries as well.

INDUSTRY ENVIRONMENT

industry environment
The general conditions for competition that influence all businesses that provide similar products and services.

Harvard professor Michael E. Porter propelled the concept of **industry environment** into the foreground of strategic thought and business planning. The cornerstone of his work first appeared in the *Harvard Business Review,* in which Porter explains the five forces that shape competition in an industry. His well-defined analytic framework helps strategic managers to link remote factors to their effects on a firm's operating environment.

With the special permission of Professor Porter and the *Harvard Business Review,* we present in this section of the chapter the major portion of his seminal article on the industry environment and its impact on strategic management.[1]

HOW COMPETITIVE FORCES SHAPE STRATEGY

The essence of strategy formulation is coping with competition. Yet it is easy to view competition too narrowly and too pessimistically. While we sometimes hear executives complaining to the contrary, intense competition in an industry is neither coincidence nor bad luck.

Moreover, in the fight for market share, competition is not manifested only in the other players. Rather, competition in an industry is rooted in its underlying economics, and competitive forces exist that go well beyond the established combatants in a particular industry. Customers, suppliers, potential entrants, and substitute products are all competitors that may be more or less prominent or active depending on the industry.

The state of competition in an industry depends on five basic forces, which are diagrammed in Exhibit 4.9. The collective strength of these forces determines the ultimate profit potential of an industry. It ranges from intense in industries like tires, metal cans, and steel, where no company earns spectacular returns on investment, to mild in industries like oil-field services and equipment, soft drinks, and toiletries, where there is room for quite high returns.

In the economists' "perfectly competitive" industry, jockeying for position is unbridled and entry to the industry very easy. This kind of industry structure, of course, offers the worst prospect for long-run profitability. The weaker the forces collectively, however, the greater the opportunity for superior performance.

Whatever their collective strength, the corporate strategist's goal is to find a position in the industry where his or her company can best defend itself against these forces or can influence them in its favor. The collective strength of the forces may be painfully apparent to all the antagonists; but to cope with them, the strategist must delve below the surface and analyze the sources of competition. For example, what makes the industry vulnerable to entry? What determines the bargaining power of suppliers?

Knowledge of these underlying sources of competitive pressure provides the groundwork for a strategic agenda of action. They highlight the critical strengths and weaknesses of the company, animate the positioning of the company in its industry, clarify the areas where strategic changes may yield the greatest payoff, and highlight the places where industry trends promise to hold the greatest significance as either opportunities or threats.

Understanding these sources also proves to be of help in considering areas for diversification.

[1]M. E. Porter, "How Competitive Forces Shape Strategy," *Harvard Business Review*, March–April 1979, pp. 137–45. Copyright © 1979 by the Harvard Business School Publishing Corporation; all rights reserved.

EXHIBIT 4.9 **Forces Driving Industry Competition**

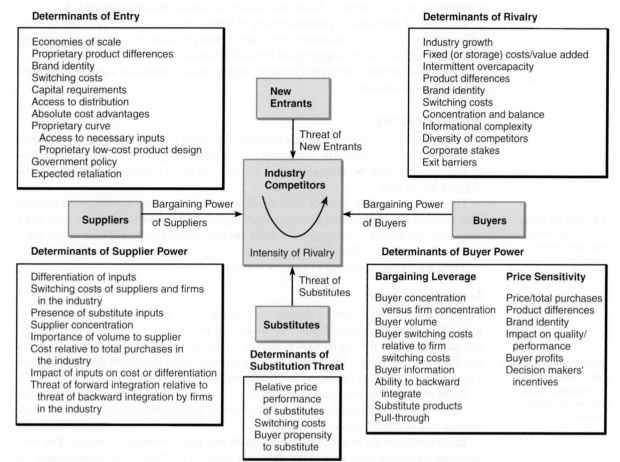

Determinants of Entry

- Economies of scale
- Proprietary product differences
- Brand identity
- Switching costs
- Capital requirements
- Access to distribution
- Absolute cost advantages
  - Proprietary curve
  - Access to necessary inputs
  - Proprietary low-cost product design
- Government policy
- Expected retaliation

Determinants of Rivalry

- Industry growth
- Fixed (or storage) costs/value added
- Intermittent overcapacity
- Product differences
- Brand identity
- Switching costs
- Concentration and balance
- Informational complexity
- Diversity of competitors
- Corporate stakes
- Exit barriers

New Entrants

Threat of New Entrants

Industry Competitors

Intensity of Rivalry

Bargaining Power of Suppliers

Suppliers

Bargaining Power of Buyers

Buyers

Threat of Substitutes

Substitutes

Determinants of Supplier Power

- Differentiation of inputs
- Switching costs of suppliers and firms in the industry
- Presence of substitute inputs
- Supplier concentration
- Importance of volume to supplier
- Cost relative to total purchases in the industry
- Impact of inputs on cost or differentiation
- Threat of forward integration relative to threat of backward integration by firms in the industry

Determinants of Substitution Threat

- Relative price performance of substitutes
- Switching costs
- Buyer propensity to substitute

Determinants of Buyer Power

Bargaining Leverage	Price Sensitivity
Buyer concentration versus firm concentration	Price/total purchases
Buyer volume	Product differences
Buyer switching costs relative to firm switching costs	Brand identity
	Impact on quality/ performance
Buyer information	Buyer profits
Ability to backward integrate	Decision makers' incentives
Substitute products	
Pull-through	

Source: Reprinted by permission of *Harvard Business Review*. Exhibit from "How Competitive Forces Shape Strategy," by M. E. Porter, March–April 1979. Copyright 1979 by the Harvard Business School Publishing Corporation; all rights reserved.

CONTENDING FORCES

The strongest competitive force or forces determine the profitability of an industry and so are of greatest importance in strategy formulation. For example, even a company with a strong position in an industry unthreatened by potential entrants will earn low returns if it faces a superior or a lower-cost substitute product—as the leading manufacturers of vacuum tubes and coffee percolators have learned to their sorrow. In such a situation, coping with the substitute product becomes the number one strategic priority.

Different forces take on prominence, of course, in shaping competition in each industry. In the ocean-going tanker industry, the key force is probably the buyers (the major oil companies), while in tires it is powerful OEM buyers coupled with tough competitors. In the steel industry the key forces are foreign competitors and substitute materials.

Every industry has an underlying structure, or a set of fundamental economic and technical characteristics, that gives rise to these competitive forces. The strategist, wanting to position his or her company to cope best with its industry environment or to influence that environment in the company's favor, must learn what makes the environment tick.

This view of competition pertains equally to industries dealing in services and to those selling products. To avoid monotony, we refer to both products and services as *products.* The same general principles apply to all types of business.

A few characteristics are critical to the strength of each competitive force. They will be discussed in this section.

Threat of Entry

New entrants to an industry bring new capacity, the desire to gain market share, and often substantial resources. Similarly, companies diversifying through acquisition into the industry from other markets often leverage their resources to cause a shake-up, as Philip Morris did with Miller beer.

barriers to entry
The conditions that a firm must satisfy to enter an industry.

The seriousness of the threat of entry depends on the barriers present and on the reaction from existing competitors that the entrant can expect. If **barriers to entry** are high and a newcomer can expect sharp retaliation from the entrenched competitors, he or she obviously will not pose a serious threat of entering.

There are six major sources of barriers to entry.

Economies of Scale

economies of scale
The savings that companies achieve because of increased volume.

These economies deter entry by forcing the aspirant either to come in on a large scale or to accept a cost disadvantage. Scale economies in production, research, marketing, and service are probably the key barriers to entry in the mainframe computer industry, as Xerox and GE sadly discovered. **Economies of scale** also can act as hurdles in distribution, utilization of the sales force, financing, and nearly any other part of a business.

Economies of scale refer to the savings that companies within an industry achieve due to increased volume. Simply put, when the volume of production increases, the long-range average cost of a unit produced will decline.

Economies of scale result from technological and nontechnological sources. The technological sources of these economies are higher levels of mechanization or automation and a greater modernization of plant and facilities The nontechnological sources include better managerial coordination of production functions and processes, long-term contractual agreements with suppliers, and enhanced employee performance arising from specialization.

Economies of scale are an important determinant of the intensity of competition in an industry. Firms that enjoy such economies can charge lower prices than their competitors. They also can create barriers to entry by reducing their prices temporarily, or permanently, to deter new firms from entering the industry.

Product Differentiation

product differentiation
The extent to which customers perceive differences among products and services.

Product differentiation, or brand identification, creates a barrier by forcing entrants to spend heavily to overcome customer loyalty. Advertising, customer service, being first in the industry, and product differences are among the factors fostering brand identification. It is perhaps the most important entry barrier in soft drinks, over-the-counter drugs, cosmetics, investment banking, and public accounting. To create high fences around their business, brewers couple brand identification with economies of scale in production, distribution, and marketing.

Capital Requirements

The need to invest large financial resources to compete creates a barrier to entry, particularly if the capital is required for unrecoverable expenditures in upfront advertising or R&D. Capital is necessary not only for fixed facilities but also for customer credit, inventories,

The Experience Curve as an Entry Barrier

In recent years, the experience curve has become widely discussed as a key element of industry structure. According to this concept, unit costs in many manufacturing industries (some dogmatic adherents say in all manufacturing industries) as well as in some service industries decline with "experience," or a particular company's cumulative volume of production. (The experience curve, which encompasses many factors, is a broader concept than the better-known learning curve, which refers to the efficiency achieved over time by workers through much repetition.)

The causes of the decline in unit costs are a combination of elements, including economies of scale, the learning curve for labor, and capital-labor substitution. The cost decline creates a barrier to entry because new competitors with no "experience" face higher costs than established ones, particularly the producer with the largest market share, and have difficulty catching up with the entrenched competitors.

Adherents of the experience curve concept stress the importance of achieving market leadership to maximize this barrier to entry, and they recommend aggressive action to achieve it, such as price cutting in anticipation of falling costs in order to build volume. For the combatant that cannot achieve a healthy market share, the prescription is usually, "Get out."

Is the experience curve an entry barrier on which strategies should be built? The answer is, not in every industry. In fact, in some industries, building a strategy on the experience curve can be potentially disastrous.

That costs decline with experience in some industries is not news to corporate executives. The significance of the experience curve for strategy depends on what factors are causing the decline.

A new entrant may well be more efficient than the more experienced competitors: if it has built the newest plant, it will face no disadvantage in having to catch up. The strategic prescription, "You must have the largest, most efficient plant," is a lot different from "You must produce the greatest cumulative output of the item to get your costs down."

Whether a drop in costs with cumulative (not absolute) volume erects an entry barrier also depends on the sources of the decline. If costs go down because of technical advances known generally in the industry or because of the development of improved equipment that can be copied or purchased from equipment suppliers, the experience curve is not an entry barrier at all—in fact, new or less-experienced competitors may actually enjoy a cost advantage over the leaders. Free of the legacy of heavy past investments, the newcomer or less-experienced competitor can purchase or copy the newest and lowest cost equipment and technology.

If, however, experience can be kept proprietary, the leaders will maintain a cost advantage. But new entrants may require less experience to reduce their costs than the leaders needed. All this suggests that the experience curve can be a shaky entry barrier on which to build a strategy.

and absorbing start-up losses. While major corporations have the financial resources to invade almost any industry, the huge capital requirements in certain fields, such as computer manufacturing and mineral extraction, limit the pool of likely entrants.

Cost Disadvantages Independent of Size

Entrenched companies may have cost advantages not available to potential rivals, no matter what their size and attainable economies of scale. These advantages can stem from the effects of the learning curve (and of its first cousin, the experience curve), proprietary technology, access to the best raw materials sources, assets purchased at preinflation prices, government subsidies, or favorable locations. Sometimes cost advantages are enforceable legally, as they are through patents. (For analysis of the much-discussed experience curve as a barrier to entry, see Exhibit 4.10, Strategy in Action.)

Access to Distribution Channels

The new boy or girl on the block must, of course, secure distribution of his or her product or service. A new food product, for example, must displace others from the supermarket shelf via price breaks, promotions, intense selling efforts, or some other means. The more

Chinese Companies Retreat from U.S. Listings as Scrutiny Mounts

Early in 2013, Chinese companies were deserting U.S. stock markets in record numbers as regulatory scrutiny mounted and the advantages of a U.S. listing slipped away. U.S. government investigations of suspect financial reports and battered share prices have for many Chinese companies wrecked the chances of raising new money in the United States and given them little reason to stay. "There's very little in [the] way of new capital flows to those companies, their valuations are low and they're encountering significant headwinds in terms of regulatory oversight," said James Feltman, a senior managing director at Mesirow Financial Consulting.

Twenty-seven China-based companies with U.S. listings announced plans to go private through buyouts in 2012, up from 16 in 2011 and just six in 2010, according to investment bank Roth Capital Partners. Before 2010, only one to two privatizations a year were typically done by China-based companies. In addition, about 50 mostly small Chinese companies "went dark," or deregistered with the U.S. Securities and Exchange Commission, ending their requirements for public disclosures. That was up from about 40 in 2011 and the most since at least 1994, when the SEC's records start.

Just three Chinese companies successfully went public on U.S. exchanges in 2012, down from 12 in 2011 and 41 in 2010. About 300 China-based companies still have shares trading in the United States on exchanges or "over-the-counter" between individual dealers. Bankers are aggressively pitching the idea of companies pulling out of the United States and relisting elsewhere, saying they can get a better share price in Hong Kong or mainland China. "The idea is that the markets here understand the China story better and will therefore hopefully assign a higher valuation to the stocks," said Mark Lehmkuhler, a partner at the law firm Davis Polk, in Hong Kong. U.S.-listed Chinese companies in the consumer staples sector, for example, were trading recently at a 67 percent discount to comparable Chinese companies on the Hong Kong Exchange, according to investment bank Morgan Joseph.

A failure by U.S. regulators to reach an agreement with China on accounting oversight was pushing more Chinese companies to abandon their U.S. listings, bankers and lawyers said. The United States had been trying to get access to audit records and permission to inspect Chinese audit firms to combat a rash of accounting scandals. China balked, leaving the future of U.S. listings for Chinese companies in doubt.

Stepping up pressure, the SEC deregistered about 50 China-based companies over the past two years. In December 2012, it charged the Chinese arms of five top accounting firms with securities violations for failing to turn over documents, raising tensions in its standoff with China.

Source: Excerpted from "Chinese Companies Retreat from U.S. Listings as Scrutiny Mounts." 2013. *Reuters Hedgeworld*, January 14.

limited the wholesale or retail channels are and the more that existing competitors have these tied up, obviously the tougher that entry into the industry will be. Sometimes this barrier is so high that, to surmount it, a new contestant must create its own distribution channels, as Timex did in the watch industry.

Government Policy

The government can limit or even foreclose entry to industries, with such controls as license requirements, limits on access to raw materials, and tax incentives. Regulated industries like trucking, liquor retailing, and freight forwarding are noticeable examples; more subtle government restrictions operate in fields like ski-area development and coal mining. The government also can play a major indirect role by affecting entry barriers through such controls as air and water pollution standards and safety regulations.

A distinctive form of government policy regulates the access of businesses to public investment in the United States. An agency of the U.S. federal government known as the Securities and Exchange Commission works with the New York Stock exchange, NASDAQ, and other corporate stock exchanges to regulate the listing of companies. As detailed in Global Strategy in Action, Exhibit 4.11, Chinese companies were backing away from pursuing membership in the exchanges by 2013. A failure by U.S. regulators to reach an agreement with China on accounting oversight was pushing Chinese companies to abandon their U.S. listings. The United States had been trying to get access to audit records and permission to inspect Chinese audit firms to combat a rash of accounting scandals. China balked, leaving the future of U.S. listings for Chinese companies in doubt and their participation in the U.S. investment industry sharply limited.

The potential rival's expectations about the reaction of existing competitors also will influence its decision on whether to enter. The company is likely to have second thoughts if incumbents have previously lashed out at new entrants, or if

The incumbents possess substantial resources to fight back, including excess cash and unused borrowing power, productive capacity, or clout with distribution channels and customers.

The incumbents seem likely to cut prices because of a desire to keep market shares or because of industrywide excess capacity.

Industry growth is slow, affecting its ability to absorb the new arrival and probably causing the financial performance of all the parties involved to decline.

Powerful Suppliers

Suppliers can exert bargaining power on participants in an industry by raising prices or reducing the quality of purchased goods and services. Powerful suppliers, thereby, can squeeze profitability out of an industry unable to recover cost increases in its own prices. By raising their prices, soft-drink concentrate producers have contributed to the erosion of profitability of bottling companies because the bottlers—facing intense competition from powdered mixes, fruit drinks, and other beverages—have limited freedom to raise their prices accordingly.

The power of each important supplier (or buyer) group depends on a number of characteristics of its market situation and on the relative importance of its sales or purchases to the industry compared with its overall business.

A *supplier* group is powerful if

1. It is dominated by a few companies and is more concentrated than the industry it sells.

2. Its product is unique or at least differentiated, or if it has built-up switching costs. Switching costs are fixed costs that buyers face in changing suppliers. These arise because, among other things, a buyer's product specifications tie it to particular suppliers, it has invested heavily in specialized ancillary equipment or in learning how to operate a supplier's equipment (as in computer software), or its production lines are connected to the supplier's manufacturing facilities (as in some manufacturing of beverage containers).

3. It is not obliged to contend with other products for sale to the industry. For instance, the competition between the steel companies and the aluminum companies to sell to the can industry checks the power of each supplier.

4. It poses a credible threat of integrating forward into the industry's business. This provides a check against the industry's ability to improve the terms on which it purchases.

5. The industry is not an important customer of the supplier group. If the industry is an important customer, suppliers' fortunes will be tied closely to the industry, and they will want to protect the industry through reasonable pricing and assistance in activities like R&D and lobbying.

Powerful Buyers

Customers likewise can force down prices, demand higher quality or more service, and play competitors off against each other—all at the expense of industry profits.

A *buyer* group is powerful if

1. It is concentrated or purchases in large volumes. Large-volume buyers are particularly potent forces if heavy fixed costs characterize the industry—as they do in metal containers, corn refining, and bulk chemicals, for example—which raise the stakes to keep capacity filled.

2. The products it purchases from the industry are standard or undifferentiated. The buyers, sure that they always can find alternative suppliers, may play one company against another, as they do in aluminum extrusion.

3. The products it purchases from the industry form a component of its product and represent a significant fraction of its cost. The buyers are likely to shop for a favorable price and purchase selectively. Where the product sold by the industry in question is a small fraction of buyers' costs, buyers are usually much less price sensitive.

4. It earns low profits, which create great incentive to lower its purchasing costs. Highly profitable buyers, however, are generally less price sensitive (i.e., of course, if the item does not represent a large fraction of their costs).

5. The industry's product is unimportant to the quality of the buyers' products or services. Where the quality of the buyers' products is very much affected by the industry's product, buyers are generally less price sensitive. Industries in which this situation exists include oil field equipment, where a malfunction can lead to large losses, and enclosures for electronic medical and test instruments, where the quality of the enclosure can influence the user's impression about the quality of the equipment inside.

6. The industry's product does not save the buyer money. Where the industry's product or service can pay for itself many times over, the buyer is rarely price sensitive; rather, he or she is interested in quality. This is true in services like investment banking and public accounting, where errors in judgment can be costly and embarrassing, and in businesses like the mapping of oil wells, where an accurate survey can save thousands of dollars in drilling costs.

7. The buyers pose a credible threat of integrating backward to make the industry's product. The Big Three auto producers and major buyers of cars often have used the threat of self-manufacture as a bargaining lever. But sometimes an industry so engenders a threat to buyers that its members may integrate forward.

Most of these sources of buyer power can be attributed to consumers as a group as well as to industrial and commercial buyers; only a modification of the frame of reference is necessary. Consumers tend to be more price sensitive if they are purchasing products that are undifferentiated, expensive relative to their incomes, and of a sort where quality is not particularly important.

The buying power of retailers is determined by the same rules, with one important addition. Retailers can gain significant bargaining power over manufacturers when they can influence consumers' purchasing decisions, as they do in audio components, jewelry, appliances, sporting goods, and other goods.

Because of its heavy reliance on a few large customers, MasterCard's corporate strategy is strongly influenced by buyer power. MasterCard Inc. generates revenue by charging fees to process payments from banks to consumers who swipe MasterCard-brand credit and debit cards, making the banks, not individual consumers, MasterCard's customers.

MasterCard issues 916 million cards through 25,000 financial institutions in more than 200 countries.

Rapid consolidation within the banking industry, combined with a 28 percent market share in global credit and debit card transactions compared with main-rival Visa's 68 percent share, means that MasterCard has to work hard to win and keep bank business. Further, MasterCard's dependence on four large customers, which make up 30 percent of annual revenues (J.P. Morgan Chase, Citigroup, Bank of America, and HSBC), makes it vulnerable to attack.

Substitute Products

By placing a ceiling on the prices it can charge, substitute products or services limit the potential of an industry. Unless it can upgrade the quality of the product or differentiate it somehow (as via marketing), the industry will suffer in earnings and possibly in growth.

Manifestly, the more attractive the price-performance trade-off offered by substitute products, the firmer the lid placed on the industry's profit potential. Sugar producers confronted with the large-scale commercialization of high-fructose corn syrup, a sugar substitute, learned this lesson.

Substitutes not only limit profits in normal times but also reduce the bonanza an industry can reap in boom times. The producers of fiberglass insulation enjoyed unprecedented demand as a result of high energy costs and severe winter weather. But the industry's ability to raise prices was tempered by the plethora of insulation substitutes, including cellulose, rock wool, and Styrofoam. These substitutes are bound to become an even stronger force once the current round of plant additions by fiberglass insulation producers has boosted capacity enough to meet demand (and then some).

Substitute products that deserve the most attention strategically are those that *(a)* are subject to trends improving their price-performance trade-off with the industry's product or *(b)* are produced by industries earning high profits. Substitutes often come rapidly into play if some development increases competition in their industries and causes price reduction or performance improvement.

Jockeying for Position

Rivalry among existing competitors takes the familiar form of jockeying for position—using tactics like price competition, product introduction, and advertising price-cutting. This type of intense rivalry is related to the presence of a number of factors:

1. Competitors are numerous or are roughly equal in size and power. In many U.S. industries in recent years, foreign contenders, of course, have become part of the competitive picture.

2. Industry growth is slow, precipitating fights for market share that involve expansion-minded members.

3. The product or service lacks differentiation or switching costs, which lock in buyers and protect one combatant from raids on its customers by another.

4. Fixed costs are high or the product is perishable, creating strong temptation to cut prices. Many basic materials businesses, like paper and aluminum, suffer from this problem when demand slackens.

5. Capacity normally is augmented in large increments. Such additions, as in the chlorine and vinyl chloride businesses, disrupt the industry's supply–demand balance and often lead to periods of overcapacity and price-cutting.

6. Exit barriers are high. Exit barriers, like very specialized assets or management's loyalty to a particular business, keep companies competing even though they may be earning low or

Global Construction Industry Forecast

Construction activity across a wide range of economies—both developed and emerging—has been going through [a] 'soft patch' by those countries' usually robust standards, reflecting weaker conditions across the wider global economy. Those affected in this way include the more developed economies of Australia and Canada, some key emerging Asian economies such as China, India and Korea, east European economies including Russia and Poland, and some Latin American economies including Brazil. However, these countries are, for the most part, less exposed to the kind of financial and fiscal difficulties facing western Europe, the United States and Japan, and also have generally stronger underlying construction growth potential reflecting the scope for wider GDP 'catch-up' and positive demographics. Forecasters envisaged a return to robust growth in all of these cases in 2013.

More specifically, construction output growth across the emerging markets group as a whole is expected to be 5 percent in 2013 and 7 percent in 2014, having slowed from 5 percent in 2011 to 4 percent in 2012. Growth in China is put at 8 percent in 2014 following two calendar years of comparatively modest 7 percent growth, while sector growth in India is put at 9 percent next year following a 12-year low of 4.2 percent in 2013. Meanwhile, sector growth in Canada is put at 4 percent in 2014 following a slowdown to 1 percent in 2013, while that in Australia is seen reviving to 4 percent in 2013—going on to 4 percent in 2014—following 2012's modest 2 percent. Finally, Japan had been enjoying a period of unusually robust construction growth by that country's own recent standards, with the construction activity index approximately 5 percent higher than in 2012.

The main downside risk to the wider global economy stemmed from the possibility of a group of member states exiting the euro, with a consequent short-term loss of GDP across the continent and beyond and added pressure on those countries not leaving the zone to tighten fiscal policy still further. Uncertainty stemming from this possibility was helping to hold back construction activity. Nevertheless, construction output around the globe was expected to be hit at least as hard, if not harder, than overall GDP in this event, reflecting the sector's highly cyclical nature and its exposure to public spending and credit availability. A further downside risk to the wider economy, though with a smaller probability attached, stemmed from the possibility of conflict in the Middle East and [a] consequent spike in oil prices. In this case construction would be adversely affected indirectly, as private spending power was squeezed.

House building is heavily dependent on trends in the wider economy, labor markets, interest rates, credit conditions and (in the long term) demographics. It can also be prone to 'booms,' with subsequent stock overhangs and/or high prices affecting conditions. As a result, recent trends have varied considerably across countries, for example being positive in Germany and negative in Italy and Spain, with the United States seeing a sharp bounce from a very low base.

Source: Excerpted from "Global Industry Forecast—Construction." Spring 2013. *Oxford Economics.*

even negative returns on investment. Excess capacity remains functioning, and the profitability of the healthy competitors suffers as the sick ones hang on. If the entire industry suffers from overcapacity, it may seek government help—particularly if foreign competition is present.

7. The rivals are diverse in strategies, origins, and "personalities." They have different ideas about how to compete and continually run head-on into each other in the process.

As an industry matures, its growth rate changes, resulting in declining profits and (often) a shakeout. In the booming recreational vehicle industry of the early 1970s, nearly every producer did well; but slow growth since then has eliminated the high returns, except for the strongest members, not to mention many of the weaker companies. The same profit story has been played out in industry after industry—snowmobiles, aerosol packaging, and sports equipment are just a few examples.

An acquisition can introduce a very different personality to an industry, as has been the case with Black & Decker's takeover of McCullough, the producer of chain saws.

Technological innovation can boost the level of fixed costs in the production process, as it did in the shift from batch to continuous-line photo finishing.

While a company must live with many of these factors—because they are built into the industry economics—it may have some latitude for improving matters through strategic shifts. For example, it may try to raise buyers' switching costs or increase product differentiation. A focus on selling efforts in the fastest growing segments of the industry or on market areas with the lowest fixed costs can reduce the impact of industry rivalry. If it is feasible, a company can try to avoid confrontation with competitors having high exit barriers and, thus, can sidestep involvement in bitter price-cutting.

An example of an industry forecast executive summary is provided in Global Strategy in Action, Exhibit 4.12. The summary gives an overview of the global construction industry as forecast in 2013. Notice at the end of the exhibit that the authors reference the influences discussed in this section of the book including labor markets, interest rates, long-term credit, demographics, economic cyclicality, and inflation.

INDUSTRY ANALYSIS AND COMPETITIVE ANALYSIS

Designing viable strategies for a firm requires a thorough understanding of the firm's industry and competition. The firm's executives need to address four questions: (1) What are the boundaries of the industry? (2) What is the structure of the industry? (3) Which firms are our competitors? (4) What are the major determinants of competition? The answers to these questions provide a basis for thinking about the appropriate strategies that are open to the firm.

Industry Boundaries

industry
A group of companies that provide similar products and services.

An **industry** is a collection of firms that offer similar products or services. By "similar products," we mean products that customers perceive to be substitutable for one another. Consider, for example, the brands of personal computers (PCs) that are now being marketed. The firms that produce these PCs, such as Hewlett-Packard, IBM, Apple, and Dell, form the nucleus of the microcomputer industry.

Suppose a firm competes in the microcomputer industry. Where do the boundaries of this industry begin and end? Does the industry include desktops? Laptops? These are the kinds of questions that executives face in defining industry boundaries.

Why is a definition of industry boundaries important? First, it helps executives determine the arena in which their firm is competing. A firm competing in the microcomputer industry participates in an environment very different from that of the broader electronics business. The microcomputer industry comprises several related product families, including personal computers, inexpensive computers for home use, and workstations. The unifying characteristic of these product families is the use of a central processing unit (CPU) in a microchip. On the other hand, the electronics industry is far more extensive; it includes computers, radios, supercomputers, superconductors, and many other products.

The microcomputer and electronics industries differ in their volume of sales, their scope (some would consider microcomputers a segment of the electronics industry), their rate of growth, and their competitive makeup. The dominant issues faced by the two industries also are different. Witness, for example, the raging public debate being waged on the future of the "high-definition TV." U.S. policy makers are attempting to ensure domestic control of that segment of the electronics industry. They also are considering ways to stimulate "cutting-edge" research in superconductivity. These efforts are likely to spur innovation and stimulate progress in the electronics industry.

Second, a definition of industry boundaries focuses attention on the firm's competitors. Defining industry boundaries enables the firm to identify its competitors and producers of substitute products. This is critically important to the firm's design of its competitive strategy.

Third, a definition of industry boundaries helps executives determine key factors for success. Survival in the premier segment of the microcomputer industry requires skills that are considerably different from those required in the lower end of the industry. Firms that compete in the premier segment need to be on the cutting edge of technological development and to provide extensive customer support and education. On the other hand, firms that compete in the lower end need to excel in imitating the products introduced by the premier segment, to focus on customer convenience, and to maintain operational efficiency that permits them to charge the lowest market price. Defining industry boundaries enables executives to ask these questions: Do we have the skills it takes to succeed here? If not, what must we do to develop these skills?

Finally, a definition of industry boundaries gives executives another basis on which to evaluate their firm's goals. Executives use that definition to forecast demand for their firm's products and services. Armed with that forecast, they can determine whether those goals are realistic.

Problems in Defining Industry Boundaries

Defining industry boundaries requires both caution and imagination. Caution is necessary because there are no precise rules for this task and because a poor definition will lead to poor planning. Imagination is necessary because industries are dynamic—in every industry, important changes are under way in such key factors as competition, technology, and consumer demand.

Defining industry boundaries is a very difficult task. The difficulty stems from three sources:

1. The evolution of industries over time creates new opportunities and threats. Compare the financial services industry as we know it today with that of the 1990s, and then try to imagine how different the industry will be in the year 2020.

2. Industrial evolution creates industries within industries. The electronics industry of the 1960s has been transformed into many "industries"—TV sets, transistor radios, micro and macrocomputers, supercomputers, superconductors, and so on. Such transformation allows some firms to specialize and others to compete in different, related industries.

3. Industries are becoming global in scope. Consider the civilian aircraft manufacturing industry. For nearly three decades, U.S. firms dominated world production in that industry. But small and large competitors were challenging their dominance by 1990. At that time, Airbus Industries (a consortium of European firms) and Brazilian, Korean, and Japanese firms were actively competing in the industry.

The challenge of defining an industry is complicated by the fact that many large companies compete in multiple industries. Further, technology can quickly redefine an industry or lead directly to the creation of a new one. Global Strategy in Action, Exhibit 4.13 provides an example of how Apple has redefined one of the traditional industries in which it competes by the way it structures its supply chain.

Developing a Realistic Industry Definition

Given the difficulties just outlined, how do executives draw accurate boundaries for an industry? The starting point is a definition of the industry in global terms; that is, in terms that consider the industry's international components as well as its domestic components.

Having developed a preliminary concept of the industry (e.g., computers), executives flesh out its current components. This can be done by defining its product segments. Executives need to select the scope of their firm's potential market from among these related but distinct areas.

How Apple Set the Standard for Its Industry

In 2012, technology titans were increasingly looking like vertically integrated conglomerates largely in an attempt to emulate the success of Apple. Google acquired mobile-device maker Motorola Mobility for $12.5 billion to manufacture smartphones and television set-top boxes. Amazon's Kindle Fire tablet represented its bridge between hardware and e-commerce. Oracle bought Sun Microsystems to champion engineered systems (integrated hardware-and-software devices). Even long-standing software giant Microsoft made hardware for its Xbox gaming system.

Vertical integration dictates that one company controls the end product as well as its component parts. In technology, Apple for 35 years had championed a vertical model, which featured an integrated hardware-and-software approach. For instance, the iPhone and iPad had hardware and software designed by Apple, which also designed its own processors for the devices. This integration allowed Apple to set the pace for mobile computing.

The tech industry's success in this type of integration was mixed. Samsung, a large technology conglomerate, thrived by making everything from LCD panels to processors, televisions and smartphones. But Sony, which attempted to meld content, TVs, and game systems like the PlayStation, had yet to find a way to make the disparate parts gel.

Although tech companies were focusing on entering areas closely aligned with their core businesses, Lawrence Hrebiniak, a Wharton management professor, noted that hardware and software require different competencies and skill sets in areas such as manufacturing, procurement and supply chains. In that respect, the challenges these firms face were similar to what many diversified multinationals deal with when managing disparate business units.

Markets that are not commoditized, such as mobile computing, smartphones and tablets, benefit most from vertical integration. However, once markets become less differentiated, a specialized approach—where each member of a supply chain has a role—makes sense. In the case of PCs, a group of companies now made different parts of the machine that are then put together to create the final product: Microsoft built operating systems, Intel made processors, Nvidia provided graphic chips and a series of companies manufactures hard drives.

Source: Excerpted from "How Apple Made 'Vertical Integration' Hot Again—Too Hot, Maybe." March 16, 2012. Knowledge@Wharton.

To understand the makeup of the industry, executives adopt a longitudinal perspective. They examine the emergence and evolution of product families. Why did these product families arise? How and why did they change? The answers to such questions provide executives with clues about the factors that drive competition in the industry.

Exhibit 4.14, Global Strategy in Action provides an example of the changing industry dynamics in the Philippine telecommunications industry in 2011. Increased rivalry resulting from the maturing of the industry, heightened price competition, and product improvements all add to the challenges of the industry's strategic planners.

Executives also examine the companies that offer different product families, the overlapping or distinctiveness of customer segments, and the rate of substitutability among product families.

To realistically define their industry, executives need to examine five issues:

1. Which part of the industry corresponds to our firm's goals?
2. What are the key ingredients of success in that part of the industry?
3. Does our firm have the skills needed to compete in that part of the industry? If not, can we build those skills?
4. Will the skills enable us to seize emerging opportunities and deal with future threats?
5. Is our definition of the industry flexible enough to allow necessary adjustments to our business concept as the industry grows?

A Year of Change in the Philippine Telecommunications Industry

To say that 2011 would be a difficult year for the Philippine telecommunications industry is an understatement. The industry's dynamics are changing dramatically. While consumers rejoice about the barrage of unlimited and bucket-priced offerings that brought down the costs of text messaging and mobile voice calls, the revenues of telecommunications companies suffered.

Globe Telecom president and CEO Ernest Cu said the company's financial results are reflective of the challenges facing the industry, whereby traffic is growing, but revenues are declining with the market's increasing preference for unlimited services. Despite an increase in traffic and overall usage, Globe's mobile revenues were lower with sustained price pressures resulting from intense competition and subscribers' increasing preference for lower-yield bucket and unlimited promotions.

Globe's Super All Txt 20 is one such bucket-priced offering. For only P20 a day, a subscriber gets to send 200 text messages to any network, which means that each SMS costs only 10 centavos. The company's Unli Txt All Day allows one to send unlimited text messages to Globe/TM subscribers for one day. Many of these promos are offered for a limited time only, but they are usually renewed.

The mobile telephony sector is now a matured one. The cellular penetration rate has now exceeded 80 percent. This triggered the search for new revenue streams and the rise of broadband Internet services as the new revenue driver.

But even the cost of mobile Internet access has significantly gone down, thanks to bucket price and unlimited offerings. For just P50 a day, a Globe subscriber is given unlimited access to the Internet using a Globe Tattoo Broadband USB or mobile phone for one day. Smart also offers unlimited mobile surfing for P50 per day while Smart Broadband has its unlimited Internet access promo at P200 good for five days. With the entry of a new player, San Miguel Corp./Liberty Telecom's Wi-Tribe, expect the cost of Internet access to go down even further.

Now here's a look at how the industry's decision makers viewed prospects for 2011:

- PLDT planned to preserve "margins by strengthening cost management given the modest top-line growth. . . . Demand for bucket and unlimited offers in the cellular space will continue. We expect that broadband will keep growing given the growing popularity of social networking and new access devices such as tablets and smartphones. PLDT will continue to invest in its network in order to fortify its market leadership."

- In 2011 "we expect further developments in 3.5G. New Android phones are also getting exciting. We are optimistic both about the telco industry and the economy in general. . . . In 2011, we are confident we can achieve robust growth in both 2G and 3.5G as we continue our strong rollout of cellsites. By end of 2011, Sun should be even in number of cellsites as the other two telco players in almost all regions of the country." —James Go, president, Digital Telecommunications Phils. Inc. (Digitel)

- "Our growth drivers next year would continue to be data and Internet services for both consumer and corporate sectors. On the consumer side, we will continue to focus on Internet services as we leverage on our cooperation within the Lopez Group to deliver relevant and compelling communication and content services. At the same time, Bayan has been strong in the corporate data sector servicing banks and BPOs, and we hope to gain on the opportunities." —Rafael Aguado, chief operations officer, Bayan Telecommunications

- "The device business will continue to grow in leaps and bounds with the mobile phones still leading the way and new affordable devices such as smart phones and tablets coming in strong in the second half of the year. MyPhone will continue to invest in expanding our retail chains and service centers to maintain its excellent quality and after-sales service reputation." —David Lim, chairman, Solid Group, makers of MyPhone

Source: Exerpted from Mary Ann L. Reyes, "2010: A Year of Changing Telecommunications Market Dynamics," *The Philippine Star*, December 30, 2010.

Power Curves

Strategic managers have a new tool that helps them assess industry structure, which refers to the enduring characteristics that give an industry its distinctive character. According to Michele Zanini of the McKinsey Group, from whose work this discussion is derived, power

EXHIBIT 4.15
Common Shape of a Power Curve

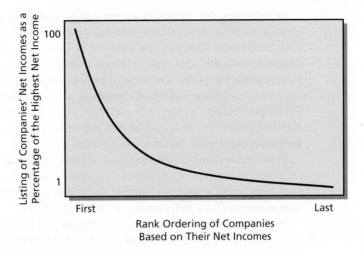

curves depict the fundamental structural trends that underlie an industry.[2] While major economic events like the worldwide recession of 2008 are extremely disruptive to business activity, they do little to change the relative position of most businesses to one another over the long term.

What would you guess is the typical shape of the distribution of companies in an industry? Is it bell shaped, with a few superlarge firms, many companies of medium size, and a few extremely small competitors? Or, is it linear, with a few large companies and progressively larger numbers of smaller firms? Do you think that company strategies should be different if one of these models is right and the other wrong?

In many industries, the top firm is best described as a mega-institution—a company of unprecedented scale and scope that has an undeniable lead over competitors. Wal-Mart, Best Buy, McDonald's, and Starbucks are examples. However, even among these firms, there is a clear difference in size and performance. When the distribution of net incomes of the global top 150 corporations in 2005 was plotted, the result was a "power curve," which implies that most companies, even in the set of superstars, are below average in performance. This power curve is shown in Exhibit 4.15.

A power curve is described as exhibiting a small set of companies with extremely large incomes, followed quickly by a much larger array of companies with significantly smaller incomes that are progressively smaller than one another, but only slightly.

As Zanini explains, low barriers to entry and high levels of rivalry are positively associated with an industry's power curve dynamics. The larger the number of competitors in an industry, the larger the gap on the vertical axis usually is between the top and median companies. When entry barriers are lowered, such as occurs with deregulation, revenues increase faster in the top-ranking firms, creating a steeper power curve. This greater openness seems to create a more level playing field at first, but greater differentiation and consolidation tend to occur over time.

Power curves are also promoted by intangible assets such as software and biotechnology, which generate increasing returns to scale and economies of scope. By contrast, more labor- or capital-intensive sectors, such as chemicals and machinery, have flatter curves.

[2]Michele Zanini, "'Using Power Curves' to Assess Industry Dynamics," *The McKinsey Quarterly*, November 2008.

In industries that display a power curve—including insurance, machinery, and U.S. banks and savings institutions—intriguing implications suggest that strategic thrusts rather than incremental strategies are required to improve a company's position significantly. Zanini defends this idea with evidence from the retail mutual fund industry. The major players at the top of the power curve can extend their lead by exploiting network effects, such as cross-selling individual retirement accounts (IRAs), to a large installed base of 401(k) plan holders as they roll over their assets. A financial crisis, like the recession of 2008, increases the likelihood of this opportunity as weakened financial institutions sell their asset-management units to raise capital.

Power curves can be useful to strategic managers in understanding their industry's structural dynamics and in benchmarking its performance. Because an industry's curve evolves over many years, a large deviation in the slope can indicate some exceptional occurrence, such as unusual firm performance or market instability.

As Zanini concludes, power curves suggest that companies generally compete against one another and against an industry structure that becomes progressively more unequal. For most companies, this possibility makes power curves an important strategic consideration.

Competitive Analysis

How to Identify Competitors

In identifying their firm's current and potential competitors, executives consider several important variables:

1. How do other firms define the scope of their market? The more similar the definitions of firms, the more likely the firms will view each other as competitors.

2. How similar are the benefits the customers derive from the products and services that other firms offer? The more similar the benefits of products or services, the higher the level of substitutability between them. High substitutability levels force firms to compete fiercely for customers.

3. How committed are other firms to the industry? Although this question may appear to be far removed from the identification of competitors, it is in fact one of the most important questions that competitive analysis must address, because it sheds light on the long-term intentions and goals. To size up the commitment of potential competitors to the industry, reliable intelligence data are needed. Such data may relate to potential resource commitments (e.g., planned facility expansions).

The idea of a power curve helps us to understand competition in the global aerospace and transport industry, as described in Strategy in Action, Exhibit 4.16. The exhibit points out that all airplane manufacturers only generally compete with one another, and that different groups of competitors are susceptible to different environmental influences, to different degrees and at different times. The result is a very uneven distribution of power among manufacturers and consequently, some very clear market segmentation.

Common Mistakes in Identifying Competitors

Identifying competitors is a milestone in the development of strategy. But it is a process laden with uncertainty and risk, a process in which executives sometimes make costly mistakes. Examples of these mistakes are:

1. Overemphasizing current and known competitors while giving inadequate attention to potential entrants.

2. Overemphasizing large competitors while ignoring small competitors.

Global Aerospace and Transport Industry Forecast

For Boeing in 2012, the push was clearly on to raise production schedules in order to fill existing orders, a stimulus which was likely to continue through to 2014 at least. European competitor Airbus' progress in filling orders early in 2012 was less impressive. Airlines and regulators were concerned about the cracks found in some wing brackets of the A380 planes, with extra inspections and fixes disrupting flight schedules and diverting management attention from other issues. In turn, Airbus' plans to ramp up production were pushed into 2013, as it dealt with problems on planes in production and already in service. In the first quarter of 2012, only four out of the 30 A380 deliveries scheduled for 2012 were achieved. Finally, the cloud over Asian orders due to disquiet about EU emission charges remained, with some airlines refusing to supply data. Nonetheless, on balance, EU 15 production growth was 6 percent in 2012, and predicted to accelerate to 8 percent in 2013 and almost 9 percent in 2014.

In terms of the drivers of demand for new aircraft, although airfreight volumes were weak in 2012, passenger load factors were encouraging despite uncertain macroeconomic conditions. Moreover, jet fuel costs came off the peaks in earlier 2012. U.S. fleet renewals plus the continued expansion of Middle East and low-cost carriers was offsetting curtailed investment plans from more established airlines (e.g., investment cuts by Air France–KLM and the likelihood Quantas would continue to focus more on its domestic rather than international routes that had meant delaying two A380 deliveries from 2013 until 2017).

Moving from the civilian to the military sector, the contrast remained stark. Firms were chasing fewer defense contracts as budgets of established military powers remained under intense pressure. Austerity measures across Europe put military procurements under the microscope. Commodity, especially oil, producers including China were set to continue building up their forces but slower GDP growth in India threatened to slow military purchases in the near term.

Less established producers than Boeing and Airbus struggled to achieve the critical mass of orders that would allow them to reap economies of scale and move on decisively to produce bigger aircraft. Makers in China (Comae), Brazil (Embraer), Russia (Irkut) and Canada (Bombardier) all wished to move beyond producing regional jets and other smaller aircraft but earlier optimism about near-term prospects was fading. Nonetheless, after weaker-than-expected growth of 6 percent in 2012, aerospace output in emerging markets was forecast to rebound. Indeed, in the medium term, a gradual shift towards production in emerging markets was projected.

There are several distinctive economic forces at play in the industry. Aerospace products are expensive, discrete items with long delivery times, breaking any immediate link between short-term economic developments and sector production. The production series can also be quite erratic. However, civilian aircraft purchases ultimately stem from increasing demands to transport people and freight by air, while military purchases are driven by threat levels, defense priorities, and government budget constraints. There is also a growing push for emerging countries to expand their own aerospace industries, in order to break the duopoly of Airbus and Boeing.

Source: Excerpted from "Global Industry Forecast—Aerospace and Transport." Summer 2012. *Oxford Economics.*

3. Overlooking potential international competitors.

4. Assuming that competitors will continue to behave in the same way they have behaved in the past.

5. Misreading signals that may indicate a shift in the focus of competitors or a refinement of their present strategies or tactics.

6. Overemphasizing competitors' financial resources, market position, and strategies while ignoring their intangible assets, such as a top management team.

7. Assuming that all of the firms in the industry are subject to the same constraints or are open to the same opportunities.

8. Believing that the purpose of strategy is to outsmart the competition, rather than to satisfy customer needs and expectations.

OPERATING ENVIRONMENT

operating environment
Factors in the immediate competitive situation that affect a firm's success in acquiring needed resources.

The **operating environment,** also called the *competitive* or *task environment,* comprises factors in the competitive situation that affect a firm's success in acquiring needed resources or in profitably marketing its goods and services. Among the most important of these factors are the firm's competitive position, the composition of its customers, its reputation among suppliers and creditors, and its ability to attract capable employees. The operating environment is typically much more subject to the firm's influence or control than the remote environment. Thus, firms can be much more proactive (as opposed to reactive) in dealing with the operating environment than in dealing with the remote environment.

Competitive Position

Assessing its competitive position improves a firm's chances of designing strategies that optimize its environmental opportunities. Development of competitor profiles enables a firm to more accurately forecast both its short- and long-term growth and its profit potentials. Although the exact criteria used in constructing a competitor's profile are largely determined by situational factors, the following criteria are often included:

1. Market share.
2. Breadth of product line.
3. Effectiveness of sales distribution.
4. Proprietary and key account advantages.
5. Price competitiveness.
6. Advertising and promotion effectiveness.
7. Location and age of facility.
8. Capacity and productivity.
9. Experience.
10. Raw materials costs.
11. Financial position.
12. Relative product quality.
13. R&D advantages position.
14. Caliber of personnel.
15. General images.
16. Customer profile.
17. Patents and copyrights.
18. Union relations.
19. Technological position.
20. Community reputation.

Once appropriate criteria have been selected, they are weighted to reflect their importance to a firm's success. Then the competitor being evaluated is rated on the criteria, the ratings are multiplied by the weight, and the weighted scores are summed to yield a numerical profile of the competitor, as shown in Exhibit 4.17.

EXHIBIT 4.17
Competitor Profile

Key Success Factors	Weight	Rating*	Weighted Score
Market share	0.30	4	1.20
Price competitiveness	0.20	3	0.60
Facilities location	0.20	5	1.00
Raw materials costs	0.10	3	0.30
Caliber of personnel	0.20	1	0.20
	1.00†		3.30

*The rating scale suggested is as follows: very strong competitive position (5 points), strong (4), average (3), weak (2), very weak (1).
†The total of the weights must always equal 1.00.

This type of competitor profile is limited by the subjectivity of its criteria selection, weighting, and evaluation approaches. Nevertheless, the process of developing such profiles is of considerable help to a firm in defining its perception of its competitive position. Moreover, comparing the firm's profile with those of its competitors can aid its managers in identifying factors that might make the competitors vulnerable to the strategies the firm might choose to implement.

Customer Profiles

Perhaps the most vulnerable result of analyzing the operating environment is the understanding of a firm's customers that this provides. Developing a profile of a firm's present and prospective customers improves the ability of its managers to plan strategic operations, to anticipate changes in the size of markets, and to reallocate resources so as to support forecast shifts in demand patterns. The traditional approach to segmenting customers is based on customer profiles constructed from geographic, demographic, psychographic, and buyer behavior information.

Enterprising companies have quickly learned the importance of identifying target segments. In recent years, market research has increased tremendously as companies realize the benefits of demographic and psychographic segmentation. Research by American Express (AMEX) showed that competitors were stealing a prime segment of the company's business, affluent business travelers. AMEX's competing companies, including Visa and Mastercard, began offering high-spending business travelers frequent flier programs and other rewards including discounts on new cars. In turn, AMEX began to invest heavily in rewards programs, while also focusing on its strongest capabilities, assets, and competitive advantage. Unlike most credit card companies, AMEX cannot rely on charging interest to make money because most of its customers pay in full each month. Therefore, the company charges higher transaction fees to its merchants. In this way, increases in spending by AMEX customers who pay off their balances each month are more profitable to AMEX than to competing credit card companies.

Assessing consumer behavior is a key element in the process of satisfying your target market needs. Many firms lose market share as a result of assumptions made about target segments. Market research and industry surveys can help to reduce a firm's chances of relying on illusive assumptions. Firms most vulnerable are those that have had success with one or more products in the marketplace and as a result try to base consumer behavior on past data and trends.

Geographic

It is important to define the geographic area from which customers do or could come. Almost every product or service has some quality that makes it variably attractive to buyers from different locations. Obviously, a Wisconsin manufacturer of snow skis should think twice about investing in a wholesale distribution center in South Carolina. On the other hand, advertising in the *Milwaukee Journal-Sentinel* could significantly expand the geographically defined customer market of a major Myrtle Beach hotel in South Carolina.

Demographic

Demographic variables most commonly are used to differentiate groups of present or potential customers. Demographic information (e.g., information on sex, age, marital status, income, and occupation) is comparatively easy to collect, quantify, and use in strategic forecasting, and such information is the minimum basis for a customer profile.

Psychographic

Personality and lifestyle variables often are better predictors of customer purchasing behavior than geographic or demographic variables. In such situations, a psychographic study is an important component of the customer profile. Advertising campaigns by soft-drink producers—Pepsi-Cola ("the Pepsi generation"), Coca-Cola ("the real thing"), and 7UP ("America's turning 7UP")—reflect strategic management's attention to the psychographic characteristics of their largest customer segment—physically active, group-oriented nonprofessionals.

Buyer Behavior

Buyer behavior data also can be a component of the customer profile. Such data are used to explain or predict some aspect of customer behavior with regard to a product or service. Information on buyer behavior (e.g., usage rate, benefits sought, and brand loyalty) can provide significant aid in the design of more accurate and profitable strategies.

Suppliers

Dependable relationships between a firm and its suppliers are essential to the firm's long-term survival and growth. A firm regularly relies on its suppliers for financial support, services, materials, and equipment. In addition, it occasionally is forced to make special requests for such favors as quick delivery, liberal credit terms, or broken-lot orders. Particularly at such times, it is essential for a firm to have had an ongoing relationship with its suppliers.

In the assessment of a firm's relationships with its suppliers, several factors, other than the strength of that relationship, should be considered. With regard to its competitive position with its suppliers, the firm should address the following questions:

Are the suppliers' prices competitive? Do the suppliers offer attractive quantity discounts?

How costly are their shipping charges? Are the suppliers competitive in terms of production standards?

In terms of deficiency rates, are the suppliers' abilities, reputations, and services competitive?

Are the suppliers reciprocally dependent on the firm?

Creditors

Because the quantity, quality, price, and accessibility of financial, human, and material resources are rarely ideal, assessment of suppliers and creditors is critical to an accurate evaluation of a firm's operating environment. With regard to its competitive position with its creditors, among the most important questions that the firm should address are the following:

Do the creditors fairly value and willingly accept the firm's stock as collateral?

Do the creditors perceive the firm as having an acceptable record of past payment?

A strong working capital position? Little or no leverage?

Are the creditors' loan terms compatible with the firm's profitability objectives?

Are the creditors able to extend the necessary lines of credit?

The answers to these and related questions help a firm forecast the availability of the resources it will need to implement and sustain its competitive strategies.

Human Resources: Nature of the Labor Market

A firm's ability to attract and hold capable employees is essential to its success. However, a firm's personnel recruitment and selection alternatives often are influenced by the nature of its operating environment. A firm's access to needed personnel is affected primarily by four factors: the firm's reputation as an employer, local employment rates, the ready availability of people with the needed skills, and its relationship with labor unions.

Reputation

A firm's reputation within its operating environment is a major element of its ability to satisfy its personnel needs. A firm is more likely to attract and retain valuable employees if it is seen as permanent in the community, competitive in its compensation package, and concerned with the welfare of its employees, and if it is respected for its product or service and appreciated for its overall contribution to the general welfare.

Employment Rates

The readily available supply of skilled and experienced personnel may vary considerably with the stage of a community's growth. A new manufacturing firm would find it far more difficult to obtain skilled employees in a vigorous industrialized community than in an economically depressed community in which similar firms had recently cut back operations.

Availability

The skills of some people are so specialized that relocation may be necessary to secure the jobs and the compensation that those skills commonly command. People with such skills include oil drillers, chefs, technical specialists, and industry executives. A firm that seeks to hire such a person is said to have broad labor market boundaries; that is, the geographic area within which the firm might reasonably expect to attract qualified candidates is quite large. On the other hand, people with more common skills are less likely to relocate from a considerable distance to achieve modest economic or career advancements. Thus, the labor market boundaries are fairly limited for such occupational groups as unskilled laborers, clerical personnel, and retail clerks.

Many manufacturers in the United States attempt to minimize the labor cost disadvantage they face in competing with overseas producers by outsourcing to lower-cost foreign locations or by hiring immigrant workers. Similarly, companies in construction and other labor-intensive industries try to provide themselves with a cost advantage by hiring temporary, often migrant, workers.

Labor Unions

Approximately 12 percent of all workers in the United States belong to a labor union; and almost half of these are government employees. The percentages are higher in Japan and western Europe at about 25 and 40 percent, respectively, and extremely low in developing nations. Unions represent the workers in their negotiations with employers through the process of collective bargaining. When managers' relationships with their employees are complicated by the involvement of a union, the company's ability to manage and motivate the people that it needs can be compromised.

EMPHASIS ON ENVIRONMENTAL FACTORS

This chapter has described the remote, industry, and operating environments as encompassing five components each. While that description is generally accurate, it may give the false impression that the components are easily identified, mutually exclusive, and equally applicable in all situations. In fact, the forces in the external environment are so dynamic and interactive that the impact of any single element cannot be wholly disassociated from the effect of other elements. For example, are increases in OPEC oil prices the result of economic, political, social, or technological changes? Or are a manufacturer's surprisingly good relations with suppliers a result of competitors,' customers,' or creditors' activities or of the supplier's own activities? The answer to both questions is probably that a number of forces in the external environment have combined to create the situation. Such is the case in most studies of the environment.

Strategic managers are frequently frustrated in their attempts to anticipate the environment's changing influences. Different external elements affect different strategies at different times and with varying strengths. The only certainty is that the effect of the remote and operating environments will be uncertain until a strategy is implemented. This leads many managers, particularly in less powerful or smaller firms, to minimize long-term planning, which requires a commitment of resources. Instead, they favor allowing managers to adapt to new pressures from the environment. While such a decision has considerable merit for many firms, there is an associated trade-off, namely that absence of a strong resource and psychological commitment to a proactive strategy effectively bars a firm from assuming a leadership role in its competitive environment.

There is yet another difficulty in assessing the probable impact of remote, industry, and operating environments on the effectiveness of alternative strategies. Assessment of this kind involves collecting information that can be analyzed to disclose predictable effects. Except in rare instances, however, it is virtually impossible for any single firm to anticipate the consequences of a change in the environment; for example, what is the precise effect on alternative strategies of a 2 percent increase in the national inflation rate, a 1 percent decrease in statewide unemployment, or the entry of a new competitor in a regional market?

Still, assessing the potential impact of changes in the external environment offers a real advantage. It enables decision makers to narrow the range of the available options and to eliminate options that are clearly inconsistent with the forecast opportunities. Environmental assessment seldom identifies the best strategy, but it generally leads to the elimination of all but the most promising options.

Exhibit 4.18 provides a set of key strategic forecasting issues for each level of environmental assessment—remote, industry, and operating. While the issues that are presented are not inclusive of all of the questions that are important, they provide an excellent set of questions with which to begin. Chapter 4 Appendix, Sources for Environmental Forecasting, is provided to help identify valuable sources of data and information from which answers and subsequent forecasts can be constructed. It lists governmental and private marketplace intelligence that can be used by a firm to gain a foothold in undertaking a strategic assessment of any level of the competitive environment.

EXHIBIT 4.18
Strategic Forecasting Issues

Key Issues in the Remote Environment Economy

What are the probable future directions of the economies in the firm's regional, national, and international market? What changes in economic growth, inflation, interest rates, capital availability, credit availability, and consumer purchasing power can be expected? What income differences can be expected between the wealthy upper middle class, the working class, and the underclass in various regions? What shifts in relative demand for different categories of goods and services can be expected?

Society and demographics

What effects will changes in social values and attitudes regarding childbearing, marriage, lifestyle, work, ethics, sex roles, racial equality, education, retirement, pollution, and energy have on the firm's development? What effects will population changes have on major social and political expectations—at home and abroad? What constraints or opportunities will develop? What pressure groups will increase in power?

Ecology

What natural or pollution-caused disasters threaten the firm's employees, customers, or facilities? How rigorously will existing environment legislature be enforced? What new federal, state, and local laws will affect the firm, and in what ways?

Politics

What changes in government policy can be expected with regard to industry cooperation, antitrust activities, foreign trade, taxation, depreciation, environmental protection, deregulation, defense, foreign trade barriers, and other important parameters? What success will a new administration have in achieving its stated goals? What effect will that success have on the firm? Will specific international climates be hostile or favorable? Is there a tendency toward instability, corruption, or violence? What is the level of political risk in each foreign market? What other political or legal constraints or supports can be expected in international business (e.g., trade barriers, equity requirements, nationalism, patent protection)?

Technology

What is the current state of the art? How will it change? What pertinent new products or services are likely to become technically feasible in the foreseeable future? What future impact can be expected from technological breakthroughs in related product areas? How will those breakthroughs interface with the other remote considerations, such as economic issues, social values, public safety, regulations, and court interpretations?

Key Issues in the Industry Environment

New entrants

Will new technologies or market demands enable competitors to minimize the impact of traditional economies of scale in the industry? Will consumers accept our claims of product or service differentiation? Will potential new entrants be able to match the capital requirements that currently exist? How permanent are the cost disadvantages (independent of size) in our industry? Will conditions change so that all competitors have equal access to marketing channels? Is government policy toward competition in our industry likely to change?

Bargaining power of suppliers

How stable are the size and composition of our supplier group? Are any suppliers likely to attempt forward integration into our business level? How dependent will our suppliers be in the future? Are substitute suppliers likely to become available? Could we become our own supplier?

(continued)

EXHIBIT 4.18
(continued)

Substitute products or services

Are new substitutes likely? Will they be price competitive? Could we fight off substitutes by price competition? By advertising to sharpen product differentiation? What actions could we take to reduce the potential for having alternative products seen as legitimate substitutes?

Bargaining power of buyers

Can we break free of overcommitment to a few large buyers? How would our buyers react to attempts by us to differentiate our products? What possibilities exist that our buyers might vertically integrate backward? Should we consider forward integration? How can we make the value of our components greater in the products of our buyers?

Rivalry among existing firms

Are major competitors likely to undo the established balance of power in our industry? Is growth in our industry slowing such that competition will become fiercer? What excess capacity exists in our industry? How capable are our major competitors of withstanding intensified price competition? How unique are the objectives and strategies of our major competitors?

Key Issues in the Operating Environment

Competitive position

What strategic moves are expected by existing rivals—inside and outside the United States? What competitive advantage is necessary in selected foreign markets? What will be our competitors' priorities and ability to change? Is the behavior of our competitors predictable?

Customer profiles and market changes

What will our customer regard as needed value? Is marketing research done, or do managers talk to each other to discover what the customer wants? Which customer needs are not being met by existing products? Why? Are R&D activities under way to develop means for fulfilling these needs? What is the status of these activities? What marketing and distribution channels should we use? What do demographic and population changes portend for the size and sales potential of our market? What new market segments or products might develop as a result of these changes? What will be the buying power of our customer groups?

Supplier relationships

What is the likelihood of major cost increases because of dwindling supplies of a needed natural resource? Will sources of supply, especially of energy, be reliable? Are there reasons to expect major changes in the cost or availability of inputs as a result of money, people, or subassembly problems? Which suppliers can be expected to respond to emergency requests?

Creditors

What lines of credit are available to help finance our growth? What changes may occur in our creditworthiness? Are creditors likely to feel comfortable with our strategic plan and performance? What is the stock market likely to feel about our firm? What flexibility would our creditors show toward us during a downturn? Do we have sufficient cash reserves to protect our creditors and our credit rating?

Labor market

Are potential employees with desired skills and abilities available in the geographic areas in which our facilities are located? Are colleges and vocational/technical schools that can aid in meeting our training needs located near our plant or store sites? Are labor relations in our industry conducive to meeting our expanding needs for employees? Are workers whose skills we need shifting toward or away from the geographic location of our facilities?

Summary

A firm's external environment consists of three interrelated sets of factors that play a principal role in determining the opportunities, threats, and constraints that the firm faces. The remote environment comprises factors originating beyond, and usually irrespective of, any single firm's operating situation—economic, social, political, technological, and ecological factors. Factors that more directly influence a firm's prospects originate in the environment of its industry, including entry barriers, competitor rivalry, the availability of substitutes, and the bargaining power of buyers and suppliers. The operating environment comprises factors that influence a firm's immediate competitive situation—competitive position, customer profiles, suppliers, creditors, and the labor market. These three sets of factors provide many of the challenges that a particular firm faces in its attempts to attract or acquire needed resources and to profitably market its goods and services. Environmental assessment is more complicated for multinational corporations (MNCs) than for domestic firms because multinationals must evaluate several environments simultaneously.

Thus, the design of business strategies is based on the conviction that a firm able to anticipate future business conditions will improve its performance and profitability. Despite the uncertainty and dynamic nature of the business environment, an assessment process that narrows, even if it does not precisely define, future expectations is of substantial value to strategic managers.

Key Terms

barriers to entry, *p. 102*
eco-efficiency, *p. 99*
ecology, *p. 96*
economies of scale, *p. 102*

external environment, *p. 88*
industry, *p. 109*
industry environment, *p. 100*
operating environment, *p. 116*

pollution, *p. 96*
product differentiation, *p. 102*
remote environment, *p. 88*
technological forecasting, *p. 95*

Questions for Discussion

1. Briefly describe two important recent changes in the remote environment of U.S. business in each of the following areas:
   a. Economic.
   b. Social.
   c. Political.
   d. Technological.
   e. Ecological.
2. Describe two major environmental changes that you expect to have a major impact on the wholesale food industry in the next 10 years.
3. Develop a competitor profile for your college and for the college geographically closest to yours. Next, prepare a brief strategic plan to improve the competitive position of the weaker of the two colleges.
4. Assume the invention of a competitively priced synthetic fuel that could supply 25 percent of U.S. energy needs within 20 years. In what major ways might this change the external environment of U.S. business?
5. With your instructor's help, identify a local firm that has enjoyed great growth in recent years. To what degree and in what ways do you think this firm's success resulted from taking advantage of favorable conditions in its remote, industry, and operating environments?
6. Choose a specific industry and, relying solely on your impressions, evaluate the impact of the five forces that drive competition in that industry.
7. Choose an industry in which you would like to compete. Use the five-forces method of analysis to explain why you find that industry attractive.
8. Many firms neglect industry analysis. When does this hurt them? When does it not?

9. The model below depicts industry analysis as a funnel that focuses on remote-factor analysis to better understand the impact of factors in the operating environment. Do you find this model satisfactory? If not, how would you improve it?

Factors in the remote environment → Industry analysis → Factors in the operating environment

10. Who in a firm should be responsible for industry analysis? Assume that the firm does not have a strategic planning department.

Chapter 4 Appendix

Sources for Environmental Forecasting

Remote and Industry Environments

A. Economic considerations:
1. *Predicasts* (most complete and up-to-date review of forecasts)
2. National Bureau of Economic Research
3. *Handbook of Basic Economic Statistics*
4. *Statistical Abstract of the United States* (also includes industrial, social, and political statistics)
5. Publications by Department of Commerce agencies:
   a. Office of Business Economics (e.g., *Survey of Business*)
   b. Bureau of Economic Analysis (e.g., *Business Conditions Digest*)
   c. Bureau of the Census (e.g., *Survey of Manufacturers* and various reports on population, housing, and industries)
   d. Business and Defense Services Administration (e.g., *United States Industrial Outlook*)
6. Securities and Exchange Commission (various quarterly reports on plant and equipment, financial reports, working capital of corporations)
7. The Conference Board
8. *Survey of Buying Power*
9. *Marketing Economic Guide*
10. *Industrial Arts Index*
11. U.S. and national chambers of commerce
12. American Manufacturers Association
13. *Federal Reserve Bulletin*
14. *Economic Indicators*, annual report
15. *Kiplinger Newsletter*
16. International economic sources:
   a. *Worldcasts*
   b. Master key index for business international publications
   c. Department of Commerce
      (1) Overseas business reports
      (2) Industry and Trade Administration
      (3) Bureau of the Census—*Guide to Foreign Trade Statistics*
17. *Business Periodicals Index*

B. Social considerations:
1. Public opinion polls
2. Surveys such as *Social Indicators and Social Reporting*, the annals of the American Academy of Political and Social Sciences
3. Current controls: Social and behavioral sciences
4. Abstract services and indexes for articles in sociological, psychological, and political journals

5. Indexes for *The Wall Street Journal, New York Times*, and other newspapers
6. Bureau of the Census reports on population, housing, manufacturers, selected services, construction, retail trade, wholesale trade, and enterprise statistics
7. Various reports from such groups as the Brookings Institution and the Ford Foundation
8. World Bank Atlas (population growth and GNP data)
9. World Bank–World Development Report

C. Political considerations:
1. *Public Affairs Information Services Bulletin*
2. CIS Index (Congressional Information Index)
3. Business periodicals
4. Funk & Scott (regulations by product breakdown)
5. Weekly compilation of presidential documents
6. *Monthly Catalog of Government Publications*
7. *Federal Register* (daily announcements of pending regulations)
8. *Code of Federal Regulations* (final listing of regulations)
9. Business International Master Key Index (regulations, tariffs)
10. Various state publications
11. Various information services (Bureau of National Affairs, Commerce Clearing House, Dow Jones)

D. Technological considerations:
1. *Applied Science and Technology Index*
2. *Statistical Abstract of the United States*
3. Scientific and Technical Information Service
4. University reports, congressional reports
5. Department of Defense and military purchasing publishers
6. Trade journals and industrial reports
7. Industry contacts, professional meetings
8. Computer-assisted information searches
9. National Science Foundation annual report
10. *Research and Development Directory* patent records

E. Industry considerations:
1. *Concentration Ratios in Manufacturing* (Bureau of the Census)
2. *Input-Output Survey* (productivity ratios)
3. *Monthly Labor Review* (productivity ratios)
4. *Quarterly Failure Report* (Dun & Bradstreet)
5. *Federal Reserve Bulletin* (capacity utilization)
6. *Report on Industrial Concentration and Product Diversification in the 1,000 Largest Manufacturing Companies* (Federal Trade Commission)
7. Industry trade publications

8. Bureau of Economic Analysis, Department of Commerce (specialization ratios)

Industry and Operating Environments

A. Competition and supplier considerations:
1. Target Group Index
2. U.S. Industrial Outlook
3. Robert Morris annual statement studies
4. Troy, Leo *Almanac of Business & Industrial Financial Ratios*
5. *Census of Enterprise Statistics*
6. Securities and Exchange Commission (10-K reports)
7. Annual reports of specific companies
8. *Fortune 500 Directory, The Wall Street Journal, Barron's, Forbes, Dun's Review*
9. Investment services and directories: Moody's, Dun & Bradstreet, Standard & Poor's, Starch Marketing, Funk & Scott Index
10. Trade association surveys
11. Industry surveys
12. Market research surveys
13. *Country Business Patterns*
14. *Country and City Data Book*
15. Industry contacts, professional meetings, salespeople
16. *NFIB Quarterly Economic Report for Small Business*

B. Customer profile:
1. *Statistical Abstract of the United States*, first source of statistics
2. *Statistical Sources* by Paul Wasserman (a subject guide to data—both domestic and international)
3. *American Statistics Index* (Congressional Information Service Guide to statistical publications of U.S. government—monthly)
4. Office of the Department of Commerce:
   a. Bureau of the Census reports on population, housing, and industries
   b. *U.S. Census of Manufacturers* (statistics by industry, area, and products)
   c. *Survey of Current Business* (analysis of business trends, especially February and July issues)
5. Market research studies (*A Basic Bibliography on Market Review*, compiled by Robert Ferber et al., American Marketing Association)

6. *Current Sources of Marketing Information: A Bibliography of Primary Marketing Data* by Gunther & Goldstein, AMA
7. *Guide to Consumer Markets*, The Conference Board (provides statistical information with demographic, social, and economic data—annual)
8. *Survey of Buying Power*
9. *Predicasts* (abstracts of publishing forecasts of all industries, detailed products, and end-use data)
10. *Predicasts Basebook* (historical data from 1960 to present, covering subjects ranging from population and GNP to specific products and services; series are coded by Standard Industrial Classifications)
11. *Market Guide* (individual market surveys of over 1,500 U.S. and Canadian cities; includes population, location, trade areas, banks, principal industries, colleges and universities, department and chain stores, newspapers, retail outlets, and sales)
12. *Country and City Data Book* (includes bank deposits, birth and death rates, business firms, education, employment, income of families, manufacturers, population, savings, and wholesale and retail trade)
13. *Yearbook of International Trade Statistics* (UN)
14. *Yearbook of National Accounts Statistics* (UN)
15. *Statistical Yearbook* (UN—covers population, national income, agricultural and industrial production, energy, external trade, and transport)
16. *Statistics of (Continents): Sources for Market Research* (includes separate books on Africa, America, Europe)

C. Key natural resources:
1. *Minerals Yearbook, Geological Survey* (Bureau of Mines, Department of the Interior)
2. *Agricultural Abstract* (Department of Agriculture)
3. Statistics of electric utilities and gas pipeline companies (Federal Power Commission)
4. Publications of various institutions: American Petroleum Institute, Atomic Energy Commission, Coal Mining Institute of America, American Steel Institute, and Brookings Institution

Chapter **Five**

The Global Environment

After reading and studying this chapter, you should be able to

1. Explain the importance of a company's decision to globalize.

2. Describe the four main strategic orientations of global firms.

3. Understand the complexity of the global environment and the control problems that are faced by global firms.

4. Discuss major issues in global strategic planning, including the differences for multinational and global firms.

5. Describe the market requirements and product characteristics in global competition.

6. Evaluate the competitive strategies for firms in foreign markets, including niche market exporting, licensing and contract manufacturing, franchising, joint ventures, foreign branching, private equity, and wholly owned subsidiaries.

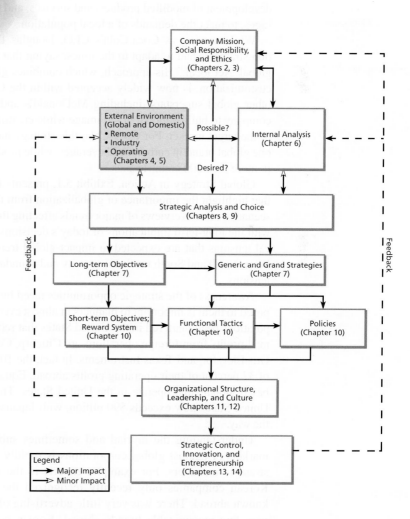

Company Mission, Social Responsibility, and Ethics (Chapters 2, 3)

External Environment (Global and Domestic)
• Remote
• Industry
• Operating
(Chapters 4, 5)

Possible?

Desired?

Internal Analysis (Chapter 6)

Strategic Analysis and Choice (Chapters 8, 9)

Long-term Objectives (Chapter 7)

Generic and Grand Strategies (Chapter 7)

Short-term Objectives; Reward System (Chapter 10)

Functional Tactics (Chapter 10)

Policies (Chapter 10)

Organizational Structure, Leadership, and Culture (Chapters 11, 12)

Strategic Control, Innovation, and Entrepreneurship (Chapters 13, 14)

Feedback

Feedback

Legend
→ Major Impact
⇢ Minor Impact

GLOBALIZATION

globalization
The strategy of pursuing opportunities anywhere in the world that enable a firm to optimize its business functions in the countries in which it operates.

Globalization refers to the strategy of pursuing opportunities anywhere in the world that enable a firm to optimize its business functions in the countries in which it operates. A company with global sales may have its high value-added software design activity done in Ireland, while it may achieve its lowest manufacturing costs by outsourcing those activities to India.

There are two main theories concerning the introduction of a product globally: standardization and customization. Standardization is the use of a common product, service, and message across all markets to create a strong brand image. The constantly improving communication technology in the twentieth century led to an ever-more-homogenous global customer base that allowed for strategic success with a standardized product. Standardization performed well until the late 1990s, when global brand owners saw their share prices drop as consumers reached for local products that were better aligned with their cultural identities. The change in customer purchase behavior was the beginning of an evolution in international strategy.

Since then, standardization is steadily being replaced by customization, which is the development of modified products and services, and the use of somewhat tailor-made messages, to meet the demands of a local population.

While serving as Coca-Cola's CEO, Douglas Daft famously argued that globalization strategies had to adapt to the times, saying that multinational firms needed to "Think global. Act local." His approach, which combines global standardization with some local customization, is now widely accepted within the Coca-Cola Corporation, as well as by other global superstars, including McDonald's and Wal-Mart. The approach allows the company to build a global brand image while creating products to meet the local demands of the target market. For Coca-Cola, this strategy has resulted in a ranking as the number one global brand in carbonated beverages, while producing more than 450 localized brands in more than 200 countries.

Global Strategy in Action, Exhibit 5.1, presents four intriguing scenarios of the future that highlight the importance of globalization from the National Intelligence Council. The scenarios offer overviews of major trends affecting the world to help leaders as they grapple with the long-term implications of today's decisions. The exhibit also discusses four critical tensions that are expected to impact global trends: organizational tensions; East and West, North and South tensions; scarcity and abundance tensions; and technology and jobs tensions.

Awareness of the strategic opportunities faced by global corporations and of the threats posed to them is important to planners in almost every domestic U.S. industry. Among corporations headquartered in the United States that receive more than 50 percent of their annual profits from foreign operations are Citicorp, Coca-Cola, ExxonMobil, Gillette, IBM, Otis Elevator, and Texas Instruments. In fact, the 100 largest U.S. globals earn an average of 37 percent of their operating profits abroad. Equally impressive is the effect of foreign-based globals that operate in the United States. Their "direct foreign investment" in the United States now exceeds $90 billion, with Japanese, German, and French firms leading the way.

Understanding the myriad and sometimes subtle nuances of competing in global markets or against global corporations is rapidly becoming a required competence of strategic managers. For example, experts in the advertising community contend that Korean companies only recently recognized the importance of making their names known abroad. There was very little advertising of Korean brands, and the country had very few recognizable brands abroad. Korean companies tended to emphasize sales

Global Strategy in Action

Exhibit 5.1

Four Scenarios for 2030

The National Intelligence Council offers an overview of major trends affecting the world, reduced to four basic scenarios. Each scenario creates valuable "memories of the future" that help leaders as they grapple with the long-term implications of today's decisions.

- The "Stalled Engines" scenario is a worst-case scenario in which the Pacific Rim is engulfed in nationalistic brinkmanship' and conflict, global growth slows, the EU disintegrates, the United States turns inward, and globalization unravels.

- In the best-case "Fusion" scenario, an interconnected East and West work together to address the globe's major challenges, innovation blossoms, and most players prosper.

- In the "Genie out of the Bottle" scenario, gaping extremes define the global stage and within countries, as the best positioned reap all the benefits of the new world order.

- In the "Non-State" scenario, cities, NGOs, global elites, terror groups, and multinationals drive global change and chaos.

The scenarios address four critical tensions that deserve much wider discussion:

1. Organizational tensions. Is the unit of analysis the traditional nation-state, invented in Europe and responsible for so much progress and pain in the nineteenth and twentieth centuries? Is the unit of analysis the global hub cities housing the "creative class" and responsible for most innovation and a large amount of the world's economic output? Is the unit of measure human networks like NGOs, movements, and multinationals?

2. East and West, North and South tensions. Assuming present trends continue, economic power will continue to shift eastward and southward. The NIC reports a relative decline of U.S. and European economic power as the BRICs (Brazil, Russia, India, and China) and the Next Eleven (South Korea, Vietnam, Indonesia, Turkey, Bangladesh, Pakistan, Egypt, Iran, Mexico, the Philippines, and Nigeria) catch up and urbanize. How will our global institutions adapt to this new, multipolar world? Will America retain a global focus?

3. Scarcity and abundance tensions. A significant focus of the NIC's report is on future scarcity of water, food, and energy. Will technological progress in genetically modified seeds, water filtration and conservation, hydraulic fracturing, and solar energy meet these needs?

4. Technology and jobs tensions. So-called "technological unemployment" is only hinted at in the NIC's report. The facts are that algorithms will automate away many process-heavy white-collar jobs (potentially including many medical professionals involved in diagnosis), and robotics will automate away most manufacturing jobs.

The creative class, highly skilled technology workers, and the intellectually agile will still thrive in this world, but what are the prospects for the others? If technological progress and change are accelerating, technological unemployment may knock many workers off the treadmill. Could technological unemployment and the accelerating rate of change slow the rise of the global middle class and lead to a highly polarized global society? Or will the creative destruction from software and robots be followed quickly by wholly new industries? The key question is if and how the displaced can retrain in an accelerating environment requiring higher levels of cognition and creativity. New categories of employment will be created, but will the displaced have the skills to step in?

Source: Excerpted from Robert Moran. 2013. "Global Trends 2030: Alternative Worlds, by the National Intelligence Council. A review." *The Futurist*, 47 (2): 54–55.

and production more than marketing. The opening of the Korean advertising market in the 1990s indicated that Korean firms had acquired a new appreciation for the strategic competencies that are needed to compete globally and created an influx of global firms like Saatchi and Saatchi, J. W. Thompson, Ogilvy and Mather, and Bozell. Many of them established joint ventures or partnerships with Korean agencies. An excellent example of such a strategic approach to globalization by Mondelez is described in Exhibit 5.2, Global Strategy in Action. The opportunities for corporate growth often seem greatest in global markets.

Yummy in the Tummy

When Irene Rosenfeld returned to Kraft Foods as [chair] and CEO for Mondelez in 2006, she found that the company was on the verge of delisting the Oreo brand in China. "We were losing money, and it was a very unattractive proposition. We had a $60 million factory in Beijing, which was sitting empty because sales had not materialized."

Rosenfeld and her team at Kraft decided to reach out to people in China before taking such a drastic move. They asked what it would take to make the Oreo brand a success in their country. "They very quickly told us that the product was too big and too sweet for the Chinese consumer," Rosenfeld says. "When we allowed our local managers to redesign our product for the local taste and local customs, we had a phenomenal turnaround."

The Chinese Oreo is smaller and less sweet and actually comes in a green tea flavor. It's not at all what American consumers want when they open their package of Oreos, but different cultures have different tastes. Rosenfeld knew in that case she needed to adapt to earn the business of the Chinese consumers.

The effort paid off thanks in part to China's own Yao Ming, a former star basketball player in the United States. "Who is the best symbol in China but Yao Ming?" Rosenfeld says. "He's our spokesman, and we actually go to the local guy. It has been a phenomenal business in China with almost $800 million of the $2 billion business from Oreo worldwide."

The willingness to adapt played a large part in the move completed in fall 2012 to split Kraft into two groups. Kraft Foods Group now holds the company's North American grocery business, which is led by iconic brands such as Oscar Mayer and Maxwell House.

Kraft Foods Inc. is now Mondelez International Inc. and focuses on high-growth global snacks. Said Rosenfeld, "The opportunity for us is to create a $36 billion start-up. It's an opportunity to take an incredible roster of brands that are household names, brands like Oreo, Ritz, Chips Ahoy, Trident and Cadbury, and put those together."

"North American grocery needs to be managed for cash and for margin," Rosenfeld says. "There is a big focus there on maintaining the moderate growth but making sure it's a very cost-focused company. Our global snacks business is all about growth. So the focus is on global platforms for each of our brands. The focus is on capabilities and the supply chain and sales, which will drive these products more rapidly around the world. The opportunity for us to be able to scale up very quickly if we are properly structured and have the proper communication from one part of the world to another is the main idea for our new company."

"The rate of consumption in the emerging markets is a fraction of what we see in developed markets," Rosenfeld says. "So the whole investment thesis behind Mondelez is this idea of a growth company because of our geographic footprint and our category participation. It's really depending on explosive growth, and we're growing at a double-digit rate in these emerging parts."

Source: Excerpted from Mark Scott. 2013. "Yummy in the Tummy." *Smart Business Chicago*, May 6: 16.

Because the growth in the number of global firms continues to overshadow other changes in the competitive environment, this section will focus on the nature, outlook, and operations of global corporations.

DEVELOPMENT OF A GLOBAL CORPORATION

The evolution of a global corporation often entails progressively involved strategy levels. The first level, which often entails export-import activity, has minimal effect on the existing management orientation or on existing product lines. The second level, which can involve foreign licensing and technology transfer, requires little change in management or operation. The third level typically is characterized by direct investment in overseas operations, including manufacturing plants. This level requires large capital outlays and the development of global management skills. Although the domestic operations of a firm at this level continue to dominate its policy, such a firm is commonly categorized as a true multinational corporation (MNC). The most involved strategy level is characterized by a substantial increase in foreign investment, with foreign assets comprising a significant portion of total assets. At this level, the firm begins to emerge as a global enterprise with global approaches to production, sales, finance, and control.

To get a more complete understanding of the many elements of a multinational environment that need to be considered by strategic planners, study the Chapter 5 Appendix. It contains lists of important competitive issues that will help you to see the complexity of the multinational landscape and to better appreciate the complicated and sophisticated nature of strategic planning.

Some firms downplay their global nature (to never appear distracted from their domestic operations), whereas others highlight it. For example, General Electric's formal statement of mission and business philosophy includes the following commitment:

> To carry out a diversified, growing, and profitable worldwide manufacturing business in electrical apparatus, appliances, and supplies, and in related materials, products, systems, and services for industry, commerce, agriculture, government, the community, and the home.

A similar global orientation is evident at IBM, which operates in 125 countries, conducts business in 30 languages and more than 100 currencies, and has 23 major manufacturing facilities in 14 countries.

The complexity of operating as a successful global corporation is complicated by the volatility of resource availability and pricing. As described in Global Strategy in Action, Exhibit 5.3, the world is undergoing a period of intensified resource stress because of soaring demand from emerging economies and tightening commodity markets. Climate change, water scarcity, and a shift in historical trading patterns, driven by new demand from developing nations, will also continue to bolster prices. The Chatham House report includes many interesting findings and forecasts. For example:

- From 2003–2012, the global share of fossil-fuel trade to China and India has more than doubled from 4.4 percent to 10.8 percent.
- Some energy exporters, such as Saudi Arabia, are fast-growing energy consumers, which may limit their ability to maintain trade volumes.
- Water and energy supplies will become increasingly interdependent, and greater competition for resources could lead to conflict and instability.
- Existing mechanisms are inadequate to deal with oil-supply shocks, particularly with the rise of new consumers.
- Increased competition for fossil fuels could lead to conflict in the East and South China Seas, the South Atlantic, the Arctic Ocean, and East Africa.

WHY FIRMS GLOBALIZE

The technological advantage once enjoyed by the United States has declined dramatically during the past 30 years. In contrast, France is making impressive advances in electric traction, nuclear power, and aviation. Germany leads in chemicals and pharmaceuticals, precision and heavy machinery, heavy electrical goods, metallurgy, and surface transport equipment. Japan leads in optics, solid-state physics, engineering, chemistry, and process metallurgy. Eastern Europe and the former Soviet Union, the so-called COMECON (Council for Mutual Economic Assistance) countries, generate 30 percent of annual worldwide patent applications. However, the United States is regaining some of its lost technological advantage. Through globalization, U.S. firms often can reap benefits from industries and technologies developed abroad. Even a relatively small service firm that possesses a distinct competitive advantage can capitalize on large overseas operations.

Volatility Is the New Normal

The world is undergoing a period of intensified resource stress because of soaring demand from emerging economies and tightening commodity markets, according to a new report by Chatham House, a London-based think tank. The report, which examines the supply and demand outlook for 19 key resources including crops, water and fossil fuels, says the world must get used to energy-price volatility. Climate change, water scarcity and a shift in historical trading patterns, driven by new demand from developing nations, will also continue to bolster prices.

With increasing oil-price volatility will come more instability in food prices. Rob Bailey, one of the authors of Chatham House's report, said the world is "just one or two bad harvests" away from a global food crisis, as climate change and failed crops have placed increasing pressure on global food stocks. The World Bank's Food Price Watch says global maize and soybean prices reached all-time peaks in July 2012, following a drought in both the United States and Eastern Europe. The dry summer in Russia, Ukraine and Kazakhstan led to wheat production losses of more than 6 million tons, the World Bank says, around 10 percent of yearly production. Countries in the Middle East and parts of Africa are most vulnerable to such shocks because of their heavy reliance on food imports.

The availability and price of one resource has a knock-on effect on supply of others, Chatham House says. The energy sector, for example, will have to compete for water with the mining, transport and agricultural industries. In Europe alone 37 percent of all water used is for cooling in energy production, according to the European Environment Agency. This is followed by agriculture, which uses around 33 percent of water extracted, water for use by the public (20 percent) and industrial use (10 percent).

The rise of consumption in Asia-Pacific, which now consumes the majority of all commodities, is putting stress on markets and shifting global trading patterns. Chinese oil and gas demand alone is likely to rise by 60 percent between 2013 and 2035. Consumption from India and the Middle East will also soar. China will increasingly depend on the Middle East, forcing it to become more involved in the region's politics, says Glada Lahn, a co-author of the Chatham House report. Iran, Vietnam, Turkey, and Thailand are also emerging as major resource consumers, helping to boost non-OECD countries' share of global energy demand from 55 percent in 2010 to 65 percent by 2035.

A wealth of new oil resources was discovered in the new millennium, including vast reserves of unconventional gas; Brazil's pre-salt oil resources; and large deposits of conventional natural gas in East and West Africa, and in the offshore eastern Mediterranean. But water scarcity could limit production. In Africa alone between 75 million and 250 million people will be exposed to increased water stress by 2020 because of climate change, the think tank says.

Source: Excerpted from H. Robertson. 2013. "Volatility Is the New Normal." *Petroleum Economist*, http://www.petroleum-economist.com/Article/3142534/Volatility-is-the-new-normal.html

Diebold Inc. once operated solely in the United States, selling automated teller machines (ATMs), bank vaults, and security systems to financial institutions. However, with the U.S. market saturated, Diebold needed to expand internationally to continue its growth. The firm's globalization efforts led to both the development of new technologies in emerging markets and opportunistic entry into entirely new industries that significantly improved Diebold's sales.

In many situations, global development makes sense as a competitive weapon. Direct penetration of foreign markets can drain vital cash flows from a foreign competitor's domestic operations. The resulting lost opportunities, reduced income, and limited production can impair the competitor's ability to invade U.S. markets. A case in point is IBM's move to establish a position of strength in the Japanese mainframe computer industry before two key competitors, Fugitsu and Hitachi, could dominate it. Once IBM had achieved a substantial share of the Japanese market, it worked to deny its Japanese competitors the vital cash and production experience they needed to invade the U.S. market.

Firms that operate principally in the domestic environment have an important decision to make with regard to their globalization: Should they act before being forced to do so by

ethnocentric orientation

When the values and priorities of the parent organization guide the strategic decision making of all its international operations.

polycentric orientation

When the culture of the country in which the strategy is to be implemented is allowed to dominate a company's international decision-making process.

regiocentric orientation

When a parent company blends its own predisposition with those of its international units to develop region-sensitive strategies

geocentric orientation

When an international firm adopts a systems approach to strategic decision making that emphasizes global integration.

competitive pressures or after? Should they (1) be proactive by entering global markets in advance of other firms and thereby enjoy the first-mover advantages often accruing to risk-taker firms that introduce new products or services or (2) be reactive by taking the more conservative approach and following other companies into global markets once customer demand has been proven and the high costs of new-product or new-service introductions have been absorbed by competitors?

Strategic Orientations of Global Firms

Multinational corporations typically display one of four orientations toward their overseas activities. They have a certain set of beliefs about how the management of foreign operations should be handled. A company with an **ethnocentric orientation** believes that the values and priorities of the parent organization should guide the strategic decision making of all its operations. If a corporation has a **polycentric orientation,** then the culture of the country in which a strategy is to be implemented is allowed to dominate the decision-making process. In contrast, a **regiocentric orientation** exists when the parent attempts to blend its own predispositions with those of the region under consideration, thereby arriving at a region-sensitive compromise. Finally, a corporation with a **geocentric orientation** adopts a global systems approach to strategic decision making, thereby emphasizing global integration.

American firms often adopt a regiocentric orientation for pursing strategies in Europe. U.S. e-tailers have attempted to blend their own corporate structure and expertise with that of European corporations. For example, Amazon has been able to leverage its experience in the United States while developing regionally and culturally specific strategies overseas. By purchasing European franchises that have had regional success, E*Trade is pursuing a foreign strategy in which they insert their European units into their corporate structure. This strategy requires the combination and use of culturally different management styles and involves major challenges for upper management.

Exhibit 5.4, Global Strategy in Action shows the effects of each of the four orientations on key activities of the firm. It is clear from the figure that the strategic orientation of a global firm plays a major role in determining the locus of control and corporate priorities of the firm's decision makers.

AT THE START OF GLOBALIZATION

External and internal assessments are conducted before a firm enters global markets. For example, Japanese investors conduct extensive assessments and analyses before selecting a U.S. site for a Japanese-owned firm. They prefer states with strong markets, low unionization rates, and low taxes. In addition, Japanese manufacturing plants prefer counties characterized by manufacturing conglomeration; low unemployment and poverty rates; and concentrations of educated, productive workers.

External assessment involves careful examination of critical features of the global environment, particular attention being paid to the status of the host nations in such areas as economic progress, political control, and nationalism. Expansion of industrial facilities, favorable balances of payments, and improvements in technological capabilities over the past decade are gauges of the host nation's economic progress. Political status can be gauged by the host nation's power in and impact on global affairs.

Understanding the political risk involved is a key element in the decision to do business in a foreign nation. Opportunities for fast growth and attractive profits often arise in countries with suspect political risk. The principal concern of foreign direct investors is whether

Orientation of a Global Firm

	Orientation of the Firm			
	Ethnocentric	**Polycentric**	**Regiocentric**	**Geocentric**
Mission	Profitability (viability)	Public acceptance (legitimacy)	Profitability and public acceptance. (viability and legitimacy)	Same as regiocentric
Governance	Top-down	Bottom-up (each subsidiary decides on local objectives)	Mutually negotiated between region and its subsidiaries	Mutually negotiated at all levels of the corporation
Strategy	Global integration	National Responsiveness	Regional integration and national responsiveness	Global integration and national responsiveness
Structure	Hierarchical product divisions	Hierarchical area divisions, with autonomous national units	Product and regional organization tied through a matrix	A network of organizations (including some competitors)
Culture Technology Marketing	Home country Mass production Product development determined by the needs of home country	Host country Batch production Local product development based on local heeds	Regional Flexible manufacturing Standardize within region but not across regions	Global Flexible manufacturing Global product, with local variations
Finance	Repatriation of profits to home country	Retention of profits in host country	Redistribution within region	Redistribution globally
Personnel Practices	People of home country developed for key positions in the world	People of local nationality developed for key positions in their own country	Regional people developed for key positions anywhere in the region	Global personnel development and placement

Source: From *Columbia Journal of World Business*, Summer 1985, by B.S. Chukravarthy and Howard V. Perlmuter, "Strategic Planning for a Global Business," p. 506. Copyright © Elsevier 1985.

the foreign government is able to implement its policies during a period of political, social, or economic upheaval. If it can, the country is judged to be stable. Stability provides investors with confidence that the country's regulatory environment will enable it to achieve the economic returns that it deserves.

A second issue that concerns investors is how the stability in a foreign nation is achieved. Strategists often place a country's openness along a simple continuum from closed to open. Closed countries maintain their stability by restricting the flow of money, goods, services, people, and information across their borders. Countries that tend toward this extreme include Cuba, Iran, and North Korea because their isolationist policies prevent their citizens from fully comprehending the conditions and options that are available in other countries.

At the other extreme, many nations achieve their stability by allowing and encouraging exchanges among their and business and public institutions, and their citizens and those of other nations. Examples include the countries in Australia, Brazil, the European zone, Japan, and the United States.

The J-Curve on Country Stability and Openness

The J-curve represents the relationship between stability and openness as shown in the accompanying figure. Each country moves along its own J-curve and the curve itself shifts up and down with fluctuations in the economy. Nations higher on the graph are more stable; those lower are less stable. Nations to the right of the dip in the J are more open; those to the left less open. As a country that is stable because it is closed becomes more open, it slides down the left side of the curve toward the dip in the J, the point of greatest instability. So, for example, if Pakistan, Myanmar, or Cuba held elections next week, political turmoil would likely erupt. If North Koreans had [had] access to South Korea media for a week, Kim Jong Il would have [had] plenty to fear.

The irony is that the energies of globalization and growth in demand for key commodities are driving more businesses to contemplate ventures in politically closed countries, particularly China. But those same energies may destabilize the ground beneath unwary businesses' feet.

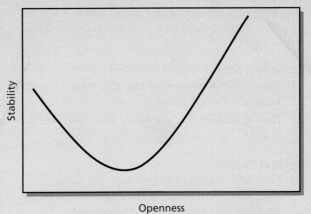

Source: From "Prepare to Lose It all? Read on . . . How to Calculate Political Risk," by Ian Bremmer, *Inc. Magazine.* Copyright © by Mansueto Ventures LLC. Reproduced with permission of Mansueto Ventures LLC via Copyright Clearance Center.

Exhibit 5.5, Global Strategy in Action, describes the J-curve, a useful approach for evaluating the relationship between stability and openness and an important element in political risk assessment.

Internal assessment involves identification of the basic strengths of a firm's operations. These strengths are particularly important in global operations, because they are often the characteristics of a firm that the host nation values most and, thus, offer significant bargaining leverage. The firm's resource strengths and global capabilities must be analyzed. The resources that should be analyzed include, in particular, technical and managerial skills, capital, labor, and raw materials. The global capabilities that should be analyzed include the firm's product delivery and financial management systems.

A firm that gives serious consideration to internal and external assessment is Business International Corporation, which recommends that seven broad categories of factors be considered. As shown in Exhibit 5.6, Global Strategy in Action, these categories include economic, political, geographic, labor, tax, capital source, and business factors.

COMPLEXITY OF THE GLOBAL ENVIRONMENT

By 2003, Coke was finally achieving a goal that it had set a decade earlier when it went to India. That goal was to take the market away from Pepsi and local beverage companies. However, when it arrived, Coke found that the Indian market was extremely complex and smaller than it had estimated. Coke also encountered cultural problems, in part because the chief of Coke India was an expatriate. The key to overcoming this cultural problem was promoting an Indian to operations chief. Coke also changed its marketing strategy by pushing their "Thums Up" products, a local brand owned by

Global Strategy in Action

Exhibit 5.6

Checklist of Factors to Consider in Choosing a Foreign Manufacturing Site

The following considerations were drawn from an 88-point checklist developed by Business International Corporation.

Economic Factors:
1. Size of GNP and projected rate of growth
2. Foreign exchange position
3. Size of market for the firm's products; rate of growth

Political Factors:
4. Form and stability of government
5. Attitude toward private and foreign investment by government, customers, and competition
6. Degree of antiforeign discrimination

Geographic Factors:
7. Proximity of site to export markets
8. Availability of local raw materials
9. Availability of power, water, gas

Labor Factors:
10. Availability of managerial, technical, and office personnel able to speak the language of the parent company
11. Degree of skill and discipline at all levels
12. Degree and nature of labor voice in management

Tax Factors:
13. Tax-rate trends
14. Joint tax treaties with home country and others
15. Availability of tariff protection

Capital Source Factors:
16. Cost of local borrowing
17. Modern banking systems
18. Government credit aids to new businesses

Business Factors:
19. State of marketing and distribution system
20. Normal profit margins in the firm's industry
21. Competitive situation in the firm's industry: do cartels exist?

Coke. Then, they began to focus their efforts on creating new products for rural areas and lowering the prices of their existing products to increase sales. Once Coke had new products in the market, they focused on a new advertising campaign to better relate to Indian consumers.

Coke's experience highlights the fact that global strategic planning is more complex than purely domestic planning. There are at least five factors that contribute to this increase in complexity:

1. Globals face multiple political, economic, legal, social, and cultural environments as well as various rates of changes within each of them. Occasionally, foreign governments work in concert with their militaries to advance economic aims even at the expense of human rights. International firms must resist the temptation to benefit financially from such immoral opportunities.

2. Interactions between the national and foreign environments are complex, because of national sovereignty issues and widely differing economic and social conditions.

3. Geographic separation, cultural and national differences, and variations in business practices all tend to make communication and control efforts between headquarters and the overseas affiliates difficult.

4. Globals face extreme competition, because of differences in industry structures within countries.

5. Globals are restricted in their selection of competitive strategies by various regional blocs and economic integrations, such as the European Economic Community, the European Free Trade Area, and the Latin American Free Trade Area.

CONTROL PROBLEMS OF THE GLOBAL FIRM

An inherent complicating factor for many global firms is that their financial policies typically are designed to further the goals of the parent company and pay minimal attention to the goals of the host countries. This built-in bias creates conflict between the different parts of the global firm, between the whole firm and its home and host countries, and between the home country and host country themselves. The conflict is accentuated by the use of various schemes to shift earnings from one country to another in order to avoid taxes, minimize risk, or achieve other objectives.

Moreover, different financial environments make normal standards of company behavior concerning the disposition of earnings, sources of finance, and the structure of capital more problematic. Thus, it becomes increasingly difficult to measure the performance of international divisions.

In addition, important differences in measurement and control systems often exist. Fundamental to the concept of planning is a well-conceived, future-oriented approach to decision making that is based on accepted procedures and methods of analysis. Consistent approaches to planning throughout a firm are needed for effective review and evaluation by corporate headquarters. In the global firm, planning is complicated by differences in national attitudes toward work measurement, and by differences in government requirements about disclosure of information.

Although such problems are an aspect of the global environment, rather than a consequence of poor management, they are often most effectively reduced through increased attention to strategic planning. Such planning will aid in coordinating and integrating the firm's direction, objectives, and policies around the world. It enables the firm to anticipate and prepare for change. It facilitates the creation of programs to deal with worldwide development. Finally, it helps the management of overseas affiliates become more actively involved in setting goals and in developing means to more effectively utilize the firm's total resources.

An example of the need for coordination in global ventures and evidence that firms can successfully plan for global collaboration (e.g., through rationalized production) is the Ford Escort (Europe), the best-selling automobile in the world, which has a component manufacturing Ford Focus.

GLOBAL STRATEGIC PLANNING

It should be evident from the previous sections that the strategic decisions of a firm competing in the global marketplace become increasingly complex. In such a firm, managers cannot view global operations as a set of independent decisions. These managers are faced with trade-off decisions in which multiple products, country environments, resource sourcing options, corporate and subsidiary capabilities, and strategic options must be considered.

The global growth challenges in the construction equipment industry are indicative of conditions often faced by strategic planners in preparing their firms for international competition, as explained in Exhibit 5.7, Strategy in Action. The shift in wealth toward emerging economies is changing the competitive landscape, providing great opportunities for companies that can overcome the challenges of working with economically developing nations.

stakeholder activism
Demands placed on a global firm by the stakeholders in the environments in which it operates.

A recent trend toward increased activism of stakeholders has added to the complexity of strategic planning for the global firm. **Stakeholder activism** refers to demands placed on the global firm by the foreign environments in which it operates, principally by foreign governments. This section provides a basic framework for the analysis of strategic decisions in this complex setting.

Caterpillar's Chinese Lessons

Caterpillar has a well-earned reputation as a global technology leader, having done a masterful job diversifying from its main construction equipment business into mining equipment, heavy-duty engines, electric power generation, and locomotives. Yet, Caterpillar's performance floundered in China, the world's largest market for its products and services. Although it opened a Beijing office in 1978, the company's market share in China in 2013 was only 7 percent, behind such local competitors as Sany and global players such as Komatsu. Caterpillar's travails yielded four important lessons for multinational companies keen to expand in China:

1. BEWARE OF THE "1.3 BILLION CUSTOMERS" SYNDROME

In devising a strategy for China, it is critical to look beyond the obvious reality of 1.3 billion customers. Corporate leaders must also strive for clarity about how they will beat equally determined and perhaps more capable competitors. In a price-conscious market dominated by low-cost players, Caterpillar, which imported 40 percent of its excavator components from Japan, was a very high-cost competitor. This was not a competitive disadvantage that Cat could overcome within a short span of time.

2. DO NOT BASE TOMORROW'S STRATEGY ON YESTERDAY'S REALITY

In 2009 and 2010, the government implemented a one-time 4 trillion yuan stimulus package aimed at helping the country survive the global financial crisis. The market for construction machinery exploded during this period, and Caterpillar found itself short of capacity. By 2011, the government had begun to close the spigots, the real estate market was beginning to cool, and the demand for commodities had started to taper off. Unfortunately for Caterpillar, this was precisely when it decided to become exceptionally aggressive in boosting production capacity in China—a clear case of developing tomorrow's strategy based on yesterday's reality.

3. WHAT'S "NORMAL" ELSEWHERE MAY NOT BE "NORMAL" IN CHINA

From 2010–2013, the U.S. Securities and Exchange Commission filed fraud cases against nearly 40 Chinese companies listed in the United States and delisted many of them. The SEC also accused Chinese affiliates of leading accounting firms with violating securities law for failing to disclose information pertaining to several Chinese companies traded on U.S. exchanges. Companies aiming to avoid missteps in China should start with the assumption that what is normal in developed markets may very well not be normal in China. It is extremely important to go well beyond normal Checks and even verify whether the company being acquired actually owns the brands, the real estate, and the equipment it claims to own.

4. ELIMINATE THE "10,000 MILE" GAP

Corporate leaders know the world's center of gravity is moving toward Asia. Yet, more often than not, leaders with the power to shape a company's future direction are far removed (psychologically, cognitively, and physically) from the new epicenters of global change. They rely primarily on information that is not merely "old" but also filtered and processed to make it palatable—in other words, information that may well be useless or even misleading. Given the complexity and importance of emerging markets, there can be no substitute for judgment based on direct observation and immersion within these societies.

Source: Excerpted from Anil K. Gupta and Haiyan Wang. 2013. "Caterpillar's Chinese Lessons." *Bloomberg Businessweek*, March 15.

Multidomestic Industries and Global Industries
Multidomestic Industries

International industries can be ranked along a continuum that ranges from multidomestic to global.

multidomestic industry
An industry in which competition is segmented from country to country.

A **multidomestic industry** is one in which competition is essentially segmented from country to country. Thus, even if global corporations are in the industry, competition in one country is independent of competition in other countries. Examples of such industries include retailing, insurance, and consumer finance.

In a multidomestic industry, a global corporation's subsidiaries should be managed as distinct entities; that is, each subsidiary should be rather autonomous, having the authority to make independent decisions in response to local market conditions. Thus, the global strategy of such an industry is the sum of the strategies developed by subsidiaries operating in different countries. The primary difference between a domestic firm and a global firm competing in a multidomestic industry is that the latter makes decisions related to the countries in which it competes and to how it conducts business abroad.

Factors that increase the degree to which an industry is multidomestic include[1]

- The need for customized products to meet the tastes or preferences of local customers.
- Fragmentation of the industry, with many competitors in each national market.
- A lack of economies of scale in the functional activities of firms in the industry.
- Distribution channels unique to each country.
- A low technological dependence of subsidiaries on R&D provided by the global firm.

An interesting example of a multidomestic strategy is the one designed by Renault-Nissan for the low-cost automobile industry. Renault's strategy involves designing cars to fit the budgets of buyers in different countries, rather than being restricted to the production of cars that meet the safety and emission standards of countries in western Europe and the United States or by their consumer preferences for technological advancements and stylish appointments.

Global Industries

global industry
An industry in which competition crosses national borders on a worldwide basis.

A **global industry** is one in which competition crosses national borders. In fact, it occurs on a worldwide basis. In a global industry, a firm's strategic moves in one country can be significantly affected by its competitive position in another country. The very rapidly expanding list of global industries includes commercial aircraft, automobiles, mainframe computers, and electronic consumer equipment. Many authorities are convinced that almost all product-oriented industries soon will be global. As a result, strategic management planning must be global for at least six reasons:

1. *The increased scope of the global management task.* Growth in the size and complexity of global firms made management virtually impossible without a coordinated plan of action detailing what is expected of whom during a given period. The common practice of management by exception is impossible without such a plan.

2. *The increased globalization of firms.* Three aspects of global business make global planning necessary: *(a)* differences among the environmental forces in different countries, *(b)* greater distances, and *(c)* the interrelationships of global operations.

3. *The information explosion.* It has been estimated that the world's stock of knowledge is doubling every 10 years. Without the aid of a formal plan, executives can no longer know all that they must know to solve the complex problems they face. A global planning process provides an ordered means for assembling, analyzing, and distilling the information required for sound decisions.

4. *The increase in global competition.* Because of the rapid increase in global competition, firms must constantly adjust to changing conditions or lose markets to competitors. The increase in global competition also spurs managements to search for methods of increasing efficiency and economy.

---

[1]Y. Doz and C. K. Prahalad, "Patterns of Strategic Control within Multinational Corporations," *Journal of International Business Studies,* Fall 1984, pp. 55–72.

5. *The rapid development of technology.* Rapid technological development has shortened product life cycles. Strategic management planning is necessary to ensure the replacement of products that are moving into the maturity stage, with fewer sales and declining profits. Planning gives management greater control of all aspects of new-product introduction.

6. *Strategic management planning breeds managerial confidence.* Like the motorist with a road map, managers with a plan for reaching their objectives know where they are going. Such a plan breeds confidence, because it spells out every step along the way and assigns responsibility for every task. The plan simplifies the managerial job.

A firm in a global industry must maximize its capabilities through a worldwide strategy. Such a strategy necessitates a high degree of centralized decision making in corporate headquarters so as to permit trade-off decisions across subsidiaries.

Among the factors that make for the creation of a global industry are

- Economies of scale in the functional activities of firms in the industry.
- A high level of R&D expenditures on products that require more than one market to recover development costs.
- The presence in the industry of predominantly global firms that expect consistency of products and services across markets.
- The presence of homogeneous product needs across markets, which reduces the requirement of customizing the product for each market. The presence of a small group of global competitors.
- A low level of trade regulation and of regulation regarding foreign direct investment.[2]

The Global Challenge

Although industries can be characterized as global or multidomestic, few "pure" cases of either type exist. A global firm competing in a global industry must be responsive, to some degree, to local market conditions. Similarly, a global firm competing in a multidomestic industry cannot totally ignore opportunities to utilize intracorporate resources in competitive positioning. Thus, each global firm must decide which of its corporate functional activities should be performed where and what degree of coordination should exist among them.

Location and Coordination of Functional Activities

Typical functional activities of a firm include purchases of input resources, operations, research and development, marketing and sales, and after-sales service. A multinational corporation has a wide range of possible location options for each of these activities and must decide which sets of activities will be performed in how many and which locations. A multinational corporation may have each location perform each activity, or it may center an activity in one location to serve the organization worldwide. For example, research and development centered in one facility may serve the entire organization.

A multinational corporation also must determine the degree to which functional activities are to be coordinated across locations. Such coordination can be extremely low, allowing each location to perform each activity autonomously, or extremely high, tightly linking the functional activities of different locations. Coca-Cola tightly links its R&D and marketing functions worldwide to offer a standardized brand name, concentrate formula, market positioning, and advertising theme. However, its operations function is more autonomous, with the artificial sweetener and packaging differing across locations.

[2]G. Hamel and C. K. Prahalad, "Managing Strategic Responsibility in the MNC," *Strategic Management Journal,* October–December 1983, pp. 341–51.

Escalating Commitments to International Markets

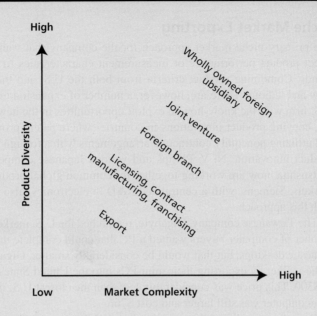

High

Product Diversity

Wholly owned foreign subsidiary

Joint venture

Foreign branch

Licensing, contract manufacturing, franchising

Export

Low   Market Complexity   High

Location and Coordination Issues

How a particular firm should address location and coordination issues depends on the nature of its industry and on the type of international strategy that the firm is pursuing. As discussed earlier, an industry can be ranked along a continuum that ranges between multidomestic at one extreme and global at the other. Little coordination of functional activities across countries may be necessary in a multidomestic industry, since competition occurs within each country in such an industry. However, as its industry becomes increasingly global, a firm must begin to coordinate an increasing number of functional activities to effectively compete across countries.

Going global impacts every aspect of a company's operations and structure. As firms redefine themselves as global competitors, workforces are becoming increasingly diversified. The most significant challenge for firms, therefore, is the ability to adjust to a workforce of varied cultures and lifestyles and the capacity to incorporate cultural differences to the benefit of the company's mission.

COMPETITIVE STRATEGIES FOR FIRMS IN FOREIGN MARKETS

Strategies for firms that are attempting to move toward globalization can be categorized by the degree of complexity of each foreign market being considered and by the diversity in a company's product line (see Exhibit 5.8, Global Strategy in Action). *Complexity* refers to the number of critical success factors that are required to prosper in a given competitive arena. When a firm must consider many such factors, the requirements of success increase in complexity. *Diversity*, the second variable, refers to the breadth of a firm's business lines. When a company offers many product lines, diversity is high.

Together, the complexity and diversity dimensions form a continuum of possible strategic choices. Combining these two dimensions highlights many possible actions.

Niche Market Exporting

The primary niche market approach for the company that wants to export is to modify select product performance or measurement characteristics to meet special foreign demands. Combining product criteria from both the U.S. and the foreign markets can be slow and tedious. There are, however, a number of expansion techniques that provide the U.S. firm with the know-how to exploit opportunities in the new environment. For example, copying product innovations in countries where patent protection is not emphasized and utilizing nonequity contractual arrangements with a foreign partner can assist in rapid product innovation. N. V. Philips and various Japanese competitors, such as Sony and Matsushita, now are working together for common global product standards within their markets. Siemens, with a centralized R&D in electronics, also has been very successful with this approach.

The Taiwanese company, Gigabyte, researched the U.S. market and found that a sizable number of computer buyers wanted a PC that could complete the basic tasks provided by domestic desktops, but that would be considerably smaller. Gigabyte decided to serve this niche market by exporting their mini-PCs into the United States with a price tag of $200 to $300. This price was considerably less than the closest U.S. manufacturer, Dell, whose minicomputer was still larger and cost $766.

Exporting usually requires minimal capital investment. The organization maintains its quality control standards over production processes and finished goods inventory, and risk to the survival of the firm is typically minimal. Additionally, the U.S. Commerce Department through its Export Now Program and related government agencies lowers the risks to smaller companies by providing export information and marketing advice.

Licensing and Contract Manufacturing

Establishing a contractual arrangement is the next step for U.S. companies that want to venture beyond exporting but are not ready for an equity position on foreign soil. Licensing involves the transfer of some industrial property right from the U.S. licensor to a motivated licensee. Most tend to be patents, trademarks, or technical know-how that are granted to the licensee for a specified time in return for a royalty and for avoiding tariffs or import quotas. Bell South and U.S. West, with various marketing and service competitive advantages valuable to Europe, have extended a number of licenses to create personal computer networks in the United Kingdom.

Another licensing strategy open to U.S. firms is to contract the manufacturing of its product line to a foreign company to exploit local comparative advantages in technology, materials, or labor.

U.S. firms that use either licensing option will benefit from lowering the risk of entry into the foreign markets. Clearly, alliances of this type are not for everyone. They are used best in companies large enough to have a combination of international strategic activities and for firms with standardized products in narrow margin industries.

Two major problems exist with licensing. One is the possibility that the foreign partner will gain the experience and evolve into a major competitor after the contract expires. The experience of some U.S. electronics firms with Japanese companies shows that licensees gain the potential to become powerful rivals. The other potential problem stems from the control that the licensor forfeits on production, marketing, and general distribution of its products. This loss of control minimizes a company's degrees of freedom as it reevaluates its future options.

Franchising

A special form of licensing is franchising, which allows the franchisee to sell a highly publicized product or service, using the parent's brand name or trademark, carefully developed procedures, and marketing strategies. In exchange, the franchisee pays a fee to the parent company, typically based on the volume of sales of the franchisor in its defined market area. The franchise is operated by the local investor who must adhere to the strict policies of the parent.

Franchising is so popular that an estimated 500 U.S. businesses now franchise to more than 50,000 local owners in foreign countries. Among the most active franchisees are Avis, Burger King, Canada Dry, Coca-Cola, Hilton, Kentucky Fried Chicken, Manpower, Marriott, Midas, Muzak, Pepsi, and ServiceMaster. However, the acknowledged global champion of franchising is Subway, which had 37,335 franchisees in 95 nations in 2013.

Foreign Branching

A foreign branch is an extension of the company in its foreign market—a separately located strategic business unit directly responsible for fulfilling the operational duties assigned to it by corporate management, including sales, customer service, and physical distribution. Host countries may require that the branch be "domesticated," that is, have some local managers in middle and upper-level positions. The branch most likely will be outside any U.S. legal jurisdiction, liabilities may not be restricted to the assets of the given branch, and business licenses for operations may be of short duration, requiring the company to renew them during changing business regulations. Gruma, Mexico's leading flour producer and the world's leading tortillas manufacturer, has manufacturing branches in 89 foreign countries and sales of $4 billion annually.

Joint Ventures

As the multinational strategies of U.S. firms mature, most will include some form of joint venture (JV) with a target nation firm. AT&T followed this option in its strategy to produce its own personal computer by entering into several joint ventures with European producers to acquire the required technology and position itself for European expansion. Because JVs begin with a mutually agreeable pooling of capital, production or marketing equipment, patents, trademarks, or management expertise, they offer more permanent cooperative relationships than export or contract manufacturing.

Compared with full ownership of the foreign entity, JVs provide a variety of benefits to each partner. U.S. firms without the managerial or financial assets to make a profitable independent impact on the integrated foreign markets can share management tasks and cash requirements often at exchange rates that favor the dollar. The coordination of manufacturing and marketing allows ready access to new markets, intelligence data, and reciprocal flows of technical information.

For example, Siemens, the German electronics firm, has a wide range of strategic alliances throughout Europe to share technology and research developments. For years, Siemens grew by acquisitions, but now, to support its horizontal expansion objectives, it is engaged in joint ventures with companies like Groupe Bull of France, International Computers of Britain, General Electric Company of Britain, IBM, Intel, Philips, and Rolm. Another example is Airbus Industries, which produces wide-body passenger planes for the world market as a direct result of JVs among many companies in Britain, France, Spain, and Germany.

JVs speed up the efforts of U.S. firms to integrate into the political, corporate, and cultural infrastructure of the foreign environment, often with a lower financial commitment than acquiring a foreign subsidiary. General Electric's (GE) 3 percent share in the European lighting market was very weak and below expectations. Significant increases in competition throughout many of their American markets by the European giant, Philips Lighting, forced GE to retaliate by expanding in Europe. GE's first strategy was an attempted joint venture with the Siemens lighting subsidiary, Osram, and with the British electronics firm, Thorn EMI. Negotiations failed over control issues. When recent events in eastern Europe opened the opportunity for a JV with the Hungarian lighting manufacturer, Tungsram, which was receiving 70 percent of revenues from the West, GE capitalized on it.

Although joint ventures can address many of the requirements of complex markets and diverse product lines, U.S. firms considering either equity- or non-equity-based JVs face many challenges. For example, making full use of the native firm's comparative advantage may involve managerial relationships where no single authority exists to make strategic decisions or solve conflicts. Additionally, dealing with host-company management requires the disclosure of proprietary information and the potential loss of control over production and marketing quality standards. Addressing such challenges with well-defined covenants agreeable to all parties is difficult. Equally important is the compatibility of partners and their enduring commitments to mutually supportive goals. Without this compatibility and commitment, a joint venture is critically endangered.

Wholly Owned Subsidiaries

Wholly owned foreign subsidiaries are considered by companies that are willing and able to make the highest investment commitment to the foreign market. These companies insist on full ownership for reasons of control and managerial efficiency. Policy decisions about local product lines, expansion, profits, and dividends typically remain with the U.S. senior managers.

Fully owned subsidiaries can be started either from scratch or by acquiring established firms in the host country. When one company buys another, the purchase is called an acquisition. The purchase can be achieved either by acquiring the seller's stock or by purchasing its assets. There are many reasons that one company might buy another, such as to grow assets quickly, deploy funds more profitably, improve the company's competitive position, bypass regulations, leverage the acquirer's competitive advantages in a new market, and gain access to cash, patents, technologies, customers, employees, locations or other physical assets, or its recognized brand. In future chapters, we will explore these reasons in greater depth. However, in the context of competitive strategies for foreign markets, it is important to know that buying a company that is already established in the market that you wish to enter may be the most attractive strategic option. U.S. firms can benefit significantly if the acquired company has complementary product lines or an established distribution or service network. For example, when Irish software giant SAS wanted to expand its law enforcement business, it acquired Memex, a Scottish firm whose software is used to combat crime and terrorism. "The Memex acquisition is a key element of our global initiative to enhance our law enforcement, criminal justice, homeland security and intelligence offerings," SAS co-founder and CEO Jim Goodnight said. Of major importance in the acquisition, Memex's customers include the Delaware, Michigan, New Hampshire and Pennsylvania state police; the Georgia Bureau of Investigation; the Los Angeles and Philadelphia police departments; the Bedfordshire, Surrey and British Transport police departments in the United Kingdom; Belize Police Department; Albania State Police; and the U.N. Office on Drugs and Crime.

PepsiCo's Eastern European Snack Attack

In 2011, PepsiCo paid $4.2 billion for Russian yogurt giant Wimm-Bill-Dann Foods, the company's biggest-ever foreign acquisition. At the time, PepsiCo CEO Indra Nooyi said she was capitalizing on growing global demand for dairy products—and left it at that.

Turns out that was just Nooyi's opening move: PepsiCo aim was to use the Russian market as a springboard to reach new consumers in former Soviet republics such as Ukraine, Turkmenistan, and Kyrgyzstan. She saw Russia, with its 142 million consumers, as a proving ground where PepsiCo could experiment with drinks and snacks targeted at a growing middle class. The company then used Wimm-Bill-Dann's distribution across the region to bring Western-style snacking in all its gluttonous glory to Eastern Europeans. Fritos, Lay's chips, and Doritos were among the company's most profitable products, in part because they were light and easy to distribute. And capturing market share early in former Soviet satellites offered the possibility of growth for decades to come.

PepsiCo in 2008 paid almost $2 billion for Lebedyansky, Russia's largest juice company. With the Wimm-Bill-Dann acquisition in 2010, the maker of sodas and snacks became the largest food and beverage maker in Russia and the former Soviet republics, putting it toe-to-toe with Denone in dairy and Coke in beverages. PepsiCo had $5 billion in annual revenue in Russia, its second-largest market after the U.S.

While Americans consume $34 billion worth of snacks each year, according to Euromonitor, Eastern Europeans are only now warming up to packaged snacks and on-the-go munching. PepsiCo hoped to shift Eastern European consumers from lower-margin dairy and juice products to "value-added" beverages such as drinkable yogurts or juices with added vitamins. In thousands of retailers' drink coolers across Russia, it aimed to replace slow-selling soft drinks in winter months with Wimm-Bill-Dann probiotic dairy drinks, which many consumers believed help stave off sickness.

Using equipment designed to make Cheetos, PepsiCo developed its own bread-based snack, Hrusteam. The brand was Russia's No. 1 packaged version of the traditional goodie, and PepsiCo planned to roll it out across the region. The company also sold Lay's chips in culturally attuned flavors such as caviar and crab. A Ruffles-like chip had become Lay's Strong, aimed at beer-drinking men. In Ukraine, temperature dials are printed on Strong's bags to highlight the power of its chili flavoring—a come-on for the region's men.

As PepsiCo introduces more product categories in individual markets throughout Eastern Europe, the real payoff of Nooyi's strategy may kick in: economies gained from shared distribution. In Ukraine, for instance, Sturrock is testing transporting juice and dairy products in the same trucks and then throwing Frito-Lay's snacks on the top—at almost no additional shipping cost.

Source: Excerpted from Duane Stanford. 2013. "PepsiCo's Eastern European Snack Attack." *Bloomberg Businessweek*, February 28.

PepsiCo pursued a similar strategy but its plan involved several more actions and required a longer timeframe. As discussed in Global Strategy in Action, Exhibit 5.9, PepsiCo decided on a strategy of securing wholly owned subsidiaries in Eastern Europe in 2008 when it purchased Lebedyansky, Russia's largest juice company. Then, in 2011, PepsiCo acquired Wimm-Bill-Dann Foods, the Russian yogurt giant. The company's cleverly coordinated and highly successful plan involving these acquisitions is explained in the exhibit.

U.S. firms seeking to improve their competitive postures through a foreign subsidiary face a number of risks to their normal mode of operations. First, if the high capital investment is to be rewarded, managers must attain extensive knowledge of the market, the host nation's language, and its business culture. Second, the host country expects both a long-term commitment from the U.S. enterprise and a portion of their nationals to be employed in positions of management or operations. Fortunately, hiring or training foreign managers for leadership positions is commonly a good policy, because they are close to both the market and contacts. This is especially important for smaller firms when markets are regional. Third, changing standards mandated by foreign regulations may eliminate a company's protected market niche. Product design and worker protection liabilities also may extend back to the home office.

For Small Businesses, the Big World Beckons

Husband-and-wife business partners Matt and Rene Greff are on track to open the first out-of-state branch of their Michigan brewpub—in Bangalore, India.

At Peter Frykman's Palo Alto, Calif., irrigation-equipment company, seven of the 20 employees are located outside the United States, in China and India, while Gangesh Ganesan's communications-chip firm, in San Jose, has about a quarter of its staffers in Istanbul, and others in Tokyo and Taipei.

While big companies have been the trailblazers of globalization, a growing number of relatively small businesses are following in their footsteps. Like their larger counterparts, they are drawn by new markets that are often growing much faster than those at home. Their forays abroad are made possible by technologies like file sharing and videoconferencing, which allow managers to communicate easily across continents. Though these technologies are not new, their price has fallen sharply over the past decade, putting them within reach of more companies.

Still, crossing borders does not come easily. Advances in technology have not done away with the need for small-business owners to spend face time with employees and clients in other countries. PharmaSecure Inc., for example, is based in Lebanon, New Hampshire, but chief executive and co-founder Nathan Sigworth says he has been spending more time in India, his primary market, than at home.

Venturing abroad also requires small companies to put a lot of care into choosing the employees or local partners who will represent their interests overseas. The task often requires bridging cultural differences and navigating complex and unfamiliar bureaucracies. The Greffs, in Ann Arbor, Michigan, were skeptical when Gaurav Sikka, a former University of Michigan student, approached them about opening a brewpub in Bangalore. Mr. Sikka, a native of India, was a regular at the couple's 200-seat Arbor Brewing Co. The couple had recently opened a small brewery in nearby Ypsilanti, and worried about stretching themselves too thin. "We said no, we don't have any time or money," recalls Mr. Greff. "He said: 'Don't rule it out of hand.'" The Greffs traveled to India, where they came to believe Mr. Sikka's idea was feasible. Now, a group of local investors, led by Mr. Sikka, is supervising arrangements for the Bangalore opening. The Greffs will have a stake in the new brewpub, and will receive consulting and licensing fees.

Though there are no hard figures available, the number of small businesses that have invested directly in overseas operations remains relatively small. But it is growing, says Larry Harding, president of High Street Partners Inc., an Annapolis, Maryland, company that helps small firms set up foreign offices. A year ago, he says, his company was working with about 200 companies; now it's working with more than 300. "There's an explosion of 50- to 100-person companies that are going overseas," he says.

Mr. Frykman, the irrigation-gear executive, helped to develop a method for making drip irrigation systems inexpensively. After testing them in Ethiopia, he formed Driptech Inc. A pilot project in India went well and caught the eye of Chinese officials. In 2009, the company made its first sales, in India and China, and began to seek angel investors. In 2010, it raised $900,000 in funding. Seven of Driptech's employees are now working in its offices in Beijing and outside of Mumbai, and Mr. Frykman expects that half of its workers will soon be overseas. Having offices in three countries is a challenge, he says, but thanks to the revolution in communications technology he is able to hand off work in the evening to his co-workers in Asia, and pick it back up in the morning.

PharmaSecure got its start in 2007 when Mr. Sigworth and a friend came up with a low-cost way to combat counterfeit drugs, a big problem in the developing world. PharmaSecure's system, which combines mobile-software apps and databases, allows customers to send text messages containing the codes printed on drug packages and get a reply indicating whether the code is legitimate. After a year of traveling, the partners decided that India, the source of much of the developing world's drug supply, was the best place to begin. Now, most of the company's 15 employees work out of New Delhi. Mr. Sigworth says the ability to communicate cheaply has been crucial. "We use [Internet telephone service] Skype a lot; we use e-mail a ton," he says, but he adds that just as important has been the company's ease and comfort working across cultures.

To videoconference, chat and work together on projects, Ubicom's offices use technology that would have been too costly for the company a decade ago, says Mr. Ganesan, the CEO. Ubicom Inc., which produces chips for products such as wireless routers, made its first international foray three years ago when it tapped a Turkish employee to start an office in Istanbul. Now about 20 of its 85 employees work there. Ubicom also has offices in Taipei and Tokyo, as well as a group of engineers in the United Kingdom.

Source: Excerpted from Justin Lahart, "For Small Businesses, the Big World Beckons," *Wall Street Journal*, January 27, 2011, p. B.1.

The strategies shown in Exhibit 5.8 may be undertaken singly or in combination. For example, a firm may engage in any number of joint ventures while maintaining an export business. Additionally, there are a number of other strategies that a firm should consider before deciding on its long-term approach to foreign markets. These will be discussed in detail in Chapter 7 under the topic of grand strategies. However, the strategies discussed in this chapter provide the most popular starting points for planning the globalization of a firm.

While big companies have been the trailblazers of globalization, a growing number of relatively small businesses are achieving success by adopting the strategic models of large firms. As described in Exhibit 5.10, Global Strategy in Action, small businesses based in the United States are locating profitable operations in such far-flung countries as China, Ethiopia, India, Japan, Turkey, and the United Kingdom.

Summary

To understand the strategic planning options available to a corporation, its managers need to recognize that different types of industry-based competition exist. Specifically, they must identify the position of their industry along the global versus multidomestic continuum and then consider the implications of that position for their firm.

The differences between global and multidomestic industries about the location and coordination of functional corporate activities necessitate differences in strategic emphasis. As an industry becomes global, managers of firms within that industry must increase the coordination and concentration of functional activities.

The Appendix at the end of this chapter lists many components of the environment with which global corporations must contend. This list is useful in understanding the issues that confront global corporations and in evaluating the thoroughness of global corporation strategies.

As a starting point for global expansion, the firm's mission statement needs to be reviewed and revised. As global operations fundamentally alter the direction and strategic capabilities of a firm, its mission statement, if originally developed from a domestic perspective, must be globalized.

The globalized mission statement provides the firm with a unity of direction that transcends the divergent perspectives of geographically dispersed managers. It provides a basis for strategic decisions in situations where strategic alternatives may appear to conflict. It promotes corporate values and commitments that extend beyond single cultures and satisfies the demands of the firm's internal and external claimants in different countries. Finally, it ensures the survival of the global corporation by asserting the global corporation's legitimacy with respect to support coalitions in a variety of operating environments.

Movement of a firm toward globalization often follows a systematic pattern of development. Commonly, businesses begin their foreign nation involvements progressively through niche market exporting, license-contract manufacturing, franchising, joint ventures, foreign branching, and foreign subsidiaries.

Key Terms

ethnocentric orientation, *p. 133*
geocentric orientation, *p. 133*
global industry, *p. 139*

globalization, *p. 128*
multidomestic industry, *p. 138*
polycentric orientation, *p. 133*

regiocentric orientation, *p. 133*
stakeholder activism, *p. 137*

Questions for Discussion

1. How does environmental analysis at the domestic level differ from global analysis?
2. Which factors complicate environmental analysis at the global level? Which factors are making such analysis easier?
3. Do you agree with the suggestion that soon all industries will need to evaluate global environments?
4. Which industries operate almost devoid of global competition? Which inherent immunities do they enjoy?
5. Explain when and why it is important for a company to globalize.
6. Describe the four main strategic orientations of global firms.
7. Explain the control problems that are faced by global firms.
8. Describe the differences between multinational and global firms.
9. Describe the market requirements and product characteristics in global competition.
10. Evaluate the competitive strategies for firms in foreign markets:
    a. Niche market exporting
    b. Licensing and contract manufacturing
    c. Franchising
    d. Joint ventures
    e. Foreign branching
    f. Private equity investment
    g. Wholly owned subsidiaries

Chapter 5 Appendix

Components of the Global Environment

Global firms must operate within an environment that has numerous components. These components include the following:

1. Government, laws, regulations, and policies of home country (United States, for example)
   a. Monetary and fiscal policies and their effect on price trends, interest rates, economic growth, and stability
   b. Balance-of-payments policies
   c. Mandatory controls on direct investment
   d. Interest equalization tax and other policies
   e. Commercial policies, especially tariffs, quantitative import restrictions, and voluntary import controls
   f. Export controls and other restrictions on trade
   g. Tax policies and their impact on overseas business
   h. Antitrust regulations, their administration, and their impact on international business
   i. Investment guarantees, investment surveys, and other programs to encourage private investments in less-developed countries
   j. Export-import and government export expansion programs
   k. Other changes in government policy that affect international business

2. Key political and legal parameters in foreign countries and their projection
   a. Type of political and economic system, political philosophy, national ideology
   b. Major political parties, their philosophies, and their policies
   c. Stability of the government
      (1) Changes in political parties
      (2) Changes in governments
   d. Assessment of nationalism and its possible impact on political environment and legislation
   e. Assessment of political vulnerability
      (1) Possibilities of expropriation
      (2) Unfavorable and discriminatory national legislation and tax laws
      (3) Labor laws and problems
   f. Favorable political aspects
      (1) Tax and other concessions to encourage foreign investments
      (2) Credit and other guarantees
   g. Differences in legal system and commercial law

   h. Jurisdiction in legal disputes
   i. Antitrust laws and rules of competition
   j. Arbitration clauses and their enforcement
   k. Protection of patents, trademarks, brand names, and other industrial property rights

3. Key economic parameters and their projection
   a. Population and its distribution by age groups, density, annual percentage increase, percentage of working age, percentage of total in agriculture, and percentage in urban centers
   b. Level of economic development and industrialization
   c. Gross national product, gross domestic product, or national income in real terms and also on a per capita basis in recent years and projections over future planning period
   d. Distribution of personal income
   e. Measures of price stability and inflation, wholesale price index, consumer price index, other price indexes
   f. Supply of labor, wage rates
   g. Balance-of-payments equilibrium or disequilibrium, level of international monetary reserves, and balance-of-payments policies
   h. Trends in exchange rates, currency stability, evaluation of possibility of depreciation of currency
   i. Tariffs, quantitative restrictions, export controls, border taxes, exchange controls, state trading, and other entry barriers to foreign trade
   j. Monetary, fiscal, and tax policies
   k. Exchange controls and other restrictions on capital movements, repatriation of capital, and remission of earnings

4. Business system and structure
   a. Prevailing business philosophy: mixed capitalism, planned economy, state socialism
   b. Major types of industry and economic activities
   c. Numbers, size, and types of firms, including legal forms of business
   d. Organization: proprietorships, partnerships, limited companies, corporations, cooperatives, state enterprises
   e. Local ownership patterns: public and privately held corporations, family-owned enterprises
   f. Domestic and foreign patterns of ownership in major industries

g. Business managers available: their education, training, experience, career patterns, attitudes, and reputations

h. Business associations and chambers of commerce and their influence

i. Business codes, both formal and informal

j. Marketing institutions: distributors, agents, wholesalers, retailers, advertising agencies, advertising media, marketing research, and other consultants

k. Financial and other business institutions: commercial and investment banks, other financial institutions, capital markets, money markets, foreign exchange dealers, insurance firms, engineering companies

l. Managerial processes and practices with respect to planning, administration, operations, accounting, budgeting, and control

5. Social and cultural parameters and their projections

a. Literacy and educational levels

b. Business, economic, technical, and other specialized education available

c. Language and cultural characteristics

d. Class structure and mobility

e. Religious, racial, and national characteristics

f. Degree of urbanization and rural-urban shifts

g. Strength of nationalistic sentiment

h. Rate of social change

i. Impact of nationalism on social and institutional change

Chapter **Six**

Internal Analysis

After reading and studying this chapter, you should be able to

1. Understand how to conduct a SWOT analysis, and be able to summarize its limitations.

2. Understand value chain analysis and how to use it to disaggregate a firm's activities and determine which are most critical to generating competitive advantage.

3. Understand the resource-based view of a firm and how to use it to disaggregate a firm's activities and resources to determine which resources are best used to build competitive advantage.

4. Use three circles analysis as a technique to examine a company's product/service attributes with those of key competitors relative to tangible customer needs.

5. Apply four different perspectives for making meaningful comparisons to assess a firm's internal strengths and weaknesses.

6. Refamiliarize yourself with ratio analysis and basic techniques of financial analysis to assist you in doing internal analysis to identify a firm's strengths and weaknesses.

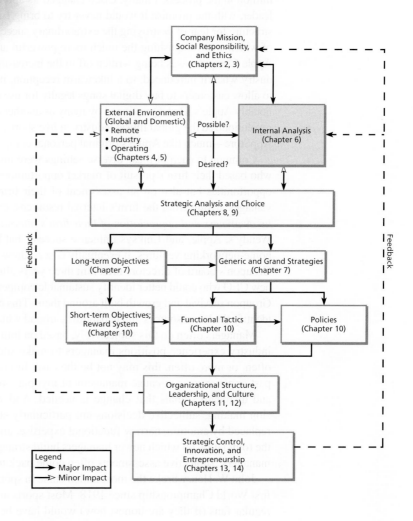

Company Mission, Social Responsibility, and Ethics (Chapters 2, 3)

External Environment (Global and Domestic)
• Remote
• Industry
• Operating
(Chapters 4, 5)

Possible?

Internal Analysis (Chapter 6)

Desired?

Strategic Analysis and Choice (Chapters 8, 9)

Long-term Objectives (Chapter 7)

Generic and Grand Strategies (Chapter 7)

Short-term Objectives; Reward System (Chapter 10)

Functional Tactics (Chapter 10)

Policies (Chapter 10)

Organizational Structure, Leadership, and Culture (Chapters 11, 12)

Strategic Control, Innovation, and Entrepreneurship (Chapters 13, 14)

Feedback

Legend
→ Major Impact
⇢ Minor Impact

Andrew Mason, 30-year-old former rock band keyboardist turned entrepreneur/CEO and creator of Groupon, was in his hometown, Chicago, trying to figure out how to chart a strategy to guide his highly successful three-year-old digital couponing startup into a rebirth of itself as "Groupon Now." The company reached over $4 billion in sales in less than five years. Mason's job was to shape a strategy that addressed massive copycat competition and Facebook competition so as to make Groupon something much more difficult to replicate. Amazingly, Mason turned down a $6 billion offer for Groupon at its second birthday, in part because of the many venture capitalists that felt Groupon could become the fastest growing company of all time. The late R. David Thomas, who could have been Mason's grandfather, had a similar albeit more negative reception when he was ridiculed by many restaurant industry veterans and analysts as he set about building "yet another" hamburger chain, named after his young daughter, Wendy. Okay with the name, these critics questioned Thomas's sanity for entering a North American market saturated with hamburger stores such as Burger King, Hardees, McDonald's, White Castle, Dairy Queen, and others. Interestingly, Wendy's became the fastest growing restaurant chain in the history of the world. Cisco, the global leader in networking equipment and switching devices linking wired and wireless computer systems worldwide, twice entered and tried to dominate the home-networking market. It failed each time, wasting more than $250 million in the process. Finally, Cisco changed its approach and acquired Linksys, the market leader, with the promise it would never try to bring Linksys into the normal Cisco company structure for fear of destroying the extraordinary success Linksys had achieved—not the least of which was vanquishing the much more powerful and wealthy Cisco twice in one decade. Apple Computer was being written off in the increasingly competitive personal computer industry when it introduced, to a lukewarm reception, its new iTunes music download service to allow customers to buy digital songs legally for use on their computer or MP3 player, most notably Apple's iPod. Questioned by many as another cute Apple fad, that modest innovation revolutionized the global music industry in five short years and led to the iPhone, the iPad, the AppStore—much like Apple's original personal computer did three decades earlier.

Common to each of these diverse settings were insightful managers and business leaders who based their firm's pursuit of market opportunities not only on the existence of external opportunities but also on an assessment of their firm's competitive advantages and disadvantages arising from the firm's internal resources, capabilities, and skills. A *sound, realistic awareness and appreciation of their firm's internally generated advantages* helped bring Wendy's, Apple, and Linksys immense success, but brought much the opposite to Cisco's home-networking ventures. It eventually cost Andrew Mason his job as Groupon CEO when Groupon's board of directors fired him three years after Groupon went public to search for a new CEO who could better identify sustainable competitive advantages and then a strategy for Groupon survival and growth built around them. This chapter, then, focuses on how managers identify the key resources and capabilities around which to build successful strategies.

Managers often do this subjectively, based on intuition and "gut feel." Years of seasoned industry experience positions managers to make sound subjective judgments. But just as often, or more often, this may not be the case. In fast-changing environments, reliance on past experiences can cause management myopia—or a tendency to accept the status quo and disregard signals that change is needed. And with managers new to strategic decision making, subjective decisions are particularly suspect. A lack of experience is easily replaced by emotion, narrow functional expertise, and the opinions of others, thus creating the foundation on which newer managers build strategic recommendations. So it is that new managers' subjective assessments often come back to haunt them.

John W. Henry broke the most fabled curse in sports when his Boston Red Sox won their first World Championship since 1918. Most sports analysts, sports business managers, and regular fans (if they are honest now) would have bet a small fortune, based on their own subjective assessment, that there was no way the Boston Red Sox, having already lost three games, would win four straight games to beat the New York Yankees and then go on to win the World Series. That subjective assessment or "feel" would have led them to believe there were just too many reasons to bet the Red Sox would fail. At the same time, a seasoned global futures market trader, John W. Henry, relied on applying his systematic global futures market approach to baseball player selection along with selected other resources and capabilities unique to the Boston area and situation in his bet that the Red Sox could win it all. His very systematic approach to internal analysis of the Boston Red Sox sports enterprise and the leveraging of his/their strengths led to the World Series championship and perhaps many more, as described in Exhibit 6.1, Global Strategy in Action. That approach was proven again in 2013 when the Red Sox went from last place the year before to win the 2013 World Series based on those same player skills previously identified but orchestrated by a new, more skill-focused manager to deploy those skills effectively.

Managers often start their internal analysis with questions like, How well is the current strategy working? What is our current situation? or What are our strengths and weaknesses? The chapter begins with a review of a long-standing, traditional approach managers have frequently used to answer these questions, SWOT analysis. This approach is a logical framework intended to help managers thoughtfully consider their company's internal capabilities and use the results to shape strategic options. Its value and continued use is found in its simplicity. At the same time, SWOT analysis has limitations that have led strategists to seek more comprehensive frameworks for conducting internal analysis.

Value chain analysis is one such framework. Value chain analysis views a firm as a "chain" or sequential process of value-creating activities. The sum of all of these activities represents the "value" the firm exists to provide its customers. So undertaking an internal analysis that breaks down the firm into these distinct value activities allows for a detailed, interrelated evaluation of a firm's internal strengths and weaknesses that improves upon what strategists can create using only SWOT analysis.

The resource-based view (RBV) of a firm is another important framework for conducting internal analysis. This approach improves upon SWOT analysis by examining a variety of different yet specific types of resources and capabilities any firm possesses and then evaluating the degree to which they become the basis for sustained competitive advantage based on industry and competitive considerations. In so doing, it provides a disciplined approach to internal analysis.

Common to all the approaches to internal analysis is the use of meaningful standards for comparison in internal analysis. We conclude this chapter by examining how managers use past performance, comparison with competitors, or other "benchmarks," industry norms, and traditional financial analysis to make meaningful comparisons.

SWOT ANALYSIS: A TRADITIONAL APPROACH TO INTERNAL ANALYSIS

SWOT analysis
SWOT is an acronym for the internal Strengths and Weaknesses of a firm, and the environmental Opportunities and Threats facing that firm. SWOT analysis is a technique through which managers create a quick overview of a company's strategic situation.

SWOT is an acronym for the internal **S**trengths and **W**eaknesses of a firm and the environmental **O**pportunities and **T**hreats facing that firm. **SWOT analysis** is a historically popular technique through which managers create a quick overview of a company's strategic situation. It is based on the assumption that an effective strategy derives from a sound "fit" between a firm's internal resources (strengths and weaknesses) and its external situation (opportunities and threats). A good fit maximizes a firm's strengths and opportunities and minimizes its weaknesses and threats. Accurately applied, this simple assumption has sound, insightful implications for the design of a successful strategy.

Environmental and industry analysis in Chapters 3 and 4 provides the information needed to identify opportunities and threats in a firm's environment, the first fundamental focus in SWOT analysis.

John W. Henry, SWOT Analysis Fixes Boston Red Sox ... Then Liverpool Football Club

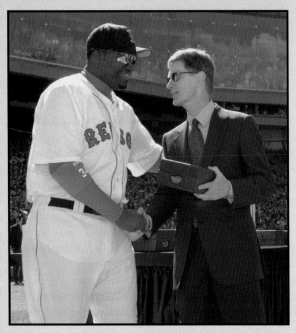

John W. Henry, principal owner of the Boston Red Sox, and slugger David "Big Papi" Ortiz

The return of pain and broken hearts for every Boston Red Sox fan with each new professional baseball season was legendary. Not since 1918 had they experienced winning the World Series, yet they had suffered through their arch nemesis, the New York Yankees, doing it 26 times over that lengthy spell. Then, suddenly, twice in the first decade of the new millennium, sports' best-known curse was broken after almost a century of trying—the Boston Red Sox won two World Series titles.

It could not have happened in a more dramatic fashion. The Red Sox were down three games to none in the American League Championship series, once again, to the hated New York Yankees . . . and playing in New York for the deciding Game 4. Somehow, the Red Sox rallied to win that game, and then the next three, allowing them to go to the World Series. They won that too. Since then, the

Sox have won another and are now in the championship hunt each year. What happened? John W. Henry became the principal owner a few years before that initial win, and he took a different approach to charting the Red Sox's future. He may well have achieved immortality, at least in the Red Sox nation.

Henry set about a careful, internal analysis to determine the Red Sox's skills, resources, capabilities, and weaknesses. He set the tone by firing the manager during the 2003 playoff series for what he thought was a critical, poor decision in a decisive game. That set a tone of seriousness—and gained fan support. Henry had previously earned his fortune developing and building a business around his proprietary global futures trading system still widely used today. So he secondly approached internal assessments of the Red Sox player possibilities in a similar manner—he used a system called *sabermetrics* to mine baseball statistics about minor league and other young players, systematically finding undervalued players to bring into the Red Sox organization while also identifying when to avoid long-term contracts with aging stars.

He further saw other underutilized capabilities, such as generating more revenue from Fenway Park, the oldest stadium in Major League Baseball, by squeezing in more seats and then charging the highest prices for home games. They always sold out. He started high-definition (HD) broadcasts of home games on their 80 percent–owned New England Sports Cable Network, broadening the fan base, increasing advertising revenue, and routinely winning regional prime-time ratings. The Red Sox quickly turned into the second-highest-earning MLB franchise, giving it the financial muscle to compete with the perennial highest payroll Yankees.

Then John Henry looked toward Europe and the world's most popular sport, soccer. Not long thereafter, he had found his next project after a thorough SWOT analysis seeking an oncore. The Liverpool Football Club woke up to learn of a new owner, an American businessman from Boston. And, starting in the second decade of the new millennium, another SWOT-based sports success story was in the making.

Opportunities

opportunity
A major favorable situation in a firm's environment.

An **opportunity** is a major favorable situation in a firm's environment. Key trends are one source of opportunities. Identification of a previously overlooked market segment, changes in competitive or regulatory circumstances, technological changes, and improved buyer or supplier relationships could represent opportunities for the firm. Sustained, growing interest in organic foods has created an opportunity that is a critical factor shaping strategic decisions at groceries and restaurants worldwide.

AT&T's decision to attempt to acquire T-Mobile in 2011 created a sudden potential opportunity for Verizon in three ways. Regulatory approval of the deal would take a lot of time and attention on AT&T; and confusion for T-Mobile customers with the future ability to continue the lower cost T-Mobile contracts when they were up for renewal creating a possibility for considerable T-Mobile customer unhappiness. Finally, the attempted acquisition came just after the Apple iPhone had finally become available through Verizon and not just AT&T, creating a major additional opportunity for Verizon.

Threats

threat
A major unfavorable situation in a firm's environment.

A **threat** is a major unfavorable situation in a firm's environment. Threats are key impediments to the firm's current or desired position. The entrance of new competitors, slow market growth, increased bargaining power of key buyers or suppliers, technological changes, and new or revised regulations could represent threats to a firm's success. Japan's sudden, massive earthquake and the tsunami it unleashed created an unanticipated opportunity for wood and building products companies still trying to emerge from the global "Great Recession." But it was a new, potentially major threat for companies like GE and others with significant new investments anticipating long-term growth in the newly revitalized nuclear energy industry. Literally overnight, as a result of this unprecedented natural disaster and its effect on several Japanese nuclear power plants, hundreds of major global companies faced a serious, unfolding long-term threat to take into account as they each reevaluated their company's capabilities in light of this new environment.

Once managers agree on key opportunities and threats facing their firm, they have a frame of reference or context from which to evaluate their firm's ability to take advantage of opportunities and minimize the effect of key threats. And vice versa: Once managers agree on their firm's core strengths and weaknesses, they can logically move to consider opportunities that best leverage their firm's strengths while minimizing the effect certain weaknesses may present until remedied.

Strengths

strength
A resource advantage relative to competitors and the needs of the markets a firm serves or expects to serve.

A **strength** is a resource or capability controlled by or available to a firm that gives it an advantage relative to its competitors in meeting the needs of the customers it serves. Strengths arise from the resources and competencies available to the firm. Southland Log Homes' southeastern plant locations (Virginia, South Carolina, and Mississippi) provide both transportation and raw material cost advantages along with ideal proximity to the United States' most rapidly growing second-home markets. Southland leveraged these strengths to take advantage of the moderate interest rates and rapidly growing baby-boomer second-home demand trend to become one of the largest log home companies in North America. This strength has continued to sustain Southland even as it navigates the recent economic depression in the U.S. housing market.[1]

Weaknesses

weakness
A limitation or deficiency in one or more resources or competencies relative to competitors that impedes a firm's effective performance.

A **weakness** is a limitation or deficiency in one or more of a firm's resources or capabilities relative to its competitors that create a disadvantage in effectively meeting customer needs. Limited financial capacity was a weakness recognized by Southwest Airlines, which charted a selective route expansion strategy to build the best profit record in a deregulated airline industry.

Using SWOT Analysis in Strategic Analysis

The most common use of SWOT analysis is as a logical framework guiding discussion and reflection about a firm's situation and basic alternatives. This often takes place as a series of managerial group discussions. What one manager sees as an opportunity, another

[1] www.SouthlandLogHomes.com

may see as a potential threat. Likewise, a strength to one manager may be a weakness to another. The SWOT framework provides an organized basis for insightful discussion and information sharing, which may improve the quality of choices and decisions managers subsequently make. Consider what initial discussions among Apple Computer's management team might have been that led to the decision to pursue the rapid development and introduction of the iPod. A brief SWOT analysis of their situation might have identified:

Strengths

Sizable miniature storage expertise

User-friendly engineering skill

Reputation and image with youthful consumers

Brand name

Web-savvy organization and people

Weaknesses

Economies of scale versus computer rivals

Maturing computer markets

Limited financial resources

Limited music industry expertise

Opportunities

Confused online music situation

Emerging file-sharing restrictions

Few core computer-related opportunities

Digitalization of movies and music

Threats

Growing global computer companies

Major computer competitors

It is logical to envision Apple managers' discussions evolving to a consensus that the combination of Apple's storage and digitalization strengths along with their strong brand franchise with "sophisticated" consumers, when combined with the opportunity potentially arising out of the need for a simple way to legally buy and download music on the Web, would be the basis for a compelling strategy for Apple to become a first mover in the emerging downloadable music industry.

Exhibit 6.2 illustrates how SWOT analysis might take managerial planning discussions into a slightly more structured approach to aid strategic analysis. The objective is identification of one of four distinct patterns in the match between a firm's internal resources and external situation. Quadrant 1 is the most favorable situation; the firm faces several environmental opportunities and has numerous strengths that encourage pursuit of those opportunities. This situation suggests growth-oriented strategies to exploit the favorable match. Our example of Apple Computer's intensive market development strategy in the online music services and the iPod is the result of a favorable match of its strong technical expertise, early entry, and reputation resources with an opportunity for impressive market growth as millions of people sought a legally viable, convenient way to obtain, download, store, and use their own customized music choices.

EXHIBIT 6.2
SWOT Analysis
Diagram

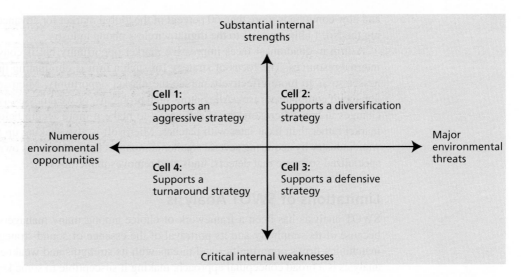

In quadrant 2, a firm that has identified several key strengths faces an unfavorable environment. In this situation, strategies would seek to redeploy those strong resources and competencies to build long-term opportunities in more opportunistic product markets. IBM, a dominant manufacturer of mainframes, servers, and PCs worldwide, has nurtured many strengths in computer-related and software-related markets for many years. Increasingly, however, it has had to address major threats that include product commoditization, pricing pressures, accelerated pace of innovation, and the like. IBM's decision to sell its PC business to the Chinese firm Lenovo and focus instead on continued development of ISSC, better known now as IBM Global Services, has allowed IBM to build a long-term opportunity in the (hopefully) more profitable, growing markets of the next decade. In the past 10 years, Global Services has become the fastest-growing division of the company, its largest employer, and the keystone of IBM's strategic future. The group does everything from running a customer's IT (information technology) department to consulting on legacy system upgrades to building custom supply-chain management applications. As IBM's hardware divisions struggle against price wars and commoditization and its software units fight to gain share beyond mainframes, it is Global Services that drives the company's growth.

Quadrant 3 is the least favorable situation, with the firm facing major environmental threats from a weak resource position. This situation clearly calls for strategies that reduce or redirect involvement in the products or markets examined by means of SWOT analysis. Texas Instruments (TI) offers a good example of a quadrant 4 firm. It was a sprawling maker of chips, calculators, laptop PCs, military electronics, and engineering software on a sickening slide toward oblivion. Rich Templeton, current chairman and CEO, rose to this position based on his success in helping to define and execute TI's strategy to focus narrowly on semiconductors for signal processing. Templeton convinced his boss at the time, Tom Engibous, to divest TI of most of the products and businesses in which it had become involved in order to rebuild TI around its core semiconductor technology, even during the worst downturn in semiconductor history. These actions ultimately reinvigorated the ailing electronics giant and turned it into one of the hottest players in signal semiconductors by betting the company on an emerging class of chips known as digital signal processors—DSPs. The chips crunch vast streams of data for an array of digital gadgets, phones, and other cellular devices. TI has experienced increasing market share every year since then, and now commands more than 60 percent of the global market for advanced DSPs, becoming the No. 1 chip supplier to the digital wireless phone industry.[2]

A firm in quadrant 4 faces impressive market opportunity but is constrained by weak internal resources. The focus of strategy for such a firm is eliminating the internal weaknesses so as to more effectively pursue the market opportunity. Microsoft has big problems with computer viruses. Alleviating such problems, or weaknesses, is driving massive changes in how Microsoft writes software—to make it more secure before it reaches the market rather than fix it later with patches. Microsoft is also shaking up the security software industry by acquiring several smaller companies to accelerate its own efforts to create specialized software that detects, finds, and removes malicious code.[3]

Limitations of SWOT Analysis

SWOT analysis has been a framework of choice among many managers for a long time because of its simplicity and its portrayal of the essence of sound strategy formulation—matching a firm's opportunities and threats with its strengths and weaknesses. But SWOT analysis is a broad conceptual approach, making it susceptible to some key limitations.

1. A SWOT analysis can overemphasize internal strengths and downplay external threats. Strategists in every company have to remain vigilant against building strategies around what the firm does well now (its strengths) without due consideration of the external environment's impact on those strengths. Apple's success with the iPod and its iTunes downloadable music Web site provides a good example of strategists who placed a major emphasis on external considerations—the legal requirements for downloading and subsequently using individual songs, what music to make available, and the evolution of the use of the Web to download music—as a guide to shaping Apple's eventual strategy. What would Apple's success have been like if its strategy had been built substantially with a focus on its technology in making the iPod device and offering it in the consumer marketplace—without bothering with the development and creation of iTunes, which also became the basis for its rapidly growing AppStore?

2. A SWOT analysis can be static and can risk ignoring changing circumstances. A frequent admonition about the downfall of planning processes says that plans are one-time events to be completed, typed, and relegated to their spot on a manager's shelf while he or she goes about the actual work of the firm. So it is not surprising that critics of SWOT analysis, with good reason, warn that it is a one-time view of a changing, or moving, situation. Microsoft, Oracle, Adobe, and other enterprise software industry giants built their empires by licensing copies to individuals or companies. This system—selling software just like cars, clothes or any other product—worked great for them. But it demanded a lot from business users, including the need for costly on-site servers and substantial upfront setup costs. While these large players benefitted from their strong software licensing position, software-as-a-service (SaaS) has rapidly moved into the enterprise software space and instead treats software as a pay-as-you-go subscription, much like cable or phone service. Hardware and software is all centrally managed by the provider on cloud-based servers, including upgrades, backups, and security. For businesses, SaaS solutions—Salesforce, Google Apps, Hubspot, and so on—often represent a clear win-win, promising both lower costs and fewer headaches than licensed alternatives. The original industry giants are now struggling to adjust to this major new reality.[4]

---

[2]http://www.ti.com/corp/docs/investor/compinfo/CEOPerspective.shtml; and "TI's Next-Gen OMAP5 Chips Are on a Whole 'Nother Level of Crazy.'" GIZMODO.com, February 8, 2011.
[3]"Microsoft Has Secretly Acquired 15 Companies in the Last Year," businessinsider.com , Oct. 2, 2010.
[4]"Behind Microsoft's Yammer Acquisition," *CNNMoney*, June 26, 2013, http://tech.fortune.cnn.com/2012/06/26/behind-microsofts-yammer-acquisition/.

3. A SWOT analysis can overemphasize a single strength or element of strategy. Dell Computer's long-dominant strength based on a highly automated, Internet, or phone-based direct sales model gave Dell, according to chairman and founder Michael Dell, "a competitive advantage [strength] as wide as the Grand Canyon." He viewed it as being prohibitively expensive for any rival to copy this source of strength. Unfortunately for Dell shareholders, Dell's reliance on that "key" strength proved to be an oversimplified basis around which to sustain the company's strategy for continued dominance and growth in the global PC industry, and the subsequent impact of cloud-enabled mobile computing devices. HP's size alone, with its reemphasis on printing and technical skills, and Lenovo's home base in the fast-growing Asian market overcame Dell's dominance in the global PC industry, while on another front Apple, Samsung, Amazon, and Google created the mobile computing explosion.

4. A strength is not necessarily a source of competitive advantage. Cisco Systems Inc. has been a dominant player in providing switching equipment and other key networking infrastructure items around which the global computer communications system has been able to proliferate. It has substantial financial, technological, and branding expertise. Cisco Systems twice attempted to use its vast strengths in these areas as the basis to enter and remain in the market for home computer networks and wireless home-networking devices. It failed both times and lost hundreds of millions of dollars in the process. It possesses several compelling strengths, but none were sources of sustainable competitive advantage in the home-computer-networking industry. After leaving that industry for several years, it recently chose to reenter it by acquiring Linksys, an early pioneer in that industry. Cisco management acknowledged that it was doing so precisely because it did not possess those sources of competitive advantage and that, furthermore, it would avoid any interference with that business lest it disrupt the advantage around which Linksys' success has been built.

In summary, SWOT analysis is a longtime, traditional approach to internal analysis among many strategists. It offers a generalized effort to examine internal capabilities in light of external factors, most notably key opportunities and threats. It has limitations that must be considered if SWOT analysis is to be the basis for any firm's strategic decision-making process. Another approach to internal analysis that emerged, in part, to add more rigor and depth in the identification of competitive advantages around which a firm might build a successful strategy is value chain analysis. We examine it next.

VALUE CHAIN ANALYSIS

value chain
A perspective in which business is seen as a chain of activities that transforms inputs into outputs that customers value.

value chain analysis
An analysis that attempts to understand how a business creates customer value by examining the contributions of different activities within the business to that value.

The term **value chain** describes a way of looking at a business as a chain of activities that transform inputs into outputs that customers value. Customer value derives from three basic sources: activities that differentiate the product, activities that lower its cost, and activities that meet the customer's need quickly. **Value chain analysis** (VCA) attempts to understand how a business creates customer value by examining the contributions of different activities within the business to that value.

VCA takes a process point of view: It divides (sometimes called disaggregates) the business into sets of activities that occur *within the business,* starting with the inputs a firm receives and finishing with the firm's products (or services) and after-sales service to customers. VCA attempts to look at its costs across the series of activities the business performs to determine where low-cost advantages or cost disadvantages exist. It looks at the attributes of each of these different activities to determine in what ways each activity that occurs between purchasing inputs and after-sales service helps differentiate the company's products and services. Proponents of VCA believe it allows managers to better identify their firm's competitive advantages by looking at the business as a process—a chain of

EXHIBIT 6.3
The Value Chain

Source: Based on Michael
Porter. *On Competition,*
1998. Harvard Business
School Press.

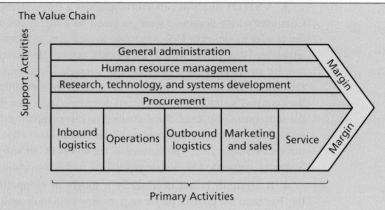

The Value Chain

Primary Activities

- **In bound logistics**—Activities, costs, and assets associated with obtaining fuel, energy, raw materials, parts components, merchandise, and consumable items from vendors; receiving, storing, and disseminating inputs from suppliers; inspection; and inventory management.
- **Operations**—Activities, costs, and assets associated with converting inputs into final product form (production, assembly, packaging, equipment maintenance, facilities, operations, quality assurance, environmental protection).
- **Outbound logistics**—Activities, costs, and assets dealing with physically distributing the product to buyers (finished goods warehousing, order processing, order picking and packing, shipping, delivery vehicle operations).
- **Marketing and sales**—Activities, costs, and assets related to sales force efforts, advertising and promotion, social media/community, market research and planning, and dealer/distributor support.
- **Service**—Activities, costs, and assets associated with providing assistance to buyers, such as installation, spare parts delivery, maintenance and repair, technical assistance, buyer inquiries, and complaints.

Support Activities

- **General administration**—Activities, costs, and assets relating to general management, accounting and finance, legal and regulatory affairs, safety and security, management information systems, social media strategy, and other "overhead" functions.
- **Human resources management**—Activities, costs, and assets associated with the recruitment, hiring, training, development, and compensation of all types of personnel; labor relations activities; development of knowledge-based skills.
- **Research, technology, and systems development**—Activities, costs, and assets relating to product R&D, process R&D, process design improvement, equipment design, computer software development, telecommunications systems, computer-assisted design and engineering, social media and community-building technologies, new database capabilities, and development of computerized support systems.
- **Procurement**—Activities, costs, and assets associated with purchasing and providing raw materials, supplies, services, and outsourcing necessary to support the firm and its activities. Sometimes this activity is assigned as part of a firm's inbound logistic purchasing activities.

primary activities
The activities in a firm
of those involved in the
physical creation of the
product, marketing and
transfer to the buyer,
and after-sale support.

activities—of what actually happens in the business rather than simply looking at it based on arbitrary organizational dividing lines or historical accounting protocol.

Exhibit 6.3 shows a typical value chain framework. It divides activities within the firm into two broad categories: primary activities and support activities. **Primary activities**

FedEx Uses Value Chain Analysis to Reinvent Itself

Stories of Fred Smith's early years creating Federal Express, like when he went to Las Vegas to gamble in order to [luckily] win $28,000 to use the next day to make payroll, are the stuff of legend. But the analysis and decision to reinvent FedEx into a logistics information company, rather than an overnight transportation company, has created a revolution in how companies around the world do business, allowing FedEx to maximize the value it adds in the process and the value it receives from doing so. FedEx becomes the logistical infrastructure for any client's business, handling every-thing from the customer order to the delivery, often including assembly and warehousing in the process.

"Moving an item from point A to point B is no longer a big deal," said James Barksdale, an early architect of the FedEx transformation. "Having the information about the item, where it is, what to connect it up with, and the best way to use that info . . . that is the value. The companies that maximize that step in their value chain will be the big winners." Fred Smith bought into that concept, envisioning a time when FedEx's value—long built on large planes and trucks—would be built on information, computers, coordination, and the FedEx brand.

That day has arrived at FedEx. It is now the linchpin of a just-in-time revolution for companies worldwide. Its planes and trucks are mobile warehouses, sometimes stopping at FedEx-operated assembling centers serving clients, all the while significantly cutting costs and increasing productivity for clients worldwide, large and small.

FedEx's value chain has dramatically shrunk the area involved with planes and trucks, while the overall logistical value added now contributes more than 90 percent of FedEx annual revenues. And, this all started with an objective, careful analysis of the FedEx value chain 10 years ago. That was followed by a visionary commitment to build that chain around activities that contribute the most value to a customer, in the process seeking to make them the core competencies upon which FedEx reinvented itself and built its future success.

Source: Various FedEx annual reports and www.fedex.com.

support activities
The activities in a firm that assist the firm as a whole by providing infrastructure or inputs that allow the primary activities to take place on an ongoing basis.

(sometimes called *line functions*) are those involved in the physical creation of the product, marketing and transfer to the buyer, and after-sale support. **Support activities** (sometimes called *staff* or *overhead functions*) assist the firm as a whole by providing infrastructure or inputs that allow the primary activities to take place on an ongoing basis. The value chain includes a profit margin because a markup above the cost of providing a firm's value-adding activities is normally part of the price paid by the buyer—creating value that exceeds cost so as to generate a return for the effort.[5]

Judgment is required across individual firms and different industries because what may be seen as a support activity in one firm or industry may be a primary activity in another. Computer operations might typically be seen as infrastructure support, for example, but may be seen as a primary activity in airlines, newspapers, or banks. Exhibit 6.4, Global Strategy in Action, describes how Federal Express reconceptualized its company using a value chain analysis that ultimately saw its information support become its primary activity and source of customer value.

Conducting a Value Chain Analysis

Identify Activities

The initial step in value chain analysis is to divide a company's operations into specific activities or business processes, usually grouping them similarly to the primary and support activity categories shown earlier in Exhibit 6.3. Within each category, a firm typically

[5] Different "value chain" or value activities may become the focus of value chain analysis. For example, companies using Hammer's *Reengineering the Corporation* might use (1) order procurement, (2) order fulfillment, (3) customer service, (4) product design, and (5) strategic planning plus support activities.

EXHIBIT 6.5   The Difference Between Traditional Cost Accounting and Activity-Based Cost Accounting

Traditional Cost Accounting in a Purchasing Department		Activity-Based Cost Accounting in the Same Purchasing Department for Its "Procurement" Activities	
Wages and salaries	$175,000	Evaluate supplier capabilities	$ 67,875
Employee benefits	57,500	Process purchase orders	41,050
Supplies	3,250	Expedite supplier deliveries	11,750
Travel	1,200	Expedite internal processing	7,920
Depreciation	8,500	Check quality of items purchased	47,150
Other fixed charges	62,000	Check incoming deliveries against	
Miscellaneous operating expenses	12,625	purchase orders	24,225
	$320,075	Resolve problems	55,000
		Internal administration	65,105
			$320,075

performs a number of discrete activities that may be key to the firm's success. Service activities, for example, may include such discrete activities as installation, repair, parts distribution, and upgrading—any of which could be a major source of competitive advantage or disadvantage. The manager's challenge at this point is to be very detailed attempting to "disaggregate" what actually goes on into numerous distinct, analyzable activities rather than settling for a broad, general categorization.

Allocate Costs

The next step is to attempt to attach costs to each discrete activity. Each activity in the value chain incurs costs and ties up time and assets. Value chain analysis requires managers to assign costs and assets to each activity, thereby providing a very different way of viewing costs than traditional cost accounting methods would produce. Exhibit 6.5 helps illustrate this distinction. Both approaches in Exhibit 6.5 tell us that the purchasing department (procurement activities) cost $320,075. The traditional method lets us see that payroll expenses are 73 percent [($175 + $57.5)/$320] of our costs with "other fixed charges" the second largest cost, 19 percent [$62/$320] of the total procurement costs. VCA proponents would argue that the benefit of this information is limited. Their argument might be the following:

> With this information we could compare our procurement costs to key competitors, budgets, or industry averages and conclude that we are better, worse, or equal. We could then ascertain that our "people" costs and "other fixed charges" cost are advantages, disadvantages, or "in line" with competitors. Managers could then argue to cut people, add people, or debate fixed overhead charges. However, they would get lost in what is really a budgetary debate without ever examining what it is those people do in accomplishing the procurement function, what value that provides, and how cost effective each activity is.

VCA proponents hold that the activity-based VCA approach would provide a more meaningful analysis of the procurement function's costs and consequent value added. The activity-based side of Exhibit 6.5 shows that approximately 21 percent of the procurement cost or value added involves evaluating supplier capabilities. A rather sizable cost, 20 percent, involves internal administration, with an additional 17 percent spent resolving problems and almost 15 percent spent on quality control efforts. VCA advocates see this information as being much more useful than traditional cost accounting information, especially when compared with the cost information of key competitors or other "benchmark" companies. VCA supporters assert the following argument that the benefit of this activity-based information is substantial:

> Rather than analyzing just "people" and "other charges," we are now looking at meaningful categorizations of the work that procurement actually does. We see, for example, that a key value-added activity (and cost) involves "evaluating supplier capabilities." The amount spent on "internal administration" and "resolving problems" seems high and may indicate a weakness or area for improvement if the other activities' costs are in line and outcomes favorable. The bottom line is that this approach lets us look at what we actually "do" in the business—the specific activities—to create customer value, and that in turn allows more specific internal analysis than traditional, accounting-based cost categories.

Recognizing the Difficulty in Activity-Based Cost Accounting

It is important to note that existing financial management and accounting systems in many firms are not set up to easily provide activity-based cost breakdowns. Likewise, in virtually all firms, the information requirements to support activity-based cost accounting can create redundant work because of the financial reporting requirements that may force firms to retain the traditional approach for financial statement purposes. The time and energy to change to an activity-based approach can be formidable and still typically involve arbitrary cost allocation decisions—trying to allocate selected asset or people costs across multiple activities in which they are involved. Challenges dealing with a cost-based use of VCA have not deterred use of the framework to identify sources of differentiation. Indeed, conducting a VCA to analyze competitive advantages that differentiate the firm is compatible with the resource-based view's examination of intangible assets and capabilities as sources of distinctive competence.

Identify the Activities That Differentiate the Firm

Scrutinizing a firm's value chain may not only reveal cost advantages or disadvantages, it may also bring attention to several sources of differentiation advantage relative to competitors. Google considers its Internet-based search algorithms (activities) to be far superior to any competitor's. Google knows it has a cost advantage because of the time and expense replicating this activity would take. But Google considers it an even more important source of value to the customer because of the importance customers place on this activity, which differentiates Google from many would-be competitors. Likewise, Federal Express, as we noted in Exhibit 6.4, considers its information management skills to have become the core competence and essence of the company because of the value these skills allow FedEx to provide its customers and the importance they in turn place on such skills. Exhibit 6.6 suggests some factors for assessing primary and support activities' differentiation and contribution.

Examine the Value Chain

Once the value chain has been documented, managers need to identify the activities that are critical to buyer satisfaction and market success. It is those activities that deserve major scrutiny in an internal analysis. Three considerations are essential at this stage in the value chain analysis. First, the company's basic mission needs to influence managers' choice of activities to be examined in detail. If the company is focused on being a low-cost provider, then management attention to lower costs should be very visible, and missions built around commitment to differentiation should find managers spending more on activities that are differentiation cornerstones. Retailer Walmart focuses intensely on costs related to inbound logistics, advertising, and loyalty to build its competitive advantage, while Nordstrom

EXHIBIT 6.6   **Possible Factors for Assessing Sources of Differentiation in Primary and Support Activities**

Support Activities

General Administration
- Capability to identify new-product market opportunities and potential environmental threats
- Quality of the strategic planning system to achieve corporate objectives
- Coordination and integration of all value chain activities among organizational subunits
- Ability to obtain relatively low-cost funds for capital expenditures and working capital
- Level of information systems support in making strategic and routine decisions
- Overall social media strategy and coordination across all value chain activities
- Relationships with public policymakers and interest groups
- Public image and corporate citizenship

Human Resource Management
- Effectiveness of procedures for recruiting, training, and promoting all levels of employees
- Appropriateness of reward systems for motivating and challenging employees
- A work environment that minimizes absenteeism and keeps turnover at desirable levels
- Relations with trade unions
- Active participation by managers and technical personnel in professional organizations
- Levels of employee motivation and job satisfaction

Technology Development
- Success of research and development activities in leading to product and process innovations
- Quality of working relationships between R&D personnel and other departments
- Timeliness of technology development activities in meeting critical deadlines
- Quality of laboratories; Qualification of lab technicians and scientists
- Use of social media as an input to technology development activities
- Ability of work environment to encourage creativity and innovation

Procurement
- Development of alternate sources for inputs to minimize dependence on a single supplier
- Procurement of raw materials (1) on a timely basis, (2) at lowest possible cost, (3) at acceptable levels of quality
- Procedures for procurement of plant, machinery, and buildings
- Development of criteria for lease-versus-purchase decisions
- Good, long-term relationships with reliable suppliers

Profit Margin

Inbound Logistics	Operations	Outbound Logistics	Marketing and Sales	Service
• Soundness of material and inventory control systems • Efficiency of raw material warehousing activities	• Productivity of equipment compared to that of key competitors • Appropriate automation of production processes • Effectiveness of production control systems to improve quality and reduce costs • Efficiency of plant layout and work-flow design	• Timeliness and efficiency of delivery of finished goods and services • Efficiency of finished goods warehousing activities	• Effectiveness of market research to identify customer segments and needs • Innovation in sales promotion and advertising • Evaluation of alternate distribution channels • Motivation and competence of sales force • Development of an image of quality and a favorable reputation • Extent of brand loyalty among customers • Vibrant digital-social media platform and connections • Online sales and support • Extent of market dominance within the market segment or overall market	• Means to solicit customer input for product improvements • Promptness of attention to customer complaints • Appropriateness of warranty and guarantee policies • Quality of customer education and training • Ability to provide replacement parts and repair services • Ease of online connection with customers

Primary Activities

Profit Margin

Source: Based on Michael Porter, *On Competition*, 1998, Harvard Business School Press.

builds its distinct position in retailing by emphasizing sales and support activities on which they spend twice the retail industry average.

Second, the nature of value chains and the relative importance of the activities within them vary by industry. Lodging firms like Marriott have major costs and concerns that involve operational activities—it provides its service instantaneously at each location—and marketing activities, while having minimal concern for outbound logistics. Yet for a distributor, such as the food distributor PYA, inbound and outbound logistics are the most critical area. Major retailer Walmart has built value advantages focusing on purchasing, inbound logistics, and large full-service outlets. Financial software giant Intuit has built value advantages by program features tied to service—ease of use, year-to-year connection of customers to data accumulated in the software program (e.g., Turbo Tax) that tie the user back to it each year, and exceptional online support with any and every question through multilevel choices (FAQs; Community Answers; Expert Answers; Answers for a charge) for that help.

Third, the relative importance of value activities can vary by a company's position in a broader value system that includes the value chains of its upstream suppliers and downstream customers or partners involved in providing products or services to end users. A producer of roofing shingles depends heavily on the downstream activities of wholesale distributors and building supply retailers to reach roofing contractors and do-it-yourselfers. Maytag manufactures its own appliances, sells them through independent distributors, and provides warranty service to the buyer. Sears outsources the manufacture of its appliances while it promotes its brand name—Kenmore—and handles all sales and service.

Finally, the Internet-driven global revolution in the way people seek information, shop, and communicate is changing the potential sources of advantage in virtually all industries. Amazon.com now challenges Walmart for dominance in mass discount retailing based on advantages derived from a set of value activities that are different in several ways from what led Walmart's rise to global dominance. News availability online; entertainment options online; mobile computing and cloud services are all value-related activities in which competitive advantage can begin to dramatically lessen the importance of traditional sources of value in many industries rather quickly in favor of rapidly changing yet substantial new sources of advantage driven by the connectivity, convenience, and service the Internet-based offerings allow.

As all of these value chain examples suggest, it is important that managers take into account their level of vertical integration when comparing their cost structure for activities on their value chain to those of key competitors. Comparing a fully integrated rival with a partially integrated one requires adjusting for the scope of activities performed to achieve meaningful comparison. It also suggests the need for examining costs associated with activities provided by upstream or downstream companies; these activities ultimately determine comparable, final costs to end users. Said another way, one company's comparative cost disadvantage (or advantage) may emanate more from activities undertaken by upstream or downstream "partners" than from activities under the direct control of that company—therefore suggesting less of a relative advantage or disadvantage within the company's direct value chain.

RESOURCE-BASED VIEW OF THE FIRM

Toyota versus Ford is a competitive situation virtually all of us recognize. Stock analysts for the last two decades have concluded that Toyota was the clear leader. They often cited Toyota's superiority in tangible assets (newer factories worldwide, R&D facilities, computerization, cash, etc.) and intangible assets (reputation, brand name awareness, quality-control culture, global business system, etc.). They also felt that Toyota led Ford in several capabilities that made use of those assets effectively—managing distribution globally, influencing labor and supplier relations, managing franchise relations, marketing savvy, and speed of decision making to take quick advantage of changing global conditions are just a few that are frequently mentioned. The combination of capabilities and assets, most analysts concluded, created several competencies that gave Toyota key competitive advantages over Ford that were durable and not easily imitated.

In the last decade, Ford has begun to reverse that view. Capitalizing on an accelerator-sticking series of incidents that uncovered surprising quality-control problems attributed to Toyota's rapid global expansion, Ford found a "glitch" in the Toyota resource base that was a major deficiency. Then Toyota compounded the impact on its quality reputation with its initially poor handling of the PR aspects and response worldwide. That massive series of recalls stymied Toyota for some time, which was happening as the worldwide recession of recent years unfolded, again weakening Toyota's financial strength and Ford's. Fortunately for Ford, that period of time called for a massive turnaround strategy, which saw Ford eliminate outdated production facilities, reduce a bloated organization, sell off or shut down unproductive product lines, and concentrate on identifying several new product offerings that were carefully and methodically conceived, designed, and built to meet valid market concerns about quality, innovative electronics, appearance, and fuel efficiency. The result saw Ford come out of the recession a dramatically changed company, with new tangible assets (manufacturing facilities, improved R&D coordination, financial strength, smaller and stronger dealer networks) and some key, improved intangible assets (reputation, market-driven focus, brand leadership in midrange sedans). Ford executives managed these new assets with considerable skill, taking quick advantage of globally changing conditions to leverage them into a dramatic improvement in Ford's position relative to Toyota by 2012.

The Toyota–Ford situation provides a useful illustration for understanding several concepts central to the **resource-based view** (RBV) of the firm. The RBV is a method of analyzing and identifying a firm's strategic advantages based on examining its distinct combination of assets, skills, capabilities, and intangibles as an organization. The RBV's underlying premise is that firms differ in fundamental ways because each firm possesses a unique "bundle" of resources—tangible and intangible assets and organizational capabilities to make use of those assets. Each firm develops competencies from these resources, and, when developed especially well, these become the source of the firm's competitive advantages. Toyota's decision to enter global markets locally and regularly invest in or build newer factory locations in those global markets gave Toyota a competitive advantage, which it leveraged against Ford and others for over 25 years into the last decade to rise to become the top global car company. Now, after an extended passage of time accompanied by a deterioration in some of Toyota's historical distinctive competencies, Ford was able to build selective resources and capabilities, while it literally sought to survive, in a manner that has made those into several clear core distinctive competencies that may well be sustainable competitive advantages versus Toyota for many years to come.

resource-based view
A method of analyzing and identifying a firm's strategic advantages based on examining its distinct combination of assets, skills, capabilities, and intangibles as an organization.

Core Competencies

core competence
A capability or skill that a firm emphasizes and excels in doing while in pursuit of its overall mission.

Executives charting the strategy of their business have more recently concentrated their thinking on the notion of a "core competence." A **core competence** is a capability or skill that a firm emphasizes and excels in doing while in pursuit of its overall mission. Core competencies that differ from those found in competing firms would be considered *distinctive competencies*. Apple's competencies in pulling together available technologies and others' software and combining this with their own product design skills and new-product introduction prowess result in an innovation competence that is different and distinct from any firm against which Apple competes. Toyota's pervasive organizationwide pursuit of quality; Wendy's systemwide emphasis on and ability to provide fresh meat daily; and the University of Phoenix's ability to provide comprehensive educational options for working adults worldwide are all examples of competencies that are unique to these firms and arguably distinctive when compared to their competitors.

Distinctive competencies that are identified and nurtured throughout the firm, allowing it to execute effectively so as to provide products or services to customers that are superior to competitor's offerings, become the basis for a lasting *competitive advantage*. Executives, enthusiastic about the notion that their job as strategists was to identify and leverage core competencies into distinctive ones that create sustainable competitive advantage, encountered difficulty applying the concept because of the generality of its level of analysis. The RBV emerged as a way to make the core competency notion and thought process more focused and measurable—creating a very important, and more meaningful, tool for internal analysis. Let's look at the basic concepts underlying the RBV.

Three Basic Resources: Tangible Assets, Intangible Assets, and Organizational Capabilities

tangible assets
The most easily identified assets, often found on a firm's balance sheet. They include production facilities, raw materials, financial resources, real estate, and computers.

intangible assets
A firm's assets that you cannot touch or see but that are very often critical in creating competitive advantage: brand names, company reputation, organizational morale, technical knowledge, patents and trademarks, and accumulated experience within an organization.

organizational capabilities
Skills (the ability and ways of combining assets, people, and processes) that a company uses to transform inputs into outputs.

The RBV's ability to create a more focused, measurable approach to internal analysis starts with its delineation of three basic types of resources, some of which may become the building blocks for distinctive competencies. These resources are defined below and illustrated in Exhibit 6.7.

Tangible assets are the easiest "resources" to identify and are often found on a firm's balance sheet. They include production facilities, raw materials, financial resources, real estate, and computers. Tangible assets are the physical and financial means a company uses to provide value to its customers.

Intangible assets are "resources" such as brand names, company reputation, organizational morale, technical knowledge, patents and trademarks, and accumulated experience within an organization. While they are not assets that you can touch or see, they are very often critical in creating competitive advantage.

Organizational capabilities are not specific "inputs" like tangible or intangible assets; rather, they are the skills—the ability and ways of combining assets, people, and processes—that a company uses to transform inputs into outputs. Apple pioneered and has subsequently leveraged its iPod, iTunes, iPhone, iPad, and AppStore successes into major leadership positions in digitalized music, entertainment, and communication on a global basis for individual consumers. Microsoft and others have attempted to copy Apple, but remain far behind Apple's diverse organizational capabilities. Apple has subsequently refined or revolutionized these devices and services to automate and individually customize a whole new level of communication and entertainment capability that combines assets, people, and processes throughout and beyond the Apple organization. Finely developed capabilities, such as Apple's Internet-based, customer-friendly iTunes and AppStore systems, can be a source of sustained competitive advantage. They enable a firm to take the same input factors as rivals (such as Microsoft, HP, Google, or Dell) and convert them into products and services, either with greater efficiency in the process or greater quality in the output, or both.

EXHIBIT 6.7
Examples of Different "Resources"

*Adapted from Robert M. Grant and Judith Jordan, *Foundations of Strategy,* John Wiley & Sons (2012). pp. 130–136.

Tangible Assets	Intangible Assets	Organizational Capabilities
Google's Campus Hdqtrs.	Google's Culture	Google's Product Innovation Process
Apple's Cash Reserves	Apple's Reputation	Apple's Supply Chain Coord.
FedEx's Plane Fleet	FedEx Cup PR value	FedEx Transportation Scheduling
Disney Theme Parks	ESPN logo/Ad value	Disney synergy with Pixar & ESPN

Ways to Classify and Measure a Firm's Resources*

Type of Resource	Its Associated Characteristics	Ways to Measure or Gauge
Tangible Resources:		
Physical resources	Physical resources are characteristics that define the firm's operational possibilities and influence its cost position and market reach. Key ones include: • The size, location, technical sophistication, and adaptability of facilities, equipment, and related fixed operational items • Location of and alternative uses for facilities, equipment, and land • Sources of key inputs, raw materials, etc. when needed	Type and age of operational/capital equipment Market value of key operational assets and capital equipment Scale available through facilities/equipment Flexibility in use of assets and equipment Interdependence with suppliers/buyers
Financial resources	The firm's available cash, its borrowing capacity, and its conservative cash flow to support its capacity for investment and sustainability under variable conditions	Short term assets; cash; credit rating Ratios: Debt/Equity; assets/liabilities Operating cash flow/free cash flow
Intangible Resources:		
Technology resources	Intellectual property: trade secrets, copyrights, patents, patent portfolio, trademarks Innovation resources like research facilities, technical personnel, capabilities, talented people, social media connections, and communities strongly linked to firm	Nature of research facilities and location R&D staff as % of total employment Social media/community innovate links # & $$ of patents; licensing; other IP
Reputation	Relationship with customers through social media, distinct virtual communities; through brands, trademarks and image-related means; continued customer relationship and reputation/perception for quality and dependability; nature of relationship with suppliers, banks, employees, investors, and those aspiring to be; with regulatory and government entities; and with communities in which the company operates	Number of social media followers; members of online and digital communities Brand recognition; ranking; equity Level of repeat customer/buyers; Objective comparative performance evaluations; company reputation survey comparisons (J. D. Powers, *Consumer Reports, Fortune;* etc.)

What Makes a Resource Valuable?

Once managers identify their firm's tangible assets, intangible assets, and organizational capabilities, the RBV applies a set of guidelines to determine which of those resources represent strengths or weaknesses—which resources generate core competencies that are sources of sustained competitive advantage. These RBV guidelines derive from the idea that resources are more valuable when they

1. Are *critical to* being able to *meet a customer's need* better than other alternatives.
2. Are *scarce*—few others if any possess that resource or skill to the degree you do.
3. *Drive* a key portion of overall *profits,* in a manner controlled by your firm.
4. Are *durable* or sustainable over time.

Before proceeding to explain each basis for making resources valuable, we suggest that you keep in mind a simple, useful idea: Resources are most valuable when they meet all four of these guidelines. We return to this point after we explain each guideline more thoroughly.

RBV Guideline 1: Is the resource or skill critical to fulfilling a customer's need better than that of the firm's competitors?

Two restaurants offer similar food, at similar prices, but one has a location much more convenient to downtown offices than the other. The tangible asset, location, helps fulfill daytime workers' lunch-eating needs better than its competitor, resulting in greater profitability and sales volume for the conveniently located restaurant. Walmart redefined discount retailing and outperformed the industry in profitability by 4.5 percent of sales—a 200 percent improvement. Four resources—store locations, brand recognition, employee loyalty, and sophisticated inbound logistics—allowed Walmart to fulfill customer needs much better and more cost effectively than Kmart and other discount retailers. In both of these examples, *it is important to recognize that only resources that contributed to competitive superiority were valuable.* At the same time, other resources such as the restaurant's menu and specific products or parking space at Walmart were essential to doing business but contributed little to competitive advantage because they did not help fulfill customer needs better than those of the firm's key competitors.

RBV Guideline 2: Is the resource scarce? Is it in short supply or not easily substituted for or imitated?

Short Supply   When a resource is scarce, it is more valuable. When a firm possesses a resource and few if any others do, and it is central to fulfilling customers' needs, then it can become the basis of a competitive advantage for the firm. Literal physical scarcity is perhaps the most obvious way a resource might meet this guideline. Very limited natural resources, a unique location, skills that are truly rare—all represent obvious types of scarce resource situations.

Availability of Substitutes   We discussed the threat of substitute products in Chapter 4 as part of the five forces model for examining industry profitability. This basic idea can be taken further and used to gauge the scarcity-based value of particular resources. Whole Foods has been an exciting growth company for several years, focused exclusively on selling wholesome, organic food. The basic idea was to offer food grown organically, without pesticides or manipulation, in a convenient grocery atmosphere. Investors were excited about this concept because of the processed, nonorganic foods offered by virtually every existing grocery chain. Unfortunately for their more recent investors, substitutes for Whole Foods's offerings are becoming easily available from several grocery chains and regional organic chains. Publix, Harris-Teeter, and even Walmart are easily adapting their grocery operations to offer organic fare. With little change to their existing facilities and operational resources, these companies are quickly creating alternatives to Whole Foods's offerings if not offering some of the same items, cheaper. So some worry about the long-term impact on Whole Foods. Investors have seen the value of their Whole Foods's stock decline as substitute resources and capabilities are readily created by existing and new entrants into the organic grocery sectors.

Imitation A resource that competitors can readily copy can only generate temporary value. It is "scarce" for only a short time. It cannot generate a long-term competitive advantage. When Wendy's first emerged, it was the only major hamburger chain with a drive-through window. This unique organizational capability was part of a "bundle" of resources that allowed Wendy's to provide unique value to its target customers: young adults seeking convenient food service. But once this resource, or organizational capability, proved valuable to fast-food customers, every fast-food chain copied the feature. Then Wendy's continued success was built on other resources that generated other distinctive competencies.

The scarcity that comes with an absence of imitation seldom lasts forever, as the Wendy's example illustrates. Competitors will match or better any resource as soon as they can. It should be obvious, then, that the firm's ability to forestall this eventuality is very important. So how does a firm create resource scarcity by making resources hard to imitate? The RBV identifies four characteristics, called **isolating mechanisms,** that make resources difficult to imitate:

isolating mechanisms
Characteristics that make resources difficult to imitate. In the RBV context these are physically unique resources, pathdependent resources, causal ambiguity, and economic deterrence.

• *Physically unique resources* are virtually impossible to imitate. A one-of-a-kind real estate location, mineral rights, and patents are examples of resources that cannot be imitated. Disney's Mickey Mouse copyright or Winter Park, Colorado's Aspen resort possess physical uniqueness. While many strategists claim that resources are physically unique, this is seldom true. Rather, other characteristics are typically what make most resources difficult to imitate.

• *"Path-dependent" resources* are very difficult to imitate because of the difficult "path" another firm must follow to create the resource. These are resources that cannot be instantaneously acquired but rather must be created over time in a manner that is frequently very expensive and always difficult to accelerate. Google's creation of proprietary search algorithms; interlocking and directly targeted online advertising; very easy to use, and also interwined, e-mail services; and an extraordinary environment to attract and retain the world's top talent have combined to create a combination of path-dependent resources that are very difficult for even the wealthiest software and Internet companies worldwide to easily emulate, acquire, or accelerate. It will take years for any competitor to develop the expertise, infrastructure, reputation, and capabilities to compete effectively with Google. Coca-Cola's brand name, Gerber Baby Food's reputation for quality, and Steinway's expertise in piano manufacture would take competitors many years and millions of dollars to match. Consumers' many years of experience drinking Coke or using Gerber or playing a Steinway would also need to be matched.

• *Causal ambiguity* is a third way resources can be very difficult to imitate. This refers to situations in which it is difficult for competitors to understand exactly how a firm has created the advantage it enjoys. Competitors can't figure out exactly what the uniquely valuable resource is or how resources are combined to create the competitive advantage. Causally ambiguous resources are often organizational capabilities that arise from subtle combinations of tangible and intangible assets and culture, processes, and organizational attributes the firm possesses. Southwest Airlines has regularly faced competition from major and regional airlines, with some like United and Continental eschewing their traditional approach and attempting to compete by using their own version of the Southwest

EXHIBIT 6.8
Degree to Which Resource Can Be Imitated

Source: © RCTrust LLC, 2014.

	Easily Imitated	Possibly Imitated	Hard to Imitate	Cannot be Imitated
Examples	Utilities	Skilled employees	Image reputation	Unique location
	Cash	Additional capacity	Customer satisfaction	Patents
	Common raw materials	Economies of scale	Employee attitudes	Unique licenses/assets
Specific example: Google	Electricity Server farms	Smart people Larger server farms	Search leadership Brand image	Patented search algorithms "Google"

approach—same planes, routes, gate procedures, number of attendants, and so on. They have yet to succeed. The most difficult thing to replicate is Southwest's "personality," or culture of fun, family, and frugal yet focused services and attitude. Just how that works is hard for United and Continental to figure out.

• *Economic deterrence* is a fourth source of inimitability. This usually involves large capital investments in capacity to provide products or services in a given market that are scale sensitive. It occurs when a competitor understands the resources that provide a competitive advantage and may even have the capacity to imitate, but chooses not to because of the limited market size that realistically would not support two players the size of the first mover.

While we may be inclined to think of the ability to imitate a resource as a yes-or-no situation, imitation is more accurately measured on a continuum that reflects difficulty and time. Exhibit 6.8 illustrates such a continuum. Some resources may have multiple imitation deterrents. For example, 3M's reputation for innovativeness may involve path dependencies and causal ambiguity.

RBV Guideline 3: Appropriability: Who actually gets the profit created by a resource?

Warren Buffett is known worldwide as one of the most successful investors of the last 25 years. One of his legendary investments was the Walt Disney Company, which he once said he liked "because the Mouse does not have an agent."[6] What he was really saying was that Disney owned the Mickey Mouse copyright, and all profits from that valuable resource went directly to Disney. Other competitors in the "entertainment" industry generated similar profits from their competing offerings, for example, movies, but they often "captured" substantially less of those profits because of the amounts that had to be paid to well-known actors or directors or other entertainment contributors seen as the real creators of the movie's value.

Disney's eventual acquisition of Pixar illustrates just the opposite situation for the home of the Mouse. Pixar's expertise in digital animation had proven key to the impressive success of several major animation films released by Disney in the past several years. While Disney apparently thought its name and distribution clout justified its sizable share of the profits this five-year joint venture generated, Steve Jobs and his Pixar team felt otherwise. Pixar's assessment was that their capabilities were key drivers of the huge profits by *Ants* and *Finding Nemo*, leading them not to renew their Disney partnership. Pixar's unmatched digitalization animation expertise quickly "appropriated" the profits generated by this key

[6]*The Harbus,* March 25, 1996, p. 12.

competitive advantage, and Disney Studios struggled to catch up. Disney eventually solved the dilemma by acquiring Pixar at a handsome premium. The movie *Cars* soon followed.[7]

Sports teams, investment services, and consulting businesses are other examples of companies that generate sizable profits based on resources (e.g., key people, skills, contacts) that are not inextricably linked to the company and therefore do not allow the company to easily capture the profits. Superstar sports players can move from one team to another or command excessively high salaries, and this circumstance could arise in other personal services business situations. It could also occur when one firm joint ventures with another, sharing resources and capabilities and the profits that result. Sometimes restaurants or lodging facilities that are franchisees of a national organization are frustrated by the fees they pay the franchisor each month and decide to leave the organization and go "independent." They often find, to their dismay, that the business declines significantly. The value of the franchise name, reservation system, and brand recognition is critical in generating the profits of the business.

RBV Guideline 4: Durability: How rapidly will the resource depreciate?

The slower a resource depreciates, the more valuable it is. Tangible assets, such as commodities or capital, can have their depletion measured. Intangible resources, such as brand names or organizational capabilities, present a much more difficult depreciation challenge. The Coca-Cola brand has continued to appreciate, whereas technical know-how in various computer technologies depreciates rapidly. In the increasingly hypercompetitive global economy of the twenty-first century, distinctive competencies and competitive advantages can fade quickly, making the notion of durability a critical test of the value of key resources and capabilities. Some believe that this reality makes well-articulated visions and associated cultures within organizations potentially the most important contributor to long-term survival.[8]

Using the Resource-Based View in Internal Analysis

To use the RBV in internal analysis, a firm must first identify and evaluate its resources to find those that provide the basis for future competitive advantage. This process involves defining the various resources the firm possesses and examining them based on the preceding discussion to gauge which resources truly have strategic value. It is usually helpful in this undertaking to

- *Disaggregate resources*—break them down into more specific competencies—rather than stay with broad categorizations. Saying that Domino's Pizza has better marketing skills than Pizza Hut conveys little information. But dividing that into subcategories such as advertising that, in turn, can be divided into national advertising, local promotions, and coupons allows for a more measurable assessment. Exhibit 6.9 provides a useful illustration of this at the United Kingdom's largest full-service restaurant operator—Whitbread's Restaurant.

- *Utilize a functional perspective.* Looking at different functional areas of the firm, disaggregating tangible and intangible assets as well as organizational capabilities that are present, can begin to uncover important value-building resources and activities that deserve further analysis. Appendix 6A lists a variety of functional area resources and activities that deserve consideration.

- *Look at organizational processes* and combinations of resources and not only at isolated assets or capabilities. While disaggregation is critical, you must also take a creative,

[7]"Disney Buys Pixar," *Money.CNN.com*, January 1, 2006.
[8]"The Power of One Person . . . And Your Corporate Culture," Scott McKain, January 19, 2011, http://mckainviewpoint.com/2011/01/the-power-of-one-person-and-your-corporate-culture/

EXHIBIT 6.9
Disaggregating Whitbread Restaurant's Customer Service Resource

Source: Andrew Campbell and Kathleen Sommers-Luchs, *Core Competency-Based Strategy* (London: International Thomson, 1997).

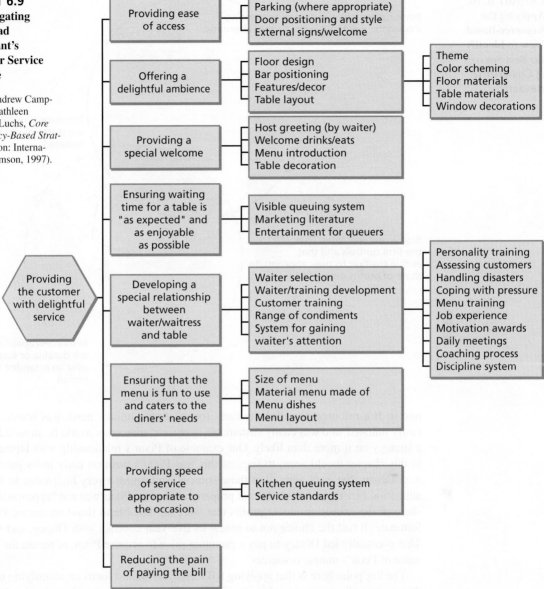

gestalt look at what competencies the firm possesses or has the potential to possess that might generate competitive advantage.

• *Use the value chain approach* to uncover organizational capabilities, activities, and processes that are valuable potential sources of competitive advantage.

Once the resources are identified, managers apply the four RBV guidelines for uncovering "valuable" resources. The objective for managers at this point is to identify resources and capabilities that are valuable for most if not all of the reasons our guidelines suggest a resource can be valuable.

If a resource creates the ability to meet a unique customer need, it has value. But if it is not scarce, or if it is easily imitated, it would be unwise to build a firm's strategy on that resource or capability unless that strategy included plans to build scarcity or inimitability

EXHIBIT 6.10
**Applying the
Resource-Based
View to Identify
the Best Sources
of Competitive
Advantage**

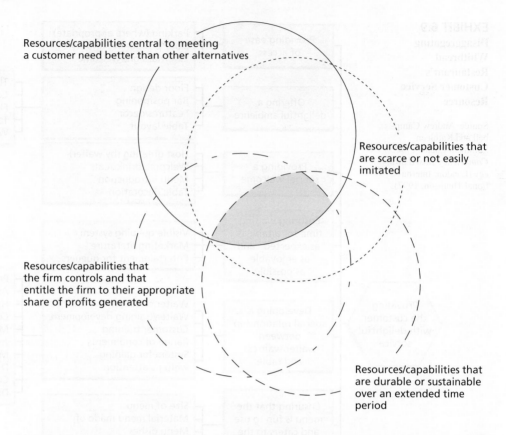

Resources/capabilities central to meeting
a customer need better than other alternatives

Resources/capabilities that
are scarce or not easily
imitated

Resources/capabilities that
the firm controls and that
entitle the firm to their appropriate
share of profits generated

Resources/capabilities that
are durable or sustainable
over an extended time
period

into it. If a resource provided the basis for meeting a unique need, was scarce, was not easily imitated, and was easily sustainable over time, managers would be attracted to build a strategy on it more than likely. Our example of Pixar's relationship with Disney earlier in this chapter would seem to suggest this was Pixar's position early in its joint venture with Disney. Yet even with all of those sources confirming a very high value in its digital animation expertise and intellectual property resources, Pixar was not "appropriating" the share of the animation movie profits that were attributable to those resources. Pixar was fortunate: It had the choice not to renew its five-year contract with Disney, and so it did. That eventually led Disney to pay a premium price to acquire Pixar, to regain the strategic value of Pixar's unique resources.

The key point here is that applying RBV analysis should focus on identifying resources that contain all sources of value identified in our four guidelines. Consider the diagram in Exhibit 6.10. Each circle in that diagram represents one way resources have value. The area where all circles intersect or overlap would represent resources that derive value in all four ways. Such resources are the ones managers applying the RBV should seek to identify. They are powerful sources around which to build competitive advantage and craft successful strategies. And resources that possess some but not all sources of value become points of emphasis by a management team able to identify ways to build the missing source of value into that resource over time much like Pixar did in its relationship with Disney.

By using RBV, value chain analysis, three circles analysis, and SWOT analysis, firms are virtually certain to improve the quality of internal analysis undertaken to help craft a company's competitive strategy. Central to the success of each technique is the strategists' ability to make meaningful comparisons. The next section examines how meaningful comparisons can be made.

INTERNAL ANALYSIS: MAKING MEANINGFUL COMPARISONS

Managers need objective standards to use when examining internal resources and value-building activities. Whether applying the SWOT approach, VCA, or the RBV, strategists typically rely on three sources of comparison—past performance, competitors, and industry success factors—to evaluate how their firms stack up on internal capabilities. This section examines each of these sources used to make meaningful comparisons.

Comparison with Past Performance

Strategists use the firm's historical experience as a basis for evaluating internal factors. Managers are most familiar with the internal capabilities and problems of their firms because they have been immersed in the financial, marketing, production, and R&D activities. Not surprisingly, a manager's assessment of whether a certain internal factor—such as production facilities, sales organization, financial capacity, control systems, or key personnel—is a strength or a weakness will be strongly influenced by his or her experience in connection with that factor. In the capital-intensive package delivery industry, for example, operating margin is a strategic internal factor affecting a firm's flexibility to add capacity. A few years ago, UPS managers viewed its declining operating margins (down from 12 percent to 9 percent by mid-decade) as a troubling weakness, limiting their flexibility to aggressively continue to expand their overnight air fleet. FedEx managers viewed a similar operating margin around the same time as a growing strength because it was a steady improvement and almost double its 5 percent level five years earlier.

Although historical experience can provide a relevant evaluation framework, strategists must avoid "tunnel vision" in making use of comparison with past performance. It can become a force for resisting change, for continuing to be satisfied with improving upon what was done last year or in the past, at the cost of not realizing that what were viewed as strengths in the past have eroded and lost relevance as the organization moves into a changing future. Speedtree.com is a "middleware" company in the video gaming and movie industries. It became well known worldwide in both industries for its exceptionally realistic tree and foliage software solutions that allow video game developers or movie producers to insert any vegetation seamlessly into the games they are designing or movies they are producing. The trees and forests in *Life of Pi, Snow White, Jack & the Giant Slayer, Avatar, Halo4, Battlefield3,* and *Tiger Woods' Golf,* to mention just a few, revolutionized that very specialized creative process in games and movies. Speedtree's management team focused on continued development of ever more sophisticated software to render these trees and forests instantly and lifelike in games that were on consoles like PS4, Xbox360, and large movie producer desktops—always looking at the strength in each new version versus the last. And it solidified Speedtree as the industry standard over a decade. However, a flood of cheap, unsophisticated mobile device games unleashed by the success of Angry Birds quickly changed the gaming landscape, making ones that could not be played on mobile devices less desirous. The result was a difficult reassessment of Speedtree's strengths and an eventual acceptance of the mobile trend, necessitating a redo of much of Speedtree's foliage rendering coding to allow for less sophisticated uses of its hallmark tree rendering expertise so that it could emerge competitive in mobile device games until their capacity can handle its more sophisticated coding ancestor.[9]

[9]www.speedtree.com.

Benchmarking: Comparison with Competitors

A major focus in determining a firm's resources and competencies is comparison with existing (and potential) competitors. Firms in the same industry often have different marketing skills, financial resources, operating facilities and locations, technical know-how, brand images, levels of integration, managerial talent, and so on. These different internal resources can become relative strengths (or weaknesses) depending on the strategy a firm chooses. In choosing a strategy, managers should compare the firm's key internal capabilities with those of its rivals, thereby isolating its key strengths and weaknesses.

In the global tech-services industry, New York–based IBM and India–based Tata Consultancy Services are major rivals. Tata has focused on large American and European companies providing lower-cost information technology (IT) services and business process simplification consulting. IBM has taken a different strategy, focusing in on helping U.S. clients cut costs while helping emerging market customers build out their technology infrastructure. Tata's strength has become its ability to offer low-cost outsourcing options to large U.S. and European firms for their information system operation needs. IBM, with a personnel cost structure that would put it at a disadvantage versus Tata in this regard, has emphasized systems design and optimization of the latest technology infrastructure to make that system perform well—building on its technical skills and computer technology expertise where it maintains a relative strength. Interestingly, this has led to a situation where Tata generates half of its revenue from U.S. clients, while IBM generates 65 percent of its revenue overseas and is the largest seller of tech services in India. Managers in both Tata and IBM have built successful strategies, yet those strategies are fundamentally different. Benchmarking each other, they have identified ways to build on relative strengths while avoiding dependence on capabilities at which the other firm excels.[10]

benchmarking
Evaluating the sustainability of advantages against key competitors. Comparing the way a company performs a specific activity with a competitor or other company doing the same thing.

Benchmarking, or comparing the way "our" company performs a specific activity with a competitor or other company doing the same thing, has become a central concern of managers in quality commitment companies worldwide. Particularly as the value chain framework has taken hold in structuring internal analysis, managers seek to systematically benchmark the costs and results of the smallest value activities against relevant competitors or other useful standards because it has proven to be an effective way to continuously improve that activity.

Global Strategy in Action, Exhibit 6.11 shows how Kodak used benchmarking of a key value chain activity in which it excelled, low-cost/high-quality inks, to differentiate its dramatic move into printers as a last-gasp basis for a strategy to avoid bankruptcy driven by the overwhelming impact of digital picture technology on its century-old dominance in traditional camera films. As you can see from this example, Kodak sought to highlight its internal benchmarking versus other ink-jet printer makers, particularly HP, but also sought in going so public to touch a long-held raw nerve they believed millions of printer customers shared—the shock they feel every time they have to buy a new printer cartridge for their HP, Canon, or Epson printer. Unfortunately for Kodak, while the benchmarking was excellent in confirming its superior ink-based skills, the ability to help it sell marginal printers never materialized, and Kodak ultimately had to declare bankruptcy.

Another way benchmarking is used is to identify the "best practices" in performing a value chain activity and to learn how lower costs, fewer defects, or other outcomes linked to excellence can be achieved. Companies committed to benchmarking attempt to isolate and identify where their costs or outcomes are out of line with what they identify as the best practices of other companies or organizations that undertake similar tasks. Once identified

[10]"The Future of Enterprise Software," http://blogs.amrresearch.com/enterprisesoftware/2008/05/ibm-vs-tata.html, July 27, 2010.

Global Strategy in Action   Exhibit 6.11

Kodak's Last Gasp: The Ink Benchmark Wars

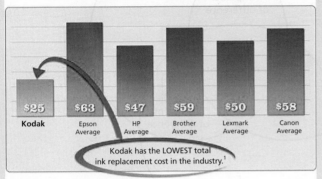

Save more every time you refill your printer with ink.
$9.99 black MSRP $14.99 color MSRP

| $25 | $63 | $47 | $59 | $50 | $58 |
| Kodak | Epson Average | HP Average | Brother Average | Lexmark Average | Canon Average |

Kodak has the LOWEST total ink replacement cost in the industry.[1]

Ink Value Comparison Chart

Kodak's promise to you is that you'll save up to 50% on everything you print compared to similar consumer inkjet printers[10]. View the information below for details on ink yield, as verified by third party test and quality assurance professionals.

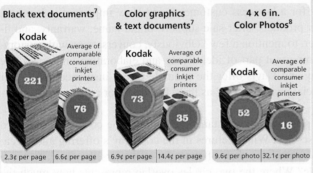

What you get for every $5 (USD) spent on ink[6]

Black text documents[7]

Kodak

221

Average of comparable consumer inkjet printers

76

2.3¢ per page | 6.6¢ per page

Color graphics & text documents[7]

Kodak

73

Average of comparable consumer inkjet printers

35

6.9¢ per page | 14.4¢ per page

4 x 6 in. Color Photos[8]

Kodak

52

Average of comparable consumer inkjet printers

16

9.6¢ per photo | 32.1¢ per photo

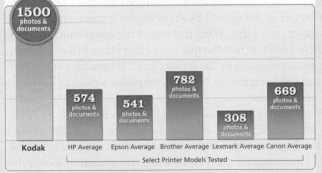

Look how much more you get a year for just $70.[5]

| 1500 photos & documents | 574 photos & documents | 541 photos & documents | 782 photos & documents | 308 photos & documents | 669 photos & documents |
| Kodak | HP Average | Epson Average | Brother Average | Lexmark Average | Canon Average |

— Select Printer Models Tested —

and studied, this allows managers to change what they do or how they do these activities to achieve the new best practices "benchmarks." General Electric sends managers to benchmark FedEx's customer service practices, seeking to compare and improve on its own practices within a diverse set of businesses none of which compete directly with FedEx. It earlier did the same thing with Motorola, leading it to embrace Motorola's Six Sigma program for quality control and continuous improvement.

Three circles analysis is a useful competitor benchmarking approach that helps visualize a firm's comparison with a key competitor based on the needs and desired attributes customers seek when buying each company's product or service.[11] Simply stated, it examines what customers want, what your company has to offer, and what a key competitor has to offer. Each of these three areas are represented by one of the three circles in the analysis. The areas of overlap among the three circles become important areas for competitive benchmarking guidance. Also, the area in the customers' desired attributes not covered by either the company or the competitor circles (each firm's respective offerings) becomes another important area for internal analysis.

> **three circles analysis**
> An internal analysis technique wherein strategists examine customers' needs, company offerings, and competitor's offerings to more clearly articulate what their company's competitive advantage is and how it differs from those of competitors.

Circle #1. The area of this circle should contain attributes, features, organizational capabilities, and so forth that customers need or desire in the product being sold to them; answers to questions like: *What benefits do they seek? Why are these benefits important? What features in the product and what capabilities do they look for in the company from whom they buy?* For example, is speedy service to

[11]Joe E. Urbany and James H. Davis, "Strategic Insights in Three Circles," *Harvard Business Review* 85, no. 11 (2007), pp. 28–30.

EXHIBIT 6.12
Three Circles Analysis

Source: Reprinted by permission of *Harvard Business Review*, Exhibit from "Strategic Insight in Three Circles," by Joel E. Urbany and James H. Davis, November 2007. Copyright © 2007 by the Harvard Business School Publishing Corporation; all rights reserved.

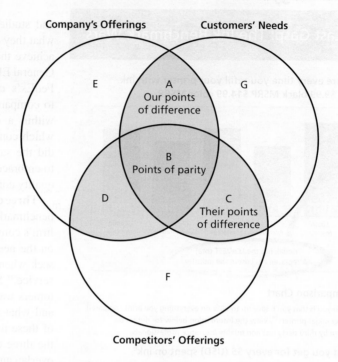

minimize inventory costs key for a business customer base? How important is location, price, compatibility with other products, after-sale support, brand name, warranty, and financial strength of the provider, to mention a few? Obviously, conversations with customers, potential or real, are an important part of identifying and elaborating on items to be included in this circle. Urbany and Davis offer the example of car insurance, citing fair coverage, fair price, and financial peace of mind as three key needs or attributes car insurance customers seek.[12]

Circle #2. The area of the second circle contains the value to the customers provided by the company's product or service. What features in the company's offering and its capabilities are what its managers perceive they offer to the customers they seek to serve represented by the initial circle? Where the two circles overlap represents how much the company's product or service overlaps what the customers' need or want.

Circle #3. The area of the third circle contains the value to the customers provided by a key competitor's product or service as envisioned by the company's management and/or suggested in interviews with target customers. What features in the competitor's offering and its capabilities are assumed or known to be what that competitor offers to the customers both companies seek to serve and represented by the initial circle? Where the competitor's circle overlaps with the customer circle represents how the competitor's product or service overlaps what the customers' need or want.

Exhibit 6.12 provides a typical three circles analysis diagram. Once these three circles are drawn and their contents envisioned, several areas of importance in benchmarking a company with its competitor that begin to enrich both internal analysis and strategic thinking start to emerge. And within that diagram areas A, B, and C are critical to identifying and building realistic value-based competitive advantages. Every unique subarea across the three circles takes on special meaning as benchmarking inputs to guide internal analysis and strategic thinking. Managers would create assumptions or hypotheses about the contents in

[12]Ibid.

each area, which they would regularly test by asking customers. Let's review each of them and the types of internal analysis and strategic thinking they call into question:

Section A—This area is the unique value the company perceives it provides to customers that its competitor doesn't—if accurate, a key source of strength and competitive advantage around which to build the company's strategy. These are key building blocks, whether they are product features, cost considerations, specific value chain activities, and so forth. Their strength and sustainability need to be realistically judged, so the importance of these features to the customer as perceived by company managers needs confirmation from customers. Urbany and Davis found that area A is often the source of the biggest surprise to company managers, with items in area A envisioned as huge by those managers turning out to be quite small in the eyes of their typical customer.[13] So questions like "how big and sustainable are our advantages?" and "are they based on unique, distinct capabilities not easily replicated?" become important in the internal analysis driven by this section.

Section B—This area is sometimes referred to as the "table stakes," or "points of parity." It is the value a company must provide "to be in the game"—the features, capabilities, need fulfillers that customers value and which other companies provide that are matched by what your company provides and vice versa. This area represents the basic features and capabilities customers expect a company to minimally provide before they will even consider the possibility of buying what that company offers. So it is not a source of competitive advantage, just a source of disadvantage or weakness, which the company needs to remedy or seek other markets or customers to serve. The key questions here are "do we offer the essential table stakes to play in this market?" and "are we delivering effectively in the area of parity?"

Section C—This area is the unique value the company perceives its competitor provides to customers that it does not—if accurate, a key source of competitive understanding around which the competitor seeks to build its strategy and which it envisions as a source of strength. Much like the items in section A, the existence, strength, and sustainability of section C items need to be realistically judged. Company managers that downplay the points of value a competitor offers risk misjudging their competitor's strength, so the importance of these features to the customer as perceived by company managers needs confirmation from customers. The key question here is obviously "how can we counter our competitor's advantages?"

An interesting *point of analysis* from Urbany and Davis is that once areas A and C are identified, the company's profitability in serving this customer base is reflected in the relative size of area A relative to area C. At the very least, each area's importance or value to the target customer base is the critical take-away for internal analysis purposes so that managers know the strengths they possess in providing value to their customers around which to build a strategy. They also know the competitor's key attributes against which they must compete effectively to survive and prosper.

Section D—This area is interesting. It is value created by both the company and the competitor's attributes, capabilities or features that are perceived as important by company managers but which may not hold any meaningful value to the target customers. So, if accurate, it is value both companies are investing resources in creating that customers do not need. Carefully identified as not being "table stakes," these items can become resources that can be better deployed toward features and desired attributes that customers truly value.

Sections E & F—Similar in some ways to section D, but not overlapping, each company has in these areas activities, features, or offerings it perceives as useful, which in reality are of no value or even negative value from the customers' perspective. For example,

[13]Urbany and Davis, ibid.

Zeneca Ag Products discovered that one of its most important distributors was wiling to do more business with the firm only if Zeneca eliminated the time-consuming promotional programs that Zeneca managers thought were an essential part of their value proposition. Instead, they were, as we see, a detriment. So again, as with section D, carefully identified as not being valued offerings, these items can become resources that can be better deployed toward features and desired attributes that customers truly value.

Section G—Finally, this area represents customers' "white space," an area composed of needs and attributes that have not been met by either the company or the competitor. They may be known to the customers, but prioritized or considered realistic. More often they are not even known to the customer, but represent significant potential value. The rapid emergences of distinct features on Apple's iPhones, or Samsung's Galaxy, like Suri or bumping, were all essentially features conceived by Apple or Samsung that customers didn't know they valued but that subsequently became invaluable features customers needed and wanted. Procter & Gamble had no consumer demand to invent the Swiffer, a product category that now contributes double-digit sales growth in P&G's home care products division. Swiffer emerged instead from P&G's careful observation of the challenges of household cleaning. So, in conducting benchmarking via three circles analysis, section G—customers' unexpressed needs—can often be a critical future source of value and growth based upon it.

The value of the three circles analysis approach to benchmarking is threefold. First, it focuses benchmarking around the needs and wants of customers and the value of what the company offers to address them. Instead of coming at internal analysis from the starting point of what the company has to sell, three circles analysis forces company managers to start the process by asking what benefits the customer is seeking to buy. Second, three circles analysis drills down to a more in-depth, one-on-one competitor analysis. So, detailed evaluation of the competitor and obtaining input from customers as well as sales and operating personnel enrich the validity of the basis for a more thorough strategic internal analysis. Third, the technique divides areas of consideration first as three broad circles but then drills down into seven different areas across the three circles, which make for a much richer and multistep internal analysis process, which, if done intently, should yield valuable strategic building blocks and insight.

Comparison with Success Factors in the Industry

Industry analysis (see Chapter 4) involves identifying the factors associated with successful participation in a given industry. As was true for the evaluation methods discussed earlier, the key determinants of success in an industry may be used to identify a firm's internal strengths and weaknesses. By scrutinizing industry competitors as well as customer needs, vertical industry structure, channels of distribution, costs, barriers to entry, availability of substitutes, and suppliers, a strategist seeks to determine whether a firm's current internal capabilities represent strengths or weaknesses in new competitive arenas. The discussion in Chapter 4 provides a useful framework—five industry forces—against which to examine a firm's potential strengths and weaknesses. General Cinema Corporation, the largest U.S. movie theater operator, determined that its internal skills in marketing, site analysis, creative financing, and management of geographically dispersed operations were key strengths relative to major success factors in the soft-drink bottling industry. This assessment proved accurate. Within 10 years after it entered the soft-drink bottling industry, General Cinema became the largest franchised bottler of soft drinks in the United States, handling Pepsi, 7UP, Dr Pepper, and Sunkist. Or consider large-scale discount retailing, where two key success factors in that industry are same-store sales growth and steady updating of store

EXHIBIT 6.13
Illustration of the Product Life Cycle

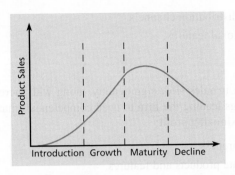

facilities or new locations. During the last decade, once-mighty Walmart saw itself begin to fall behind its key rivals in same-store sales growth and age/quality of 60 percent of its U.S. stores. These two critical success factors drive and indicate the relative health of large discount retail firms. Firms with solid same-store sales growth indicate wise choices in location, attractiveness of their stores, and the merchandise inside them. Likewise, aging and probably substandard store facilities are typically not as efficient as newer ones, nor are they as inviting to shoppers. So Walmart, Target, and other discount retailers conduct internal analyses in part by comparing themselves on these two (and surely others) critical success factors to interpret their strength or weakness relative to factors that drive industry success. Today, the steadily increasing impact of Amazon.com on traditional "big box" retailers is adding the ease of use of that traditional retailer's newer Web site–based "store" offering as a new critical success factor now monitored for its critical role in driving industry success.

Product Life Cycle

Product life cycle (PLC) is one way to identify success factors against which executives can evaluate their firm's competencies relative to its key product or products. The **product life cycle** is a concept that describes a product's sales, profitability, and competencies that are key drivers of the success of that product as it moves through a sequence of stages from development, introduction to growth, maturity, decline, and eventual removal from a market. Exhibit 6.13 illustrates the "typical" product life cycle.

Core competencies associated with success are thought to vary across different stages of the product life cycle. Those competencies might include the following.

product life cycle
A concept that describes a product's sales, profitability, and competencies that are key drivers of the success of that product as it moves through a sequence of stages from development, introduction to growth, maturity, decline, and eventual removal from a market.

Introduction Stage

During this stage the firm needs competence in building product awareness and market development along with the resources to support initial losses:

- Ability to create product awareness.
- Good channel relationships in ways to get the product introduced quickly, gaining a first-mover advantage.
- Premium pricing to "skim" profitability if few competitors exist.
- Solid relationships with and access to trendsetting early adopters.
- Financial resources to absorb an initial cash drain and lack of profitability.

Growth

During this stage market growth accelerates rapidly, with the firm seeking to build brand awareness and establish/increase market share:

- Brand awareness and ability to build brand.
- Advertising skills and resources to back them.
- Product features that differentiate versus increased competitive offerings.
- Establishing and stabilizing market shares.

- Access to multiple distribution channels.
- Ability to add additional features.

Maturity

This stage sees growth in sales slow significantly, along with increased competition and similar product offerings leading the firm to need competencies that allow it to defend its market share while maximizing profit:

- Sustained brand awareness.
- Ability to differentiate products and features.
- Resources to initiate or sustain price wars.
- Operating advantages to improve slimming margins.
- Judgment to know whether to stay in or exit saturated market segments.

Decline

At this point the product and its competitors start to experience declining sales and increased pressure on margins. Competencies needed are:

- Ability to withstand intense price-cutting.
- Brand strength to allow reduced marketing.
- Cost cutting capacity and slack to allow it.
- Good supplier relationships to gain cost concessions.
- Innovation skills to create new products or "re-create" existing ones.

The PLC is an interesting concept or framework against which executives might gauge the strength of relevant competencies. Caution is necessary in its use beyond that purpose, however. In reality, very few products follow exactly the cycle portrayed in the PLC model. The length in each stage can vary, the length and nature of the PLC for any particular product can vary dramatically, and it is not easy to tell exactly what stage a product might be in at any given time. Not all products go through each stage. Some, for example, go from introduction to decline. And movement from one stage to the next can be accelerated by strategies or tactics executives emphasize. For example, price-cutting can accelerate the movement from maturity to decline.

Product life cycles can describe a single product, a category of products, or an industry segment. Applying the basic idea to an industry segment (category of products) rather than a specific product has been a more beneficial adaptation of the PLC concept, providing executives with a conceptual tool to aid them in strategic analysis and choice in the context of the evolution of an industry segment in which their firm competes. So we examine the concept of stages of evolution of an industry segment or category of products as a tool of strategic analysis and choice in Chapter 8.

Summary

This chapter looked at several ways managers achieve greater objectivity and rigor as they analyze their company's internal resources and capabilities. Managers often start their internal analysis with questions like, How well is the current strategy working? What is our current situation? What are our strengths and weaknesses? SWOT analysis is a traditional approach that has been in use for decades to help structure managers' pursuit of answers to these questions. A logical approach still used by many managers today, SWOT analysis has limitations linked to the depth of its analysis and the risk of overlooking key considerations.

Three techniques for internal analysis have emerged that overcome some of the limitations of SWOT analysis, offering more comprehensive approaches that can help managers identify and assess their firm's internal resources and capabilities in a more systematic, objective, and measurable manner. Value chain analysis has managers look at and disaggregate their business as a chain of activities that occur in a sequential manner to create the products or services they sell. The value chain approach breaks down the firm's activities into primary and support categories of activities, then breaks these down further into specific types of activities with the objective to disaggregate activity into as many meaningful subdivisions as possible. Once done, managers attempt to attribute costs to each. Doing this gives managers very distinct ways of isolating the things they do well and not so well, and it isolates activities that are truly key in meeting customer needs—true potential sources of competitive advantage. Three circles analysis provides an additional technique, simple yet insightful, for applying a customer needs perspective that should help improve the quality of a management team's internal analysis in understanding potential value-based sources of competitive advantage at the firm's disposal.

The third approach covered in this chapter was the resource-based view (RBV). RBV is based on the premise that firms build competitive advantage based on the unique resources, skills, and capabilities they control or develop, which can become the basis of unique, sustainable competitive advantages that allow them to craft successful competitive strategies. The RBV provides a useful conceptual frame to first inventory a firm's potential competitive advantages among its tangible assets, intangible assets, and its organizational capabilities. Once inventoried, the RBV provides four fundamental guidelines that managers can use to "value" these resources and capabilities. Those with major value, defined as ones that are valuable for several reasons, become the bases for building strategies linked to sustainable competitive advantages.

Finally, this chapter covered three ways objectivity and realism are enhanced when managers use meaningful standards for comparison regardless of the particular analytical framework they employ in internal analysis. This chapter is followed by two appendixes. The first provides a useful inventory of the types of activities in different functional areas of a firm that can be sources of competitive advantage. The second appendix covers traditional financial analysis to serve as a refresher and reminder about this basic internal analysis tool.

When matched with management's environmental analyses and mission priorities, the process of internal analysis provides the critical foundation for strategy formulation. Armed with an accurate, thorough, and timely internal analysis, managers are in a better position to formulate effective strategies. The next chapter describes basic strategy alternatives that any firm may consider.

Key Terms

benchmarking, *p. 176*
core competence, *p. 166*
intangible assets, *p. 167*
isolating mechanisms, *p. 170*
opportunity, *p. 154*
organizational capabilities, *p. 167*

primary activities, *p. 160*
product life cycle, *p. 181*
resource-based view, *p. 166*
strength, *p. 155*
support activities, *p. 161*
SWOT analysis, *p. 153*
tangible assets, *p. 167*

threat, *p. 155*
three circles analysis, *p. 177*
value chain, *p. 159*
value chain analysis, *p. 159*
weakness, *p. 155*

Questions for Discussion

1. Describe SWOT analysis as a way to guide internal analysis. How does this approach reflect the basic strategic management process?

2. What are potential weaknesses of SWOT analysis?

3. Describe the difference between primary and support activities using value chain analysis.

4. How is VCA different from SWOT analysis?

5. What is three circles analysis, and how might it help doing internal analysis?

6. What is the resource-based view? Give examples of three different types of resources.

7. What are three ways resources become more valuable? Provide an example of each.

8. Explain how you might use VCA, RBV, three circles analysis, and SWOT analysis to get a better sense of what might be a firm's key building blocks for a successful strategy.

9. Attempt to apply SWOT, VCA, RBV, and three circles analysis to yourself and your career aspirations. What are your major strengths and weaknesses? How might you use your knowledge of these strengths and weaknesses to develop your future career plans?

Chapter 6 Appendix A

Key Resources across Functional Areas

MARKETING

Firm's products-services: breadth of product line
Concentration of sales in a few products or to a few customers
Ability to gather needed information about markets
Market share or submarket shares
Product-service mix and expansion potential: life cycle of key products; profit-sales balance in product-service
Channels of distribution: number, coverage, and control
Effective sales organization: knowledge of customer needs
Internet usage; Web presence; e-commerce
Product-service image, reputation, and quality
Imaginativeness, efficiency, and effectiveness of sales promotion and advertising
Pricing strategy and pricing flexibility
Procedures for digesting market feedback and developing new products, services, or markets
After-sale service and follow-up
Goodwill—brand loyalty

FINANCIAL AND ACCOUNTING

Ability to raise short-term capital
Ability to raise long-term capital; debt-equity
Corporate-level resources (multibusiness firm)
Cost of capital relative to that of industry and competitors
Tax considerations
Relations with owners, investors, and stockholders
Leverage position; capacity to utilize alternative financial strategies, such as lease or sale and leaseback
Cost of entry and barriers to entry
Price-earnings ratio
Working capital; flexibility of capital structure
Effective cost control; ability to reduce cost
Financial size
Efficiency and effectiveness of accounting system for cost, budget, and profit planning

PRODUCTION, OPERATIONS, TECHNICAL

Raw materials' cost and availability, supplier relationships
Inventory control systems; inventory turnover
Location of facilities; layout and utilization of facilities
Economies of scale
Technical efficiency of facilities and utilization of capacity
Effectiveness of subcontracting use
Degree of vertical integration; value added and profit margin
Efficiency and cost-benefit of equipment
Effectiveness of operation control procedures: design, scheduling, purchasing, quality control, and efficiency
Costs and technological competencies relative to those of industry and competitors
Research and development—technology—innovation
Patents, trademarks, and similar legal protection

PERSONNEL

Management personnel
Employees' skill and morale
Labor relations costs compared with those of industry and competitors
Efficiency and effectiveness of personnel policies
Effectiveness of incentives used to motivate performance
Ability to level peaks and valleys of employment
Employee turnover and absenteeism
Specialized skills
Experience

QUALITY MANAGEMENT

Relationship with suppliers, customers
Internal practices to enhance quality of products and services
Procedures for monitoring quality

INFORMATION SYSTEMS

Timeliness and accuracy of information about sales, operations, cash, and suppliers
Relevance of information for tactical decisions
Information to manage quality issues: customer service
Ability of people to use the information that is provided
Linkages to suppliers and customers

INTERNET AND WIRELESS CAPABILITIES

Web site quality and functionality
Online sales and marketing
Customer connectivity
Use of social networking
Facebook, Twitter, LinkedIn, etc.
Wireless relevance; apps
Global cultural and language connection via the Web

ORGANIZATION AND GENERAL MANAGEMENT

Organizational structure
Firm's image and prestige
Firm's record in achieving objectives
Organization of communication system
Overall organizational control system (effectiveness and utilization)

Organizational climate; organizational culture
Use of systematic procedures and techniques in decision making

Top-management skill, capabilities, and interest
Strategic planning system
Intraorganizational synergy (multibusiness firms)

Chapter 6 Appendix B

Using Financial Analysis

One of the most important tools for assessing the strength of an organization within its industry is financial analysis. Managers, investors, and creditors all employ some form of this analysis as the beginning point for their financial decision making. Investors use financial analyses in making decisions about whether to buy or sell stock, and creditors use them in deciding whether or not to lend. They provide managers with a measurement of how the company is doing in comparison with its performance in past years and with the performance of competitors in the industry.

Although financial analysis is useful for decision making, some weaknesses should be noted. Any picture that it provides of the company is based on past data. Although trends may be noteworthy, this picture should not automatically be assumed to be applicable to the future. In addition, the analysis is only as good as the accounting procedures that have provided the information. When making comparisons between companies, one should keep in mind the variability of accounting procedures from firm to firm.

There are four basic groups of financial ratios: liquidity, leverage, activity, and profitability.

Depicted in Exhibit 6.B1 are the specific ratios calculated for each of the basic groups. Liquidity and leverage ratios represent an assessment of the risk of the firm. Activity and profitability ratios are measures of the return generated by the assets of the firm. The interaction between certain groups of ratios is indicated by arrows.

Typically, two common financial statements are used in financial analyses: the balance sheet and the income statement. Exhibit 6.B2 is a balance sheet and Exhibit 6.B3 an income statement for the ABC Company. These statements will be used to illustrate the financial analyses.

LIQUIDITY RATIOS

Liquidity ratios are used as indicators of a firm's ability to meet its short-term obligations. These obligations include any current liabilities, including currently maturing long-term debt. Current assets move through a normal cash cycle of inventories—sales—accounts receivable—cash. The firm then uses cash to pay off or reduce its current liabilities. The best-known liquidity ratio is the current ratio: current assets divided by current liabilities. For the ABC Company, the current ratio is calculated as follows:

$$\frac{\text{Current assets}}{\text{Current liabilities}} = \frac{\$4,125,000}{\$2,512,500} = 1.64 \ (2016)$$

$$= \frac{\$3,618,000}{\$2,242,250} = 1.161 \ (2015)$$

Most analysts suggest a current ratio of 2 to 3. A large current ratio is not necessarily a good sign; it may mean that an organization is not making the most efficient use of its assets. The optimum current ratio will vary from industry to industry, with the more volatile industries requiring higher ratios.

Because slow-moving or obsolescent inventories could overstate a firm's ability to meet short-term demands, the quick ratio is sometimes preferred to assess a firm's liquidity. The quick ratio is current assets minus inventories, divided by current liabilities. The quick ratio for the ABC Company is calculated as follows:

$$\frac{\text{Current assets} - \text{Inventories}}{\text{Current liabilities}} = \frac{\$1,950,000}{\$2,512,500} = 0.78 \ (2016)$$

$$= \frac{\$1,618,000}{\$2,242,250} = 0.72 \ (2015)$$

A quick ratio of approximately 1 would be typical for American industries. Although there is less variability in the quick ratio than in the current ratio, stable industries would be able to operate safely with a lower ratio.

LEVERAGE RATIOS

Leverage ratios identify the source of a firm's capital—owners or outside creditors. The term *leverage* refers to the fact that using capital with a fixed interest charge will "amplify" either profits or losses in relation to the equity of holders of common stock. The most commonly used ratio is total debt divided by total assets. Total debt includes current liabilities and long-term liabilities. This ratio is a measure of the percentage of total funds provided by debt. A total debt–total assets ratio higher than 0.5 is usually considered safe only for firms in stable industries.

$$\frac{\text{Total debt}}{\text{Total assets}} = \frac{\$3,862,500}{\$7,105,000} = 0.54 \ (2016)$$

$$= \frac{\$3,667,250}{\$6,393,000} = 0.57 \ (2015)]$$

EXHIBIT 6.B1   **Financial Ratios**

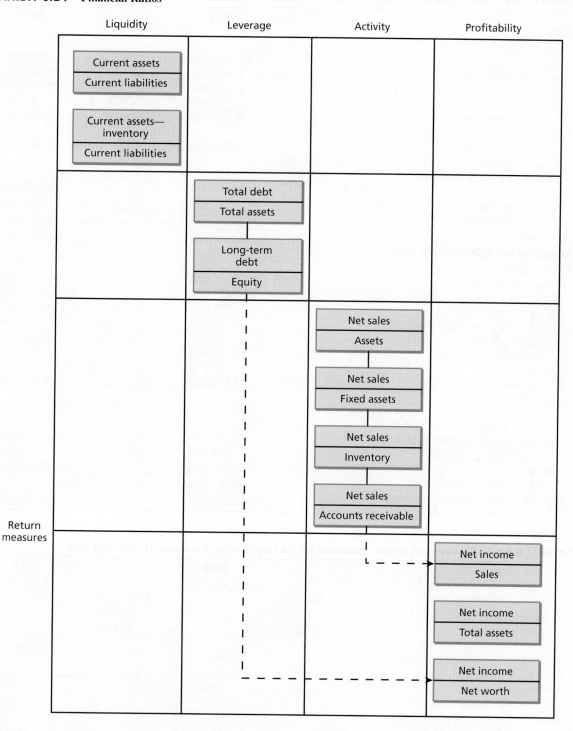

EXHIBIT 6.B2 ABC Company Balance Sheet as of December 31, 2015 and 2016

		2016		2015
Assets				
Current assets:				
Cash		$ 140,000		$ 115,000
Accounts receivable		1,760,000		1,440,000
Inventory		2,175,000		2,000,000
Prepaid expenses		50,000		63,000
Total current assets		4,125,000		3,618,000
Fixed assets:				
Long-term receivable		1,255,000		1,090,000
Property and plant	$2,037,000		$2,015,000	
Less: Accumulated depreciation	862,000		860,000	
Net property and plant		1,175,000		1,155,000
Other fixed assets		550,000		530,000
Total fixed assets		2,980,000		2,775,000
Total assets		$7,105,000		$6,393,000
Liabilities and Stockholders' Equity				
Current liabilities:				
Accounts payable		$1,325,000		$1,225,000
Bank loans payable		475,000		550,000
Accrued federal taxes		675,000		425,000
Current maturities (long-term debt)		17,500		26,000
Dividends payable		20,000		16,250
Total current liabilities		2,512,500		2,242,250
Long-term liabilities		1,350,000		1,425,000
Total liabilities		3,862,500		3,667,250
Stockholders' equity:				
Common stock				
(104,046 shares outstanding in 2016;				
101,204 shares outstanding in 2015)		44,500		43,300
Additional paid-in-capital		568,000		372,450
Retained earnings		2,630,000		2,310,000
Total stockholders' equity		3,242,500		2,725,750
Total liabilities and stockholders' equity		$7,105,000		$6,393,000

EXHIBIT 6.B3 ABC Company Income Statement for the Years Ending December 31, 2015 and 2016

		2016		2015
Net sales		$8,250,000		$8,000,000
Cost of goods sold	$5,100,000		$5,000,000	
Administrative expenses	1,750,000		1,680,000	
Other expenses	420,000		390,000	
Total		7,270,000		7,070,000
Earnings before interest and taxes		980,000		930,000
Less: Interest expense		210,000		210,000
Earnings before taxes		770,000		720,000
Less: Federal income taxes		360,000		325,000
Earnings after taxes (net income)		$ 410,000		$ 395,000
Common stock cash dividends		$ 90,000		$ 84,000
Addition to retained earnings		$ 320,000		$ 311,000
Earnings per common share		$ 3.940		$ 3.90
Dividends per common share		$ 0.865		$ 0.83

The ratio of long-term debt to equity is a measure of the extent to which sources of long-term financing are provided by creditors. It is computed by dividing long-term debt by the stockholders' equity:

$$\frac{\text{Long-term debt}}{\text{Stockholder's Equity}} = \frac{\$1,350,000}{\$3,242,500} = 0.42 \text{ (2016)}$$

$$= \frac{\$1,425,000}{\$2,725,750} = 0.52 \text{ (2015)}$$

Another ratio helpful in examining a company's use of leverage is the ratio of total assets to stockholder's equity, known as the *equity multiplier ratio*. Total assets is the sum of assets financed through stockholder's equity, and debt. So this equity multiplier ratio is another way of looking at the use of debt versus equity financing, in this case by calculating the multiple of equity being used to create the company's total asset base. The higher the equity multiplier ratio, the more a company is using debt relative to equity to finance its asset base.

Typically, the equity multiplier ratio is calculated by dividing a company's *average total assets* by its *average stockholder's equity* for a specific year. *Average total assets* would be determined by dividing the sum of total assets at the beginning of the year plus total assets at the end of the year by two (2). *Average stockholder's equity* would similarly be determined by dividing the sum of total stockholder's equity at the beginning of the year plus total stockholder's equity at the end of the year by two (2). The calculations to determine ABC Company's equity multiplier ratio would be as follows:

Average total assets = ($7,105,000 + $6,393,000)/2

= $6,749,000

Average stockholder's equity = ($3,242,000 + $2,725,750)/2

= $2,984,125

Equity multiplier ratio = $6,749,000 / $2,984,125 = 2.262

ACTIVITY RATIOS

Activity ratios indicate how effectively a firm is using its resources. By comparing revenues with the resources used to generate them, it is possible to establish an efficiency of operation. The asset turnover ratio indicates how efficiently management is employing total assets. Asset turnover is calculated by dividing sales by total assets. For the ABC Company, asset turnover is calculated as follows:

$$\text{Asset turnover} = \frac{\text{Sales}}{\text{Average Total Assets}}$$

$$= \frac{\$8,250,000}{\$7,105,000} = 1.16 \text{ (2016)}$$

$$= \frac{\$8,000,000}{\$6,393,000} = 1.25 \text{ (2015)}$$

The ratio of sales to fixed assets is a measure of the turnover on plant and equipment. It is calculated by dividing sales by net fixed assets.

$$\begin{array}{l}\text{Fixed asset} \\ \text{turnover}\end{array} = \frac{\text{Sales}}{\text{Net fixed assets}} = \frac{\$8,250,000}{\$2,980,000} = 2.77 \text{ (2016)}$$

$$= \frac{\$8,000,000}{\$2,775,000} = 2.88 \text{ (2015)}$$

Industry figures for asset turnover will vary with capital-intensive industries, and those requiring large inventories will have much smaller ratios.

Another activity ratio is inventory turnover, estimated by dividing sales by average inventory. The norm for U.S. industries is 9, but whether the ratio for a particular firm is higher or lower normally depends on the product sold. Small, inexpensive items usually turn over at a much higher rate than larger, expensive ones. Because inventories normally are carried at cost, it would be more accurate to use the cost of goods sold in place of sales in the numerator of this ratio. Established compilers of industry ratios, such as Dun & Bradstreet, however, use the ratio of sales to inventory.

$$\begin{array}{l}\text{Inventory} \\ \text{turnover}\end{array} = \frac{\text{Sales}}{\text{Inventory}} = \frac{\$8,250,000}{\$2,175,000} = 3.79 \text{ (2016)}$$

$$= \frac{\$8,000,000}{\$2,000,000} = 4.00 \text{ (2015)}$$

The accounts receivable turnover is a measure of the average collection period on sales. If the average number of days varies widely from the industry norm, it may be an indication of poor management. A too-low ratio could indicate the loss of sales because of a too-restrictive credit policy. If the ratio is too high, too much capital is being tied up in accounts receivable, and management may be increasing the chance of bad debts. Because of varying industry credit policies, a comparison for the firm over time or within an industry is the only useful analysis. Because information on credit sales for other firms generally is unavailable, total sales must be used. Because not all firms have the same percentage of credit sales, there is only approximate comparability among firms:

$$\text{Accounts receivable turnover} = \frac{\text{Sales}}{\text{Accounts receivable}}$$

$$= \frac{\$8,250,000}{\$1,760,000} = 4.69 \text{ (2016)}$$

$$= \frac{\$8,000,000}{\$1,440,000} = 5.56 \text{ (2015)}$$

$$\text{Average collection period} = \frac{360}{\text{Accounts receivable turnover}}$$

$$= \frac{360}{4.69} = 77 \text{ days (2016)}$$

$$= \frac{360}{5.56} = 65 \text{ days (2015)}$$

PROFITABILITY RATIOS

Profitability is the net result of a large number of policies and decisions chosen by an organization's management. Profitability ratios indicate how effectively the total firm is being managed. The profit margin for a firm is calculated by dividing net earnings by sales. This ratio is often called *return on sales* (ROS). There is wide variation among industries, but the average for U.S. firms is approximately 5 percent.

$$\frac{\text{Net income}}{\text{Sales}} = \frac{\$410,000}{\$8,250,000} = 0.0497 \text{ (2016)}$$

$$= \frac{\$395,000}{\$8,000,000} = 0.0494 \text{ (2015)}$$

A second useful ratio for evaluating profitability is the return on total assets—or ROA, as it is frequently called—found by dividing net earnings by average total assets. The ABC Company's ROA is calculated as follows:

$$\frac{\text{Net income}}{\text{Average total assets}} = \frac{\$410,000}{\$7,105,000} = 0.0577 \text{ (2016)}$$

$$= \frac{\$395,000}{\$6,393,000} = 0.0618 \text{ (2015)}$$

ROA is sometimes calculated for a given year where the denominator, total assets, is measured as *average* total assets for that year. *Average total assets* would be determined by dividing the sum of total assets at the beginning of the year plus total assets at the end of the year by two. The DuPont Financial Analysis approach employs *average total assets* in its calculations of asset turnover and equity multiplier as shown in Exhibit 6.B4 and explained in the next section. The calculation of the average total assets at ABC Company would be:

$$\text{Average total assets} = (\$7,105,000 + \$6,393,000) / 2$$
$$= \$6,749,000$$

The ratio of net earnings to net worth is a measure of the rate of return or profitability of the stockholders' investment. It is calculated by dividing net earnings by net worth, the common stock equity and retained earnings account. ABC Company's *return on net worth or return on equity*, also called ROE, is calculated as follows:

$$\frac{\text{Net income}}{\text{Stockholder's Equity}} = \frac{\$410,000}{\$3,242,500} = 0.1264 \text{ (2016)}$$

$$= \frac{\$395,000}{\$2,725,750} = 0.1449 \text{ (2015)}$$

DuPont Financial Analysis. It is often difficult to determine causes for low ROE and/or a lack of profitability. The DuPont system of financial analysis provides management with clues to the lack of success of a firm. This financial tool brings together activity, profitability, and leverage measures and shows how these ratios interact to determine the overall profitability of the firm. A depiction of the system is set forth in Exhibit 6.B4.

The right side of the exhibit develops the turnover ratio. This section breaks down total assets into current assets (cash, marketable securities, accounts receivable, and inventories) and fixed assets. Sales divided by these total assets gives the turnover on assets.

The left side of the exhibit develops the profit margin on sales. The individual expense items plus income taxes are subtracted from sales to produce net profits after taxes. Net profits divided by sales gives the profit margin on sales. When the asset turnover ratio on the right side of Exhibit 6.B4 is multiplied by the profit margin on sales developed on the left side of the exhibit, the product is the return on assets (ROA) for the firm. This can be shown by the following formula:

$$\frac{\text{Sales}}{\text{Average total assets}} \times \frac{\text{Net income}}{\text{Sales}}$$

$$= \frac{\text{Net income}}{\text{Avg. total assets}} = \text{ROA}$$

The last step in the DuPont analysis is to multiply the rate of return on assets (ROA) by the equity multiplier, which is the ratio of assets to common equity, to obtain the rate of return on equity (ROE). This percentage rate of return, of course, could be calculated directly by dividing net income by common equity. However, the DuPont analysis demonstrates how the return on assets and the use of debt interact to determine the return on equity.

The DuPont system can be used to analyze and improve the performance of a firm. On the left, or profit, side of the exhibit, attempts to increase profits and sales could be investigated. The possibilities of raising prices to improve profits (or lowering prices to improve volume) or seeking new products or markets, for example, could be studied. Cost accountants and production engineers could investigate ways to reduce costs. On the right, or turnover, side, financial officers could analyze the effect of reducing investment in various assets as well as the effect of using alternative financial structures.

There are two basic approaches to using financial ratios. One approach is to evaluate the corporation's performance over several years. Financial ratios are computed for different years, and then an assessment is made about whether there has been an improvement or deterioration over time. Financial ratios also can be computed for projected, pro forma, statements and compared with present and past ratios.

The other approach is to evaluate a firm's financial condition and compare it with the financial conditions of similar firms or with industry averages in the same period. Such

EXHIBIT 6.B4   **DuPont's Financial Analysis**

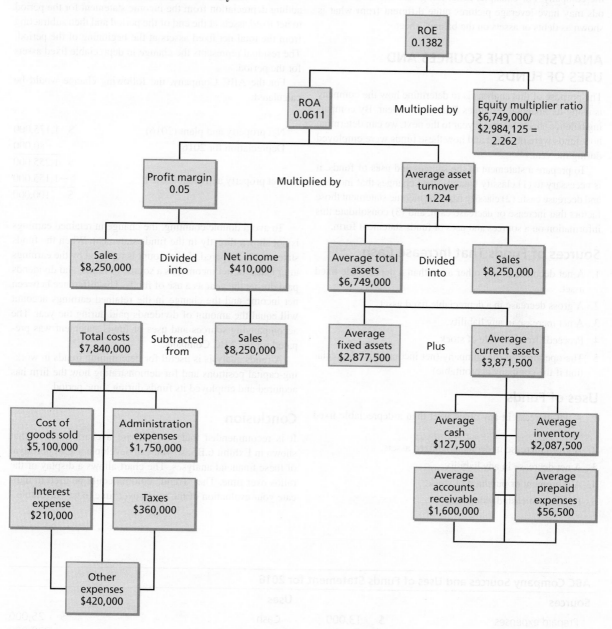

a comparison gives insight into the firm's relative financial condition and performance. Financial ratios for industries are provided by Robert Morris Associates, Dun & Bradstreet, Prentice Hall, and various trade association publications. (Associations and their addresses are listed in the *Encyclopedia of Associations* and in the *Directory of National Trade Associations*.) Information about individual firms is available through *Moody's Manual,* Standard & Poor's manuals and surveys, annual reports to stockholders, and the major brokerage houses.

To the extent possible, accounting data from different companies must be so standardized that companies can be compared or so a specific company can be compared with an industry average. It is important to read any footnotes of financial statements, because various accounting or management practices can have an effect on the financial picture of the company. For example, firms using sale-leaseback methods may have leverage pictures quite different from what is shown as debts or assets on the balance sheet.

ANALYSIS OF THE SOURCES AND USES OF FUNDS

The purpose of this analysis is to determine how the company is using its financial resources from year to year. By comparing balance sheets from one year to the next, we can determine how funds were obtained and how these funds were employed during the year.

To prepare a statement of the sources and uses of funds, it is necessary to (1) classify balance sheet changes that increase and decrease cash, (2) classify from the income statement those factors that increase or decrease cash, and (3) consolidate this information on a sources and uses of funds statement form.

Sources of Funds That Increase Cash

1. A net decrease in any other asset than a depreciable fixed asset.
2. A gross decrease in a depreciable fixed asset.
3. A net increase in any liability.
4. Proceeds from the sale of stock.
5. The operation of the company (net income, and depreciation if the company is profitable).

Uses of Funds

1. A net increase in any other asset than a depreciable fixed asset.
2. A gross increase in depreciable fixed assets.
3. A net decrease in any liability.
4. A retirement or purchase of stock.
5. Payment of cash dividends.

We compute gross changes to depreciable fixed assets by adding depreciation from the income statement for the period to net fixed assets at the end of the period and then subtracting from the total net fixed assets at the beginning of the period. The residual represents the change in depreciable fixed assets for the period.

For the ABC Company, the following change would be calculated:

Net property and plant (2016)	$ 1,175,000
Depreciation for 2016	+80,000
	$ 1,255,000
Net property and plant (2015)	−1,155,000
	$ 100,000

To avoid double counting, the change in retained earnings is not shown directly in the funds statement. When the funds statement is prepared, this account is replaced by the earnings after taxes, or net income, as a source of funds, and dividends paid during the year as a use of funds. The difference between net income and the change in the retained earnings account will equal the amount of dividends paid during the year. The accompanying sources and uses of funds statement was prepared for the ABC Company.

A funds analysis is useful for determining trends in working-capital positions and for demonstrating how the firm has acquired and employed its funds during some period.

Conclusion

It is recommended that you prepare a chart, such as that shown in Exhibit 6.B5, so you can develop a useful portrayal of these financial analyses. The chart allows a display of the ratios over time. The "Trend" column could be used to indicate your evaluation of the ratios over time (e.g., "favorable,"

ABC Company Sources and Uses of Funds Statement for 2016

Sources		Uses	
Prepaid expenses	$ 13,000	Cash	$ 25,000
Accounts payable	100,000	Accounts receivable	320,000
Accrued federal taxes	250,000	Inventory	175,000
Dividends payable	3,750	Long-term receivables	165,000
Common stock	1,200	Property and plant	100,000
Additional paid-in capital	195,550	Other fixed assets	20,000
Earnings after taxes (net income)	410,000	Bank loans payable	75,000
Depreciation	80,000	Current maturities of long-term debt	8,500
Total sources	$1,053,500	Long-term liabilities	75,000
		Dividends paid	90,000
		Total uses	$1,053,500

EXHIBIT 6.B5   **A Summary of the Financial Position of a Firm**

Ratios and Working Capital	2012	2013	2014	2015	2016	Trend	Industry Average	Interpre-tation
Liquidity: Current								
Quick								
Leverage: Debt-assets								
Debt-equity								
Equity Multiplier								
Activity: Asset turnover								
Fixed asset ratio								
Inventory turnover								
Accounts receivable turnover								
Average collection period								
Profitability: ROS								
ROI								
ROE								
Working-capital position								

"neutral," or "unfavorable"). The "Industry Average" column could include recent industry averages on these ratios or those of key competitors. These would provide information to aid interpretation of the analyses. The "Interpretation" column could be used to describe your interpretation of the ratios for this firm. Overall, this chart gives a basic display of the ratios that provides a convenient format for examining the firm's financial condition.

Finally, Exhibit 6.B6 is included to provide a quick reference summary of the calculations and meanings of the ratios discussed earlier.

EXHIBIT 6.B6   **A Summary of Key Financial Ratios**

Ratio	Calculation	Meaning
Liquidity Ratios:		
Current ratio	$\dfrac{\text{Current assets}}{\text{Current liabilities}}$	The extent to which a firm can meet its short-term obligations.
Quick ratio	$\dfrac{\text{Current assets–inventory}}{\text{Current liabilities}}$	The extent to which a firm can meet its short-term obligations without relying on the sale of inventories.
Leverage Ratios:		
Debt-to-total-assets ratio	$\dfrac{\text{Total debt}}{\text{Total assets}}$	The percentage of total funds that are provided by creditors.
Debt-to-equity ratio	$\dfrac{\text{Total debt}}{\text{Total stockholders' equity}}$	The percentage of total funds provided by creditors versus the percentage provided by owners.
Long-term-debt-to-equity ratio	$\dfrac{\text{Long-term debt}}{\text{Total stockholders' equity}}$	The balance between debt and equity in a firm's long-term capital structure.

(continued)

EXHIBIT 6.B6 *(continued)*

Ratio	Calculation	Meaning
Times-interest-earned ratio	$\dfrac{\text{Profits before interest and taxes}}{\text{Total interest charges}}$	The extent to which earnings can decline without the firm becoming unable to meet its annual interest costs.
Equity Multiplier Ratio	$\dfrac{\text{Average total assets}}{\text{Avg. stockholders' equity}}$	The use of debt financing to leverage a company's stockholders equity.
Activity Ratios:		
Inventory turnover	$\dfrac{\text{Sales}}{\text{Inventory of finished goods}}$	Whether a firm holds excessive stocks of inventories and whether a firm is selling its inventories slowly compared to the industry average.
Fixed assets turnover	$\dfrac{\text{Average sales}}{\text{Fixed assets}}$	Sales productivity and plant equipment utilization.
Total assets turnover	$\dfrac{\text{Sales}}{\text{Average total assets}}$	Whether a firm is generating a sufficient volume of business for the size of its assets investment.
Accounts receivable turnover	$\dfrac{\text{Annual credit sales}}{\text{Accounts receivable}}$	In percentage terms, the average length of time it takes a firm to collect on credit sales.
Average collection period	$\dfrac{\text{Accounts receivable}}{\text{Total sales/365 days}}$	In days, the average length of time it takes a firm to collect on credit sales.
Profitability Ratios:		
Gross profit margin	$\dfrac{\text{Sales} - \text{Cost of goods sold}}{\text{Sales}}$	The total margin available to cover operating expenses and yield a profit.
Operating profit margin	$\dfrac{\text{Earnings before interest and taxes (EBIT)}}{\text{Sales}}$	Profitability without concern for taxes and interest.
Net profit margin	$\dfrac{\text{Net income}}{\text{Sales}}$	After-tax profits per dollar of sales.
Return on total assets (ROA)	$\dfrac{\text{Net income}}{\text{Avg. total assets}}$	Ratio of annual net income to average total assets during a financial year—indicator of profitable use assets.
Return on stockholders' equity (ROE)	$\dfrac{\text{Net income}}{\text{Total stockholders' equity}}$	After-tax profits per dollar of stock-holders' investment in the firm.
Earnings per share (EPS)	$\dfrac{\text{Net income}}{\text{Number of shares of common stock outstanding}}$	Earnings available to the owners of common stock.
Growth Ratios:		
Sales	Annual percentage growth in total sales	Firm's growth rate in sales.
Income	Annual percentage growth in profits	Firm's growth rate in profits.
Earnings per share	Annual percentage growth in EPS	Firm's growth rate in EPS.
Dividends per share	Annual percentage growth in dividends per share	Firm's growth rate in dividends per share.
Price-earnings ratio	$\dfrac{\text{Market price per share}}{\text{Earnings per share}}$	Faster-growing and less risky firms tend to have higher price-earnings ratios.

Chapter **Seven**

Long-Term Objectives and Strategies

After reading and studying this chapter, you should be able to

1. Discuss seven different topics for long-term corporate objectives.

2. Describe the five qualities of long-term corporate objectives that make them especially useful to strategic managers.

3. Explain the generic strategies of low-cost leadership, differentiation, and focus.

4. Discuss the importance of the value disciplines.

5. List, describe, evaluate, and give examples of the 15 grand strategies that decision makers use as building blocks in forming their company's competitive plan.

6. Understand the creation of sets of long-term objectives and grand strategies options.

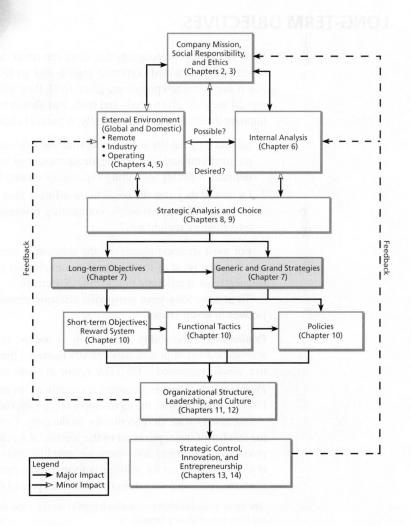

The company mission was described in Chapter 2 as encompassing the broad aims of the firm. The most specific statement of aims presented in that chapter appeared as the goals of the firm. However, these goals, which commonly dealt with profitability, growth, and survival, were stated without specific targets or time frames. They were always to be pursued but could never be fully attained. They gave a general sense of direction but were not intended to provide specific benchmarks for evaluating the firm's progress in achieving its aims. Providing such benchmarks is the function of objectives.[1]

The first part of this chapter will focus on long-term objectives. These are statements of the results a firm seeks to achieve over a specified period, typically three to five years. The second part will focus on the formulation of grand strategies. In combination, these two components of long-term planning provide a comprehensive general approach in guiding major actions designed to accomplish the firm's long-term objectives.

The chapter has two major aims: (1) to discuss in detail the concept of long-term objectives, the topics they cover, and the qualities they should exhibit; and (2) to discuss the concept of grand strategies and to describe the 15 principal grand strategy options that are available to firms singly or in combination, including three newly popularized options that are being used to provide the basis for global competitiveness.

LONG-TERM OBJECTIVES

Strategic managers recognize that short-run profit maximization is rarely the best approach to achieving sustained corporate growth and profitability. An often repeated adage states that if impoverished people are given food, they will eat it and remain impoverished; however, if they are given seeds and tools and shown how to grow crops, they will be able to improve their condition permanently. A parallel choice confronts strategic decision makers:

1. Should they eat the seeds to improve the near-term profit picture and increase dividend payments through cost-saving measures such as laying off workers during periods of slack demand, reducing marketing expense, or cutting back on research and development?
2. Or should they sow the seeds in the effort to reap long-term rewards by reinvesting profits in growth opportunities, committing resources to employee training, or increasing advertising expenditures?

For most strategic managers, the solution is clear—distribute a small amount of profit now but sow most of it to increase the likelihood of a long-term supply. This is the most frequently used rationale in selecting objectives.

To achieve long-term prosperity, strategic planners commonly establish long-term objectives in seven areas.

Profitability The ability of any firm to operate in the long run depends on attaining an acceptable level of profits. Strategically managed firms characteristically have a profit objective, usually expressed in EBITDA, return on assets, return on investment, and return on equity.

Productivity Strategic managers constantly try to increase the productivity of their systems. Firms that can improve the input-output relationship normally increase profitability. Thus, firms almost always state an objective for productivity. Commonly used productivity objectives are the number of items produced or the number of services rendered per unit of input. However, productivity objectives sometimes are stated in terms of desired cost decreases. For example, objectives may be set for reducing defective items, customer complaints leading to litigation, or overtime. Achieving such objectives increases profitability if unit output is maintained.

[1]The terms *goals* and *objectives* are each used to convey a special meaning, with goals being the less specific and more encompassing concept.

Competitive Position One measure of corporate success is relative dominance in the marketplace. Larger firms commonly establish an objective in terms of competitive position, often using total sales or market share as measures of their competitive position. An objective with regard to competitive position may indicate a firm's long-term priorities. For example, Gulf Oil set a five-year objective of moving from third to second place as a producer of high-density polypropylene. Total sales were the measure.

Employee Development Employees value education and training, in part because they lead to increased compensation and job security. Providing such opportunities often increases productivity and decreases turnover. Therefore, strategic decision makers frequently include an employee development objective in their long-range plans. For example, PPG has declared an objective of developing highly skilled and flexible employees and, thus, providing steady employment for a reduced number of workers.

Employee Relations Whether or not they are bound by union contracts, firms actively seek good employee relations. In fact, proactive steps in anticipation of employee needs and expectations are characteristic of strategic managers. Strategic managers believe that productivity is linked to employee loyalty and to appreciation of managers' interest in employee welfare. They, therefore, set objectives to improve employee relations. Among the outgrowths of such objectives are safety programs, worker representation on management committees, and employee stock option plans.

Technological Leadership Firms must decide whether to lead or follow in the marketplace. Either approach can be successful, but each requires a different strategic posture. Therefore, many firms state an objective with regard to technological leadership. For example, Caterpillar Tractor Company established its early reputation and dominant position in its industry by being in the forefront of technological innovation in the manufacture of large earthmovers. E-commerce technology officers will have more of a strategic role in the management hierarchy of the future, demonstrating that the Internet has become an integral aspect of corporate long-term objective setting. In offering an e-technology manager higher-level responsibilities, a firm is pursuing a leadership position in terms of innovation in computer networks and systems. Officers of e-commerce technology at GE and Delta Air Lines have shown their ability to increase profits by driving down transaction-related costs with Web-based technologies that seamlessly integrate their firms' supply chains. These technologies have the potential to "lock in" certain suppliers and customers and heighten competitive position through supply chain efficiency.

Social Responsibility Managers recognize their responsibilities to their customers and to society at large. In fact, many firms seek to exceed government requirements. They work not only to develop reputations for fairly priced products and services but also to establish themselves as responsible corporate citizens. For example, they may establish objectives for charitable and educational contributions, minority training, public or political activity, community welfare, or urban revitalization. In an attempt to exhibit their public responsibility in the United States, Japanese companies, such as Toyota, Hitachi, and Matsushita, contribute more than $500 million annually to American educational projects, charities, and nonprofit organizations.

Qualities of Long-Term Objectives

What distinguishes a good objective from a bad one? What qualities of an objective improve its chances of being attained? These questions are best answered in relation to five criteria that should be used in preparing long-term objectives: flexible, measurable over time, motivating, suitable, and understandable.

Flexible Objectives should be adaptable to unforeseen or extraordinary changes in the firm's competitive or environmental forecasts. Unfortunately, such flexibility usually is increased at the expense of specificity. One way of providing flexibility while minimizing its negative effects is to allow for adjustments in the level, rather than in the nature, of objectives. For example, the personnel department objective of providing managerial development training for 15 supervisors per year over the next five-year period might be adjusted by changing the number of people to be trained.

Measurable Objectives must clearly and concretely state what will be achieved and when it will be achieved. Thus, objectives should be measurable over time. For example, the objective of "substantially improving our return on investment" would be better stated as "increasing the return on investment on our line of paper products by a minimum of 1 percent a year and a total of 5 percent over the next three years." A great example is provided by IAG (Insurance Australia Group), which offers a wide range of commercial and personal insurance products. IAG stated its annual financial objective as a return on equity of 1.5 times the weighted average cost of capital.

A second example shows that measurable objectives can include nonfinancial targets. Aegerion Pharmaceuticals, Inc. is a biopharmaceutical company dedicated to the development and commercialization of innovative, life-altering therapies for patients with debilitating, often fatal, rare diseases.[2] It announced the following objectives for 2013 in January of that year:

- Aegerion expects global net revenues of $15 million to $25 million for FY 2013.
- 250 to 300 patients on Aegerion's drug (JUXTAPID) for treating patients with homozygous familial hypercholesterolemia by year-end 2013.
- Generate global net revenue at a $100 million annualized run rate at 18 months post approval of JUXTAPID in the EU.
- Achieve cash flow breakeven from operations.

Motivating People are most productive when objectives are set at a motivating level—one high enough to challenge but not so high as to frustrate or so low as to be easily attained. The problem is that individuals and groups differ in their perceptions of what is high enough. A broad objective that challenges one group frustrates another and minimally interests a third. One valuable recommendation is that objectives be tailored to specific groups. Developing such objectives requires time and effort, but objectives of this kind are more likely to motivate.

Objectives must also be achievable. This is easier said than done. Turbulence in the remote and operating environments affects a firm's internal operations, creating uncertainty and limiting the accuracy of the objectives set by strategic management. To illustrate, a recessionary economy makes objective setting extremely difficult, particularly in such areas as sales projections.

MasterCard provides a good example of well-constructed company objectives. In September 2012, MasterCard Incorporated provided 2013–2015 longer-term performance objectives, on a constant currency basis and excluding future acquisitions.[3] The company said it assumed there would not be any further deterioration in the U.S. economy or more significant problems within the Eurozone. MasterCard's financial objectives included:

- Net revenue compound annual growth rate, or CAGR, is expected to be in the range of 11 percent–14 percent.
- Annual operating margin of a minimum of 50 percent.
- Earnings per share CAGR of at least 20 percent.

[2]This example was excerpted from "Aegerion Pharmaceuticals Announces Key Business and Financial Objectives for 2013 as the Company Prepares for U.S. Launch of JUXTAPID™ (lomitapide) Capsules." NASDAQ OMX's News Release Distribution Channel. New York, January 7, 2013.

[3]This example was excerpted from "MasterCard Provides 2013–2015 Performance Objectives." RTTNews, Williamsville. September 20, 2012.

- Net revenue growth in the early part of the 2013–2015 period may be slightly below the 11 percent–14 percent range.
- In part of the 2013–2015 period, net revenue growth could be at the higher end of the range, assuming that the global economy could return to a more stable environment.

Suitable Objectives must be suited to the broad aims of the firm, which are expressed in its mission statement. Each objective should be a step toward the attainment of overall goals. In fact, objectives that are inconsistent with the company mission can subvert the firm's aims. For example, if the mission is growth oriented, the objective of reducing the debt-to-equity ratio to 1.00 would probably be unsuitable and counterproductive.

Understandable Strategic managers at all levels must understand what is to be achieved. They also must understand the major criteria by which their performance will be evaluated. Thus, objectives must be so stated that they are as understandable to the recipient as they are to the giver. Consider the misunderstandings that might arise over the objective of "increasing the productivity of the credit card department by 20 percent within two years." What does this objective mean? Increase the number of outstanding cards? Increase the use of outstanding cards? Increase the employee workload? Make productivity gains each year? Or hope that the new computer-assisted system, which should improve productivity, is approved by year 2? As this simple example illustrates, objectives must be clear, meaningful, and unambiguous.

The Balanced Scorecard

balanced scorecard
A set of four measures directly linked to a company's strategy: financial performance, customer knowledge, internal business processes, and learning and growth.

The **balanced scorecard** is a set of measures that are directly linked to the company's strategy. It directs a company to link its own long-term strategy with tangible goals and actions. The scorecard allows managers to evaluate the company from four perspectives: financial performance, customer knowledge, internal business processes, and learning and growth.

The balanced scorecard, as shown in Exhibit 7.1, contains a concise definition of the company's vision and strategy. Surrounding the vision and strategy are four additional boxes; each box contains the objectives, measures, targets, and initiatives for one of the four perspectives:

- The box at the top of Exhibit 7.1 represents the financial perspective and answers the question "To succeed financially, how should we appear to our shareholders?"
- The box to the right represents the internal business process perspective and addresses the question "To satisfy our shareholders and customers, what business processes must we excel at?"
- The learning and growth box at the bottom of Exhibit 7.1 answers the question "To achieve our vision, how will we sustain our ability to change and improve?"
- The box at the left reflects the customer perspective and responds to the question "To achieve our vision, how should we appear to our customers?"

All of the boxes are connected by arrows to illustrate that the objectives and measures of the four perspectives are linked by cause-and-effect relationships that lead to the successful implementation of the strategy. Achieving one perspective's targets should lead to desired improvements in the next perspective, and so on, until the company's performance increases overall.

A properly constructed scorecard is balanced between short- and long-term measures, financial and nonfinancial measures, and internal and external performance perspectives.

The balanced scorecard is a management system that can be used as the central organizing framework for key managerial processes. Chemical Bank, Mobil Corporation's U.S. Marketing and Refining Division, and CIGNA Property and Casualty Insurance have used the balanced scorecard approach to assist in individual and team goal setting, compensation, resource allocation, budgeting and planning, and strategic feedback and learning.

EXHIBIT 7.1   **The Balanced Scorecard**

The balanced scorecard provides a framework to translate a strategy into operational terms

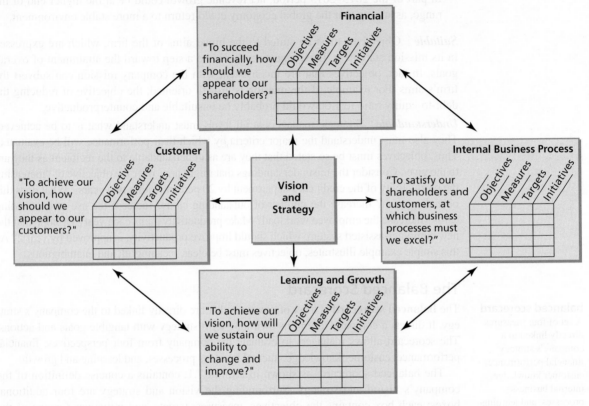

Source: Reprinted by permission of *Harvard Business Review,* Exhibit from "Using the Balanced Scorecard as a Strategic Management System," by Robert S. Kaplan and David P. Norton, February 1996. Copyright 1996 by the Harvard Business School Publishing Corporation; all rights reserved.

The Balanced Scorecard offers more than a way to think about the priorities of a company; it can also serve as a vehicle to help the company achieve those priorities. Exhibit 7.2, Strategy in Action provides nine steps for strategic managers to follow to succeed in implementing a Balanced Scorecard approach.

GENERIC STRATEGIES

Many planning experts believe that the general philosophy of doing business declared by the firm in the mission statement must be translated into a holistic statement of the firm's strategic orientation before it can be further defined in terms of a specific long-term strategy. In other words, a long-term or grand strategy must be based on a core idea about how the firm can best compete in the marketplace.

generic strategy
A core idea about how a firm can best compete in the marketplace.

The popular term for this core idea is **generic strategy.** From a scheme developed by Michael Porter, many planners believe that any long-term strategy should derive from a firm's attempt to seek a competitive advantage based on one of three generic strategies:

1. Striving for overall *low-cost leadership* in the industry.

2. Striving to create and market unique products for varied customer groups through *differentiation*.

3. Striving to have special appeal to one or more groups of consumer or industrial buyers, *focusing* on their cost or differentiation concerns.

Implementing a Balanced Scorecard: Nine Steps to Success

1. Assess the organization's mission and vision, challenges, and values. Prepare a change management plan for the organization.

2. Develop elements of the organization's strategy, including strategic results, strategic themes, and perspectives to focus attention on customer needs and the organization's value proposition.

3. Decompose the strategic elements developed in steps one and two into strategic objectives. Objectives should be initiated and categorized on the strategic theme level, categorized by perspective, linked in cause-effect linkages (strategy maps) for each strategic theme, and then later merged to produce one set of strategic objectives for the entire organization.

4. Formalize the cause and effect linkages between the enterprise-wide strategic objectives in an enterprise-wide strategy map.

5. Develop performance measures for each of the enterprise-wide strategic objectives. Identify leading and lagging measures, establish targets, thresholds, and baseline and benchmarking data.

6. Develop strategic initiatives that support the strategic objectives. Build accountability throughout the organization by assigning ownership of performance measures and strategic initiatives to the appropriate staff and documented in data definition tables.

7. Begin the implementation process by applying performance measurement software to get the right performance information to the right people at the right time. Automation adds structure and discipline when implementing the balanced scorecard system, helps transform disparate corporate data into information and knowledge, and helps communicate performance information. In short, automation helps people make better decisions because it offers quick access to actual performance data.

8. Cascade the enterprise-level scorecard down into business and support unit scorecards, meaning the organizational level scorecard (the first tier) is translated into business unit or support unit scorecards (the second tier) and then later to team and individual scorecards (the third tier). Cascading translates high-level strategy into lower level objectives, measures, and operational details and is the key to organization alignment around strategy. Team and individual scorecards link day-to-day work with department goals and corporate vision. Performance measures are developed for all objectives at all organizational levels. As the scorecard management system is cascaded down through the organization, objectives and performance measures become more operational and tactical. Accountability follows the objectives and measures, as ownership is defined at each level. An emphasis on the results and the strategies needed to produce results is communicated throughout the organization.

9. Evaluate the completed scorecard to answer questions such as, "Are our strategies working?", "Are we measuring the right things?", "Has our environment changed?" and "Are we budgeting our money strategically?"

Source: Excerpted from Ashu Sharma, "Implementing Balanced Scorecard for Performance Measurement," *IUP Journal of Business Strategy*, March 2009, 6(1): 7–16.

Advocates of generic strategies believe that each of these options can produce above-average returns for a firm in an industry. However, they are successful for very different reasons.

Low-Cost Leadership

Low-cost leaders depend on some fairly unique capabilities to achieve and sustain their low-cost position. Examples of such capabilities are having secured suppliers of scarce raw materials, being in a dominant market share position, or having a high degree of capitalization. Low-cost producers usually excel at cost reductions and efficiencies. They maximize economies of scale, implement cost-cutting technologies, stress reductions in overhead and in administrative expenses, and use volume sales techniques to propel themselves up the earning curve.

A low-cost leader is able to use its cost advantage to charge lower prices or to enjoy higher profit margins. By so doing, the firm effectively can defend itself in price wars, attack competitors on price to gain market share, or, if already dominant in the industry, simply benefit from exceptional returns. As an extreme case, it has been argued that National Can Company, a corporation in an essentially stagnant industry, is able to generate attractive and improving profits by being the low-cost producer.

In the wake of the tremendous successes of such low-price leaders as Walmart and Target, only a rare few companies can ignore the mandate to reduce costs. Yet, doing so without compromising the key attributes of a company's products or services is a difficult challenge. One company that has succeeded in its efforts to become a low-cost leader while maintaining quality is IAG. The company's CEO, Michael Wilkins, expresses the principle of the company's focus on low costs in its mission statement by saying: "IAG's large scale allows us to manage costs across our brands through access to volume discounts throughout the supply chain, without sacrificing quality, thereby keeping costs per policy down."

Differentiation

Strategies dependent on differentiation are designed to appeal to customers with a special sensitivity for a particular product attribute. By stressing the attribute above other product qualities, the firm attempts to build customer loyalty. Often such loyalty translates into a firm's ability to charge a premium price for its product. Cross-brand pens, Brooks Brothers suits, Porsche automobiles, and Chivas Regal Scotch whiskey are all examples.

The product attribute also can be the marketing channels through which it is delivered, its image for excellence, the features it includes, and the service network that supports it. As a result of the importance of these attributes, competitors often face "perceptual" barriers to entry when customers of a successfully differentiated firm fail to see largely identical products as being interchangeable. For example, General Motors hopes that customers will accept "only genuine GM replacement parts."

Because advertising plays a major role in a company's development and differentiation of its brand, many strategists use celebrity spokespeople to represent their companies. These spokespeople, most often actors, models, and athletes, help give the company's products and services a popular, successful, trendy, modern cachet.

Focus

A focus strategy, whether anchored in a low-cost base or a differentiation base, attempts to attend to the needs of a particular market segment. Likely segments are those that are ignored by marketing appeals to easily accessible markets, to the "typical" customer, or to customers with common applications for the product. A firm pursuing a focus strategy is willing to service isolated geographic areas; to satisfy the needs of customers with special financing, inventory, or servicing problems; or to tailor the product to the somewhat unique demands of the small- to medium-sized customer. Focusing firms profit from their willingness to serve otherwise ignored or underappreciated customer segments. A classic example is cable television. An entire industry was born because of a willingness of cable firms to serve isolated rural locations that were ignored by traditional television services. Brick producers that typically service a radius of less than 75 miles and commuter airlines that serve regional geographic areas are other examples of industries where a focus strategy has yielded above-average industry profits.

THE VALUE DISCIPLINES

International management consultants Michael Treacy and Fred Wiersema propose an alternative approach to generic strategy that they call the value disciplines.[4] They believe that strategies must center on delivering superior customer value through one of three value disciplines: operational excellence, customer intimacy, or product leadership.

---

[4]The ideas and examples in this section are drawn from Michael Treacy and Fred Wiersema, "Customer Intimacy and Other Value Disciplines," *Harvard Business Review* 71, no. 1 (1993), pp. 84–94.

Operational excellence refers to providing customers with convenient and reliable products or services at competitive prices. Customer intimacy involves offerings tailored to match the demands of identified niches. Product leadership, the third discipline, involves offering customers leading-edge products and services that make rivals' goods obsolete.

Companies that specialize in one of these disciplines, while simultaneously meeting industry standards in the other two, gain a sustainable lead in their markets. This lead is derived from the firm's focus on one discipline, aligning all aspects of operations with it. Having decided on the value that must be conveyed to customers, firms understand more clearly what must be done to attain the desired results. After transforming their organizations to focus on one discipline, companies can concentrate on smaller adjustments to produce incremental value. To match this advantage, less focused companies require larger changes than the tweaking that discipline leaders need.

Operational Excellence

Operational excellence is a specific strategic approach to the production and delivery of products and services. A company that follows this strategy attempts to lead its industry in price and convenience by pursuing a focus on lean and efficient operations. Companies that employ operational excellence work to minimize costs by reducing overhead, eliminating intermediate production steps, reducing transaction costs, and optimizing business processes across functional and organizational boundaries. The focus is on delivering products or services to customers at competitive prices with minimal inconvenience.

Operational excellence is also the strategic focus of General Electric's large appliance business. Historically, the distribution strategy for large appliances was based on requiring that dealers maintain large inventories. Price breaks for dealers were based on order quantities. However, as the marketplace became more competitive, principally as a result of competition multibrand dealers like Sears, GE recognized the need to adjust its production and distribution plans.

The GE system addresses the delivery of products. As a step toward organizational excellence, GE created a computer-based logistics system to replace its in-store inventories model. Retailers use this software to access a 24-hour online order processing system that guarantees GE's best price. This system allows dealers to better meet customer needs, with instantaneous access to a warehouse of goods and accurate shipping and production information. GE benefits from the deal as well. Efficiency is increased since manufacturing now occurs in response to customer sales. Additionally, warehousing and distribution systems have been streamlined to create the capability of delivering to 90 percent of destinations in the continental United States within one business day.

Firms that implement the strategy of operational excellence typically restructure their delivery processes to focus on efficiency and reliability, and use state-of-the art information systems that emphasize integration and low-cost transactions.

Customer Intimacy

Companies that implement a strategy of customer intimacy continually tailor and shape products and services to fit an increasingly refined definition of the customer. Companies excelling in customer intimacy combine detailed customer knowledge with operational flexibility. They respond quickly to almost any need, from customizing a product to fulfilling special requests to create customer loyalty.

Customer-intimate companies are willing to spend money now to build customer loyalty for the long term, considering each customer's lifetime value to the company, not the profit of any single transaction. Consequently, employees in customer-intimate companies go to great lengths to ensure customer satisfaction with low regard for initial cost.

Home Depot implements the discipline of customer intimacy. Home Depot clerks spend the necessary time with customers to determine the product that best suits their needs, because the company's business strategy is built around selling information and service in addition to home-repair and improvement items. Consequently, consumers concerned solely with price fall outside Home Depot's core market.

Companies engaged in customer intimacy understand the difference between the profitability of a single transaction and the profitability of a lifetime relationship with a single customer. The company's profitability depends in part on its maintaining a system that differentiates quickly and accurately the degree of service that customers require and the revenues their patronage is likely to generate. Firms using this approach recognize that not every customer is equally profitable. For example, a financial services company installed a telephone-computer system capable of recognizing individual clients by their telephone numbers when they call. The system routes customers with large accounts and frequent transactions to their own senior account representative. Other customers may be routed to a trainee or junior representative. In any case, the customer's file appears on the representative's screen before the phone is answered.

The new system allows the firm to segment its services with great efficiency. If the company has clients who are interested in trading in a particular financial instrument, it can group them under the one account representative who specializes in that instrument. This saves the firm the expense of training every representative in every facet of financial services. Additionally, the company can direct certain value-added services or products to a specific group of clients that would have interest in them.

Businesses that select a customer intimacy strategy have decided to stress flexibility and responsiveness. They collect and analyze data from many sources. Their organizational structure emphasizes empowerment of employees close to customers. Additionally, hiring and training programs stress the creative decision-making skills required to meet individual customer needs. Management systems recognize and utilize such concepts as customer lifetime value, and norms among employees are consistent with a "have it your way" mind set.

Product Leadership

Companies that pursue the discipline of product leadership strive to produce a continuous stream of state-of-the-art products and services. Three challenges must be met to attain that goal. Creativity is the first challenge. Creativity is recognizing and embracing ideas usually originating outside the company. Second, innovative companies must commercialize ideas quickly. Thus, their business and management processes need to be engineered for speed. Product leaders relentlessly pursue new solutions to problems. Finally, firms utilizing this discipline prefer to release their own improvements rather than wait for competitors to enter. Consequently, product leaders do not stop for self-congratulation; they focus on continual improvement.

For example, Johnson & Johnson's organizational design brings good ideas in, looks for ways to improve them, and puts them into production quickly. The president of J&J's Vistakon Inc., a maker of specialty contact lenses, provided an example when he received a tip concerning an ophthalmologist who had conceived of a method to manufacture disposable contact lenses inexpensively. Vistakon purchased the rights to the technology, assembled a management team to oversee the product's development, and built a state-of-the-art facility in Florida to manufacture disposable contact lenses called Acuvue. Vistakon and its parent, J&J, were willing to incur high manufacturing and inventory costs before a single lens was sold. A high-speed production facility helped give Vistakon a six-month head start over the competition that, taken off guard, never caught up.

Like other product leaders, J&J creates and maintains an environment that encourages employees to share ideas. Additionally, product leaders continually scan the environment for new-product or service possibilities and rush to capitalize them. Product leaders also avoid bureaucracy because it slows commercialization of their ideas. In a product leadership company, a wrong decision often is less damaging than one made late. As a result, managers make decisions quickly, their companies encouraging them to decide today and implement tomorrow. Product leaders continually look for new methods to shorten their cycle times.

The strength of product leaders lies in reacting to situations as they occur. Shorter reaction times serve as an advantage in dealings with the unknown. For example, when competitors challenged the safety of Acuvue lenses, the firm responded quickly and distributed data combating the charges to eye care professionals. This reaction created goodwill in the marketplace.

Product leaders act as their own competition. These firms continually make the products and services they have created obsolete. Product leaders believe that if they do not develop a successor, a competitor will. So, although Acuvue is successful in the marketplace, Vistakon continues to investigate new material that will extend the wearability of contact lenses and technologies that will make current lenses obsolete. J&J and other innovators recognize that the long-run profitability of an existing product or service is less important to the company's future than maintaining its product leadership edge and momentum.

GRAND STRATEGIES

grand strategy
A master long-term plan that provides basic direction for major actions for achieving long-term business objectives.

Grand strategies, sometimes called master or business strategies, provide basic direction for strategic actions. They are the basis of coordinated and sustained efforts directed toward achieving long-term business objectives.

The purpose of this section is twofold: (1) to list, describe, and discuss 15 grand strategies that strategic managers should consider and (2) to present approaches to the selection of an optimal grand strategy from the available alternatives.

Grand strategies indicate the time period over which long-range objectives are to be achieved. Thus, a grand strategy can be defined as a comprehensive general approach that guides a firm's major actions.

The 15 principal grand strategies are concentrated growth, market development, product development, innovation, horizontal acquisition, vertical acquisition, concentric diversification, conglomerate diversification, turnaround, divestiture, liquidation, bankruptcy, joint ventures, strategic alliances, and consortia. Any one of these strategies could serve as the basis for achieving the major long-term objectives of a single firm. But a firm involved with multiple industries, businesses, product lines, or customer groups—as many firms are—usually combines several grand strategies. For clarity, however, each of the principal grand strategies is described independently in this section, with examples to indicate some of its relative strengths and weaknesses.

1. Concentrated Growth

Many of the firms that fell victim to merger mania were once mistakenly convinced that the best way to achieve their objectives was to pursue unrelated diversification in the search for financial opportunity and synergy. By rejecting that "conventional wisdom," such firms as Martin-Marietta, KFC, Compaq, Avon, Hyatt Legal Services, and Tenant have demonstrated the advantages of what is increasingly proving to be sound business strategy.

concentrated growth
A grand strategy with which a firm directs its resources to the profitable growth of a single product, in a single market, with a single dominant technology.

These firms are just a few of the majority of businesses worldwide firms that pursue a concentrated growth strategy by focusing on a dominant product-and-market combination. **Concentrated growth** is the strategy of the firm that directs its resources to the profitable growth of a dominant product, in a dominant market, with a dominant technology. The main rationale for this approach, sometimes called a market penetration strategy, is that by thoroughly developing and exploiting its expertise in a narrowly defined competitive arena, the company achieves superiority over competitors that try to master a greater number of product and market combinations.

Rationale for Superior Performance

Concentrated growth strategies lead to enhanced performance. The ability to assess market needs, knowledge of buyer behavior, customer price sensitivity, and effectiveness of promotion are characteristics of a concentrated growth strategy. Such core capabilities are a more important determinant of competitive market success than are the environmental forces faced by the firm. The high success rates of new products also are tied to avoiding situations that require undeveloped skills, such as serving new customers and markets, acquiring new technology, building new channels, developing new promotional abilities, and facing new competition.

A major misconception about the concentrated growth strategy is that the firm practicing it will settle for no growth. This is certainly not true for a firm that correctly utilizes the strategy. A firm employing concentrated growth grows by building on its competencies, and it achieves a competitive edge by concentrating in the product-market segment it knows best. A firm employing this strategy is aiming for the growth that results from improved productivity, better coverage of its product-market segment, better-defined marketing, and more efficient use of its technology.

Conditions That Favor Concentrated Growth

Specific conditions in the firm's environment are favorable to the concentrated growth strategy. The first is a condition in which the firm's industry is resistant to major technological advancements. This is usually the case in the late growth and maturity stages of the product life cycle and in product markets where product demand is stable and industry barriers, such as capitalization, are high. Machinery for the paper manufacturing industry, in which the basic technology has not changed for more than a century, is a good example.

An especially favorable condition is one in which the firm's targeted markets are not product saturated. Markets with competitive gaps leave the firm with alternatives for growth, other than taking market share away from competitors. The successful introduction of traveler services by Allstate and Amoco demonstrates that even an organization as entrenched and powerful as the AAA could not build a defensible presence in all segments of the automobile club market.

A third condition that favors concentrated growth exists when the firm's product markets are sufficiently distinctive to dissuade competitors in adjacent product markets from trying to invade the firm's segment. John Deere scrapped its plans for growth in the construction machinery business when mighty Caterpillar threatened to enter Deere's mainstay, the farm machinery business, in retaliation. Rather than risk a costly price war on its own turf, Deere scrapped these plans.

A fourth favorable condition exists when the firm's inputs are stable in price and quantity and are available in the amounts and at the times needed. Maryland-based Giant Foods is able to concentrate in the grocery business largely due to its stable long-term arrangements with suppliers of its private-label products. Most of these suppliers are makers of the national brands that compete against the Giant labels. With a high market share and aggressive retail distribution, Giant controls the access of these brands to the consumer. Consequently, its suppliers have considerable incentive to honor verbal agreements, called bookings, in which they commit themselves for a one-year period with regard to the price, quality, and timing of their shipments to Giant.

The pursuit of concentrated growth also is favored by a stable market—a market without the seasonal or cyclical swings that would encourage a firm to diversify. Night Owl Security, the District of Columbia market leader in home security services, commits its customers to initial four-year contracts. In a city where affluent consumers tend to be quite transient, the length of this relationship is remarkable. Night Owl's concentrated growth strategy has been reinforced by its success in getting subsequent owners of its customers' homes to extend and renew the security service contracts. In a similar way, Lands' End reinforced its growth strategy by asking customers for names and addresses of friends and relatives living overseas who would like to receive Lands' End catalogs.

A firm also can grow while concentrating, if it enjoys competitive advantages based on efficient production or distribution channels. These advantages enable the firm to formulate advantageous pricing policies. More efficient production methods and better handling of distribution also enable the firm to achieve greater economies of scale or, in conjunction with marketing, result in a product that is differentiated in the mind of the consumer. Graniteville Company, a large South Carolina textile manufacturer, enjoyed decades of growth and profitability by adopting a "follower" tactic as part of its concentrated growth strategy. By producing fabrics only after market demand had been well established, and by featuring products that reflected its expertise in adopting manufacturing innovations and in maintaining highly efficient long production runs, Graniteville prospered through concentrated growth.

Finally, the success of market generalists creates conditions favorable to concentrated growth. When generalists succeed by using universal appeals, they avoid making special appeals to particular groups of customers. The net result is that many small pockets are left open in the markets dominated by generalists, and that specialists emerge and thrive in these pockets. For example, hardware store chains, such as Home Depot, focus primarily on routine household repair problems and offer solutions that can be easily sold on a self-service, do-it-yourself basis. This approach leaves gaps at both the "semiprofessional" and "neophyte" ends of the market—in terms of the purchaser's skill at household repairs and the extent to which available merchandise matches the requirements of individual homeowners. Strategy in Action, Exhibit 7.3 provides an example of Shutterfly, which provided more than a decade of solid financial performance, by relying on a grand strategy of concentrated growth to fend off such competitors as Walmart Stores, Eastman Kodak, and Yahoo!.

Risk and Rewards of Concentrated Growth

Under stable conditions, concentrated growth poses lower risk than any other grand strategy; but, in a changing environment, a firm committed to concentrated growth faces high risks. The greatest risk is that concentrating in a single product market makes a firm particularly vulnerable to changes in that segment. Slowed growth in the segment would jeopardize the firm because its investment, competitive edge, and technology are deeply entrenched in a specific offering. It is difficult for the firm to attempt sudden changes if its product is threatened by near-term obsolescence, a faltering market, new substitutes, or changes in technology or customer needs. For example, the manufacturers of IBM clones faced such a problem when IBM adopted the OS/2 operating system for its personal computer line. That change made existing clones out of date.

The concentrating firm's entrenchment in a specific industry makes it particularly susceptible to changes in the economic environment of that industry. For example, Mack Truck, the second-largest truck maker in America, lost $20 million as a result of an 18-month slump in the truck industry.

Exhibit 7.3

Shutterfly's Improbably Long Survival

Shutterfly, the Redwood City, California–based company was making money by turning digital snapshots into tangible things: Sales of custom photo books, calendars, greeting cards, wedding invitations, and even wall decals totaled an estimated $600 million in 2012. Yet there was a feeling that the company had been passed. After all, investors valued Shutterfly at $1 billion—the same price Facebook paid for Instagram, a startup with no revenue. Despite its solid financial performance, Shutterfly had a roller-coaster stock history, reflecting investors' continuing concerns that it would be edged out by potential new competitors, including Facebook, Apple, and Amazon.

Founded in 1999, Shutterfly was surrounded by naysayers for much of its existence. The company had faced off against 1,000 (yes, really) startups in the online photo market as well as giants such as Walmart Stores, Walgreens, Hewlett-Packard, Eastman Kodak, and

Yahoo!. Its odds of survival seemed low, but Shutterfly chalked up 47 straight quarters of revenue growth. Sales multiplied elevenfold. Having absorbed the customers from the defunct digital photo businesses of Kodak, Fujifilm, and Yahoo, Shutterfly was home to 70 petabytes' worth of cherished family pictures—making it the largest service of its kind.

Women accounted for 80 percent of Shutterfly's business, and more than half of the company's revenue came around December as these CMOs turn photos into gifts. To secure its edge over rivals, Shutterfly invested in technology, such as algorithms that could scan a photo album and arrange the pictures into a well-crafted book, as well as high-quality materials like double-thick paper.

Source: Excerpted from Ashlee Vance. January 3, 2013. "Shutterfly's Improbably Long Survival (and Success)." *Bloomberg Businessweek.*

Entrenchment in a specific product market tends to make a concentrating firm more adept than competitors at detecting new trends. However, any failure of such a firm to properly forecast major changes in its industry can result in extraordinary losses. Numerous makers of inexpensive digital watches were forced to declare bankruptcy because they failed to anticipate the competition posed by Swatch, Guess, and other trendy watches that emerged from the fashion industry.

A firm pursuing a concentrated growth strategy is vulnerable also to the high opportunity costs that result from remaining in a specific product market and ignoring other options that could employ the firm's resources more profitably. Overcommitment to a specific technology and product market can hinder a firm's ability to enter a new or growing product market that offers more attractive cost-benefit trade-offs. Had Apple Computers maintained its policy of making equipment that did not interface with IBM equipment, it would have missed out on what have proved to be its most profitable strategic options.

Concentrated Growth Is Often the Most Viable Option

Examples abound of firms that have enjoyed exceptional returns on the concentrated growth strategy. Such firms as McDonald's, Goodyear, and Apple Computers have used firsthand knowledge and deep involvement with specific product segments to become powerful competitors in their markets. For example, between 2013–2015, 600 Wendy's restaurants in North America will be remodeled to include fireplaces.[5] Tré Musco, the chief executive of Tesser, who heads the design firm that is handling the remodeling jobs, says that Wendy's is looking for a way to make its restaurants more inviting so that the fast-food experience will slow down. A longer dining experience benefits Wendy's because customers typically spend more than when they order takeout or drive-through. Sales at the renovated stores increased 25 percent over their prior year.

[5]Excerpted from Venessa Wong. February 28, 2013. "Let's Go to Wendy's and Cuddle by the Fireplace." *Bloomberg Businessweek.*

The limited additional resources necessary to implement concentrated growth, coupled with the limited risk involved, also make this strategy desirable for a firm with limited funds. For example, through a carefully devised concentrated growth strategy, medium-sized John Deere & Company was able to become a major force in the agricultural machinery business even when competing with such firms as Ford Motor Company. While other firms were trying to exit or diversify from the farm machinery business, Deere spent $2 billion in upgrading its machinery, boosting its efficiency, and engaging in a program to strengthen its dealership system. This concentrated growth strategy enabled it to become the leader in the farm machinery business despite the fact that Ford was more than 10 times its size.

The firm that chooses a concentrated growth strategy directs its resources to the profitable growth of a narrowly defined product and market, focusing on a dominant technology. Firms that remain within their chosen product market are able to extract the most from their technology and market knowledge and, thus, are able to minimize the risk associated with unrelated diversification. The success of a concentration strategy is founded on the firm's use of superior insights into its technology, product, and customer to obtain a sustainable competitive advantage. Superior performance on these aspects of corporate strategy has been shown to have a substantial positive effect on market success.

A grand strategy of concentrated growth allows for a considerable range of action. Broadly speaking, the firm can attempt to capture a larger market share by increasing the usage rates of present customers, by attracting competitors' customers, or by selling to nonusers. In turn, each of these options suggests more specific options, some of which are listed in the top section of Exhibit 7.4.

When strategic managers forecast that their current products and their markets will not provide the basis for achieving the company mission, they have two options that involve moderate costs and risk: market development and product development.

2. Market Development

market development

A grand strategy of marketing present products, often with only cosmetic modification, to customers in related marketing areas.

Market development commonly ranks second only to concentration as the least costly and least risky of the 15 grand strategies. It consists of marketing present products, often with only cosmetic modifications, to customers in related market areas by adding channels of distribution or by changing the content of advertising or promotion. Several specific market development approaches are listed in Exhibit 7.4. Thus, as suggested by the exhibit, firms that open branch offices in new cities, states, or countries are practicing market development. Likewise, firms are practicing market development if they switch from advertising in trade publications to advertising in newspapers or if they add jobbers to supplement their mail-order sales efforts.

Market development allows firms to leverage some of their traditional strengths by identifying new uses for existing products and new demographically, psychographically, or geographically defined markets. Frequently, changes in media selection, promotional appeals, and distribution signal the implementation of this strategy. Du Pont used market development when it found a new application for Kevlar, an organic material that police, security, and military personnel had used primarily for bulletproofing. Kevlar now is being used to refit and maintain wooden-hulled boats, since it is lighter and stronger than glass fibers and has 11 times the strength of steel. Kenner Products introduced the classic light bulb–powered Easy-Bake Oven in 1963, in the color turquoise.[6] As early ads made clear, the company was primarily targeting future female homemakers with its imaginary feasts. Then, in 2012, Hasbro unveiled a "unisex" version of its Easy-Bake Oven at the New York

[6]This example was excerpted from Venessa Wong. December 21, 2012. "Toymakers See Profit in Going 'Gender Neutral.'" *Bloomberg Businessweek.*

EXHIBIT 7.4
Specific Options under the Grand Strategies of Concentration, Market Development, and Product Development

Source: Adapted from Philip Kotler and Kevin Keller, *Marketing Management,* 14th Edition, 2012. Reprinted by permission of Pearson Education, Upper Saddle River, NJ.

Concentration (increasing use of present products in present markets):

1. Increasing present customers' rate of use:
   a. Increasing the size of purchase.
   b. Increasing the rate of product obsolescence.
   c. Advertising other uses.
   d. Giving price incentives for increased use.
2. Attracting competitors' customers:
   a. Establishing sharper brand differentiation.
   b. Increasing promotional effort.
   c. Initiating price cuts.
3. Attracting nonusers to buy the product:
   a. Inducing trial use through sampling, price incentives, and so on.
   b. Pricing up or down.
   c. Advertising new uses.

Market development (selling present products in new markets):

1. Opening additional geographic markets:
   a. Regional expansion.
   b. National expansion.
   c. International expansion.
2. Attracting other market segments:
   a. Developing product versions to appeal to other segments.
   b. Entering other channels of distribution.
   c. Advertising in other media.

Product development (developing new products for present markets):

1. Developing new-product features:
   a. Adapt (to other ideas, developments).
   b. Modify (change color, motion, sound, odor, form, shape).
   c. Magnify (stronger, longer, thicker, extra value).
   d. Minify (smaller, shorter, lighter).
   e. Substitute (other ingredients, process, power).
   f. Rearrange (other patterns, layout, sequence, components).
   g. Reverse (inside out).
   h. Combine (blend, alloy, assortment, ensemble; combine units, purposes, appeals, ideas).
2. Developing quality variations.
3. Developing additional models and sizes (product proliferation).

Toy Show. The oven became available in new colors of silver, black, and blue, and boys were featured in the new ads and packaging. In a gender-segmented industry, Hasbro was hoping that crossing the gender divide would result in increased sales. Because Hasbro is a top seller of toys for boys, including Transformers, Nerf, and G.I. Joe, it had brand reputation and experience on its side. In 2012, Hasbro's revenue from boys' toys was approximately three times the revenue from girls' toys or $2 billion.

The medical industry provides other examples of new markets for existing products. The National Institutes of Health's report of a study showing that the use of aspirin may lower the incidence of heart attacks was expected to boost sales in the $2.2 billion analgesic market. It was predicted that the expansion of this market would lower the market share of nonaspirin brands, such as industry leaders Tylenol and Advil. Product extensions currently planned include Bayer Calendar Pack, 28-day packaging to fit the once-a-day prescription for the prevention of a second heart attack.

Another example is Chesebrough-Ponds, a major producer of health and beauty aids, which decided several years ago to expand its market by repacking its Vaseline Petroleum Jelly in pocket-size squeeze tubes as Vaseline "Lip Therapy." The corporation decided to place a strategic emphasis on market development, because it knew from market studies that its petroleum-jelly customers already were using the product to prevent chapped lips. Company leaders reasoned that their market could be expanded significantly if the product were repackaged to fit conveniently in consumers' pockets and purses.

Apple has also been successful with a market development strategy. As reported in *Bloomberg Businessweek*, Indians preferred low-cost Android smartphones or basic handsets to the far more expensive iPhone.[7] Apple ranked 10th in Indian smartphone sales in 2013. Because overall consumer spending was forecasted by Boston Consulting Group to almost quadruple to $3.6 trillion by 2020, Apple needed a more aggressive approach. Apple placed iPhone ads in national Indian newspapers offering interest-free payment plans, trade-in offers, and discounted service agreements. In September 2012, the company signed deals with electronics distributors Redington (India) and Ingram Micro to strengthen iPhone supplies throughout the country. While the new iPhone5, priced at 44,000 rupees, sold at low volumes, sales of the newly discounted iPhone4 increased very dramatically.

A more complete example of marketing development is provided in Global Strategy in Action, Exhibit 7.5. In 2013, Google developed plans to open showrooms in the United States to highlight its devices running the Android and Chrome operating systems, to introduce Google Glass, and potentially to offer customer service to small and medium-size business owners on advertising products like Adwords.

3. Product Development

product development
A grand strategy that involves the substantial modification of existing products that can be marketed to current customers.

Product development involves the substantial modification of existing products or the creation of new but related products that can be marketed to current customers through established channels. The product development strategy often is adopted either to prolong the life cycle of current products or to take advantage of a favorite reputation or brand name. The idea is to attract satisfied customers to new products as a result of their positive experience with the firm's initial offering. The bottom section in Exhibit 7.4 lists some of the options available to firms undertaking product development. A revised edition of a college textbook, a new car style, and a second formula of shampoo for oily hair are examples of the product development strategy.

Pepsi changed its strategy on beverage products by creating new products to follow the industry movement away from mass branding. This new movement was designed to attract a younger, hipper customer segment. Pepsi's new products include a version of Mountain Dew, called Code Red, and new Pepsi brands, called Pepsi Twist and Pepsi Blue.

Similarly, in 2013, Pizza Hut added mini pizzas to its menu, called Big Pizza Sliders. As reported by *Bloomberg Businessweek*, this was an odd name, since they were neither big nor sliders.[8] Each pizza had a 3.5 inch diameter and weighed about the same as a slice of a large pie. While sizing down helped the chain control costs since the cost of the

---

[7]Kartikay Mehrotra and Bruce Einhorn. January 24, 2013. "Why Apple Is Giving iTunes Discounts in India." *Bloomberg Businessweek*.

[8]Venessa Wong. February 6, 2013. "To Add Variety and Control Cost, Fast Foods Go Small." *Bloomberg Businessweek*.

Google Eyes Apple Stores and Considers Retail

As malls closed, big-box stores tried to shrink, and the overall prospects of physical retail ranged from stagnant to apocalyptic, one sector of the market was enjoying an unlikely growth spurt in 2013: stores opened by the big technology companies. Apple spawned about 400 Apple Stores in the prior decade, Microsoft was opening new locations, and Google was developing plans to open showrooms in the United States to highlight its devices running the Android and Chrome operating systems.

Google was doing just fine without the hassle of being a merchandiser: It had the most-trafficked real estate on the Web and enjoys healthy distribution at electronics outlets like Best Buy. It also had close relationships with its carrier partners, such as Verizon and AT&T, which had their own ubiquitous stores.

But over the past few years, Google was making more of its own hardware, and it could have used additional help reaching customers. It started selling many of its Nexus smartphones and Nexus 7 small tablets itself, primarily online. These devices were modest successes, but as Apple showed, having a direct channel to the customer could help immeasurably.

Google was making more of its own hardware, via its Motorola, Android, and Chrome divisions; a physical store would cast those devices in the best possible light. The company was experimenting with temporary pop-up stores in airports and store-within-a-store configurations in Best Buys.

The best reason to open stores may have been all the secret projects still gestating at Google's far-out think tank, Google X. Google Glass, the Internet-connected eyewear being touted by co-founder Sergey Brin, was the most obvious example. The eyeglasses place a tiny voice-controlled computer screen in the corner of the wearer's periphery. By opening its own stores, Google was able to control the demo experience for Glass rather than relying on Best Buy blue-shirts in noisy box stores. In the future, Google might use these locations to offer customer service to small and medium-size business owners on advertising products like Adwords.

Source: Excerpted from Brad Stone. February 19, 2013. "Google Eyes Apple Stores and Considers Retail." *Bloomberg Businessweek*.

---

three sliders was less than the cost for a large pizza, the real benefit for Pizza Hut is that the sliders provide more customization, because customers could choose up to three different sliders with up to three toppings on each. The sliders are also priced attractively for a lunch menu at $10 for nine or $5 for three.

The product development strategy is based on the penetration of existing markets by incorporating product modifications into existing items or by developing new products with a clear connection to the existing product line. The telecommunications industry provides an example of product extension based on product modification. To increase its estimated 8 to 10 percent share of the $5 to $6 billion corporate user market, MCI Communication Corporation extended its direct-dial service to 146 countries, the same as those serviced by AT&T, at lower average rates than those of AT&T. MCI's addition of 79 countries to its network underscores its belief in this market, which it expects to grow 15 to 20 percent annually. Another example of expansions linked to existing lines is Gerber's decision to engage in general merchandise marketing. Gerber's recent introduction included 52 items that ranged from feeding accessories to toys and children's wear. Likewise, Nabisco Brands seeks competitive advantage by placing its strategic emphasis on product development. With headquarters in Parsippany, New Jersey, the company is one of three operating units of RJR Nabisco. It is the leading producer of biscuits, confections, snacks, shredded cereals, and processed fruits and vegetables. To maintain its position as leader, Nabisco pursues a strategy of developing and introducing new products and expanding its existing product line. Spoon Size Shredded Wheat and Ritz Bits crackers are two examples of new products that are variations on existing products.

How Disney Hopes to Game the Console Market

Console video games sales were falling in 2013, but a hit game could still out-gross most movies. So what should a large entertainment company do if it wants a piece of this risky business? The future model could be the one that Disney designed for Disney Infinity, a video-game platform that enabled fans to choose characters from the company's many different worlds and deploy them simultaneously in a sandbox-like environment. In Disney's initial demonstration of the product, Capt. Jack Sparrow of *Pirates of the Caribbean* mingles with Sulley of *Monsters Inc.* and *The Incredibles*' Mr. Incredible. This was a departure for Disney, which had historically kept its characters from disparate franchises away from each other.

What's more intriguing is how Infinity breaks from the traditional strategy most studios follow. Instead of creating games for each movie or television show,

Disney introduced them into Infinity. Fans could purchase the $74.99 Infinity starter kit, which came with the Infinity Base. The device looked a little like a futuristic set-top box, and could be plugged into most video-game consoles and mobile devices. The starter pack came with three character figurines. Gamers activated their characters in the Infinity sandbox by attaching them to the Infinity Base. Disney, of course, had many characters and worlds; fans who wanted to populate their Infinity universe with them have to pay extra. The same was true of the "play-set packs," which unlocked virtual worlds from the company's franchises.

Source: Excerpted from Devin Leonard. January 17, 2013. "How Disney Hopes to Game the Console Market." *Bloomberg Businessweek.*

Global Strategy in Action, Exhibit 7.6, describes how Disney planned to use Disney Infinity, a video-game platform, to break from the traditional strategy most studios follow. Instead of creating games for each movie or television show, Disney will introduce them into Infinity as a way to leverage its product development.

4. Innovation

innovation

A grand strategy that seeks to reap the premium margins associated with creation and customer acceptance of a new product or service.

In many industries, it has become increasingly risky not to innovate. Both consumer and industrial markets have come to expect periodic changes and improvements in the products offered. As a result, some firms find it profitable to make **innovation** their grand strategy. They seek to reap the initially high profits associated with customer acceptance of a new or greatly improved product. Then, rather than face stiffening competition as the basis of profitability shifts from innovation to production or marketing competence, they search for other original or novel ideas. The underlying rationale of the grand strategy of innovation is to create a new product life cycle and thereby make similar existing products obsolete. Thus, this strategy differs from the product development strategy of extending an existing product's life cycle. For example, Intel, a leader in the semiconductor industry, pursues expansion through a strategic emphasis on innovation. Companies under pressure to innovate often supplement their own R&D efforts by partnering with other firms in their industry that have complementary needs.

Walmart is a prime example of a corporation that innovates through partners. The retailing giant works with Indian vendors such as TCS, Infosys, Wipro and multinationals such as IBM, Accenture, Cognizant, UST Global, and SofTec to broaden its technology supplier vendor base and speed up technology innovation.[9] With increasing number of customers preferring to shop online in the United States and competition coming from

[9]"Walmart eyes Indian vendors to speed up tech innovation." February 14, 2013. *Businessline* [Chennai], Kasturi and Sons Ltd.

EXHIBIT 7.7
Decay of New Product Ideas

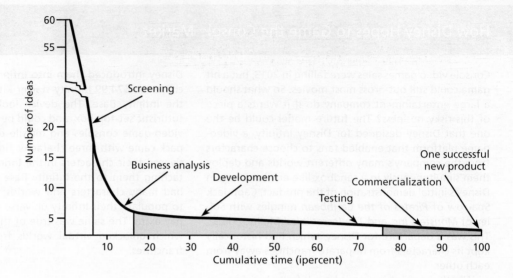

Amazon, Walmart is trying to leapfrog existing technology with the help of its high-tech partners. These efforts supplement Walmart's in-house technology operations. In 2012, Walmart expanded its WalmartLabs in Bangalore and hired 100 software developers to become the company's center for creating platforms and products around social and mobile commerce.

While most growth-oriented firms appreciate the need to be innovative, a few firms use it as their fundamental way of relating to their markets. An outstanding example is Polaroid, which heavily promoted each of its new cameras until competitors were able to match its technological innovation; by then, Polaroid normally was prepared to introduce a dramatically new or improved product. For example, it introduced consumers in quick succession to the Swinger, the SX-70, the One Step, and the Sun Camera 660.

Few innovative ideas prove profitable because the research, development, and premarketing costs of converting a promising idea into a profitable product are extremely high. A study by the Booz Allen Hamilton management research department provides some understanding of the risks. As shown in Exhibit 7.7, Booz Allen found that fewer than 2 percent of the innovative projects initially considered by 51 companies eventually reached the marketplace. Specifically, out of every 58 new product ideas, only 12 pass an initial screening test that finds them compatible with the firm's mission and long-term objectives, only 7 remain after an evaluation of their potential, and only 3 survive development attempts. Of the three survivors, two appear to have profit potential after test marketing and only one is commercially successful.

McKinsey Global Institute provides some insight into some of the areas where innovative product successes will appear in Global Strategy in Action, Exhibit 7.8. McKinsey identifies 12 technologies that it forecasts will have significant potential to drive economic impact and disruption by 2025, including mobile Internet, automation of knowledge work, intelligent software systems, and cloud technology.

horizontal acquisition
A grand strategy based on growth through the acquisition of similar firms operating at the same stage of the production-marketing chain.

5. Horizontal Acquisition

When a firm's long-term strategy is based on growth through the acquisition of one or more similar firms operating at the same stage of the production-marketing chain, its grand strategy is called **horizontal acquisition.** Such acquisitions eliminate competitors and provide the acquiring firm with access to new markets. One example is Warner-Lambert's

Global Strategy in Action

Disruptive Technologies: Advances That Will Transform Life, Business, and the Global Economy

According to the McKinsey Global Institute important technologies can come in any field or emerge from any scientific discipline, but they share four characteristics: high rate of technology change, broad potential scope of impact, large economic value that could be affected, and substantial potential for disruptive economic impact. Many technologies have the potential to meet these criteria eventually, but leaders need to focus on technologies with potential impact that is near enough at hand to be meaningfully anticipated and prepared for. Therefore, McKinsey focused on 12 technologies that have significant potential to drive economic impact and disruption by 2025:

1. Mobile Internet: Increasingly inexpensive and capable mobile computing devices and Internet connectivity.

2. Automation of knowledge work: Intelligent software systems that can perform knowledge work tasks involving unstructured commands and subtle judgments.

3. Internet of things: Networks of low-cost sensors and actuators for data collection, monitoring, decision making, and process optimization.

4. Cloud technology: Use of computer hardware and software resources delivered over a network or the Internet, often as a service.

5. Advanced robotics: Increasingly capable robots with enhanced senses, dexterity, and intelligence used to automate tasks or augment humans.

6. Autonomous and near-autonomous vehicles: Vehicles that can navigate and operate with reduced or no human intervention.

7. Next-generation genomics: Fast, low-cost gene sequencing, advanced big data analytics, and synthetic biology ("writing" DNA).

8. Energy storage: Devices or systems that store energy for later use, including batteries.

9. 3D printing: Additive manufacturing techniques to create objects by printing layers of material based on digital models.

10. Advanced materials: Materials designed to have superior characteristics (e.g., strength, weight, conductivity) or functionality.

11. Advanced oil and gas exploration and recovery: Exploration and recovery techniques that make extraction of unconventional oil and gas economical.

12. Renewable energy: Generation of electricity from renewable sources with reduced harmful climate impact.

Source: Excerpted from "Disruptive technologies: Advances That Will Transform Life, Business, and the Global Economy." *McKinsey Global Institute*, May 2013, pp. 1–4.

---

acquisition of Parke Davis, which reduced competition in the ethical drugs field for Chilcott Laboratories, a firm that Warner-Lambert previously had acquired. Another example is the long-range acquisition pattern of White Consolidated Industries, which expanded in the refrigerator and freezer market through a grand strategy of horizontal acquisition, by acquiring Kelvinator Appliance, the Refrigerator Products Division of Bendix Westinghouse Automotive Air Brake, and Frigidaire Appliance from General Motors. Nike's acquisition in the dress shoes business and N. V. Homes's purchase of Ryan Homes have vividly exemplified the success that horizontal acquisition strategies can bring.

The attractions of a horizontal acquisition strategy are many and varied.[10] However every benefit provides the parent firm with critical resources that it needs to improve overall profitability. For example, the acquiring firm that uses a horizontal acquisition can quickly expand its operations geographically, increase its market share, improve its production capabilities and economies of scale, gain control of knowledge-based resources, broaden its product line, and increase its efficient use of capital. An added attraction of horizontal acquisition is that these benefits are achieved with only moderately increased risk, because the success of the expansion is principally dependent on proven abilities.

[10]This section was drawn from John A. Pearce II and D. Keith Robbins, "Strategic Transformation as the Essential Last Step in the Process of Business Turnaround," *Business Horizons* 50, no. 5 (2008).

A horizontal acquisition can provide the firm with an opportunity to offer its customers a broader product line. This motivation has sparked a series of acquisitions in the security software industry. Because Entrust purchased Business Signatures, the consolidated company is able to offer banks a full suite of antifraud products. Similarly, Verisign's acquisitions of m-Qube and Snapcentric enabled Verisign to expand its cross-marketing options by offering password-generating software, transaction monitoring software, and identity protection. RSA Security's horizontal acquisitions started with the purchase of PassMark, which reduced competitors in the authentication software space. RSA Security then acquired Cyota to provide its customers with both transaction monitoring and authentication software. As a final example, Symantec bought both Veritas Software and WholeSecurity to provide its customers of storage with additional features, such as antivirus software.

The motivation to gain market share has prompted the financial industry to feature horizontal merger strategies. The acquisition of First Coastal Bank by Citizens Business Bank provided new bases of operation in Los Angeles and Manhattan for Citizens Business Bank. The merger of Raincross Credit Union with Visterra Credit Union enabled these credit unions to achieve the size to justify the expansion of services their customers were demanding.

In a deal that created a dominant supplier of computer disk drives, Western Digital Corp. purchased Hitachi Ltd.'s disk-drive business for $4.3 billion in 2011. The transaction reduced the number of hard drive makers to four giants. Western Digital's share of global shipments after adding Hitachi's operations became nearly 50 percent, compared with about 30 percent for No. 2, Seagate Technology PLC. Because Hitachi was the industry's price aggressor, the merger greatly reduced the cutthroat price cutting that characterized the industry's rivalry.

For example, Trauson Holdings Co. paid Stryker Corp. $764 million in cash in 2013 in a horizontal acquisition to acquire the Chinese maker of orthopedic implants. Orthopedic implant sales in China were projected to double to $2.7 billion by 2015.[11] As reported by *Bloomberg.com*, profit before taxes at Trauson, the nation's largest maker of pelvic reconstruction plates and other products used in trauma surgery, more than tripled to 182 million yuan ($29 million) from 2008 through 2011. Its gross margins were estimated to be in the high 60 percent range. Kalamazoo, Michigan–based Stryker paid 33 times Changzhou, China–based Trauson's 2011 net income, about half the median of six comparable deals globally in the past six years, according to data compiled by *Bloomberg*. Stryker was attracted by Trauson's low production costs in China and its network of more than 663 distributors covering 3,840 Chinese hospitals.

Strategy in Action, Exhibit 7.9, provides a great example of a successful horizontal acquisition. Tyco International merged its flow control unit with Pentair Inc. in 2012, creating a new powerhouse in the business of industrial pumps and valves. The combined company had 30,000 employees and became the clear leader in a very fragmented industry.

An example of an efficiency-driven merger is one between Constellation and FPL, which saves between $1.5 and $2.1 billion by eliminating overlapping operations. Another example is the acquisition of Green Mountain Power by Gaz Metro, a subsidiary of Northern New England Energy Power for $187 million. The merger was prompted by Green Mountain Power's expiring supplier contracts that threatened it with high costs of going to suppliers who were out of its geographic region—but within the region of Gaz Metro. The horizontal acquisition enabled Green Mountain Power to avail itself of Gaz Metro's suppliers.

Deutsche Telekom's growth strategy was horizontal acquisition. Deutsche Telekom was a dominant player in the European wireless services market, but without a presence in the fast-growing U.S. market. To correct this limitation, Deutsche Telekom horizontally integrated by purchasing the American firm VoiceStream Wireless, a company that was

[11]Kim McLaughlin, and Michelle Fay Cortez. January 18, 2013. "Trauson Jumps by Record after $764 Million Stryker Offer." *Bloomberg. com*.

Tyco Merges Flow Unit with Pentair in All-Stock Deal

Tyco International merged its flow control unit with Pentair Inc. in an all-stock deal in 2012, creating a new powerhouse in the business of industrial pumps and valves. Under the terms of the merger, Tyco spun off its flow business as an independent company. Pentair then immediately merged with the new stand-alone entity, in a deal that gave Tyco shareholders 52.5 percent of the company and Pentair investors the remainder. Pentair also assumed $275 million in debt of the flow business. The transaction valued Tyco Flow Control at $4.9 billion. Pentair has a market value of about $4 billion. The combined corporation kept the Pentair name, and was led by Pentair's chief executive, Randall J. Hogan. It retained the Pentair board, though it added two directors named by Tyco. Pentair kept its main headquarters in Switzerland, where Tyco is based, with its American offices in Minnesota. The new company has 30,000 employees, with half coming from each of its parents, and is the clear number one leader in a very fragmented industry.

Source: Michael De La Merced. March 28, 2012. "Tyco to Merge Flow Unit with Pentair in All-Stock Deal." *Deal Book.*

growing faster than most domestic rivals and that owned spectrum licenses providing access to 220 million potential customers.

Finally, through a horizontal acquisition designed to take advantage of the multiple strengths of the grand strategy, Aon acquired its top rival Benfield. The new company, Aon Benfield, became a world leader in reinsurance brokerage and benefited from significant cost reductions, increased efficiencies, and stronger presence in the reinsurance market.

6. Vertical Acquisition

vertical acquisition
A grand strategy based on the acquisition of firms that supply the acquiring firm with inputs or new customers for its outputs.

When a firm's grand strategy is to acquire firms that supply it with inputs (such as raw materials) or are customers for its outputs (such as warehousers for finished products), **vertical acquisition** is involved. To illustrate, if a shirt manufacturer acquires a textile producer—by purchasing its common stock, buying its assets, or exchanging ownership interests—the strategy is vertical acquisition. In this case, it is *backward* vertical integration, because the acquired firm operates at an earlier stage of the production-marketing process. If the shirt manufacturer had merged with a clothing store, it would have been *forward* vertical acquisition—the acquisition of a firm nearer to the ultimate consumer.

Amoco emerged as North America's leader in natural gas reserves and products as a result of its acquisition of Dome Petroleum. This backward acquisition by Amoco was made in support of its downstream businesses in refining and in gas stations, whose profits made the acquisition possible.

The principal attractions of a horizontal acquisition grand strategy are readily apparent. The acquiring firm is able to greatly expand its operations, thereby achieving greater market share, improving economies of scale, and increasing the efficiency of capital use. In addition, these benefits are achieved with only moderately increased risk, because the success of the expansion is principally dependent on proven abilities.

The reasons for choosing a vertical acquisition grand strategy are more varied and sometimes less obvious. The main reason for backward acquisition is the desire to increase the dependability of the supply or quality of the raw materials used as production inputs. That desire is particularly great when the number of suppliers is small and the number of competitors is large. In this situation, the vertically integrating firm can better control its costs and, thereby, improve the profit margin of the expanded production-marketing system. Forward acquisition is a preferred grand strategy if great advantages accrue to stable production. A firm can increase the predictability of demand for its output

Henry Schein Completes Three Acquisitions to Advance Strategic Plan

Henry Schein, Inc., the world's largest provider of health care products and services to office-based dental, medical, and animal health practitioners, completed three acquisitions that advanced key priorities of the company's 2012–2014 strategic plans. Together these acquisitions represented annual sales of approximately $61 million and were neutral to the company's 2012 diluted EPS.

Henry Schein enhanced its position in the dental specialty market through the acquisition of Ortho Technology, Inc., a $24 million orthodontics business. It furthered its strategy of helping medical practitioners operate more efficient and profitable practices by strengthening its U.S. physician office laboratory presence through the acquisition of Modern Laboratory Services, a $22 million medical distributor. Finally, it expanded its geographic footprint in Asia through a merger with Accord, a $15 million full-service dental dealer in Thailand, the 26th country in which Henry Schein had operations or affiliates.

"The addition of Ortho Technology, Modern Laboratory Services and Accord furthers our strategic priority of global growth in important market segments and new geographies," said Stanley M. Bergman, chairman and chief executive officer of Henry Schein.

ORTHO TECHNOLOGY

Ortho Technology, Inc. was a distributor of orthodontics products primarily to orthodontists. The company is based in Tampa, Florida, was founded in 1991, had approximately 90 team members and posted 2011 sales of approximately $24 million. Ortho Technology offered a complete line of orthodontic supplies, including brackets, bands, buccal tubes, archwires, adhesives, laboratory supplies, and patient accessories. The company served more than 10,000 customers worldwide via direct sales from the United States and distributors across the globe.

"Specialty dental markets including orthodontics are important components of our growth strategy. In December 2008 we acquired Ortho Organizers and with this transaction we are further penetrating the $1.25 billion global orthodontics market with a company that has been gaining market share for several years," said Mr. Bergman.

"We envision multiple synergies between these two organizations, including leveraging Ortho Organizers'

manufacturing of certain key products and Ortho Technology's aesthetic brackets and its best-in-class direct marketing expertise," added Mr. Bergman.

MODERN LABORATORY SERVICES

Based in Bakersfield, California, and founded in 1984, MLS was one of the leading distributors in the western United States for products and services for physician office laboratories, such as laboratory equipment and supplies. MLS represented many of the most important suppliers in the clinical laboratory business including serving as the exclusive distributor for the Siemens' Dimension® chemistry analyzer product line.

With 2011 sales of approximately $22 million, MLS served approximately 700 customers through 36 team members. "The acquisition of MLS reflects Henry Schein's continued commitment to physicians and the clinical laboratory market, and strengthens our position in the West Coast, which is an area of exciting growth for us," said Mr. Bergman. "This transaction advances our goal of gaining market share and adding knowledgeable management through strategic acquisitions within important business areas."

ACCORD

Based in Bangkok, Accord recorded 2011 sales of approximately $15 million. Founded in 1976, Accord has approximately 115 team members, including 45 sales representatives, and more than 5,000 customers, including private office-based dental practitioners, public and private hospitals, dental schools, and public health authorities. Henry Schein acquired 75 percent of Accord. The Accord founder's family retained the remaining 25 percent of the company.

"Thailand, with an estimated market size of more than $100 million, is the fifth largest dental market in Asia. In addition to establishing our presence in that important market, Accord also will serve as an anchor for further expansion into Southeast Asia, which represents an incremental $150 million market opportunity," said Mr. Bergman.

Source: Excerpted from "Henry Schein Completes Three Acquisitions to Advance Strategic Plan." July 17, 2012. *PR Newswire*, New York.

through forward acquisition; that is, through ownership of the next stage of its production-marketing chain.

Global Strategy in Action, Exhibit 7.10 provides a detailed example of a vertical merger. In 2012, Henry Schein, Inc., the world's largest provider of health care products and services to office-based dental, medical, and animal health practitioners, completed three acquisitions that advanced key priorities of the company's 2012–2014 strategic plan. Henry Schein enhanced its position in the dental specialty market through the acquisition of Ortho Technology, Inc., a orthodontics business; furthered its strategy of strengthening its U.S. physician office laboratory presence through the acquisition of Modern Laboratory Services, a medical distributor; and expanded its geographic footprint in Asia through a merger with Accord, a full-service dental dealer in Thailand.

Some increased risks are associated with both types of acquisition. For horizontally acquired firms, the risks stem from increased commitment to one type of business. For vertically acquired firms, the risks result from the firm's expansion into areas requiring strategic managers to broaden the base of their competencies and to assume additional responsibilities.

7. Concentric Diversification

concentric diversification
A grand strategy that involves the operation of a second business that benefits from access to the first firm's core competencies.

Concentric diversification involves the acquisition of businesses that are related to the acquiring firm in terms of technology, markets, or products. With this grand strategy, the selected new businesses possess a high degree of compatibility with the firm's current businesses. The ideal concentric diversification occurs when the combined company profits increase the strengths and opportunities and decrease the weaknesses and exposure to risk. Thus, the acquiring firm searches for new businesses whose products, markets, distribution channels, technologies, and resource requirements are similar to but not identical with its own, whose acquisition results in synergies but not complete interdependence.

Abbott Laboratories pursues an aggressive concentric growth strategy. Abbott seeks to acquire a wide range of businesses that have some important connection to its basic business. In recent years, this strategy has led the company to acquire pharmaceuticals, a diagnostic business, and a medical device manufacturer.

Under Armour is another firm that bases its grand strategy on concentric diversification. As discussed in Global Strategy in Action, Exhibit 7.11, Under Armour jumped into the heavily contested field of fitness monitoring in 2013 with its Armour39 system. The Under Armour brand was synonymous with exercise clothing, so the addition of monitoring devices represented a marked departure but one that was clearly related to its core business.

8. Conglomerate Diversification

conglomerate diversification
A grand strategy that involves the acquisition of a business because it presents the most promising investment opportunity available.

Occasionally a firm, particularly a very large one, plans to acquire a business because it represents the most promising investment opportunity available. This grand strategy is commonly known as **conglomerate diversification.** The principal concern, and often the sole concern, of the acquiring firm is the profit pattern of the venture. Unlike concentric diversification, conglomerate diversification gives little concern to creating product-market synergy with existing businesses. What such conglomerate diversifiers as ITT, Textron, American Brands, Litton, U.S. Industries, Fuqua, and I. C. Industries seek is financial synergy. For example, they may seek a balance in their portfolios between current businesses with cyclical sales and acquired businesses with countercyclical sales, between high-cash/low-opportunity and low-cash/high-opportunity businesses, or between debt-free and highly leveraged businesses.

Global Strategy in Action

Exhibit 7.11

Under Armour Unveils Its Nike FuelBand-killer

Under Armour jumped into the heavily contested field of fitness monitoring in 2013 with its Armour39 system. Armour39 consisted of a sensor-equipped strap worn around the chest (or right below it); it included a center sleeve for a "bug," which acts as a computer in storing and moving fitness data to the cloud via Bluetooth. Users could check their progress on a watch or by way of an app on the smartphone. The system consisted of a strap and bug for $149.99, and an optional watch accessory for $199.99. In moving into this field, the sports apparel manufacturer took on large companies such as Nike and its FuelBand, as well as established fitness monitoring players such as FitBit and JawBone.

The market for fitness-monitoring devices exploded in 2012 with a number of companies linking small motion sensors to smartphones and Web sites, allowing users to get a more complete picture of their workout regimen and progress. Companies also added a social element, allowing people to compete and share their workout stats.

Armour39, which is named for the style number for Under Armour's first white undershirt, measures heart rate, calories burned, and intensity, and comes up with a combined score that quantifies how hard and intense the session can be. Under Armour started with an iOS app linked to Armour39, but with no Android app available. Nike had a similar competitive stance, having dropped its planned support of Android, potentially ignoring a huge market of potential users.

For Nike and Under Armour, these devices represent a marked departure from their core business. Neither were known as hardware companies, and Nike had to prove itself with the FuelBand, which generally got strong reviews for its design and features. While Under Armour had a lot of momentum behind it, the company still had an uphill climb in its attempt to breach the already crowded fitness-monitoring market.

Source: Excerpted from Roger Cheng. February 12, 2013. "Under Armour Unveils Its Nike FuelBand-killer. *CNet News*.

A good example of the use of conglomerate diversification as a grand strategy is provided in Strategy in Action, Exhibit 7.12. In 2013, Warren Buffett's Berkshire Hathaway Inc. and 3G Capital teamed up to buy ketchup maker H.J. Heinz Co. The deal represented a rare partnership for Berkshire, which has traditionally worked alone to acquire leading companies in a number of industries, including automobile insurer Geico, paint maker Benjamin Moore, underwear company Fruit of the Loom, and Dairy Queen stores.

The principal difference between the two types of diversification is that concentric diversification emphasizes some commonality in markets, products, or technology, whereas conglomerate diversification is based principally on profit considerations.

Several of the grand strategies discussed above, including concentric and conglomerate diversification and horizontal and vertical acquisition, often involve the purchase or acquisition of one firm by another.

Motivation for Diversification

Grand strategies involving either concentric or conglomerate diversification represent distinctive departures from a firm's existing base of operations, typically the acquisition or internal generation (spin-off) of a separate business with synergistic possibilities counterbalancing the strengths and weaknesses of the two businesses. For example, Head Ski sought to diversify into summer sporting goods and clothing to offset the seasonality of its "snow" business. Additionally, diversifications occasionally are undertaken as unrelated investments, because of their high profit potential and their otherwise minimal resource demands.

Regardless of the approach taken, the motivations of the acquiring firms are the same:

- Increase the firm's stock value. In the past, mergers often have led to increases in the stock price or the price-earnings ratio.
- Increase the growth rate of the firm.

220

Berkshire, 3G Capital Buying Heinz for $23B

Warren Buffett's Berkshire Hathaway Inc. and 3G Capital teamed up to buy ketchup maker H.J. Heinz Co. in a $23 billion deal, one of the largest-ever acquisitions in the food industry. The deal represented a rare partnership for Mr. Buffett, who has used Berkshire's vast resources in the past to acquire top brands across a range of industries without teaming up with others. Mr. Buffett said that Berkshire was providing about $12 billion to $13 billion in cash for the deal, but that 3G—a Brazilian investment firm that took over Burger King in 2010—would be "in charge of things."

Including debt, the $28 billion deal would rank as the largest-ever takeover for a pure food company, topping the 2000 acquisition of Bestfoods for $23.2 billion by consumer-brand conglomerate Unilever NV. That deal brought brands such as Lipton tea, Knorr Soups, and Lever soaps under the Unilever umbrella.

While the partnership with 3G is unusual, the Heinz deal is in other ways a typical one for Mr. Buffett and Berkshire. Mr. Buffett has said he values powerful brands and strong management, and in the statement he praised Heinz for its "strong, sustainable growth potential based on high quality standards, continuous innovation, excellent management, and great tasting products."

Berkshire already owns car insurer Geico, paint-maker Benjamin Moore, underwear company Fruit of the Loom, and the Dairy Queen stores, among other brands. In Heinz, he will get a stake in a packaged-foods company known for its iconic ketchup brand, albeit one that is now battling weaker North American sales. The deal is the largest for Berkshire since Mr. Buffett agreed to acquire railroad Burlington Northern Santa Fe for more than $25 billion in 2009.

Source: Excerpted from Erik Holm and Lauren Pollock. February 14, 2013. "Berkshire, 3G Capital Buying Heinz for $23B." *LBO Wire*, Dow Jones & Company, Inc.

- Make an investment that represents better use of funds than plowing them into internal growth.
- Improve the stability of earnings and sales by acquiring firms whose earnings and sales complement the firm's peaks and valleys.
- Balance or fill out the product line.
- Diversify the product line when the life cycle of current products has peaked.
- Acquire a needed resource quickly (e.g., high-quality technology or highly innovative management).
- Achieve tax savings by purchasing a firm whose tax losses will offset current or future earnings.
- Increase efficiency and profitability, especially if there is synergy between the acquiring firm and the acquired firm.[12]

9. Turnaround

For any one of a large number of reasons, a firm can find itself with declining profits. Among these reasons are economic recessions, production inefficiencies, and innovative breakthroughs by competitors. In many cases, strategic managers believe that such a firm can survive and eventually recover if a concerted effort is made over a period of a few years to fortify its distinctive competencies. This grand strategy is known as **turnaround**. It typically is begun through one of two forms of retrenchment, employed singly or in combination:

turnaround
A grand strategy of cost reduction and asset reduction by a company to survive and recover from declining profits.

1. *Cost reduction.* Examples include decreasing the workforce through employee attrition, leasing rather than purchasing equipment, extending the life of machinery, eliminating

[12]Godfrey Devlin and Mark Bleackley, "Strategic Alliances—Guidelines for Success," *Long Range Planning,* October 1988, pp. 18–23.

221

elaborate promotional activities, laying off employees, dropping items from a production line, and discontinuing low-margin customers.

In 2009, electronics giant Sony took major steps to reduce staff and supply chain costs. It reduced its reliance on a high-priced, high-tech approach in favor of more popular low-cost items. Consequently, Sony reduced the number of its suppliers by 50 percent to cut costs, and laid off 8,000 of its 186,000 employees.

2. *Asset reduction.* Examples include the sale of land, buildings, and equipment not essential to the basic activity of the firm and the elimination of "perks," such as the company airplane and executives' cars.

Alcoa, one of the world's largest aluminum makers, sold several unprofitable business lines in 2009 and stopped all "noncritical" capital investment programs to try to conserve cash in response to the continuing economic downturn that followed the recession of 2007–2009. Alcoa reduced output by 18 percent and cut its head count by 13 percent, or 13,500 employees. Facing a steep decline in demand for its fabricated goods, Alcoa believed that the moves were necessary for the firm to try to conserve cash and reduce costs. Alcoa also froze all hiring and salaries for one year.

Interestingly, the turnaround most commonly associated with this approach is in management positions. In a study of 58 large firms, researchers found that turnaround almost always was associated with changes in top management.[13] Bringing in new managers was believed to introduce needed new perspectives on the firm's situation, to raise employee morale, and to facilitate drastic actions, such as deep budgetary cuts in established programs.

Strategic management research provides evidence that the firms that have used a *turnaround strategy* have successfully confronted decline. The research findings have been assimilated and used as the building blocks for a model of the turnaround process shown in Exhibit 7.13, Strategy in Action.

The model begins with a depiction of external and internal factors as causes of a firm's performance downturn. When these factors continue to detrimentally impact the firm, its financial health is threatened. Unchecked decline places the firm in a turnaround situation.

A *turnaround situation* represents absolute and relative-to-industry declining performance of a sufficient magnitude to warrant explicit turnaround actions. Turnaround situations may be the result of years of gradual slowdown or months of sharp decline. In either case, the recovery phase of the turnaround process is likely to be more successful in accomplishing turnaround when it is preceded by planned retrenchment that results in the achievement of near-term financial stabilization. For a declining firm, stabilizing operations and restoring profitability almost always entail strict cost reduction followed by a shrinking back to those segments of the business that have the best prospects of attractive profit margins. The need for retrenchment often arises when companies face an economic recession. The United States has experienced 12 economic recessions since the end of WWII in 1945. During this period, the average business cycle was 70 months or roughly one full cycle every 5.8 years. The average expansion period has been 59 months, and the average recession has been 11 months. However, statistical patterns often fail to provide useful guidance in predicting the specifics of a recession.

---

[13]D. Schendel, R. Patton, and J. Riggs, "Corporate Turnaround Strategies: A Study of Profit Decline and Recovery," *Journal of General Management* 3, no. 3 (1976), pp. 3–11.

A Model of the Turnaround Process

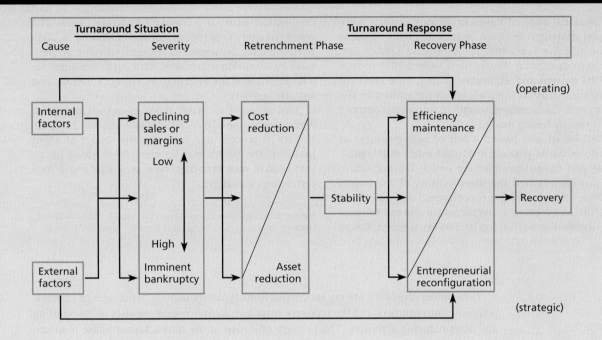

Turnaround Situation		Turnaround Response	
Cause	Severity	Retrenchment Phase	Recovery Phase

For example, economists failed to predict the "great recession" of 2007–2009, which resulted in massive layoffs and high levels of unemployment. Roughly 8.5 million jobs were lost during the recession, and it is predicted that these jobs might not fully return until 2018. In addition, from 2007 to 2009 the rate at which new business establishments were started fell 13.3 percent.

During the 2007–2009 recession, pretax corporate profits fell for three consecutive years. In 2006, pretax corporate profits, with inventory valuation and capital consumption adjustments, reached an all-time high of $1.6083 trillion. However, these corporate profits dropped to $1.5106 trillion in 2007, $1.2628 trillion in 2008, and $1.258 trillion in 2009. By the end of 2009, pretax corporate profits were 27 percent lower than the 2006 high.

Managers benefit from understanding the factors that foreshadow an economic downturn. Companies that are able to understand the economic uncertainties facing their industry and make timely adjustments to their company will outperform their competitors.

The immediacy of the resulting threat to company survival posed by the turnaround situation is known as *situation severity*. Severity is the governing factor in estimating the speed with which the retrenchment response will be formulated and activated. When severity is low, a firm has some financial cushion. Stability may be achieved through cost retrenchment alone. When turnaround situation severity is high, a firm must immediately stabilize the decline or bankruptcy is imminent. Cost reductions must be supplemented with more drastic asset reduction measures. Assets targeted for divestiture are those determined to be underproductive. In contrast, more productive resources are protected from cuts and represent critical elements of the future core business plan of the company (i.e., the intended recovery response).

National Bank Diversifies in New Turnaround Strategy

The National Bank of Kenya undertook a major turn-around strategy with hopes of attaining tier one status in the next five years. NBK plans included a major cash call from its existing shareholders by mid-2013 to support its growth and expansion strategy scheduled for completion in 2017. The plan, which was crafted by the bank's new management, sought to restore its foothold on its rapidly fading market share.

NBK board also passed a raft of new measures to transform the 44-year-old institution into a highly profitable and competitive banking entity. The restructuring process included the diversification of the bank's balance, which has highly concentrated on retail banking. NBK also created a new corporate and institutional banking division to rival top lenders like Barclays, Kenya Commercial Bank, and Standard Chartered Bank. The move reduced its reliance on consumer lending. In addition, the bank revamped its customized value prepositions by venturing into Islamic banking in the quest for a larger share of the debt market, currency trading, and custody business.

NBK planned to invest more in branch expansion with plans to open 10–15 additional outlets in 2013, automate its process, and fast-track the rollout of agent banking. The bank's management then scaled up investment in new branches, new products, and a new technological platform.

Source: Excerpted from James Anyanzwa. April 2, 2013. "National Bank Diversifies in New Turnaround Strategy." *Standard Digital.*

Turnaround responses among successful firms typically include two stages of strategic activities: retrenchment and the recovery response. *Retrenchment* consists of cost-cutting and asset-reducing activities. The primary objective of the retrenchment phase is to stabilize the firm's financial condition. Situation severity has been associated with retrenchment responses among successful turnaround firms. Firms in danger of bankruptcy or failure (i.e., severe situations) attempt to halt decline through cost and asset reductions. Firms in less severe situations have achieved stability merely through cost retrenchment. However, in either case, for firms facing declining financial performance, the key to successful turnaround rests in the effective and efficient management of the retrenchment process.

The primary causes of the turnaround situation have been associated with the second phase of the turnaround process, the *recovery response*. During the first year of the 2007–2009 recession, many firms retrenched sharply to avoid financial failure. For firms that declined primarily as a result of external problems, turnaround most often has been achieved through creative new entrepreneurial strategies. For firms that declined primarily as a result of internal problems, turnaround has been most frequently achieved through efficiency strategies. *Recovery* is achieved when economic measures indicate that the firm has regained its predownturn levels of performance.

Global Strategy in Action, Exhibit 7.14 provides an example of a company's plan to implement a grand strategy of turnaround. The National Bank of Kenya's plans included a major cash call to support its growth and expansion scheduled for completion in 2017. Its restructuring process included the diversification of the bank's balance, the creation of a corporate and institutional banking division, reduced reliance on consumer lending, inclusion of Islamic banking, and branch expansion.

divestiture strategy
A grand strategy that involves the sale of a firm or a major unit of a firm as a going concern.

10. Divestiture

A **divestiture strategy** involves the sale of a firm or a major component of a firm. Sara Lee Corp. provides a good example. It sells everything from Wonderbras and Kiwi shoe polish to Endust furniture polish and Chock Full o' Nuts coffee. The company used a conglomerate diversification strategy to build Sara Lee into a huge portfolio of disparate brands. A new president, C. Steven McMillan, faced stagnant revenues and earnings. So he consolidated, streamlined, and focused the company on its core categories—food, underwear, and household products. He divested 15 businesses, including Coach leather goods, which together equaled more than 20 percent of the company's revenue, and laid off 13,200 employees, nearly 10 percent of the workforce. McMillan used the cash from asset sales to snap up brands that enhanced Sara Lee's clout in key categories, like the $2.8 billion purchase of St. Louis–based breadmaker Earthgrains Co. to quadruple Sara Lee's bakery operations. In another case of divestitures, Kraft Foods found that it could improve its overall operations by selling some of its best-known brands, including Cream of Wheat.

When retrenchment fails to accomplish the desired turnaround, or when a nonintegrated business activity achieves an unusually high market value, strategic managers often decide to sell the firm. However, because the intent is to find a buyer willing to pay a premium above the value of a going concern's fixed assets, the term *marketing for sale* is often more appropriate. Prospective buyers must be convinced that because of their skills and resources or because of the firm's synergy with their existing businesses, they will be able to profit from the acquisition.

The reasons for divestiture vary. They often arise because of partial mismatches between the acquired firm and the parent corporation. Some of the mismatched parts cannot be integrated into the corporation's mainstream activities and, thus, must be spun off. A second reason is corporate financial needs. Sometimes the cash flow or financial stability of the corporation as a whole can be greatly improved if businesses with high market value can be sacrificed. The result can be a balancing of equity with long-term risks or of long-term debt payments to optimize the cost of capital. A third, less frequent reason for divestiture is government antitrust action when a firm is believed to monopolize or unfairly dominate a particular market.

Although examples of the divestiture grand strategy are numerous, CBS Inc. provides an outstanding example. In a two-year period, the once diverse entertainment and publishing giant sold its Records Division to Sony, its magazine publishing business to Diamandis Communications, its book publishing operations to Harcourt Brace Jovanovich, and its music publishing operations to SBK Entertainment World. Other firms that have pursued this type of grand strategy include Esmark, which divested Swift & Company, and White Motors, which divested White Farm.

Many times, the reason for a divestiture is profit taking, the ability to cash in on a successful investment. This was the case when OM Group, Inc. divested its Advanced Materials business, including the sale of its downstream business, to a joint venture held by Freeport-McMoRan Copper & Gold Inc., Lundin Mining Corporation, and La Generale des Carrieres et des Mines.[14] OM Group received cash consideration of $325 million, plus approximately $30 million for cash retained in the business, upon the closing of the transaction. The sale agreements also provided for potential future cash consideration of up to an additional $110 million based on the business achieving certain revenue targets over a period of three years.

Global Strategy in Action, Exhibit 7.15 provides a final example of successful divestiture. In 2013, Dow Chemical Co. was accelerating its divestiture of noncore businesses. The company planned to shut 20 facilities and eliminate 2,400 jobs in Europe, the United States, and Japan. It was also trimming capital expenditure as part of efforts to boost cost savings. Dow's actions were evidence of its rigorous focus on return on capital and were squarely in line with its public commitments.

---

[14]This example was excerpted from "OM Group Inc. Completes Divestiture of Its Cobalt Business for $325 Million in Cash." March 29, 2013. *Yahoo Finance.*

Dow Chemical Divestitures

Dow Chemical Co. was accelerating its divestiture of non-core businesses in 2013 and was targeting nearly $1.5 billion of proceeds by mid-2014. The world's second-largest chemical producer by revenue planned to shut 20 facilities and eliminate 2,400 jobs in Europe, the United States, and Japan. It was also trimming capital expenditure as part of efforts to boost cost savings to $2.5 billion from a target that had already been doubled to $1.5 billion over 2012. Dow had divested noncore businesses representing about $8 billion in revenue since 2009.

Dow's actions were evidence of its rigorous focus on return on capital, and were squarely in line with its public commitments. In general, chemical makers were wrestling with the impact of destocking as well as weak construction and electronics markets. Dow executives had been bearish on China in the second half of 2012, but saw signs of improvement and switched attention back to the weak economic outlook for Europe, where Dow's revenue fell in 2012.

Source: This example was excerpted from Melodie Warner. March 14, 2013. "Dow Accelerates Noncore Business Divestitures." *Downstream Today.*

11. Liquidation

liquidation

A grand strategy that involves the sale of the assets of the business for their salvage value.

When **liquidation** is the grand strategy, the firm typically is sold in parts, only occasionally as a whole—but for its tangible asset value and not as a going concern. In selecting liquidation, the owners and strategic managers of a firm are admitting failure and recognize that this action is likely to result in great hardships to themselves and their employees. For these reasons, liquidation usually is seen as the least attractive of the grand strategies. As a long-term strategy, however, it minimizes the losses of all the firm's stockholders. Faced with bankruptcy, the liquidating firm usually tries to develop a planned and orderly system that will result in the greatest possible return and cash conversion as the firm slowly relinquishes its market share. Planned liquidation can be worthwhile. For example, Columbia Corporation, a $130 million diversified firm, liquidated its assets for more cash per share than the market value of its stock. Similarly, a federal bankruptcy judge finalized the liquidation of Hostess Brands in November 2012 after 82 years in business.[15] This followed a failed attempt to mediate a dispute between the company and its bakery workers' union over wage and benefit cuts imposed through bankruptcy court. With the Teamsters union membership of bakers overwhelmingly opposed to the concessions agreed to by other Hostess employees, the bakers walked off the job on November 9, 2012. Hostess filed for liquidation a week later, resulting in the judicial decision to accept Hostess' liquidation request.

More commonly, liquidation is the companion to Chapter 7 bankruptcy. For example, in 2011 the bankrupt Robb & Stucky furniture chain started a court-ordered liquidation sale of all inventory just hours after being bought in court by an investment fund that specializes in winding down bankrupt stores. Like most retail shutdowns, the sale followed the pattern of escalating discounts until all inventory, store fixtures, and equipment were sold. The sale of $90 million in inventory ended 96 years in business for the Florida-based upscale furniture seller. After the liquidation sale, all 20 Robb & Stucky stores were closed. The corporation filed bankruptcy following a rapid expansion of new stores into Nevada and Texas that suffered some of the worst of a housing downturn, with resulting massive losses for the furniture retailer.

As discussed in Strategy in Action, Exhibit 7.16, large competitors are not immune from the risk of liquidation. In 2013, a federal bankruptcy judge approved the multiyear liquidation plan for Dewey & LeBoeuf, a law firm that had employed more than 1,000

[15]James O'Toole. November 29, 2012. "Judge OKs Bonuses for Execs in Hostess Liquidation." *CNN Money.*

Largest Law Firm in the United States Files for Liquidation

A federal bankruptcy judge approved the liquidation plan for Dewey & LeBoeuf in 2013, a milestone in the winding down of the collapsed law firm that paved the way for creditors to recover tens of millions of dollars. Dewey & LeBoeuf, which once employed more than 1,000 lawyers in 26 offices worldwide, in 2012 became the largest U.S. law firm to file for bankruptcy. Its demise was largely attributed to compensation guarantees the firm's leaders made to many partners.

Under the bankruptcy plan, more than 450 former partners agreed to pay the estate at least $71.5 million in exchange for a release from potential litigation. Those funds went to satisfy secured lenders such as JPMorgan Chase & Co., which had a total of $262 million in claims against Dewey, and an unknown amount from unsecured creditors. One unsecured creditor, the

Pension Benefit Guarantee Corp., had a $120 million claim. The estate potentially could also collect money from the firm's $50 million management liability insurance policy, which covered the actions of Dewey's former leaders.

Secured lenders received 80 percent of the initial $67.5 million the estate collected from partners, while unsecured creditors, which included landlord Paramount Group and Thomson Reuters Corp. for legal research, received 20 percent of that amount, according to the plan. Any payments by partners to the settlement after the $67.5 million mark was met were to be split between secured and unsecured creditors.

Source: This example was excerpted from Casey Sullivan (of Reuters). February 27, 2013. "Judge Approves Dewey & LeBoeuf Liquidation Plan." *Yahoo News*.

lawyers in 26 offices worldwide. Under the bankruptcy plan, more than 450 former partners agreed to pay the estate at least $71.5 million. Those funds went to satisfy lenders such as JPMorgan Chase & Co, the Pension Benefit Guarantee Corp., Paramount Group, and Thomson Reuters Corp.

12. Bankruptcy

bankruptcy
When a company is unable to pay its debts as they become due.

Business failures are playing an increasingly important role in the American economy. In an average week, more than 300 companies fail and file for **bankruptcy.** More than 75 percent of these financially desperate firms file for a *liquidation bankruptcy*—they agree to a complete distribution of their assets to creditors, most of whom receive a small fraction of the amount they are owed. Liquidation is what the layperson views as bankruptcy: the business cannot pay its debts, so it must close its doors. Investors lose their money, employees lose their jobs, and managers lose their credibility. In owner-managed firms, company and personal bankruptcy commonly go hand in hand.

The other 25 percent of these firms refuse to surrender until one final option is exhausted. Choosing a strategy to recapture its viability, such a company asks the courts for a *reorganization bankruptcy*. The firm attempts to persuade its creditors to temporarily freeze their claims while it undertakes to reorganize and rebuild the company's operations more profitably. The appeal of a reorganization bankruptcy is based on the company's ability to convince creditors that it can succeed in the marketplace by implementing a new strategic plan, and that when the plan produces profits, the firm will be able to repay its creditors, perhaps in full. In other words, the company offers its creditors a carefully designed alternative to forcing an immediate, but fractional, repayment of its financial obligations. The option of reorganization bankruptcy offers maximum repayment of debt at some specified future time if a new strategic plan is successful.

Strategy in Action, Exhibit 7.17 provides a good example of bankruptcy used as a grand strategy to revive a financially endangered company. RG Steel LLC, the fourth-biggest U.S. flat-rolled steelmaker, sought bankruptcy protection. The company listed assets and

RG Steel Seeks Bankruptcy Protection

RG Steel LLC, the fourth-biggest U.S. flat-rolled steel-maker, sought bankruptcy protection in May 2012. The company notified employees and the United Steelworkers union, which represents 88 percent of RG Steel's 4,000 employees, that it would start firing workers in one week as the final steelmaking orders were completed.

RG Steel, based in Sparrows Point, Maryland, listed assets and debts of more than $1 billion each in Chapter 11 documents filed in U.S. Bankruptcy Court in Wilmington, Delaware. Seven affiliates also sought protection from creditors, including WP Steel Venture LLC.

Renco Group Inc. bought the three-plant steelmaker from Russia's OAO Severstal in 2011 for $1.2 billion, less than three years after Severstal acquired it for $2.2 billion. Renco created RG Steel to buy the mills, which could produce 8.2 million tons of steel a year. The steelmaker arranged a $50 million bankruptcy loan from a group of existing lenders to help fund operations while it sought a buyer.

Source: Dawn McCarty and Michael Bathon. May 31, 2012. "RG Steel Seeks Bankruptcy Protection, Plans to Sell Mills." *Bloomberg*.

debts of more than $1 billion each in Chapter 11 documents filed in U.S. Bankruptcy Court. The steelmaker arranged a $50 million bankruptcy loan from a group of existing lenders to help fund operations while it sought a buyer.

The Bankruptcy Situation

Imagine that your firm's financial reports have shown an unabated decline in revenue for seven quarters. Expenses have increased rapidly, and it is becoming difficult, and at times not possible, to pay bills as they become due. Suppliers are concerned about shipping goods without first receiving payment, and some have refused to ship without advanced payment in cash. Customers are requiring assurances that future orders will be delivered and some are beginning to buy from competitors. Employees are listening seriously to rumors of financial problems and a higher than normal number have accepted other employment. What can be done? What strategy can be initiated to protect the company and resolve the financial problems in the short term?

Chapter 7: The Harshest Resolution

If the judgment of the owners of a business is that its decline cannot be reversed, and the business cannot be sold as a going concern, then the alternative that is in the best interest of all may be a liquidation bankruptcy, also known as Chapter 7 of the Bankruptcy Code. The court appoints a trustee, who collects the property of the company, reduces it to cash, and distributes the proceeds proportionally to creditors on a pro rata basis as expeditiously as possible. Because all assets are sold to pay outstanding debt, a liquidation bankruptcy terminates a business. This type of filing is critically important to sole proprietors or partnerships. Their owners are personally liable for all business debts not covered by the sale of the business assets unless they can secure a Chapter 7 bankruptcy, which will allow them to cancel any debt in excess of exempt assets. Although they will be left with little personal property, the liquidated debtor is discharged from paying the remaining debt.

The shareholders of corporations are not liable for corporate debt and any debt existing after corporate assets are liquidated is absorbed by creditors. Corporate shareholders may simply terminate operations and walk away without liability to remaining creditors. However, filing a Chapter 7 proceeding will provide for an orderly and fair distribution of assets to creditors and thereby may reduce the negative impact of the business failure.

Chapter 11: A Conditional Second Chance

A proactive alternative for the endangered company is reorganization bankruptcy. Chosen for the right reasons, and implemented in the right way, reorganization bankruptcy can provide a financially, strategically, and ethically sound basis on which to advance the interests of all of the firm's stakeholders.

A thorough and objective analysis of the company may support the idea of its continuing operations if excessive debt can be reduced and new strategic initiatives can be undertaken. If the realistic possibility of long-term survival exists, a reorganization under Chapter 11 of the Bankruptcy Code can provide the opportunity. Reorganization allows a business debtor to restructure its debts and, with the agreement of creditors and approval of the court, to continue as a viable business. Creditors involved in Chapter 11 actions often receive less than the total debt due to them but far more than would be available from liquidation.

A Chapter 11 bankruptcy can provide time and protection to the debtor firm (which we will call the *Company*) to reorganize and use future earnings to pay creditors. The Company may restructure debts, close unprofitable divisions or stores, renegotiate labor contracts, reduce its workforce, or propose other actions that could create a profitable business. If the plan is accepted by creditors, the Company will be given another chance to avoid liquidation and emerge from the bankruptcy proceedings rehabilitated.

Seeking Protection of the Bankruptcy Court

If creditors file lawsuits or schedule judicial sales to enforce liens, the Company will need to seek the protection of the Bankruptcy Court. Filing a bankruptcy petition will invoke the protection of the court to provide sufficient time to work out a reorganization that was not achievable voluntarily. If reorganization is not possible, a Chapter 7 proceeding will allow for the fair and orderly dissolution of the business.

If a Chapter 11 proceeding is the required course of action, the Company must determine what the reorganized business will look like, if such a structure can be achieved, and how it will be accomplished while maintaining operations during the bankruptcy proceeding. Will sufficient cash be available to pay for the proceedings and reorganization? Will customers continue to do business with the Company or seek other more secure businesses with which to deal? Will key personnel stay on or look for more secure employment? Which operations should be discontinued or reduced?

Emerging from Bankruptcy

Bankruptcy is only the first step toward recovery for a firm. Many questions should be answered: How did the business get to the point at which the extreme action of bankruptcy was necessary? Were warning signs overlooked? Was the competitive environment understood? Did pride or fear prevent objective analysis? Did the business have the people and resources to succeed? Was the strategic plan well designed and implemented? Did financial problems result from unforeseen and unforeseeable problems or from bad management decisions?

Commitments to "try harder," "listen more carefully to the customer," and "be more efficient" are important but insufficient grounds to inspire stakeholder confidence. A recovery strategy must be developed to delineate how the company will compete more successfully in the future.

An assessment of the bankruptcy situation requires executives to consider the causes of the Company's decline and the severity of the problem it now faces. Investors must decide whether the management team that governed the company's operations during the downturn can return the firm to a position of success. Creditors must believe that the company's managers have learned how to prevent a recurrence of the observed and similar problems.

Alternatively, they must have faith that the company's competencies can be sufficiently augmented by key substitutions to the management team, with strong support in decision making from a board of directors and consultants, to restore the firm's competitive strength.

The 12 grand strategies just discussed, used singly and much more often in combinations, represent the traditional alternatives used by firms in the United States. Recently, three new additional grand types fit under the broad category of corporate combinations. These grand strategies deserve special attention and consideration—especially by companies that operate in global, dynamic, and technologically driven industries. They are joint ventures, strategic alliances, and consortia.

13. Joint Ventures

Occasionally two or more capable firms lack a necessary component for success in a particular competitive environment. For example, no single petroleum firm controlled sufficient resources to construct the Alaskan pipeline. Nor was any single firm capable of processing and marketing all of the oil that would flow through the pipeline. The solution was a set of **joint ventures,** which are commercial companies (children) created and operated for the benefit of the co-owners (parents). These cooperative arrangements provided both the funds needed to build the pipeline and the processing and marketing capacities needed to profitably handle the oil flow.

joint venture
A grand strategy in which companies create a co-owned business that operates for their mutual benefit.

The particular form of joint ventures discussed above is *joint ownership*. In recent years, it has become increasingly appealing for domestic firms to join foreign firms by means of this form. For example, Diamond-Star Motors was the result of a joint venture between a U.S. company, Chrysler Corporation, and Japan's Mitsubishi Motors Corporation. Located in Normal, Illinois, Diamond-Star was launched because it offered Chrysler and Mitsubishi a chance to expand on their long-standing relationship in which subcompact cars (as well as Mitsubishi engines and other automotive parts) were imported to the United States and sold under the Dodge and Plymouth names.

Similarly, as discussed in Global Strategy in Action, Exhibit 7.18, GE and Toshiba Corporation formed a global joint venture in 2013. Its purpose is to enable the two companies to jointly develop select combined-cycle power generation projects around the world.

The joint venture extends the supplier-consumer relationship and has strategic advantages for both partners. For Chrysler, it presented an opportunity to produce a high-quality car using expertise brought to the venture by Mitsubishi. It also gave Chrysler the chance to try new production techniques and to realize efficiencies by using the workforce that was not included under Chrysler's collective bargaining agreement with the United Auto Workers. The agreement offered Mitsubishi the opportunity to produce cars for sale in the United States without being subjected to the tariffs and restrictions placed on Japanese imports.

As a second example, Bethlehem Steel acquired an interest in a Brazilian mining venture to secure a raw material source. The stimulus for this joint ownership venture was grand strategy, but such is not always the case. Certain countries virtually mandate that foreign firms entering their markets do so on a joint ownership basis. India and Mexico are good examples. The rationale of these countries is that joint ventures minimize the threat of foreign domination and enhance the skills, employment, growth, and profits of local firms.

Relatively small firms also see the advantages of joint ventures and cooperative arrangements. The British law firm of Barlow Lyde & Gilbert entertained the options of a merger, alliance, or the launch of an independent office with partners relocating from London in its search for ways to explore international opportunities aggressively.

Strategic managers are wary of joint ventures. Admittedly, joint ventures present new opportunities with risks that can be shared. On the other hand, joint ventures often limit the

GE and Toshiba Establish Joint Venture

GE and Toshiba Corporation formed a global joint venture, under which the two companies jointly develop select combined-cycle power generation projects around the world. In addition, the two companies committed to explore the formation of a strategic joint venture for the development of next-generation combined-cycle power projects with higher levels of thermal efficiency.

Toshiba and GE have cooperated in gas turbine combined-cycle power generation systems since 1982 and have existing agreements to pursue 50-Hz and 60-Hz projects together in Japan and in key regions in Asia. This JV builds on that history of collaboration by targeting projects around the world that the companies can jointly develop and by exploring joint development of future combined-cycle technology.

GE and Toshiba won a contract in 2012 to supply the new FlexEfficiency technology to Chubu Electric Power's Nishi Nagoya Thermal Power Plant in Japan. This system is being jointly configured to achieve the world's highest thermal efficiency of 62 percent. Combined-cycle power generation systems combine gas turbines and steam turbines to achieve very high fuel efficiency and reduced CO_2 emissions as compared to conventional thermal power plants. Exhaust heat from the gas turbine is recovered and used to produce steam that drives the steam turbine and generates more electricity.

GE's FlexEfficiency technology portfolio harnesses natural gas and enables greater use of renewable energy. The FlexEfficiency portfolio combines high efficiency, which will reduce emissions and save money, along with flexibility, which will enable utilities to deliver power quickly when it is needed and to ramp down when it is not, balancing the grid cost-effectively.

Source: Excerpted from Kevin Gomez. January 2013. "GE and Toshiba Establish Joint Venture in Combined-Cycle Power Projects and Technology." *PACE*, Reed Business Information Pty Ltd.

discretion, control, and profit potential of partners, while demanding managerial attention and other resources that might be directed toward the firm's mainstream activities. Nevertheless, increasing globalization in many industries may require greater consideration of the joint venture approach, if historically national firms are to remain viable.

Collaborative Growth in China through Joint Ventures[16]

A prime example of the value of joint ventures is seen in their use by foreign businesses that seek to do business in China. Until very recently, China enthusiastically invited foreign investment to help in the development of its economy. However, in the early 2000s, China increased its regulations on foreign investment to moderate its economic growth and to ensure that Chinese businesses would not be at a competitive disadvantage when competing for domestic markets. The new restrictions require local companies to retain control of Chinese trademarks and brands, prevent foreign investors from buying property that is not for their own use, limit the size of foreign-owned retail chains, and restrict foreign investment in selected industries.[17] With these increasing regulations, investment in China through joint ventures with Chinese companies has become a prominent strategy for foreign investors who hope to circumvent some of the limitations on their strategies, therefore more fully capitalizing on China's economic growth.

In China, a host country partner can greatly facilitate the acceptance of a foreign investor and help minimize the costs of doing business in an unknown nation. Typically, the foreign partner contributes financing and technology, while the Chinese partner provides

[16]This section was drawn from Pearce II and Robbins, "Strategic Transformation as the Essential Last Step in the Process of Business Turnaround."

[17]E. Kurtenbach, "China Raising Stakes for Foreign Investment," *Philadelphia Inquirer*, September 24, 2006.

the land, physical facilities, workers, local connections, and knowledge of the country.[18] In a wholly owned venture, the foreign company is forced to acquire the land, build the workspace, and hire and train the employees, all of which are especially expensive propositions in a country in which the foreign company lacks *guanxi*.[19] *Guanxi* is a network of relationships a person cultivates through the exchange of gifts and favors to attain mutual benefits. It is based on friendship and affection, and on a reciprocal obligation to respond to requests for assistance. People who share a *guanxi* network are committed to one another by an unwritten code. Disregarding this commitment can destroy a business executive's prestige and social reputation.

For example, *guanxi* networks bind millions of Chinese firms into social and business webs, largely dictating their success. In China, enterprises are built on long-lasting links with political party administrative leaders and executives in other companies. Through connections with people who are empowered to make decisions, Chinese executives obtain vital information and assistance. Many Chinese entrepreneurs rely almost exclusively on their "old friends" to obtain material and financial resources, skilled personnel, and even tax considerations. Because *guanxi* is based on reciprocity, executives implicitly accept an obligation to "return a favor" in the unspecified future whenever they benefit from the *guanxi* network. Thus, developing and expanding *guanxi* is a form of social investment that enriches the executive's current resources and future potential.

Foreign partners in equity joint ventures benefit from speed of entry to the Chinese market, tax incentives, motivational and competitive advantages of a mutual long-term commitment, and access to the resources of its Chinese partner. Two large joint ventures in the media industry were created when Canada's AGA Resources partnered with Beijing Tangde International Film and Culture Co and when the United States' Sequoia Capital formed a joint venture with Hunan Greatdreams Cartoon Media.[20] Joint ventures in China's asset management industry include the partnerships between Italy's Banca Lombarda, the United States' Lord Abbett, and Chinese companies.

Similar opportunities exist for international joint ventures in the construction and operation of oil refineries, in the building of the nation's railroad transportation system, and in the development of specific geographic areas. In special economic zones, foreign firms operate businesses with Chinese joint venture partners. The foreign companies receive tax incentives in the form of rates that are lower than the standard 30 percent corporate tax rate. For example, in the Shanghai Pudong New Area, a 15 percent tax rate applies.[21]

The number of international joint ventures is increasing because of China's admission to the World Trade Organization (WTO). Under the conditions of its membership, China is expanding the list of industries that permit foreign investment.[22] As of 2007, for example, foreign investors that participate with Chinese partners in joint ventures are permitted to hold an increased share of JVs in several major industries: banks (up to 20 percent), investment funds (33 percent), life insurance (50 percent), and telecommunications (25 percent).

[18]Ying Qui,"Problems of Managing Joint Ventures in China's Interior: Evidence from Shaanxi," *Advanced Management Journal* 70, no. 3 (2005), pp. 46–57.

[19]J. A. Pearce II and R. B. Robinson Jr., "Cultivating Guanxi as a Corporate Foreign-Investor Strategy," *Business Horizons* 43, no. 1 (2000), pp. 31–38.

[20]Andrew Bagnell,"China Business," *China Business Review* 33, no. 5 (2006), pp. 88–92.

[21]N. P. Chopey, "China Still Beckons Petrochemical Investments," *Chemical Engineering* 133, no. 8 (2006) pp. 19–23.

[22]"China's WTO Scorecard: Selected Year-Three Service Commitments," *The US-China Business Council* (2005), pp. 1–2.

14. Strategic Alliances

strategic alliances
Contractual partnerships because the companies involved do not take an equity position in one another

Strategic alliances are distinguishable from joint ventures because the companies involved do not take an equity position in one another. In many instances, strategic alliances are *partnerships* that exist for a defined period during which partners contribute their skills and expertise to a cooperative project. For example, one partner provides manufacturing capabilities while a second partner provides marketing expertise. In other situations, a strategic alliance can enable similar companies to combine their capabilities to counter the threats of a much larger or new type of competitor.

A strategic alliance produced Spotify's first connected-car appearance at the 2013 Mobile World Congress.[23] Ford and Spotify had joined in the strategic alliance to make it possible for the subscription music service to be available over the Sync AppLink platform, and integrated with the Sync's voice command system in Ford vehicles in the United States, Europe, and Australia. According to *Bloomberg Businessweek*, iPhone and Android apps were able to pair with the dashboard AppLink system, streaming music through the car's entertainment systems. Users were able to play their songs, playlists, and radio stations by voice commands. Within the first month of operation through Ford's new open development platform, 2,500 developers had signed up and downloaded the SDK. Many of those developers had already completed apps, submitted them to Ford, and received final approval.

In December 2012, Nokia unveiled a strategic alliance with China's dominant cellular operator, China Mobile, to offer the Lumia 920T, Nokia's new Windows-based smartphone, to China Mobile subscribers, as discussed in Global Strategy in Action, Exhibit 7.19. China Mobile's leadership foresaw a problem as the Chinese market rapidly matures. China Mobile relied on low-end 2G users far more than its smaller rivals do. Lagging in 3G smartphones would not do at a time when the Chinese market was quickly moving away from the feature-phone business.

Strategic alliances are sometimes undertaken because the partners want to develop in-house capabilities to supplant the partner when the contractual arrangement between them reaches its termination date. Such relationships are tricky because, in a sense, the partners are attempting to "steal" each other's know-how.

In other instances, strategic alliances are synonymous with *licensing agreements*. Licensing involves the transfer of some industrial property right from the U.S. licensor to a motivated licensee in a foreign country. Most tend to be patents, trademarks, or technical know-how that are granted to the licensee for a specified time in return for a royalty and for avoiding tariffs or import quotas. Bell South and U.S. West, with various marketing and service competitive advantages valuable to Europe, have extended a number of licenses to create personal computers networks in the United Kingdom. Another example of licensing is UTEK Corporation's successful strategy for licensing discoveries resulting from research efforts at universities.

Another licensing strategy is to contract the manufacturing of its product line to a foreign company to exploit local comparative advantages in technology, materials, or labor. MIPS Computer Systems licensed Digital Equipment Corporation, Texas Instruments, Cypress Semiconductor, and Bipolar Integrated Technology in the United States and Fujitsu, NEC, and Kubota in Japan to market computers based on its designs in the partner's country.

Service and franchise-based firms—including Anheuser-Busch, Avis, Coca-Cola, Hilton, Hyatt, Holiday Inns, Kentucky Fried Chicken, McDonald's, and Pepsi—have long

[23]Kevin Fitchard. February 25, 2013. "Spotify Joins Ford's Roster of In-Car Music Apps." *Bloomberg Businessweek*.

Nokia Strategic Alliance Is Just the Beginning for China Mobile

In December 2012, Nokia unveiled a strategic alliance with China's dominant cellular operator, China Mobile, to offer the Lumia 920T, Nokia's new Windows-based smartphone, to the more than 700 million Chinese who are China Mobile subscribers. The Lumia partnership was not the only new strategic move for China Mobile. The company also introduced its own-brand cell phones and a mobile Internet subsidiary.

China Mobile's leadership foresaw a problem as the Chinese market rapidly matures. The company is by far the biggest mobile operator in China, but China Mobile relied on low-end 2G users far more than its smaller rivals do, China Unicom and China Telecom. Only 11 percent of China Mobile subscribers subscribe to 3G, compared with China Unicom's 30 percent and China Telecom's 40 percent. While China Mobile had a 50 percent share among total cell-phone users, the three state-owned companies were about evenly matched in 3G market share.

Lagging in 3G would not do at a time when the Chinese market was quickly moving away from the feature-phone business that had long been China Mobile's bread and butter. Smartphone sales rose 197 percent in the second quarter of 2012, and for the first time smartphone demand outpaced feature phones. China accounted for 29 percent of global smartphone shipments in the second quarter of 2012, up from 14 percent a year earlier.

As smartphone sales increased, more Chinese were signing up for 3G services. Nineteen percent of Chinese cellular subscribers used 3G, according to a November 2012 report by Kary Sei, an analyst in Hong Kong with ICBC International Research. At the start of 2011, 3G subscribers accounted for just 6.1 percent of the market. The shift to 3G made China Mobile an even more attractive partner for Western companies, such as Qualcomm, trying to build sales in the country. The average selling price for 3G phones was $364. For 2.5G, it was just $38.

Source: Excerpted Bruce Einhorn. December 7, 2012. "Nokia Deal Is Just the Beginning for China Mobile." *Bloomberg Businessweek.*

engaged in licensing arrangements with foreign distributors as a way to enter new markets with standardized products that can benefit from marketing economies.

Outsourcing is a basic approach to strategic alliances that enables firms to gain a competitive advantage. Significant changes within many segments of American business continue to encourage the use of outsourcing practices. Within the health care arena, an industry survey recorded 67 percent of hospitals using provider outsourcing for at least one department within their organization. Services such as information systems, reimbursement, and risk and physician practice management are outsourced by 51 percent of the hospitals that use outsourcing.

Another successful application of outsourcing is found in human resources. A survey of human resource executives revealed 85 percent have personal experience leading an outsourcing effort within their organization. In addition, it was found that two-thirds of pension departments have outsourced at least one human resource function. Within customer service and sales departments, outsourcing increases productivity in such areas as product information, sales and order taking, sample fulfillment, and complaint handling.

15. Consortia, *Keiretsus*, and *Chaebols*

consortia
Large interlocking relationships between businesses of an industry.

keiretsu
A Japanese consortia of businesses that is coordinated by a large trading company to gain a strategic advantage.

chaebol
A Korean consortia financed through government banking groups to gain a strategic advantage.

Consortia are defined as large interlocking relationships between businesses of an industry. In Japan such consortia are known as **keiretsus;** in South Korea as **chaebols.**

In Europe, consortia projects are increasing in number and in success rates. Examples include the Junior Engineers' and Scientists' Summer Institute, which underwrites cooperative learning and research; the European Strategic Program for Research and Development in Information Technologies, which seeks to enhance European competitiveness in fields related to computer electronics and component manufacturing; and EUREKA, which

Japan's Consortium with Myanmar

Myanmar's government agreed to a deal with a Japanese keiretsu in 2012 to develop jointly a special economic zone on the edge of the commercial capital, Yangon, to expand industry and bring in much-needed investment. Mitsubishi Corp. Marubeni Corp., and Sumitomo Corp., teamed up for a 49 percent share in the 5,900-acre estate in Thilawa, close to a deep-sea port, with the government set to invite private domestic firms to get involved.

The Japanese government provided financial assistance to support the development of infrastructure for the industrial zone, which included factories and a gas-fired power plant. Japanese firms were eager to get in early and expand their footprint in an underdeveloped country strategically located for their business. Japan was a big investor in neighboring Thailand, with car manufacturing plants and factories for high-tech industries, and planned to connect Myanmar to Thai industrial zones and ports.

Japan moved quickly into fast-changing Myanmar to capitalize on an improving investment climate and urgent infrastructure needs, just as European Union sanctions were suspended in response to reforms by its civilian-led government. As part of the arrangement, Japan waived 303.5 billion yen ($3.72 billion) of Myanmar's debt and agreed to restart development loans. The Daiwa Securities Group also agreed to help Myanmar develop a stock exchange and committed to invest $380 million to build an information technology backbone for the government in partnership with major Japanese tech companies. Sumitomo Mitsui Banking Corp. agreed to provide management help to Myanmar's Kanbawza Bank, the country's biggest private bank, with a view to business deals.

Source: Excerpted from Aung Hia Tun. August 28, 2012. "Myanmar Signs Industrial Zone Pact with Japan Consortium." *Reuters.*

is a joint program involving scientists and engineers from several European countries to coordinate joint research projects.

A Japanese *keiretsu* is an undertaking involving up to 50 different firms that are joined around a large trading company or bank and are coordinated through interlocking directories and stock exchanges. It is designed to use industry coordination to minimize risks of competition, in part through cost sharing and increased economies of scale. Examples include Sumitomo, Mitsubishi, Mitsui, and Sanwa.

A recent example of a keiretsu is provided in Global Strategy in Action, Exhibit 7.20. It describes how Myanmar's government agreed to a deal with a Japanese keiretsu in 2012 to develop jointly a special economic zone to expand industry and bring in much-needed investment. Mitsubishi Corp., Marubeni Corp., and Sumitomo Corp. teamed up for a 49 percent share in the 5,900-acre estate in Thilawa, with the government set to invite private domestic firms to get involved. The Japanese government provided financial assistance to support the development of infrastructure for the industrial zone. Japanese firms were eager to get in early and expand their footprint in an underdeveloped country strategically located for their business.

A South Korean *chaebol* resembles a consortium or keiretsu except that it is typically financed through government banking groups and is largely run by professional managers trained by participating firms expressly for the job.

SELECTION OF LONG-TERM OBJECTIVES AND GRAND STRATEGY SETS

At first glance, the strategic management model seems to suggest that strategic choice decision making leads to the sequential selection of long-term objectives and grand strategies. In fact, however, strategic choice is the simultaneous selection of long-range objectives and grand strategies. When strategic planners study their opportunities, they try to determine

A Profile of Strategic Choice Options

	Six Strategic Choice Options					
	1	2	3	4	5	6
Interactive opportunities	West Coast markets present little competition		Current markets sensitive to price competition		Current industry product lines offer too narrow a range of markets	
Appropriate long-range objectives (limited sample):						
Average 5-year ROI.	15%	19%	13%	17%	23%	15%
Company sales by year 5.	+50%	+40%	+20%	+0%	+35%	+25%
Risk of negative profits.	.30	.25	.10	.15	.20	.05
Grand strategies	Horizontal integration	Market development	Concentration	Selective retrenchment	Product development	Concentration

which are most likely to result in achieving various long-range objectives. Almost simultaneously, they try to forecast whether an available grand strategy can take advantage of preferred opportunities so the tentative objectives can be met. In essence, then, three distinct but highly interdependent choices are being made at one time. Several triads, or sets, of possible decisions are usually considered.

A simplified example of this process is shown in Exhibit 7.21, Strategy in Action. In this example, the firm has determined that six strategic choice options are available. These options stem from three interactive opportunities (e.g., West Coast markets that present little competition). Because each of these interactive opportunities can be approached through different grand strategies—for options 1 and 2, the grand strategies are horizontal acquisition and market development—each offers the potential for achieving long-range objectives to varying degrees. Thus, a firm rarely can make a strategic choice only on the basis of its preferred opportunities, long-range objectives, or grand strategy. Instead, these three elements must be considered simultaneously, because only in combination do they constitute a strategic choice.

In an actual decision situation, the strategic choice would be complicated by a wider variety of interactive opportunities, feasible company objectives, promising grand strategy options, and evaluative criteria. Nevertheless, Exhibit 7.21 does partially reflect the nature and complexity of the process by which long-term objectives and grand strategies are selected.

In the next chapter, the strategic choice process is fully explained. However, knowledge of long-term objectives and grand strategies is essential to understanding that process.

SEQUENCE OF OBJECTIVES AND STRATEGY SELECTION

The selection of long-range objectives and grand strategies involves simultaneous, rather than sequential, decisions. While it is true that objectives are needed to prevent the firm's direction and progress from being determined by random forces, it is equally true that objectives can be achieved only if strategies are implemented. In fact, long-term objectives and grand strategies are so interdependent that some business consultants do not distinguish between them. Long-term objectives and grand strategies are still combined under the heading of company strategy in most of the popular business literature and in the thinking of most practicing executives.

However, the distinction has merit. Objectives indicate what strategic managers want but provide few insights about how they will be achieved. Conversely, strategies indicate what types of actions will be taken but do not define what ends will be pursued or what criteria will serve as constraints in refining the strategic plan.

Does it matter whether strategic decisions are made to achieve objectives or to satisfy constraints? No, because constraints are themselves objectives. The constraint of increased inventory capacity is a desire (an objective), not a certainty. Likewise, the constraint of an increase in the sales force does not ensure that the increase will be achieved, given such factors as other company priorities, labor market conditions, and the firm's profit performance.

DESIGNING A PROFITABLE BUSINESS MODEL

business model
A clear understanding of how the firm will generate profits and the strategic actions it must take to succeed over the long term.

The process of combining long-term objectives and grand strategies produces a **business model.** Creating an effective model requires a clear understanding of how the firm will generate profits and the strategic action it must take to succeed over the long term.

Adrian Slywotzky, David Morrison, and Bob Andelman identified 22 business models—designs that generate profits in a unique way.[24] They present these models as examples, believing that others do or can exist. The authors also believe that in some instances profitability depends on the interplay of two or more business models. Their study demonstrates that the mechanisms of profitability can be very different but that a focus on the customer is the key to the effectiveness of each model.

Slywotzky, Morrison, and Andelman suggest that the two most productive questions asked of executives are these:

1. What is our business model?
2. How do we make a profit?

The classic strategy rule suggested: "Gain market share and profits will follow." This approach once worked for some industries. However, because of competitive turbulence caused by globalization and rapid technological advancements, the once-popular belief in a strong correlation between market share and profitability has collapsed in many industries.

How can businesses earn sustainable profits? The answer is found by analyzing the following questions: Where will the firm make a profit in this industry? How should the business model be designed so that the firm will be profitable? Slywotzky, Morrison, and Andelman describe the following profitability business models as ways to answer those questions.

1. *Customer development customer solutions profit model.* Companies that use this business model make money by finding ways to improve their customers' economics and investing in ways for customers to improve their processes.

---

[24]This section is excerpted from A. J. Slywotzky, D. J. Morrison, and B. Andelman, *The Profit Zone; How Strategic Business Design Will Lead You To Tomorrow's Profits* (New York: Times Books, 1997).

2. *Product pyramid profit model*. This model is effective in markets where customers have strong preferences for product characteristics, including variety, style, color, and price. By offering a number of variations, companies can build so-called product pyramids. At the base are low-priced, high-volume products, and at the top are high-priced, low-volume products. Profit is concentrated at the top of the pyramid, but the base is the strategic firewall (i.e., a strong, low-priced brand that deters competitor entry), thereby protecting the margins at the top. Consumer goods companies and automobile companies use this model.

3. *Multicomponent system profit model*. Some businesses are characterized by a production/marketing system that consists of components that generate substantially different levels of profitability. In hotels, for example, there is a substantial difference between the profitability of room rentals and that of bar operations. In such instances, it often is useful to maximize the use of the highest-profit components to maximize the profitability of the whole system.

4. *Switchboard profit model*. Some markets function by connecting multiple sellers to multiple buyers. The switchboard profit model creates a high-value intermediary that concentrates these multiple communication pathways through one point or "switchboard" and thereby reduces costs for both parties in exchange for a fee. As volume increases, so too do profits.

5. *Time profit model*. Sometimes, speed is the key to profitability. This business model takes advantage of first-mover advantage. To sustain this model, constant innovation is essential.

6. *Blockbuster profit model*. In some industries, profitability is driven by a few great product successes. This business model is representative of movie studios, pharmaceutical firms, and software companies, which have high R&D and launch costs and finite product cycles. In this type of environment, it pays to concentrate resource investments in a few projects rather than to take positions in a variety of products.

7. *Profit multiplier model*. This business model reaps gains, repeatedly, from the same product, character, trademark capability, or service. Think of the value that Michael Jordan Inc. creates with the image of the great basketball legend. This model can be a powerful engine for businesses with strong consumer brands.

8. *Entrepreneurial profit model*. Small can be beautiful. This business model stresses that diseconomies of scale can exist in companies. They attack companies that have become comfortable with their profit levels with formal, bureaucratic systems that are remote from customers. As their expenses grow and customer relevance declines, such companies are vulnerable to entrepreneurs who are in direct contact with their customers.

9. *Specialization profit model*. This business model stresses growth through sequenced specialization. Consulting companies have used this design successfully.

10. *Installed base profit model*. A company that pursues this model profits because its established user base subsequently buys the company's brand of consumables or follow-on products. Installed base profits provide a protected annuity stream. Examples include razors and blades, software and upgrades, copiers and toner cartridges, and cameras and film.

11. *De facto standard profit model*. A variant of the installed base profit model, this model is appropriate when the installed base model becomes the de facto standard that governs competitive behavior in the industry.

Summary

Before we learn how strategic decisions are made, it is important to understand the two principal components of any strategic choice; namely, long-term objectives and the grand strategy. The purpose of this chapter was to convey that understanding.

Long-term objectives were defined as the results a firm seeks to achieve over a specified period, typically five years. Seven common long-term objectives were discussed: profitability, productivity, competitive position, employee development, employee relations, technological leadership, and public responsibility. These, or any other long-term objectives, should be flexible, measurable over time, motivating, suitable, and understandable.

Grand strategies were defined as comprehensive approaches guiding the major actions designed to achieve long-term objectives. Fifteen grand strategy options were discussed: concentrated growth, market development, product development, innovation, horizontal acquisition, vertical acquisition, concentric diversification, conglomerate diversification, turnaround, divestiture, liquidation, bankruptcy, joint ventures, strategic alliances, and consortia.

Key Terms

balanced scorecard, *p. 191*
bankruptcy, *p. 227*
business model, *p. 237*
chaebol, *p. 234*
concentrated growth, *p. 206*
concentric diversification, *p. 219*
conglomerate diversification, *p. 219*

consortia, *p. 234*
divestiture strategy, *p. 224*
generic strategy, *p. 200*
grand strategy, *p. 205*
horizontal acquisition, *p. 214*
innovation, *p. 213*
joint venture, *p. 230*
keiretsu, *p. 234*

liquidation, *p. 226*
market development, *p. 209*
product development, *p. 211*
strategic alliances, *p. 233*
turnaround, *p. 221*
vertical acquisition, *p. 217*

Questions for Discussion

1. Identify firms in the business community nearest to your college or university that you believe are using each of the 15 grand strategies discussed in this chapter.
2. Identify firms in your business community that appear to rely principally on 1 of the 15 grand strategies. What kind of information did you use to classify the firms?
3. Write a long-term objective for your school of business that exhibits the seven qualities of long-term objectives described in this chapter.
4. Distinguish between the following pairs of grand strategies:

   a. Horizontal and vertical acquisition.
   b. Conglomerate and concentric diversification.
   c. Product development and innovation.
   d. Joint venture and strategic alliance.

5. Rank each of the 15 grand strategy options discussed in this chapter on the following three scales:

High	Low
	Cost

High	Low
	Risk of failure

High	Low
	Potential for exceptional growth

6. Identify firms that use the eight specific options shown in Exhibit 7.4 under the grand strategies of concentration, market development, and product development.

Business Strategy

After reading and studying this chapter, you should be able to

1. Determine why a business would choose a low-cost, differentiation, or speed-based strategy.

2. Explain the nature and value of a market focus strategy.

3. Illustrate how a firm can pursue both low-cost and differentiation strategies.

4. Identify requirements for business success at different stages of industry evolution.

5. Determine good business strategies in fragmented and global industries.

6. Decide when a business should diversify.

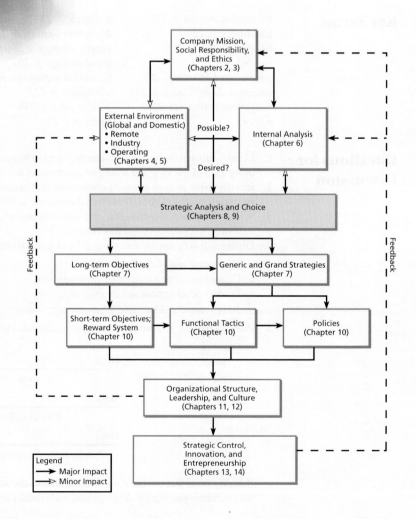

Strategic analysis and choice is the phase of the strategic management process in which business managers examine and choose a business strategy that allows their business to maintain or create a sustainable competitive advantage. Their starting point is to evaluate and determine which competitive advantages provide the basis for distinguishing the firm in the customer's mind from other reasonable alternatives. Businesses with a dominant product or service line must also choose among alternate grand strategies to guide the firm's activities, particularly when they are trying to decide about broadening the scope of the firm's activities beyond its core business. This chapter examines strategic analysis and choice in single- or dominant-product/service businesses by addressing two basic issues:

1. What strategies are most effective at building sustainable competitive advantages for single business units? For example, Scania, the most productive truck manufacturer in the world, joins its major rival Volvo as two anchors of Sweden's economy. Scania's return on sales of 9.9 percent far exceeds Mercedes (2.6 percent) and Volvo (2.5 percent), a level it has achieved most of the last 60 years. Scania has built a sustainable competitive advantage with a strategy of focusing solely on heavy transport vehicles in three geographic markets—Europe, Latin America, and Asia—by providing vehicles customized to specific tasks yet built using modularized components (20,000 components per vehicle versus 25,000 for Volvo and 40,000 for Mercedes). Scania is a low-cost producer of a differentiated heavy transport vehicle that can be custom-manufactured quickly and sold to a regionally focused market.

2. Should dominant-product/service businesses diversify to build value and competitive advantage? For example, Dell and Coca-Cola managers have examined the question of diversification and apparently concluded that continued concentration on their core products and services and development of new markets for those same core products and services are best. IBM and Pepsi examined the same question and concluded that concentric diversification and vertical acquisition were best. Why?

EVALUATING AND CHOOSING BUSINESS STRATEGIES: SEEKING SUSTAINED COMPETITIVE ADVANTAGE

Business managers evaluate and choose strategies that they think will make their business successful. Businesses become successful because they possess some advantage relative to their competitors. The two most prominent sources of competitive advantage can be found in the business's cost structure and its ability to differentiate the business from competitors. DisneyWorld in Orlando offers theme park patrons several unique, distinct features that differentiate it from other entertainment options. Costco offers retail customers the lowest prices on popular consumer items because they have created a low-cost structure that results in a competitive advantage over most competitors.

Businesses that create competitive advantages from one or both of these sources usually experience above-average profitability within their industry. Businesses that lack a cost or differentiation advantage usually experience average or below-average profitability. Two well-recognized studies found that businesses that do not have either form of competitive advantage perform the poorest among their peers, while businesses that possess both forms of competitive advantage enjoy the highest levels of profitability within their industry.[1]

The average return on investment for more than 2,500 businesses across seven industries looked like this:

Differentiation Advantage	Cost Advantage	Overall Average ROI across Seven Industries
High	High	35.0%
Low	High	26.0
High	Low	22.0
Low	Low	9.5

Initially, managers were advised to evaluate and choose strategies that emphasized one type of competitive advantage, often referred to as generic strategies. Firms were encouraged to become either a differentiation-oriented or low-cost-oriented company. In so doing, it was logical that organizational members would develop a clear understanding of company priorities and, as these studies suggest, likely experience profitability superior to competitors without either a differentiation or low-cost orientation.

The studies mentioned here, and the experience of many other businesses, indicate that the highest profitability levels are found in businesses that possess both types of competitive advantage at the same time. In other words, businesses that have one or more resources/capabilities that truly differentiate them from key competitors and also have resources/capabilities that let them operate at a lower cost will consistently outperform their rivals that don't. Southwest Airlines has followed a low-cost strategy by simplifying reservations, eliminating reserved seats, not serving meals, and cutting operating costs by flying only 737 aircraft. It has simultaneously emphasized differentiation by creating a fun experience for customers, unique commercials, baggage flying for free, and an unusual culture that customers can see and "feel."

Starting during the "Great Recession" and continuing today, Facebook has followed a combination low-cost and differentiation strategy to solidify its position as the top social media platform worldwide. While others cut costs, Facebook invested significantly to expand its user base worldwide by taking developers off ad revenue generation to create versions in languages like Arabic, French Canadian, Tagalog, and Xhosa, to mention a few, as well as by acquiring competitive sites in Brazil, India, Germany, and Japan. Though it was foregoing needed revenue, these moves allowed Facebook to build scale and with it

[1]G. A. Shinkle, A. P. Kriauciunas, and G. Hundley (2013), "Why Pure Strategies May Be Wrong for Transition Economy Firms," *Strategic Management Journal*, Vol. 34, No.2, p. 206; Richard Makadok and David Gaddis Ross (2013), "Taking Industry Structuring Seriously: A Strategic Perspective on Product Differentiation," *Strategic Management Journal*, Vol. 34, No.5, pp. 509–532; Mas Bambang Baroto and Muhammad Madi Bin Abdullah (2012), "The Application of Cost, Differentiation and Hybrid Strategy in Business Operations: Will Hybrid Strategy Become the New Competitive Strategy?" *International Journal of Business and Management*, Vol. 20, No.7, pp. 120–132; Aqsa Siddiqui (2012), *IKEA: Making a Success of Being "Stuck in the Middle"?*, Munich, GRIN Publishing GmbH, http://www.grin.com/en/e-book/20684; Bauer E. Sumpio (2013), "Application of Porter's Five Forces Model and Generic Strategies for Vascular Surgery: Should Be Stuck in the Middle?" *Vascular, The Royal Society of Medicine Journal*, Vol. 21, No. 2, pp. 170–178; Shiv S. Mathur and Alfred Kenyon (2012), *Creating Valuable Business Strategies,* Elsevier/Butterworth-Heinemann, London; and foundation research from R. B. Robinson and J. A. Pearce (1988), "Planned Patterns of Strategic Behavior and their Relationship to Business Unit Performance," *Strategic Management Journal*, Vol. 9, No. 1, pp. 43–60, followed by G. G. Dess and G. T. Lumpkin, "Emerging Issues in Strategy Process Research," in *Handbook of Strategic Management,* M. A. Hitt, R. E. Freeman, and J. S. Harrison (eds) (Oxford: Blackwell, 2001), pp. 3–34.

EXHIBIT 8.1

Evaluating a Business's Cost Leadership Opportunities

Source: Based on Michael Porter, *On Competition*, 1998, Harvard Business School Press.

A. Skills and Resources That Foster Cost Leadership

Sustained capital investment and access to capital
Process engineering skills
Intense supervision of labor or core technical operations
Products or services designed for ease of manufacture or delivery
Low-cost distribution system

B. Organizational Requirements to Support and Sustain Cost Leadership Activities

Tight cost control
Frequent, detailed control reports
Continuous improvement and benchmarking orientation
Structured organization and responsibilities
Incentives based on meeting strict, usually quantitative targets

C. Examples of Ways Businesses Achieve Competitive Advantage via Cost Leadership

					Profit Margin
Technology Development	Process innovations lower production costs		Product redesign reduces the number of components		
Human Resource Management	Safety training for all employees reduces absenteeism, downtime, and accidents				
General Administration	Reduced levels of management cut corporate overhead		Computerized, integrated information system reduces errors and administrative costs		
Procurement	Favorable long-term contracts; captive suppliers or key customer for supplier.				
	Global, online suppliers provide automatic restocking of orders based on our sales.	Economy of scale in plant reduces equipment costs and depreciation.	Computerized routing lowers transportation expense.	Cooperative advertising with distributors creates local cost advantage in buying media space and time.	Subcontracted service technicians repair product correctly the first time or they bear all costs.
	Inbound logistics	**Operations**	**Outbound logistics**	**Marketing and Sales**	**Service**

an unparalleled cost advantage to advertisers in reaching audiences on a global basis, or a narrowly targeted geographic one. Simultaneously, Facebook has emphasized differentiation in the myriad of distinct features built into its user experience—simple design, ways to increase user interaction, privacy and trust, and market size, while enabling differentiation in its offering to advertising customers for the variety of ways it can target and reach specific groups of customers among Facebook users. So, as Southwest and Facebook suggest, the challenge facing today's executives in their strategic decision making is often to choose strategies based on core competencies that will sustain both a cost leadership position as well as a differentiation one too.

Evaluating Cost Leadership Opportunities

Business success built on cost leadership requires the business to be able to provide its product or service at a cost below what its competitors can achieve. And it must be a sustainable cost advantage. Through the skills and resources identified in Exhibit 8.1, a business must

Taking the "LOW" Cost Road

The Apple vs. Samsung battle was big news a few years ago. Apple was on top, or perceived so. It had won a large patent infringement lawsuit, at least in the United States, related to features and design patents on the iPhone and iPad vs. Samsung's Galaxy. Samsung paid its bill, made a few adjustments, and continued on, soon outselling Apple with its new Galaxy model at the time, and leading it in sales and profitability. Why?

Samsung's strategy has long been to build economies of scale in its vast, fully integrated Korean production capabilities. Once a company assembling clunky transistor radios, Samsung now sells more memory chips, smartphones, high-resolution TVs, and flat-panel displays than any other company in the world. Samsung has always sought not to lead, rather to follow, doing it cheaper and better, after a sophisticated competitor

has proven a new or refined product/market. It has let Apple, Motorola, Nokia, or Blackberry . . . or Sony, Sharp, or Panasonic introduce a new product and have initial sales that prove the offering. Then, Samsung moves to build a similar product, a little better, at a much lower cost.

Samsung's view of the U.S. patent litigation loss . . . just the cost of doing business. It was already through selling that model anyway. Samsung makes not only hardware like the phone, but also all of its components; it is Apple's biggest parts supplier, while also its fiercest smartphone competitor. Bottom line, Apple's presence in the business simply helps Samsung lower its cost and find new product ideas—both reinforcing an incredibly successful, low-cost-driven sustainable competitive advantage.

---

be able to accomplish one or more activities in its value chain activities—procuring materials, processing them into products, marketing the products, and distributing the products or support activities—in a more cost-effective manner than that of its competitors or it must be able to reconfigure its value chain so as to achieve a cost advantage. Exhibit 8.1 provides examples of such **low-cost strategies.**

low-cost strategies
Business strategies that seek to establish long-term competitive advantages by emphasizing and perfecting value chain activities that can be achieved at costs substantially below what competitors are able to match on a sustained basis. This allows the firm, in turn, to compete primarily by charging a price lower than competitors can match and still stay in business.

Strategists examining their business's value chain for low-cost leadership advantages evaluate the sustainability of those advantages by benchmarking (refer to Chapter 6 for a discussion of this comparison technique) their business against key competitors and by considering the effect of any cost advantage on the five forces in their business's competitive environment. Low-cost activities that are sustainable and that provide one or more of these advantages relative to key industry forces should become a key basis for the business's competitive strategy:

Low-cost advantages that reduce the likelihood of pricing pressure from buyers When key competitors cannot match prices from the low-cost leader, customers pressuring the leader risk establishing a price level that drives alternate sources out of business.

Truly sustained low-cost advantages may push rivals into other areas, lessening price competition Intense, continued price competition may be ruinous for all rivals, as seen occasionally in the airline industry. Exhibit 8.2 shows how Samsung has used this approach to cause rivals to seek other competitive tactics conceding Samsung's cost leadership in mass markets.

New entrants competing on price must face an entrenched cost leader without the experience to replicate every cost advantage EasyJet, a British start-up with a Southwest Airlines copycat strategy, entered the European airline market with much fanfare and low-priced, city-to-city, no-frills flights.

Analysts have cautioned for some time that British Airways, KLM's no-frills off-shoot (Buzz), and Virgin Express will simply match fares on easyJet's key routes and let high landing fees and flight delays take their toll on the British upstart. To their surprise, first mover easyJet has sustained and nurtured its low-cost leadership advantage by using the same model for all its planes, providing only short-haul travel, no in-flight meals, and rapid turnaround, and more recently, cutting out travel agents, having no tickets, selling on the Internet, and selling food/drink on the planes. These are all cost-savings tactics that most of the larger competitors don't do, and therefore they can't survive if they just lower their prices.[2]

Low-cost advantages should lessen the attractiveness of substitute products A serious concern of any business is the threat of a substitute product in which buyers can meet their original need. Low-cost advantages allow the holder to resist this happening because it allows them to remain competitive even against desirable substitutes, and it allows them to lessen concerns about price facing an inferior, lower-priced substitute.

Higher margins allow low-cost producers to withstand supplier cost increases and often gain supplier loyalty over time Sudden, particularly uncontrollable increases in the costs suppliers face can be more easily absorbed by low-cost, higher-margin producers. Severe droughts in California quadrupled the price of lettuce—a key restaurant demand. Some chains absorbed the cost; others had to confuse customers with a "lettuce tax." Furthermore, chains that worked well with produce suppliers gained a loyal, cooperative "partner" for possible assistance in a future, competitive situation.

Once managers identify opportunities to create cost advantage–based strategies, they must consider whether key risks inherent in cost leadership are present in a way that may mediate sustained success. The key risks with which they must be concerned are discussed next.

Many cost-saving activities are easily duplicated Computerizing certain order entry functions among hazardous waste companies gave early adopters lower sales costs and better customer service for a brief time. Rivals quickly adapted, adding similar capabilities with similar effects on their costs.

Exclusive cost leadership can become a trap Firms that emphasize lowest price and can offer it via cost advantages where product differentiation is increasingly not considered must truly be convinced of the sustainability of those advantages. Particularly with commodity-type products, the low-cost leader seeking to sustain a margin superior to lesser rivals may encounter increasing customer pressure for lower prices with great damage to both leader and lesser players.

Obsessive cost cutting can shrink other competitive advantages involving key product attributes Intense cost scrutiny can build margin, but it can reduce opportunities for or investment in innovation, processes, and products. Similarly, such scrutiny can lead to the use of inferior raw materials, processes, or activities that were previously viewed by customers as a key attribute of the original products. Some mail-order computer companies that sought to maintain or enhance cost advantages found reductions in telephone service personnel and automation of that function backfiring with a drop in demand for their products even though their low prices were maintained.

Cost differences often decline over time As products age, competitors learn how to match cost advantages. Absolute volumes sold often decline. Market channels and suppliers mature. Buyers become more knowledgeable. All of these factors present opportunities to lessen the value or presence of earlier cost advantages. Said another way, cost advantages that are not sustainable over a period of time are risky.

Once business managers have evaluated the cost structure of their value chain, determined activities that provide competitive cost advantages, and considered their inherent risks, they

---

[2]"easyJet Defies Sir Stelios with Plans for New Aircraft," www.Telegraph.co.uk, April 20, 2013.

start choosing the business's strategy. Those managers concerned with differentiation-based strategies, or those seeking optimum performance incorporating both sources of competitive advantage, move to evaluating their business's sources of differentiation.

Evaluating Differentiation Opportunities

differentiation
A business strategy that seeks to build competitive advantage with its product or service by having it be "different" from other available competitive products based on features, performance, or other factors not directly related to cost and price. The difference would be one that would be hard to create and/or difficult to copy or imitate.

Differentiation requires that the business have sustainable advantages that allow it to provide buyers with something uniquely valuable to them. A successful differentiation strategy allows the business to provide a product or service of perceived higher value to buyers at a "differentiation cost" below the "value premium" to the buyers. In other words, the buyer feels the additional cost to buy the product or service is well below what the product or service is worth compared with other available alternatives.

Differentiation usually arises from one or more activities in the value chain that create a unique value important to buyers. Perrier's control of a carbonated water spring in France, Stouffer's frozen food packaging and sauce technology, Apple's control of iTunes download software that worked solely with iPods, iPhones, and iPads at first, American Greeting Card's automated inventory system for retailers, and Federal Express's customer service capabilities are all examples of sustainable advantages around which successful differentiation strategies have been built. A business can achieve differentiation by performing its existing value activities or reconfiguring in some unique way. And the sustainability of that differentiation will depend on two things: a continuation of its high perceived value to buyers and a lack of imitation by competitors.

Exhibit 8.3 provides examples of the types of key skills and resources on which managers seeking to build differentiation-based strategies would base their underlying, sustainable competitive advantages. Examples of value chain activities that provide a differentiation advantage are also provided.

Strategists examining their business's resources and capabilities for differentiation advantages evaluate the sustainability of those advantages by benchmarking (refer to Chapter 6 for a discussion of this comparison technique) their business against key competitors and by considering the effect of any differentiation advantage on the five forces in their business's competitive environment. Sustainable activities that provide one or more of the following opportunities relative to key industry forces should become the basis for differentiation aspects of the business's competitive strategy:

Rivalry is reduced when a business successfully differentiates itself   BMW's Z4, made in Greer, South Carolina, does not compete with Saturns made in central Tennessee. A Harvard education does not compete with an education from a local technical school. Both situations involve the same basic needs—transportation or education. However, one rival has clearly differentiated itself from others in the minds of certain buyers. In so doing, they do not have to respond competitively to that competitor.

Buyers are less sensitive to prices for effectively differentiated products   The Highlands Inn in Carmel, California, and the Ventana Inn along the Big Sur charge a minimum of $750 and $1,000, respectively, per night for a room with a kitchen, fireplace, hot tub, and view. Other places are available along this beautiful stretch of California's spectacular coastline, but occupancy rates at these two locations remain over 90 percent. Why? You can't get a better view and a more relaxed, spectacular setting to spend a few days on the Pacific Coast. Similarly, buyers of differentiated products tolerate price increases low-cost-oriented buyers would not accept. The former become very loyal to certain brands. Harley-Davidson motorcycles continue to rise in price, and its buyer base continues to expand worldwide, even though many motorcycle alternatives more reasonably priced are easily available.

EXHIBIT 8.3
Evaluating a Business's Differentiation Opportunities

Source: Based on Michael Porter, *On Competition*, 1998, Harvard Business School Press.

A. Skills and Resources That Foster Differentiation

Strong marketing abilities
Product engineering
Creative talent and flair
Strong capabilities in basic research
Corporate reputation for quality or technical leadership
Long tradition in an industry or unique combination of skills drawn from other businesses
Strong cooperation from channels
Strong cooperation from suppliers of major components of the product or service

B. Organizational Requirements to Support and Sustain Differentiation Activities

Strong coordination among functions in R&D, product development, and marketing
Subjective measurement and incentives instead of quantitative measures
Amenities to attract highly skilled labor, scientists, and creative people
Tradition of closeness to key customers
Some personnel skilled in sales and operations—technical and marketing

C. Examples of Ways Businesses Achieve Competitive Advantage via Differentiation

Technology Development	Use cutting-edge production technology and product features to maintain a "distinct" image and actual product.
Human Resource Management	Develop programs to ensure technical competence of sales staff and a marketing orientation of service personnel.
General Administration	Develop comprehensive, personalized database to build knowledge of groups of customers and individual buyers to be used in "customizing" how products are sold, serviced, and replaced.
Procurement	Maintain quality control presence at key supplier facilities; work with suppliers' new-product development activities.

Inbound logistics	Operations	Outbound logistics	Marketing and Sales	Service
Purchase superior quality, well-known components, raising the quality and image of final products.	Carefully inspect products at each step in production to improve product performance and lower defect rate.	Coordinate JIT with buyers; use own or captive transportation service to ensure timeliness.	Build brand image with expensive, informative advertising and promotion.	Allow service personnel considerable discretion to credit customers for repairs.

Profit Margin

Brand loyalty is hard for new entrants to overcome   Many new beers are brought to market in the United States, but Budweiser continues to gain market share. Why? Brand loyalty is hard to overcome! And Anheuser-Busch has been clever to extend its brand loyalty from its core brand into newer niches, such as nonalcohol brews, that other potential entrants have pioneered. Perhaps few if any companies match the brand loyalty Apple has built over the years. Global Strategy in Action, Exhibit 8.4, examines some of the core capabilities Apple management has long closely monitored to allow it to commit to a user experience–based differentiation strategy built upon hardware design, a dynamic product line, careful marketing and promotion, and closely coordinated software with hardware.

Managers examining differentiation-based advantages must take potential risks into account as they commit their business to these advantages. Some of the more common ways risks arise are discussed next.

Apple Pursues Differentiation-Based Business Strategy

Hardware design. Apple has built in its practices, its culture, its image, and its core a passion for simple, clean, elegant, and compact hardware design packed with features and user experience–focused.

Dynamic product line. Apple has repeatedly created an initial product that defines a new user experience solution, then builds over time on that same product, adding new features and upgrades as the customers' needs evolve.

Marketing and promotion. Simple, elegant, clean, and compact in visual offering and message content.

Software and hardware. Core, unique software capabilities integrated over time with hardware.

Where is it going from here? In the post-Jobs era, many question how well Apple will do in following this differentiation strategy based on these core sources of differentiation. Apple loyalists, employees, and its leader suggest it will continue to do this as it moves into TVs, watches, or other products that allow it to create a unique hardware design, following it with an unfolding, dynamic product line, supporting it with classic Apple marketing and promotion, and ensuring a tightly integrated software and hardware experience. What do you think?

Imitation narrows perceived differentiation, rendering differentiation meaningless AMC pioneered the Jeep passenger version of a truck 40 years ago. Ford created the Explorer, or luxury utility vehicle, in 1990. It took luxury car features and put them inside a jeep. Ford's payoff was substantial. The Explorer became Ford's most popular domestic vehicle. However, virtually every vehicle manufacturer offered a luxury utility a few years later, resulting in customers beginning to be hard pressed to identify clear distinctions between lead models. Ford's Explorer managers have sought to shape a new business strategy for the next decade that relies both on new sources of differentiation and placing greater emphasis on low-cost components in their value chain.

Technological changes that nullify past investments or learning   Consider the strategic decisions of numerous companies committed to differentiation strategies just a few years ago as they also tried to extrapolate the implications of the Internet and social media on how to build competitive advantages that enabled greater differentiation. Blockbuster sought to ensure convenient location and first-to-have new movie releases as key ways to build in differentiation. Borders, the differentiated pioneer of the book superstore business model, and the niche-focused Waldenbooks chain entered bankruptcy in 2011. Numerous regional newspaper chains committed for years to differentiate themselves with excellent regional coverages followed a similar fate in the last few years. Google—the incredible Internet-based story of the last ten years, built on unmatched search algorithms differentiating them from all others as the starting point for most people connecting to the Internet—is suddenly faced with the reality that Facebook's simple sharing of pictures and personal information with friends will revolutionize how people first come to the Internet and as a result how advertisers might best link to their interests. All of these examples are ones where the fundamental underpinnings of companies' differentiation-based advantages—best locations, best selection, unique atmosphere, and even the reason you go onto the Internet—have changed suddenly and dramatically due to a technological change or shift. The result in each case is a company-threatening reality for the business as it is or was operating; with the reality that what had been a stellar and powerful differentiation strategy suddenly is becoming a potential death-trap.

The cost difference between low-cost competitors and the differentiated business becomes too great for differentiation to hold brand loyalty   Buyers may begin to choose to sacrifice some of the features, services, or image possessed by the differentiated business for large cost savings. The rising cost of a college education, particularly at several "premier" institutions, has caused many students to opt for lower-cost destinations that offer very similar courses without image, frills, and professors who seldom teach undergraduate students anyway.

Evaluating Speed as a Competitive Advantage

The success of Samsung in challenging and overtaking Apple in the smartphone market is an example of the role of speed in building competitive advantage. Samsung's calculated choice of a follower strategy in huge global consumer product markets requires an accurate evaluation of its ability to respond quickly—to have unmatched speed—allowing it to be able to build something similar, make it better, at a sustainable lower cost, but critically in a very quick fashion before the market cycle for that product version matures and profits fall. Samsung determines whether its rapidly created version of the current innovative product leader is better in some key way, or equal but able to be profitably priced much lower. If it answers "yes," Samsung pounces, deploying its vast integrated production capabilities, then flooding the market with a wide range of models constantly updated with a speed that its rivals find hard to match. Said James Song of KDB Securities, "What Samsung did in smartphones was brilliant, no one can beat Samsung in playing catch-up." After its court patent battle loss, Samsung saw Apple lawyers filing injunctions against sales of Galaxy smartphones in the United States. For Samsung, those products had already lived through their life cycles. Already anticipating those injunctions, with characteristic speed Samsung had already retooled its latest Galaxy S III smartphones to stay ahead of the patent battle and grew 150 percent to a record 35 percent of the market, with Apple coming in selling roughly half the number of smartphones as Samsung. Said Anthony Miller, "Koreans do things quicker than almost anyone . . . this allows them to change models, go from design to production faster than anyone at the present time." Said Mr. Song, "Despite the patent verdict the fight for the smartphone market is over and has been decided in Samsung's favor."[3] Speed works!

speed-based strategies
Business strategies built around functional capabilities and activities that allow the company to meet customer needs directly or indirectly more rapidly than its main competitors.

Speed-based strategies, or rapid responses to customer requests or market and technological changes, have become a major source of competitive advantage for numerous firms in today's intensely competitive global economy. Speed is certainly a form of differentiation, but it is more than that. Speed involves the *availability of a rapid response* to a customer by providing current products quicker, accelerating new-product development or improvement, quickly adjusting production processes, and making decisions quickly. While low cost and differentiation may provide important competitive advantages, managers in tomorrow's successful companies will base their strategies on creating speed-based competitive advantages. Facebook is perhaps the perfect example of speed-based strategic choice, becoming the fourth largest "country" in the world, with over 500 million users in three years, and its breakneck continuous introduction of new features, capabilities, even sometimes "borking up the site," as one blogger now making a living covering Facebook's constant new features[4] asserts. And Facebook's acquisition of Snaptu, the Israeli mobile applications for feature phones company, foretells a yet faster pace.[5]

---

[3]"After Verdict, Assessing the Samsung Strategy in South Korea," *The New York Times,* September 2, 2012.
[4]Zack Whittaker, "Facebook's New Features, But Borking Up the Site in the Process," *ZDNet.com,* March 20, 2011.
[5]Ben Parr, "Facebook Acquires Snaptu to Bring Social Networking to Feature Phones," *mashable.com,* March 20, 2011.

Building Ryanair with an Emphasis on SPEED

A few years ago, founder Michael O'Leary was pushing the idea of a quick, low-cost, international flight service from Europe to America . . . fly across the pond last minute for $55. Vintage O'Leary. Years earlier he drove a World War II tank to England's Luton airport demanding access to "attack" rival easyJet and liberate the public from easyJet's high fares. O'Leary even called customers that forget or don't get their boarding passes printed out before arriving at the airport "idiots." Behind it all is a strategy built around SPEED.*

SPEED1: Ryanair uses small, secondary airports outside major cities. They allow Ryanair to fly into and out of an area quicker, turn around faster, and get customers on their way with far less time lost compared to regular airlines and airports. These airports also cost less to use, get people close to big city destinations, and get planes back in the air in 25 minutes—half the time competitors experience. This allows Ryanair to provide more frequent flights,

adding timesaving convenience for both leisure and business travelers.

SPEED2: Ryanair has made large bulk purchases of Boeing's newest 737 airplanes. These planes require less maintenance and are easy to handle in smaller airports—all leading to speedier operations on a daily basis and quicker in and out maintenance downtimes.

SPEED3: Ryanair sells more than 98 percent of its tickets on Ryanair.com—allowing for quicker, more accessible service for customers seeking simplicity, speed, and convenience. It also sells hotels, car rentals, and various other offerings at the same Web site, further simplifying and saving considerable time [think speed] for customers.

*Felix Billette, "Ryanair's O'Leary: The Duke of Discomfort," *Bloomberg Business Week*, September 2, 2010; and Brad Tuttle, "That's Some Quirky Marketing Strategy: CEO Calls His Customers 'Idiots'," www.business.time.com.Sept.11, September 11, 2012.

Exhibit 8.5, Global Strategy in Action tells how Irishman Michael O'Leary built Ryanair using a speed-based competitive strategy. Exhibit 8.6 describes and illustrates key skills and organizational requirements that are associated with speed-based competitive advantage. Jack Welch, the now-retired CEO who transformed General Electric from a fading company into one of Wall Street's best performers over the past 25 years, had this to say about speed:

> Speed is really the driving force that everyone is after. Faster products, faster product cycles to market. Better response time to customers. . . . Satisfying customers, getting faster communications, moving with more agility, all these things are easier when one is small. And these are all characteristics one needs in a fast-moving global environment.[6]

Speed-based competitive advantages can be created around several activities:

Customer Responsiveness   All consumers have encountered hassles, delays, and frustration dealing with various businesses from time to time. The same holds true when dealing business to business. Quick response with answers, information, and solutions to mistakes can become the basis for competitive advantage—one that builds customer loyalty quickly.

Product Development Cycles   Japanese automakers have focused intensely on the time it takes to create a new model because several experienced disappointing sales growth in the last decade in Europe and North America competing against new vehicles like Ford's Explorer and Renault's Megane. VW had recently conceived, prototyped, produced, and marketed a totally new 4-wheel-drive car in Europe within 12 months. Honda, Toyota, and Nissan lowered their product development cycle from 24 months to 9 months from conception to production. This capability is old hat to 3M Corporation, which is so successful at speedy product development that one-fourth of its sales and profits each year are from products that didn't exist five years earlier.

[6]"Jack Welch: A CEO Who Can't Be Cloned," *BusinessWeek*, September 17, 2001.

EXHIBIT 8.6 **Evaluating a Business's Rapid Response (Speed) Opportunities**

A. Skills and Resources That Foster Speed

Process engineering skills
Excellent inbound and outbound logistics
Technical people in sales and customer service
High levels of automation
Corporate reputation for quality or technical leadership
Flexible manufacturing capabilities
Strong downstream partners
Strong cooperation from suppliers of major components of the product or service

B. Organizational Requirements to Support and Sustain Rapid Response Activities

Strong coordination among functions in R&D, product development, and marketing.
Major emphasis on customer satisfaction in incentive programs
Strong delegation to operating personnel
Tradition of closeness to key customers
Some personnel skilled in sales and operations—technical and marketing
Empowered customer service personnel

C. Examples of Ways Businesses Achieve Competitive Advantage via Speed

Technology Development	Use companywide technology sharing activities and autonomous product development teams to speed new-product development.				
Human Resource Management	Develop self-managed work teams and decision making at the lowest levels to increase responsiveness.				
General Administration	Develop highly automated and integrated information processing system. Include major buyers in the "system" on a real-time basis.				
Procurement	Integrate preapproved online suppliers into production.				
	Work very closely with suppliers to include their choice of warehouse location to minimize delivery time.	Standardize dies, components, and production equipment to allow quick changeover to new or special orders.	Ensure very rapid delivery with JIT delivery plus partnering with express mail services.	Use of laptops linked directly to operations to speed the order process and shorten the sales cycle.	Locate service technicians at customer facilities that are geographically close.
	Inbound logistics	Operations	Outbound logistics	Marketing and Sales	Service

Profit Margin

Product or Service Improvements Like development time, companies that can rapidly adapt their products or services and do so in a way that benefits their customers or creates new customers have a major competitive advantage over rivals that cannot do this.

Speed in Delivery or Distribution Firms that can get you what you need when you need it, even when that is tomorrow, realize that buyers have come to expect that level of responsiveness. Federal Express's success reflects the importance customers place on speed in inbound and outbound logistics.

Information Sharing and Technology Speed in sharing information that becomes the basis for decisions, actions, or other important activities taken by a customer, supplier, or partner has become a major source of competitive advantage for many businesses. Telecommunications, the Internet, and networks are but a part of a vast infrastructure that is being used by knowledgeable managers to rebuild or create value in their businesses via information sharing.

These rapid response capabilities create competitive advantages in several ways. They create a way to lessen rivalry because they have *availability* of something that a rival may not have. It can allow the business to charge buyers more, engender loyalty, or otherwise enhance the business's position relative to its buyers. Particularly where impressive customer response is involved, businesses can generate supplier cooperation and concessions because their business ultimately benefits from increased revenue. Finally, substitute products and new entrants find themselves trying to keep up with the rapid changes rather than introducing them.

While the notion of speed-based competitive advantage is exciting, it has risks managers must consider. First, speeding up activities that haven't been conducted in a fashion that prioritizes rapid response should only be done after considerable attention to training, reorganization, and/or reengineering. Second, some industries—stable, mature ones that have very minimal levels of change—may not offer much advantage to the firm that introduces some forms of rapid response. Customers in such settings may prefer the slower pace or the lower costs currently available, or they may have long time frames in purchasing such that speed is not that important to them.

Evaluating Market Focus as a Way to Competitive Advantage

market focus
This is a generic strategy that applies a differentiation strategy approach, or a low-cost strategy approach, or a combination—and does so solely in a narrow (or "focused") market niche rather than trying to do so across the broader market. The narrow focus may be geographically defined or defined by product type features, or target customer type, or some combination of these.

Small companies, at least the better ones, usually thrive because they serve narrow market niches. This is usually called **market focus,** the extent to which a business concentrates on a narrowly defined market. Consider the story of Soho Beverages, a small beverage company in New York that Seagram bought to augment liquor sales, adapted with a price increase, and pulled into the regular Seagram sales approach. Within 18 months, steadily losing sales, Seagram sold it to a group led by Tom Cox, a former Pepsi manager, for pennies on the dollar compared to what Seagram paid two years earlier. The tiny brand, once a healthy niche product in New York and a few other East Coast locations, languished within Seagrams because its sales force was unused to selling in delis. Cox was able to double sales in one year. He did this on a lean marketing budget that didn't include advertising or database marketing. He hired Korean- and Arabic-speaking college students and had his people walk into practically every deli in Manhattan in order to reacquaint owners with the brand, spot consumption trends, and take orders. He provided rapid stocking services to all Manhattan-area delis, regardless of size. The business continued to grow sales year after year. Why? Cox attributed it to focusing on a niche market—delis; continually differentiating the product using a unique sales force; rapidly responding to any deli-owner request, and keeping costs low in promotion and delivery.

Two things are important in this example. First, this business focused on a narrow niche market in which to build a strong competitive advantage. But focus alone was not enough to build competitive advantage. Rather, Cox created several capabilities, resources, and value chain activities that achieved differentiation, low-cost, and rapid response competitive advantages within this niche market that would be hard for other firms, particularly mass market—oriented firms, to replicate. Exhibit 8.7, Global Strategy In Action, describes how surfer Nicholas Woodman used a passion for action sports and his wrist-mounted camera to build what is now a social phenomenon via a narrow focus strategy, selling to like-minded action sports enthusiasts and any others that wish to join them in documenting more and more of their lives, their work, or their fun.

Market focus allows some businesses to compete on the basis of low cost, differentiation, and rapid response against much larger businesses with greater resources. Focus lets a business "learn" its target customers—their needs, special considerations they want

Nicholas Woodman joined the Forbes World Billionaires List, being one of the 30 youngest members, based on the worth of his interest in Woodman Labs, maker of GoPro cameras. A passionate athlete and surfer, Woodman turned his initial idea to tether cameras to athletes' wrists into a social video phenomenon. Often asked whether selling tiny, rugged cameras so divers, surfers, skiers, and skydivers can record their exploits is just a "niche" business, Woodman responds that "It's becoming the norm to document more and more of our lives . . . if that is a niche, it's a very big one." Fire departments now use them for training, the U.S. Army puts them on Humvees and drones, marine biologists use them for undersea research.

Woodman will no doubt experience increased joiners in this niche as GoPro goes more and more mainstream. Large traditional camera makers like Sony and Nikon are scrambling to address the growth of the "niche" Woodman has pioneered. But at his core Woodman has a passionate, aggressive focus on making and refining cameras and tethers that allow action-sports enthusiasts to take professional-quality videos. He has maintained that focus intensely for twelve years since he created his first camera attached to his wrist while surfing. To get GoPro started he moved back in with his parents, worked 20/7, and wrote off a personal life. He gave himself four years to make something of the idea, driven by two prior business failures, and he hooked up with Chinese manufacturer Hotax, working from its $3.05 film camera—FedExing designs back and forth weekly. He then lived out of his 1971 Volkswagen bus, driving up and down the California coast to approach people on the beach and at concerts, selling imported belts from Indonesia to fund his development, and then tediously visited surf, bike, and running shops to sell the earliest GoPro versions.

He now has an in-house product design group of about 150 engineers. He has remained adamant about following the Apple approach—stick with a core product genre and continuously refine it, selling regular new versions. That now means exceptional digital versions, tie-in with cloud computing storage, and 14-megapixel video exceeding 60 frames per second. Ever wary that you evolve or die, Woodman remains hyper-vigilant on a continued focus strategy, continuously refining the product offered in a simple let-the-product-sell-itself marketing program, hitting key price points that work to keep large competitor copycats at bay.

accommodated—and establish personal relationships in ways that "differentiate" the smaller firm or make it more valuable to the target customer. Low costs can also be achieved, filling niche needs in a buyer's operations that larger rivals either do not want to bother with or cannot do as cost effectively. Cost advantage often centers around the high level of customized service the focused, smaller business can provide. And perhaps the greatest competitive weapon that can arise is rapid response. With enhanced knowledge of its customers and intricacies of their operations, the small, focused company builds up organizational knowledge about timing-sensitive ways to work with a customer. Often the needs of that narrow set of customers represent a large part of the small, focused business's revenues. Exhibit 8.7 tells the story of Nicholas Woodman's stunning success pursuing a strategy focused on a narrow initial market, global in scope, and doing so with extraordinary attention to product design, continuous redesign, exceptional quality, and careful price points.

The risk of focus is that you attract major competitors who have waited for your business to "prove" the market. Domino's proved that a huge market for pizza delivery existed and now faces serious challenges. Likewise, publicly traded companies built around focus strategies become takeover targets for large firms seeking to fill out a product portfolio. And perhaps the greatest risk of all is slipping into the illusion that it is focus itself, and not some special form of low cost, differentiation, or rapid response, that is creating the business's success.

EXHIBIT 8.8 Sources of Distinctive Competence at Different Stages of Industry Evolution

Functional Area	Introduction	Growth	Maturity	Decline
Marketing	Resources/skills to create widespread awareness and find acceptance from customers; advantageous access to distribution	Ability to establish brand recognition, find niche, reduce price, solidify strong distribution relations, and develop new channels	Skills in aggressively promoting products to new markets and holding existing markets; pricing flexibility; skills in differentiating products and holding customer loyalty	Cost-effective means of efficient access to selected channels and markets; strong customer loyalty or dependence; strong company image
Production operations	Ability to expand capacity effectively, limit number of designs, develop standards	Ability to add product variants, centralize production, or otherwise lower costs; ability to improve product quality; seasonal subcontracting capacity	Ability to improve product and reduce costs; ability to share or reduce capacity; advantageous supplier relationships; subcontracting	Ability to prune product line; cost advantage in production, location, or distribution; simplified inventory control; subcontracting or long production runs
Finance	Resources to support high net cash overflow and initial losses; ability to use leverage effectively	Ability to finance rapid expansion, to have net cash outflows but increasing profits; resources to support product improvements	Ability to generate and redistribute increasing net cash inflows; effective cost control systems	Ability to reuse or liquidate unneeded equipment; advantage in cost of facilities; control system accuracy; streamlined management control

Managers evaluating opportunities to build competitive advantage should link strategies to resources, capabilities, and value chain activities that exploit low cost, differentiation, and rapid response competitive advantages. When advantageous, they should consider ways to use focus to leverage these advantages. One way business managers can enhance their likelihood of identifying these opportunities is to consider several different "generic" industry environments from the perspective of the typical value chain activities most often linked to sustained competitive advantages in those unique industry situations. The next section discusses key generic industry environments and the value chain activities most associated with success.

Stages of Industry Evolution and Business Strategy Choices

The requirements for success in industry segments change over time. Strategists can use these changing requirements, which are associated with different stages of industry evolution, as a way to isolate key competitive advantages and shape strategic choices around them. Exhibit 8.8 depicts four stages of industry evolution and the typical functional capabilities that are often associated with business success at each of these stages.

EXHIBIT 8.8 *(continued)*

Functional Area	Introduction	Growth	Maturity	Decline
Personnel	Flexibility in staffing and training new management; existence of employees with key skills in new products or markets	Existence of an ability to add skilled personnel; motivated and loyal workforce	Ability to cost effectively, reduce workforce, increase efficiency	Capacity to reduce and reallocate personnel; cost advantage
Engineering and research and development	Ability to make engineering changes, have technical bugs in product and process resolved	Skill in quality and new feature development; ability to start developing successor product	Ability to reduce costs, develop variants, differentiate products	Ability to support other grown areas or to apply product to unique customer needs
Key functional area and strategy focus	Engineering: market penetration	Sales: consumer loyalty; market share	Production efficiency; successor products	Finance; maximum investment recovery

Competitive Advantage and Strategic Choices in Emerging Industries

emerging industry
An industry that has growing sales across all the companies in the industry based on growing demand for the relatively new products, technologies, and/or services made available by the firms participating in this industry.

Emerging industries are newly formed or re-formed industries that typically are created by technological innovation, newly emerging customer needs, or other economic or sociological changes. **Emerging industries** of the last decade have been the Internet social networking, satellite radio, surgical robotics, and online services industries.

From the standpoint of strategy formulation, the essential characteristic of an emerging industry is that there are no "rules of the game." The absence of rules presents both a risk and an opportunity—a wise strategy positions the firm to favorably shape the emerging industry's rules.

Business strategies must be shaped to accommodate the following characteristics of markets in emerging industries:

- Technologies that are mostly proprietary to the pioneering firms and technological uncertainty about how product standardization will unfold.
- Competitor uncertainty because of inadequate information about competitors, buyers, and the timing of demand.
- High initial costs but steep cost declines as the experience curve takes effect.
- Few entry barriers, which often spurs the formation of many new firms.
- First-time buyers requiring initial inducement to purchase and customers confused by the availability of a number of nonstandard products.

- Inability to obtain raw materials and components until suppliers gear up to meet the industry's needs.
- Need for high-risk capital because of the industry's uncertainty prospects.

For success in this industry setting, business strategies require one or more of these features:

1. The ability to *shape the industry's structure* based on the timing of entry, reputation, success in related industries or technologies, and role in industry associations.
2. The ability to *rapidly improve product quality* and performance features.
3. *Advantageous relationships* with key suppliers and promising distribution channels.
4. The ability to *establish the firm's technology as the dominant one* before technological uncertainty decreases.
5. The early acquisition of *a core group of loyal customers* and then the expansion of that customer base through model changes, alternative pricing, and advertising.
6. The ability to *forecast future competitors* and the strategies they are likely to employ.

A firm that has had repeated successes with business in emerging industries is 3M Corporation. In each of the past 20 years, more than 25 percent of 3M's annual sales have come from products that did not exist five years earlier. Start-up companies enhance their success by having experienced entrepreneurs at the helm, a knowledgeable management team and board of directors, and patient sources of venture capital. Steven Jobs's dramatic unveiling of Apple's iPod, iPhone, and then iPad came to be seen by many as the catalysts for the emergence of a new personalized digital post-PC world. Jobs and Apple certainly took advantage by building a strategy that shaped the industry's structure, established the firm's technology as a dominant one, endeared themselves to a core group of loyal customers, and rapidly improved each product's quality and wireless, Web-based functionality.

Competitive Advantages and Strategic Choices in Growing Industries

growth industry strategies
Business strategies that may be more advantageous for firms participating in rapidly growing industries and markets.

Rapid growth brings new competitors into the industry. Oftentimes, those new entrants are large competitors with substantial resources who have waited for the market to "prove" itself before they committed significant resources. At this stage, **growth industry strategies** that emphasize brand recognition, product differentiation, and the financial resources to support both heavy marketing expenses and the effect of price competition on cash flow can be key strengths. Accelerating demand means scaling up production or service capacity to meet the growing demand. Doing so may place a premium on being able to adapt product design and production facilities to meet rapidly increasing demand effectively. Increased investment in plant and equipment, in research and development (R&D), and especially marketing efforts to target specific customer groups along with developing strong distribution capabilities place a demand on the firm's capital resources.

For success in this industry setting, business strategies require one or more of these features:

1. The ability to *establish strong brand recognition* through promotional resources and skills that increase selective demand.
2. The ability and resources to *scale up to meet increasing demand*, which may involve production facilities, service capabilities, and the training and logistics associated with that capacity.
3. *Strong product design skills* to be able to adapt products and services to scaled operations and emerging market niches.
4. The ability to *differentiate the firm's product[s]* from competitors entering the market.

5. *R&D resources and skills* to create product variations and advantages.

6. The ability to *build repeat buying from established customers* and attract new customers.

7. Strong capabilities in *sales and marketing*.

IBM entered the personal computer market—which Apple pioneered in the growth stage—and was able to rapidly become the market leader with a strategy based on its key strengths in brand awareness and possession of the financial resources needed to support consumer advertising. Many large technology companies today prefer exactly this approach: to await proof of an industry or product market and then to acquire small pioneer firms with first-mover advantage as a means to obtain an increasingly known brand, or to acquire technical know-how and experience behind which the firms can put its resources and distribution strength to build brand identity and loyalty. When the PC market matured, IBM sold its PC division to China's Lenovo and has exited the personal computer industries.

Competitive Advantages and Strategic Choices in Mature Industry Environments

mature industry strategies
Strategies used by firms competing in markets where the growth rate of that market from year to year has reached or is close to zero.

As an industry evolves, its rate of growth eventually declines. This "transition to maturity" is accompanied by several changes in its competitive environment: Competition for market share becomes more intense as firms in the industry are forced to achieve sales growth at one another's expense. Firms working with the **mature industry strategies** sell increasingly to experienced, repeat buyers who are now making choices among known alternatives. Competition becomes more oriented to cost and service as knowledgeable buyers expect similar price and product features. Industry capacity "tops out" as sales growth ceases to cover up poorly planned expansions. New products and new applications are harder to come by. International competition increases as cost pressures lead to overseas production advantages. Profitability falls, often permanently, as a result of pressure to lower prices and the increased costs of holding or building market share.

These changes necessitate a fundamental strategic reassessment. Strategy elements of successful firms in maturing industries often include the following:

1. *Product line* pruning, or dropping unprofitable product models, sizes, and options from the firm's product mix.

2. *Emphasis on process innovation* that permits low-cost product design, manufacturing methods, and distribution synergy.

3. *Emphasis on cost reduction* through exerting pressure on suppliers for lower prices, switching to cheaper components, introducing operational efficiencies, and lowering administrative and sales overhead.

4. *Careful buyer selection* to focus on buyers who are less aggressive, more closely tied to the firm, and able to buy more from the firm.

5. *Horizontal acquisition* to acquire rival firms whose weaknesses can be used to gain a bargain price and that are correctable by the acquiring firms.

6. *International expansion* to markets where attractive growth and limited competition still exist and the opportunity for lower-cost manufacturing can influence both domestic and international costs.

Milliken, the world's largest private textile company and a chemical company, offers a notable example of a company making solid strategic choices in what are often considered mature industries. Milliken's choice has been to emphasize technology and process innovation, integrate textiles capabilities and chemical capabilities, achieve international expansion, and promote careful buyer selection—thus serving major consumer and industrial industry

Milliken's Strategic Choice to Reduce Its Environmental Impact

Milliken personnel responsible for cost-control strategic choices related to waste and environmental impact management communicate the essence of those choices in the interesting triangular "Waste Management Pyramid" shown here. The least desirable option for Milliken facilities to handle manufacturing waste is to dispose of it in a secure, legal landfill. Milliken sees this as the most costly option, both directly and in liability terms. Reuse is the most desirable option—least liability and least costly. Shown also are the results Milliken achieved in 2010: a 7 percent reduction in waste over the previous year, with only 0.008 percent of its waste going to landfills, none incinerated, 24 percent converted to energy at Milliken facilities, 60 percent recycled, and 16 percent reused.

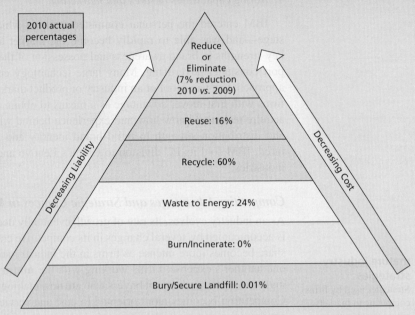

2010 actual percentages

Reduce or Eliminate (7% reduction 2010 vs. 2009)

Reuse: 16%

Recycle: 60%

Waste to Energy: 24%

Burn/Incinerate: 0%

Bury/Secure Landfill: 0.01%

Decreasing Liability

Decreasing Cost

Source: Estimate based on Innoventure Sustainability Forum, Moore School of Business, University of South Carolina, presentation by Milliken Sustainability Team; and Milliken.com.

---

buyers with significant fabric-related needs. Milliken also includes constant emphasis on cost reduction along with environmental impact reduction. Taken together, these strategic choices regularly result in Milliken being named one of the top global companies in many recognition forums, plus being named one of the world's most ethical companies by Ethisphere.com—all this in two "mature" industries that have seen numerous well-known companies exit or lose out to low-cost competitors in emerging economies. Exhibit 8.9, Global Strategy in Action, illustrates just one strategic choice at Milliken—minimizing its environmental impact while also endeavoring to save costs and limit future waste-related liability.

Business strategists in maturing industries must avoid several pitfalls. First, they must make a clear choice among the three generic strategies and avoid a middle-ground approach, which would confuse both knowledgeable buyers and the firm's personnel. Second, they must avoid sacrificing market share too quickly for short-term profit. Finally, they must avoid waiting too long to respond to price reductions, retaining unneeded excess capacity, engaging in sporadic or irrational efforts to boost sales, and placing their hopes on "new" products, rather than aggressively selling existing products.

Competitive Advantages and Strategic Choices in Declining Industries

Declining industries are those that make products or services for which demand is growing slower than demand in the economy as a whole or is actually declining. This slow growth or decline in demand is caused by technological substitution (such as the substitution of electronic calculators for slide rules), demographic shifts (such as the increase in

declining industry
An industry in which the trend of total sales as an indicator of total demand for an industry's products or services among all the participants in the industry have started to drop from the last several years with the likelihood being that such a trend will continue indefinitely.

the number of older people and the decrease in the number of children), and shifts in needs (such as the decreased need for red meat).

Firms in a declining industry should choose strategies that emphasize one or more of the following themes:

1. *Focus* on segments within the industry that offer a chance for higher growth or a higher return.

2. *Emphasize product innovation and quality improvement*, where this can be done cost effectively, to differentiate the firm from rivals and to spur growth.

3. *Emphasize production and distribution efficiency* by streamlining production, closing marginal production facilities and costly distribution outlets, and adding effective new facilities and outlets.

4. *Gradually harvest the business*—generate cash by cutting down on maintenance, reducing models, and shrinking channels and make no new investment.

Strategists who incorporate one or more of these themes into the strategy of their business can anticipate relative success, particularly where the industry's decline is slow and smooth and some profitable niches remain. Penn Tennis, the nation's no. 1 maker of tennis balls, watched industrywide sales steadily decline over the last decade. In response it started marketing tennis balls as "dog toys" in the rapidly growing pet products industry. It secondly made Penn balls the official ball at major tournaments. Third, it created three different quality levels; then, as sales revived, Penn Sports sold its tennis ball business to Head Sports.

Competitive Advantage in Fragmented Industries

Fragmented industries are another setting in which identifiable types of competitive advantages and the strategic choices suggested by those advantages can be identified. A **fragmented industry** is one in which no firm has a significant market share and can strongly influence industry outcomes. Fragmented industries are found in many areas of the economy and are common in such areas as professional services, retailing, distribution, wood and metal fabrication, and agricultural products. The funeral industry is an example of a highly fragmented industry. Business strategists in fragmented industries pursue low-cost or differentiation strategies or focus competitive advantages in one of five ways:

fragmented industry
An industry in which there are numerous competitors (providers of the same or similar products or services the industry involves) such that no single firm or small group of firms controls any significant share of the overall industry sales.

Tightly Managed Decentralization   Fragmented industries are characterized by a need for intense local coordination, a local management orientation, high personal service, and local autonomy. Recently, however, successful firms in such industries have introduced a high degree of professionalism into the operations of local managers.

"Formula" Facilities   This alternative, related to the previous one, introduces standardized, efficient, low-cost facilities at multiple locations. Thus, the firm gradually builds a low-cost advantage over localized competitors. Fast-food and motel chains have applied this approach with considerable success.

Increased Value Added   The products or services of some fragmented industries are difficult to differentiate. In this case, an effective strategy may be to add value by providing more service with the sale or by engaging in some product assembly that is of additional value to the customer.

Specialization   Focus strategies that creatively segment the market can enable firms to cope with fragmentation. Specialization can be pursued by

1. *Product type.* The firm builds expertise focusing on a narrow range of products or services.

2. *Customer type.* The firm becomes intimately familiar with and serves the needs of a narrow customer segment.

3. *Type of order.* The firm handles only certain kinds of orders, such as small orders, custom orders, or quick turnaround orders.

4. *Geographic area.* The firm blankets or concentrates on a single area.

Although specialization in one or more of these ways can be the basis for a sound focus strategy in a fragmented industry, each of these types of specialization risks limiting the firm's potential sales volume.

Bare Bones/No Frills   Given the intense competition and low margins in fragmented industries, a "bare bones" posture—low overhead, minimum wage employees, tight cost control—may build a sustainable cost advantage in such industries.

Competitive Advantage in Global Industries

global industry
Industry in which competition crosses national borders.

Global industries present a final setting in which success is often associated with identifiable sources of competitive advantage. A **global industry** is one that comprises firms whose competitive positions in major geographic or national markets are fundamentally affected by their overall global competitive positions. To avoid strategic disadvantages, firms in global industries are virtually required to compete on a worldwide basis. Oil, steel, automobiles, apparel, motorcycles, televisions, and computers are examples of global industries.

Global industries have four unique strategy-shaping features:

- Differences in prices and costs from country to country due to currency exchange fluctuations, differences in wage and inflation rates, and other economic factors.
- Differences in buyer needs across different countries.
- Differences in competitors and ways of competing from country to country.
- Differences in trade rules and governmental regulations across different countries.

These unique features and the global competition of global industries require that two fundamental components be addressed in the business strategy: (1) the approach used to gain global market coverage and (2) the generic competitive strategy. Three basic options can be used to pursue global market coverage:

1. *License* foreign firms to produce and distribute the firm's products.
2. *Maintain a domestic production base* and export products to foreign countries.
3. *Establish foreign-based plants and distribution* to compete directly in the markets of one or more foreign countries.

Along with the market coverage decision, strategists must scrutinize the condition of the global industry features identified earlier to choose among four generic global competitive strategies:

1. *Broad-line global competition*—directed at competing worldwide in the full product line of the industry, often with plants in many countries, to achieve differentiation or an overall low-cost position.
2. *Global focus* strategy—targeting a particular segment of the industry for competition on a worldwide basis.
3. *National focus* strategy—taking advantage of differences in national markets that give the firm an edge over global competitors on a nation-by-nation basis.
4. *Protected niche* strategy—seeking out countries in which governmental restraints exclude or inhibit global competitors or allow concessions, or both, that are advantageous to localized firms.

Nineteenth-Century French Steelmaker Crafts a Global Focus Strategy

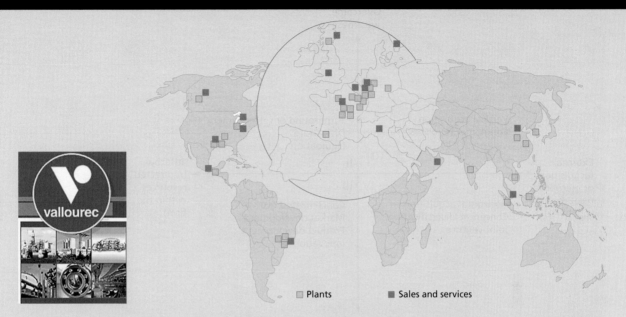

☐ Plants   ■ Sales and services

Vallourec's beginnings go back to the late 1800s in northern France with construction, engineering, metallurgy, and steelmaking. Early the next century, it began making welded and eventually seamless tubes (round pipe). As it prepared to enter the twenty-first century, with all of its plants in Europe, its management decided to sell off various parts of its businesses and commit instead to a global focus strategy providing seamless steel pipes, primarily to the oil and gas and electric power industries.

Vallourec acquired MSA in Brazil in 2000, and, by the beginning of this decade, had moved over half its manufacturing capacity outside Europe, shown in the accompanying world map. It is the world leader in

the global seamless steel tube market. Its global focus strategy is reinforced by a decentralized organizational structure, where regional subsidiaries enjoy considerable autonomy to work closely with clients in their target markets. The global focus strategy must be working well, as evidenced in by more than 20,000 employees—more than 74 percent of its workforce—choosing to buy 1.2 million shares of Vallourec stock, in globally recovering equity and oil markets, at the current market price. At the ground level of a global focus strategy, that is a strong vote of confidence.

Source: www.vallourec.com

Competing in a global context has become a reality for most businesses in virtually every economy around the world. So most firms must consider among the global competitive strategies identified above. Exhibit 8.10, Global Strategy in Action, describes how an "Old World" French steelmaker did just this to craft a global focus strategy selling steel pipe worldwide and in the process become the world leader in seamless steel tubing.

DOMINANT PRODUCT/SERVICE BUSINESSES: EVALUATING AND CHOOSING TO DIVERSIFY TO BUILD VALUE

McDonald's has frequently looked at numerous opportunities to diversify into related businesses or to acquire key suppliers. Its decision has consistently been to focus on its core business using the grand strategies of concentration, market development, and product development. Rival Yum Brands, on the other hand, has chosen to diversify into related

EXHIBIT 8.11   **Grand Strategy Selection Matrix**

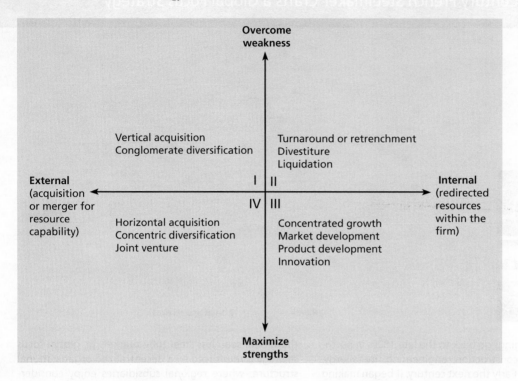

grand strategy selection matrix
A four-cell guide to strategies based upon whether the business is (1) operating from a position of strength or weakness and (2) rely on its own resources versus having to acquire resources via merger or acquisition.

vertical acquisition
Acquisition of firms that supply inputs such as raw materials, or customers for its outputs, such as warehouses for finished products.

conglomerate diversification
Acquiring or entering businesses unrelated to a firm's current technologies, markets, or products.

businesses and vertical acquisition as the best grand strategies for it to build long-term value. Both firms experienced unprecedented success during the last 20 years.

Many dominant product businesses face this question as their core business proves successful: What grand strategies are best suited to continue to build value? Under what circumstances should they choose an expanded focus (diversification, vertical acquisition); steady continued focus (concentration, market or product development); or a narrowed focus (turnaround or divestiture)? This section examines two ways you can analyze a dominant product company's situation and choose among 12 of the 15 grand strategies identified in Chapter 7.

Grand Strategy Selection Matrix

One valuable guide to the selection of a promising grand strategy is the **grand strategy selection matrix** shown in Exhibit 8.11. The basic idea underlying the matrix is that two variables are of central concern in the selection process: (1) the principal purpose of the grand strategy and (2) the choice of an internal or external emphasis for growth or profitability.

In the past, planners were advised to follow certain rules or prescriptions in their choice of strategies. Now, most experts agree that strategy selection is better guided by the conditions of the planning period and by the company strengths and weaknesses. It should be noted, however, that even the early approaches to strategy selection sought to match a concern over internal versus external growth with a desire to overcome weaknesses or maximize strengths.

retrenchment
Cutting back on products, markets, operations because the firm's overall competitive and financial situation cannot support commitments needed to sustain or build its operations.

divestiture
The sale of a firm or a major component.

liquidation
Closing down the operations of a business and selling its assets and operations to pay its debts and distribute any gains to stockholders.

concentrated growth
Aggressive market penetration where a firm's strong position and favorable market growth allow it to "control" resources and effort for focused growth.

market development
Selling present products, often with only cosmetic modification, to customers in related marketing areas by adding channels of distribution or by changing the content of advertising or promotion.

product development
The substantial modification of existing products or the creation of new but related products that can be marketed to current customers through established channels.

innovation
A strategy that seeks to reap the initially high profits associated with customer acceptance of a new or greatly improved product.

The same considerations led to the development of the grand strategy selection matrix. A firm in quadrant I, with "all its eggs in one basket," often views itself as overcommitted to a particular business with limited growth opportunities or high risks. One reasonable solution is **vertical acquisition,** which enables the firm to reduce risk by reducing uncertainty about inputs or access to customers. Another is **conglomerate diversification,** which provides a profitable investment alternative with diverting management attention from the original business. However, the external approaches to overcoming weaknesses usually result in the most costly grand strategies. Acquiring a second business demands large investments of time and sizable financial resources. Thus, strategic managers considering these approaches must guard against exchanging one set of weaknesses for another.

More conservative approaches to overcoming weaknesses are found in quadrant II. Firms often choose to redirect resources from one internal business activity to another. This approach maintains the firm's commitment to its basic mission, rewards success, and enables further development of proven competitive advantages. The least disruptive of the quadrant II strategies is **retrenchment,** pruning the current activities of a business. If the weaknesses of the business arose from inefficiencies, retrenchment can actually serve as a *turnaround* strategy—that is, the business gains new strength from the streamlining of its operations and the elimination of waste. However, if those weaknesses are a major obstruction to success in the industry and the costs of overcoming them are unaffordable or are not justified by a cost-benefit analysis, then eliminating the business must be considered. **Divestiture** offers the best possibility for recouping the firm's investment, but even **liquidation** can be an attractive option if the alternatives are bankruptcy or an unwarranted drain on the firm's resources.

A common business adage states that a firm should build from strength. The premise of this adage is that growth and survival depend on an ability to capture a market share that is large enough for essential economies of scale. If a firm believes that this approach will be profitable and prefers an internal emphasis for maximizing strengths, four grand strategies hold considerable promise. As shown in quadrant III, the most common approach is **concentrated growth,** that is, market penetration. The firm that selects this strategy is strongly committed to its current products and markets. It strives to solidify its position by reinvesting resources to fortify its strengths.

Two alternative approaches are **market development** and **product development.** With these strategies, the firm attempts to broaden its operations. Market development is chosen if the firm's strategic managers feel that its existing products would be well received by new customer groups. Product development is chosen if they feel that the firm's existing customers would be interested in products related to its current lines. Product development also may be based on technological or other competitive advantages. The final alternative for quadrant III firms is **innovation.** When the firm's strengths are in creative product design or unique production technologies, sales can be stimulated by accelerating perceived obsolescence. This is the principle underlying the innovative grand strategy.

Maximizing a firm's strengths by aggressively expanding its base of operations usually requires an external emphasis. The preferred options in such cases are shown in quadrant IV. **Horizontal acquisition** is attractive because it makes possible a quick increase in output capability. Moreover, in horizontal acquisition, the skills of the managers of the original business often are critical in converting newly acquired facilities into profitable contributors to the parent firm; this expands a fundamental competitive advantage of the firm—its management.

Concentric diversification is a good second choice for similar reasons. Because the original and newly acquired businesses are related, the distinctive competencies of the diversifying firm are likely to facilitate a smooth, synergistic, and profitable expansion.

EXHIBIT 8.12   Model of Grand Strategy Clusters

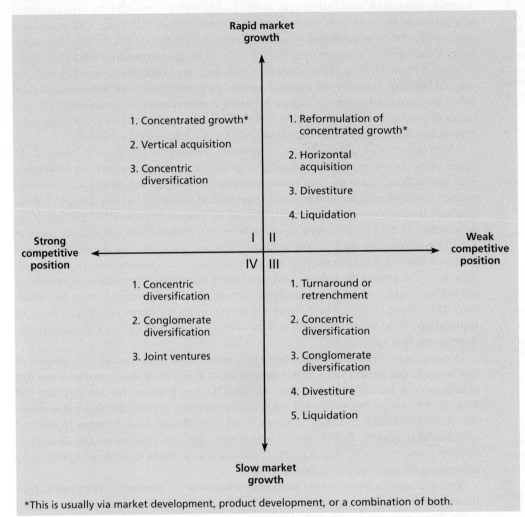

Rapid market growth

I

1. Concentrated growth*

2. Vertical acquisition

3. Concentric diversification

II

1. Reformulation of concentrated growth*

2. Horizontal acquisition

3. Divestiture

4. Liquidation

Strong competitive position ←   → Weak competitive position

IV

1. Concentric diversification

2. Conglomerate diversification

3. Joint ventures

III

1. Turnaround or retrenchment

2. Concentric diversification

3. Conglomerate diversification

4. Divestiture

5. Liquidation

Slow market growth

*This is usually via market development, product development, or a combination of both.

horizontal acquisition
Growth through the acquisition of one or more similar firms operating at the same stage of the production-marketing chain.

concentric diversification
Acquisition of businesses that are related to the acquiring firm in terms of technology, markets, or products.

The final alternative for increasing resource capability through external emphasis is a **joint venture** or **strategic alliance.** This alternative allows a firm to extend its strengths into competitive arenas that it would be hesitant to enter alone. A partner's production, technological, financial, or marketing capabilities can reduce the firm's financial investment significantly and increase its probability of success.

Model of Grand Strategy Clusters

A second guide to selecting a promising strategy is the **grand strategy cluster** shown in Exhibit 8.12. The figure is based on the idea that the situation of a business is defined in terms of the growth rate of the general market and the firm's competitive position in that market. When these factors are considered simultaneously, a business can be broadly categorized in one of four quadrants: (I) strong competitive position in a rapidly growing market, (II) weak position in a rapidly growing market, (III) weak position in a slow-growth market, or (IV) strong position in a slow-growth market. Each of these quadrants suggests a set of promising possibilities for the selection of a grand strategy.

joint ventures
Commercial companies created and operated for the benefit of the co-owners; usually two or more separate companies that form the venture.

strategic alliances
Partnerships that are distinguished from joint ventures because the companies involved do not take an equity position in one another.

grand strategy clusters
Strategies that may be more advantageous for firms to choose under one of four sets of conditions defined by market growth rate and the strength of the firm's competitive position.

Firms in quadrant I are in an excellent strategic position. One obvious grand strategy for such firms is continued concentration on their current business as it is currently defined. Because consumers seem satisfied with the firm's current strategy, shifting notably from it would endanger the firm's established competitive advantages. McDonald's Corporation has followed this approach for 25 years. However, if the firm has resources that exceed the demands of a concentrated growth strategy, it should consider vertical acquisition. Either forward or backward acquisition helps a firm protect its profit margins and market share by ensuring better access to consumers or material inputs. Finally, to diminish the risks associated with a narrow product or service line, a quadrant I firm might be wise to consider concentric diversification; with this strategy, the firm continues to invest heavily in its basic area of proven ability.

Firms in quadrant II must seriously evaluate their present approach to the marketplace. If a firm has competed long enough to accurately assess the merits of its current grand strategy, it must determine (1) why that strategy is ineffectual and (2) whether it is capable of competing effectively. Depending on the answers to these questions, the firm should choose one of four grand strategy options: formulation or reformulation of a concentrated growth strategy, horizontal acquisition, divestiture, or liquidation.

In a rapidly growing market, even a small or relatively weak business often is able to find a profitable niche. Thus, formulation or reformulation of a concentrated growth strategy is usually the first option that should be considered. However, if the firm lacks either a critical competitive element or sufficient economies of scale to achieve competitive cost efficiencies, then a grand strategy that directs its efforts toward horizontal acquisition is often a desirable alternative. A final pair of options involves deciding to stop competing in the market or product area of the business. A multiproduct firm may conclude that it is most likely to achieve the goals of its mission if the business is dropped through divestiture. This grand strategy not only eliminates a drain on resources but also may provide funds to promote other business activities. As an option of last resort, a firm may decide to liquidate the business. This means that the business cannot be sold as a going concern and is at best worth only the value of its tangible assets. The decision to liquidate is an undeniable admission of failure by a firm's strategic management and, thus, often is delayed—to the further detriment of the firm.

Strategic managers tend to resist divestiture because it is likely to jeopardize their control of the firm and perhaps even their jobs. Thus, by the time the desirability of divestiture is acknowledged, businesses often deteriorate to the point of failing to attract potential buyers. The consequences of such delays are financially disastrous for firm owners because the value of a going concern is many times greater than the value of its assets.

Strategic managers who have a business in quadrant III and expect a continuation of slow market growth and a relatively weak competitive position will usually attempt to decrease their resource commitment to that business. Minimal withdrawal is accomplished through retrenchment; this strategy has the side benefits of making resources available for other investments and of motivating employees to increase their operating efficiency. An alternative approach is to divert resources for expansion through investment in other businesses. This approach typically involves either concentric or conglomerate diversification because the firm usually wants to enter more promising arenas of competition than acquisition or concentrated growth strategies would allow. The final options for quadrant III businesses are divestiture, if an optimistic buyer can be found, and liquidation.

Quadrant IV businesses (strong competitive position in a slow-growth market) have a basis of strength from which to diversify into more promising growth areas. These businesses have characteristically high cash flow levels and limited internal growth needs. Thus, they are in an excellent position for concentric diversification into ventures that utilize their proven acumen.

A previous example in this chapter described how the no. 1 tennis ball maker, Penn Racquet Sports, chose concentric diversification from humans to dogs as their best option. A second option is conglomerate diversification, which spreads investment risk and does not divert managerial attention from the present business. The final option is joint ventures, which are especially attractive to multinational firms. Through joint ventures, a domestic business can gain competitive advantages in promising new fields while exposing itself to limited risks.

Opportunities for Building Value as a Basis for Choosing Diversification or Acquisition

The grand strategy selection matrix and model of grand strategy clusters are useful tools to help dominant product company managers evaluate and narrow their choices among alternative grand strategies. When considering grand strategies that would broaden the scope of their company's business activities through acquisition, diversification, or joint venture strategies, managers must examine whether opportunities to build value are present. Opportunities to build value via diversification, acquisition, or joint venture strategies are usually found in market-related, operating-related, and management activities. Such opportunities center around reducing costs, improving margins, or providing access to new revenue sources more cost effectively than traditional internal growth options via concentration, market development, or product development. Major opportunities for sharing and value building as well as ways to capitalize on core competencies are outlined in the next chapter, which covers strategic analysis and choice in diversified companies.

Dominant product company managers who choose diversification or acquisition eventually create another management challenge. That challenge is charting the future of a company that becomes a collection of several distinct businesses. These distinct businesses often encounter different competitive environments, challenges, and opportunities. The next chapter examines ways managers of such diversified companies attempt to evaluate and choose corporate strategy. Central to their challenge is the continued desire to build value, particularly shareholder value.

Summary

This chapter examined how managers in businesses that have a single or dominant product or service evaluate and choose their company's strategy. Two critical areas deserve their attention: (1) their business's value chain, and (2) the appropriateness of 12 different grand strategies based on matching environmental factors with internal capabilities.

Managers in single-product-line business units examine their business's value chain to identify existing or potential activities around which they can create sustainable competitive advantages. As managers scrutinize their value chain activities, they are looking for three sources of competitive advantage: low cost, differentiation, and rapid response capabilities. They also examine whether focusing on a narrow market niche provides a more effective, sustainable way to build or leverage these three sources of competitive advantage.

Managers in single- or dominant-product/service businesses face two interrelated issues: (1) They must choose which grand strategies make best use of their competitive advantages. (2) They must ultimately decide whether to diversify their business activity. Twelve grand strategies were identified in this chapter along with three frameworks that aid managers in choosing which grand strategies should work best and when diversification or acquisition should be the best strategy for the business. The next chapter expands the coverage of diversification to look at how multibusiness companies evaluate continued diversification and how they construct corporate strategy.

Key Terms

concentrated growth, *p. 263*
concentric diversification, *p. 264*
conglomerate diversification, *p. 262*
declining industry, *p. 258*
differentiation, *p. 246*
divestiture, *p. 263*
emerging industry, *p. 255*
fragmented industry, *p. 259*

global industry, *p. 260*
grand strategy clusters, *p. 265*
grand strategy selection matrix, *p. 262*
growth industry strategies, *p. 256*
horizontal acquisition, *p. 264*
innovation, *p. 263*
joint ventures, *p. 265*
liquidation, *p. 263*

low-cost strategies, *p. 244*
market development, *p. 263*
market focus, *p. 252*
mature industry strategies, *p. 257*
product development, *p. 263*
retrenchment, *p. 263*
speed-based strategies, *p. 249*
strategic alliances, *p. 265*
vertical acquisition, *p. 262*

Questions for Discussion

1. What are three activities or capabilities a firm should possess to support a low-cost leadership strategy? Use Exhibit 8.1 to help you answer this question. Can you give an example of a company that has done this?

2. What are three activities or capabilities a firm should possess to support a differentiation-based strategy? Use Exhibit 8.3 to help you answer this question. Can you give an example of a company that has done this?

3. What are three ways a firm can incorporate the advantage of speed in its business? Use Exhibit 8.6 to help you answer this question. Can you give an example of a company that has done this?

4. Do you think it is better to concentrate on one source of competitive advantage (cost versus differentiation versus speed) or to nurture all three in a firm's operation?

5. How does market focus help a business create competitive advantage? What risks accompany such a posture?

6. Using Exhibits 8.11 and 8.12, describe situations or conditions under which horizontal acquisition and concentric diversification would be preferred strategic choices.

Chapter **Nine**

Multibusiness Strategy

After reading and studying this chapter, you should be able to

1. Understand the portfolio approach to strategic analysis and choice in multibusiness companies.

2. Understand and use three different portfolio approaches to conduct strategic analysis and choice in multibusiness companies.

3. Identify the limitations and weaknesses of the various portfolio approaches.

4. Understand the synergy approach to strategic analysis and choice in multibusiness companies.

5. Evaluate the parent company role in strategic analysis and choice to determine whether and how it adds tangible value in a multibusiness company.

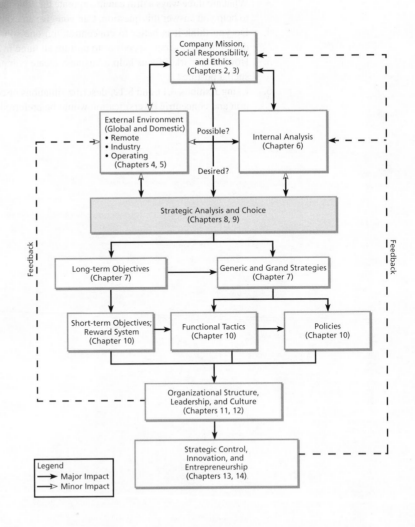

Legend
→ Major Impact
⇢ Minor Impact

Company Mission, Social Responsibility, and Ethics (Chapters 2, 3)

External Environment (Global and Domestic)
• Remote
• Industry
• Operating
(Chapters 4, 5)

Possible?

Desired?

Internal Analysis (Chapter 6)

Strategic Analysis and Choice (Chapters 8, 9)

Long-term Objectives (Chapter 7)

Generic and Grand Strategies (Chapter 7)

Short-term Objectives; Reward System (Chapter 10)

Functional Tactics (Chapter 10)

Policies (Chapter 10)

Organizational Structure, Leadership, and Culture (Chapters 11, 12)

Strategic Control, Innovation, and Entrepreneurship (Chapters 13, 14)

Feedback

Feedback

Marissa Mayer left Google to be CEO, president, and director of Yahoo!, and immediately created a stir by rescinding Yahoo's work-at-home policies. While controversial, the real challenge facing Ms. Mayer was how to craft a relevant corporate strategy for an "old" sprawling Internet conglomerate with everything from a top finance service to movie listings to a news hub, search engine, and a photo-sharing social network, just to name a few. Her swift answer started to unfold by selling off or closing several existing offerings, and yet making many numerous acquisitions starting with Summly, then Tumblr, and next Hulu. That process is still unfolding as we write this paragraph, with the noticable avalanche of observers, bloggers, pundits, and analysts weighing in both pro and con. Ms. Mayer seems indifferent to all the commentators. Instead, as a talented technology executive with excellent Google-based experience over 18 years, she is fast at work with her executive team trying to decide on a sound corporate strategy to rebirth an aging Yahoo! into a serious young player in the mobile-dominated future dramatically unfolding worldwide.

Jeff Immelt, entering his second decade as General Electric CEO and chairman, survived two recessions and accelerated global competition with a portfolio of underperforming legacy businesses his highly respected mentor and predecessor, Jack Welch, had put into place when financial services and TV-network-based entertainment were "hot" sectors. But the worse recession since the Great Depression, driven by the swift collapse of the global finance system, wars on two continents, and radical changes in TV-like entertainment options forced Immelt and his executive team to determine which businesses GE should remain in, which to exit, where to add businesses, and how to do so confidently under painfully disappointing financial performance results, casting widespread doubt about his leadership.

Apple CEO Tim Cook, the Apple veteran selected by Steve Jobs as his replacement prior to Jobs' death, was struggling a year later with how to revitalize an innovation-based corporate strategy across numerous lines of business worldwide. Samsung's success in copying plus in some ways one-upping the iPhone, the growing dominance of Android-based devices, along with other political and legal factors combined to challenge Apple's post-Jobs leadership and its ability to still make corporate strategy decisions that would lead to dramatic new products and lines of business.

British-born American Sir Howard Stringer, Sony Corporation's first non-Japanese leader, recently turned over the helm to Kazuo Hirai, longtime head of Sony's video-game unit. After four straight years losing money, culminating in Sony's biggest loss in its 67-year history, Stringer said in announcing his retirement that he was "pleased to hand the reins to Kazuo Hirai because I saw in him the right mix of skills to lead Sony," and that he knew it was "the right time for a generational change." Sony, once the darling of consumer electronics, challenges Hirai's corporate strategy skills as he tries to reverse those losses in a diversified electronics and entertainment conglomerate with an organizational culture based on consensus decision making being overwhelmed by more focused, leaner competitors: Apple and Samsung in mobile communication; Nintendo, EArts, and Microsoft in games; Canon in cameras; and so forth. What should Hirai do? Should he emphasize certain businesses? Sell others? Should he stay in electronics or outsource that and concentrate on entertainment? Where will he get the resources he needs to do whatever he chooses?

Meg Whitman, president and CEO of Hewlett-Packard, faced pressure related to HP corporate strategy decisions that many thought should be rather a decision to break the technology icon into two different companies—printers and computers—rather than trying to craft a corporate strategy based on keeping them both together. Her prior position as eBay CEO had ended with what some called "Whitman's Folly" when she acquired Skype at eBay as part of a corporate diversification strategy her replacement CEO, John Donahue, quickly reversed once he was on board.

Each of these examples show the challenge all multibusiness company leaders face—the challenge of crafting a corporate strategy to determine what businesses they should be in, which they should not, and how to provide resources and other forms of support to help them compete successfully. They must create an overarching strategy that guides a company with numerous, often unrelated businesses, and inevitably make hard, contentious decisions in doing so. And all of this in a twenty-first century where change is the only constant, and which happens faster than ever with the capacity to fundamentally change most industries' competitive advantage drivers very quickly.

Faced with this ever-increasing rate of change across multiple industries in which their businesses compete, multibusiness company leaders must still examine and choose which businesses to own and which ones to forgo or divest. They must consider business managers' plans to capture and exploit competitive advantage in each business, and then decide how to allocate resources among those businesses. This chapter covers ways managers in multibusiness companies analyze and choose what businesses to be in and how to allocate resources across those businesses.

The portfolio approach was one of the early approaches for charting strategy and allocating resources in multibusiness companies. This approach, with its appealing fundamental logic, was initially popularized by consulting groups like the Boston Consulting Group and McKinsey and Company as they helped corporate clients pursue and "rationalize" diversification strategies. Inevitably, some corporate managers, concerned with possible shortcomings in this type of approach, welcomed new options. Yet, while some companies moved on to other techniques, the portfolio approach remains a useful way of evaluating corporate strategy options. Interestingly, GE pioneered one form of the approach, which was subsequently abandoned under Jack Welch, only to now have successor Jeff Immelt bring it back as part of GE's corporate strategy vocabulary and decision making.

Immelt's comments as he entered his second decade show the prominence the portfolio approach played as he led GE's strategic decision-making through two recessions, two wars, and a global technology revolution:

> I would ask investors to think about the progress we have made with our portfolio [of businesses] . . . We have executed a disciplined portfolio strategy to aggressively reshape GE . . . We exited all or most of our insurance, materials, equipment services, mortgage origination, personal loans, significant ancillary financial services as well as entertainment, TV/cable and plastics . . . at the same time, we have acquired the equivalent of a Fortune 30 company investing in infrastructure, renewable energy, and fast-growing markets like life sciences, health care IT, . . . created a new business called Enterprise Solutions . . . and acquired Vector Gray, a subsea platform for Oil & Gas; Smith Aerospace creating an avionics platform. Now about one-third of our infrastructure revenues come from businesses we weren't in a decade ago.[1]

Global Strategy in Action, Exhibit 9.1 summarizes the businesses GE was in as Immelt assumed the leadership role along with its portfolio of businesses headed into 2014.

Immelts comments on GE's portfolio decision making undertaken to make and shape GE's corporate strategy included the following:

> Strategy is about making choices, building competitive advantage, and planning for the future. Strategy is not set through one act or one deal. Rather, we build it sequentially through making decisions and enhancing capability. I took over a great company, but one where we had a lot of work to do to position GE to win in the twenty-first century. Despite our high valuation, we were in businesses where we could not sustain competitive advantage, like plastics and insurance. Our team rolled up their sleeves. Ultimately, we exited half of our

[1] Drawn from various GE Letters to Shareholders, 2000–2013.

GE's Changing Business Portfolio

2000—*The end of the Glory Days under Jack Welch. GE's business portfolio was:*
$130B/$12.7B/$15B*

Power Systems   Aircraft Engines   NBC Universal   Medical Systems   Appliances   Lighting Industrial Systems   Transportation Systems   Plastics   Aviation Services   GE Capital   GE Equity   Global Consumer Finance   Employers Reinsurance   Financial Assurance   Mortgage Insurance   Real Estate   Card Services   Commercial Finance   Structured Finance   Commercial Equipment Finance

2013—*Immelt's "Reset Era" business portfolio entering his second decade at GE:*
$147B/$16B/$18B*

Power and Water   Oil and Gas   Aviation   Health Care Transportation   Energy Management   Home and Business Solutions   GE Capital (Equipment Finance for GE clients)

*GE's consolidated financial results in $Billions:
Total sales/Operating earnings/Cash flow that year.

portfolio. We invested in infrastructure businesses like oil and gas, life sciences, renewable energy, avionics, molecular medicine, and water. We restored our manufacturing muscle. We dramatically simplified GE. The last major portfolio move we made was exiting NBC Universal. The first phase we sold 51 percent for $11 billion we used to purchase new platforms in energy and oil and gas. A subsequent disposition of the remainder of NBCU provided an additional $18 billion for value creation and investment in growth. And we have dramatically reduced and focused GE Capital so that it serves our industrial clients and returns significant dividends annually to the parent [GE] to reinvest into infrastructure opportunities.[2]

Summarizing the results of almost 15 years of using a determined portfolio approach to manage multibusiness GE, Immelt concluded:

We like the way GE is positioned: a great portfolio of world-class, technology-leading businesses; a strong position in fast-growing global markets; leading-edge service technologies that achieve customer productivity; high visibility with a backlog of $210 billion; and a strong financial position.[3]

GE is a 135-year-old company that is the seventh most valuable company in the world as of this writing. Some see GE and argue, particularly in recent economic times, that it and several other companies are too big and complicated to achieve success compared to what could be achieved if their various businesses operated separately. Others argue that GE (and others like it) has produced impressive innovation and growth over those years, and that its individual businesses benefit from the synergies and support gained from one another in a variety of ways. Both perspectives have legitimate points. Regardless, where managers in a company like GE with multiple diverse businesses need to be able to examine and develop corporate-level strategies, the need to look at the "whole" as a portfolio of different business remains to this day a frequently used approach to accomplish that task.[4]

[2]Drawn from various GE Letters to Shareholders, 2000–2013.
[3]2013 Comment to Shareholders and analysts.
[4]"Corporate Strategy and Portfolio Management," www.bcg.com, 2014; "Strategic Portfolio Management," www.mckinsey.com, 2014; Ronald Klingebiel and Christian Rammer, "Resource Allocation Strategy for Innovation Portfolio Management," *Strategic Management Journal*, May 22, 2013; Freek Vermeulen, "Corporate Strategy Is a Fool's Errand," *Harvard Business Review*, www.hbr.org, March 20, 2013.

Improvement on the portfolio approach focused on ways to broaden the rationale behind pursuit of diversification strategies. This approach centered on the idea that at the heart of effective diversification is the identification of core competencies in a business or set of businesses to then leverage as the basis for competitive advantage in the growth of those businesses and the entry in or divestiture of other businesses. This notion of leveraging core competencies as a basis for strategic choice in multibusiness companies has been a popular one for the past 20 years. Meg Whitman's leadership role at both eBay and more recently Hewlett-Packard saw her facing this issue in both firms. At eBay, her acquisition of Skype as part of the eBay portfolio gained it the moniker "Whitman's Folly" from people that saw little synergy or leverageable core competencies between the online market businesses of eBay and VOIP phone/video calling. And her HP challenges have a similar theme with many critics challenging the wisdom of keeping a commodity computer company and a high-tech printer company as one company. We will come back to this in a Strategy in Action later in this chapter.

Recent evolution of strategic analysis and choice in this setting has expanded on the core competency notion to focus on a series of fundamental questions that multibusiness companies should address in order to make diversification work. With both the accelerated rates of change in most global markets and trying economic conditions, multibusiness companies have adapted the fundamental questions into an approach called "patching" to map and remap their business units swiftly against changing market opportunities. Finally, as companies have embraced lean organizational structures, strategic analysis in multibusiness companies has included careful assessment of the corporate parent, its role, and value or lack thereof in contributing to the stand-alone performance of their business units. This chapter will examine each of these approaches to shaping multibusiness corporate strategy.

THE PORTFOLIO APPROACH: A HISTORICAL STARTING POINT

portfolio techniques
An approach pioneered by the Boston Consulting Group that attempted to help managers "balance" the flow of cash resources among their various businesses while also identifying their basic strategic purpose within the overall portfolio.

market growth rate
The projected rate of sales growth for the market being served by a particular business.

relative competitive position
The market share of a business divided by the market share of its largest competitor.

The past 30 years we have seen a virtual explosion in the extent to which single-business companies seek to acquire other businesses to grow and to diversify. There are many reasons for this emergence of multibusiness companies: Companies can enter businesses with greater growth potential; enter businesses with different cyclical considerations; diversify inherent risks; increase vertical integration, and thereby reduce costs; capture value added; and instantly have a market presence rather than slower internal growth. As businesses jumped on the diversification bandwagon, their managers soon found a challenge in managing the resource needs of diverse businesses and their respective strategic missions, particularly in times of limited resources. Responding to this challenge, the Boston Consulting Group (BCG) pioneered an approach called **portfolio techniques** that attempted to help managers "balance" the flow of cash resources among their various businesses while also identifying their basic strategic purpose within the overall portfolio. Three of these techniques are reviewed here. Once reviewed, we will identify some of the problems with the portfolio approach that you should keep in mind when considering its use.

The BCG Growth-Share Matrix

Managers using the BCG matrix plotted each of the company's businesses according to market growth rate and relative competitive position. **Market growth rate** is the projected rate of sales growth for the market being served by a particular business. Usually measured as the percentage increase in a market's sales or unit volume over the two most recent years, this rate serves as an indicator of the relative attractiveness of the markets served by each business in the firm's portfolio of businesses. **Relative competitive position** usually

EXHIBIT 9.2
The BCG Growth-Share Matrix

Source: The growth-share matrix was originally developed by the Boston Consulting Group.

Description of Dimensions

Market share: Sales relative to those of other competitors in the market (dividing point is usually selected to have only the two to three largest competitors in any market fall into the high market share region)

Growth rate: Industry growth rate in constant dollars (dividing point is typically the GNP's growth rate)

is expressed as the market share of a business divided by the market share of its largest competitor. Thus, relative competitive position provides a basis for comparing the relative strengths of the businesses in the firm's portfolio in terms of their positions in their respective markets. Exhibit 9.2 illustrates the growth-share matrix.

stars
Businesses in rapidly growing markets with large market shares.

The **stars** are businesses in rapidly growing markets with large market shares. These businesses represent the best long-run opportunities (growth and profitability) in the firm's portfolio. They require substantial investment to maintain (and expand) their dominant position in a growing market. This investment requirement is often in excess of the funds that they can generate internally. Therefore, these businesses are often short-term, priority consumers of corporate resources.

cash cows
Businesses with a high market share in low-growth markets or industries.

Cash cows are businesses with a high market share in low-growth markets or industries. Because of their strong competitive positions and their minimal reinvestment requirements, these businesses often generate cash in excess of their needs. Therefore, they are selectively "milked" as a source of corporate resources for deployment elsewhere (to stars and question marks). Cash cows are yesterday's stars and the current foundation of corporate portfolios. They provide the cash needed to pay corporate overhead and dividends and provide debt capacity. They are managed to maintain their strong market share while generating excess resources for corporatewide use. But corporations with great cash cows need be careful not to stagnate enjoying the cash cow as its future can change over the years without being sensed until it is too late. Exhibit 9.3 tells the story of Kodak and how this reality, even while it invented the digital camera, led to its bankruptcy 30 years later.

dogs
Low market share and low market growth businesses.

Low market share and low market growth businesses are the **dogs** in the firm's portfolio. Facing mature markets with intense competition and low profit margins, they are managed for short-term cash flow (e.g., through ruthless cost cutting) to supplement corporate-level resource needs. According to the original BCG prescription, they are divested or liquidated once this short-term harvesting has been maximized.

question marks
Businesses whose high growth rate gives them considerable appeal but whose low market share makes their profit potential uncertain.

Question marks are businesses whose high growth rate gives them considerable appeal but whose low market share makes their profit potential uncertain. Question marks are cash guzzlers because their rapid growth results in high cash needs, while their small market share results in low cash generation. At the corporate level, the concern is to identify the question marks that would increase their market share and move into the star group if extra corporate resources were devoted to them. Where this long-run shift from question mark to star is unlikely, the BCG matrix suggests divesting the question mark and repositioning its resources more effectively in the remainder of the corporate portfolio.

Kodak and a Case of Cash Cow-itis

Kodak recently emerged from bankruptcy. Kodak was once a technology giant that was inventing a new film-related product every 3 days. Kodak engineer Steve Sasson pitched an electronic camera to upper management in 1975. Sasson's toaster-size prototype took photos with a resolution of 0.01 megapixels. He later told the *New York Times* that Kodak's management responded, "That's cute, but don't tell anyone about it." The U.S. arrival of Fuji's less expensive film a few years earlier, which Kodak execs dismissed as well, was the first forewarning.

What happened? The portfolio approach would have had Kodak investing some of the excess cash from the cash cow into "stars" and possibilities. It appears that Kodak, the consummate innovator, became complacent, relying too heavily on its highly profitable cash cow, the film business. That made it fearful and skeptical of new disruptive technologies, such as the digital camera. Sadly, that decision in 1975 and the mindset it reflected sealed the fate of Kodak, one-time innovator extraordinaire.

The Industry Attractiveness–Business Strength Matrix

Corporate strategists found the growth-share matrix's singular axes limiting in their ability to reflect the complexity of a business's situation. Therefore, some companies adopted a matrix with a much broader focus. This matrix, developed by McKinsey & Company at General Electric, is called the industry attractiveness–business strength matrix. This matrix uses multiple factors to assess industry attractiveness and business strength rather than the single measures (market share and market growth, respectively) employed in the BCG matrix. It also has nine cells as opposed to four—replacing the high/low axes with high/medium/low axes to make finer distinctions among business portfolio positions.

The company's businesses are rated on multiple strategic factors within each axis, such as the factors described in Exhibit 9.4. The position of a business is then calculated by "subjectively" quantifying its rating along the two dimensions of the matrix. Depending on the location of a business within the matrix as shown in Exhibit 9.5, one of the following strategic approaches is suggested: (1) invest to grow, (2) invest selectively and manage for earnings, or (3) harvest or divest for resources. The resource allocation decisions remain quite similar to those of the BCG approach.

Although the strategic recommendations generated by the industry attractiveness–business strength matrix are similar to those generated by the BCG matrix, the industry attractiveness–business strength matrix improves on the BCG matrix in three fundamental ways:

1. The terminology associated with the industry attractiveness–business strength matrix is preferable because it is less offensive and more understandable.
2. The multiple measures associated with each dimension of the business strength matrix tap many factors relevant to business strength and market attractiveness besides market share and market growth.
3. In turn, this makes for broader assessment during the planning process, bringing to light considerations of importance in both strategy formulation and strategy implementation.

BCG's Strategic Environments Matrix

BCG's latest matrix offering (see Exhibit 9.6) took a different approach, using the idea that it was the nature of competitive advantage in an industry that determined the strategies available to a company's businesses, which in turn determined the structure of

EXHIBIT 9.4
Factors Considered
in Constructing
an Industry
Attractiveness–
Business Strength
Matrix

Industry Attractiveness	Business Strength
Nature of Competitive Rivalry	**Cost Position**
Number of competitors Size of competitors Strength of competitors' corporate parents Price wars Competition on multiple dimensions	Economies of scale Manufacturing costs Overhead scrap/waste/rework Experience effects Labor rates Proprietary processes
Bargaining Power of Suppliers/ Customers	**Level of Differentiation**
Relative size of typical players Numbers of each Importance of purchases from or sales to Ability to vertically integrate	Promotion effectiveness Product quality Company image Patented products Brand awareness
Threat of Substitute Products/ New Entrants	**Response Time**
Technological maturity/stability Diversity of the market Barriers to entry Flexibility of distribution system	Manufacturing flexibility Time needed to introduce new products Delivery times Organizational flexibility
Economic Factors	**Financial Strength**
Sales volatility Cyclicality of demand Market growth Capital intensity	Solvency Liquidity Break-even point Cash flows Profitability Growth in revenues
Financial Norms	**Human Assets**
Average profitability Typical leverage Credit practices	Turnover Skill level Relative wage/salary Morale Managerial commitment Unionization
Sociopolitical Considerations	**Public Approval**
Government regulation Community support Ethical standards	Goodwill Reputation Image

the industry. Their idea was that such a framework could help ensure that individual businesses' strategies were consistent with strategies appropriate to their strategic environment. Furthermore, for corporate managers in multiple-business companies, this matrix offered one way to rationalize which businesses they are in—businesses that share core competencies and associated competitive advantages because of similar strategic environments.

The matrix has two dimensions. The number of sources of competitive advantage could be many with complex products and services (e.g., automobiles, financial services) and few with commodities (chemicals, microprocessors). Complex products offer multiple

EXHIBIT 9.5   The Industry Attractiveness–Business Strength Matrix

		Business Strength		
		Strong	**Average**	**Weak**
Industry Attractiveness	**High**	***Premium—invest for growth:*** • Provide maximum investment • Diversify worldwide • Consolidate position • Accept moderate near-term profits • Seek to dominate	***Selective—invest for growth*** • Invest heavily in selected segments • Share ceiling • Seek attractive new segments to apply strengths	***Protect/refocus— selectively invest for earnings:*** • Defend strengths • Refocus to attractive segments • Evaluate industry revitalization • Monitor for harvest or divestment timing • Consider acquisitions
	Medium	***Challenge—invest for growth:*** • Build selectively on strengths • Define implications of leadership challenge • Avoid vulnerability—fill weaknesses	***Prime—selectively invest for earnings:*** • Segment market • Make contingency plans for vulnerability	***Restructure—harvest or divest:*** • Provide no unessential commitment • Position for divestment or • Shift to more attractive segment
	Low	***Opportunistic— selectively invest for earnings:*** • Ride market and maintain overall position • Seek niches, specialization • Seek opportunity to increase strength (for example through acquisition) • Invest at maintenance levels	***Opportunistic—preserve for harvest:*** • Act to preserve or boost cash flow • Seek opportunistic sale or • Seek opportunistic rationalization to increase strengths • Prune product lines • Minimize investment	***Harvest or divest:*** • Exit from market or prune product line • Determine timing so as to maximize present value • Concentrate on competitor's cash generators

Source: Reprinted by permission of the publisher, from *Strategic Market Planning* by Bernard A. Rausch, AMACOM, division of American Management Association, New York, 1982, www.amanet.org.

EXHIBIT 9.6
BCG's Strategic Environments Matrix

Source: From R.M. Grant, *Contemporary Strategy Analysis,* Blackwell Publishing, 2001, p. 327. Reprinted with permission of Wiley-Blackwell.

Sources of Advantage			
Many	**Fragmented** apparel, housebuilding, jewelry retailing, sawmills	**Specialization** pharmaceuticals, luxury cars, chocolate confectionery
Few	**Stalemate** basic chemicals, volume-grade paper, ship owning (VLCCs), wholesale banking	**Volume** jet engines, supermarkets, motorcycles, standard microprocessors
	Small	**Big**
	Size of Advantage	

opportunities for differentiation as well as cost, while commodities must seek opportunities for cost advantages to survive.

The second dimension is size of competitive advantage. How big is the advantage available to the industry leader? The two dimensions then define four industry environments as follows:

volume businesses
Businesses that have few sources of advantage, but the size is large—typically the result of scale economies.

stalemate businesses
Businesses with few sources of advantage, most of them small. Skills in operational efficiency, low overhead, and cost management are critical to profitability.

fragmented businesses
Businesses with many sources of advantage, but they are all small. They typically involve differentiated products with low brand loyalty, easily replicated technology, and minimal scale economies.

specialization businesses
Businesses with many sources of advantage. Skills in achieving differentiation (product design, branding expertise, innovation, and perhaps scale) characterize winning specialization businesses.

- **Volume businesses** are those that have few sources of advantage, but the size is large—typically the result of scale economies. Advantages established in one such business may be transferable to another as Honda has done with its scale and expertise with small gasoline engines.
- **Stalemate businesses** have few sources of advantage, with most of those small. This results in very competitive situations. Skills in operational efficiency, low overhead, and cost management are critical to profitability.
- **Fragmented businesses** have many sources of advantage, but they are all small. This typically involves differentiated products with low brand loyalty, easily replicated technology, and minimal scale economies. Skills in focused market segments, typically geographic, the ability to respond quickly to changes, and low costs are critical in this environment.
- **Specialization businesses** have many sources of advantage and find those advantages potentially sizable. Skills in achieving differentiation—product design, branding expertise, innovation, first-mover, and perhaps scale—characterize winners here.

BCG viewed this matrix as providing guidance to multibusiness managers to determine whether they possessed the sources and size of advantage associated with the type of industry facing each business and allowed them a framework to realistically explore the nature of the strategic environments in which they competed or were interested in entering.

Limitations of Portfolio Approaches

Portfolio approaches made several contributions to strategic analysis by corporate managers convinced of their ability to transfer the competitive advantage of professional management across a broad array of businesses. They helped convey large amounts of information about diverse business units and corporate plans in a greatly simplified format. They illuminated similarities and differences between business units and helped convey the logic behind corporate strategies for each business with a common vocabulary. They simplified priorities for sharing corporate resources across diverse business units that generated and used those resources. They provided a simple prescription that gave corporate managers a sense of what they should accomplish—a balanced portfolio of businesses—and a way to control and allocate resources among them. While these approaches offered meaningful contributions, they had several critical limitations and shortcomings:

- A key problem with the portfolio matrix was that it did not address how value was being created across business units—the only relationship between them was cash. Addressing each business unit as a stand-alone entity ignores common core competencies and internal synergies among operating units.
- Truly accurate measurement for matrix classification was not as easy as the matrices portrayed. Identifying individual businesses, or distinct markets, was not often as precise as underlying assumptions required. Comparing business units on only two fundamental dimensions can lead to the conclusion that these are the only factors that really matter and that every unit can be compared fairly on those bases.
- The underlying assumption about the relationship between market share and profitability—the experience curve effect—varied across different industries and market

segments. Some have no such link. Some find that firms with low market share can generate superior profitability with differentiation advantages.

- The limited strategic options, intended to describe the flow of resources in a company, came to be seen more as basic strategic missions, which creates a false sense of what each business's strategy actually entails. What do we actually "do" if we're a star? A cash cow? This becomes even more problematic when attempting to use the matrices to conceive strategies for average businesses in average-growth markets.

- The portfolio approach portrayed the notion that firms needed to be self-sufficient in capital. This ignored capital raised in capital markets.

- The portfolio approach typically failed to compare the competitive advantage a business received from being owned by a particular company with the costs of owning it. The 1980s saw many companies build enormous corporate infrastructures that created only small gains at the business level. The reengineering and deconstruction of numerous global conglomerates in the past 10 years reflects this important omission. We will examine this consideration in greater detail later in this chapter.

- Recent research by well-known consulting firm Booz Allen Hamilton suggests that "conventional wisdom is wrong. Corporate managers often rely on accounting metrics [based on past performance] to make business decisions." They go on to argue that "past performance is a poor predictor of the future. When performance is assessed over time, greater shareholder value can be created by improving the operations of the company's worst-performing businesses." "The way to thrive," they say, "is to love your dogs." Their point, backed up by impressive research, is that a corporate manager can learn to identify "value assets," hold and nurture them, and produce superior performance ultimately leading to increased shareholder value more so than can be achieved by acquiring and trying to add value to an overvalued "star."[5]

Constructing business portfolio matrices must be undertaken with these limitations in mind. Perhaps it is best to say that they provide one form of input to corporate managers seeking to balance financial resources. While limitations have meant portfolio approaches are seen as mere historical concepts, others appear to find them useful in evaluating strategic options as we saw happening in the chapter introduction example about General Electric's current efforts to manage its diverse business portfolio in the rapidly changing global economy of the twenty-first century. A recent comprehensive study of over 200 large, global companies found that over 90 percent of these firms continue to actively use the corporate portfolio management (CPM) techniques we have been discussing in this chapter. Forty years after the introduction of the BCG growth-share matrix, the study found that corporate portfolio management continues to be a topic that is very relevant and challenging for twenty-first-century corporate leaders. Managing and developing the corporate portfolio was still found to be a top strategic priority in most major firms worldwide. Yet, while acknowledging its importance, the majority of the companies studied were not satisfied with their current CPM approaches and processes. There was a noticeable gap between the effort that many companies put into corporate portfolio management and its impact on corporate-level decisions.[6]

---

[5]A comprehensive discussion of these ideas to include their research examining the performance of "falling stars" and "rising dogs" can be found at Harry Quaris, Thomas Pernsteiner, and Kasturi Rangan, "Love your 'Dogs,'" *Strategy+Business Magazine*, Booz Allen Hamilton, www.strategy-business.com/resiliencereport/resilience/rr00030, 2007.

[6]Ulrich Pidun, Harald Rubner, Matthias Kruhlerr, and Michael Nippa, "Corporate Portfolio Management: Theory and Practice," *Journal of Applied Corporate Finance* 23, no. 1 (Winter, 2011), p. 75.

The study identified the following twelve "best practices" thought to address many of the short-comings found in the study and in the academic criticism we noted above regarding traditional corporate portfolio management techniques:[7]

- Analyze the businesses in your corporate portfolio from all relevant perspectives, including the market-based view (market attractiveness and competitive position), the value-based view (current and anticipated financial returns), and the resource-based view (parenting advantage).

- Rather than integrating the different perspectives in a single matrix, keep the various perspectives distinct and let the integration happen in the strategy discussion. In most cases, the process is more important than the final matrix representation. CPM can help you ask the right questions, but it will not give you definitive answers. It supports strategic thinking but should not replace it.

- Do not focus your analysis solely on the individual strategic business units. Portfolio management is about creating a total that is more than the sum of its parts, which can only be assessed at the portfolio level, not at the level of individual SBUs.

- Think like your shareholders and measure the quality of the portfolio against your corporate goals. What is the short-term versus long-term value creation profile of the portfolio? What is its balance along critical dimensions such as risk versus return, cash generation versus cash use, and growth versus profitability?

- Do not apply CPM as a deterministic exercise but rather as a means of facilitating thinking in scenarios and discussing portfolio strategy in terms of risk and uncertainty in the context of alternative portfolio development options.

- Establish corporate portfolio management as a regular process that is clearly driven top-down by the center but also ensures strong SBU involvement both in generating the data and in drawing conclusions. Successful CPM processes tend to be rather formal and standardized, without becoming overly complex and inefficient.

- Apply CPM not only as a corporate development instrument (such as for identifying divestiture and acquisition candidates) but also as an instrument for steering the SBUs—setting strategic as well as financial targets and allocating resources such as capital, human resources, and management attention.

- Treat generic portfolio roles with respect: They are a double-edged sword. Many boards still love to classify their businesses into simple roles—such as explore, attack, grow, defend, or harvest—with role-specific strategic goals and financial performance targets. This can be an effective approach for reducing the complexity of a broad portfolio. But beware of oversimplification. Consider corporate portfolio management as a mind set, not a tool. It should be not a one-time or once-a-year exercise but an ongoing process—and ultimately a way of thinking—that is fully integrated into other corporate processes.[8]

This study foretells a continued use of the portfolio approach, recognizing its limitations, to provide a picture of the "balance" of resource generators and users, to test underlying assumptions about these issues and the individual SBUs in more involved corporate planning efforts, and to leverage core competencies to build sustained competitive advantages. Indeed, two key findings in this comprehensive study included the importance of looking at the multibusiness company's corporate strategy from the perspective of leveraging core

[7] Ibid, pp. 75–76.
[8] Ibid, pp. 75–76.

competencies across a company's portfolio of businesses, and secondly to examine the corporate "parenting" role as a vehicle for doing so. The following two sections of this chapter look at those two considerations. We will first examine the next major approach in multibusiness strategic analysis, leveraging shared capabilities and core competencies.

THE SYNERGY APPROACH: LEVERAGING CORE COMPETENCIES

Opportunities to build value via diversification, integration, or joint venture strategies are usually found in market-related, operations-related, and management activities. Each business's basic value chain activities or infrastructure become a source of potential synergy and competitive advantage for another business in the corporate portfolio. Mars (the M&M company) acquired Wrigley (the gum company) a few years ago based on what both legendary companies saw as multiple opportunities for synergy leveraging core competencies in the global confectionery market. Cadbury Schweppes, the European confectionary global powerhouse, was looking to acquire Wrigley, but Mars achieved the "deal" in part because of what executives from both companies saw as the strongest leveraging capability across key sales, marketing, distribution, and manufacturing synergies between Mars and Wrigley. There were numerous opportunities for shared operating capabilities—sales forces that could immediately add a variety of products to their daily sales calls; the ability to blend marketing events, materials, and promotions again leveraging the gap-filling ability to reach across both product offerings. Management talents in both companies were complementary in many regions and product lines and in functional areas—gaps in one company's talent pool found support from the other company's people strengths. Cost-saving and cost-sharing opportunities were quickly targeted across manufacturing facilities, sometimes location driven and other times based on innovative and/or newer operating equipment and skill. Some of the more common opportunities to share value chain activities and build value are identified in Exhibit 9.7.

Strategic analysis is concerned with whether or not the potential competitive advantages expected to arise from each value opportunity have materialized. Where advantage has not materialized, corporate strategists must take care to scrutinize possible impediments to achieving the synergy or competitive advantage. We have identified in Exhibit 9.6 several impediments associated with each opportunity, which strategists are well advised to examine. Good strategists assure themselves that their organization has ways to avoid or minimize the effects of any impediments, or they recommend against further integration or diversification and consider divestiture options.

Two elements are critical in meaningful shared opportunities:

1. The shared opportunities must be a significant portion of the value chain of the businesses involved. Disney acquired Pixar, or it is perhaps better to say Pixar joined Disney, and in so doing acted on two simple shared opportunities that were significant portions of the value chain of both businesses. One critical part of the value chain for movie-related excellence in the twenty-first-century entertainment industry is excellence and innovative talent in digital animation, digital artisan skill, and advanced visualization wizardry. Disney was still a bit "old fashioned," and falling behind the new breed in creating animations for twenty-first-century young audiences. Pixar had that capability "nailed" as perhaps the most innovative animation house in that space. Meanwhile, Disney had a vast distribution and proprietary brand name and entertainment breadth upon which to build new offerings, new niches, a whole spectrum to monetize an animation of existing Disney stars or totally new animated characters through deals with its own

EXHIBIT 9.7 **Value Building in Multibusiness Companies**

Opportunities to Build Value or Sharing	Potential Competitive Advantage	Impediments to Achieving Enhanced Value
Market-Related Opportunities		
Shared sales force activities, shared sales office, or both	Lower selling costs Better market coverage Stronger technical advice to buyers Enhanced convenience for buyers (can buy from single source) Improved access to buyers (have more products to sell)	• Buyers have different purchasing habits toward the products. • Different salespersons are more effective in representing the product. • Some products get more attention than others. • Buyers prefer to multiple-source rather than single-source their purchases.
Shared after-sale service and repair work	Lower servicing costs Better utilization of service personnel (less idle time) Faster servicing of customer calls	• Different equipment or different labor skills, or both, are needed to handle repairs. • Buyers may do some in-house repairs.
Shared brand name	Stronger brand image and company reputation Increased buyer confidence in the brand	• Company reputation is hurt if quality of one product is lower.
Shared advertising and promotional activities	Lower costs Greater clout in purchasing ads	• Appropriate forms of messages are different. • Appropriate timing of promotions is different.
Common distribution channels	Lower distribution costs Enhanced bargaining power with distributors and retailers to gain shelf space, shelf positioning, stronger push and more dealer attention, and better profit margins	• Dealers resist being dominated by a single supplier and turn to multiple sources and lines. • Heavy use of the shared channel erodes willingness of other channels to carry or push the firm's products.
Shared order processing	Lower order processing costs One-stop shopping for buyer to enhance service and, thus, differentiation	• Differences in ordering cycles disrupt order-processing economies.
Operating Opportunities		
Joint procurement of purchased inputs	Lower input costs Improved input quality Improved service from suppliers	• Input needs are different in terms of quality or other specifications. • Inputs are needed at different plant locations, and centralized purchasing is not responsive to separate needs of each plant.
Shared manufacturing and assembly facilities	Lower manufacturing/assembly costs Better capacity utilization, because peak demand for one product correlates with valley demand for the other Bigger scale of operation to improve access to better technology, resulting in better quality	• Higher changeover costs in shifting from one product to another. • High-cost special tooling or equipment is required to accommodate quality differences or design differences.
Shared inbound or out-bound shipping and materials handling	Lower freight and handling costs Better delivery reliability More frequent deliveries, such that inventory costs are reduced	• Input sources or plant locations, or both, are in different geographic areas. • Needs for frequency and reliability of inbound/outbound delivery differ among the business units.

(continued)

EXHIBIT 9.7   *(continued)*

Opportunities to Build Value or Sharing	Potential Competitive Advantage	Impediments to Achieving Enhanced Value
Operating Opportunities (cont.)		
Shared product and process technologies, technology development, or both	Lower product or process design costs, or both, because of shorter design times and transfers of knowledge from area to area More innovative ability, owing to scale of effort and attraction of better R&D personnel	• Technologies are the same, but the applications in different business units are different enough to prevent much sharing of real value.
Shared administrative support activities	Lower administrative and operating overhead costs	• Support activities are not a large proportion of cost, and sharing has little cost impact (and virtually no differentiation impact).
Management Opportunities		
Shared management know-how, operating skills, and proprietary information	Efficient transfer of a distinctive competence—can create cost savings or enhance differentiation More effective management as concerns strategy formulation, strategy implementation, and understanding of key success factors	• Actual transfer of know-how is costly or stretches the key skill personnel too thinly, or both. • Increased risks that proprietary information will leak out.

Source: Based on Michael Porter, *On Competition*, Harvard Business School Press.

theme parks, TV programs, preteen entertainment star factories, and ongoing relationships with every fast-food outlet globally.

2. The businesses involved must truly have shared needs—need for the same activity—or there is no basis for synergy in the first place. Skype is a pioneering success story of the use of the Internet for telephone and video communication between any two computer locations worldwide. eBay acquired Skype, anticipating numerous synergies with its worldwide online auction business—but such synergies failed to emerge. eBay management took quite a lot of criticism for the price it paid and, after three successive Skype CEOs failed to uncover any shared needs common to both businesses leading to any meaningful synergy, a fourth Skype CEO installed by eBay sought to "harvest" Skype. Josh Silverman's first step was to operate Skype as a separate business and sell off 70 percent of eBay's interest in it. Subsequently, in 18 months, he and that investment group succeeded in selling Skype to Microsoft for $8.5 billion.[9]

Corporate strategies have repeatedly rushed into diversification only to find perceived opportunities for sharing were nonexistent because the businesses did not really have shared needs.

The most compelling reason companies should diversify can be found in situations where core competencies—key value-building skills—can be leveraged with other products or into markets that are not a part of where they were created. Where this works well, extraordinary value can be built. Managers undertaking diversification strategies should dedicate a significant portion of their strategic analysis to this question.

[9]Hermantha Abeywardena, "Sale of Skype: Business Hype and Ground Realities," AsianTribune.com, London, May 14, 2011. http://www.asiantribune.com/news/2011/05/14/sale-skype-business-hype-and-ground-realities

General Cinema was a company that grew from drive-in theaters to eventually dominate the multicinema, movie exhibition industry. Next, they entered soft-drink bottling and became the largest bottler of soft drinks (Pepsi) in North America. Their stock value rose 2,000 percent in 10 years. They found that core competencies in movie exhibition—managing many small, localized businesses; dealing with a few large suppliers; applying central marketing skills locally; and acquiring or crafting a "franchise"—were virtually the same in soft-drink bottling. eBay CEO Meg Whitman bought Skype. Then her replacement, to his great relief, got it sold to Microsoft in a two-step process that raised the obvious question—where does Skype leverage core competencies better—eBay or Microsoft? You can explore this question in the next section and in Exhibit 9.8.

Each Core Competency Should Provide a Relevant Competitive Advantage to the Intended Businesses

The core competency must assist the intended business in creating strength relative to key competition. This could occur at any step in the business's value chain. But it must represent a major source of value to be a basis for competitive advantage—and the core competence must be transferable. Honda of Japan viewed itself as having a core competence in manufacturing small, internal combustion engines. It diversified into small garden tools, perceiving that traditional electric tools would be much more attractive if powered by a lightweight, mobile, gas combustion motor. Their core competency created a major competitive advantage in a market void of gas-driven hand tools. When Coca-Cola added bottled water to its portfolio of products, it expected its extraordinary core competencies in marketing and distribution to rapidly build value in this business. Ten years later, Coke sold its water assets, concluding that the product did not have enough margin to interest its franchised bottlers and that marketing was not a significant value-building activity among many small suppliers competing primarily on the cost of "producing" and shipping water. In the last few years, however, Coke has reversed its decision and added the Dasani water brand because a rapidly increasing consumer demand has made the value of its extensive distribution network a relevant competitive advantage to the Dasani water product line.

Businesses in the Portfolio Should Be Related in Ways That Make the Company's Core Competencies Beneficial

Related versus unrelated diversification is an important distinction to understand as you evaluate the diversification question. "Related" businesses are those that rely on the same or similar capabilities to be successful and attain competitive advantage in their respective product markets. Earlier, we described General Cinema's spectacular success in both movie exhibition and soft-drink bottling. Seemingly unrelated, they were actually very related businesses in terms of key core competencies that shaped success—managing a network of diverse business locations, localized competition, reliance on a few large suppliers, and centralized marketing advantages. Thus, the products of various businesses do not necessarily have to be similar to leverage core competencies. While their products may not be related, it is essential that some activities in their value chains require similar skills to create competitive advantage if the company is going to leverage its core competence(s) in a value-creating way. Exhibit 9.8 offers a look at whether eBay's acquisition of Skype, or Microsoft's acquisition of Skype from eBay's group, was the better addition to the company's business portfolio from a leveraging of competencies point of view. eBay was excited to add a new technology to its business group, and envisioned numerous eBay buyers and sellers worldwide taking advantage of Skype through eBay to engage in buying and selling. While that was an intriguing concept, it was little used, and any notion that skills, expertise, and relationships involved in operating numerous domestic and global online marketplaces,

Leveraging Core Competencies with Skype? Was eBay or Microsoft wisest?

This "map" from eBay shows the evolution of its "business portfolio" from a collection of about 24 different businesses to what became viewed as its "3-Legged Stool" business portfolio—a division of those 24 businesses based on related aspects of these businesses into Online Commerce, Payments, or Communications. Many analysts, eBay sellers, and increasingly eBay managers questioned the rationale for having Skype in the business mix. They saw Skype as having snookered former CEO Meg Whitman into paying $3.1 billion in 2005 for "synergies" that have never materialized, thus the name "Whitman's Folly." eBay took a $1.4 billion write-down two years later, and Skype's fourth president since the acquisition, Josh Silverman, started trying to increase Skype's financial value to eBay by separating it from eBay as a part of the eBay portfolio; selling a 70 percent interest to an investment group led by Marc Andreessen for $2 billion in cash; and 18 months later in 2011 that group sold it to Microsoft for $8.5 billion in cash. So now the eBay portfolio is a two-legged stool, logically interrelated, and energized by getting

approximately $5 billion in cash "back" for its trouble. Now Skype is Microsoft's opportunity, or problem.

eBay was lucky to salvage excess resources from the sale of Skype, doubly so because its core competencies—online global marketplace expertise and online payments expertise—offered no synergy and value-added to Skype, nor did Skype's VOIP telephony provide any synergy or value-added in return.

Microsoft might have done better leveraging core competencies; even if its premium price doesn't prove too excessive. Microsoft gets a client base and set of technologies that can integrate easily with its business software and new Xbox360 household entertainment center. It could use foreign cash reserves in Europe to buy Skype. Microsoft can leverage its powerful distributors/resellers/integration partners network. Skype strengthens Microsoft's capabilities as an OTT player, increases partnerships with telecom operators, mobile phone operators, and OSS, and of course it is already in Nokia, Android OS, and iOS. Skype is well known, and well known with a youthful demographic that helps Microsoft.

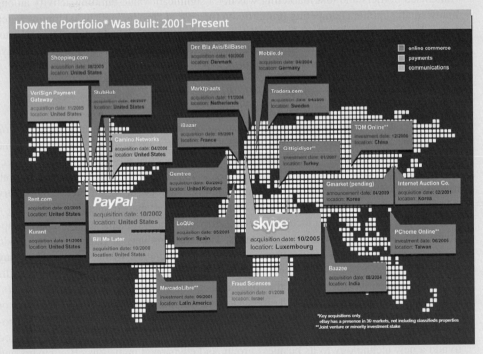

Source: Fair Use per EBay

or expertise and knowhow in proving online payment services and processing, had any synergistic contribution to Skype, and vice versa. On the other hand, it appears Microsoft, though paying a steep price, has several solid reasons that competencies from Microsoft can leverage to Skype's advantage, and capabilities as well as brand and clientele brought from Skype add value to Microsoft in several ways.

Situations that involve "unrelated" diversification occur when no real overlapping capabilities or products exist other than financial resources. We refer to this as *conglomerate diversification* in Chapter 7. Recent research indicates that the most profitable firms are those that have diversified around a set of resources and capabilities that are specialized enough to confer a meaningful competitive advantage in an attractive industry, yet adaptable enough to be advantageously applied across several others. The least profitable are broadly diversified firms whose strategies are built around very general resources (e.g., money) that are applied in a wide variety of industries, but that are seldom instrumental to competitive advantage in those settings.[10]

Any Combination of Competencies Must Be Unique or Difficult to Recreate

Skills that corporate strategists expect to transfer from one business to another, or from corporate to various businesses, may be transferable. They may also be easily replicated by competitors. When this is the case, no sustainable competitive advantage is created. Sometimes strategists look for a combination of competencies, a package of various interrelated skills, as another way to create a situation where seemingly easily replicated competencies become unique, sustainable competitive advantages. 3M Corporation has the enviable record of having 25 percent of its earnings always coming from products introduced within the last five years. 3M has been able to "bundle" the skills necessary to accelerate the introduction of new products so that it consistently extracts early life-cycle value from adhesive-related products that hundreds of competitors with similar technical or marketing competencies cannot touch.

All too often companies envision a combination of competencies that make sense conceptually. This vision of synergy develops an energy of its own, leading CEOs to relentlessly push the merger of the firms involved. But what makes sense conceptually and is seen as difficult for competitors to recreate often proves difficult if not impossible to create in the first place.

THE CORPORATE PARENT ROLE: CAN IT ADD TANGIBLE VALUE?

Realizing synergies from shared capabilities and core competencies is a key way value is added in multibusiness companies. Research suggests that figuring out if the synergies are real and, if so, how to capture those synergies is most effectively accomplished by business unit managers, not the corporate parent.[11] Multibusiness CEOs all face the same constant

---

[10]David J. Collis and Cynthia A. Montgomery, *Corporate Strategy* (New York: McGraw-Hill/Irwin, 2005), p. 88; "Why Mergers Fail," *McKinsey Quarterly Report*, 2001, vol. 4; and "Deals That Create Value," *McKinsey Quarterly Report*, 2001, vol. 1.

[11]See most recently Ulrich Pidun, Harald Rubner, Matthias Kruhlerr, and Michael Nippa, "Corporate Portfolio Management: Theory and Practice," *Journal of Applied Corporate Finance* 23, no. 1 (Winter, 2011), pp. 63, 68–69, for a recent study of 200 global companies' parenting approaches; and, as an earlier foundation to this perspective on "parenting" as a framework for understanding the corporate role in multibusiness companies, see Michael Goold, Andrew Campbell, and Marcus Alexander, "The Quest for Parenting Advantage," *Harvard Business Review*, March–April 1995; and Michael Goold, Andrew Campbell, and Marcus Alexander, "How Corporate Parents Add Value to the Stand-Alone Performance of Their Businesses," *Business Strategy Review*, Winter 1994.

expectation—how is their corporate center adding value to their portfolio of businesses so that the whole is worth more than the sum of its parts? That expectation comes from outside analysts, banks, and investors. It comes from inside—their boards and their business units that have to pay toward corporate overhead. All ask essentially the same question: What is the corporate parent doing to add value to its business units and how might it do it better? We want to acquaint you with three perspectives to use to answer that question: the parenting opportunities framework, corporate center parenting strategies, and the patching approach.

The Parenting Opportunities Framework

parenting opportunities framework

The perspective that the role of corporate headquarters (the "parent") in multibusiness (the "children") companies is that of a parent sharing wisdom, insight, and guidance to help develop its various businesses to excel.

The **parenting opportunities framework** perspective sees multibusiness companies as creating value by influencing—or parenting—the businesses they own. The best parent companies create more value than any of their rivals do or would if they owned the same businesses. To add value, a parent must improve its businesses. Obviously there must be room for improvement. Advocates of this perspective call the potential for improvement within a business "a parenting opportunity." They identify 10 places to look for parenting opportunities, which then become the focus of strategic analysis and choice across multiple businesses and their interface with the parent organization.[12] Let's look at each briefly.

Size and Age

Old, large, successful businesses frequently engender entrenched bureaucracies and overhead structures that are hard to dismantle from inside the business. Doing so may add value, and getting it done may be best done by an external catalyst, the parent. Small, young businesses may lack some key functional skills, or outgrow their top managers' capabilities, or lack capital to deal with a temporary downturn or accelerated growth opportunity. Where these are relevant issues within one or more businesses, a parenting opportunity to add value may exist.

Management

Does the business employ managers superior in comparison with its competitors? Is the business's success dependent on attracting and keeping people with specialized skills? Are key managers focused on the right objectives? Ensuring that these issues are addressed and objectively assessed and assisting in any resolution may be a parenting opportunity that could add value.

Business Definition

Business unit managers may have a myopic or erroneous vision of what their business should be, which, in turn, has them targeting a market that is too narrow or broad. They may employ too much vertical integration or not enough. Accelerated trends toward outsourcing and strategic alliances are changing the definitions of many businesses. All of this creates a parenting opportunity to help redefine a business unit in a way that creates greater value.

Predictable Errors

The nature of a business and its unique situation can lead managers to make predictable mistakes. Managers responsible for previous strategic decisions are vested in the success of those decisions, which may prevent openness to new alternatives. Older, mature businesses

---

[12]These 10 areas of opportunity are taken from an insert entitled "Ten Places to Look for Parenting Opportunities" on page 126 of the *Harvard Business Review* article by Goold, Campbell, Alexander (footnote 10).

often accumulate a variety of products and markets, which becomes excessive diversification within a particular business. Cyclical markets can lead to underinvestment during downturns and overinvestment during the upswing. Lengthy product life cycles can lead to overreliance on old products. All of these are predictable errors a parent can monitor and attempt to avoid, creating, in turn, added value.

Linkages

Business units may be able to improve market position or efficiency by linking with other businesses that are not readily apparent to the management of the business unit in question. Whether apparent or not, linkages among business units within or outside the parent company may be complex or difficult to establish without parent company help. In either case, an opportunity to add value may exist.

Common Capabilities

Fundamental to successful diversification, as we have discussed earlier, is the notion of sharing capabilities and competencies needed by multiple business units. Parenting opportunities to add value may arise from time to time through regular scrutiny of opportunities to share capabilities or add shared capabilities that would otherwise go unnoticed by business unit managers closer to daily business operations.

Specialized Expertise

There may be situations in which the parent company possesses specialized or rare expertise that may benefit a business unit and add value in the process. Unique legal, technical, or administrative expertise critical in a particular situation or decision point, which is quickly and easily available, can prove very valuable.

External Relations

Does the business have external stakeholders—governments, regulators, unions, suppliers, shareholders—the parent company could manage more effectively than individual business units? If so, a natural parenting opportunity exists that should add value.

Major Decisions

A business unit may face difficult decisions in areas for which it lacks expertise—for example, making an acquisition, entering China, a major capacity expansion, divesting and outsourcing a major part of the business's operations. Obtaining capital externally to fund a major investment may be much more difficult than doing so through the parent company—GE proved this could be a major parenting advantage in the way it developed GE Capital into a major source of capital for its other business units as well as to finance major capital purchases by customers of its own business units.

Major Changes

Sometimes a business needs to make major changes in ways critical to the business's future success yet which involve areas or considerations in which the business unit's management has little or no experience. A complete revamping of a business unit's information management process, outsourcing all that capability to India, or shifting all of a business unit's production operations to another business unit in another part of the world—these are just a few examples of major changes in which the parent may have extensive experience with what feels like unknown territory to the business's management team.

Overlap in some of these 10 sources of parenting opportunities may exist. For example, specialized expertise in China and a major decision to locate or outsource operations there may be the same source of added value. And that decision would involve a major change. The fact that overlap or redundancy may exist in classifying sources of parenting opportunity is a minor consideration, however, relative to the value of the parenting opportunities framework for strategic analysis in multibusiness companies. The portfolio approaches focus on how businesses' cash, profit, and growth potential create a balance within the portfolio. The core competence approach concentrates on how business units are related and can share technical and operating know-how and capacity. The parenting opportunities perspective adds to these approaches and the strategic analysis in a multibusiness company because it focuses on competencies of the parent organization and on the value created from the relationship between the parent and its businesses.

For example, Exhibit 9.9, Global Strategy in Action highlights how Xerox chairwoman and CEO Ursula Burns went about crafting a corporate parenting role focused on business definition, major urgent decisions, and major changes. Her team's parenting effort sought to realign Xerox businesses from ones that dominated the office of yesterday with copiers, laser printers, and fax machines to a strong role in the offices of the future. This involved leading the negotiation and integration of a major acquisition, which instantly and dramatically accelerated Xerox's new integrated services vision, while also reinforcing the long-treasured "Xerox family" culture. She did the latter by emphasizing with every outside managerial candidate the privileges they can enjoy if they pass her "parental test." That test, a pop quiz of sorts, is described in Exhibit 9.9.

The Parenting Strategy Approach[13]

Parenting Strategy Approach
An approach to crafting the best corporate role in a multi-business company created by BCG based on the "levers" corporate parents can use to influence business units. Six parenting strategy types are identified by BCG based on their emphasis on different levers they influence.

BCG's legacy working with multibusiness companies has it increasingly working with large global companies on this issue of value added by the parenting provided from the corporate center. BCG has done some excellent empirical and best practices research seeking to learn with a variety of clients how corporate centers can add the most value. One conclusion they recently reported—corporate stakeholders (analysts, boards, business managers) have shifted their focus from individual businesses' competitive advantages, a given, to the competitive advantage at the corporate level. BCG research suggests that understanding how corporate parents add value is a first step in devising a corporate parenting strategy. Then, their ongoing research suggests six basic parenting strategies based on the level of direct engagement between the parent and the business units.

Corporate parents, BCG suggests, add value via five types of "levers": corporate functions and resources, strategy development, financing advantages, business synergies, and operational engagement. Specific "levers" within each of these five types are listed in Exhibit 9.10. The relevance of any particular lever for a corporate center to use in adding value to one or more of its business units varies from company to company. But identification of the levers that are most relevant in a particular business unit or set of units becomes a logical manner with which to craft a parenting strategy that more intentionally adds value.

BCG found that there was no single "right" corporate parenting strategy.[14] What was best for one corporate center client might not be useful for another company, even when that company is otherwise a close rival with similar businesses. Their suggestion instead was twofold. First, to draw on the advice of Hippocrates that guides physicians even today, "First, do no harm." Second, a corporate center with its stakeholders should systematical assess these fundamental

---

[13]This section draws on the research by the Boston Consulting Group as reported in www.bcgperspectives.com; Fabruce Roghe, Ulrich Pidun, Sebastian Stange, and Mathias Kruhler, "Designing the Corporate Center: How to Turn Strategy into Structure," *bcg.perspectives*, May 13, 2013; "First Do No Harm: How to Be a Good Corporate Parent," *bcg.perspectives*, March, 2012. For much more elaborate coverage, visit www.bcgperspectives.com.

[14]See *First Do No Harm: How to Be a Good Corporate Parent*, Boston Consulting Group, March, 2012.

Ursula Burns, Chairwoman and CEO, Xerox

Ursula Burns joined Xerox over 30 years ago in New York as a young mechanical engineer summer intern. Twenty years later she celebrated the dawn of the twenty-first century as Xerox's new V.P. for Global Manufacturing. Xerox, though, was heading into a precipitous decline led by a new, non-Xerox outsider CEO's misguided strategies and eventual related challenges—SEC accounting irregularities, substantial debt, excessive bureaucracy, senior management drama, and echoes of bankruptcy.

Ms. Burns, frustrated with what was happening to Xerox, almost left. A board member convinced her that abandoning Xerox would signal the company was unsalvageable. She stayed. Anne Mulcahy, another Xerox lifer, soon thereafter became CEO, replacing the "outsider." She then went about stabilizing Xerox and rebuilding the maligned, dedicated Xerox family.

Burns became a key part of Mulcahy's corporate team, and eventually heir apparent. She and Mulcahy approached the salvaging and rebirth of the Xerox family of businesses as parental siblings, sisters, stabilizing this business "family" and creating for it a better future. They both in effect assumed the roles of corporate parents to Xerox's different businesses and its people. Mulcahy focused on the immediate situation—managing external relations with key stakeholders to help different parts of Xerox stabilize; to identify predictable errors currently affecting Xerox businesses, like overreliance on old products, and fix them; to gain better efficiencies sharing common capabilities; and to balance the precious, precarious capital resources.

Burns took the corporate parenting role focused on the future—foremost being a "bet-the-company" acquisition by Xerox to move up-market into more profitable services—business services handling all a company's documents, packaging, work flow, utilization planning, and related business process needs. She personally led the acquisition team, and she focused on the soft side of due diligence: "'Are we gonna like these guys?' Back when there was a *them* and *us,* 'Do they have a soul that was good for Xerox's culture?'" So she decided to put into place a clear hurdle for any Xerox outsider, including any among *them* at the time, as they were being considered for a Xerox management position—they must answer to her satisfaction "What is it that you see in Xerox that you love—that you can love—you can grow to love?"As a good corporate "parent," the answer lets her protect and carefully rebuild the right "Xerox family."

Even though ACS had 74,000 employees and Xerox 54,000, Ms. Burns sought to retain and imbed the existing Xerox family culture into the new entity driven by ACS's capabilities. "Xerox was dead in the water. It had no future." said a former top ACS executive. "With ACS, it has a future, but it has to make something of it." Apparently this executive didn't join the Xerox family. But, is it making something of it?

Nearly four years later, Xerox is no longer a just a synonym for copier. More than half of its $25 billion in 2014 revenue came from services built on ACS' legacy. If you've booked an airline ticket, run through a toll booth, paid a parking ticket, filed a health insurance claim, or applied for a car loan, chances are Xerox handled the back-end processing. By 2017, business services and IT outsourcing that stem from ACS are expected to account for two of every three dollars Xerox brings in.

Lynn Blodgett, former ACS CEO and now president of Xerox Services, said he and Burns shared a vision of how to mesh two large organizations. "Ursula has done a terrific job of getting the right level of integration and at the same time preserving the entrepreneurial spirit that made ACS such a great company," he said. That hasn't been easy, Burns said. "We essentially doubled the revenue growth of the ACS portion of the company. That's hard to do and keep control when you're talking in billions." Spoken like a wise, thoughtful parent!

Sources: Adam Bryant, "Xerox's New Chief Tries to Redefine Its Culture," The New York Times, February 21, 2010; See also, "CEO Leads Xerox in a New Direction with ACS Deal," www.*DallasNews. com,* May 4, 2013; "Q&A with Ursula Burns," *MIT Technology Review,* February 20, 2013; and Adam Bryant, "Xerox's New Chief Tries to Redefine Its Culture," *The New York Times,* February 21, 2013.

EXHIBIT 9.10   **Levers a Corporate Center Might Use to Create Value**[15]

Corporate function and resource levers:

- *Central functions*—cost advantages through these functions, or bundled services like IT, accounting, legal, and procurement services
- *Corporate assets*—such as brands, distinct capabilities, technologies, or facilities
- *People advantages*—helping recruit talented people attracted by strong brands, broader career opportunities, job rotation opportunities

Strategy development levers:

- *Strategic direction*—helping develop, analyze, and shape a business unit's strategy
- *Active M&A*—experienced deal-making team to help analyze and execute M&As
- *Superior governance*—sound support, knowhow, and execution in doing things right

Financing advantage levers:

- *External funding*—access to capital at lower rates than stand-alone competitors
- *Internal funding*—steady operational cash flows may be shared; less dependence on external capital markets
- *Tax optimization*—benefit from tax optimizaton across business units; tax help

Operational engagement levers:

- *Corporate intervention*—taking over management of dysfunctional operating activities
- *Operational monitoring*—influence unit operating objectives by establishing thorough criteria and procedures for business unit investment approvals necessitating major monitoring of performance across all units
- *Fostering cooperation*—actively enabling cooperation between business units

Business Synergies:

- *Operational Synergies*—shared facilities, logistics, process & product technologies, & admin support
- *Sales Synergies*—shared sales force, activities, after sale support, brand name, promotion, distribution channels, and order processing
- *Managerial Synergies*—Special management knowhow, relationships, contacts, expertise.

levers with which a corporate parent creates value and devise the use or nonuse of each based on the thoughtful relevance each brings to truly add value to individual business units.

While they found no one ideal corporate parenting strategy, BCG's research suggested six archetypal or prevailing parenting strategies that most corporate centers could be at least implicitly characterized as following. They ranged from very engaged corporate centers, which BCG calls "Hands-on Manager," to minimally engaged ones they call "Hands-off Owner." The six parenting strategy types are as follows:[16]

Hands-off Owner corporate centers exert no central control over the individual businesses they own. They essentially are investors developing an investment portfolio, buying businesses to add to their portfolio while divesting others to generate funds for reinvestment. This is a careful, conservative approach, which has the parenting strategy using mainly corporate function levers during deal negotiation and structure and fiduciary governance. BCG suggests state-owned investment funds as a typical example of the type of corporate entity following this parenting strategy.

Financial Sponsor corporate centers exist primarily to provide financing advantages and governance oversight to the business units—corporate function and financial resource levers, with minimal involvement in strategy and operations. This parenting

[15]Adapted from "Designing the Corporate Center: How to Turn Strategy into Structure," Boston Consulting Group, May 13, 2013, www.bcg.com.
[16]"Designing the Corporate Center: How to Turn Strategy Into Structure," ibid.

strategy is one step more involved than the hands-off owner approach. For example, this approach might typically be found in private sector investment companies like traditional private-equity firms and financial holding companies.

Family Builder corporate centers are another step more involved with their business units to help accelerate value building across the portfolio. BCG said this is frequently seen in diversified, fast-moving consumer goods companies with limited but intense focus on financial resource levers and business synergy levers. For example, providing or arranging significant financing for a new facility or strategic acquisition that benefits multiple businesses within the portfolio would be a family builder parenting strategy. Evaluating and helping bring together or acquiring companies that have intrinsically similar needs in production, or that sell through similar channels, would also be common in this approach.

Strategic Guide corporate centers take the involvement level up a significant notch. Their parenting role frequently plays an active role through strategy development levers and business synergy levers to actively help formulate the strategies of business units and the overall corporation. At the same time, this parenting strategy would have minimal involvement with other phases of each individual business. So this parenting strategy is what we typically associate with diversified, multibusiness companies where the corporate center takes a major interest in each business's strategy, and in seeing that the synergies envisioned when bringing the companies into a related business portfolio come to fuition. The parent seeks to have top-level oversight through this strategy, with in effect a strategy-based means to evaluate each business and its team that all have bought into and accept as the basis for accountability.

Functional Leader corporate centers are typically concerned with core functional excellence, or a cost-leadership bundling of services around their growing number of business units. So the parenting strategy of the corporate center is to protect and promote that functional expertise or cost-leadership service bundling to keep it constantly improving, state of the art, and safe from the market/competitive dynamics in any one business unit's particular domain. This strategy is most often seen at large, integrated multibusiness companies. Samsung stands out in consumer electronics for its core, rapidly adjusting mass production capabilities; UPS for its bundling of services supporting logistics-based businesses; and Amazon.com for the core technology it continuously makes second to none, supporting a variety of businesses and partners worldwide.

Hands-on Manager corporate centers are the most engaged corporate parents. Their parenting strategy has the center actively involved in the management and operations of each business unit. They deploy potentially all corporate value-creating levers, but particularly operational engagement and business synergy levers. They make sure what is to be done, who is to do it, when, and how it is to be done. Managers in each business unit may be involved in developing those key answers during the corporate-led planning session, but the managers' main job and responsibility is essentially execution. This parenting strategy is most appropriate for companies with a related portfolio of businesses operating in maturing industries.

How Corporate Parents Reduce Business Unit Value

Even when the parenting strategy is enabling the corporate center to engage levers that add value to business units, there is the risk that it could also in other ways be destroying value. BCG's research identified five types of value destroyers that corporate centers should and can manage.[17]

---

[17]"First Do No Harm: How to Be a Good Corporate Parent," The Boston Consulting Group, www.bcgperspectives.com, March 2012.

Insufficient expertise and skills regarding a business unit's specific requirements and the drivers of its success can be a real frustration for hard-pressed operating executives. Accomodating a corporate parent's managers who don't understand key operating considerations in a particular business inevitably interferes with a corporate manager's ability to meaningfully ensure corporate policies, requirements, and services add value to the business unit's potential to succeed. This concern—they don't understand what we do and how we have to do it—is often top on operating managers, frustration list.

Inefficient processes are a frequent complaint by business unit managers referring to their "corporate parent." Time is a precious commodity, and following processes and procedures that seem unnecessary, confusing, and even poorly explained eat up that precious commodity. Processes for approval of decisions significant to a business unit manager but that are one of many approval decisions to be made by a corporate parent are ripe for conflict, delay, confusion, and frustration. Review meetings, where operating managers expect outcomes or decisions and leave without being certain about "what just happened" or what to do can waste time and effort.

Cost of complexity can destroy value when the desire for cooperation and/or synergy between different business units is complicated to manage and made more so by corporate protocol. Further, doing so to coordinate input on corporate policies and shaping critical decisions that will affect future resources gets further complicated by interunit competition for resources and influence.

Resource shortages can arise for successful business units having to subsidize less successful business units, reducing their available capital for investment and management talent. Also, a business unit's role in the corporate portfolio may call on them to share financial, people, or capabilities that reduce their ability to maximize their performance.

Conflict of goals may arise when the corporate parent has objectives that conflict with the optimum performance of individual business units. For example, the corporate parent may prioritize certain sales channels, cash management procedures, incentive programs, or market regions on a corporate-wide strategy basis, which may work to the detriment of individual business units with changing sales channel needs, access to cash timing considerations, certain proven incentive approaches, or strong preference to prioritize other market regions. The result is possible value reduction for individual business units as a result of corporate center decisions.

The challenge for corporate parent strategy is to be exceptionally alert to the potential for these types of value destroyers that may come from the actions of the corporate center. At the very least, they should become a filter to periodically revisit with unit managers to minimize or ideally do no harm as the corporate center for a multibusiness company. It's a difficult task, no doubt, because they start from being a cost center and net drag on each business unit. Many business unit managers will say that corporate functions and corporate-level bosses are more often a hindrance than a help.

The value of the corporate-parent strategy approach is its improved framing of that issue. What are specific ways corporate centers add value here for us as levers potentially relevant in doing so? Second, with no one best way to use those levers, what are nonetheless typical patterns of parenting strategy that make use of these levers in different ways, defined now for us around level of involvement with the business units? Finally, in what key ways do corporate managers typically become "a hindrance," or destroy value so that, in knowing what to look out for, they at least do no harm and, ideally, start to add value through intentional lever usage and a parental strategy approach that fits with a business unit's market realities?

The Patching Approach

patching
The process by which corporate executives routinely "remap" their businesses to match rapidly changing market opportunities—adding, splitting, transferring, exiting, or combining chunks of businesses.

Another approach that focuses on the role and ability of corporate managers to create value in the management of multibusiness companies is called "patching."[18] **Patching** is the process by which corporate executives routinely remap businesses to match rapidly changing market opportunities. It can take the form of adding, splitting, transferring, exiting, or combining chunks of businesses. Patching is not seen as critical in stable, unchanging markets. When markets are turbulent and rapidly changing, patching is seen as critical to the creation of economic value in a multibusiness company.

Proponents of this perspective on the strategic decision-making function of corporate executives say it is the critical, and arguably only, way corporate executives can add value beyond the sum of the businesses within the company. They view traditional corporate strategy as creating defensible strategic positions for business units by acquiring or building valuable assets, wisely allocating resources to them, and weaving synergies among them. In volatile markets, they argue, this traditional approach results in business units with strategies that are quickly outdated and competitive advantages rarely sustained beyond a few years.[19] As a result, they say, strategic analysis should center on **strategic processes** more than **strategic positioning.** In these volatile markets, patchers' strategic analysis focuses on making quick, small, frequent changes in parts of businesses and organizational processes that enable dynamic strategic repositioning rather than building long-term defensible positions. Exhibit 9.11 compares differences between traditional approaches to shaping corporate strategy with the patching approach.

strategic processes
Decision making, operational activities, and sales activities that are critical business processes.

strategic positioning
The way a business is designed and positioned to serve target markets.

To be successful with a patching approach to corporate strategic analysis and choice in turbulent markets, Eisenhardt and Sull suggest that managers should flexibly seize opportunities—as long as that flexibility is disciplined. Effective corporate strategists, they argue, focus on key processes and *simple rules.* The following example at Miramax helps illustrate the notion of strategy as simple rules:

> Miramax—well known for artistically innovative movies such as *The Crying Game, Life is Beautiful*, and *Pulp Fiction*—has boundary rules that guide the all-important movie-picking process: First, every movie must revolve around a central human condition, such as love *(The Crying Game)* or envy *(The Talented Mr. Ripley)*. Second, a movie's main character must be appealing but deeply flawed—the hero of *Shakespeare in Love* is gifted and charming but steals ideas from friends and betrays his wife. Third, movies must have a very clear story line with a beginning, middle, and end (although in *Pulp Fiction* the end comes first). Finally, there is a firm cap on production costs. Within the rules, there is flexibility to move quickly when a writer or director shows up with a great script. The result is an enormously creative and even surprising flow of movies and enough discipline to produce superior, consistent financial results. *The English Patient,* for example, cost $27 million to make, grossed more than $200 million, and grabbed nine Oscars.[20]

[18]J. A. Martin and K. M. Eisenhardt, "Rewiring: Cross-Business-Unit Collaborations in Multibusiness Organizations," *The Academy of Management Journal* 53, no. 2 (April, 2010), pp. 265–301; K. M. Eisenhardt, "Has Strategy Changed?" *MIT Sloan Management Review* (Winter, 2002), pp. 88–91; K. M. Eisenhardt and S. L. Brown, "Patching: Restitching Business Portfolios in Dynamic Markets," *Harvard Business Review* (May–June, 1999), pp. 72–82; K. M. Eisenhardt and D. N. Sull, "Strategy as Simple Rules," *Harvard Business Review* (January, 2001), pp. 104–112; S. A. Zahra, R. S. Sisodia, and S. R. Das, "Technological Choices within Competitive Strategy Types: A Conceptual Integration," *International Journal of Technology Management* 9, no. 2 (May 2009), pp. 172–195; and M. Garbuio, A. W. King, and D. Lovallo, "Looking Inside: Psychological Influences on Structuring a Firm's Portfolio of Resources," *Journal of Management* 37, no. 3 (May, 2011), pp. 651–681.

[19]Eisenhardt and Brown, "Patching," p. 76.

[20]Ibid., Eisenhardt and Sull, p. 111.

EXHIBIT 9.11   Three Approaches to Strategy

Managers competing in business can choose among three distinct ways to fight. They can build a fortress and defend it; they can nurture and leverage unique resources; or they can flexibly pursue fleeting opportunities within simple rules. Each approach requires different skill sets and works best under different circumstances.

	Position	Resources	Patching [Simple Rules]
Strategic logic	Establish position	Leverage resources	Pursue opportunities
Strategic steps	Identify an attractive market	Establish a vision Build resources	Jump into the confusion Keep moving
	Locate a defensible position	Leverage across markets	Seize opportunities Finish strong
	Fortify and defend		
Strategic question	Where should we be?	What should we be?	How should we proceed?
Source of advantage	Unique, valuable position with tightly integrated activity system	Unique, valuable, inimitable resources	Key processes and unique simple rules
Works best in	Slowly changing, well-structured markets	Moderately changing, well-structured markets	Rapidly changing, ambiguous markets
Duration of advantage	Sustained	Sustained	Unpredictable
Risk	Too difficult to alter position as conditions change	Too slow to build new resources as conditions change	Too tentative in executing promising opportunities
Performance goal	Profitability	Long-term dominance	Growth

Source: Reprinted by permission of *Harvard Business Review*. Exhibit from "Strategy as Simple Rules," by Kathleen M. Eisenhardt and Donald M. Sull, January 2001. Copyright 2001 by the Harvard Business School Publishing Corporation; all rights reserved.

Different types of rules help managers and strategists manage different aspects of seizing opportunities. Exhibit 9.12 explains and illustrates five such types of rules. These rules are called "simple" rules because they need to be brief, be axiomatic, and convey fundamental guidelines to decisions or actions. They need to provide just enough structure to allow managers to move quickly to capture opportunities with confidence that the judgments and commitments they make are consistent with corporate intent. At the same time, while they set parameters on actions and decisions, they are not thick manuals or rules and policies that managers in turbulent environments may find paralyze any efforts to quickly capitalize on opportunities.

The patching approach then relies on simple rules unique to a particular parent company that exist to guide managers in the corporate organization and its business units in making rapid decisions about quickly reshaping parts of the company and allocating time as well as money to capitalize on rapidly shifting market opportunities. The fundamental argument of this approach is that no one can predict how long a competitive advantage will last, particularly in turbulent, rapidly changing markets. While managers in stable markets may be able to rely on complex strategies built on detailed predictions of future trends, managers in complex, fast-moving markets—where significant growth and wealth creation may occur—face constant unpredictability; hence, strategy must be simple, responsive, and dynamic to encourage success.

EXHIBIT 9.12 Simple Rules, Summarized

In turbulent markets, managers should flexibly seize opportunities—but flexibility must be disciplined. Smart companies focus on key processes and simple rules. Different types of rules help executives manage different aspects of seizing opportunities.

Type	Purpose	Example
How-to rules	Spell out key features of how a process is executed—"What makes our process unique?"	Akami's rules for the customer service process: Staff must consist of technical gurus, every question must be answered on the first call or e-mail, and R&D staff must rotate through customer service.
Boundary rules	Focus on which opportunities can be pursued and which are outside the pale.	Cisco's early acquisitions rule: Companies to be acquired must have no more than 75 employees, 75 percent of whom are engineers.
Priority rules	Help managers rank the accepted opportunities.	Intel's rule for allocating manufacturing capacity: Allocation is based on a product's gross margin.
Timing rules	Synchronize managers with the pace of emerging opportunities and other parts of the company.	Nortel's rules for product development: Project teams must know when a product has to be delivered to the customer to win, and product development time must be less than 18 months.
Exit rules	Help managers decide when to pull out of yesterday's opportunities.	Oticon's rule for pulling the plug on projects in development: If a key team member—manager or not—chooses to leave the project for another within the company, the project is killed.

Source: Reprinted by permission of *Harvard Business Review.* Exhibit from "Strategy as Simple Rules," by Kathleen M. Eisenhardt and Donald M. Sull, January 2001. Copyright 2001 by the Harvard Business School Publishing Corporation; all rights reserved.

Summary

This chapter examined how managers make strategic decisions in multibusiness companies. One of the earliest approaches was to look at the company as a portfolio of businesses. This portfolio was then examined and evaluated based on each business's growth potential, market position, and need for and ability to generate cash. Corporate strategists then allocated resources, divested, and acquired businesses based on the balance across this portfolio of businesses or possible businesses.

The notion of synergy across business units—sharing capabilities and leveraging core competencies—has been another very widely adopted approach to making strategic decisions in multibusiness companies. Sharing capabilities allows for greater efficiencies, enhanced expertise, and competitive advantage. Core competencies that generate competitive advantage can often be leveraged across multiple businesses, thereby expanding the impact and value added from that competitive advantage.

Globalization, rapid change, outsourcing, and other major forces shaping today's economic landscape have ushered in multibusiness strategic decision making that also focuses on the role and value-added contributions, if any, of the parent company itself. Does the parent company add or could it add value beyond the sum of the businesses it owns? Three perspectives that have gained popularity in multibusiness companies' strategic decision making are the parent opportunities framework, the parenting strategy approach, and the patching approach. The parenting opportunities framework focuses on 10 areas of opportunity managers should carefully explore to find ways the parent organization might add value to one or more businesses and the overall company. BCG's parent strategy approach focuses on five types of "levers" that corporate parents selectively use to shape a customized parent strategy that should add value to each business unit within their business portfolio. Those levers are: corporate functions and resources, strategy development, financing advantages, business synergies, and operational engagement. Similarly, there are five related types of value destroyers identified in this chapter that BCG suggests corporate parents should be careful to avoid. The patching approach concentrates on multibusiness companies in turbulent markets of the twenty-first century, where managers need to make quick, small shifts and adjustments in processes, markets, and products, and offers five types of "simple rules" that managers use as guidelines to structure quick decisions throughout a multibusiness company on a continuous basis.

Key Terms

cash cows, *p. 273*
dogs, *p. 273*
fragmented businesses, *p. 277*
market growth rate, *p. 272*
parenting opportunities framework, *p. 286*

parenting strategy approach, *p. 288*
patching, *p. 293*
portfolio techniques, *p. 272*
question marks, *p. 273*
relative competitive position, *p. 272*

specialization businesses, *p. 277*
stalemate businesses, *p. 277*
stars, *p. 273*
strategic positioning, *p. 293*
strategic processes, *p. 293*
volume businesses, *p. 277*

Questions for Discussion

1. How does strategic analysis at the corporate level differ from strategic analysis at the business unit level? How are they related?
2. When would multibusiness companies find the portfolio approach to strategic analysis and choice useful?
3. What are three types of opportunities for sharing that form a sound basis for diversification or vertical integration? Give an example of each from companies you have read about.
4. Describe three types of opportunities through which a corporate parent could add value beyond the sum of its separate businesses.
5. Identify five types of levers corporate parents should consider in shaping a corporate parenting strategy.
6. What are five key ways corporate parents destroy value among their business units?
7. What does "patching" refer to? Describe and illustrate two rules that might guide managers to build value in their businesses.

Strategy Implementation, Control, and Innovation

Strategic management has two equally important parts, interrelated in life but separated here to aid your study of what it involves. It is an important caveat to remember. Up to this point we have covered one part—strategy formulation. Now we turn your attention to the second part, strategy implementation. As we do so by conceptually separating them to aid your process of learning about both parts, it is important to keep in mind that they are often intertwined, not distinct and separate in practice.

For a strategy's ultimate success, it must become effective in organizational and individual action. This means that

1. The strategy must be translated into guidelines for the daily activities of the firm's members.
2. The strategy and the firm must become one—that is, the strategy must be reflected in
   a. The way the firm organizes its activities.
   b. The key organization leaders.
   c. The culture of the organization.
3. The company's managers must put into place "steering" controls that provide strategic control and the ability to adjust strategies, commitments, and objectives in response to ever-changing future conditions.
4. Increasingly, organizations must make a serious commitment to be innovative and must consider bringing the entrepreneurship process into their company to survive, grow, and prosper in a vastly more competitive and rapidly changing global business arena.

Chapter 10 explains how organizational action is successfully initiated through four interrelated steps:

1. Creation of clear *short-term objectives* and *action plans*.
2. Development of specific *functional tactics,* to include *outsourcing,* that create competitive advantage.
3. Empowerment of operating personnel through *policies* to guide decisions.
4. Implementation of effective *reward systems*.

Short-term objectives and action plans guide implementation by converting long-term objectives into short-term actions and targets. Functional tactics, whether done internally or outsourced to other partners, translate the business strategy into activities that build advantage. Policies empower operating personnel by defining guidelines for making decisions. Reward systems encourage effective results.

Today's competitive environment requires careful analysis in designing the organizational structure most suitable to build and sustain competitive advantage. Chapter 11 examines traditional organizational structures—their pros and cons. It looks at the pervasive trend toward outsourcing, along with outsourcing's pros and cons. It concludes with examination of the latest developments in creating ambidextrous, virtual, boundaryless organizations designed to adapt in a highly interconnected, lightning-speed, global business environment.

There can be no doubt that effective organizational leadership and the consistency of a strong organizational culture reinforcing norms and behaviors best suited to the organization's mission are two central ingredients in enabling successful execution of a firm's strategies and objectives. Chapter 12 examines leadership, the critical things good leaders do, and how to nurture effective operating managers as they become outstanding future organizational leaders. Chapter 12 then examines the organizational culture, how it is shaped, and creative ways of managing the strategy-culture relationship.

Because the firm's strategy is implemented in a changing environment, successful implementation requires strategic control—an ability to "steer" the firm through an extended future time period when premises, sudden events, internal implementation efforts, and general economic and societal developments will be sources of change not anticipated or predicted when the strategy was conceived and initiated. Chapter 13 examines how to set up strategic controls to deal with the important steering function during the implementation process. The chapter also examines operational control functions and the balanced scorecard approach to integrating strategic and operational control.

The overriding concerns in executing strategies and leading a company are survival, growth, and prosperity. In a global economy that allows everyone everywhere instant information and instant connectivity, change often occurs at lightning speed. Thus, leaders are increasingly encouraging their firms to embrace innovation and entrepreneurship as key ways to respond to such overwhelming uncertainty. Chapter 14 examines innovation in general, different types of innovation, and the best ways to bring more innovative activity into a firm. It examines the entrepreneurship process as another way to build innovative responsiveness and opportunity recognition into a firm, both in new-venture settings and in large business organizations.

Implementation is "where the action is." It is the arena that most students enter at the start of their business careers. It is the strategic phase in which staying close to the customer, achieving competitive advantage, and pursuing excellence become realities. These five chapters in Part Three will help you understand how this is done and how to prepare to take your place as a future leader of successful, innovative business organizations.

Implementation

After reading and studying this chapter, you should be able to

1. Understand how short-term objectives are used in strategy implementation.

2. Identify and apply the qualities of good short-term objectives to your own experiences.

3. Illustrate what is meant by functional tactics and understand how they are used in strategy implementation.

4. Gain a general sense of what out-sourcing is and how it becomes a choice in functional tactics decisions for strategy implementation.

5. Understand what policies are and how to use policies to empower operating personnel in implementing business strategies and functional tactics.

6. Understand the use of financial reward in executive compensation.

7. Identify different types of executive compensation and when to use each in strategy implementation.

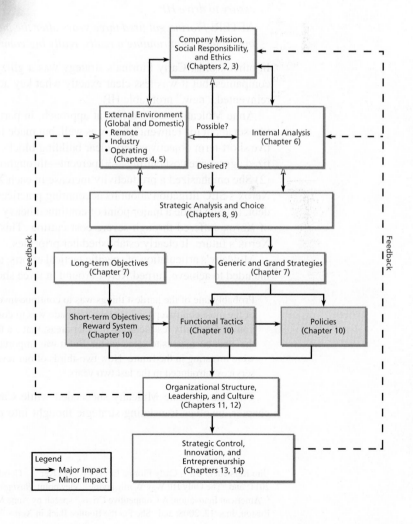

Xerox and Hewlett-Packard faced difficult times during the last decade. For Xerox, bankruptcy was a real possibility given its $14 billion debt and its serious problems with the U.S. Securities and Exchange Commission. Hewlett-Packard was falling behind in the computer business while living solely on profits from its printer division. Anne Mulcahy became Xerox CEO during this time. Carly Fiorina became HP's CEO. Five years later, Anne Mulcahy was celebrated for the success of her strategy at Xerox while Carly Fiorina was dismissed for the failure of the path she chose. Two legendary technology companies and two celebrated CEOs who shattered the "glass ceiling" in being selected to lead two legendary companies back to glory: Why did one succeed and the other fail?

Analysts suggest that the "devil is in the detail." Fiorina's strategy was to acquire Compaq, build the size of HP's PC business, and use profits from HP's venerable printer business to sustain a reorganization of the combined companies. CNET and former *PC Week* Senior Editor Jim Kerstetter and Mark Anderson, an investment analyst who had followed HP for over 20 years when he listened to her pitch, shared these before and after thoughts about Carly Fiorina's strategy:[1]

> BEFORE: *I would say it stinks, but it isn't even a strategy. A few bullet points don't make a strategy. Such an approach lacks the technical and market understanding necessary to drive HP . . .*
>
> AFTER: *Fiorina got fired three years after the merger because she was better at selling an idea than running a really, really big company.*

In other words, Carly Fiorina's strategy was a glitzy combination of two large computer companies, but it was less clear exactly what key actions and tactics would bring about a reinvented, "new," profitable HP.

Anne Mulcahy took a different approach, in part reflecting her 28 years inside Xerox. She set about to "reinvent" Xerox as well, but made four functional tactics and their respective short-term objectives very clear building blocks for reinventing Xerox: (1) She prioritized aggressive cost cutting—30 percent—throughout the company to restore profitability. (2) She emphasized a productivity increase in each Xerox division. (3) She quickly settled Xerox's SEC litigation about its accounting practices, and she refinanced Xerox's massive debt. (4) She made a major point of continued heavy R&D funding even as every other part of Xerox suffered through severe cost cutting. This, she felt, sent a message of belief in Xerox's future. It clearly established her priorities.

Mulcahy's articulation of specific tactical efforts, and the short-term objectives they were intended to achieve, turned Xerox around in three short years. As she proudly pointed out:

> Probably one of the hardest things was to continue investing in the future, in growth. One of the most controversial decisions we made was to continue our R&D investment. When you're drastically restructuring in other areas, that's a tough decision. It makes it harder for the other businesses to some extent. But it was important for the Xerox people to believe we were investing in the future. Now two-thirds of our revenue is coming from products and services introduced in the last two years.[2]

The reason Anne Mulcahy succeeded while Carly Fiorina did not, the focus of this chapter, involves translating strategic thought into organizational action. In the words of

---

[1]Jim Kerstetter, "HP's Carly Fiorina Era Is Finally Over . . . Good Riddance," www.news.cnet.com, August 19, 2011; and "The Only HP Way Worth Trying," Viewpoint, *BusinessWeek*, March 9, 2005.

[2] "American Innovation: A Competitive Crisis," speech by Anne M. Mulcahy at The Chief Executive's Club of Boston, June 12, 2008; and "She Put the Bounce Back in Xerox," *BusinessWeek*, January 10, 2005.

Silicon Valley Serial Entrepreneur Dirk Brown Shares His Secret of Success

CEO and co-founder Dirk Brown is hard at work building his fourth Silicon Valley technology company, Pandoodle, after an earlier career at ADM. Pandoodle has a proprietary technology that is likely to change how advertising is monetized on video, streaming movies, and games. But that's another story. Dirk has a secret that keeps investors wanting in on what he's building, and talented people scrambling to try to get a chance to be in his next company.

What we wanted to know from Dr. Brown is what drives his success at being able to create a team, engage major investors, and build a fledgling start-up into a large company over time. That process often includes challenges like "pivoting" when initial product/sales efforts stall, running lean to start, and managing tight financial constraints that mean he has to have a way to keep control while encouraging quick-thinking action and results. So, what is his secret?

Dirk says a key part of his repeat success building companies has been his belief in the importance of short-term objectives to help him with his management team, and the team with their people, to guide strategy implementation under challenging circumstances. He views short-term objectives as key levers to guide how you are performing "now," and also as valuable talent windows that show how you will or will not fit in over the next several years as the effort to build the company gains serious momentum.

"I am an engineer by training, so I like objectives or outcomes we can measure. I find I can lead and guide my E-team better with short range targets are measurable." "As an entrepreneur," Brown said, "we're always faced with pivoting, shifting, and adjusting." So knowing when to do so, in his opinion, "is dependent upon short term targets, objectives, and outcomes you can measure, monitor, and trust your inclination to act."

Brown also emphasizes simplicity in setting short term objectives with his E-team. "Time is precious, money is being spent with little reserve to count on" Brown continued, "it boils down to having a few key objectives that everyone understands—that are simple—and that drive what everyone focuses on doing every day."

two well-worn phrases, they move from "planning their work" to "working their plan." Anne Mulcahy successfully made this shift at Xerox when she did these five things well:

1. Identify short-term objectives.
2. Initiate specific functional tactics.
3. Outsource nonessential functions.
4. Communicate policies that empower people in the organization.
5. Design effective rewards.

Short-term objectives translate long-range aspirations into this year's targets for action. If well developed, these objectives provide clarity, a powerful motivator and facilitator of effective strategy implementation. In Exhibit 10.1, Global Strategy in Action. Action, Serial Silicon Valley Entrepreneur Dirk Brown describes how critical short term objectives are to his success in building each of the four companies he has started.

Functional tactics translate business strategy into daily activities people need to execute. Functional managers participate in the development of these tactics, and their participation, in turn, helps clarify what their units are expected to do in implementing the business's strategy.

301

Outsourcing nonessential functions normally performed in-house frees up resources and the time of key people to concentrate on leveraging the functions and activities critical to the core competitive advantages around which the firm's long-range strategy is built.

Policies are empowerment tools that simplify decision making by empowering operating managers and their subordinates. Policies can empower the "doers" in an organization by reducing the time required to decide and act.

Rewards that align manager and employee priorities with organizational objectives and shareholder value provide very effective direction in strategy implementation.

SHORT-TERM OBJECTIVES

short-term objective
Measurable outcomes achievable or intended to be achieved in one year or less.

Chapter 7 described various long range strategies and attributes of accompanying types of long-term objectives that are critically important in charting a successful future for any company. To make them become a reality, however, the people in an organization who actually "do the work" of the business need guidance in exactly what they need to do. Short-term objectives help do this. **Short-term objectives** are measurable outcomes achievable or intended to be achieved in one year or less. They are specific, usually quantitative, results operating managers set out to achieve in the immediate future.

Short-term objectives help implement strategy in at least three ways:

1. Short-term objectives "operationalize" long-term objectives. If we commit to a 20 percent gain in revenue over five years, what is our specific target or objective in revenue during the current year, month, or week to indicate we are making appropriate progress?

2. Discussion about and agreement on short-term objectives help raise issues and potential conflicts within an organization that usually require coordination to avoid otherwise dysfunctional consequences. Exhibit 10.2 illustrates how objectives within marketing, manufacturing, and accounting units within the same firm can be very different even when created to pursue the same firm objective (e.g., increased sales, lower costs).

EXHIBIT 10.2
Potential Conflicting Objectives and Priorities

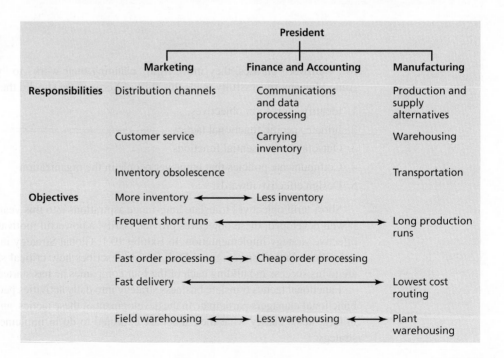

	Marketing	Finance and Accounting	Manufacturing
Responsibilities	Distribution channels	Communications and data processing	Production and supply alternatives
	Customer service	Carrying inventory	Warehousing
	Inventory obsolescence		Transportation
Objectives	More inventory ←——→	Less inventory	
	Frequent short runs ←—————————————→		Long production runs
	Fast order processing ←——→	Cheap order processing	
	Fast delivery ←————————————————————→		Lowest cost routing
	Field warehousing ←——→	Less warehousing ←——→	Plant warehousing

3. Finally, short-term objectives assist strategy implementation by identifying measurable outcomes of action plans or functional activities, which can be used to make feedback, correction, and evaluation more relevant and acceptable.

Short-term objectives are usually accompanied by action plans, which enhance these objectives in three ways. First, action plans usually identify functional tactics and activities that will be undertaken in the next week, month, or quarter as part of the business's effort to build competitive advantage. The important point here is *specificity*—what exactly is to be done. We will examine functional tactics in a subsequent section of this chapter. The second element of an action plan is a clear *time frame for completion*—when the effort will begin and when its results will be accomplished. A third element action plans contain is identification of *who is responsible* for each action in the plan. This accountability is very important to ensure action plans are acted upon.

Qualities of Effective Short-Term Objectives

Measurable

Short-term objectives are more consistent when they clearly state *what* is to be accomplished, *when* it will be accomplished, and *how* its accomplishment will be *measured*. Such objectives can be used to monitor both the effectiveness of each activity and the collective progress across several interrelated activities. Exhibit 10.3 illustrates several effective and ineffective short-term objectives. Measurable objectives make misunderstanding less likely among interdependent managers who must implement action plans. It is far easier to quantify the objectives of *line* units (e.g., production) than of certain *staff* areas (e.g., personnel). Difficulties in quantifying objectives often can be overcome by initially focusing on *measurable activity* and then identifying *measurable outcomes*.

EXHIBIT 10.3
Creating Measurable Objectives

Examples of Deficient Objectives	Examples of Objectives with Measurable Criteria for Performance
To improve morale in the division (plant, department, etc.)	To reduce turnover (absenteeism, number of rejects, etc.) among sales managers by 10 percent by January 1, 2014. *Assumption:* Morale is related to measurable outcomes (i.e., high and low morale are associated with different results).
To improve support of the sales effort	To reduce the time lapse between order data and delivery by 8 percent (two days) by June 1, 2014. To reduce the cost of goods produced by 6 percent to support a product price decrease of 2 percent by December 1, 2014. To increase the rate of before- or on-schedule delivery by 5 percent by June 1, 2014.
To improve the firm's image	To conduct a public opinion poll using random samples in the five largest U.S. metropolitan markets to determine average scores on 10 dimensions of corporate responsibility by May 15, 2014. To increase our score on those dimensions by an average of 7.5 percent by May 1, 2014.

Priorities

Although all annual objectives are important, some deserve priority because of a timing consideration or their particular impact on a strategy's success. If such priorities are not established, conflicting assumptions about the relative importance of annual objectives may inhibit progress toward strategic effectiveness. Anne Mulcahy's turnaround of Xerox described at the beginning of this chapter emphasized several important short-term objectives. But it was clear throughout Xerox that her highest priority in the first two years was to dramatically lower overhead and production costs so as to satisfy the difficult challenge of continuing to invest heavily in R&D while also restoring profitability.

Priorities are established in various ways. A simple ranking may be based on discussion and negotiation during the planning process. However, this does not necessarily communicate the real difference in the importance of objectives, so such terms as primary, top, and secondary may be used to indicate priority. Some firms assign weights (e.g., 0 to 100 percent) to establish and communicate the relative priority of objectives. Whatever the method, recognizing priorities is an important dimension in the implementation value of short-term objectives.

Cascading: From Long-Term Objectives to Short-Term Objectives

The link between short-term and long-term objectives should resemble cascades through the firm from basic long-term objectives to specific short-term objectives in key operation areas. The cascading effect has the added advantage of providing a clear reference for communication and negotiation, which may be necessary to integrate and coordinate objectives and activities at the operating level.

Milliken, a U.S.–based global leader and innovator in the global textile industry, provides a good example of cascading objectives. One of Milliken's long-term priorities is sustainability—being an exemplary corporate steward of its global environment. That strategic commitment has been in existence almost 20 years—since Roger Milliken set forth four strategic principles and goals for all of Milliken's plants and facilities:

- Complete regulatory compliance.
- Strive for zero waste generation.
- Conserve natural resources.
- Continuously develop new environmental solutions.

Exhibit 10.4 shows how Milliken's Sustainability Team translates the four long-range goals into cascading and more specific, measurable short-term objectives for one year. This cascading approach gives solid guidance to Milliken "associates" at all its plants and facilities worldwide—cascading downward in specificity and also, ultimately, cascading upward to consolidate and evaluate Miliken's overall improvement in global environmental stewardship.[3]

FUNCTIONAL TACTICS THAT IMPLEMENT BUSINESS STRATEGIES

functional tactics
Detailed statements of the "means" or activities that will be used by a company to achieve short-term objectives and establish competitive advantage.

Functional tactics are the key, routine activities that must be undertaken in each functional area—marketing, finance, production/operations, R&D, and human resource management—to provide the business's products and services. In a sense, functional tactics translate thought (grand strategy) into action designed to accomplish specific short-term objectives. Every value chain activity in a company executes functional tactics that support the business's strategy and help accomplish strategic objectives.

---

[3] "Enhancing Sustainability at Milliken," SwampFox Sustainability Forum, Moore School of Business, University of South Carolina, Columbia, SC.

EXHIBIT 10.4
Milliken Global Environmental Objectives

Source: "Enhancing Sustainability at Milliken," presentation at SwampFox Sustainability Forum, Moore School of Business, University of South Carolina, Columbia, SC.

Strategic Priority	Functional Tactic	This Year's Objectives
Complete compliance	Zero serious environmental incidents	Number of serious incidents: 0 20% fewer significant incidents
Zero waste to landfill	Reduce solid waste	Zero waste to landfill 5% less solid waste/pound Increase reuse/recycle 75% to 78%
Conserve national resources	Reduce energy use	10% less energy consumed per pound
Conserve national resources	Reduce water use	10% less water consumed per pound
Zero emissions to air	Zero net greenhouse gas emissions	5% reduction greenhouse gas emit per pound
Environmental education	100% plant coverage worldwide	100% plant coverage worldwide
Quality control	ISO-14001 registration	ISO regulations for St. George; Gillespie; Autotex; Brazil; Zhangliangang; China

We said at the beginning of this part of the book that, while formulation and implementation are conceptually separated to aid your process of learning about them, it is important to keep in mind that they are often and inevitably intertwined in practice. Shaping tactics at the operating level that implement business strategy is a key juncture where that should happen. Getting tactics clarified and in sync with the business strategy can provide benefits and add value. Some of those benefits include:

- Giving operating personnel a better understanding of their role and how what they do fits with the unit's mission and strategy.
- The process of developing them, when done right, can be a forum for raising and resolving conflicts between strategic intent and operational realities due to operational issues not immediately known to higher management.
- Working through tactics and functional plans provides a basis for developing budgets, schedules, trigger points, critical factors to monitor, and other aspects that will inform strategic control.
- Generating and creating functional tactics and plans can be powerful motivators, especially when those doing them participate in the process of doing so.
- They can also become powerful motivators when connected to the reward system.

Differences between Business Strategies and Functional Tactics

Exhibit 10.5, Global Strategy in Action, illustrates the difference between functional tactics and business strategy. It also shows that functional tactics are essential to implement business strategy. It explains the situation at the leading U.K. restaurant company, where consultants were brought in to identify specific tactical things employees needed to do or deal with to implement an overall business strategy to differentiate the growing chain from many other restaurant competitors. The business strategy outlined the competitive posture of its operations in the restaurant industry. To increase the likelihood that these strategies would be successful, specific functional tactics were needed for the firm's operating components. These functional tactics clarified the business strategy, giving specific, short-term guidance to operating managers and employees in the areas of marketing, operations, and finance.

The Nature and Value of Specificity in Functional Tactics versus Business Strategy

A European restaurant business was encountering problems. Although its management had agreed unanimously that it was committed to a business strategy to differentiate itself from other competitors based on concept and customer service rather than price, the multilocation business continued to encounter inconsistencies across different store locations in how well it did this. Consultants indicated that the customer experience varied greatly from store to store. The conclusion was that while the management understood the "business strategy," and the employees did too in general terms, the implementation was inadequate because of a lack of specificity in the functional tactics—what everyone should do every day in the restaurant—to make the vision a reality in terms of the customers' dining experience. The following breakdown of part of their business strategy into specific functional tactics just in the area of customer service helps illustrate the value specificity in functional tactics brings to strategy implementation.

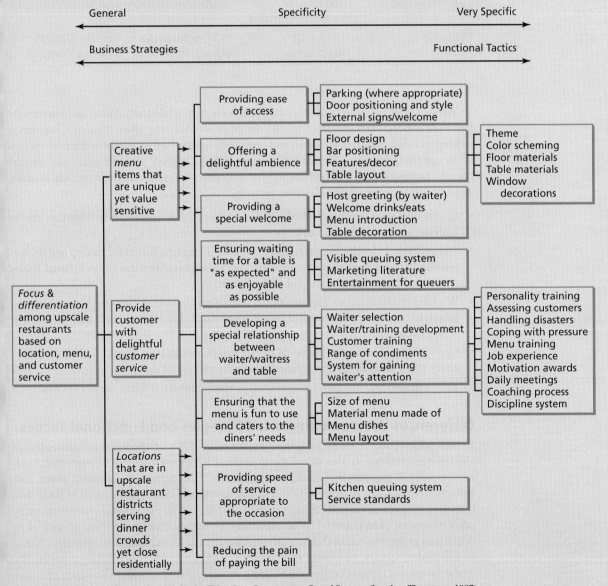

Source: Adapted from A. Campbell and K. Luchs, Eds., *Core Competency – Based Strategy* (London: Thompson, 1997).

Functional tactics are different from business or corporate strategies in three fundamental ways:

1. Specificity.
2. Time horizon.
3. Participants who develop them.

Specificity

Functional tactics are more specific than business strategies. Business strategies provide general direction. Functional tactics identify the specific activities that are to be undertaken in each functional area and thus allow operating managers to work out *how* their unit is expected to pursue short-term objectives. Exhibit 10.5, Global Strategy in Action, illustrates the nature and value of specificity in functional tactics versus business strategy at the United Kingdom's leading restaurant chain.

Specificity in functional tactics contributes to successful implementation by

- Helping ensure that functional managers know what needs to be done and can focus on accomplishing results.
- Clarifying for top management how functional managers intend to accomplish the business strategy, which increases top management's confidence in and sense of control over the business strategy.
- Facilitating coordination among operating units within the firm by clarifying areas of interdependence and potential conflict.

Time Horizon

Functional tactics identify activities to be undertaken "now" or in the immediate future. Business strategies focus on the firm's posture three to five years out. Exhibit 10.6, Global Strategy in Action, describes how Apple CEO Tim Cook won his "spurs" early on at Apple when he initially joined Apple's Operations Fixer and implemented immediate functional tactics to quickly turn around that company's broken manufacturing operations shortly after Steve Jobs brought him on board specifically to help do just that.

The shorter time horizon of functional tactics is critical to the successful implementation of a business strategy for two reasons. First, it focuses the attention of functional managers on what needs to be done *now* to make the business strategy work. Second, it allows functional managers like those at Apple to adjust to changing current conditions.

Participants

Different people participate in strategy development at the functional and business levels. Business strategy is the responsibility of the general manager of a business unit. That manager typically delegates the development of functional tactics to subordinates charged with running the operating areas of the business. The manager of a business unit must establish long-term objectives and a strategy that corporate management feels contributes to corporate-level goals. Similarly, key operating managers must establish short-term objectives and operating strategies that contribute to business-level goals. Just as business strategies and objectives are approved through negotiation between corporate managers and business managers, so, too, are short-term objectives and functional tactics approved through negotiation between business managers and operating managers.

Involving operating managers in the development of functional tactics improves their understanding of what must be done to achieve long-term objectives and, thus, contributes

Tim Cook: Did "the Apple" Fall Too Far from "the Tree"?

Tim Cook has had some dramatic challenges the last few years as Steve Jobs hand-picked replacement as the best CEO to lead Apple in the post-Jobs era. Jobs saw in Cook the same attention to detail, the tactical and operation tenacity, and the utter dedication to Apple he saw in himself.

While Cook's other side, an Auburn (1982) graduate and passion for the outdoors, cycling and Auburn football were perhaps related in some way to Jobs zen-like perspective, it was his passion for detail in operational tactics and strategies that Jobs' loved. Many of his past decisions Jobs' probably knew paved the foundation for Apple's success under Jobs. For example:

- Cook was reported to have prepaid Apple suppliers Hynix and Samsung over $1.25 billion for all their year's production of flash memory production when Apple introduced the iPod nano. Cook's tactic here effectively cornered the supply of the new flash memory chips for two years before competitions could find a supplier.

- Jobs initially hired Cook away from Compaq Computer to fix Apple's sprawling complex of company-owned manufacturing facilities and warehouses haphazardly developed over the early years at Apple. Cook's tactic—within months he had closed factories, sold off warehouses, and established tight relationships with outside manufacturers. His operational tactics led Apple to match the best in the industry for manufacturing efficiency, with Apple's days in inventory falling 95% from months to days.*

*Helft, Miguel, "The Understudy Takes the Stage at Apple," The New York Times, January 23, 2011.

to successful implementation. It also helps ensure that functional tactics reflect the reality of the day-to-day operating situation. And perhaps most important, it can increase the commitment of operating managers to the strategies developed.

OUTSOURCING FUNCTIONAL ACTIVITIES

A generation ago, it was conventional wisdom that a business has a better chance of success if it controls the doing of everything necessary to produce its products or services. Referring back to Chapter 6's value chain approach, the "wise" manager would have sought to maintain control of virtually all the "primary" activities and the "support" activities associated with the firm's work. Not any longer. Starting for most firms with the outsourcing of producing payroll each week, companies worldwide are embracing the idea that the best way to implement their strategies is to retain responsibility for executing some functions while seeking outside people and companies to do key support and key primary activities where they can do so more effectively and more inexpensively. **Outsourcing,** then, is acquiring an activity, service, or product necessary to provide a company's products or services from "outside" the people or operations controlled by that acquiring company.

outsourcing
Obtaining work previously done by employees inside the companies from sources outside the company.

DuPont Co. has always run corporate training and development out of its Wilmington (Delaware) head office. But these days, Boston-based Forum Corp. handles it instead. In Somers, New York, PepsiCo Inc. employees, long used to receiving personal financial planning from their employer, now get that service from KPMG Peat Marwick. Denver's TeleTech Holdings Inc. is taking customer-service calls from AT&T customers and books seat reservations for Continental Airlines.

Relentless cost-cutting was an early driver behind the trend to outsource. When Tim Cook first came to Apple from Compaq Computer, he was a 16-year computer industry veteran with 12 years at IBM. His mandate at Apple was to clean up the atrocious state of Apple's

EXHIBIT 10.7
**Outsourcing Is
Increasing**

Source: Estimated based
on various articles
in *BusinessWeek* on
outsourcing.

ORDERING OUT . . . Companies That Say They Outsource Some Functional Activity		
	Yes	No
2015	99%	1%
2010	98	2
2000	75	25
1995	52	48
1990	23	77

. . . FOR EVERYTHING Functional Activities Most Frequently Outsourced	
Payroll	75%
Manufacturing	72
Maintenance	68
Warehousing/transportation/distribution	62
Information technology	52
Travel	48
Temporary service	48
HR activities (varied)	40
Product design	35
R&D	25
Marketing	22

manufacturing, distribution, and supply apparatus. He quickly closed factories and warehouses around the world and instead established relationships with contract manufacturers. By outsourcing almost all of its manufacturing and warehousing, Apple cut its inventory costs by a substantial amount (see Exhibit 10.6 Global Strategy in Action, on page 308).

Outsourcing now occurs across every function in a business—marketing, product design, and computer operations are just a few functions other than typical rote functions that have been regularly outsourced by many companies. Infosys, the India-based bastion of early call center outsourcing followed by many types of outsourcing, is itself now outsourcing to IPsoft, a New York–based firm that automates IT infrastructure management, the sort of dreadfully dull stuff IT personnel in Bangalore don't want to do anymore.[4] Exhibit 10.7 shows how rapidly outsourcing has become commonplace in today's global economy. And Exhibit 10.8 Global Strategy in Action, seriously addressing the age-old question "does size matter," provides a fun but very serious example of how Delta Airlines answered that question. In creating the functional tactics that would help implement its companywide revenue growth strategy, Delta outsourced a key tactical activity to Boeing. It involved increasing revenue capacity inside the 737-900 aircraft. Boeing in turn outsourced a key part of it to B/E Aerospace. Their answer: "size does matter—smaller is better," and doable. It all comes down to the loo, and improved head space in the process.[5]

[4]Leo Mirani, "This Indian Outsourcing Giant Is Outsourcing Its Own Jobs—to Computers," *QUARTZ*, April 30, 2013.
[5]If you want to read more about this interesting story, go to Scott McCartney, "Airlines Lavs Shrink to Fit More Seats," *Wall Street Journal,* March 29, 2013; or go to http://blogs.wsj.com/middleseat/2013/03/29/airlines-lavs-shrink-to-fit-in-more-seats/.

Is Size Really Important? Yes, Especially When . . .

Yes it is, especially when you are looking for tactical actions that help in implementing an airline's revenue growth strategy. On commercial airplanes, it is all about how you use the "real estate" that drives revenue generated per flight, or revenue per available seat mile (RASM). RASM is a key measure used industrywide to evaluate the revenue-generating effectiveness and success of different airlines. RASM tells you how effective an airline has been in selling its available seating, but it is ultimately the amount of available seating that allows an airline, along with pricing decisions, to generate more revenue. So, the more seats a plane has available, the more revenue it can potentially generate per flight.

Does size matter? Well, larger planes can have more seats and generate more revenue per flight than smaller planes given the same pricing and occupancy levels. But that part is complicated and depends on the routes and volume of likely passengers for particular routes and so forth. So that is not the size we are talking about. RASM helps adjust for plane size anyway by comparing the

same measure, RASM, for any flight regardless of plane size. So how does size really matter for airlines?

Well, it all seems to boil down to the size of the plane's loo, or lavatory. Delta Airlines is the first customer for Boeing's new 737-900 plane, chosen in part because they will be the first to include B/E Aerospace's SIZE MATTERS innovation—a slightly shrunken (from the 80-year-old 3' × 3' standard) coach-class lavatory offered with its own toilet. B/E Aerospace, "flush" with pride, won the 737 contract over incumbent Zodiac Aerospace. This new, smaller loo will not be noticeably smaller, as it harvested wasted space behind the sink, allowing a sculpted exterior wall that will enable the seats in front of it to decline. And, where size really matters, it will allow Delta to add four more seats, bringing the total to 180 coach seats in the 737-900. That's 2.5 percent more RASM potential in every 737-900 flight. Redesigning/shrinking the coach-class lavatory footprint is a key tactical strategy implementing Delta's companywide revenue growth strategy for the next decade or more.

The embrace of outsourcing's benefits, however, can obscure the potential for numerous problems. Boeing's 787 Dreamliner was three years late before finally being delivered to its early customers because of repeated production and design mistakes as well as problems related to quality and response time from a large number of outsourced partners around the globe. Communication glitches, production delays, and routine design adjustments required in any major production effort can be a real problem when they occur with outsourced partners halfway around the globe, rather than when the project is all done under one roof. Southern Pacific Railroad suffered through numerous computer breakdowns, delays, and scheduling mistakes after outsourcing its internal computer network to IBM.

The important point to recognize at this point is that functional activities long associated with doing the work of any business organization are increasingly subject to be outsourced if they can be done more cost effectively by other providers. So it becomes critical for managers implementing strategic plans to focus company activities on functions deemed central to the company's competitive advantage and to seek others outside the firm's structure to provide the functions that are necessary, but not within the scope of the firm's core competencies. And, increasingly, this decision considers every organizational activity fair game—even marketing, product design, innovation. We will explore this in greater detail in Chapter 11.

EMPOWERING OPERATING PERSONNEL: THE ROLE OF POLICIES

Specific functional tactics provide guidance and initiate action implementing a business's strategy, but more is needed. Supervisors and personnel in the field have been charged in today's competitive environment with being responsible for customer value—for being the "front line" of the company's effort to truly meet customers' needs. Meeting customer needs is a buzzword regularly cited as a key priority by most business organizations. Efforts to do so often fail because employees that are the real contact point between the business and its customers are not empowered to make decisions or act to fulfill customer needs. One solution has been to empower operating personnel by pushing down decision making to their level. General Electric allows appliance repair personnel to decide about warranty credits on the spot, a decision that used to take several days and multiple organizational levels. American Air Lines allows customer service personnel and their supervisors wide range in resolving customer ticket pricing decisions. Federal Express couriers make decisions and handle package routing information that once involved five management levels in the U.S. Postal Service.

empowerment
The act of allowing an individual or team the right and flexibility to make decisions and initiate action.

Empowerment is the act of allowing an individual or team the right and flexibility to make decisions and initiate action. It is being expanded and widely advocated in many organizations today. Training, self-managed work groups, eliminating whole levels of management in organizations, and aggressive use of automation are some of the ways and ramifications of this fundamental change in the way business organizations function. At the heart of the effort is the need to ensure that decision making is consistent with the mission, strategy, and tactics of the business while at the same time allowing considerable latitude to operating personnel. One way operating managers do this is through the use of policies.

policies
Broad, precedent-setting decisions that guide or substitute for repetitive or time-sensitive managerial decision making.

Policies are directives designed to guide the thinking, decisions, and actions of managers and their subordinates in implementing a firm's strategy. Sometimes called *standard operating procedures,* policies increase managerial effectiveness by standardizing many routine decisions and clarifying the discretion managers and subordinates can exercise in implementing functional tactics. Logically, policies should be derived from functional tactics (and, in some instances, from corporate or business strategies) with the key purpose of aiding strategy execution.[6] Exhibit 10.9, Global Strategy in Action, illustrates selected policies of several well-known firms.

Creating Policies That Empower

Policies communicate guidelines to decisions. They are designed to control decisions while defining allowable discretion within which operational personnel can execute business activities. They do this in several ways:

1. *Policies establish indirect control over independent action* by clearly stating how things are to be done *now*. By defining discretion, policies in effect control decisions yet empower employees to conduct activities without direct intervention by top management.

2. *Policies promote uniform handling of similar activities.* This facilitates the coordination of work tasks and helps reduce friction arising from favoritism, discrimination, and the disparate handling of common functions—something that often hampers operating personnel.

[6] The term *policy* has various definitions in management literature. Some authors and practitioners equate policy with strategy. Others do this inadvertently by using "policy" as a synonym for company mission, purpose, or culture. Still other authors and practitioners differentiate policy in terms of "levels" associated, respectively, with purpose, mission, and strategy. "Our policy is to make a positive contribution to the communities and societies we live in" and "Our policy is not to diversify out of the hamburger business" are two examples of the breadth of what some call policies. This book defines *policy* much more narrowly as specific guides to managerial action and decisions in the implementation of strategy. This definition permits a sharper distinction between the formulation and implementation of functional strategies. And, of even greater importance, it focuses the tangible value of the policy concept where it can be most useful—as a key administrative tool to enhance effective implementation and execution of strategy.

Selected Policies That Aid Strategy Implementation

Google has a personnel policy, the ITO (**Innovation Time Out) policy,** which encourages Google employees to spend 80 percent of their time on core projects and roughly 20 percent (or one day per week) on "innovation" activities to examine and develop ideas they have that might lead to something new at Google or related to Google. (This policy helps implement two strategic priorities at Google—creating new product/service offerings or improvements in those that exist; and keeping employees challenged and engaged in ways that aid retention and keep staff learning and growing.)

IBM has an ever-changing set of social computing policies, which they call "social computing guidelines," with one such guideline being that "if you publish content online relevant to IBM in your personal capacity use a disclaimer such as this: 'The postings on this site are my own and don't necessarily represent IBM's positions, strategies or opinions.' " (IBM has a strategic priority that IBMers are encouraged to engage in online social computing as a key way to keep IBM innovative and technology savvy. This guideline is one of many that have emerged to help IBMers individually manage their online social networking in a way that is consistent with IBM's overall strategy.)

Prior to its acquisition by AMC, General Cinema had a financial policy that required annual capital investment in movie theaters not exceed annual depreciation. (This policy supported General Cinema's financial strategy at the time to maximize cash flow for growth

area investment, and to increase its valuation. It also helped implement the financial strategy that area managers would use leasing as much as possible.)

Fundamental to Wendy's concept and strategy was to offer fresh meat and produce in its core products, to ensure the best taste possible. It established early-on a policy that gave local managers the authority to buy fresh meat and produce locally, rather than from regionally or nationally designated suppliers like all of its competitors did to reduce costs. (This policy supported the Wendy's product strategy of having fresh, unfrozen, "juicy" hamburgers daily.)

Zappos, the online shoe company, has a P-E-C "policy," more like an expected attitude, for its call center personnel. That Personal Emotional Connection or P-E-C "policy" allows, indeed expects, online customer service reps to make decisions on their own, like a refund. They are supposed to send a dozen or so personal notes to customers every day. An example Zappos founder Ton Hsieh likes to share is about a woman in New York whose husband died in a car accident after she had ordered boots for him from Zappos. The day after she called Zappos for help with a refund, she received a flower delivery. The call center rep had ordered the flowers and billed them to the company without checking with a supervisor. At the funeral, the widow told her friends and family about the experience. "Not only did she become a customer for life," said Hsieh, "but so were the 30–40 people at the funeral."

innovation time out policy
Innovation Time Out policy refers to what is usually an official company guideline, or policy, establishing an amount of time during each work week an employee, or specific types of employees (e.g. engineers) can at their choice set aside from their regular assignment to work on innovative, new ideas they are thinking about.

3. *Policies ensure quicker decisions* by standardizing answers to previously answered questions that otherwise would recur and be pushed up the management hierarchy again and again—something that requires unnecessary levels of management between senior decision makers and field personnel.

4. *Policies institutionalize basic aspects of organization behavior.* This minimizes conflicting practices and establishes consistent patterns of action in attempts to make the strategy work—again, freeing operating personnel to act.

5. *Policies reduce uncertainty in repetitive and day-to-day decision making,* thereby providing a necessary foundation for coordinated, efficient efforts and freeing operating personnel to act.

6. *Policies counteract resistance to or rejection of chosen strategies by organization members.* When major strategic change is undertaken, unambiguous operating policies clarify what is expected and facilitate acceptance, particularly when operating managers participate in policy development.

7. *Policies offer predetermined answers to routine problems.* This greatly expedites dealing with both ordinary and extraordinary problems—with the former, by referring to

Make Sure Policies Aren't Used to Drive Away Customers

Every year *Inc.* magazine sponsors a conference for the 500 fastest growing companies in the United States to share ideas, hear speakers, and network. A conference in Palm Springs, CA, included a talk by Martha Rogers, co-author of *The One to One Future.* Here is an interesting anecdote about policies she used in her talk:

> The story was about a distinguished-looking gentleman in blue jeans who walked into a bank and asked a teller to complete a transaction. The teller said she was sorry, but the person responsible was out for the day. The man would have to come back.

He then asked to have his parking receipt validated. Again, she said she was sorry, but under bank policy she could not validate a parking receipt unless the customer completed a transaction. The man pressed her. She did not waver. "That's our policy," she said.

So the man completed a transaction. He withdrew all $1.5 million from his account. It turned out he was John Akers, then chairman of IBM.

The moral: Give employees information about the value of customers, not mindless policies.

these answers; with the latter, by giving operating personnel more time to cope with them.

8. *Policies afford managers a mechanism for avoiding hasty and ill-conceived decisions in changing operations.* Prevailing policy can always be used as a reason for not yielding to emotion-based, expedient, or temporarily valid arguments for altering procedures and practices.

Policies may be written and formal or unwritten and informal. Informal, unwritten policies are usually associated with a strategic need for competitive secrecy. Some policies of this kind, such as promotion from within, are widely known (or expected) by employees and implicitly sanctioned by management. Managers and employees often like the latitude granted by unwritten and informal policies. However, such policies may detract from the long-term success of a strategy. Formal, written policies have at least seven advantages:

1. They require managers to think through the policy's meaning, content, and intended use.
2. They reduce misunderstanding.
3. They make equitable and consistent treatment of problems more likely.
4. They ensure unalterable transmission of policies.
5. They communicate the authorization or sanction of policies more clearly.
6. They supply a convenient and authoritative reference.
7. They systematically enhance indirect control and organizationwide coordination of the key purposes of policies.

The strategic significance of policies can vary. At one extreme are such policies as travel reimbursement procedures, which are really work rules and may not have an obvious link to the implementation of a strategy. Exhibit 10.10, Strategy in Action, provides an interesting example of how the link between a simple policy and strategy implementation regarding customer service can have serious negative consequences when it is neither obvious to operating personnel nor well thought out by bank managers. At the other extreme are organizationwide policies that are virtually functional strategies, such as Wendy's requirement that every location invest 1 percent of its gross revenue in local advertising.

Policies can be externally imposed or internally derived. Policies regarding equal employment practices are often developed in compliance with external (government) requirements, and policies regarding leasing or depreciation may be strongly influenced by current tax regulations.

Regardless of the origin, formality, and nature of policies, the key point to bear in mind is that they can play an important role in strategy implementation. Communicating specific policies will help overcome resistance to strategic change, empower people to act, and foster commitment to successful strategy implementation.

Policies empower people to act. Compensation, at least theoretically, rewards their action. The last decade has seen many firms realize that the link between compensation, particularly executive management compensation, and value-building strategic outcomes within their firms was uncertain. The recognition of this uncertainty has brought about increased recognition of the need to link management compensation with the successful implementation of strategies that build long-term shareholder value. The next section examines this development and major types of executive bonus compensation plans.

BONUS COMPENSATION PLANS[7]

Major Plan Types

Company shareholders typically believe that the goal of a bonus compensation plan is to motivate executives and key employees to achieve maximization of shareholder wealth. Because shareholders are both owners and investors of the firm, they desire a reasonable return on their investment. Because they are absentee landlords, shareholders expect their board of directors to ensure that the decision-making logic of their firm's executives is concurrent with their own primary motivation.

However, the goal of shareholder wealth maximization is not the only goal that executives may pursue. Alternatively, executives may choose actions that increase their personal compensation, power, and control. Therefore, an executive compensation plan that contains a bonus component can be used to orient management's decision making toward the owners' goals. The success of bonus compensation as an incentive hinges on a proper match between an executive bonus plan and the firm's strategic objectives. Recent research suggests that compensation committees that link executive rewards (compensation) to the unique nature of their firm's strategy achieve better outcomes."[8] Exhibit 10.11 summarizes five types of executive compensation plans we will now explore in more detail.

Stock Options

stock options
The right, or "option," to purchase company stock at a fixed price at some future date.

A common measure of shareholder wealth creation is appreciation of company stock price. Therefore, a popular form of bonus compensation is stock options. Stock options have typically represented more than 50 percent of a chief executive officer's average pay package, and remain the most significant component of CEO pay even after the recent Great Recession and the criticism they took from a variety of supposed faults.[9] **Stock options** provide the executive with the right to purchase company stock at a fixed price in the future. The precise amount of compensation is based on the difference, or "spread," between the option's initial price and its selling, or exercised, price. As a result, the executive receives a

[7] We wish to thank Roy Hossler for his assistance on this section.
[8] Steven Balsam, Guy Fernando, and Arindam Tripathy, "The Impact of Firm Strategy on Performance Measures in Executive Compensation," *Journal of Business Research* 64 (2011), pp. 187–193.
[9] Richard A. Booth, "Why Stock Options Are the Best Form of Executive Compensation," *New York University Journal of Law and Business* 6 (Spring, 2010), p. 281.

EXHIBIT 10.11   **Types of Executive Bonus Compensation**

Bonus Type	Description	Rationale	Shortcomings
Stock option grants	Right to purchase stock in the future at a price set now. Compensation is determined by "spread" between option price and exercise price.	Provides incentive for executive to create wealth for shareholders as measured by increase in firm's share price.	Movement in share price does not explain all dimensions of managerial performance.
Restricted stock plan	Shares given to executive who is prohibited from selling them for a specific time period. May also include performance restrictions.	Promotes longer executive tenure than other forms of compensation.	No downside risk to executive, who always profits unlike other shareholders.
Golden handcuffs	Bonus income deferred in a series of annual installments. Deferred amounts not yet paid are forfeited with executive resignation.	Offers an incentive for executive to remain with the firm.	May promote risk-averse decision making due to downside risk borne by executive.
Golden parachute	Executives have right to collect the bonus if they lose position due to takeover, firing, retirement, or resignation.	Offers an incentive for executive to remain with the firm.	Compensation is achieved whether or not wealth is created for shareholders. Rewards either success or failure.
Cash based on internal business performance using financial measures	Bonus compensation based on accounting performance measures such as return on equity.	Offsets the limitations of focusing on market-based measures of performance.	Weak correlation between earnings measures and shareholder wealth creation. Annual earnings do not capture future impact of current decisions.

bonus only if the firm's share price appreciates. If the share price drops below the option price, the options become worthless.

Stock options were the source of extraordinary wealth creation for executives, managers, and rank-and-file employees in the technology boom of the 1990s. Behind using options as compensation incentives was the notion that they were essentially free. Although they dilute shareholders' equity when they're exercised, taking the cost of stock options as an expense against earnings was not required. That, in turn, helped keep earnings higher than actual costs to the company and its shareholders. The bear market and corporate scandals of the last few years brought increased scrutiny on the use of and accounting for stock options. Recent changes in SEC guidelines have established rules for expensing stock options to more accurately reflect company performance. The following table shows the effect expensing stocks options would have on the net earnings of Standard & Poor's (S&P) 500 firms between 1996 and 2005. "Stock options were a free resource, at BankOne and because of that, they were used freely," said JPMorgan Chase's James Dimon, who voluntarily began to expense stock options in 2003. "But now," he said, "when you have to expense options, you start to think, 'Is it an effective cost? Is there a better way?'" Legendary investor Warren Buffett argued for years that many companies enticed executives and managers with lower-than-market salaries because they also offered options. This inflated the companies' profits because of the lower salaries—hence lower expenses on the income statement.

The other side of the argument has been that it is very difficult to value stock options when issued below current values, or when a company is very new. To settle this matter, the Financial Accounting Standards Board issued a ruling in 2004 that required expensing of stock options beginning in 2006. Although challenged in the U.S. Congress, the changes were upheld and companies now expense options.[10]

A Big Hit to Earnings

If options had been expensed between 1996 and 2005, earnings would have been whacked as their popularity grew as shown below:

Options Expense as a Percent of Net Earnings for S&P 500 Companies

1996	1998	2000	2002	2005
2%	5%	8%	23%	22%

Source: *The Analysis Accounting Observer*, R. G. Associates Inc.

Microsoft shocked the business world during this time by announcing it would discontinue stock options, eliminating a form of pay that made thousands of Microsoft employees millionaires and helped define the culture of the tech industry. Starting in September 2003, the company began paying its 54,000 employees with restricted stock, a move that will let employees make money even if the company's share price declines. Like options, the restricted stock will vest gradually over a five-year period, and grants of restricted stock are counted as expenses and charged against earnings. Said CEO Steven Ballmer, "We asked: Is there a smarter way to compensate our people, a way that would make them feel even more excited about their financial deal at Microsoft and at the same time be something that was at least as good for the shareholders as today's compensation package?" At the time of Ballmer's announcement, more than 20,000 employees who had joined Microsoft in the past three years held millions of stock options that were "under water," meaning the market value of Microsoft stock was far below the stock price of their stock options.

Restricted stock has the advantage of offering employees more certainty, even if there is less potential for a big win. It also means shareholders don't have to worry about massive dilution after employees exercise big stock gains, as happened in the 1990s. Another advantage is that grants of restricted stock are much easier to value than options because restricted stock is equivalent to a stock transfer at the market price. That improves the transparency of corporate accounting.[11]

Research suggests that stock option plans lack the benefits of plans that include true stock ownership. Stock option plans provide unlimited upside potential for executives, but limited downside risk because executives incur only opportunity costs. Because of the tremendous advantages to the executive of stock price appreciation, there is an incentive for

---

[10] U.S. GAAP (generally accepted accounting principles) required expensing of stock options using one of two acceptable valuation methods starting in the first fiscal year after June 15, 2005. (www.wikipedia .org/wikiemployee_stock_options); and Karen Berman and Joe Knight, "Expensing Stock Options: The Controversy," Blogs; HBR.org, *Harvard Business Review*, August 28, 2009.

[11] Many argue that stock options are critical to start-up firms as a way to motivate and retain talented employees with the promise of getting rich should the new venture succeed. Among them appear to be recently retired FASB chairman Robert Herz, who favors sentiment to make special exceptions in the expensing of options in pre-IPO firms.

the executive to take undue risk. Thus, supporters of stock ownership plans argue that direct ownership instills a much stronger behavioral commitment, even when the stock price falls, because it binds executives to their firms more than do options.[12] Additionally, "Executive stock options may be an efficient means to induce management to undertake more risky projects."[13]

Options may have been overused and indeed abused in the last two bull markets,[14] but evidence suggests that the smart use of options and other incentive compensation does boost performance. Companies that spread ownership throughout a large portion of their workforce deliver higher returns than similar companies with more concentrated ownership. If options seemed for a time to be the route that enriched CEOs, employees, and investors alike, it still appears they will be used, although with less emphasis than a mix of options, restricted stock, and cash bonuses. Whatever the exact mix, they are likely to be more closely tied to achieving specific operating goals. The next section examines restricted stock and cash bonuses in greater detail.

Restricted Stock

restricted stock
Stock given to an employee who is prohibited or "restricted" from selling the stock for a certain time period and not at all if they leave the company before that time period.

A **restricted stock** plan is designed to provide benefits of direct executive stock ownership. In a typical restricted stock plan, an executive is given a specific number of company stock shares. The executive is prohibited from selling the shares for a specified time period. Should the executive leave the firm voluntarily before the restricted period ends, the shares are forfeited. Therefore, restricted stock plans are a form of deferred compensation that promotes longer executive tenure than other types of plans.

In addition to being contingent on a vesting period, restricted stock plans may also require the achievement of predetermined performance goals. Price-vesting restricted stock plans tie vesting to the firm's stock price in comparison to an index or to reaching a predetermined goal or annual growth rate. If the executive falls short on some of the restrictions, a certain amount of shares are forfeited. The design of these plans motivates the executive to increase shareholder wealth while promoting a long-term commitment to stay with the firm.

If the restricted stock plan lacks performance goal provisions, the executive needs only to remain employed with the firm over the vesting period to cash in on the stock. Performance provisions make sure executives are not compensated without achieving some level of shareholder wealth creation. Like stock options, restricted stock plans offer no downside risk to executives because the shares were initially gifted to the executive. Unlike options, the stock retains value tied to its market value once ownership is fully vested. Shareholders, on the other hand, do suffer a loss in personal wealth resulting from a share price drop.

---

[12] Jeffrey Pfeffer, "Seven Practices of Successful Organizations," *California Management Review*, Winter 1998; John Barron and Glen Waddell, "Work Hard, Not Smart: Stock Options in Executive Compensation," *Journal of Economic Behavior and Organization* 66, no. 3 (June 2008), pp. 767–790; and Yan Wendy Wu, "Optimal Executive Compensation: Stock Options or Restricted Stock," *International Review of Economics & Finance* 32 (January 2011), pp. 45–64.

[13] William Gerard Sanders and Donald C. Hambrick, "Swinging for the Fences: The Effects of CEO Stock Options on Company Risk-Taking and Performance," *Academy of Management Journal* (October–November 2007); and Z. Dong and C. Wong, "Do Executive Stock Options Induce Excessive Risk Taking?" *Journal of Banking and Finance* 34, no. 10 (October 2010), pp. 2518–2529.

[14] Z. Dong and C. Wong, "Do Executive Stock Options Induce Excessive Risk Taking?" *Journal of Banking and Finance* 34, no. 10 (October 2010), pp. 2518–2529. This review of several studies found that over 30 percent of all U.S. publicly traded firms apparently manipulated (backdated) stock option grants to increase the payoff to executives receiving the grants.

Golden Handcuffs

golden handcuffs
A form of executive compensation where compensation is deferred (either a re-stricted stock plan or bonus income deferred in a series of annual installments).

The rationale behind plans that defer compensation forms the basis for another type of executive compensation called golden handcuffs. **Golden handcuffs** refer to either a re-stricted stock plan, where the stock compensation is deferred until vesting time provisions are met, or to bonus income deferred in a series of annual installments. This type of plan may also involve compensating an executive a significant amount upon retirement or at some predetermined age. In most cases, compensation is forfeited if the executive volun-tarily resigns or is discharged before certain time restrictions.

Many boards consider their executives' skills and talents to be their firm's most valu-able assets. These "assets" create and sustain the professional relationships that generate revenue and control expenses for the firm. Research suggests that the departure of key executives is unsettling for companies and often disrupts long-range plans when new key executives adopt a different management strategy.[15] Thus, the golden handcuffs approach to executive compensation is more congruent with long-term strategies than short-term performance plans, which offer little staying-power incentive.

Firms may turn to golden handcuffs if they believe stability of management is critical to sustained growth. Jupiter Asset Management recently tied 10 fund managers to the firm with golden handcuffs. The compensation scheme calls for a cash payment in addition to base salaries if the managers remain at the firm for five years. In the first year of the plan, the firm's pretax profits more than doubled, and their assets under management increased 85 percent. The firm's chairman has also signed a new incentive deal that will keep him at Jupiter for four years.

Deferred compensation is worrisome to some executives. In cases where the compensa-tion is payable when the executives are retired and no longer in control, as when the firm is acquired by another firm or a new management hierarchy is installed, the golden handcuff plans are considerably less attractive to executives.

Golden handcuffs may promote risk averseness in executive decision making due to the huge downside risk borne by executives. This risk averseness could lead to mediocre performance results from executives' decisions. When executives lose deferred compensa-tion if the firm discharges them voluntarily or involuntarily, the executive is less likely to make bold and aggressive decisions. Rather, the executive will choose safe, conservative decisions.

Golden Parachutes

golden parachute
A form of bonus com-pensation that guaran-tees a substantial cash payment if the executive quits, is fired, or simply retires.

Golden parachutes are a form of bonus compensation that guarantees a substantial cash payment to an executive if the executive quits, is fired, or simply retires. In addition, the golden parachute may also contain covenants that allow the executive to cash in on nonin-vested stock compensation.

The popularity of golden parachutes grew with the increased popularity of takeovers, which often led to the ouster of the acquired firm's top executives. In these cases, the golden parachutes encouraged executives to take an objective look at takeover offers. The executives could decide which move was in the best interests of the shareholders, having been personally protected in the event of a merger. The "parachute" helps soften the fall of

[15] William E. Hall, Brian J. Lake, Charles T. Morse, and Charles T. Morse Jr., "More Than Golden Handcuffs," *Journal of Accountancy* 184, no. 5 (1997), pp. 37–42; R. L. Heneman, J. W. Tansky, and S. Michael Camp, "Human Resource Strategies of High-Growth Entrepreneurial Firms," in *International Handbook of Entrepreneurship and HRM*, Chapter 8, Edward Elgar Publishing, 2008; and David DeLong and Steve Trautman, *The Executive Guide to High-Impact Talent Management* (New York: McGraw-Hill, 2011).

the ousted executive. It is "golden" because the size of the cash payment often varies from several to tens of millions of dollars.

Golden parachutes caused quite an uproar in the financial services industry during the recent Great Recession. Financial engineering and several highly leveraged, marginally regulated practices associated with several major firms in that setting ended up releasing top executives, which in turn brought attention to their significant golden parachutes. Those exit commitments for ten of the largest financial firms involved in the financial meltdown were:

Million-Dollar Exit Amounts for CEOs in Key Financial Services Firms Dismissed during the Great Recession

Cash, pension, benefits, accelerated stock and options and other compensation for CEOs of financial firms and mortgage lenders:

Company	CEO	Total
Merrill Lynch	Stanley O'Neal	$161,000,000
Citigroup	Charles Prince	$105,000,000
Washington Mutual	Kerry Killinger	$44,000,000
Wachovia	Ken Thompson	$42,000,000
Lehman Bros.	Richard Fuld	$24,000,000
Washington Mutual	Alan Fishman	$19,000,000
Freddie Mac	Richard Syron	$16,000,000
Bear Stearns	James Cayne	$13,000,000
Merrill Lynch	John Thain	$9,000,000
Fannie Mae	Daniel Mudd	$8,000,000

Golden parachutes typically pay ousted CEOs three times annual pay, bonuses and pensions and often include perks lasting well into retirement. They similarly cover typical key executives and company officers. Intended originally to attract executive talent, plus protect them in the case of an acquisition or takeover, golden parachutes include making the executives "whole" on restricted stock grants and options that would have been available over the three-year period in question. Should an acquisition or hostile takeover come to fruition, the executives would receive the total value of the restricted stock even if it was not yet vested. The stock options would also become available immediately. Some of the restricted stock was performance restricted. Under normal conditions this stock would not be available without the firm reaching certain performance levels.

Golden parachutes are designed in part to anticipate hostile takeovers. In the event such a situation arises, the executives' position is to lead the firm's board of directors in deciding if the hostile offer is in the long-term interests of shareholders. Because the executives are compensated heavily whether the company is taken over or not, the golden parachute has helped remove the temptation they could have of not acting in the best interests of shareholders.

Cash

Executive bonus compensation plans that focus on accounting measures of performance are designed to offset the limitations of market-based measures of performance. This type of plan is most usually associated with the payment of periodic (quarterly or annual) cash bonuses. Market factors beyond the control of management, such as pending legislation, can keep a firm's share price repressed even though a top executive is exceeding the performance expectations of the board. In this situation, a highly performing executive loses bonus compensation due to the undervalued stock. However, accounting measures of performance correct for this problem by tying executive bonuses to improvements in internally measured performance. Traditional accounting measures, such as net income, earnings per share, return on equity, and return on assets, are used because they are easily understood, are familiar to senior management, and are already tracked by firm data systems.

Critics argue that because of inherent flaws in accounting systems, basing compensation on these figures may not result in an accurate gauge of managerial performance. Return on equity estimates, for example, are skewed by inflation distortions and arbitrary cost allocations. Accounting measures are also subject to manipulation by firm personnel to artificially inflate key performance figures. Firm performance schemes, critics believe, need to be based on a financial measure that has a true link to shareholder value creation. This issue led to the creation of the Balanced Scorecard, which emphasizes not only financial measures, but also such measures as new-product development, market share, and safety as discussed in Chapter 7.

Matching Bonus Plans and Corporate Goals

Exhibit 10.12 matches a company's strategic goal with the most likely compensation plan. On the vertical axis are common strategic goals. The horizontal axis lists the main compensation types that serve as incentives for executives to reach the firm's goals. A rationale is provided to explain the logic behind the connection between the firm's goal and the suggested method of executive compensation.

Researchers emphasize that fundamental to these relationships is the importance of incorporating the level of strategic risk of the firm into the design of the executive's compensation plan. Incorporating an appropriate level of executive risk can create a desired behavioral change commensurate with the risk level of strategies shareholders and their firms want.[16] To help motivate an executive to pursue goals of a certain risk-return level, the compensation plan can quantify that risk-return level and reward the executive accordingly.

The links we show between bonus compensation plans and strategic goals were derived from the results of prior research. The basic principle underlying Exhibit 10.12 is that different types of bonus compensation plans are intended to accomplish different purposes; one element may serve to attract and retain executives; another may serve as an incentive to encourage behavior that accomplishes firm goals.[17] Although every strategy option has probably been linked to each compensation plan at some time, experience shows that there may be scenarios where a plan type best fits a strategy option. Exhibit 10.12 attempts to display the "best matches."

The global financial crisis and the accompanying "Great Recession" resulted in the passage of the Dodd-Frank Wall Street Reform and Consumer Protection Act in the United States. It resulted in a mandatory "say-on-pay" shareholder vote for most U.S. public companies starting in 2011. It included a requirement to take effect in 2015 that these companies must also report the relationship between executive compensation "actually paid" and the company's financial performance.

Many companies have chosen to voluntarily start reporting "pay for performance" results in advance of being required to do so. They are doing their own analyses so that they

[16] Carola Frydman and Raven Saks, "Executive Compensation: A New View from a Long-Term Perspective, 1936–2005," *The Review of Financial Studies* 23, no. 5 (2010), pp. 2099–2138.
[17] Ibid.

EXHIBIT 10.12 **Compensation Plan Selection Matrix**

	Type of Bonus Compensation					
Strategic Goal	**Cash**	**Golden Handcuffs**	**Golden Parachutes**	**Restricted Stock Plans**	**Stock Options**	**Rationale**
Achieve corporate turnaround					X	Executive profits only if turnaround is successful in returning wealth to shareholders.
Create and support growth opportunities					X	Risk associated with growth strategies warrants the use of this high-reward incentive.
Defend against unfriendly takeover			X			Parachute helps takeover remove temptation for executive to evaluate takeover based on personal benefits.
Evaluate suitors objectively			X			Parachute compensates executive if job is lost due to a merger favorable to the firm.
Globalize operations					X	Risk of expanding overseas requires a plan that compensates only for achieved success.
Grow share price incrementally	X					Accounting measures can identify periodic performance benchmarks.
Improve operational efficiency	X					Accounting measures represent observable and agreed-upon measures of performance.
Increase assets under management				X		Executive profits proportionally as asset growth leads to long-term growth in share price.
Reduce executive turnover		X				Handcuffs provide executive tenure incentive.
Restructure organization					X	Risk associated with major change in firm's assets warrants the use of this high-reward incentive.
Streamline operations				X		Rewards long-term focus on efficiency and cost control.

can better understand, in their company, the relationship between executive pay and company performance. It also lets them get a head start on telling their executives' pay for performance story, hopefully in the most accurate fashion, before they are told how to do so.

Global Strategy in Action, Exhibit 10.13 reports the early trends in response to the Dodd-Frank legislation, placing greater scrutiny and transparency on executive compensation in U.S.-based public companies. One issue is, of course, what metrics you use, or prioritize, to define the company's "financial performance." This exhibit shows what metrics U.S. firms

U.S. Public Company Performance Metrics and Executive Compensation Trends Post Dodd-Frank and the Great Recession

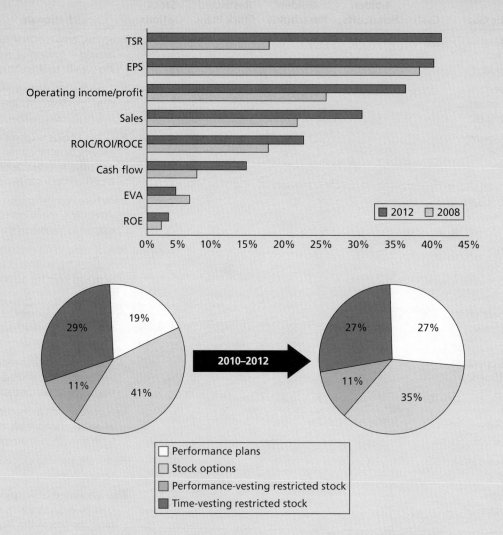

Source: Katharine Turner, Dan Perrett, and Richard Latham, "US Trends in Executive Compensation," *Executive Compensation Market Watch,* Towers Watson Newsletter, United Kingdom, April 15, 2013.

prioritized, or used exclusively, to define performance in 2008 vs. 2012. The second part of the exhibit shows the change in executive compensation programs in light of the coming requirement to show a relationship between executives' "actual pay" and the company's financial performance. Total Stockholder Return (TSR) is becoming used more often as a metric of choice to comply with Dodd-Frank. Use of stock options has started since Dodd-Frank was enacted, but they are still quite popular. Performance-based compensation, either by cash and/or performance-based vesting restricted stock, is increasing in importance.

Summary

The first concern in the implementation of business strategy is to translate that strategy into action throughout the organization. This chapter discussed five considerations for accomplishing this.

Short-term objectives are derived from long-term objectives, which are then translated into current actions and targets. They differ from long-term objectives in time frame, specificity, and measurement. To be effective in strategy implementation, they must be integrated and coordinated. They also must be consistent, measurable, and prioritized.

Functional tactics are derived from the business strategy. They identify the specific, immediate actions that must be taken in key functional areas to implement the business strategy.

Outsourcing of selected functional activities has become a central tactical agenda for virtually every business firm in today's global economy. Can we get that activity done more effectively—and more inexpensively—outside our company? This question has become a regular one managers ask as they seek to make their business strategies work.

Employee empowerment through policies provides another means for guiding behavior, decisions, and actions at the firm's operating levels in a manner consistent with its business and functional strategies. Policies empower operating personnel to make decisions and take action quickly.

Compensation rewards action and results. Once the firm has identified strategic objectives that will best serve stockholder interests, there are five bonus compensation plans that can be structured to provide the executive with an incentive to work toward achieving those goals.

Objectives, functional tactics, policies, and compensation represent only the start of the strategy implementation. The strategy must be institutionalized—it must permeate the firm. The next chapter examines this phase of strategy implementation.

Key Terms

empowerment, *p. 311*
functional tactics, *p. 304*
golden handcuffs, *p. 318*
golden parachute, *p. 318*
Innovation Time Out
policy, *p. 312*

outsourcing, *p. 308*
policies, *p. 311*
restricted stock, *p. 317*
short-term objective, *p. 302*
social computing, *p. 325*

Social Computing
Guidelines, *p. 326*
stock options, *p. 314*

Questions for Discussion

1. How does the concept "translate thought into action" bear on the relationship between business strategy and operating strategy? Between long-term and short-term objectives?
2. How do functional tactics differ from corporate and business strategies?
3. What key concerns must functional tactics address in marketing? finance? production/operations management? personnel?
4. What is "outsourcing?" Why has it become a key element in shaping functional tactics within most business firms today?
5. How do policies aid strategy implementation? Illustrate your answer.
6. Use Exhibits 10.11 and 10.12 to explain five executive bonus compensation plans.
7. Illustrate a policy, an objective, and a functional tactic in your personal career strategy.
8. Why are short-term objectives needed when long-term objectives are already available?

Chapter 10 Appendix

Functional Tactics

FUNCTIONAL TACTICS THAT IMPLEMENT BUSINESS STRATEGIES

Functional tactics are the key, routine activities that must be undertaken in each functional area—marketing, finance, production/operations, R&D, and human resource management—to provide the business's products and services. In a sense, functional tactics translate thought (grand strategy) into action designed to accomplish specific short-term objectives. Every value chain activity in a company executes functional tactics that support the business's strategy and help accomplish strategic objectives.

The next several sections will highlight key tactics around which managers can build competitive advantage and add value in each of the various functional areas.

FUNCTIONAL TACTICS IN PRODUCTION/OPERATIONS

Basic Issues

Production/operations management (POM) is the core function of any organization. That function converts inputs

(raw materials, supplies, machines, and people) into value-enhanced output. The POM function is most easily associated with manufacturing firms, but it also applies to all other types of businesses (e.g., service and retail firms). POM tactics must guide decisions regarding (1) the basic nature of the firm's POM system, seeking an optimum balance between investment input and production/operations output, and (2) location, facilities design, and process planning on a short-term basis. Exhibit 10.A1 highlights key decision areas in which the POM tactics should provide guidance to functional personnel.

POM facility and equipment tactics involve decisions regarding plant location, size, equipment replacement, and facilities utilization that should be consistent with grand strategy and other operating strategies. In the mobile home industry, for example, the facilities and equipment tactic of Winnebago was to locate one large centralized, highly integrated production center (in Iowa) near its raw materials. On the other extreme, Fleetwood Inc., a California-based competitor, located dispersed, decentralized production facilities near markets and emphasized maximum equipment life and less-integrated, labor-intensive production processes. Both firms are leaders in the mobile home industry, but have taken very different tactical approaches.

The interplay between computers and rapid technological advancement has made flexible manufacturing systems (FMS) a major consideration for today's POM tacticians.

EXHIBIT 10.A1   Key Functional Tactics in POM

Functional Tactic	Typical Questions That the Functional Tactic Should Answer
Facilities and equipment	How centralized should the facilities be? (One big facility or several small facilities?)
	How integrated should the separate processes be?
	To what extent should further mechanization or automation be pursued?
	Should size and capacity be oriented toward peak or normal operating levels?
Sourcing	How many sources are needed?
	How should suppliers be selected, and how should relationships with suppliers be managed over time?
	What level of forward buying (hedging) is appropriate?
Operations planning and control	Should work be scheduled to order or to stock?
	What level of inventory is appropriate?
	How should inventory be used, controlled, and replenished?
	What are the key foci for control efforts (quality, labor cost, downtime, product use, other)?
	Should maintenance efforts be oriented to prevention or to breakdown?
	What emphasis should be placed on job specialization? Plant safety? The use of standards?

FMS allows managers to automatically and rapidly shift production systems to retool for different products or other steps in a manufacturing process. Changes that previously took hours or days can be done in minutes. The result is decreased labor cost, greater efficiency, and increased quality associated with computer-based precision.

Sourcing has become an increasingly important component in the POM area. Many companies now accord sourcing a separate status like any other functional area. Sourcing tactics provide guidelines about questions such as: Are the cost advantages of using only a few suppliers outweighed by the risk of overdependence? What criteria (e.g., payment requirements) should be used in selecting vendors? Which vendors can provide "just-in-time" inventory, and how can the business provide it to our customers? How can operations be supported by the volume and delivery requirements of purchases?

POM planning and control tactics involve approaches to the management of ongoing production operations and are intended to match production/operations resources with longer-range, overall demand. These tactical decisions usually determine whether production/operations will be demand oriented, inventory oriented, or outsourcing oriented to seek a balance between the two extremes. Tactics in this component also address how issues such as maintenance, safety, and work organization are handled. Quality control procedures are yet another focus of tactical priorities in this area.

Just-in-time (JIT) delivery, outsourcing, and statistical process control (SPC) have become prominent aspects of the way today's POM managers create tactics that build greater value and quality in their POM system. JIT delivery was initially a way to coordinate with suppliers to reduce inventory carrying costs of items needed to make products. It also became a quality control tactic because smaller inventories made quality checking easier on smaller, frequent deliveries. It has become an important aspect of supplier-customer relationships in today's best businesses.

Outsourcing, or the use of a source other than internal capacity to accomplish some task or process, has become a major operational tactic in today's downsizing-oriented firms. Outsourcing is based on the notion that strategies should be built around the core competencies that add the most value in the value chain and that functions or activities that add little value or that cannot be done cost effectively should be done outside the firm—outsourced. When done well, the firm gains a supplier that provides superior quality at lower cost than it could provide itself. JIT and outsourcing have increased the strategic importance of the purchasing function. Outsourcing must include intense quality control by the buyer. ValuJet's tragic 1996 crash in the Everglades was caused by poor quality control over its outsourced maintenance providers.

social computing
Social computing refers to the area of computer science that is concerned with the intersection of social behavior and computation systems. It typically refers to software that contributes to compelling and effective social interactions.

The Internet and e-commerce have begun to revolutionize functional tactics in operations and marketing. How we sell, where we make things, how we logistically coordinate what we do—all of these basic business functions and questions have new perspectives and ways of being addressed because of the technological effect of the globally emerging ways we link together electronically, quickly, and accurately.

FUNCTIONAL TACTICS IN MARKETING

The role of the marketing function is to achieve the firm's objectives by bringing about the profitable sale of the business's products/services in target markets. Marketing tactics should guide sales and marketing managers in determining who will sell what, where, to whom, in what quantity, and how. Marketing tactics at a minimum should address four fundamental areas: products, price, place, and promotion. Exhibit 10.A2 highlights typical questions marketing tactics should address.

In addition to the basic issues raised in Exhibit 10.A2, marketing tactics today must guide managers addressing the effect of the communication revolution and the increased diversity among market niches worldwide. The Internet and the accelerating blend of computers and telecommunications has facilitated instantaneous access to several places around the world. A producer of plastic kayaks in Easley, South Carolina, receives orders from somewhere in the world about every 30 minutes over the Internet without any traditional distribution structure or global advertising. It fills the order within five days without any transportation capability. Speed linked to the ability to communicate instantaneously is causing marketing tacticians to radically rethink what they need to do to remain competitive and maximize value.

Diversity has accelerated because of communication technology, logistical capability worldwide, and advancements in flexible manufacturing systems. The diversity that has resulted is a virtual explosion of market niches—adaptations of products to serve hundreds of distinct and diverse customer segments that would previously have been served with more mass-market, generic products or services. Where firms used to rely on volume associated with mass markets to lower costs, they now encounter smaller niche players carving out subsegments they can serve more timely *and* more cost effectively. These new, smaller players lack the bureaucracy and committee approach that burdens the larger firms. They make decisions, outsource, incorporate product modifications, and make other agile adjustments to niche market needs before their larger competitors get through the first phase of committee-based decision making.

FUNCTIONAL TACTICS IN SOCIAL COMPUTING

The role of **social computing**—blogs, wikis, networks, virtual worlds, and social media—has become a key aspect of

EXHIBIT 10.A2 Key Functional Tactics in Marketing

Functional Tactic	Typical Questions That the Functional Tactic Should Answer
Product (or service)	Which products do we emphasize? Which products/services contribute most to profitability? What product/service image do we seek to project? What consumer needs does the product/service seek to meet? What changes should be influencing our customer orientation?
Price	Are we competing primarily on price? Can we offer discounts on other pricing modifications? Are our pricing policies standard nationally, or is there regional control? What price segments are we targeting (high, medium, low, and so on)? What is the gross profit margin? Do we emphasize cost/demand or competition-oriented pricing?
Place	What level of market coverage is necessary? Are there priority geographic areas? What are the key channels of distribution? What are the channel objectives, structure, and management? Should the marketing managers change their degree of reliance on distributors, sales reps, and direct selling? What sales organization do we want? Is the sales force organized around territory, market, or product?
Promotion	What are the key promotion priorities and approaches? Which advertising/communication priorities and approaches are linked to different products, markets, and territories? Which media would be most consistent with the total marketing strategy?

implementing a firm's strategy in today's global economy. Sites like Facebook, MySpace, Twitter, Second Life, and Web-based blogs are part of the daily routine and means of connecting with others in our personal and work environments. So it is important to incorporate this phenomenon in strategy implementation with tactics and guidelines for company personnel to use when working on behalf of and representing the company.

IBM is deeply involved in information technology–based assistance to clients worldwide. In so doing, it has long embraced the rapidly growing Web-based social computing developments as an important arena for organizational and individual development and connection with colleagues, clients, partners, stakeholders, and virtually every part of a company's external environment. So they decided very quickly in the last decade to create tactical guidelines for social

Social Computing Guidelines

Social Computing Guidelines are a set of norms and shared rules designed to guide behavior when involved in social computing activities, like blogs, social websites, etc.

computing, which are regularly updated and adapted so as to keep pace with the rapidly developing and ever changing social computer scene on the Web. Twelve fundamental **Social Computing Guidelines** (or tactics) IBM uses with its people and openly shares for others to consider using are:

1. Know and follow IBM's *Business Conduct Guidelines*.[1]

2. IBMers are personally responsible for the content they publish on-line, whether in a blog, social computing site or any other form of user-generated media. Be mindful that what you publish will be public for a long time—protect your privacy and take care to understand a site's terms of service.

3. Identify yourself—name and, when relevant, role at IBM—when you discuss IBM or IBM-related matters, such as IBM products or services. You must make it clear that you are speaking for yourself and not on behalf of IBM.

4. If you publish content online relevant to IBM in your personal capacity, use a disclaimer such as this: "The postings on this site are my own and don't necessarily represent IBM's positions, strategies or opinions."

[1] See http://www.ibm.com/investor/governance/business-conduct-guidelines.wss for details on IBM's Business Conduct Guidelines. Obviously any company making use of these guidelines would do so in that company's name, not IBM's.

5. Respect copyright, fair use, and financial disclosure laws.

6. Don't provide IBM's or another's confidential or other proprietary information and never discuss IBM business performance or other sensitive matters publicly.

7. Don't cite or reference clients, partners or suppliers without their approval. When you do make a reference, link back to the source. Don't publish anything that might allow inferences to be drawn which could embarrass or damage a client.

8. Respect your audience. Don't use ethnic slurs, personal insults, obscenity, or engage in any conduct that would not be acceptable in IBM's workplace. You should also show proper consideration for others' privacy and for topics that may be considered objectionable or inflammatory—such as politics and religion.

9. Be aware of your association with IBM in online social networks. If you identify yourself as an IBMer, ensure your profile and related content is consistent with how you wish to present yourself with colleagues and clients.

10. Don't pick fights, be the first to correct your own mistakes.

11. Try to add value. Provide worthwhile information and perspective. IBM's brand is best represented by its people and what you publish may reflect on IBM's brand.

12. Don't use IBM logos or trademarks unless approved to do so.

An excellent, detailed discussion of each of these guidelines can be found at IBM Social Computing Guidelines, http://www.ibm.com/blogs/zz/en/guidelines.html. A video slide show from IBM to its employees about social computing guidelines, which IBM shares with clients and organizations interested in what it does and how it communicates doing so with its employees, can be found at http://www.ibm.com/blogs/zz/en/social_computing_guidelines.html. Tactics in marketing and sales related to social media are particularly important—using Facebook to connect with current and potential customers; to build your brand; using Twitter to maintain frequent connection with key people and partners. For some businesses, particularly locally focused retailers and service providers, using Groupon and other instant digital coupon providers has become another important social media tactic to manage. Using virtual worlds to build global "virtual" teams or train to do so; using B2B sites to develop supply chain relationships worldwide; simple e-mail, texting, video conferencing . . . all are rapidly developing social media–related means to work together and "do business" leveraging what the Web enables. Use of social computing also carries with it greater security responsibilities for your company as your IT system inevitably stores confidential information on employees, customers, clients, and so forth. Breaches in this responsibility can be harmful if not catastrophic to your company and those affected, so tactics and policies to manage this responsibility are an essential part of this new, exciting strategic reality. Overall, in every aspect of social computing, it is critical for a company, in implementing its strategy, to create useful guidelines in the use of these tools that help employees know how to use them effectively as they represent the business and do the things that make its strategies and tactics more successful.

FUNCTIONAL TACTICS IN ACCOUNTING AND FINANCE

While most functional tactics guide implementation in the immediate future, the time frame for functional tactics in the area of finance varies because these tactics direct the use of financial resources in support of the business strategy, long-term goals, and annual objectives. Financial tactics with longer time perspectives guide financial managers in long-term capital investment, debt financing, dividend allocation, and leveraging. Financial tactics designed to manage working capital and short-term assets have a more immediate focus. Exhibit 10.A3 highlights some key questions that financial tactics must answer.

Accounting tactics increasingly emphasize more accurately identifying a meaningful basis from which managers can determine the relative value of different activities undertaken throughout the company contribute to the company's overall success. Traditional cost accounting approaches proved inadequate in doing this, as we discussed in Chapter 6. So, in addition to accounting tactics centered on positioning the company to accurately comply with securities, tax, and regulatory considerations, considerable accounting tactical attention centers on providing value-based accounting of the costs of creating and providing the business' products and services so that managers in different units—as well as company executives—can more truly understand the value of activities undertaken in, between, and among those units. See Exhibit 6.5 in Chapter 6 for a refresher explanation of activity-based versus traditional cost accounting tactics.

FUNCTIONAL TACTICS IN RESEARCH AND DEVELOPMENT

With the increasing rate of technological change in most competitive industries, research and development has assumed a key strategic role in many firms. In the technology-intensive computer and pharmaceutical industries, for example, firms typically spend between 4 and 6 percent, respectively, of their sales dollars on R&D. In other industries, such as the hotel/motel and construction industries, R&D spending is less than 1 percent of sales. Thus, functional R&D tactics may be more critical instruments of the business strategy in some industries than in others.

Exhibit 10.A4 illustrates the types of questions addressed by R&D tactics. First, R&D tactics should clarify whether basic research or product development research will be emphasized. Several major oil companies now have solar energy

EXHIBIT 10.A3   **Key Functional Tactics in Finance and Accounting**

Functional Tactic	Typical Questions That the Functional Tactics Should Answer
Acquiring capital	What is the optimal balance between external and internal funding?
	What proportion of debt should be long-term versus short-term? How should leasing be used?
	What levels of common versus preferred equity would be best? What ownership restrictions apply?
	What is a target cost of capital?
Using/allocating capital	What are priorities for allocating capital across different parts of the business and key projects?
	What approval processes and what levels should be allowed to make capital allocation decisions?
	How should competing demands for capital be resolved?
Working capital management	What levels of cash flow are needed? What are maximum/minimum cash flow requirements and balances?
	What should the credit policies be? How might client-specific changes be determined?
	What are payment terms, limits on credit, and what collection steps/procedures are needed?
	What are our payment policies, terms, and timing procedures?
Dividends	Are dividends important in support of the company's overall strategy?
	What portion of earnings, or range, should be used to set dividend payout levels?
	When can dividends be raised or lowered? How important is dividend stability?
	Should dividends be exclusively cash? What other things other than cash are appropriate?
Accounting	How can we best account for the costs of creating and providing our business's products and services?
	What is the "value" of each activity within different parts of our business versus traditional cost categories?

Source: © RC Trust, LLC, 2010.

EXHIBIT 10.A4   **Key Functional Tactics in R&D**

R&D Decision Area	Typical Questions That the Functional Tactics Should Answer
Basic research versus product and process development	To what extent should innovation and breakthrough research be emphasized? In relation to the emphasis on product development, refinement, and modification?
	What critical operating processes need R&D attention?
	What new projects are necessary to support growth?
Time horizon	Is the emphasis short term or long term?
	Which orientation best supports the business strategy? The marketing and production strategy?
Organizational fit	Should R&D be done in-house or contracted out?
	Should R&D be centralized or decentralized?
	What should be the relationship between the R&D units and product managers? Marketing managers? Production managers?
Basic R&D posture	Should the firm maintain an offensive posture, seeking to lead innovation in its industry?
	Should the firm adopt a defensive posture, responding to the innovations of its competitors?

subsidiaries in which basic research is emphasized, while the smaller oil companies emphasize product development research.

The choice of emphasis between basic research and product development also involves the time horizon for R&D efforts. Should these efforts be focused on the near term or the long term? The solar energy subsidiaries of the major oil companies have long-term perspectives, while the smaller oil companies focus on creating products now in order to establish a competitive niche in the growing solar industry.

R&D tactics also involve organization of the R&D function. For example, should R&D work be conducted solely within the firm, or should portions of that work be contracted out? A closely related issue is whether R&D should be centralized or decentralized. What emphasis should be placed on process R&D versus product R&D?

Decisions on all of these questions are influenced by the firm's R&D posture, which can be offensive or defensive, or both. If that posture is offensive, as is true for small high-technology firms, the firm will emphasize technological innovation and new-product development as the basis for its future success. This orientation entails high risks (and high payoffs) and demands considerable technological skill, forecasting expertise, and the ability to quickly transform innovations into commercial products.

A defensive R&D posture emphasizes product modification and the ability to copy or acquire new technology.

Converse Shoes is a good example of a firm with such an R&D posture. Faced with the massive R&D budgets of Nike and Reebok, Converse placed R&D emphasis on bolstering the product life cycle of its prime products (particularly canvas shoes).

Large companies with some degree of technological leadership often use a combination of offensive and defensive R&D strategy. GE in the electrical industry, IBM in the computer industry, and Du Pont in the chemical industry all have a defensive R&D posture for currently available products *and* an offensive R&D posture in basic, long-term research.

FUNCTIONAL TACTICS IN HUMAN RESOURCE MANAGEMENT

The strategic importance of human resource management (HRM) tactics received widespread endorsement in the 1990s. HRM tactics aid long-term success in the development of managerial talent and competent employees, the creation of systems to manage compensation or regulatory concerns, and guiding the effective utilization of human resources to achieve both the firm's short-term objectives and employees' satisfaction and development. HRM tactics are helpful in the areas shown in Exhibit 10.A5. The recruitment, selection, and orientation should establish the basic parameters for bringing new people into a firm and adapting them to "the way things are done" in the firm. The career development and training component

EXHIBIT 10.A5   Key Functional Tactics in HRM

Functional Tactic	Typical Questions That HRM Tactics Should Answer
Recruitment, selection, and orientation	What key human resources are needed to support the chosen strategy?
	How do we recruit these human resources?
	How sophisticated should our selection process be?
	How should we introduce new employees to the organization?
Career development and training	What are our future human resource needs?
	How can we prepare our people to meet these needs?
	How can we help our people develop?
Compensation	What levels of pay are appropriate for the tasks we require?
	How can we motivate and retain good people?
	How should we interpret our payment, incentive, benefit, and seniority policies?
Evaluation, discipline, and control	How often should we evaluate our people? Formally or informally?
	What disciplinary steps should we take to deal with poor performance or inappropriate behavior?
	In what ways should we "control" individual and group performance?
Labor relations and equal opportunity requirements	How can we maximize labor-management cooperation?
	How do our personnel practices affect women/minorities?
	Should we have hiring policies?

should guide the action that personnel take to meet the future human resources needs of the overall business strategy. Merrill Lynch, a major brokerage firm whose long-term corporate strategy is to become a diversified financial service institution, has moved into such areas as investment banking, consumer credit, and venture capital. In support of its long-term objectives, it has incorporated extensive early-career training and ongoing career development programs to meet its expanding need for personnel with multiple competencies. Larger organizations need HRM tactics that guide decisions regarding labor relations; Equal Employment Opportunity Commission requirements; and employee compensation, discipline, and control.

Current trends in HRM parallel the reorientation of managerial accounting by looking at their cost structure anew. HRM's "paradigm shift" involves looking at people expense as an investment in human capital. This involves looking at the business's value chain and the "value" of human resource components along the various links in that chain. One of the results of this shift in perspective has been the downsizing and outsourcing phenomena of the last quarter century. While this has been traumatic for millions of employees in companies worldwide, its underlying basis involves an effort to examine the use of "human capital" to create value in ways that maximize the human contribution. This scrutiny continues to challenge the HRM area to include recent major trends to outsource some or all HRM activities not regarded as part of a firm's core competence. The emerging implications for human resource management tactics may be a value-oriented perspective on the role of human resources in a business's value chain as suggested here:

Traditional HRM Ideas	Emerging HRM Ideas
Emphasis solely on physical skills	Emphasis on total contribution to the firm
Expectation of predictable, repetitious behavior	Expectation of innovative and creative behavior
Comfort with stability and conformity	Tolerance of ambiguity and change
Avoidance of responsibility and decision making	Accepting responsibility for making decisions
Training covering only specific tasks	Open-ended commitment; broad continuous development
Emphasis placed on outcomes and results	Emphasis placed on processes and means
High concern for quantity and throughput	High concern for total customer value
Concern for individual efficiency	Concern for overall effectiveness
Functional and subfunctional specialization	Cross-functional integration
Labor force seen as unnecessary expense	Labor force seen as critical investment
Workforce is management's adversary	Management and workforce are partners

Source: From A. Miller and G. Dess, *Strategic Management*, 2002, p. 400. Reprinted with permission of The McGraw-Hill Companies, Inc.

To summarize, functional tactics reflect how each major activity of a firm contributes to the implementation of the business strategy. The specificity of functional tactics and the involvement of operating managers in their development help ensure understanding of and commitment to the chosen strategy. A related step in implementation is the development of policies that empower operating managers and their subordinates to make decisions and to act autonomously.

Chapter **Eleven**

Organizational Structure

After reading and studying this chapter, you should be able to

1. Identify five traditional organizational structures and the pros and cons of each.

2. Describe the product-team structure and explain why it is a prototype for a more open, agile organizational structure.

3. Explain five ways improvements have been sought in traditional organizational structures.

4. Describe what is meant by agile, virtual organizations.

5. Explain how outsourcing can create agile, virtual organizations, along with its pros and cons.

6. Describe boundaryless organizations and why they are important.

7. Explain why organizations of the future need to be ambidextrous learning organizations.

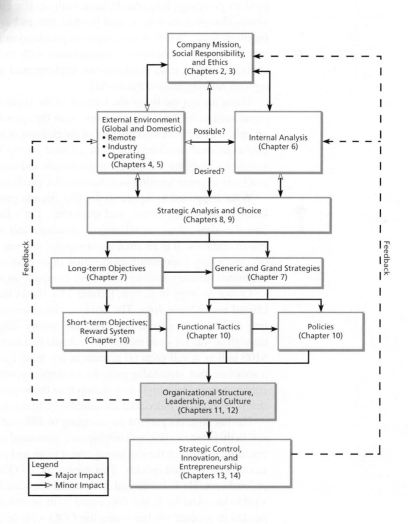

Company Mission, Social Responsibility, and Ethics (Chapters 2, 3)

External Environment (Global and Domestic)
- Remote
- Industry
- Operating
(Chapters 4, 5)

Possible?

Internal Analysis (Chapter 6)

Desired?

Strategic Analysis and Choice (Chapters 8, 9)

Feedback

Long-term Objectives (Chapter 7)

Generic and Grand Strategies (Chapter 7)

Short-term Objectives; Reward System (Chapter 10)

Functional Tactics (Chapter 10)

Policies (Chapter 10)

Organizational Structure, Leadership, and Culture (Chapters 11, 12)

Strategic Control, Innovation, and Entrepreneurship (Chapters 13, 14)

Feedback

Legend
→ Major Impact
⇢ Minor Impact

The implementation process is initiated through the creation of action plans detailing tactics and actions to be taken that initiate long-term strategies through the work of the organization. Getting that work done involves a simple but nonetheless serious and sometimes contentious question about the organization's structure—how can we best get the work of the business done efficiently and effectively so as to make the chosen strategy work?

The core question is: What is the best way to organize people, tasks, and resources to execute the strategy most effectively? A simple question, but one that demands other questions as its answer will usually be the key determinant of the effectiveness by which the organization accomplishes its mission. Questions like: What changes in how we are currently organized might improve our success? Should we organize around our product lines, or would doing so geographically make us more responsive to regional or international differences? Is it mission-critical to keep some specific activities "in-house," in one location or at the corporate level? Are there activities better "outsourced," even though we will lose control of the underlying skill set and expertise over time? With the rapid growth we are projecting, how can we design or redesign our organization to ensure better coordination between sales and manufacturing or operations so as to avoid problems arising with new customers unfamiliar with our product or service? Logic says we should combine several product groupings into one division with similar customer characteristics, but that necessitates changing the way several product groups have been organized and done good work for many years. Will that cause serious problems or resistance? How can we reorganize the way in which remote teams communicate with their functional home bases to get quick decisions before team solutions are implemented with the customers they are serving in regions halfway around the world?

These are but the tip of the iceberg of the types of questions arising every day in most organizations as they come to grips with the question of how to organize the work done on behalf of a business on behalf of its customers so as to create profitable, lasting value. Organizational structure can seem a rather boring notion, but it is far from that. It is the setting for enabling the energy of the people and capabilities and excellence a company has available to come together in a meaningful, profitable, exciting manner.

What happened at Apple so far this decade provides an interesting example of these kinds of questions, issues, and outcomes. Let's look at that story a bit before jumping into the ideas about organizational structure and ways to use them to improve strategy implementation. It is an amazing company, and one for which organizational structure has become a very important consideration in its post-Jobs ability to successfully implement a continued industry-leading innovative company strategy.

Global Strategy in Action, Exhibit 11.1 shows the organizational structure at Apple that existed under Steve Jobs. The obvious characteristic drawn from this rather simple structure is that every critical decision, and history suggests many noncritical ones too, went through or was Jobs's to make. While Apple had over 50,000 employees and sales exceeding $100 billion, it still grew 60 percent in one year. Existing and former employees talk about a structure that repeatedly eschews modern corporate convention in a manner that lets it continue more like a high-tech startup than the huge consumer-electronics global company it still is. Simplicity. Individual accountability. Specialization to enable exceptional expertise.

Having different parts of the company in different "silos," so that expertise compounds itself in that narrow slice, and relying on a command and control where ideas are shared at the top, filtered through the top management team and especially through Jobs. Decisions, once made, were enacted quickly. That means the CFO is concerned with finance, not the head of hardware. He is concerned with world-class design, on time, competitively unmatched worldwide. And he is not concerned with inventory and integration of the supply chain needed to produce his hardware; the COO with deep supply chain expertise is responsible

Apple's Organization Chart under Steve Jobs

As Apple was introducing the iPad and becoming the most valuable company in the world, journalists interested in how Apple works "inside" reported this organizational structure that guided Apple employees on "Who Does What" inside Apple. Even facing inevitable death, Steve Jobs remained at the center of the whole Apple organization and the conduit through which any major and often minor decisions needed to pass. Here is the organizational chart offered to explain "who does what" in Apple at that time. What problems could arise in this structure, particularly after Jobs's death? See Strategy in Action, Exhibit 11.2 to learn what problems arose, and what happened as a result, after Jobs's death.

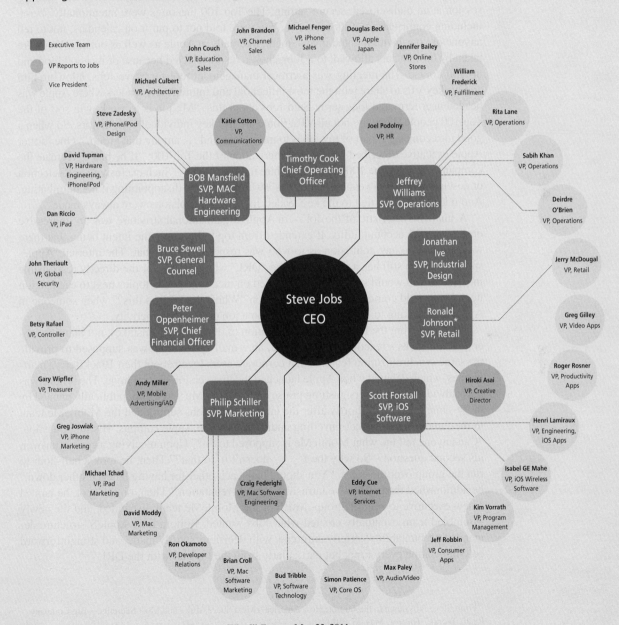

Source: Adam Lashinsky, "Apple's Core: Who Does What?" *Fortune*, May 23, 2011.

for doing that for hardware. The powerful chief of retail sales doesn't control his inventory levels, the COO does, while the retail sales VP is expected to build ever more sales-capable people, facilities, locations, and results. Software for the iMac, iPhone, and iPad is strictly someone else's role, with any need to talk with hardware run through the CEO, Steve Jobs. No committees. No general management level. Everyone focused on his or her "little" part, exercising the "power of picking the things you don't do" as Jobs called it, enabling exceptional focus and constantly improving best-in-class, specialized skills and capabilities.

This simple, functional structure, unprecedented for a giant consumer products company, allowed Apple and its organization to institutionalize the entrepreneurial trait of focus. Jobs would gather a small group at Apple, called the Top 100, for an intense three-day strategy session at an undisclosed, secure setting. The Top 100 meetings were intentionally secret, including confirmation of its existence. You were told not to put it on calendars, not to tell anyone of your invitation and involvement, internally at Apple as well as outside. You were taken by bus, no cars allowed, to a Jobs-chosen resort selected because of its good food and no golf course. The meeting was a critical management tool for Steve Jobs, allowing him and his key VPs to share with the most influential and future Apple leaders where Apple was headed near-term and long-term. Said Jobs about this: "My job is to work with sort of the Top 100 people. They are not all VPs. Some are just key individual contributors. So when a good idea comes, . . . part of my job is to move it around . . . among that group."[1] One former Apple executive described Jobs's characterization of the Top 100: "If he had to recreate the company, these are the 100 people he'd hire to bring along."[2] Such exclusivity and selection or deselection year-to-year based on Jobs's whims could be disappointing if not humiliating. And it kept everyone tied to the key leader, Jobs, where decisions were always made.

A final characteristic of the Jobs-era Apple organizational structure was an impressive obsession with accountability. It extended from top to bottom—the intent being that there was never to be any confusion as to who was responsible for what. The internal "Apple-speak" or lingo still has a name for it, the "DRI," which stands for the directly responsible individual. You would see that person named on meeting agenda topics next to each action item. You would commonly hear the question "Who's the DRI on this?" when someone in Apple was seeking to get the right contact on a job or project or activity.

Accompanying the DRI was the expectation of owning your mistakes, not blaming others. Here is Jobs's reaction to MobileMe, an e-mail system that was supposed to provide the same synchronization features that corporate users loved about their BlackBerry smartphones, which debuted when Apple launched the first version of its iPhone. The iPhone was a worldwide hit, reviewers gushing praise on it. MobileMe was a dud, publically panned by those same reviewers. Shortly after the launch event, Jobs summoned the MobileMe team to the famous new product unveiling auditorium on the Apple campus. His first question: "Can anyone tell me what MobileMe is supposed to do?" Upon receiving a correct answer, his second question: "So why the f _ _ _ doesn't it do that?" Then, he took a half-hour to run the group over the coals. "You should hate each other for having let each other down," he admonished them. "You've tarnished Apple's reputation." Then, on the spot, he named a new executive to run the group. Much of the MobileMe team disbanded, and the newly assembled team eventually created what Jobs wanted. Bottom line, Apple's structure demanded accountability, strictly enforced, with decisions swiftly made, and straightforward communication every time, but particularly from the top and with the DRI.

---

[1]"From Steve Jobs down to the Janitor: How America's Most Successful—and Most Secretive—Big Company Really Works," *Fortune,* May 23, 2011.
[2]Ibid.

Simplicity was the key. Straightforward structure, with no dotted-line or matrixed responsibilities. There were no committees, the notion of "general management" was frowned upon, and only one person—the CFO—has a "P&L" responsibility—a distraction in Jobs's Apple organization only the CFO needed to worry about. When *Jobs was in charge, everything flowed through him.* He hosted a series of weekly meetings without fail—Mondays he met with the executive management team to discuss results and strategy as well as to review nearly every important project in the company; on Wednesday he would hold a marketing and communications meeting. "We don't have a lot of process at Apple, but we do these Monday and Wednesday meetings just to all stay on the same page," said Jobs. He also demanded and used these meetings to reinforce *strict accountability.* There was never any confusion about who was responsible for what—the DRI in Applespeak, originated by Jobs, which refers to the "directly responsible individual." *The DRI was identified on every action* item, in every meeting, always.

Specialization was Jobs's mantra—Apple executives weren't exposed to functions outside their area of expertise. Jobs saw specialization as a process of having best-in-class employees in every role, and had no patience for building managers for the sake of managing. Creating "well-rounded" executives was a total waste in Jobs's eyes, leading to a path that creates fiefdoms, and making Jobs's Apple the polar opposite of Microsoft or GE. The result, "*constant course correction,*" focused on a few things, and occasional last-minute course corrections that kept Apple nimble and entrepreneurial. Jobs comparing Apple to competitors: "Sony had too many divisions to create the iPod. Apple instead has functions. It's not synergy that makes it work, it's that we're a unified team." Part of the "team" was accountability. And Jobs himself was the glue that held that unique approach together.

So, the obvious problem—*What happens when Jobs dies?* Initial unity, but soon some increasing infighting, politics, and a phase of concern about the leadership vacuum that the central messianic leader left.

Answer? Better collaboration. A major change in the organizational structure, combining software and hardware under Jony Ive to increase collaboration in design and function; having Craig Federighi lead the OSX and iOS teams, because they need to work seamlessly; and Bob Mansfield taking over wireless and silicon technologies, which are related mobile growth areas. Cook fired longtime Jobs software guru Scott Forstall, saying, "We have to have the courage to say when we're wrong [Apple Maps]; and there is no room for politics in this company." "To go higher at Apple," said Cook, "we have to be an A-plus in collaboration." "No politics. No bureaucracy. We want this fast-moving, agile company where there are no politics, no agendas, with a deep belief that collaboration is essential for innovation."

Background: Steve Jobs said about Jonathan "Jony" Ive to Jobs's biographer Walter Isaacson, "If I had a spiritual partner at Apple, it's Jony."

Apple's decision to stay with a simple, functional structure enabled a unique entrepreneurial and innovative organization even as it grew ever larger and more comprehensive. Global Strategy in Action, Exhibit 11.2 highlights why it did so while also asking the question about how well it would work post-Jobs. That structure enabled several advantages, which in turn Apple used to implement strategies with dramatic success, make changes, and shift quickly and successfully. It enabled Apple to overcome mistakes to minimize damage, build specialized talent, and have secrecy that was the envy of the commercial world. But a key ingredient, some say the essential ingredient to making this organizational structure work was Steve Jobs himself. Corporate dictator, technology renaissance man, antimanagement leader, obsessively passionate owner/creator, the truth is that Jobs himself was the glue that was able to hold this simple, unique organizational structure together and enable it to "do magic." So, what to do after he died?

That question was on everyone's mind with any connection to or interest in Apple. While Tim Cook had been anointed by Jobs as his self-selected replacement, the lingering question was who was going to fill the giant void Jobs left behind in making the organization that was Apple keep Apple uniquely successful. For a year, the answer was always "a committee of executives." But rumors of discord began to emerge. Two key executives, one software and one hardware, with whom Jobs had worked so closely over many years, became increasingly frustrated working together. Observers were counting the days that had passed since Apple had announced a new product compared to the same longest stretch in the Jobs era. People were concerned that Tim Cook's supply chain and operations expertise, while exceptional, were not matched by an equally deep technology understanding that was second nature to Jobs.

Tim Cook acted a year after Jobs's passing. The focus was on whom he dismissed and whom he retained. The more subtle key was organizational. He concluded that a post-Jobs Apple needed to change its organizational structure if it had a chance of retaining the innovative magic associated with the Jobs era. He knew that he alone, or an executive committee, could not replace what Jobs did as the organizational structure's glue and decision maker. Rather, Cook had to remake the organization in a way that would have a chance of enabling an organizational structure like what Jobs did through sheer will and persona.

Global Strategy in Action, Exhibit 11.2 summarizes that move. Its essence was to structure in more collaboration by combining key functional silos previously run separately through Jobs with an executive in charge that offered the best hope of keeping the innovative magic alive. Combining hardware and software design—the "look" of the hardware and the "look" of the software—was his key focus. And that meant, ultimately, firing Jobs's longtime favored software leader, Scott Forstall, who created the iOS for mobile software that ran iPads and iPhones. Forstall had been a problem post-Jobs, attempting to politick for himself and his ideas at others' expense. This even occurred as the Apple Maps disaster, for which he was the ultimate DRI, brought Apple great public pain. The other key Apple executives continued to complain to Cook and insist they would meet with him only if Cook were included. Eventually, Cook fired Forstall, stating that it was due to "my deep belief that collaboration is essential for innovation." Cook reorganized Apple so that Forstall's software function was moved under hardware guru Jonathan Ive, long credited with the amazing design success of Apple's key products. Ive was also Jobs's technology design soulmate. But Ive had little software experience. Cook's thought was that Ive's appreciation and understanding of simplicity, targeting younger users, was the key needed there too anyway. When Apple finally broke its new product announcement drought, it was Ive's new software for iPhones and iPads, with a simpler, contemporary look much different from the original iOS dating back to 2007 under Forstall. It suggests Cook's expectation that Ive's magic in hardware would spill over into software innovation may just have been the first organizational structure step in keeping the Apple magic alive.

Cook similarly pulled two sets of units, previously autonomous silos under Jobs, together under one executive. The OSX and iOS teams were brought together under one leader, and the wireless and silicon technologies under another to accelerate innovation there too. Again, Cook was making a significant change in Apple's functional organizational structure to increase collaboration. Finally, Cook reinforced some of the organizational rules on accountability and antimanagement dogma that seem to keep old Apple themes very much intact, saying, "The thing that ties us all is we are brought together by values. We want to do the right thing. We want to be honest and straightforward. We admit when we're wrong and have the courage to change." Cook went on to say, "I despise politics. There is no room for it in a company. My life is going to be way too short to deal with that. No bureaucracy. We want this fast-moving, agile company where there are no politics, no agendas."[3]

[3]Jay Yarow, "Tim Cook: Why I Fired Scott Forstall," *businessinsider.com,* December 6, 2012.

Today's fast-changing, global economy demands ever-increasing productivity, speed, and flexibility from companies that seek to survive, perhaps thrive. To do so, companies must change their organizational structures dramatically, retaining the best of their traditional (hierarchical) structures while embracing radically new structures that leverage the value of the people who generate ideas, collaborate with colleagues and customers, innovate and therein generate future value for the company. So this chapter seeks to familiarize you with both perspectives on organizational structure and the major trends in structuring business organizations today. Let's start by looking at what have been traditional ways to organize, along with the advantages and disadvantages of each organizational structure.

TRADITIONAL ORGANIZATIONAL STRUCTURES AND THEIR STRATEGY-RELATED PROS AND CONS

You may be one of several students who choose to start your own business rather than take a job with an established company when you finish your current degree program. Or perhaps you are currently in a full-time job position but soon plan to leave that job and start your own company. Like millions of others who have done or will soon do the same thing, usually with a few other "partners," your group will be faced with the question of how to organize your work and the activities and tasks necessary to do the work of your new company. What you are looking for is an organizational structure. We do not mean, here, the "legal" structure of your company such as a proprietorship, corporation, limited liability corporation, or limited partnership to mention a few. **Organizational structure** refers to the formalized arrangement of interaction between and responsibility for the tasks, people, and resources in an organization. It is most often seen as a chart, often a pyramidal chart, with positions or titles and roles in cascading fashion. The organizational structure you and your partners would have in this start-up of which you are a part would most likely be a "simple" organization.

organizational structure
Refers to the formalized arrangements of interaction between and responsibility for the tasks, people, and resources in an organization.

Simple Organizational Structure

simple organizational structure
Structure in which there is an owner and a few employees and where the arrangement of tasks, responsibilities, and communication is highly informal and accomplished through direct supervision.

In the smallest business enterprise, a simple structure usually prevails. A **simple organizational structure** is one where there is an owner and, usually, a few employees and where the arrangement of tasks, responsibilities, and communication is highly informal and accomplished through direct supervision. All strategic and operating decisions are made by the owner, or a small owner-partner team. Because the scope of the firm's activities are modest, there is little need to formalize roles, communication, and procedures. With the strategic concern primarily being survival, and the likelihood that one bad decision could seriously threaten continued existence, this structure maximizes the owner's control. It can also allow rapid response to product/market shifts and the ability to accommodate unique customer demands without major coordination difficulties. This is in part because the owner is directly involved with customers on a regular basis. Simple structures encourage employees to multitask, and they are efficacious in businesses that serve a simple, local product/market or narrow niche.

The simple structure can be very demanding on the owner-manager. If it is successful, and starts to grow, this can cause the owner-manager to give increased attention to day-to-day concerns, which may come at the expense of time invested in stepping back and examining strategic questions about the company's future. At the same time, the company's reliance on the owner as the central point for all decisions can limit the development of future managers capable of assuming duties that allow the owner time to be a strategist.

And, this structure usually requires a multitalented, resourceful owner, good at producing and selling a product or service—and at controlling scarce funds.

Most businesses in this country and around the world are of this type. Many survive for a period of time, then go out of business because of financial, owner, or market conditions. Some grow, having been built on an idea or capability that taps a great need for what the company does. As they grow, the need to "get organized" is increasingly heard among owners and a growing number of employees in the growing company. That fortunate circumstance historically led to the need for a functional organizational structure.

Functional Organizational Structure

functional organizational structure

Structure in which the tasks, people, and technologies necessary to do the work of the business are divided into separate "functional" groups (e.g., marketing, operations, finance) with increasingly formal procedures for coordinating and integrating their activities to provide the business's products and services.

Continuing our example, you and your partners, no doubt being among the successful ones, find increased demand for your product or service. Your sales have grown substantially—and so have the number of people you employ to do the work of your business. Once you reach 15 to 25 people in the organization, you will experience a need to have some people handle sales, some operations, a financial accounting person or two—that is, you will need to have different people focus on different functions within the business to become better organized and efficient, and to achieve control and coordination. A **functional organizational structure** is one in which the tasks, people, and technologies necessary to do the work of the business are divided into separate "functional" groups (such as marketing, operations, finance) with increasingly formal procedures for coordinating and integrating their activities to provide the business's products and services.

Functional structures predominate in firms with a single or narrow product focus and that have experienced success in their marketplace, leading to increased sales and an increased number of people needed to do the work behind those sales. Such firms require well-defined skills and areas of specialization to build competitive advantages in providing their products or services. Dividing tasks into functional specialties enables the personnel of these firms to concentrate on only one aspect of the necessary work. This allows use of the latest technical skills and develops a high level of efficiency.

Product, customer, or technology considerations determine the identity of the parts in a functional structure. A hotel business might be organized around housekeeping (maids), the front desk, maintenance, restaurant operations, reservations and sales, accounting, and personnel. An equipment manufacturer might be organized around production, engineering/quality control, purchasing, marketing, personnel, and finance/accounting. Two examples of functional organizations are illustrated in Exhibit 11.3.

The strategic challenge presented by the functional structure is effective coordination of the functional units. The narrow technical expertise achieved through specialization can lead to limited perspectives and to differences in the priorities of the functional units. Specialists may see the firm's strategic issues primarily as "marketing" problems or "production" problems. The potential conflict among functional units makes the coordinating role of the chief executive critical. Integrating devices (such as project teams or planning committees) are frequently used in functionally organized firms to enhance coordination and to facilitate understanding across functional areas.

Divisional Structure

When a firm diversifies its product/service lines, covers broad geographic areas, utilizes unrelated market channels, or begins to serve heterogeneous customer groups, a functional structure rapidly becomes inadequate. If a functional structure is retained under these circumstances, production managers may have to oversee the production of numerous and varied

EXHIBIT 11.3
Functional Organization Structures

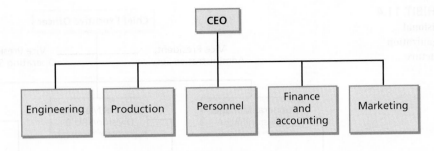

A process-oriented functional structure (an electronics distributor):

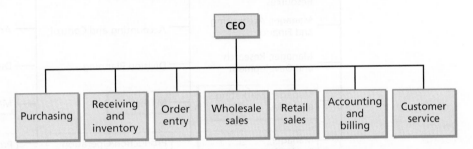

Strategic Advantages	Strategic Disadvantages
1. Achieves efficiency through specialization	1. Promotes narrow specialization and functional rivalry or conflict
2. Develops functional expertise	2. Creates difficulties in functional coordination and interfunctional decision making
3. Differentiates and delegates day-to-day operating decisions	3. Limits development of general managers
4. Retains centralized control of strategic decisions	4. Has a strong potential for interfunctional conflict—priority placed on functional areas, not the entire business
5. Tightly links structure to strategy by designating key activities as separate units	5. May cost more to do a function than it does "outside" the company, unless outsourced

divisional organizational structure
Structure in which a set of relatively autonomous units, or divisions, are governed by a central corporate office but where each operating division has its own functional specialists who provide products or services different from those of other divisions.

products or services, marketing managers may have to create sales programs for vastly different products or sell through vastly different distribution channels, and top management may be confronted with excessive coordination demands. A new organizational structure is often necessary to meet the increased coordination and decision-making requirements that result from increased diversity and size, and the divisional structure is the form often chosen.

A **divisional organizational structure** is one in which a set of relatively autonomous units, or divisions, are governed by a central corporate office but where each operating division has its own functional specialists who provide products or services different from those of other divisions. For many years, global automobile companies have used divisional structures organized by product groups. Manufacturers often organize sales into divisions based on differences in distribution channels.

A divisional structure allows corporate management to delegate authority for the strategic management of distinct business entities—the division. This expedites decision making in response to varied competitive environments and enables corporate management to concentrate on corporate-level strategic decisions. The division usually is given profit responsibility, which

EXHIBIT 11.4
Divisional
Organization
Structure

Strategic Advantages	Strategic Disadvantages
1. Forces coordination and necessary authority down to the appropriate level for rapid response	1. Fosters potentially dysfunctional competition for corporate-level resources
2. Places strategy development and implementation in closer proximity to the unique environments of the division	2. Presents the problem of determining how much authority should be given to division managers
3. Frees chief executive officer for broader strategic decision making	3. Creates a potential for policy inconsistencies among divisions
4. Sharply focuses accountability for performance	4. Presents the problem of distributing corporate overhead costs in a way that's acceptable to division managers with profit responsibility
5. Retains functional specialization within each division	5. Increases costs incurred through duplication functions
6. Provides good training ground for strategic managers	6. Creates difficulty maintaining overall corporate image
7. Increases focus on products, markets, and quick response to change	

facilitates accurate assessment of profit and loss. Exhibit 11.4 illustrates a divisional organizational structure and specifies the strategic advantages and disadvantages of such structures.

Strategic Business Unit

Some firms encounter difficulty in controlling their divisional operations as the diversity, size, and number of these units continues to increase. Corporate management may encounter difficulty in evaluating and controlling its numerous, often multi-industry divisions. Under these conditions, it may become necessary to add another layer of management in order to improve implementation, promote synergy, and gain greater control over the

strategic business unit
An adaptation of the divisional structure in which various divisions or parts of divisions are grouped together based on some common strategic elements, usually linked to distinct product/market differences.

diverse business interests. The **strategic business unit** (SBU) is an adaptation of the divisional structure whereby various divisions or parts of divisions are grouped together based on some common strategic elements, usually linked to distinct product/market differences. General Foods, after originally organizing itself along product lines (which served overlapping markets), created an SBU organization along menu lines with SBUs for breakfast foods, beverages, main meals, desserts, and pet foods. This change allowed General Foods to adapt a vast divisional organization into five strategic business areas with a distinct market focus for each unit and the divisions each contained.

The advantages and disadvantages of the SBU form are very similar to those identified for divisional structures in Exhibit 11.4. Added to its potential disadvantages would be the increased costs of coordination with another "pricy" level of management. Exhibit 11.5.

EXHIBIT 11.5
Matrix Organizational Structure

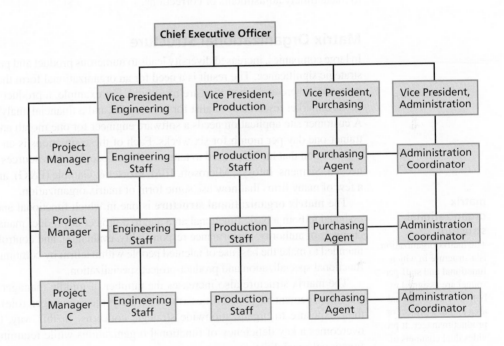

Strategic Advantages	Strategic Disadvantages
1. Accommodates a wide variety of project-oriented business activities	1. May result in confusion and contradictory policies
2. Provides good training ground for strategic managers	2. Necessitates tremendous horizontal and vertical coordination
3. Maximizes efficient use of functional managers	3. Can proliferate information logjams and excess reporting
4. Fosters creativity and multiple sources of diversity	4. Can trigger turf battles and loss of accountability
5. Gives middle management broader exposure to strategic issues	

Holding Company

holding company structure

Structure in which the corporate entity is a broad collection of often unrelated businesses and divisions such that it (the corporate entity) acts as financial overseer "holding" the ownership interest in the various parts of the company, but has little direct managerial involvement.

A final form of the divisional organization is the **holding company structure,** where the corporate entity is a broad collection of often unrelated businesses and divisions such that it (the corporate entity) acts as financial overseer "holding" the ownership interest in the various parts of the company but has little direct managerial involvement. Berkshire Hathaway owns a wide variety of businesses in full or in part. Essentially, at the corporate level, it provides financial support and manages each of these businesses, or divisions, through financial goals and annual review of performance, investment needs, and so forth. Otherwise, strategic and operating decisions are made in each separate company or division, which operates autonomously. The corporate office acts simply as a holding company.

This approach can provide a cost savings over the more active SBU approach since the additional level of "pricy" management is not that much. The negative, of course, becomes the degree to which the corporate office is dependent on each business unit's management team and the lack of control over the decisions those managers make in terms of being able to make timely adjustments or corrections.

Matrix Organizational Structure

In large companies, increased diversity leads to numerous product and project efforts of major strategic significance. The result is a need for an organizational form that provides skills and resources where and when they are most vital. For example, a product development project needs a market research specialist for two months and a financial analyst one day per week. A customer site application needs a software engineer for one month and a customer service trainer one day per month for six weeks. Each of these situations is an example of a matrix organization that has been used to temporarily put people and resources where they are most needed. Siemens, Infosys, Microsoft, IBM, Procter & Gamble (P&G), and Accenture are just a few of many firms that now use some form of matrix organization.

matrix organizational structure

The matrix organization is a structure in which functional and staff personnel are assigned to both a basic functional area and to a project or product manager. It provides dual channels of authority, performance responsibility, evaluation, and control.

The **matrix organizational structure** is one in which functional and staff personnel are assigned to both a basic functional area and to a project or product manager. It provides dual channels of authority, performance responsibility, evaluation, and control. The matrix form is intended to make the best use of talented people within a firm by combining the advantages of functional specialization and product-project specialization.

The matrix structure also increases the number of middle managers who exercise general management responsibilities (through the project manager role) and, thus, broaden their exposure to organizationwide strategic concerns. In this way, the matrix structure overcomes a key deficiency of functional organizations while retaining the advantages of functional specialization.

Although the matrix structure is easy to design, it is difficult to implement. Dual chains of command challenge fundamental organizational orientations. Negotiating shared responsibilities, the use of resources, and priorities can create misunderstanding or confusion among subordinates. These problems are heightened in an international context with the complications introduced by distance, language, time, and culture. Global Strategy in Action, Exhibit 11.6 describes how GE is experimenting with changes in the matrix structure it uses for all its global businesses, which was very similar to the traditional matrix structure used by most multinational corporations (MNCs). GE decided to drop the matrix structure for India and Germany, but keep it in China and virtually every other country in which it operates. GE found, as we have noted above, that potential for conflict is built into its matrix structure: dual reporting, where business heads have two bosses, both playing a role in performance reviews. Second, the country head plays a role as a link between various businesses, which compete for resources but seldom speak to each other directly.

GE's Matrix Structure Experiment in Its Global Business Structure

The matrix structure is a very typical structure used by multinational corporations (MNCs) with multiple businesses and/or functions spread throughout many different countries. The core issue is centralization of power. Typically, there is a "country head" of that MNC's businesses in a particular country with overall "responsibility" for all those separate businesses or functions. But, in typical matrix form, those individual business heads or major functional heads in far-off geographic regions report directly to the bosses at HQ running their particular specialized function or business globally, with the business head having a "dotted line" responsibility to the country head. This means the individual operation is tightly integrated with the global strategy, leaving minimal leeway for the country head to direct the business or key functional operation. Control still vests with the HQ executive for a business or function, and the country head is typically a generalist face of the MNC in that country—custodian of the relationships, reputation, and overall country strategy—much like an ambassador, with no operational role in the business. Emerson, Shell Oil, HSBC, Standard Bank, IBM, and Siemens are but a few examples that work this way across all their various businesses that operate globally.

GE has taken a different, hybrid approach. It put John Flannery in charge of GE-India as president and CEO of that country's GE businesses and operations. Rather than the traditional matrix structure described above, GE's matrix structure for India was dismantled, a first for GE, and everyone reports to the country head.

Flannery, with a finance background, had to convince all the India business heads—specialists in high-tech areas like aviation, health care, transportation, and energy—that they were better off reporting to a generalist who would now be their sole link to GE-HQ and its global business heads for each technology area. Those HQ CEOs are understandably worried that GE-India could produce a domino effect, causing them to lose control of their business operations in other countries. Said Flannery, "I have to convince everyone that this is not a zero-sum game. We want to localize the business but also want to know what projects and technologies are developing at HQ so we can get these into India."

GE-China still uses the traditional matrix structure. China represents 15 percent of GE's global business, and India only 1 percent, making it a good place to experiment with the new structure. GE is already changing GE-Germany to the India model, where it competes with Siemens. It has no plans to do so elsewhere. At this time, GE is the only MNC in India to have made this change. This decision was in part driven by John Flannery, considered a star at GE, which helps his credibility when he has to persuade HQ business bosses to give GE-India the resources it needs. And, he said, "I would be personally frustrated in an ambassadorial job where you can see what needs to be done, but can't actually do it."

Source: Adapted from Dibeyendu Ganguly, "Matrix Evolutions: How GE Underwent a Fundamental Change in Its Organizational and Matrix Structure," *The Economic Times*, February 17, 2012.

While GE-India is underway with its country-by-country de-matrix experiment, most other MNCs in India are not interested. Emerson, one of GE's closest competitors, has 12 different business entities in India. Emerson country head Pradipta Sen is not sold. He says, "Integrating operational responsibilities at the country head level is not such a good idea. Anything operational, by definition, is short-term focused, whereas large, multi-technology, multi-business companies like Emerson require long-term planning for fast-growing emerging markets."[4]

Product-Team Structure

To avoid the deficiencies that might arise from a permanent matrix structure, some firms are accomplishing particular strategic tasks, by means of a "temporary" or "flexible" *overlay structure*. This approach, used recently by such firms as Motorola, Matsushita, Philips, and Unilever, is meant to take *temporary* advantage of a matrix-type team while preserving an

[4]Dibeyendu Ganguly, "Matrix Evolutions: How GE Underwent a Fundamental Change in Its Organizational and Matrix Structure," *The Economic Times*, February 17, 2012.

EXHIBIT 11.7
The Product-Team Structure

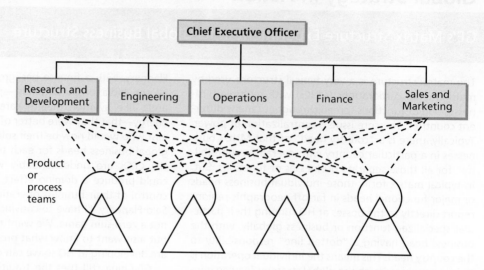

product-team structure

Assigns functional managers and specialists to a new product, project, or process team that is empowered to make major decisions about their product. Team members are assigned permanently in most cases.

underlying divisional structure. This adaptation of the matrix approach has become known as the "product-team structure." The **product-team structure** seeks to simplify and amplify the focus of resources on a narrow but strategically important product, project, market, customer, or innovation. Exhibit 11.7 illustrates how the product-team structure looks.

The product-team structure assigns functional managers and specialists (e.g., engineering, marketing, financial, R&D, operations) to a new product, project, or process team that is empowered to make major decisions about their product. The team is usually created at the inception of the new-product idea, and they stay with it indefinitely if it becomes a viable business. Instead of being assigned on a temporary basis, as in the matrix structure, team members are assigned permanently to that team in most cases. This results in much lower coordination costs and, because every function is represented, usually reduces the number of management levels above the team level needed to approve team decisions.

It appears that product teams formed at the beginning of product-development processes generate cross-functional understanding that irons out early product or process design problems. They also reduce costs associated with design, manufacturing, and marketing, while typically speeding up innovation and customer responsiveness because authority rests with the team allowing decisions to be made more quickly. That ability to make speedier, cost-saving decisions has the added advantage of eliminating the need for one or more management layers above the team level, which would traditionally have been in place to review and control these types of decisions. While seemingly obvious, it has only recently become apparent that those additional management layers were also making these decisions with less firsthand understanding of the issues involved than the cross-functional team members brought to the product or process in the first place. Exhibit 11.8, Global Strategy in Action, gives examples of a product-team approach at two well-known companies and some of the advantages that appear to have accrued.

THE NEW MILLENNIUM

BusinessWeek had an interesting issue as the world moved into the twenty-first century. That issue focused on "Twenty-first Century Companies." One thing they did was to predict what they thought would be the key differences in the "typical" global twenty-first century company compared to the "typical" large twentieth-century company. Many of the attributes they focused on inevitably relate to an organization's structure and the nature of how it goes about getting its work done. We have included those predictions by *BusinessWeek* in Exhibit 11.9.

Cross-Functional Teams Add Value at Monsanto and IBM in Implementing Innovative Strategies

Monsanto CEO Hugh Grant took over Monsanto when it was a chemical conglomerate, selling for $10 per share. Five years later, it had become a global leading producer of biotech seeds. Within the first 100 days at Monsanto, Grant's management team made the decision to reduce staff and product lines in its chemicals businesses and redirect resources to the new but still unprofitable biotech seeds business. Furthermore, they decided to abandon wheat and focus on corn, soybeans, and cotton. All were very risky bets.

To help enable this transformation of Monsanto to more high-tech, fast-changing lines of business, Grant introduced the extensive use of cross-functional teams. These teams would draw on people from five or six different functional specialties within Monsanto and focus on a specific problem related to new seeds, markets, or similar issues. That structure accelerated to an ability to commercialize the newest seed technologies, ultimately becoming a strategic advantage at Monsanto. Formerly an agriculture chemical company before Hugh Grant and his cross-functional teams, Monsanto entered 2013 as the world's largest seed company for four years running. Much of that success is attributed to Grant's aggressive strategic bet and the organizational structure of cross-functional teams in implementing it from the beginning.

IBM uses cross-functional teams consisting of hundreds of people to implement its new Smart Planet strategy.

These teams are constantly being combined, dismantled and reconfigured to work on anything from the Stockholm traffic system to a smart electric grid for the island of Malta. This constant assembly and disassembly of cross-functional teams is commonplace at IBM. Responding to the complexity of a global economy, IBM has returned to a functional structure and assembles teams to address all dimensions, whether they are products, countries, new businesses, or Smart Planet solutions. IBM can then restructure itself around any dimension. Bentley College business graduate turned **IBM** Workplace Domain Engineer Sally McSwiney is a prime example of IBM's extensive use of cross-functional teams to become more competitive in a global computer services marketplace. She said this about her role on a cross functional team: "As part of a cross-functional software product development team, I manage product requirements by working with clients, analysts, and experts to adapt the product and strengthen its position. I have regular meetings and discussions with my cross-functional team members located in North Carolina, Massachusetts, and China. And as external communicator for my team, I talk with customers, press, analysts—and provide product demos to audiences worldwide—regularly."

Source: Jay R. Galbraith, "The Multi-Dimensional and Reconfigurable Organization," 2010 Working paper accessible at http://ceo.usc.edu; and, http: www.monsanto.com/careers/Pages/meet-our-people.aspx, 2013.

Now, 15 years later, how accurate would you say their predictions have proven to be? It appears to us that they were rather accurately identifying the attributes that many companies have adopted to enable successful strategy execution today versus what was common just a few years ago. Successful organizations once required an internal focus, structured interaction, self-sufficiency, a top-down approach. Today and tomorrow, organizational structure reflects an external focus, flexible interaction, interdependency, and a bottom-up approach, just to mention a few characteristics associated with strategy execution and success. Three fundamental trends are driving decisions about effective organizational structures in the twenty-first century: globalization, the Internet, and speed of decision making.

Globalization

Pulitzer Prize–winning author Thomas Friedman[5] described the first 10 years of the twenty-first century as "Globalization 3.0." This, he says, is a whole new era in which the world is shrinking from a size "small" to a size "tiny" and flattening the global playing field for everyone at the same time. He describes it as follows:

[5]Thomas L. Friedman, *The World Is Flat* (New York: Farrar, Straus and Giroux, 2005).

EXHIBIT 11.9
What a Difference a Century Can Make

Source: From "21st Century Companies," *BusinessWeek*. Reprinted from August 28, 2000 issue of *BusinessWeek* by special permission. Copyright © 2000 by The McGraw-Hill Companies, Inc.

Contrasting Views of the Corporation		
Characteristic	**20th Century**	**21st Century**
Organization	The pyramid	The Web or network
Focus	Internal	External
Style	Structured	Flexible
Source of strength	Stability	Change
Structure	Self-sufficiency	Interdependencies
Resources	Atoms—physical assets	Bits—information
Operations	Vertical integration	Virtual integration
Products	Mass production	Mass customization
Reach	Domestic	Global
Financials	Quarterly	Real time
Inventories	Months	Hours
Strategy	Top-down	Bottom-up
Leadership	Dogmatic	Inspirational
Workers	Employees	Employees and free agents
Job expectations	Security	Personal growth
Motivation	To compete	To build
Improvements	Incremental	Revolutionary
Quality	Affordable best	No compromise

Globalization 1.0 was countries globalizing;

Globalization 2.0 was companies globalizing;

Globalization 3.0 is the newfound power for *individuals*

To collaborate and compete globally, instantly;

Individuals from every corner of the flat world are

Being empowered to enter a wide open, global marketplace.[6]

This means that companies in virtually every industry either operate globally (e.g., computers, aerospace) or will soon do so. In the past 20 years, the percentage of sales from outside the home market for these five companies grew dramatically:

	1995	2000	2005	2010	2015 est.
General Electric	16%	35%	41%	55%	75%
Walmart	0	14	22	32	50
McDonald's	46	65	71	75	80
Siemens	53	62	75	85	90
Toyota	44	53	61	75	85

The need for global coordination and innovation is forcing constant experimentation and adjustment to get the right mix of local initiative, information flow, leadership, and corporate culture. At Swedish-based Ericsson, top managers scrutinize compensation schemes to make managers pay attention to global performance and avoid turf battles, while also attending to their local operations. Companies such as Dutch electronics giant Philips regularly move headquarters for different businesses to the hottest regions for new trends—the "high voltage" markets. Its TV and home theater business is now in California; its audio business moved from Europe to Hong Kong.[7]

[6]Ibid, p. 10.
[7]www.philips.com.

Global once meant selling goods in overseas markets. Next was locating operations in numerous countries. Today companies will call on talents and resources wherever they can be found around the globe, just as they now sell worldwide. Such companies may be based in the United States, do their software programming in New Delhi, their engineering in Germany, and their manufacturing in Indonesia. Philips, the Amsterdam-based health care, lighting, and consumer products company, has manufacturing sites in 28 countries and sales outlets in 150 countries and is one of the largest multinationals in China. And that is fast becoming the norm. The ramifications for organizational structures are revolutionary.

The Internet

The World Wide Web gives everyone in the organization, or working with it—from the lowest clerk to the CEO to any supplier or customer—the ability to access a vast array of information—instantaneously, from anywhere. Ideas, requests, and instructions zap around the globe in the blink of an eye. The Net allows the global enterprise with different functions, offices, and activities dispersed around the world to be seamlessly connected so that far-flung customers, employees, and suppliers can work together in real time. The result—coordination, communication, and decision-making functions are accomplished quickly and easily, making traditional organizational structures look slow, inefficient, and noncompetitive. Take www.speedtree.com, a South Carolina–based maker of virtual foliage for video games and movies, like the tree-intense movie *Avatar*. Its largest geographic niche market for inserting trees into new video games has become Korea, even though none of its personnel have ever been there. That was all accomplished via the Internet. The ramifications of the Internet for typical business functions and the organizational structures needed to carry them out are, once again, revolutionary.

Speed

Technology, or digitization, means removing human minds and hands from an organization's most routine tasks and replacing them with computers and networks. Digitizing everything from employee benefits to accounts receivable to product design cuts cost, time, and payroll, resulting in cost savings and vast improvements in speed. "Combined with the Internet, the speed of actions, deliberations, and information will increase dramatically," predicted Intel's Andy Grove. "You are going to see unbelievable speed and efficiencies," said Cisco's John Chambers, "with many companies about to increase productivity 20 percent to 40 percent per year." Leading-edge technologies will enable employees throughout the organization to seize opportunity as it arises. These technologies will allow employees, suppliers, and freelancers anywhere in the world to converse in numerous languages online without need for a translator to develop markets, new products, new processes. Again, the ramifications for organizational structures are revolutionary.

Whether technology assisted or not, globalization of business activity creates a potential velocity of decision making that challenges traditional hierarchical organizational structures. A company like Cisco, for example, may be negotiating 50 to 60 alliances at one time due to the nature of its diverse operations. The speed at which these negotiations must be conducted and decisions made requires a simple and accommodating organizational structure lest the opportunities may be lost.

Faced with these and other major trends, what are managers doing to structure effective organizations? Let's examine this question two ways. First, we will summarize some key ways managers are changing traditional organizational structures to make them more responsive to this new reality. Second, we will examine current ideas for creating agile, virtual organizations.

INITIAL EFFORTS TO IMPROVE THE EFFECTIVENESS OF TRADITIONAL ORGANIZATIONAL STRUCTURES

Major efforts to improve traditional organizational structures seek to reduce unnecessary control and focus on enhancing core competencies, reducing costs, and opening organizations more fully to outside involvement and influence. One key emphasis in large organizations has been corporate headquarters.

Redefine the Role of Corporate Headquarters from Control to Support and Coordination

The role of corporate management in multibusiness and multinational companies increasingly face a common dilemma: how can the resource advantages of a large company be exploited, while ensuring the responsiveness and creativity found in the small companies against which each of their businesses compete? This dilemma constantly presents managers with conflicting priorities or adjustments as corporate managers:[8]

- Rigorous financial controls and reporting enable cost efficiency, resource deployment, and autonomy across different units; flexible controls are conducive to responsiveness, innovation and "boundary spanning."

- Multibusiness companies historically gain advantage by exploiting resources and capabilities across different businesses and markets, yet competitive advantage in the future increasingly depends on the creation of new resources and capabilities.

- Aggressive portfolio management seeking maximum shareholder value is often best achieved through independent businesses; the creation of competitive advantage increasingly requires the management—recognition and coordination—of business interdependencies.

Increasingly, globally engaged, multibusiness companies are changing the role of corporate headquarters from one of control, resource allocation, and performance monitoring to one of coordinator of linkages across multiple businesses, supporter, and enabler of innovation and synergy. One way this has been done is to create an executive council comprised of top managers from each business, usually including four to five of their key managers, with the council then serving as the critical forum for corporate decision, discussions, and analysis. IBM's CEO Virginia Rometty uses this approach at IBM to cross-fertilize ideas and opportunities across its software, enterprise services, chip design, and now virtual world business activities. These councils replace the traditional corporate staff function of overseeing and evaluating various business units, replacing it instead with a forum to share business unit plans, to discuss problems and issues, to seek assistance and expertise, and to foster cooperation and innovation. Exhibit 11.10, Global Strategy in Action provides an example of the need for trade-offs in control versus coordination between a global corporate headquarters and a regional part of the same company.

John Chambers's experiment at Cisco provides a useful example. He realized that Cisco's hierarchical structure was precluding it from moving quickly into new markets, so he began to group executives like cross-functional teams. Chambers figured that putting together managers in sales and leaders in engineering would break down walls. It then expanded to be a means to replace corporate executives with "councils" or "boards" composed of three to seven managers from various Cisco businesses and functional areas to quickly find synergies, opportunities, and expedite decisions.[9]

---

[8]Robert M. Grant, *Contemporary Strategy Analysis* (Oxford: Blackwell, 2001), p. 503.
[9]"Cisco Systems Layers It On," *Fortune*, December 3, 2008.

Toyota vs. Ford on Reexamining the Need for Control versus Coordination

Toyota's legendary safety challenges and eventual recalls that started with sticking accelerator pedals and went much further caused much pain for the "top quality" automobile global leader. When Jim Lentz, the American head of Toyota Motor Sales in North America, was called before a congressional committee about handling their defective automobiles, he testified under oath that he had no power to order the recall of a vehicle. Stating a longstanding fact of life at Toyota, Lentz had neither the authority nor the information to do so. Executives at other automakers were reportedly stunned. Said one top manager, "Jim Lentz saying the American management team had no say in recalls was the thing that surprised me the most. There was not a lot of cross-divisional communication."*

Toyota, some argue, has basically the same underlying functional organization it had when it first began selling cars in the United States over 50 years ago. None of its operations outside Japan are functionally integrated. Rather, they all—sales, engineering, manufacturing, and purchasing—report independently back to their functional chain of command in Japan. Some observers even reported action was delayed because of a power struggle between the powerful U.S. sales unit and other functional divisions of the global company. Lentz's predecessor, Jim Press, reportedly stepped down in 2007 after sensing he had become a "window worker," a Japanese term for an older employee with no responsibilities, when his requests to Toyota's board asking for the North American operation to be improved by strengthening communication with Toyota Motor Sales, Toyota Engineering and Manufacturing, and company headquarters in Japan were ignored.**

Meanwhile, Ford, long suffering under internal competition among executives across different functional and divisional fiefdoms as the company descended close to failing in the global recession, seemed to do just the opposite. New CEO Alan Mulally initiated weekly meetings, every Thursday, attended by all of his top functional managers, at which they were expected to share information. That way, when problems arose like a sticking accelerator or a dealership sales issue or a product design question, implications across different functions could be relayed and cooperation initiated so that a solution could be found that worked across functions more quickly. That balanced demand for integration while preserving relevant control is cited as a major reason for Ford's rebirth as a significant global automotive company once again.

*Alex Taylor III, "What's Really behind the Toyota Debacle," *Fortune*, April 14, 2010.

**Ibid.

Balance the Demands for Control/Differentiation with the Need for Coordination/Integration

Specialization of work and effort allows a unit to develop greater expertise, focus, and efficiency. So it is that some organizations adopt functional, or similar, structures. Their strategy depends on dividing different activities within the firm into logical, common groupings—sales, operations, administration, or geography—so that each set of activities can be done most efficiently. Control of sets of activities is at a premium. Dividing activities in this manner, sometimes called "differentiation," is an important structural decision. At the same time, these separate activities, however they are differentiated, need to be coordinated and integrated back together as a whole so the business functions effectively. Demands for control and the coordination needs differ across different types of businesses and strategic situations. Exhibit 11.10, Global Strategy in Action provides an interesting contrast between how this need for control versus coordination led Toyota into a major, seemingly unnecessary safety-driven setback in North America while its crippled rival, Ford, switched to a more functionally integrative approach that led to its dramatic turnaround coming out of the recent global recession.

The rise of a consumer culture around the world has led brand marketers to realize they need to take a multidomestic approach to be more responsive to local preferences. Coca-Cola, for example, used to control its products rigidly from its Atlanta headquarters. But managers have found in some markets consumers thirst for more than Coke, Diet Coke, and

Sprite. So Coke has altered its structure to reduce the need for control in favor of greater coordination/integration in local markets where local managers independently launch new flavored drinks. At the same time, GE, the paragon of new-age organization, had altered its GE Medical Systems organization structure to allow local product managers to handle everything from product design to marketing. This emphasis on local coordination and reduced central control of product design led managers obsessed with local rivalries to design and manufacture similar products for different markets—a costly and wasteful duplication of effort. So GE reintroduced centralized control of product design, with input from a worldwide base of global managers and their customers, resulting in the design of several single global products produced quite cost competitively to sell worldwide. GE's need for control of product design outweighed the coordination needs of locally focused product managers.[10] At the same time, GE obtained input from virtually every customer or potential customer worldwide before finalizing the product design of several initial products, suggesting that it rebalanced in favor of more control, but organizationally coordinated input from global managers and customers so as to ensure a better potential series of medical scanner for hospitals worldwide. Virtually all companies serving global markets face a similar organizational puzzle—how does the company integrate itself with diverse markets yet ensure adequate control and differentiation of internal units so that it executes profitably and effectively? We will examine some ways to do so later in this chapter.

Restructure to Emphasize and Support Strategically Critical Activities

restructuring

Redesigning an organizational structure with the intent of emphasizing and enabling activities most critical to a firm's strategy to function at maximum effectiveness.

Restructuring is redesigning an organizational structure with the intent of emphasizing and enabling activities most critical to the firm's strategy to function at maximum effectiveness. At the heart of the restructuring trend is the notion that some activities within a business's value chain are more critical to the success of the business's strategy than others. Walmart's organizational structure is designed to ensure that its impressive logistics and purchasing competitive advantages operate flawlessly. Coordinating daily logistical and purchasing efficiencies among separate stores lets Walmart lead the industry in profitability yet sell retail for less than many competitors buy the same merchandise at wholesale. Qualcomm's organizational structure is designed to protect and nurture its legendary R&D and new-product development capabilities—spending over twice the industry average in R&D alone each year. Qualcomm's R&D emphasis continually spawns proprietary technologies that support its technology-based competitive advantage. Coca-Cola emphasizes the importance of distribution activities, advertising, and retail support to its bottlers in its organizational structure. All three of these companies emphasize very different parts of the value chain process, but they are extraordinarily successful in part because they have designed their organizational structures to emphasize and support strategically critical activities. Two developments that have become key ways many of these firms have sought to improve their emphasis and support of strategic activities are business process reengineering and downsizing/self-management.

business process reengineering

A customer-centric restructuring approach. It involves fundamental rethinking and radical redesigning of a business process so that a company can best create value for the customer by eliminating barriers that create distance between employees and customers.

Business process reengineering (BPR) was originally advocated by consultants Michael Hammer and James Champy[11] as a "customer-centric" restructuring approach. BPR is intended to place the decision-making authority that is most relevant to the customer closer to the customer, in order to make the firm more responsive to the needs of the customer. This is accomplished through a form of empowerment, facilitated by revamping organizational structure.

---

[10]"Innovation," 2010 GE Annual Report, access through www.ge.com.
[11]Michael Hammer, *The Agenda* (New York: Random House, 2001); and Michael Hammer and James Champy, *Reengineering the Corporation* (New York: HarperBusiness, 1993).

Business reengineering reduces fragmentation by crossing traditional departmental lines and reducing overhead to compress formerly separate steps and tasks that are strategically intertwined in the process of meeting customer needs. This "process orientation," rather than a traditional functional orientation, becomes the perspective around which various activities and tasks are then grouped to create the building blocks of the organization's structure. This is usually accomplished by assembling a multifunctional, multilevel team (the product-team approach discussed earlier) that begins by identifying customer needs and how the customer wants to deal with the firm. Customer focus must permeate all phases. Companies that have successfully reengineered their operations around strategically critical business processes have pursued the following steps:[12]

- Develop a flowchart of the total business process, including its interfaces with other value chain activities.

- Try to simplify the process first, eliminating tasks and steps where possible and analyzing how to streamline the performance of what remains.

- Determine which parts of the process can be automated (usually those that are repetitive, time-consuming, and require little thought or decision); consider introducing advanced technologies that can be upgraded to achieve next-generation capability and provide a basis for further productivity gains down the road.

- Evaluate each activity in the process to determine whether it is strategy-critical or not. Strategy-critical activities are candidates for benchmarking to achieve best-in-industry or best-in-world performance status—and ones to emphasize in reengineered organizational structures.

- Weigh the pros and cons of outsourcing activities that are noncritical or that contribute little to organizational capabilities and core competencies.

- Design a structure for performing the activities that remain; reorganize the personnel and groups who perform these activities into the new structure.

IBM provides a good example of reengineering. As globalization started to take hold in the world's economy, IBM was struggling to survive. To do so, it embraced reengineering—with efforts designed to simplify its enormous complexity associated with its highly decentralized organization. Said its CEO at the time, "It's called reengineering. It's called getting competitive. It's called reducing cycle time and cost, flattening organizations, increasing customer responsiveness. All of this requires close collaboration with the customer, with suppliers, and with vendors." That effort helped save IBM from a steady, PC-maker-based decline. Aspects of that effort, which centered on reengineering processes and approaches at IBM for more closely collaborating with its customers and within itself as it did so, continue to this day as a new IBM division. CEO Sam Palmisano made the following observation about that reengineering as it was gaining significant traction within IBM:

> IBM has developed a system that lets it shift work to the areas with available skills at the lowest-available costs. The goal is to deliver higher-quality services at competitive prices. Clearly one opportunity associated with globalization is costs. You have access to expertise wherever it is in the world—if you have the infrastructure and the relationships to take advantage of it.[13]

From those lessons it learned on itself, Palmisano and his team sought to create a services capability within IBM to adapt its own reengineering experiences into a new business

---

[12]Alexis Leon, *ERP Demystified*, 2nd. ed. (New Delhi, India: Tata McGraw-Hill, 2008), pp. 99–208.
[13]Steve Hamm, "Big Blue Wields the Knife Again," *BusinessWeek*, May 30, 2007.

Exhibit 11.11

From Reengineering to Reinvention: The IBM Journey from Reengineering Itself to Becoming an "On Demand Business" to IBM Global Business Services

Facing a challenge of sheer survival, IBM looked intensely at all of its business processes. Eventually, IBM leveraged the Internet and global connectivity to simplify access to information and enable simple, Web-based transactions. The company integrated processes both within the business and among a group of core clients, partners, and suppliers. For example, IBM created a master database, dubbed the "Blue Monster," of all its service employees—where they were, what they worked on, what their expertise and experiences were, and so on. While IBM reaped enormous efficiency gains from these efforts, it saw opportunities to continuously reengineer and challenge long-accepted practices, processes, and organizational structures that limited its—and most other companies'—options in the face of globalization, industry consolidation, and disruptive technologies.

This became a real business opportunity at IBM. Dubbing it "On Demand Business," IBM committed itself to becoming not simply a case study, but a living laboratory for figuring out what business services could be shaped into services it would be able to offer on demand inside IBM and eventually outside to large businesses and other organizations immediately after being asked to do so. The company identified key business characteristics—horizontally integrated, flexible, and responsive—and the IT infrastructure needed to

produce its enterprise transformation—integrated, open, virtualized, and autonomic. IBM focused on tackling the complex issues surrounding significant changes to essential business processes, organizational culture, and IT infrastructure and worked to find new ways to access, deploy, and finance solutions. IBM's on demand experiment became IBM Global Business Services.

Today, IBM is hitting a new stride. A powerful combination of innovation and value creation is driving top-line revenue growth. Client satisfaction is climbing. And the company continues to operate in a highly disciplined manner, focusing on increased productivity and IT optimization to drive bottom-line earnings. Because this is precisely the type of growth that tops the majority of CEOs' agendas, many will find IBM's story particularly timely and relevant. IBM has gone from doing this for its top 25 clients in seven countries to over 2,500 global companies and organizations generating more than $20 billion in sales in 2013 from Global Business Services alone. And that number is steadily rising as IBM Global Business Services leverages its expertise in an increasingly digital world.

Source: http://www-03.ibm.com/industries/healthcare/doc/content/resource/insight/1591291105.html? g_type=rssfeed_leaf; and Carl, "IBM Achieves $100 bn in Sales in 2010," www.KitGuru.net, January 19, 2011.

---

downsizing
Eliminating the number of employees, particularly middle management, in a company.

self-management
Allowing work groups or work teams to supervise and administer their work as a group or team without a direct supervisor exercising the supervisory role. These teams set parameters of their work, make decisions about work-related matters, and perform most of the managerial functions previously done by their direct supervisor.

seeking to sell that know how to other global companies. Starting with 25 key clients buying IBM's "On Demand Business" service, that has now become its Global Business Services division, a major growth area for IBM, as described in Exhibit 11.11, Global Strategy in Action. Downsizing and self-management at operating levels are additional ways companies restructure critical activities. **Downsizing** is eliminating the number of employees, particularly middle management, in a company. The arrival of a global marketplace, information technology, and intense competition caused many companies to reevaluate middle management activities to determine just what value was really being added to the company's products and services. The result of this scrutiny, along with continuous improvements in information processing technology, has been widespread downsizing of the number of management personnel in thousands of companies worldwide. Bloomberg Businessweek Executive Editor John Byrne has spent years observing and writing about downsizing, delayering, and self-management in leading global companies over the course of a distinguished business journalism and consulting career. A synthesis of his observations about these organizational structure considerations is provided in Global Strategy in Action, Exhibit 11.12.

One of the outcomes of downsizing was increased **self-management** at operating levels of the company. Cutbacks in the number of management people left those who remained with more work to do. The result was that remaining managers had to give up a good measure of control to operating personnel. Spans of control, traditionally thought to

Delayering and empowering—what are some key questions, and answers?

Question	Answer
How many management layers between the CEO and the work level?	Many large companies had up to 12; most have cut that to 4 or 5; above 6 is seen as excess now.
What is the new span of control?	Many companies see up to 1 manager for 30 subordinates; 1: 8 or less is seen as excess now.
How much work or how many tasks are cut when delayering and empowering?	Part of delayering is eliminating unnecessary or redundant work. Should see management tasks reduced by 25 percent to 50 percent in a successful effort.
What skills are key for remaining managers and work teams?	The skill to accept more responsibility and the ability to identify and eliminate unneeded work.
How large should your largest profit center be?	Some argue, even in the biggest firm, that breaking operating units into less than 500 people is wise . . . gaining entrepreneurial tendencies and losing bureaucracy.
What should happen at corporate headquarters given fewer layers?	Surprisingly, to some, the largest reductions on a percentage basis should come at corporate headquarters. It is typically overstaffed, and far from customers.

virtual organization
A temporary network of independent companies—suppliers, customers, subcontractors, and even competitors—linked primarily by information technology to share skills, access to markets, and costs.

maximize at under 10 people, have become much larger due to information technology, running "lean and mean," and delegation to lower levels. Ameritech, for example, has seen its spans of control rise to as much as 30 to 1 in some divisions because most of the people who did staff work—financial analysts, assistant managers, and so on—have disappeared. This delegation, also known as *empowerment,* is accomplished through concepts such as self-managed work groups, reengineering, and automation. It is also seen through efforts to create distinct businesses within a business—conceiving a business as a confederation of many "small" businesses, rather than one large, interconnected business. Whatever the terminology, the idea is to push decision making down in the organization by allowing major management decisions to be made at operating levels. The result is often the elimination of up to half the levels of management previously existing in an organizational structure.

CREATING AGILE, VIRTUAL ORGANIZATIONS

Corporations today are increasingly seeing their "structure" become an elaborate network of external and internal relationships. This organizational phenomenon has been termed the **virtual organization,** which is defined as a temporary network of independent companies—suppliers, customers, subcontractors, even competitors—linked primarily by information

agile organization
A firm that identifies a set of business capabilities central to high-profitability operations and then builds a virtual organization around those capabilities.

technology to share skills, access to markets, and costs.[14] An **agile organization** is one that identifies a set of business capabilities central to high-profitability operations and then builds a virtual organization around those capabilities, allowing the agile firm to build its business around the core, high-profitability information, services, and products. Creating an agile, virtual organization structure involves outsourcing, strategic alliances, a boundaryless structure, an ambidextrous learning approach, and Web-based organization. Let's examine each of the approaches to creating a virtual organization in more detail.

Outsourcing—Creating a Modular Organization

outsourcing
Obtaining work previously done by employees inside the companies from sources outside the company.

Outsourcing was an early driving force for the virtual organization trend. Dell does not make PCs. Cisco doesn't make its world renowned routers. Motorola doesn't make cell phones. **Outsourcing** is simply obtaining work previously done by employees inside the companies from sources outside the company. Managers have found that as they attempt to restructure their organizations, particularly if they do so from a business process orientation, numerous activities can often be found in their company that are not "strategically critical activities." This has particularly been the case with numerous staff activities and administrative control processes previously the domain of various middle management levels in an organization. But it can also refer to primary activities that are steps in their business's value chain—purchasing, shipping, manufacturing, and so on. Further scrutiny has led managers to conclude that these activities either add little or no value to the product or services, or that they can be done much more cost effectively (and competently) by other businesses specializing in these activities. If this is so, then the business can enhance its competitive advantage by outsourcing the activities.

modular organization
An organization structured via outsourcing where the organization's final product or service is based on the combination of several companies' self-contained skills and business capabilities.

Choosing to outsource activities has been likened to creating a "modular" organization. A **modular organization** provides products or services using different, self-contained specialists or companies brought together—outsourced—to contribute their primary or support activity to result in a successful outcome. Dell is a "modular" organization because it uses outsourced manufacturers and assemblers to provide parts and assemble its computers. It also uses outsourced customer service providers in different parts of the world to provide most of its customer service and support activities. These outsourced providers are independent companies, many of which offer similar services to other companies including, in some cases, Dell's competitors. Dell remains the umbrella organization and controlling organization in fact and certainly in the customers' mind, yet it is able to do so based on putting together a variety of "modules" or parts because of its ability to provide computers and related services through extensive dependence on outsourcing.

Many organizations long ago started outsourcing functions like payroll and benefits administration—routine administrative functions more easily and cost effectively done by a firm specializing in that activity. But outsourcing quickly moved into virtually every

---

[14]Early identification of the rise of the "virtual organization" was found in W. H. Davidow and M. S. Malone, *The Virtual Corporation* (New York: Harper, 1992); and Steven Goldman, *Agile Competitors and Virtual Organizations* (New York: Van Nostrand Reinhold, 1995). As virtual organizations have become mainstream, additional coverage of use for further reading can be found in books like Malcolm Warner and Morgen Witzel, *Managing in Virtual Organizations* (London: Thomson, 2008), *The Economist's* "The Virtual Organisation," Nov. 23, 2009; or research like Rene Algesheimer, Utpal M. Dholakia, and Calin Gurau, "Virtual Team Performance in a Highly Competitive Environment," *Group Organization Management* 36, no. 2 (March 15, 2011), pp. 161–190. It is interesting that NSF allocates research attention to evolving virtual organizations with a program called "VOSS: Virtual Organizations as Sociotechnical Systems," allocating $3 million for annual research; see NSF 09 Jan 2013 solicitation from its Office of Cyber Infrastructure; and, finally the focus on virtual organizations has become academic mainstream as evidenced by the University of Phoenix's use of "virtual organizations" as a way to customize business education as can be seen at: http://www.phoenix.edu/students/how-it-works/innovative_education_technology/virtual-organizations.html, 2012.

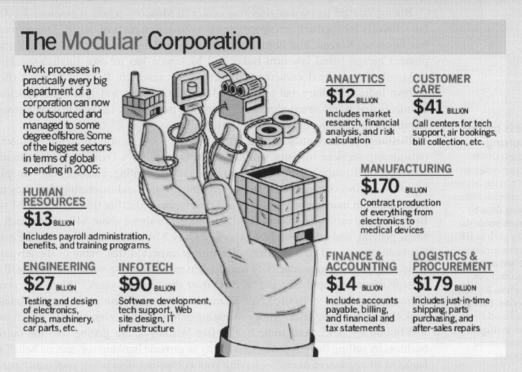

The Modular Corporation

Work processes in practically every big department of a corporation can now be outsourced and managed to some degree offshore. Some of the biggest sectors in terms of global spending in 2005:

HUMAN RESOURCES

$13 BILLION

Includes payroll administration, benefits, and training programs.

ENGINEERING

$27 BILLION

Testing and design of electronics, chips, machinery, car parts, etc.

INFOTECH

$90 BILLION

Software development, tech support, Web site design, IT infrastructure

ANALYTICS

$12 BILLION

Includes market research, financial analysis, and risk calculation

CUSTOMER CARE

$41 BILLION

Call centers for tech support, air bookings, bill collection, etc.

MANUFACTURING

$170 BILLION

Contract production of everything from electronics to medical devices

FINANCE & ACCOUNTING

$14 BILLION

Includes accounts payable, billing, and financial and tax statements

LOGISTICS & PROCUREMENT

$179 BILLION

Includes just-in-time shipping, parts purchasing, and after-sales repairs

Source: "The Modular Corporation," *BusinessWeek.* Reprinted from January 30, 2006 issue of *BusinessWeek* by special permission. Copyright © 2006 by The McGraw-Hill Companies.

aspect of what a business does to provide the products and services it exists to provide. Global Strategy in Action, Exhibit 11.13 shows the biggest sectors for outsourcing 10 years ago when outsourcing and creating modular organizations started to take hold in just U.S.-based companies. These levels have increased five to 10 times since then. Just think, the UK's Virgin Group briefly held 5 percent of the British cola market with just five employees. This was achieved by narrowly focusing on Virgin's core competence—marketing. Everything else, from making the drink to distribution and delivery, was done by other companies.[15] And not only large companies are involved. A New York insurance company was once started from scratch by someone whose overriding aim was to employ no one but himself.[16] Veteran entrepreneur and co-founder of Celestial Seasonings, Wyck Hay, having sold that company to Kraft Foods for $40 million, returned from retirement several years later to build a new company, Kaboom Beverages, in California. Seeking to avoid the hassle of managing people directly, Hay built a totally modular company, outsourcing every function in the company except the owner/manager role to a variety of specialists and specialized companies. Today, the Web has made this even easier. As we write, Elance.com had 200,000 programmers, 22,000 mobile developers, 150,000 designers, 200,000 writers, and 50,000 marketers offering their services as freelancers through that one site, with over

[15]"The Virtual Organization," *The Economist*, Nov. 23, 2009.
[16]Ibid.

100,000 companies posting "jobs" each month. Elance.com is part of a global fabric making modular organizations ever easier to build, combining world-class talent wherever it resides, into a company's ability to deliver the best product and service it can.

Boeing opened its own engineering center in Moscow, where it employs 1,100 skilled but relatively inexpensive aerospace engineers to design parts of the 787 Dreamliner. It also has Japanese, Korean, and European companies making various parts of that critical new plane. Chicago-based law firm Baker and Mckenzie has its own English-speaking team in Manila that drafts documents and does market research. Bank of America (BoA) has its own India subsidiary, but also teamed up with InfoSys and Tata Consultancies—BoA estimates that it has saved almost $200 million in IT work in their first two years, while improving product quality at the same time.

Business process outsourcing (BPO) is the most rapidly growing segment of the outsourcing services industry worldwide. BPO includes a broad array of administrative functions—HR, supply procurement, finance and accounting, customer care, supply-chain logistics, engineering, research and development, sales and marketing, facilities management and even management training and development. Earlier this decade, IBM strategist Bruce Harreld estimated that the world's companies spend about $19 trillion each year on sales, general, and administrative expenses. Only $14 trillion-worth of this, he estimated, has been outsourced to other firms. He further expected that many of the advantages in scale, wage rates, and productivity found when manufacturing was outsourced will quickly emerge driving a rapid increase in BPO over the next 10 years.[17] Many big companies estimate they could outsource half or more of this work currently done in-house. U.S. banks are outsourcing back-office processing duties at an accelerated rate, which exceeded $70 billion by 2015. And some banks, like Wachovia, are getting into the outsourcing business by selling their expertise and ability to provide banking services on behalf of other banks in an aggressive manner—having your competitor also being your outsource partner in some aspects of your banking business.[18] Yet banking services currently deliver less than 10 percent of their services remotely—a major global outsourcing opportunity.

Perhaps the more controversial outsourcing trends involve product design and even innovation activities. Particularly in consumer electronics markets, companies such as Dell, Motorola, and Philips are buying complete designs of some digital devices from Asian developers, tweaking them to their own specifications, and just adding their brand name before selling or having a more effective sales channel sell the product for them. This trend seems to be spreading. Boeing works with an Indian software company to develop its software for landing gear, navigation systems, and cockpit controls in its newest planes. Procter & Gamble, the consummate innovator, targeted and reached half of its new-product ideas by 2010 to come from outside the company—outsourced R&D or innovation—versus 20 percent five years earlier. Eli Lilly has outsourced selected biotech research for new drugs to an Asian biotech research firm. Consider this admonition in a still widely referenced *BusinessWeek* article:

> The result is a rethinking of the structure of the modern corporation. What, specifically, has to be done in-house anymore? At a minimum, most leading Western companies are turning toward a new model of innovation, one that employs global networks of partners. These can include U.S. chipmakers, Taiwanese engineers, Indian software developers, and Chinese factories. IBM is even offering the smarts of its famed research labs and a new global team of 1,200 engineers to help customers develop future products using next-generation

business process outsourcing
Having an outside company manage numerous routine business management activities previously done by employees inside the company such as HR, supply procurement, finance and accounting, customer care, supply-chain logistics, engineering, R&D, sales and marketing, facilities management, and management/development.

[17]J. Bruce Harreld, Senior Lecturer, Harvard Business School.
[18]Bob Gach, "Banks Outsourcing: New Routes to Bottom Line," *Financial News,* June 12, 2013.

technologies. When the whole chain works in sync, there can be a dramatic leap in the speed and efficiency of product development.[19]

Outsourcing as a means to create an agile, virtual organization has many potential advantages:

1. *It can lower costs incurred when the activity done in-house is outsourced.*

An accountant with a masters degree from UGA working for Ernst & Young in Atlanta, Georgia, costs E&Y at least $75,000 annually. Her colleague with the same education, returning to her native Philippines to live, works on a similar E&Y audit team in Southeast Asia and via the Internet in the United States—$7,000 annual salary.

2. *It can reduce the amount of capital a firm must invest in production or service capacity.*

Lenovo will cover the capital expenditure for its new Chinese PC manufacturing facilities; IBM will not. IBM will sell Lenovo its existing PC manufacturing facilities around the world, freeing up that capital for investment in IBM's development of its Global Business Services core competencies, and just buy PCs very cheaply from Lenovo as it needs them. It will include a markup in doing so to pass along to its IT management services clients.

3. *The firm's managers and personnel can concentrate on mission-critical activities.*

As noted in the preceding example, not only does IBM free up capital, but it frees up its people and remaining capital to focus more intensely on its new emphasis on IT systems, BPO, and consulting.

4. *This concentration and focus allow the firm to control and enhance the source of its core competitive advantage.*

Dell outsources the manufacture of its computers. It carefully controls and continuously improves its Web-based direct sales capability so that it increasingly distances itself from the closest competitors. It is able to build such a strong direct sales capability because that is virtually all it concentrates on, even though it is a computer company.

5. *Careful selection of outsourced partners allows the firm to potentially learn and develop its abilities through ideas and capabilities that emerge from the growing expertise and scope of work done by the outsource partner for several firms.*

Outsourced cell phone manufacturers in Korea and Taiwan have become large providers to several large, global cell phone companies. Their product design prototypes and improvements for one client quickly find their way to the attention of other clients. Their improvement in logistics with some firms becomes knowledge incorporated in their dealings with another client.

Outsourcing is not without its "cons," however. There are several:

1. *Outsourcing involves loss of some control and reliance on "outsiders."*

By definition, outsourcing places control of that function or activity "outside" the requesting firm. This loss of control can result in many future problems such as delays, quality issues, customer complaints, and loss of competitor-sensitive information. Recent thefts of personal ID information from U.S.–based bank clients using major information management outsourcing services from Indian companies have caused major problems for the banks obtaining these services.

---

[19]Pete Engardio and Bruce Einhorn, "Outsourcing Innovation," *BusinessWeek*, March, 2005; see Michael A. Stanko, Johnathan D. Bohlmann, and Roger J. Calantone, "Outsourcing Innovation," *The Wall Street Journal*, June 14, 2002 for a more in-depth treatment of this issue.

2. *Outsourcing can create future competitors.*

Companies that supply the firm with basic IT services or software programming assistance or product design services may one day move "up the chain" to undertake the higher level work the firm was attempting to reserve for itself. IBM has outsourced considerable work to Indian companies related to its "value-added" IT system management services—its strategic future. It now is experiencing competition from some of these former suppliers of programming support that have become multi-billion-dollar software and IT service providers in their own right.

3. *Skills important to a product or service are "lost."*

While things a company does may not be considered essential to its core competency, they still may be quite important. And as it continues over time to outsource that activity, it loses any capacity in the firm of being able to do it effectively. That, potentially, leaves the company vulnerable.

4. *Outsourcing may cause negative reaction from the public and investors.*

Outsourcing manufacturing, tech support, and back-office work may make sense to investors, but product design and innovation? Asking what value the company is providing and protecting will be an obvious potential reaction. Publicly, the loss of jobs from home country to low-cost alternative locations represents difficult job losses and transitions for people who bring political heat.

5. *Crafting good legal agreements, especially for services, is difficult.*

When outsourced manufacturers send product, you take delivery, inspect, and pay. When service providers supply a service, it is a continuous process. Bottom line: it takes considerable trust and cross-cultural understanding to work.

6. *The company may get locked into long-term contracts at costs that are no longer competitive.*

Multiyear IT management contracts can be both complex and based on costs that are soon noncompetitive because of other sources providing much more cost-effective solutions.

7. *Costs aren't everything: What if my supplier underbids?*

EDS (Dallas, Texas) has a multiyear contract as an outsource provider to the U.S. Navy to provide IT services and consolidate 70,000 different IT systems. Two years into the contract, in 2005, it was $1.5 billion in the red. It hopes to make that heavy loss up over the life of the contract. But what if it was a smaller company and couldn't afford to carry a loss for a contract it poorly bid?

8. *Outsourcing can lead to increasingly fragmented work cultures where low-paid workers get the work done with little initiative or enthusiasm.*

"A mercenary may shoot a gun the same as a soldier, but he will not create a revolution, build a new society, or die for the homeland," said a Silicon Valley manager who objects to his company's turning to contract workers for services.[20]

9. *Intellectual property development and ownership can be complicated.*

Several manufacturers outsourcing work to some Asian manufacturers have experienced these companies seeking ways to incrementally improve the products and processes by which they make them over time. Who owns those improvements? May the manufacturer also become its own seller of the incrementally improved, yet now "their" own version of and competitor to the original product? And progressive development and protection of intellectual property often comes from the daily processes of making, assembling, and simply figuring out ways to do current activities, processes, and products or services

[20]"Time to Bring It Back," *The Economist*, March 3, 2005.

better—incremental innovation. So giving up control of that aspect of a product or services creation can result in lost future value.[21]

Its potential disadvantages not withstanding, outsourcing has become a key, standard means by which agile, virtual organization structures are built. It has become an essential building block; most firms in any market anywhere in the world structure some of their business activities to allow them to remain cost competitive, dynamic, and able to develop their future core competencies. As outsourcing moves from sourcing manufacturing and IT management to all business management processes, careful attention and efforts to build trust and cross-cultural understanding will be important as will effective contractual arrangements to govern multiyear, ongoing relationships.

Strategic Alliances

strategic alliances
Alliances with suppliers, partners, contractors, and other providers that allow partners in the alliance to focus on what they do best, farm out everything else, and quickly provide value to the customer.

Strategic alliances are arrangements between two or more companies in which they both contribute capabilities, resources, or expertise to a joint undertaking, usually with an identity of its own, with each firm giving up overall control in return for the potential to participate in and benefit from the joint venture relationship. They are different from outsourcing relationships because the requesting company usually retains control when outsourcing, whereas strategic alliances involve firms giving up overall control to the joint entity, or alliance, in which they become a partner. Texas-based EDS was awaiting word at the time of this writing on whether the "Atlas Consortium" would be awarded a 10-year, $7.6 billion contract to manage 150,000 computers and networking software for British military personnel. The Atlas Consortium is a strategic alliance, formed by EDS as the "lead" firm with the Dutch firm LogicaCMG and a British subsidiary of the defense company, EADS, as full partners. While EDS is the "lead" member of the alliance, final control of the alliance rests not in EDS but in the governance that all three partners have the right to influence and shape.

This is a good example of a strategic alliance—three different firms all with other major business commitments and activities. They have joined together, investing time, analysis resources, and negotiations so as to be in a position to bid as a team (or alliance) on a major 10-year contract. In a few weeks they will know. If they get the contract, then their alliance will have a lengthy commitment to the British military and their firms to the Atlas Consortium. If they don't, then they may or may not work together to pursue other deals. But this relationship allowed each firm to seek work it could not have otherwise pursued independently because of restrictions imposed by the British government, the limitations of each firm individually, or both. It expanded the exposure of each firm to the other, to selected markets, to the building of relationships that may be usefully leveraged in each company's interests in the future.

Strategic alliances can be for long-term or for very short periods. Engaging in alliances, whether long-term or one time, lets each participant take advantage of fleeting opportunities quickly, usually without tying up vast amounts of capital. Strategic alliances allow companies with world-class capabilities to partner together in a way that combines different core competencies so that within the alliance each can focus on what they do best, but the alliance can pull together what is necessary to quickly provide superior value to the customer. FedEx and the U.S. Postal Service have formed an alliance—FedEx planes carry USPS next-day letters and USPS delivers FedEx ground packages—to allow both to challenge their common rival, UPS.

[21]Subroto Roy and K. Sivakumar, "Managing Intellectual Property in Global Outsourcing for Innovation Generation," *The Journal of Product Innovation Management* 28, no. 1 (2011).

Strategic alliances have the following pros and cons for firms seeking agile, responsive organizational structures:

Advantages

1. *Leverages several firms' core competencies.*

This allows alliance members to be more competitive in seeking certain project work or input.

2. *Limits capital investment.*

One partner firm does not have to have all the resources necessary to do the work of the alliance.

3. *Is flexible.*

Alliances allow a firm to be involved yet continue to pursue its other, "regular" business opportunities.

4. *Leads to networking and relationship building.*

Alliances get companies together, sometimes even competitors. They allow key players to build relationships that are valuable, even if the present alliance doesn't "pan out." Alliance partners learn more about each others' capabilities and gain advantage or benefit from referrals and other similar behaviors, creating win–win situations.

Disadvantages

1. *Can result in loss of control.*

A firm in an alliance by definition cedes ultimate control to the broader alliance for the undertaking for which the alliance is formed. This can prove problematic if the alliance doesn't work out as planned—or is not well planned.

2. *Can be hard to establish good management control of the project—loss of operational control.*

Where multiple firms have interrelated responsibilities for a sizable joint project, it should not be difficult to imagine problems arising as the players go about implementing a major project as in the example of EDS and its Dutch and British partners in the Atlas Consortium. It requires good up-front planning and use of intercompany project team groups early on in the bidding process.

3. *Can distract a participating company's management and key players.*

One strategic alliance can consume the majority attention of key players essential to the overall success of the "home" company. Whether because of their technical skills, managerial skills, key roles, or all three, the potential for lost focus or time to devote to key responsibilities exists.

4. *Raises issues of control of proprietary information and intellectual property.*

Where technology development is the focus of the alliance, or maybe part of it, firms partnered together may also compete in other circumstances. Or they may have the potential to do so. So partnering together gives each the opportunity to learn much more about the other, their contacts, capabilities, and unique skills or trade secrets.

Strategic alliances have proven a very popular mechanism for many companies seeking to become more agile competitors in today's dynamic global economy. They have proven a major way for small companies to become involved with large players to the benefit of both—allowing the smaller player to grow in a way that builds its future survival possibilities and the larger player to tap expertise and knowledge it can no longer afford to retain or develop in-house.

Toward Boundaryless Structures

boundaryless organization
Organizational structure that allows people to interface with others throughout the organization without need to wait for a hierarchy to regulate that interface across functional, business, and geographic boundaries.

horizontal boundaries
Rules of communication, access, and protocol for dealing with different departments or functions or processes within an organization.

vertical boundaries
Limitations on interaction, contact, and access between operations and management personnel; between different levels of management; and between different organizational parts like corporate versus divisional units.

geographic boundaries
Limitations on interaction and contact between people in a company based on being at different physical locations domestically and globally.

external interface boundaries
Formal and informal rules, locations, and protocol that separate and/or dictate the interaction between members of an organization and those outside the organization—customers, suppliers, partners, regulators, associations, and even competitors.

Management icon Jack Welch[22] is recognized worldwide for his success as a global executive, his teaching of management and leadership, and his insight into making organizations more effective. When he was leading General Electric, he coined the term **boundaryless organization** to characterize his vision of what he wanted GE to become: to be able to generate knowledge, share knowledge, and get knowledge to the places it could be best used to provide superior value. A key component of this concept was erasing internal divisions so the people in the company could work across functional, business, and geographic boundaries to achieve an integrated diversity—the ability to transfer the best ideas, the most developed knowledge, and the most valuable people quickly, easily, and freely throughout the organization.

Boundaries, or borders, arise in four "directions" based on the ways we traditionally structure and run organizations:

1. **Horizontal boundaries**—between different departments or functions in a firm. Salespeople are different from administrative people or operating people or engineering people. One division is separate from another.
2. **Vertical boundaries**—between operations and management, and levels of management; between "corporate" and "division," in virtually every organization.
3. **Geographic boundaries**—between different physical locations; between different countries or regions of the world (or even within a country) and between cultures.
4. **External interface boundaries**—between a company and its customers, suppliers, partners, regulators, and, indeed, its competitors.

Outsourcing, strategic alliances, product-team structures, reengineering, restructuring—all are ways to move toward boundaryless organization. Culture and shared values across an organization that value boundaryless behavior and cooperation help enable these efforts to work.

As we noted at the beginning of this section, globalization has accelerated many changes in the way organizations are structured, and that is certainly driving the recognition by many organizations of their need to become more boundaryless, to become an agile, virtual organization. Technology, particularly driven by the Internet, has and will be a major driver of the boundaryless organization. Commenting on technology's effect on Cisco, John Chambers observed that with all its outsourcing and strategic alliances, roughly 90 percent of all orders come into Cisco without ever being touched by human hands. "To my customers, it looks like one big virtual plant where my suppliers and inventory systems are directly tied into our virtual organization," he said. "That will be the norm in the future. Everything will be completely connected, both within a company and between companies. We will become boundaryless. The people who get that will have a huge competitive advantage."[23]

The Web's contribution electronically has simultaneously become the best analogy in explaining the future boundaryless organization. And it is not just the Web as in the Internet, but a weblike shape of successful organizational structures in the future. If there are a pair of images that symbolize the vast changes at work, they are the pyramid and the web. The organizational chart of large-scale enterprise had long been defined as a pyramid of ever-shrinking layers leading to an omnipotent CEO at its apex. The twenty-first-century corporation, in contrast, is far more likely to look like a web: a flat, intricately woven form that links partners, employees, external contractors, suppliers, and customers in various collaborations. The players will grow more and more interdependent. Fewer companies

---

[22]www.welchway.com.
[23]http://blogs.cisco.com/collaboration, 2011.

EXHIBIT 11.14

From Traditional Structure to B-Web Structure

Source: Reprinted by permission of Harvard Business School Publishing. Exhibit from *Digital Capital: Harnessing the Power of Business Webs,* by Don Tapscott, David Ticoll and Alex Lowy. Copyright 2000 by the Harvard Business School Publishing Corporation; all rights reserved.

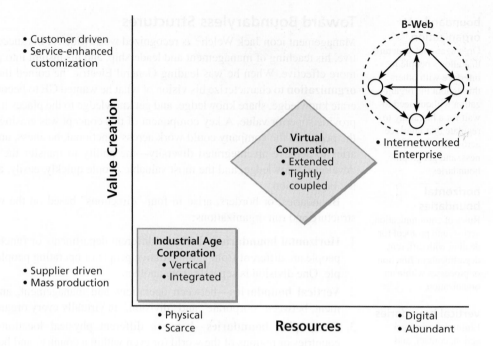

will try to master all the disciplines necessary to produce and market their goods but will instead outsource skills—from research and development to manufacturing—to outsiders who can perform those functions with greater efficiency.[24]

Exhibit 11.14 illustrates this evolution in organization structure to what it predicted would become the B-Web, a truly Internet-driven form of organization designed to deliver speedy, customized, service-enhanced products to savvy customers from an integrated boundaryless B-Web organization, pulling together abundant, world-class resources digitally. Take Colgate-Palmolive. The company needed a more efficient method for getting its toothpaste into the tube—a seemingly straightforward problem. When its internal R&D team came up empty-handed, the company posted the specs on InnoCentive, one of many new marketplaces that link problems with problem-solvers. A Canadian engineer named Ed Melcarek proposed putting a positive charge on fluoride powder, then grounding the tube. It was an effective application of elementary physics, but not one that Colgate-Palmolive's team of chemists had ever contemplated. Melcarek was duly rewarded with $25,000 for a few hours' work. Today, some 120,000 scientists like Melcarek have registered with Inno-Centive and hundreds of companies pay annual fees of roughly $80,000 to tap the talents of a global scientific community. Launched as an e-business venture by U.S. pharmaceutical giant Eli Lilly, the company now provides on-demand solutions to innovation-hungry titans such as Boeing, Dow, DuPont, P&G, and Novartis.[25]

Managing this intricate network of partners, spin-off enterprises, contractors, and freelancers will be as important as managing internal operations. Indeed, it will be hard to tell the difference. All of these constituents will be directly linked in ways that will make it nearly impossible for outsiders to know where an individual firm begins and where it ends. "Companies will be much more molecular and fluid," predicted futurist Don Tapscott, co-author

[24]John Byrne, Executive Editor, Bloomberg Businessweek.
[25]www.innocentive.com. See also Don Tapscott, *grown up digital* (New York: McGraw-Hill, 2008); and Don Tapscott and Anthony D. Williams, *MacroWikinomics* (New York: The Penguin Group, 2010).

of *Digital Capital* and more recently, *MacroWikinomics*. "They will be autonomous business units connected not necessarily by a big building but across geographies all based on networks. The boundaries of the firm will be not only fluid or blurred but in some cases hard to define.[26] Just as events in Northern Africa and the Middle East in 2011 amazed the world, they also showed the power for change enabled by social media and Internet connections to bring individual to individual yet simultaneous collective action on a mass scale, instantaneously. Tapscott and Williams suggest that such developments are also images of the nature and speed of collaboration and action and idea exchange enabled by the Web in B-Web organizational structures, or what they now call Enterprise 2.0. Rapid sharing of information, ideas, action, and movement in all aspects of an enterprise are taken quickly rather than the plodding dinosaur-like action of their not so old predecessor organizational structures.[27]

Ambidextrous Learning Organizations

The evolution of the virtual organizational structure as an integral mechanism managers use to implement strategy has brought with it recognition of the central role knowledge plays in this process. *Knowledge* may be in terms of operating know-how, relationships with and knowledge of customer networks, technical knowledge upon which products or processes are based or will be, relationships with key people or a certain person that can get things done quickly, and so forth. Consulting firm McKinsey's organizational expert, Lowell Bryan, and co-author Claudia Joyce, describe the role of knowledge in effective organizational structures this way:

> We believe that the centerpiece of corporate strategy for most large companies should become the redesign of their organizations. We believe this for a very simple reason—it's where the money is.
>
> Let us explain. Most companies today were designed for the 20th century. By remaking them to mobilize the mind power of their 21st century workforces, these companies will be able to tap into the presently underutilized talents, knowledge, relationships, and skills of their employees, which will open up to them not only new opportunities but also vast sources of new wealth.[28]

Bryan and Joyce see this shaping future organizational structure with managers becoming knowledge "nodes" through which intricate networks of personal relationships—inside and outside the formal organization—are constantly coordinated to bring together relevant know-how and successful action. Cathleen Benko and Molly Anderson's book, *The Corporate Lattice*, takes the notion of "nodes" with knowledge a major step forward, identifying the reality in many organizations that relevant knowledge exists with many organizational members other than just managers. Their book and the research that underlies it help document this phenomenon of networks of relationships as a multidirectional and almost randomly natural latticework, which describes the reality of the nature of work today, and the way a workplace in many organizations large and small really works. Rather than the usual "ladder" metaphor to describe communication and career processes in organizations, they suggest that an organization today is more like a **lattice**—a three-dimensional structure extending infinitely vertically, horizontally, and diagonally. People are less tethered to offices, even to tradition career patterns—with major technological advances, globalization, and different options for where, when and how work gets done. So the work of a lattice-functioning organization gets done in a virtual, dynamic, typically project-based manner

corporate lattice
Corporate lattice is a model of how work, careers and communication get done in twenty-first century organizations up, down and across organizational levels and positions versus a "corporate ladder" tradition that views work, careers and communication as predominantly hierarchical driven.

lattice
A metaphor used to describe the reality of the nature & structure of work in organizations today—a 3-dimensional structure extending vertically, horizontally, and diagonally whereby people communicate and work with others anywhere, anytime, to provide answers, ideas, form teams, and solve problems.

[26]www.innocentive.com; and Tapscott and Williams, *MacroWikinomics*
[27]Tapscott and Williams, *MacroWikinomics*
[28]Lowell L. Bryan, and Claudia I. Joyce (McKinsey and Company), *Mobilizing Minds* (New York: McGraw-Hill, 2007), p. 1.

The Corporate Lattice—A Social Media Organizational Structure at AT&T

John Donovan, AT&T's chief technology officer, was looking for a nonhierarchical approach to harness the rich depth of knowledge and creativity inside the multibillion-dollar firm. Leveraging social media, Donovan created a mass participation approach to innovation that, by design, would not replicate the company's existing functional or hierarchical organizational structure.

This approach features a Web site that allows anyone (and Donovan is quick to underscore anyone) to contribute an idea, become a collaborator on someone else's idea, provide encouragement and critical feedback, assess a concept's marketability, challenge its engineering and affordability, and the like. Each employee can also vote on the caliber of the insights and rate additional postings of suggestions and comments, earning the contributors reputation points. "This is meritocracy at its best—a highly diverse set of people, in every sense of the word, crowd-sourcing and crowd-storming," says Donovan.

By the end of its third quarter, the site had more than 24,000 members, 2,000 ideas, and more than a million page views and was still growing. The first season's winners have been funded and are moving from PowerPoint to prototype.

Source: Cathleen Benko and Molly Anderson, *The Corporate Lattice* (Cambridge, Mass: Harvard Business Review Press, 2010), www.thecorporatelattice.com

---

learning organization

Organization structured around the idea that it should be set up to enable learning, to share knowledge, to seek knowledge, and to create opportunities to create new knowledge. It would move into new markets to learn about those markets rather than simply to bring a brand to it, or find resources to exploit in it.

ambidextrous organization

Organization structure most notable for its lack of structure wherein knowledge and getting it to the right place quickly are the key reasons for organization. Managers become knowledge "nodes" through which intricate networks of personal relationships— inside and outside the formal organization— are constantly, and often informally, coordinated to bring together relevant know-how and successful action.

resembling nodes on a network, each with the possibility of connecting anywhere and anytime to others to provide answers, ideas, form teams, or communities. With strong horizontal along with diagonal and vertical supports, the visual image of an organization is one far less reliant on or constrained by top-down hierarchy. This broader, sometimes unexpected pattern of participation enables interaction, gets involvement, spreads ideas and knowhow throughout an organization regardless of exact levels and roles in an organizational chart.[29] Exhibit 11.15, Global Strategy in Action provides an example about AT&T from their book to illuminate both the lattice view and the boundaryless, Web-enabled fluid organizations through which strategies are enabled today.

A shift from what Subramanian Rangan called *exploitation to exploration* indicated the growing importance of organizational structures that enable a **learning organization** to allow global companies the chance to build competitive advantage.[30] Rather than going to markets to exploit brands or for inexpensive resources, in Rangan's view, the smart ones were going global to learn. This shift in the intent of the structure, then, is to seek information, to create new competences. Demand in another part of the world could be a new-product trendsetter at home. So a firm's structure needs to be organized to enable learning, to share knowledge, to create opportunities to create it. Others look to companies like 3M or Procter & Gamble that allow slack time, new-product champions, manager mentors—all put in place in the structure to provide resources, support, and advocacy for cross-functional collaboration leading to innovation in new-product development, and the generation and use of new ideas. This perspective is similar to the boundaryless notion—accommodate the speed of change and therefore opportunity by freeing up historical constraints found in traditional organizational approaches. So having structures that emphasize coordination over control, that allow flexibility (are **ambidextrous**), that emphasize the value and importance of informal relationships and interaction over formal systems, techniques, and controls are all characteristics associated with what are seen as effective structures for the twenty-first century.

[29]Cathleen Benko and Molly Anderson, *The Corporate Lattice* (Cambridge, Mass: Harvard Business Review Press, 2010), www.thecorporatelattice.com.
[30]Subramanian Rangan, "Making Sustainability Profitable: Lessons from Emerging Markets," *Harvard Business Review*, Vol. 91, No. 3–4, pp. 132–135, 2013.

Summary

This chapter has examined ways organizations are structured and ways to make those structures most effective. It described five traditional organizational structures–simple organization, functional structure, divisional structure, matrix structure, and product-team structure. Simple structures are often found in small companies, where tight control is essential to survival. Functional structures take advantage of the specialization of work by structuring the organization into interconnected units like sales, operations, and accounting/finance. This approach generates more efficiency, enhances functional skills over time, and is perhaps the most pervasive organizational structure. Coordination and conflict across functional units are the perpetual challenge in functional structures.

As companies grow they add products, services, and geographic locations, which leads to the need for divisional structures which divide the organization into units along one or more of these three lines. This division of the business into units with common settings increases focus and allows each division to operate more like an independent business itself. That in turn can generate competition for corporate-level resources and potentially loose consistency and image corporatewide. Companies that work intensely with certain clients or projects created the matrix organization structure to temporarily assign functional specialists to those activities while having them remain accountable to their "home" functional unit. The product-team structure has evolved from the matrix approach, where functional specialists' assignments can be for an extended time and usually center around creating a functionally balanced team to take charge of a new-product idea from generation to production, sales, and market expansion. This approach has been found to create special synergy, teamwork, and cooperation because these specialists are together building a new revenue stream from its inception through its success and expansion.

The twenty-first century has seen an accelerating move away from traditional organizational structures toward hybrid adaptations that emphasize an external focus, flexible interaction, interdependency, and a bottom-up approach. Organizations have sought to adapt their traditional structures in this direction by redefining the role of corporate headquarters, rebalancing the need for control versus coordination, adjusting and reengineering the structure to emphasize strategic activities, downsizing, and moving toward self-managing operational activities.

More successful organizations are becoming agile, virtual organizations—temporary networks of independent companies linked by information technology to share skills, markets, and costs. Outsourcing has been a major way organizations have done this. They retain certain functions, while having other companies take full responsibility for accomplishing other functions necessary to provide the product or services of this host organization. Strategic alliances are arrangements between two or more companies who typically contribute resources or skills to a joint undertaking where the joint entity is a separate, distinct organization itself and usually created to seek a particular contract or activities that represent too great an undertaking for any one player in the alliance.

Twenty-first century leaders have increasingly spoken about making their organizations boundaryless, by which they mean the absence of internal and external "boundaries" between units, levels, and locations that lessen their company's ability to generate knowledge, share knowledge, and get knowledge to the places it can be best used to create value. Forward thinkers describe ambidextrous learning organizations as ones that innately share knowledge, enable learning within and across organizations, and nurture informal relationships within and outside organizations to foster opportunities to be at the forefront of creating new knowledge.

Key Terms

agile organization, *p. 354*
ambidextrous organization, *p. 364*
boundaryless organization, *p. 361*
business process outsourcing, *p. 356*
business process reengineering, *p. 350*
corporate lattice, *p. 363*
divisional organizational structure, *p. 339*
downsizing, *p. 352*

external interface boundaries, *p. 361*
functional organizational structure, *p. 338*
geographic boundaries, *p. 361*
holding company structure, *p. 342*
horizontal boundaries, *p. 361*
lattice, *p. 363*
learning organization, *p. 364*
matrix organizational structure, *p. 342*
modular organization, *p. 354*

organizational structure, *p. 337*
outsourcing, *p. 354*
product-team structure, *p. 344*
restructuring, *p. 350*
self-management, *p. 352*
simple organizational structure, *p. 337*
strategic alliances, *p. 359*
strategic business unit, *p. 341*
vertical boundaries, *p. 361*
virtual organization, *p. 353*

Questions for Discussion

1. Explain each traditional organizational structure.
2. Select a company you have worked for or research one in the business press that uses one of these traditional structures. How well suited is the structure to the needs and strategy of the organization? What seems to work well, and what doesn't?
3. What organizations do you think are most likely to use product-team structures? Why?
4. Identify an organization that operated like a twentieth-century organization but has now adopted a structure that manifests twenty-first-century characteristics. Explain how you see or detect the differences.
5. How would you use one or more of the ways to improve traditional structures to improve the company you last worked in? Explain what might result.
6. What organization are you familiar with that you would consider the most agile, virtual organization? Why?
7. What situation have you personally seen outsourcing benefit?
8. What "boundary" would you first eliminate or change in an organization you are familiar with? Explain what you would do to eliminate it or change it and how that should make it more effective.
9. What would be the advantages of a corporate lattice–type organization? Are there disadvantages? How is it similar or different from the "grapevine" notion?

Chapter Twelve

Leadership and Culture

After reading and studying this chapter, you should be able to

1. Describe what good organizational leadership involves.

2. Explain how vision and performance help leaders clarify strategic intent.

3. Explain the value of passion and selection/development of new leaders in shaping an organization's culture.

4. Briefly explain seven sources of power and influence available to every manager.

5. Define and explain what is meant by organizational culture, and how it is created, influenced, and changed.

6. Describe four ways leaders influence culture.

7. Explain four strategy-culture situations.

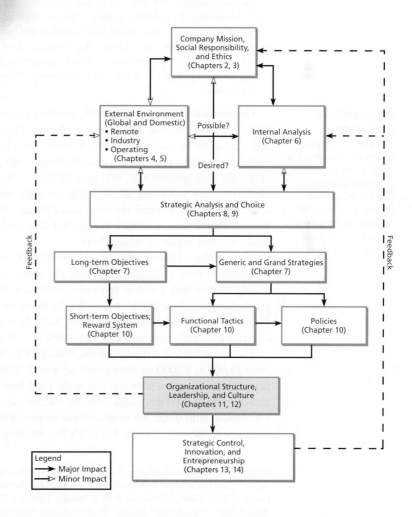

Company Mission, Social Responsibility, and Ethics (Chapters 2, 3)

External Environment (Global and Domestic)
• Remote
• Industry
• Operating
(Chapters 4, 5)

Possible?

Internal Analysis (Chapter 6)

Desired?

Strategic Analysis and Choice (Chapters 8, 9)

Long-term Objectives (Chapter 7)

Generic and Grand Strategies (Chapter 7)

Short-term Objectives; Reward System (Chapter 10)

Functional Tactics (Chapter 10)

Policies (Chapter 10)

Organizational Structure, Leadership, and Culture (Chapters 11, 12)

Strategic Control, Innovation, and Entrepreneurship (Chapters 13, 14)

Feedback

Feedback

Legend
→ Major Impact
⇢ Minor Impact

The job of leading a company has never been more demanding, and it will only get more challenging amidst the global dynamism businesses face today. The CEO will retain ultimate authority, but the corporation will depend increasingly on the skills of the CEO and key executives to lead, coordinate, make decisions, and act quickly. The accelerated pace and complexity of business will continue to force corporations to push authority down through increasingly horizontal, flattened management structures. As we saw in the last chapter, these organizations will also need to be more and more open, agile, and boundaryless. This will require all the more emphasis on able leadership and a strong culture to shape decisions that must be made quickly, even when the stakes are big. In the future, every line manager will have to exercise leadership's prerogatives—and bear its burdens—to an extent unthinkable 20 years ago.[1]

John Kotter, a widely recognized leadership expert, predicted this evolving role of leadership in an organization when he distinguished between management and leadership:

> Management is about coping with complexity. Its practices and procedures are largely a response to one of the most significant developments of the twentieth century: the emergence of large organizations. Without good management, complex enterprises tend to become chaotic in ways that threaten their very existence. Good management brings a degree of order and consistency to key dimensions like the quality and profitability of products.
>
> Leadership, by contrast, is about coping with change. Part of the reason it has become so important in recent years is that the business world has become more competitive and more volatile. . . . The net result is that doing what was done yesterday, or doing it 5 percent better, is no longer a formula for success. Major changes are more and more necessary to survive and compete effectively in this new environment. More change always demands more leadership.[2]

organizational leadership
The process and practice by key executives of guiding and shepherding people in an organization toward a vision over time and developing that organization's future leadership and organization culture.

Organizational leadership, then, involves action on two fronts. The first is in guiding the organization to deal with constant change. This requires CEOs who embrace change, and who do so by clarifying strategic intent, who build their organization and shape their culture to fit with opportunities and challenges change affords. The second front is in providing the management skill to cope with the ramifications of constant change. This means identifying and supplying the organization with operating managers prepared to provide operational leadership and vision as never before. Thus, organizational leadership is guiding and shepherding toward a vision over time and developing that organization's future leadership and organizational culture.

Consider the challenge that faced Ford Motor Company CEO Alan Mulally as he sought to transform Ford's culture and return the company to profitability after years of accelerating decline and a severe economic downturn. He was brought in by CEO Bill Ford, great-grandson of the founder, who finally threw up his arms in frustration and concluded that an insider could no longer fix Ford. Mulally was not Bill Ford's first choice, but Ford concluded Mulally was someone who knew how to shake the company to its foundations.

Mulally inherited virtually all the managers he had to work through. Ford was losing from $3,000 to $5,000 on most every car it sold. There was a legacy within the company of placing a premium on personal ties to the Ford family, sometimes trumping actual performance in promotion decisions. Mulally had no experience in the automobile industry and was viewed with suspicion as an outsider in a town that places a premium on lifelong association with the industry. On Mulally's first meeting with his inherited management team,

[1]Ram Charan, *Global Tilt: Leading Your Business Through the Great Economic Power Shift* (London: Crown Business, 2013); Paul J. H. Schoemaker, Steve Knepp, and Samantha Howland, "Strategic Leadership: The Essential Skills," *Harvard Business Review*, January–February, 2013.
[2]John P. Kotter, "Accelerate!" *Harvard Business Review,* November–December, 2012.

one manager asked: "How are you going to tackle something as complex and unfamiliar as the auto business when we are in such tough financial shape?"

Wall Street was skeptical early on. Of 15 analysts surveyed by Bloomberg.com at the time, only two rated it a buy. The other 13's opinion: fixing Ford would require much more than simply whacking expenses and replacing a few key people. The company had to figure out how to produce more vehicles consumers actually wanted. And doing that required addressing the most fundamental problem of all: Ford's dysfunctional, often defeatist, culture. Once a model of efficiency, it had degenerated into a symbol of inefficiency, and its managers seemed comfortable with the idea of losing money.

If you were Alan Mulally, how would you have led the dramatic change that appeared to be needed at Ford Motor Company? How would you have dated to move Ford's 300,000-plus employees and managers in a direction that abandoned ingrained, and to some "sacred," cultural and leadership norms, quickly?

Consider another example. Jeff Immelt took the reins of leadership of GE from Jack Welch, recognized worldwide as one of the truly great business leaders of the twentieth century, and faced a leadership and organizational culture challenge quite different in some ways from what Alan Mulally was addressing. GE under Welch built more value for its stockholders than any other company in the history of global commerce. That legacy alone would be pressure enough on a new leader, wouldn't you think?

Fortunately, some would quickly answer, Immelt had trained for many years under and in Welch's shadow. He was Welch's choice as successor. He was deeply schooled in the GE way and the Jack Welch leadership approach, as were all the other 300,000 GE employees over the prior 20 years. That Welch/GE way valued, above all, executives who could cut costs, cut deals, and generate continuous improvement in their business units. They were evaluated personally by Welch on an annual basis, in front of each other at the GE School.

But a storm was brewing. Shortly after Immelt became CEO, the 9/11 tragedy unfolded. A major recession and stock market drop soon followed. The option to continue mega deal making was slowing down with fewer candidates. The ability to generate GE-caliber earnings growth via sales growth combined with relentless efficiency was slowing down. The reach of GE's huge financial services business holdings Welch built that were revered as the key instruments of his golden touch were now a deadly albatross for Immelt and GE. So Immelt concluded that he could not continue with the old strategy. Rather, he would have to embark on virtually a new direction at GE that would dramatically change what he needed GE executives as leaders to prioritize and become. Instead of being experts in deal making and continuous improvement, they needed, in Immelt's vision, to become creative, innovators of internal growth generated by identifying new markets and technologies and needs as yet unknown.

With a slower-growing domestic economy, less tolerance among investors for buying your way to growth, and more global competitors, Immelt, like many of his peers, is being forced to shift the emphasis from deals and cost-cutting to new products, services, and markets. "It's a different world," Immelt has repeatedly said, than the one Welch knew. Immelt inherited one of the world's greatest companies yet faced a situation he concluded required dramatic changes in the way GE would be led, in the nature of the culture it needed, and in the fundamental priorities with which its managers would build GE's future. The dramatic 2008–2010 financial services initiated global economic collapse further underscored the challenge Immelt faced.

If you were Jeff Immelt, how would you lead such a change? How would you seek to move GE's 300,000 people in a direction that abandons "sacred" cultural and leadership norms that were well used and entrenched under Welch's watch to make GE great? How would you quickly and convincingly lead those people to accept massive change throughout this special company and very quickly have that uncertain change produce the growth and profitability investors understandably expect?

The challenges Immelt and Mulally faced were different, but both were nothing short of a revolution. Fortunately for Ford and GE, Mulally and Immelt focused intensely and aggressively on the organizational leadership and organizational culture elements we will now examine.

STRATEGIC LEADERSHIP: EMBRACING CHANGE

The blending of telecommunications, computers, the Internet, and one global marketplace has increased the pace of change exponentially during the past 10 years. All business organizations are affected. Change has become an integral part of what leaders and managers deal with daily. The opening example about Jeff Immelt shows a manager normally able to celebrate 20 years of historically unmatched accomplishment, only to face the need to virtually abandon what drove it and commit to unprecedented, dramatic change at GE.

The leadership challenge is to galvanize commitment among people within an organization as well as stakeholders outside the organization to embrace change and implement strategies intended to position the organization to succeed in a vastly different future. Leaders galvanize commitment to embrace change through three interrelated activities: clarifying strategic intent, building an organization, and shaping organizational culture.

Clarifying Strategic Intent

strategic intent
Leaders' clear sense of where they want to lead their company and what results they expect to achieve.

Leaders help their company embrace change by setting forth their **strategic intent**—a clear sense of where they want to lead the company and what results they expect to achieve. They do this by concentrating simultaneously and very clearly on two very different issues: vision and performance.

Vision

leader's vision
An articulation of a simple criterion or characterization of what a leader sees the company must become in order to establish and sustain global leadership.

A leader needs to communicate clearly and directly a fundamental vision of what the business needs to become. Traditionally, the concept of vision has been a description or picture of what the company could be that accommodates the needs of all its stakeholders. The intensely competitive, rapidly changing global marketplace has refined this to be targeting a very narrowly defined **leader's vision**—an articulation of a simple criterion or characterization of what the leader sees the company must become to establish and sustain global leadership. Former IBM CEO Lou Gerstner is a good example of a leader in the middle of trying to shape strategic intent when he began to try to change IBM from a computer company to a business solutions management company. He said at the time: "One of the great things about this industry is that every decade or so, you get a chance to redefine the playing field." He further commented, "We're in that phase of redefinition right now, and winners or losers are going to emerge from it. We've got to become the leader in 'network-centric computing.' It's a shift brought about by telecommunications-based change that is changing IBM more than semiconductors did in the last decade." Said Gerstner, "I sensed there were too many people inside IBM who wanted to fight the war we lost," referring to PCs and PC software, so he aggressively instilled network-centric computing as the strategic intent for IBM in the next several decades. Gerstner's vision is shaping IBM well beyond his time there. His successor, Sam Palmisano, sold IBM's PC business to China's Lenovo, creating in it the world's third-largest PC company. At the same time, Palmisano agressively pushed his IBMers to concentrate on newer IBM businesses in IT services, software, and servers—where they would leverage the online digital revolution worldwide. Palmisano's successor, Virginia Rometty, carries on Gerstner's vision today, saying recently after a record performance that "it reflects the impact of a distinct choice we have made about IBM's business and technology model. IBM is an innovation company, both in what we do and how we do it—we pursue continuous transformation."

Keep the Vision Simple Mark Zuckerberg and Facebook have, in a few short years, dramatically changed the paradigm of how people worldwide interface with the Internet. Instead of search and e-mail as the main reasons individuals log onto the Internet, Zuckerberg's simple vision for Facebook—*Facebook helps you connect and share with the people in your life*—has become the initial connecting point with the Web for over a billion people worldwide. John Donahoe, taking over for the well-known Meg Whitman at eBay, has sold off several prior acquisitions, like Skype, with a vision to reconnect eBay with its roots—*to remain the world's largest online marketplace, where practically anyone can buy and sell practically anything.* In the annals of business leadership, Coca-Cola's legendary former chairman and CEO, Roberto Goizueta, was known for reinvigorating Coke at a key point in its history by articulating a very simple, powerful strategic vision for Coke when he said, *"Our company is a global business system for which we raise capital to make concentrate and sell it at an operating profit. Then we pay the cost of that capital. Shareholders pocket the difference."* Coke averaged 27 percent annual return on stockholder equity for 18 years under his leadership. Global Strategy in Action, Exhibit 12.1 shows how Michael Bloomberg, recently having completed his third and final term as New York City's top leader, articulated a radical yet simple vision of New York City that resonated with its famously critical citizenry through 9/11, strikes, and efforts to ban smoking, large sodas, and guns. They continued to give him high approval ratings, often topping 75 percent. All four of these organizations are very different, but their leaders were each effective in shaping and communicating a vision that clarified strategic intent in a way that helped everyone understand, or at least have a sense of, where the organization needed to go and, as a result, created a better sense of the rationale behind any new, and often radically changing, strategy.

Performance

Clarifying strategic intent must also ensure the survival of the enterprise as it pursues a well-articulated vision, and after it reaches the vision. So a key element of good organizational leadership is to make clear the performance expectations a leader has for the organization, and managers in it, as they seek to move toward that vision.

Oftentimes this can create a bit of a paradox, because the vision is a future picture and performance is now and tomorrow and next quarter and this year. Larry Page, Google cofounder, stepped back in to assume the CEO role in mid-2011. A major reason for doing so was his belief, and many others, that Google was at risk to lose its global dominance as a key entry point to the Internet, and therefore eventually ad revenue, to the fast-rising Facebook. He moved immediately to tie vision and performance. His immediate sense of vision was simple—*Google needs to go "social" to compete.* To that end, Page sent out a company-wide memo his first week as CEO alerting all Google employees that 25 percent of their annual bonus would be tied to the success or failure of Google's social strategy that year. Page told employees that were not directly involved in Google's social efforts that they, too, would be held accountable. He wrote that employees must test the products and give feedback; that they should push Google's social products on their "family and friends."[3] So Larry Page was directly clarifying Google's strategic intent by focusing on a simple vision—social—and linking performance immediately and in the near future for *every* Google employee on the success of that vision. Just a few months after Page's social

[3] Read more: http://www.businessinsider.com/larry-page-just-tied-employee-bonuses-to-the-success-of-the-googles-social-strategy-2011-4#ixzz1IxMq2Sg6

Mike Bloomberg, New York's Three-Time CEO Leader

Michael Bloomberg is in his third and final term as mayor of New York City, and he has had extraordinary entrepreneurship success building Bloomberg LP, of which he still owns 88 percent, after being fired by Salomon Brothers in 1982. On becoming NYC's mayor shortly after 9/11, Bloomberg's leadership approach was based on a businesslike view of NYC—NYC is the company; its citizens are its customers; its public servants NYC's talent; and Bloomberg the CEO responsible for results. Here's his leadership approach.

BE BOLD AND TAKE RISKS

Bloomberg's first major decision was to raise property taxes to put NYC in a better financial condition. Overwhelmingly advised this was political suicide, Bloomberg saw only two choices, reduce services or increase taxes. The risk paid off. NYC's finances improved—and economic activity in the city improved in the process. At the same time, he sought to have NYC win the 2012 Winter Olympics. He lost to London. Bloomberg's reaction: "In business, you reward people for taking risks. When it doesn't work out, you promote them because of their willingness to try new things. If people come back and tell me they skied all day and never fell down, I tell them to try a different mountain." What did he do? Go about stopping smoking, large sodas, and guns.

BE OPEN ABOUT PERFORMANCE AND RESULTS

He insisted that employees, and customers, see decision making in action and regularly see results. So he first changed doors on key meeting rooms and offices from wood to glass, so people could look inside the city's administrative activities. He created semiannual reports about NYC's revenues and expenses, giving everyone a detailed financial picture of what each agency of NYC's government does, and costs.

COMMUNICATE WITH CUSTOMERS

Bloomberg has long been obsessed with constant customer contact and feedback. So as mayor, he immediately established a 311 telephone and Web-based system so that any citizen or guest of NYC could call, 24/7, to comment on any- and everything being done in NYC. Bloomberg personally reviewed weekly summaries of all calls to get a feeling for key citizen concerns. The number of calls reached 50 million within the first 16 months resulting in numerous improvements in services and actions solving problems or complaints. It has also reduced dramatically the number of 911 calls, by more than 1 million annually, meaning critical first-responders are used more for real emergencies, while nonemergency concerns get addressed in a more appropriate manner.

RECRUIT TOP OPERATIONAL TALENT

Most politicians fill top jobs with people owed political patronage. Not Bloomberg. He views as critical to his success as a leader, regardless of whether he is leading a business or a government, the priority of filling key operating positions with the best talent he can get. And he wants that talent to be able to identify targets for their units, and then lead their people in achieving them. For example, he immediately hired Katherine Oliver, a talented executive with Bloomberg—the business operation in London—to build first-class film and TV operations in NYC. She set impressive targets, and her results exceeded them.

Bloomberg has maintained a very high approval rating in perhaps the world's most cynical city populace. He just finished an unprecedented third and final term as NYC mayor. His open, dedicated performance-linked leadership has won him the approval of his citizenry, his NYC employees, and admiration worldwide as a proven leader in both business and government settings.

Sources: "Michael Bloomberg," *The New York Times, Times Topics,* June 14, 2013; "The CEO Mayor," *BusinessWeek,* June 25, 2007.

vision, while starting with Google+, Page elaborated that Google's social vision would be less about building a popular social network than it was to transform users' experience with the company and its litany of products. "Think about it this way," Page said back then. "Last quarter we shipped the Plus; now we're going to [get ready to] ship the Google part." Two years later, it appeared Page's effort to match performance with vision paid off. Google's I/O developers conference opened with four hours by one Google executive after another discussing changes coming to major products like Google Maps and Google Search, making all of these products more personal and social for every Google user. "This means," said Page in a surprise appearance, "baking identity and sharing into all of our products so that we build a 'real' relationship with our users. Sharing on the Web will be like sharing in real life across all your stuff."[4]

Jim McNerney, Boeing CEO and GE alumnus, described how he handled this paradox at Boeing and 3M as a contrast between an encouraging style (visioning) and setting expectations (performance).

> I think the harder you push people, the more you have to encourage them. Some people feel you either have a demanding, command-and-control management style or you have a nurturing, encouraging management style. I believe you have to have both. If you're only demanding, without encouraging, eventually that runs out of gas. And if you're only encouraging, without setting high expectations, you're not getting as much out of people. It's not either/or. You can't have one without the other.[5]

A real challenge for Alan Mulally at Ford was changing managers' mindsets about being profitable. When he was reviewing Ford's product line as the new CEO facing an unprecedented global recession, he was told that Ford loses close to $3,000 every time a customer buys a Focus compact. "Why haven't you figured out a way to make a profit?" he asked. Executives explained that Ford needed the high sales volume to maintain the company's CAFÉ, or corporate average fuel economy, rating and that the plant that made the car was a high-cost UAW factory in Michigan. "That's not what I asked," he shot back. "I want to know why no one figured out a way to build this car at a profit, whether it has to be built in Michigan or China or India, if that's what it takes." Nobody had a good answer.[6]

Building an Organization

The previous chapter examined alternative structures to use in designing the organization necessary to implement strategy. Leaders spend considerable time shaping and refining their organizational structure and making it function effectively to accomplish strategic intent. Because leaders are attempting to embrace change, they are often rebuilding or remaking their organization to align it with the ever-changing environment and needs of a new strategy. And because embracing change often involves overcoming resistance to change, leaders find themselves addressing problems such as the following as they attempt to build or rebuild their organization:

- Ensuring a common understanding about organizational priorities.
- Clarifying responsibilities among managers and organizational units.
- Empowering newer managers and pushing authority lower in the organization.

[4]Sharon Gaudin, "Google Weaves Larry Page's Social Strategy into Maps, Search," *ComputerWorld,* May 16, 2013.
[5]Maria Bartiromo, "Facetime with Boeing's Jim McNerney," *BusinessWeek*, May 10, 2008; and "Alumni Interview Series: Jim McNerney, CEO, the Boeing Company," www.HARBUS.org, Harvard Business School, April 16, 2013.
[6]David Kiley, "New Heat on Ford," *BusinessWeek*, June 4, 2007.

- Uncovering and remedying problems in coordination and communication across the organization and across boundaries inside and outside the organization.
- Gaining the personal commitment to a shared vision from managers throughout the organization.
- Keeping closely connected with what's going on inside and outside the organization and with its customers.

There are three ways good leaders go about building the organization they want and dealing with problems and issues like those listed: education, perseverance, and principles.

leadership development
The effort to familiarize future leaders with the skills important to the company and to develop exceptional leaders among the managers employed.

Education and **leadership development** is the effort to familiarize future leaders with the skills important to the company and to develop exceptional leaders among the managers you employ. Jack Welch was legendary for the GE education center in Croton-on-Hudson, New York, and its role in allowing the GE leader to educate current and future GE managers on the ways of GE and the vision of its future. It allowed a leader to shape future leaders, thereby building an organization. His successor, Jeff Immelt, uses the same facility to interact with and discuss GE's future with a new crop of future leaders.

Leaders do this in many ways. Larry Bossidy, former chairman of Honeywell and co-author of the best seller, *Execution,* spent 50 percent of his time each year flying to Allied Signal's various operations around the world, meeting with managers and discussing decisions, results, and progress. While still CEO at Microsoft, Bill Gates reportedly spent two hours each day reading and sending e-mail to any of Microsoft's 36,000 employees who wanted to contact him. All managers adapt structures, create teams, implement systems, and otherwise generate ways to coordinate, integrate, and share information about what their organization is doing and might do. Once again, here is what Jim McNerney had to say:

> It comes down to personal engagement. I spend a lot of time out with our people. I probably do 30 major events a year with 100 people or more, where I spend time debating things and pushing my ideas, telling them what I am thinking and soliciting feedback. Most CEOs are smart enough to figure out where to go with a company. The hard work is engaging everyone in doing it. That's the hard work in leadership.[7]

Others create customer advisory groups, supplier partnerships, R&D joint ventures, and other adjustments to build an adaptable, learning organization that buys into the leader's vision and strategic intent and the change driving the future opportunities facing the business. These, in addition to the fundamental structural guidelines described in the previous chapter for restructuring to support strategically critical activities, are key ways leaders constantly attempt to educate and build a supportive organization.

perseverance (of a leader)
The capacity to see a commitment through to completion long after most people would have stopped trying.

Perseverance is the capacity to see a commitment through to completion long after most people would have stopped trying. Global Strategy in Action, Exhibit 12.2 describes how Jeff Bezos personifies perseverance in leading Amazon.com. The opening example about Jeff Immelt conjures up images of some people in GE being hesitant to follow him because of their longtime loyalty to Jack Welch and his ways. Immelt will need to have patience and perseverance to deal with these people, to help them gradually shift their loyalty and accept the new. The example also conjures up another image, one of people excited to embrace Immelt's effort to take GE in a new direction—just because of the excitement of the moment along with some sense that a change is needed. But imagine that the first signs are not good, that it is unclear whether the radical new approach will work or not. It is relatively easy to then imagine a significant negative shift in the enthusiasm and faith of this group—again, Immelt must call on considerable perseverance to simply continue to bring them along and build their commitment over the long term.

[7]Ibid.

Jeff Bezos, Amazon.com Founder/CEO . . . Perserverance Personified

Since starting Amazon.com, Jeff Bezos was often in Wall Street's doghouse. The main reason was his insistence on building capacity to support new services his team has determined Amazon's customers need, even as their stock price steadily declines or fluctuates wildly. Asked about his seemingly consistent ability to ignore Wall Street's criticism, Bezos offered these thoughts: "We don't claim that our long-term approach is the right approach. We just claim it's ours. Our approach has been to be as clear as we can be about what kind of company we are and let investors choose." To his employees, Bezos repeatedly makes it clear that Amazon's vision is to find ways that make Amazon's operations more efficient and lower its costs so that it can make its customer experience more value-added while also less costly. And, Bezos notes, "I've taken repeated criticism about our stock price, but never about our customer experience." He goes on to describe that he has repeatedly sat with harsh critics discussing fluctuations in Amazon's stock price yet its insistence on innovation investments, and then, he notes, they would end the meeting saying "I am a huge [Amazon] customer."

Bezos also describes how he clarifies this simple vision to his employees—continuously improving on providing what Amazon customers need. "We have three all-hands meetings a year, and I'll tell people that if the stock is up 30%, please don't feel you are 30% smarter. Because when the stock is 30% down, it's not good to feel 30% dumber." The key is to continuously focus on ways to improve the ways we provide customers what they need. "Companies get skills-focused, instead of customer-needs-focused. When they look at growing their business into some new area, the first question is 'why should we do that—we don't have any skills in that area.'" That approach, Bezos believes, leads eventually to a company's decline because the world constantly changes and a company's current skills eventually become less important. So he leads Amazon by focusing on one simple question, "What do our customers need?" From there he urges his managers to determine if Amazon has the skills to meet the needs and, if not, to go out and hire the people that do. Bezos cites Amazon's Kindle, and electronic books, as a clear example of doing just that, hiring people who know how to build hardware devices, creating a whole new book-reading-related competency in the process. His principles and perseverance to stick with that simple question as Amazon's foundation have proven, over time, to provide solid leadership. Judging from Amazon's upward stock price, Bezos's perserverance may be winning over many investors.

Source: "Bezos on Innovation," BusinessWeek, April 17, 2008; and "The Montessouri Mafia," Wall Street Journal, April 5, 2011.

"When the going gets tough, the tough get going" is a mantra often heard in sports and in U.S. Marine Corps leadership training. The real point in this is perseverance. Three times NYC mayor and business leader Michael Bloomberg's perspective on risk described in Exhibit 12.1 reflects an emphasis on perseverance. The capacity to take a risk, to make a tough decision, to commit to a new vision, and then to stick with that decision even when it doesn't appear "right" early on is a scenario often found in the history of effective leadership that ultimately creates a favorable future. A broad panel of U.S. historians recently rated Abraham Lincoln the best American president—based in large part on his perseverance in preserving the union. Winston Churchill's perseverance was perhaps his most compelling trait as he successfully led England through World War II.

**Principles
(of a leader)**
A leader's fundamental personal standards that guide her sense of honesty, integrity, and ethical behavior.

Principles are your fundamental personal standards that guide your sense of honesty, integrity, and ethical behavior. If you have a clear moral compass guiding your priorities and those you set for the company, you will be a more effective leader. This observation is repeatedly one of the first thing effective leaders interviewed by researchers, business writers, and students mention when they answer a question about what they think is most important in

Test *YOUR* Principles

A few years ago, the dean of Duke's Fuqua School of Business announced that 10 percent of its MBA class had been caught cheating on a take-home final exam and would be dismissed. These MBAs were "cream of the crop" students with six years of corporate experience and careers under way in the new "wiki" world of online collaboration and aggregation of others,' knowledge via the Web as an emerging key source of competitive advantage. So they collaborated in crafting answers to the take-home final exam, sharing insights and ideas, and so forth. Their professors saw the similarity in answers, and, looking to evaluate individual performance, found the collaboration unethical, dishonest, lacking integrity, and fundamentally wrong. So they were dismissed for cheating.

Three years later, Centenary College, a small Hackettstown, New Jersey-based institution, ended its MBA program for Chinese-speaking students after finding "evidence of widespread plagiarism," the school said in a statement posted on its Web site. The China MBA program was based in Beijing, Shanghai, and Taiwan. All 400 students were given the choice of accepting a tuition refund—as much as $1,400—or taking a comprehensive exam to earn a degree.*

According to the statement, all but two students decided to take a refund. The college also noted in the statement that students who cheat are ordinarily dismissed from the school, but the China MBA students are being given more leniency "in an effort to afford students every fair possibility."*

A *BusinessWeek* Commentary took issue with the Duke decision—and saw a different interpretation. Their point: the new world order is about teamwork, shared information. Social networking, a new culture of shared information, postmodern learning wiki style. Text messaging, downloading essays, getting questions answered from others, often unknown, via the Web. All of these are the new ways we work today. We function in an interdependent world, where success often hinges on creative collaboration, networking, and "googling" to tap a literal world of information and expertise available at the click of a keyboard or a cell phone.

Others, starting with their Duke professors, viewed these students collaborating on a take-home exam as a conscious effort to break the rules, or at least, gain unauthorized advantage. And maybe, they apparently thought, this was a good situation about which to make an example in order to rein in an increasingly rudderless business culture.

What do you think? Is what these students did ethical, principled leadership? Is it "cheating," or simply collaborative learning?

* Michelle Conlin, "Commentary: Cheating—or Postmodern Learning?" *BusinessWeek*, May 14, 2007; and Geoff Gloeckler, "MBA Program Withdraws from China due to 'Widespread Plagiarism,' Other Issues," Bloomberg-Businessweek, www.businessweek.com, July 26, 2010.

explaining their success as leaders and the success of leaders they admire. Steven Reinemund, Wake Forest Business School dean, former Pepsico chairman, and member of the board of directors for Walmart, Marriott, American Express, Exxon Mobil, Ocean Park Hotels, and Johnson & Johnson, described the role of principles in leadership this way:

> It starts with basic beliefs and values. It's important to make clear to the people in the organization what those are, so you're transparent. They have to be consistent with the values of the organization, or there will be a problem. If you look at all the issues that have happened in the corporate world of the last few years, … it all boils down to a basic lack of a moral compass and checks and balances among leaders. We as leaders have to check each other. We're going to make mistakes. If we don't check each other on them, you get in trouble. Most of the companies that got into trouble had a set of stated principles, but the leaders didn't check each other on those principles.[8]

Principle boils down to a personal philosophy we all deal with at an individual level—choices involving honesty, integrity, ethical behavior. Indeed Exhibit 12.3, Global Strategy in Action, gives you the chance to "test" *your* personal principles in comparison with the actions of some of your business school peers at Duke University's MBA program and at

[8]Sommer Saadi, "How I Got Here: Steven Reinemund," *BloombergBusinessweek*, March 12, 2012; "Steven S. Reinemund: Leadership for a 21st Century Multinational Corporation," www.ethix.org and Kelsey Perry, "Pepsi CEO Defines Leadership," www.asuwebdeveilarchieve.asu.edu.

Centenary College's China MBA program, along with BusinessWeek's thoughts on the subject too. The key thing to remember as a future leader is that your personal philosophies, or choices, manifest themselves exponentially for you or any key leaders of any organization. The people who do the work of any organization watch their leaders and what their leaders do, sanction, or stand for. So do people outside that organization who deal with it. These people then reflect those principles in what they do or come to believe is the way to do things in or with that organization. An effective organization is better built—is stronger—when its leaders show by example what they want their people to do and the principles they want their people to operate by on a day-to-day basis and in making decisions shaped by values and principles—a clear sense of right or wrong. "Values," "Lead by example," "Do as I say AND as I do"—these are very basic notions that good leaders find great strength in using. *BusinessWeek*'s "The Ethics Guy" says simply that principles should boil down to "five easy principles," which are:[9]

1. Do no harm.
2. Make things better.
3. Respect others.
4. Be fair.
5. Be compassionate.

The value of that kind of clarity, and transparency, as Wake Forest Dean Reinemund described it, can become a major force by which a leader will shape and move his or her organization.

Shaping Organizational Culture

Leaders know well that the values and beliefs shared throughout their organization will shape how the work of the organization is done. And when attempting to embrace accelerated change, reshaping their organization's culture is an activity that occupies considerable time for most leaders. Elements of good leadership—vision, performance, perseverance, principles, which have just been described—are important ways leaders shape organizational culture as well. Leaders shape organizational culture through their passion for the enterprise and the selection/development of talented managers to be future leaders. We will examine these two ideas and then cover the notion of organizational culture in greater detail.

passion (of a leader)
A highly motivated sense of commitment to what you do and want to do.

    Passion, in a leadership sense, is a highly motivated sense of commitment to what you do and want to do. The late Steve Jobs, perhaps more so than most any business leader of the last 25 years, is an excellent example of the role of passion in the recipe of good organizational leadership. What he said when he returned as CEO of Apple after a 12-year absence, the company close to bankruptcy, is very instructive about understanding passion as a leader. Those first few months Apple was being written off by the business media, and employees were unsure too. Mr. Jobs held an informal staff meeting, and what he said is as instructive today as it was then:

> Marketing is about values. This is a very complicated world. It's a very noisy world. We're not going to get a chance for people to remember a lot about us. No company is. So we have to be really clear about what they want them to know about us. Our customers want to know what we stand for. What we're about is not making boxes for people to get their jobs done. Although we do that very well. Apple is about more than that. We believe that people with passion can change the world for the better. That's what we believe.[10]

[9]Bruce Weinstein, "Five Easy Principles," *BusinessWeek*, January 10, 2007.
[10]Carmine Gallo, "Steven Jobs: People with Passion Can Change the World," Jan. 17, 2011, http://blogs.forbes.com/carminegallo/2011/01/17/steve-jobs-people-with-passion-can-change-the-world/.

Over the next decade Steve Jobs not only helped revitalize Apple through the passion ever present in his leadership, he turned Apple into one of the most important brands of our time. Like many other traits of good leaders, passion is best seen through the leader's intermittent behaviors while in the throws of the challenging times of the organizations they lead. They must use special moments to convey a sincere passion for and delight in the work of the company they lead. These observations by and about Ryanair founder Michael O'Leary about competing in the increasingly competitive European airline industry and archrival easyJet provide a useful example:

> It was vintage Michael O'Leary. On May 13, the 42-year-old CEO of Dublin-based discount airline Ryanair outfitted his staff in full combat gear, drove an old World War II tank to England's Luton airport, an hour north of London, then demanded access to the base of archrival easyJet Airline Co. With the theme to the old television series *The A-Team* blaring, O'Leary declared he was "liberating the public from easyJet's high fares." When security—surprise!—refused to let the Ryanair armor roll in, O'Leary led the troops in his own rendition of a platoon march song: "I've been told and it's no lie. easyJet's fares are way too high!" So it is that there are new rivals for O'Leary to conquer. "When we were a much smaller company, we compared ourselves to British Airways. But they are such a mess, most people just feel sorry for them," O'Leary says. "Now we're turning the guns on easyJet."[11]

It was readily apparent to anyone on this scene that O'Leary was passionate about Ryanair, and that example sent a clear message that he wanted an organizational culture that was aggressive, competitive, and somewhat freewheeling in order to take advantage of change in the European airline industry. He did this by passionate example, by expectations felt by his managers, and in the way decision making is approached within Ryanair.

Sam Walton used to lead cheers at every Walmart store he visited each year before and long after Wal-Mart was an overwhelming success. Ursula Burns, the first African-American woman CEO of a Fortune 500 company, has made sure her 30-year colleagues at Xerox sense her passion for the candor she was most known for in Xerox, as a way to build its future, and not all the sudden accolades she is getting for her "first." In building her management team, she set a clear hurdle for anyone Xerox is considering from outside the company. Their skills already vetted, her main question is: "What do you see in this company that you love—that you can love—you can grow to love?"[12] She's looking for underlying passion for Xerox as an essential leadership skill. GE's Jeff Immelt is described by a board member as a natural salesman who still happily recounts the days when he drove around his territory in a Ford Taurus while at GE Plastics. "He knows the world looks to GE as a harbinger of future trends," says Ogilvy & Mather Worldwide CEO Rochelle Lazarus, who sits on the board. "He really feels GE has a responsibility to the world to get out in front and play a leadership role." Immelt, it would seem, is passionate about GE and its future opportunities. Indeed, at a recent gathering of GE's top 650 executives, amidst a situation where GE stock price is down more than 70 percent since he became CEO, Immelt insisted that "there's never been a better day, a better time, or a better place to be," meaning than GE. That's passion.

Leaders also use reward systems, symbols, and structure among other means to shape the organization's culture. Travelers' Insurance Co.'s notable turnaround was accomplished in part by changing its "hidebound" culture through a change in its agent reward system. Employees previously on salary with occasional bonuses were given rewards that involved substantial cash bonuses and stock options. A major Travelers' customer and risk management director at drug-maker Becton Dickinson said: "They're hungrier now. They want to make deals. They're different than the old, hidebound Travelers' culture." Jeff Immelt is

---

[11]"Michael O'Leary's Most Memorable Quotes: Parts One–Five," *The Telegraph,* June, 2013; and "Ryanair Rising," *Businessweek*, June 2, 2003.

[12]Adam Bryant, "Xerox's New Chief Tries to Redefine Its Culture," *The New York Times*, Feb. 21, 2010.

doing something similar to reshape the ingrained GE culture—tying executive compensation to their ability to come up with new ideas that show improved customer service, generate cash growth, and boost sales instead of simply meeting bottom-line targets.[13]

As leaders clarify strategic intent, build an organization, and shape their organization's culture, they look to one key element to help—their management team throughout their organization. As Honeywell's chairman Larry Bossidy candidly observed when asked about how after 42 years at General Electric, Allied Signal, and now Honeywell, with seemingly drab businesses, he could expect exciting growth: "There's no such thing as a mature market. What we need is mature executives who can find ways to grow."[14] Leaders look to managers they need to execute strategy as another source of leadership to accept risk and cope with the complexity that change brings about. So selection and development of key managers become major leadership roles.

Recruiting and Developing Talented Operational Leadership

Fundamental to a leader's responsibility in developing operational talent is to serve as a role model to younger managers. The purpose of doing so is to model behaviors and habits that become instinctive ways those younger managers address issues and make decisions. This has been particularly critical in the dramatic global economic downturn—which virtually every business has been dealing with the past few years. It has required leadership that is lean and focused at every level, and particularly at operating levels of the organization.

Modeling behavior and desired habits is particularly relevant in the depressed economic times most companies have been facing for the past few years and that many still face today. In many cases, their very survival may be at stake. Thus, modeling and ensuring these specific leadership habits can be absolutely critical.

As we noted at the beginning of this section on organizational leadership, the accelerated pace and complexity of business beyond the immediate economic contraction will also increase pressure on corporations to push authority down in their organizations, ultimately meaning that every line manager will have to exercise leadership's prerogatives to an extent unthinkable a generation earlier. We also defined one of the key roles of good organizational leadership as building the organization by educating and developing new leaders. They will each be global managers, change agents, strategists, motivators, strategic decision makers, innovators, and collaborators if the business is to survive and prosper. So we want to examine this more completely by looking at key competencies these future managers need to possess or develop. Exhibit 12.4, Global Strategy in Action provides an interesting interview with IBMer Helen Cheng about her introduction to the *World of Warcraft* online game and how it is now a key way IBM is using online multiplayer games to develop its young managers of global teams into better team leaders and future global leaders for the reality of today's fast-paced, global marketplace.

Today's need for fluid learning organizations capable of rapid response, sharing, and cross-cultural synergy place sizeable demands on young managers to bring competencies to the organization. Leadership consultants and researchers Ruth Williams and Joseph Cothrel drew the conclusion that the "new" competencies needed today represented a shift from competencies often seen as masculine to ones seen as feminine:

> Today's competitive environment requires a different set of management competencies than we traditionally associate with the role. The balance has clearly shifted from attributes traditionally thought of as masculine (strong decision making, leading the troops, driving strategy, waging competitive battle) to more feminine qualities (listening, relationship-building, and nurturing). The model today is not so much "take it on your shoulders" as it is to "create the environment

---

[13]"Jeff Immelt on Pay, His AAA Rating, and Taking the Train," *Businessweek*, February 1, 2009.
[14]Larry Bossidy and Ram Charan, *Execution: The Discipline of Getting Things Done*, as reviewed in http://bookreviewsummaries.wordpress.com/2008/03/30/execution-by-larry-bossidy-ram-charan/.

IBM Goes with MMORG to Develop Its Managers into Future Global Leaders

MMORPGs (massively multiplayer online role-playing games) like *World of Warcraft* are perhaps the most realistic setting for leadership training and development in our new "wiki" world, according to IBM leadership development researchers. "It's not a stretch to think that résumés that include detailed gaming experience will be landing on the desks of *Fortune* 500 executives in the very near future. Those hiring managers would do well to look closely at that experience, and not disregard it as a mere hobby. After all, that gamer may just be your next CEO."* Reading the experience of Helen Cheng helps explain why IBM is moving aggressively into the use of MMORPGs as a basis for leadership selection and development at IBM, as well as at client businesses worldwide. Helen Cheng got her first taste of online gaming three years ago, when a friend got her to join up with *Star Wars Galaxies*™. "I was pretty skeptical," she recalled. "I mean, fighting dragons in a fantasy world? Sounds kinda nerdy." Three days later Cheng was hooked. She soon moved on to *World of Warcraft*™, an online game that counts more than 8 million members. She moved quickly up the ranks and spent six months as a level-60 guild leader, the highest level of leadership in the game. Here are some of her leadership lessons gleaned from the game:

Q: Do you consider yourself a natural leader?

A: I'm pretty quiet. The first time I thought I could be a leader was during a raid that involved 40 people. The raid went bad, and everybody died. The designated raid leader went silent. Everyone was waiting for instruction. I pushed my button to talk and rallied the troops. It was me, a girl, talking to 39 guys. To my surprise, everyone complied, and we got going. That was a defining moment for me, eventually leading to me becoming a guild leader.

Q: What was it about the environment that made it easy for you to try a leader role?

A: The speed at which things happens contributes to that. You don't have a lot of time, and decisions have to be made. Also, there are different forms of communication. You can send instant messages, use a chat channel, speak over VOIP [Voice Over Internet Protocol], even leave messages on the Web site. These different communications mediums affort opportunities to lead.

Q: What is it like managing people you never see in person?

A: Not that different from real life. I've had my share of personality conflicts that I had to mediate. In my last guild, we had a raid officer who was extremely capable. He was great leading 40-man raids in real time. But he was extremely practical and did not care about other guild members' feelings, or guild unity. On the other hand, we had a recruiting officer who was very friendly and gung ho about building relationships. They often went head-to-head on issues. I found it difficult to mediate between them. So eventually I left to go raid with another guild that was more advanced.

Q: Kind of like climbing the corporate ladder?

A: Something like that.

Source: "Gaming and Leadership Report: Virtual Worlds, Real Leaders," A Global Innovation Outlook 2.0 Report, www.ibm.com/ibm/gio/us/en/gaming.html, 2013.

that will enable others to carry part of the burden." The focus is on unlocking the organization's human asset potential.[15]

Researcher Ronald Riggio suggested that senior leaders seeking to develop their operational leaders should focus on their development of competencies on three levels—self/personal leadership; interpersonal leadership; and leading teams and organizations. Three competencies associated with each level respectively are as follows:[16]

Self/Personal Leadership

- Self-Awareness—It is key for a leader to have a deep understanding of oneself, one's strengths and challenges.

[15]Ruth Williams and Joseph Cothrel, *Current Trends in Strategic Management* (New York: Blackwell Publishing, 2007).

[16]Ronald E. Riggio, "Core Leadership Competencies: Which Do You Possess?" *Psychology Today: Cutting-Edge Leadership,* March 25, 2013.

- Strong and Positive Character—Trust is key for any leader; trust starts with self, and at the personal level that is character driven.
- Sense of Purpose—Your motivation and ability to lead increases when you believe in your purpose.

Interpersonal Leadership

- Ability to Communicate—Good leaders are inevitably good verbal and emotional communicators.
- Building and Maintaining Relationships—Empowering and developing others, managing conflict, and fostering cooperation.
- Influence and Motivation—Consistent capacity to motivate others, to persuade, to get people to do things and to focus on outcomes.

Leading Teams and Organizations

- Understanding and Facilitating Group/Team Processes—articulating a group's purpose; a vision; stimulating effort, results, and creativity.
- Understanding Organizational Processes and Dynamics—Skills to handle political and social dynamics.
- Global Mindset—Engendering trust through genuine awareness and openness to people from diverse backgrounds.

position power
The ability and right to influence and direct others based on the power associated with your formal position in the organization.

A key way these competencies manifest themselves in a manager's routine activities is found in the way they seek to get the work of their unit or group done over time. How do they use power and influence to get others to get things done? Effective leaders seek to develop managers who understand they have many sources of power and influence, and that relying on the power associated with their position in an organization is often the least effective means to influence people to do what is needed. Managers have available seven sources of power and influence:

reward power
The ability to influence and direct others that comes from being able to confer rewards in return for desired actions or outcomes.

Organizational Power	Personal Influence
Position power	Expert influence
Reward power	Referent influence
Information power	Peer influence
Punitive power	

information power
The ability to influence others based on your access to information and your control of dissemination of information that is important to subordinates and others yet not otherwise easily obtained.

Organizational sources of power are derived from a manager's role in the organization. **Position power** is formally established based on the manager's position in the organization. By virtue of holding that position, certain decision-making authorities and responsibilities are conferred that the manager is entitled to use to get things done. It is the source of power many new managers expect to be able to rely on, but often the least useful. **Reward power** is available when the manager confers rewards in return for desired actions and outcomes. This is often a power source. **Information power** can be particularly effective and is derived from a manager's access to and control over the dissemination of information that is important to subordinates yet not easily available in the organization. **Punitive power** is the power exercised via coercion or fear of punishment for mistakes or undesired actions by a manager's subordinates.

punitive power
Ability to direct and influence others based on your ability to coerce and deliver punishment for mistakes or undesired actions by others, particularly subordinates.

Leaders today increasingly rely on their personal ability to influence others perhaps as much, if not more so, than organizational sources of power. Personal influence, a form of

EXHIBIT 12.5
Management Processes and Levels of Management

Source: S. Ghoshal, in R. M. Grant, *Contemporary Strategy Analysis* (Oxford: Blackwell, 2005), p. 501.

	RENEWAL PROCESS	
Attracting resources and capabilities and developing the business	Developing operating managers and supporting their activities; maintaining organizational trust	Providing institutional leadership through shaping and embedding corporate purpose and challenging embedded assumptions
	INTEGRATION PROCESS	
Managing operational interdependencies and personal networks	Linking skills, knowledge, and resources across units; reconciling short-term performance and long-term ambition	Creating corporate direction; developing and nurturing organizational values
	ENTREPRENEURIAL PROCESS	
Creating and pursuing opportunities; managing continuous performance improvement	Reviewing, developing, and supporting initiatives	Establishing performance standards
Front-Line Management	Middle Management	Top Management

expert influence
The ability to direct and influence others because they defer to you based on your expertise or specialized knowledge that is related to the task, undertaking, or assignment in which they are involved.

referent influence
The ability to influence others derived from their strong desire to be associated with you, usually because they admire you, gain prestige or a sense of purpose by that association, or believe in your motivations.

peer influence
The ability to influence individual behavior among members of a group based on group norms, a group sense of what is the right thing or right way to do things, and the need to be valued and accepted by the group.

"power," comes mainly from three sources. **Expert influence** is derived from a leader's knowledge and expertise in a particular area or situation. This can be a very important source of power in influencing others. **Referent influence** comes from having others want to identify with the leader. We have all seen or worked for leaders who have major influence over others based simply on their charisma, personality, empathy, and other personal attributes. And finally, **peer influence** can be a very effective way for leaders to influence the behavior of others. Most people in organizations and across an organization find themselves put in groups to solve problems, serve customers, develop innovations, and perform a host of other tasks. Leaders can use the assignment of team members and the charge to the team as a way to enable peer-based influence to work on key managers and the outcomes they produce.

Effective leaders make use of all seven sources of power and influence, very often in combination, to deal with the myriad situations they face and need others to handle. The exact best source(s) of power and influence are often shaped by the nature of the task, project, urgency of an assignment, or the unique characteristics of specific personnel, among myriad factors. Organizational leaders such as Jeff Immelt at GE draw on all these sources and, equally important, seek to develop their organizations around subordinate leaders and managers who insightfully and effectively make use of all their sources of power and influence.

One final perspective on the role of organizational leadership and management selection is found in the work of Bartlett and Ghoshal. Their study of several of the most successful global companies suggests that combining flexible responsiveness with integration and innovation requires rethinking the management role and the distribution of management roles within a twenty-first-century company. They see three critical management roles: the *entrepreneurial process* (decisions about opportunities to pursue and resource deployment), the *integration process* (building and deploying organizational capabilities), and the *renewal process* (shaping organizational purpose and enabling change). Traditionally viewed as the domain of top management, their research suggests that these functions need to be shared and distributed across three management levels as suggested in Exhibit 12.5.[17]

[17]R. M. Grant, *Contemporary Strategic Management* (Oxford: Blackwell, 2005), p. 500.

THE BIG PICTURE

THINK YOUR WORKPLACE is like a sitcom?
In an online survey, Staffing.org, a performance research firm, asked 300 people to describe their company's culture using one of four fictional touchstones. The results:

"A lot like *The Office*" 57%	"More like *Dilbert* than I'd like to admit" 24%	"*M*A*S*H*, on a good day" 14%	"Like *Leave It to Beaver*" 5%

Source: From "The Big Picture," *BusinessWeek*. Reprinted from May 25, 2007 issue of *BusinessWeek* by special permission. Copyright © 2007 by The McGraw-Hill Companies, Inc.

ORGANIZATIONAL CULTURE

organizational culture
The set of important assumptions and beliefs (often unstated) that members of an organization share in common.

Organizational culture is the set of important assumptions (often unstated) that members of an organization share in common. Every organization has its own culture. An organization's culture is similar to an individual's personality—an intangible yet ever-present theme that provides meaning, direction, and the basis for action. In much the same way as personality influences the behavior of an individual, the shared assumptions (beliefs and values) among a firm's members influence opinions and actions within that firm. Exhibit 12.6, Strategy in Action, shows the results of a *BusinessWeek* survey conducted by Staffing.org to identify how employees view their company's culture in the context of various TV shows or cartoon characters.

A member of an organization can simply be aware of the organization's beliefs and values without sharing them in a personally significant way. Those beliefs and values have more personal meaning if the member views them as a guide to appropriate behavior in the organization and, therefore, complies with them. The member becomes fundamentally committed to the beliefs and values when he or she internalizes them; that is, comes to hold them as personal beliefs and values. In this case, the corresponding behavior is *intrinsically rewarding* for the member—the member derives personal satisfaction from his or her actions in the organization because those actions are congruent with corresponding personal beliefs and values. *Assumptions become shared assumptions through internalization among an organization's individual members.* And those shared, internalized beliefs and values shape the content and account for the strength of an organization's culture.[18]

[18]Edgar H. Shein, *Organizational Culture and Leadership* 4th ed. (San Francisco: Jossey-Bass), 2010.

The Role of the Organizational Leader in Organizational Culture

The previous section of this chapter covered organizational leadership in detail. Part of that coverage discussed the role of the organizational leader in shaping organizational culture. Several points in that discussion apply here. We will not repeat them, but it is important to emphasize that the leader and the culture of the organization she or he leads are inextricably intertwined. The leader is the standard bearer, the personification, the ongoing embodiment of the culture (Mark Zuckerberg at Facebook; Indra Nooyi at Pepsico), or the new example of a desired new culture (Alan Mulally at Ford; Marissa Mayer at Yahoo!) for long existing and well-known companies. As such, several of the aspects of what a leader does or should do represent influences on the organization's culture, either to reinforce it or to exemplify the standards and nature of what it needs to become. How the leader behaves and emphasizes those aspects of being a leader become what all the organization sees are "the important things to do and value."

Build Time in the Organization

Some leaders have been with the organization for a long time. If they have been in the leader role for an extended time, then their association with the organization is usually strongly entrenched. They continue to reinforce the current culture, are empowered by it, and understandably go to considerable lengths to reinforce it as a key element in sustaining continued success. The problematic long-time leaders are those who have built a successful enterprise that also sustains a culture that appears unethical or worse. Either type of long-time leader is often a widely known figure in today's media-intense business world. And in their setting, while the culture may be exceptionally strong, their role in creating it usually means they seemingly hold sway over the culture rather than the other way around.

Many leaders in recent years, and inevitably in any organization, are new to the top post of the organization. Their relationship with the organization's culture is perhaps more complex. Those who built a management career within that culture—Jeff Immelt at GE, Ursula Burns at Xerox, Tim Cook at Apple—have the benefit of knowledge of the culture and credibility as an "initiated" member of that culture. This may be quite useful in helping engender confidence as they take on the task of leader of that culture or, perhaps more difficult (as with these three), as change agent for parts of that culture as the company moves forward.

In the other situation, a new leader who is not an "initiated" member of the culture or tribe faces a much more challenging task. Quite logically, they must earn credibility with the "tribe," which is usually somewhat resistant to change. And, very often, they are being brought in with a board of directors desiring change in the strategy, company, and usually culture. That becomes a substantial challenge for these new leaders to face. Some make it happen, others find the strength of the organization's culture far more powerful than their ability to change it.

"Cultural awareness is one of the most neglected and yet most powerful predictors of executive success and it's also one of the things [incoming new] executives know the least about," says Kenneth Siegel, a managerial psychologist with Beverly Hills–based Impact Group, who works with boards and executive teams to improve performance.[19] The employment site Glassdoor's spokesman Scott Dobroski says the site has found "a significant rise in questions asked about cultural fit" over the last several years in companies hiring new managers, among other positions. Dobroski reports that job seekers cite company

---

[19]"Culture Club," *BusinessWeek*, March 3, 2008.

culture as their second-highest priority, "almost tied with salary."[20] Northwestern professor Lauren Rivera concludes that companies are making hiring decisions "in a manner more closely resembling the choice of friends or romantic partners." Rivera found that apparently off-topic questions about leisure pursuits have become central to the hiring process. "These leisure pursuits were crucial for assessing someone as a cultural fit," Rivera says, and often means "employers don't necessarily hire the most skilled candidates."[21] Siegel says it works both ways in terms of seeking a cultural fit, especially when hiring new managers for key positions.

Why? Because a cultural mismatch could disrupt organizational performance for years to come as well as have a major impact on the executive's future career options. That makes the decision of bringing in an outsider as a new leader or manager as important to the executive as it is to the hiring organization. And the conundrum with "cultural fit" can get even more complicated. Management selection processes seeking someone that "fits" a given culture can inevitably, whether intentionally or not, let it become a rationale for sameness—selecting people that are like "we" are. That, in turn, can reduce diversity, which may otherwise benefit the organization significantly over time. We will examine that in an upcoming section.

Exhibit 12.7, Global Strategy in Action, provides an interesting example of these two perspectives as viewed through the experience of the same founder/CEO of successful companies with two very different cultures. It explains how Netflix founder and CEO Reed Hastings sought to dramatically change the culture and way of doing things at Netflix, his second company, after his experience with the nature of the culture that his first start-up, Pure Software, grew into as it became a part of IBM through a series of acquisitions and mergers. Hastings said of Pure, "We got more bureaucratic as we grew," and that it went from being a place that was fast-paced and the "where-everybody-wanted-to-be" place to a "dronish, when-does-the-day-end" software factory. After leaving Pure, Hastings spent about two years thinking about how to build a culture in his next start-up that would not have "big company creep."

At Netflix, Hastings has instilled a very unique "freedom and responsibility" culture that seeks to revolutionize both the way people rent movies and, perhaps more important to Hastings, how his managers work. Facing Blockbuster, Wal-Mart, Amazon, the cable companies, and Apple, Hastings created a culture so unique at Netflix that it is an "A" talent magnet, ensuring the best players in the business line up to help Netflix outsmart these very sizable competitors. And in doing so, Hastings is a "new" leader of a new company with a different business model that is trying to outlast and outcompete other, well established, major players in selling movie rentals. Blockbuster became Netflix's first victim, recently filing for bankruptcy and languishing over a year before finally being bought out of bankruptcy very cheaply. It would appear that Hastings, and his unique Netflix culture, is building a lasting presence based on his experiences and inclinations as a successful entrepreneur and innovator in similarly competitive, large, firmly competitor-entrenched industry niches.

When "new" leaders come into a company with a mandate to consider adjusting / changing its culture, another important approach is through an infusion of "outsiders." The basic underpinning is that shared assumptions can be changed by changing the dominant groups or coalitions within an organization. Obviously such a key group would be composed of the key executives leading the company. And so it is often the case that a new CEO will bring in his or her "own people" to replace existing executives, even and often particularly those with long

[20]Logan Hill, "Job Applicants' Cultural Fit Can Trump Qualifications," *BloombergBusinessweek,* January 3, 2013.
[21]Lauren Rivera, "Hiring as Cultural Matching," *American Sociological Review,* December, 2012.

Reed Hastings Builds a Unique, Revolutionary Culture at Netflix

"I had the great fortune of doing a mediocre job at my first company," said Netflix founder Reed Hastings. He was talking about his software startup, Pure Software, which was a very successful debugging software maker acquired by Rational Software for $750 million, which was later acquired by IBM. Hastings had two observations on that time: "We got more bureaucratic as we grew," but "it was so different how they [Rational Software] operated—the level of trust and the quality of interaction between them was impressive, . . . something I wanted to grow toward."*

Hastings cashed out and spent the next two years thinking about his next start-up and the type of culture he wanted that company to embrace. A $40 late fee on a DVD movie rental and the subsequent hassle germinated the next venture, Netflix. Then it was on to figure out, in creating Netflix, how to create a culture that would revolutionize the way managers and employees worked as well as the way people rent movies. His initial step was to convince two key colleagues from his Pure days to leave Rational/IBM and join him—Neil Hunt and Patty McCord. Today, Neil Hunt remains chief product officer and Patty McCord chief talent officer. They joined Hastings in crafting from the very start a dramatically different culture, even for Silicon Valley standards.

Priority one from day one—make Netflix a place Hastings, Hunt, and McCord enjoyed coming to every day, with people who pushed them intellectually, and in a company they were proud of. They carefully added to the executive team, and that team has now been with the company since its beginning, with the trust and quality of interaction they have with each other a key to Netflix's success, a key foundation to its culture, and an accomplishment Reed set for his future when he observed the Rational Software core team in his first venture.

The Netflix culture they created is like no other. It was called from the beginning the "Freedom and Responsibility Culture." Hastings believed understanding it in detail is so important that he created a 128-slide Power-Point presentation to help new employees understand it in detail. In 2009 he even made it public on the Web, with entrepreneurs and managers worldwide immediately absorbing its every detail. (You can too . . . go to http://www.slideshare.net/reed2001/culture-1798664 or http://blog.summation.net/2009/08/reed-hastings-on-corp-culture.html). Fundamental to the Netflix culture is the belief shared by Hastings, Hunt, and McCord, which McCord dedicatedly oversees, that Netflix requires "talent density" to survive and thrive. That in turn means that Netflix wants only "A" talent, not average. And its approach to do this, its culture, and the policies that drive it, all seek to enable this talent-dense "A" team approach to work masterfully.

At Netflix, there is no vacation policy, or as Hastings would say, "no policy on vacation." Employees take what they need as long as they get their job done. Compensation is flexible, there are no strict compensation rules. Salaries are typically higher than Silicon Valley standards; "we're unafraid to pay high," said Hastings.** Employees typically choose their stock-to-cash compensation ratios. Pay increase is not tied to performance reviews, or a raise pool, but rather to the job market.

Formal titles are few. Perks are minimal. "If you are looking for perks, this the wrong place. The fun we have here is all about building products," offered McCord.† "We hire a lot of seasoned people but we don't have all the perks—cubes, not offices, very few assistants, small staffs, no traditional HR support," said Hastings in a recent interview.‡ Formal titles are few. Parties are few—there are no Friday afternoon bands or beer bashes.

There is also the concept that "We're not a family, we're a professional sports team. Therefore, we're going to try to have the best players at every position, and that means that folks who are B-players are going to be working elsewhere."§ Translated, Netflix seeks to have the best team possible, and get their players placed in the role that best leverages their talents and potential. Said Hastings, "It's an honest and candid environment, and as a result, most employees that don't work out say thank you when they leave. And severances are generous."§§

Finally, Hastings sees Netflix managers' role as a leader being to educate people on what they're trying to do, giving context, and not guiding every specific action. In his mind that "context" includes finding a talented person who would come up with the right decision in most situations. So poor performance to Hastings mostly reflects back on the Netflix manager/leader. What context did they fail to set that led to a poor hire? In the Netflix culture, that might just lead to a major bonus for one manager, and maybe a generous severance for both another manager and the poorly performing employee they hired. Why such generous severances? Because Hastings is of the opinion that otherwise managers might feel too guilty to let someone go.§§§

*"Netflix Flees to the Max," *BusinessWeek*, September 24, 2007; and Michael Copeland, "Reed Hastings: Leader of the pack," *Fortune*, November 18, 2010.

**Ibid, "Netflix Flees . . ."

†Ibid, Copeland.

‡Hastings, http://www.businessinsider.com/netflix-ceo-reed-hastings-interview-2011-4?page=5.

§Ibid, Hastings.

§§Ibid, Hastings.

§§§Ibid, "Netflix Flees."

tenure in the organization. This creates the perception of replacing those representing the old and seemingly ineffective way of doing things, starting the process of new culture formation.[22] Interestingly, referring back to Reed Hastings and Netflix in Exhibit 12.7, Hastings persuaded two key executives, Neil Hunt and Patty McCord, to leave the first company he was a part of building to join him in building Netflix, with a particular emphasis on doing so with a unique culture.[23]

ethical standards
A person's basis for differentiating right from wrong.

Ethical standards are a person's basis for differentiating right from wrong. An earlier section of this chapter emphasized the importance of "principles" in defining what a leader needs to incorporate in his or her recipe to become an effective leader. We need not repeat those points in the context of being a leader, but it is critical to recognize that the culture of an organization, and particularly the link between the leader and the culture's very nature, is inextricably tied to the ethical standards of behavior, actions, decisions, and norms that leader personifies. Enron, Merrill Lynch, WorldCom, Bear Sterns, Madoff, are companies, people, and situations we discussed in Chapter 3—they are all imprinted in each of our minds. They speak volumes about this very point: leaders, and their key associates, play a key role in shaping and defining the ethical standards that become absorbed into and shape the culture of the organizations they lead. Those ethical standards then become powerful, informal guidelines for the behaviors, decisions, and dealings of members of that culture or tribe.

Leaders use every means available to them as an organizational leader to influence an organization's culture and their relationship with it. It bears repeating in this regard that reward systems, assignment of new managers from within versus outside the organization, composition of the firm's board of directors, reporting relationships, and organizational structure—each of these fundamental elements of executing a company's vision and strategy are also a leader's key "levers" for attempting to shape organizational culture in a direction she or he sees it needing to go. Because we have already discussed these levers, we move on to other ways leaders have sought to shape and reinforce their organization's culture.

Emphasize Key Themes or Dominant Values

Businesses build strategies around distinct competitive advantages they possess or seek. Quality, differentiation, cost advantages, and speed are four key sources of competitive advantage. Insightful leaders nurture key themes or dominant values within their organization that reinforce competitive advantages they seek to maintain or build. Key themes or dominant values may center around wording in an advertisement. They are often found in internal company communications. They are most often found as a new vocabulary used by company personnel to explain "who we are." At Xerox, the key themes include respect for the individual and services to the customer. At Procter & Gamble (P&G), the overarching value is product quality; McDonald's uncompromising emphasis on QSCV—quality, service, cleanliness, and value—through meticulous attention to detail is legendary; Southwest Airlines is driven by the "family feeling" theme, which builds a team spirit and nurtures each employee's cooperative attitude toward others, cheerful outlook toward life, and pride in a job well done. Du Pont's safety orientation—a report of every accident must be on the chairman's desk within 24 hours—has resulted in a safety record that was 27 times better than the chemical industry average and 68 times better than the all-manufacturing average.

[22]Edgar H. Schein, *Organizational Culture and Leadership* (San Francisco: Josey-Bass), 2010, p. 287.
[23]Ashlee Vance, "The Man Who Ate the Internet," *Bloomberg Businessweek,* May 19, 2013.

Encourage Dissemination of Stories and Legends about Core Values

Companies with strong cultures are enthusiastic collectors and tellers of stories, anecdotes, and legends in support of basic beliefs. Frito-Lay's zealous emphasis on customer service is reflected in frequent stories about potato chip route salespeople who have slogged through sleet, mud, hail, snow, and rain to uphold the 99.5 percent service level to customers in which the entire company takes great pride. Milliken (a textile leader) holds "sharing" rallies once every quarter at which teams from all over the company swap success stories and ideas. Typically, more than 100 teams make five-minute presentations over a two-day period. Every rally is designed around a major theme, such as quality, cost reduction, or customer service. No criticisms are allowed, and awards are given to reinforce this institutionalized approach to storytelling. L.L.Bean tells customer service stories; 3M tells innovation stories; P&G, Johnson & Johnson, IBM, and Maytag tell quality and innovation stories. These stories are very important in developing an organizational culture, because organization members identify strongly with them and come to share the beliefs and values they support.

Institutionalize Practices That Systematically Reinforce Desired Beliefs and Values

Companies with strong cultures are clear on what their beliefs and values need to be and take the process of shaping those beliefs and values very seriously. Most important, the values espoused by these companies underlay the strategies they employ. For example, McDonald's has a yearly contest to determine the best hamburger cooker in its chain. First, there is a competition to determine the best hamburger cooker in each store; next, the store winners compete in regional championships; finally, the regional winners compete in the "All-American" contest. The winners, who are widely publicized throughout the company, get trophies and All-American patches to wear on their McDonald's uniforms. As noted earlier in Exhibit 12.7, Netflix's founder Reed Hastings created a 128-slide PowerPoint presentation shared with all Netflix employees and aspirants to explain Netflix beliefs and values that drive its culture in simple, clear, unambiguous terms. He has also made it available to anyone via the Web, further institutionalizing and reinforcing the culture he views as essential to Netflix's future success. Facebook COO Sheryl Sanberg recently said of Reed Hastings's Netflix Culture presentation, "it may well be the most important document ever to come out of Silicon Valley.[24]

Adapt Some Very Common Themes in Their Own Unique Ways

The most typical beliefs that shape organizational culture include (1) a belief in being the best (or, as at GE, "better than the best"); (2) a belief in superior quality and service; (3) a belief in the importance of people as individuals and a faith in their ability to make a strong contribution; (4) a belief in the importance of the details of execution, the nuts and bolts of doing the job well; (5) a belief that customers should reign supreme; (6) a belief in inspiring people to do their best, whatever their ability; (7) a belief in the importance of informal communication; and (8) a belief that growth and profits are essential to a company's well-being. Every company implements these beliefs differently (to fit its particular situation), and every company's values are the handiwork of one or two legendary figures in leadership positions. Accordingly, every company has a distinct culture that it believes no other company can copy successfully. And in companies with strong cultures, managers and workers either accept the norms of the culture or opt out from the culture and leave the company.

[24]*GQ Magazine*, February, 2013.

The stronger a company's culture and the more that culture is directed toward customers and markets, the less the company uses policy manuals, organization charts, and detailed rules and procedures to enforce discipline and norms. The reason is that the guiding values inherent in the culture convey in crystal-clear fashion what everybody is supposed to do in most situations. Poorly performing companies often have strong cultures. However, their cultures are dysfunctional, being focused on internal politics or operating by the numbers as opposed to emphasizing customers and the people who make and sell the product.

Organizational Culture in a Global Organization[25]

The importance of "cultural fit," and making sure new hires "fit" an existing culture, can present a problem in that it can lead to too much "sameness" and less diversity among an organization's people, even as the world grows ever smaller and customers increasingly diverse. This reality is particularly important in today's global organizations, be they well-known multinational corporations or newer startups with a small, but culturally diverse employee base. *Social norms* create differences across national boundaries that influence how people interact, read personal cues, and otherwise interrelate socially. *Values* and *attitudes* about similar circumstances also vary from country to country. Where individualism is central to a North American's value structure, the needs of the group dominate the value structure of their Japanese counterparts. *Religion* is yet another source of cultural differences. Holidays, practices, and belief structures differ in very fundamental ways that must be taken into account as one attempts to shape organizational culture in a global setting. Finally, *education,* or ways people are accustomed to learning, differs across national borders. Formal classroom learning in the United States may teach things that are only learned via apprenticeship in other cultures. Because the process of shaping an organizational culture often involves considerable "education," leaders should be sensitive to global differences in approaches to education to make sure their cultural education efforts are effective. Henning Kagermann, former CEO of German-based global software company SAP, spoke to this issue when he said: "If you are a big company, you need to tap into the global talent pool. It's foolish to believe the smartest people are in one nation. In Germany, we now have this big public debate about there being a shortage of engineers in the country. Well, I don't care, or at least not as CEO of SAP. We are a collection of talented engineers in Germany, India, China, the U.S., Israel, Brazil, and the diversity therein represented enriches the culture, creativity, and market responsiveness of SAP."[26] Kagermann was seeking significant representation of cultures and communities worldwide so that SAP truly reflected the vast global settings in which it does business.

Manage the Strategy-Culture Relationship

Managers find it difficult to think through the relationship between a firm's culture and the critical factors on which strategy depends. They quickly recognize, however, that key components of the firm—structure, staff, systems, people, style—influence the ways in which key managerial tasks are executed and how critical management relationships are formed. And implementation of a new strategy is largely concerned with adjustments in these components to accommodate the perceived needs of the strategy. Consequently, managing the strategy-culture relationship requires sensitivity to the interaction between the

[25]Differing backgrounds, often referred to as *cultural diversity*, is something that most managers will certainly see more of, both because of the growing cultural diversity domestically and the obvious diversification of cultural backgrounds that result from global acquisitions and mergers. For example, Harold Epps, manager of a computer keyboard plant in Boston, manages 350 employees representing 44 countries of origin and 19 languages.
[26]"Tapping Global Talent in Software," *BusinessWeek*, June 9, 2007.

EXHIBIT 12.8
Managing the Strategy-Culture Relationship

Changes in key organizational factors that are necessary to implement the new strategy

	High	Low
Many	Link changes to basic mission and fundamental organizational values 1	Reformulate strategy or prepare carefully for long-term, difficult cultural change 4
Few	2 Synergistic—focus on reinforcing culture	3 Manage around the culture

High   **Low**
Potential compatibility of changes with existing culture

changes necessary to implement the new strategy and the compatibility or "fit" between those changes and the firm's culture. Exhibit 12.8 provides a simple framework for managing the strategy-culture relationship by identifying four basic situations a firm might face.

Link to Core Values

A firm in cell 1 is faced with a situation in which implementing a new strategy requires several changes in structure, systems, managerial assignments, operating procedures, or other fundamental aspects of the firm. However, most of the changes are potentially compatible with the existing organizational culture. Firms in this situation usually have a tradition of effective performance and are either seeking to take advantage of a major opportunity or are attempting to redirect major product-market operations consistent with proven core capabilities. Such firms are in a very promising position: they can pursue a strategy requiring major changes but still benefit from the power of cultural reinforcement.

Four basic considerations should be emphasized by firms seeking to manage a strategy-culture relationship in this context:

1. *Key changes should be visibly linked to the basic company mission.* Because the company mission provides a broad official foundation for the organizational culture, top executives should use all available internal and external forums to reinforce the message that the changes are inextricably linked to it.

2. *Emphasis should be placed on the use of existing personnel* where possible to fill positions created to implement the new strategy. Existing personnel embody the shared values and norms that help ensure cultural compatibility as major changes are implemented.

3. *Care should be taken if adjustments in the reward system are needed.* These adjustments should be consistent with the current reward system. If, for example, a new product-market thrust requires significant changes in the way sales are made, and, therefore, in incentive compensation, common themes (e.g., incentive oriented) should be emphasized. In this way, current and future reward approaches are related, and the changes in the reward system are justified (encourage development of less familiar markets).

4. *Key attention should be paid to the changes that are least compatible with the current culture,* so current norms are not disrupted. For example, a firm may choose to subcontract an important step in a production process because that step would be incompatible with the current culture.

P&G's shift to open innovation under Alan Lafley, not once but twice hiring him as CEO, offers an example (described in Global Strategy in Action Exhibit 12.9) of a company in this situation. P&G's long-standing core value as a consumer products company had been one of

Rebirthing P&G Twice—Is this Corporate Reincarnation?*

For most of the first decade of the twenty-first century, Alan Lafley was CEO of P&G. An insider, he nonetheless dramatically changed the culture at P&G by interpreting the organization's 170-year-old values in light of the dramatically changing twenty-first-century consumer and competitive landscape. Lafley followed Dirk Jager, an aggressive outside change agent who launched new brands, openly criticized P&G's "internally focused culture," and sought to change that culture. P&G was built on a culture that emphasized internally focused, "invented here" innovation; incremental innovation; and intense loyalty to its core brands—Tide, Crest, and Pampers. Poor earnings and employee resistance to change resulted in Jager's departure. Lafley, a comfortable insider, nonetheless agreed with Jager's assessment. He just took a different approach. Said Lafley, "At P&G we're purpose driven and values led. Focusing first on what would *not* change—the company's core purpose and values—made it easier to ask the organization to take on what I knew would be fairly dramatic changes elsewhere. The challenge was to understand and embrace the values that had guided P&G over generations—trust, integrity, ownership, leadership and a passion for winning—while reorienting them toward the outside and translating them for current and future relevance."

Before he retired, Lafley had opened up P&G far beyond what anyone expected. He has made innovation from folks outside P&G a key priority, started new product lines, and outsourced key functions like IT and soap manufacturing. Lafley described his perspective in an interview early in his reign: "Durk and I had believed very strongly that the company had to change and make fundamental changes. . . . There are two simple differences: One is I'm very externally focused. I expressed the change in the context of how we're going to serve consumers better, how we're going to win with the retailer, and how we're going to defeat the competitor in the marketplace.

The most important thing—I didn't attack. I avoided saying P&G people are bad. I thought that was a big mistake [on Jager's part]. The difference is, I preserved the core of the culture and pulled people where I wanted to go. I enrolled them in change. I didn't tell them. And, I was lucky when you have a mess, you have a chance to make more changes.**

BACK TO THE FUTURE

Five years after his retirement, Lafley was suddenly brought back, replacing CEO Bob McDonald, Lafley's replacement. Lafley's task—turn around a faltering P&G.

McDonald, a 33-year P&G veteran, ran into problems with the global recession that saw previous P&G brand loyalists opting for cheaper Unilever and store brands, which they continued with after the recession passed. McDonald's vision—"living a life driven by purpose is more meaningful and rewarding than meandering through life without direction. My life's purpose is to improve lives"—seemed more like a sermon than a vision pitch employees could use to sell toothpaste, skin creams, and detergents. Plus, it was a different vision from Lafley's unwavering devotion to understanding how customers live and feel—trying to grasp what "jobs" they were "hiring" P&G products to do.[†] Lafley's first comments to P&G employees:

> I will be getting up to speed on the business in the next several weeks. In the meantime, here are a few of my core beliefs: The consumer is boss—at the heart of everything we do. We create and build brands that improve consumers' lives. Innovation is our lifeblood. Every P&Ger is an owner and a leader—we are one team, with one dream, collaborating internally and competing externally. I look forward to working with you in the days and weeks ahead.

Will it work? Lafley has quite a challenge. P&G has not had a meaningful innovation since the Swiffer, which was created on his previous watch. Obviously the board selecting Lafley is a sign of how much the company values continuity, company knowledge, and company roots—a "cultural fit." But rebirthing P&G yet one more time seems Lafley's repeat challenge, and many feel he is just the leader for the challenge.

*Sarah Green, "What A. G. Lafley's Return Means for P&G," www.blogs.hbr.org May 24, 2013; Hal Gregersen, "A. G. Lafley's Innovation Skills Will Weather P&G's Storm," *Bloomberg Businessweek*, June 3, 2013; Lauren Coleman-Lochner and Carol Hymowitz, "Lafley's CEO oncore at P&G Puts Rock Star Legacy at Risk: Retail," www.bloomberg.com, May 28, 2013; and Jay Greene, "P&G: New & Improved," *BusinessWeek*, July 7, 2003.

**Jay Greene, "P&G: New & Improved," *BusinessWeek*, July 7, 2003.

†Gregersen, 2013, ibid.; and Coleman-Lochner, 2013, ibid.

innovative product design and development. Alan Lafley was very careful to push for a more open culture in terms of who would help P&G innovate more effectively, but he was also emphatic about linking these new efforts at changing how the "great innovator" innovated with the core notion that P&G people, and P&G's 170-year-old tradition or mission was still *THE* global consumer products innovator. He linked changes to the basic P&G values. Lafley next emphasized speaking positively about P&G people and getting them to buy in to the changes he sought. He placed emphasis on existing personnel. Third, he included new rewards to encourage acceptance of the different way of doing things. And fourth, he made sure on changes that were "stretching people too much" to use what he called an accelerator and a throttle approach. He identified himself as the accelerator, pushing aggressively for change. And he assigned his managers as his throttle, to regularly meet and discuss and perhaps alter the pace of change, depending on their assessment of whether the changes were taking or whether people were being pushed to change too quickly. So in this way Lafley made sure to monitor changes least compatible with P&G's current culture.

Maximize Synergy

A firm in cell 2 needs only a few organizational changes to implement its new strategy, and those changes are potentially quite compatible with its current culture. A firm in this situation should emphasize two broad themes:

1. *Take advantage of the situation to reinforce and solidify the current culture.*
2. *Use this time of relative stability to remove organizational roadblocks to the desired culture.*

3M's efforts to reacquire its culture of innovation illustrates this situation. Earlier this decade, James McNerney became the first outsider to lead 3M in its 100-year history. He had barely stepped off the plane before he announced he would change the DNA of the place. His playbook was classic pursuit of efficiency: he axed 8,000 workers (about 11 percent of the workforce), intensified the performance-review process, tightened the purse strings, and implemented a Six Sigma program to decrease production defects and increase efficiency. Five years later, McNerney abruptly left for a bigger opportunity—Boeing. 3M turned to Briton George Buckley, then CEO of Brunswick Corporation, to lead 3M. Buckley's question: had the relentless emphasis on efficiency made 3M a less innovative company? His assessment: "Operating margins had risen from 17.5 percent to 23.5 percent under McNerney—an unnatural rise for a company as large as 3M. Organic growth was only half the market level, so 3M was losing market share; the new product vitality index percent of sales derived from products introduced the previous five years had dropped from 30 percent to 8 percent; customer and employee satisfaction was rapidly deteriorating; yet the financials looked magnificent. This company looked magnificent on the surface, but it was in reality on a glide path to disaster.[27]

Those results are not coincidental. Efficiency programs such as Six Sigma are designed to identify problems in work processes—and then use rigorous measurement to reduce variation and eliminate defects. When these types of initiatives become ingrained in a company's culture, as they did at 3M, creativity can easily get squelched. After all, a breakthrough innovation is something that challenges existing procedures and norms. "Invention is by its very nature a disorderly process," says CEO Buckley, who has dialed down some key McNerney initiatives as he attempts to return 3M to its roots and its culture of innovation. "You can't put a Six Sigma process into that area and say, well,

[27]Steve Johnson, "Retired 3M Chief Finds a New Life in Sustainability," *Financial Times,* January 20, 2013.

I'm getting behind on invention, so I'm going to schedule myself for three good ideas on Wednesday and two on Friday. That's not how creativity works." While process excellence demands precision, consistency, and repetition, innovation calls for variation, failure, and serendipity.[28] Buckley took advantage of this difficult situation to reinforce and solidify 3M's "re"-embrace of its former, innovation culture by bringing back flexible funding for innovative ideas among other traditions. At the same time, he used the general embrace of a return to its old culture to make some key changes in manufacturing practices and plant locations outside the United States to make 3M more cost effective and competitive in a global economy. Buckley recently retired as CEO to be replaced by his COO, Swede Inge Thulin, a 33-year 3M veteran. Said Thulin, "We will continue to look for acquisitions and keep investing in new products, continuing the pattern of research and development that accelerated under George Buckley."

Manage around the Culture

A firm in cell 3 must make a few major organizational changes to implement its new strategy, but these changes are potentially inconsistent with the firm's current organizational culture. The critical question for a firm in this situation is whether it can make the changes with a reasonable chance of success.

A firm can manage around the culture in various ways: create a separate firm or division; use task forces, teams, or program coordinators; subcontract; bring in an outsider; or sell out. These are a few of the available options, but the key idea is to create a method of achieving the change desired that avoids confronting the incompatible cultural norms. As cultural resistance diminishes, the change may be absorbed into the firm.

IBM's sale of its PC business to China's Lenovo, creating the third-largest global PC firm behind Dell and HP, was a strategic decision it took three years to conclude. IBM management became increasingly concerned with the problem that the PC business, and the culture surrounding it, were incompatible with the culture and direction IBM's core business had been taking for some time. The conflict, and the inability to reconcile different cultural needs, led IBM executives to explore the sale of the PC division to Lenovo. At the time IBM's PC division was in disarray and losing $400 million annually. Lenovo's reaction was to send IBM packing out of China with a sense they had tried to take Lenovo's executives for fools who would buy a "pig in a poke." But IBM executives, still desperately concerned about the fundamental and cultural difference between the PC business and the rest of IBM set about an intense 18-month effort to wring costs out of the PC's supply chain, bring it back to profitability, and then go to call on Lenovo again. They achieved both in 18 months and, in their next business, found a more receptive Lenovo management team—ultimately concluding the deal a few months later. In so doing, IBM worked feverishly even to include creating a profitable global PC business only to then sell it quickly and cheaply so that it could "manage around a culture" in the sense of allowing IBM to unify around a different business model and remove the business it was most known for, the IBM-PC business, from its organization along with the cultural incompatibility it represented.

Reformulate the Strategy or Culture

A firm in cell 4 faces the most difficult challenge in managing the strategy-culture relationship. To implement its new strategy, such a firm must make organizational changes that are

---

[28]"At 3M, a Struggle Between Efficiency and Creativity," *BusinessWeek*, June 11, 2007; and Marc Gunther, "3M's Innovation Revival," *Fortune*, September 24, 2010.

incompatible with its current, usually entrenched, values and norms. A firm in this situation faces the complex, expensive, and often long-term challenge of changing its culture; it is a challenge that borders on impossible.

When a strategy requires massive organizational change and engenders cultural resistance, a firm should determine whether reformulation of the strategy is appropriate. Are all of the organizational changes really necessary? Is there any real expectation that the changes will be acceptable and successful? If these answers are yes, then massive changes are often necessary. Alan Mulally's actions at Ford over the last few years saw him making major changes in an attempt to change Ford's culture to suit its new strategy: bringing outsiders in as top execs, changing long-standing executive compensation programs, emphasizing sales and marketing over the traditional, patronage-based culture as, sadly, Ford's most "prized" cultural element. These are elements through which Ford, under Mulally, is undergoing massive change as he tries to build a different culture compatible with a new vision and strategy.

The John Deere company faced a growing challenge in a globally competitive farm equipment industry as it moved into the twenty-first century. Its financial performance was marginal, and it retained a "family" culture borne out of its century-long roots in the land and farm setting it served. New CEO at the time Bob Lane first developed a new strategy that placed straightforward emphasis on improving Deere's efficient use of its assets and clear profitability targets. Pursuing this strategy required several organizational changes at Deere, which were received relatively easily in a tradition-laden company. But Lane quickly found that a greater challenge needed confronting—and that was Deere's "family" culture, which manifests itself in what he called a "best efforts mentality." That mentality drove the culture that had many Deere managers often satisfied with making earnest efforts and doing "pretty good." Lane had to change that culture, or change his new results-driven strategy. He chose to change the culture, which meant moving from the commonly heard expression of "the John Deere family" to one that prioritized high-performance teams. As Lane described it, "We're changing from being a family to being a high-performance team. To use an American football analogy, some people prefer to play intramurals. That's okay, but they are no longer a good fit for John Deere. It was as if you could always count on Deere to move the ball at least six or seven yards. And when we got to that point, we could say 'good work, good enough'—even though we hadn't reached the first-down marker." Now, Deere people are expected to have exhausted every legitimate effort to move the ball farther and meet the goal, and then move the ball farther again. The management team, decided to stick with the strategy and reformulate Deere's culture.[29] The cultural changes and emphasis on profitability from high-performance teams took hold. John Deere achieved successive years of record earnings over the final five years Lane was CEO. Lane's replacement, Sam Allen, recently announced the "John Deere Strategy 2018" as a continuation of the transformative strategy that propelled the company's performance in the last 10 years under former Chief Executive Robert Lane, emphasizing a "Shareholder Value-Added" operating model focusing the company on generating cash by driving out waste and inefficiency from Deere's operations, aligning equipment production to retail demand to avoid inventory overhangs, and increasing the company's global focus. "By all accounts, it worked exceeding well," Allen said. "Now it's time to build on that strong foundation of achievement."[30]

[29]"Leading Change," *McKinsey on Organization*, McKinsey and Company, December 2006.
[30]http://www.foxbusiness.com/industries/2011/02/23/deere-wants-nearly-double-sales-50-billion-2018/.

Summary

This chapter has examined organizational leadership and organization culture—two factors essential to the successful implementation and execution of a company's strategic plan. Organizational leadership is guiding and shepherding an organization over time and developing that organization's future leadership and its organization culture.

We saw that good organizational leadership involves three considerations: clarifying strategic intent, building an organization, and shaping the organization's culture. Strategic intent is clarified through the leader's vision, a broad picture of where he or she is leading the firm, and candid attention to and clear expectations about performance.

Leaders use education, principles, and perseverance to build their organization. Education involves familiarizing managers and future leaders with an effective understanding of the business and the skills they need to develop. Perseverance, the ability to stick to the challenge when most others falter, is an unquestionable tool for leaders to instill faith in the vision they seek when times are hard. Principles are the leader's personal standards that guide her or his sense of honesty, integrity and ethical behavior. They are more essential than ever in today's world as key building blocks for the type of organization for which a leader's principles reflect and are watched with great interest by every manager, employee, customer, and supplier of the organization.

Leaders start to shape organizational culture by the passion they bring to their role, and their choice and development of young managers and future leaders. Passion, a highly motivated sense of commitment to what you do and want to do, is a force that permeates attitudes throughout an organization and helps them buy into your cultural aspirations. Combining those with the skills, aspirations, and inclinations you seek to make the vision a reality—and then helping them develop—is a key way to build a culture over the long term. One of the key skills of these rising leaders is to learn how to motivate, lead, and get others to do what they need.

Understanding seven sources of power and influence, rather than just the power of position and punishment, is a critical skill for effective future leaders to grasp.

Organizational culture is the set of important assumptions, values, beliefs, and norms that members of an organization share in common. The organizational leader plays a critical role in developing, sustaining, and changing organizational culture. Ethical standards, the leader's basis for differentiating right from wrong, quickly spread as a centerpiece between the leader and the organization's culture. Leaders use many means to reinforce and develop their organization's culture—from rewards and appointments to storytelling and rituals. Managing the strategy-culture relationship requires different approaches, depending on the match between the demands of the new strategy and the compatibility of the culture with that strategy. This chapter examined four different scenarios.

Key Terms

ethical standards, *p. 387*
expert influence, *p. 382*
information power, *p. 381*
leadership development, *p. 374*
leader's vision, *p. 370*
organizational culture, *p. 383*

organizational leadership, *p. 368*
passion (of a leader), *p. 377*
peer influence, *p. 382*
perseverance (of a leader), *p. 374*
position power, *p. 381*

principles (of a leader), *p. 375*
punitive power, *p. 381*
referent influence, *p. 382*
reward power, *p. 381*
strategic intent, *p. 370*

Questions for Discussion

1. Think about any two leaders you have known, preferably one good and one weak. They can be businesspersons, coaches, someone you work(ed) with, and so forth. Make a list of five traits, practices, or characteristics that cause you to consider one good and the other weak. Compare the things you chose with the seven factors used to differentiate effective organizational leadership in the first half of this chapter.

2. This chapter describes seven attributes that enable good leadership—vision, performance, principles, education of subordinates, perseverance, passion, and leader selection/development. Which one have you found to be the most meaningful to you in the leaders you respond to the best?

3. Consider the following situation and determine whether the VC group is engaging in something that would violate your principles, or be totally acceptable to you. Explain why.

    Who likes those ubiquitous online pop-up ads planted by intrusive spyware? Technology Crossover Ventures is betting few do. The Silicon Valley venture-capital firm helped to finance the anti-spyware company Webroot Software. But it appears to hedge that bet with a sizable investment in Claria, a company vilified for spreading spyware.

    More than 40 million Web surfers viewed Claria ads. TCV pumped at least $13 million into Claria, but it has removed the company from a list of investments on its Web site.

    Critics wonder why TCV would make dual investments. "Users are rubbed the wrong way by even the suggestion that the same companies that made this mess are now profiting from helping to clean it up," says Harvard University researcher and spyware expert Ben Edelman. TCV declined to comment. There is a similar element in both ventures: the potential to make money.

4. Read Exhibit 12.3. What would you do if you were asked to serve as an Ethics Review Arbitrator and render a decision on what should happen to the Duke MBA students? The Centenary College Chinese MBA program? Summarize the key reasons supporting your ruling.

5. Do you think new-old P&G CEO Alan Lafley was a good organizational leader? What was his most important contribution to his organizational culture in your opinion?

6. What is your opinion of the Netflix organizational culture crafted by Reed Hastings? What pros and cons do you detect?

7. What three sources of power and influence are best suited to you as a manager?

8. Describe two organizations you have been a part of based on differences in their organizational cultures.

9. What key things did Alan Mulally do as an organizational leader to shape Ford's organizational culture? Do you think he succeeded? Why?

Chapter **Thirteen**

Strategic Control

After reading and studying this chapter, you should be able to

1. Describe and illustrate four types of strategic control.

2. Summarize the balanced score-card approach and how it integrates strategic and operational control.

3. Illustrate the use of controls to guide and monitor strategy implementation.

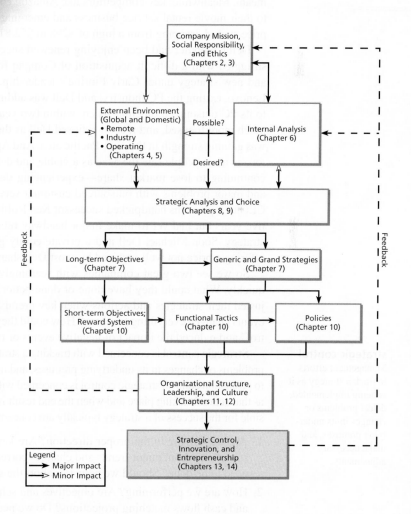

Company Mission, Social Responsibility, and Ethics (Chapters 2, 3)

External Environment (Global and Domestic)
• Remote
• Industry
• Operating
(Chapters 4, 5)

Possible?

Internal Analysis (Chapter 6)

Desired?

Strategic Analysis and Choice (Chapters 8, 9)

Long-term Objectives (Chapter 7)

Generic and Grand Strategies (Chapter 7)

Short-term Objectives; Reward System (Chapter 10)

Functional Tactics (Chapter 10)

Policies (Chapter 10)

Organizational Structure, Leadership, and Culture (Chapters 11, 12)

Strategic Control, Innovation, and Entrepreneurship (Chapters 13, 14)

Feedback

Feedback

Legend
→ Major Impact
⇢ Minor Impact

STRATEGIC CONTROL

Strategies are forward looking, designed to be accomplished several years into the future. They are based on management assumptions about numerous events that have not yet occurred. How should executives "control" a strategy, and its execution?

Consider the experiences of Netflix and Dell Computer over the last decade. Netflix, having overwhelmed Blockbuster and other DVD movie rental businesses with its DVD-by-mail rental service, experienced impressive early success. Seeing its stock price continue to climb above $200 per share, and an increase above 30 million in the subscriber base, Netflix was flourishing. Founder Reed Hastings and his team saw the emerging Web-based video streaming technology as an inevitable development that would become a key way current customers would want to watch movies. Trying to stay ahead of that innovation curve, Hastings and his team introduced a Netflix strategy that included raising its prices for renting videos and dividing the company into two separate companies—a DVD mailer company called Qwikster and a streaming entity under the original Netflix name. The result? Customer outrage. Netflix quickly started losing millions of customers over the price increase and the way it was handled. Others were reacting to confusion over what the two approaches meant. Meanwhile, key competitors like Amazon.com were aggressively adding customers to their movie rental service business and emerging streaming offering too. Netflix's stock price started dropping from a high of $298 to $52.81 in a matter of months.

Dell Computer had been enjoying renewed success after its rival Hewlett-Packard had struggled with a difficult acquisition of Compaq followed by a confusing reorganization and new strategy under Carly Fiorina's leadership. IBM sold its PC business to China's Lenovo, exiting the PC industry, and Dell was adding more printers and electronic devices to its PC-outsourced pipeline. Then, within two years, HP's new CEO Mark Hurd had HP much more focused, and it soon eclipsed Dell as the world's largest seller of PCs. Lenovo was gaining strength in the Asia-Pacific area. And Apple's renewal was putting pressure on, too, as more people saw the Mac as a viable and desirable option to PCs. Dell found itself continuing to lose market share—experiencing declining profitability, excess inventory, and major problems with outsourced customer service. Founder Michael Dell returned as CEO to replace his handpicked successor Ken Rollins, who had worked as CEO more than five years but had yet to make major headway rebuilding Dell and any newly successful strategy. Soon Michael Dell and a private equity group were trying to take Dell private, offering a price not well received by most Dell shareholders.

So we see two great companies with seemingly solid strategies that deteriorated very quickly. What could they have done or done better? How could Netflix and Dell have adjusted their strategies and actions when key premises, technology, competitors, or sudden events changed everything for them? How could they have established better "strategic control" and reduced the impact of negative events or taken advantage of new opportunities?

strategic control
Management efforts to track a strategy as it is being implemented, detect problems or changes in its underlying premises, and make necessary adjustments.

Strategic control is concerned with tracking a strategy as it is being implemented, detecting problems or changes in its underlying premises, and making necessary adjustments. In contrast to postaction control, strategic control is concerned with guiding action on behalf of the strategy as that action is taking place and when the end result is still several years off. Managers responsible for the success of a strategy typically are concerned with two sets of questions:

1. Are we moving in the proper direction? Are key things falling into place? Are our assumptions about major trends and changes correct? Are we doing the critical things that need to be done? Should we adjust or abort the strategy?

2. How are we performing? Are objectives and schedules being met? Are costs, revenues, and cash flows matching projections? Do we need to make operational changes?

The rapidly accelerating level of change in the global marketplace has made the need for strategic control key in managing a company. This chapter examines strategic control.

ESTABLISHING STRATEGIC CONTROLS

The control of strategy can be characterized as a form of "steering control." As time elapses between the initial implementation of a strategy and achievement of its intended results, investments are made and numerous projects and actions are undertaken to implement the strategy. Also, during that time, changes are taking place in both the environmental situation and the firm's internal situation. Strategic controls are necessary to steer the firm through these events. They must provide the basis for adapting the firm's strategic actions and directions in response to these developments and changes. The four basic types of strategic control summarized in Exhibit 13.1 are

1. Premise control.
2. Strategic surveillance.
3. Special alert control.
4. Implementation control.

Premise Control

premise control
Management process of systematically and continuously checking to determine whether premises upon which the strategy is based are still valid.

Every strategy is based on certain planning premises—assumptions or predictions. **Premise control** is the systematic recognition and analysis of assumptions upon which a strategic plan is based, to determine if those assumptions remain valid in changing circumstances and in light of new information. If a vital premise is no longer valid, the strategy may have to be changed. The sooner an invalid premise can be recognized and rejected, the better are the chances that an acceptable shift in the strategy can be devised. Planning premises are primarily concerned with environmental and industry factors.

Environmental Factors

Although a firm has little or no control over environmental factors, these factors exercise considerable influence over the success of its strategy, and strategies usually are based on key premises about them. Inflation, technology, interest rates, regulation, and demographic/social changes are examples of such factors.

The third-generation Internet, Web 3.0, with cloud computing, virtualization, and ultra mobility, is spawning an instantaneously connected global youth culture that presents both a challenge to the old ways of doing business and an opportunity to gain tremendous leverage via the right goods and services. "Flying blind" is how some executives describe their effort to adapt to it: the tens of millions of digital elite who are the vanguard of a fast-emerging global culture based on smartphones, blogs, text messaging, social networks, YouTube, Twitter, Facebook, iPhone apps, to mention a few. These highly influential young people are sharing ideas and information across borders that will drive products, employment, services, food, fashion, and ideas—rapidly. Savvy companies are recognizing this phenomenon as perhaps the most critical environmental factor/phenomenon they need to monitor and understand.[1]

Netflix, the introductory example in this chapter, had been monitoring rather closely developments regarding cloud computing, streaming of video content, and the potential combination of the two as a business model changer for a company like Netflix. Their

[1]Steve Hamm, "Children of the Web," *BusinessWeek*, July 2, 2007.

EXHIBIT 13.1
**Four Types of
Strategic Control**

Source: From *Academy
of Management Review*
by G. Schreyogg and H.
Steinmann. Reproduced
with permission of Acad-
emy of Management via
Copyright Clearance
Center.

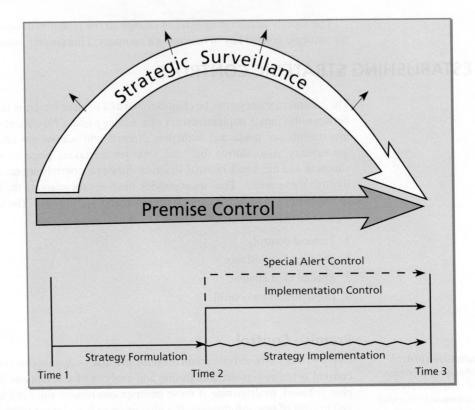

Characteristics of the Four Types of Strategic Control

	Types of Strategic Control			
Basic Characteristics	**Premise Control**	**Implementation Control**	**Strategic Surveillance**	**Special Alert Control**
Objects of control	Planning premises and projections	Key strategic thrusts and milestones	Potential threats and opportunities related to the strategy	Occurrence of recognizable but unlikely events
Degree of focusing	High	High	Low	High
Data acquisition:				
Formalization	Medium	High	Low	High
Centralization	Low	Medium	Low	High
Use with:				
Environmental factors	Yes	Seldom	Yes	Yes
Industry factors	Yes	Seldom	Yes	Yes
Strategy-specific factors	No	Yes	Seldom	Yes
Company-specific factors	No	Yes	Seldom	Seldom

Source: From *Academy of Management Review* by G. Schreyogg and H. Steinmann. Reproduced with permission of Academy of
Management via Copyright Clearance Center.

premise was that its acceptance would rapidly accelerate, with early evidence they monitored reinforcing that premise. So while they faced a very difficult strategic situation when they started seeing several million customers drop the DVD-mailing service under the Qwikster brand, their continued monitoring of streaming, cloud-enhanced technology convinced them to stick with their plan to move in that direction. That took considerable courage given the drop in subscriptions and stock price they experienced, but they also issued a flurry of apologies and pricing accomodations to deal with DVD-mailing-comfortable customers as they moved forward with the streaming plan.

Industry Factors

The performance of the firms in a given industry is affected by industry factors. Competitors, suppliers, product substitutes, and barriers to entry are a few of the industry factors about which strategic assumptions are made.

Returning again to Netflix, Hastings and his executive team were closely monitoring Amazon.com as a key premise control aspect of their strategy. Their strategy to move into streaming included the premise that they could do this by leasing cloud computing space and service from Amazon to save on Netflix's capital costs of moving into streaming, along with the key premise that Amazon would prove a dependable supplier even though it was also a significant competitor on its retail side renting and/or selling movies.

Netflix decided to gradually lease cloud space from Amazon to "test" their premise as they also leased space from Microsoft and several other cloud space providers. They also worked directly with key Amazon IT people as they wrote and used the code necessary to make sure the interface between Netflix's online connection with their customer receiving the streaming movie actually stored on the Amazon server flowed seamlessly to the Netflix customer watching the movie on their TV, computer, or other device. This offered further "testing" of the premise and increased confidence that they could increase the amount of Amazon cloud space they leased. In two years, Netflix is now Amazon's largest cloud services customer. Amazon and Netflix have developed software to not only manage flawless streaming to real-time customers, but also software to translate underlying digital movie data into a manner that flows seamlessly to a variety of different devices with different operating systems.

Strategies are often based on numerous premises, some major and some minor, about environmental and industry variables. Tracking all of these premises is unnecessarily expensive and time consuming. Managers must select premises whose change (1) is likely and (2) would have a major impact on the firm and its strategy.

Strategic Surveillance

strategic surveillance
Management efforts to monitor a broad range of events inside and more often outside the firm that are likely to affect the course of its strategy over time.

By their nature, premise controls are focused controls; strategic surveillance, however, is unfocused. **Strategic surveillance** is designed to monitor a broad range of events inside and outside the firm that are likely to affect the course of its strategy. The basic idea behind strategic surveillance is that important yet unanticipated information may be uncovered by a general monitoring of multiple information sources.

Strategic surveillance must be kept as unfocused as possible. It should be a loose "environmental scanning" activity. Trade magazines, *The Wall Street Journal*, trade conferences, conversations, and intended and unintended observations are all subjects of strategic surveillance. Despite its looseness, strategic surveillance provides an ongoing, broad-based vigilance in all daily operations that may uncover information relevant to the firm's strategy. P&G's widely admired former and recently returned new CEO Alan Lafley used "commercial anthropology," his way of describing strategic surveillance, to identify and monitor developments that were central to the success of its ongoing innovation strategy to provide products that meet basic needs better and do so repeatedly. In Global

Alan Lafley, P&G's Former New CEO's Secret to Good Innovation

Alan Lafley turned P&G into a global juggernaut once. He has recently been brought back to do it again. Some 4 billion people, more than half the world's population, use a P&G product each day. Lafley's philosophy on how to do that is very simple: observe people going about their daily lives, identify their unmet needs, and come up with new products that meet them.

He tells the story of how he had managers in Mexico study the daily washing rituals of low-income women to help kick start P&G sales in that country. He once described another time doing this himself: "I have sat with my legs in the water of a rural village in China talking with an interpreter to an older woman and her daughter doing her laundry in the river. I have probably done laundry in 25 countries. It is like being a social anthropologist." He went on to say it is really "commercial" rather than social or academic anthropology, but

clarifying that in saying, "We are observing because we believe that if we don't do anything to improve the life then we don't do anything to deserve to reap the commercial rewards."

Lafley's insistence on strategic surveillance, or commercial anthropology, takes place in many forums. P&G managers in Europe noticed the accelerated growth of private-label consumer products due to the rapid growth of discount retailers like Germany's Aldi and France's Leader Price. While other leading brands were hurt, P&G's manager had been following articles in European publications looking at consumer lifestyles. "We have studied this trend for some time, and concluded that discounters can be a real opportunity." Good strategic surveillance, or commercial anthropology? Lafley was no doubt very proud of P&G's efforts the first time. Now we get to see if he returns to his anthropological roots in his second reign at P&G.

Source: "A. G. Lafley's Innovation Skills Will Weather P&G's Storm," *Bloomberg BusinessWeek*, June 3, 2013; "Lafley's CEO Encore at P&G Puts Rock Star Legacy at Risk," www.bloomberg.com, May 28, 2013. See an excellent extended YouTube video discussion by Lafley, which includes a few examples of commercial anthropology early in the video, at http://www.youtube.com/watch?v=Stz9HkKdRS8.

Strategy in Action, Exhibit 13.2, Lafley talks about watching women wash clothes in rivers in China, watching others doing laundry in Mexico, and having European managers study consumer preferences in buying diapers from German and French discount retailers—all examples of strategic surveillance, Alan Lafley style.

Special Alert Control

special alert control
Management actions undertaken to thoroughly, and often very rapidly, reconsider a firm's strategy because of a sudden, unexpected event.

Another type of strategic control, really a subset of the other three, is special alert control. A **special alert control** is the thorough, and often rapid, reconsideration of the firm's strategy because of a sudden, unexpected event. The tragic events following the sudden 2011 earthquake and tsunami in Japan; an outside firm's sudden acquisition of a leading competitor; an unexpected product difficulty, like the fingertip in a bowl of Wendy's chili—events of these kinds can drastically alter the firm's strategy.

Such an event should trigger an immediate and intense reassessment of the firm's strategy and its current strategic situation. In many firms, crisis teams handle the firm's initial response to unforeseen events that may have an immediate effect on its strategy. IBM's shock at the precipitous decline in the sales growth and profitability of its core IT services business resulted in a special alert and ongoing focus on this business's strategy to allow it to immediately adjust by cutting staff or changing services frequently each quarter.

The sudden media drama involving Charlie Sheen, star of CBS TV's most profitable sitcom, *Two and a Half Men*, dominated Web-based, cable, and traditional TV for many months. CBS chose to cancel the series and fire Mr. Sheen, and Sheen chose to take on CBS and societal convention, dominating celebrity TV and Web-based coverage for almost a year. That series was the most profitable and popular sitcom for CBS, which in turn caused a lengthy special alert control for CBS. A few years earlier, the sudden release of a photo of Olympic gold medalist Michael Phelps at a South Carolina fraternity house party using a special pipe often associated with smoking marijuana caused an instant crisis for several companies paying Phelps as a celebrity sports endorser of their products after his unprecedented eight gold medals in the Olympics held months earlier in China. Kellogg chose to cancel his contract with their cereals, while Speedo chose to continue their association with Phelps. While others pondered what to do, it showed vividly why a process of special alert controls has become a key for companies using celebrity endorsers as described in Global Strategy in Action Exhibit 13.3.

Implementation Control

Strategy implementation takes place as a series of steps, programs, investments, and moves that occur over an extended time. Special programs are undertaken. Functional areas initiate strategy-related activities. Key people are added or reassigned. Resources are mobilized. In other words, managers implement strategy by converting broad plans into the concrete, incremental actions and results of specific units and individuals.

Implementation control is the type of strategic control that must be exercised as those events unfold. **Implementation control** is designed to assess whether the overall strategy should be changed in light of the results associated with the incremental actions that implement the overall strategy. The two basic types of implementation control are (1) monitoring strategic thrusts and (2) milestone reviews.

Monitoring Strategic Thrusts or Projects

As a means of implementing broad strategies, narrow strategic projects often are undertaken—projects that represent part of what needs to be done if the overall strategy is to be accomplished. These **strategic thrusts** provide managers with information that helps them determine whether the overall strategy is progressing as planned or needs to be adjusted.

Although the utility of strategic thrusts seems readily apparent, it is not always easy to use them for control purposes. It may be difficult to interpret early experience or to evaluate the overall strategy in light of such experience. One approach is to agree early in the planning process on which thrusts or which phases of thrusts are critical factors in the success of the strategy. Managers responsible for these implementation controls will single them out from other activities and observe them frequently. Another approach is to use stop/go assessments that are linked to a series of meaningful thresholds (time, costs, research and development, success, and so forth) associated with particular thrusts. Global Strategy in Action, Exhibit 13.3 describes Boeing's challenge to do this as it coordinates globally diverse outsourcing partners' production of various parts of the revolutionary new 787 Dreamliner fuselage and its components.

Milestone Reviews

Managers often attempt to identify significant milestones that will be reached during strategy implementation. These milestones may be critical events, major resource allocations, or simply the passage of a certain amount of time. The **milestone reviews** that then take place usually involve a full-scale reassessment of the strategy and of the advisability of continuing or refocusing the firm's direction.

A useful example of implementation control based on milestone review is offered by an earlier Boeing's product-development strategy of entering the supersonic transport (SST)

---

implementation control
Management efforts designed to assess whether the overall strategy should be changed in light of results associated with the incremental actions that implement the overall strategy. These are usually associated with specific strategic thrusts or projects and with predetermined milestone reviews.

strategic thrusts or projects
Special efforts that are early steps in executing a broader strategy, usually involving significant resource commitments yet where predetermined feedback will help management determine whether continuing to pursue the strategy is appropriate or whether it needs adjustment or major change.

milestone reviews
Points in time, or at the completion of major parts of a bigger strategy, where managers have predetermined they will undertake a go–no go type of review regarding the underlying strategy associated with the bigger strategy.

PREMISE CONTROL AT NEWSCRED.COM

NewsCred.com started out as a Web-based company seeking to build advertising revenue and content success around the global obsession with news coverage. The premise underlying NewsCred.com's strategy was that people around the world would visit its site to rank the credibility of a whole host of news sources, from mainstream to bloggers, with the result being that the most credible—accurate, believable, and honest—will rise to the top of the community rankings. Some observers argue that in a politically polarized society and world, some people will trash the publications they disagree with. So, for example, *The Wall Street Journal* or *The New York Times* could be relegated to mediocre status, while media outlets and blogs barely known will rise to the top. That premise proved incorrect. So NewsCred.com pivoted to focus on excelling at providing continuously updated, full text articles, picture and video content from 1000+ sources globally to clients (world's top publishers, marketers, and brands) seeking help to engage and grow their online audiences with unique, on-demand content experiences. And it acquired Daylife.com, which had cutting-edge publisher tools that can transform any Web destination in just a few clicks, to add depth to its pivot in doing so.

IMPLEMENTATION CONTROL

Boeing was scheduled to be delivering its first 787 Dreamliners in 2008. It did not until 2011. Boeing was forced to delay the 787 program four times due to problems with a shortage of parts, the need to redesign parts of the aircraft, and incomplete work by suppliers. For example, Boeing found out in early 2009 that tens of thousands of fasteners on several aircraft had apparently been incorrectly installed after mechanics at Boeing's Seattle plant misunderstood installation instructions. Boeing's ambitious worldwide outsourcing strategy—combined with the 787 being the largest, lightest, biggest plane in history—clearly necessitated careful, coordinated implementation planning and control to meet the milestones and deadline Boeing promised its many customers.

Virgin Atlantic is one typical example. Virgin committed to buy 15 of the new aircraft, at prices approaching $200 million each. This necessitated deposits of notable sums, plus plans and commitments on Virgin's part in working these planes into its fleet, its schedules, its decisions about existing aircraft and routes. Expecting delivery in April 2011, Virgin was still waiting for its first delivery in late 2013.

The consolation that Boeing will pay them some compensation for the impact of these delays offers Virgin little solace. What they want from Boeing is better control of the implementation of its Dreamliner strategy. That, and a safe aircraft, seem like reasonable expectations for a $200 million price tag each.

airplane market. Boeing had invested millions of dollars and years of scarce engineering talent during the first phase of its SST venture, and competition from the British/French Concorde effort was intense. Because the next phase represented a billion-dollar decision, Boeing's management established the initiation of the phase as a milestone. The milestone reviews greatly increased the estimates of production costs; predicted relatively few passengers and rising fuel costs, thus raising the estimated operating costs; and noted that the Concorde, unlike Boeing, had the benefit of massive government subsidies. These factors led Boeing's management to scrap its SST strategy in spite of high sunk costs, pride, and patriotism. Only an objective, full-scale strategy reassessment could have led to such a decision. A similar decision by Boeing regarding its strategic "bet" on the new 787 Dreamliner is very unlikely as it nears final assembly and initial test flights of this revolutionary, next-generation, composite airplane (see Exhibit 13.3).

In the SST example, a milestone review occurred at a major resource allocation decision point. Milestone reviews may also occur concurrently when a major step in a strategy's implementation is being taken or when a key uncertainty is resolved. Managers even may set an arbitrary period, say, two years, as a milestone review point. Whatever the basis for

Exhibit 13.3 continued

Examples of Strategic Control

STRATEGIC SURVEILLANCE AT WELLS FARGO

Wells Fargo, and most other banks large and small via the American Bankers Association, aggressively fought and lobbied against Walmart's application for a bank charter. They didn't like the idea of losing credit card processing fees. They won the lobbying battle and Walmart withdrew its application to open a bank in the United States.

According to Walmart's management at the time of their application, their primary motivation was to reduce the cost of allowing customers to buy on credit every time they used a Discover, MasterCard, or Visa branded charge card. Every time a customer uses one of these cards, Walmart pays a small processing fee to the bank that processes the payment. And so, from Walmart's perspective, why should they give that fee to Wells Fargo or others when they could just as easily handle the processing through their own bank? They could then pass that fee back to their customer, thereby saving them money.

Wells Fargo is now carefully engaging in strategic surveillance of Walmart's activities related to banking because of this situation—and because Walmart now has banking operations in 38 Mexican Walmarts with plans to increase that number 10-fold with new "banking booths" over the next few years. Walmart has filed an application in Canada seeking to open a pocket bank for its Canadian subsidiary. So is Walmart going to enter the U.S. bank market from its new foreign bases? You can bet Wells Fargo and others have ongoing strategic surveillance of Walmart's Mexican and Canadian banking activities so as to be ready to act.

SPECIAL ALERT CONTROL FOR CELEBRITY ENDORSEMENT COMPANIES

Critical to the strategies, and the success of many companies is the use of celebrity endorsements to promote their products and the perception of that product in the buyer's mind. Tiger Woods was almost always believable as a user of everything he endorses. Nike and Michael Jordan, Bill Cosby and Jell-O, Dan Marino and NutriSystem. But Paris Hilton's ads for Carl's Jr. and Hardees? Peyton Manning for Oreo Cookies? Catherine Zeta Jones for T-Mobile? Jason Alexander for KFC? Or Michael Phelps for Frosted Flakes? Or even Tiger Woods for Buick (subsequently dropped) or Tag Heuer?

Bottom line: any company that uses the celebrity endorsement approach to build its brand and image has committed to a part of "borrowed equity," meaning they define their product by borrowing the equity, image, and reputation of the celebrity as a user/endorser. In so doing, they are well advised to maintain a careful special alert control for changes that might immediately or gradually erode the connection with that celebrity.

---

selecting that point, the critical purpose of a milestone review is to thoroughly scrutinize the firm's strategy so as to control the strategy's future.

Implementation control is also enabled through operational control systems like budgets, schedules, and key success factors. While strategic controls attempt to steer the company over an extended period (usually five years or more), operational controls provide postaction evaluation and control over short periods—usually from one month to one year. To be effective, operational control systems must take four steps common to all postaction controls:

1. Set standards of performance.
2. Measure actual performance.
3. Identify deviations from standards set.
4. Initiate corrective action.

Exhibit 13.4 illustrates a typical operational control system. These indicators represent progress after two years of a five-year strategy intended to differentiate the firm as a customer-service–oriented provider of high-quality products. Management's concern is to compare

EXHIBIT 13.4 **Monitoring and Evaluating Performance Deviations**

Key Success Factors	Objective, Assumption, or Budget	Forecast Performance at This Time	Current Performance	Current Deviation	Analysis
Cost control: Ratio of indirect overhead cost to direct field and labor costs	10%	15%	12%	+3 (ahead)	Are we moving too fast, or is there more unnecessary overhead than was originally thought?
Gross profit	39%	40%	40%	0%	
Customer service: Installation cycle in days	2.5 days	3.2 days	2.7 days	+0.5 (ahead)	Can this progress be maintained?
Ratio of service to sales personnel	3.2	2.7	2.1	−0.6 (behind)	Why are we behind here? How can we maintain the installation-cycle progress?
Product quality: Percentage of products returned	1.0%	2.0%	2.1%	−0.1% (behind)	Why are we behind here? What are the ramifications for other operations?
Product performance versus specification	100%	92%	80%	−12% (behind)	
Marketing: Monthly sales per employee	$12,500	$11,500	$12,100	+$600 (ahead)	Good progress. Is it creating any problems to support?
Expansion of product line	6	3	5	+2 products (ahead)	Are the products ready? Are the perfect standards met?
Employee morale in service area: Absenteeism rate	2.5%	3.0%	3.0%	(on target)	Looks like a problem!
Turnover rate	5%	10%	15%	−8% (behind)	Why are we so far behind?
Competition: New-product introductions (average number)	6	3	6	−3 (behind)	Did we underestimate timing? What are the implications for our basic assumptions?

progress to date with *expected progress*. The *current deviation* is of particular interest because it provides a basis for examining *suggested actions* (usually suggested by subordinate managers) and for finalizing decisions on changes or adjustments in the firm's operations.

From Exhibit 13.4, it appears that the firm is maintaining control of its cost structure. Indeed, it is ahead of schedule on reducing overhead. The firm is well ahead of its delivery cycle target, while slightly below its target service-to-sales personnel ratio. Its product returns look OK, although product performance versus specification is below standard. Sales per employee and expansion of the product line are ahead of schedule. The absenteeism rate in the service area is on target, but the turnover rate is higher than that targeted. Competitors appear to be introducing products more rapidly than expected.

After deviations and their causes have been identified, the implications of the deviations for the ultimate success of the strategy must be considered. For example, the rapid product-line expansion indicated in Exhibit 13.4 may have been a response to the increased rate of competitors' product expansion. At the same time, product performance is still low, and, while the installation cycle is slightly above standard (improving customer service), the ratio of service to sales personnel is below the targeted ratio. Contributing to this substandard ratio (and perhaps reflecting a lack of organizational commitment to customer service) is the exceptionally high turnover in customer service personnel. The rapid reduction in indirect overhead costs might mean that administrative integration of customer service and product development requirements have been cut back too quickly.

This information presents operations managers with several options. They may attribute the deviations primarily to internal discrepancies. In that case, they can scale priorities up or down. For example, they might place more emphasis on retaining customer service personnel and less emphasis on overhead reduction and new-product development. On the other hand, they might decide to continue as planned in the face of increasing competition and to accept or gradually improve the customer service situation. Another possibility is reformulating the strategy or a component of the strategy in the face of rapidly increasing competition. For example, the firm might decide to emphasize more standardized or lower-priced products to overcome customer service problems and take advantage of an apparently ambitious salesforce.

This is but one of many possible interpretations of Exhibit 13.4. The important point here is the critical need to monitor progress against standards and to give serious in-depth attention to both the causes of observed deviations and the most appropriate responses to them. After the deviations have been evaluated, slight adjustments may be made to keep progress, expenditure, or other factors in line with the strategy's programmed needs. In the unusual event of extreme deviations—generally because of unforeseen changes—management is alerted to the possible need for revising the budget, reconsidering certain functional plans related to budgeted expenditures, or examining the units concerned and the effectiveness of their managers.

balanced scorecard
A management control system that enables companies to clarify their strategies, translate them into action, and provide quantitative feedback as to whether the strategy is creating value, leveraging core competencies, satisfying the company's customers, and generating a financial reward to its shareholders.

The Balanced Scorecard Methodology

An alternative approach linking operational and strategic control, developed by Harvard Business School professors Robert Kaplan and David Norton, is a system we briefly discussed in Chapter 7 that was named the **balanced scorecard.** Recognizing some of the weaknesses and vagueness of previous implementation and control approaches, the balanced scorecard approach was intended to provide a clear prescription as to what companies should measure in order to "balance" the financial perspective in implementation and control of strategic plans.[2] The global consulting firm Bain and Company estimated that more than 60 percent of all large global companies are using the balanced scorecard.[3]

---

[2]This methodology is covered in great detail in a number of books and articles by R. S. Kaplan and D. P. Norton. It is also the subject of frequent special publications by the *Harvard Business Review,* providing updated treatment of uses and improvements in the balanced scorecard methodology. See, for example, "Harvard Business Review Balanced Scorecard Report," *Harvard Business Review,* monthly, 2002 to present; Robert S. Kaplan, and David P. Norton, "The Balanced Scorecard: Measures That Drive Performance," *Harvard Business Review,* July 2005, pp. 71–79; Robert S. Kaplan, and David P. Norton, *Alignment: Using the Balanced Scorecard to Create Corporate Synergies* (Boston: Harvard Business School Press, 2008); Paul R. Niven, *Balanced Scorecard Step-by-Step: Maximizing Performance and Maintaining Results,* 2nd ed. (New York: John Wiley & Sons, 2006). Numerous Web sites also exist such as www.bscol.com and www.balancedscorecard.org.
[3]Darrell Rigby, "Management Tools. An Executive's Guide," Bain and Company, 2009.

The balanced scorecard is a management system (not only a measurement system) that enables companies to clarify their strategies, translate them into action, and provide meaningful feedback. It provides feedback around both the internal business processes and external outcomes in order to continuously improve strategic performance and results. When fully deployed, the balanced scorecard is intended to transform strategic planning from a separate top management exercise into the nerve center of an enterprise. Kaplan and Norton describe the innovation of the balanced scorecard as follows:

> The balanced scorecard retains traditional financial measures. But financial measures tell the story of past events, an adequate story for industrial age companies for which investments in long-term capabilities and customer relationships were not critical for success. These financial measures are inadequate, however, for guiding and evaluating the journey that information age companies must make to create future value through investment in customers, suppliers, employees, processes, technology, and innovation.[4]

The balanced scorecard methodology adapts the total quality management (TQM) ideas of customer-defined quality, continuous improvement, employee empowerment, and measurement-based management/feedback into an expanded methodology that includes traditional financial data and results. The balanced scorecard incorporates feedback around internal business process *outputs,* as in TQM, but also adds a feedback loop around the *outcomes* of business strategies. This creates a "double-loop feedback" process in the balanced scorecard. In doing so, it links together two areas of concern in strategy execution—quality operations and financial outcomes—that are typically addressed separately yet are obviously critically intertwined as any company executes its strategy. A system that links shareholder interests in return on capital with a system of performance management that is linked to ongoing, operational activities and processes within the company is what the balanced scorecard attempts to achieve.

Exhibit 13.5 illustrates the balanced scorecard approach drawing on the traditional Du Pont formula discussed in Chapter 6 and historically used to examine drivers of stockholder-related financial performance across different company activities. The balanced scorecard seeks to "balance" shareholder goals with customer goals and operational performance goals, and Exhibit 13.5 shows that they are interconnected: shareholder value creation is linked to divisional concerns for return on capital employed, which, in turn, is driven by functional outcomes in sales, inventory, capacity utilization, that, in turn, come about through the results of departments' and teams' daily activities throughout the company. The balanced scorecard suggests that we view the organization from four perspectives and to develop metrics, collect data, and analyze it relative to each of these perspectives:

1. *The learning and growth perspective: How well are we continuously improving and creating value?* The scorecard insists on measures related to innovation and organizational learning to gauge performance on this dimension—technological leadership, product development cycle times, operational process improvement, and so on.

2. *The business process perspective: What are our core competencies and areas of operational excellence?* Internal business processes and their effective execution as measured by productivity, cycle time, quality measures, downtime, and various cost measures, among others, provide scorecard input here.

[4]Another useful treatment of various aspects of the balanced scoreboard that includes further learning opportunities you may wish to explore, especially with regard to the use of this approach with governmental organizations, may be found at www.balancedscorecard.org. Chapter 7 in this book describes how the balanced scorecard approach is used to help create measurable objectives linked directly to the company's strategy.

EXHIBIT 13.5
Integrating Shareholder Value and Organizational Activities across Organizational Levels

Source: From R.M. Grant, *Contemporary Strategy Analysis,* Blackwell Publishing, 2001, p. 56. Reprinted with permission of Wiley-Blackwell.

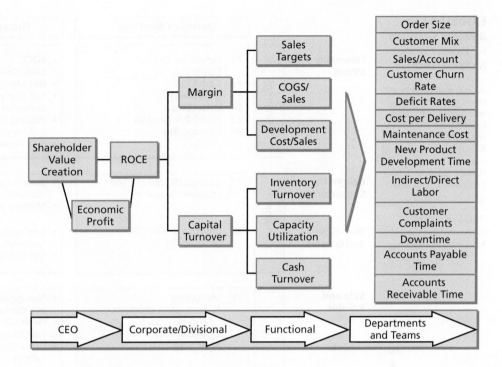

3. *The customer perspective: How satisfied are our customers?* A customer satisfaction perspective typically adds measures related to defect levels, on-time delivery, warranty support and product development, among others, that come from direct customer input and are linked to specific company activities.

4. *The financial perspective: How are we doing for our shareholders?* A financial perspective typically uses measures like cash flow, return on equity, sales, and income growth.

Through the integration of goals from each of these four perspectives, the balanced scorecard approach enables the strategy of the business to be linked with shareholder value creation while providing several measurable short-term outcomes that guide and monitor strategy implementation. The integrating power of the balanced scorecard can be seen at Exxon Corporation's North American Marketing and Refining business (NAM&R). NAM&R's scorecard is shown in Exhibit 13.6. Assisted by Kaplan and Norton, an unprofitable NAM&R adopted the scorecard methodology to better link its strategy with financial objectives and to translate these into operating performance targets tailored to outcomes in each business unit, functional departments, and operating process within them. They included measures developed with key customers from their perspective. The result was an integrated system in which scorecards provided measurable outcomes through which the performance of each department and operating unit, team, or activity within NAM&R was monitored, adjusted, and used to determine performance-related pay bonuses.[5]

dashboard
A user interface that organizes and presents information from multiple digital sources simultaneously in a user-designed format on the computer screen.

Executives and CEOs are increasingly monitoring specific measurable outcomes related to the execution of their strategies. Now, thanks to the Internet and new Web-based software tools known as **dashboards,** accessing this type of specific information is as easy as

[5]Charles E. Davis and Elizabeth Davis, *Managerial Accounting* (New York: John Wiley & Sons, Inc., 2012), p. 583.

EXHIBIT 13.6
Balanced Scorecard for Exxon Corp's NAM&R[1] Division

Source: Reprinted by permission of Harvard Business School Publishing. Exhibit from *The Strategy Focused Organization,* by Robert Kaplan and David Norton. Copyright by the Harvard Business School Publishing Corporation; all rights reserved.

[1]NAM&R stands for North American Marketing and Refining

		Strategic Objectives	Strategic Measures
Financially Strong	Financial	F1 Return on Capital Employed F2 Cash Flow F3 Profitability F4 Lowest Cost F5 Profitable Growth F6 Manage Risk	• ROCE • Cash Flow • Net Margin • Full cost per gallon delivered to customer • Volume growth rate vs. industry • Risk index
Delight the Consumer **Win–Win Relationship**	Customer	C1 Continually delight the targeted consumer C2 Improve dealer/distributor profitability	• Share of segment in key markets • Mystery shopper rating • Dealer/distributor margin on gasoline • Dealer/distributor survey

Safe and Reliable
 	
Competitive Supplier
 	
Good Neighbor
 	
On Spec On Time
	Internal	I1 Marketing
		  1. Innovative products and services
		  2. Dealer/distributor quality
		
		I2 Manufacturing
		  1. Lower manufacturing costs
		  2. Improve hardware and performance
		
		I3 Supply, Trading, Logistics
		  1. Reducing delivered cost
		  2. Trading organization
		  3. Inventory management
		
		I4 Improve health, safety, and environmental performance
		I5 Quality
			• Non-gasoline revenue and margin per square foot
			• Dealer/distributor acceptance rate of new programs
			• Dealer/distributor quality ratings
			• ROCE on refinery
			• Total expenses (per gallon) vs. competition
			• Profitability index
			• Yield index
			Delivered cost per gallon vs. competitors
			• Trading margin
			• Inventory level compared to plan and to output rate
			• Number of incidents
			• Days away from work
			• Quality index

Motivated and Prepared	Learning and growth	L1 Organization involvement L2 Core competencies and skills L3 Access to strategic information	• Employee survey • Strategic competitive availability • Strategic information availability

clicking a mouse. Global Strategy in Action, Exhibit 13.7 shows how dashboards are used by two executives with well-known companies as well as by the Richmond, Virginia police department, which uses real-time data about crime and weather to better assign patrol officers to address and deter crime. So, for example, an executive at Exxon Corporation might now use a dashboard to monitor updated information on where the company stands on some of the key measures generated through their balanced scorecard process as shown in Exhibit 13.6. The opportunity to react, take action, ask questions, and so forth approaches

Examples of the Use of Dashboards for Strategic Control

LARRY ELLISON, ORACLE

A fan of dashboards, Ellison uses them to track sales activity at the end of a quarter, the ratio of sales divided by customer service requests, and the number of hours that technicians spend on the phone solving customer problems.

RICHMOND, VIRGINIA POLICE DEPARTMENT

The police department of the City of Richmond, Virginia implemented an operational dashboard that uses analytical models to predict crime throughout the city in eight-hour cycles. The models are fed with real-time data about crime and

weather, helping to position patrol personnel in the right places at the right time to deter crime.

JEFF RAIKES MICROSOFT AND, NOW, GATES FOUNDATION

Jeff Raikes, while president of Microsoft's Office Division, said that more than half of Microsoft Division's employees use dashboards. "Every time I go to see Balmer, or now Gates, it was an expectation that I bring my dashboard." Ballmer, he says, reviews the dashboards of his seven business heads in one-on-one meetings to focus on sales, customer satisfaction, and the status of key product development.

real time with the advent of the dashboard software options. That is, of course, when there is a high level of confidence in the reliability of the data that appear—both for the Business executives and in the Richmond police leadership who take action in real time with limited resources based on what the dashboard indicates.

Strategic controls and comprehensive control programs like the balanced scorecard bring the entire management task into focus. Organizational leaders can adjust or radically change their firm's strategy based on feedback from a balanced scorecard approach as well as other strategic controls. Other, similar approaches like Six Sigma, which is described in Chapter 14, can also be sources of information and specific measurable outcomes useful in strategic and operational control efforts. The overriding goal is to enable the survival and long-term success of the business. In addition to using controls, leaders are increasingly embracing innovation and entrepreneurship as a way to accomplish this overriding goal in rapidly changing environments. They look to young business graduates, like you, to bring a fresh sense of innovativeness and entrepreneurship with you as you join their companies. We will examine innovation and entrepreneurship in the next chapter.

Summary

Strategies are forward looking, usually designed to be accomplished over several years into the future. They are often based in part on management assumptions about numerous events and factors that have not yet occurred. Strategic controls are intended to steer a company toward its long-term strategic goals under uncertain, often changing, circumstances.

Premise controls, strategic surveillance, special alert controls, and implementation controls are four types of strategic controls. All four types are designed to meet top management's needs to track a strategy as it is being implemented; to detect underlying problems, circumstances, or assumptions surrounding that strategy; and to make necessary adjustments. These strategic controls are linked to environmental assumptions and the key operating requirements necessary for successful strategy implementation. Ever-present forces of change fuel the need for and focus of strategic control.

Operational control systems require systematic evaluation of performance against predetermined standards and targets. A critical concern here is identification and evaluation of performance deviations, with careful attention paid to determining the underlying reasons for and strategic implications of observed deviations before management reacts. Approaches like the balanced scorecard and Six Sigma (discussed in the next chapter) have emerged as comprehensive control systems that integrate strategic goals, operating outcomes, customer satisfaction, and continuous improvement into an ongoing strategic management system.

The emergence of the Internet has led to innovative software that further assists executives in more closely and carefully monitoring outcomes in real time as a strategy is being implemented. This allows executives and managers to have *dashboards* on their computers, laptops, or mobile devices that further enhance their ability to control and adjust strategies as they are being executed.

A central goal with any strategy is the survival, growth, and improved competitive position of the company in the face of ever-accelerating rates of change. Executives, as they seek to control the execution of their strategy, are also increasingly aware of the need for innovation and entrepreneurial thinking as a companion to their emphasis on control as a means to accomplish these key goals in the face of rapid global change. The next chapter will examine innovation and entrepreneurship.

Key Terms

balanced scorecard, *p. 407*
dashboard, *p. 409*
implementation control, *p. 403*
milestone reviews, *p. 403*

premise control, *p. 399*
special alert control, *p. 402*
strategic control, *p. 398*
strategic surveillance, *p. 401*

strategic thrusts or
projects, *p. 403*

Questions for Discussion

1. Distinguish between strategic control and operating control. Give an example of each.
2. Select a business whose strategy is familiar to you. Identify what you think are the key premises of the strategy. Then select the key indicators that you would use to monitor each of these premises.
3. Explain the differences between implementation controls, strategic surveillance, and special alert controls. Give an example of each.
4. Why are budgets, schedules, and key success factors essential to operations control and evaluation?
5. What are the key considerations in monitoring deviations from performance standards?
6. How is the balanced scorecard related to strategic and operational control?
7. What is a dashboard?

Innovation and Entrepreneurship

After reading and studying this chapter, you should be able to

1. Summarize the difference between incremental and breakthrough innovation.

2. Explain what is meant by continuous improvement and how it contributes to incremental innovation.

3. Summarize the risks associated with an incremental versus a breakthrough approach to innovation.

4. Describe the three key elements of the entrepreneurship process.

5. Explain intrapreneurship and how to enable it to thrive.

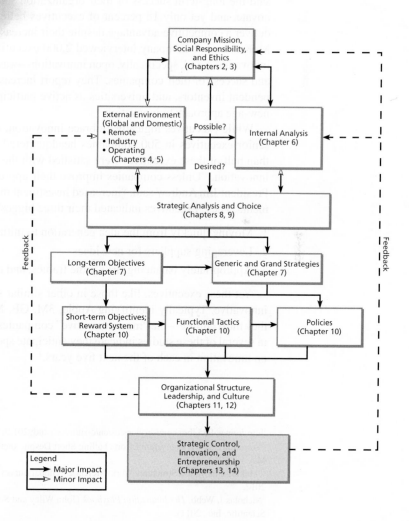

Company Mission, Social Responsibility, and Ethics (Chapters 2, 3)

External Environment (Global and Domestic)
- Remote
- Industry
- Operating
(Chapters 4, 5)

Possible?

Internal Analysis (Chapter 6)

Desired?

Strategic Analysis and Choice (Chapters 8, 9)

Long-term Objectives (Chapter 7)

Generic and Grand Strategies (Chapter 7)

Short-term Objectives; Reward System (Chapter 10)

Functional Tactics (Chapter 10)

Policies (Chapter 10)

Organizational Structure, Leadership, and Culture (Chapters 11, 12)

Strategic Control, Innovation, and Entrepreneurship (Chapters 13, 14)

Feedback

Feedback

Legend
→ Major Impact
⇒ Minor Impact

Survival and long-term success in a business enterprise eventually come down to two outcomes: sales growth or lower costs, and hopefully both. Rapid change, globalization, and connectivity in the global economy have led to impressive growth across many sectors of the global economy. Most companies have spent the last decade or two putting continuous pressure on their organizations to drive out excessive costs and inefficiencies so as to compete in this increasingly price sensitive global arena. Increasingly, executives in these same companies see growth, particularly growth via innovation, as the key priority to their firm's long-term survival and prosperity.

Recent studies by four prominent consulting organizations have documented the critical importance of innovation for CEOs of companies large and small around the globe as these CEOs seek to chart the destinies of their companies into the next decade. IBM's study of almost 1,100 CEOs found innovation in three ways to be the central focus among today's CEOs: product/service/market innovation, business model innovation, and operational innovation. They further found that collaborating with other companies to do so was more important than ever before.[1] Accenture's 2013 survey of 519 companies across more than 12 industry sectors in France, the United Kingdom, and the United States showed that 51 percent of participating companies report increased funding for innovation, 93 percent said the long-term success of their organization's strategy depends on their ability to innovate, and yet only 18 percent of executives believe their company's innovation efforts deliver a competitive advantage despite their increased business investment in innovation.[2] McKinsey and Company interviewed 2,000 executives and found accelerated embrace of innovation—and, specifically, open innovation—was deemed essential to the future growth and success of their companies. They report increasing use of customers, suppliers, independent inventors, and universities as active participants in their innovation efforts as the new-age approach to innovation.[3]

While executives logically embrace innovation, a Boston Consulting Group survey of senior executives in 500 companies headquartered across 47 countries found that fewer than half of these executives were satisfied with the returns on their investments to date in innovation. "Unless companies improve their approach to innovation," BCG Senior Vice President Jim Andrew said, "increased investment may in fact lead to increased disappointment." These executives indicated their three biggest problems with innovation were

1. Moving quickly from the idea generation to initial sales.
2. Leveraging suppliers for new ideas.
3. Appropriately balancing risks, time frames, and returns.

Yet these executives, like those in other similar studies, were anxious to become more innovative. Typically identifying Apple, 3M, GE, Microsoft, and Sony as the innovators they most admire—the "most innovative" companies worldwide, the majority of executives in several of these studies indicate they anticipate spending more time and money resources on innovation in each of the next five years.[4]

---

[1] http://www-935.ibm.com/services/us/en/c-suite/ceostudy2012/, 2013.

[2] "Accenture Study: Innovation Efforts Falling Short Despite Increased Investment," *Accenture Latest Thinking,* May 13, 2013.

[3] "Making Innovation Structures Work: McKinsey Global Survey Results," *McKinsey Quarterly,* September 2012.

[4] Nicholas J. Webb, *The Innovation Playbook* (John Wiley and Sons, Inc., Hoboken, New Jersey: Lassen Scientific, Inc., 2011).

WHAT IS INNOVATION?

invention
The creation of new products or processes through the development of new knowledge or from new combinations of knowledge.

innovation
The initial commercialization of invention by producing and selling a new product, service, or process.

Common to the vocabulary of most business executives is a distinction between *invention* and *innovation*. We define the two using this common perspective:

Invention is the creation of new products or processes through the development of new knowledge or from new combinations of existing knowledge. The jet engine was patented in 1930, yet the first commercial jet airplane did not fly until 1957. Computers were based on three different sets of knowledge created decades before the first computer.

Innovation is the initial commercialization of invention by producing and selling a new product, service, or process. As executives across each of the surveys summarized earlier typically put it, "Innovation is turning ideas into profits."[5]

Apple's iPod, iPhone, and then iPad were three successive *product innovations* that applied, among other things, Apple's chip storage technology with sleek device styling to create three blockbuster products within a short time frame in each instance. After creating the iPod, Steven Jobs then worked intensely for almost two years negotiating digital music rights with a recalcitrant music industry, culminating in the launching of iTunes in 2003—a music download *service innovation* with an initial 200,000 digital songs to choose from for your iPod and subsequently your iPhone. In five short years, that became 3 million songs and more than $5 billion in annual revenue added to the business, allowing Apple in the process to replace Walmart as the world's largest music retailer. Starbucks added the simple service of wireless access free to its customers at most of its 8,000 stores in what turned out to be a highly successful *service innovation* that resulted in customers using the service staying nine times longer than regular customers, and doing so during off-peak hours.

While these two leading innovators are creating profitable product and service innovations, Toyota is a widely acknowledged and studied business *process innovator* worldwide due to its meticulous attention to business and operating processes. Several years ago, Toyota made one change to its production lines, using a single brace to hold auto frames together instead of the 50 it previously took. While a minute part of Toyota's overall production process, this "global body line" system slashed 75 percent off the cost of refitting a production line. It is the reason behind Toyota's ability to make different models on a single production line, estimated to save Toyota more than $3 billion annually.

To some business managers, "innovation seems as predictable as a rainbow and as manageable as a butterfly. Penicillin, Teflon, Post-it-notes—they sprang from such accidents as moldy Petri dishes, a failed coolant, and a mediocre glue." Not surprisingly, many managers forgo trying to harness innovation systematically. "Our approach has always been very simple, which is to try not to manage innovation," said Michael Moritz, a partner with world-renowned venture capital firm Sequoia Capital. "We prefer to just let the market manage it."[6] For those managers who try to manage innovation, it is important to distinguish two types of innovations: incremental innovation and breakthrough innovation.

Incremental Innovation

incremental innovation
Simple changes or adjustments in existing products, services, or processes.

Incremental innovation refers to simple changes or adjustments in existing products, services, or processes. There is growing evidence that companies seeking to increase the payoff from innovation investments best do so by focusing on incremental innovations. We will examine the payoff research more completely in a subsequent section on risks associated with innovation. First, however, we need to examine how companies are seeking

[5]www.innovationcoach.com, 2013.
[6]Charlie Rose, "Charlie Rose Talks to Sequoia Capital's Michael Moritz," *Bloomberg Businessweek*, February 7, 2013.

Global Strategy in Action

Exhibit 14.1

Taiichi Ohno . . . Toyota's Quiet Perfectionist Who Changed the World

All we are doing is looking at the time line, from the moment the customer gives us an order to the point when we collect the cash. And we are reducing the time line by reducing the non-value-adding wastes.

—*Taiichi Ohno*

Why not make the work easier and more interesting so that people do not have to sweat? The Toyota style is not to create results by working hard. It is a system that says there is no limit to people's creativity. People don't go to Toyota to "work," they go there to "think."

—*Taiichi Ohno*

Every 20-year-old factory worker, or designer, and every Toyota executive reveres the heritage bestowed upon them by Taiichi Ohno. Sixty years ago, after observing Henry Ford's work, and American grocery stores, he set about creating in-house precepts at Toyota's production facilities to eliminate waste while improving efficiency, which became JIT; continuous improvement (*kaizen*); mistake proofing (*pokayoke*); and regular brainstorming sessions among suppliers, designers, engineering, and sales personnel. The result has revolutionized car manufacturing.

Toyota's plants are high-tech marvels, building multiple car models on the same production line with parts descending on time from above and below via numerous conveyor belts like a manufacturing ballet. While sophisticated, Ohno's spirit is ever present, seeking creative frugality—reducing the use of PowerPoint handouts in meetings to save

on ink costs, or lessening heating during working hours at company dormitories, or pushing suppliers to reduce the number of side-view mirror sizes from 50 to 3 for all Toyota cars. All these actions and many, many more reflect Ohno's passion for continuous, simple innovation borne out of the minds of Toyota's employees going about their daily work, building the best cars and trucks in the world.

Source: http://www.kellogg.northwestern.edu/course/opns430/modules/lean_operations/ohno-tps.pdf; and quotes courtesy of www.matthrivnak.com

---

incremental innovation. A major driver of incremental innovation in many companies the last several years has come from programs aimed at continuous improvement, cost reduction, and quality management.

continuous improvement
The process of relentlessly trying to find ways to improve and enhance a company's products and processes from design through assembly, sales, and service. It is called *kaizen* in Japanese. It is usually associated with incremental innovation.

Continuous improvement, what in Japanese is called *kaizen,* is the process of relentlessly trying to find ways to improve and enhance a company's products and processes from design through assembly, sales, and service. This approach, or really an operating philosophy, seeks to always find slight improvements or refinements in every aspect of what a company does so that it will result in lower costs, higher quality and speed, or more rapid response to customer needs.[7]

A few years ago Toyota responded to incidents of potentially defective accelerator systems with a companywide, humble reaffirmation of the philosophy of the father of its long-famous production system, Taiichi Ohno. Mr. Ohno's original system for Toyota is summarized in Global Strategy in Action, Exhibit 14.1. That system, credited with leading Toyota to become one of the world's leading automobile companies, is one good example of a cost-oriented continuous improvement effort called **CCC21** (Construction of Cost Competitiveness for the 21st Century). Toyota embarked on this intense scrutiny of every product it purchases or builds to include in the assembly of its automobiles in response to growing concern about the relative cost advantage to be derived from a surge

CCC21
A world-famous, cost-oriented continuous improvement program at Toyota (Construction of Cost Competitiveness for the 21st Century).

---

[7]TQM, total quality management, is the initial continuous improvement philosophy used worldwide to focus managers and employees on customer defined quality since starting in Japan in the 1970s.

in global automobile company mergers starting with Daimler-Chrysler. The result: a stunning $20 billion in cost savings over the last decade in the parts it buys, while also improving quality significantly. Taking the Japanese perspective, 1,001 small innovations or improvements together have become something transformative. A good example would be Toyota engineers disassembling the horns made by a Japanese supplier and finding ways to eliminate 6 of 28 horn components, saving 40 percent in costs and improving quality. Or, interior assist grips above each door—once there were 35 different grips but now, across 90 different Toyota models, there are only 3. Toyota engineers call this process *kawaita zokin wo shiboru,* or "wringing drops from a dry towel," which means an excruciating, unending process essential to Toyota's continuous improvement success.

Six Sigma is another continuous improvement approach widely used by many companies worldwide to spur incremental innovation in their businesses. Six Sigma is a rigorous and analytical approach to quality and continuous improvement with an objective to improve profits through defect reduction, yield improvement, improved consumer satisfaction, and best-in-class performance. Six Sigma complements TQM philosophies such as management leadership, continuous education, and customer focus while deploying a disciplined and structured approach of hard-nosed statistics.[8]

Companies such as Honeywell, Motorola, BMW, GE, SAP, IBM, and Texas Instruments have adopted the Six Sigma discipline as a major business initiative. Many of these companies invested heavily in and pursued this model initially to create products and services that were of equal and higher quality than those of its competitors and to improve relationships with customers. A Six Sigma program at many organizations simply means a measure of quality that strives for near perfection in every facet of the business including every product, process, and transaction:

Six Sigma
A continuous improvement program adopted by many companies in the last two decades that takes a very rigorous and analytical approach to quality and continuous improvement with an objective to improve profits through defect reduction, yield improvement, improved customer satisfaction, and best-in-class performance.

How the Six Sigma Statistical Concept Works

Six Sigma means a failure rate of 3.4 parts per million or 99.9997 percent. At the sixth standard deviation from the mean under a normal distribution, 99.9996 percent of the population is under the curve with not more than 3.4 parts per million defective. The higher the sigma value, the less likely a process will produce defects as excellence is approached.

If you played 100 rounds of golf per year and played at:
2 Sigma: You'd miss 6 putts per round.
3 Sigma: You'd miss 1 putt per round.
4 Sigma: You'd miss 1 putt every 9 rounds.
5 Sigma: You'd miss 1 putt every 2.33 years.
6 Sigma: You'd miss 1 putt every 163 years!

Source: From John Petty, Lecturer, Accounting, University of Technology Sydney, Australia. John.Petty@UTS.edu.au. Reprinted with permission of the author.

Many frameworks, management philosophies, and specific statistical tools exist for implementing the Six Sigma methodology and its objective to create a near-perfect process or service. One such method for improving a system for existing processes falling below specification while looking for incremental improvement is the DMAIC process (define, measure, analyze, improve, control) shown in Exhibit 14.2.

Incremental innovation via continuous improvement programs is viewed by most proponents as virtually a new organizational culture and way of thinking. It is built around an

[8]ISO certification, from the International Standards Organization, is another widely used means of encouraging rigorous and analytically based assessment and confirmation of meeting quality and building continuous improvement into the way the organization functions.

EXHIBIT 14.2   The DMAIC Six Sigma Approach

Define

- Project definition
- Project charter
- Gathering voice of the customer
- Translating customer needs into specific requirements

Measure

- Process mapping (as-is process)
- Data attributes (continuous vs. discrete)
- Measurement system analysis
- Gauge repeatability and reproducibility
- Measuring process capability
- Calculating process sigma level
- Visually displaying baseline performance

Analyze

- Visually displaying data (histogram, run chart, Pareto chart, scatter diagram)

- Value-added analysis
- Cause-and-effect analysis (a.k.a. Fishbone, Ishikawa)
- Verification of root causes
- Determining opportunity (defects and financial) for improvement
- Project charter review and revision

Improve

- Brainstorming
- Quality function deployment (house of quality)
- Failure modes and effects analysis (FMEA)
- Piloting your solution
- Implementation planning
- Culture modification planning for your organization

Control

- Statistical process control (SPC) overview
- Developing a process control plan
- Documenting the process

intense focus on customer satisfaction; on accurate measurement of every critical variable in a business's operation; on continuous improvement of products, services, and processes; and on work relationships based on trust and teamwork. One useful explanation of the continuous improvement philosophy suggests 10 essential elements that lead to meaningful incremental innovation:

1. *Define quality and customer value.* Rather than be left to individual interpretation, company personnel should have a clear definition of what *quality* means in the job, department, and throughout the company. It should be developed from your customer's perspective and communicated as a written policy. Thinking in terms of customer value broadens the definition of *quality* to include efficiency and responsiveness. Said another way, quality to your customer often means that the product performs well; that it is priced competitively (efficiency); and that you provide it quickly and adapt it when needed (responsiveness). Customer value is found in the combination of all three—quality, price, and speed.

2. *Develop a customer orientation.* Customer value is what the customer says it is. Don't rely on secondary information—talk to your customers directly. Also recognize your "internal" customers. Usually less than 20 percent of company employees come into contact with external customers, while the other 80 percent serve internal customers—other units with real performance expectations—in a process that looks like this:

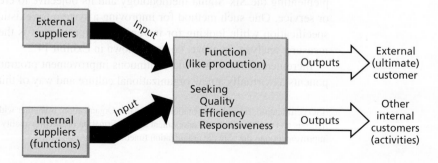

3. *Focus on the company's business processes.* Break down every minute step in the process of providing the company's product or service, and look at ways to improve it, rather than focusing simply on the finished product or service. Each process contributes value in some way, which can be improved or adapted to help other processes (internal customers) improve. Here are several examples of ways customer value is enhanced across business processes in several functions:

	Quality	**Efficiency**	**Responsiveness**
Marketing	Provides accurate assessment of customer's product preferences to R&D	Targets advertising campaign at customers, using cost-effective medium	Quickly uncovers and reacts to changing market trends
Operations	Consistently produces goods matching engineering design	Minimizes scrap and rework through high-production yield	Quickly adapts to latest demands with production flexibility
Research and development	Designs products that combine customer demand and production capabilities	Uses computers to test feasibility of idea before going to more expensive full-scale prototype	Carries out parallel product/process designs to speed up overall innovation
Accounting	Provides the information that managers in other functions need to make decisions	Simplifies and computerizes to decrease the cost of gathering information	Provides information in "real time" (as the events described are still happening)
Purchasing	Selects vendors for their ability to join in an effective "partnership"	Given the required vendor quality, negotiates prices to provide good value	Schedules inbound deliveries efficiently, avoiding both extensive inventories and stock-outs
Personnel	Trains workforce to perform required tasks	Minimizes employee turnover, reducing hiring and training expenses	In response to strong growth in sales, finds large numbers of employees and quickly teaches needed skills

4. *Develop customer and supplier partnerships.* Organizations have a destructive tendency to view suppliers and even customers adversarily. It is better to understand the horizontal flow of a business—outside suppliers to internal suppliers/customers (a company's various departments) to external customers. This view suggests suppliers are partners in meeting customer needs, and customers are partners by providing input so the company and suppliers can meet and exceed those expectations.

Ford Motor Company's Dearborn, Michigan, plant is linked electronically with supplier Allied Signal's Kansas City, Missouri, plant. A Ford computer recently sent the design for a car's connecting rod to an Allied Signal factory computer, which transformed the design into instructions that it fed to a machine tool on the shop floor. The result: quality, efficiency, and responsiveness.

5. *Take a preventive approach.* Many organizations reward "fire fighters" not "fire preventers" and identify errors after the work is done. Management, instead, should be rewarded for being prevention oriented and seeking to eliminate non-value-added work as CCC21 does quite well at Toyota.

6. *Adopt an error-free attitude.* Instill an attitude that "good enough" is not good enough anymore. "Error free" should become each individual's performance standard, with managers taking every opportunity to demonstrate and communicate the importance of this Six Sigma–type imperative.

7. *Get the facts first.* Continuous improvement–oriented companies make decisions based on facts, not on opinions. Accurate measurement, often using readily available statistical techniques, of every critical variable in a business's operation—and using those measurements to trace problems to their roots and eliminate their causes—is a better way.

8. *Encourage every manager and employee to participate.* Employee participation, empowerment, participative decision making, and extensive training in quality techniques, statistical techniques, and measurement tools are the ingredients continuous improvement companies employ to support and instill a commitment to customer value.

9. *Create an atmosphere of total involvement.* Quality management cannot be the job of a few managers or of one department. Maximum customer value cannot be achieved unless all areas of the organization apply quality concepts simultaneously.

10. *Strive for continuous improvement.* Stephen Yearout, director of Ernst & Young's Quality Management Center, recently observed that "Historically, meeting your customers' expectations would distinguish you from your competitors. The twenty-first century will require that you anticipate customer expectations and deliver quality service faster than the competition."

Quality, efficiency, and responsiveness are not one-time programs of competitive response because they create a new standard to measure up to. Organizations quickly find that continually improving quality, efficiency, and responsiveness in their processes, products, and services is not just good business; it's an excellent means to identify incremental innovations that become foundations for long-term survival.

Disciplines like Six Sigma are systematic ways to improve customer service and quality; the added benefit that emerged has been its effectiveness in cutting costs and improving profitability. That has made it a powerful tool, but the notion that Six Sigma is a survival cure-all is subsiding. Once a company has created incremental innovations that maximize profitability, some argue that "kick-starting the top line" becomes paramount, which in turn means acquisition or dramatic, revenue-generating product or service innovations. And that, they argue, calls less for Six Sigma's "define, measure, analyze, improve, control" regimen and more for a "fuzzier" front-end, creative-idea-generation type of orientation.[9] That calls for a more disruptive form of innovation, which we call *breakthrough innovation.*

Breakthrough Innovation

Clayton Christensen of Harvard Business School makes the distinction between "sustaining" technologies, which are incremental innovations that improve product or process performance, and "disruptive" technologies, which revolutionize industries and create new ones.[10] Rather than an innovation that reduces the cost of a mirror on a car by 40 percent, Christensen is focusing when speaking of disruptive technologies on the product idea that works 10 times better than existing ones or costs less than half what the existing ones do to make—a breakthrough innovation. A **breakthrough innovation,** then, is an innovation in a product, process, technology, or the cost associated with it that represents a quantum leap forward in one or more of these ways.

breakthrough innovation
An innovation in a product, process, technology, or the cost associated with it that represents a quantum leap forward in one or more of these ways.

[9]Brian Hindo and Brian Grow, "Six Sigma: So Yesterday?" *BusinessWeek,* June 11, 2007.
[10]see Christensen's thoughts on disruptive innovation at www.claytonchristensen.com/key-concepts

EXHIBIT 14.3
From Idea to
Profitable Reality

Source: Industrial
Research Institute,
Washington, D.C.

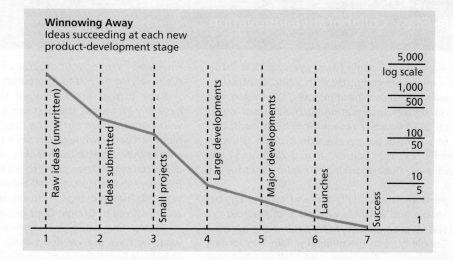

Winnowing Away
Ideas succeeding at each new
product-development stage

Apple's innovation with iPod and iTunes is a breakthrough innovation. It was not an incremental improvement in Apple's computer offerings. It was an application of the microprocessor technology associated with Apple's computers, applied in a totally different industry. Apple, which only has a 2 percent market share in the personal computer industry, now has positioned itself as a dominant force in the emerging digital music and entertainment industries based on this breakthrough innovation, becoming the top music retailer worldwide in five short years after it introduced iTunes.

Breakthrough innovations, which Christensen calls "disruptive," often shake up the industries with which they are associated, even though many times they may come from totally different origins or industry settings than the industry to start with. Apple seems to make a habit of creating new industries; Apple's original innovation 20 years earlier in Jobs's and Wozniak's garage that created the first Apple computer was viewed as a toy by most players in the computer industry at the time, but it quickly tore the mainstream computer industry apart and almost brought down the mighty IBM. Texas Instrument's digital watch resulted in the virtual destruction of the dominant Swiss watch industry. Breakthrough innovations can also be appreciated by some fringe (often new) customer group for features such as being cheap, simple, easy to use, or smaller, which is seen as underperforming the mainstream products. San Disk's memory stick, Walmart's discount retailing, and Netflix's use of competitor Amazon.com's cloud capacity as its largest customer to stream movies are all examples of breakthrough innovations that ultimately caused the demise of or significant reduction in key industry participants. Former Digital Equipment Company CEO Ken Olsen, a leading industry figure and a leading computer manufacturer at the time, said of Apple and the idea of a personal computer in your home when the early Apple computers were being sold: "I can think of no reason why an individual should wish to have a computer in his own home."[11]

Breakthrough approaches to innovation are inherently more risky than incremental innovation approaches. The reason can be seen in Exhibit 14.3, which is provided by the Industrial Research Institute in Washington, D.C. Their conclusion is that firms committed to breakthrough innovation must first have the ability to explain clearly to all employees, at every level, just how critical the breakthrough project is to the company's future. The

[11]Robert M. Grant, *Contemporary Strategic Analysis* (Oxford: Blackwell, 2002), p. 330.

Google Glass: Collaborative Innovation

Google introduced Google Glass, eyewear that incorporates a miniature computer with a display attached to its frame, which can shoot pictures, take video, run apps, and deliver information such as travel directions, activated by voice recognition, head nods, and swipes of a control bar on the side. Google Glass introduced its "Explorer Edition" in mid-2013 for $1,500 to software developers looking to explore uses for the eyewear.

Google Glass is essentially a grand experiment between Google and a sizable ecosystem of Android operating system programmers to help refine the eyewear before Google goes to the general public. Tim Jordan, Project Glass' senior developer, said "Tell us what your dreams are for Glass" at the Google I/O conference targeting key Android programmers/developers. "Our goal is to get happy users using Glass," said CEO Larry Page, and "a lot of your experiences can move to Glass. We're relying on you to figure that out."

Page further acknowledged that Google doesn't have any idea what the best use is for Glass or how it will ultimately turn out. Some skeptics say it is a fad for high-tech nerds, while others say a slow initial approach with knowledgeable users makes innovative and developmental sense. They point to early cell phone users in medicine and real estate well before a mass market developed. Then too, legal, cultural, and ethical issues will emerge if use of Google Glass grows.

Bottom line, Google's techno-crowdsourced "here is what we have but we don't know what to do with it, so help us figure that out" approach to product innovation with Google Glass may be just the right way to let its eventual place in the innovative technology product space ramp up slowly over time.

second is to set next-to-impossible goals for those involved. The third is to target only "rich domains"—areas of investigation where plenty of answers are still waiting to be found. The fourth, and maybe the most important, is to move people regularly between laboratories and business units, to ensure that researchers fully understand the needs of the marketplace. These thoughts, of course, apply more to larger firms and particularly ones where breakthrough efforts are concentrated in laboratories and other separate R&D units.

Smaller firms are often sources for breakthrough innovation because they have less invested in serving a large, established customer base and gradually improving on the products, services, or processes used to serve them. Google is one company that doesn't adhere to this large firm pattern, as has been seen with many of its innovation attempts, which we see in Global Strategy in Action, Exhibit 14.4 on the Google Glass. We will explore these differences more completely in the section on entrepreneurship. Regardless of the size of a firm, it is important to consider risks associated with incremental versus breakthrough innovation.

Risks Associated with Innovation[12]

Innovation involves creating something that doesn't now exist. It may be a minor creation or something monumental. In either case, there is risk associated with it. Exhibit 14.3 shows the conclusions of the Industrial Research Institute's examination of breakthrough innovation

[12]See Robert C. Merton, "Innovation Risk: How to Make Smarter Decisions," *Harvard Business Review*, April 2013, for a look at five rules-of-thumb for making decisions related to risk/reward trade-offs in new product and service decisions. Geoff Tuff, "How Hot Is Your Next Innovation?" *Harvard Business Review*, May 2011, offers a means to assess an innovation idea on two dimensions: its ability to respond to competitive pressures, and the economic value it can deliver to users. A related study by CPA Global Limited called "Closing the Innovation Value Gap," wherein it examined in detail the risk/reward differences across 11 global industries, which executives need to take into account as they address the process of taking ideas from intellectual property into commercially viable products and services quickly. www.cpaglobal.com, 2011. Finally, see Morten Hansen and Julian Birkinshaw, "The Innovation Value Chain," *Harvard Business Review*, June 2007, for an interesting use of a value chain "breakdown" of innovation to use in assessing risks and sources of problems in innovation efforts.

outcomes, which suggests that you need to start with 3,000 "bright" ideas, which are winnowed down to four product launches, then one major success emerges. Long odds for sure.

The *Economist* regularly studies global innovation and offers annual awards acknowledging it. While a recent study it offers takes a rather pessimistic look at the risks, asking whether the global "ideas machine has broken down," it concludes there remains much reason for optimism. And its earlier study that looked at 197 product innovations—111 successes and 86 failures—was perhaps more informative for understanding innovation risks. They first sought to examine what was common to successful innovations and what was common to failing innovations. First, they found that successful innovations had some, or all, of the following five characteristics:[13]

- Moderately new to the marketplace.
- Based on tried and tested technology.
- Saved money for users of the innovation.
- Reportedly met customer needs.
- Supported existing practices.

In contrast, product innovations that failed were based on cutting-edge or untested technology, followed a "me-too" approach, or were created with no clearly defined problem or solution in mind.

The second set of findings from this study emerged from the researchers' examination of what they called "idea factors." Idea factors were concerned with how the idea for the innovation originated. They identified six idea factors:

- *Need spotting*—actively looking for an answer to a known problem.
- *Solution spotting*—finding a new way of using an existing technology.
- *Mental inventions*—things dreamed up in the head with little reference to the outside world.
- *Random events*—serendipitous moments when innovators stumbled on something they were not looking for but immediately recognized its significance.
- *Market research*—traditional market research techniques to find ideas.
- *Trend following*—following demographic and other broad trends and trying to develop ideas that may be relevant and useful.

The researchers then compared the "success-to-failure" ratio of these six idea factors to see which idea factors were more often associated with success or failure of the related innovation. The two most failure-prone idea factors were trend following and mental inventions, both producing three times as many failures as successes. Need spotting produced twice as many successes as failures. Market research produced four times as many, and solution spotting seven times more successes than failures. Taking advantage of random

---

[13]"Has the Ideas Machine Broken Down?" The Economist, January 12, 2013; and earlier "Expect the Unexpected," *The Economist,* September 4, 2004. Similar and more recent findings were found in a study reported by McKinsey and Company that surveyed 300 employees at 28 companies across North America and Europe working on a variety of new product innovation projects over time. Their findings support what is reported above in the *Economist* study, with particular emphasis on the importance of maintaining close contact with customers through a project's duration, nurturing a strong project culture in their workplace, and having clear project goals early on. Divided into successful vs. unsuccessful project outcomes, product innovation teams McKinsey studied that embraced these three aspects were 17 times more likely to have projects come in on time, five times more likely to be on budget, and twice as likely to meet the company's ROI targets. Read more at Mike Gordon, Chris Musso, Eric Rebentisch, and Nisheeth Gupta, "The Path to Successful New Products,"*McKinsey Quarterly*, January, 2010.

EXHIBIT 14.5 **Risks Associated with Innovation**

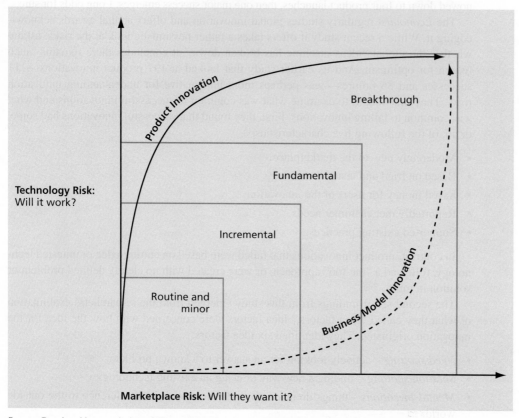

Source: Reprinted by permission of *Harvard Business Review*. Exhibit from "Innovation as a Last Resort," by Michael Treacy, July 1, 2004. Copyright 2004 by the Harvard Business School Publishing Corporation; all rights reserved.

events was the clear winner, generating 13 times more successes than failures. Their conclusion: focus on eliminating bad ideas early in the process, emphasize market research and technology application/solution spotting efforts, while being open to serendipitous outcomes in the process.

Inherent in their analysis is the presence of two key risks associated with innovation—market risks and technology risks. Market risks come from uncertainty with regard to the presence of a market, its size, and its growth rate for the product or service in question: do customers exist and will they buy it? Technology risks derive from uncertainty about how the technology will evolve and the complexity through which technical standards and dominant designs or approaches emerge: will it work?

Research by Michael Treacy of GEN3 Partners reported in the *Harvard Business Review* suggests that incremental innovation is far more effective than breakthrough innovation in managing the market and technology risk associated with innovation. Exhibit 14.5 provides an early visual portrayal of his research.[14] In it he suggests that technology risk is primary

[14]Alan Martinovich, Rob Bell, and John Roberts, "The Need to Focus on Organic Revenue Growth to Drive Shareholder Value," Treacy & Company INSIGHTS, March 2012; and Michael Treacy, "Innovation As a Last Resort," *Harvard Business Review,* July 1, 2004. See also http://www.youtube.com/user/treacyandcompany#p/a/u/0/a7D25Ub95yc, and http://www.youtube.com/watch?v=bRTQRS1rJaQ, to have Dr. Michael Treacy explain his perspective on *Growth Through Innovation*. And you can visit his Web site, http://treacyandco.com/aboutus/our-leadership/michael-treacy/, and explore his new book, *Growth Through Innovation*, 2013.

and marketplace risk secondary in product innovations; the reverse is true for business model or process innovations.

The point that emerges from this graph is that breakthrough innovation, while glamourous and exciting, is very risky compared with incremental innovation. Breakthrough innovations, according to Treacy's examination of much of the research to date on innovation, usually get beaten down or outperformed by the slow and steady approach of incremental innovation. He makes several useful points about managing the resulting risks:

• Remember, *the point of innovation is growth.* So ask the question, Can I increase revenue without innovation? Retain existing customers and improve targeted coverage of existing and similar new customers, where innovation isn't necessary to keep existing customers.

• *Get the most out of minimum innovation.* Tweaking a business process doesn't incur much technology risk. Incremental product or service innovation does not incur nearly the market risk that a radical one would. So emphasize an incremental approach to most innovation efforts.

• Incremental product innovations can be particularly good at *locking in existing customers.* Every saved customer is an additional source of revenue.

• Incremental business process innovations can *generate more revenue gain or cost savings with less risk* than radical ones. The earlier example about Toyota's single brace to hold auto frames is a dramatic example of the payoff—$2.6 billion annually—from one simple, incremental business process innovation.

• Radical innovations are often *too radical for existing markets,* and customers will balk at paying for that new approach, product, process, or technology. So it will fail with existing customers.

• The time to launch breakthrough innovations is not when they are necessary, important, or of interest to your business, but *when they are essential to the marketplace.* And that usually takes time, like the 10 years it has taken for car buyers to become interested in the electric/hybrid vehicles that have been available for more than 10 years.

The case for incremental innovation as a less risky approach than breakthrough innovation is widely advocated. Clayton Christensen offers a word of caution in this regard, arguing that as important as incremental improvements are, steady improvements to a company's product do not conquer new markets. Nor do they guarantee survival. He argues that while **disruptive** (breakthrough) **innovations** may underperform established products in mainstream markets, they often offer features or capabilities appreciated by some fringe (usually new) customer group—like being easier to use, cheaper, smaller, or more versatile. Often, his research suggests, those fringe customers swell in numbers to become the mainstream market, absorbing the newly informed old mainstream in the process. And in so doing, they "disrupt" or bring about the downfall of leading existing industry players.

Not surprisingly, many companies are experimenting with new ways to lower risks and improve chances for failure regardless of the innovation approach they use. For years the idea of product teams and cross-functional groups within the company has played a major role in trying to improve the odds that innovations will succeed, or that bad ideas are eliminated much earlier in the innovation management process. This approach broadens to include several more:

• *Joint ventures* with other firms that have an interest in the possible innovation share the costs and risks associated with the effort. Toyota undertook a joint venture with General Motors to share its hybrid vehicle technology for the Prius and jointly build a manufacturing facility in the United States to lower both companies' risk associated with this innovation.

disruptive innovation
A term to characterize breakthrough innovation popularized by Harvard Professor Clayton Christensen; usually shakes up or revolutionizes industries with which they are associated even though they often come from totally different origins or industry settings than the industry they "disrupt."

Google Acquires Dodgeball to Innovate, Then Drops the Ball

Dodgeball started life as a Manhattan company providing a cell phone service aimed at young barhoppers wanting to let their friends know where they were hanging out. Founders Dennis Crowley and Alex Rainert sold it to Google in 2005, providing a good payday for them and a potential basis for a social networking niche innovation for Google. Within two years, Crowley and Rainert left Google, frustrated by what they reported as minimal support from Google.* Crowley stayed in New York City to run the operation, but had trouble competing for the attention of other Google engineers to expand the service. "If you're a product manager, you have to recruit people from their '20 percent time,'" said Crowley,† who then started building a new location-based service called FourSquare.

Google, for its part, found the concepts behind Dodgeball interesting and adapted those concepts to create *Latitude,* a more sophisticated add-on to Google Maps that lets people share their location with friends and family automatically, while including different privacy and communication options. Said Google's senior engineering vice president, "Maybe it worked in Manhattan. It didn't fly in Chicago, or St. Louis, or Denver, or the rest of the world."‡ Still, Google appears to have found innovations worth adapting, as its new Latitude service seems to indicate.

* See their Flickr departure posting at http://www.flickr.com/photos/dpstyles/460987802/.
† Vindu Goel, "How Google Decides to Pull the Plug," *The New York Times,* February 15, 2009.
‡ Ibid.

- *Cooperation with lead users* is increasingly used in both types of innovation. Nike tests new shoes with inner-city street gangs; software companies beta-test their new software with loyal users; GE works with railroad companies to create a new, ecofriendly locomotive.

- *"Do it yourself"* innovation allows a company to work directly with key existing or expected customers, further allowing these customers to play a lead role in developing a product, service, or process—not just get a sense of their reaction to developments. This approach allows a company to go beyond the traditional market research model or simply cooperating with lead users. Instead, it has customers actually conceptualize or make design proposals which become the starting point for developing a new innovation. BMW sent 1,000 customers a "toolkit" that let them develop ideas, showing how the firm could take advantage of telematics and in-car online services. BMW chose 15 submissions, brought them to Germany from all over the world, and worked further with them to flesh out those ideas. Four ideas are now in the prototype stage, and BMW anticipates several will emerge in new models along with an increased use of this new customer-innovation effort.

- *Acquiring innovation* has become a major way larger companies bring innovation into their firm while mitigating the risk/reward trade-off in the process. Cisco has built itself into a dominant player in the computer and networking equipment industries in large part by buying smaller companies that had developed and tentatively proven new market niches but who needed capital and distribution to rapidly exploit the new technological advantage. Cisco acquired these companies for a premium using stock, but it invested little or nothing in the early development of the technology. Thus, the smaller firm bore all the early risk of failure, and those that succeeded were rewarded in the price of the sale of their company, but Cisco got to avoid the losses associated with the majority of the innovations attempted but not successful. Global Strategy in Action, Exhibit 14.6, describes how Google does something similar in acquiring innovation and how the results are not always to the liking of the entrepreneur company founders they acquire in the process.

- *Outsourcing innovation,* particularly product design, has become a major part of the "modular" organizational structure of today's global technology companies. Nokia,

Samsung, and Motorola—cell phone giants—get proposed new-product design prototypes from HTC, Flextronics, and Cellon—unknown global, billion-dollar-plus companies that create new designs and sell them to cell phone and other electronics brand-name companies annually at the biggest trade shows around the world. To Nokia and its competitors, this shifts the risk of product design innovation to these emerging technology outsourcing powerhouses.

Procter & Gamble, under Alan Lafley, radically changed that company's culture so that it accepts as a matter of corporate strategy that 50 percent of its consumer product innovations will come from outside P&G. The resulting growth and profitability due to new-product innovations at P&G over the last five years of Lafley's first CEO tenure made it the new model of open source product/service/market Innovation worldwide. And, after five years, Lafley's back to do it all over again.[15]

ideagoras

Web-enabled, virtual marketplaces which connect people with unique ideas, talents, resources, or capabilities with companies seeking to address problems or potential innovations in a quick, competent manner.

Ideagoras, defined as places where millions of ideas and solutions change hands in something akin to an eBay for innovation, reflects one of the newest approaches to open innovation, which leverages the value of the Internet to access talent worldwide, instantly. Also referred to as "crowdsourcing" and "open innovation," companies seeking solutions to seemingly insoluble problems can tap the insights of hundreds of thousands of enterprising scientists without having to employ any of them full time. Take, for example, Colgate-Palmolive, which needed a more efficient method for getting its toothpaste into the tube—a seemingly straightforward problem. When its internal R&D team came up empty-handed, the company posted the specs on InnoCentive, one of many ideagoras or marketplaces that link problems with problem solvers. A Canadian engineer named Ed Melcarek proposed putting a positive charge on fluoride powder, then grounding the tube. It was an effective solution, an application of elementary physics, but not one that Colgate-Palmolive's team of chemists had ever contemplated.[16] Melcarek earned $25,000 for a few hours' work, and a timely innovation from outside the company accrued to another client company.

Today more than 160,000 scientists like Melcarek have registered with InnoCentive, and hundreds of companies pay annual fees of roughly $80,000 to tap the talents of this global scientific community. Launched as an e-business by Eli Lilly in 2001, InnoCentive was spun off in 2005, enabling it to expand its offerings and serve clients in a variety of industries. The company now provides solutions to some of the world's most well-known

[15]Hal Gergersen, "A.G. Lafley's Innovation Skills Will Weather P&G's Storm," *Bloomberg BusinessWeek,* June 3, 2013; earlier, "Lafley Leaves Big Shoes to Fill at P&G," Bloomberg-BusinessWeek, June 8, 2009; http:// www.businessweek.com/bwdaily/dnflash/content/jun2009/db2009068_155480.htm. An excellent 3-minute video with Alan Lafley a year after he retired talking about his approach to open innovation at P&G can be found on YouTube at http://www.youtube.com/watch?v=_7mMToRlAxs. Another, longer YouTube video (14 minutes) with Lafley describes in more detail the P&G approach to innovation, particularly their customer or end consumer–focused innovation driver. This 14-minute video was done during the last year of Lafley's leadership at P&G prior to retiring: http://www.youtube.com/watch?v=xvIUSxXrffc&feature=related. It covers more specifics of how they make innovation happen.

[16]Don Tapscott and Anthony D. Williams, "Ideagora, a Marketplace for Minds," *BusinessWeek,* February 15, 2007; a quick video to explain InnoCentive that won the 2010 InnoCentive Idea competition: http://www .youtube.com/user/innocentiveinc#p/c/A81E23D5AC6511C3/2/cac-XdXL-Qk; an explanation of The Power of Open Innovation and Crowdsourcing by Dwayne Spradlin, CEO, InnoCentive, in 2010 at Columbia Business School: http://www.youtube.com/watch?v=phA_NSApxrQ. Another excellent example of the value of crowdsourcing, or an ideagora, is the well-known story of Goldcorp's use of crowdsourcing to turn a $1 million investment into a $6+ billion payoff for Goldcorp: http://www.youtube.com/watch?v=EQca _xH3BVI&feature=relmfu; it is very good for seeing the value of youthful input into corporate innovation decision making.

and innovation-hungry companies. The reason? Mature companies cannot keep up with the speed of innovation nor the demands for growth by relying on internal capabilities alone. This approach creates a much more flexible, free-market mechanism; secondly, it taps a vastly changing global landscape where the talent to generate disruptive or path-breaking innovation will increasingly reside in China, India, Brazil, Eastern Europe, or Russia. P&G figures that for every one of its 9,000 top-notch scientists, there are another 200 outside who are just as good. That's a total of 1.8 million talented people it could potentially tap, using ideagoras to seek out ideas, innovations, and uniquely qualified minds on a global scale quickly, efficiently, and productively.[17]

Such openness in seeking new, key innovations that determine a company's future survival and growth—as opposed to doing innovation on a closely guarded, internal basis—is viewed with skepticism and as a risk that cuts at the very core of what a company essentially exists to do. Product design, major innovations, even incremental innovations, have long been viewed as key, secret core competencies and competitive advantages that generate the long-term success of the company that possesses them. Outsourcing these activities, or doing so via ideagoras, puts the whole firm at risk in the minds of observers opposed to this open type of innovation. That said, the impressive progress Dwayne Spratlin has engineered at InnoCentive, described in Global Strategy in Action, Exhibit 14.7, seems to be reflective of a broadening embrace of Web-enabled, wide-open collaboration in breakthrough innovation.

Another way of looking at the notion of innovation, and an organization's ability to manage it effectively, is found in the argument that innovation is associated with entrepreneurial behavior. And so, to be more innovative, a firm has to become more entrepreneurial.

The examples of Cisco and Google, as they used the "acquiring innovation" approach illustrate the useful ways some companies deal with the reality that breakthrough innovation occurs very often in the smallest of firms, where focus, intensity, and total survival depend on that innovation succeeding. Advocates of this perspective make the point that many industry-creating and paradigm-changing breakthrough innovations (e.g., personal computers; digital file sharing), as well as seemingly obvious incremental innovations ignored by large industry players (e.g., Paychex serving small businesses), came from start-up or small companies—entrepreneurs—that have since become major industry leaders.

Taking this perspective has led some other forward-thinking large companies to seek ways to make themselves more entrepreneurial and to enable their "entrepreneurs within" to emerge and succeed in building new businesses around innovative ideas. Such people, termed "intrapreneurs" in the business and academic press, have proven to be effective champions of innovation-based growth in many companies that have sincerely encouraged their emergence. But whether it is through the entrepreneurs within, or becoming or teaming with independent entrepreneurs, ensuring the presence of entrepreneurship in an organization is central to innovation, long-term survival, and renewal.

---

[17] Simon Schneider, "The Power of the Crowd," *Alliance Magazine,* March 2013; Debi Lewis, "Where Do New Ideas Come From: Crowdsourcing Innovation," http://www.verizonwireless.com/news/article/2013/04/crowdsourcing-innovation.html, April 29, 2013; Carolyn Y. Johnson, "Thorny Research Problems, Solved by Crowdsourcing," *Boston Globe,* February 11, 2013; and Dwayne Spradlin, "Are You Solving the Right Problem?" *Harvard Business Review,* September 2012.

Dwayne Spradlin, CEO, InnoCentive—Harnessing the Power of the Crowd Worldwide

InnoCentive is an open-innovation marketplace in the world, where corporations and non-profits ("seekers") post their toughest research problems and a global network of 160,000 "solvers" takes a crack at solving them for cash rewards. Dwayne Spradlin was a co-founder of InnoCentive, based on his passionate belief that crowdsourcing—allowing experts around the world to help solve problems and create innovation—would easily become a powerful tool for more efficient and speedy problem solving, allowing clients to develop new commercial solutions and allowing many opportunities for more effectively doing good. Spradlin says of this approach, "In this prize-based world, companies and organizations [those pursuing a crowdsourcing approach] are paying predominantly for success. Most innovation efforts fail. With the monolithic view of R&D and innovation, one of the main reasons it's insufficient is that you're paying for failure. In this [crowdsourcing, open-innovation] InnoCentive model, you're paying only for the winning solutions."

He offers a few recent examples: Oil Spill Recovery Institute out of Cordova, Alaska, needed to find a new and novel way to get oil off the bottom of Prince William Sound from the Exxon Valdez spill. For 15 years, that oil has been sitting down there at the bottom of the ocean. They could get the oil off the bottom and onto the barges, but the surface temperature drops so dramatically that the oil almost solidifies and they can't pump it through the barge system.

The solver ended up being an engineer out of the Midwest, and he recognized a way to solve that problem using technology that is fairly common in the construction industry. He recognized that was very similar to the problem of keeping cement liquid when pouring a foundation. They used commercial-grade vibrating equipment on the barges to keep the oil fluid enough so they could process it through the system.

Prize4Life, which is focused on ALS, also known as Lou Gehrig's disease, wanted to find a biomarker to help identify and treat Lou Gehrig's disease patients. They decided to run the challenge in multiple phases. The first phase was a prize to anyone on Earth who can come up with a new and novel way of identifying where a promising biomarker might be.

What's amazing about this was that solutions were coming not necessarily from the medical field—computer scientists; experts in bioinformatics, who were suggesting algorithmic approaches; and machine manufacturers, who knew enough about the disease to say the following kind of approach might provide a highly predictive model of who might be susceptible to this disease were all participating. They were getting solutions from outside the establishment that ended up generating some of the most innovative thinking in that field in recent years.

Crowdsourcing works in other settings too. Toronto-based Goldcorp, a gold mining company heavily in debt, facing labor strikes and high costs, was about to fold. In desperation, CEO Rob McEwen published all their proprietary geological data, a usually carefully guarded company secret in the mining industry, on the Web—400 megabytes of data about 55,000 acres. McEwen made $575,000 in prize money available to anyone who could propose the best methods of finding gold and estimating the likely find.

Within weeks, submissions came from around the world, ultimately resulting in several awards and, for Goldcorp, totally new ways to prospect. The company has now reached more than $6 billion in gold sales by applying the solutions "problem-solvers" from around the world helped them find: $100 invested in Goldcorp in 1993 is worth more than $6,000 today.

Swiss drugmaker Novartis has done something similar, again unheard of in the world of large pharmaceuticals. It decided to share online, after investing millions in secret proprietary research, all of its raw data regarding its efforts to unlock the genetic basis for type 2 diabetes. Among the most challenging and potentially lucrative areas of broad public health needs, Novartis and its partners at MIT decided that the problem is still sufficiently complex that Novartis hopes to leverage the talents and training of a global scientific community to speed the development of gene-related interventions to help solve the type 2 diabetes challenge.

Source: www.innocentive.com. A short video of Rob McEwen on his use of crowdsourcing at Goldcorp can be found at: http://www .youtube.com/watch?v=EQca_xH3BVI&feature=relmfu.

EXHIBIT 14.8
Who Is the
Entrepreneur?

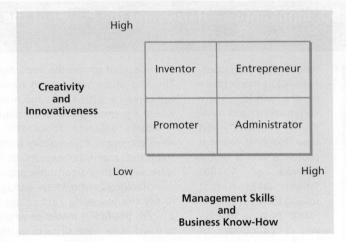

WHAT IS ENTREPRENEURSHIP?

The Global Entrepreneurship Monitor estimates that 15 percent of all working adults are self-employed, a number they project is steadily growing.[18] New entrepreneurial ventures are recognized globally as key drivers of economic development, job creation, and innovation. So what is entrepreneurship? What does it involve?

entrepreneurship
The process of bringing together the creative and innovative ideas and actions with the management and organizational skills necessary to mobilize the appropriate people, money, and operating resources to meet an identifiable need and create wealth in the process.

Entrepreneurship is the process of bringing together creative and innovative ideas and actions with the management and organizational skills necessary to mobilize the appropriate people, money, and operating resources to meet an identifiable need and create wealth in the process. Whether the process is undertaken by a single individual or a team of individuals, there is mounting evidence that growth-minded entrepreneurs possess not only a creative and innovative flair but also solid management skills and business know-how—or they ensure the presence of both in the fledgling organizations they start. Exhibit 14.8 illustrates the fundamental skills associated with being entrepreneurial versus those suitable for promoters, managers, and inventors.

Inventors are exceptional for their technical talents, insights, and creativity. But their creations and inventions often are unsuccessful in becoming commercial or organizational realities because their interests and skills are lacking in terms of reading a market and bringing products or services to creation and then marketing and selling them effectively. *Promoters* are in some way just the opposite—clever at devising schemes or programs to push a product or service, but aimed more at a quick payoff than a profitable, business-building endeavor for the longer term.

Administrators, the good ones, develop strong management skills, specific business know-how, and the ability to organize people. They usually take pride in overseeing the smooth, efficient functioning of operations largely as they are. Their administrative talents are focused on creating and maintaining efficient routines and organization—creative and innovative behavior may actually be counterproductive within the organizations they operate.

---

[18] The Global Entrepreneurship Monitor is a not-for-profit research consortium that is the largest single study of entrepreneurial activity in the world. Initiated in 1999 by Babson College and London Business School, it now involves research teams at universities and other organizations worldwide. It provides annual and quarterly GEM updates at www.gemconsortium.org.

Fred. W. Smith: Blackjack Gambler and Entrepreneur Extraordinaire

Frederick W. Smith, a Yale economics major, first laid out his idea for an express delivery service in what is now the most infamous term paper in business school settings. Legend has it he received a low C, though Smith is rather vague on that folklore. Whatever the professorial critique, he was undeterred. After a stint with the Marines in Vietnam, he returned to hawk the idea to venture capitalists, ultimately getting a significant investment to which he added his family's holdings. He purchased a used aircraft company in Little Rock, Arkansas, and used it to start Federal Express in Memphis, Tennessee.

Smith apparently had transportation in his blood. His grandfather was a steamboat captain; his father built a regional bus service from scratch, ultimately selling it to Greyhound Bus System. Smith learned to fly on weekends as a charter pilot while attending Yale. FedEx's first night's run involved just seven packages.

The postal monopoly was a big headache early in the effort to start FedEx. Smith, desperate and on the verge of bankruptcy with only $5,000 in the bank—not enough to fuel FedEx's planes any further—took the money, flew to Las Vegas, played blackjack, won $27,000—then wired the $32,000 back to Memphis to cover fuel and payroll at that critical moment in the company's survival. Shortly after that, he got an additional $11 million investment, and FedEx started to take off as America came to rely on its overnight delivery. Merrill Lynch excutives came to find that employees even used it to deliver documents overnight between floors of its Manhattan headquarters because it was more reliable and faster than interoffice mail.

Today, FedEx is a global supply chain linchpin for global companies worldwide. It carries more than 8 million shipments in 240 countries every day. All because a young college student first sensed a need for overnight delivery others couldn't or didn't see.

The ideal *entrepreneur* has that unusual combination of talent: strength in both creativity and management. In a new venture, these strengths enable the entrepreneur to conceive and launch a new business as well as make it grow and succeed. In a large organization, these talents enable strong players to emerge and build new ideas into impressive new revenue streams and profitability for a larger company. Because these strengths so rarely coexist in one individual, entrepreneurship is increasingly found to involve teams of people that combine their strengths to build the business they envision. Global Strategy in Action, Exhibit 14.9, tells the story of just such a rare entrepreneur, Fred Smith, founder and chairman of Federal Express.

New ventures and small, growth-oriented business entrepreneurs are able to achieve success from effectively managing three elements central to the entrepreneurial process in creating and sustaining new ventures. Those three elements are opportunity, the entrepreneurial team, and resources:

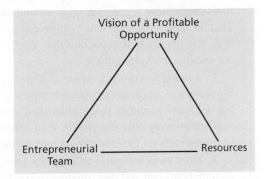

Source: RCTrust, LLC, © 2014.

Opportunity

The most frequent cause of failure of new ventures, as reported by Dun & Bradstreet (D&B) in its yearly failure record, is lack of sales; the second is competitive weakness. Both causes stem from the lack of appreciation of the necessity for a market orientation as the basis of any new venture. In other words, failure among new ventures is heavily linked to ventures started because someone had the idea for such a business but did not identify a concrete market opportunity.

Entrepreneurs doomed to learn from their all too frequent failure conceive an idea for a product or service and immediately become enamored of it. They invest time, money, and energy in developing the idea into a commercial reality. And, tragically, they make only a minimum investment in identifying the customers, the customers' needs, and their willingness to buy the product or service as an answer to those needs. Such entrepreneurs are focused inward, perhaps satisfying their own personal ego needs. The result is often a product or service that few customers will buy. The customers are seeking to buy benefits, and the ineffective entrepreneur is consumed with selling his or her product.

The effective entrepreneur is more likely to assume a marketing orientation and look outward at a target market to identify or confirm the presence of a specific need or desired solution. Here the entrepreneur is focused on potential customers and on seeking to understand their need. The effective entrepreneur seeks to confirm an opportunity defined by what the customer wants and is willing to pay. It is interesting that the most effective approach in the way firms seek to innovate is to bring customers into the innovation process to help shape the solution they seek. In essence, customers define what they want. The design of an effective entrepreneur's product or service comes in response to an opportunity, not the other way around.

Another way to determine if an entrepreneur is focused on simply an idea or a good opportunity is to apply the same criteria venture capitalists use to evaluate new venture investment opportunities. It is important to recognize that these criteria are applied by investors interested primarily in high-growth ventures. The criteria for smaller ventures would be less demanding in scope (e.g., a minimum $250 million market) but similar in the types of concerns that should be addressed in an effort to determine whether the opportunity is a good one. Let's look at each criterion individually:

1. *The venture team can clearly identify its customers and the market segment(s) it plans to capture.* Exactly who are the target customers? Who makes the buying decision? Does the entrepreneur have evidence that these customers are enthusiastic about the product or service and will act favorably (e.g., pay in advance) on that enthusiasm? Firm purchase orders or other tangible purchase commitments help confirm the timing is right.

2. *A minimum market as large as $250 million.* A market this size suggests that the firms can achieve significant sales without having to attain a dominant share of its market. That, in turn, means the new venture can grow without attracting much competitive reaction. It is important to recognize that this threshold pertains to high-growth opportunities, not smaller, lifestyle ventures.

3. *A market growing at a rate of 30 to 50 percent.* This is another indicator that the timing is right to act on an opportunity; it means new entrants can enter the fray without evoking defensive reactions from established competitors. On the other hand, if the market is static or growing only marginally, then either the opportunity must offer a realistic chance of revolutionizing the industry—a rare occurrence—or the timing is bad.

4. *High gross margins (selling price less direct, variable costs) that are durable.* When entrepreneurs can sell their product or service at gross margins in the 50+ percent range, there is an attractive cushion built in that covers the mistakes they are likely to make while developing a new enterprise. When margins are small, the margin for error is too.

5. *There is no dominant competitor in the market segments representing the venture opportunity.* A market share of 40 to 60 percent usually translates into significant power over suppliers, customers, pricing, and costs. The absence of such a competitor means more room for the newcomer to maneuver, without fear of serious retaliation.

6. *A significant response time, or lead time, in terms of technical superiority, proprietary protection, distribution, or capacity.* When a new venture possesses this type of legitimate "unfair advantage," the new firm should be able to create barriers to entry or expansion by others who are aware of the profitable opportunity. When an entrepreneur can take advantage of this sort of proprietary edge, and the edge will last, the timing is right.

7. *An experienced entrepreneur or team capable of enthusiastically and professionally building a company to exploit the profitable opportunity.* Venture capitalists universally identify this as an essential ingredient for the timing to be right to invest in a proposed venture. Aspiring entrepreneurs should likewise use it as a criterion for whether it is wise to pursue the new venture opportunity they are considering. Let's examine this last point more fully.

Entrepreneurial Teams

Successful entrepreneurs and entrepreneurial teams bring several competencies and characteristics to their new ventures. Let's examine both.

• *Technical competence.* The entrepreneur or team must possess the knowledge and skill necessary to create the products or services the new venture will provide. It may be that some of those competencies exist outside the entrepreneur or team, in which case meaningful arrangements to outsource them become part of the technical competence equation. But know-how and capability are essential to success.

• *Business management skills.* The survival and growth of a technically viable new venture depend on the ability of the entrepreneur to understand and manage the economics of the business. Financial and accounting know-how in areas of cash flow, liquidity, costs and contributions, record keeping, pricing, structuring debt, and asset acquisition are essential. People management skills, marketing, organizational skills, sales, computer literacy, and planning skills are just some of those essential to success.

Technical and business skills being critical, they alone are not enough. Observers identify several behavioral and psychological characteristics that are usually associated with successful entrepreneurs:

• *Endless commitment and determination.* Ask any number of entrepreneurs the secret of their success, and they inevitably cite this one. Entrepreneurs' level of commitment can usually be gauged by their willingness to jeopardize personal economic well-being, to tolerate a lower standard of living than they would otherwise enjoy early in the enterprise, and even to sacrifice time with their family.

• *A strong desire to achieve.* Need to achieve is a strong entrepreneurial motivator. Money is a way to keep score, but outdoing their own expectations is an almost universal driver.

• *Orientation toward opportunities and goals.* Good entrepreneurs always like to talk about their customers and their customers' needs. They can readily respond when asked what their goals are for this week, month, and year.

• *An internal locus of control.* Successful entrepreneurs are self-confident. They believe they control their own destiny. To use a sports analogy, they want the ball for the critical last-second shot.

- *Tolerance for ambiguity and stress.* Start-up entrepreneurs face the need to meet payroll when revenue has yet to be received, jobs are constantly changing, customers are ever new, and setbacks and surprises are inevitable.

- *Skills in taking calculated risks.* Entrepreneurs are like pilots: they take calculated risks. They do everything possible to reduce or share risks. They prepare or anticipate problems; confirm the opportunity and what is necessary for success; create ways to share risk with suppliers, investors, customers, and partners; and are typically obsessed with controlling key roles in the execution of the firm's operations.

- *Little need for status and power.* Power accrues to good entrepreneurs, but their focus is on opportunities, customers, markets, and competition. They may use that power in these settings, but they do not often seek status for the sake of having it.

- *Problem solvers.* Good entrepreneurs seek out problems that may affect their success and methodically go about overcoming them. Not intimidated by difficult situations, they are usually decisive and capable of enormous patience.

- *A high need for feedback.* "How are we doing?" The question is ever-present in an entrepreneur's mind. They seek feedback. They nurture mentors to learn from and expand their network of contacts.

- *Ability to deal with failure.* Entrepreneurs love to win, but they accept failure and aggressively learn from it as a way to better manage their next venture.

- *Boundless energy, good health, and emotional stability.* Their challenges are many, so good entrepreneurs seem to embrace their arena and pursue good health to build their stamina and emotional well-being.

- *Creativity and innovativeness.* New ways of looking at things, tinkering, staying late to talk with a customer or employee—all these are typical of entrepreneurs' obsession with doing things better, more efficiently, and so forth. They see an opportunity instead of a problem, a solution instead of a dilemma.

- *High intelligence and conceptual ability.* Good entrepreneurs have "street smarts," a special sense for business, and the ability to see the big picture. They are good strategic thinkers.

- *Vision and the capacity to inspire.* The capacity to shape and communicate a vision in a way that inspires others is a valuable skill entrepreneurs need in themselves or from someone in their core team.

Resources

The third element in new venture entrepreneurship involves *resources*—money and time. Let's summarize money first. A vital ingredient for any business venture is the capital necessary to acquire equipment, facilities, people, and capabilities to pursue the targeted opportunity. New ventures do this in two ways. **Debt financing** is money provided to the venture that must be repaid at some point in time. The obligation to pay is usually secured by property or equipment bought by the business, or by the entrepreneur's personal assets. **Equity financing** is money provided to the venture that entitles the provider to rights or ownership in the venture and which is not expected to be repaid. It entitles the source to some form of ownership in the venture, for which the source usually expects some future return or gain on that investment.

Debt financing is generally obtained from a commercial bank to pay for property, equipment, and maybe provide working capital—all available only after there is proven revenue coming into the business. Family and friends are debt sources, as are leasing companies, suppliers, and companies that lend against accounts receivable. Entrepreneurs benefit when

debt financing
Money "loaned" to an entrepreneur or business venture that must be repaid at some point in time.

equity financing
Money provided to a business venture that entitles the provider to rights or ownership in the venture and which is not expected to be repaid.

using debt capital because they retain ownership and increase the return on their investment if things go as planned. If not, debt financing can be a real problem for new ventures because rapid growth requires steady cash flow (to pay salaries, bills, interest), which creates a real dilemma if interest rates rise and sales slow down. Most new ventures find early debt capital hard to get anyway, so gradually nurturing a relationship with a commercial lender, letting them get to know the entrepreneur and the business, is a wise approach for the new entrepreneur.

Crowdsourced lending has become another way small entrepreneurial ventures can get debt financing. Web sites like www.prosper.com and www.lendingclub.com aggregate small individual "lenders" with ventures and individuals seeking loans. These loans can range from $500 to over $10,000—rather small amounts but a steadily proliferating global model for replacing traditional lenders with crowdsourced individuals seeking to lend money for a modest return.

Equity financing is usually obtained from one or more of three sources: friendly sources, informal venture investors, or professional venture capitalists. In each case, it is often referred to as "patient money," meaning it does not have to be paid back immediately or on any particular schedule. *Friendly sources* are prevalent early in many new ventures—friends, family, wealthy individuals who know the entrepreneur. *Informal venture investors,* usually wealthy individuals, or what are now called "angel" investors (for obvious reasons), are increasingly active and accessible as possible equity investors. *Professional venture capitalists* seek investment in the truly high-growth potential ventures. They have stringent criteria as we have seen, and expect a return of five times their money in three to five years! A fourth source of equity capital, *public stock offerings,* is available for a very select few new ventures. They are usually firms that have gone through the other three sources first.

Crowdsourced equity investment has emerged as a Web-enabled, broad-based way to reach individual investors seeking to help finance entrepreneurial ventures. It exists in Europe regardless of an individual investor's financial condition. Legislation passed in the United States has authorized the Securities and Exchange Commission to write rules that would apply to it in the United States while protecting investors that are not "accredited investors."[19] Once those new rules are finalized, sites like www.earlyshares.com and many others are ready to allow average individuals worldwide to join others investing in entrepreneurial ventures by buying equity in those firms online through their site. Kickstarter (www.kickstarter.com) is a well-known example of sites[20] that have helped many ventures and entrepreneurs raise money for artists and private and social ventures by getting people to give money in a crowdsourcing format in return for gifts or rewards, but not equity in those ventures.

Regardless of the source, equity capital is money that does not have to be repaid on an immediate, regular basis as debt capital requires. So when a firm is rapidly growing and needs to use all its cash flow to grow, not having to repay makes equity more attractive than debt. The unattractive aspect of equity financing for some people is that it constitutes selling part of the ownership of the business and, with it, a say in the decisions directing the venture.

The other resource is time—time of the entrepreneur(s) and key players in the business venture's chance for success. The entrepreneur is the catalyst, the glue that holds the fledgling business together and oftentimes the critical source of energy to make success happen. As we noted earlier, determination is a key characteristic of entrepreneurs. And time is the

---

[19]Individual persons with incomes greater than $200,000 annually and a net worth exceeding $1 million not counting residence were considered "accredited investors" according to Reg. D in 2013 in the United States.
[20]See, for example, www.indiegogo.com; www.crowdrise.com; www.profounder.com

most critical resource, combined with determination, to virtually "will" the new venture's success at numerous junctures in its early development.

Successful entrepreneurs are impressive growth and value building innovators. Their success often comes at the expense of large firms with which they compete, do business, obtain supplies, and such. Their success in commercializing new ideas has drawn the attention of many larger companies leading to the question, Can a big firm be more entrepreneurial? The conclusion has been a tentative yes, that larger firms can increase their level of innovation and subsequent commercialization success if they encourage entrepreneurship and entrepreneurs within their organizations. Understanding and encouraging entrepreneurship in large organizations to improve future survival and growth has become a major agenda in thousands of large companies today. The ideas behind these efforts, which have been called *intrapreneurship,* are examined in the next section.

Intrapreneurship

intrapreneurship
A term associated with entrepreneurship in large, established companies; the process of attempting to identify, encourage, enable, and assist entrepreneurship within a large, established company so as to create new products, processes, services, or improvements that become major new revenue streams and/or sources of cost savings for the company.

Intrapreneurship, or entrepreneurship in large companies, is the process of attempting to identify, encourage, enable, and assist entrepreneurship within a large, established company so as to create new products, processes, or services that become major new revenue streams and sources of cost savings for the company. Gordon Pinchot, founder of a school for intrapreneurs and creator of the phrase itself, suggests 10 **freedom factors** that need to be present in large companies seeking to encourage intrapreneurship:

1. *Self-selection.* Companies should give innovators the opportunity to bring forth their ideas, rather than making the generation of new ideas the designated responsibility of a few individuals or groups.

2. *No hand-offs.* Once ideas surface, managers should allow the person generating the idea to pursue it rather than instructing him or her to turn it over ("hand it off") to someone else.

3. *The doer decides.* Giving the originator of an idea some freedom to make decisions about its further development and implementation, rather than relying on multiple levels of approval for even the most minor decision, enhances intrapreneurship.

4. *Corporate "slack."* Firms that set aside money and time ("slack") facilitate innovation.

5. *End the "home run" philosophy.* Some company cultures foster an interest in innovative ideas only when they represent major breakthroughs. Intrapreneurship is restricted in that type of culture.

intrapreneurship freedom factors
Ten characteristics identified by Dr. Gorden Pinchot and elaborated upon by others that need to be present in large companies seeking to encourage and increase the level of intrapreneurship within their company.

6. *Tolerance of risk, failure, and mistakes.* Where risks and failure are damaging to their careers, managers carefully avoid them. But innovations inherently involve risks, so calculated risks and some failures should be tolerated and chalked up to experience.

7. *Patient money.* The pressure for quarterly profits in many U.S. companies stifles innovative behavior. Investment in intrapreneurial activity may take time to bear fruit.

8. *Freedom from turfness.* In any organization, people stake out turf. Boundaries go up. Intrapreneurship is stifled by this phenomenon because cross-fertilization is often central to innovation and successful entrepreneurial teams.

9. *Cross-functional teams.* Organizations inhibit cross-functional interaction by insisting that communication flow upward. That inhibits sales from learning from operations and company people from interacting with relevant outsiders.

10. *Multiple options.* When an individual with an idea has only one person to consult or one channel to inquire into for developing the idea, innovation can be stifled. Intrapreneurship is encouraged when people have many options for discussing or pursuing innovative ideas.

When you read Pinchot's 10 freedom factors, they sound very much like characteristics associated with entrepreneurs or the nature of the types of resources—money and time—that we identified as being central to the entrepreneurship process. And that, obviously, is exactly what intrapreneurship is trying to do—replicate the presence of entrepreneurs (small undertakings) inside a large enterprise that offers the potential advantage of easier money, expertise, facilities, distribution, and so forth. Global Strategy in Action, Exhibit 14.10 describes a variety of intrapreneurial successes with companies you should readily recognize. Nine specific ways companies are attempting to enable intrapreneurs and intrapreneurship to flourish in their companies are given here:[21]

- *Designate intrapreneurship "sponsors."* Formally identify several people with credibility and influence in the company to serve as facilitators of new ideas. These "sponsors" usually have discretionary funds to allocate on the spot to help innovators develop their ideas.

- *Allow innovation time.* 3M was know for its "15 percent rule," which means that members of its engineering group can spend 15 percent of their time tinkering with whatever idea they think has market potential. Google gives employees one day a week to work on their own projects.

- *Accommodate intrapreneurial teams.* 3M calls it "tin cupping." American Cement calls it "innovation volunteers." P&G sets up teams across product divisions to intentionally cross-pollinate new business. The idea is for companies to give managers interdepartmental or unit flexibility to let informal idea-development teams (a marketing person, an engineer, and an operations person) interact about promising ideas and develop them as though they were an independent business.

- *Provide intrapreneurial forums.* Owens Corning calls them "skunkworks, innovation boards, and innovation fairs." 3M has "technical forums," annual "technical review fairs," and "sales clubs." P&G, eBay, and Amazon bring in outsiders, customers especially, to help form the basis for interaction about new ideas where ones that gain traction can quickly move to more serious pursuit using other specific ways described here.

- *Use intrapreneurial controls.* Quarterly profit contribution does not work with intrapreneurial ventures at their early stages. Milestone reviews like we discussed earlier in this chapter—key timetables, resource requirements—provide a type of control more suited to early, innovative activity.

- *Provide intrapreneurial rewards.* Recognition for success, financial bonuses if successful, and most importantly the opportunity to "do it again," with even greater freedom in developing and implementing the next idea are extremely important to this type of venture.

- *Articulate specific innovation objectives.* Clearly setting forth organizational objectives that legitimize and indeed call for intrapreneurship and innovation helps encourage an organizational culture to support this activity. 3M is the "granddaddy" of this approach, having long held to a corporate objective, which they have hit every year since 1970, that "25 percent of annual sales each year will come from products introduced within the last five years." P&G has a corporate goal that 50 percent of its innovations originate outside the company to encourage collaborative, "open," innovative behavior.

[21]"Unhappy at Work? Be an Intrapreneur," www.wired.com, May 13, 2013; "5 Must-Have Skills for Intrapreneurs," www.boardofinnovation.com, April 19, 2013; "Richard Branson Hails Top 'Intrapreneurs,'" www.virgin .com/entrepreneur, April 9, 2013; Niko Karvounis, "The Intrapreneur's Playbook," http://www.fastcompany .com/3002459/intrapreneurs-playbook, October 31, 2012; David Armano, "Move Over Entrepreneurs, Here Come the Intrapreneurs," *Forbes,* May 21, 2012; and www.businessweek.com/innovation-and-design.

Intrapreneurs—They Are Everywhere!
Just Give Them Time to Blossom

Google encourages all its employees to spend 20 percent of their time on ideas that they would like to develop or feel passionate about. This is the reason Google is constantly introducing new products such as Gmail, Google Earth, and Google Apps. Google Adsense and Adwords were created by an employee who was paid $10 million for his internal-entrepreneurial effort.

Arthur Fry, 53, a 3M chemical engineer, used to get annoyed at how pieces of paper that marked his church hymnal always fell out when he stood up to sing. He knew that Spencer Silver, a scientist at 3M, had accidentally discovered an adhesive that had very low sticking power. Normally that would be bad, but for Fry it was good. He figured that markers made with the adhesive might stick lightly to something and would come off easily. Since 3M allows employees to spend 15 percent of their office time on independent projects, he began working on the idea. Fry made samples and then distributed the small yellow pads to company secretaries. They were delighted. 3M eventually began selling it under the name **Post-it.** Sales last year were more than **$100 million.**

Ken Kutaragi was working in Sony's sound labs when he bought his daughter a Nintendo game console. Watching her play, he was dismayed by the system's primitive sound effects. With Sony's blessing, Kutaragi worked with Nintendo to develop a CD-ROM–based Nintendo. But Nintendo decided not to go forward with it, so Kutaragi helped Sony develop its own gaming system, which became the PlayStation. The first PlayStation made Sony a major player in the games market, but the PlayStation 2 did even better, becoming the best-selling game console of all time. Kutaragi founded Sony Computer Entertainment, one of the Sony's most profitable divisions.

W.L. Gore, known primarily as the maker of Gore-Tex rain gear, encourages employees to develop new ideas through its "dabble time" policy: 10 percent of a workday can be devoted to personal projects. A few years ago, the company was experimenting with ePTFE, a chemical cousin to Teflon, to coat push-pull cables for use in animatronics. Dave Myers, an associate in the company's medical unit, thought the coating might be good for guitar strings and recruited both marketing and manufacturing personnel to work on the project. Myers's team originally believed that the coating's appeal would be in making strings more comfortable to use. But extensive market research, piloted by John Spencer, and more than 15,000 guitar-player field tests led the team to realize their real selling point: better sound. The coated strings were only nominally more comfortable than noncoated strings, but they kept their tone longer than conventional guitar strings. W.L. Gore launched them under the brand name ELIXIR Strings, now the No. 1 seller of acoustic guitar strings and the overall No. 2 seller in the guitar string market.

There's an engineer in Dallas whose "wasteful" tinkering with a flow problem he had to deal with every day almost got him fired. Now his oil delivery spout invention is used by almost every major oil company in the world.

Caterpillar took its own internal logistics problem and created Caterpillar Logistics, which now spans 25 countries and six continents.

Alicia Ledlie, co-manager at a Walmart store in Long Island, New York, attended a conference at the company's Arkansas headquarters and heard about a possible new venture: in-store health clinics. It was Ledlie's idea to include drug-testing services for Walmart job applicants in the clinics' scope of services. Ledlie knew that all new hires had to have a drug test within 24 hours of receiving a job offer. "Working in the stores, I'd seen how this requirement created a challenge for recruits who relied on public transportation," she says. "Adding this service to the clinics' roster was a quick win. Store managers raved about the effect it had on helping them keep new recruits." Walmart has added over 2,000 sites in the last three years.

Jim Lynch's big idea came out of the most ordinary of activities—cleaning the gutters on his suburban Massachusetts home. "It occurred to me that this was a perfect job for a robot," Lynch says, "because it fit into our company's three criteria: dumb, dirty, and dangerous." A senior electrical engineer at Burlington, Massachusetts–based iRobot, Lynch began tinkering with different models and built a prototype using a spaghetti ladle and an electric screwdriver. His chance to present it came when the company held its first-ever "idea bake-off," where employees got 10 minutes each to pitch an idea for a new product. Lynch's project was green-lighted by the company brass, and the new gutter-cleaning robot, named "Looj" (after the Olympic sport), launched on schedule last year.

Source: www.bnet.com/2403-1313070_23-196888.htm, and 23-196890.htm.

• *Create a culture of intrapreneurship.* Jeff Bezos of Amazon.com calls it a "culture of divine discontent," in which everyone itches to improve things. P&G calls it letting outsiders into P&G to innovate, and returning CEO Lafley looks to reestablish the P&G norm that more than half of P&G new products will come from outsiders teamed with inside intrapreneurs. GE's Immelt hires successful intrapreneurs from other companies to become leaders in a usually insider-promoted organization, both to get the intrapreneur involved and even more importantly to send a message of fundamental cultural change toward intrapreneurship. Other firms create internal "banks" to invest in new internal start-ups. Intel has its own venture capital arm investing aggressively in entrepreneurial ventures inside and outside the company, often spinning them off.

• *Encourage innovation from without as well as within.* Apple is widely assumed to be an innovator "within." In fact, its real skill lies in stitching together its own ideas with technologies from outside and then wrapping the results in elegant software and simple, stylish designs.

Innovation and entrepreneurship are intertwined phenomena and processes. Organizations seeking to control their destiny, which most all seek to do, increasingly "get it" that even having a destiny may be the issue. And to have that opportunity or chance, organizations need leaders who embrace the importance of being innovative and entrepreneurial to give their companies the chance to find ways to adapt, be relevant, to position themselves in a future that, to use a trite phrase, has but one real constant—change.

Summary

A central goal with any strategy is the survival, growth, and improved competitive position of the company in the future. Executives seek ways to make their organizations innovative and entrepreneurial because these are increasingly seen as essential capabilities for survival, growth, and relevance. Incremental innovation—where companies increasingly, in concert with their customers, seek to steadily refine and improve their products, services, and processes—has proven to be a very effective approach to innovation. The continuous improvement philosophy, and programs such as CCC21 and Six Sigma, are key ways firms make incremental innovation a central part of their organization's ongoing work activities.

Breakthrough innovation involves far more risk than the incremental approach yet brings high reward when successful. Firms with this approach need a total commitment and are often going against mainstream markets in the process. Large, well-known global companies are increasingly embracing "open" approaches to innovation, including breakthrough innovation, in ways that would have been unthinkable 20 years ago. They have embraced the outsourcing of much product design innovation in recent years and are rapidly adopting Web-enabled forums for tapping expertise located around the globe to gain assistance and collaboration in generating breakthrough innovation. They also increasingly look to innovate by acquiring small, entrepreneurial firms that often generate breakthrough innovations because they have a narrow focus, tolerate risks, have a passion for what they are doing, and benefit greatly if they succeed.

Entrepreneurship is central to making businesses innovative and fresh. New-venture entrepreneurship is the source of much innovation, and it is really a process involving opportunity, resources, and key people. Opportunity is focusing intensely on solving problems and benefits to customers rather than product or service ideas someone just dreams up. Resources involve money and time. Key people, the entrepreneurial team, need to bring technical skill, business skill, and key characteristics to the new venture endeavor for it to succeed.

Intrapreneurship is entrepreneurship in large organizations. Many firms now claim that they seek to encourage intrapreneurship. For intrapreneurship to work, individual intrapreneurs need freedom and support to pursue perceived opportunities, be allowed to fail, and do more of the same more easily if they succeed.

Key Terms

breakthrough innovation, *p. 420*
CCC21, *p. 416*
continuous improvement, *p. 416*
debt financing, *p. 434*
disruptive innovation, *p. 425*

entrepreneurship, *p. 430*
equity financing, *p. 434*
ideagoras, *p. 427*
incremental innovation, *p. 415*
innovation, *p. 415*

intrapreneurship, *p. 436*
intrapreneurship freedom
factors, *p. 436*
invention, *p. 415*
Six Sigma, *p. 416*

Questions for Discussion

1. What is the difference between incremental and breakthrough innovation? What risks are associated with each approach?
2. Why is continuous improvement, and programs such as CCC21 and Six Sigma, a good way to develop incremental innovation?
3. What is an ideagora?
4. How are big, global companies looking "outward" to accelerate their innovativeness and breakthrough innovations?
5. Why do most breakthrough innovations occur in smaller firms?
6. What are the three key elements in the entrepreneurship process in new ventures?
7. What is intrapreneurship, and how is it best enabled?

Cases

Guide to Strategic Management Case Analysis

Guide to Strategic Management Case Analysis

THE CASE METHOD

Case analysis is a proven educational method that is especially effective in a strategic management course. The case method complements and enhances the text material and your professor's lectures by focusing attention on what a firm has done or should do in an actual business situation. Use of the case method in a strategic management course offers you an opportunity to develop and refine analytical skills. It also can provide exciting experience by allowing you to assume the role of the key decision maker for the organizations you will study.

When assuming the role of the general manager of the organization being studied, you will need to consider all aspects of the business. In addition to drawing on your knowledge of marketing, finance, management, production, and economics, you will be applying the strategic management concepts taught in this course.

The cases in this book are accounts of real business situations involving a variety of firms in a variety of industries. To make these opportunities as realistic as possible, the cases include a variety of quantitative and qualitative information in both the presentation of the situation and the exhibits. As the key decision maker, you will need to determine which information is important, given the circumstances described in the case. Keep in mind that the results of analyzing one firm will not necessarily be appropriate for another since every firm is faced with a different set of circumstances.

PREPARING FOR CASE DISCUSSION

The case method requires an approach to class preparation that differs from the typical lecture course. In the typical lecture course, you can still benefit from each class session, even if you did not prepare, by listening carefully to the professor's lecture. This approach will not work in a course using the case method. For a case course, proper preparation is essential.

Suggestions for Effective Preparation

1. *Allow adequate time in preparing a case.* Many of the cases in this text involve complex issues that are often not apparent without careful reading and purposeful reflection on the information in the cases.

2. *Read each case twice.* Because many of these cases involve complex decision making, you should read each case at least twice. Your first reading should give you an overview of the firm's unique circumstances and the issues confronting the firm. Your second reading allows you to concentrate on what you feel are the most critical issues and to understand what information in the case is most important. Make limited notes identifying key points during your first reading. During your second reading, you can add details to your original notes and revise them as necessary.

3. *Focus on the key strategic issue in each case.* Each time you read a case you should concentrate on identifying the key issue. In some cases, the key issue will be identified by the case writer in the introduction. In other cases, you might not grasp the key strategic issue until you have read the case several times. (Remember that not every piece of information in a case is equally important.)

4. *Do not overlook exhibits.* The exhibits in these cases should be considered an integral part of the information for the case. They are not just "window dressing." In fact, for many cases you will need to analyze financial statements, evaluate organizational charts, and understand the firm's products, all of which are presented in the form of exhibits.

5. *Adopt the appropriate time frame.* It is critical that you assume the appropriate time frame for each case you read. If the case ends in 2009, that year should become the present for you as you work on that case. Making a decision for a case that ends in 2009 by using data you could not have had until 2011 defeats the purpose of the case method. For the same reason, although it is recommended that you do outside reading on each firm and industry, you should not read material written after the case ended unless your professor instructs you to do so.

6. *Draw on all of your knowledge of business.* As the key decision maker for the organization being studied, you will need to consider all aspects of the business and industry. Do not confine yourself to strategic management concepts presented in this course. You will need to determine if the key strategic issue revolves around a theory you have learned in a functional area, such as marketing, production, finance, or economics, or in the strategic management course.

USING THE INTERNET IN CASE RESEARCH

The proliferation of information available on the Internet has direct implications for business research. The Internet has become a viable source of company and industry data to assist those involved in case study analysis. Principal sources of useful data include company Web sites, U.S. government Web sites, search engines, investment research sites, and online data services. This section will describe the principal Internet sources of case study data and offer means of retrieving that data.

Company Web Sites

Virtually every public and private firm has a Web site that any Internet user can visit. Accessing a firm's Web site is easy. Many firms advertise their Web address through both TV and print advertisements. To access a site when the address is known, enter the address into the address line on any Internet service provider's homepage. When the address is not known, use of a search engine will be necessary. The use of a search engine will be described later. Often, but not always, a firm's Web address is identical to its name, or is at least an abbreviated form of its name.

Company Web sites contain data that are helpful in case study analysis. A firm's Web site may contain descriptions of company products and services, recent company accomplishments and press releases, financial and stock performance highlights, and an overview of a firm's history and strategic objectives. A company's Web site may also contain links to relevant industry Web sites that contain industry statistics as well as current and future industry trends. The breadth of data available on a particular firm's Web site will vary but in general larger, global corporations tend to have more complete and sophisticated Web sites than do smaller, regional firms.

U.S. Government Web Sites

The U.S. government allows the public to access virtually all of the information that it collects. Most of this information is available online to Internet users. The government collects a great range of data types, from firm-specific data the government mandates all publicly traded firms to supply to highly regarded economic indicators. The usefulness of many U.S. government Web sites depends on the fit between the case you are studying and the data located on the Web site. For example, a study of an accounting firm may be supplemented with data supplied by the Internal Revenue Service Web site, but not the Environmental Protection Agency Web site. A sampling of prominent government Web sites and their addresses is shown here:

Environmental Protection Agency: www.epa.gov

General Printing Office: www.gpo.gov

Internal Revenue Service: www.irs.ustreas.gov

Libraries of Congress: www.loc.gov

National Aeronautics and Space Administration: www.hq.nasa.gov

SEC's Edgar Database: www.sec.gov/edgarhp.htm

Small Business Administration: www.sba.gov

STAT-USA: www.stat-usa.gov

U.S. Department of Commerce: www.doc.gov

U.S. Patent and Trademark Office: www.uspto.gov

U.S. Department of Treasury: www.ustreas.gov

One of the most useful sites for company case study analysis is the Securities and Exchange Commission's EDGAR database. The EDGAR database contains the documents that the government mandates all publicly traded firms to file including 10-Ks and 8-Ks. A Form 10-K is the annual report that provides a comprehensive overview of a firm's financials in addition to discussions regarding industry and product background. Form 8-K reports the occurrence of any material events or corporate changes that may be of importance to investors. Examples of reported occurrences include key management personnel changes, corporate restructures, and new debt or equity issuance. This site is very user friendly and requires the researcher to provide only the company name in order to produce a listing of all available reports.

Search Engines

Search engines allow a researcher to locate information on a company or industry without prior knowledge of a specific Internet address. Generally, to execute a search the search engine requires the entering of a keyword, for example, a company name. However, each search engine differs slightly in its search capabilities. For example, to narrow a search on one search engine may be accomplished differently than narrowing a search on another.

The information retrieved by search engines typically includes articles and other information that contain the entered keyword or words. Because the search engine has retrieved data that contain keywords does not necessarily mean that the information is useful. Internet data are unfiltered, meaning they may not be checked for accuracy before the data are posted online. However, data copyrighted or published by a reputable source may greatly increase the chance that the data are indeed accurate. Popular search options like google.com, bing.com, yahoo.com, and ask.com should work just fine to allow you to do basic research on the companies and industries discussed in the cases.

Investment Research Sites

Investment research sites provide company stock performance data including key financial ratios, competitor identification, industry data, and links to research reports and SEC filings. These sites provide support for the financial analysis portion of a case study, but only for publicly traded businesses. Most investment research sites also contain macro market data that may not be company specific, but may still affect many investors of equities.

Investment research sites usually contain a search mechanism if a desired stock's ticker symbol is not known. In this case, the company name is entered to enable the site to find the corresponding equity. Because these sites are geared toward traders who want recent stock prices and data, searching for data relevant to a case may require more elaborate investigations at multiple sites. The following list includes many popular investment research sites:

American Stock Exchange: www.amex.com

CBS Market Watch: www.cbsmarketwatch.com

CNN FinancialNews: www.money.cnn.com

DBC Online: www.esignal.com

Hoover's Online: www.hoovers.com

InvestorGuide: www.investorguide.com

Wall Street Research Net: www.wsrn.com

Market Guide: www.marketguide.com

Money Search: www.moneysearch.com

MSN Money: www.moneycentral.msn.com

NASDAQ: www.nasdaq.com

New York Stock Exchange: www.nyse.com

PC Financial Network: www.csfbdirect.com

Quote.Com: www.finance.lycos.com

Stock Smart: www.stocksmart.com

www.Yahoo.com/finance

Wright Investors' Service on the World Wide Web: www.wisi.com

The Wall Street Journal Online: www.online.wsj.com/public/us

Zacks Investment Research: www.my.zacks.com

One site that conveniently contains firm, industry, and competitor data is Hoover's Online. Hoover's also provides financials, stock charts, current and archived news stories, and links to research reports and SEC filings. Yahoo!'s "Finance" option is another excellent resource for company-related research. Some of these data, most notably the lengthy research reports produced by analysts, are fee-based and must be ordered.

Online Data Sources

Online data sources provide wide access to a huge volume of business reference material. Information retrieved from these sites typically includes descriptive profiles, stock price performance, SEC filings, and newspaper, magazine, and journal articles related to a particular company, industry, or product. Online data services are popular with educational and financial institutions. While some services are free to all users, to utilize the entire array of these sites' services, a fee-based subscription is usually necessary.

Accessing these sites requires only the source's address, or the use of a search engine to find the address. The source's homepage will clearly indicate the nature of the information available and describe how to search for and access the data. Most sites have help screens to assist in locating the desired information.

One of the most useful online sources for business research is the Lexis-Nexis Universe. This source provides a wide array of news, business, legal, and reference information. The information is categorized into dozens of topics including general news; company and industry news; company financials that include SEC filings; government and political news; accounting, auditing, and tax data; and legal research. One particularly impressive service is a search mechanism that allows a user to locate a particular article when the specific citation is known. A list of several notable online data sources is shown here:

ABI/Inform (Proquest Direct): www.il.proquest.com/proquest

American Express: www.americanexpress.com

Bloomberg Financial News Services: www.bloomberg.com

BusinessWeek Online: www.businessweek.com or www.bloombergbusinessweek.com

Dow Jones News Retrieval: http://bis.dowjones.com

EconLit: www.econlit.org

Lexis-Nexis Universe: www.lexis-nexis.com

PARTICIPATING IN CLASS

Because the strategic management course uses the case method, the success and value of the course depend on class discussion. The success and value of the class discussion, in turn, rely on the roles both you and your professor perform. Following are aspects of your role and your professor's that, if kept in mind, will enhance the value and excitement of this course.

Students as Active Learners

The case method requires your active participation. This means your role is no longer one of sitting and listening.

1. *Attend class regularly.* Not only is your grade likely to depend on your involvement in class discussions, but the benefit you derive from this course is directly related to your involvement in and understanding of the discussions.

2. *Be prepared for class.* The need for adequate preparation already has been discussed. You will benefit more from the discussions, will understand and participate in the exchange of ideas, and will avoid the embarrassment of being called on when not prepared. By all

means, bring your book to class. Not only is there a good chance you will need to refer to a specific exhibit or passage from the case, you may need to refresh your memory of the case (particularly if you made notes in the margins while reading).

3. *Participate in the discussion.* Attending class and being prepared are not enough; you need to express your views in class. You can participate in a number of ways: by addressing a question asked by your professor, by disagreeing with your professor or your classmates (by all means, be tactful), by building on an idea expressed by a classmate, or by simply asking a relevant question.

4. *Participate wisely.* Although you do not want to be one of those students who never raises his or her hand, you also should be sensitive to the fact that others in your class will want to express themselves. You have probably already had experience with a student who attempts to dominate each class discussion. A student who invariably tries to dominate the class discussion breeds resentment.

5. *Keep a broad perspective.* By definition, the strategic management course deals with the issues facing general managers or business owners. As already mentioned, you need to consider all aspects of the business, not just one particular functional area.

6. *Pay attention to the topic being discussed.* Focus your attention on the topic being discussed. When a new topic is introduced, do not attempt to immediately introduce another topic for discussion. Do not feel you have to have something to say on every topic covered.

Your Professor as Discussion Leader

Your professor is a discussion leader. As such, he or she will attempt to stimulate the class as a whole to share insights, observations, and thoughts about the case. Your professor will not necessarily respond to every comment you or your classmates make. Part of the value of the case method is to get you and your classmates to assume this role as the course progresses.

The professor in a strategic management case course performs several roles:

1. *Maintaining focus.* Because multiple complex issues need to be explored, your professor may want to maintain the focus of the class discussion on one issue at a time. He or she may ask you to hold your comment on another issue until a previous issue is exhausted. Do not interpret this response to mean your point is unimportant; your professor is simply indicating there will be a more appropriate time to pursue that particular comment.

2. *Getting students involved.* Do not be surprised if your professor asks for input from volunteers and nonvolunteers alike. The value of the class discussion increases as more people share their comments.

3. *Facilitating comprehension of strategic management concepts.* Some professors prefer to lecture on strategic management concepts on a "need-to-know" basis. In this scenario, a lecture on a particular topic will be followed by an assignment to work on a case that deals with that particular topic. Other professors will have the class work through a case or two before lecturing on a topic to give the class a feel for the value of the topic being covered and for the type of information needed to work on cases. Still other professors prefer to cover all of the theory in the beginning of the course, thereby allowing uninterrupted case discussion in the remaining weeks of the term. All three of these approaches are valued.

4. *Playing devil's advocate.* At times your professor may appear to be contradicting many of the comments or observations being made. At other times your professor may adopt a position that does not immediately make sense, given the circumstances of the case. At other times your professor may seem to be equivocating. These are all examples

of how your professor might be playing devil's advocate. Sometimes the professor's goal is to expose alternative viewpoints. Sometimes he or she may be testing your resolve on a particular point. Be prepared to support your position with evidence from the case.

ASSIGNMENTS

Written Assignments

Written analyses are a critical part of most strategic management courses. Each professor has a preferred format for these written analyses, but a number of general guidelines will prove helpful to you in your written assignments.

1. *Analyze.* Avoid merely repeating the facts presented in the case. Analyze the issues involved in the case and build logically toward your recommendations.

2. *Use headings or labels.* Using headings or labels throughout your written analysis will help your reader follow your analysis and recommendations. For example, when you are analyzing the weaknesses of the firm in the case, include the heading Weaknesses. Note the headings in the cases that follow.

3. *Discuss alternatives.* Follow the proper strategic management sequence by *(a)* identifying alternatives, *(b)* evaluating each alternative, and *(c)* recommending the alternative you think is best.

4. *Use topic sentences.* You can help your reader more easily evaluate your analysis by putting the topic sentence first in each paragraph and following with statements directly supporting the topic sentence.

5. *Be specific in your recommendations.* Develop specific recommendations logically and be sure your recommendations are well defended by your analysis. Avoid using generalizations, clichés, and ambiguous statements. Remember that any number of answers are possible and so your professor is most concerned about how your reasoning led to your recommendations and how well you develop and support your ideas.

6. *Do not overlook implementation.* Many good analyses receive poor evaluations because they do not include a discussion of implementation. Your analysis will be much stronger when you discuss how your recommendation can be implemented. Include some of the specific actions needed to achieve the objectives you are proposing.

7. *Specifically state your assumptions.* Cases, like all real business situations, involve incomplete information. Therefore, it is important that you clearly state any assumptions you make in your analysis. Do not assume your professor will be able to fill in the missing points.

Oral Presentations

Your professor is likely to ask you and your classmates to make oral presentations on a particular case. Oral presentations usually are done by groups of students. In these groups, each member will typically be responsible for one aspect of the overall case. Keep the following suggestions in mind when you are faced with an oral presentation:

1. *Use your own words.* Avoid memorizing a presentation. The best approach is to prepare an outline of the key points you want to cover. Do not be afraid to have the outline in front of you during your presentation, but do not just read the outline.

2. *Rehearse your presentation.* Do not assume you can simply read the outline you have prepared or that the right words will come to you when you are in front of the class making

your presentation. Take the time to practice your speech, and be sure to rehearse the entire presentation with your group.

3. *Use visual aids.* The adage "a picture is worth a thousand words" contains quite a bit of truth. The people in your audience will more quickly and thoroughly understand your key points—and will retain them longer—if you use visual aids. Think of ways you and your team members can use the blackboard in the classroom; a graph, chart, or exhibit on a large posterboard; or, if you will have a number of these visual aids, a flip chart.

4. *Be prepared to handle questions.* You probably will be asked questions by your classmates. If questions are asked during your presentation, try to address those that require clarification. Tactfully postpone more elaborate questions until you have completed the formal phase of your presentation. During your rehearsal, try to anticipate the types of questions that you might be asked.

Working as a Team Member

Many professors assign students to groups or teams for analyzing cases. This adds more realism to the course, since most strategic decisions in business are addressed by a group of key managers. If you are a member of a group assigned to analyze a case, keep in mind that your performance is tied to the performance of the other group members, and vice versa. The following are some suggestions to help you be an effective team member:

1. *Be sure the division of labor is equitable.* It is not always easy to decide how the workload can be divided equitably, since it is not always obvious how much work needs to be done. Try breaking down the case into the distinct parts that need to be analyzed to determine if having a different person assume responsibility for each part is equitable. All team members should read and analyze the entire case, but different team members can be assigned primary responsibility for each major aspect of the analysis. Each team member with primary responsibility for a major aspect of the analysis also will be the logical choice to write that portion of the written analysis or to present it orally in class.

2. *Communicate with other team members.* This is particularly important if you encounter problems with your portion of the analysis. Because, by definition, the team members are dependent on each other, it is critical that you communicate openly and honestly with each other. Therefore, it is essential that your team members discuss problems, such as some members not doing their fair share of work or members insisting that their point of view dominate the team's report.

3. *Work as a team.* A group's output should reflect a combined effort, so the whole group should be involved in each part of the analysis, even if different individuals assume primary responsibility for different parts of the analysis. Avoid having the marketing major do the marketing portion of the analysis, the production major handle the production issues, and so forth. This will both hamper the group's aggregate analysis and do all of the team members a disservice by not giving each member exposure to decision making involving the other functional areas. The strategic management course provides an opportunity to look at all aspects of the business situation, to develop the ability to see the big picture, and to integrate the various functional areas.

4. *Plan and structure team meetings.* When you are working with a group on case analysis, it is impossible to achieve the team's goals and objectives without meeting outside of class. As soon as the team is formed, establish mutually convenient times for regular meetings, and be sure to keep this time available each week. Be punctual in going to the meetings, and manage the meetings so they end at a predetermined time. Plan several shorter meetings, as opposed to one longer session right before the case is due. (This, by the way,

is another way realism is introduced in the strategic management course. Planning and managing your time is essential in business, and working with others to achieve a common set of goals is a critical part of life in the business world.)

SUMMARY

The strategic management course is your opportunity to assume the role of a key decision maker in a business organization. The case method is an excellent way to add excitement and realism to the course. To get the most out of the course and the case method, you need to be an active participant in the entire process.

The case method offers you the opportunity to develop your analytical skills and to understand the interrelationships of the various functional areas of business; it also enables you to develop valuable skills in time management, group problem solving, creativity, organization of thoughts and ideas, and human interaction.

Case 1

Bristol-Myers Squibb's Growth through Addition, Subtraction, and Sharing

John A. Pearce II and Richard B. Robinson Jr.

1   Bristol-Myers Squibb underwent a tremendous strategic transformation in the seven years between 2007 and 2013, acquiring important new companies and spinning off others to become a pure-play pharmaceutical company.

2   As Bristol and other pharmaceutical companies lost significant revenue from expiring patents of blockbuster drugs, mergers played a large role in filling the holes in the drug pipelines. Bristol's strategy, dubbed the "string of pearls," was formulated in 2007 when the company hired James Cornelius as CEO. The strategy centered on Bristol restocking its product pipeline by acquiring small and medium-sized businesses that had promising products in development.

3   The top-choice acquisitions that Bristol sought complemented the company's main drug lines including treatments for HIV/AIDS and neurological disorders. However, Bristol also looked beyond its core disease areas to especially promising new formulations such as those for congestive heart failure and fibrosis for deal-making.

4   The acquisition of companies that had new pharmaceutical breakthroughs saved Bristol small fortunes in R&D costs, but they cost the company huge fortunes to buy patentable products with blockbuster sales potential. The purchase prices were so high that with every deal Bristol felt obligated to assure stockholders and investment analysts of its goals to take minimal risk and not overspend on the acquisition.

5   The company's first acquisition under its new strategy was Adnexus Therapeutics in 2007. Adnexus developed Adnectins, a new therapeutic class of biologics. The deal was valued at $430 million. It helped Bristol improve its product offerings on biologics across multiple areas of its therapeutic division.

6   Bristol also entered into strategic alliance agreements with AstraZeneca and Pfizer to co-develop and co-commercialize investigational compounds that had previously been discovered by Bristol. The agreement with AstraZeneca involved Onglyza and dapagliflozin, two compounds that are used for the treatment of diabetes. The Pfizer agreement focused on an anticoagulant used for the prevention and treatment of various arterial thrombotic and venous conditions.

7   In 2008, Bristol advanced its strategy through an acquisition and a strategic alliance. First, Bristol purchased Kosan Biosciences for $190 million. Kosan, a cancer therapeutics company, added to Bristol's pipeline by providing two classes of anticancer agents: inhibitors and epothilones. Then, a collaboration agreement with Exelixis brought Bristol two novel molecules to fight cancer. The $195 million agreement gave Bristol the development and commercialization rights for both molecules.

8   In 2009, Bristol acquired Medarex for $2.3 billion. This acquisition added to Bristol's biologics capabilities and expanded its oncology pipeline. The purchase of Medarex also

gave Bristol full rights to ipilimumab, an immunotherapy being studied for melanoma, prostate cancer, and lung cancer.

9   Bristol continued to acquire businesses in 2010 with the purchase of ZymoGenetics. The deal gave Bristol full rights to a number of investigational biologics, including an investigational compound for the hepatitis-C virus. This acquisition marked the first time during the "string of pearls" strategy that Bristol secured an existing product. The product was Recothrom, which controlled bleeding during surgery.

10   Acquisitions in 2011 included Ambrx, Inc. and Amira Pharmaceuticals Inc. Acquired for $24 million, Ambrx produced drugs for congestive heart failure and diabetes. Amira, purchased for $325 million, developed pharmaceuticals for fibrosis, an area that complemented Bristol's therapeutic research efforts.

11   After Bristol's patent protection on the blood thinner drug Plavix ended in 2012, generic versions began to be manufactured. These generic manufacturers dramatically lowered the price of the drug and overnight most of the sales volume from Bristol. A drug that once accounted for a third of Bristol's total revenue was gone. Bristol soon thereafter lost patent protection on its Plavix drug, resulting in a decline of over $3.5 billion in annual sales.

12   Understandably, Bristol intensified its search for ways to replace lost sales. In 2013, the company looked into purchasing Biogen Idec Inc., a producer of neurological disease medication for multiple sclerosis. It also tried to acquire Shire PLC, whose products include medication for attention-deficit disorder and hyperactivity disorder. However, the two companies had a combined market value of over $57 billion, almost equaling the size of Bristol, and the outcomes of the negotiations were uncertain.

13   However, if successful, these acquisitions would fit well with the strategic combinations that Bristol had made since 2007. In combination, the acquisitions made by Bristol enabled the company to modernize and reorganize how it identified, contacted, secured, and managed the relationships it had with third parties.

14   While acquisitions were the primary strategic focus for Bristol, a second emphasis was to spin off business units. Large corporations sometime have a unit that is different from the other parts in some important ways. As a result, the unit may be underemphasized in the strategic planning of the parent corporation and underappreciated by investors and financial analysts. Additionally, its inclusion under the corporate umbrella can confuse stakeholders about the corporation's mission of the corporation with regard to industry, investment priorities, growth and profit potential, primary customers, principal competitors, and a number of other important considerations. One remedy for such a situation is for the parent to spin off the unit as an independent business, freed of all obligations except those of any other corporation.

15   With a spin-off, a corporation takes a unit, whether it is a company, subsidiary, or division, and uses it to form an independent company. Shares of the spun-off company are distributed to the parent company's shareholders, as well as being sold, often through a stock exchange. The parent corporation's stockholders then own shares of the parent and shares of the spun-off company. Theoretically, at the instant of the stock transfer, no value has been gained or lost. The parent's hope, of course, is that the newly independent company will thrive and enrich its stockholders. Experience shows that many spinoffs benefit through capital appreciation, perhaps because their potential is better understood as a stand-alone company.

16   Spin-offs can also be used to free a corporation of a troubled unit, perhaps one with regulatory problems. The spin-off will be left to fend for itself, hopefully freeing the parent of any negative associations.

17   In Bristol's case, the reason for spinning off a unit was to take advantage of upside market potential. Bristol was looking to become more focused on BioPharma, so its business units that produced ultrasound machines, baby formula, and surgical bandages were

expendable. However, because Bristol considered the businesses to have profit potential far beyond the benefit that could be derived from their sale, the company preferred to spin them off. Notable spin-offs for Bristol included Tyco, ADT, and Zimmer. Overall, by 2013, the spin-offs resulted in a 50 percent reduction in the number of Bristol manufacturing plants and two-thirds the number of employees over the time frame of the new strategy.

18   In the pharmaceutical industry, two competitors of Bristol also used spin-offs during this time to sharpen their market focus and improve their investment performance. In 2012, Pfizer, Inc. spun off its animal-health business into a newly formed company, Zoetis. In 2013, Abbott Laboratories split into two separate publicly traded companies: AbbVie, Inc. and Abbott Laboratories. AbbVie retained big-name drugs, such as Tricor, Niaspan, and Humira. The newly formed Abbott Laboratories marketed health care products that ranged from baby formula to laboratory testing equipment.

19   Bristol's corporate strategy was not limited to acquisitions and spin-offs; strategic alliances were also important. For example, in early 2013 Bristol signed an agreement with Reckitt Benckiser for $438 million. The terms of the strategic alliance gave Reckitt the exclusive rights to sell, distribute, and market seven different products for Bristol for three years. The products included Tempra, a pain reliever, and Dermodex, an antirash cream. The collaboration enabled Bristol to gain market share in significant Latin American markets, such as Brazil and Mexico, where these products were primarily marketed.

20   That same year, Bristol expanded its strategic relationship with Simcere Pharmaceutical Group, one of the leading pharmaceutical companies in China. Under the agreement the two companies worked together to develop and commercialize Orencia in China. The drug, which was already on the markets in the United States, Europe, and Japan, was a treatment for rheumatoid arthritis. While many of the previous moves by Bristol focused on early-stage drug development activities, this partnership with Simcere centered on the clinical development and commercialization of an existing Bristol product.

21   Bristol partnered with Samsung BioLogics in 2013 on a 10-year agreement for the Korean-based company to manufacture a commercial antibody cancer drug. The deal helped Bristol by increasing its biologic manufacturing capacity while ensuring an adequate supply of the antibody in the long term.

22   In the first seven years of Bristol's "string of pearls" strategy, significant changes led to a more focused organization. Through acquisitions, joint ventures, and strategic alliances, the company focused on the development and commercialization of products both in-house and through partnerships. The financial results from these changes produced an overall upward trend, but with promising results in some years and disappointing results in others. In 2007, net sales reached over $18 billion. The following year sales jumped to $20.6 billion. Then, hit by the economic crisis in 2009, sales dropped to $18 billion for the fiscal year, before rising again to over $19 billion in 2010. As the U.S. economy improved, so did Bristol's financial results. By 2011 sales reached over $21 billion. But sales saw a large slump in 2012, dropping to $17 billion. Even with considerable volatility in global sales, Bristol's stock steadily improved from 2008 to 2013, reaching its postrecession peak at $49.57 in early 2013.

23   With patent protection expiring on products and generic competition taking away a huge percentage of unprotected sales, Bristol was forced to reinvent itself in an attempt to maintain its foothold as a dominant pharmaceutical company in the industry. Through acquisitions and spin-offs, the company became more focused on its key areas of business. From a possible takeover target seven years earlier, Bristol managed an impressive transformation by 2013. However, the corporation had also increased its financial risk by concentrating its investments, weakened its R&D capabilities by choosing to buy rather than develop new products, and virtually eliminated its potential for blockbuster sales in nonpharmaceuticals, all while facing major changes in the health care industry.

Case 2

Competing for New York's Best Lobster Roll:
Failed Trade Protection

David E. Desplaces
College of Charleston

Roxane M. Delaurell
College of Charleston

Laquita C. Blockson
College of Charleston

1   Pearl Oyster Bar owner Rebecca Charles walked out of her attorney's office in Manhattan confused about what could be happening to her business. Even though Rebecca was visiting her attorney to right a wrong she believed had happened to her, she actually began wondering if what she had done was in fact wrong. She had worked so hard to establish herself in New York over the previous ten years as the best lobster roll restaurant, yet it appeared that she could lose both the recognition and her restaurant's identity to a copycat. How could this happen? Could she have done things differently?

REBECCA CHARLES AND PEARL OYSTER BAR

2   Pearl Oyster Bar, founded in 1997, established a reputation in Manhattan for serving one of the best lobster rolls on the Island of Manhattan in New York City. Owner Rebecca Charles built this reputation by creating a unique atmosphere with such specialty menu items as "The Pearl Lobster Roll with Shoestring Fries." Rebecca claimed she built recognition and her reputation through various endeavors going back to 1972. Such activities included working at top-rated restaurants in Maine and New York and writing a cookbook entitled "Lobster Rolls & Blueberry Pie" with co-author Deborah DiClementi.[1]

3   As she worked to build Pearl Oyster Bar's reputation, Rebecca hired Ed McFarland in 2003 as a line cook. Ed was a good employee and was promoted to *sous chef* within his first two months of employment. Ed was then in a position of trust and confidence with access to all confidential and propriety information about the restaurant, its cuisine and its operations till his departure in 2007.[2]

THE RESTAURANT INDUSTRY IN NEW YORK CITY

4   According to both the National Restaurant[3] and the New York State Restaurant Associations' data,[4] there were 24,600 restaurant and food service establishments in New York City in 2006. These establishments employed over 225,000 individuals in the Big Apple

Source: *The CASE Journal* 6, no. 2 (Spring 2010). ©2010 by the author and *The CASE Journal*. Contact the author at desplacesd@cofc.edu. No part of this publication may be copied, stored, transmitted, reproduced or distributed in any form or medium whatsoever without the permission of the copyright owner. This case is intended to be used as the basis for class discussion rather than to illustrate either effective or ineffective handling of a management situation. The case was compiled from public domain information about the legal case including news media coverage of the lawsuit.

[1]*Pearl Oyster Bar vs. Ed McFarland and Ed's Lobster Bar, 2007.* 07-cv-06036 (2007).
[2]*Pearl Oyster Bar vs. Ed McFarland and Ed's Lobster Bar, 2007.* 07-cv-06036 (2007).
[3]National Restaurant Association (n.d.).
[4]Hunt, E. C. (n.d.).

generating gross annual sales of $12 billion. Although this translated into 3.3 restaurants per 1,000 residents, the restaurant industry historically had been plagued by a 60 percent failure rate within the first five years[5] especially where competition was most fierce in lower Manhattan. Owners and chefs alike had to compete on price, talent, location, quality of product, and many other important factors to gain competitive advantage and increase their chances of survival. How far would these business people be willing to go to compete or mirror the competition?

COMPETITION OR COPYCAT?

5   Rebecca's attorney filed suit in Federal District Court in the Southern District of New York against Ed McFarland for opening a competing restaurant, Ed's Lobster Bar, using her trade dress, her recipes and her good reputation.

6   With the restaurants located only nine blocks apart (see Exhibit 1), Rebecca alleged that Ed had infringed on her restaurant identity by copying her business' overall look, and claimed that then *sous chef* Ed violated his fiduciary obligation to keep the secrets of her business including the recipes and identity of her restaurant. Rebecca charged that Ed copied "each and every element" of Pearl Oyster Bar.

7   Rebecca alleged that Ed had requested permission several times to reproduce Pearl's success on the upper east side of Manhattan, something Rebecca said she refused categorically. Rebecca claimed that Ed owed her a fiduciary duty of undivided loyalty, good faith and fidelity. Furthermore, Rebecca alleged that Ed purposely deceived her when asked upon announcing his departure from Pearl Oyster Bar, if he would open a "Pearl Knockoff" and he denied having such plans. Furthermore, she alleged that "each and every element" of Pearl Oyster Bar was ripped off, including the bar, the furniture, the paint job (see Exhibit 2), and even the Caesar salad dressing (see copies of the menus in Exhibit 3). Rebecca was not proud of the fact that Ed never signed any documents upon gaining employment with her.

8   Ed did not defend against any of the allegations made by Rebecca at a press conference he held in his restaurant, which according to local news media, was "deeply reminiscent of

EXHIBIT 1   **Restaurant Locations**

You can view the distance between the two restaurants using Google maps.

1.   Open a browser and type http://maps.google.com
2.   Select "Get directions"
3.   Type in A: Pearl's Oyster Bar, New York, NY
4.   Type in B: Ed's Lobster Bar, New York, NY
5.   Click "Get Directions"

Or you can type in the following URL into a Web browser:

http://www.google.com/maps?f=d&source=s_d&saddr=pearl's+oyster+bar, +new+york,+ny&daddr=Ed's+Lobster+bar,+new+york,+ny&hl=en&geocode =FUaDbQIdstGWyGRV12DLY3-0SkhmGjHk1nCiTGdsjMmw5pRLw%3BFcFebQIdieKW- yGhwcc6WzHv0ymXuNXXiFnCiTE1912NsVDjMw&mra=ls&sll=37.0625,-95.677068&sspn =37.136668,53.349609&ie=UTF8&z=15

[5]Parsa, H. G., Self, J. T., Njite, D., & King, T. (2005), pp. 304–322.

EXHIBIT 2   Restaurant Interiors

You can view pictures of the inside of each of the restaurants by viewing pictures available on the Web using the following instructions:

1. Type in the following URL into your Web browser:
   http://ny.eater.com/archives/2007/06/pearl_v_eds.php

2. Review each of the pictures, compare and identify any similarities (if any) by putting pictures side by side.

EXHIBIT 3   Pearl Oyster and Ed's Lobster Bar Menus[6]

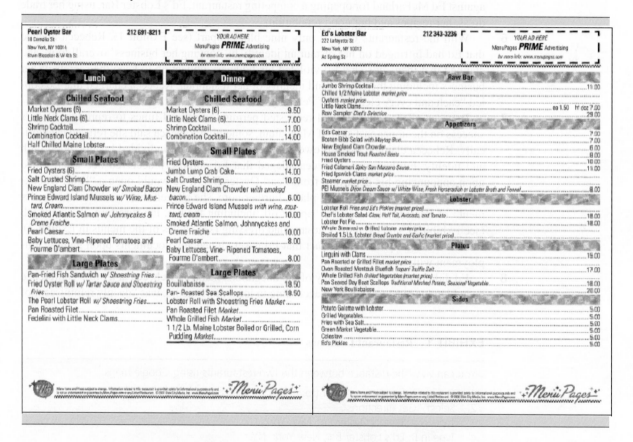

Pearl Oyster Bar."[7] He did acknowledge that the restaurants were similar, but would not say that his was a copy.[8] Furthermore, Ed's lawyer scoffed, "I didn't know Caesar salads and lobsters are protected under the intellectual-property laws."[9] The questions remained: Were they? What was protected? What could have been protected?

[6]Menu Pages (n.d.).
[7]Grub Street New York (n.d).
[8]Wells, P. (2007).
[9]Grub Street New York (n.d.).

REFERENCES

Grub Street New York (n.d). Ed's Lobster Bar to Pearl Oyster Bar: Step Off!. Retrieved on November 4, 2009, http://newyork.grubstreet.com/2007/06/eds_lobster_bar_calls_a_press.html

Hunt, E. C. (n.d.) Tips for opening & running a restaurant in New York City. New York State Restaurant Association. Retrieved on February 4, 2010, http://legacy.www.nypl.org/research/sibl/smallbiz/qt6/OpeningRestrInNYC.ppt

Menu Pages (n.d.). Retrieved November 17, 2007 on http://www.menupages.com

National Restaurant Association (n.d.). New York Restaurant Industry at a glance. Retrieved on February 4, 2010: Url: http://www.restaurant.org/pdfs/research/state/newyork.pdf

Parsa, H. G., Self, J. T., Njite, D., & King, T. (2005) Why Restaurant Fail. Quarterly Cornell Hotel and Restaurant Administration, 46 (3): 304–322.

Pearl Oyster Bar vs. Ed McFarland and Ed's Lobster Bar, 2007. 07-cv-06036 (2007). Retrieved on February 4, 2010. http://docs.justia.com/cases/federal/districtcourts/new-york/nysdce/1:2007cv06036/309166/11/0.pdf

Wells, P. (2007). Chef Sues Over Intellectual Property (the Menu). Retrieved on November 17, 2009, http://www.nytimes.com/2007/06/27/nyregion/27pearl.html?_r=1&scp=1&sq=PETE+WELLS+2007+june&st=nyt

Case 3

JCPenney's Uncertain Turnaround

John A. Pearce II and Richard B. Robinson Jr.

1   Investors in JCPenney experienced a great deal of uncertainty in the past few years. Penney's replaced its CEO in 2011 and again in 2013, and made major alterations to its corporate strategy each time. The company also dramatically changed its pricing and sales approaches. During the same period, profits were negative, the availability of funds decreased, and the company's stock price was volatile while trending down.

2   Penney's success throughout prior years was driven by discounts, promotions, and clearance aisles. The company's pricing model centered on setting high regular prices, then offering discounts on those prices to create the impression of great sales. The feeling of finding discounted items appealed greatly to moderate-income shoppers who were attached to sales and coupons. This marketing tactic worked for many years. By the end of fiscal year 2007, Penney's had reached annual sales of over $19 billion. The company had over 1,000 stores, opening an additional 50 in 2007 alone. On February 21, 2007, Penney's stock reached its all-time high price of over $86 per share.

3   However, as the recession took hold, Penney's success began to fade. Consumers began to feel the effects of a weakening economy and store sales for Penney's began to decline. Sales dropped to $18.4 billion in 2008 and to $17.5 billion in 2009. By the end of 2009, Penney's stock had dropped nearly 70 percent to just over $26 a share.

4   When the economy began to recover from the economic recession that ended in June 2009, Penney's saw only a marginal improvement. Sales increased 1.2 percent to $17.7 billion for fiscal year 2010. The slight improvement in sales did not stir investor confidence. By the end of 2010 the stock price had only increased to a respectable but unremarkable $30 per share.

5   The number of new store openings paralleled the multiyear decline in sales. In 2008, the company opened 35 stores, followed by only 17 store openings in 2009, and just two new store openings in 2010.

6   The company's financial situation became worse in 2011. Sales dropped by 2.8 percent to $17.2 billion. Citing the continuing pattern of financial decline, Penney's fired CEO Mike Ullman in 2011. His replacement was Apple executive Ron Johnson. The new CEO was praised for his work as the head of retail operations at Apple. He had created the unique style of Apple stores and had pioneered the Genius Bar. The financial markets reacted very positively to the news when the change of CEO was announced. Penney's stock rose by 17.5 percent on the day that Johnson was hired.

7   Penney's hoped to utilize Johnson's innovative ideas to recreate the Penney's brand. Johnson's first change involved introducing "everyday low prices" instead of sales and discounts. To make up for the lack of sales prices, the company advertised their products more aggressively. The company turned away from special promotions, believing that promotions encouraged consumers to look for price breaks on products, which ultimately detracted from customers' loyalty to the Penney's brand. This was an approach that Johnson brought from Apple. He believed that consumers would buy more from Penney's when they were loyal to the company rather than simply looking for a good deal.

8   Johnson also began the process of changing the look of stores by creating in-store boutiques with higher-end fashion brands. The stores were transformed to appeal to a more youthful demographic. The Apple stores were viewed as a place consumers went to hang out, and Johnson wanted to bring that characteristic to Penney's stores.

9   The changes were implemented by Johnson on a nearly simultaneous company-wide basis. Instead of using the traditional small test-market approach to gauge how successful the new tactics would be, all Penney's stores introduced the untested changes at the same time. The steady decline in company performance led Penney's strategic planners to believe that delaying a full rollout for testing purposes would allow the financial problems to grow and would rob the company of the positive buzz surrounding Johnson's much anticipated changes. However, the all-in approach put the company at greater risk, and it was a gamble that did not pay off.

10   One year after the plans were implemented, Penney's revenues had dropped by 25 percent and the company was unprofitable. By the end of 2012, the company's stock had dropped below $20 per share. Penney's store closures continued to rise, albeit slowly. Perhaps most discouraging, Johnson's new store designs and change in prices were ineffective. Same-store sales were 30 percent lower than the previous year.

11   The decline of sales and increased costs of remodeling stores combined to drain Penney's cash.[1] In January 2013, Penney's had $930 million in cash and short-term investments. This figure had dropped by over $2 billion in two years. Closer inspection revealed that nearly 10 percent of the cash on hand was from deferring $85 million in payments to suppliers. The lack of cash led the company to draw $850 million from its revolving credit line of $1.85 billion in April 2013.

12   In that same month, the company made another change of CEO, bringing back Mike Ullman to his previous position. Several possible explanations for Johnson's failure to turn around sales at Penney's were given. First, he might have misjudged customers' preference for discounts and promotions over everyday low prices. Second, customers might have been confused by the changes in pricing policies. Third, a combination of changes at Penney's, not just its pricing policies, might have displeased customers. Fourth, the consequences of the economic recession and the subsequent period of no or low growth might have affected Penney's more than analysts understood. Finally, Johnson's lack of presence at the company's headquarters in Plano, Texas was viewed very negatively. Johnson chose not to relocate from California, and instead spent three days a week at the headquarters and worked remotely the remainder of the time.

13   With Ullman back at the helm, Penney's looked to return to its former operations model. Ullman began by adding a greater variety of clothing styles and sizes, in contrast to former CEO Johnson who had stopped selling larger sized clothing, focusing more on a trendier, younger shopper. However, Ullman's major change as CEO was to restore the discounts and promotions offered by the company. He believed strongly that Penney's shoppers wanted to buy items at promotional prices. Ullman promised to bring back 26 annual event promotions, with most occurring around the holidays when there is a greater presence of shoppers in the stores. Interestingly, Ullman's reintroduction of promotional prices and discount coupons occurred just as consumer retail sales began to pick up in earnest nationwide, and as consumers measurably decreased their couponing in clothing stores.

14   Additionally, not everyone was pleased with Penney's return to its old pricing tactics. In response to a July 2013 article in *Today* that was critical of JCPenney for initially pricing items artificially high, then dropping the prices to a competitive level and calling them "sale prices," the company released the following statement:[2]

---

[1]Lahart, J. 2013. "Not Much Future in Penney's Past." *Wall Street Journal,* April 17: C.16.
[2]Rossen, J., and A. Patel. 2013. "Some of JCPenney's Big Sales Are Misleading, Say Employees." TODAY, July 24.

Last year [2012] we implemented an everyday low pricing structure that was ultimately rejected by JCPenney's core customer. We learned that our customers are motivated by promotions and prefer to receive discounts through sales and coupons applied at checkout. As such, we have returned to the promotional pricing model employed often in the retail industry. This shift requires us to make pricing changes on much of the merchandise to remain competitive. In addition, under this promotional pricing model, any time an item is put on sale the item must have been previously sold at its original or regular price for a reasonable period of time. While we understand this transition back to promotional pricing may cause some temporary confusion, the Company remains committed to delivering the quality, price and value that customers expect from JCPenney.

15   Penney's also started focusing more on its "new home" department, which included bedding, cookware, and furniture. The company partnered with exclusive designers and home décor specialists, such as Michael Graves and Martha Stewart. Ullman felt the need to reverse the company's performance in 2012, when home goods sales dropped by $1 billion. Home goods sales were critically important because they represented 12 percent of overall sales, down from 15 percent in 2011.[3]

16   U-turn changes were also made to the company's online offerings. During Johnson's short stint as CEO, the company had changed the design of its Web site, which many consumers complained had been made too difficult to navigate. In 2012, Web traffic fell compared to 2011, leading to online sales dropping double-digits. Part of the new approach involved restoring online promotions to the company's social media platforms. During April and May of 2013 Penney's posted discounts on its Facebook page for the first time in more than a year.[4]

17   However, Penney's did not return to all of its previous tactics. The company is continuing with its approach of creating in-store boutiques for specific brands. This was a tactic Ullman had implemented with Sephora products during his first tenure as CEO. The company also continued to try to expand its customer base by trying to attract a younger, more stylish demographic, but without alienating its already established consumers.

18   Part of this plan involved expanding Penney's brand offerings. The company partnered with Canadian-based apparel maker Joe Fresh to drive up traffic to stores. The Joe Fresh products were available in nearly 700 Penney's stores. Even though the Joe Fresh brand made up only a small portion of the overall inventory, results showed that customers were starting to return.

19   Near the end of Johnson's run as CEO, JCPenney's stock dropped to near record low levels, at less than $15 per share. By mid-2013, the stock recovered slightly to just above $16 as the new changes took hold. Whether the return to Ullman's traditional model, which customers had abandoned less than two years earlier, would attract them to return as active supporters and enthusiastic buyers would determine Penney's survival.

[3]Cheng, A. 2013. "JCPenney Pins Hopes on New Home Department." *MarketWatch.com*, June 7.
[4]Heine, C. 2013. "JCPenney Returns to Sales Strategy Online, but Struggles Persist." *AdWeek*, May 8.

Case 4

Livestrong: *Cycling Around Lance Armstrong*

1   Doug Ulman, CEO of the nonprofit LIVESTRONG Foundation (LIVESTRONG), sat in his office in a renovated warehouse in Austin, Texas, surrounded by his leadership team in yet another "emergency" meeting. Phone calls, primarily from journalists, had been flooding in all morning, and Ulman and his team needed to return them. Reporters from the *New York Times*, the *Wall Street Journal*, *Fortune*, and other publications, all wanted to know what Lance Armstrong, the founder and public face of LIVESTRONG, was going to say in his televised interview with renowned talk-show host Oprah Winfrey, which was scheduled for the next day.

2   Ulman most dreaded returning the call from Leslie Lane, head of the Nike Foundation, one of LIVESTRONG's biggest supporters. Despite the performance-enhancing drug (PED) scandal that had engulfed Armstrong over the last year, Nike had continued to support the foundation. Had something changed? Ulman and his team had to decide how to proceed and what conversations to have in the coming days to minimize the damage to LIVESTRONG from the controversy. Ulman knew that, on Oprah's program, Armstrong would finally confess to doping. He worried that this admission, along with the controversial rumors that had plagued Armstrong for more than a decade, threatened the future and sustainability of LIVESTRONG. Ulman himself was a cancer survivor—most of LIVESTRONG's employees were—and he knew the important work that LIVESTRONG had done. Ulman and his team could not stay locked in their offices ignoring the press, the public, and the nonprofit's supporters. But how to proceed in addressing the further controversy that was at their doorstep, and how to keep this controversy from adversely affecting the millions of cancer survivors who had benefitted—and those cancer sufferers who would benefit in the future—from LIVESTRONG?

LANCE ARMSTRONG

3   World-famous cyclist Lance Armstrong was born in 1971, in Plano, Texas. His first athletic love was swimming, until his participation at age 13 in an Iron Kids Triathlon (which he won) sparked his interest in cycling. At 16, Armstrong entered the world of professional triathlons, winning a number of championships until turning professional in cycling in 1992. He immediately began winning one-day events and stage races, and chalked up his first Tour de France stage win[1] in 1993. Many wins followed over the next several years, and in August 1996, he signed a two-year, $2 million deal with the French cycling team Cofidis.

Source: This case was prepared by Erika Hayes James, Senior Associate Dean for Executive Education and Professor of Business Administration, and Jenny Mead, Senior Researcher. It was written as a basis for class discussion rather than to illustrate effective or ineffective handling of an administrative situation. Copyright © 2013 by the University of Virginia Darden School Foundation, Charlottesville, VA. All rights reserved. *To order copies, send an e-mail to* sales@dardenbusinesspublishing.com. *No part of this publication may be reproduced, stored in a retrieval system, used in a spreadsheet, or transmitted in any form or by any means—electronic, mechanical, photocopying, recording, or otherwise—without the permission of the Darden School Foundation.*

[1]The Tour de France, an annual 20-stage bicycle race in France and parts of adjoining countries, took place over 23 days and covered more than 2,000 miles. Because there were multiple stages, it was possible for a different rider to win each stage.

Briefly Sidelined by Cancer

4   In 1996, the 25-year-old Armstrong was diagnosed with testicular cancer, which had metastasized to his brain, lungs, and abdomen. He underwent surgery to remove the brain tumors and a testicle, then had extensive chemotherapy. Armstrong was declared cancer-free in February 1997. At that point, the Cofidis team had dropped him, but the U.S. Postal Service team subsequently took him on at $200,000 a year. In 1999, Armstrong had what was to be the first of seven consecutive Tour de France wins. In the 2005 Tour, Armstrong clocked the fastest pace in the race's history: an average speed of 26 miles per hour. Immediately afterwards, Armstrong announced that he was retiring from professional cycling. He came out of retirement in 2008 specifically to participate again in the Tour de France. While he saw some success in his return, Armstrong did not win another Tour and was plagued by falls and injuries, including a broken collarbone during a race in Spain. His final Tour ride was in 2010, with Team RadioShack. In early 2011, Armstrong announced that he was finished with competitive cycling.

5   In 2000, Armstrong chronicled his struggle with cancer in a memoir, *It's Not About the Bike: My Journey Back to Life*, which chronicled his struggle with cancer. He followed that with *Every Second Counts* in 2003, which covered his first several Tour de France wins as well as the birth of his twin daughters and being chosen *Sports Illustrated*'s Sportsman of the Year in 2002. Armstrong had become, as the CEO of the American Cancer Society said, "the most famous cancer survivor in the world."[2]

THE CONTROVERSY[3]

6   Allegations of doping had plagued Armstrong since his first Tour de France victory in 1999, when a French lab test detected traces of a synthetic corticoid in his urine. Armstrong's explanation was that he was using an authorized skin cream to treat saddle sores. Angry over the French newspaper *Le Monde*'s intense interest in the controversy, Armstrong lashed out at the press, calling himself " 'persecuted' and a victim of 'vulture journalism.' "[4] Rumors persisted over the years, but Armstrong continued to deny the accusations. He even mocked the rumors in a 2001 Nike television spot that showed him working out and riding, with his voiceover: "Everybody wants to know what I'm on. What am I on? I'm on my bike, busting my ass six hours a day. What are *you* on?"[5]

7   Right before the 2004 Tour de France, sports journalists Pierre Ballester (*Agence France-Presse*) and David Walsh (the *Sunday Times*) released a book called *L.A. Confidentiel: Les Secrets de Lance Armstrong*.[6] The book contained reputed incidents and events surrounding Armstrong's doping activities, but the most damning allegations came from Armstrong's former masseuse, Emma O'Reilly, who detailed trips to pick up and drop off doping material. Armstrong reacted furiously, suing the book's authors and its publisher,

---

[2]Chuck Salter, "Can LIVESTRONG Survive Lance Armstrong and a Doping Scandal?" *Fast Company*, October 18, 2010, http://www.fastcompany.com/1693641/can-livestrong-survive-lance-armstrong-and-doping-scandal (accessed January 31, 2013).

[3]For an extensive index of the Lance Armstrong doping controversy, see Laura Weislo, "Index of Lance Armstrong Doping Allegations Over the Years," Cyclingnews.com, January 16, 2013, http://www.cyclingnews.com/features/index-of-lance-armstrong-doping-allegations-over-the-years (accessed on March 20, 2013).

[4]Samuel Abt, "Armstrong Is Engulfed by a Frenzy Over Salve," *New York Times*, July 22, 1999, http://www.nytimes.com/1999/07/22/sports/cycling-armstrong-is-engulfed-by-a-frenzy-over-salve.html (accessed March 19, 2013).

[5]"Lance Armstrong's 2001 Anti-Doping Ad for Nike," YouTube video, 0:34, posted by "NewsPoliticsToday," January 16, 2013, http://www.youtube.com/watch?v=v4nHQsrUrZg (accessed March 19, 2013).

[6]The title translates to *L.A. Confidential: Lance Armstrong's Secrets*. The book was only published in French.

as well as the *Sunday Times*, which eventually settled, paying Armstrong (British pounds sterling) GBP300,000. In 2005, former personal assistant Mike Anderson publicly stated that he had found the steroid androstenone in Armstrong's bathroom. In 2006, former teammate Frankie Andreu and his wife Betsy claimed in a *Le Monde* article that Armstrong had admitted to them, in 1996, that he had used PEDs.

8   The chorus of critics and accusations continued. In May 2010, cyclist Floyd Landis, who had been stripped of his 2006 Tour de France title after testing positive for PEDs, and who had maintained his innocence, finally admitted to doping and told cycling officials that Armstrong had doped when the two of them were on the U.S. Postal Service team. Landis also filed a whistle-blower suit against Armstrong, claiming that "Armstrong and his associates defrauded the federal government by accepting roughly $30 million in sponsorship money to bankroll a U.S. Postal Service Pro Cycling team that was fueled by performance-enhancing drugs."[7] The U.S. government began an investigation into the matter. In a 2011 *60 Minutes* interview, former Armstrong teammate Tyler Hamilton detailed Armstrong's use from 1999 to 2001 of erythropoietin, a performance-enhancing hormone. Other former teammates confirmed Hamilton's account, and this ground swell of accusations began to erode Armstrong's credibility.

9   In the meantime, the United States Anti-Doping Agency (USADA) had been investigating Armstrong and the U.S. Postal Service team. In June 2012, the USADA charged Armstrong with doping and trafficking of drugs, based on blood sample evidence from 2009 and 2010, and suspended him from any cycling events. Armstrong filed a countersuit, which was thrown out. Finally, in August 2012, Armstrong announced that he would no longer fight the charges. Shortly afterward, the USADA stripped him of his seven Tour de France victories and banned him from further competition in any Olympic sport. In October, the organization released a 1,000-page report about Armstrong and other members of the U.S. Postal Service team doping. The practice was referred to as, "the most sophisticated, professionalized and successful doping program that sport has ever seen."[8]

LIVESTRONG

10   In 1997, with the help of his sports agent, Bill Stapleton, Armstrong established the Lance Armstrong Foundation to help and support people affected by cancer. The kick-off was marked by the foundation's first cycling race, which evolved into the Ride for the Roses (modeled on the Susan G. Komen Foundation's Ride for the Cure). With corporate and grassroots support, the nonprofit grew rapidly. Initially, it was focused on medical resources for patients, but the foundation leadership soon realized that many people contacting them were more interested in sharing their stories and getting emotional support. In 1999, the foundation shifted its focus to the area of survivorship: "programs and services aimed at easing the personal and practical hardships that come with cancer."[9]

11   Ulman, who had been hired in 2001, worked with the U.S. Centers for Disease Control and Prevention and the National Cancer Institute to study the needs of survivors. The three organizations awarded grants to various cancer centers that wanted to set up programs dealing with the aftereffects of cancer: relapse, long-term side effects of chemotherapy, and

[7]Liz Clarke, "Floyd Landis Whistleblower Suit Targets More Than Lance Armstrong," *Washington Post,* January 17, 2003.
[8]"Statement from USADA CEO Travis T. Tygart Regarding The U.S. Postal Service Pro Cycling Team Doping Conspiracy," USADA's U.S. Postal Service Pro Cycling Team Investigation site, October 10, 2012, http://cyclinginvestigation.usada.org/ (accessed March 19, 2013).
[9]Stephanie Saul, "Armstrong's Business Brand, Bound Tight with His Charity," *New York Times*, January 13, 2013.

emotional struggles. Many doctors and others in the medical field applauded the foundation's strategy. As an oncologist at the esteemed Dana-Farber Cancer Institute said, "We were entirely focused on making the cancer go away. We weren't looking at people's long-term problems. It's hard . . . to think of another organization that has done things like this, so seriously, in an academic and scientific way."[10]

11   The foundation's early years saw phenomenal growth, from revenues of $9 million in 2001 to $40 million in 2004. The peak of financial growth was in 2005, when Armstrong won his seventh Tour de France title; that year saw revenue of $52.5 million. It also came up with a new motto, "Live Strong," which eventually became the foundation's name, in part to shift the focus away from and rely less on the celebrity of Lance Armstrong. Among the hottest fundraising items were "LIVESTRONG yellow" (the color of the Tour de France leader's jersey) silicone gel wristbands, which riders wore at the Tour de France, as did athletes at the 2004 Summer Olympics. After Armstrong appeared on Oprah Winfrey's show to promote the bands, sales shot through the roof, temporarily clogging Internet servers. At one point, sales of the $1 bands topped 100,000 a day. The organization took a financial hit when Armstrong retired in 2006, but rebounded when he announced his return to the Tour de France in 2008.

12   LIVESTRONG continued to expand its reach. After Ulman had a conversation with Bill Clinton on the former president's private jet in 2008, the foundation did an international launch at the Clinton Global Initiative. While many in the United States focused on cancer in their own country, the fact was that the developing world had 60 percent of cancer deaths and only 5 percent of the cancer resources. In addition, those with cancer were stigmatized in the developing countries and thus kept their illnesses to themselves. In response, LIVESTRONG worked with NGOs in Mexico and South Africa on antistigma campaigns. As part of a campaign to reach the Hispanic community, LIVESTRONG brought on Mexican actress and singer Lorena Rojas as a global envoy.

13   In 2013, LIVESTRONG had grown to be one of the largest cancer charities in the United States. Since its inception, the charity had raised over $480 million and, according to its Web site, "81 percent of those funds have gone directly to support our programs and services for survivors."[11] Because of this ratio of program expenses versus administrative costs, LIVESTRONG had been consistently given stellar ratings by CharityNavigator.org, the nonprofit monitor, and had been favorably reported on by the Better Business Bureau's Wise Giving Alliance. The charity had taken another financial hit in 2010, when the doping allegations had multiplied—donations fell 27 percent—but had rebounded over the next few years.

14   Indeed, much to Ulman's surprise, donations had risen in the fall of 2012, after Armstrong's Tour de France titles had been stripped from him. As of September 2012, year-to-date revenues had risen 2.1 percent above those in 2011. The number of donations was up 5.4 percent and the average dollar amount of each donation was up 5.7 percent—from $74.88 the previous year to $79.15.[12] 2012 had seen revenues of $46.8 million. Nonetheless, donations had dropped after USADA released its 1,000-page report in October, and 2013 might prove to be an even bumpier ride with Armstrong's impending admission. Ulman was aware of the hits that other eponymous charities had taken when their founders encountered bad publicity; after Tiger Woods's admission of infidelity in 2009, for example, donations to the Tiger Woods Foundation, which promoted education for underserved children, had fallen 45 percent.

[10]Salter.

[11]"Where the Money Goes," LIVESTRONG's website, http://www.livestrong.org/What-We-Do/Our-Approach/Where-the-Money-Goes (accessed March 19, 2013).

[12]Darrell Rovell, "Armstrong's Foundation Still Thriving," ESPN.com, October 10, 2012, http://espn.go.com/blog/playbook/dollars/post/_/id/1986/armstrongs-foundation-still-thriving (accessed March 19, 2013).

15   Over the years, many people had been critical of Armstrong creating a cancer foundation (although not of LIVESTRONG itself), claiming that it was intended only to burnish the cyclist's image, particularly in the face of dogged rumors and accusations. Others believed that Armstrong was sincere, that he had what was termed "the obligation of the cured."[13]

The Fallout

16   To minimize the damage to LIVESTRONG, Armstrong had resigned as board chair in October, then stepped down from the board entirely in November 2012. On the same day that Armstrong stepped down as chair of LIVESTRONG, he was dropped by two sponsors, Nike and Anheuser-Busch. Shortly after, Armstrong was dropped by Honey Stinger (a natural energy food company), Trek Bicycle Corporation, 24 Hour Fitness, Oakley apparel, and FRS (a supplement maker).

CONFRONTING THE FUTURE

17   The ongoing controversy had been a huge distraction for LIVESTRONG and its leadership team during 2012, who suddenly found a lot of their time taken up with fielding calls and questions. Ulman and the others prided themselves on being direct and straightforward, and although the foundation was about cancer, not cycling, they believed they needed to address the torrent of questions that came their way from every possible source. Although they invariably referred questions to Armstrong's publicist, the LIVESTRONG leadership team believed that, at the very least, they could not refuse to talk to those wanting information. They thought that they needed to maintain a dialogue, not a monologue, with the press and others. Particularly burdensome was the amount of disinformation floating around in the newspapers; each new sloppy and inaccurate piece of information that emerged in the papers wasted even more of the foundation's time and energy.

18   Nonetheless, one of the foundation's biggest assets—the Lance Armstrong connection—had now become a major liability, and Ulman was conflicted and worried about the future of LIVESTRONG. Would Armstrong's admission hurt the organization? It was not just the doping; stories had emerged over the years about Armstrong's ruthlessness—some suggesting he'd even gone so far as bullying—in dealing with his critics. He had often said he would "take people down," and he did on several occasions, bringing libel lawsuits and chasing some of his competitors away from the cycling world. Ulman and the LIVESTRONG leadership team were able to separate the man from the cause, but they knew that many other people could not.

19   The immediate future promised only a variety of challenges: a continued drain on the organization's time and energy, bad publicity, media scrutiny, and the erosion of financial support. What immediate steps could LIVESTRONG take to deflect criticism and controversy? Should it make a bold statement or lay low for a while? What was the best strategy to pursue at this critical point? And how could it continue to maintain a straightforward dialogue with all stakeholders while maintaining focus on the organization's most important stakeholders: those with cancer?

[13]Salter.

Case 5

A "World's Top Company": *Southern New Hampshire University*

Richard B. Robinson Jr. and John A. Pearce II

1   *Fast Company* magazine recently named SNHU to its annual "World's Most Innovative Company List" in 2012, even though it is not a company. It is the first carbon-neutral campus in New Hampshire, among the few nationwide. The largest university in New Hampshire, it has been reinventing its campus lately with an average of one new building every year, including a gorgeous new dining hall, a state-of-the-art academic building, new dorms, a new Learning Commons/Library, and a 300-bed dormitory. "Welcome to Southern New Hampshire University, one of the fastest growing and most dynamic private, nonprofit universities in the country," says President Paul J. LeBlanc. What's going on? While most small private colleges are struggling, SNHU is thriving. Why? *BloombergBusinessweek* went to see. Here's what they found:[1]

> Southern New Hampshire University's quaint red-brick New England campus is home to 2,750 undergraduates, making it the size of some high schools. A casual visitor would never suspect that another 25,000 students are also enrolled online. That's roughly how many are in the bachelor's program at the University of California at Berkeley.
>
> Harvard, Stanford, and the Massachusetts Institute of Technology have gained attention with their MOOCs, or massive open online courses, which are free and feature famed professors. Critics of these programs say that with no business model, they're little more than a branding exercise. Southern New Hampshire's College of Online and Continuing Education is no vanity project. The school's management forecasts that revenue will reach $200 million in the next academic year–four times what it took in for 2010–11—making it one of the biggest and fastest-growing online operations at any not-for-profit college in the U.S. "They are one of the most important players in the online space," says Robert Lytle, co-head of the education practice at Parthenon Group, a Boston-based management consulting firm. "They've painted a pathway for other schools."
>
> Online, Southern New Hampshire offers standardized courses, a factory-style approach that has as much in common with Henry Ford as John Harvard. Classes are designed by so-called subject-matter experts—a professor of English or accounting—but taught by part-time instructors typically paid $2,500 per course. Classes don't meet; students read online materials or watch a video of a lecture, which they can do at night of during their lunch hour. A classroom discussion translates into posts on a discussion board. The total price of Southern New Hampshire's online bachelor's degree, $38,000, isn't cheap, but it's far less than the $112,000—not including housing or meals—the university charges undergrads for four years at the brick-and-mortar college.
>
> For the current academic year, the university is projecting a $29 million profit from the online college, which amounts to a 22 percent margin. Some of the money is being plowed back into the online operation, which will soon have a dedicated faculty of 25 full-time professors. There's still plenty left over for a campus building boom. A new student center features a pub, big-screen televisions, and exposed stone walls, while a revamped dining hall boasts a sushi bar. The school will soon inaugurate a 308-student dorm and break ground on a 50,000-square-foot library, also largely paid for by profit from the online operation. "This is why college is so expensive," says President Paul LeBlanc, as he leads a reporter on a campus tour.

[1]John Hechinger, "A Little College That's a Giant Online," *BloombergBusinessweek,* May 13–19, 2013, © 2013, BloombergBusinessweek, All Rights Reserved.

As the architect of the university's online strategy, LeBlanc has been deeply influenced by the ideas of Clayton Christensen, the Harvard Business School professor who coined the phrase "disruptive innovation" to describe the process by which companies at the bottom of the market use new technologies to displace more established competitors. In Christensen's view, higher education, with its sky-rocketing costs, is ripe for a revolution; he predicts that in 15 years, half of all universitites will be out of business.

LeBlanc sees no contradiction in using the fruits of the Internet to lavish attention on the 80-year-old university. Many students, particularly recent high school graduates, are looking for what he calls "a residential coming-of-age experience." Southern New Hampshire's real-life campus is also key to its virtual success. It's a way to distinguish the online college from for-profit institutions such as Apollo Group's University of Phoenix, whose high student-loan default rates and aggressive marketing have drawn scrutiny from Congress as well as state and federal authorities. LeBlanc says prospective applicants to the online college are often sold when they learn that the school is a full-service university, complete with a basketball team—even if they'll never watch it play.

The college's Web site and 24-hour call center bear more than a passing resemblance to those of the University of Phoenix, the nation's largest for-profit chain. "We have borrowed shamelessly," LeBlanc says. "We don't mind saying so." Like the for-profits, Southern New Hampshire markets itself aggressively, spending $20 million a year on television ads. For its online operations, which are housed in an old textile mill several miles from the regular campus, LeBlanc has hired veterans from Kaplan, the for-profit higher-education unit of Washington Post Co., and Education Management, the second-largest for-profit chain. At the same time, LeBlanc is undercutting for-profits on price, charging half as much for some types of degrees.

Concerns about quality hang over online college education. Recent Columbia University studies of tens of thousands of community college students in Virginia and Washington State found that those taking online courses earned lower grades and were more likely to fail or withdraw. Using profits from the online college to subsidize the regular college suggests the nonprofit institution could be charging online students less, says Kevin Carey, an education expert at the New America Foundation. The Internet enables vast cost savings, he says. "Who benefits from that savings? So far, the students haven't."

Even some of the beneficiaries of Southern New Hampshire's online push are uneasy. John Wescott, a 19-year-old sophomore at the physical campus, expects to graduate with only $15,000 in student debt thanks to financial aid. Yet he recalls a spirited discussion at a student-government meeting: "There was a sense that we were turning into the University of Phoenix and the value of our degree was going down."

Southern New Hampshire is offering a $5,000 two-year associate degree, a stripped-down online offering that lets working adults earn a diploma for showing competency, rather than for class credits. The Obama administration in April made Southern New Hampshire the first school eligible for federal financial aid using that approach.

To fight the notoriously high attrition rates in online programs, LeBlanc relies on a corps of 131 "academic sherpas." The guides monitor students' progress, calling them if they see a poor grade or if they fail to log on to their computer for days at a time. Dean Young, a 23-year-old from Skowhegan, Me., whose parents didn't graduate from high school, credits his counselor with helping him keep up with the demands of his forensic-psychology bachelor's program. Without that prodding, Young says, "I probably would have given up."

2   President LeBlanc, perhaps cognizant that some question his game-changing strategy for a small private university, offered an impressive summary in a recent online letter:

> Most important are our academic programs. We offer a wide range of majors across all degree levels in a wide variety of formats from traditional face-to-face instruction on a semester schedule, 8- and 11-week options and online, a nationally known three-year bachelor's degree and College Unbound—an experiential learning program.

We serve every kind of student from traditional-age undergraduates usually on our main campus, graduate students in evening and online programs, working adults, more veterans than any NH institution and deployed military students, and the largest population of international students in NH representing 60 countries. We are the most affordable NH private university; one of the most affordable online, and with aid often more affordable than most public institutions.

Innovation allows us to keep our tuition costs low. Now in the first tier among regional universities, we combine quality with low cost for a degree of which you can be proud. Most importantly, we are committed to a high level of personal attention to our students. No large lecture halls with hundreds of students listening to lectures from a distant stage. Every course, on campus or online, has small enrollments; every student is assigned an advisor who remains with them throughout their program.

Case 6

Wal-Mart Online—What to Do about Amazon.com?

Richard B. Robinson Jr. and John A. Pearce II

1   While the "online thing" has been exploding worldwide in the last 15 years, the world's largest retailer, Wal-Mart, has until recently not even broken out its online sales, preferring instead to look at overall sales and at the growing trend of shoppers ordering using its rather simple online site and picking up in its thousands of stores. And why not? Wal-Mart will exceed a half-trillion in sales this year. As the world's largest retailer and the United States' largest employer, it has reason to preserve and grow its concept of sell everything to everyone, close by. Consider these facts:

- Wal-Mart will soon reach 5,000 stores in the United States alone.
- Two-thirds of the United States population live within 5 miles of a Wal-Mart store.
- Its global presence, particularly in Asia and Central America, is rapidly expanding organically and through acquisition and joint ventures.
- Its global supply chain skills and resulting pricing power are unmatched.
- Its move into groceries has been quite successful in the United States and elsewhere.

2   Still, Wal-Mart's executive team is asking the question, "What's with this Amazon.com thing?" Amazon.com sells much of what Wal-Mart sells, other than groceries. Rumor has it they are looking into that. Amazon.com has gone from modest sales to almost $75 billion in 2013, steadily growing. It is even moving toward store locations via "locker" relationships with other former competitors, like Staples, which will have Amazon lockers in their stores for Amazon customers to pick up the things they have bought. Meanwhile, Amazon's ever-expanding customer base seems to do so because of the convenience of looking, clicking, and having it come to their front door without getting out of the house, into a car, and so forth—to the tune of, real soon, $100 billion annually. Yet, the Wal-Mart executives no doubt ponder, while they have long been the retailer of choice for the price-conscious, convenience-seeking customer, why do they only have $9 billion in sales through their Web site offering essentially the same products? What have they done wrong? What can they do to right it? How can they grab back a big chunk, say $50 billion, of the sales of "their things" that have gone through Amazon.com, instead of Wal-Mart or www.walmart.com? Neil Ashe, CEO of Wal-Mart's e-commerce unit, said in 2013 that "we can build e-commerce equivalent to anyone in the world." Mixing the company's expanding online capabilities with its knowledge from running stores for 50+ years "creates a commerce experience that no one else can do." While that may be so, $100 billion versus $9 billion still legitimately calls the question.

3   What would you advise them to do to solve this "problem"? Should they not bother with it, and instead continue with where they have long been—consider the online thing a fad; have and improve their Web site, but continue to build more stores, increase locational convenience, and keep prices low with unmatched selection? Or should they aggressively attack Amazon.com, build not only their Web site but other ways to sell online and support online sales? What should they do?

4   Wal-Mart executives seem to have sought to do both, continuing with the latter strategy while expanding their tiptoeing into Amazon.com's space. Executives favoring more than the tiptoe approach have proposed the following tactics:

1. The Locker Tactic. This idea is to have special lockers in every Wal-Mart store—a customer buys something online, selects a Wal-Mart (or Sam's) store closest to them (remember the 5-mile proximity thing), and can stop by that store to check with the customer service desk and pick up the purchase for a quick in-and-out purchasing process. Wal-Mart's supply system, JIT capabilities, and point-of-sales linked with distribution system capabilities mean it can do this without any additional net costs on its end—the result is more sales, customer convenience, and increased incremental profit . . . and one less Amazon.com customer.

   Wal-Mart thinks its network of physical stores, married with customers increasingly using smartphones as they shop, will easily drive them to use the locker fullfilment option, competing in the process with Amazon's successful Prime subscription service. That service gives free two-day shipping anywhere in the United States for $79 per year.

2. The Online Grocery Purchase and Delivery Service Offering. Wal-Mart is experimenting at several stores with grocery offerings whereby customers can enter their grocery purchases online, pay online, and have those purchases delivered directly to their house or other indicated location by Wal-Mart grocery delivery personnel. They envision a minimum purchase total that would avoid any delivery fee; or otherwise have a modest fee if purchases fall below that minimum. The executives advocating this idea say it can use the existing www.walmart.com site setup; that it fits well with the 5-mile proximity to every Wal-Mart customer from a cost control point of view, and starting it with groceries makes it a regular purchasing activity with regular customers to build a steady pattern of purchasing over time that could expand from groceries to other items much like what they would otherwise buy from Amazon.com.

3. Create a "Wal-Mart to Go" Service, Partnering with FedEx or UPS. Here Wal-Mart would partner with one or both of these well-known delivery services to have items bought online from walmart.com delivered in metro areas to the purchasers. The idea here is to essentially match what Amazon.com now does with the same services and have packages at key Wal-Mart distribution centers close to major urban areas routed into this delivery system much like Amazon.com now does. Wal-Mart executives advocating this approach now have five experimental sites in major U.S. cities experimenting with this idea.

4. Crowdsourcing. Have regular Wal-Mart customers offer delivery services to fellow customers. Wal-Mart executives, starting with U.S. CEO Joel Anderson, were considering an idea that would have Wal-Mart jump into the middle of the global "crowdsourcing" or "sharing economy" phenomenon by letting its customers that want to earn a little extra income offer to deliver purchases to other customers from stores the deliverer frequently goes to anyway. So, under this idea, you regularly come to Wal-Mart store XXX to make item or grocery purchases; then you could register as a deliverer to customers in the area where you reside. Then, you pick up your purchase plus a set of packages for other customers in your home destination area. You deliver their packages to them directly and receive cash or store credit from Wal-Mart for doing so. Wal-Mart has millions of customers visiting every store each week. Some of these shoppers could tell Wal-Mart where they live and sign up to drop off packages for online customers who live on their route back home, according to Mr. Anderson. Wal-Mart would offer a credit or something similar, which would, in effect, cover their cost of coming to Wal-Mart to shop. Anderson sees this as just tapping into a major trend unfolding in the "sharing economy" where ventures like Zipments, TaskRabbit, Fiverr, and Airbnb are just a few that let individuals rent out their time, their car, their house or expertise, looking for a little extra income while using the time, car, or home they already own to do so.

5 Wal-Mart CEO Joel Anderson posited, regardless of the option, that all have a core advantage. "It is really efficient to use our stores. We've been picking and putting items in boxes for years." Continuing, "Ship to or from the store is no different. We are just picking items off the shelves and putting them in a box."

6 So, Wal-Mart executives look to you for advice. They realize you are a part of the generation more comfortable with what Amazon.com offers, with aspects of some of these options, and yet you know Wal-Mart. What would you advise them to do in order to meaningfully make a dent in the online sales Amazon.com "takes away" from Wal-Mart? Would you do all of these options, or just some of them? If more than one, which would you prioritize as most important? What potential revenue possibility would you expect within three years from the ones you think best? What pros and cons would you see with each option?

Case 7

Wells Fargo's Remarkable Ascent

John A. Pearce II, Steven T. Woods, and
Richard B. Robinson Jr.

1   In a five-year period ending in 2013, Wells Fargo & Company, an American multinational banking and financial services holding company with operations worldwide, grew rapidly to become the largest bank in the United States as measured by market capitalization and the fourth largest bank based on assets. Its ascendance was rapid but never certain.

2   The December 2007 to June 2009 financial crisis in the United States changed the landscape of mortgage lending. Leading up to the recession, many banks issued subprime and adjustable-rate mortgages. With a greater availability of credit and the belief that housing prices never declined, customers were increasingly borrowing maximum amounts from banks to purchase homes, often with very small or no down payment. Seemingly, every applicant qualified. One analyst quipped that any mortgage applicant who could "show breath on a mirror" qualified for a loan. When the housing bubble burst and the financial crisis took hold in late 2007, many borrowers had trouble paying their mortgages, and a number of banks and financial institutions suffered such great losses that they were forced to merge to avoid bankruptcy.

3   One of the largest mergers in the banking industry involved San Francisco–based Wells Fargo's purchase of Wachovia Corporation for $15 billion in 2008. With this purchase, Wells Fargo became the third largest bank in the United States as measured by total deposits. The acquisition also created the largest corporate network of branch banks in the United States and added considerably to Wells Fargo's portfolio of mortgages. While the purchase of Wachovia involved sizable risks, Wells Fargo was eventually able to improve its newly combined mortgage business and become one of the top performing banks in the United States.

4   Wachovia became the target for a takeover by competitors, including Wells Fargo, when its financial performance plummeted because of its massive exposure to bad mortgage debt. The prelude to Wachovia's troubles occurred in 2006 when the company purchased the California-based mortgage lender Golden West Financial Corp. for $25.5 billion in order to expand its mortgage business. With housing sales booming in California and Florida at the time, Wachovia looked for growth in those markets through the purchase. However, in 2008, when the housing bubble started to burst, Wachovia's mortgage portfolio was exposed to reveal an extremely high risk level.

5   Because of the depth of Wachovia's financial trouble, it engaged in merger talks with Morgan Stanley. When the negotiations failed, the federal government moved in and pushed Citigroup to purchase the struggling company. A central element of the proposed government-brokered deal to have Citigroup acquire Wachovia was a provision that guaranteed that the government would absorb any loan losses that Citigroup might incur over a $42 billion cap. The proposed deal was praised by Citigroup investors, but was not favorable for taxpayers because it put their dollars at risk.

6   Although the deal was being negotiated for Citigroup to purchase Wachovia, Wells Fargo stepped in and successfully purchased Wachovia by offering a higher price. The acquisition added considerably to Wells Fargo's mortgage business, which in 2008 accounted for

11.2 percent of mortgages in the United States. Wachovia shareholders received 0.1991 share of Wells Fargo stock per one share of Wachovia stock, which put the value of Wachovia at $5.87 per share. When Wachovia purchased Golden West in 2006, the company's stock was at $59.39 per share. The drop in stock price marked a 90 percent decrease in market capitalization.

7   Unlike many of the large bank competitors that had bundled their loans into mortgage securities and then resold them to investors, Wachovia retained many of the mortgage loans. By keeping the loans it wrote, Wachovia had considerably lower returns than its largest competitors but much greater control over the majority of its mortgage-related investments. Consequently, Wells Fargo was able to restructure many of the Wachovia loans so that customers would not default. Wells Fargo also had more stringent credit standards for the mortgage loans that it approved, which decreased the number of risky loans it had issued that in turn led to a lower rate of foreclosures.

8   The financial crisis caused extreme economic stress on the U.S. market in 2007–2008, and declining interest rates beginning in 2009. Nevertheless, by adding 3,400 new retail branches to its network, Wells Fargo was able to achieve such high levels of market penetration and operational efficiencies that it was able to optimally benefit from any pockets or types of borrowing that occurred. Furthermore, complementing the U.S. federal government's tightening of the banking industry's standards for lending, Wells Fargo altered its operations to be a more "old-fashioned bank" by making loans that it would hold on its own books. This policy disciplined the company to improve its lending criteria and make less risky loans.

9   In addition to Wells Fargo's improvements in its mortgage business, the company also undertook changes in a number of other areas. Unfortunately, these changes would not be viewed as favorably.[1] Customers who had free checking at Wachovia faced a $7 monthly fee when their accounts converted to Wells Fargo, which they interpreted as a shortcoming of Wells Fargo. Customers also took issue with a declining level of customer service at Wells Fargo. This perception led J.D. Power and Associates to downgrade Wells Fargo's customer service rating to below average among its competitors. Even employees from Wachovia who were retained by Wells Fargo were disgruntled when they lost some of their paid holidays as a result of the merging of management philosophies.

10   Despite selected instances of employee and customer dissatisfaction, Wells Fargo thrived. Analysts Shayndi Raice and Nick Timiraos conducted an analysis of the company's mortgage loan business, which explored Wells Fargo's progress and provided details on its impressive inroads into the New York and San Francisco markets.[2] They found that in 2012, Wells Fargo's mortgage business accounted for 28.8 percent of home loans issued nationwide, making it the largest lender in the country. Its portfolio of loans accounted for over $524 billion, the largest annual total ever for one bank. This amount was greater than the combined loans issued by the next five largest banks. A result was net income of $18.9 billion for 2012, two times greater than Wells Fargo's profit in 2007.

11   Contributing to Wells Fargo's comparative progress was the lack of success by its competitors. For example, shortly after its purchase of Countrywide Financial in 2008, Bank of America (BOA) was the largest lender. But with hundreds of thousands of defaulted loans, BOA's share of the mortgage business dropped from 21.6 percent in 2009 to 4.3 percent in 2012. Citigroup and Ally Financial also lost market share during this period, enabling Wells Fargo to take over as the nation's top lender.

[1]Dunn, A. 2012. "1 Year in, Change Visible at Wells Fargo." *Charlotte Observer*, October 13.
[2]Raice, S., and N. Timiraos. 2013. "Mortgage Gamble Pays Off for Wells." *Wall Street Journal*, April 3: A.1.

12   The challenge for Wells Fargo in 2013, as Raice and Timiraos reported, was to maintain its success in mortgage lending. With interest rates rising and forecast to increase further in 2014, fewer loan initiations and fewer mortgage refinances were anticipated. Such declines would hurt Wells Fargo's profits, since more than 65 percent of its mortgage production in 2012 came from refinancing.

13   Therefore, Wells Fargo altered its plans. The company cultivated relationships with real-estate agents and developers in an effort to persuade them to use Wells Fargo as their preferred lender, enabling the bank to increase its mortgage loans in preferred markets. This move helped produce Wells Fargo's market share lead in mortgage loans in 2012. In that year, the bank issued over 20 percent of new home loans in both the New York and San Francisco markets, equaling the new home loan issuance of its two largest competitors combined.

14   Wells Fargo saw portfolio lending in New York, San Francisco, and other expensive markets as a way to access high net worth borrowers, who provided disproportionally high per capita profits for the bank. To make inroads against its competition, Wells Fargo studied the nuances of each market. For example, Raice and Timiraos reported that in San Francisco an industry-high percentage of young technology entrepreneurs were buying multimillion-dollar homes in 2013, when only months earlier they had been paying less than $3,000 a month in rent. When these buyers faced a monthly mortgage payment of $30,000 on their new homes, Wells Fargo could not utilize its previous approval process and standards to get their loans approved. Adopting an uncharacteristically aggressive posture, the bank revamped its approval standards to accommodate the changing competitive pressures.

15   With the anticipated loss in revenue from reduced refinancing activity, Wells Fargo pushed for new business in new markets. In 2001, Wells Fargo had 150 loan salespeople in San Francisco. But with its push for more mortgages in the Bay Area, Wells Fargo brought in an additional 450 salespeople to bring the total to 600 by 2013.

16   The New York market was far more complex than the one in San Francisco, as Raice and Timiraos reported. With a unique mix of co-op apartments and expensive condominiums, national mortgage lenders had difficulty gaining penetration in New York. In its specialized market segments, a lender had to assess the financial strength of the borrower and the building, adding to the complexity of the loan process. The makeup of the borrowers was also different in New York from other markets. Many high net worth mortgage applicants had resources committed to investments in unique business partnerships, had lower percentile incomes than their very high total assets might suggest, and were self-employed.

17   An indication of its success in working with real-estate agents and developers, in Raice and Timiraos's view, was that Wells Fargo became the preferred lender of Brown Harris Stevens and Halstead Property, two of the largest brokerages in New York City. Wells Fargo also created DE Capital as a joint venture with Douglas Elliman, the largest brokerage in New York City. The benefit was that 50 percent of Douglas Elliman clients applied for their mortgages through Wells Fargo.

18   Other tactics that led Wells Fargo to be successful in the New York market included creating a clearinghouse of information for New York loan officers. The database provided information on whether loans qualified for backing from Fannie, Freddie, and the Federal Housing Administration. If the loans were eligible for backing, the process for buyers to purchase units was accelerated for certain condo developments.

19   Wells Fargo overhauled its operations to reduce costs and improve the bank's technology. To cut costs in its branches, the bank improved its online and mobile banking operations. With its improved technology, customers needed less retail branch assistance, which decreased the need for retail branch employees.

20   With its dominance in the mortgage business, Wells Fargo doubled its return on assets between 2010 and 2013. Its profits for 2013 were projected to exceed 20 percent principally because of its increased effectiveness in generating profits from lending. Its mid-year price in 2013 was a historic high for the company of $43 a share.

21   While the large market share held by Wells Fargo was expected to decline as it increasingly shifted its focus on low-risk home buyers, the company's turnaround strategy had enabled it to thrive following the financial crisis in 2008. By 2013, Wells Fargo seemed well positioned to continue to strengthen its profitable operations.

Case 8

Wendy Aust, Senior Strategic Analyst, Global Strategy Advisors, LLC

Richard B. Robinson Jr., Ryan Maltba, and John A. Pearce II

1   Ms. Wendy Aust celebrated her tenth year at Global Strategy Advisors, LLC (GSA) by taking Jim Warren, her newly hired financial analyst, to lunch in Atlanta's swanky Buckhead area to discuss his new job. Jim was excited to have joined GSA, given its impressive reputation as a strategic advisory group headquartered in Atlanta with offices in Boston, Denver, Geneva, and Hong Kong. Jim had just finished his MBA through APEI's American Public University and his CFP through the University of Phoenix after serving in the U.S. Army for three years. He graduated with honors from Georgia Tech in industrial management prior to entering the Army.

2   The lunch gave Ms. Aust an informal chance to give Jim a clearer understanding about the focus strategy at Global Strategy Advisors, which had, she felt, established the foundation of GSA's impressive success since its founding 25 years earlier. That strategy had as its core a commitment to focus on only 10 basic "industries" or business sectors. The specialized expertise developed over time was thought to enable GSA to consistently help client companies become more successful than they were prior to GSA's involvement with them. She smiled as she thought about the assignment she was about to give Jim Warren, remembering back to the time when she was given the exact same assignment when she joined GSA. It was a tradition at Global Strategy Advisors that every new associate was given the assignment during their first week on the job, with that tradition also being to keep the assignment unknown to new hires until that first GSA immersion week, which always took place at GSA's Atlanta headquarters.

3   Once their food arrived, Ms. Aust started by telling Jim about GSA's longtime focus strategy, sharing numerous stories of how GSA's exceptional sector expertise had helped several large global companies on repeated occasions. The core foundation to absorbing that expertise, she said, was a sound understanding of the financial fundamentals of each sector and various firms that operated in each sector. Jim was aware of some of the top global companies GSA had assisted over the years, but he was a little surprised that a firm with such a global reach would focus only on ten sectors. Ms. Aust then, with a more serious tone in her voice, told Jim that every new associate was given an assignment considered of the utmost importance by the sector directors at Global Strategy Advisors. As she gave Jim an attractive thin brochure, which contained seven sheets of crisp parchment paper, she told Jim of the importance of this exercise in any new associate's future with the firm. She then started to explain the packet. The first page was a welcome message with a list of the ten "industries" or sectors that comprised GSA's strategic focus. The second and third pages contained two similar financial spreadsheets with ten columns, each column containing financial information—balance sheet and a variety of financial ratios—describing one unnamed company and former or current GSA client.

4   The next two pages contained the numbers 1 through 10 with the words "Please explain why?" under each number, and a blank space enough to write a few sentences or bullet points in answer to that question. "ASSIGNMENT A" was listed at the top of these pages.

Source: ©2014, RCTrust LLC.

The final page listed two additional, related assignments Jim was being given. A copy of what Jim saw is provided below. As Jim thumbed through the pages, Ms. Aust continued, "Jim, you are to complete this assignment this evening and then you will be expected in the boardroom promptly tomorrow morning at 7:30 a.m. for your first meeting with the ten GSA sector directors. After a brief meet and greet, you will be expected to make a presentation to that group answering the questions asked in Assignments A, B and C. This set of assignments and the presentation meeting with the sector directors is one every new GSA associate undertakes during their first week here in the Atlanta headquarters. Those that show a solid intuitive understanding of the basic financial underpinnings of our ten chosen sectors during this first meeting with the sector directors, as well as an intuitive and fact-based ability to explain the often dramatic performance difference between two companies in the same industry, receive an immediate $25K increase in their basic compensation plan. Those associates that don't both forego the compensation increase and, historically, approximately 70 percent will leave GSA within their first two years."

5   Jim tried to remain relaxed as Ms. Aust returned to friendly chatter about her first ten years at GSA, and her anxiety when she was given this assignment. Her expressions of confidence in Jim were minimally reassuring. Later that evening, shortly after Jim got back to his hotel room around the corner from the GSA headquarters, he pulled out the brochure and started to read the assignment in earnest.

ASSIGNMENT FOR MR. JIM WARREN

6   Jim, welcome to Global Strategy Advisors. We are extremely pleased that you have chosen to join us. Global Strategy Advisors focuses exclusively on the follow ten industries as a means of building deep expertise, which in turn has allowed us to build a competitive advantage no other firm can match in the success of our investments, acquisitions, and advisory services. What we started 25 years ago as an experiment has continued to prove perhaps the best indicator of a new associate's future success at quickly contributing to and continuing that result. That experiment was the assignment you will undertake this evening and conclude early tomorrow morning, giving us a clearer view of your intuitive appreciation for the underlying financial dynamics of the industries we serve. It also lets us listen to your rationale and view a presentation of your strategic insights that you think might explain performance differences between two competitors in each industry we serve.

GSA's Fortune 500-Based INDUSTRY CHOICES:

A.	Computers	F.	Internet Services
B.	Commercial Banks	G.	Petroleum Refining
C.	Entertainment	H.	Pharmaceuticals
D.	Food Services	I.	Telecommunications
E.	General Merchandise	J.	Utilities

Financial Information

7   Included on the next two pages are Spreadsheets #1 and #2 which contain financial informations on two sets of companies that compete in the ten Fortune 500–based industries GSA focuses on. Refer to Chapter 6, Appendix B, "Using Financial Analysis" to refamiliarize yourself with the definition of these ratios and how to interpret them as a helpful primer for this assignment.

SpreadSheet#1	1	2	3	4	5	6	7	8	9	10
Year end:	31 DEC 2012	01 JAN 2013	31 DEC 2012	31 DEC 2012	27 DEC 2012	30 DEC 2012	30 SEPT 2012	31 DEC 2012	31 DEC 2012	01 JAN 2013
Assets:										
Cash/Equivalents	7.08%	3.83%	51.27%	2.97%	4.48%	15.21%	4.52%	0.96%	1.79%	26.88%
Accts.Receiv.	4.05%	3.33%	8.41%	10.48%	3.54%	11.48%	8.21%	5.49%	4.65%	13.94%
Inventory	0.35%	21.57%	0.54%	4.36%	0.90%	6.16%	2.05%	0.80%	0.00%	2.91%
Other CA	1.87%	0.78%	4.24%	1.50%	0.25%	0.00%	3.52%	1.13%	1.90%	15.10%
Total Current Assets:	13.35%	29.51%	64.45%	19.31%	9.16%	32.84%	18.30%	8.37%	8.34%	58.83%
Net PP&E	69.22%	57.45%	12.64%	67.99%	85.21%	15.10%	28.72%	65.37%	40.31%	4.47%
Goodwill	8.04%	10.09%	11.23%	0.00%	0.00%	11.43%	33.53%	1.04%	25.62%	19.57%
Intangibles/Other	4.33%	0.00%	9.54%	2.30%	1.68%	33.74%	10.34%	23.56%	23.26%	12.50%
LT investments	5.07%	2.95%	2.14%	10.40%	3.94%	6.88%	9.12%	1.66%	2.47%	4.63%
Total	**100%**	**100%**	**100%**	**100.00%**	**100.00%**	**100.00%**	**100.01%**	**100.00%**	**100.00%**	**100.00%**
Liabilities:										
Accts Pay.	2.91%	18.75%	2.15%	15.20%	5.13%	13.22%	6.17%	3.94%	NA	24.36%
ST Debt	1.11%	6.10%	2.72%	1.09%	2.55%	4.07%	4.83%	3.14%	1.28%	8.08%
Other	6.61%	10.51%	10.42%	2.92%	0.92%	0.00%	6.12%	2.50%	10.40%	16.86%
Total Current Liabilities:	10.64%	35.36%	15.28%	19.22%	8.59%	17.29%	17.12%	9.57%	11.68%	49.30%
LT Debt	36.78%	18.90%	3.19%	2.37%	29.61%	15.31%	14.28%	24.42%	24.37%	11.03%
Other	8.96%	8.16%	5.08%	26.98%	32.40%	17.44%	15.53%	37.20%	30.04%	17.20%
Total Liabilities:	56.38%	62.41%	23.54%	48.57%	70.60%	50.04%	46.93%	71.20%	66.09%	77.53%
Equity:										
Common Stock	0.07%	0.16%	24.34%	2.89%	3.34%	1.68%	42.37%	0.08%	2.39%	26.41%
Retained Erngs	111.27%	35.93%	51.54%	109.57%	29.03%	37.67%	57.36%	19.41%	8.26%	63.80%
Treasury Stock	-85.70%	0.00%	0.00%	-59.12%	0.00%	-23.29%	-42.29%	-2.52%	-12.08%	-67.62%
Capital Surplus	16.63%	0.00%	0.00%	0.00%	0.09%	38.30%	0.00%	12.11%	33.42%	0.00%

	1	2	3	4	5	6	7	8	9	10
Other Stock. Eq.	1.36%	1.49%	0.57%	-1.91%	-3.06%	-4.41%	-4.36%	-0.28%	1.92%	-0.12%
Total Equity:	43.62%	37.59%	76.46%	51.43%	29.40%	49.96%	53.08%	28.80%	33.91%	22.47%
Total Liab. & Equity:	**100%**	**100%**	**100%**	**100%**	**100%**	**100%**	**100%**	**100.00%**	**100%**	**100%**
ROS	**19.80%**	**3.60%**	**20.60%**	**4.20%**	**10.00%**	**13.00%**	**14.30%**	**9.30%**	**5.70%**	**4.20%**
Asset Turnover	*0.78*	*2.33*	*0.55*	*0.05*	*1.34*	*0.45*	*0.53*	*0.30*	*0.47*	*1.19*
ROA	**15.40%**	**8%**	**11.40%**	**0.20%**	**13.40%**	**5.80%**	**7.60%**	**2.80%**	**2.70%**	**5.00%**
Financial Leverage	*2.32*	*2.65*	*1.32*	*9.00*	*2.02*	*2.00*	*1.88*	*3.43*	*2.93*	*4.44*
ROE	**35.70%**	**22.30%**	**15.00%**	**1.80%**	**27.10%**	**11.60%**	**14.30%**	**9.60%**	**7.90%**	**22.20%**
Current Ratio	1.45	0.83	4.22	NA	1.01	1.9	1.07	0.87	0.71	1.19
Quick Ratio	1.09	0.2	3.95	NA	0.69	1.3	0.77	0.6	0.55	0.97
Debt/Equity	0.89	0.54	0.04	1.26	0.05	0.3	0.28	0.85	0.72	0.49
Receivables Turnover	20.34	73.85	7.54	NA	14.83	5.93	7.14	10.39	9.7	8.69
Inventory Turnover	140.47	8.34	NA	NA	22.73	2.57	21.34	11.33	NA	32.13
Dividend Payout	53.5%	31.7%	NA	16.00%	22.50%	84.50%	NA	62.7	141.6	11.9
Revenue Growth	2.08%	4.97%	32.37%	-10.83%	-0.85%	4.97%	3.39%	-5.80%	0.56%	-8.27%
Gross Margin	39.20%	24.87%	58.90%	NA	29.94%	65.21%	19.20%	68.11	56.67	21.4
R & D Ratio	NA	NA	13.54	NA	NA	17.28%	NA	NA	NA	1.88

SpreadSheet#2	1	2	3	4	5	6	7	8	9	10
Year end:	30 DEC 2012	30 SEP 2012	31 DEC 2012	31 DEC 2012	30 SEP 2012	30 SEP 2012	01 JAN 2013	30 DEC 2012	30 DEC 2012	30 DEC 2012
Assets:										
Cash/Equivalents	44.31%	3.81%	1.54%	1.58%	16.54%	24.78%	1.63%	63.74%	31.76%	3.87%
Receiv. Accts.	4.64%	11.38%	2.39%	5.58%	6.21%	5.91%	0.00%	4.76%	58.31%	18.00%
Inventory	5.05%	3.74%	2.83%	0.48%	0.45%	15.11%	16.41%	0.00%	0.00%	13.43%
Other CA	3.47%	2.88%	2.13%	1.79%	9.55%	5.29%	15.99%	6.11%	2.17%	1.71%
Total Current Assets:	57.47%	21.81%	8.89%	9.43%	32.75%	51.09%	34.03%	74.61%	92.24%	37.01%
Net PP&E	9.81%	4.80%	60.21%	39.36%	8.78%	32.35%	63.64%	15.83%	0.66%	59.13%
Goodwill	23.32%	49.64%	14.37%	10.72%	0.64%	4.86%	0.00%	3.89%	1.80%	0.00%
Intangibles/Other	21.86%	1.47%	14.14%	38.66%	54.72%	9.94%	0.00%	5.30%	1.40%	0.48%
LT investments	-12.46%	22.28%	2.39%	1.83%	3.11%	1.76%	2.33%	0.38%	3.90%	3.38%
Total Assets:	100.00%	100.00%	100.00%	100.00%	100.00%	100.00%	100.00%	100%	100.00%	100.00%
Liabilities: Accts Pay.	1.67%	1.15%	2.15%	0.00%	12.03%	4.84%	14.65%	0.43%	70.49%	21.02%
Debt ST	4.60%	0.08%	3.66%	1.94%	9.86%	NA	6.22%	5.22%	4.02%	2.17%
Other	8.82%	15.98%	3.00%	10.03%	0.00%	22.05%	8.26%	1.32%	0.00%	3.64%
Total Current Liabilities:	15.09%	17.21%	8.81%	11.97%	21.89%	26.89%	29.13%	6.97%	74.51%	26.83%
Debt LT	44.26%	36.55%	31.93%	21.14%	1.50%	6.69%	30.43%	9.93%	8.95%	0.00%
Other	5.55%	12.77%	23.37%	52.17%	9.46%	4.27%	6.06%	5.27%	5.46%	32.63%
Total Liabilities:	64.90%	66.53%	64.11%	85.28%	32.85%	37.85%	65.62%	22.17%	88.92%	59.46%
Equity: Common Stock	54.03%	0.02%	0.08%	0.13%	0.00%	0.01%	0.11%	0.00%	0.96%	0.02%

Retained Earnings	-19.20%	1.66%	-1.66%	57.53%	61.40%	27.31%	10.98%	5.46%	38.29%
Treasury Stock	0.00%	0.00%	-1.81%	0.00%	0.00%	0.00%	0.00%	-0.46%	-14.47%
Capital Surplus	0.00%	34.50%	16.87%	9.33%	0.48%	8.15%	66.83%	5.18%	16.46%
Other	0.27%	-0.35%	1.19%	0.29%	0.28%	-1.19%	0.02%	-0.06%	0.24%
Stock. Eq. Total Equity:	35.10%	35.89%	14.72%	67.15%	62.17%	34.38%	77.83%	11.08%	40.54%
Total Liab. & Equity:	100.00%	100.00%	100.00%	100.00%	100%	100.00%	100%	100%	100.00%
ROS	25.20%	9.00%	0.80%	26.70%	10.40%	4.10%	1.00%	20.70%	1.50%
Asset Turnover	0.32	0.18	0.50	0.89	1.62	1.51	0.40	0.06	3.13
ROA	8.00%	1.60%	0.40%	23.70%	16.80%	6.2%	0.40%	1.30%	4.70%
Financial Leverage	2.85	2.69	6.50	1.49	1.61	2.92	1.25	9.23	2.47
ROE	22.80%	4.30%	2.60%	35.30%	27.10%	18.10%	0.50%	12.00%	11.60%
Current Ratio	3.81	1.01	1.01	1.5	1.9	1.17	10.71	NA	1.38
Quick Ratio	3.24	0.45	0.69	1.24	1.14	0.06	10.26	NA	0.84
Debt/Equity	1.26	0.89	0.05	NA	0.11	0.89	0.17	0.88	0.36
Receivables Turnover	6.38	11.21	14.83	19.2	30.49	24.73	8.04	NA	16.67
Inventory Turnover	1.12	3.15	22.73	112.12	5.27	6.45	NA	NA	22.76
Dividend Payout	31.70%	100.7	22.5	6	38%	29.2%	NA	23.20%	17.30%
Revenue Growth	10.80%	35.07%	-0.85%	44.58%	13.67%	4.92%	5.94%	6.35%	10.53%
Gross Margin	83.10%	61.43	29.9	43.87	56.29%	30.38%	73.20%	NA	5.24%
R & D Ratio	19.58	NA	NA	2.16	NA	NA	27.49	NA	NA

Assignment A

8   Review the financial information in each spreadsheet, then please list which industry your intuition tells you is associated with the company in each column of data, for each spreadsheet. Make notes or bullet points in the space provided after each number that help explain why you chose to associate each column's data with that particular industry. Do this separately for each spreadsheet.

Sheet 1: *Assignment A1*—Chosing among the ten Fortune 500–based sectors GSA focuses on, please list the industry you think is best associated with the financial information in each column of Sheet #1:

1. This column is the _____ industry, because
2. This column is the _____ industry, because
3. This column is the _____ industry, because
4. This column is the _____ industry, because
5. This column is the _____ industry, because
6. This column is the _____ industry, because
7. This column is the _____ industry, because
8. This column is the _____ industry, because
9. This column is the _____ industry, because
10. This column is the _____ industry, because

Sheet 2: *Assignment A2*—Chosing among the ten Fortune 500–based sectors GSA focuses on, please list the industry you think is best associated with the financial information in each column of Sheet #1:

1. This column is the _____ industry, because
2. This column is the _____ industry, because
3. This column is the _____ industry, because
4. This column is the _____ industry, because
5. This column is the _____ industry, because
6. This column is the _____ industry, because
7. This column is the _____ industry, because
8. This column is the _____ industry, because
9. This column is the _____ industry, because
10. This column is the _____ industry, because

Assignment B

9   What specific financial and ratio information in each spreadsheet leads you to conclude that a particular column is the sector you have concluded it represents? Please prepare to explain your thinking.

Assignment C

10   The senior director [your instructor] will now tell you who the firms are that correspond to each column on both spreadsheets, and their annual sales for the year reported. After receiving this information, please re-compare the financial information for the two firms in each sector, along with your general knowledge about those firms. What additional support

for your interpretation of differences between the two firms on key ratios or other financial indicators occurs to you? Does the support for your interpretation lessen in any way once you know the firm's name, and annual sales? And, now that you know who the firms are and their sales volume for that column year, does it change what differences in either firm's strategy, tactics, and internal capabilities explain the differences you see between those two firms based on their ratios and financial information in their respective columns? Prepare to explain your points orally and quickly once your senior director [your instructor] gives you the information on which company is associated with which column.

11   Jim grabbed the spreadsheets, made a hot cup of tea, and set them on the kitchen counter to begin preparing for his assignments. He turned to Pearce and Robinson's *Chapter 6, Appendix B, "Using Financial Analysis"* to refamiliarize himself with the definition of these ratios and how to interpret them as a helpful primer for this assignment. It was only 9 p.m. so he was confident he had plenty of time to be ready for tomorrow morning. Jim laid out his suit and accessories he'd wear in the morning when he went over to join Ms. Aust for breakfast an hour before the scheduled 7:30 a.m. meeting with the directors. He very quickly returned to the kitchen counter to get started.

Case 9

Absolut Vodka

1   You found it inserted in the December 1988 issues of *LA Style* and *New York* magazines: two sheets of plastic, one clear and attached at the edges; inside, a viscous liquid containing floating snow droplets. You could shake it and, like an old-fashioned paperweight of a Christmas scene, snow swirled around a bottle of Absolut vodka—"Absolut Wonderland." The industry, advertisers, publishers, and news media took note. Was this (the second in Absolut's blockbuster Christmas ads) the establishment of a tradition? What next?

BACKGROUND OF THE ALCOHOLIC BEVERAGE INDUSTRY

2   The 21st Amendment, which marked the end of Prohibition in the United States, allowed each state to regulate the sale of alcoholic beverages. More than 50 years later, their sale was still highly regulated and taxed.[1] Some states had licensed private package stores, some had state-controlled stores, and the regulation of on-premise drinking laws varied considerably. A three-tiered system of distribution was strictly followed, however: producers/importers, wholesalers, and retailer/on-premise licensees. Wholesalers were allowed to operate only within one state. All retail and on-premise licensed vendors (bars, restaurants, and clubs) were required to buy from wholesalers. Eighteen states were "control" states, that is, the state owned and operated the majority of retail outlets. In these states, bar and restaurant owners received a discount on buys but had to make all of their purchases through state stores. "Noncontrol" states required licensing but allowed competitive pricing.

3   Alcoholic beverages (distilled spirits, wine, and beer) were a $170 billion global market in the mid-1980s; global advertising expenditures, excluding other promotional devices such as sports sponsorships, were estimated at about $2 billion. One-half of this spending was estimated to occur in the United States.[2]

4   Industry classification broke down the distilled-spirit group into (1) brown goods (or whiskey) such as bourbon, blends, Scotch, Canadian and Irish whiskeys; (2) white goods such as gin, vodka, rum, and tequila; and (3) specialties such as brandy, cordials, liqueurs, and premixed cocktails. By 1986, the distilled-spirits industry had been on a downward slide for some five years.

---

[1]Federal excise taxes went to $12.50 a proof/gallon (i.e., higher-proof beverages had higher taxes) at the producer level in 1985 from the $10.50 it had been since 1976. State taxes averaged $2.63 a proof/gallon in 1976; $3.06 in 1984. The advertising of distilled liquor on television or radio was prohibited.

[2]This and information on marketing strategies primarily from John Cavanagh and Frederick F. Clairmonte, *Alcoholic Beverages: Dimensions of Corporate Power* (New York: St. Martin's Press, 1985), 129–130.

Source: This case was prepared from publicly available sources by Bette Collins, under the supervision of Professor Paul W. Farris. It was written as a basis for class discussion rather than to illustrate effective or ineffective handling of an administrative situation. Copyright © 1989 by the University of Virginia Darden Business Publishing Darden School of Business ATTN: Stephen Momper PO Box 6550 Charlottesville, VA 22906 Permissions@dardenbusinesspublishing.com. *No part of this publication may be reproduced, stored in a retrieval system, used in a spreadsheet, or transmitted in any form or by any means—electronic, mechanical, photocopying, recording, or otherwise—without the permission of the Darden School Foundation.* Rev. 9/90.

TABLE 1   Distilled Spirit Industry Sales, 1975 and 1986

	1975		1986	
	Cases* Sold (in millions)	Share of Market(%)	Cases* Sold (in millions)	Share of Market(%)
Brown goods	101	53.7	65	38.9
White goods	65	34.6	71	42.4
Vodka	37	19.7	39	23.4
Specialties	21	11.2	32	8.8

*A case was defined as 9 liters.

5   One product that bucked the sliding figures throughout the rest of the distilled-spirits industry was imported vodka. Vodka was distilled from any grain material at 190 proof or above. When bottled, without aging, it was usually between 80 and 100 proof. After distillation, it was charcoal-filtered to remove any flavor or aroma. In 1982, while total vodka sales were down 3.8 percent, imported vodka was up 17 percent. Big losers were domestic giants Smirnoff (sales down 8 percent in 1981, 0.7 percent in 1982) and Wolfschmidt (sales down 10.1 percent in 1982); big winners were import leader Stolichnaya, and newcomer, Absolut.

6   One author summarized the marketing strategies of distillers at this time as follows:

1. Targeting of women as a rising consumer group (with new brands or redefinition of old brands, which was successfully carried out by various vodka brands as well as Jack Daniels)
2. Capturing of the youth market, although "youth" had to be redefined, as states raised drinking ages from 18 to 21 in order to receive federal highway construction monies
3. Capturing of specific ethnic markets
4. Capitalizing on a trend toward lightness
5. Focusing on super premiums at the "summit of the income pyramid." Absolut vodka was an example of such a super premium brand.

7   Selected price information on vodkas is presented in Exhibit 1.

THE LAUNCH OF ABSOLUT IN THE UNITED STATES

8   Absolut vodka was owned and produced by the Swedish government. It was introduced in the United States in 1979, by Carillon Importers, a division of International Distillers and Vintners, Ltd. (IDV), the U.S. marketing subsidiary of the British alcoholic-beverage marketing firm, Grand Metropolitan. Carillon sales stood at $52 million at that time, and it was the smallest of Grand Metropolitan's import and distribution subsidiaries. (Later in the decade, IDV bought Heublein, sellers of the domestic vodka brands Smirnoff and Popov, and the third-ranked import brand, Finlandia.)

9   Before the rise of Absolut as Carillon's star product, the company had focused on the orange-flavored liqueur, Grand Marnier. Grand Marnier (and later Creme de Grand Marnier) consistently grew about 8 percent a year. Carillon also sold Bombay, the imported gin.

10   The key to Absolut's story was Michel Roux. A Frenchman, Roux had earned a degree in hotel management and enology, the study of wines; however, Roux stated that more influential to his career was his stint as a paratrooper in the French army.

EXHIBIT 1   **ABSOLUT VODKA**   **Selected Price Information, August 1989**

A. Commonwealth of Virginia Alcoholic Beverage Control Prices (for 750-ml bottles, except as noted; all prices include 20% state tax)

Domestic Vodka	Price	Imported Vodka	Price
Aristocrat*	$6.00	*Canada:*	
Bowman's Virginia	4.70	Seagram's	$6.80
Fleischmann's Royal	5.00	*Denmark:*	
Gilbey's	5.40	Danzka	11.95
Glenmore*	6.25	Denaka	13.20
Gordon's	5.65	*England:*	
Kamchatka	4.80	Tanqueray Sterling	12.90
Mr. Boston's Riva	4.80	*Finland:*	
Mohawk Peach (70 pf)	5.35	Finlandia	13.30
Nikolai	5.30	*Iceland:*	
Odesse	5.80	Elduris	12.85
Ostrova*	6.50	Icy	13.00
Popov	5.05	*Holland:*	
Relsky	4.90	Olifant	8.40
Senator's Club	4.65	*Poland:*	
Simka Kosher	6.90	Luksusowa	11.35
Skol	4.90	*Russia:*	
Skyline (Va.)	4.65	Stolichnaya	12.85
Smirnoff #21	7.15	1.75	26.00
#57*	9.10	1.00*	14.95
Stitzel-Weller	5.50	*Sweden:*	
Tvarscki-Cherry	9.10	Absolut	13.20
Vladimir	4.60	1.75	26.65
Wolfschmidt	$5.50	1.00*	$14.95

B. Plain Old Pearson's (Washington, D.C.) Comparative Advertising of Vodka Specials, August 14, 1989 (1.75-liter bottles; available rebates in parentheses)

	State of VA	Montgomery Co., MD	State of PA	Everyday Prices	Extra Special Low Prices
Absolut	$26.85	$22.99	$24.37	$19.99	—
Bowman's	10.10	9.39	—	8.99	—
Finlandia	—	22.85	24.14	18.99	$17.49
Fleischmann's	10.70	9.55	11.36	8.49	—
Gilbey's	11.40	10.85	12.08	8.99	—
Gordon's ($1.50)	12.50	11.39	13.01	8.99	—
Kamchatka	10.30	9.85	11.00	8.19	—
Popov	11.20	10.29	11.75	8.79	—
Smirnoff ($2.00)	15.70	13.89	15.85	11.29	9.99
Stolichnaya ($3.00)	26.00	22.19	24.30	19.99	—
Wolfschmidt ($2.00)	$11.90	$10.85	$12.49	$ 8.99	$7.99

*100 proof; proofs other than 80 or 100 noted in parentheses.

11   Roux went to the United States when he was 24. With no plans, he headed for "booming" Texas and worked a series of routine jobs at hotels and clubs. In 1967, he opened a French restaurant in Dallas. By the time he heard Carillon was looking for its first salesperson, however, he decided both his strengths and the big money were in sales. Roux joined Carillon and, by the late 1970s, became their director of marketing.

12   In 1979, with U.S. vodka sales rising, the Swedish government was looking for a United States importer for Absolut. Roux recalled, "Larger distillers wanted time to mull over the project, but Carillon leapt at the chance."[3] Roux redesigned the bottle—giving it a short neck, contemporary look, and a silver and blue label—and had the label printed directly on the glass. He priced Absolut at "half again as much as domestic brands."

13   At the time, Stolichnaya, marketed by Monsieur Henri, had an 80 percent share of the imported vodka market. Market research evaluations of Roux's changes were devastating:

> With its off-beat bottle and name, combined with its unlikely origins, the researchers predicted disaster. People wondered if Roux was losing his touch. Roux himself had doubts—but not for long.
>
> "We had never had market research before, and we said, 'You know, we've been very successful at what we've done in the past. So why should we listen to it now?'"

14   Roux ascribed the problem to a mismatch between market-research techniques and the Absolut marketing strategy; traditional market research asked the wrong people. The wealthy don't volunteer for tests. He decided that conventional wisdom was right—that the best way to sell a luxury item was by marketing it as a status symbol, but the "status" buyer for Absolut was unconventional—the young and the hip. Roux believed they were not open to snob appeal, but they were open to wit.

15   The target market for Absolut was described variously as "anyone under 35," to "the top of the pyramid," "the upper end, trend-setting, artsy crowd," to "the ferociously hip." Roux said that he used demographics when he was planning but described the target market as "everyone 21 and older with the ability to drink. I have a whole spectrum."[4]

THE ABSOLUT ADVERTISING STRATEGY

16   The first advertising campaign stressed Absolut's Swedish origins. Then, a year later, Carillon's advertising firm was acquired by an agency handling Brown-Forman's competitive brands, and Carillon began searching for a separate agency to handle its Absolut account. The company looked at 94 agencies and finally narrowed the field down to a small group who were asked to do "speculative" advertising. In 1981, TBWA (which one observer dubbed as "feisty") won the account and proceeded to "break all the rules in liquor advertising."

17   To make sure that TBWA didn't discard any ideas, Roux told them to bring him what was in their garbage cans, the resting place of the "Absolut Impression" ad before its rescue. He welcomed all ideas and suggestions; a staffer's 11-year-old child was the origin for an "Absolut Magic" ad.

18   Roux was dogged about motivating for creativity. He once took the sales staff on the Orient Express, another time hot-air ballooning, and he flew them on the Supersonic Transport Aircraft—all because he believed that new experiences were the greatest reward one could give as a motivator, and because he believed inspiration was the key ingredient to success. Gloria Steinem was the keynote speaker at a 1983 sales meeting.

---

[3]This and the majority of information and quotations on Roux from Michele B. Morse, "Absolut Truths," *Review*, December 1988.
[4]Brian Bagot, "Neat Shot," *Marketing and Media Decisions*, March 1989.

Copy and Media

19   Wit, intrigue, and subtlety became the focus of the first TBWA Absolut ad campaign. Punning on "absolute," the ads used the superlative and, usually, a single other word, such as the image of a chained bottle with the caption, "Absolut Security." Turning the weakness of an odd bottle into a strength, they played with the traditional liquor ad, which for some reason usually consisted of the bottle and a glass or the bottle alone. Roux said, "When somebody reads an art magazine, they are reading for leisure. Their state of mind is not the same as when they're reading a weekly magazine. The brand becomes part of the enjoyment and the ads are more conducive to the state of mind."

20   From the beginning, advertising outlets included not only the newsweeklies and the established glossies (*Vanity Fair, Rolling Stone, Esquire, Sports Illustrated*), but also off-beat magazines such as *Spy, Details, LA Style,* and *Interview*. Carillon was one of the original advertisers in *Ms.* and in *The Advocate* (a gay magazine). Roux believed that if the campaign got to the trendsetters, the masses would follow. Ads, which generally appeared as full pages 8 to 10 times a year, were sometimes tailored to fit the magazine genre, even to the extent of asking advertising reps of magazines for ideas. The emphasis was on the medium, but the bottle was the focus, even when it took other forms. The Absolut ad used in *Vogue* in 1988 pictured the Absolut label emblazoning a tight silver T-shirt dress designed by David Cameron on a woman who, in effect, became the bottle—"Absolut Cameron." TBWA noted, "The idea is to make the bottle the hero in a whimsical fashion. It's always the headliner." The ad later became part of an eight-page insert in *Vogue* of Absolut dresses created by new designers.

Special Events and Promotions

21   Music, art, and fashion were consistent themes for Absolut promotion and advertising. Roux said, "The artists and the people who buy art are the trend-setters in this world."[5]

22   Carillon sponsored an "Absolut Grappelli" concert at Carnegie Hall in 1988, for the violinist Stéphane Grappelli's 80th birthday. An "Absolut Concert" was scheduled for late 1989 at Lincoln Center's Avery Fisher Hall, to feature four modern composers conducting their own pieces. It was to end with an "Absolut Fanfare." Such special event sponsorships generally absorbed 20 percent of the product's advertising and promotion budget.

23   Carillon commissioned an original song by Brazilian Antonio Carlos Jobim (singer of "Bossa Nova" and "Girl from Ipanema") to run in *Rolling Stone*—"Absolut Jobim." Others were: "Downtown" and "Uptown" images: billboards tied to the locale, as on Rodeo Drive in Beverly Hills—"Absolut Drive"; billboards in Chicago with the letters in "Absolut Chicago" blowing in the wind; trucks roaming the streets of New York in 1988 with reproductions of the bottle, on ice, on their backs, and similar "outdoor" advertising for San Francisco and Washington, D.C.

24   In 1988, the advertising image changed slightly from whimsical treatments of the actual bottle to recreations of the bottle. In addition to fashion designers and photographers, Roux and TBWA hired painters and sculptors to create Absolut bottles for ads. Bottle renditions were commissioned from pop artist Andy Warhol (the drawing was later donated to the Whitney Museum), and artists Kenny Scharf and Ed Ruscha, who created an "Absolut L.A." ad. In it, the bottle became a pool of crystal blue water surrounded by a white terrace. It won the 1988 MPA Kelly Award for "Best in Magazine Advertising" and ran free in *Newsweek*'s June 12, 1989, issue.

---

[5]Andrea Adelson, "Unusual Ads Help a Foreign Vodka to the Top," *The New York Times*, November 28, 1988.

TABLE 2 Distilled Spirit Industry Advertising Budgets, 1988

Class Brand	No. of Brands Combined	Dollars (thousands)	Percentage of Class
Seagram's liquors	10	26,380.9	11.3
Dewars' Scotch whiskeys	2	11,498.9	4.9
Johnnie Walker Scotch	3	9,481.8	4.1
Kahlua liqueurs	3	8,151.1	3.5
Absolut vodka	2	7,686.9	3.3
Bacardi rums	5	7,547.7	3.2
Puerto Rican rums	2	7,498.1	3.2
Chivas	2	7,195.4	3.1
Tanqueray	1	7,054.9	3.0
J&B Scotch whiskeys	1	6,522.9	2.8
Top 10 total		99,018.6	42.4
Class total		233,554.2	100.0

Budgets

25 According to BAR/LNA, Grand Metropolitan, IDV, and Carillon spent $6.7 million dollars on advertising Absolut in 1987. The Absolut advertising budget was set at $18 million for 1988, which was believed to be the highest budget for spirits in U.S. history, and the budget was estimated to between $22.5 and $23 million for 1989. (Carillon's fiscal year ended in October.) BAR/LNA comparative figures for January–December 1988 are given in Table 2.

26 Figures for Absolut early in the 1980s were not available; the brand was too small at that time. But Carillon was not alone in turning to advertising to reverse declining liquor sales in the early years. When Smirnoff sales fell by 8 percent in 1981, its advertising jumped 34 percent to $9.9 million; sales were off by only 0.7 percent in 1982. Wolfschmidt spent $3.4 million, but its sales were down 10.1 percent. Some industry-watchers blamed problems with Russian vodka on the boycott of the Olympics.

Advertising Production and Costs

27 Carillon produced expensive ads; the "Absolut Impression" ad mentioned previously was a costly, no-print, embossed white-on-white magazine insert. But the most expensive were the Christmas special ads; the first, appearing in 1987, was reported to have cost over $1 million to produce. When the ad was opened, a microchip recording played three songs, including "Santa Claus Is Coming to Town." This ad was inserted in *The New Yorker* and *New York*—"Have an Absolut Ball."

28 Christmas 1988 and "Absolut Wonderland" was also reported to have cost over $1 million to produce. Another source said the cost was $1 each, with a total of $750 thousand for two of the magazines. Carillon had been planning the ad for almost a year but was stymied by how to make the snow drift, how to keep the liquid from freezing, how to bind the edges, and how it would withstand magazine mail-handling. The company experimented with 15 to 20 prototypes, finally settling on a liquid composed of water, oil, and antifreeze (said to be, however, nontoxic). Rounded snowflakes were used, because they didn't puncture the plastic and they drifted better than others, and the amount of snow was eventually reduced

because it obscured the bottle. Copies were mailed around the country to test the ad's durability. *The Washington Post* printed the following description by Jeff Greenberg, vice president and print-production director for TBWA:

> The production key to this pricey undertaking is incredibly cheap Asian labor. You couldn't do it here. You couldn't pay for it.
>
> The insert required hand-assembly by 300 workers, mostly teen-agers who put in 20-hour days in non-air-conditioned factories at a salary equivalent to $50 a month. The workers are incredible—they never lift their heads up. I'm not meaning to sound like it's slave labor.

29   The three-dimensional snow ad ran in *LA Style*, *New York*, and *MarketWatch*. One million were printed at around $.75 each, according to one source. "Absolut Wonderland" generated a huge amount of media coverage. Some 300 newspapers ran stories on the ad as did 40 TV news programs.

APPROACHING 1990

30   The marriage of Carillon and TBWA was a boon for both partners. TBWA U.S. offices were billing $127 million midway through 1988, and the firm had added 12 new accounts during those six months alone. *The New York Times* noted the influence of the Absolut campaigns, saying it was "advertising that is so good it attracts new business to the agency." Richard Costello, president and CEO of TBWA, called Roux "the best client I ever had." Carillon sales for 1988 were $200 million.

31   Absolut vodka sales grew an average 22 percent a year for a decade. It became the number one imported vodka in 1985, when it overtook Stolichnaya—perhaps partly as a result of a boycott of Soviet goods following the shooting of the Korean Airlines plane in September 1983.

32   At the end of 1988, Absolut had between 51 percent and 56 percent of the imported vodka market in the United States, 5 percent of the total market. Its recent case sales had grown from 1.1 million in 1986 to 1.8 million in 1988. Over two million cases were expected to be sold in 1989. Rival Stolichnaya had 30 percent of the import market, which represented 3.2 million cases (8 percent) of a total 1988 spirits market of 38 million cases. Vodka leader Smirnoff, however, was pulling in $600 million versus Absolut's $260 million.

33   Although total distilled-spirit volume sales were off 3.3 percent in 1988 (even imports were down 0.7 percent), *Advertising Age* noted (February 26, 1989) that "Imported vodka again outperformed all other categories, and domestic vodka followed on the imports' success." Exhibit 2 gives estimated case sales and the 1988 rank of top brands. Absolut was listed 18th in 1987, 35th in 1986.

34   In the United States, adult drinkers constituted a market of 170 million people in 1988; distilled-spirit consumption per capita was 2.2 gallons a year (2.3 gallons in 1987). Vodka accounted for 24 percent of those figures. The average cost of distilled spirits was $39.90 a gallon; the average American spent $83.26 on them in 1988. Exhibit 3 presents data as of spring 1987, on vodka consumers.

35   By the end of the decade, brown spirits were also attempting to cash in on trends toward lower calories and lower alcohol content or higher premiums. Seagram's Mount Royal Light boasted that its reduced calories came from a special process rather than the usual watering down. Schenley relaunched the classic Pinch Scotch with the restored wire mesh on the bottle (dropped in the 1960s because of cost) as a super-premium liquor, aged 15 years, and Schenley planned to spend $20 million advertising it over three years. Jack Daniels introduced a $20 bottle of Gentleman Jack.

EXHIBIT 2   ABSOLUT VODKA   Liquor Industry Scoreboard*

	1988 Rank	Marketer	Sales (thousands of cases)			Five-Year Growth Rate
			1988	1987	1986	
Rum						
Bacardi	1	Bacardi	7,350	7,330	7,120	0.2%
Ron Castillo	49	Bacardi	720	720	740	(3.2)
Vodka						
Smirnoff	2	Heublein	5,900	5,510	6,100	(0.7)
Popov	5	Heublein	3,250	3,060	3,410	1.6
Gordon's	18	Schenley	1,650	1,610	1,650	(1.7)
Kamchatka	21	Jim Beam	1,490	1,600	1,570	(3.1)
Absolut	22	Carillon	1,410	1,110	900	25.1**
Skol	27	Glenmore	1,170	1,070	1,030	7.9
Gilbey's	28	Jim Beam	1,160	1,130	1,130	(2.3)
Stolichnaya	38	Monsieur Henri	900	790	740	14.7
Wolfschmidt	39	Seagram	890	890	870	(1.4)
Fleischmann's	43	Glenmore	800	850	1,000	(4.4)
Barton	50	Barton Brands	660	600	610	1.0
McCormick	51	McCormick	630	590	610	13.7
Relska	58	Heublein	590	600	690	(2.8)
Blended/Canadian Whiskey						
Seagram's 7-Crown	3	Seagram	3,840	3,900	3,950	(4.5)
Canadian Mist	4	Brown-Forman	3,370	3,410	3,560	0.0
Canadian Club	10	Hiram Walker	2,350	2,300	2,250	(1.8)
Seagram's VO	11	Seagram	2,200	2,230	2,250	(5.5)
Windsor Supreme	13	Jim Beam	1,900	1,920	1,990	(2.2)
Black Velvet	16	Heublein	1,730	1,690	1,740	(1.9)
Crown Royal	23	Seagram	1,310	1,220	1,200	5.0
Kessler	32	Seagram	1,090	1,090	1,140	(4.6)
Lord Calvert	34	Seagram	1,030	1,020	1,070	(0.9)
Canadian Ltd.	54	Glenmore	600	670	720	(0.8)
Calvert Extra	59	Seagram	570	620	710	(8.9)
Bourbon/Tennessee						
Jim Beam	6	Jim Beam	3,200	3,250	3,240	(0.3)
Jack Daniel	7	Brown-Forman	3,180	3,030	2,960	0.2
Early Times	29	Brown-Forman	1,150	1,200	1,330	(4.8)
Ancient Age	35	Age International	960	900	930	1.9
Ten High	40	Hiram Walker	880	1,030	1,000	(4.0)
Old Crow	52	Jim Beam	620	520	480	(5.6)
Evan Williams	56	Heaven Hill	600	580	590	(1.7)

(Continued)

EXHIBIT 2   (*Continued*)

	1988 Rank	Marketer	Sales (thousands of cases)			Five-Year Growth Rate
			1988	1987	1986	
Gin						
Seagram's	8	Seagram	3,150	2,970	2,920	3.9
Gordon's	15	Schenley	1,740	1,650	1,750	(3.9)
Tanqueray	26	Schieffelin/ Somerset	1,180	1,150	1,100	4.9
Gilbey's	31	Jim Beam	1,130	1,190	1,150	(8.7)
Beefeater	37	Buckingham Wile	930	950	980	(4.5)
Fleischmann's	53	Glenmore	610	700	680	(2.0)
Cordial/Brandy/Cocktail						
DeKuyper Cordials	9	Jim Beam	2,550	3,100	3,370	(13.0)**
E&J	14	E&J Gallo	1,850	1,790	1,670	9.1
Hiram Walker	17	Hiram Walker	1,690	1,680	1,650	7.5
Kahlua	19	Maidstone	1,550	1,580	1,470	2.4
Southern Comfort	25	Brown-Forman	1,190	1,150	1,100	3.5
Christian Brothers	30	Christian Bros.	1,150	1,190	1,160	(2.2)
Bailey's	36	Paddington	950	920	890	4.8
Golden Spirits	41	Seagram	850	1,350	910	(3.2)**
Club Cocktails	42	Heublein	840	930	880	(2.2)**
Arrow Cordials	44	Heublein	750	850	1,000	(8.6)
Leroux Cordials	45	Seagram	750	810	950	(1.3)
Hennessy Cognac	47	Schieffelin/ Somerset	740	730	750	3.5
Courvoisier Cognac	60	W.A. Taylor	550	580	540	6.1
Scotch						
Dewar's	12	Schenley	2,100	2,070	2,160	(0.9)
J&B	24	Paddington	1,260	1,320	1,300	(5.3)
Johnnie Walker Red	33	Schieffelin/ Smt.	1,060	1,120	1,150	(1.2)
Chivas Regal	46	Seagram	740	750	750	(2.2)
Cutty Sark	48	Buckingham Wile	730	760	770	(7.0)
Old Smuggler	55	W.A. Taylor	600	730	750	(3.7)
Scoresby	57	Glenmore	600	630	590	8.4
Tequila						
Jose Cuervo	20	Heublein	1,500	1,250	1,150	12.0

*Estimates of retail sales, rounded to nearest 10,000 mixed cases, from Jobson Beverage Alcohol Group.
**1986–1988.

EXHIBIT 3   **ABSOLUT VODKA**   Vodkas and Media-Use Profiles (base: 172,957,000 adults; index: all adults = 100)

A. Vodka Consumption

	Percentage of all	Share of users	Share of volume
Total drunk in last six months	13.8		
Vodka brands: Absolut	1.2	6.4	5.6
Crown Russe	0.2	0.8	0.6
Finlandia	0.4	1.9	0.6
Fleischmann's	0.5	2.8	1.5
Gilbey's	1.0	5.0	5.5
Gordon's	1.3	7.1	3.6
Hiram Walker	0.3	1.4	0.6
Mr. Boston	0.3	1.8	1.6
Nikolai	0.3	1.7	1.9
Popov	1.9	10.2	19.8
Relska	0.2	0.9	1.2
Schenley	0.2	0.9	1.6
Seagrams Imported	0.6	2.9	1.7
Smirnoff	6.3	33.2	30.9
Stolichnaya	1.0	5.5	3.0
Vikin Fjord	—	0.2	0.2
Wolfschmidt	0.7	3.7	4.3
Unspecified brand @ bar/restaurant	1.8	9.5	8.5
Other	0.8	4.3	7.5
Drinks or glasses in last 30 days:			
Light: none	4.4	41.7	1.7
1	1.3		
Medium: 2	1.6	31.0	17.9
3	0.9		
4	1.0		
5	0.8		
Heavy: 6	0.6	27.4	80.4
7	0.3		
8	0.3		
9 or more	2.7		

B. Total and Selected Brands

	All vodka All Drinkers Index	Brand not specified Heavy Drinkers* Index	Absolut All Drinkers Index	Popov All Drinkers Index	Smirnoff All Drinkers Index	Stolichnaya All Drinkers Index	At Bar/ Restaurant All Drinkers Index
Men	109	114**	111**	122	118	139	83
Women	92	87	90	80	84	65	116
Graduated college	140	128	182	180	116	215	171
Attended college	127	116	164	132	124	143	154
Graduated high school	95	98	75	78	102	76	82

(Continued)

EXHIBIT 3   *(Continued)*

	All vodka All Drinkers Index	Brand not specified Heavy Drinkers* Index	Absolut All Drinkers Index	Popov All Drinkers Index	Smirnoff All Drinkers Index	Stolichnaya All Drinkers Index	At Bar/Restaurant All Drinkers Index
Ages 18–24	116	122	189	138	137	135	142
Ages 25–34	109	96	152	76	117	149	116
Ages 35–44	109	77	89	88	101	125	113
Ages 45–54	105	124	64	102	106	73	71
Ages 55–64	92	108	32	128	76	58	97
Ages 65 or over	62	84	30	88	51	20	45
House.inc.$50,000 or more	137	134	179	135	126	161	121
$40,000–49,999	123	126	120	146	124	158	130
$35,000–39,999	98	109	100	72	93	124	79
$25,000–34,999	98	92	92	109	104	76	125
$15,000–24,999	80	94	48	75	83	53	77
Marketing reg.: N. England	145	161	155	111	129	171	151
Middle Atlantic	130	132	237	64	125	134	132
East Central	72	57	67	147	70	48	52
West Central	94	98	38	85	97	76	139
South East	84	82	60	74	83	69	65
South West	93	90	69	81	113	101	57
Pacific	105	110	87	150	102	140	120
Single	121	120	195	115	131	146	130
Married	97	94	75	97	94	81	90
Other	86	97	72	91	82	109	97
White	101	104	102	111	99	103	111
Black	89	63	87	17	108	59	22
Home owned	100	100	81	96	95	85	97
Daily newspapers: Read any	109	112					
Read one daily	104	105					
Read two or more dailies	128	135					
Sunday newspapers: Read any	114	110					
Read one Sunday	114	112					
Read two or more Sundays	116	97					
Heavy magazines/heavy TV	100	109					
Heavy magazines/light TV	120	104					
Light magazines/heavy TV	85	94					
Light magazines/light TV	95	93					

(Continued)

EXHIBIT 3 *(Continued)*

C. Magazine Use of Heavy Vodka Drinkers (selected magazines only)	
Travel & Leisure	270
Wall Street Journal	219
Nation's Business	210
Golf Digest	206
Guns & Ammo.	206
Scientific American	198
PC World	194
Fortune	193
Inc.	190
Penthouse	184
Vogue	157
The New Yorker	110
Sports Illustrated	109
Rolling Stone	106
Newsweek	99
Ms.	85
Esquire	80
New York Magazine	68
Home	60
Runner's World	60
Barron's	56
Colonial Homes	56
Health	56
Mother Earth News	51
Byte	48
Seventeen	48
True Story	43
Working Woman	35

*More than 5 drinks or glasses in last 30 days.
**To be read: men are 14% more likely than women to be heavy users of vodka; 11% more likely to drink Absolut Vodka

Source: Adapted from Mediamark Research, Inc.

36   Foreign vodkas' 22 percent growth attracted a rush of new imports. Seagram introduced a Polish vodka, Wybrowa; brands called Elduris and Denaka appeared. Elduris was Icelandic vodka going for $12 to $14 a bottle. Brown-Forman spent $15 million to launch Icy (from Iceland) and planned on 4.5 million cases by 1992. They opened its advertising with an ad featuring the bottle and the words, "Absolute Improvement." Carillon got a court order to stop the ad, and Roux said "There is room for people who don't try to imitate others. They have to create their own image and quality."[6] In August 1989, the Denaka vodka ad (in *Business Week*, for example) featured a woman with flowing red-brown locks leaning

[6]"What Stirs the Spirit Makers: Vodka, Vodka, Vodka," *Business Week* (June 12, 1989).

on a pool table by a bottle and glass. She was saying, "When I said vodka, I meant Denaka," and the caption read, "In a world of absolutes, Denaka excels."

37   Within vodka products at the end of the decade, one trend was toward flavors, particularly pepper. The trend appeared to have started when a marketer (reportedly, Carillon) noted that restaurant managers marinated peppercorns in vodka for drinks such as Bloody Mary's, although the tradition of peppered vodka was centuries old in Europe. Many believed the niche would grow because of a perceived trend toward spicy foods and full-tasting drinks. The demand was said to be coming from upscale, 25-to-50-year-old, metropolitan types. One of Carillon's competitors said, however, that the pepper-drinkers were minimum-age consumers who downed them in shot glasses at nightclubs but that marketers didn't want to focus on this fact: "Vodka marketers don't want to admit that people are doing shots any more than the cognac marketers advertise that a lot of people drink cognac with Coke, because it's looked to be downscale." [7]

38   Stolichnaya introduced Zubrowka, a musky-tasting vodka with north European buffalo grass that never caught on and was dropped; Pertsovka with pepper (in 1985), Ohkotnichya with ginger, cloves, juniper, anise, and lemon peel; and Limonnaya in 1986. Carillon's Absolut Pepper ad in 1987 showed the bottle, with just the brand name, in a jungle of peppers hanging from vines. The brand grew slowly to 20,000 cases by the end of 1988, with plans by Roux for it to grow to 500,000 by the end of 1989. Citron Absolut in early 1989 was selling 10,000 cases a month.

39   Adding flavors to vodka raised the long-standing issue of whether vodkas varied by taste or quality. The U.S. Bureau of Alcohol, Tobacco, and Firearms had always maintained that it did not, by definition. The bureau had always objected to use of the word "taste" in advertising. Many people, however, maintained that the premium imported vodkas did, in fact, have a distinctive taste. Smirnoff tested the bureau's stance in 1989 with an ad claiming it was "so superior, you can taste it." The marketers claimed their labs had confirmed a taste difference in vodkas. The bureau ruled that it would look at the context of the word's use: that vodka has no distinctive taste but one vodka "can taste different from another vodka."[8] Carillon and TBWA planned to avoid the question altogether.

40   A more publicized issue facing the alcoholic-beverages industry was the question of alcohol's effects on society. U.S. Surgeon General, in 1988, C. Everett Koop had called together a workshop on drunken driving, the report of which was released in late 1988. The workshop called for restrictions on advertising and promotion and the raising of excise taxes that were primarily directed at the beer and wine segments. It also, however, called for higher excise taxes on liquor, a decrease in tax deductions allowable for alcohol ads, and the placement of warnings on print advertising. (Warnings on bottle labels had already been mandated by Congress.) Reaction from the alcoholic-beverage industry and broadcasters was swift, vocal, and highly critical.

41   The workshop and ensuing flap focused attention on a fundamental, long-standing issue of the role of advertising in consumption—its influence in general, through the advertising of adults-only products, and the influence of advertising on "abuse" versus "use." Critics of the report noted that it was based on conjecture and anecdotal evidence and that it assumed a causal link between advertising and alcohol abuse (drunk driving) that had never been established by research. A 1987 study in the *Journal of Advertising*, for example, summarized

[7]Patricia Winters, "New Flavors Spice Up Vodka Category," *Advertising Age* (February 16, 1987).
[8]"U.S. May Let Vodka Advertisers Use 'Taste' but in a Limited Way," *Wall Street Journal*, June 28, 1989.

findings as follows: "Advertising has not generally been shown to *substantially* affect primary demand, relative to other influences."

42   Nevertheless, in June 1989, Anheuser-Busch announced increased spending on its "Know when to say when" campaign. Expenditures were to be approximately $30 million a year, equivalent to its brand advertising, up from a $22 million average in recent years. Coors and Philip Morris's Miller Beer announced similar increases to responsible drinking programs. The Beer Institute, the industry trade group, planned to spend $2.5 million to publicize the programs already in place.

NEW DIRECTIONS

43   In October 1989, the holiday season and the possibility for another "blockbuster" advertising execution were drawing nearer. Recent ads included a tag-line, "For gift delivery of Absolut Vodka (except where prohibited by law) call 1-800-243-3787," a reminder that the holiday party season would involve the giving, receiving, and consumption of spirits.

Case 10

Amazon.com, Inc: *Retailing Giant to High-Tech Player?*

Alan N. Hoffman Bentley University

OVERVIEW

1   Founded by Jeff Bezos, online giant Amazon.com, Inc. (Amazon) was incorporated in the state of Washington in July 1994 and sold its first book in July 1995. In May 1997, Amazon (AMZN) completed its initial public offering, and its common stock was listed on the NASDAQ Global Select Market. Amazon quickly grew from an online bookstore to the world's largest online retailer, greatly expanding its product and service offerings through a series of acquisitions, alliances, partnerships, and exclusivity agreements. Amazon's financial objective was to achieve long-term sustainable growth and profitability. To attain this objective, Amazon maintained a lean culture focused on increasing its operating income through continually increasing revenue and efficiently managing its working capital and capital expenditures, while tightly managing operating costs.

2   The name "Amazon" was evocative for founder Jeff Bezos of his vision of Amazon as a huge natural phenomenon, like the longest river in the world. The company would be "Earth's most customer-centric company . . . a place where people can come to find and discover anything they might want to buy online."[1]

3   By 2008 Amazon had become a global brand (see Exhibit 1), with web sites in Canada, the United Kingdom, Germany, France, China, and Japan, with order fulfillment in more than 200 countries.[2] Its operations were organized into two principal segments: North America and International Operations, which grew to include Italy in 2010 and Spain in 2011. By 2012, Amazon employed more than 56,200 people around the world working in the corporate office in Seattle and in software development, order fulfillment, and customer service centers in North America, Latin America, Europe, and Asia.

RETAIL OPERATIONS/AMAZON'S SUPERIOR WEB SITE

4   As people became more comfortable shopping online, Amazon developed its web site to take advantage of increased Internet traffic and to serve its customers most effectively.[3] The hallmarks of Amazon's appeal were ease of use; speedy, accurate search results; selection,

The author would like to thank Barbara Gotfried, Jodi Germann, Lauren-Ashley Higson, Faith Naymie, Faina Shakarova, Jamal Ait Hammou, Muntasir Alam, Shaheel Dholakia, Xinxin Zhu, and Will Hoffman for their research and contributions to this case. Please address all correspondence to: Dr. Alan N. Hoffman, Dept. of Management, Bentley University, 175 Forest Street, Waltham, MA 02452-4705, voice (781) 891-2287, ahoffman@bentley.edu. Printed by permission of Alan N. Hoffman.

[1]Amazon.com FAQs. December 2011. http://phx.corporate-ir.net/phoenix.zhtml?c=97664&p=irol-faq
[2]D. Chaffey. *Amazon.com Case Study.* http://www.davechaffey.com/E-commerce-Internet-marketing-case-studies/Amazon-case-study/
[3]Mind Tools. *PEST Analysis—Problem-Solving Training from MindTools.com.* Management Training, Leadership Training and Career Training. Mind Tools Ltd. December 12, 2011. http://www.mindtools.com/pages/article/newTMC_09.htm

EXHIBIT 1   **Amazon's Online Visitor Breakout**

Country	Percent of Visitors
United States	66.8%
India	2.6%
United Kingdom	2.2%
Canada	2.1%
Japan	1.4%
China	1.4%
Australia	1.3%
Germany	1.3%
Mexico	1.3%
Venezuela	1.2%

Source: Alexa.com

price, and convenience; a trustworthy transaction environment; timely customer service; and fast, reliable fulfillment[4]; all enabled by the sophisticated technology the company encouraged its employees to develop to better serve its customers. The site, which offered a huge array of products sold both by itself and by third parties, was particularly designed to create a personalized shopping experience that helped customers discover new products and make efficient, informed buying decisions.

5   Key to Amazon's success was continual web site improvement. A huge part of the technological work done for Amazon was dedicated to identifying problems, developing solutions, and enhancing customers' online experience. Jacob Lepley, in his "Amazon Marketing Strategy: Report One," notes that, "when you visit Amazon . . . you can use [it] to find just about any item on the market at an extremely low price. Amazon has made it very simple for customers to purchase items with a simple click of the mouse. . . . When you have everything you need, you make just one payment and your orders are processed."[5] This simple system is the same whether a customer purchases directly from Amazon or from one of its associates.

6   Pursuing perfection, Amazon was aggressive in analyzing its web site's traffic and modifying the web site accordingly. Amazon particularly excelled at customer tracking,

[4]D. Chaffey. *Amazon.com Case Study.* http://www.davechaffey.com/E-commerce-Internet-marketing-case-studies/Amazon-case-study/
[5]Marketing Plan. *Marketing Strategies of Amazon.com.* http://www.marketingplan.net/amazon-com-marketing-strategies/

collecting data from every visit to its web site. Utilizing the information, Amazon then directed users to products it surmised they might be interested in because the item was either:[6]

- similar to what the user was currently searching for (on-the-fly recommendations)
- related to what the user had searched for or clicked on at any time in the past, or
- had been purchased by other people who had searched or bought the same item the user was searching for.

7   Recommendations were also customized based on the information customers provided about themselves and their interests, and their ratings of prior purchases. Amazon also collected data on those who had never visited any of its web sites, but who had received gifts from those who had used the site.

8   One of Amazon's most distinctive features was the community created based on the ratings/reviews provided by private individuals to help others make more informed purchasing decisions. Anyone could provide a narrative review and rate a product on a scale of 1–5 stars, and/or comment on others' reviews. Individuals could also create their own "So You'd Like . . ." guides and "Listmania" lists based on Amazon's products offerings and post them or send them to friends and family. To streamline customer research, Amazon also consolidated different versions of a product (i.e., DVD, VHS, Blu-Ray of a video) into a single product available for commentary that simplified commentary and user accessibility.[7]

9   To further target potential customers Amazon engaged in permission marketing, eliciting permission to e-mail customers regarding specific production promotions based on prior purchases on the assumption that a targeted e-mail was more likely to be read than a blanket e-mail. This strategy was hugely appreciated by Amazon customers, further contributing to Amazon's success.

10   In addition, Amazon purchased pay-per-click advertisements on search engines such as Google to direct browsing customers to its web sites. The ads appeared on the left-hand side of the search list results, and Amazon paid a fee for each visitor who clicked on its sponsored link.

11   At the same time, as "TV and billboard ads were roughly ten times less effective when compared to direct or online marketing when concerning customer acquisition costs,"[8] according to the Marketing Plan, Amazon reduced its offline marketing. The strategy was simple: as customers shopped online, online marketing was key. However, in 2010, Amazon initiated a small television advertising campaign to increase brand awareness.

12   Finally, to round out its customer care, Amazon expedited shipping by strategically locating its fulfillment centers near airports[9] where rents were also cheaper, giving Amazon the two-pronged advantage of speed and low cost over its competitors. Furthermore, in the United States, the United Kingdom, Germany, and Japan, Amazon offered subscribers to Amazon Prime the added convenience of free express shipping. Amazon Prime's 2-day delivery endeared it to Amazon customers, again contributing to the customer loyalty that was key to Amazon's success. Amazon Prime cost $79 annually to join and included free access to Amazon Instant Video. The overarching objective of the company was to offer low prices, convenience, and a wide selection of merchandise, a pared-down, yet wide-reaching strategy that made Amazon such a huge success.

[6]D. Chaffey. *Amazon.com Case Study.* http://www.davechaffey.com/E-commerce-Internet-marketing-case-studies/Amazon-case-study/
[7]J. Layton. *How Amazon Works.* Retrieved from *How Stuff Works,* http://money.howstuffworks.com/amazon3
[8]Marketing Plan. *Marketing Strategies of Amazon.com.* http://www.marketingplan.net/amazon-com-marketing-strategies/
[9]Amazon.com. *2010 Annual Report.* April 2011.

DIVERSIFIED PRODUCT OFFERINGS

13   Amazon diversified its product portfolio well beyond simply offering books, which in turn allowed it to diversify its customer mix. In 2007, Amazon successfully launched the Kindle, its $79 e-book reader, which offered users more than one million reasonably priced books and newspapers easily accessed on its handheld device. Competitor Apple, Inc., then introduced the iPad, the first tablet computer, in January 2010, sparking further development of mobile e-readers. E-book sales took off immediately, increasing by more than 100 percent, according to the Association of American Publishers. Eager to compete in a market for which it was uniquely positioned, Amazon quickly developed its own low-cost tablet, the Kindle Fire, an Android-based tablet with a color touch screen priced at $199, more than $300 lower than the iPad, sacrificing profit margins in search of sales volume and market-share gains. Other tech giants such as RIMM and HP were unable to compete with the iPad. Only the Sony Nook, the Amazon Kindle and Kindle Fire, and the Samsung Galaxy and Series 7 tablets challenged Apple's consistent 60 percent market share. Ultimately, however, Amazon's huge growth derived not simply from the sale of Kindle hardware and the growth of e-book sales, but from its diversification and the continual expansion of the easy web site access created by mobile devices.

14   By 2010, 43 percent of Amazon net sales were from media, including books, music, DVDs/video products, magazine subscriptions, digital downloads, and video games. More than half of all Amazon sales came from computers, mobile devices including the Kindle, Kindle Fire, and Kindle Touch, and other electronics, as well as general merchandise from home and garden supplies to groceries, apparel, jewelry, health and beauty products, sports and outdoor equipment, tools, and auto and industrial supplies.

15   Amazon also offered its own credit card, a form of co-branding, which benefited all parties: Amazon, the credit card company (Chase Bank), and the consumer. Amazon benefited because it received money from the credit card company both directly from Amazon purchases and indirectly from fees generated from non-Amazon purchases. In addition Amazon benefited from the company loyalty generated by having its own credit card the consumer sees and uses every day. The credit card company gained from Amazon's high visibility, increasing its potential customer base and transactions. And the consumer earned credit toward gift certificates with each use of the card.

PARTNERSHIPS

16   Amazon leveraged its expertise in online order taking and order fulfillment (see Exhibit 2) and developed partnerships with many retailers whose web sites it hosted and managed, including (currently or in the past) Target, Sears Canada, Bebe Stores, Timex Corporation, and Marks & Spencer. Amazon offered services comparable to those it offered customers on its own web sites, thus freeing those retailers to focus on the nonweb site, nontechnological aspects of their operations.[10]

17   In addition, Amazon Marketplace allowed independent retailers and third-party sellers to sell their products on Amazon by placing links on their web sites to Amazon.com or to specific Amazon products. Amazon was "not the seller of record in these transactions, but instead earn[ed] fixed fees, revenue share fees, per-unit activity fees, or some combination thereof."[11] Linking to Amazon created visibility for these retailers and individual sellers, adding

---

[10]Marketing Plan. *Marketing Strategies of Amazon.com.* http://www.marketingplan.net/amazon-com-marketing-strategies/
[11]Amazon.com. *2010 Annual Report.* April 2011.

EXHIBIT 2 Fulfillment by Amazon

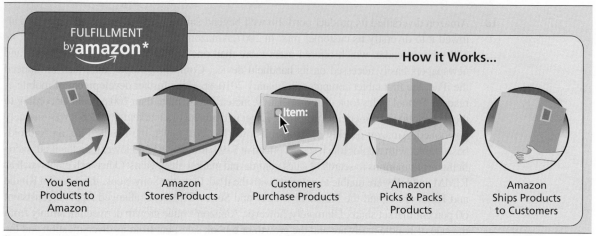

Source: Amazon.com

value to their web sites, increasing their sales, and enabling them to take advantage of Amazon's convenience and fast delivery. Sellers shipped their products to an Amazon warehouse or fulfillment center, where the company stored it for a fee, and when an order was placed, shipped out the product on the seller's behalf. This form of affiliate marketing came at nearly no cost to Amazon. Affiliates used straight text links leading directly to a product page, and they also offered a range of dynamic banners, which featured different content.

WEB SERVICES

18   As a major tech player, Amazon developed a number of Web services, including e-commerce, database, payment and billing, Web traffic, and computing. These Web services provided access to technology infrastructure that developers were able to utilize to enable various types of virtual businesses. The Web services (many of which were free) created a reliable, scalable, and inexpensive computing platform that revolutionized small business' online presence. For instance, Amazon's e-commerce Fulfillment By Amazon (FBA) program allowed merchants to direct inventory to Amazon's fulfillment centers; after products were purchased, Amazon packed and shipped. This freed merchant from a complex ordering process while allowing them control over their inventory. Amazon's Fulfillment Web Service (FWS) added to FBA's program. FWS let retailers embed FBA capabilities straight into their own sites, vastly enhancing their business capabilities.

19   In 2012, Amazon announced a cloud storage solution (Amazon Glacier) from Amazon Web Services (AWS), a low-cost solution for data archiving, backups, and other long-term storage projects where data not accessed frequently could be retained for future reference. Companies often incurred significant costs for data archiving in anticipation of growing backup demand, which led to underutilized capacity and wasted money. With Amazon Glacier, companies were able to keep costs in line with actual usage, so managers could know the exact cost of their storage systems at all times. With Amazon Glacier, Amazon continued to dominate the space of cold storage, which had first come into prominence in 2009, amidst competitors such as Rackspace and Microsoft offering their own solutions.

20 By 2012, Amazon Web Services were a crucial facet of Amazon's profit base, and Amazon was one of the lead players in the fast-growing retail e-commerce market. Seeing huge growth potential Amazon made the decision to expand Amazon Web Services (AWS) internationally and invested heavily in technology infrastructure to support the rapid growth in AWS. Though its investments in e-commerce threatened to suppress its near-term margin growth, Amazon expected to benefit in the long term, given the significant growth potential in domestic and, even more so, in international e-commerce.

AMAZON'S ACQUISITION OF ZAPPOS, QUIDSI, LIVINGSOCIAL, AND LOVEFILM

21 On July 22, 2009, Amazon acquired Zappos, the online shoe and clothing retailer, for $1.2 billion. At that time Zappos was reporting over $1 billion in annual sales without any marketing or advertising. According to founder Tony Hsieh, the secret to Zappos' success was superior customer service, from its 365-day return guarantee to the company tours with which it regaled visitors, picking them up at the airport, then returning them to the airport afterward. Zappos' employees were also very well treated, earning it a place at the top of the list of the "best companies to work for." Announcing Zappos' acquisition by Amazon, Tony Hsieh told his employees that he was excited because it was "a huge opportunity to accelerate the growth of the Zappos brand and culture, and . . . Amazon is the best partner to help us get there faster."[12]

22 On November 8, 2010, Amazon announced the acquisition of Quidsi, the parent company of Diapers.com, an online baby care specialty site, and Soap.com, an online site for everyday essentials. Amazon paid $500 million in cash and assumed $45 million in debt and other obligations. As Jeff Bezos explained, "This acquisition brings together two companies who are committed to providing great prices and fast delivery to parents, making one of the chores of being a parent a little easier and less expensive."[12]

23 On December 2, 2010, Amazon announced that it had invested $175 million in Groupon competitor LivingSocial, a site whose up-to-the-minute research offered users immediate access to the hottest restaurants, shops, activities, and services in a given area while saving them 50 percent to 70 percent through special site deals.

24 On January 20, 2011, Amazon acquired Lovefilm for £200 million, a 1.6-million-subscriber-strong European Web-based DVD rental service based in London. Lovefilm had followed Netflix's business model, offering unlimited DVD rentals by mail for a monthly subscription fee of £9.99, but planned to challenge Netflix and expand its digital media business by entering the live-streaming subscription business.

COMPETITORS

25 Competition was fierce for Amazon on all fronts, from catalogue and mail-order houses to retail stores, from book, music, and video stores to retailers of electronics, home furnishings, auto parts, and sporting goods. Amazon's Kindle contended with Apple's iPad among many lesser competitors. And Amazon's competitors in the service sector included other e-commerce and Web service providers. The company faced direct competition from companies such as eBay, Apple, Barnes & Noble, Overstock.com, MediaBay, Priceline. com, PCMall.com, and RedEnvelope.com. Amazon had to compete with companies that provided their own products or services, sites that sold or distributed digital content such as

[12]From the "Letter to Shareholders" by Jeff Bezos in the 2009 and 2010 Amazon Annual Reports, respectively.

iTunes and Netflix, and media companies such as the *New York Times*. Many of the company's competitors had greater resources (eBay), longer histories (Barnes & Noble), more customers (Apple), or greater brand recognition (iTunes).

26   The companies offering the most direct threat to Amazon were eBay and Metro AG. Pierre Omidyar founded eBay in 1995, a web site that connected individual buyers and sellers including small businesses to buy and sell virtually anything. In 2010, the total value of goods sold on eBay was $62 billion, making eBay the world's largest online marketplace serving 39 markets with more than 97 million active users worldwide. eBay and Amazon subscribed to similar growth strategies: each acquired a broad spectrum of companies. Over the 15 years from 1995–2010 eBay acquired PayPal, Shopping.com, StubHub, and Bill Me Later, which have brought new e-commerce efficiencies to eBay.

27   Metro AG, headquartered in Dusseldorf, Germany, one of the world's leading international retail and wholesale companies, was formed through the merger of retail companies Asko Deutsche Kaufhaus AG, Kaufhof Holding AG, and Deutsche SB-Kauf AG. In 2010, the total value of goods sold by Metro AG was €67 billion.[13] Serving 33 countries, Metro AG offered a comprehensive range of products and services designed to meet the specific shopping needs of private and professional customers. Metro AG, like Amazon, focused on customer orientation, efficiency, sustainability, and innovation.

28   Amazon had to be vigilant, negotiating more favorable terms from suppliers, adopting more aggressive pricing, and devoting more resources to technology, infrastructure, fulfillment, and marketing. To maintain competitiveness, Amazon also strengthened its edge by entering into alliances with other businesses (i.e., Amazon Marketplace). Nevertheless, growing competition from global and domestic players continually threatened to erode Amazon's desired share of the market. Across the industries in which it competed, however, Amazon fought to maintain its edge based on its core principles of "selection, price, availability, convenience, information, discovery, brand recognition, personalized services, accessibility, customer service, reliability, speed of fulfillment, ease of use, and ability to adapt to changing conditions, as well as . . . customers' overall experience and trust."[14]

FRUSTRATION FREE PACKAGING

29   To stay current, Amazon took the initiative to reduce its carbon footprint by implementing a "Frustration Free Packaging" program. Recyclable Frustration Free Packaging came without excess packaging such as hard plastic clamshell casings, plastic bindings, and wire ties (see Exhibit 2) and was designed to be opened "without . . . a box cutter or knife."[15] Amazon then went one step further and worked with the original manufacturers to package products in Frustration Free Packaging right off the assembly line, further reducing the use of plastic and paper. Units shipped that utilized Frustration Free Packaging have increased very rapidly, from 1.3 million in 2009 to 4.0 million in 2010[16] (see Exhibit 3). Amazon also utilized software to determine the right size box for any product the company shipped, achieving a dramatic reduction in the number of packages shipped in oversized boxes and significantly reducing waste.

[13]Metro Group. *Corporate Srategy*. 2011. http://www.metrogroup.de/internet/site/metrogroup/node/10781/Len/index.html

[14]D. Chaffey. *Amazon.com Case Study*. http://www.davechaffey.com/E-commerce-Internet-marketing-case-studies/Amazon-case-study/

[15]Amazon.com. *Amazon Certified Frusturation-Free Packaging FAQ* (2011). http://www.amazon.com/gp/help/customer/display.html?nodeId=200285450

[16]Amazon.com. *Amazon Annual Meeting of Shareholders Presentation (10Q)*. June 2011. http://phx.corporate-ir.net/phoenix.zhtml?c=97664&p=irol-presentations

EXHIBIT 3   **Frustration Free Packaging Growth**

Source: Amazon.com 10Q

FINANCIAL OPERATIONS

30   Amazon sales doubled from 2009 to 2011, growing from $24,509 million (2009) to $48,077 million (2011) (see Exhibits 4a and 4b), growth attributable especially to increased sales in electronics and other general merchandise, and the adoption of a new accounting standard update, reduced prices including free shipping offers, increased in stock inventory availability, and the impact of the acquisition of Zappos in 2009.[17]

31   Amazon's annual net income for 2009, 2010, and 2011 was $902 million, $1,152 million, and $631 million respectively. The significant increase from 2009 to 2010 was due in large part to aggressive net sales growth and a large portion of its expenses and investments being fixed. Management explained that net income decreased from 2010 to 2011 as a result of (1) selling Kindle hardware at a market price slightly below the cost of manufacture; (2) increased spending on technology infrastructure; and (3) increased payroll expenses.

CHALLENGES FOR AMAZON

32   Amazon developed very quickly into a major player in the online retail market, yet challenges hovered:

1. From its inception Amazon was not required to collect state or local sales or use taxes, an exemption upheld by the U.S. Supreme Court. However, in 2012, states began to consider superseding the Supreme Court decision.[18] If the states were to prevail, Amazon would be forced to collect sales and use tax, creating administrative burdens for it and putting it at a competitive disadvantage "if similar obligations are not imposed on all of its online competitors, potentially decreasing its future sales."[19] Massachusetts and other states were motivated both by the desire to tap into new sources of revenues for their state budgets and to protect local retailers. According to the *Boston Globe*:

[17]Amazon.com. *2010 Annual Report.* April 2011.
[18]Amazon.com. *2010 Annual Report.* Pp. 13–14. April 2011.
[19]Amazon.com. *2010 Annual Report.* P. 14. April 2011.

EXHIBIT 4a Income Statement and Balance Sheet

Income Statement Currency in (Millions of US Dollars)	As of:	Dec 31 2008	Dec 31 2009	Dec 31 2010	Dec 31 2011
Revenues		19,166.0	24,509.0	34,204.0	48,077.0
Total Revenues		**19,166.0**	**24,509.0**	**34,204.0**	**48,077.0**
Cost of Goods Sold		14,896.0	18,978.0	26,561.0	37,288.0
Gross Profit		**4,270.0**	**5,531.0**	**7,643.0**	**10,789.0**
Selling General & Admin Expenses, Total		2,419.0	3,060.0	4,397.0	6,864.0
R&D Expenses		1,033.0	1,240.0	1,734.0	2,909.0
Other Operating Expenses		29.0	51.0	106.0	154.0
Other Operating Expenses, Total		**3,481.0**	**4,351.0**	**6,237.0**	**9,927.0**
Operating Income		**789.0**	**1,180.0**	**1,406.0**	**862.0**
Interest Expense		−71.0	−34.0	−39.0	−65.0
Interest and Investment Income		83.0	37.0	51.0	61.0
Net Interest Expense		**12.0**	**3.0**	**12.0**	**−4.0**
Income (Loss) on Equity Investments		−9.0	−6.0	7.0	−12.0
Currency Exchange Gains (Loss)		23.0	26.0	75.0	64.0
Other Non-Operating Income (Expenses)		22.0	−1.0	3.0	8.0
Ebt, Excluding Unusual Items		**837.0**	**1,202.0**	**1,503.0**	**918.0**
Gain (Loss) on Sale of Investments		2.0	4.0	1.0	4.0
Gain (Loss) on Sale of Assets		53.0	—	—	—
Other Unusual Items, Total		—	−51.0	—	—
Legal Settlements		—	−51.0	—	—
EBT, Including Unusual Items		**892.0**	**1,155.0**	**1,504.0**	**922.0**
Income Tax Expense		247.0	253.0	352.0	291.0
Earnings from Continuing Operations		645.0	902.0	1,152.0	631.0
Net Income		**645.0**	**902.0**	**1,152.0**	**631.0**
Net Income to Common Including Extra Items		**645.0**	**902.0**	**1,152.0**	**631.0**
Net Income to Common Excluding Extra Items		**645.0**	**902.0**	**1,152.0**	**631.0**

EXHIBIT 4b Balance Sheet

Balance Sheet Currency in Millions of US Dollars	As of:	Dec 31 2008	Dec 31 2009	Dec 31 2010	Dec 31 2011
Assets					
Cash and Equivalents		2,769.0	3,444.0	3,777.0	5,269.0
Short-Term Investments		958.0	2,922.0	4,985.0	4,307.0
Total Cash And Short Term Investments		**3,727.0**	**6,366.0**	**8,762.0**	**9,576.0**
Accounts Receivable		827.0	988.0	1,587.0	2,571.0
Total Receivables		**827.0**	**988.0**	**1,587.0**	**2,571.0**
Inventory		1,399.0	2,171.0	3,202.0	4,992.0
Deferred Tax Assets, Current		204.0	272.0	196.0	351.0
Total Current Assets		**6,157.0**	**9,797.0**	**13,747.0**	**17,490.0**
Gross Property Plant and Equipment		1,078.0	1,517.0	2,769.0	5,143.0
Accumulated Depreciation		−396.0	−418.0	−587.0	−1,075.0

EXHIBIT 4b *(Continued)*

Balance Sheet Currency in Millions of US Dollars	As of:	Dec 31 2008	Dec 31 2009	Dec 31 2010	Dec 31 2011
Net Property Plant And Equipment		682.0	1,099.0	2,182.0	4,068.0
Goodwill		438.0	1,234.0	1,349.0	1,955.0
Deferred Tax Assets, Long Term		145.0	18.0	22.0	28.0
Other Intangibles		332.0	758.0	795.0	996.0
Other Long-Term Assets		560.0	907.0	702.0	741.0
Total Assets		**8,314.0**	**13,813.0**	**18,797.0**	**25,278.0**
Liabilities & Equity					
Accounts Payable		3,594.0	5,605.0	8,051.0	11,145.0
Accrued Expenses		632.0	901.0	1,357.0	2,106.0
Current Portion of Long-Term Debt/Capital Lease		59.0	—	—	395.0
Current Portion of Capital Lease Obligations		—	—	—	395.0
Unearned Revenue, Current		461.0	858.0	964.0	1,250.0
Total Current Liabilities		**4,746.0**	**7,364.0**	**10,372.0**	**14,896.0**
Long-Term Debt		409.0	109.0	184.0	255.0
Capital Leases		124.0	143.0	457.0	1,160.0
Other Non-Current Liabilities		363.0	940.0	920.0	1,210.0
Total Liabilities		**5,642.0**	**8,556.0**	**11,933.0**	**17,521.0**
Common Stock		4.0	5.0	5.0	5.0
Additional Paid in Capital		4,121.0	5,736.0	6,325.0	6,990.0
Retained Earnings		−730.0	172.0	1,324.0	1,955.0
Treasury Stock		−600.0	−600.0	−600.0	−877.0
Comprehensive Income and Other		−123.0	−56.0	−190.0	−316.0
Total Common Equity		**2,672.0**	**5,257.0**	**6,864.0**	**7,757.0**
Total Equity		**2,672.0**	**5,257.0**	**6,864.0**	**7,757.0**
Total Liabilities and Equity		**8,314.0**	**13,813.0**	**18,797.0**	**25,278.0**

Massachusetts Governor Deval Patrick may require Amazon.com to start collecting sales tax on purchases made in Massachusetts, a move that would raise prices for online shoppers, but generate as much as $45 million in annual revenue for the state, according to several people briefed on the matter. Traditional shop owners say Amazon's exemption has put them at a competitive disadvantage by providing online customers with a built-in discount. Other states grappling with deficits have looked to Amazon, the world's largest Internet retailer, as a source of additional revenue. Last week, the Seattle-based company said it would begin collecting and paying state sales tax in New Jersey, and the merchant recently struck deals to do the same in Indiana, Nevada, South Carolina, Tennessee, and Virginia. Amazon—which for years resisted such efforts—has offices, distribution centers, or other operations in all of those states. (June 6, 2012)

In 2012 reports had it that Amazon was making deals to collect sales tax in all 50 states so that it could open warehouses near population centers and provide same-day delivery, a major shift in its business model that would ratchet up competition with big box stores like Best Buy and Target as well as local retailers. However, there were no guarantees of the profitability of same-day delivery given the added warehouse and delivery costs.

2. With the new social trend of "buying local," Amazon faced the threat of some regular consumers preferring to buy from their local stores rather than from an online retailer.[20]

3. Amazon always had to grapple with the threat of customer preference for instant gratification, customer desire to get a product immediately in the store, rather than waiting several days for the product to be shipped to them.

4. Breaches of security from outside parties trying to gain access to its information or data were a continual threat for Amazon.[21] As of 2012, Amazon had systems and processes in place that were designed to counter such attempts; however, failure to maintain these systems or processes could be detrimental to the operations of the company.

5. As more media products were sold in digital formats, Amazon's relatively low-cost physical warehouses and distribution capabilities no longer provided the same competitive advantages. In addition, Amazon had felt that its worldwide free shipping offers and Amazon Prime were effective worldwide marketing tools and intended to offer them indefinitely, yet it began to suffer from soaring shipping expenses cutting into profits. In quarter three of 2011, Amazon's shipping fees generated $360 million in revenue, which was dwarfed by $918 million in shipping expenses.

6. Amazon had to contend with absorbing losses from its unsuccessful ventures such as its A9 search engine, Amazon Auctions, and Unbox, Amazon's original video-on-demand service.

7. Recent hires from Microsoft, Robert Williams, former senior program manager, and Brandon Watson, head of Windows Phone development, prompted speculation that Amazon was developing a smartphone, possibly a Kindle-branded device. Bloomberg reported that Amazon had gone so far as to strike a manufacturing deal with Foxconn, the controversial Taiwanese company responsible for assembling Apple's iPhone and Google Android devices. Amazon has not commented on the reports. A smartphone would have given Amazon another mobile device to sell, but some analysts felt it wouldn't have made sense for Amazon to enter into the already crowded smartphone arena. "Since tablets skew more heavily toward media consumption than smartphones, they are a natural fit for Amazon's commerce and media platform," said Baird & Co. analyst Colin Sebastian in a research note. "In contrast, smartphones require specialized native apps (e.g., maps, voice, search, e-mail) that would be costly for Amazon to replicate." Sebastian also noted that hardware is a low-margin business. Amazon's Kindle Fire sold for $199, a price that some analysts believed was below cost, suggesting Amazon hoped the Kindle Fire would more than pay for itself by boosting sales of e-books and other digital content.[22]

33 Thus, by 2012 Amazon had proved itself as a retail giant, yet as with any vibrant company, faced continual challenges, particularly regarding the overarching questions of whether to spend its money developing media products such as the Kindle smartphone, or to stick with its strengths as an online retailer, perhaps acquiring more holdings such as Zappos, and pushing for same-day delivery despite the added cost to compete with other online retailers and with the big box stores as well.

[20]John Tozzi. "To Beat Recession, Indies Launch Buy-Local Push." *Businessweek.* Bloomberg L.P., February 2009. http://www.businessweek.com/smallbiz/content/feb2009/sb20090226_752622.htm
[21]Amazon.com. *2010 Annual Report.* P. 15. April 2011.
[22]Colin Sebastian, Senior Research Analyst, Baird 2012 *Research Note on Amazon.com.*

34 By 2012, Bezos had assembled a small, experienced leadership team to help him take Amazon to become the world's largest retailer. Those members of his leadership team are described in Exhibit 5. They soon found that Amazon was at a crossroads. It needed to decide if it should invest in the infrastructure for same-day delivery and take on local retailers, or invest in high technology and compete at a deeper level with Sony, Apple, and Samsung.

EXHIBIT 5 **Corporate Officers and Board of Directors**

Corporate Officers

Jeffrey P. Bezos
President, Chief Executive Officer and Chairman of the Board

Jeff Bezos founded Amazon.com in 1994. Amazon's mission is to be Earth's most customer-centric company. Amazon offers low prices and fast delivery on millions of items, designs and builds the best-selling Kindle hardware, and empowers companies and governments in over 190 countries around the world with the leading cloud computing infrastructure through its Amazon Web Services offering. Bezos is also the founder of aerospace company Blue Origin, which is working to lower the cost and increase the safety of space flight so that humans can better continue exploring the solar system.

Bezos graduated summa cum laude, Phi Beta Kappa in electrical engineering and computer science from Princeton University in 1986 and was named TIME Magazine's Person of the Year in 1999.

Senior Vice President, Business Development
Jeffrey M. Blackburn

Mr. Blackburn has served as Senior Vice President, Business Development, since April 2006. From June 2004 to April 2006, he was Vice President, Business Development; from July 2003 to June 2004, he was Vice President, European Customer Service; and from November 2002 to July 2003, he was Vice President, Operations Integration.

Sebastian J. Gunningham
Senior Vice President, Seller Services

Senior Vice President, Amazon Web Services
Andrew R. Jassy

Andy Jassy leads the Amazon Web Services business (AWS) and the Technology Infrastructure organization for Amazon.com. AWS is a subsidiary of Amazon.com that provides software developers and businesses with cloud-based infrastructure services that are inexpensive, reliable, scalable, comprehensive, and flexible.

Senior Vice President, Worldwide Digital Media
Steven Kessel

Mr. Kessel has served as Senior Vice President, Worldwide Digital Media, since April 2006. From April 2004 to April 2006, he was Vice President, Digital and from July 2002 to April 2004, he was Vice President, U.S. Books, Music, Video, and DVD. Prior to joining Amazon.com in 1999, Mr. Kessel was a consultant to Internet companies.

Kessel received his bachelor's degree in computer science from Dartmouth College and an MBA from Stanford's Graduate School of Business.

Senior Vice President, Worldwide Operations
Marc A. Onetto

(Continued)

EXHIBIT 5 *(Continued)*

Mr. Onetto has served as Senior Vice President, Worldwide Operations, since joining Amazon.com in December 2006. Prior to joining Amazon.com, Mr. Onetto was Executive Vice President, Worldwide Operations, at Solectron Corporation, an electronics manufacturing and technology company, from June 2003 to June 2006, and, prior to Solectron, he held various positions at GE, including Vice President, European Operations, GE Europe.

Senior Vice President, International Consumer Business
Diego Piacentini

Mr. Piacentini has served as Senior Vice President, International Consumer Business, since February 2012. From January 2007 until February 2012, Mr. Piacentini served as Senior Vice President, International Retail, and from November 2001 until December 2006, he served as Senior Vice President, Worldwide Retail and Marketing.

Vice President, Worldwide Controller and Principal Accounting Officer
Shelley L. Reynolds

Ms. Reynolds has served as Vice President, Worldwide Controller, and Principal Accounting Officer since April 2007. From February 2006 to April 2007, she was Vice President, Finance and Controller.

Senior Vice President and Chief Financial Officer
Thomas J. Szkutak

After more than 20 years with GE, Mr. Szkutak joined Amazon.com in October 2002 to serve as the company's chief financial officer and senior vice president. As CFO he oversees the company's overall financial activities, including controllership, tax, treasury, analysis, investor relations, internal audit, and financial operations.

Before joining Amazon.com, Szkutak served as CFO for GE Lighting.

Senior Vice President, Ecommerce Platform
H. Brian Valentine

Mr. Valentine has served as Senior Vice President, E-commerce Platform since joining Amazon.com in September 2006. Prior to joining Amazon.com, Mr. Valentine held various positions with Microsoft Corporation, including Senior Vice President, Windows Core Operating System Division, from January 2004 to September 2006 and Senior Vice President, Windows, from December 1999 to January 2004.

Senior Vice President, Consumer Business

Jeffrey A. Wilke

Mr. Wilke has served as Senior Vice President, Consumer Business, since February 2012. From January 2007 until February 2012, Mr. Wilke served as Senior Vice President, North American Retail, and from January 2002 until December 2006, he was Senior Vice President, Worldwide Operations. Jeff Wilke joined Amazon.com as Vice President and General Manager, Operations in September, 1999.

Senior Vice President, General Counsel, Secretary

L. Michelle Wilson

Ms. Wilson joined Amazon.com in March 1999 as Associate General Counsel for finance and mergers and acquisitions. In July 1999, Michelle was promoted to become Amazon.com's Vice President and General Counsel, overseeing all legal and policy affairs. Michelle also serves as the Corporate Secretary.

EXHIBIT 5 *(Continued)*

Board of Directors

Jeffrey P. Bezos
President, Chief Executive Officer, and Chairman of the Board

Jeffrey P. Bezos has been Chairman of the Board since founding the Company in 1994 and Chief Executive Officer since May 1996. Mr. Bezos served as President from founding until June 1999 and again from October 2000 to the present.

Tom A. Alberg
Madrona Venture Group

John Seely Brown
Visiting Scholar and Advisor to the Provost at USC

William B. (Bing) Gordon
Kleiner Perkins Caufield & Byers

Jamie S. Gorelick
Wilmer Cutler Pickering Hale and Dorr LLP

Blake G. Krikorian
id8 Group Productions, Inc.

Alain Monié
Ingram Micro Inc.

Jonathan Rubinstein
Former Chairman and CEO, Palm, Inc.

Thomas O. Ryder
Former Chairman and CEO, Reader's Digest Association, Inc.

Patricia Q. Stonesifer
Smithsonian Institution

Case 11

Apple v. Samsung: *Intellectual Property and the Smartphone Patent Wars*[1]

It is unfortunate that patent law can be manipulated to give one company a monopoly over rectangles with rounded corners, or technology that is being improved every day by Samsung and other companies.

—Official Statement by Samsung Electronics[2]

We value originality and innovation and pour our lives into making the best products on earth. And we do this to delight our customers, not for competitors to flagrantly copy.

—Memo to Apple employees from Tim Cook, CEO of Apple, Inc.[3]

1   On August 24, 2012, Apple, Inc. (Apple) chief executive officer (CEO) Tim Cook sent a memo to the company's 12,000 employees in Cupertino, California, celebrating the successful outcome of the company's patent infringement case against Samsung Electronics (Samsung) (see Exhibit 1). Earlier in the day, a San Francisco jury awarded $1.05 billion to Apple for Samsung's willful copying of Apple's iPhone and iPad. "For us, this lawsuit has always been about something much more important than patents or money," explained Cook. "It's about values."[4]

2   Meanwhile, more than 5,000 miles away in Seoul, South Korea, Samsung's leadership was in crisis. "This is absolutely the worst-case scenario for us," said one executive, after the unexpected verdict.[5] Samsung's head of corporate strategy, Choi Gee-sung, called a

Source: David Wesley wrote this case under the supervision of Professors Gloria Barczak and Susan Montgomery solely to provide material for class discussion. The authors do not intend to illustrate either effective or ineffective handling of a managerial situation. The authors may have disguised certain names and other identifying information to protect confidentiality.

This publication may not be transmitted, photocopied, digitized or otherwise reproduced in any form or by any means without the permission of Ivey Publishing, the exclusive representative of the copyright holder. Reproduction of this material is not covered under authorization by any reproduction rights organization. To order copies or request permission to reproduce materials, contact Ivey Publishing, Ivey Business School, Western University, London, Ontario, Canada, N6G 0N1; (t) 519.661.3208; (e) cases@ivey.ca; www.iveycases.com.

Copyright © 2013, Northeastern University, D'Amore-McKim School of Business   Version: 2013-04-30

Richard Ivey School of Business
The University of Western Ontario

IVEY

[1]This case has been written on the basis of published sources only. Consequently, the interpretation and perspectives presented in this case are not necessarily those of Apple, Inc., Samsung Electronics or any of their employees.
[2]Sam Kim, "Eric Schmidt Defends Google, Mourns Jobs' Death," *Associated Press*, November 8, 2011, http://finance.yahoo.com/news/Eric-Schmidt-defends-Google-apf-1664680727.html, accessed September 21, 2012.
[3]Mark Gurman, "Tim Cook Tells Apple Employees That Today's Victory 'Is about Values'," *9-to-5Mac*, August 24, 2012, http://allthingsd.com/20120824/wall-street-reacts-to-apples-legal-win-over-samsung-maybe-lets-not-kill-all-the-lawyers/, accessed October 17, 2012.
[4]Ibid.
[5]Yoo-chiu Kim, "Samsung Scrambles to Recover after Uppercut," *Korea Times*, August 26, 2012, http://www.koreatimes.co.kr/www/news/opinon/2012/08/133_118242.html, accessed October 17, 2012.

EXHIBIT 1   Memo from Tim Cook, CEO of Apple, Inc., to Apple Employees

To:	Undisclosed Recipients
From:	Tim Cook
CC:	
Date:	8/24/2012
Re:	Verdict
Comments:	Today was an important day for Apple and for innovators everywhere.

Many of you have been closely following the trial against Samsung in San Jose for the past few weeks. We chose legal action very reluctantly and only after repeatedly asking Samsung to stop copying our work. For us this lawsuit has always been about something much more important than patents or money. It's about values. We value originality and innovation and pour our lives into making the best products on earth. And we do this to delight our customers, not for competitors to flagrantly copy.

We owe a debt of gratitude to the jury who invested their time in listening to our story. We were thrilled to finally have the opportunity to tell it. The mountain of evidence presented during the trial showed that Samsung's copying went far deeper than we knew.

The jury has now spoken. We applaud them for finding Samsung's behavior willful and for sending a loud and clear message that stealing isn't right.

I am very proud of the work that each of you do.

Today, values have won and I hope the whole world listens.

Tim

Source: Replica of the original memo as described in Mark Gurman, "Tim Cook Tells Apple Employees That Today's Victory 'Is about Values'," *9-to-5 Mac*, August 24, 2012, http://9to5mac.com/2012/08/24/tim-cook-tells-apple-employees-that-todays-victory-is-about-values/, accessed October 17, 2012.

meeting with the head of the company's mobile division, Shin Jong-kyun, and the head of marketing, Lee Don-joo, to plan the company's next move. One option was to appeal the case to U.S. Supreme Court, arguing that "the verdict was based on protectionism."[6]

BACKGROUND

I will spend my last dying breath if I need to, and I will spend every penny of Apple's $40 billion in the bank, to right this wrong. I'm going to destroy Android.

—Steve Jobs, March 2010[7]

[6]Ibid.
[7]Walter Isaacson, *Steve Jobs*, Simon & Schuster, New York, 2011, p. 251.

3 In recent years, spending on smartphone patent litigation and acquisition of intellectual property rights reached an estimated $10 billion[8] per year. In 2011, Apple and Google spent more on lawsuits than on research and development.[9] Such situations led federal appeals court justice Richard Allen Posner to make the following comment about patents:

> They are not an ideal solution to the problem [of creating adequate incentives for invention]; instead they are part of the problem. Although they are supposed to be limited to inventions that are novel, useful, and non-obvious, they are granted rather promiscuously by the Patent and Trademark Office. And while they can be challenged in court, jurors tend to be biased in favor of patent holders. That is one reason that even a patent granted for a minor invention of little value can be a potent competitive weapon. Patent "trolls," as they are called, purchase large numbers of patents in the hope of using the threat of a patent-infringement suit to extort a patent-license fee from a company that makes a similar product; the product may or may not infringe, which is often very difficult to determine, but the alleged infringer may decide to pay the licensee fee, if it is not too large, to avoid the cost of litigation.[10]

4 In response to such criticism, United States Patent and Trademark Office Director David Kappos retorted that critics of the patent system were engaging in "flippant rhetoric" instead of "thoughtful discussion."[11]

5 Apple had been involved in dozens of lawsuits over intellectual property. Recently, it had become embroiled in legal disputes with most of its competitors, including Motorola, HTC, Amazon, Google and Nokia, in what had become known as "the smartphone wars" (see Exhibit 2). However, Apple was reluctant to take legal action against Samsung, given its key role in supplying chips and components that made up as much as 26 percent of the manufacturing cost of the iPhone.[12] In 2010, Apple purchased a total of $6 billion in components from Samsung, which accounted for 4 percent of Samsung's total revenue.[13]

6 In August 2010, Steve Jobs and Tim Cook contacted their counterparts at Samsung to express concerns that Samsung's adoption of the Android mobile phone operating system violated several Apple software patents. They followed up by sending a team of Apple attorneys to Korea to meet with Samsung's legal team and express their dismay that "a trusted partner could build a copycat product."[14]

7 Apple was particularly concerned about the Samsung Galaxy S smartphone, a product that closely mirrored the iPhone in appearance and function (see Exhibit 3). In a PowerPoint presentation titled "Samsung's Use of Apple Patents in Smartphones," Apple's legal team showed their Samsung counterparts side-by-side pictures of the iPhone and Galaxy S

[8]All currency amounts are shown in U.S. dollars unless otherwise noted.
[9]Charles Duhigg and Steve Lohr, "The Patent, Used as a Sword," *The New York Times*, October 8, 2012, p. A1.
[10]Richard A. Posner, "Patent Trolls Be Gone," *Slate*, October 15, 2012, http://www.slate.com/articles/news_and_politics/view_from_chicago/2012/10/patent_protection_how_to_fix_it.html, accessed November 23, 2012.
[11]David Kappos, "An Examination of Software Patents," Address at the Center for American Progress, Washington, DC, November 20, 2012, http://www.uspto.gov/news/speeches/2012/kappos_CAP.jsp, accessed November 26, 2012.
[12]Miyoung Kim, "Analysis: Friend and Foe; Samsung, Apple Won't Want to Damage Parts Deal," *Reuters*, August 27, 2012, http://www.reuters.com/article/2012/08/27/us-samsung-apple-supply-idUSBRE87Q06N20120827, accessed October 11, 2012.
[13]Yukari Iwatane Kane and Ian Sherr, "Apple: Samsung Copied Design," *The Wall Street Journal*, April 19, 2011, http://online.wsj.com/article/SB10001424052748703916004576271210109389154.html, accessed October 11, 2012.
[14]Philip Elmer-Dewitt, "Steve Jobs Offered Samsung Apple's Crown Jewels for $250M," *CNNMoney*, August 11, 2012, http://tech.fortune.cnn.com/2012/08/11/steve-jobs-offered-samsung-apples-crown-jewels-for-250m/, accessed March 21, 2013.

EXHIBIT 2 Smartphone Patent and Trademark Lawsuits

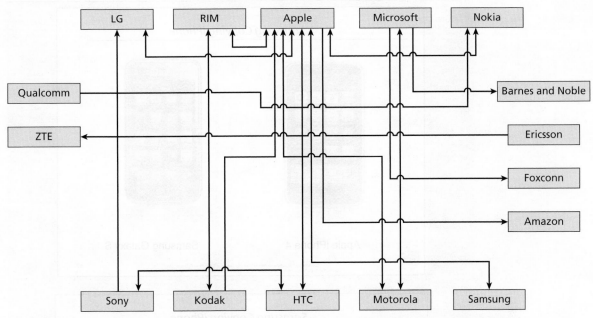

Note: The above chart was compiled by the case writers from multiple sources. It reflects a sample of the many cases filed in the "smartphone patent wars." Space did not permit a complete listing of lawsuits involving software and hardware component suppliers, such as Gemalto, Interdigital, Pantech, and Open Wave, to name a few.
Sources: Forbes, Reuters, news reports

EXHIBIT 3 Mobile phone Timeline, 2005–2011

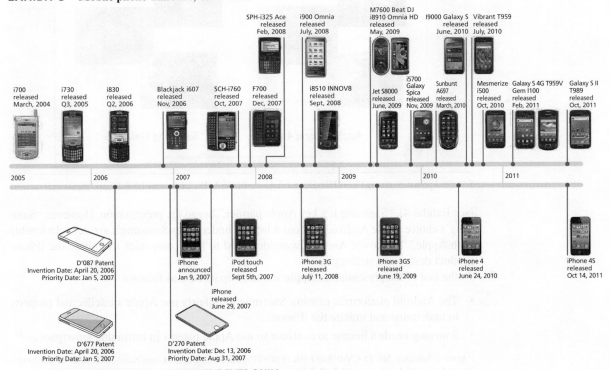

HIGHLY CONFIDENTIAL - ATTORNEYS EYES ONLY
Source: Apple v. Samsung Court Filings, case 5:11-cv-01846-LHK, Document 1570-2, p. 14.

EXHIBIT 4   **Apple PowerPoint Presentation to Samsung, August 2010**

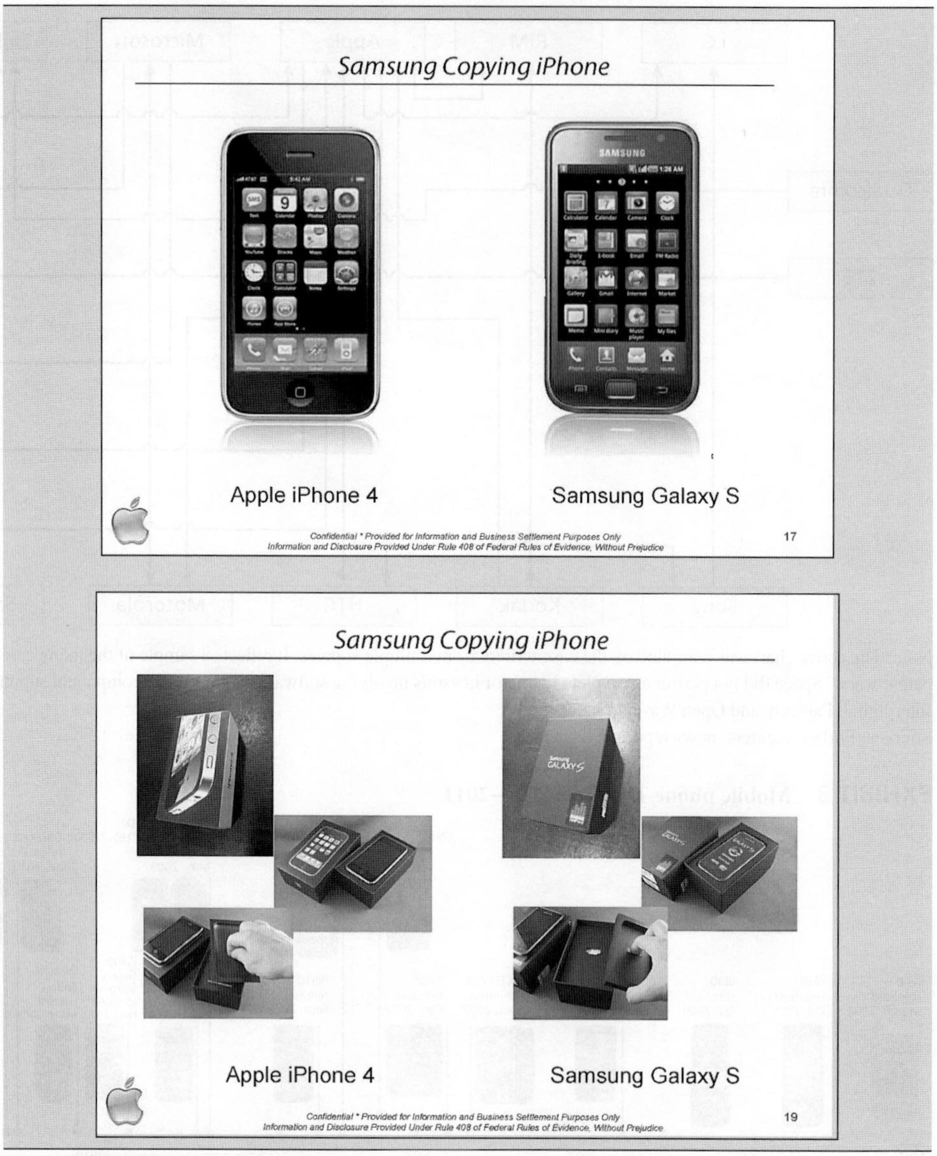

Source: Apple v. Samsung Court Filings, case 5:11-cv-01846-LHK, Document 1988-18, pp. 18, 20.

(see Exhibit 4). "Samsung is a key Apple partner," began the presentation. However, "Samsung's choice to use Android without a license undermines Samsung's greater relationship with Apple." Moreover, Android was "designed to lead companies to imitate the iPhone product design and strategy."

8   At the end of the presentation, Apple summed up its case as follows:

- The Android platform is causing Samsung to unfairly use Apple's intellectual property to undermine and imitate the iPhone.

- Samsung needs a license to continue to use Apple patents in infringing smartphones.[15]

[15]*Apple v. Samsung*, No. 11-CV-01846-LHK (PSG) (United States District Court Northern District of California 2012), Plaintiff's Exhibit No. 52.2, filed September 21, 2012.

9 Apple was also troubled by Samsung's plans to introduce a tablet similar to the iPad in late 2010. The Galaxy Tab, a 10-inch Android-based tablet computer so closely resembled Apple's iPad that more than half the consumers who saw the device mistook it for an Apple product, while only 16 percent recognized it as a Samsung product, according to Samsung market research conducted in January 2011.[16] After failing to reach a cross-licensing agreement, Samsung released the Galaxy Tab, and Apple filed a patent infringement suit against Samsung in a San Jose, California, federal court in April 2011.

Apple v. Samsung

10 Apple's intellectual property strategy developed out of a decade-old conflict with Singapore-based Creative Technology (Creative) over Creative's patent for "a portable music playback device," commonly known today as an MP3 player. When Apple launched the iPod in late 2001, Creative sued for patent infringement. The companies eventually settled for $100 million, but Jobs had vowed to become more protective of his company's intellectual property. When Apple began development on the iPhone, Jobs called a meeting with his senior management team and told them, "we're going to patent it all."[17] From that point on, patents would become a critical piece of Apple's competitive strategy.

11 In its initial petition to the U.S. District Court, Apple argued that "Samsung [had] chosen to slavishly copy Apple's innovative technology," thus infringing on Apple's intellectual property (IP) and diminishing the company's image as a product and design innovator in the minds of consumers. As noted in Apple's statement, not only had Samsung copied the overall look and feel of the iPhone but it had also copied other design features, from the retail packaging to the icons used to represent software applications:

> Of significant concern for Apple is that Apple devotes a tremendous amount of resources—technical research and development and design resources—to develop its cutting edge products. Part of the cachet of Apple products is the very fact that they consistently stand out from all of the other products on the market. Apple's goodwill among consumers is closely tied to its position as an outlier in technology and communications products, which causes each release of a new product to be highly anticipated among consumers who want to be among the early adopters of the newest Apple product.
>
> Samsung's flagrant and relentless copying of Apple's intellectual property rights in its Galaxy family of products not only allows Samsung to reap benefits from Apple's investment, it also threatens to diminish the very important goodwill that Apple has cultivated with its products.[18]

12 Samsung likewise claimed that the iPhone had borrowed heavily from Samsung's own innovations, included patented technologies "for transmission optimization and reduction of power usage during data transmission, 3G technology for reducing data-transmission errors and a method of tethering a mobile phone to a PC to enable the PC to utilize the phone's wireless data connection."[19] In its defense, Samsung asserted that many of the iPhone's design features were obvious and that many of Apple's patents should never have been granted.

13 In the same lawsuit, Samsung counterclaimed for infringement of its patents based on Apple's unlicensed use of its technology. Whereas Apple's claims focused on the user

---

[16]Greg Sandoval and Josh Lowensohn, "Samsung Studies Show People Confused Galaxy Tab with iPad," *CNet News*, August 8, 2012, http://news.cnet.com/8301-13579_3-57489289-37/samsung-studies-show-people-confused-galaxy-tab-with-ipad/, accessed October 11, 2012.
[17]Charles Duhigg and Steve Lohr, "The Patent, Used as a Sword," *The New York Times*, October 8, 2012, p. A1.
[18]*Apple v. Samsung*, No. sf-2981926 (United States District Court Northern District of California 2011), pp. 24–25.
[19]Evan Ramstad, "Samsung Sues Apple on Patents," *The Wall Street Journal*, April 22, 2011, http://online.wsj.com/article/SB10001424052748703983704576277863329446914.html, accessed October 11, 2012.

interface, appearance and overall look and feel of its products, Samsung focused more on technical features that improved functionality, but were not immediately apparent to end users. The claims and counterclaims were primarily in three broad categories, namely utility patents, design patents and trademarks.

Utility Patents

14   When the average person thought about patents, what typically came to mind were utility patents. Utility patents covered inventions of new, useful devices, processes and materials. Familiar examples included computers, pharmaceuticals and light bulbs. For a particular electronic device, one or more utility patents could cover the useful, functional features and method of using the device. Each utility patent gave the holder the right to exclude others from making, selling or using the invention for a period of 20 years from the date of the application.

15   A patent did not address what the patent owner could do, but what the owner could prevent others from doing—namely, infringing the claims in the patent. In a patent application to the U.S. Patent Office, the inventor was required to describe the invention in detail, typically through a combination of explanatory text, drawings and specific claims. The applicant was also required to identify any relevant, preexisting technology (i.e., any "prior art") and to respond to an examiner's questions and grounds for rejecting the application.

16   Apple claimed that Samsung had infringed on several utility patents, including U.S. Patent No. 7,469,381, titled "List scrolling and document translation, scaling, and rotation on a touch-screen display." This patent was 62 pages long and contained 20 claims, 38 diagrams and more than 20,000 words of text (see Exhibit 5 for an excerpt).

EXHIBIT 5   First and Last Two Pages of U.S. Patent No. 7,469,381

US007469381B2

(12) **United States Patent** Ording	(10) **Patent No.: US 7,469,381 B2** (45) **Dale of Patent: Dec. 23, 2008**
(54) **LIST SCROLLING AND DOCUMENT TRANSLA-TION, SCALING, AND ROTATION ON A TOUCH-SCREEN DISPLAY**	(51) **Int. Cl.** *G06F 3/01* (2006.01)
(75) Inventor: **Bas Ording**, San Francisco, CA (US)	(52) **U.S. Cl.......................................715/702**;715/764; 715/863; 715/864; 715/769

(73) Assignee: **Apple Inc.**, Cupertino, CA (US)	(58) **Field of Classification Search**............... 715/764,
	          715/769, 702, 863, 864
	     See application file for complete search history.

(*) Notice: Subject to any disclaimer, the term of this patent is extended or adjusted under 35 U.S.C. 154(b) by 0 days.	(56) **References Cited** U.S. PATENT DOCUMENTS
(21) Appl. No.: **11/956,969**	5,495,566 A 2/1996 Kwatinetz............... 395/157
(22) Filed: **Dec. 14, 2007**	5,844,547 A 12/1998 Minakuchi et al. 345/173
(65) **Prior Publication Data** US 2008/0168404 A1 Jul. 10, 2008	5,867,158 A 2/1999 Murasaki et al. ....345/341 6,034,688 A 3/2000 Greenwood et al. 345/353
Related U.S. Application Data	6,489,951 B1 12/2002 Wong et al. 345/173

(60) Provisional application No. 60/937,993, filed on Jun. 29, 2007, provisional application No. 60/946,971 filed on Jun. 28, 2007, provisional application No. 60/945,858, filed on Jun. 22, 2007, provisional application No. 60/879,469, filed on Jan. 8, 2007, provisional application No. 60/883,801, filed on Jan. 7, 2007, provisional application No. 60/879,253, filed on Jan. 7, 2007.	6,567,102 B2 5/2003 Kung 345/660
	
	          (Continued)
	
	     FOREIGN PATENT DOCUMENTS
	 EP 0 635 779 A1 1/1995
	
	          (Continued)
	
	     OTHER PUBLICATIONS
	 Microsoft Word 2003 Screen Shots.*

(Continued)

EXHIBIT 5 *(Continued)*

(Continued)

Primary Examiner—Boris Pesin

(74) *Attorney, Agent, or Firm*—Morgan, Lewis & Bockius LLP

(57) **ABSTRACT**

In accordance with some embodiments, a computer-implemented method for use in conjunction with a device with a touch screen display is disclosed. In the method, a movement of an object on or near the touch screen display is detected. In response to detecting the movement, an electronic document displayed on the touch screen display is translated in a first direction. If an edge of the electronic document is reached while translating the electronic document in the first direction while the object is still detected on or near the touch screen display, an area beyond the edge of the document is displayed. After the object is no longer detected on or near the touch screen display, the document is translated in a second direction until the area beyond the edge of the document is no longer displayed.

20 Claims, 38 Drawing Sheets

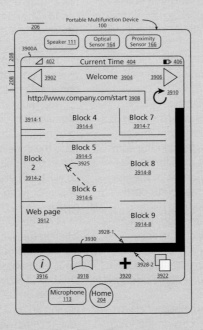

U.S. PATENT NO. 7,469,381 (CLAIMS)

35

programs, modules, and data structures analogous to the programs, modules, and data structures stored in the memory **102** of portable multifunction device **100** (FIG. **1**), or a subset thereof. Furthermore, memory **1770** may store additional programs, modules, and data structures (not shown) not present in the memory **102** of portable multifunction device **100**.

Each of the above identified elements in FIG. **17** may be stored in one or more of the previously mentioned memory devices. Each of the above identified modules corresponds to a set of instructions for performing a function described above. The above identified modules or programs (i.e., sets of instructions) need not be implemented as separate software programs, procedures or modules, and thus various subsets of these modules may be combined or otherwise re-arranged in various embodiments. In some embodiments, memory **1770** may store a subset of the modules and data structures identified above. Furthermore, memory **1770** may store additional modules and data structures not described above.

The foregoing description, for purpose of explanation, has been described with reference to specific embodiments. However, the illustrative discussions above are not intended to be exhaustive or to limit the invention to the precise forms disclosed. Many modifications and variations are possible in view of the above teachings. The embodiments were chosen and described in order to best explain the principles of the invention and its practical applications, to thereby enable others skilled in the art to best utilize the invention and various embodiments with various modifications as are suited to the particular use contemplated.

What is claimed is:

1. A computer-implemented method, comprising:
at a device with a touch screen display:

EXHIBIT 5   *(Continued)*

displaying a first portion of an electronic document; 35
detecting a movement of an object on or near the
    touch screen display;
in response to detecting the movement, translat-
    ing the electronic document displayed on the
    touch screen display in a first direction to display 40
    a second portion of the electronic document,
    wherein the second portion is different from the
    first portion;
in response to an edge of the electronic document
    being reached while translating the electronic 45
    document in the first direction while the object is
    still detected on or near the touch screen display:
    displaying an area beyond the edge of the docu-
        ment, and
    displaying, a third portion of the electronic docu- 50
        ment, wherein the third portion is smaller
        than the first portion; and
    in response to detecting that the object is no
        longer on or near the touch screen display,
        translating the electronic document in a sec- 55
        ond direction until the area beyond the edge
        of the electronic document is no longer dis-
        played to display a fourth portion of the elec-
        tronic document, wherein the fourth portion
        is different from the first portion. 60

2. The computer-implemented method of claim
1, wherein the first portion of the electronic document, the second portion of the electronic document,
the third portion of the electronic document, and the
fourth portion of the electronic document are displayed 65
at the same magnification.

3. The computer-implemented method of claim
1, wherein the movement of the object is on the touch
screen display.

4. The computer-implemented method of claim **1**, 70
wherein the object is a finger.

36

5. The computer-implemented method of claim **1**,
wherein the first direction is a vertical direction, a horizontal direction, or a diagonal direction.

6. The computer-implemented method of claim **1**,
wherein the electronic document is a web page.

7. The computer-implemented method of claim **1**,
wherein the electronic document is a digital image.

8. The computer-implemented method of claim **1**,
wherein the electronic document is a word processing,
spreadsheet, email or presentation document.

9. The computer-implemented method of claim
1, wherein the electronic document includes a list of
items.

10. The computer-implemented method of claim **1**,
wherein the second direction is opposite the first
direction.

11. The computer-implemented method of claim **1**,
wherein translating in the first direction prior lo reaching an edge of the document has an associated speed
of translation that corresponds to a speed of movement of the object.

12. The computer-implemented method of claim
1, wherein translating in the first direction is in accordance with a simulation of an equation of motion having friction.

13. The computer-implemented method of claim **1**,
wherein the area beyond the edge of the document is
black, gray, a solid color, or white.

14. The computer-implemented method of claim **1**,
wherein the area beyond the edge of the document is
visually distinct from the document.

15. The computer-implemented method of claim **1**,
wherein translating the document in the second direction is a damped motion.

16. The computer-implemented method or claim **1**,
wherein changing from translating in the first direction
to translating in the second direction until the area beyond the edge of the document is no longer displayed
makes the edge of the electronic document appear to
be elastically attached to an edge of the touch screen
display or to an edge displayed on the touch screen
display.

17. The computer-implemented method of claim **1**,
wherein translating in the first direction prior to reaching the edge of the electronic document has a first
associated translating distance that corresponds to a
distance of movement of the object prior to reaching
the edge of the electronic document; and wherein displaying an area beyond the edge of the electronic document comprises translating the electronic document
in the first direction for a second associated translating
distance, wherein the second associated translating distance is less than a distance of movement of the object
after reaching the edge of the electronic document.

18. The computer-implemented method of claim **1**,
wherein translating in the first direction prior to reaching the edge of the electronic document has a first associated translating speed that corresponds to a speed
of movement of the object, and wherein displaying
an area beyond the edge of the electronic document
comprises translating the electronic document in the
first direction at a second associated translating speed,
wherein the second associated translating speed is
slower than the first associated translating speed.

19. A device, comprising:
a touch screen display;
one or more processors;
memory; and
one or more programs, wherein the one or
    more programs are stored in the memory and

EXHIBIT 5 *(Continued)*

configured to be executed by the one or more processors, the programs including: instructions for displaying a first portion of an electronic document;

37

instructions for detecting a movement of an object on or near the touch screen display; instructions for translating the electronic document displayed on the touch screen display in a first direction to display a second portion of the electronic document, wherein the second portion is different from the first portion, in response to detecting the movement; instructions for displaying an area beyond an edge of the electronic document and displaying a third portion of the electronic document, wherein the third portion is smaller than the first portion, in response to the edge of the electronic document being reached while translating the electronic document in the first direction while the object is still detected on or near the touch screen display; and instructions for translating the electronic document in a second direction until the area beyond the edge of the electronic document is no longer displayed to display a fourth portion of the electronic document, wherein the fourth portion is different from the first portion, in response to detecting that the object is no longer on or near the touch screen display.

20. A computer readable storage medium having stored herein instructions, which when executed by a device with a touch screen display, cause the device to:

38

display a first portion of an electronic document: detect a movement of an object on or near the touch screen display; translate the electronic document displayed on the touch screen display in a first direction to display a second portion of the electronic document, wherein the second portion is different from the first portion, in response to detecting the movement; display an area beyond an edge of the electronic document and display a third portion of the electronic document, wherein the third portion is smaller than the first portion, if the edge of the electronic document is reached while translating the electronic document in the first direction while the object is still detected on or near the touch screen display; and translate the electronic document in a second direction until the area beyond the edge of the electronic document is no longer displayed to display a fourth portion of the electronic document, wherein the fourth portion is different from the first portion, in response to detecting that the object is no longer on or near the touch screen display.

*   *   *   *   *

Source: U.S. Patent No. 7,469,381.

17   Despite the length of the patent, Apple's right to exclude Samsung from infringing patent 7,469,381 was limited to the specific claims for a particular method of causing a page to appear to bounce in the opposite direction when a user reached the end of the document, commonly referred to as the "bounce back" feature.

18   In patent infringement cases, the accused infringer could seek to avoid liability by arguing that it was not infringing the specific claims or the patent was invalid, or both. Both parties sought to invalidate the other party's utility patents, which could occur in one of four ways, as explained by Justice Koh in her instructions to the jury:

1. "A utility patent claim is invalid if the patent does not contain an adequate written description of the claimed invention."

2. The existence of "prior art": A patent was invalid if the invention was not new (see Exhibit 6).

   - Statutory bars: Patents were invalid if the application was not filed on time, which could result in several ways: "If the claimed invention was already patented or

EXHIBIT 6 Justice Koh's Jury Instructions on Prior Art

FINAL JURY INSTRUCTION NO. 31
UTILITY PATENTS—ANTICIPATION

A Utility patent claim is invalid if the claimed invention is not new. For the claim to be invalid because it is not new, all of its requirements must have existed in a single device or method that predates the claimed invention, or must have been described in a single previous publication or patent that predates the claimed invention. In patent law, these previous devices, methods, publications or patents are called "prior art references." If a patent claim is not new we say it is "anticipated" by a prior art reference.

The description in the written reference does not have to be in the same words as the claim, but all of the requirements of the claim must be there, either stated or necessarily implied, so that someone of ordinary skill in the field looking at that one reference would be able to make and use the claimed invention.

Here is a list of the ways that either party can show that a patent claim was not new:

–If the claimed invention was already publicly known or publicly used by others in the United States before the date of conception of the claimed invention;

–If the claimed invention was already patented or described in a printed publication anywhere in the world before the date of conception of the claimed invention. A reference is a "printed publication" if it is accessible to those interested in the field, even if it is difficult to find;

–If the claimed invention was already made by someone else in the United States before the date of conception of the claimed invention, if that other person had not abandoned the invention or kept it secret;

If the patent holder and the alleged infringer dispute who is a first inventor, the person who first conceived of the claimed invention and first reduced it to practice is the first inventor. If one person conceived of the claimed invention first, but reduced to practice second, that person is the first inventor only if that person (a) began to reduce the claimed invention to practice before the other party conceived of it, and (b) continued to work diligently to reduce it to practice. A claimed invention is "reduced to practice" when it has been tested sufficiently to show that it will work for its intended purpose or when it is fully described in a patent application filed with the PTO.

–If the claimed invention was already described in another issued U.S. patent or published U.S. patent application that was based on a patent application filed before the patent holder's application filing date or the date of conception of the claimed invention.

Since certain of them are in dispute, you must determine dates of conception for the claimed inventions and prior inventions. Conception is the mental part of an inventive act and is proven when the invention is shown in its complete form by drawings, disclosure to another, or other forms of evidence presented at trial.

5:11-CV-01846-LHK
FINAL JURY INSTRUCTIONS

United States District Court
For the Northern District of California

1
2
3
4
5
6
7
8
9
10
11
12
13
14
15
16
17
18
19
20
21
22
23
24
25
26
27
28

described in a printed publication anywhere in the world more than one year before the effective filing date of the patent application. . . ."

- "If the claimed invention was already being openly used in the United States more than one year before the effective filing date of the patent application. . . ."
- "If a device or method using the claimed invention was sold or offered for sale in the United States, and that claimed invention was ready for patenting, more than one year before the effective filing date of the patent application;"
- "If the patent holder had already obtained a patent on the claimed invention in a foreign country before filing the original U.S. application, and the foreign application was filed at least one year before the U.S. application."

3. If the invention was "obvious to a person of ordinary skill in the field at the time of invention."

19   An inventor could use several methods to prove that an invention was not obvious. For example, the inventor could prove that, at the time of the application, a perceived need had led others to try to invent a similar product, but they failed. Also, the commercial success of a product or the praise and recognition by others in the field were considered to be signs that an invention was not obvious. However, the absence of these conditions was not sufficient to prove that an invention was obvious. Koh pointed out that the alleged infringer must also identify "a reason that would have prompted a person of ordinary skill in the field to combine the elements or concepts from the prior art in the same way as in the claimed invention."

20   If the jury found a patent to be valid, then the patent was considered to have been infringed if the jury found that the device performed either as specifically claimed in the patent (i.e., a literal infringement) or, under the doctrine of equivalents, "as of the time of the alleged infringement, the part or software instructions [had to perform] substantially the same function, in substantially the same way, to achieve substantially the same result as the requirement in the patent claim."[20] If it did not, then no infringement had occurred.

Design Patents

21   Design patents covered both the new, original, ornamental design of a product and the decorative, non-utilitarian features of a product. Although a product could have both functional and ornamental features, the scope of a design patent was limited to the product's ornamental features. The ornamentation requirement was satisfied when the appearance of the design was not solely dictated by utilitarian necessity. A design was determined to be ornamental if it could be demonstrated that other designs could accomplish the same tasks equally well.

22   Although utility patents can have numerous, precisely worded claims, "a design patent can only have one claim," explained Justice Koh. "That claim covers all the [drawings] in the patent. . . . The scope of the claim encompasses the design's visual appearance as a whole." Rather than words, the single claim is shown in one or more drawings. For example, Apple's Patents D'677, D'087, and D'889 covered "the ornamental design of an electronic device" that would become the iPhone (see Exhibit 7).

23   As with a utility patent, Samsung could avoid liability by proving either invalidity or non-infringement, or both. Samsung sought to prove that its products did not infringe on Apple's design patents by showing the jury that the appearance of each of its Galaxy line

[20]Jury Instructions, *Apple v. Samsung*, United States District Court, Northern District of California, San Jose Division, Case 5:11-cv-01846-LHK, August 21, 2012.

EXHIBIT 7
Patent for "Ornamental Design of an Electronic Device"

Source: Patent for "ornamental design of an electronic device"

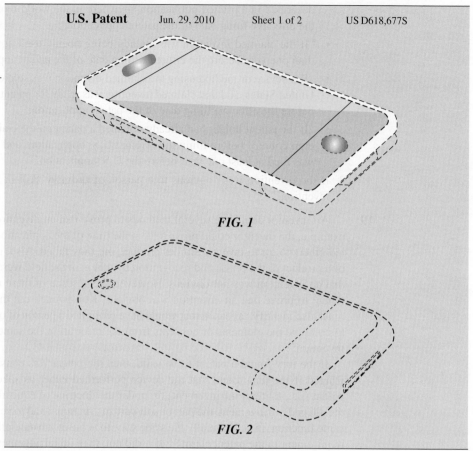

U.S. Patent   Jun. 29, 2010   Sheet 1 of 2   US D618,677S

FIG. 1

FIG. 2

of phones and tablets was not substantially the same as Apple's patented designs. Justice Koh explained that "two designs are substantially the same if, in the eye of an ordinary observer, giving such attention as a purchaser usually gives, the resemblance between the two designs is such as to deceive such an observer, inducing him to purchase one supposing it to be the other."

24   Samsung also sought to invalidate Apple's patents for lack of required originality by producing evidence of preexisting designs or prior art, stating:

> In general, prior art includes things that existed before the claimed design, that were publicly known in this country, or used in a publicly accessible way in this country, or that were patented or described in a publication in any country. . . . For a claimed design patent to be invalid because it is anticipated, Samsung must prove by clear and convincing evidence that there is a single prior art reference that is substantially the same as the claimed design patent.[21]

25   Finally, in much the same way as a utility patent (see above), a design patent for an electronic device could be deemed obvious and thus invalid if the claimed design would have been deemed obvious to a designer of ordinary skill who designed that type of device.

---

[21]Ibid.

EXHIBIT 8 Apple Trademark Claim

66. In addition to copying Apple's Product Trade Dress, Samsung has also copied numerous application icons in which Apple had valid trademark rights, as shown below:

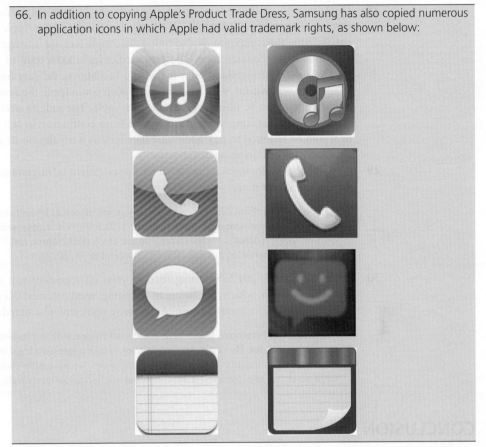

Source: *Apple v. Samsung*, No. sf-2981926 (United States District Court Northern District of California 2011), pp. 22–23. Due to space limitations, some icons were excluded from the exhibit.

Trademarks

26   A trademark is a word, logo or other indication of source, such as the word marks APPLE® and SAMSUNG®. Neither party claimed the other had infringed its word mark. In this case, Apple claimed infringement of icons it had registered as trademarks, including the Phone, Notes and Utilities icons (see Exhibit 8). Two important requirements for trademark protection were the owner's first use as a trademark and distinctiveness (i.e., the capacity of the mark to distinguish the owner's products from another's same, similar or related products). While registration has its advantages, unlike patents, registration is not required for trademark protection.

27   Apple claimed trademark infringement of several icons representing basic functions, such as placing calls, changing phone settings and accessing contacts. "For example, U.S. Registration No. 3,886,196 covers an icon that is green in color with a white silhouette of a phone handset arranged at a 45 degree angle and centered on the icon that represents the application for making telephone calls," noted the complaint.[22]

[22]*Apple v. Samsung*, No. sf-2981926 (United States District Court Northern District of California 2011), pp. 22–23.

Verdicts, Appeals, and Countersuits

28   On August 24, 2012, after weeks of trial and only 21 hours of deliberation, the jury found that Samsung had willfully infringed many, but not all, of the Apple utility and design patents listed in the complaint. It also found that Apple had not infringed the Samsung patents identified in the counterclaim. The jury verdict included a total of $1.05 billion damages for Samsung's infringement prior to the suit. In addition, the jury found that Samsung's infringement was willful, which meant Judge Koh could triple the amount when she decided on the damages to be ultimately awarded to Apple. The judge's decision would also determine whether Samsung would be enjoined from continuing to sell the infringing devices or would be required to pay additional damages as a royalty on its continuing sales in the United States of infringing devices.[23]

29   Although the damages represented the largest patent infringement award in U.S. history, Apple had sought more:

> a further $400 million damage award for design infringement by Samsung; $135 million for willful infringement of its utility patents; $121 million in supplemental damages based on Samsung's product sales not covered in the jury's deliberation; and $50 million of prejudgment interest on damages through [December 31, 2012].[24]

30   On October 5, 2012, Samsung filed its own infringement suit against Apple's newly released iPhone 5, which, according to Samsung, used patented 4G communications technology without a Samsung license. A Samsung representative noted:

> We have always preferred to compete in the marketplace with our innovative products, rather than in courtrooms. However, Apple continues to take aggressive legal measures that will limit market competition. Under these circumstances, we have little choice but to take the steps necessary to protect our innovations and intellectual property rights.[25]

CONCLUSION

31   In the second quarter of 2012, worldwide smartphone sales topped 400 million units. The largest device maker by far was Samsung with unit sales of 90 million, followed by Nokia at 83 million and Apple at 29 million.[26] Samsung also posted record earnings of $7 billion for the quarter, driven largely by sales of its Galaxy smartphones (see Exhibit 9 for historical financial data). Samsung's mobile earnings were double the previous year's earnings

---

[23]Both the amount of damages awarded and the scope of any injunction awarded were often the subject of post-verdict motions to the trial judge and appeals to higher courts. The two parties in this case continued to litigate the case with both post-trial motions to Judge Koh and appeals. Given the amounts at stake and the impact on brand image, this process is expected to continue, meaning that the damages and injunction may not be finalized or known for many years.

[24]Miyoung Kim, "Apple Seeks U.S. Samsung Sales Ban, $707 Million More in Damages," *Reuters*, September 22, 2012, http://www.reuters.com/article/2012/09/22/us-apple-samsung-idUSBRE88L04B20120922, accessed October 21, 2012.

[25]Todd Wasserman, "Samsung Adds iPhone 5 to Patent Lawsuits," *Mashable.com*, September 20, 2012, http://mashable.com/2012/09/20/samsung-iphone-lawsuit/, accessed October 21, 2012.

[26]Ingrid Lunden, "Gartner: Global Mobile Sales Down 2%, Smartphones Surge 43%, Apple Stalls as Fans Hold Out for New iPhone," *Techcrunch*, August 14, 2012, http://techcrunch.com/2012/08/14/gartner-global-mobile-sales-down-2-smartphones-surge-43-apple-stalls-as-fans-hold-out-for-new-iphone/, accessed September 22, 2012.

EXHIBIT 9   **Samsung Consolidated Financial Summaries, 2006–2011 (In Billions of Korean Won)**

- **Consolidated**

(✕ ~ 08 figures are based on K-GAAP, while '09 figures are K-IFRS based)

	2006	2007	2008	2009	2010	2011
Balance Sheet						
Assets	81,366	93,375	105,301	112,180	134,289	155,631
Cash etc*	9,785	11,817	13,388	20,884	22,480	26,878
A/R	9,089	11,125	12,044	17,819	19,153	21,882
Inventory	6,753	7,969	9,493	9,839	13,365	15,717
Liabilities	33,426	37,403	42,377	39,135	44,940	53,786
Debt	14,477	14,514	17,455	9,395	10,775	14,647
Shareholders' Equity	47,940	55,972	62,924	73,045	89,349	101,845
Income Statement						
Sales	85,426	98,508	121,294	136,324	154,630	165,002
—COGS	59,652	70,881	89,762	94,595	102,667	112,145
Gross Profit	25,773	27,627	31,532	41,729	51,964	52,857
(Margin)	30.2%	28.0%	26.0%	30.6%	33.6%	32.0%
—SG&A	16,766	18,654	25,500	23,362	26,243	27,422
—R&D	✕R&D Included SG&A in K-GAAP			7,387	9,099	9,980
Operating Profit	9,008	8,973	6,032	10,925	17,297	16,250
(Margin)	10.5%	9.1%	5.0%	8.0%	11.2%	9.8%
Income before tax	9,828	9,633	6,578	12,192	19,329	17,159
(Margin)	11.5%	9.8%	5.4%	8.9%	12.5%	10.4%
—Income tax expense	1,634	1,710	688	2,431	3,182	3,425
Net Income	7,926	7,421	5,526	9,761	16,147	13,734
(Margin)	9.3%	7.5%	4.6%	7.2%	10.4%	8.3%

Note: US$1 = Approx. 1,100 KRW

Source: http://www.samsung.com/us/aboutsamsung/samsung_group/our_performance/samsung_profile_old.html, accessed October 23, 2012.

and accounted for approximately 60 percent of the company's profits.[27] Samsung's leadership in smartphones also helped give Android a solid lead in smartphone operating systems (see Exhibit 10).

32   Samsung stepped up its campaign against Apple by running television and print ads touting the superiority of the Galaxy S3 over the iPhone 5. In a television advertisement that became a social media sensation, Samsung ridiculed Apple users who waited in line at the Apple store for the iPhone 5. "The headphone jack is going to be on the bottom!" says one. "I heard you have to have an adapter to use the dock on the new one," says another.

[27]"Galaxy S3 Brings Record Profits for Samsung," *The Telegraph* (UK), July 27, 2012, http://www.telegraph.co.uk/technology/samsung/9431621/Galaxy-S3-brings-record-profits-for-Samsung.html, accessed April 10, 2012.

EXHIBIT 10 U.S. Smartphone Marketshare, 2006–2012

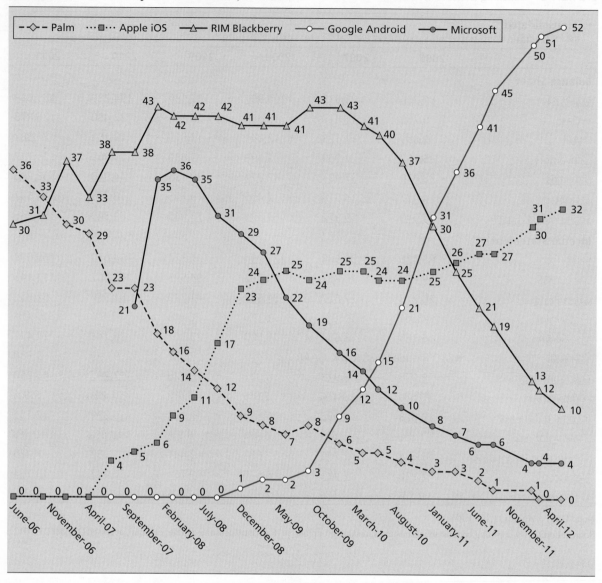

Sources: Data compiled by case writer from various sources including Canalys, Silicon Valley Insider, ComScore, and Gartner.

"Yeah, but they make the coolest adapters," a dedicated Apple fan replies. Just then, a Samsung owner arrives and strikes up a conversation with the people in line as he explains the benefits of the Galaxy S3 over the iPhone 5, such as a bigger screen and the ability to send e-mail while watching a video. "This one's 4G," says an Apple user. "Yeah, we've had that for a while," replies the Samsung owner. The advertisement ends with the tagline, "The next big thing is already here. The Samsung Galaxy S3."

Case 12

American Public Education, Inc. (A)[1]

Richard B. Robinson Jr. and John A. Pearce II

1   For active duty soldiers, the price can't be beat. American Public Education's (APEI) courses are free to military personnel, thanks to government tuition benefits. But the government doesn't pay that much, just $750 per three-credit course. That forced the for-profit educator to keep its expenses low.

2   But those low prices, often half what some competitors charge, gave APEI a leg up on the civilian side. "Convenience and cost, that's what working adults are looking for," said Harry T. Wilkens, APEI's executive vice president and chief financial officer. The school saw revenue climb 55 percent in 2008. It grew by double-digits in each quarter since APE went public in 2007. Enrollment jumped 50 percent in 2008 to 45,200 students.

CIVILIAN SURGE

3   More than two-thirds of them were military personnel. But the civilian side is growing fast. Wilkens thinks teachers, police officers and other civilians could make up half or more of the student body in three or four years. The recession that started in 2008 gave the entire for-profit education sector a boost as workers scramble to update their skills and burnish resumes.

4   But the military side has legs, too. It grew faster than expected in the fourth quarter of 2008 in part due to an expanded partnership with the U.S. Navy. The number of active duty and reserve personnel in the U.S. services has held relatively constant for decades at a little above 2.1 million. But there's a churn of about 300,000 new soldiers a year replacing retiring ones.

5   The DoD's [Department of Defense's] tuition program has become a key Pentagon recruiting and retention tool. APEI assumed that more soldiers would be applying that tuition credit to online schools. It calculated that it had about 12 percent of the military education market in 2012, up from 10 percent a year earlier. Wilkens said APEI is committed to keeping the course free to military personnel.

6   A typical three-credit undergraduate course costs about $750. A graduate-level course costs $850. The company throws in the books to make sure there are no out-of-pocket expenses for military personnel. But with its DNA firmly rooted in that military cost structure, it can deliver that same cheap education to the civilian sector.

7   A full four-year degree totals about $30,000, far less than a brick-and-mortar university. And a masters in business administration costs about $10,000 total, vs. $20,000 to $25,000 at other online institutions, such as Capella Education, Apollo Group's University of Phoenix, and Strayer Education.

8   Those institutions instead push the quality of their education, support programs they offer, and their longer histories. "But in the end of the day, if consumers are unwilling to

[1]Source: The APEI (A) case was developed by the author from "Commercial Online School Keeps Costs Low for Military Personnel," *Investor's Business Daily*, March 24, 2009. © Investor's Business Daily, Inc. 2009. Reprinted with permission of *Investor's Business Daily*.

take on more debt looking for a postsecondary education, then American Public wins," Barrington Research's Alexander Paris Jr. said. Barrington has done banking business with APEI.

9   West Virginia–based American Public was formed in 1991 by retired Marine Corps Major Jim Etter. He had taught at the Corps' Amphibious Warfare School and wanted to help service personnel continue their educations. The school, then known as American Military University, enrolled its first students in January 1993. Over the years, it built up its course offerings and earned the accreditations necessary to grant degrees.

10   In 2002, it formed a second university, American Public University, to better appeal to the civilian market. It created American Public Education as the parent over the two institutions. With shared faculty and administration, the two universities have a combined 74 degree and 51 certificate programs in areas such as national security, military studies, criminal justice, technology, business administration, education, and liberal arts. American Public Education, Inc., went public in 2005 [symbol APEI].[2]

11   Now, it's actively reaching out to police, teachers and other civilian-sector groups, where education can bolster careers, but costs are still a concern. The programs became eligible for federal Title IV loans in late 2006, opening the doors wider to the civilian students.

12   But to keep costs under the DoD reimbursement rate, American Public Education has had to watch costs. It pays its professors based on the number of students enrolling, for instance. So if enrollment dips, so do expenses.

WORD OF MOUTH

13   APEI was also very modest in its market expenses. It relied instead on word-of-mouth marketing. About 55 percent of students heard about the school from another student, which analysts said was tops in the industry. One "strategic" challenge will be keeping that cost of acquiring students down as it expands beyond the civilian market. So far, APEI has been able to do so. And the DoD hasn't raised its tuition reimbursement rate in years. Should it do so, which should happen with the new GI bill, that would allow APEI to raise tuitions.

PROFITABILITY

14   APEI [earnings] per share [was] 86 cents in 2008, up from 64 cents in 2007. The company projected 2009 EPS to come in between $1.16 and $1.20. Stock market analysts were even more optimistic, expecting a minimum of $1.21 per share.

15   American Public's low-cost model could give it traction against its civilian-focused competitors, analysts think. "It's pretty interesting and potentially disruptive in that marketplace," said Trace Urdan, an analyst with Signal Hill. "But we haven't really seen it take off yet. I guess it's still in the category of promising." And, as APEI entered its third year, 2009, as a public company its management team wondered what a deepening global recession would mean for their future.

[2]An eventual step after APEI created American Public University (APU) was to create an academic administrative entity to oversee its two universities—APU and AMU. That entity, or educational "system," was named American Public University System (APUS). APUS' charge was and is to oversee and provide sound independent governance to ensure the academic integrity, quality, and accreditation of APU and AMU. APUS is wholly owned by APEI, as are APU and AMU. To simplify references using the APUS and APEI acronyms, this case simply uses one—APEI.

Learn—That's an Order

American Public Education has grown by providing online education to U.S. military personnel. But its ability to live within the government's tuition reimbursement rates means it can offer those same degrees to civilians at less cost than competitiors.

Total registration

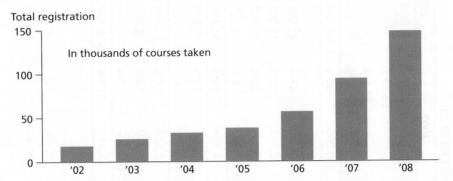

In thousands of courses taken

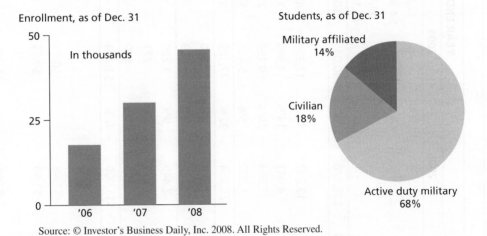

Source: © Investor's Business Daily, Inc. 2008. All Rights Reserved.

CONSOLIDATED STATEMENTS OF INCOME

	2005		2006		2007		2008	
			YEAR ENDED DECEMBER 31,					
Total Enrollment	11,000		17,000		32,000		45,200	
Growth: Year over Year	50%		54.55%		88.24%		41.25%	
Total Registrations [# of courses taken]	37,506		54,828		94,846		147,124	
Growth: Year over Year	15.20%		46.18%		72.99%		55.12%	
Revenues (In thousands, except per share amounts)	$28,178	100%	$40,045	100%	$69,095	100%	$107,147	100%
Costs and expenses:								
Instructional costs and services	13,247	47%	17,959	45%	29,479	43%	43,561	41%
Selling and promotional	4,043	14%	4,895	12%	6,765	10%	12,361	12%
General and administrative	7,364	26%	9,150	23%	15,335	22%	21,302	20%
Depreciation and amortization	1,300	5%	5,101	13%	2,825	4%	4,235	4%
Total costs and expenses	25,954	92%	37,105	93%	54,404	79%	81,459	76%
Income before interest income and income taxes	2,224	8%	2,940	7%	14,691	21%	25,688	24%
Interest income, net	225	1%	289	1%	888	1%	706	1%
Income from operations before income taxes	2,449	9%	3,229	8%	15,579	23%	26,394	25%
Income tax expense	1,061	4%	771	2%	6,829	10%	10,207	10%
Investment loss, net of tax	−303	−1%	−660	−2%	—	0%	—	0%
Net income	−$11,900	−42%	$1,798	4%	$8,750	13%	$16,187	15%
Net income attributable to common stockholders per common share:								
Basic	−$1.48		$0.15		$0.69		$0.91	
Diluted	−$1.48		$0.15		$0.64		$0.86	
Weighted average number of shares outstanding:								
Basic	8,055		11,741		12,758		17,840	
Diluted	8,055		12,177		13,600		18,822	

CONSOLIDATED BALANCE SHEETS

AS OF DECEMBER 31,

(In thousands, except per share amounts)	2005		2006		2007		2008	
Assets								
Current assets:								
Cash and cash equivalents	$6,000	27.3%	$11,678	40.6%	$26,951	55.0%	$47,714	60.5%
Accounts receivable, net of allowance of $263 in 2006 and $385 in 2007	4000	18.2%	5448	18.9%	4896	10.0%	6188	7.9%
Prepaid expenses	—	0.0%	679	2.4%	1089	2.2%	2156	2.7%
Income tax receivable	2000	9.1%	856	3.0%	1596	3.3%	1306	1.7%
Deferred income taxes	—	0.0%	299	1.0%	309	0.6%	640	0.8%
Total current assets	12000	54.5%	18960	65.9%	34841	71.1%	58004	73.6%
Property and equipment, net	10000	45.5%	9363	32.6%	13364	27.3%	19622	24.9%
Note receivable	—	0.0%	—	0.0%	—	0.0%	—	0.0%
Investment	—	0.0%	—	0.0%	—	0.0%	—	0.0%
Other assets	—	0.0%	427	1.5%	775	1.6%	1187	1.5%
Total assets	$22,000	100.0%	$28,750	100.0%	$48,980	100.0%	$78,813	100.0%
Liabilities and Stockholders' Equity								
Current liabilities:								
Accounts payable	$1,000	4.3%	$1,502	5.2%	$2,471	5.0%	$4,946	6.3%
Accrued liabilities	—	0.0%	3,165	11.0%	4,323	8.8%	7,075	9.0%
Deferred revenue and student deposits	5,000	21.7%	3,881	13.5%	6,614	13.5%	9,626	12.2%
Total current liabilities	6,000	26.1%	8,548	29.7%	13,408	27.4%	21,647	27.5%
Deferred income taxes & other LTD	2,000	8.7%	3,381	11.8%	2,065	4.2%	3,691	4.7%
Total liabilities	8,000	34.8%	11,929	41.5%	15,473	31.6%	25,338	32.1%
Commitments and contingencies								
Stockholders' equity:								
Class A, $0.01 par value:								
Authorized shares = 9,412,071; Issued and outstanding shares 9,256,258 in 2006 and none in 2007	—	0.0%	93	0.3%	—	0.0%	—	0.0%
Common stock, $0.01 par value:								
Authorized shares—100,000,000; 2,542,342 issued and outstanding in 2006 and 17,687,952 in 2007	—	0.0%	25	0.1%	177	0.4%	180	0.2%
Additional paid-in capital	26,000	113.0%	26,378	91.7%	128,005	261.3%	132,078	167.6%
Retained earnings (accumulated deficit)	−11,000	−47.8%	−9,675	−33.7%	−94,675	−193.3%	−78,193	−99.2%
Total stockholders' equity	15,000	65.2%	16,821	58.5%	33,507	68.4%	53,475	67.9%
Total liabilities and stockholders' equity	$23,000	100.0%	$28,750	100.00%	$48,980	100.0%	$78,813	100.0%

CONSOLIDATED STATEMENTS OF CASH FLOWS

(In thousands, % of Net Income)

	2005		2006		2007		2008	
					YEAR ENDED DECEMBER 31			
Operating activities								
Net income	-$11,597	-210.4%	$2,458	21.0%	$8,750	32.5%	$16,187	33.9%
Adjustments to reconcile net income to net cash provided by operating activities								
Increase in allowance for doubtful accounts	-467	-8.5%	-307	-2.6%	121	0.4%	152	0.3%
Depreciation and amortization	1,300	23.6%	1,953	16.7%	2,825	10.5%	4,235	8.9%
Stock-based compensation	1,198	21.7%	284	2.4%	1,033	3.8%	1,674	3.5%
Loss on disposal	—	0.0%	3,148	27.0%	—	0.0%	—	0.0%
Investment loss	—	0.0%	—	0.0%	—	0.0%	—	0.0%
Stock issued for director compensation	12,985	235.6%	—	0.0%	—	0.0%	196	0.4%
Deferred income taxes	864	15.7%	-599	-5.1%	618	2.3%	1,295	2.7%
Changes in operating assets and liabilities:								
Accounts receivable	-505	-9.2%	-989	-8.5%	430	1.6%	-1,443	-3.0%
Prepaid expenses and other assets	-71	-1.3%	-324	-2.8%	-739	-2.7%	-560	-1.2%
Income tax receivable	-730	-13.2%	589	5.0%	-410	-2.3%	-217	-0.5%
Accounts payable	450	8.2%	390	3.3%	969	3.6%	2,474	5.2%
Accrued liabilities	14	0.3%	1,339	11.5%	1,157	4.3%	2,752	5.8%
Deferred revenue and student deposits	219	4.0%	987	8.5%	2,763	10.3%	3,012	6.3%
Net cash provided by operating activities	**3,660**	**66.4%**	**8,929**	**76.5%**	**17,517**	**64.2%**	**29,757**	**62.4%**
Investing activities								
Capital expenditures	-4,613	-83.7%	-4,475	-38.3%	-6,827	-25.3%	-10,009	-21.0%
Investment	-360	-6.5%	—	0.0%	—	0.0%	—	0.0%
Note receivable	—	0.0%	—	0.0%	—	0.0%	—	0.0%
Capitalized program development costs and other assets	-377	-6.8%	-459	-3.9%	-347	-1.3%	-896	-1.9%
Net cash used in investing activities	**-5,350**	**-97.1%**	**-4,934**	**-42.3%**	**-7,174**	**-26.6%**	**-10,905**	**-22.9%**
Financing activities								
Cash paid for repurchase of common/restricted stock	-18,615	-337.8%	1,980	17.0%	-2,028	-7.5%	-295	-0.6%
Cash received from issuance of common stock, net of issuance costs	18,596	337.4%	199	1.7%	6,186	23.0%	770	1.6%
Excess tax benefit from stock based compensation	-30	-0.5%	—	0.0%	772	2.9%	1,436	3.0%
Net cash used in financing activities	**-49**	**-0.9%**	**2,172**	**18.7%**	**4,930**	**18.3%**	**1,911**	**4.0%**
Total Cash								
Net increase (decrease) in cash and cash equivalents	-1,739	-31.6%	6,167	52.8%	15,273	56.7%	20,763	43.5%
Cash and cash equivalents at beginning of period	7,250	131.6%	5,511	47.2%	11,678	43.3%	26,951	56.5%
Cash and cash equivalents at end of period	**$5,511**	**100.0%**	**$11,678**	**100.0%**	**$26,951**	**100.0%**	**$47,714**	**100.0%**
Supplemental disclosures of cash flow information								
Income taxes paid	$596	10.8%	$436	3.7%	$6,005	22.3%	$8,023	16.8%

AEPI—Key Financial Ratios	AS OF DECEMBER 31,			
	2005	2006	2007	2008
Profitability % of Sales				
*Return on Sales (net margin) %	−42.23	4.49	12.66	15.11
*Asset Turnover	1.26	1.56	1.78	1.68
*Return on Assets %	−53.02	7.02	22.51	25.33
*Financial Leverage	1.54	1.71	1.46	1.47
*Return on Equity %	−81.85	11.47	34.77	37.22
Gross Margin %	52.99	55.15	57.34	59.34
Operating Margin %	7.89	7.34	21.26	23.97
* Dupont Ratios				
Growth				
Revenue				
Year over Year	21.88	42.11	72.54	55.07
3-Year Average	—	31.13	44.04	56.08
Operating Income				
Year over Year	—	32.19	399.69	74.86
3-Year Average	—	16.74		126.05
Net Income				
Year over Year	−52.56	65.71	386.65	84.99
3-Year Average	—	102.35	56.4	146.18
EPS				
Year over Year	—	—	326.67	34.38
3-Year Average	—	55.36	42.75	—
Liquidity/Financial Health				
Current Ratio	1.96	2.22	2.6	2.68
Quick Ratio	1.82	2.08	2.46	2.55
Financial Leverage	1.54	1.71	1.46	1.47
Debt / Equity	—	—	—	—
Efficiency				
Days Sales Outstanding	53.77	43.75	27.32	18.88
Receivables Turnover	6.79	8.34	13.36	19.33
Fixed Assets Turnover	2.96	4.24	6.08	6.5
Asset Turnover	1.26	1.56	1.78	1.68

American Public Education, Inc. (B)[3]

Richard B. Robinson Jr. and John A. Pearce II

16 The last five years may have traumatized most companies facing the global "Great Recession," but not, it would seem, APEI. Instead, APEI has experienced continued growth. Net course registrations, tuition revenue, and income before taxes have virtually doubled since 2008. Total revenue increased from $107.1M in 2008 to $313.5M in 2012, which represents a compounded annual growth rate (CAGR) of 30.8 percent. Net course registrations will have increased from 147,000 in 2008 to almost 450,000 in 2013, a 200 percent increase over five recessionary years. Earnings before interest and taxes increased 167 percent (29.9M in 2008 to 79.9M in 2012), and net income improved to $42.3M in 2012 from net income of $16.2M in 2008.

17 Entering 2013, APEI was serving around 127,000 adult students, most holding full-time employment. They are living in all 50 states and the District of Columbia and are enrolled in 87 different degree programs and 69 different certificate programs taught by 1,570 adjunct faculty and 430 full-time faculty members considered top professionals in their respective fields, teaching from locations around the world.

18 Approximately 57 percent of APEI students serve in the United States military on active duty. The remainder of their student population is generally civilians with careers in public service, such as federal, national, and local law enforcement personnel or other first responders, or they are civilians who are military-affiliated professionals, such as veterans, reservists, or National Guard members. APEI's programs are primarily designed to help these and other students advance in their current professions or prepare for their next career. Their exclusively online method of instruction is well suited to these particular students, many of whom serve in positions requiring extended and irregular schedules, are on-call for rapid response missions, participate in extended deployments and exercises, travel or relocate frequently, and have limited financial resources.

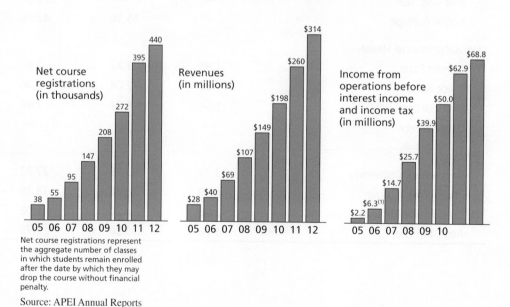

Net course registrations represent the aggregate number of classes in which students remain enrolled after the date by which they may drop the course without financial penalty.

Source: APEI Annual Reports

[3]2014. RCT, LLC, Developed based on publicly available information and APEI Annual Reports and 10-Ks.

APEI'S STRATEGIC ASSESSMENT AND GROWTH STRATEGIES TOWARD 2025

19 *Core Competencies.* The APEI executive team believed they had the following core competencies and competitive strengths in 2013 upon which to build a successful strategy:

- *Exclusively Online Education*—All of the courses and programs at APEI's two schools, American Military University and American Public University, have been specifically designed via a proprietary system for online delivery, and APEI recruits and trains faculty exclusively for online instruction. Since their students are located in 100 countries around the globe, APEI has focused on asynchronous, interactive instruction that provides students the flexibility to study and interact during the hours of the day or days of the week that suit their situation and schedules.

- *Emphasis on Military and Public Services Communities*—Since its founding, APEI's culture has reflected its devotion to its mission of *Educating Those Who Serve*™. They have designed every one of their academic programs, policies, marketing strategies, and tuition specifically to meet the needs of the military and public service communities.

- *Affordable Tuition*—AMU and APU tuition, fees, and books are less for undergraduate, and graduate students than the average in-state cost at public universities. Tuition was established at a competitive rate whereby DoD tuition assistance programs fully cover the cost of undergraduate course tuition and over 75 percent of the cost of graduate course tuition. APEI's two universities have not increased their undergraduate tuition of $250 per credit hour since 2000 and have no current intention to do so.

- *Commitment to Academic Excellence*—APEI academic programs are overseen by their Board of Trustees, which counts as members two former college presidents, active accreditation peer evaluators, a former commandant of the Marine Corps, and a former Department of the Army inspector general. APEI claims an exceptional commitment to continuously improving its academic programs and services, as evidenced by the level of attention and resources they apply to instruction and educational support. That includes intermittent, national standardized competency tests, which they have administered during and after related classes to help "JIT" monitor learning outcomes and teaching effectiveness. It also includes continuous monitoring of employers of APEI graduates to see if they would hire another APEI student. The recent results of this survey as reported in their recent annual report were as follows: Ninety-nine percent of APUS alumni employers surveyed would hire another graduate from APUS.[4]

- *Proprietary Information Systems and Processes*—APEI's proprietary PAD— "Partnership At a Distance" system provides students 24/7 access to APEI services, such as admission, orientation, course registrations, tuition payments, book requests, grades, transcripts and degree progress, and various other inquiries. APEI has also created management tools based on the data from the PAD system that help them in their efforts to continuously improve APEI academic quality, student support services, and marketing efficiency. A key benefit they find with these proprietary systems and processes is that they allow APEI to seamlessly manage the complexities involved in starting over 3,100 classes in over 1,250 unique courses starting the first Monday of each month in either 8- or 16-week formats; adapted also to semester and academic year formats to assist students using Title IV programs meet eligibility requirements. APEI's proprietary systems and processes will allow them to support a much larger student

[4] APEI 2012 Annual Report.

body at minimal incremental costs, which in turn they believe provides them with important future competitive and cost advantages. They obtained patent protection on their PAD system in 2010.

- *Highly Scalable and Profitable Business Model*—APEI executives believe that their exclusively online education model, their proprietary management information systems, their relatively low student acquisition costs, and their variable faculty cost model have enabled them to expand APEI operating margins. Related, they often note that their narrow market focus (and quality offerings) created a satisfied tightly-knit base of students that has been a significant source of referrals over time, which they believe has led to lower marketing costs, particularly among the military and police/first responder groups of their student populations.

20   **Growth Strategies.** APEI believes these six core competencies, along with (1) high student satisfaction and referral rates; (2) regional accreditation; (3) increasing acceptance of distance learning within their targeted markets; and (4) variety and affordability of APEI programs will lead to considerably higher growth to 2020 and beyond. APEI's executive has identified six primary strategies to grow APEI that build on these core competencies:

- *Expand in APEI's Core Military Market*—APEI has focused on the needs of the military community since its founding, and this community has been responsible for the vast majority of APEI growth to date. The combination of their online model, focused curriculum and outreach to the military has enabled APEI to gain share from more established schools that have served this market for longer periods, many of which are traditional brick and mortar schools.

- *Broaden APEI's Acceptance in the Public Service and Civilian Markets*—APEI believes its curriculum is directly relevant to federal, state, and local law enforcement, first responders, and other public service professionals. Historically this market was limited because, outside the federal government, only a few agencies or departments have the tuition reimbursement plans critical to fund continuing adult education. APEI students can now obtain Title IV grants or low-cost student loans, so APEI will increase its focus on these markets. APEI believes that the affordability and diversity of its academic program offerings, including its liberal arts degrees, attracts civilian students.

- *Add New Degree Programs*—APEI will expand its degree offerings to meet students' needs and marketplace demands with a focus on new programs in fields exhibiting higher than average growth. APEI is also currently preparing itself academically and culturally to potentially offer doctoral programs within the next few years.

- *Pursue and Expand Strategic Partnerships*—APEI believe that articulation agreements and partnerships with institutions of higher learning, corporations, professional associations, and other organizations are important to enrollment growth and to expanding access to higher education.

- *Provide Education Hosting and Support Services*—APEI has recently begun to offer hosting and support services to traditional universities and other institutions of higher learning to support online offerings. They believe the growth of online programs at traditional universities, combined with the attractiveness of APEI's proprietary distance learning platform, represents an attractive business opportunity to provide such services to smaller universities as a low-cost, high-quality provider of online education.

- *Explore International Opportunities*—APEI is developing partnerships and other initiatives aimed at expanding international access to its affordable online programs that will further increase the diversity of the APEI student population, enhance the learning environment, and diversify APEI's tuition funding sources. APEI plans to pursue other relationships, partnerships, and business opportunities that may expand its international reach, including the development of new international relationships, corporate training programs, and nondegree certifications.

COMPETITION

21   More than 4,000 U.S. colleges and universities serve traditional college-age students and adult students. Competition is highly fragmented and varies by geography, program offerings, delivery method, ownership, quality level, and selectivity of admissions. No one institution has a significant share of the total postsecondary market. Within APEI's primary military market, there are more than 1,000 institutions that serve military students and receive tuition assistance funds.

22   APEI executives believe for-profit (proprietary) schools, particularly the publicly traded ones, may increasingly be seeking to attract military students. One major reason, they surmise, is that these schools, such as the University of Phoenix, may well see increasing their number of active military personnel as students can be helpful in their efforts to comply with the "90/10 rule." The 90/10 rule[5] says that a proprietary university will not be able to receive Title IV funds (federal student loan funds or loan funds guaranteed by the federal government) if more than 90 percent of its tuition revenue comes from such funds. Currently Dept. of Defense tuition assistance and veterans education benefits do not count towards the 90 percent limit. So that, in turn, can become attractive to companies like the UOP, whose large adult student population using Title IV funding has put the UOP at approximately 88 percent in 2011, 84 percent in 2012, and 85 percent in 2013. UOP executives continued to caution that it could move higher, given the high borrowing levels of recent years and the heavy competition for students not needing Title IV support.

23   Whatever the cause, something was happening with APEI's growth rate among active duty military students as APEI managers examined their enrollment data starting in late 2010. Said one executive:

> Beginning with registrations for the 3rd quarter of 2010, we observed that the growth of our net course registrations from active duty military students slowed more than we expected. We do not know all of the factors that caused this to occur, and we cannot determine whether over time net course registrations from active duty military students will return to our previous expectations, continue to grow more slowly than expected, remain flat or decline. We believe that the changes in net course registrations from active duty military students were in part due to increased operations activity and overseas deployments across all branches of the U.S. military, particularly the level of activity in the United States Marine Corps.

24   Another manager pointed to numerous pictures of military personnel in uniform prominently displayed on Web sites and promotional material from key competitors as evidence it might be competitors enrolling more active duty military students, and at an increasing rate of growth. Since, APEI's overall participation in federal student aid programs under Title IV constituted only 23.9 percent of its net registrations in 2010, APEI executives felt

[5]Under the Higher Education Opportunity Act, a proprietary institution is prohibited from deriving from Title IV funds, on a cash accounting basis (except for certain institutional loans) for any fiscal year, more than 90 percent of its revenues. Under the terms of HEOA, a proprietary institution that violates the 90/10 rule for any fiscal year will be placed on provisional status for two fiscal years. Proprietary institutions of higher education that violate the 90/10 rule for two consecutive fiscal years will become ineligible to participate in Title IV programs for at least two fiscal years and will be required to demonstrate compliance with Title IV eligibility and certification requirements for at least two fiscal years prior to resuming Title IV program participation. (Read the "Adult Education Market" section provided in Case 3 on the Apollo Group to understand the 90/10 rule in more detail.)

their ability to participate in these programs was important to APEI's growth, especially given their signification margin relative to the 90/10 rule compared to other proprietary institutions at the time.

25   ***Student Loan Defaults*** have become another significant financial factor shaping the competitive landscape among proprietary universities. Under the recent Higher Education Act, a proprietary educational institution may lose its eligibility to participate in some or all of the Title IV programs if, for three consecutive federal fiscal years, 25 percent or more of its students who were required to begin repaying their student loans in the relevant federal fiscal year default on their payment by the end of the next federal fiscal year. For each federal fiscal year, a rate of student defaults (known as a "cohort default rate") is calculated for each institution with 30 or more borrowers entering repayment in a given federal fiscal year by determining the rate at which borrowers who become subject to their repayment obligation in that federal fiscal year default by the end of the next federal fiscal year. If the Department of Education notifies an institution that its cohort default rates for each of the three most recent federal fiscal years are 25 percent or greater, the institution's participation in all Title IV and Pell Grant programs ends 30 days after the notification. An institution whose participation ends under these provisions may not participate in the relevant programs for the remainder of the fiscal year in which the institution receives the notification, as well as for the next two fiscal years.

26   This will certainly increase competition among proprietary schools to enroll students that have or will have solid capacity to repay Title IV loans they incur to pay for attending that school. APEI executives express some concern, given that the majority of APEI's students and target students are typically fully employed and often have company/employer tuition reimbursement assistance, which in turn makes them better credit risks that competitors will aggressively seek to enroll.

27   Prior to 2006, APEI did not even participate in Title IV programs. But with its opening of American Public University to be its civilian counterpart to its American Military University, APEI has increased its population of Title IV–using students. Still, in carefully monitoring its cohort default rate, APEI reports that its rates for federal fiscal years 2007 and 2008 are 0.0 percent and 5.2 percent, respectively. These rates are considerably better than those of its major competitors, although some APEI executives report expecting the rate to rise as more civilian students are added to its student body. At the same time, competitors will inevitably see adding military and public service students able to take advantage of tuition reimbursement benefits as a way to ultimately drive down their cohort default rates. Students at proprietary colleges represent 12 percent of higher education enrollment, yet they take out 26 percent of all student loans and represented 46 percent of all student-loan dollars in default in 2011.

28   By 2013 that default rate was approaching 60 percent among for-profit school students that had used Title IV–enabled loans. While APEI had seen its students' use of Title IV loans and loan guarantees rise by 2013 to a 35 percent share of its tuition, it still had an attractively employed student population at low risk of becoming loan default problems in the future. That fortunate reality also had a negative consequence—those types of students were increasingly becoming students of interest to other for-profit competitors, especially the bigger ones.

29   ***Gainful Employment*** has become a third significant financial factor shaping the competitive landscape among proprietary universities. The U.S. Department of Education will soon publish final regulations defining "gainful employment" to take effect on July 1, 2012. Those regulations will set a third financial hurdle facing proprietary colleges and universities that is intended to make sure the jobs their graduates can get provide the earning capacity sufficient to allow the student to repay the loans taken to pay the cost of attending that

school. Currently, the gainful employment regulation will deny federal aid to programs that fail three "tests" of gainful employment three times in a four-year span:

- Are at least 35 percent of former students actively paying down their loans? In other words, roughly a third of ex-students must make payments that lower the loan balance by at least a dollar in a given year.
- Are graduates spending 30 percent or less of their discretionary income on loan payments? This test seeks to ensure that loan payments are not eating up too much of the money left after graduates pay for basic needs.
- Are graduates spending 12 percent or less of their total income on loan payments? This standard, related to the previous test, establishes that loan bills should not consume more than about an eighth of total earnings.

30   Programs that pass any of the three tests would retain eligibility to participate in federal aid initiatives, enabling qualified students to secure federal grants or loans. And, with recent intense lobbying by proprietary school proponents, a three-year grace period until 2015 has been tentatively incorporated instead of an immediate enforcement should a school not meet these three tests.

31   APEI executives evidenced little concern about this impacting its two universities in 2011. At the same time, concern among some of those executives about it driving other powerful proprietary university competitors into its target market was rising. Another wind of change with serious consequences for APEI had entered the picture by 2013—proposed federal legislation to make DOD educational benefits and VA educational benefits count in the "90 percent" of the 90/10 rule rather than in the "10 percent" part. Powerful senators supported doing so, saying those funds came from the federal government too. Opponents said that they were not borrowed money, but rather benefits contractually given to voluntary servicemen and women in a time of war in return for their service in the armed forces. As such, they were those people's private monies to do with as they pleased; not something the federal government had the right to oversee via the ability to remove a for-profit school from Title IV lending partication where it violated the 90/10 rule. The issue was expected to be decided in late 2013 or 2014, with some strong support in Congress for counting it in the 90-side of that formula. APEI's student body in 2013 got their funding to pay for the APEI courses through the following sources:

2013 APEI Registrations by Primary Funding Source	% of Total
Federal Student Aid (Title IV)	35%
Department of Defense Tuition Assistance (TA)	39%
Veterans Benefits (VA)	15%
Cash and Other Sources	11%

32   Part of that strong support in Congress also saw increasing energy for considering going back to an 85/15 rule rather than the current 90/10 rule for the amount of federal student loan money that could make up a proprietary university's tuition revenue base. So APEI executives, and those of its competitors, had seen a very significant concern affecting their core revenue source take center stage as the great recession, and the war in Afghanistan, appeared to be fading in importance.

33   **Lead Generation and Student Recruitment** is the lifeblood of proprietary schools, which in turn makes it a driver influencing the competitive landscape. APEI has historically focused mainly on a relationship-based marketing strategy, striving to build long-term, mutually beneficial relationships with organizations and individuals in the military and public service communities. APEI's assumption is that people working in these fields tend to be tightly knit affinity groups, which greatly facilitates personal referrals from influential members as well as from current students and alumni to prospective students. They believe this approach enables APEI universities to achieve student acquisition costs that are substantially less than the industry average. APEI also supplement this approach with multifaceted interactive marketing campaigns (organic search; pay-per-click and banner advertising; participation in online social communities) to help build brand awareness and drive inquiries. APEI has recently experienced increases in student acquisition costs, which they primarily attribute to APEI's APU expansion in nonmilitary markets. As a result, APEI executives have alerted stockholders that, as it continues to grow in size and diversity, its student acquisition costs may continue to increase. An APEI marketing executive recently made this observation:

> To continue to grow our enrollment, we expect to continue to increase the amounts that we spend on marketing and advertising as our traditional approach to marketing and advertising may not be able to sustain meaningful growth rates. However, because we are smaller than most of our competitors and because our tuition is generally lower, we have fewer dollars available to spend on marketing and advertising than they do. Accordingly, we may find it increasingly difficult to continue to compete and grow our enrollments.[6]

34   The UOP spent $1.2 billion last year in selling and promo expenditures—6 times APEI's total revenue, 24 times APEI's PBTax, and 35 times APEI's selling and promotional expenditures last year.

35   ***Incentive Payment Rules.*** As part of an institution's program participation agreement with the Department of Education and in accordance with the Higher Education Act, an institution may not provide any commission, bonus, or other incentive payment to any person or entity engaged in any student recruitment, admissions, or financial aid awarding activity based directly or indirectly on success in securing enrollments or financial aid. Failure to comply with the incentive payment rule could result in termination of participation in Title IV programs, limitation on participation in Title IV programs, or financial penalties.

36   The wave of DOE Title IV-related regulatory attention sweeping Washington has not ignored proprietary colleges' lead generation and student recruitment practices either. The immediate focus in all of this attention, indeed, the practice that ignited the flame of attention, was undercover scrutiny of "enrollment counseling" and recruitment practices undertaken by the Department of Education. The results were damaging to the industry, particularly the large public proprietary schools, even those including APEI that weren't targeted or indicted relative to their practices. Most actions were settled before extended litigation, with the most meaningful change being the implementation of a regulation that barred proprietary college or university students from receiving Title IV funding if that school paid bonuses or financial incentives to recruiters or enrollment counselors. That, in turn, has caused a fundamental change in how key large proprietary colleges and universities go about their lead generation and recruitment efforts. That has caused some significant organization and compensation adjustments for the biggest APEI competitors, which APEI has not had to do.

37   **Tuition, Books, and Fees.** APEI's ability to provide affordable programs is one of its competitive strengths. As noted earlier, APEI has maintained its undergraduate tuition costs in line with public, in-state rates and within the DoD tuition ceilings—$250 per semester credit hour, or $750 per three-credit course, DoD's maximum tuition assistance levels per

[6]APEI 2012 10-K.

semester credit hour. Since 2000, APEI has not raised undergraduate tuition rates per semester credit hour, and they anticipate no tuition increase for undergraduate students for the foreseeable future. A full 121-semester hour undergraduate degree may be earned for $30,250.

38   Eligible undergraduate students also receive their textbooks at no cost to them through APEI's book grant program, which represents a potential average student savings over the course of a degree of approximately $4,500 when compared to four-year colleges according to The College Board Study, Annual Survey of Colleges report. Most students transfer in a significant amount of prior credit earned, which also reduces the cost and time of earning their degree.

39   Graduate tuition is $325 per semester hour, or $975 per three-credit hour course. For military students, the service branch pays $750 of the tuition costs per three-semester credit hour course, and students have the option of paying the remainder out of pocket or applying their GI Bill entitlements to cover the cost above $750. At these tuition rates, including the planned tuition increase, students may earn a graduate degree for less than $12,000 in tuition costs.

40   Despite being an open enrollment institution, APEI does not charge an admission fee, nor does it charge fees for services such as registration, technology, course drops, and similar events that trigger fees at many institutions. In addition, as a total distance learning institution, there are no resident fees, such as for parking, food service, student union, and recreation. While APEI charges a fee for transfer credit evaluation for non–active duty military students, unlike transfer credit fees at many institutions, the fee is a one-time fee that does not increase as more credits are transferred.

41   **Other competitive forces.** APEI competes with not-for-profit public and private two-year and four-year colleges as well as other for-profit schools, particularly those that offer online learning programs similar to those that APEI offers. These public institutions receive substantial government subsidies, and public and private institutions have access to government and foundation grants, tax-deductible contributions, and other financial resources generally not available to for-profit schools. Accordingly, public and private institutions may have instructional and support resources that are superior to those in the for-profit sector. In addition, says an APEI marketing executive, "some of our competitors, including both traditional colleges and universities and other for-profit schools, have substantially greater name recognition and financial and other resources than we have, which may enable them to compete more effectively for potential students. We are also continuing to see increasing differentiation between the way in which our competitors are delivering online offerings, which impacts the ability to attract students, facilitate access to education, and provide convenience to learners."

42   In addition, APEI faces new competition from various emerging nontraditional, credit-bearing, and non-credit-bearing education programs provided by proprietary, not-for-profit, and public providers, including massively open online courses (MOOCs) offered worldwide without charge by traditional educational institutions and other direct-to-consumer education services, as well as other offerings at low costs to students. These MOOCs are offered by some of the most well-known universities in the United States, Canada, Europe, and Asia. Within the last year, many public and private schools are considering or starting to give academic credit for having successfully taken these free courses.

43   While APEI faces many old and new competitive forces, APEI's top marketing executive said that "the primary competitive factors for institutions targeting working adult students include specific degree program offerings; affordability, including tuition and fees and rates of increase; convenience and flexibility, including availability of online courses and the use of education related technology; reputation and academic quality; and marketing effectiveness."

THE FUTURE FOR APEI

44 Dr. Wallace Boston, a certified public accountant and certified management accountant who earned an AB degree in history from Duke University, an MBA in marketing and accounting from Tulane University's Freeman School of Business Administration, and a doctorate in higher education management from the University of Pennsylvania's Graduate School of Education, had these thoughts to share looking toward APEI's future as its president and CEO:

> Since our founding in 1991 by recently retired USMC Major Jim Etter, we have earned a reputation for best practices in online higher education, won increasing recognition for academic excellence and innovation, and established APEI as a distance-learning leader. Today, according to the research and consulting firm Eduventures, we are the second-largest, fully online provider of higher education in the United States. In 2013, *U.S. News & World Report* ranked APEI 22nd among the nation's 237 schools offering online bachelor's degree programs, or in the top 10 percent overall.
>
> Higher education is a national priority. The United States alone is expected to require 22 million new workers with college degrees by 2018—and the nation faces a projected shortfall of 3 million. In an economic environment where the cost of higher education exceeds the reach of many students, and prospective students have become increasingly discerning, APEI offers a compelling value proposition—access to respected and affordable online degree programs. For undergraduates, the combined cost of tuition, fees, and books at APEI is roughly 19 percent lower than the average in-state cost of a public university; for graduate students, it is 33 percent lower. Among the 10 leading providers of online education, APEI is, on average, 42 percent lower for undergraduates and 33 percent lower for graduate students.
>
> APEI has built an efficient, asset-rich platform for organic growth, as well as for addressing new and emerging growth opportunities in higher education. With over $125 million in cash and equivalents and no long-term debt, APEI looks to 2014 with significant financial resources. We have developed a strategic plan to leverage our strengths and expand internationally, to offer new degree programs in high-demand professional fields, to provide cost-effective and innovative education hosting and support services, and to enter into new market segments.

CONSOLIDATED STATEMENTS OF INCOME

	YEAR ENDED DECEMBER 31,									
	2008		2009		2010		2011		2012	
Total Enrollment	45,200		63,732		83,100		111,000		127,000	
Growth: Year over Year	50%		41%		30.39%		33.57%		14.41%	
Net Course Registrations [# of courses taken]	147,124		198,392		259,389		341,669		402,205	
Growth: Year over Year	55%		34.85%		30.75%		31.72%		17.72%	
Revenues (In thousands, except per share amounts)	$107,147	100%	$148,998	100%	$198,174	100%	$260,377	100%	$313,516	100%
Costs and expenses:										
Instructional costs and services	43,561	41%	58,383	39%	75,309	38%	95,216	37%	110,192	35%
Selling and promotional	12,361	12%	20,479	14%	34,296	17%	44,713	17%	59,761	19%
General and administrative	21,302	20%	25,039	17%	32,045	16%	48,350	19%	63,615	20%
Depreciation and amortization	4,235	4%	5,231	4%	6,502	3%	9,239	4%	11,146	4%
Total costs and expenses	81,459	76%	109,132	73% ;	148,152	75%	197,518	76%	244,714	78%
Income before interest income and income taxes	25,688	24%	39,866	27%	50,022	25%	62,859	24%	68,802	22%
Interest income, net	706	1%	94	0%	111	0%	109	0%	135	0%
Income from operations before income taxes	26,394	25%	39,960	27%	50,133	25%	62,968	24%	68,937	22%
Income tax expense	10,207	10%	16,017	11%	20,265	10%	22,211	9%	26,528	8%
Investment loss, net of tax	—		—		—		—		-86	
Net income	$16,187	15%	$23,943	16%	$29,868	15%	$40,757	16%	$42,323	13%
Net income attributable to common stockholders per common share:										
Basic	$0.91		$1.32		$1.63		$2.28		$2.38	
Diluted	$0.86		$1.27		$1.59		$2.23		$2.35	
Weighted average number of shares outstanding:										
Basic	17,840		18,167		18,281		17,877		17,772	
Diluted	18,822		18,906		18,837		18,295		18,041	

CONSOLIDATED BALANCE SHEETS

AS OF DECEMBER 31,

(In thousands, except per share amounts)	2008		2009		2010		2011		2012	
Assets										
Current assets:										
Cash and cash equivalents	$47,714	60.5%	$74,866	64.7%	$81,352	57.4%	$119,006	59.8%	$114,901	48.4%
Accounts receivable, net of allowance of $4,996 in 2011 and $11,106 in 2012	6,188	7.9%	8,664	7.5%	10,269	7.2%	9,499	4.8%	10,428	4.4%
Prepaid expenses	2,156	2.7%	2,990	2.6%	4,233	3.0%	4,961	2.5%	4,290	0.0%
Income tax receivable	1,306	1.7%	863	0.8%	780	0.6%	1,603	0.8%	4,953	3.9%
Deferred income taxes	640	0.8%	999	0.9%	1,369	1.0%	3,653	1.8%	6,502	2.7%
Total current assets	58,004	73.6%	88,382	76.4%	98,003	69.1%	138,722	69.8%	141,074	59.4%
Property and equipment, net	19,622	24.9%	25,294	21.9%	42,415	29.9%	58,759	29.5%	82,840	34.9%
Note receivable	—	0.0%	—	0.0%	—	0.0%	—	0.0%	—	0.0%
Investment	—	0.0%	—	0.0%	—	0.0%	—	0.0%	6,664	2.8%
Other assets	1,187	1.5%	2,077	1.8%	1,421	1.0%	1,410	0.7%	1,025	3.0%
Total assets	$78,813	100.0%	$115,753	100.0%	$141,839	100.0%	$198,891	100.0%	$237,603	100.0%
Liabilities and Stockholders' Equity										
Current liabilities:										
Accounts payable	$4,946	6.3%	$6,756	5.8%	$9,422	6.6%	$16,318	8.2%	$17,251	7.3%
Accrued liabilities	7,075	9.0%	8,003	6.9%	9,349	6.6%	14,486	7.3%	12,042	5.1%
Deferred revenue and student deposits	9,626	12.2%	14,204	12.3%	18,815	13.3%	25,884	13.0%	25,777	10.9%
Total current liabilities	21,647	27.5%	28,963	25.0%	37,586	26.5%	56,688	28.5%	55,070	23.2%
Deferred income taxes	3,691	4.7%	4,772	4.1%	6,953	4.9%	8,370	4.2%	11,380	4.8%
Total liabilities	25,338	32.2%	33,735	29.1%	44,539	31.4%	65,058	32.7%	66,450	28.0%
Commitments and contingencies (Note 3 and 7)										
Stockholders' equity:										
Preferred Stock, $.01 par value; Authorized shares—10,000; no shares issued or outstanding	—		—		—		—		—	
Common Stock, $.01 par value; Authorized shares—100,000; 17,844 issued and outstanding in 2011; 17,752 issued and outstanding in 2012	180	0.2%	183	0.2%	186	0.1%	178	0.1%	178	0.1%
Additional paid-in capital	132,078	167.6%	136,380	117.8%	121,791	100.0%	147,053	73.9%	157,449	66.3%
Retained earnings (accumulated deficit)	−78,193	−100.0%	−54,545	−47.1%	−24,677	−31.5%	−13,398	−6.7%	13,526	5.7%
Total stockholders' equity	53,475	67.9%	82,018	70.9%	97,300	68.6%	133,833	67.3%	171,153	72.0%
Total liabilities and stockholders' equity	$78,813	100.0%	$115,753	100.0%	$141,839	100.0%	$198,891	100.0%	$237,603	100.0%

CONSOLIDATED STATEMENTS OF CASH FLOWS

YEAR ENDED DECEMBER 31,

(In thousands, % of Net Income)	2008		2009		2010		2011		2012	
Operating activities										
Net income	$16,187	33.9%	$23,943	32.0%	$29,868	36.7%	$40,757	34.2%	$42,323	36.8%
Adjustments to reconcile net income to net cash provided by operating activities										
Increase in allowance for doubtful accounts	152	0.3%	359	0.5%	154	0.2%	3,946	3.3%	6,110	5.3%
Depreciation and amortization	4,235	8.9%	5,231	7.0%	6,502	8.0%	9,239	7.8%	11,146	9.7%
Stock-based compensation	1,674	3.5%	2,223	3.0%	2,805	3.4%	3,189	2.7%	3,818	3.3%
Loss on disposal	—	0.0%	5	0.0%	129	0.2%	44	0.0%	91	0.1%
Investment loss	—	0.0%	—	0.0%	—	0.0%	—	0.0%	86	0.1%
Stock issued for director compensation	196	0.4%	186	0.2%	174	0.2%	139	0.1%	116	0.1%
Deferred income taxes	1,295	2.7%	722	0.1%	1,811	2.2%	−867	−0.7%	161	0.1%
Changes in operating assets and liabilities:										
Accounts receivable	−1,443	−3.0%	−2,835	−3.8%	−1,759	−2.2%	−3,176	−2.7%	−7,039	−6.1%
Prepaid expenses and other assets	−560	−1.2%	−837	−1.1%	−1,312	−1.6%	−1,112	−0.9%	1,080	0.9%
Income tax receivable	−217	−0.5%	443	0.6%	83	0.2%	−823	−0.7%	−3,350	−2.9%
Accounts payable	2,474	5.2%	1,810	2.4%	2,666	3.3%	6,896	5.8%	933	0.8%
Accrued liabilities	2,752	5.8%	928	1.2%	1,346	1.7%	5,137	4.3%	−2,444	−2.1%
Deferred revenue and student deposits	3,012	6.3%	4,578	6.1%	4,611	5.7%	7,069	5.9%	−107	−0.1%
Net cash provided by operating activities	**29,757**	**62.4%**	**36,756**	**49.1%**	**47,078**	**57.9%**	**70,438**	**59.2%**	**52,924**	**46.1%**
Investing activities										
Capital expenditures	−10,009	−21.0%	−10,758	−14.4%	−22,454	−27.6%	−24,925	−20.9%	−35,014	−30.5%
Investment	—	0.0%	—	0.0%	—	0.0%	—	0.0%	−6,750	−5.9%
Note receivable	—	0.0%	—	0.0%	—	0.0%	—	0.0%	−6,000	−5.2%
Capitalized program development costs and other assets	−896	−1.9%	−1,037	−1.4%	−573	−0.7%	−307	−0.3%	−328	−0.3%
Net cash used in investing activities	**−10,905**	**−22.9%**	**−11,795**	**−15.8%**	**−23,027**	**−28.3%**	**−25,232**	**−21.2%**	**−48,092**	**−41.9%**
Financing activities										
Cash paid for repurchase of common/restricted stock	−295	−0.6%	−220	−0.3%	−20,240	−24.9%	−9,745	−8.2%	−15,861	−13.8%
Cash received from issuance of common stock, net of issuance costs	770	1.6%	640	0.9%	1,121	1.4%	910	0.8%	4,058	3.5%
Excess tax benefit from stock based compensation	1,436	3.0%	1,771	2.4%	1,554	1.9%	1,283	1.1%	2,866	2.5%
Net cash used in financing activities	**1,911**	**4.0%**	**2,191**	**2.9%**	**−17,565**	**−21.6%**	**−7,552**	**−6.3%**	**−8,937**	**−7.8%**
Total Cash										
Net increase (decrease) in cash and cash equivalents	20,763	43.5%	27,152	36.3%	6,486	8.0%	37,645	31.6%	−4,105	−3.6%
Cash and cash equivalents at beginning of period	26,951	56.5%	47,714	63.7%	74,866	92.0%	81,352	68.4%	119,006	1036%
Cash and cash equivalents at end of period	**$47,714**	**100.0%**	**$74,866**	**100.0%**	**$81,352**	**100.0%**	**$119,006**	**100.0%**	**$114,901**	**100.0%**
Supplemental disclosures of cash flow information										
Income taxes paid	$8,023	16.8%	$12,932	17.3%	$16,819	20.7%	$22,619	19.0%	$26,851	23.4%

CONSOLIDATED STATEMENT OF STOCKHOLDERS' EQUITY

(In thousands, except shares)	PREFERRED STOCK		COMMON STOCK		REPURCHASED STOCK		ADDITIONAL PAID-IN CAPITAL	ACCU-MULATED DEFICIT	TOTAL STOCK-HOLDERS' EQUITY
	SHARES	AMOUNT	SHARES	AMOUNT	SHARES	AMOUNT	AMOUNT	SHARES	AMOUNT
Balance as of December 31, 2009	—	$—	18275655	$183	—	$—	$136,380	-$54,545	$82,018
Stock issued for cash	—	—	322134	3	—	—	1,118	—	1,121
Stock issued for director compensation	—	—	4,424	—	—	—	174	—	174
Repurchased shares of common and restricted stock from stockholders	—	—	-9,625	—	-682046	-19,966	-274	—	-20,240
Stock-based compensation	—	—	—	—	—	—	2,805	—	2,805
Repurchased and retired shares of common stock	—	—	—	—	—	—	—	—	—
Excess tax benefit from stock based compensation	—	—	—	—	—	—	1,554	—	1,554
Net income	—	—	—	—	—	—	—	29,868	29,868
Balance as of December 31, 2010	—	—	18592588	186	-682046	-19,966	141757	-24,677	97,300
Stock issued for cash	—	—	155472	1	—	—	909	—	910
Stock issued for director compensation	—	—	3,540	—	—	—	139	—	139
Repurchased shares of common and restricted stock from stockholders	—	—	-6,050	—	-219208	-9,521	-224	—	-9,745
Stock-based compensation	—	—	—	—	—	—	3,189	—	3,189
Repurchased and retired shares of common stock	—	—	-901254	-9	901254	29,487	—	-29,478	—
Excess tax benefit from stock based compensation	—	—	—	—	—	—	1,283	—	1,283
Net income	—	—	—	—	—	—	—	40,757	40,757
Balance as of December 31, 2011	—	—	17844296	178	—	—	147053	-13,398	133833
Stock issued for cash	—	—	408739	5	—	—	4,053	—	4,058
Stock issued for director compensation	—	—	3,098	—	—	—	116	—	116
Repurchased shares of common and restricted stock from stockholders	—	—	-10,697	—	-493491	-15,399	-457	—	-15,856
Stock-based compensation	—	—	—	—	—	—	3,818	—	3,818
Repurchased and retired shares of common stock	—	—	-493491	-5	493491	15,399	—	-15,399	-5
Excess tax benefit from stock based compensation	—	—	—	—	—	—	2,866	—	2,866
Net income	—	—	—	—	—	—	—	42,323	42,323
Balance as of December 31, 2012	$—	—	17751945	$178	—	$—	$157449	$13,526	$171153

APEI—Key Financial Ratios	AS OF DECEMBER 31,							
	2005	2006	2007	2008	2009	2010	2011	2012
Profitability % of Sales								
*Return on Sales (net margin) %	−42.23	4.49	12.66	15.11	16.07	15.07	15.65	13.5
*Asset Turnover	1.26	1.56	1.78	1.68	1.53	1.54	1.53	1.44
*Return on Assets %	−53.02	7.02	22.51	25.33	24.61	23.19	23.92	19.39
*Financial Leverage	1.54	1.71	1.46	1.47	1.41	1.46	1.49	1.39
*Return on Equity %	−81.85	11.47	34.77	37.22	35.34	33.31	35.27	27.75
Gross Margin %	52.99	55.15	57.34	59.34	60.82	62	63.43	64.85
Operating Margin %	7.89	7.34	21.26	23.97	26.76	25.24	24.14	21.95

* Dupont Ratios

	2005	2006	2007	2008	2009	2010	2011	2012
Growth								
Revenue								
Year over Year	21.88	42.11	72.54	55.07	39.06	33	31.39	20.41
3-Year Average	—	31.13	44.04	56.08	54.96	42.08	34.44	28.14
Operating Income								
Year over Year	—	32.19	399.69	74.86	55.19	25.48	25.66	9.45
3-Year Average	—	16.74	—	126.05	138.46	50.44	34.76	19.95
Net Income								
Year over Year	−52.56	65.71	386.65	84.99	47.92	24.75	36.46	3.84
3-Year Average	—	102.35	56.4	146.18	137.03	50.57	36.04	20.91
EPS								
Year over Year	—	—	326.67	34.38	47.67	25.2	40.25	5.38
3-Year Average	—	55.36	42.75	—	103.82	35.44	37.38	22.77
Liquidity/Financial Health								
Current Ratio	1.96	2.22	2.6	2.68	3.05	2.61	2.45	2.5
Quick Ratio	1.82	2.08	2.46	2.55	2.91	2.46	2.3	2.37
Financial Leverage	1.54	1.71	1.46	1.47	1.41	1.46	1.49	1.39
Debt/Equity	—	—	—	—	—	—	—	—
Efficiency								
Days Sales Outstanding	53.77	43.75	27.32	18.88	18.19	17.44	13.86	11
Receivables Turnover	6.79	8.34	13.36	19.33	20.06	20.93	26.34	31.47
Fixed Assets Turnover	2.96	4.24	6.08	6.5	6.63	5.85	5.15	4.43
Asset Turnover	1.26	1.56	1.78	1.68	1.53	1.54	1.53	1.44

Case 13

The Apollo Group, Inc. [University of Phoenix]   Richard B. Robinson

1   A 55-year-old college professor at San Jose State University with a PhD from Cambridge University and previous teaching jobs at Maryland, Ohio State, and Northern Illinois, John Sperling was a surprise entrepreneur when he started the Apollo Group, parent company of the University of Phoenix, in 1976. Ambitious, his goal was to revolutionize conventional higher education. Most people would say that Sperling, recently celebrating his 91st birthday, has done just that.

2   Rather than catering to 18- to 22-year-olds looking to find themselves, Sperling focused on the then-neglected market of working adults. And he recruited working professionals as teachers, rather than tenured professors. UOP (on-campus and online) has more than 32,000 faculty members with less than 5 percent being full-time. Most radical of all, while nearly all other universities are nonprofits, Sperling ran his university to make money. Those ideas sparked overwhelming resistance from the education establishment, which branded UOP a "diploma mill." The result? "We faced failure every day for the first 10 years," said founder Sperling, who turned 93 in 2014.

3   From an IPO adjusted price of $0.76 to a mid-2005 high of $98, Apollo's stock reflected a company *BusinessWeek* once considered among the top 50 performing companies on Wall Street. The Phoenix-based company, whose day-to-day operations were still generating average annual revenue growth exceeding 30 percent over that time, saw its revenues reach $4.3 billion in 2012 with net income exceeding $393 million. It has also joined the S&P 500.

4   Tuition at Apollo averages only $12,000 a year, 60 percent of what a typical private college charges. A key factor, says Sperling, is that universities for the young require student unions, sports teams, student societies, and so on. The average age of a UOP student is 35, so UOP doesn't have those expenses. It also saves by holding classes in leased office spaces around the country, and online, By 2012, over 75 percent of UOP students studied at University of Phoenix Online.

5   UOP has become the dominant player in the online education market that still has lots of potential for growth. The bricks-and-mortar University of Phoenix was one of the first institutions to identify and serve the burgeoning market for educating working adults. In the late 1980s, long before the Web debuted, the school began to experiment with offering its classes online. It got off to a slow start, "and we lost money for a number of years," recalled Brian Mueller, Apollo's former president.

6   As a result of this head start, however, UOP's online option was ready to capitalize on an online-education market that began exploding in the mid-1990s. Today, it is estimated that over 10 percent of the U.S. students earning a degree via the Net are enrolled through the UOP's online option. UOP's online option also garners an outsize share of the industry's revenues—about one-third of the total. That's because as the market leader, it can charge higher tuition than most rivals. Undergraduates pay a little more than $12,000 a year at UOP, while students seeking a master's degree pay nearly $22,000. "They're by far the giant in this industry," says Eduventure market analyst Sean Gallagher. The

Source: ©2014, RCT, LLC. This case was developed based on publicly available information from the Apollo Group, Inc., the University of Phoenix, interviews with UOP students and professors, and selected reports as cited.

average 2013 undergraduate tuition + fees was $29,056 at private colleges, $8,651 for state residents at public colleges, and $21,706 for out-of-state residents attending public universities.

7   Online education is rapidly growing, but it is still just getting started. "There are 70 million working adults in this country who don't have a college degree," says Gallagher. Increasingly, they realize that they need a degree to get ahead. But because they often have a family as well as a job, studying online is the most convenient solution. Howard Block, an analyst at Banc of America Securities, predicts "dramatic enrollment growth" for UOP's online option. He expects that half of the students in postsecondary education will one day make at least some use of the Internet to earn their degrees.

GLOBAL OUTREACH

8   UOP began to seriously tap the international market with its online option in 2005, initially "bringing in about 500 students a month," said Mueller. "But that's just the tip of the iceberg." Though the UOP started offering online classes only in English, it has begun to offer courses in Spanish and plans to introduce Mandarin soon as well. Ironically, UOP has done all this with plain-vanilla technology. While other companies charged into online education with dazzling digital content, UOP has historically offered primarily a text-heavy format that can easily be accessed with dial-up modems.

9   This might sound like a recipe for failure. But UOP realized that interaction with humans—the professor and other students in the class—was far more important to success than interaction with the digital content. Thus, UOP keeps its classes small, averaging just 12 students. And to combat the Achilles heel of distance education—a high dropout rate—it offers its students plenty of hand-holding, including round-the-clock tech support. The result: 65 percent of its students go on to graduate.

10   Some see plain technology as a potential negative for the virtual college. "At some point, UOP online will need to upgrade the sophistication of its platform," warned Trace Urdan, an analyst with ThinkEquity Partners, a boutique investment bank. That will require more spending on research and development and information technology, he warns, which could crimp margins. Still, any extra spending could be easily offset if UOP bumped up its class size to 15 students, argueed Block. Even with today's small classes, operating profit margins now top 20 percent. As if listening to them, the UOP now has an excellent, visual explanation of how this type of multifaceted online educational approach works.[1]

THE ONLINE TREND

11   The dot-com bubble may have burst in the world of commerce, but the promise of harnessing the Internet for paradigm-changing growth—and even profits—still thrives in the halls of academia.

12   A decade after the dot-com fizzle began, e-learning has emerged from the wreckage as one of the Internet's most useful applications. Nearly 90 percent of the 4,000 major colleges and universities in the United States now offer classes over the Internet or use the Web to enhance campus classes, according to market researcher International Data Corp. About 7 million students took online classes from U.S. higher-ed institutions in 2012 according to John G. Flores, head of the U.S. Distance Learning Assn., a nonprofit trade group outside

[1]www.phoenix.edu/students/how-it-works.html.

Boston. And it's not just a U.S. phenomenon: students from developing countries are jumping online, too.

13   These classes continue to open new horizons for the fastest-growing segment of higher education: working adults, who often find it difficult to juggle conventional classes with jobs and families. Adults over 25 now represent nearly half of higher-ed students; most are employed and want more education to advance their careers.

14   E-learning is an influence in the traditional college class as well. Online classes won't replace the college experience for most 18- to 24-year-olds. But from the Massachusetts Institute of Technology to Wake Forest University in North Carolina, colleges are using the Web in on-campus classes to augment textbooks and boost communication. And students, far more technology savvy than many of their professors or administrators, are using Web-based tools, social media, and many other approaches to morph Web-based capabilities into their academic experience with or without their university following along, or even approving.

MASS MARKET?

15   Quality is a problem, which is a key reason why many online students drop out. That will force a further shakeout, eliminating mediocre players. Many colleges grapple with such issues as how much time their faculty should devote to e-teaching. And long-established rules make it difficult for online students to get financial aid. Even as these problems are resolved, "online learning will never be as good as face-to-face instruction," argues Andy DiPaolo, director of the Stanford Center for Professional Development, which offers online graduate classes to engineers.

16   Ultimately, the greatest e-learning market may lie in the developing world, where the population of college-age students is exploding. Just as cell phones leapfrogged land-based telephones in many developing countries, so may e-learning help to educate the masses in countries that lack the colleges to meet demand—and can't afford to build them.

COST-EFFECTIVE

17   E-learning is a good fit with the military, where frequent transfers complicate pursuing a degree. The U.S. Army awarded PWC Consulting a $453 million, five-year contract to create an electronic university that allows soldiers to be anywhere and study at Kansas State University or any of the 24 colleges involved in the program.

18   eArmyU already has changed the perspective of soldiers like Sergeant Jeremy Dellinger, 22, who had been planning to leave the Army to go back to school when his basic enlistment ends. Then he enrolled in eArmyU to earn his bachelor's degree from Troy State University in Alabama. "Now I can get my degree and still do the work I love" as a supply sergeant, says the Fort Benning (Ga.)-based soldier. Like Dellinger, about 15 percent of those who have signed up so far have reenlisted or extended their commitment. By cutting turnover, "eArmyU could almost pay for itself," says program director Lee Harvey, since it costs nearly $70,000 to train green recruits.

19   Corporations, too, see e-learning as a cost-effective way to get better-educated employees. Indeed, corporate spending on e-learning is expected to more than quadruple by 2015, to $35 billion, estimates IDC. At IBM, some 500,000 employees received education or training online last year, and 75 percent of the company's Basic Blue class for new managers is online. The move cut IBM's training bill by $750 million last year, because online classes don't require travel.

CAUTIOUS ELITES

20 Phoenix Online aside, the big e-learning winners so far are the traditional nonprofit universities. They initially captured nearly 95 percent of online enrollments, figures A. Frank Mayadas, head of e-learning grants at the Alfred P. Sloan Foundation. Most active are state and community colleges that started with strong brand names, a faculty, and accreditation, says Mayadas, as well as a tradition of extension programs.

21 By contrast, many elite universities have been far more cautious about diluting the value of their name. Harvard Business School believes it would be impossible to replicate its classroom education online. "We will never offer a Harvard MBA online," vows professor W. Earl Sasser, chairman of HBS Interactive, which instead develops e-learning programs for companies. MIT faculty nixed teaching classes online, fearing "it would detract from the residential experience," says former faculty chair Steven Lerman.

22 That didn't stop MIT from embracing the Internet in a different way. Over the next five years, MIT plans to post lecture notes and reading assignments for most of its 2,000 classes on the Web for free, calling the effort "OpenClassWare." Lerman says "it's a service to the world," but he says it's no substitute for actual teaching, so faculty aren't worried about a threat to classroom learning.

23 A few other top schools see profit-making opportunities. Since 1996, Duke University's Fuqua School of Business has been offering MBAs for working executives. In these blended programs, some 65 percent of the work is done online and just 35 percent in classes held during required residencies that consume 9 to 11 weeks over two years. Duke charges well over $95,000 for these programs—vs. $75,000 for its traditional residential MBA. Yet they have been so popular that by next year, "we'll have more students in nontraditional programs than the daytime program," according to Fuqua's dean. The extra revenues are helping Fuqua to double its faculty.

The Adult Education Market

24 The adult education market is a significant and growing component of the postsecondary education market, which is estimated by the U.S. Department of Education to be a more than $450 billion industry. According to the U.S. Department of Education, over 7 million, or 45 percent of all students enrolled in higher education programs are over the age of 24. This number is projected to reach 8.5 million in 2015. The market for adult education in the United States is expected to increase as working adults seek additional education and training to update and improve their skills, to enhance their earnings potential, and to keep pace with the rapidly expanding knowledge-based economy.

25 Many working adults are seeking accredited degree programs that provide flexibility to accommodate the fixed schedules and time commitments associated with their professional and personal obligations. President Obama, with the United States trying to gain traction coming out of the "Great Recession," said in his 2012 State of the Union address that having no degree is really no longer an option:

> Many people watching tonight can probably remember a time when finding a good job
> meant showing up at a nearby factory or a business downtown. You didn't always need a
> degree, and your competition was pretty much limited to your neighbors. If you worked
> hard, chances are you'd have a job for life, with a decent paycheck, good benefits, and the
> occasional promotion. Maybe you'd even have the pride of seeing your kids work at the same
> company. That world has changed. And for many, the change has been painful. I've seen it
> in the shuttered windows of once booming factories, and the vacant storefronts of once busy
> Main Streets. I've heard it in the frustrations of Americans who've seen their paychecks

dwindle or their jobs disappear—proud men and women who feel like the rules have been changed in the middle of the game.

26 His point: the rules of the game have changed. And, it would seem, the for-profit (industry participants prefer "proprietary") collegiate education sector has grown to reflect the new reality that access to a higher education is no longer the province of the privileged few, but a prerequisite to "owning our future" as individuals, or as he sees it, a country.

27 The need for more options in higher education to ensure more people gain the education necessary in a knowledge-based economy is greater today than ever before. Demographics, and a changing global economy, say it is a need that will only grow.

28 Dr. Bruce Chaloux, president of the Sloan Consortium, estimates that there are more than 50 *million* working-age adults with some college credit but no degree, or who have a high school diploma but never entered college. Chaloux says that many of these adults would like to get their college degrees, but only if they're given practical "adult-friendly" alternatives to traditional, campus-based programs. He identified eight key factors that influence an adult learner's decision to attend college:[2]

- Convenient time and place for classes
- Flexible pacing for completing the program
- Ability to transfer credits
- Reputation of institution as being adult friendly
- Need the degree for current or future job
- Receive credit for life/work experiences
- Financial aid or employer assistance
- Child care

29 The Southern Regional Education Board in turn offers four guiding principles it finds essential to meeting the needs of adult college students:[3]

- Online or blended delivery
- Accelerated (or compressed) terms
- Adult-friendly policies
- Supportive credit transfer and prior learning assessment

30 Traditional colleges and universities have been slow to address the unique requirements of working adult students. First John Sperling, and now a global chorus of observers, has cited the following attributes of traditional, not-proprietary education institutions:

- Traditional universities and colleges were designed to fulfill the educational needs of conventional, full-time students aged 18 to 24, who remain the primary focus of these universities and colleges.
- This focus has resulted in a capital-intensive teaching/learning model in typical state and private colleges and universities that may be characterized by:
  - a high percentage of full-time tenured faculty with doctoral degrees;
  - fully configured library facilities and related full-time staff;
  - dormitories, student unions, and other significant plant assets to support the needs of younger students;
  - often major investment in and commitment to comprehensive sports programs;

[2]http://sloanconsortium.org.
[3]http://sreb.org.

- major administrative overhead for all the various university functions;
- politically-based funding;
- major resistance to change in any academic programs, even in the face of rapid global change across disciplines and professions;
- an emphasis on research and the related staff and facilities; and
- faculty with PhDs and a research focus but limited practical experience, even in key programs like business and other working-related professions.

- The majority of accredited colleges and universities continue to provide the bulk of their educational programming from September to mid-December and from mid-January to May. As a result, most full-time faculty members only teach during that limited period of time.
- While this structure serves the needs of the full-time 18- to 24-year-old student, it limits the educational opportunity for working adults who must delay their education for up to five months during these spring, summer, and winter breaks.
- Traditional universities and colleges are also limited in their ability to market to or provide the necessary customer service for working adult students because it requires the development of additional administrative and enrollment infrastructure.

31   Traditional colleges and universities, born out of a centuries old academic model and tradition, have seen adult and continuing education as awkard institutional fits for their mission—ancillary, less rigorous, yet subtly necessary activities to serve their state or local population needs but not rooted in the institution's core academic tradition.

32   The UOP's format since its inception has focused on working adult students by providing an accredited collegiate education that enables them to attend classes and complete classwork in a schedule and manner more convenient to the constraints their work life imposes on their ability to obtain a college or advanced degree. It may well be that proprietary schools such as the UOP have proved more adaptable, if not more creative, in responding to this twenty-first century, knowledge-economy adult student reality.

THE PROPRIETARY (FOR-PROFIT) COLLEGE AND UNIVERSITY SECTOR

33   Undergraduate enrollments in the United States increased by more than a third to 17.6 million in the first decade of the twenty-first century, with the most dramatic growth occurring at proprietary colleges. It was the fastest decade of growth since the 1970s. Proprietary colleges enrolled 10 percent of all undergraduates in 2010, up from 3 percent in 2000. Proprietary enrollments increased fivefold to 1.2 million at four-year colleges, and nearly doubled to 385,000 at two-year institutions, according to Jack Buckley, Commissioner, National Center for Education Statistics. The *Chronicle of Higher Education* says it is even higher— 10 percent of all students enrolled full-time in degree-granting institutions, and rising by an average rate of 9 percent annually over the last 30 years. "We are seeing a shift" that has "created additional opportunities . . . (and) brought to light differences in how students pursue and pay for that education," Buckley said, adding that higher education "may look quite different" in 2020, when enrollments are projected to reach 20 million.[4]

34   Thirty-five years ago, approximately 90,000 students attended proprietary colleges and universities. The sector was populated primarily by small, privately owned businesses; "mom and pop" enterprises that looked little like their traditional, four-year counterparts. The colleges—most started primarily in east coast cities like New York, Philadelphia, and

[4]Susan Aud, William Hussar, and Grace Kena, *The Condition of Education 2011*, http://nces.ed.gov, May, 2011.

Boston—taught skills for front-line jobs in high-demand fields, including business, health care, cosmetology, food, and secretarial services. They enrolled people that traditional higher education tended to ignore: working-class adults with children of their own who needed more skills to get better-paying jobs but couldn't take time out to attend a traditional campus.[5]

35   Proprietary institutions maintain much of the same mission today, amid a market that has seen sweeping changes, now populated by over 3,000 proprietary institutions. Forty percent are owned by one of 13 large, publicly traded companies. Half of those institutions offer associate, bachelor, or professional degrees today, versus less than 10 percent having done so in 1990. Over 90 percent of students at proprietary institutions are now enrolled in degree programs. Interestingly, only about 30 percent attend part-time. As the sector expands, it is attracting students who might otherwise have attended community colleges or even four-year institutions. "They are clearly a threat for both public and private schools," says Jim Scannell, president of the higher-education consulting group Scannell & Kurz, "especially for adult students returning to get a B.A. or going part time to get a master's."[6]

36   The NCES study entitled *The Condition of Education 2011*, offered these summary observations:[7]

- Enrollments and the number of degrees conferred by proprietary institutions increased faster than in the nonprofit sector, which includes public and private universities. Proprietary institutions awarded 5 percent of all bachelor's degrees in 2008–2009, and 10 percent of all master's degrees.

- For-profit colleges were more likely to enroll full-time students 25 and older, and to enroll students in distance education such as online courses. Nearly one in five students (19 percent) attending proprietary four-year colleges were enrolled entirely in distance education.

- The average price of attendance, including tuition, books, and living costs, for students enrolled full-time for a full year was highest at proprietary colleges after average grants were factored in. Students at proprietary colleges paid $30,900 on average in 2007–2008, compared with $26,600 at private, nonprofit colleges and $15,600 at public institutions.

- Proprietary institutions spent an average $2,659 on instruction per student in 2008–2009, compared with $9,418 at public colleges and $15,289 at private nonprofits. They spent more per student ($9,101) than public institutions ($6,647) but less than privates ($14,118) on student services and other types of support, including administrative and marketing salaries.

- Among four-year colleges, retention and graduation rates were lower at proprietary schools, which enroll about 1.2 million students compared with their nonprofit counterparts, which enroll about 8.9 million students.

- Among two-year colleges, retention and graduation rates were higher at proprietary colleges, which enrolled 385,000 students, than at public community colleges, where enrollments reached 7.1 million.

- Students at proprietary colleges were more likely to take out larger loans and to default on them. The average annual loan amount for all students was $7,000; the average was $9,800 at four-year proprietary institutions and $7,800 at two-year proprietary institutions.

37   Many small schools, particularly private liberal-arts colleges, are seeing drops in enrollment. After initially trying tuition increases as a solution, which has only driven students away in many cases, some of these schools are attempting to make up tuition revenue by

[5]Robin Wilson, "For-Profit Colleges Change Higher Education's Landscape," *Chronicle of Higher Education*, Feb. 7, 2010.
[6]Ibid.
[7]Aud et al., 2011.

increasing their adult student enrollment. In so doing, they are competing directly with proprietary colleges; and a recent trend has been for some of those colleges to be acquired by larger proprietary education companies as a way to enter certain geographic areas, or re-brand the small college, or leverage its brand across multiple locations. And public colleges feel the heat too. Students who have been rejected by budget-strapped public colleges, and others who find the public university bureaucracy often too much of a hassle to deal with, are being aggressively recruited by the proprietary sector. It's not clear whether this shift of students from public institutions to proprietary universities will be permanent, industry analysts say, but it continues to increase the size and legitimacy of the proprietary sector.[8]

38　Amazingly, even while facing constant budget cuts, layoffs, dwindling state support, and turning students away, most professors and administrators at traditional public colleges and universities remain dismissive of proprietary colleges. Some see proprietary institutions as a second-class education; others as too costly, or consuming too much of federal student aid; and some even arrogantly see them as trivial wannabe sideshows amid the real business of research-based education. Increasingly though, thoughtful observers of traditional universities see folly in their leaders' loyalty to a 200+ year-old model of higher education that has changed little, creating blinders for leaders of the typical public college or university. They point to the typical pattern where a two-year community college often evolves to seek accreditation as a four-year degree granting institution; and eventually, with proper political support, seeks to become an advanced degree-granting university institution with a larger "research" mission for the new faculty it starts to hire, and with appropriately credentialed expensive, additional in-state presidents, provosts, and chancellors, among other administrative layers.

39　Critics often point out to the observation that at these traditional college and university campuses, the focus is foremost on the faculty members. Tenure, seniority, obsessive reliance on faculty committee-based decision-making, lengthy deliberation to alter a curriculum, or even whether or not a class typically offered on "Tu-Th" at 10 a.m. could be offered on other days, or a Saturday, become serious, administratively intense issues. The application process, and time to a decision, can take months. It often is a tedious affair to talk with someone in the admissions process. Availability of classes, timing of required subjects, and accessibility of professors and/or advisors is often a concern cited by students at many traditional colleges and universities.

40　Leading proprietary institutions tend to point out with pride that they take a different approach on some of these issues, which their advocates argue is born out of a core focus on "the student" as their customer, and what that student needs/seeks to accomplish in attending that school. Faculty members are not tenured, but rather are hired based on expertise, experience, and qualifications. They are retained based on student demand. Course timing is oriented toward accommodating the special scheduling needs of the student. Some proprietary institutions use block times and concentrate courses in those blocks. So, for example, where a traditional college student might have a class at 9 a.m., another at noon, and a third at 4 p.m. or 10 a.m. the next day, the proprietary would set course offerings in four-hour blocks so students could get all classwork done in efficient timing sequences compatible with their work life. Others, following an approach pioneered by the University of Phoenix, let students concentrate on one or two courses maximum at a time. They last 5–6 weeks, include online or on-campus options, and allow students to concentrate their topical focus as well as the efficient use of their time. And it is not unusual to have early Saturday classes at several of these schools, because it is a convenient time for their student populations. Plus, classes start anew every month at most proprietary institutions, making availability and planning or sequencing courses very different from a traditional college or university.

[8]Wilson, 2010.

41   In admissions, the timetable at a proprietary is entirely different from its traditional counterpart. Expression of interest is quickly followed up, with that person to work with you to complete an application, figure out what program makes sense for you, and take you through the application process. Part of this activity has received considerable regulatory scrutiny in recent years as a pressure sales process. That sales process and the pressure to sign up new students versus the patient accuracy of the information provided by the "counselor" to the prospective student, to include financial aid information, has come under intense federal regulatory scrutiny in recent years. Nonetheless, the speed of attention to the inquiry from prospective students, and the effort to explain what is offered and the nature of the education process at a proprietary is typically in marked contrast to that process in a traditional college or university.

CHALLENGES FACING THE PROPRIETARY EDUCATION PROVIDERS

42   Speaking in a 2011 conference call with reporters, U.S. Secretary of Education Arne Duncan said of the proprietary education industry, "The quality here has been very uneven. There have been some absolute superstars. And there have been some players whose intentions, quite frankly, we doubt." So other notable employers, such as Intel, have recently adopted policies in recruitment that eliminate employment consideration for graduates of most of the better known proprietary schools. Harkening back to the 50 percent rule in the early 1990s,[9] recent regulatory changes have sought to address widespread growing concerns with this "quality" issue as well as others' concern with the proprietary industry's disproportionate reliance on federal student loans as a source of revenue used by its students to pay for their education at proprietary schools. Two regulations created by federal law have been put into place seeking, according to their supporters, to address these concerns—the gainful employment rule and the 90/10 rule.

43   **The Gainful Employment Rule.** This rule denies federal aid to programs that fail three "tests" of gainful employment three times in a four-year span:

- *Are at least 35 percent of former students actively paying down their loans?* The test: Do a third of ex-students make payments that lower their student loan balance by at least a dollar in a given year?

- *Are graduates spending 30 percent or less of their discretionary income on loan payments?* The test: Student loan payments are not costing too much of the money left after graduates pay for basic needs. (In other words, the proprietary's education leads to a job paying sufficiently well so as to justify the costs to the students for which they took out student loans arranged by the school.)

- *Are graduates spending 12 percent or less of their total income on loan payments?* This test, related to the previous test, is another way based on total income which establishes that loan bills should not consume more than an amount regulators believe is the appropriate level of student loan costs after graduation—about an eighth of total earnings.

44   Programs that pass any of the three tests would retain eligibility to participate in federal aid initiatives, enabling qualified students to secure federal grants or loans. The rule effectively would shut down proprietary programs that repeatedly fail to show, through measures associated with these three rules, that graduates are earning enough to pay down the loans taken out to attend those programs. Advocates say it addresses the chief complaint

[9]The 50 percent rule (federal law) mandated that students at universities providing more than 50 percent of their courses online couldn't qualify for Title IV Higher Education Act financial assistance as a means to address what they considered false advertising by "diploma mills" from online and correspondence schools. It was repealed in 2006.

against proprietary schools that students emerge from them with too much debt and too little earning power. Proprietary defenders have aggressively opposed the measure, with lobbyists alleging the Education Department was unjustly swayed by short-sellers with a financial interest in seeing the publicly traded school operators suffer. They also say the rule will limit access to higher education, particularly for minorities. And, they argue it regulates them based on behavior and actions over which they have no control. A handful of lawsuits were quickly filed by numerous parties on issues related to the rule.

45   **The 90/10 Rule.** This is a Higher Education Act rule that makes a proprietary institution of higher education ineligible to participate in Title IV (student loan) programs if for any two consecutive fiscal years it derives more than 90 percent of its cash basis revenue from Title IV programs. An institution that derives more than 90 percent of its revenue from Title IV programs for any single fiscal year will be automatically placed on provisional certification for two fiscal years and will be subject to possible additional sanctions determined to be appropriate under the circumstances by the U.S. Department of Education in the exercise of its broad discretion. An institution that derives more than 90 percent of its revenue from Title IV programs for two consecutive fiscal years will be ineligible to participate in Title IV programs for at least two fiscal years.

46   Proponents of the 90/10 rule see it as a way to ensure quality and discourage fraud at proprietary colleges by requiring students to invest some of their own money in tuition, just as homebuyers make down payments on their mortgages. Opponents argue that it penalizes low-income recipients that do not have the savings or family income to pay educational costs without receiving a full loan. Traditional universities increasingly argue that proprietary institutions are taking a disproportionate share of the student loan funds.

47   Proprietary colleges as a whole were approaching the 90 percent cap in 2012 as the Education Department has increased the availability of student loans and Pell Grants, according to Harris Miller, president of the Association of Private Sector Colleges & Universities, a Washington-based trade group. He argued that Congress needs to act so the schools can continue to operate and students can stay in class. Industry leader University of Phoenix sent out an e-mail saying it "believes 90/10 is not a good measure of quality, which is better assessed through graduation rates, default rates, compliance audits, financial ratios, etc." The UOP reported that federal student grants and loans made up almost 84 percent of the college's revenue in its 2012 fiscal year.

48   **Student Loan Defaults—Student Loan Cohort Default Rate Rule.** To remain eligible to participate in Title IV programs, educational institutions must maintain student loan cohort default rates below specified levels. Each cohort is the group of students who first enter into student loan repayment during a federal fiscal year (ending September 30). Under the Higher Education Act, as reauthorized, the currently applicable cohort default rate for each cohort is the percentage of the students in the cohort who default on their student loans prior to the end of the following two federal fiscal years, which represents a three-year measuring period.

49   Beginning with the 2011 three-year cohort default rate published in September 2014, the three-year rates will be applied for purposes of measuring compliance with the requirements as follows:

- *Annual test.* If the 2011 three-year cohort default rate exceeds 40 percent, the institution will cease to be eligible to participate in Title IV programs; and
- *Three consecutive years test.* If the institution's three-year cohort default rate exceeds 30 percent for three consecutive years, beginning with the 2009 cohort, the institution will cease to be eligible to participate in Title IV programs.

50   **A Pending Student Loan Crisis?** A growing concern that "echoes" as background with these rules is the dramatically increasing level of student debt in the United States. Entering 2011, total student loan debt, at $1 trillion, exceeded total U.S. credit card debt, itself bloated to what some call a bubble level of $827 billion. Student loan debt was estimated to be growing at the rate of $90 billion a year. The younger generation appears to have begun to mortgage its future earnings in the form of student loan debt. And student loans are not dischargeable in bankruptcy—meaning future wages, tax refunds, and so forth can be garnished to recoup these obligations. Only 40 percent of that student debt is actively being repaid. The rest is in default, or in deferment (when a student requests temporary postponement of payment because of economic hardship), which means payments and interest are halted, or in forbearance. Interest on government loans is suspended during deferment, but continues to accrue on private loans. As tuitions increase, loan amounts increase; private loan interest rates averaged 11 percent in 2012. Among the top private lenders: Citigroup, Wells Fargo, and JPMorgan Chase.[10] Recent statistics indicate that student debt was held by 62 percent of students from public universities, 72 percent from private nonprofit schools, and a whopping 96 percent from private proprietary schools.

51   **It Is, After All, "Proprietary."** Whatever one's opinion of the proprietary university model, "it's been a tremendous growth story," says Jeffrey M. Silber, a stock analyst and managing director of BMO Capital Markets, which figures the proprietary sector brought in $35 billion in 2012. Most of that was earned by 13 large publicly traded companies that now dominate the market.

52   The biggest player among those is the Apollo Group. Its flagship University of Phoenix has morphed from an institution with 25,100 students in 1995 to one with over 300,000 today. That means that 25 years ago Phoenix was about the same size as George Washington University. Now it is larger than the entire undergraduate enrollment of the Big Ten.[11] Phoenix's enrollment dwarfs that of each of the other 12 publicly traded companies, including Education Management Corporation, with over 157,000 students; American Public Education, Inc. with over 110,000 students; Career Education Corporation, with about 75,000 students; and DeVry Inc., with 133,000 students. While Kaplan Higher Education is one of the country's largest proprietary companies, with approximately 65,000 students, it is owned by the Washington Post Company and so is not one of the 13 large publicly traded proprietary universities. The proprietary sector is not only more robust than the rest of higher education, it is helping to force some changes in the way traditional colleges do business. Yet while some traditional colleges are reaching out to adult students, starting online programs, and saving money by rejecting tenure in favor of hiring professors by the class, traditional higher education characteristically remains far from being nimble and quick to change. It has been operating in roughly the same way for hundreds of years, so by its very nature it may continue to be ill-suited to respond to competition from the proprietary sector. The Apollo Group's leadership put it this way amidst the growing scrutiny of the proprietary sector's offerings, value, and reliance on student loans:[12]

> These factors—a greater number of individuals now wanting to pursue a college degree and students having a higher number of risk factors—are placing burdens on a higher education system that was not built to accommodate the needs of nontraditional students. The higher education system must significantly expand capacity to reach greater numbers of students

[10]Alan Nasseu and Kelly Norman, "The Student Loan Debt Bubble," www.globalresearch.ca, June 5, 2011.
[11]The "Big Ten" conference name remains, even though there are actually 11 universities in the Big Ten—Illinois, Indiana, Iowa, Michigan, Michigan State, Minnesota, Northwestern, Ohio State, Penn State, Purdue, and Wisconsin.
[12]The Apollo Group, Inc., 2010 Annual Report, p. 4.

and provide a higher level of academic and student support services in order to successfully educate nontraditional students.

These burdens come at a time when public funding for higher education is under pressure and budgets and capacity are being cut at traditional schools. Delivering quality education at traditional institutions generally relies upon a high fixed-cost, ground-based system of learning, and whether by design, or due to resource constraints, the traditional higher education system is rigid and inflexible. As such, the economics underlying the traditional university system's asset-intensive, high cost structure have been essentially unchanged over time.

THE APOLLO GROUP, INC.

53   Apollo Group, Inc. is one of the world's largest private education providers and has been in the education business for almost 40 years. Echoing a president's speech and the role it views itself as playing as an innovator for nontraditional students (73 percent of all U.S. college student candidates, it believes) in today's global economy, the Apollo Group's Annual Report released in 2011 had this interesting statement toward the front of the document:

> Traditional colleges and universities are the backbone of the U.S. higher education system, but they alone cannot meet the country's needs. This system, which is exclusive by design, was built to meet the needs of a different era when only a small portion of the nation's workforce needed a college degree. Today's globally competitive, knowledge-based economy requires a more broadly educated society. We believe innovation and new alternatives are required to adapt to our rapidly changing world. Accredited, degree-granting proprietary [meaning "proprietary"] institutions play a critical role in the future of education. . . . Apollo Group is committed to leading the way in meeting the evolving needs of millions of nontraditional learners and producing graduates necessary to achieve the world's collective educational goals.

54   The Apollo Groups schools, led by the University of Phoenix (UOP), served a student enrollment exceeding 328,000 in 2012. Apollo Group provides educational programs and services both online and on-campus at the undergraduate, master, and doctoral levels through wholly-owned subsidiaries:

- **The University of Phoenix, Inc. (UOP)**—the largest private university in the United States, and source of over 91 percent of the Apollo Group's revenue.
- **Institute for Professional Development**—provides adult education program development, administration, and management consulting services to private U.S. colleges and universities.
- **The College for Financial Planning Institutes**—one of the nation's leading providers of financial services education and certification for individuals and corporations in the financial services industry.
- **Meritus University**—offers degree programs online to working learners throughout Canada.

55   In addition, Apollo Group formed a joint venture with The Carlyle Group in late 2007 called Apollo Global, Inc., to pursue investments in the international education services industry. Apollo Group owns 86 percent of Apollo Global; Carlyle owns the remaining 14 percent. Consolidated into the Apollo Group's financial statements, Apollo Global currently operates the following educational institutions:

- **BPP Holdings** in the United Kingdom.
- **Western International** University in the China, India, and the Netherlands.
- **Universidad de Artes,** Ciencias y Comunicación in Chile.
- **Universidad Latinoamericana** in Mexico.

56   Revenue at the Apollo Group grew impressively through 2010, and then declined the next two fiscal years as follows:

	Revenue [$ in millions]				
Source of the Revenue	2012	2011	2010	2009	2008
University of Phoenix	$3,883.0	$4,322.7	$4,498.3	$3,766.6	$2,987.7
Apollo Global:					
BPP	—	—	$ 251.7	13.1	—
Other			$ 78.3	76.1	42.3
Total Apollo Global	295.0	298.0	$ 330.0	89.0	42.3
Other Schools	75.3	90.4	95.7	95.0	93.6
Corporate	—	—	1.8	2.8	9.8
Net Revenue	$4,253.3	$4,711.1	$4,925.8	$3,953.6	$3,133.4

57   Apollo Group executives gave a hint of a global focus when they said in a recent letter to shareholders:

> We are committed to strengthening and capitalizing on Apollo Group's position as a leading provider of high quality, accessible education for individuals around the world. This means putting the student first as we focus on academic quality and the student experience. To that end, we are intensely focused on leveraging our core capabilities and expertise—developed over our 35-plus year history—to, first and foremost, maximize the long-term value of University of Phoenix, which is our top investment priority for Apollo Group, and then, to expand intelligently beyond University of Phoenix.

58   It would appear that, over time, Apollo Global will become the organizational mechanism to take all that is known and learned from the University of Phoenix truly global, in due time. For the University of Phoenix, Apollo executives translated this vision into three priorities:

1. *Growing the UOP the right way* by identifying and attracting students who are willing to put in the effort to succeed and who UOP believes can benefit from UOP programs.
2. *Delivering a high-value, energizing and compelling learning experience* for UOP students through quality, convenience, relevant academic programs, innovative content delivery, engaging instruction, and student-centric services and protections.
3. *Increasing the efficiency of UOP operations* via scalability and process innovation.

59   They add that the fundamental Apollo Group strategic plan emphasizes two core themes:

1. Maximize the value of the core UOP business, and
2. Expand intelligently beyond the UOP.

THE UNIVERSITY OF PHOENIX STRATEGY

60   The UOP's 2007 strategic plan prioritized six core "strategies." UOP's plan heading into 2012 is noticeably different in the core strategies it emphasizes in its 10-K and other key documents.

61   The 2007 plan highlighted six key elements in order of priority:

1. **Establish New UOP Campuses and Learning Centers**—be in every state and every major U.S. metro area.
2. **International Expansion**—accommodate working adults abroad that want a U.S. education without the hassle of coming to the United States.
3. **Enhance Existing Educational Programs**—add more accredited degree programs, increase pedagogical/instructional excellence, and keep tuition down.
4. **Expand the Types of Educational Programs**—master's and doctoral programs.
5. **Serve a Broader Student Age Group**—by targeting the 18–23-year-old group.
6. **Market Aggressively**—spend over 20 percent of revenue [~$600,000] on intensive marketing to build enrollments to in turn build revenue growth.[13]

62   The results from that strategic plan were impressive. UOP revenues grew 150 percent from just over $2B in 2006 to virtually $5B in 2010. And that included the Great Recession of 2008–2009.

63   The UOP's 2011 strategic plan for the next five years was remarkably different in order of priority and emphasis. Key elements of that strategic plan in presumed order of priority as outlined in 2011 were, all echoing a UOP theme of "transitioning the UOP to more effectively support our students and improve their educational outcomes":

1. **Student Education Financing Decisions**—Adopt new tools to better support students' educational financing decisions in enrolling and staying at the UOP. Emphasize the new UOP's Responsible Borrowing Calculator, and help prospective and current students use it to help them calculate the amount of student borrowing necessary to achieve their educational objectives; and to not incur unnecessary student loan debt.
2. **Responsible Target Marketing**—Transition the UOP marketing approaches to more effectively identify students who have the ability to succeed in UOP educational programs, including reduced emphasis on the use of third parties for lead generation.
3. **Improved New Student Orientation**—Require all students who enroll in UOP with fewer than 24 incoming credits to first attend a free, three-week University Orientation program designed to help the inexperienced prospective student understand the rigors of higher education prior to enrollment.
4. **Prioritize Student Success over Financial Incentives in Employees' Compensation**—Better align UOP enrollment, admissions, and other employees to UOP students' success by redefining roles and responsibilities, resetting individual objectives and measures, and implementing new compensation structures, including eliminating factors in UOP admissions personnel compensation structures.

[13]Apollo Group agreed to pay a fine of $9.8 million to the U.S. Education Dept. in 2005 to close an investigation of aggressive recruiting practices in which its UOP was depicted as a high-pressure sales culture that resembled a telemarketing boiler room more than a university admissions office. "Phoenix recruiters soon find out that UOP bases their salaries solely on the number of students they recruit," the report charged. That's prohibited by federal law. One recruiter who started at $28,000, for instance, was bumped to $85,000 after recruiting 151 students in six months. But another who started at the same level got just a $4,000 raise after signing up 79 students. Ultimately, such violations could have led the government to bar Phoenix from the federal student loan program, crippling the university. Apollo's CEO called the report "very misleading and full of inaccuracies." But he says he decided to settle rather than wage a protracted fight. Apollo agreed to change its compensation system and pay a $9.8 million fine without admitting guilt. Still, Apollo's defenders note that the point of the law is to prevent for-profits from luring unqualified students. If Phoenix is doing that, it hadn't showed up in student-loan default rates, which were a low 6% at the time.

5. **Upgrading UOP Learning and Data Platforms**—Continue to improve online learning platforms and e-pedagogies; and ensure state-of-the-art computer equipment and operational software to continuously enhance the student experience online and on-campus. All class materials are delivered electronically, making both its online and on-campus consistent, easy to use, and up-to-date electronic educational services.

64   Commenting on these five somewhat new, key elements of the UOP's 2015 strategy, Apollo executives offered the following:

> We believe that the changes in our marketing approaches and the University Orientation pilot program contributed to the 9.8 percent reduction in University of Phoenix New Degreed Enrollment in the fourth quarter of FY 2010 compared to the fourth quarter of the previous year. We expect that the continuing changes in our marketing approaches and the implementation of the additional initiatives described above will significantly reduce University of Phoenix New Degreed Enrollment and will adversely impact our net revenue, operating income and cash flow. However, we believe that these efforts are in the best interests of our students and, over the long-term, will improve student persistence and completion rates, reduce bad debt expense, reduce the risks to our business associated with our regulatory environment, and position us for more stable long-term growth in the future.[14]

65   Other elements of UOP's previous strategy remain a part of its strategic agenda toward 2015. The difference would seem to be in emphasis, focus, and/or scope.

6. **Selectively Establish New Locations and/or Learning Centers**—UOP is now in 40 states and virtually all major U.S. metro areas. It is within 10 miles of 87 million Americans. So UOP's need for aggressively seeking new locations has passed. Plus, it is now an online leader, with a proprietary online learning system, small online classes, mandatory participation requirements for faculty and students, and flexibility to attend both online and on-campus class sessions. Its aggressive growth and purchasing of new locations in areas targeted for growth is no longer critical to its growth, or survival.

7. **International Expansion**—UOP will play an eventual essential role in partnership with the new Apollo Global developing the capabilities to take the UOP-proven approaches to comprehensive postsecondary education global. This strategic element appears to be emerging as the key vector for the Apollo Group's long-term growth. Executives had this comment about international expansion, which they appear to be approaching cautiously, and with an appreciation for local market considerations and customs:

> We believe we can capitalize on opportunities to utilize our core expertise and organizational capabilities to grow in areas outside of UOP's current markets, both domestically and internationally. In particular, we have observed a growing demand for high quality postsecondary and other education services outside of the U.S., including in Europe, Latin America and Asia, and we believe that we have the capabilities and expertise to provide these services beyond our current reach. We intend to actively pursue quality opportunities to partner with or acquire existing institutions of higher learning where we believe we can achieve attractive long-term growth and value creation.[15]

66   UOP has as the assumption guiding its increased emphasis on preparing for global expansion that proprietary education is playing an important role in advancing the development of education, specifically higher education and lifelong learning, in many countries around the world. While primary and secondary education outside the United States are still funded mainly through government expenditures, postsecondary education outside the

---

[14]Apollo Group Annual Reports.
[15]Ibid.

United States is experiencing governmental funding constraints that create opportunities for a broader proprietary sector role. UOP and Apollo executives cite several trends driving their international market optimism:

- Unmet demand for education.
- Insufficient public funding to meet demand for education.
- Shortcomings in the quality of higher education offerings, resulting in the rise of supplemental training to meet industry demands in the developing world.
- Worldwide appreciation of the importance that knowledge plays in economic progress.
- Globalization of education.
- Increased availability and role of technology in education, broadening the accessibility and reach of education.

8. **Make UOP a Comprehensive University Based on Accredited Degrees Offered**—The quality and comprehensiveness of UOP's degree offerings are critical to further establishing it as the "gold standard" among proprietary universities, and all universities, in order to allow it to deal with and separate itself from perceived low-quality and "lite" offerings that plague the industry. UOP now offers degrees in the follow program areas, all accredited:

Associate's	Bachelor's	Master's	Doctoral
• Arts and Sciences • Business and Management • Criminal Justice and Security • Education • Health Care • Human Services • Psychology • Technology	• Arts and Sciences • Business and Management • Criminal Justice and Security • Education • Health Care • Human Services • Nursing • Psychology • Technology	• Business and Management • Counseling • Criminal Justice and Security • Education • Health Care • Nursing • Psychology • Technology	• Business and Management • Education • Health Care • Nursing • Psychology • Technology

67   This breadth of accredited offerings makes the UOP, degree-wise, the equal of virtually any traditional comprehensive public or private, nonprofit university.

9. **Emphasize Input from Employers of UOP Students**—The UOP has long placed an emphasis on maintaining a close relationship with employers of its students. They are solicited for curriculum input; for project-type issues and problems, which can be used to have coursework in appropriate classes include student teams working on current, relevant applications of topics and course content they are covering. These relationships with major global employers have led to pedagogical innovations, like UOP's "Virtual Organizations." Created by subject matter experts and relevant professionals, six composite businesses, schools, health care, and government organizations provide virtual settings that allow students and their instructors to immerse themselves inside virtual real-world settings. These settings provide a more realistic form of experiential learning, UOP claims, than case studies and simulations while also fostering critical thinking and resourcefulness skills.

68   Employer closeness also helps financially, since over 60 percent of UOP's working students have historically had some level of tuition assistance from their employers. And it typically helps manage course timing and scheduling issues.

UNIVERSITY OF PHOENIX STUDENT DEMOGRAPHICS

69   As noted previously, a majority of UOP's students have been working adults employed full-time, and having been on the job at least six years. Some characteristics of UOP's student population over the last five years are shown below:

UOP Student Demographics:	2012	2011	2010	2009	2008
Gender					
Female	67.2%	67.7%	67.7%	66.0%	66.0%
Male	32.8%	32.3%	32.3%	34.0%	34.0%
	100.0%	100.0%	100.0%	100.0%	100.0%
Age (1)					
22 and under	12.3%	12.3%	12.1%	14.9%	14.0%
23 to 29	31.8%	32.0%	32.6%	34.3%	34.0%
30 to 39	32.9%	32.8%	32.7%	31.0%	31.0%
40 to 49	16.5%	16.4%	16.2%	14.5%	15.0%
50 & over	6.4%	6.5%	6.4%	5.3%	6.0%
	100.0%	100.0%	100.0%	100.0%	100.0%
Race/Ethnicity (1)					
African-American	28.8%	28.0%	28.1%	27.7%	25.0%
Asian/Pacific Islander	3.2%	3.2%	3.3%	3.6%	4.1%
Caucasian	48.7%	50.7%	51.9%	52.2%	53.8%
Hispanic	13.3%	12.4%	11.6%	11.6%	12.0%
Native Amr./Alaskan	1.2%	1.2%	1.2%	1.3%	1.3%
Other/Unknown	4.8%	4.5%	3.9%	3.6%	3.8%
	100.0%	100.0%	100.0%	100.0%	100.0%

(1) Based on New Degreed Enrollment students

Degreed Enrollment:					
Associates	163,500	204,200	200,800	201200	146500
Bachelors	186,000	678,400	193,600	163600	141800
Masters	61,700	70,800	68,700	71200	67700
Doctoral	7,500	7,400	7,700	7000	6100
	418,700	460,900	470,800	443,000	362,100
Degreed Enrollment as % of total:					
Associates	39.1%	44.3%	42.7%	45.4%	40.5%
Bachelors	44.4%	38.7%	41.1%	36.9%	39.2%
Masters	14.7%	15.4%	14.6%	16.1%	18.7%
Doctoral	1.8%	1.6%	1.6%	1.6%	1.7%
	100.0%	100.0%	100.0%	100.0%	100.0%

FINANCIAL PICTURE FOR THE APOLLO GROUP AND THE UNIVERSITY OF PHOENIX

70 A consolidated summary of the Apollo Group's business for the last five years is as follows:

	As of August 31,				
	2012	**2011**	**2010**	**2009**	**2008**
($ in thousands)					
Consolidated Balance Sheets Data:					
Cash and cash equivalents.............................	$1,276,375	$1,571,664	$1,284,769	$ 968,246	$ 483,195
Restricted cash and cash equivalents..................	$ 318,334	$ 379,407	$ 444,132	$ 432,304	$ 384,155
Long-term restricted cash and cash equivalents.....	$ —	$ —	$ 126,615	$ —	$ —
Total assets...	$2,868,322	$3,269,706	$3,601,451	$3,263,377	$1,860,412
Current liabilities...	$1,655,039	$1,655,287	$1,793,511	$1,755,278	$ 865,609
Long-term debt...	81,323	179,691	168,039	127,701	15,428
Long-term liabilities...	207,637	190,739	251,161	155,785	133,210
Total equity..	924,323	1,243,989	1,388,740	1,224,613	846,165
Total liabilities and shareholders' equity.....	$2,868,322	$3,269,706	$3,601,451	$3,263,377	$1,860,412

	Year Ended August 31,				
	2012	**2011**	**2010**	**2009**	**2008**
(In thousands, except per share data)					
Consolidated Statements of Income Data:					
Net revenue..	$4,253,337	$4,711,049	$4,906,613	$ 3,953,566	$ 3,133,436
Costs and expenses:					
Instructional and student advisory..................	1,800,569	1,759,986	1,720,059	1,333,919	1,177,991
Marketing..	663,442	654,399	622,848	497,568	416,551
Admissions advisory......................................	383,935	415,386	466,358	437,908	374,175
General and administrative..........................	344,300	355,548	301,116	277,887	204,793
Depreciation and amortization.....................	177,804	157,686	142,337	108,828	88,349
Provision for uncollectible accounts receivable..	146,742	181,297	282,628	151,021	104,201
Restructuring and other charges..................	38,695	22,913	—	—	—
Goodwill and other intangibles impairment...	16,788	219,927	184,570	—	—
Litigation charge (credit), net.......................	4,725	(11,951)	177,982	80,500	—
Total costs and expenses............................	3,577,000	3,755,191	3,897,898	2,887,631	2,366,060
Operating income..	676,337	955,858	1,008,715	1,065,935	767,376
Interest income...	1,187	2,884	2,920	12,591	30,078
Interest expense...	(11,745)	(8,931)	(11,864)	(4,448)	(3,450)
Other, net..	476	(1,588)	(685)	(7,151)	6,772
Income from continuing operations before income taxes...	666,255	948,223	999,086	1,066,927	800,776
Provision for income taxes...............................	(283,072)	(419,136)	(463,619)	(456,720)	(314,025)
Income from continuing operations............	383,183	529,087	535,467	610,207	486,751

Income (loss) from discontinued operations, net of tax	33,823		6,709		(13,886)		(16,377)		(10,824)
Net income	417,006		535,796		521,581		593,830		475,927
Net loss attributable to noncontrolling interests	5,672		36,631		31,421		4,489		598
Net income attributable to Apollo	$ 422,678		$ 572,427		$ 553,002		$ 598,319		$ 476,525

71   Components of Net Revenue were as follows over those five years:

($ in millions)	2012		2011		2010		2009		2008	
					Year Ended August 31,					
Tuition and educational services revenue	$ 4,124,629	97%	$4,549,010	96%	$ 4,738,712	96%	$3,815,000	96%	$2,988,600	96%
Educational materials revenue	294,499	7%	320,780	7%	324,951	7%	226,400	6%	184,400	6%
Services revenue	56,981	1%	76,500	2%	84,185	2%	83,200	2%	77,700	2%
Other revenue	33,192	1%	23,139	—%	22,414	—	28,300	1%	43,900	1%
Gross revenue	4,509,301	106%	4,969,429	105%	5,170,262	105%	4,152,900	105%	3,294,600	105%
Less: Discounts	(255,964)	(6)%	(258,380)	(5%)	(263,649)	(5)%	(199,300)	(5)%	(161,200)	(5)%
Net revenue	$ 4,253,337	100%	$ 4,711,049	100%	$ 4,906,613	100%	$3,953,600	100%	$3,133,400	100%

72   The following table details the 90/10 Rule percentages for University of Phoenix and Western International University for fiscal years 2012, 2011 and 2010:

	2012	2011	2010
	90/10 Rule Percentages for Fiscal Years Ended August 31,		
University of Phoenix	84%	86%	88%
Western International University	68%	66%	62%

Although the University of Phoenix 90/10 Rule percentage for fiscal year 2012 has decreased from fiscal years 2011 and 2010, the 90/10 Rule percentage for University of Phoenix has increased materially over the years prior to fiscal year 2010. This prior increase was primarily attributable to the increase in student loan limits affected by the Ensuring Continued Access to Student Loans Act of 2008 and expanded eligibility for and increases in the maximum amount of Pell Grants.

73   The decrease in the University of Phoenix 90/10 Rule percentage in fiscal year 2012 compared to fiscal years 2011 and 2010 is primarily attributable to the reduction in the proportion of students who are enrolled in the UOP's associate's degree programs, which historically have had a higher percentage of Title IV funds applied to eligible tuition and fees, and emphasizing employer-paid and other direct-pay education programs. The UOP has also implemented in recent years various other measures intended to reduce the percentage of University of Phoenix's cash basis revenue attributable to Title IV funds, including encouraging students to carefully evaluate the amount of necessary Title IV borrowing and continued focus on professional development and continuing education programs. Still, the UOP has substantially no control over the amount of Title IV student loans and grants sought by or awarded to its students.

74   Based on recent trends, the 90/10 Rule percentage for University of Phoenix should not exceed 90 percent for the next few fiscal years. However, the 90/10 Rule percentage for University of Phoenix remains near 90 percent and could exceed 90 percent in the future depending on the degree to which its various initiatives are effective, the impact of future changes in its enrollment mix, and regulatory and other factors outside its control, including any reduction in Military Benefit programs or changes in the treatment of such funding for purposes of the 90/10 Rule calculation.

75   Various legislative proposals have been introduced in Congress that would heighten the requirements of the 90/10 Rule. For example, in January 2012, the Protecting Our Students and Taxpayers Act was introduced in the U.S. Senate and, if adopted, would reduce the 90 percent maximum under the rule to the pre-1998 level of 85 percent, cause tuition derived from Military Benefit programs to be included in the 85 percent portion under the rule instead of the 10 percent portion as is the case today, and impose Title IV ineligibility after one year of noncompliance rather than two. If these or other proposals are adopted as proposed, University of Phoenix may be required to increase efforts and resources dedicated to reducing the percentage of cash basis revenue attributable to Title IV funds, which could materially and adversely affect its business.[16]

76   The other way this student loan derived revenue creates a potential problem involves loan defaults as was discussed earlier in this case, called the "cohort default rate." If an institution's two year cohort default rate exceeds 25 percent for three consecutive years, it will become ineligible to participate in Title IV programs. Apollo's two-year cohort default rates as of FY2012 were:

	Two-Year Cohort Default Rates for Cohort Years Ended September 30,		
	2010	**2009**	**2008**
University of Phoenix[(1)]	17.9%	18.8%	12.9%
Western International University[(1)]	7.7%	9.3%	10.7%
All proprietary postsecondary institutions[(1)]	12.9%	15.0%	11.6%

[(1)]Based on information published by the U.S. Department of Education.

77 Apollo Group said in this regard:

> While we expect that the challenging economic environment will continue to put pressure on our student borrowers, we believe that our ongoing efforts to shift our student mix to a higher proportion of bachelor's and graduate level students, the full implementation of our University Orientation program in November 2010 and our investment in student protection initiatives and repayment management services will continue to stabilize and over time favorably impact our rates. As part of our repayment management initiatives, effective with the 2009 cohort, we engaged third party service providers to assist our students who are at risk of default. These service providers contact students and offer assistance, which includes providing students with specific loan repayment information such as repayment options and loan servicer contact information, and they attempt to transfer these students to the relevant loan servicer to resolve their delinquency. In addition, we are intensely focused on student retention and enrolling students who have a reasonable chance to succeed in our programs, in part because the rate of default is higher among students who do not complete their degree program compared to students who graduate. Based on the available preliminary data, we do not expect the University of Phoenix or Western International University 2011 two-year cohort default rates to equal or exceed 25 percent.[17]

[16]Ibid.
[17]2012 Annual Report.

78   Related, Apollo Group Annual Reports included this footnote to its balance sheet about allowances for doubtful accounts receivable the last five years:

Note 6. Accounts Receivable, Net

Accounts receivable, net consist of the following as of August 31:

($ in thousands)	2012	2011	2010	2009	2008
Student accounts receivable.........................	$ 287,619	$ 324,324	$ 419,714	$ 380,226	$ 279,841
Less allowance for doubtful accounts...........	(107,230)	(128,897)	(192,857)	(110,420)	(78,362)
Net student accounts receivable...............	180,389	195,427	226,857	269,806	201,479
Other receivables....................................	17,890	20,140	37,520	28,464	20,440
Total accounts receivable, net...............	$ 198,279	$ 215,567	$ 264,377	$ 298,270	$ 221,919

79   The issue of student educational debt, leading to the 90/10 rule and the cohort rule, in turn has proprietary universities like the Apollo Group extra vigilant related to borrowing, payment, and repayment. That situation appears to be common across the Title IV loan program, which in turn is drawing regulatory attention to it. Fears of another credit bubble have been raised. A generation that has grown up adding this debt to their financial picture just as they begin their adult life is acutely aware of the seriousness of the obligation to repay those loans, especially when they start working and begin paying their loan payments. The feature of these loans that has them excluded from bankruptcy protection further reinforces that burden. And interest rates on delinquent and/or unmade payments, particularly from private loan providers, can rival the levels on higher interest credit cards. All of this makes the issue of defaults and the regulatory CDRs or cohort default rates a major issue industry-wide and for the country as a whole.

80   The Apollo Group's "Marketing and Admissions Advisory" expenses for the last five years were as follows:

(in thousands $)	2012	2011	2010	2009	2008
Marketing...	$ 663	$ 654	$ 623	—	—
Admissions Advisory........................	$ 384	$ 415	466	—	—
Total..	$1,047	$1,069	$1,069	$953	$801

81   The Apollo Group/University of Phoenix offered an impressive white paper called "Higher Education at the Crossroads" in August 2010, which examined issues related to higher education and the knowledge-economy needs envisioned by educational goals set forth by the Obama administration. The research in that report demonstrated the significant challenge of goals like every American having at least one year of college education equivalence and the reality of how critical the "proprietary" university sector will be to that challenge. They quoted U.S. Education Secretary Arne Duncan to emphasize the point:

Let me be crystal clear: proprietary institutions play a vital role in training young people and adults for jobs. They are critical to helping America meet the President's 2020 goal. They are helping us meet the explosive demand for skills that public institutions cannot always meet.

—*Secretary of Education Arne Duncan, May 11, 2010*

82 And the Apollo white paper offers some interesting challenges by comparing the University of Phoenix to more tradition (and all) colleges and universities on three central issues:

1. Marketing and promotion expenditures. UOP is not excessive in its marketing and enrollment expenditures; and like other colleges and universities it has a duty to inform.

Average Marketing Spend per New Enrollment

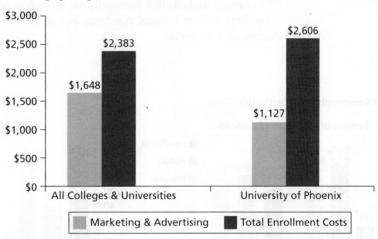

Source: National Association for College Admission Counseling, 2009 State of College Admission, and Apollo Group SEC filings and internal data.

2. Quality of education based on evaluation of learning outcomes.

Percentage Improvement in MAPP Scores: Freshmen to Seniors

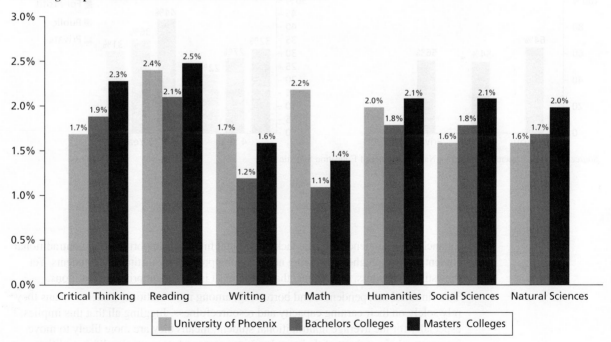

Source: Educational Testing Service (ETS), Measure of Proficiency and Progress (MAPP).
Note: Master's Universities reference institutions that offer baccalaureate through graduate degrees.

3. To meet U.S. educational goals, the U.S. higher education system will have to educate nontraditional students. But their demographic characteristics make them more at risk for graduation/completion rates (although UOP has a higher graduation rate than its most appropriate comparison, community colleges).

Student demographics by institution types show that proprietary institutions have more 25+ year-old students that financially are more dependent upon themselves to pay for college without parental assistance and are more likely to be a minority—African American or Hispanic.

Student Demographics by Institution Type

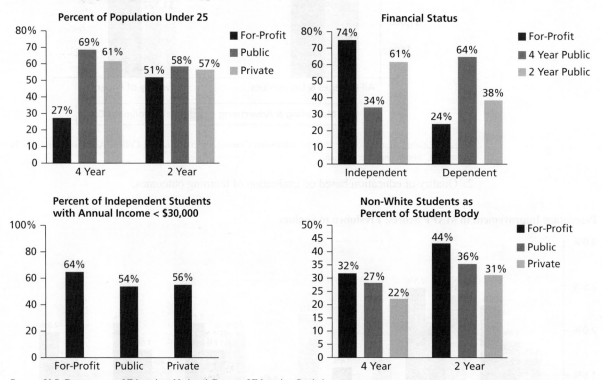

Source: U.S. Department of Education, National Center of Education Statistics.

Financial independence (aka the lack of parental financial support) among nontraditional students leads to higher borrowing needs among proprietary institutions' students. Yet they still borrow less, on average, than students at independent private institutions.

This financial independence, and borrowing, among nontraditional students means they rely solely on their earning capacity and resourcefulness. Juggling all that this implies, especially for the average nontraditional student, means they are more likely to move intermittently in and out of their academic programs while managing life's realities. That in turn affects the graduation/completion rates and timing as a population.

Average Student Debt Levels by Institution Type

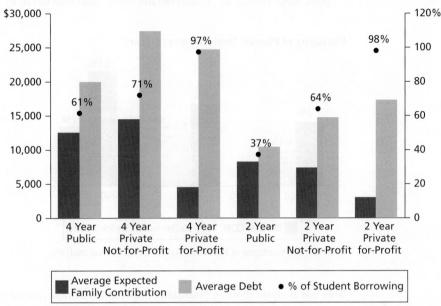

Source: U.S. Department of Education, National Center for Education Statistics, 2007–2008 National Postsecondary Student Aid Study (NPSAS: 08).

Completion Rates by Various Demographic Characteristics

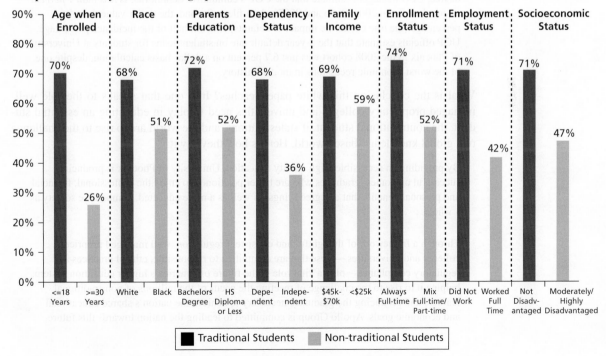

Source: U.S. Department of Education, National Center for Education Statistics.

4. And those factors then affect potential to default on loans, or as an aggregate student pool, make for higher "cohort default rates," also referred to by the acronym "CDR."

University of Phoenix Default Rates (2-Year)

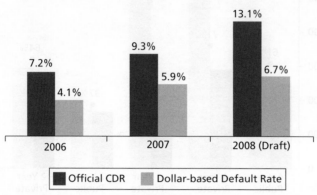

Source: U.S. Department of Education, Apollo Group internal analysis.

This last analysis shows a potentially important argument related to the regulatory environment and manner in which student loan default is monitored/regulated. UOP's point:

> The official CDR metric is a measure of default incidence, not a measure of dollar default. Students who drop out drive CDRs and drop-outs have lower debt levels as individuals who drop tend to do so early in their programs. As a result, two additional data points are worth noting. First, if you only look at students who have graduated with a University of Phoenix degree, UPO managers estimate that the UOP's cumulative default rate is *less than 1 percent* (using the official 2005, 2006 and 2007 cohort files). Second, the dollar value default percentage (the true economic impact of defaults) is about half of the incidence percentage. UOP officials estimate that the 2-year default rate on student loans for students at University of Phoenix in the 2008 cohort was just 6.7 percent on a dollar-basis calculation, despite one of the worst economic recessions in modern history.

What is the conclusion this white paper reaches? It is one that speaks to the role well-managed proprietary colleges and universities need to play in educating an essential student, the nontraditional student, if states, nations, and the world are to rise to the challenge of a global knowledge-based world. Here is how they say it:

> By providing an accessible, high quality education, University of Phoenix is producing successful outcomes–graduates who are better positioned to enjoy the professional, financial and personal benefits that a degree brings, as well as a more educated, competitive society as a whole. . . .

> Through a framework of thoughtful and consistent regulation, well managed proprietary colleges and universities—those that are committed to responsible, ethical practices and regulatory compliance—play a vital role in the future of America's higher education system, helping it to rise to the challenge of meeting the needs of the millions of non-traditional learners and producing the graduates necessary to achieve the nation's shared educational and economic goals. Apollo Group is committed to leading the nation towards this future.

Case 14

Barnes & Noble, Inc.: *The Yucaipa Proxy Challenge*[1]

1   On September 4, 2010, Leonard Riggio, the founder and chief executive officer (CEO) of Barnes & Noble (BN), the U.S.-based bookseller, learned that Ronald Burkle had filed a "Definitive Proxy Statement" through his Yucaipa Fund for the upcoming Annual Stockholder Meeting on September 28. The Yucaipa proxy (see Exhibit 1) was a challenge to the set of nominees recommended by BN to be elected to the company's board, and the proxy made a case for the election of Yucaipa's own nominees instead.[2] For Riggio, this was the second piece of disconcerting news concerning Yucaipa in the last two days. On September 2, Burkle had announced that he was appealing the Delaware Chancery Court's rejection of his challenge to a BN poison pill.[3]

2   As Riggio examined in detail the contents of the Yucaipa proxy, he realized that he and BN's board of directors would have to address this challenge prior to the Annual Stockholder Meeting. As the owner of 18 percent of BN stock and a vociferous critic of Riggio's strategy for BN,[4] Burkle's intention to appeal the Delaware ruling and challenge the company's board nominees warranted a response from Riggio, lest he lose control of the company he had founded.

BARNES & NOBLE

3   BN was a New York–based bookstore chain (NAICS 451211, SIC 5942) that engaged in the sale of trade books (hardcover and paperback mass-market fiction and nonfiction), children's books, e-books and other digital content, e-readers and related accessories, bargain books, magazines, gifts, café products and services, music, and movies to consumers through

Source: Professor Ram Subramanian wrote this case solely to provide material for class discussion. The author does not intend to illustrate either effective or ineffective handling of a managerial situation. The author may have disguised certain names and other identifying information to protect confidentiality.

Richard Ivey School of Business Foundation prohibits any form of reproduction, storage or transmission without its written permission. Reproduction of this material is not covered under authorization by any reproduction rights organization. To order copies or request permission to reproduce materials, contact Ivey Publishing, Richard Ivey School of Business Foundation, The University of Western Ontario, London, Ontario, Canada, N6A 3K7; phone (519) 661-3208; fax (519) 661-3882; e-mail cases@ivey.uwo.ca.

Copyright © 2011, Richard Ivey School of Business Foundation   Version: 2011-11-16

[1]This case has been written on the basis of published sources only. Consequently, the interpretation and perspectives presented in this case are not necessarily those of Barnes & Noble Inc. or any of its employees.
[2]Barnes & Noble, SEC Filings, September 2, 2010.
[3]Reuters, "Timeline—Ron Burkle's Proxy Fight for Barnes & Noble," http://www.reuters.com/article/2010/09/28/us-barnesandnoble-factbox-idUSTRE68R4QQ20100928. A poison pill is an anti-takeover measure. In this case, the poison pill prevented any shareholder from acquiring more than 20 percent of Barnes & Noble's common stock.
[4]Richard Siklos, "Mr. Hollywood and Barnes & Noble," *The New York Observer,* August 10, 2010, www.observer.com/print/130607, accessed March 12, 2011.

Richard Ivey School of Business
The University of Western Ontario
IVEY

School of Business
D'Amore-McKim
Northeastern University

EXHIBIT 1   Selected Excerpts from the Yucaipa Proxy Form DFAN14A Filed on 09/02/2010

- "The Yucaipa Companies today announced that it filed its notice of appeal from the decision by the Delaware Court of Chancery dismissing Yucaipa's challenge to Barnes & Noble, Inc.'s poison pill rights plan."
- "We believe that the important stockholders' rights at issue in our suit against the Riggio-dominated Barnes & Noble Board—equal treatment of stockholders and the rights of stockholders to freely and effectively vote to elect independent directors—should be decided by the Delaware Supreme Court"—statement made by a Yucaipa spokesperson.
- "Barnes & Noble stockholders will have the opportunity at the September 28, 2010, annual stockholder meeting to vote on Yucaipa's proposal to amend the Board-approved poison pill rights plan to eliminate the special treatment for Leonard Riggio and his family and to vote to elect Yucaipa's slate of three new independent director nominees."

Source: Barnes & Noble, Inc. Investors Web site. http://barnesandnobleinc.com/for_investors/for_investors.html, accessed March 10, 2011.

EXHIBIT 2   Summary of Barnes & Noble's Financial Performance ($ Millions, Except Store Count)

	Fiscal 2010	13 weeks till May 2, 2009	13 weeks till May 3, 2008	Fiscal 2008	Fiscal 2007
Revenues	5,810,564	1,105,152	1,155,882	5,121,804	5,286,674
Operating Profit	73,246	(3,244)	(1,747)	143,331	202,151
Net Earnings	36,676	(2,693)	(2,224)	75,920	135,799
Store Count	720	726	717	726	713

The company announced a change in fiscal year effective September 2009 to better align the business cycles of Barnes & Noble and Barnes & Noble College.

The company had long-term debt of $260 million in fiscal 2010, $87 million in the fiscal period ending May 3, 2008, and zero in fiscal 2008 and 2007.

Source: Barnes & Noble 2010 annual report.

its bookstores or online. It operated through two business segments: B&N Retail and B&N College. As of May 2010, B&N Retail owned and operated 720 bookstores that ranged in size from 3,000 square feet to 60,000 square feet, with an average store size of 26,000 square feet. This segment also included Barnes & Noble.com and Sterling Publishing (the company's publishing operation that produced SparkNotes and other books). As of May 2010, B&N College sold textbooks, school supplies and gifts, both online and through 637 stores that ranged in size from 500 square feet to 48,000 square feet. For fiscal 2010, BN reported revenues of $5.811 billion and net income of $36.68 million[5] (see Exhibit 2 and Exhibit 3).

4   In the late 1960s, Leonard Riggio was employed as a student clerk at the New York University (NYU) bookstore in New York. He made $1.10 an hour. Riggio dropped out of NYU and quit his job in 1971. He bought the Barnes & Noble store on New York's Fifth Avenue and immediately began to expand. He made a comment to *Forbes* magazine in 1976 that captured his strategy succinctly: "There are 30,000 mini-delicatessens in American bookselling, and we are the only supermarket."[6]

[5]http://barnesandnobleinc.com, accessed March 9, 2011.

[6]Andrew Rice, "The Billionaire and the Book Lover," *New York,* August 22, 2010, http://nymag.com/print/?/news/features/67636/, accessed March 12, 2011.

EXHIBIT 3   Barnes & Noble Stock Price History (Selected Dates)

Date	High	Low
1/2/2008	34.89	26.24
6/2/2008	30.65	24.43
1/2/2009	20.00	14.81
6/1/2009	26.96	19.78
1/4/2010	20.74	17.18
6/1/2010	20.00	12.80
7/1/2010	13.94	11.89
8/2/2010	16.74	12.70
9/1/2010	17.92	15.11
9/2/2010	16.50	15.48
9/3/2010	16.87	16.28
9/7/2010	16.00	15.57

Source: Yahoo Finance.

5   Using discounts (BN discounted bestsellers by 40 percent) and mass buying, and by increasing the retail space in each store, Riggio built BN into a national chain. Its sales per square foot stood at $244.33 (nearly 50 percent greater than that of the average independent bookstore) in 2003. That number had declined to $231.03 by 2010. BN went public through an initial public offering (IPO) in 1993, and in 1996, Riggio privately acquired the video-game retailer GameStop for $59 million, later selling it to BN for $218 million in 1999. BN invested $400 million in GameStop and then spun it off in an IPO. In 2002, Leonard Riggio stepped down as BN's CEO and was replaced by his brother, Stephen. On March 18, 2010, BN announced that William Lynch, an executive with a background in e-commerce, would become BN's new CEO, with Leonard Riggio as its chairman and Stephen Riggio as its vice-chairman[7] (see Exhibit 4).

THE BOOKSELLING INDUSTRY[8]

6   In 2010, retail bookselling was a $24 billion market that was fragmented in spite of national chains such as BN and Borders and the leading Internet retailer of books, Amazon. Bookstore chains operated in the "Specialty Retail" segment of the retailing industry. Standard & Poors forecasted that the bookselling industry was mature in 2010 and that due to declining adult readership of books, industry growth was expected to be either nonexistent or at best, in low single digits. Further, Standard & Poors indicated that e-books (which, in 2010, accounted for $500 million in sales) would cannibalize the sales of hardcopy books. The announcement of the bankruptcy of Borders was seen as a favorable trend for BN since the two chains competed for customers who bought books from bricks-and-mortar stores. Standard & Poors believed that major players such as BN and Amazon would use their buying power with book publishers to increase their gross margins.

[7]http://barnesandnobleinc.com, accessed March 9, 2011.

[8]Value Line and Mergent Online, www.valueline.com and www.mergentonline.com, accessed March 14, 2011.

EXHIBIT 4 Barnes & Noble's Board of Directors

Name	Primary Company	Age (Years)	Board Tenure (Years)
Leonard Riggio	Chairman, Barnes & Noble	69	25
Stephen Riggio	Vice Chairman, Barnes & Noble	55	18
George Campbell Jr.	President, The Cooper Union	64	3
William Dillard, III	Chairman and CEO, Dillard, Inc.	65	18
David G. Golden	Partner and Executive Vice President, Revolution LLC	N/A	1
Patricia L. Higgins	Former President and Chief Executive Officer, Switch and Data Facilities Inc.	59	5
Irene R. Miller	Chief Executive Officer, Akim, Inc.	57	18
Margaret T. Monaco	Principal, Probus Advisors	62	16
David A. Wilson	President and Chief Executive Officer, Graduate Management Admissions Council	68	1

Audit Committee: Higgins (Chair), Monaco, and Wilson

Compensation Committee: Campbell (Chair), Dillard, II, and Golden

Corporate Governance and Nominating Committee: Dillard, III (Chair), Higgins, and Monaco

Source: http://barnesandnobleinc.com/for_investors/for_investors.html and www.mergentonline, accessed March 10, 2011.

7   The two major competitors in the bookselling market were BN and Amazon. Amazon, an Internet-based retailer, was launched in 1995. BN launched its own Internet Web site in 1997. In 2010, analysts believed that Amazon was the leader in the bookselling industry, with an overall market share of 15 percent. Leveraging the trend toward e-books, Amazon had set itself the goal of obtaining a 50 percent market share by 2012.

8   Amazon launched the Kindle e-reader in November 2007. In response, BN launched the Nook in October 2009. In 2010, Kindle had a market share of 70 percent to 80 percent. In addition, Apple launched its iPad, which had an e-reader feature. The economics of e-books was different from that of hardcopy books. Retailers such as BN and Amazon typically paid $13 for a hardcopy book that retailed for $26. In contrast, in an electronic format, that same book would sell at a profit margin of around $3 or $4.

BURKLE AND RIGGIO

9   In 1986, Burkle founded a Los Angeles, California–based holding company—The Yucaipa Companies (Yucaipa)—in order to invest in underperforming businesses and create value through mergers and acquisitions and strategic repositioning. In 2010, Yucaipa owned stakes in about 35 companies, using the more than $30 billion in contributions from investors (principally pension funds). Yucaipa made its name by focusing on the grocery retail industry, wherein it acquired and merged Fred Meyer, Ralphs, and Jurgensen's to create value for its investors. In 2010, Yucaipa's investments included significant stakes in A&P and Whole Foods.[9]

[9]www.yucaipaco.com, accessed March 12, 2011.

10   On November 24, 2008, Yucaipa made its first investment in BN by buying 75,200 shares. On November 10, 2009, Yucaipa bought an additional 1 million shares, and in the same week, made further purchases to increase its stake in BN to 16.8 percent.[10]

11   Just prior to Yucaipa's initial investment in BN, Burkle called Leonard Riggio to indicate his interest in becoming a BN investor. The two men knew each other well, primarily because Riggio had made a multimillion-dollar investment in Source Interlink (which filed for bankruptcy protection in 2009 and went private shortly thereafter), a wholesale company that was controlled by Burkle[11] and was BN's main supplier of music, videos, magazines, and newspapers. Following his November 2008 investment, Burkle met Riggio for lunch in New York City, at which time he had two strategic suggestions for BN. The first was to cede ground to Amazon and its Kindle e-book reader and instead partner with Microsoft and Hewlett-Packard, using BN's store floor space to showcase their devices. The second was to acquire Borders, a bookstore chain that was rumoured to be close to bankruptcy. Recounting his reaction to the conversation, Riggio later stated in court:

> Ron Burkle is a dealmaker. He likes to put things together. I told him that I didn't want him buying Barnes & Noble stock, and while there was nothing I could do about that, I certainly wasn't going to take his strategic advice about Borders. I didn't want to sink money into bricks-and-mortar retail, not when the book business was going through sweeping change.[12]

12   On September 30, 2009, the BN board approved the company's $596 million purchase of the 624 Barnes & Noble college bookstores owned privately by Riggio and his wife. Justifying BN's purchase of the college bookstore chain, Riggio argued that:

> College bookstores operate in a separate niche that has proven resistant to recessionary cycles. While it made sense in the 1980s to keep the mass market and college bookstores as separate corporate entities, it makes sense to consolidate them now. The world is blurred now because book buyers may soon be carrying everything they read—textbooks, novels, magazines—on a single e-reader. It is important to reunite the company for the purpose of having a single platform.[13]

13   BN stockholders expressed outrage at this move, which they felt enriched the Riggios at the expense of the company, and left the company indebted and "deeply invested in the one sector of the market, textbooks, that appeared most likely to go digital in the short term."[14] In the aftermath of this transaction, BN stock dropped 20 percent, and several institutional stockholders filed suit. While Burkle expressed outrage, he did not join the lawsuit.[15]

14   In response to Yucaipa increasing its stake to 16.8 percent in November 2009, the BN board met via conference call to insert a "poison pill" into the corporate bylaws. The poison pill called for a rights plan to take effect once an outsider acquired a 20 percent interest in the company. As per the rights plan, existing shareholders could buy stock at a 50 percent discount without board approval when that threshold was reached. On May 5, 2010, Yucaipa bought 100,000 additional shares in BN, thereby increasing its stake to nearly

[10]Reuters, "Timeline—Ron Burkle's Proxy Fight for Barnes & Noble," www.reuters.com/assets/print?aid=USNO310522720100903, accessed March 11, 2011.

[11]Dawn McCarthy, "Source Interlink Files for Bankruptcy, Will Privatize," April 28, 2009, www.bloomberg.com/apps/news?pid=newsarchive&sid=aDmRedq9AdQo, accessed March 13, 2011.

[12]Andrew Rice, "The Billionaire and the Book Lover," *New York,* August 22, 2010, http://nymag.com/print/?/news/features/67636/, accessed March 12, 2011.

[13]Ibid.

[14]Phil Milford and Matt Townsend, "Yucaipa's Ron Burkle Fights Barnes & Noble's Poison Pill in Delaware Court," July 8, 2010, www.bloomberg.com/news/print/2010-07-08/yucaipa, accessed March 13, 2011.

[15]Ibid.

20 percent. At the same time, it filed a lawsuit in the Delaware Chancery Court in order to challenge BN's poison pill. In its filing, Yucaipa made various allegations against Riggio and the BN board:

> Barnes & Noble directors are engineering a self-dealing scheme designed to entrench the Riggio family and stymie Ron Burkle's efforts to gain seats on the board. The Riggios used Barnes & Noble as a personal piggy bank, authorizing a deal for the college chain at an above-market price. In addition, Barnes & Noble has an agreement to leases in which the Riggios have interests at an annual rent of more than $5 million, the company purchases $8.25 million in textbooks from a Riggio affiliate, and contracts freight services from Riggio interests for shipping to retail stores. The board's near obsession with activist stockholders as a threat shows its determination to frustrate the exercise of the stockholder franchise.[16]

15 B&N defended the poison pill in court papers:

> The company's board, reasonably fearing a hostile attack, set up the poison pill on the advice of legal and financial advisers after learning that Burkle had bought up almost 18 percent of the stock. The plan, designed to make a hostile takeover prohibitively expensive, is intended to protect our shareholders from actions that are inconsistent with their best interests.[17]

BARNES & NOBLE'S DIGITAL STRATEGY

16 In response to changes in the bookselling industry, BN embarked on a multichannel retail strategy. From a store-based model, it repositioned its business to a multichannel model centered on Internet and digital commerce. In July 2009, BN launched an e-bookstore and digital newsstand that had more than a million e-books, magazines, and newspapers available for sale. The company began selling Nook in BestBuy and BestBuy.com in addition to its own retail stores and Web site. It enabled its e-books to be read on a variety of digital platforms, such as Apple and BlackBerry. CEO William Lynch, who had worked at the Home Shopping Network prior to joining BN, captured the company's digital strategy:

> My appointment is a not-subtle signal about the company's future. We're morphing into a retail and technology company. We're purveyors of content, and I don't think anybody at this company would say we sell physical books. We do sell that, but that's not how we define ourselves.[18]

17 Riggio reiterated the significance of the company's strategy shift and his own ambivalence about it:

> The thing that excites me most about the digital revolution is the possibility of further democratization of the worlds of knowledge and literature. But I still can't imagine that the bookstore—or what I would like to call the "cultural piazza"—is replicated by a piece of plastic. We believe bookstores will exist all during and after this revolution. We're just absolutely convinced, both as citizens and as business people that bookstores are going to be important to the American culture.[19]

[16]Ibid.

[17]Phil Milford and Matt Townsend, "Yucaipa's Ron Burkle Fights Barnes & Noble's Poison Pill in Delaware Court," July 8, 2010, www.bloomberg.com/news/print/2010-07-08/yucaipa, accessed March 13, 2011.

[18]Andrew Rice, "The Billionaire and the Book Lover," *New York,* August 22, 2010, http://nymag.com/print/?/news/features/67636/, accessed March 12, 2011.

[19]Ibid.

BURKLE'S RESPONSE TO BARNES & NOBLE'S DIGITAL STRATEGY

18   Burkle summed up Yucaipa's investment strategy:

> We always try to buy companies that are doing OK but that have some issues. We buy at a price that if they just muddle through, we don't go broke. And if they do better, we make a lot.[20]

19   More specifically, Burkle believed that BN fit Yucaipa's metrics for an investment:

> Everybody was afraid the world was coming to an end. I wasn't. This is an opportunity. We can buy a phenomenal company and brand at a ridiculous price.[21]

20   In his testimony in the Delaware Chancery Court, Burkle indicated his strategy for BN:

> We invest in promising companies because we want to try to make them better companies. At the same time, we wouldn't want to keep them forever. Instead of chasing Amazon's technological lead, I think BN should forge alliances with Hewlett-Packard and Microsoft to offer electronics in retail stores and to print paperback books on-demand, without having to maintain large inventories. The keys for BN are its formidable brand name and its valuable real estate.[22]

THE DECISION

21   In his letter to BN's shareholders for the company's 2010 Annual Report, Leonard Riggio reiterated Barnes & Noble's emphasis on the Nook and on the digital marketplace for books:

> In less than a year (of the launch of the Nook), the Company achieved a 20 percent share of the e-book marketplace, larger than even its current 17 percent share of the physical book marketplace. . . . A survey of our Members (our very best customers) shows they have increased their combined physical and digital spend with us by 17 percent since purchasing a Nook and by a phenomenal 70 percent in total units. In addition, we've already begun to see the halo effect of Nook, both online at BN.com and in our stores. For example, a quarter of Nook owners are new to BN.com, which means we've been able to attract a significant number of new online customers to the Company through our strategic marketing efforts.[23]

22   Yucaipa's filing of a Definitive Proxy to challenge the company's nominees to the board signaled the intention of Ronald Burkle to shape Barnes & Noble's long-term strategy through his own personal board appointees. Riggio, the founder, chairman, and largest stockholder of Barnes & Noble, not only had to respond to the immediate proxy threat at the September 28 stockholder meeting but also come up with an action plan to retain control of the company in the long run. Would taking the company private represent the ideal solution, or was there an alternative approach for retaining control?

[20]Ibid.

[21]Ibid.

[22]Andrew Rice, "The Billionaire and the Book Lover," *New York,* August 22, 2010, http://nymag.com/print/?/news/features/67636/, accessed March 12, 2011.

[23]2010 Annual Report, http://barnesandnobleinc.com, accessed March 9, 2011.

Case 15

Blue Nile, Inc.: *"Stuck in the Middle" of the Diamond Engagement Ring Market*

Alan N. Hoffman *Bentley University and Rotterdam School of Management, Erasmus University*

1   Built on the premise of making engagement ring selection simpler, Blue Nile, Inc. (formerly known as Internet Diamonds, Inc.) has developed into the largest online retailer of diamond engagement rings. Unlike traditional jewelry retailers, Blue Nile operates completely storefront-free, without in-person consultation services. The business conducts all sales online or by phone and sales include both engagement (70%) and non-engagement (30%) categories. Therefore, the company focuses on perfecting its online shopping experience and "providing extraordinary jewelry, useful guidance, and easy-to-understand jewelry education to help you find the jewelry that's perfect for your occasion."[1]

2   Blue Nile's vision is to educate its customer base so that customers can make an informed, confident decision no matter what event they are celebrating.[2] It wants to make the entire diamond-buying process easy and hassle-free.[3] In addition, an important part of Blue Nile's vision, as CEO Diane Irvine said in a recent webinar with Kaihan Krippendorf, is for the company to be seen as the "smart" way to buy diamonds, while saving 20–40% more than one would in the typical jewelry store. Blue Nile is working to become "the Tiffany for the next generation."[4]

COMPANY BACKGROUND

3   Blue Nile started in Seattle, Washington in 1999, when Mark Vadon, the founder of the company, decided to act upon his and his friends' dissatisfaction with their experience in searching for an engagement ring. As a result, to battle their concerns, he created a company that offered customers education, guidance, quality and value, allowing customers to shop with confidence.[5]

4   Blue Nile operates its business through its three Web sites: www.bluenile.com, www.bluenile.co.uk, and www.bluenile.ca. Customers from the UK and all the member states of the European Union are served by Blue Nile's subsidiary, Blue Nile Worldwide, through the UK Web site. Canadian customers are served through the Canadian Web site, and the U.S. customers along with 14 additional countries worldwide are directed to the primary Web site. In addition, Blue Nile owns another subsidiary in Dublin, Ireland named Blue Nile Jewelry, Ltd., which acts as a customer service and fulfillment center.

Source: The author would like to thank Abdullah Al-Hadlaq, Rashid Alhamer, Chris Harbert, Sarah Martin, Adnan Rawji, and Will Hoffman for their research. Please address all correspondence to Dr. Alan N. Hoffman, Dept. of Management, Bentley University, 175 Forest Street, Waltham, MA 02452; ahoffman@bentlev.edu. Printed by permission of Dr. Alan N. Hoffman.

[1]Blue Nile, Inc. Datamonitor. www.datamonitor.com. September 10, 2010.
[2]http://www.bluenile.com/blue-nile-advantage
[3]http://www.bluenile.com/about-blue-nile
[4]http://www.kaihan.net/vpw_login.php?img=blue-nile
[5]http://www.bluenile.com/blue-nile-history

5   Furthermore, in order to enhance and facilitate the purchasing process to serve both local and foreign demand, Blue Nile has given customers the choice to purchase their products in 22 foreign currencies, as well as in the U.S. dollar.[6] As of the beginning of 2010, the company has offered sales to customers in over 40 countries worldwide.[7]

6   Not being built as a traditional brick-and-mortar jewelry company, Blue Nile uses its Web sites to exhibit its fine jewelry offerings, which include diamond, gold, gemstone, platinum, and sterling silver as well as rings, earrings, pendants, wedding bands, bracelets, necklaces, and watches. Blue Nile's revolutionary and innovative ways of restructuring industry standards did not just stop with its lack of a physical presence. The company offers a "Diamond Search" tool that lets customers examine their entire directory of diamonds to choose the right one in seconds. It also offers the popular "Build Your Own" tool that helps customers customize their own diamond jewelry and then view it on the computer before executing the order. Moreover, Blue Nile offers customers financing options, insurance for the jewelry, a 30-day return policy, and free shipping.[8]

7   Diamond sales represent the majority of Blue Nile's business and revenues. Diamonds, which are certified for high quality by an "independent diamond grading lab,"[9] are differentiated based on "shape, cut, color, clarity and carat weight."[10] Blue Nile uses a just-in-time ordering system from its suppliers, which is initiated once a diamond purchase is made on the Web site, eliminating the burden and the costs of keeping high-ticket items in inventory. However, the company does keep in inventory rings, earrings, and pendants that it uses as a base to attach the diamond to, in order to be able to customize diamond jewelry to customer requirements. In order to succeed in this industry, Blue Nile maintains a strong relationship with over 40 suppliers.

8   After its IPO in 2004, Blue Nile shares traded on the NASDAQ (ticker NILE). The company has been awarded the Circle of Excellence Platinum Award, which customers use to rank the best online company in customer service, by Bizrate.com since 2002. Being the only jeweler to be recognized for this excellence is a true testament to Blue Nile's solid business.[11]

STRATEGIC DIRECTION

9   Blue Nile is in the business of offering "high-quality diamonds and fine jewelry at outstanding prices."[12] It is a publicly traded company, making its ultimate business objective to achieve the highest return possible for its shareholders. In order to do this, Blue Nile focuses on the following:

1. Cause disruption in the diamond industry by creating a "two-horned dilemma." According to Kaihan Krippendorff, Blue Nile has been able to effectively put its competitors in a position where if they try to compete with Blue Nile directly, they compromise an area of their own business (one edge of the horn), and if they do not choose to compete with Blue Nile, they slowly lose market share and competitive positioning (the other edge of the horn). Blue Nile's decision to offer the highest quality diamonds in spite of operating in an online environment where it could easily position itself purely

[6]http://www.reuters.com/finance/stocks/companyProfile?symbol=NILE.O
[7]http://www.reuters.com/finance/stocks/companyProfile?symbol=NILE.O
[8]http://www.bluenile.com/blue-nile-history
[9]http://www.bluenile.com/about-blue-nile
[10]http://www.reuters.com/finance/stocks/companyProfile?symbol=NILE.O
[11]http://www.bluenile.com/about-blue-nile
[12]http://www.bluenile.com/blue-nile-advantage

as a "discounter" has been key to creating this dilemma. Competitors with brick-and-mortar locations are then left to decide whether they should sell their product online at a lower cost than a customer would find in a store in order to compete (knowing that this could negatively impact the brick and mortar location) or not go head-to-head with Blue Nile online.[13] This dilemma helps Blue Nile keep its stronghold as the largest online jewelry retailer.

2. Keep the consumer in mind and establish relationships with customers during a very important time in their lives. The idea for Blue Nile was born during an unpleasant shopping experience. The company remains focused on perfecting its user experience by investing in online education tools and resources within its Web site to help customers make educated decisions.[14] Blue Nile is not able to show its customers diamonds in person before a purchase is made so it must reassure customers by providing a comprehensive Web site, a 30-day return policy, and providing grading reports on their diamonds from two independent diamond grading laboratories—GIA or AGSL.[15]

3. Capture market share and emerge after the recession in a strong competitive position. Some competitors have pulled back during the recession by closing locations, while others have closed their doors altogether.[16] Blue Nile has been investing in its Web site and is working to aggressively grow its market share.[17]

THE JEWELRY INDUSTRY

10   It is estimated that 2010 U.S. jewelry sales finished at $49.3 billion for the year, a 2.6 percent growth over 2009.[18] According to First Research.com, the U.S. retail jewelry industry is considered to be fragmented as "the top 50 jewelry chains generate less than half of (total) revenue" and there are 28,800 specialty stores that generate around $30 billion in revenue. Diamond jewelry and loose diamonds account for approximately 45 percent of total jewelry store sales.[19]

11   A closer look at this industry reveals that 17.2 percent of total U.S. jewelry sales took place in non-store retailers. Still though, retail locations continue to be the primary source of jewelry sales, accounting for 50 percent of total U.S. jewelry sales in 2009 in spite of these sales decreasing by 7.8 percent between 2007 and 2009.[20]

12   According to Compete.com, Blue Nile controls 4.3 percent[21] of Internet jewelry sales and as of 2009 Blue Nile had about 4 percent of the engagement ring business in the U.S.,[22] which is 50 percent of the American online engagement jewelry market.[23]

[13]Krippendorff, Kaihan. "Creating a Two-Horned Dilemma." Fast Company.com. September 8, 2010.

[14]http://www.kaihan.net/vpw_login.php?img=blue-nile

[15]http://www.bluenile.com/why-choose-blue-nile

[16]Blue Nile, Inc. Datamonitor. www.datamonitor.com. September 10, 2010.

[17]Douglas MacMillan. "How Four Rookie CEO's Handled the Great Recession." Bloomberg_Businessweek. February 18, 2010.

[18]Mintel. Accessed May 8, 2011. http://academic.mintel.com/sinatra/oxygen_academic/search_results/show&/display/id=482738/display/id=540585#hit1

[19]Jewelry Retail Industry Profile. First Research.com. February 14, 2011.

[20]Mintel. Accessed May 8, 2011. http://academic.mintel.com/sinatra/oxygen_academic/search_results/show&/display/id=482738/display/id=540590#hit1

[21]Dimitra DeFotis. "No Diamond in the Rough." Barron's. February 15, 2010.

[22]Kate Plourd. "I Like Innovative, Disruptive Businesses." CFO Magazine. February 1, 2009.

[23]Blue Nile, Inc. Datamonitor. www.datamonitor.com. September 10, 2010.

BLUE NILE'S COMPETITORS

13   Blue Nile's many competitors include various different retail outlets like department stores, major jewelry store chains, independently owned jewelry stores, online retailers, catalogue retailers, television shopping retailers, discount superstores, and lastly wholesale clubs. Many local jewelers have great relations with their clientele in smaller communities, which poses a challenge for Blue Nile to achieve greater market share. Online retailers include Amazon, Overstock.com and Bidz.com, which are well known for their discounting, creating tremendous competition for Blue Nile. Most major firms who specialize in jewelry have their own online presence as well, such as Zales, Signet, Tiffany and Helzberg.

DeBeers

14   DeBeers, which owns 40 percent of the world's diamond supply,[24] is establishing its presence online as a trusted advisor as Blue Nile has done. Upon visiting DeBeers' Web site, it is clear that Blue Nile's consultative approach online has made an impression on DeBeers, as the Web site has an "Advice" section under Bridal rings and an "Art of Diamond Jewelry" section that both educates and serves as a source of confidence of quality.

Tiffany & Co.

15   Tiffany & Co., one of the best known luxury brand names, had revenues in 2010 of $2.9 billion, compared to Blue Nile's $302 million.[25] Tiffany & Co. continues to stand out in the jewelry sector by opening stores in urban America and has shown to be a success as there are many consumers who are willing to pay extra for a well-known brand name. Tiffany also offers great service at its stores through product information. Lastly, owning a piece of jewelry from Tiffany's—and receiving the iconic blue box—has an air of prestige all its own that Blue Nile cannot replicate.[26] In spite of the value associated with the Tiffany name, due to its lean business model, Blue Nile's return on capital is three to four times better than Tiffany's.[27]

16   Blue Nile's many powerful competitors require the business to compete through differentiation and Blue Nile gains an advantage over its competition through its unique operating structure. Its strategy, distribution channel, and supply chain help to keep Blue Nile in the market as it also creates barriers to entry. Some competitive advantages include its partnership with Bill Me Later® and its direct contracts with major diamond suppliers. Blue Nile partners with Bill Me Later®[28] in order to offer financing for fine jewelry and diamond purchases. Blue Nile also has direct contracts with major diamond suppliers, which in turn allow the company to sell stones online at lower prices than brick and mortar locations because it has lower overhead costs and fewer distribution interceptions.

Guild Jewelers

17   It is difficult to find a competitor that can be compared directly to Blue Nile because of the unique way in which the business operates. While Guild Jewelers are not necessarily a united force that Blue Nile must respond to, Blue Nile CEO Diane Irvine considers Guild

[24]Jewelry Retail Industry Profile. First Research.com. February 14, 2011.
[25]Dimitra DeFotis. "No Diamond in the Rough." *Barron's*. February 15, 2010.
[26]https://collab.itc.virginia.edu/access/content/group/dff17973-f012-465d-9e73-a05fa4456644/Research/Memos/MII%20Memos/Archive/Short/S%20-NILE_2.pdf
[27]http://www.kaihan.net/vpw_login.php?img=blue-nile
[28]http://www.bluenile.com/services_channel.jsp

Jewelers to be the company's major competitor because Guild has the local relationships with potential customers that are difficult for Blue Nile to establish online.[29]

BARRIERS TO ENTRY/IMITATION

18   Barriers to entry in the jewelry industry are high as the following are needed: capital, strong supplier relationships, and reputation. With regard to capital, traditional jewelry stores must fund their brick-and-mortar locations, on-site inventory, and store labor. Supplier relationships with diamond cutters and distributors are also key and as seen with Blue Nile can greatly impact the profitability of a given retailer. Finally, due to the expense associated with jewelry purchases, Blue Nile's "average ticket" is $2,000;[30] customers are looking for a trusted source with a strong reputation.

19   In regard to imitation, Blue Nile leverages a few unique systems and services that are hard for the competition to imitate. First, Blue Nile's "build your own" functionality online differentiates it from competitors by allowing the customer to personally create their ideal diamond ring, earring, pendant, multiple stone rings, and/or multiple stone pendants. The consumer also has access to an interactive search function, which references an inventory of 50,000 diamonds, including signature diamonds that are hand-selected and cut with extreme precision.[31]

20   Second, Blue Nile has its own customer service team of diamond and jewelry consultants that offer suggestions and assist customers with their purchases. This online interactive customer service approach creates a barrier to entry as the information technology platform for these functions is complex.

21   Lastly, Blue Nile also offers exclusive colored diamonds, which include rare diamonds that are red and pink.[32] It has a more diversified product range than its competitors because it does not have to hold inventory in stock.

22   The threat of new entrants is always a concern, but Blue Nile has been successful thus far at staying ahead of new entrants and has established a reputation as a quality, reputable online service.

23   One of the most significant resources for jewelers is diamonds and with DeBeers owning 40% of the world's jewelry supply, diamonds are considered scarce and unique. Large diamond suppliers like DeBeers are not as powerful as they were once were—DeBeers at one time sold 80% of the world's diamonds[33]—but their presence is still felt. In addition, diamonds are generally obtained in politically unstable regions of the world, like Africa, and companies must be aware of the risk of obtaining conflict diamonds. The diamond trade is complex with regard to politics and legal issues, as the majority of diamond mines exist in underdeveloped countries, where corruption is prevalent and the rule of law is not easily enforced. Many of the diamond mines are located in African countries such as Botswana, which currently produces 27% of the global diamond supply.[34] However, recent global initiatives, including the Clean Diamond Trade Act of 2003, and the Kimberly Process Certification Scheme of 2002 have made significant impacts on violence and illegal trade in the last decade.[35]

[29]http://www.kaihan.net/vpw_login.php?img=blue-nile
[30]"Blue Nile-CEO interview." CEO Wire. November 29, 2010. http://ezp.bentley.edu/login?url=http://search.proquest.com/?url=http://search.proquest.com/docview/814841480?accountid=8576
[31]http://www.bluenile.com/why-choose-blue-nile
[32]http://www.bluenile.com/diamonds/fancy-color-diamonds?keyword_search_value=colored+diamonds
[33]Joshua Levine. "A Beautiful Mine." *The New York Times*. April 17, 2011.
[34]"Diamonds: Kimberley Process Effective." *Africa Research Bulletin: Economic, Financial and Technical Series*, 44: 17640A–17641A (2008).
[35]http://www.kimberleyprocess.com/background/index_en.html

24   The lack of legal and political stability in many of the diamond source countries represents a threat to Blue Nile and the industry as a whole. With unstable changes in leadership and power, threats to the global supply chain of a valuable commodity are possible, and perhaps even likely to occur. Takeover of diamond mines by militia groups, government claims of eminent domain, diamond smuggling, and obsolescing contract negotiations with foreign governments all have potential deleterious impacts on the jewelry industry.

25   Finally, given the increased valuation of gold in recent years, this jewelry material has become harder to obtain. In April 2011, *The Times* (London) reported, "Gold prices hit a record $1,500 an ounce as investors continued to seek a safe haven."[36]

SOCIAL AND DEMOGRAPHIC TRENDS

26   There are a number of social and demographic trends that offer opportunities for Blue Nile. First, the average age of first-time newlyweds is increasing in the United States, currently 28[37] for men and 26[38] for women.

27   A *USA TODAY* analysis of the Census figures shows that just 23.5 percent of men and 31.5 percent of women ages 20–29 were married in 2006. (The analysis excludes those who are married but separated.) Both the number and percentage of those in their 20s fell from 2000, when 31.5 percent of men and 39.5 percent of women were married.[39]

28   Higher marrying ages tend to translate into greater spending power for marriage-related items, such as engagement rings.

29   Next, people nowadays are more receptive to handheld technologies and apps. These on-the-go technologies are an opportunity for Blue Nile to reach busy customers who do not have time to drop by a jewelry store to research their product choices and make a purchase. Mobile sites and apps allow a customer with a smartphone to make purchases on his or her own schedule, without adhering to a brick-and-mortar schedule. As this generation ages and people become comfortable with technology, Blue Nile will have more segments to cater to and a broader reach. With online purchases becoming more of a cultural norm, with less associated negative stigma, and as higher percentages of the global population gain reliable access to the Internet, Blue Nile is poised to capitalize on its Web-only strategy.

30   Finally, with historical events like the marriage of Prince William and Kate Middleton dominating the media, Blue Nile and other jewelry retailers reap the benefits of Kate's sapphire ring being displayed and/or mentioned in countless media venues throughout the world. Jewelers could not have planned that great of a publicity stunt for making jewelry top of mind, and have the opportunity to ride the wave for a while.

31   One social threat Blue Nile faces is tied to issues of Internet fraud and online security in today's environment. The relatively high purchase price for quality jewelry increases the perceived risk for consumers making online purchases.

32   Another threat is that with each new generation, traditions (such as the purchase and giving of engagement rings) risk becoming outdated or out of fashion. While the giving of jewelry is highly entrenched in many cultures around the world, it is possible that potential customers in Generation Y or later may perceive lower value in this giving tradition.

[36]"Gold at $1,500." *The Times* (London). April 20, 2011.
[37]http://factfinder.census.gov/servlet/GRTTable?_bm=y&-geo_id=01000US&-_box_head_nbr=R1204&-ds_name=ACS_2009_1YR_G00_&-redoLog=false&-mt_name=ACS_2005_EST_G00_R1204_US30&-format=US-30
[38]http://factfinder.census.gov/servlet/GRTTable?_bm=y&-geo_id=D&_box_head_nbr=R1205&ds_name=ACS_2009_1YR_G00_&-_lang=en&-redoLog=false&format=D&mt_name=ACS_2009_1YR_G00_R1204_US30
[39]Anthony DeBarros and Sharon Jayson. "Young Adults Delaying Marriage; Data Show 'Dramatic' Surge in Single Twentysomethings." *USA Today*. September 12, 2007.

GLOBAL OPPORTUNITIES

33   Blue Nile wants to expand internationally as it sees great potential in the global market-place. Currently non-U.S. sales represent 13 percent of the total sales at Blue Nile.[40] Blue Nile's international sales have continuously been growing. Recent numbers show that in 2010 the sales figure grew by 30.4 percent compared to the previous year.[41] It is a high priority to grow internationally at Blue Nile. It is important for Blue Nile to monitor online purchasing rates globally, and expand to those countries accordingly.

34   One major global threat for Blue Nile is the lack of adoption of online purchasing. Many countries have not yet advanced to the American consumer habits. Developed countries are continuing to adopt this as they have realized the efficiency, effectiveness, and overall con-venience. Lack of consumer confidence for high-value online purchases may continue to follow Blue Nile as it expands internationally until it has built a reputation in each foreign country of operations, which may delay return on investment for international expansion programs.

35   Many consumers in developing nations do not have reliable access to the Internet. Blue Nile currently has no way to tap the buying power of these would-be customers. Sending huge sums of money and receiving valuable goods when they clear customs is a risk many people are not willing to take, knowing its ramifications. Many countries around the world are corrupt, and thus one cannot be sure that the product has reached the customer safely.

BLUE NILE'S FINANCES

36   Net sales have been strong each year for Blue Nile since 2006, except in 2008 when the financial crisis impacted the company's performance, as seen in Exhibit 1. (All data in Exhibits 1–8 come from the *2010 Blue Nile Annual Report.*) Sales have grown by $81.3 mil-lion since 2006, a 32 percent increase. Growth was most substantial in 2007 (26.9 percent) due to the huge increase in demand for diamond and fine jewelry products ordered through the Web site. International sales contributed significantly to the surge in demand in 2007, with an increase of 104.8 percent, due mainly to the new product offerings and the ability of U.K. and Canadian customers to purchase in their local currency.[42] Sales decreased by 7.5 percent in 2008, primarily due to the sluggish economy, which negatively impacted the popularity of luxury goods, and due to the increase in diamond prices worldwide.[43] In 2009, sales rebounded slightly with an increase of 2.3 percent, due mostly to an increase of 20 percent in Q4 year-over-year. The increase in Q4 is attributed to the boost in interna-tional sales, which represented 1.9 percent of the 2.3 percent total growth, as a result of the new Web site enhancements and the ability to purchase in 22 other foreign currencies.[44]

37   In 2010, sales returned to double-digit growth with an increase of 10.2 percent. Both U.S. sales and international sales grew considerably with 7.7 percent and 30.4 percent respectively, due mainly to a better economy, which led to increased consumer spend-ing. Marketing spend, better brand recognition, and the favorable exchange rate of foreign currencies against the U.S. dollar contributed to the strong sales in Q4, which reached an

---

[40]*2010 Blue Nile Annual Report.* P. 27.
[41]*2010 Blue Nile Annual Report.* P. 27.
[42]*Annual Report 2008.* P. 31.
[43]*Annual Report 2008.* P. 30.
[44]*Annual Report 2010.* P. 31.

EXHIBIT 1   **Blue Nile Net Sales 2006–2010 (In Thousands)**

Year	2006	2007	2008	2009	2010
Net Sales	$251,587.00	$319,264.00	$295,329.00	$302,134.00	$332,889.00
Growth		26.90%	−7.50%	2.30%	10.18%

all-time record of $114.8 million.[45] However, although Q1, Q2, and Q4 numbers are growing annually due to events such as Valentine's Day, Mother's Day, Christmas, and New Year's, Q3 continues to present a challenge due to the lack of a special holiday or event.

38   Net income levels from 2006 to 2010 tracked the performance of net sales, but were more severe as seen in Exhibits 2 and 3. Net income increased by 33.64 percent in 2007, 10.06 percent in 2009, and 10.48 percent in 2010, but decreased by −33.39 percent in 2008. Not including the decrease in earnings during the financial meltdown, the net income numbers are considered healthy for a company that was started 12 years ago.

39   Gross profit has grown similar to net sales from 2006–2010 as can be seen in Exhibit 4. However, the most telling difference is in year 2009, where it outpaced net sales growth with an increase of 8.91 percent. The growth was a result of cost savings achieved with regard to sourcing and selling products, which increased the gross profit margin from 20.2 percent to 21.6 percent as can be seen in Exhibit 4. Blue Nile's increasing gross profit margin is a good sign for the company since it shows strict financial management and an emphasis on the bottom line.

40   Blue Nile has no long-term debt. The company only has lease obligations that it needs to pay every year. The lease obligations decreased from $880,000 in 2007 to $748,000 in 2010.[46] Long-term debt to equity ratio is effectively zero as a result, and even if we include lease obligations, then it is minimal with a value of 0.01, meaning that equity can cover the remaining debt obligations.

41   Cash at the company is generated mostly through ongoing operations. The increase in cash from 2009 is a result of an increase in accounts payable and the tax benefits received from the execution of stock options. Investing activities also increased the cash amount with the expiration of short-term investment maturity dates. In addition, a slight increase can be attributed to the financing activities coming from the profits of the stock option execution.[47]

[45]*Annual Report 2010.* P. 30.
[46]*Annual Report 2010.* P. 33.
[47]*Annual Report 2010.* P. 32.

EXHIBIT 2   Blue Nile Net Income 2006–2010 (In Thousands)

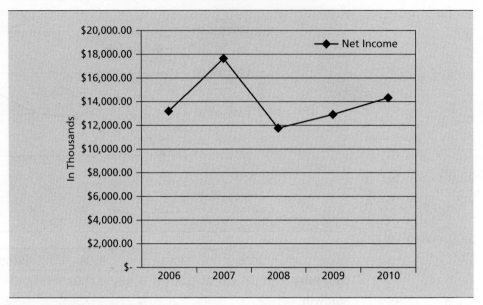

Year	2006	2007	2008	2009	2010
Net Income	$13,064.00	$17,459.00	$11,630.00	$12,800.00	$14,142.00
Growth		33.64%	−33.39%	10.06%	10.48%

EXHIBIT 3   Blue Nile Net Sales vs. Net Income (Percentage change)

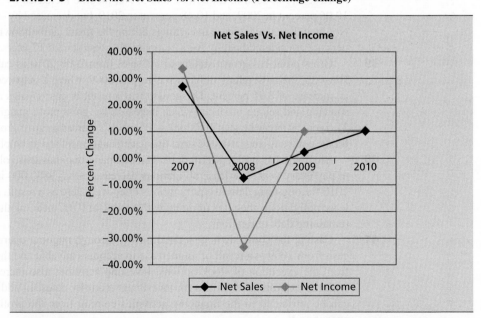

Growth	2007	2008	2009	2010
Net Sales	26.90%	−7.50%	2.30%	10.18%
Net Income	33.64%	−33.39%	10.06%	10.48%

EXHIBIT 4   Gross Profit Margin and Operating Margin

Year	2006	2007	2008	2009	2010
Gross Profit Margin	20.2%	20.4%	20.3%	21.6%	21.6%
Operating Margin	6.600%	7.00%	5.400%	6.400%	6.400%

42   In 2011, Blue Nile had only $79 million in cash. In 2008 the company purchased back 1.6 million shares of stock ($66.5 million) in order to increase consumer confidence in the stock and because Blue Nile's management team believed the stock was being undervalued.

43   Blue Nile acquires the majority of its inventory on a just-in-time basis. Moreover, the company is successful in growing cash because its uses for it are minimal, such as improving the Web site and maintaining facilities and warehouses.[48]

MARKETING

44   Blue Nile's marketing strengths include its use of technology to enhance the customer experience, its dedication to making the diamond-buying-process as easy and hassle-free as possible, and its ability to capture market share in spite of the recession.

45   First, in regard to its use of technology, Blue Nile has been investing in introducing and perfecting online technology that enhances the customer experience. For example, the Blue Nile App, which was launched in September 2010, gives customers instant access to its inventory of 70,000 diamonds and allows a customer to customize a particular diamond or gem with the ideal setting "while standing at a rival's counter."[49]

46   Likewise, Blue Nile has also developed its own mobile site that caters to customers wishing to shop using their iPhone, iPod Touch, and Android mobile devices. "The mobile version, launched in spring 2010, is smaller than the PC site in scope, with quick tabs to find diamonds, engagement rings, and other gift ideas. The company reports that more than 20 percent of its shoppers are using the mobile site."[50]

47   Finally, Blue Nile has done an excellent job of makings its Web site educational, easy to navigate, and a trusted advisor for potential diamond buyers. The company completely revamped its Web site in 2009 in order to include larger images, better zoom functionality, and enhanced product filtering features.[51] The site also utilizes interactive search tools that few other online retailers can match.[52] The Build Your Own Ring® component of the site is extremely easy to use, while also being fun. Blue Nile provides step-by-step guidance on the components of the ring a person can personalize, and based on filling out specifications on shape, color, quality, and size, builds the ideal ring right before its customer's eyes.

48   Next, another marketing strength for Blue Nile has been its ability to home in on the obstacles that might deter a customer from making a jewelry purchase online, and then

[48]*Annual Report 2010.* P. 33.
[49]Jonathan Birchall. "Smartphone Apps: Competition Set to Intensify for Online Retailers." *FT.com.* November 13, 2010.
[50]Blue Nile, Inc. Overview. *Hoovers.* http://cobrands.hoovers.com/global/cobrands/proquest/overview .xhtml?ID=100858
[51]Byron Acohido and Edward C. Baig. "Blue Nile Gets a New Look." *USA Today.* September 2, 2009.
[52]Blue Nile, Inc. Datamonitor. www.datamonitor.com. September 10, 2010.

providing assurances against those barriers. Policies like these all work to build confidence in the online purchasing experience, which works in Blue Nile's favor:

1. Offering a 30-day money-back guarantee;[53]
2. Orders being shipped fully insured to the customer;
3. Providing grading reports for all certified diamonds and professional appraisals for diamond, gemstone, and pearl jewelry over $1,000.[54]

49   Finally, in spite of the trying economic environment, Blue Nile has been able to capture market share while many other jewelry sellers have had to close their doors. According to CEO Diane Irvine, the company saw U.S. sales growth of 23 percent year over year in November and December of 2009, while its competitors ranged from 12 percent to a 12 percent decline in the same time frame.[55] In trying economic times, customers have valued the 20–40 percent reduced price found at Blue Nile in comparison to brick-and-mortar retailers.

50   Although Blue Nile has done a good job of anticipating and catering to the barriers that exist in purchasing an expensive piece of jewelry online, the fact still remains that Blue Nile operates with no storefront locations. This means that customers cannot physically touch and inspect their piece of jewelry before making a purchase. There are traditionally minded members of the jewelry market that are not comfortable with this limitation and will not consider Blue Nile a viable alternative. It is also more difficult to develop a lasting, long-term relationship with the customer when the transaction lacks the face-to-face experience found at brick-and-mortar stores. Blue Nile's business is completely dependent on online or phone transactions, making it subject to the adjustment period consumers must go through in order to be comfortable with this purchasing experience.

51   Building on this weakness is the fact that Blue Nile's online traffic and site visits have been in decline. According to 2010 data from Compete.com, Blue Nile saw its number of unique site visitors decrease year over year in the majority of months, while one of its main competitors, Tiffany's, saw its online traffic increase. Similarly, Compete.com reports that when viewing Blue Nile's unique visitor trend between 2007 and 2009, the company has seen a 36 percent decrease in unique visitors.[56]

OPERATIONS AND LOGISTICS

52   Blue Nile aims to offer a wide range of finished and partially customizable jewelry products to online shoppers, made from ethically sourced materials, via a convenient, hassle-free experience. The company looks to leverage its sourcing power to offer exclusive jewels to exclude competition and retain high selling prices, while maximizing profitability through implementation of just-in-time manufacturing tactics to minimize inventory costs.

53   Blue Nile employs a flexible manufacturing strategy in its operations. The company heavily advertises the ability to customize your desired product—"Build Your Own Ring®" is an example of how Blue Nile allows a customer to pick a diamond and an engagement ring setting and get a unique product.[57] Blue Nile also offers a similar type of customization for earrings, pendants, and other jewelry items.

[53]Blue Nile, Inc. Datamonitor. www.datamonitor.com. September 10, 2010.
[54]"Blue Nile Unwraps Cyber Monday Promotions." *Information Technology Newsweekly*. December 8, 2009.
[55]Dimitra DeFotis. "No Diamond in the Rough." *Barron's*. February 15, 2010.
[56]Dimitra DeFotis. "No Diamond in the Rough." *Barron's*. February 15, 2010.
[57]http://www.bluenile.com/build-your-own-diamond-ring?track=head

54   On the one hand, it seems as though the company would be utilizing an "intermittent job shop" approach. However, while the company does offer full customization through a special-order service, the "customization" service is basically allowing online shoppers to pick from a predetermined list of jewels and settings. The jewels are listed from a Blue Nile database (maintained in partnership with its source providers), and the materials are prefabricated en masse production-style to minimize cost.[58]

55   Using the same methods, Blue Nile makes both finished goods (noncustomizable products for direct sale over the Web), and customer-directed finished goods. By using the same supply chain and methods, Blue Nile is able to achieve rapid turnaround of "customized" products, adding value to the service offering.[59]

56   Blue Nile partners with FedEx for both shipping and returns of all of its products. By maintaining one carrier partnership, the company is able to reach economies of scale in shipping expenditures, and also take advantage of FedEx's international shipping capabilities (other carriers, such as UPS or USPS, are more limited in their international shipping offers). Also, by partnering with FedEx, Blue Nile is able to take advantage of FedEx's best-in-class shipment tracking functions, which alleviates potential customer concerns about expensive online purchases being "lost in the mail."[60]

57   Although the majority of revenues for Blue Nile come from the sale of diamonds, it typically does not receive diamonds into inventory until an order is placed, following a just-in-time manufacturing strategy. Instead, Blue Nile partners with its diamond sources, many of them in an exclusive agreement, to provide up-to-date records of available diamond inventory. When a customer places an order for a particular diamond, Blue Nile in turn ordered the specified diamond from its supplier, receives the stone, finishes the good, enters the product into inventory, and ships to the customer.[61]

58   Financially, this puts the company in a strong position, since it does not have to maintain high inventory carrying costs for the diamonds, which can be valued at several hundred to several thousand dollars each. The company actually produces a positive cash flow of approximately 30–45 days, depending on its contract with a particular supplier.[62]

59   While partnering with a single distribution partner does provide economic and logistical benefits to the company, it also puts Blue Nile at some degree of risk. Although FedEx has yet to experience a strike by its employees, its rival UPS faced this situation some years ago.[63] If the same situation should occur with FedEx, Blue Nile may be hard-pressed to quickly develop new distribution channels, both domestically and abroad.

60   In addition, there are also risks associated with Blue Nile's just-in-time inventory approach. First, this approach requires that Blue Nile establish and maintain a direct and accurate path of visibility to its suppliers' diamond inventory. Since many of its diamond suppliers are in less developed regions of the world, this is not an insignificant feat.[64]

61   Second, since the diamonds are not actually in the possession of Blue Nile at the time the customer places an order, it is possible that any type of geo-political disruption (natural disaster, governmental turmoil, etc.) could interrupt the flow of the customer's product and require subsequent customer service follow-up and potential product replacement.

[58]http://www.glassdoor.com/Reviews/Blue-Nile-Reviews-E11944.htm
[59]http://www.glassdoor.com/Reviews/Blue-Nile-Reviews-E11944.htm
[60]http://www.fedex.com/us/track/index.html
[61]http://www.reuters.com/finance/stocks/companyProfile?symbol=NILE.O
[62]http://seekingalpha.com/article/11593-the-bull-and-bear-cases-for-blue-nile-nile
[63]http://www.businessweek.com/smallbiz/news/date/9811/e981119.htm
[64]http://seekingalpha.com/article/11593-the-bull-and-bear-cases-for-blue-nile-nile

62   Despite these risks, Blue Nile's success in establishing exclusive sourcing agreements with diamond suppliers and cutters has yielded significant benefits and is one source of competitive advantage for the organization. By negotiating directly with diamond suppliers and cutters, rather than operating through wholesalers, Blue Nile is able to reduce its diamond procurement costs by more than 20 percent, compared to other diamond retailers.[65] It is therefore able to offer lower prices than its competition, while simultaneously achieving higher profit margins on its products. Blue Nile's exclusive contracts do offer the company opportunities to be a "sole source" for particular diamond cuts or rare colors, although many diamond retailers have also followed this trend, and each major retailer appears to have its own "exclusive" diamonds.[66]

HUMAN RESOURCES AND ETHICS

63   Blue Nile employees 193 full-time workers, with 26 of these full-time positions listed at the executive level.[67] The company maintains employee testimonials on its Web site as part of its career section, with several comments from employees who have been with the organization for 10 years or more.[68] However, when looking for examples of Blue Nile employee satisfaction outside of the company's own Web site, the picture is not as rosy. The most common complaints pertain to employee development and retention. Unverified reports of hyper-control by senior management, instead of empowerment and distribution of responsibility to managerial staff, if true, may have a significant impact on Blue Nile's ability to attract and retain high-performance employees, and as a result, grow its business.[69] While the company has made a significant leap forward compared to other jewelry retailers, both brick-and-mortar and Internet-based, if the company focuses exclusively on technology and not on human talent development, it has little chance to continue its recent growth trends.

64   While Blue Nile has a significant section of its Web site devoted to its policies around the ethical sourcing of its diamonds and other materials, the company does not detail any of its policies regarding the handling of its own employees. There are no statements regarding employee diversity, the cultural environment, or employee training/advancement programs. Despite listing nine senior managers in the company's investor relations section of its Web site, not one of the nine is involved in human resource management.[70] This absence, taken with the company's wordage from its corporate reports, paints a picture that suggests attention to human assets is limited at Blue Nile, Inc.

STUCK IN THE MIDDLE

65   Operating in a niche segment, Blue Nile is "stuck in the middle" of the diamond engagement ring market. It is not at the top end of the jewelry retail market with the likes of Tiffany & Co. or DeBeers. It is neither at the low end of the market with the likes of Amazon or Overstock.com. Blue Nile has found a strong growth market by providing high-quality

---

[65]http://seekingalpha.com/article/11593-the-bull-and-bear-cases-for-blue-nile-nile
[66]http://www.diamondsnews.com/hearts_on_fire.htm
[67]http://www.hoovers.com/company/Blue_Nile_Inc/rffxhxi-1.html
[68]http://www.bluenile.com/employee_testimonials.jsp
[69]http://www.glassdoor.com/Reviews/Blue-Nile-Reviews-E11944.htm
[70]http://investor.bluenile.com/management.cfm

jewelry at discounted prices. Unfortunately, as the company increasingly grows its market share, competitors at the high end and the low end will look to squeeze into the middle niche that Blue Nile currently dominates. Tiffany & Co. and DeBeers have already begun to infuse their online presence with aspects of Blue Nile's approach. Amazon and Over-stock.com are likely to look to add higher priced jewels to their offerings, as broad market acceptance of purchasing jewelry online increases. Michael Porter states that the middle is the worst place to be. The challenge for Blue Nile is how to move up the ladder and become a "high end" diamond retailer—not an easy task for an "online only" retailer.*The author would like to thank Abdullah Al-Hadlaq, Rashid Alhamer, Chris Harbert, Sarah Martin, Adnan Rawji and Will Hoffman for their research. Please address all correspondence to Dr. Alan N. Hoffman, Dept. of Management, Bentley University, 175 Forest Street, Waltham, MA 02452; ahoffman@bentley.edu. Printed by permission of Dr. Alan N. Hoffman.*

Case 16

BMW of North America: *Dream It. Build It. Drive It.*

Dmitry Alenuskin
Andreas Schotter

Any customer can have a car painted any color that he wants so long as it is black.

—Henry Ford

INTRODUCTION

1   In early January 2012, Joseph Wierda, BMW's X3 product manager, reviewed the latest sales numbers of the popular X3 Series compact SUV. He was, in particular, interested in the effects of BMW's customization program called "Dream It. Build It. Drive It." on both unit sales and overall profitability. This new integrated sales and marketing program allowed customers to create a fully customized BMW X3 SUV and have it delivered to their driveway in only a few weeks. The program scored some important points with the media. For example, Martha Stewart, a U.S. TV personality, customized her X3 live on her popular show called *The Martha Stewart Show*.

2   Just two years earlier, in 2009, the idea of the customization program came at a time when the global financial crisis had hit consumers hard, and most households were putting large ticket item purchases on hold. During the same period, fuel prices reached $4 per gallon. Consequently, BMW's North American overall sales had plummeted by 30 percent compared to 2008, and SUV sales were down a staggering 55 percent.

3   The new customization program was a departure from the traditional North American car purchasing model, where consumers were accustomed to buying a car and driving it off the dealership's lot right away, after typically receiving some generous discounts or other incentives. Wierda wondered if the program should be extended across all BMW product lines and, if so, what this meant for the regional and global manufacturing strategy, sales and distribution strategy, and the overall competitive positioning of BMW in North America. He needed to make up his mind before the next management meeting at the end of the month where he had to present the proposal to Ludwig Willisch, the recently appointed CEO of BMW North America. This proposal would have far-reaching internal and external effects.

THE U.S. AUTOMOTIVE INDUSTRY

4   The automotive industry had traditionally been the largest manufacturing sector in the United States, averaging about 3.6 percent of total GDP. Sales data for new cars in America represented one of the key economic indicators. In 2011, the U.S. auto industry was estimated to be a $500 billion industry, employing more than eight million people.

THUNDERBIRD
SCHOOL OF GLOBAL MANAGEMENT

Source: Copyright © 2012 Helen Grassbaugh Thunderbird School of GlobalManagement casesseries@thunderbird.edu. All rights reserved.
This case was prepared by Dmitry Alenuskin and Andreas Schotter for the purpose of classroom discussion only, and not to indicate either effective or ineffective management.

5   Just three years earlier, in December 2008, American auto sales dropped by 37 percent compared to the year before as a result of the 2007/08 global financial crisis. During the same month, the "Big Three" auto companies (General Motors, Ford Motor Company, and Chrysler) applied for emergency loans totaling $34 billion combined. The argument was that these loans would help avoid laying off up to three million people. In January 2009, the U.S. Congress approved this unprecedented emergency bailout. Most of the money was used to provide consumer loans and new consumer incentive programs in order to stimulate sales.

6   In exchange for government loans, the "Big Three" promised to consolidate operations and accelerate production of more fuel-efficient (greener) vehicles. Most of the loans were scheduled for cash repayment, but some of the debt was converted into government-owned equity. Many legendary brands subsequently disappeared, including Pontiac, Mercury, Saturn, and Hummer. Germany's Daimler AG announced that it would discontinue its ultra-luxury Maybach brand. The bankruptcy of Chrysler in May 2009, and its subsequent acquisition by Fiat Group of Italy, opened a new era of foreign ownership in the U.S. automotive industry.

7   In 2010/11, the U.S. auto market showed some signs of recovery. While only 10.4 million new cars and trucks were purchased in 2009, the worst year since 1982, the recent sales increases were mainly credited to serving pent-up demand, a strengthening labor market, and increased consumer credit availability. In 2011, U.S. sales of new vehicles reached 12.7 million units, the best result since 2007.[1] Sales for 2012 were projected to reach 13.8 million units, close to what many experts considered a nonbubble sales volume of around 14–15 million cars.[2]

8   In terms of local manufacturing volume, the U.S. was third in the world with a record low of 5.7 million new motor vehicles produced in 2009. During the same year, Japan built 7.9 million cars and China 13.7 million. Just a decade earlier, however, in 1999, the U.S. dominated the global car industry, manufacturing more than 13 million new vehicles, more than Japan and China combined at the time.[3]

9   Recent volume increases in China were mostly driven by first-time buyers, government incentives, rural subsidies, and reduced sales tax for fuel-efficient vehicles. While the Chinese market was growing at an impressive rate of 40% annually,[4] major U.S. carmakers were still struggling at home.

U.S. AUTO FLEET

10   In 2011, the United States had 254 million registered passenger vehicles and 205 million licensed drivers.[5] The number of cars, along with the average age of the U.S. fleet, had increased steadily since 1960, indicating an increasing number of vehicles per household.

11   Recently, however, changes in consumer behavior could be observed. Price-sensitive Americans tended to keep their cars longer. The average age of vehicles in the United States was approaching a record of 11 years. Although a government-run $3 billion "Cash for

---

[1]Carlos Gomez, "Global Auto Report," *Scotia Economics*, Dec. 22, 2011. www.scotiacapital.com/English/bns_econ/bns_auto.pdf (retrieved on Jan. 17, 2012).

[2]Tom Krisher, "US Auto Industry to Post Good Sales Year," *Associated Press*, Jan. 2, 2012.

[3]"2011 Production Statistics," *International Organization of Motor Vehicle Manufacturers*. http://oica.net/category/production-statistics/ (retrieved on Jan. 17, 2012).

[4]"China Overtakes US as World's Biggest Car Market," *The Guardian*, Jan. 8, 2010. http://www.guardian.co.uk/business/2010/jan/08/china-us-car-sales-overtakes (retrieved on Jan. 17, 2012).

[5]"National Transportation Statistics 2011," *Bureau of Transportation Statistics, U.S. Department of Transportation*. www.bts.gov/publications/national_transportation_statistics/pdf/entire.pdf (retrieved on Jan. 17, 2012).

Clunkers" vehicle replacement program had a temporary effect on new car sales in 2009, most of the U.S. fleet was still aging.[6]

12   With 6.5 million new light-duty trucks on the road, the pickup truck was the most popular vehicle in America. It remained the best-selling category with an increase of 11.6 percent from 2010 compared to the car and SUV categories.

13   In 2011, the best-selling vehicle in the United States was the Ford F-Series pickup (584,917 units sold). Another popular American workhorse was the Chevrolet Silverado (415,130). Heavy sales hitters among sedans were the Toyota Camry (308,510) and Nissan Altima (268,981). Ford Escape (254,293) was a favorite among compact SUV buyers.

14   Although only 647,943 midsize SUVs were sold during 2011, this segment saw the largest year-on-year increase with a 45 percent jump. On the other hand, large luxury cars (such as the BMW X5) sold 68,211 units throughout the year, showing a 23 percent decrease.[7]

15   In 2011, BMW outsold its long-time rival Mercedes-Benz and became the top-selling U.S. luxury brand. Throughout the year, BMW sold 247,907 cars and SUVs, 2,676 more than Mercedes. Both automakers saw their sales rise about 13 percent for the full year.[8] Toyota's Lexus (198,552 units sold in 2011) was the top-selling luxury car brand in 2010, as it had been since 2000.

16   The average transaction price for new vehicles in the United States fluctuated from $29,000 to $31,000 depending on the month, according to TrueCar.com, the authority on new-car pricing. Winter months tended to yield higher prices due to increased shopping activity, manufacturer incentives, and clearance sales.

U.S. CAR DISTRIBUTION

18   In 2011, the U.S. was home to 17,000 new passenger car and truck dealers with approximately 37,500 points of sale (franchises). Direct manufacturer car sales were prohibited in most states because of stringent franchise and distributorship laws based on a regulatory system that dated back to the 1950s. In fact, it was a criminal act for any manufacturer to sell a new vehicle through anyone other than one of state-licensed new-car dealers. State franchise laws protected dealers' substantial investment in real estate and assets like showrooms and service facilities.[9]

19   However, senators in some states recognized the need for change facing the auto industry and proposed to revise the law. These resolutions had not been passed yet, but it was a popular topic generously supported by the Alliance of Automobile Manufacturers.

20   Auto dealers operated on relatively low gross profit margins in the 7 percent–15 percent range for new vehicles, and manufactures often restricted dealers' markups over the invoice cost. Inventory was usually paid for by a low-interest loan from manufacturers. Also, dealers were financially supported by "holdbacks," which were additional discounts of around 1 percent to 2 percent of the vehicle's wholesale price. A holdback was designed to provide better vehicle availability by reimbursing the cost of the loan in order to keep the car in inventory, a critical enabler of the traditional car purchasing process.

[6]Lacey Plache, "Auto Sales Forecast 2011," *Edmunds Auto Observer*. www.autoobserver.com/assets/Auto%20 Sales%20Forecast%202011.pdf (retrieved on Apr. 12, 2012).

[7]"Auto Sales Market Data Center," *The Wall Street Journal*. http://online.wsj.com/mdc/public/page/2_3022-autosales.html?mod=mdc_h_econhl (retrieved on Jan. 19, 2012).

[8]"BMW Beats Mercedes in Luxury-Sales Showdown," *Driver's Seat Blog, WSJ.com*. http://blogs.wsj.com/drivers-seat/2012/01/05/bmw-beats-mercedes-in-luxury-sales-showdown/ (retrieved on Jan. 20, 2012).

[9]Gerald R. Bodisch, "Economic Effects of State Bans on Direct Manufacturer Sales to Car Buyers," *Economic Analysis Group (EAG), Antitrust Division, U.S. Department of Justice*, May 2009. www.justice.gov/atr/public/eag/246374.htm (retrieved on Jan. 22, 2012).

21   The Internet changed the way people bought cars. One-click access to information about the features of comparable cars and the best available prices put pressure on dealers' profitability. In late 2011, more than 70 percent of purchases originated from online research, and it became much easier for consumers to shop around.

22   In recent years, people drove fewer miles and less frequently overall because of a combination of high costs, increased urbanization, improved alternative travel options, and changing perspectives on car ownership. One of the most fundamental social trends affecting the future of the automobile was the declining interest in cars among young people, who were becoming increasingly more environmentally conscious and unresponsive to traditional advertising. Walking, cycling, and riding public transit travel became more socially acceptable, and in some groups even prestigious.[10]

BMW BACKGROUND

23   BMW AG or Bayerische Motoren Werke (Bavarian Motor Company) was established in 1918 as a successor of Rapp Motorenwerke, an engine supplier for military aircraft. The first BMW engines set more than 30 world flight records, and this achievement became a symbol of the company. In fact, the existing BMW logo was first introduced in 1920 as a circular design of an aircraft propeller using the two Bavarian national colors: blue and white.

24   The Treaty of Versailles, signed in 1918 following World War I, put BMW out of the aircraft engine business for three years. As a post-WWI disarming measure, German manufacturers were not permitted to produce armed aircraft, tanks, or armored cars.[11]

25   Although BMW returned to aircraft engine manufacturing in 1922, the Versailles ban inspired product line extensions that included air brakes, motorcycles, and railway cars. The first BMW motorcycle, named R 32, was built in 1923. The fast-growing popularity of cars based on Henry Ford's pioneering efforts (also in Germany) triggered an expansion into automotive manufacturing. The compact three-cylinder, 15-horsepower Dixi was the first BMW car in 1928. It sold more than 18,000 units. This achievement marked a new chapter in BMW history.

26   During World War II, BMW manufactured motorcycles, aircraft engines, and missiles for the German army. After the war was over, the company lay in ruins. Most of the factories were destroyed during air raids. The remaining plant in Eisenach was nationalized during the Soviet occupation and for seven years manufactured copycat BMWs, mainly pre-war 326 models carrying BMW's logo but without involvement of the Bavaria-based company.

27   Another three-year ban on engine production following WWII caused a serious downsizing of BMW's manufacturing capacity. Agreements with the U.S. army restricted BMW operations to bicycles, spare parts, and agricultural equipment, yet BMW provided repairs for U.S. army vehicles.

28   BMW returned to motorcycle production in 1948 and cars in 1951 but with little success. In the 1950s, BMW came close to being acquired by Daimler-Benz. Under the leadership of Herbert Quandt and the support of factory workers, BMW remained independent and entered into the so-called roaring' 60s with a strong product line. The company's flagship 1600 model sold more than 330,000 units.

[10]"The Future Isn't What It Used to Be," *Victoria Transport Policy Institute*, Nov. 6, 2011. www.vtpi.org/future.pdf (retrieved on Jan. 22, 2012).

[11]"The Avalon Project: Documents in Law, History, Diplomacy," *Yale Law School, Lillian Goldman Law Library*. http://avalon.law.yale.edu/subject_menus/versailles_menu.asp (retrieved on Jan. 24, 2012).

29   In the 1970s, the famous BMW 3, 5, and 7 Series were introduced. BMW's product strategy changed by requiring each update to include major technological improvements rather than simply design modifications.

30   In 1990, BMW formed a joint venture with Rolls Royce. Eight years later, BMW purchased all rights to the Rolls Royce logo and brand name but no other assets from the Volkswagen Group, which had acquired the plants and facilities and the Bentley name in a bidding war shortly before. In 1994, BMW bought British Rover Group PLC as part of an expansion strategy into new market segments, including SUVs and compact cars. After six years of losses, BMW sold Rover to Ford for a symbolic price of ten pounds. BMW kept the rights for the MINI brand and successfully relaunched the iconic model in 2002 with a revolutionary marketing strategy based on fashion, trendiness, and total customization. By 2011, BMW had successfully expanded the previously single-model brand by also offering MINI convertibles, MINI station wagons, and MINI SUVs.

31   BMW took a stand in environmental leadership by introducing its "Efficient Dynamics Concept" in 2000. According to this new initiative, all engines produced by the BMW Group had to have lower emissions than their predecessor generations.

32   By late 2011, the BMW Group was a large multinational company with a global presence and a market capitalization of €45 billion. The Quandt family owns 47 percent of the company stock and the remaining 53 percent is publicly traded on the Frankfurt Stock Exchange. Headquartered in Munich, BMW sold cars in 130 countries and had 25 manufacturing facilities in 14 countries. In the same year, BMW Group posted the highest unit sales ever, selling more than 1.6 million cars.[12] See Exhibits 1 and 2 regarding sales trends and Exhibit 3 for the BMW Group's performance indicators.

EXHIBIT 1   BMW Group Sales of vehicles by Region and Market, in 1,000 Units

	2007	2008	2009	2010	2011
Rest of Europe	443.6	432.2	357.3	369.3	405.7
Asia*	159.5	165.7	183.1	286.3	375.5
North America	364.0	331.8	271.0	298.3	341.3
Germany	280.9	280.9	267.5	267.2	285.3
Great Britain	173.8	151.5	137.1	154.8	167.5
Other markets	78.9	73.8	70.3	85.3	93.7
Total	1,500.7	1,435.9	1,286.3	1,461.2	1,669.0

*Including automobiles from the joint venture BMW Brilliance
Source: BMW Group 2011 Annual Report.

EXHIBIT 2   BMW Group Revenue by Region, in Millions

	2007	2008	2009	2010	2011
Rest of Europe	22,395	20,693	16,989	18,581	20,956
Asia/Oceania	7,353	7,523	8,495	14,776	19,216
North America	12,161	12,461	11,724	12,966	12,905
Germany	11,918	10,739	11,436	11,207	12,895
Other markets	2,191	1,781	2,037	2,947	2,885
Total	56,018	53,197	50,681	60,477	68,857

Source: BMW Group 2011 Annual Report.

[12]"BMW Group Annual Report 2011." www.press.bmwgroup.com/pressclub/p/pcgl/download.html?textId=1523 61&textAttachmentId=186357 (retrieved on Apr. 12, 2012).

EXHIBIT 3   BMW Group Key Financial Indicators

	2011	2010
Gross margin, %	21.1	18.1
EBITDA margin, %	16.9	14.5
EBIT margin, %	11.7	8.5
Pre-tax return on sales, %	10.7	8.0
Post-tax return on sales, %	7.1	5.4
Pre-tax return on equity, %	30.9	23.4
Post-tax return on equity, %	20.5	15.6
Equity ratio—Group, %	22.0	21.7
Automotive, %	41.1	40.9
Financial services, %	8.7	7.1
Coverage of intangible assets, PPE by equity, %	160.2	145.4
Return on capital employed		
Group, %	25.6	19.1
Automotive, %	77.3	40.2
Motorcycles, %	10.2	18.0
Return on equity		
Financial services, %	29.4	26.1
Cash inflow from operating activities, € million	5,713	4,319
Cash outflow from operating activities, € million	−5,499	−5,190
Free cash flow of automotive segment, € million	2,133	4,471
Net financial assets of automotive segment, € million	12,287	11,286

Source: BMW Group 2011 Annual Report.

BMW OF NORTH AMERICA

33   BMW established its U.S. office in Woodcliff Lake, New Jersey, in 1975. From simple distribution functions, it quickly advanced to full-scale operations. In 2011, BMW of North America sold the full product line of all three BMW Group brands, provided financial services, marketing, R&D, and manufactured six different models locally.

34   North America was the biggest market for the BMW Group. Sales results for 2011 were impressive across all three brands. Three hundred and five thousand BMWs, Rolls-Royces, and MINIs rolled to new owners in the United States. BMW X3 was the most popular model of the year in the luxury compact SUV segment, selling 27,793 units, which reflected a record year-on-year increase of a whopping 450 percent. For 2012, BMW was planning to introduce 14 new models—the biggest product rollout in company history.

BMW DEALERSHIPS

35   In 2011, the BMW dealer network in the U.S. consisted of independent companies operating under strict BMW brand guidelines. The company used the term "BMW Passenger Car Centers and BMW Sports Activity Vehicle Centers (SAV)" to describe its sales centers.

Altogether, there were 338 passenger car and SAV centers, 138 motorcycle retailers, 104 MINI, and 30 Rolls-Royce Motor dealers. BMW of North America also operated its own dealership in Manhattan that served as a national flagship sales center.

36   Partnerships between the dealers and BMW were based on financial incentives, marketing support, and corporate training. For example, the average discount percentage on a new BMW in December 2011 was 11.2 percent off the manufacturer's suggested retail price (MSRP), which averaged $3,694 per vehicle.[13] Apart from discounts, all dealers regularly received sales and service training and marketing support. Point-of-sales advertising for the BMW brand usually included a cash budget assigned to a dealer along with a partial reimbursement of direct advertising expenses.

37   Unlike many other car manufacturers, BMW used a push distribution system based on territorial quotas, which were assigned annually depending on the previous sales performance of each franchise dealer. For example, Mercedes Benz (Daimler AG), in addition to franchise dealerships, used a network of its own vertically integrated retailers who shared the same inventory without territorial quotas.

38   Mercedes accepted customized orders and embedded its desired features in standard vehicles planned for production. For example, a GLK compact SUV scheduled for assembly in Bremen, Germany, for May 5 could get any number of customized add-ons until May 1 and be delivered to a customer in North America by late June.

MARKETING AT BMW

39   BMW had an evolutionary approach to marketing and advertising. It often used movies to promote its latest vehicle. For instance, in the James Bond movie *Golden Eye* (1995), the sporty Z3 was featured for a few minutes, marking the first public appearance of this model. The subsequent interest in the new Bond car was enormous, and the company ended up selling 300,000 Z3s.[14] In the next Bond movie, titled *Tomorrow Never Dies* (1997), a flagship executive sedan BMW 750iL was shown multiple times, but here it was also operated via a futuristic mobile phone. The car became a key element of the story. Then, in *The World Is Not Enough* (1999), BMW put 007 behind the wheel of a Z8 luxury convertible. Although James Bond met his match in this roadster, the $128,000 Z8 sold only 5,703 cars. This marked the end of BMW's James Bond engagement.

40   From 2001–2003, BMW continued using the movie industry for promotion and released *The Hire*, a series of short films directed by several renowned filmmakers. Hollywood star Clive Owen played the lead character in eight episodes. Each series featured the story of a professional driver who tests the performance of various BMW models in extreme situations. The project became an instant success while being viewed more than 100 million times. However, in 2005 the project was suspended due to its high production costs.

41   In 2011, BMW came back to Hollywood in the latest episode of a popular blockbuster, *Mission Impossible 4—Ghost Protocol,* where BMW featured the X3 and 6 Series convertible and also showed the i8, the futuristic concept car scheduled for production in 2014.

42   While BMW of Europe was participating in F1 sponsorship, BMW of North America focused on yachting. For eight years, BMW was involved in the America's Cup, one of the world's most recognizable yacht races. In 2010, BMW's ORACLE Racing trimaran won the 33rd Cup. The benefits of this involvement went beyond marketing. Both companies

[13]"Edmunds.com's December True Cost of Incentives®: BMW and Mercedes-Benz Make Final Plays for Luxury Sales Crown." http://www.edmunds.com/about/press/edmundscoms-december-true-cost-of-incentives-bmw-and-mercedes-benz-make-final-plays-for-luxury-sales-crown.html (retrieved on Jan. 25, 2012).

[14]"5th Gear—James Bond Cars Special." www.youtube.com/watch?v=Flodhus_I8U (retrieved on Jan. 25, 2012).

developed breakthrough solutions in the fields of carbon composite construction and structural engineering that were then directly applied to automotive development.

43   In 2006, a BMW dealer in Los Angeles, California, got involved in a billboard battle with Audi. In response to Audi's challenging "Your Move BMW" campaign, BMW of Santa Monica put up a billboard featuring the M3 Coupe with a headline "Checkmate." The content of billboards quickly became viral and was reproduced in blogs and on social media.

44   The battle moved to national TV campaigns with the "Joy of Riding" from BMW and the "Supply and Demand" campaign from Audi. BMW ads also included frisky comparisons with Mercedes and Jaguar. The TV commercial dueling between Subaru, Audi, and Bentley became classics.

45   In 2012, BMW's global marketing planned to reinvigorate the tagline "Joy," whereas BMW of North America planned on adopting the slogan "The Ultimate Driving Machine" that was first introduced in the 1970s.

46   As a part of hands-on brand experience, BMW of North America offered courses at its Performance Center Driving School in Spartanburg, South Carolina. For tuition of up to $5,000, anybody could take various driving courses for top-line BMW cars or motorcycles.

BMW MANUFACTURING

47   The BMW Group Production Network consisted of 25 sites across 14 countries on five continents. The main BMW manufacturing sites were located in Germany. The home of MINI and Rolls Royce production was in Great Britain. BMW's sport and touring motorcycles were manufactured in Berlin under the BMW Motorrad brand, and motocross and enduro bikes were manufactured in Italy at Husquvarna, a subsidiary acquired in 2007 for €93 million. The company had local assembly operation for the 3, 5, 7 Series and X3 using completely knocked-down (CKD) components in Thailand, Russia, Egypt, Indonesia, Malaysia, and India.

PLANT SPARTANBURG

48   BMW's plant in Spartanburg, South Carolina, was opened in July 1994 to manufacture the 3 Series vehicles for a quickly growing North American market. Since then, the BMW Group had invested more than $6 billion in the Spartanburg facility over the years. The facility became the second largest BMW production plant outside of Germany. In 2005, the plant was redesigned to accommodate a new production system line called "OneLine" that enabled the production of SUVs, roadsters, and sedans on the same assembly line. In 2011, the plant employed more than 7,000 workers with an average daily production of 1,000 cars.

49   Plant Spartanburg produced six different BMW models: the 318i, Z3, Z4, X5, X6, X3, and their variants. The U.S. plant was the only X3 and X6 production site in the world. The company also announced that in 2014 it would expand the X-model family with the X4, a sport activity crossover based on the X3 SUV.

50   In 2011, the BMW plant in Spartanburg produced 276,065 vehicles for local and export sales. This represented an increase of 73 percent over the previous year. More than 70 percent of the vehicles produced in Spartanburg (192,813) were exported, making the BMW Group the largest automotive exporter to the non-NAFTA countries. A new round of investment in 2012–2013 was scheduled to increase plant capacity to 350,000 vehicles per year.

51   The global footprint reduced the negative impact of the economic downturn for BMW since it could partially shift some of its volume to less-affected emerging markets. The ability to react quickly and increase or decrease production for various markets was a major factor for BMW North America in turning the recession year 2008 into the highest production volume year ever in its history. "With flexible production processes and a flexible supply chain, we were able to increase the daily production volume by more than 30 percent to meet demand," said Josef Kerscher, president of BMW Manufacturing.[15]

52   The Spartanburg plant was a state-of-the-art engineering facility that generated its own power, and offered fully equipped medical facilities including an on-site pharmacy. It also provided 24-hour security and firefighting personnel.

53   In the past five years, the plant had lowered energy consumption by 48 percent, halved water consumption, reduced CO_2 emissions by 44 percent, and waste output by 65 percent.[16]

MASS CUSTOMIZATION

54   Mass customization was commonly known as "using flexible processes and organizational structures to produce varied and individually customized products and services at the price of standardized mass-produced alternatives."[17] For the automotive industry, mass customization meant simultaneous combination of large-scale volume production with the flexibility of a large variety of made-to-order runs involving a large number of small lot sizes.

55   As the automotive industry matured, almost all the major brands had tried to combine the benefits of high-volume mass production and configuration variety offerings to satisfy the individualistic needs of consumers at lower costs. However, only a few carmakers had been successful.

56   For example, in 1999 GM launched its Yellowstone program in Brazil aiming to build small cars by using mass customization and co-design with suppliers. The program failed in less than a year due to strong resistance from the United Auto Workers union, who saw modularity as a potential threat to U.S.-based jobs by making it potentially easier to shift production to low-labor-cost countries.

57   Nevertheless, the concept of mass customization was appealing. It allowed manufacturers to customize products at lower costs, reduced overheads, and produced higher margins. For customers, it heralded the benefit of finding exactly what they wanted without paying exorbitant premium prices. Dealers would not have to finance large inventories. Joseph Wierda explained: "When customers buy a vehicle off the lot, it is likely that they have to pay for something that they don't really want. For example, a navigation system—a customer doesn't want it—they have their own portable one—but the car in a color they like at the dealer's lot is only available with navigation. With mass customization, customers get exactly what they want for the price they expect."

58   BMW sensed that as consumers became more informed, they also shifted to more personalized individualistic products, seeking manufacturers that could provide precisely what they wanted. Tailored solutions became a new dimension in the marketing, where buyers could select among a high number of optional features to fit their individual needs using Web-based purchasing systems.

[15]"BMW Plant Spartanburg A Transforming Factory Speaker: Josef Kerscher, President, BMW Manufacturing." Automotive News Manufacturing Conference, September 6, 2009 www.autonews.com/assets/html/09_anmc/pdf/pres_kerscher.pdf (retrieved on Jan. 25, 2012)

[16]"BMW Group Expands U.S. Plant in South Carolina," *BMW Group Corporate News,* January 12, 2012. https://www.press.bmwgroup.com/pressclub/p/pcgl/pressDetail.html?outputChannelId=6&id=T0124314EN (retrieved on Jan. 25, 2012).

[17]C. W. Hart (1996). *Made to Order. Marketing Management,* 5(2), 12–22.

59 "The situation today is determined by: Here's a car, where's the customer for it?" said Holger Groitzsch, a BMW executive. He further stated; "We want to turn it around and say 'Here's the customer, where's the car for him?'"[18]

60 Many experts considered mass customization to be a truly customer-driven initiative that represented an organic evolution from traditional market-driven inventory-based systems. However, there were a number of supply chain issues that, so far, had been hard to solve for most manufacturers.

61 Critical success factors in achieving the vehicle customization at lower costs included flexible manufacturing systems, product modularity, and reconfigurability in order to reduce time-to-market, enhance product appeal, and maintain costs at the lowest possible level.[19,20]

62 Another operational challenge was managing the pool of suppliers who had to be able to combine flexibility and short lead times for customized products at reasonable costs. At the same time, the potential range of optional choices had to be carefully monitored in order not to explode the number of product variants beyond a manageable or cost efficient number.

63 A successful transition to customer-driven business also involved the ability to streamline communication between everyone involved in manufacturing and to solve supply problems in real time. Rapid communication with strategic trading partners had to include the intelligence to direct relevant data to assigned units and respond immediately to orders, changes in configuration, and fluctuating demand.[21,22]

CUSTOMIZATION AT BMW

64 BMW has been in the mass customization business since 1992 when it first launched the BMW Individual Program, which was later followed by an introduction of the KOVP concept. KOVP, or "customer-oriented sales and production process," was first introduced in 2000. This initiative enabled on-schedule vehicle deliveries and afforded a high degree of flexibility in making vehicle equipment changes until very late in the production process (see Exhibit 4).

65 The heart of the KOVP concept rested in the transparency of the production chain. BMW used a vehicle identification and location system that made it possible to automatically identify, collect, and document vehicle movement during and after the assembly process. Each vehicle transmitted a location identification signal every four minutes, which was acquired by in-house antennas. As a result, vehicles could be located on a workstation display, allowing adherence to schedules and last-minute modifications if needed.

66 BMW's Individual Program offered individual trimmings for the high-end 7 Series sedans and 850 sport coupes. Since then, this program had been extended in order to serve the needs of clients who wanted to deviate from standard specifications, particularly with interior designs and colors of their cars. "The BMW Individual Program caters more to high-end customers who order something that is beyond what is typically available," said Wierda.

[18]John Reed, "Benefits of a Showroom Bypass," *Financial Times,* May 2, 2011. www.ft.com/intl/cms/s/0/300b6f90-74e6-11e0-a4b7-00144feabdc0.html (retrieved on Jan. 30, 2012).

[19]J. Mula, R. Poler, J. P. García (2004). "Supply Chain Production Planning in a Mass Customization Environment," *Second World Conference on POM.* http://lcl.uniroma1.it/dspace/bitstream/123456789/84/1/File_569.pdf (retrieved on Feb. 1, 2012).

[20]Peter Frederikson, "Flexibility and Rigidity in Customization and Build-to-Order Production," *Industrial Marketing Management,* #34, 2005. www.sciencedirect.com/science/journal/00198501/34/7 (retrieved on Feb. 1, 2012).

[21]Jerry Wind, "Customerization: The Next Evolution in Mass Customization," *Journal of Interactive Marketing,* Vol. 15, Issue 1, Winter 2001. www.sciencedirect.com/science/article/pii/S1094996801701715 (retrieved on Feb. 1, 2012).

[22]Frank Piller, "Mass Customization: Providing Custom Products and Services with Mass Production Efficiency," *TUM Business School.* www.downloads.mass-customization.de/joft06.pdf (retrieved on Feb. 1, 2012).

EXHIBIT 4 Customer-Oriented Sales and Production Process (KOVP)

New Vehicle Location System

A new vehicle location system—up to now in use at the Dingolfing and Munich plants—will now be introduced at all vehicle plants of the BMW Group.

Satisfied customers are a must for a premium manufacturer such as the BMW Group. For about three years now, the so-called customer-oriented sales and production process (KOVP) has been in operation at the BMW Group, which enables on-schedule vehicle deliveries and affords a high degree of flexibility in making vehicle equipment changes till the very end.

Even vehicle movements outside of the actual production areas can be reliably registered. The magnetic field of the ports causes the transponder to transmit a signal to the nearest antennas. They in turn supply vehicle position information to the localization server in the form of a time signal. The server then computes the location of the vehicles from the individual time information of the antennas.

Location at the Push of a Button

Transparency during the whole process of the production chain is a major KOVP component. And here is where the vehicle location again provides a considerable advancement. The new vehicle identification and location system makes it possible to automatically identify, collect, and document vehicle movements during and after the production process. Parked vehicles or vehicles removed from the line can thus be located quickly and safely—within the production as well as in the entire area from F1 (initial engine activation) to F2 (transfer to sales). Transponders in the vehicles transmit an identification signal every four minutes for the location, which is acquired by antennas. So-called ports are mounted above the shop floor doors and at the plant entrances.

Workers at the assembly line can locate vehicles via the Intranet screen on their workstation display—so to speak—at the push of a button. The system has been field-tested in Dingolfing since the beginning of 2003; in the fall of last year, this was followed by the Munich plant. The results were positive: Thanks to the new location system, the realization of the strived-for adherence to schedules could be supported lastingly. In Regensburg, the system is just being commissioned as of this writing; the plant in Leipzig is equipped with it from the very beginning. At the end of last year, it was decided to also expand this KOVP measure to the international plants. As a result, all assembly areas will have the necessary prerequisites to ensure a 95 percent adherence to schedules by all worldwide plants starting in 2006.

Source: Siemens AG, www.automation.siemens.com/simatic-sensors-static/ftp/bmw_ortung_e.pdf (retrieved on May. 25, 2012).

67   Wierda explained that in Europe the BMW Individual Program was available for any model, but in the U.S. only for the 6 and 7 Series. "In Europe, customers who buy these kinds of vehicles are willing to spend. The same model that retails for $60,000 in North America retails for €60,000 in Europe. Europeans are accustomed to pay more for cars and they are likely to order more trimmings," he explained.

68   The most common BMW Individual trimming options included expensive leather and wood for the interior, advanced sound and video systems, aerodynamic exterior enhancements, and unique body colors.

69   While all the advantages of preplanned customized orders seemed obvious for car manufacturers, they were hard to achieve, simply because most American car buyers did not have the patience to wait.

70   For example, only 2 percent of Toyota's top-selling models in the U.S. were sold on a preordered basis. In general, the customized approach worked much better for premium brands. Lexus sold all of its flagship models in the U.S. on a custom-order basis only. When Audi succeeded in promoting its "Exclusive Program" that allowed customers to choose nonstandard colors and certain other features, Audi's preordered volume increased to 14 percent in 2010, up from 5.4 percent a year earlier.

71   However, Audi of America did not build its future strategy on mass customization. The company believed that significant business success from introducing discipline in the complexity of offerings was critical. "Too much complexity makes it difficult for individual dealers to stock the cars customers want at any given moment. We don't eliminate choice, but we don't let it spiral out of control," Brad Stertz, Audi's corporate communications manager, wrote in an e-mail statement. "Most customers, based on our experience, are happy with the available options packages or the Audi Exclusive Program. Hence, we will continue with our current strategies." (See Exhibit 5 for total Lux SUV sales in the U.S.)

THE BMW X3

72   The X3 was a compact crossover SUV with a 5-door wagon body style. The first generation of the X3 (E83) was introduced in 2003. In 2011, the redesigned F25 model replaced it.

73   The F25 X3 was available in the U.S. with a 3.0-liter inline six-cylinder gasoline engine, either normally aspirated or with a twin scroll turbocharger only. The premium xDrive35i model ($42,700 MSRP) used a 300-horsepower turbocharged engine, and the xDrive28i ($37,100 MSRP) had 240 horsepower. According to the U.S. Environmental Protection Agency (EPA) estimation, the base six-cylinder engine operated at 25 mpg and the turbo version at 26 mpg. All U.S. market vehicles came with an 8-speed automatic transmission. All X3s were equipped with BMW's xDrive all-wheel drive system.

74   BMW used parts from the 3 Series sedan in making the X3. For example, its rear suspension system came from the E46 330xi all-wheel drive model.

75   Wierda described the target customers for the X3: "There are a few different types of typical X3 buyers: you have people who are new to the luxury market. It could be people in their 20s, 30s, or 40s who are stepping out of domestic or nonpremium SUVs, and BMW falls in their price range. Then you have young families who need an SUV with space but they don't need a large one because their kids are still too little. Then you have empty nesters who are downsizing their SUVs because they no longer need all the extra space, but have money to afford luxury."

DREAM IT. BUILD IT. DRIVE IT.

76   Out of 242,000 BMWs sold in the U.S. in 2009, only 15 percent were customized. In Europe, about half of all BMWs were built according to buyers' specifications. The new strategy devised by BMW's U.S. headquarters promised to increase this number to 40 percent by 2015.[23]

---

[23]Chris Reiter, "BMW Hopes Impulsive Americans Order Cars a la Carte," *Bloomberg,* May 14, 2010. www .bloomberg.com/news/2010-05-13/ipod-adapter-1-350-moonroof-bmw-tries-a-la-carte-with-impatient-america .html (retrieved on Feb. 4, 2012).

EXHIBIT 5   Luxury Compact SUV, U.S. Sales in 2011 (Selected Models)

Model	Specs	MSRP (min)	Image	Units Sold in 2011, CAGR, %
BMW X3	4 WD (included) 3.0L engine 240 or 300 h.p. 8-speed AT	$37,100 or $42,700		27,793 (+457%)
Mercedes GLK 350 SUV	4 WD (included) 3.5L V6 engine 268 h.p. 7-speed AT	$38,755		24,310 (+16%)
Audi Q5	AWD, Quattro (included) 2.0L or 3.2 L TFSI engine 211 h.p. or 270 h.p. 8-speed AT	$36,950 or $43,000		24,908 (+5.9%)
Acura RDX	AWD (included) 2.3L engine 240 h.p. 5 speed AT	$32,895		15,195 (+1.04%)
Infinity EX 35	RWD 3.5L V6 engine 297 h.p. 7-speed AT	$35,800		6,030 (−27.4%)
Lincoln MKX	FWD or AWD 3.7L V6 engine 305 h.p. 6-speed AT	$39,545 or $41,395		23,395 (+6.6%)

Source: Photo, specs, and sales statistics: company courtesy.

77   The new marketing program introduced for the X3 model in 2010 was called: "Dream It. Build It. Drive It." and it was meant to be a completely new way to connect with customers.

78   Patrick McKenna, communications manager at BMW, explained why BMW chose the X3 for this project: "We picked the X3 for this project because it was a new product, and because any new BMW only comes every seven years so the lifecycle is pretty long. When you consider adding something to a product, you can only do so when there is a completely new product involved."

79   "This program encourages customers to customize their own vehicles. Americans are very different from the rest of the world. Especially in the area when you want something, you want it immediately. That's why we had to create something different as compared to the European custom strategy. We needed something different," added Wierda.

80   On the other hand, car dealers claimed that corporate executives overestimated the actual customer impatience factor. "It's an issue that has been created mostly by the dealers and hypercompetitive nature of our business. It's all about a sense of urgency and now, now, now. My experience is that customers actually do not mind waiting," said Dimitri Kotsalis, general manager of a BMW dealership in Vancouver, BC.

81   The concept of BMW's new campaign included the engagement of customers at all three stages of the sales process: from the initial surfing on the Internet, where customers "dream" about the car; to the second stage, which involved individual customizing—or "building"—and finally the last stage, which culminated in delivery and, finally, "driving" it.

82   The Web site interaction included features for individual online customization for the future vehicle in the form of a wish list. Potential customers could experience the excitement of not only buying his or her new car, but also building it. For example, BMW offers 500 side-mirror combinations, 1,300 front bumpers, 5,000 seat combinations, or 9,000 center consoles. This, of course, was a major challenge for production because parts came from more than 170 suppliers located in the U.S. and abroad.[24]

83   Online customization was not new to the automotive industry. Most manufacturers offered a Web site where customers could design their own vehicles and then send the configuration to local dealers for order processing.

85   However, most customers did not have the opportunity to actually see their vehicles being built. BMW decided to go the extra mile and extend the concept of online customization in order to address the issue of impatience in American car buyers by making the wait a more pleasurable experience. BMW decided to install video cameras along the assembly line and broadcast the process of how an X3 comes to life. By being able to access a Web site called "Your X3 on the Assembly Line," BMW buyers could trace seven major assembly stages of their new vehicle at the factory at South Carolina.

86   "We really tried to create something special that had never been done before. The technology of stitching all these camera shots was something truly unique," commented Ken Bracht, customer relations manager at BMW of North America. "Providing a video like this is a great way for keeping people excited about the process and waiting for the arrival of this new vehicle," he said.[25]

87   BMW recorded the assembly process of 450 vehicles a day using 14 cameras, and the videos needed a few days of processing, including checking them for errors.

89   "We had concerns about the bandwidth and we wanted to ensure that the bandwidth the cameras need is not going to cause any problems with the production and quality control systems. Tests proved to be successful and showed us that we can do it for every car on a production line for the U.S. market," said McKenna.

90   Once the video quality was deemed fully acceptable, it automatically went to the personal pages of the individual customers hosted on BMW of North America's Web site. Customers could view the footage by creating a "My BMW" account on bmwusa.com and

[24]Joann Muller, "BMW's Push for Made-to-Order Cars," *Forbes Magazine*, September 27, 2010. www.forbes.com/forbes/2010/0927/companies-bmw-general-motors-cars-bespoke-auto.html (retrieved on Feb. 4, 2012).
[25]"The Story Behind the Building of your BMW X3." www.youtube.com/watch?v=5g-hbqAhaL8 (retrieved on Feb. 3, 2012).

entering their X3 order number or VIN. The video did not have an expiration date, giving consumers round-the-clock access to the assembly footage, and the video could also be downloaded and shared with interested friends and family members.

91   Implementation of the "Dream It. Drive It. Build It." program required significant adjustments at the plant in Spartanburg, in BMW's supply chain, and its IT system. Apart from installing cameras on the assembly line, BMW moved the complete production of the redesigned X3 from Europe in order to reduce the delivery time for the U.S.

92   Magna Steyr Fahrzeugtechnik, a division of Magna International that had been building X3s for BMWs for five years at its Graz, Austria, plant, was no longer manufacturing this model. With a $750 million investment, the assembly line for X3 was moved to South Carolina and was completely integrated into the existing manufacturing facility.

93   As a result, the delivery time for the new X3 in the U.S. dropped from seven to two-to-three weeks. Wierda commented: "In theory, a new car showed up two weeks after it was ordered. But it could be longer if we needed to ship it, for example, to Seattle. This would mean an extra ten days. This was a dramatic improvement from 2009 when it would have taken another five weeks of ocean and other transit time, making a customization program for BMW's U.S. customers just not attractive. Now we took the transit time out of the equation."

94   Audi and Mercedes offered similar customization programs, but their waiting times for delivery in the U.S. varied between 8 and 16 weeks.

95   On the other hand, German buyers now had to wait at least an extra month or more for their X3s because of the production relocation to South Carolina. In 2012, delivery times in Germany took up to five months, whereas U.S. customers got their orders in just a few weeks, according to consumer reports.

96   The main reasons behind the decision to choose X3 as the only model for the "Dream It. Drive It. Build It." marketing initiative were the dramatically dropping U.S. sales for the previous generation of X3 and the new value proposition for the all-new model. For example, at the end of 2009, the X3 sales were the worst among all BMW models—the overall compact SUV group had declined by 86 percent, and dealers had sold only 182 cars in October, a far cry from the usual 1,200–1,600 units previously.

Source: Anthony Monahan (www.anthonymonahan.com).

97   Wierda explained: "For some people, the design of the interior of the previous X3 was not luxurious enough. Although we made some changes on the previous model, the new generation gave us the opportunity to make really big improvements. We came out with a completely new interior—more spacious, more functional more luxurious. New functionality, high performance at a lower price was our catch phrase."

98   This seemed to work, since the new X3 became one of the best-selling models for the BMW Group in 2011. "This project increased customer pride and the excitement that comes with the car even before they take the delivery. Among all X3s produced for the U.S. market in 2011 (27,793 cars), 42 percent of the customers had an active account to access the video, and of those 42 percent, 50 percent shared their video on Facebook," said McKenna.

99   To further the success of this project, BMW focused on new media, and targeted women. The new X3 launch became the biggest project for building a new online presence. Apart from developing an interactive Web site for potential X3 buyers, BMW also created an app for Apple's mobile advertising network called iAD. The interactive app allowed iPhone and iPod touch users to configure and customize their vehicles directly on their mobile devices.

100   Other marketing channels included women's glossy magazines, and TV appearances with celebrity Martha Stewart. Women's campaigns targeted empty nesters and women executives who were looking for a new car but had no need to put children in the back.

101   "In 2010–2011 we were able to take advantage of cars being produced locally and give customers an opportunity to spec their cars exactly as they want it and get it delivered fast," Wierda said, discussing how the X3 became one of the most successful compact luxury SUVs in North America. (See Exhibit 6 for summary of BMW North American sales by product type, and Exhibit 7 for BMW's X3 sales in North America.)

102   But not everyone was happy with the custom-build options from BMW, especially at some of the dealerships. "The majority of our customized vehicles are the result of the lack of supply rather than of customer demand. Yes, our profits would be higher for customized vehicles, but you have to be careful here. Of course, you can custom build a vehicle and make it a unique value proposition, but any other dealer can order the same vehicle and make it the same unique value proposition. The same rules apply to all dealers and everybody would happily take a deal away from me for a few hundred dollars. When somebody comes in and wants to customize a vehicle and a salesperson has the opportunity to move him to something that is already available, which is slightly different than the desirable option, the salesperson will always try to do so. Because a salesperson wants to make sure he secures a deal today. If you have an opportunity to do that with the vehicle that is on the ground, you can get a deposit or a credit application on the same day and the deal is done," said dealership GM Kotsalis.

103   However, Kotsalis agreed with the potential benefits of the "Dream It. Build It. Drive It." program by reducing his inventory costs and property footprint. "It would be great for urban dealers and especially in places with insane real estate prices like Vancouver, New York, or San Francisco. From that perspective, everything that we can do to lessen the footprint, and to decrease the number of vehicles we have to keep in stock, and the amount of money that we spend on interest for maintaining the inventory will drive our business forward."

104   Joseph Wierda was contemplating: should the BMW of North America Group expand its "Dream It. Build It. Drive It." campaign to its flagship X5 full-size SUVs in order to revitalize the models declining sales? Or should BMW use the campaign for the new X4 launch planned for 2014? Maybe use the Facebook "match" game for X3 with a BMW Superbowl ad once again for the X5 (see Exhibit 8)? Was the personalization aspect overrated? How many more SUVs could we sell with gas prices potentially reaching $5 a gallon?

EXHIBIT 6   BMW North America Sales Performance 2009–2011

	Y 2009	Y 2010	1Q2011	2Q2011	3Q2011	4Q2011	Y 2011
1 Series	11,182	13,132	2,383	2,210	1,979	2,260	8,832
3 Series	90,960	100,910	19,138	24,724	26,704	23,805	94,371
Z4 Roadster and Coupe	3,523	3,804	584	1,450	898	547	3,479
5 Series	40,109	39,488	13,053	12,234	12,709	13,495	51,491
6 Series	3,549	2,418	255	857	1,105	1,686	3,903
7 Series	9,254	12,253	2,762	2,688	2,300	3,549	11,299
BMW passenger cars	**158,577**	**172,005**	**38,175**	**44,163**	**45,695**	**45,342**	**173,375**
X3	6,067	6,075	5,710	7,015	6,442	8,626	27,793
X5	27,071	35,776	7,694	8,201	10,152	14,500	40,547
X6	4,787	6,257	1,037	1,710	1,685	1,760	6,192
BMW light trucks SUV	**37,925**	**48,108**	**14,441**	**16,926**	**18,279**	**24,886**	**74,532**
BMW brand	**196,502**	**220,113**	**52,616**	**61,089**	**63,974**	**70,228**	**247,907**
Cooper /S Hardtop	28,129	29,658	6,476	8,629	5,740	7,222	28,067
Cooper /S Convertible	6,206	7,022	1,018	1,597	1,380	969	4,964
Cooper /S Clubman	10,890	8,398	1,546	2,404	1,567	1,327	6,844
Coupe	0	0	0	0	0	953	953
Crossover	0	575	3,301	4,845	3,132	5,405	16,683
MINI brand	**45,225**	**45,653**	**12,341**	**17,475**	**11,819**	**15,876**	**57,511**
TOTAL North America	**241,727**	**265,766**	**64,957**	**78,564**	**75,793**	**86,104**	**305,418**

Source: BMW North America.

EXHIBIT 7   BMW X3 Sales, 2009–2011, Units

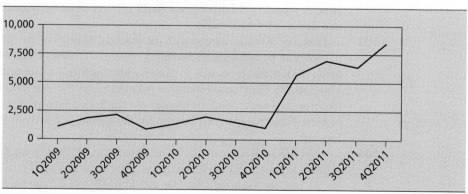

Source: BMW North America.

EXHIBIT 8 X3 Matchup*

*The X3 Matchup was a Facebook game that let people guess the configuration they'd seen featured in the Superbowl TV spot to win an X3 of their own.
Source: Anthony Monahan (www.anthonymonahan.com).

Case 17

Of Orangutans and Chainsaws: *Cargill, Inc. Confronts The Rainforest Action Network Advocacy* [1]

1 On September 30, 2011, the Roundtable on Sustainable Palm Oil (RSPO) issued a press release announcing that Indonesia was withdrawing its membership from the organization to start its own palm oil monitoring body. In addition, just two days earlier, the Girl Scouts of America had made a public statement about sourcing sustainable palm oil for its iconic cookies. The Rainforest Action Network (RAN), a nongovernmental organization (NGO) that advocated environmentalism, had targeted Cargill, Inc., the U.S.-based agribusiness company, since 2007 to force the company to switch to sustainable palm oil. RAN had successfully pressurized some of Cargill's leading customers such as General Mills, Nestle and Unilever to procure only sustainable palm oil and would continue its advocacy against the company. RAN's past actions against Cargill were high profile and embarrassing to the company and were detrimental to its overall reputation in the marketplace. Cargill's 2010 response refuting every claim made by RAN had not satisfied the NGO. Cargill and its chief executive officer (CEO), Gregory Page, had to come up with a plan of action to respond to RAN's demands.

PROFILE OF CARGILL [2]

2 Founded in 1865, Cargill was a privately held, U.S.-based agribusiness company, which had its global headquarters in Minneapolis and employed 130,000 people in 63 countries. The company's 75 businesses were organized into four major segments: agriculture, food, financial and industrial. The agriculture segment bought, processed and distributed grain, oilseeds and other commodities to food and animal nutrition products manufacturers. The food segment sold various food ingredients and meat and poultry products to food and beverage manufacturers. The financial segment provided risk management and financial solutions to the customers. The industrial segment sold energy, salt, starch and steel products and also developed and marketed sustainable products made from agriculture feedstocks.

Source: Professor Ram Subramanian wrote this case solely to provide material for class discussion. The authors do not intend to illustrate either effective or ineffective handling of a managerial situation. The authors may have disguised certain names and other identifying information to protect confidentiality.

Richard Ivey School of Business Foundation prohibits any form of reproduction, storage or transmission without its written permission. Reproduction of this material is not covered under authorization by any reproduction rights organization. To order copies or request permission to reproduce materials, contact Ivey Publishing, Richard Ivey School of Business Foundation, The University of Western Ontario, London, Ontario, Canada, N6A 3K7; phone (519) 661-3208; fax (519) 661-3882; e-mail cases@ivey.uwo.ca.

Copyright © 2012, Richard Ivey School of Business Foundation Version: 2012-06-27

Richard Ivey School of Business
The University of Western Ontario   **IVEY**

[1]This case has been written on the basis of published sources only. Consequently, the interpretation and perspectives presented here are not necessarily those of Cargill, Inc. or any of its employees.
[2]This section was based on Cargill: 2011 Fact Sheet, www.cargill.com/wcm/groups/public/@ccom/documents/document/na3048877.pdf, accessed on October 4, 2011.

3   Cargill reported revenues of $119.469 billion in 2011 (versus $101.308 billion in 2010) and earnings of $2.693 billion in 2011 (compared to $1.989 billion in 2010). While the company released limited financial information because it was privately owned, *Fortune* magazine stated that if Cargill were publicly held, it would rank 51 in the list of the largest (in terms of revenues) companies in the world.

4   Geographically, Cargill operated in North America (44 percent of gross investment, 56,000 employees), Europe/Africa (27 percent, 21,000 employees), Latin America (17 percent, 21,000 employees) and Asia/Pacific (12 percent, 32,000 employees). Cargill indicated that it focused on four performance measures: engaged employees, enriched communities, satisfied customers and profitable growth. In 2010, the company won 11 awards, including awards for food safety leadership, energy efficiency, community service and community engagement and corporate social responsibility. In addition, in 2010, Cargill won the Mc-Donald's Sustainability Award for its "ability to balance long-term sustainability goals with the need to perform competitively."[3]

5   Page, Cargill's chairman and CEO since 2007, had joined the company as a trainee in its Feeds Division in 1974 and had worked in the company's U.S. and Singapore operations. In its 2010 corporate social responsibility report titled, "Growing Together," Cargill addressed responsible supply chains.[4] Specifically, in this section of the report, Cargill talked about its membership in the RSPO and its goal of procuring 60 percent of its palm oil from RSPO members by the end of 2010. It noted that one of its Indonesian plantations, PT Hindoli in Sumatra, had already obtained RSPO certification and that it was working on obtaining similar certification for its Harapan Sawit Lestari plantation located in West Kalimantan.

Palm Oil

6   In 2011, palm oil was a leading agricultural crop used in a wide variety of food and nonfood applications. The oil palm (botanical name *Elaeis guineensis*), which originated in West Africa, yielded two types of oil. Palm oil came from the flesh of the fruit and palm kernel oil from the kernel at the fruit's core. Palm oil and palm kernel oil food applications ranged from use as shortening, as cooking oil, in margarine and in confectionery products. Their nonfood uses were in soaps, plastics, candles, lotions, body oils, shampoos, skin care products, rubber and cleaning products. About 80 percent of oil palm product was used in food applications and 20 percent in non-food products.[5] Palm oil was a cholesterol-free vegetable oil and was considered a good replacement for partially hydrogenated oils because it was free of trans fat and rich with antioxidants. From a commercial point of view, palm oil's advantages included its odorless and tasteless nature and the fact it facilitated a product's long shelf life.

7   Oil palm was a tropical plant that was grown in 17 countries. The top palm oil–producing countries were Indonesia, Malaysia, Thailand, Nigeria and Colombia. Indonesia and Malaysia accounted for 85 percent of the world's production of palm oil, and in these two countries, 4.5 million people earned a living from it. While a quarter of the palm oil produced was used domestically (where it was produced), the rest was exported. Asia, the European Union and Africa were the main importers of palm oil. In 2008, India and China accounted for 33 percent of the 34 million tons of exported palm oil, and the European Union took 15 percent. Of the total vegetable oil production of 144 million tons in 2008 (the most recent year for which figures were reported), palm oil accounted for 47 million tons. Palm oil and soy oil made up 60 percent of the world vegetable oil production.[6] In the

[3]Ibid.
[4]www.cargill.com/wcm/groups/public/@ccom/documents/document/na3035282.pdf, accessed October 7, 2011.
[5]American Palm Oil Council, www.americanpalmoil.com, accessed October 7, 2011.
[6]www.greenpalm.org, accessed October 7, 2011.

United States, palm oil benefited from a 2006 Food and Drug Administration regulation that required food products to label their trans fat content. Many food processors switched to palm oil as a result.

8   Oil palm was grown as an industrial plantation crop in both Indonesia and Malaysia. In Indonesia, about 50 percent of the oil palm plantations were owned by private companies, the state owned 17 percent and smallholders owned 33 percent.[7] Smallholders were farmers who owned a few acres each in a section of a large company's plantation and depended on the company for both inputs (fertilizers, pesticides) and for sale of their output. In both countries, the national government made large tracts of land available for private companies to establish oil palm plantations. A 2003 report indicated that oil palm plantations constituted 11 percent of Malaysia's total land area and 62 percent of all the cultivated agricultural land.[8]

9   Rainforests were the earth's oldest living ecosystems. While covering only 6 percent of the earth in terms of area, they contained more than half (around 30 million) of the earth's plant and animal species. Rainforests were typically dense jungles made up of tall trees that got a very high amount of rainfall every year. The hot and humid climate of rainforests necessitated adaptation by the animals and plants to thrive there. The Amazon jungle was the earth's largest rainforest area, followed by Central Africa. Over the years, much of the rainforest areas of Central America, Central Africa and Southern Asia were cleared to facilitate cattle ranching and plantations of various kinds. Environmentalists strongly opposed further destruction of rainforests because of the adverse impact on plants and animals.[9]

10   The bulk of the land area in Indonesia, an archipelago of more than 10,000 islands, was in the islands of Sumatra, Java, Borneo, Sulawesi and Western New Guinea. Sumatra, where oil palm was first planted in 1911, was the largest producer of palm oil, followed by Borneo. Indonesia shared the island of Borneo with Malaysia and Brunei. The Indonesian part of Borneo was called Kalimantan. While Sumatra accounted for 70 to 80 percent of oil palm plantations in Indonesia, Kalimantan saw rapid development in recent years. From the mid-1990s onward, a surge in planting activity took place there that resulted in this area becoming an important contributor of palm oil by 2010. The Indonesian government claimed that oil palm was a powerful tool for poverty alleviation since both smallholders and those employed in large oil palm plantations increased their income significantly and benefited from better living conditions and improved access to health care.[10]

11   A variety of environment and sustainability-focused NGOs pointed out that increased oil palm cultivation came at the expense of rainforests. For example, one study pointed out that in Indonesia from 1982 to 1999, more than 16,000 square miles of tropical forests were cleared to make way for oil palm (7,000 square miles), timber, coconut and other plantations. The same report stated that around 5,600 square miles of rainforests in Malaysia were cleared between 1990 and 2002 to provide for oil palm plantations. Environmentalists identified deforestation, endangered wildlife, habitat destruction and fragmentation, pollution (of soil, air and water) and toxic contamination as the adverse effects of clearing rainforests for plantations. In addition, critics pointed out that rainforest clearing caused social conflict and displacement of indigenous communities.[11]

[7]www.cspinet.org/palm/PalmOilReport.pdf, accessed Oct 11, 2011.
[8]Ibid.
[9]www.srl.caltech.edu/personnel/krubal/rainforest/Edit560s6/www/what.html, accessed October 12, 2011.
[10]www.cspinet.org/palm/PalmOilReport.pdf, accessed October 11, 2011.
[11]Greenpeace International, "How the Palm Oil Industry Is Cooking the Climate," www.greenpeace.org, accessed September 30, 2011; and Rainforest Action Network, "Cargill's Problems with Palm Oil: A Burning Threat in Borneo," www.ran.org, accessed September 30, 2011.

THE ROUNDTABLE ON SUSTAINABLE PALM OIL[12]

12   In an effort to stem the tide of criticism against rainforest destruction, the global palm oil industry created the Roundtable on Sustainable Palm Oil (RSPO) in 2004. The RSPO, an organization set up under the Swiss Civil Code, consisted of major palm oil players, consumer goods manufacturers, retailers, banks and investors, environmental and nature conservation NGOs and social/development NGOs. The main objective of the RSPO was "to promote the growth and use of sustainable palm oil through co-operation with the supply chain and open dialogue between its stakeholders." Its founding president, Jan Kees Vis of Unilever NV, stated, "If we all work hard, the RSPO could become the platform where all stakeholders in the palm oil chain, from plantation workers to retailers and from manufacturers to nature conservationists, can work together to shape a sustainable future for palm oil."

13   The governance structure of the RSPO was set up in such a way that seats on the executive board and project level working groups were fairly allocated among the various stakeholders. This was to enable the RSPO to "live out the philosophy of the 'roundtable' by giving equal rights to each stakeholder group to bring group-specific agendas to the roundtable, facilitating traditionally adversarial stakeholders and business competitors to work towards a common objective and making decisions by consensus." In 2011, the RSPO's secretariat was in Kuala Lumpur, Malaysia.

14   RSPO's key output was the supply chain certification process conducted by UTZ Certified, an independent not-for-profit certification body. RSPO certified palm oil complied with the RSPO Principles and Criteria, and this compliance was independently verified by the approved certification body. Three types of certification were available via the RSPO: identity preserved, segregation and mass balance. In identity preserved, sustainable oil was kept apart and was traceable to the plantation from which it originated. In segregation, batches of certified sustainable palm oil were blended. In mass balance, certified sustainable palm oil was mixed with conventional palm oil, but sustainable oil was monitored administratively. A fourth classification, "book and claim," did not track, trace or monitor sustainable palm oil but, instead, allowed suppliers to sell certificates to users. An independent organization, GreenPalm, managed the certificates in book and claim. Exhibit 1 provides a visual depiction of the traditional palm oil supply chain, and Exhibit 2 presents the major types of sustainability certification.

EXHIBIT 1   **Traditional Palm Oil Supply Chain**

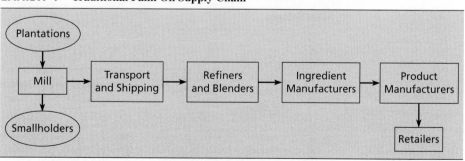

Source: Adapted from "RSPO Supply Chain Systems Overview," www.rspo.com, accessed October 4, 2011.

[12]This section is from www.rspo.org, accessed October 5, 2011. All direct quotes in this section are from this site unless otherwise noted.

EXHIBIT 2   Major Types of Sustainability Certification

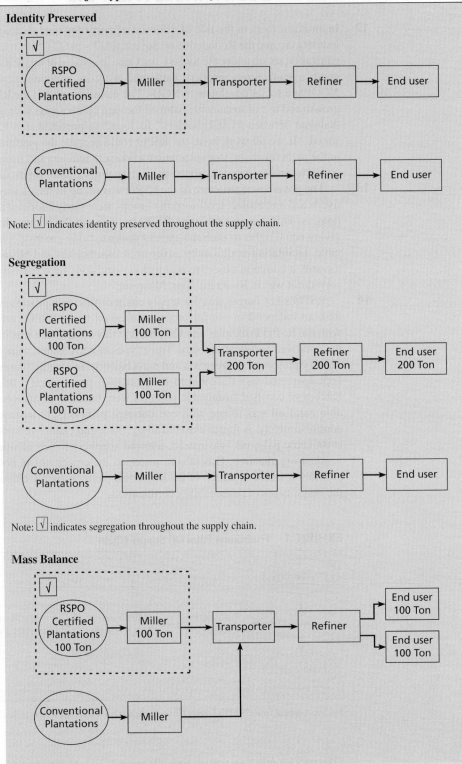

Identity Preserved

Note: ☑ indicates identity preserved throughout the supply chain.

Segregation

Note: ☑ indicates segregation throughout the supply chain.

Mass Balance

EXHIBIT 2 *(Continued)*

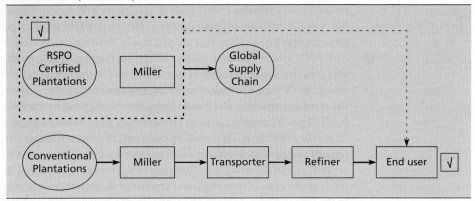

Note: In "book and claim," there was no tracking, tracing, or monitoring of palm oil. Growers and end users tracked volume credits online. The program was managed by GreenPalm that issued "GreenPalm" certificates.

Source: The Roundtable on Sustainable Palm Oil.

Adapted from "RSPO Supply Chain Systems Overview," www.rspo.com, accessed October 4, 2011.

15   In mid-2011, Malaysia accounted for 48 percent of global sustainable palm oil and Indonesia 40 percent.[13] On September 30, 2011, the RSPO announced that the Indonesian Palm Oil Association (GAPKI) had withdrawn its membership. GAPKI chairman Fadhil Hasan said that withdrawal from RSPO was to enable Indonesian palm oil producers to form their own organization, Indonesian Sustainable Palm Oil (ISPO), which had been set up by the government. Joining had been made mandatory for all local firms. In providing a rationale for this move, Hasan stated:

> We want to be neutral and accommodate all interests, as some of our members participate in the RSPO while the rest do not. Since membership in the RSPO was voluntary, such withdrawals were normal and did not imply that GAPKI was not committed to sustainability. Indonesian firms will continue to produce sustainable palm oil, which at present reaches around 1.95 million tons (Indonesia produced a total of 21 million tons in 2010) per year.[14]

16   An analyst cited in a Malaysian newspaper said that there was "dissatisfaction among members of the RSPO, as it was skewed towards the rights of the non-governmental organizations on such issues as growing oil palm at the expense of deforestation."[15]

THE RAINFOREST ACTION NETWORK[16]

17   The Rainforest Action Network (RAN), a prominent environmental NGO based in the United States, focused on businesses' adverse impact on the plants and animals that thrived in rainforests. Started in 1985 and based in San Francisco, RAN was a volunteer-driven organization whose mission was to "campaign for the forests, their inhabitants and the natural systems that sustain life by transforming the global marketplace through education, grassroots organizing and non-violent direct action."[17] Its tactics included strategic negotiating, policy analysis and development, legislative campaigns, Web-based social network campaigns, public demonstrations, public education and community organizing.

[13]http://biz.thestar.com.my/news/story.asp?file=/2011/10/5/business/9630501&sec=business
[14]www.thejakartapost.com/news/2011/10/05/gapki-withdraws-rspo-support-ispo.html, accessed October 6, 2011.
[15]Tee Lin Say, "Indonesia's Withdrawal Puts Roundtable on Sustainable Palm Oil on Shaky Ground," http://biz.thestar.com.my/news/story.asp?file=/2011/10/5/business/9630501&sec=business, accessed October 8, 2011.
[16]www.ran.org, accessed September 26, 2011.
[17]http://ran.org/content/about-ran, accessed October 10, 2011.

It employed what it called an "Inside-Outside Strategy," which combined high-pressure public pressure tactics with private negotiations with governments and focal organizations. RAN saw its role as "arguing for the solutions that will actually protect the earth's ecosystems, as opposed to steps that are politically or strategically 'feasible.'"

18   RAN's *modus operandi* was to identify a major corporation that it (i.e., RAN) held responsible for the destruction of rainforests and demand that the corporation take corrective action. RAN used a variety of attention-grabbing techniques to both cause embarrassment to the focal organization and also to bring public attention to the issue. For example, in 1997, RAN began a campaign against Home Depot (a U.S.-based home improvement chain) and its practice of selling old growth (wood from endangered areas) wood products. RAN's volunteers staged demonstrations at the company's headquarters in Atlanta, Georgia; sought the support of the company's institutional stockholders; challenged the company's expansion plans at city council meetings; and organized demonstrations at hundreds of company stores in the United States, Canada and Chile. In one instance, RAN volunteers commandeered the public address system at a Home Depot store and made a series of announcements about the company's use of wood from endangered areas. In all, in the Home Depot campaign, RAN delivered more than 250,000 faxes, e-mails, phone calls and letters from the public and staged more than 700 demonstrations.[18] The campaign succeeded when in 1999 the company announced that it would cease carrying old growth wood in its stores.

RAN AND PALM OIL ADVOCACY[19]

19   RAN's campaign against palm oil was launched on October 8, 2007 and was targeted against three major U.S. agribusiness players: Archer Daniels Midland (ADM), Cargill and Bunge. A full-page advertisement in the *Chicago Tribune* was followed by a giant banner the next day atop the Chicago Board of Trade that said, "ADM, Bunge, and Cargill: The ABCs of Rainforest Destruction." Buoyed by a November 2007 Greenpeace publication titled "How the Palm Oil Industry Is Cooking the Climate," RAN stepped up its campaign and in order to gain more focused exposure began to single out Cargill. RAN's actions included unfurling a banner on a sailboat in Lake Minnetonka (where many Cargill executives lived), pressuring General Mills (a major Cargill customer), delivering 5,000 petitions to the company and conducting a lockdown at the company's headquarters where RAN volunteers chained themselves to a stairwell and shouted protests amidst a din of chainsaws symbolizing the cutting down of rainforests (Exhibit 3 provides a timeline and summary of RAN's actions against Cargill). As a symbol of the rainforest, RAN isolated the Sumatran orangutan, a species that was 85,000 strong in 1900 and that had fewer than 6,600 in 2011 and publicized their extinction as a result of rainforest destruction. The orangutan was featured prominently in all RAN's publicity campaigns against Cargill.

20   The essence of RAN's protest against Cargill was captured in a May 2010 publication, "Cargill's Problems with Palm Oil: A Burning Threat in Borneo." The publication was an output of an investigation conducted by RAN in partnership with Kontak Masyarakat Borneo (KMB), an Indonesian NGO, between July 2009 and March 2010. In the report, RAN identified Cargill's two-part business model for palm oil: owning and operating oil palm plantations in Indonesia and purchasing and trading palm oil worldwide. The report alleged that Cargill operated two undisclosed oil palm plantations in West Kalimantan, Indonesia and that these plantations were "actively burning and clearing rainforests, causing conflict with

[18]Craig Warkentin, *Reshaping World Politics,* Rowman & Littlefield Publishers, Lanham, Maryland, 2001.
[19]www.ran.org, accessed October 1, 2011.

EXHIBIT 3   Timeline and Description of Ran's Major Actions Against Cargill

Date	Action
Oct 2007	Full-page advertisement in the *Chicago Tribune*. Banner: "ADM, Bunge, Cargill: The ABCs of Rainforest Destruction" banner unfurled at the Chicago Board of Trade.
Sep 2008	Banner: "Cargill: Biofueling Climate Change" on sailboat in Lake Minnetonka, in close proximity to Cargill's world headquarters.
Dec 2009	Holiday delivery of 5,000 signed petitions to Cargill.
Jan 2010	Unfurling of 30 × 70-foot banner "Warning: General Mills Destroys Rainforests" on the lawn of the company's headquarters. General Mills was a high-profile palm oil customer of Cargill.
May 2010	Lockdown by 10 RAN activists at Cargill's private executive mansion. Volunteers engaged in a "lockdown" (refusing to move) in a staircase inside the main lobby of the building and demanded an audience with the company's CEO. They refused to unlock themselves when a Cargill public relations official offered to speak to them. The lockdown made major media headlines.
Aug 2010	Reacted to the adverse report of one of Sinar Mas's auditors and demanded that Cargill cease doing business with Sinar Mas.
Sep 2010	Unfurled two large banners bearing the identical message "Cargill: #1 Supplier of Rainforest Destruction" on top of the Minneapolis Exchange Skyway during rush-hour traffic.
Sep 2010	During a baseball game between the Minnesota Twins and the Texas Rangers in Minneapolis, RAN activists unfurled a banner that said "Destroys Rainforests" next to a Cargill billboard so that the advertisement now read "Cargill Destroys Rainforests."

Source: Compiled by author from www.ran.org, accessed October 8, 2012.

local communities, destroying peatlands and operating in violation of the RSPO's Principles and Criteria and outside of Indonesian law."[20] The report pointed out that while Cargill was a member of the RSPO and was publicly asserting that it produced palm oil according to RSPO Principles and Criteria, in reality it was flouting them. The report stated that Cargill purchased palm oil from SALCRA and Sinar Mas Group, two palm oil suppliers who were accused of actively destroying rainforests. RAN demanded that Cargill, being the "most influential palm oil producer and trader in the U.S., reduce the negative impacts of its palm oil operations and establish an important precedent for agribusiness throughout the world." The report also called for the RSPO to investigate and take disciplinary action against Cargill for violating its Principles and Criteria and also for Cargill's palm oil customers such as General Mills to cancel their purchase contracts. RAN hoped that by pressuring Cargill, its customers and the RSPO, the palm oil global supply chain would adhere to good sustainability practices.

21   In September 2010, General Mills announced that it would stop buying palm oil from companies accused of destroying rainforests and that "it would try to get all of its palm oil from responsible and sustainable sources by 2015."[21] This announcement came on the heels of similar announcements by Unilever, Nestle, Kraft, and Burger King. In

[20]"Cargill's Problems with Palm Oil: A Burning Threat in Borneo," www.ran.org, accessed October 1, 2011.
[21]http://content.usatoday.com/communities/greenhouse/post/2010/09/general-mills-palm-oil-rainforest-destruction/1, accessed October 8, 2011.

July 2010, Cargill announced a new agreement to supply its customer, Unilever (both Cargill and Unilever were members of the RSPO), with palm oil that was certified as segregated at every step of the supply chain. In response, RAN made the following statement:

> While segregated palm oil is a step in the right direction, it is only part of the solution. Cargill needs to demonstrate that their segregated palm oil is from a credible and responsible source. Additionally, we encourage Cargill to clean up its entire supply chain, and to make certified segregated palm oil available to all of their customers, particularly those in the U.S. This is particularly important because today's Unilever commitment accounts for only 10,000 metric tons, a tiny percentage of the total volumes of palm oil that Cargill trades every year.[22]

22   An Indonesian palm oil supplier, Sinar Mas, came into the spotlight as a result of Greenpeace's campaign against Nestle. Urged by Greenpeace, two independent certification bodies conducted an audit of Sinar Mas's PT SMART and Golden Agri Resources Limited Holdings regarding destruction of rainforests and creating social conflict. PT SMART released the audit report in August 2010 claiming that the two companies of Sinar Mas were exonerated of all charges. Cargill announced that because of the favorable audit report, it would continue to do business with Sinar Mas. One of the two auditors involved in the Sinar Mas audit, however, released a statement a few days later that the report had been miscommunicated and that, in fact, PT SMART had contravened the RSPO Principles and Criteria and had also broken Indonesian law. However, Cargill did not change its stance regarding Sinar Mas.

23   After a five-year campaign by Madison Vorva and Rhiannon Tomtishen, two Girl Scouts, on September 28, 2011, the Girl Scouts of America announced that it was directing its bakers (who made the more than 200 million boxes of cookies annually that were a major fundraising source and an iconic symbol of youthful entrepreneurism) to "use as little palm oil as possible, and only in recipes where there (was) no alternative and to move to a segregated, certified palm oil source by 2015."[23] The Girl Scouts of America also stated that they were henceforth supporting GreenPalm certificates that paid a premium for sustainable palm oil. While welcoming the move from a well-known organization, RAN's Lindsey Allen said that more needed to be done and invoked the Girl Scouts' best-selling cookie brand:

> The production of palm oil is causing some of the world's most precious rainforests to disappear faster than a box of Thin Mints. While what the two young girls did was amazing, unfortunately, nothing in today's statement ensures that palm oil connected to rainforest destruction will no longer be found in Girl Scout cookies.[24]

CARGILL'S RESPONSE TO RAN'S ACTIONS

24   In response to RAN's May 2010 publication, "Cargill's Problems with Palm Oil: A Burning Threat in Borneo," Cargill categorically stated that it did not operate any undisclosed oil palm properties in Indonesia and that it disclosed to the RSPO the plantations that it did own. In response to RAN's claims about deforestation, Cargill said:

> RAN claims Cargill has cleared rainforests and primary forests. This is categorically untrue. It is our policy to not expand or develop new plantations in areas of high conservation value forests and we have not cleared or developed any land that can be categorized as rainforest

[22]www.ran.org, accessed October 8, 2011.

[23]www.msnbc.msn.com/id/44718393/ns/world_news-world_environment/t/girl-scouts-pledge-limit-palm-oil-use-cookies/, accessed October 9, 2011.

[24]www.ran.org, accessed October 9, 2011.

or primary forest. The entire area where our properties are located in Kalimantan were destroyed by loggers more than 10 years ago, which was before we acquired the plantations. The land was logged and then converted to oil palm plantations. There is no rainforest or primary forest in, or anywhere in the vicinity, of our plantation.[25]

25   Cargill's statement refuted every allegation made by RAN in its May 2010 report and added that it encouraged all their suppliers to become RSPO members and work toward obtaining certification. In a letter written to RAN in July 2010, Cargill invited RAN to communicate directly with their sustainability auditors who were conducting an audit of the two plantations owned by Cargill in Singapore. In addition to these public statements responding to RAN's claims, Cargill officials visited RAN's headquarters in October 2009 to identify their Indonesian oil palm holdings.

[25]www.cargill.com/corporate-responsibility/pov/palm-oil/response-to-ran/index.jsp, accessed October 10, 2011.

Case 18

Chipotle: Mexican Grill, Inc.: *Food With Integrity**

1   On October 18, 2012, Steven Ells, the founder, chairman of the board, and co-chief executive officer (CEO) of the Denver, Colorado-based restaurant chain, Chipotle Mexican Grill (CMG), completed the conference call following the release of the company's third quarter 2012 results. While the reported results were positive, analysts picked on the slowing down of same-stores sales (a key metric for restaurant chains), the competition from Yum Brands' Taco Bell and their recent launch of the Cantina Bell menu and CMG's announcement that food costs were expected to increase in the near future. Following the announcement of third quarter results, CMG's stock went down by nearly 12 percent in intra-day trading to finally stabilize at a 4 percent drop over the previous day's price. At the end of trading on October 18, CMG's stock price was at $285.93, a significant decline from a 52-week high of $442.40.[1] CMG had been the darling of both Wall Street and its customer base ever since the company's founding in 1993 and its 2006 initial public offering (IPO). Investors were attracted to CMG for its fast growth and sizeable profit margins, while customers responded favorably to its "Food with Integrity" mission of serving good-quality food with inputs sourced using sustainable farming practices. Both Ells and his co-CEO, Montgomery F. Moran, had to respond to the challenges confronting the company.

THE U.S. RESTAURANT INDUSTRY[2]

Profile

2   For the year 2012, the National Restaurant Association projected total U.S. restaurant sales of $631.8 billion (compared to $379 billion in 2000 and $239.3 in 1990), which represented nearly 4 percent of the gross domestic product. There were 970,000 restaurant locations, and the industry employed 12.9 million people (10 percent of the total workforce). The restaurant industry's share of the food dollar was 48 percent in 2012 compared to 25 percent in 1955.[3]

Source: Ram Subramanian wrote this case solely to provide material for class discussion. The author does not intend to illustrate either effective or ineffective handling of a managerial situation. The author may have disguised certain names and other identifying information to protect confidentiality.

This publication may not be transmitted, photocopied, digitized or otherwise reproduced in any form or by any means without the permission of the copyright holder. Reproduction of this material is not covered under authorization by any reproduction rights organization. To order copies or request permission to reproduce materials, contact Ivey Publishing, Ivey Business School, Western University, London, Ontario, Canada, N6G 0N1; (t) 519.661.3208; (e) cases@ivey.ca; www.iveycases.com.

Copyright © 2013, Richard Ivey School of Business Foundation   Version: 2013-06-11

*This case has been written on the basis of published sources only. Consequently, the interpretation and perspectives presented in this case are not necessarily those of Chipotle Mexican Grill or any of its employees.
[1]Yahoo Finance, accessed October 18, 2012.
[2]Unless otherwise indicated, the information in this section is based on *Standard & Poor's Industry Surveys: Restaurants*, June 7, 2012.
[3]National Restaurant Association, "Restaurants by the Numbers," www.restaurant.org, accessed October 10, 2012.

3   The restaurant industry consisted of a number of segments such as eating places, bars and taverns and lodging place restaurants. The three largest segments were full service, quick service and fast casual. Full service restaurants offered table ordering, and the average check (revenue per customer) was the highest of the three segments. While national chains such as Darden Restaurants (operator of Red Lobster, Olive Garden and Long Horn Steakhouse) and Dine Equity (IHOP and Applebee's) existed in this segment, the majority of operators were individuals, families or limited partnerships. This segment accounted for 31.7 percent of industry revenues in 2011.

4   The quick service segment (previously referred to as "fast food") consisted of restaurants that offered fast counter service and meals to eat in or take out. This segment was further broken down into outlets that specialized in selected menu items such as hamburgers, pizza, sandwiches and chicken. Because of this segment's focus on quick service and price (the average check was the lowest of the three segments), large chains tended to dominate. Accounting for about $168.5 billion in revenues in 2011, this segment held a 28 percent share of the restaurant market.

5   The fast casual segment was the smallest of the three, accounting for about 4 percent in market share and $24 billion in 2011 revenues. Operators in this segment offered portable convenient food and focused on fresh healthful ingredients and customizable made-to-order dishes. The average check in this segment ranged between $7 and $10, price points typically lower than the full service segment and higher than the quick service segment. Fast casual was the fastest growing of the three segments, with an 11 percent growth rate between 2007 and 2011. The NPD Group, an industry research firm, indicated that as this segment was in its growth phase, it faced intense competition from both the quick service and the full service segments. Buoyed by the growth in fast casual restaurants, several full service operators had recently entered this segment. For example, P.F. Chang's opened their Pei Wei locations, and Ruby Tuesday planned to increase the number of its Lime Fresh eateries to 200 locations by the end of 2012. Panera Bread, CMG, Five Guys Burgers and Qdoba (owned by Jack-in-the-Box) were the leading fast casual players.

Industry Economics

6   Restaurant running costs varied by segment. In addition, costs were a function of size and location. Upscale formats (typically full service restaurants and some fast casual chains) made higher investments in interior design and also incurred higher input costs. Many chain restaurants typically chose locations with high population density or a large geographic draw. Food and beverage, labor and real estate costs were the three largest expense categories for restaurants. Typically, both food and beverage and labor costs accounted for around 30 percent each of revenues, while real estate costs were around 5 percent. Marketing and general administrative overhead were the significant non–operating expense categories. The National Restaurant Association reported that in 2010 the average income before income taxes of a restaurant operator ranged between 3 and 6 percent of revenues.

7   To control the cost of inputs, many large national and regional chains negotiated directly with their suppliers (to benefit both company-owned and franchisee-owned restaurants) to ensure competitive prices. Many chains also engaged in forward pricing to ensure stability in input costs. The National Restaurant Association reported that beef prices hit record levels in 2011 and were expected to be even higher when the prices for 2012 were finally tallied. Beef prices rose 53 percent in 2012 above 2009 levels as the three largest exporters of beef to the United States—Australia, Canada and New Zealand—all reduced their shipments due to a variety of global factors. While the price of various dairy items (milk, butter, cheese) had remained fairly stable over the last few years, the price of grains such as wheat and corn had fluctuated due to changes in supply and demand as well as weather-related factors. The price of a bushel of wheat went up from $6.48 in 2007 to $7.30 in 2011, after falling to $4.87 in 2009. Similarly, while the average price of a bushel of corn was $4.20 in 2007, it rose to $6.20 in 2011 after falling to $3.55 in 2009.[4]

Key Competitors

8   A former CEO of Taco Bell, the Mexican food chain owned by Yum Brands, captured the competition in the restaurant industry in the following observation: "We are all competing for a share of the customer's stomach."[5]

9   Players in the restaurant industry competed not only with their segment's players but also with those of other segments. In addition, they competed with meals prepared at home as well as frozen or packaged food items available in supermarkets. While restaurants accounted for about 48 percent of the dollar amount spent on food in 2012, the economy played a major role in this. In a 2011 National Household Survey reported in *Standard & Poor's Industry Surveys*, 21 percent of those surveyed indicated that they would increase their eating out spending in 2012, while 42 percent would decrease it slightly and 37 percent would reduce it significantly.

10   CMG faced two major competitors in the Mexican food category of the restaurant industry. While Taco Bell was a player in the quick service segment, Qdoba competed, like CMG, in the fast casual segment.

Qdoba[6]

11   Qdoba was a wholly owned subsidiary of the San Diego, California–based Jack-in-the-Box chain and in 2012 had 600 restaurants in 42 U.S. states and the District of Columbia. Qdoba was founded in Boulder, Colorado in 1995 and grew nationally by featuring Mission-style burritos (made famous first in San Francisco). After Jack-in-the-Box acquired Qdoba in 2003, it expanded the brand rapidly. Of the 600 restaurants in the chain in 2012, around 350 were franchisee-owned and the rest were company-owned. A franchisee spoke about his rationale for launching a Qdoba restaurant:

> What attracted us to the chain was quality. What brought us to this is that everything is hand-crafted and made daily. We consider ourselves to be an artisan fast food chain. We come in every morning about three hours prior to opening and start cooking our meals. We start our slow-roasted pork and shredded beef that cooks for 6 to 8 hours. Our chicken is marinated in adobo spices for 24 hours before we serve it. We have an artisan table where we make our pico de gallo salsa, mix our cilantro with rice and prepare our guacamole as customers watch. What makes us stand out is the quality of the ingredients we use and our signature flavors. I believe being fast, friendly and fresh is what makes us successful in business.[7]

12   The company reported an average check of $9.74 in fiscal 2011 for company-operated restaurants. The average yearly revenue per restaurant was $961,000 in 2011, an increase of 5.3 percent over 2010. Jack-in-the-Box had revenues of $2.17 billion and net income

[4]John T. Barone, "Commodity Outlook 2012," National Restaurant Association, www.restaurant.org, accessed October 10, 2012.
[5]Thomas O. Jones and W. Earl Sasser, Jr., "Why Satisfied Customers Defect," *Harvard Business Review*, November–December 1995, pp. 88–99.
[6]Jack-in-the-Box, 2011 10-K.
[7]Paul Sebert, "Good Eats: San Francisco Style Hits Huntington with Qdoba," www.herald-dispatch.com/entertainment/x1543286410/San-Francisco-style-hits-Huntington-with-Qdoba?i=0, accessed October 11, 2012.

of $67.83 million in 2011. The company stated that there was long-term potential to open 1,600 to 2,000 units across the United States.[8]

Taco Bell

13   Taco Bell was part of Yum Brands, Inc., which also owned the KFC and Pizza Hut chains. Yum Brands was the world's largest restaurant company in terms of units, with nearly 38,000 restaurants in 120 countries. In fiscal 2011, Yum Brands reported revenues of $12.626 billion and a net income of $1.319 billion. At the end of fiscal 2011, there were 5,670 Taco Bell restaurants in the United States, of which 27 percent were company-owned. Taco Bell reported a 50 percent market share in the U.S. Mexican quick service segment. For fiscal 2011, the average annual revenues per restaurant were $1.284 million.[9]

14   In March 2012, Taco Bell began testing a new menu called "Cantina Bell" in 75 U.S. restaurants. It worked with a Miami-based chef and television personality, Lorena Garcia, to create a new line of upscale menu items including CMG staples such as black beans, cilantro rice and corn salsa. Greg Creed, Taco Bell's president, talked about the motivation behind Cantina Bell:

> Chipotle is an opportunity because what it's done has expanded the trial and usage of Mexican food. It's got people to believe they can pay $8 for a bowl or a burrito. Taco Bell can make food every bit as good as Chipotle and instead charge less than $5.[10]

15   Taco Bell's target market was an 18- to 24-year-old value-conscious male. Creed saw Cantina Bell as helping Taco Bell appeal to an older and less value-conscious group of customers. The Cantina Bell launch (and subsequent expansion nationwide in July 2012) was cited as one of the reasons for Taco Bell's same-store sales growth of 7 percent for third quarter 2012 (compared to the similar period in 2011).[11] Exhibit 1 presents the summary of a Zagat comparison survey of Cantina Bell and CMG in New York City.

EXHIBIT 1   **Zagat Comparison of Cantina Bell and CMG in New York City**

	Price	
Item	**Cantina bell**	**CMG**
Burrito bowl with chicken	$ 5.99	$ 9.88
Steak burrito	$ 5.99	$ 10.34
Overall assessment: For practically half the price, the Cantina Bell menu is a definite value, but you get what you pay for, and the overall quality and taste of Chipotle still has an edge over Taco Bell.		

Source: http://blog.zagat.com/2012/07/taco-bell-vs-chipotle-taste-testing.html., accessed October 19, 2012

[8]Jack-in-the-Box, 2011 10-K.
[9]Yum Brands, Inc. 2011 10-K.
[10]"Taco Bell Takes on Chipotle with New Menu," www.brandchannel.com/home/post/2012/01/24/Taco-Bell-vs-Chipotle-012412.aspx, accessed October 11, 2012.
[11]Yum Brands, Inc. Press Release, October 9, 2012

CHIPOTLE MEXICAN GRILL'S HISTORY AND PROFILE

Origin and Early Growth

16   In 1990, after graduating from the Culinary Institute of America in New York City, Colorado-born Steven Ells moved to San Francisco to work as a sous chef at a restaurant. In 1993, he opened a *taqueria* (a Spanish word meaning "taco shop") in Denver, Colorado, using $85,000 as capital obtained from his father. His goal was to reinvent Mexican food. He reflected on the origins of his first restaurant:

> I wanted layers of bold flavors that had nuance and depth, not just hot, not just spicy: cumin, cilantro, cloves, fresh oregano, lemon, and lime. It looked, smelled, and tasted different from traditional fast food. And it didn't take long before there was a line of people waiting to get in. So I thought, maybe I'll open one more. I was always quite rebellious and did things my own way. Friends said Mexican food is cheap—you can't charge $5 for a burrito. But I said this is real food, the highest-quality food. Friends said you can't have an open kitchen, but I wanted the restaurant to be like a dinner party, where everyone's in the kitchen watching what's going on. They said people have to order their meal by number. But I said no, you have to go through the line and select your ingredients. And everyone gave me grief over the name: Nobody will be able to pronounce it.[12]

17   Ells opened a second restaurant using the profits from the first and a third (all in Denver, Colorado) with a loan from the Small Business Administration. When he had opened 16 restaurants by 1998, McDonald's Corporation (the global leader in fast food in terms of revenue) made an initial investment to help fund the company's growth. The company quickly grew to more than 500 units in 2005 (primarily using McDonald's $360 million capital infusion) and on January 26, 2006 made its IPO. In October 2006, McDonald's fully divested its holdings in CMG for a value of $1.5 billion. Ells talked about CMG and McDonald's: "They funded our growth, which allowed us to open 535 restaurants. We learned from each other, but we use different kinds of food, and we aim for a different kind of experience and culture altogether. So we ended up going our separate ways."[13]

The Push to Sustainable Sourcing

18   Ells happened to read an article by Edward Behr that told the story of an Iowa farmer who raised pigs without using antibiotics or confining them. Behr went on to add that the meat tasted much better than the mass-market meat that was served in most restaurants. The Behr article led Ells to learn about concentrated animal feeding operations (CAFOs).[14] In many developed countries, the dominant method of raising livestock for commercial purposes was through CAFOs, starting with poultry in the 1950s and extending to cattle and pork by the 1970s. A CAFO enabled raising livestock by using limited space. The U.S. Environmental Protection Agency (EPA) defined a CAFO as "an animal feeding operation that confines animals for more than 45 days during the growing season in an area that does not produce vegetation and meets certain size thresholds."[15]

---

[12]Margaret Heffernan, "Dreamers: Chipotle Founder Steve Ells," www.rd.com/advice/work-career/dreamers-chipotle-founder-steve-ells/, accessed October 12, 2012.
[13]Ibid.
[14]Chipotle Web site, "About Us," www.chipotle.com/en-us/company/about_us.aspx, accessed October 11, 2012.
[15]www.epa.gov/region7/water/cafo/, accessed October 11, 2012.

19   CAFO confined large number of animals in a limited space and substituted man-made structures (for feeding, temperature and manure control) for natural ones. A study[16] reported that while it took 1 million farms in 1966 to house 57 million pigs, through CAFO it took only 80,000 farms in 2001 to house the same number of pigs. CAFOs had a negative impact on water and air quality and hence were regulated by the EPA. In addition, many commercial CAFOs established agricultural water treatment plants to control manure, which had a negative impact on the environment.[17] After Ells visited several CAFOs, he decided to source from open-range pork suppliers starting in 2000, naturally raised chicken from 2002 and naturally raised beef soon after. The company formalized its sourcing policy in 2001 when it launched its "Food with Integrity" mission statement:

> Food with integrity is our commitment to finding the very best ingredients raised with respect for the animals, the environment and the farmers. It means serving the very best sustainably raised food possible with an eye to great taste, great nutrition, and great value.[18]

20   CMG owned and operated 1,316 restaurants in June 2012, of which four were in Canada, three in the United Kingdom, one in France and the rest in the United States. It reported revenues of $2.270 billion and a net income of $215 million in fiscal 2011. It employed 28,370 hourly workers and 2,570 salaried employees. Ells was CMG's CEO till January 1, 2009, when Montgomery F. Moran (who had been the company's chief operating officer since March 2005) was appointed co-CEO along with Ells. Ells, however, retained his title as chairman of the board.[19]

BUSINESS OPERATIONS

Restaurant Operations

21   All of CMG's restaurants were company-owned. They were either end-caps (at the end of a line of retail outlets), in-lines (in a line of retail outlets) or free-standing. A typical restaurant ranged in size between 1,000 and 2,800 square feet depending on the market and cost $850,000 to open. The smaller restaurants were called "A Model" restaurants, the first of which was opened in 2010 to serve less densely trafficked areas. Restaurants served a limited menu of burritos, tacos, burrito bowls (a burrito without the tortilla) and salads, all prepared with fresh ingredients. Customers placed their order (burrito or taco) at the beginning of a line and added ingredients of their choice as they moved along the line. None of the restaurants had freezers, microwave ovens, or can openers.[20]

22   Given their higher than average food costs, CMG focused on operational efficiency at the restaurant level. The restaurant size was typically smaller than those of its peers, and it economized on labor by keeping their menu options limited and by using an assembly-line

[16]Polly Walker, Pamela Rhubart-Berg, Shawn McKenzie, Kristin Kelling, and Robert S. Lawrence, "Public Health Implications of Meat Production and Consumption," Public Health Nutrition, 8(4): 348–356, 2005, www.jhsph.edu/sebin/y/h/PHN_meat_consumption.pdf, accessed October 11, 2012.
[17]Ibid.
[18]Chipotle 2011 10-K.
[19]Chipotle 2011 10-K.
[20]Thomson Reuters, Chipotle Mexican Grill, Inc. Stock Report, https://research.scottrade.com/qnr/Stocks/GetPDF?docKey=1581-AB585-6CJHB2E4R1H0C6R0PI1L9MO8A6, accessed October 9, 2012.

system for food preparation. Chris Arnold, CMG's communication director, spoke about the company's efficiency focus:

> We are big believers in what author Jim Collins calls "the genius of and."[21] You can serve great food made with ingredients from more sustainable sources and do it at a reasonable price. You can have higher food costs than your peers and still have strong margins. It just takes the discipline to figure it out.[22]

23   In 2009, the company entered into a partnership with a company to install solar panels in its restaurants. CMG aimed to be the largest direct producer of solar energy in the restaurant industry in the next five years. Ells talked about this:

> Our effort to change the way people think about and eat fast food began with our commitment to serving food made with ingredients from more sustainable sources, and that same kind of thinking now influences all areas of our business. Today, we're following a similar path in the way we design and build restaurants, looking for more environmentally friendly building materials and systems that make our restaurants more efficient.[23]

24   CMG's rationale for using solar panels was to reduce the restaurant's traditional energy consumption during the peak period of 11:00 a.m. to 7:00 p.m. Solar panels also reduced the company's carbon footprint. Starting with a restaurant in Illinois, CMG began to obtain LEED certification (Leadership in Energy and Environmental Design, a certification program of different levels) by using on-site wind turbines and cisterns for rainwater harvesting. It was the first restaurant to obtain the highest level (platinum) of LEED certification.[24] By 2012, three of its restaurants were LEED certified.

Supply Chain

25   CMG's supply chain was closely tied to the company's "Food with Integrity" mission. The company's 22 independently owned and operated distribution centers served restaurants in a specific geographic area. These centers sourced inputs from suppliers who were evaluated on quality and understanding of the company's mission. Key ingredients included various meats; vegetables such as lettuce, cilantro and tomatoes; and dairy items such as sour cream and cheese.

26   In 2008, the company embarked on a program to increase local (grown within 350 miles of the restaurant) sourcing to 35 percent of at least one bulk produce item. The seasonal produce program was meant to cut down on fossil fuels used to transport produce, give local family farms a boost and improve the taste of the food served to customers by using ingredients during their peak season. CMG created a network of 25 local farms to supply some of its romaine lettuce, green bell peppers, jalapeno peppers, red onions, and oregano to area restaurants.[25] The local sourcing program resulted in five million pounds of produce in 2009 and 10 million pounds by 2012.[26]

[21]Jim Collins was the author of two popular business books: *Good to Great* (Harper Business, New York, 2001) and *Great by Choice* (Harper Business, New York, 2011). In the former book, Collins introduced the notion that most companies are ruled by the tyranny of "or" where they choose between options rather than attempting to do both, the "and."

[22]"Chipotle's Unique Take on Sustainable Sourcing," www.cokesolutions.com/BusinessSolutions/Pages/Site%20Pages/DetailedPage.aspx?ArticleURL=/BusinessSolutions/Pages/Articles/ChipotlesUniqueTakeonSustainableSourcing.aspx&smallImage=yes&LeftNav=Customer+Spotlight+, accessed October 12, 2012.

[23]"Chipotle Plans Major Solar Power Initiative," *Business Wire*, October 20, 2009, www.thefreelibrary.com/Chipotle+Plans+Major+Solar+Power+Initiative.-a0210101557, accessed October 12, 2012.

[24]Ibid.

[25]"Chipotle Expands Locally Grown Produce Program," *Food Business Week*, June 4, 2007.

[26]Chipotle Press Release, July 30, 2012.

27   In 2012, 100 percent of CMG's pork, 80 percent of its chicken and 50 percent of its beef were classified as "naturally raised" meat—defined as open-range, antibiotic free and fed with a vegetarian diet. Forty percent of CMG's beans were organically grown, while all of its sour cream and cheese were made from milk that came from cows that were not given rBGH (recombinant bovine growth hormone). In addition, a substantial percentage of the milk for sour cream and cheese was sourced from dairies that provided pasture access for their cows.[27]

28   Organic agriculture[28] was still in its infancy in the United States in 2012. Less than 1 percent of the total agricultural area was managed organically. Of that, the percentage was highest for produce, followed by livestock and then poultry. Starting in the 1990s, the demand for organic food drove the conversion of traditional farms to organic at a rapid rate (for example, 14 percent in 2007–2008). The U.S. Department of Agriculture (USDA) reported that the average annual profitability of organic farms in 2011 was $45,697 versus $25,448 for traditional farms. However, the downturn in the economy that started in 2008 slowed down the conversion to organic farming to 6 percent between 2009 and 2011.[29] Retail chains such as Whole Foods and Trader Joe's competed with full service restaurants and other restaurant chains for organic inputs, often driving up the prices well above those for conventional inputs. Ells commented on the pricing challenges and continuing availability of organic inputs: "The supply chain has yet to catch up, organic ingredients are still pricey, and supply is limited. What we are doing is an 'incremental revolution.' If we went all-organic and natural now, a burrito would be like $17 or $18."[30]

Marketing

29   CMG's marketing budget was $32 million in 2011 versus $26 million in 2010 and $21 million in 2009. The company had reduced its advertising spending more than three years from $7.9 million in 2009 to $7.5 million in 2010 and $5.8 million in 2011.[31] It stated its policy on advertising in its annual report: "Our marketing has always been based on the belief that the best and most recognizable brands aren't built through advertising or promotional campaigns alone, but rather through all of the ways people experience the brand. Our main method of promotion is word-of-mouth publicity."[32]

30   When CMG hired Mark Crumpacker as its first chief marketing officer in 2009, the first decision that he made was to bring the company's advertising in-house rather than use the services of an outside agency. He also made the decision not to advertise in

[27]Chipotle, 2012 Third Quarter 10-Q.

[28]While the terms "organic" and "sustainable" are used interchangeably, the two are different. Organic products can be unsustainably produced on large industrial farms, and farms that are not certified organic can produce food using methods that can sustain the farm's productivity for a long time. The term "organic" is used to mean products produced or grown at a facility that is certified as such, while sustainable is more a philosophy or way of life. Since organic farming generally falls within the accepted definition of sustainable agriculture and since data is collected on organic rather than sustainable agriculture, most observers believed that organic was a good proxy for sustainable.

[29]United States Department of Agriculture, Alternative Farming Systems Information Center, http://afsic.nal.usda.gov/organic-production, accessed October 19, 2012.

[30]Sarah Rose, "A Fast Organic Nation?" *Plenty*, October/November 2005, pp. 70–75.

[31]Jim Edwards, "How Chipotle's Business Model Depends on Never Running TV Ads," *Business Insider*, March 16, 2012, http://articles.businessinsider.com/2012-03-16/news/31199897_1_chipotle-advertising-marketing, accessed October 19, 2012.

[32]Chipotle 2011 10-K.

traditional media such as TV and instead rely on various loyalty programs. He gave his rationale for it:

> The alternative is to switch to the type of marketing that every other fast-food company uses with these new menu items and big ad campaigns to promote them. I think once you get on that model, I think it's very, very hard to get off. I want to try to do this [loyalty programs] as long as I can.[33]

31   One loyalty program was called "Farm Team." This was an invitation-only online program that quizzed users on sustainability, organic farming and humane food sourcing and rewarded them when they shared the knowledge with others via social media. Arnold talked about the program: "This is a passion program. Through Farm Team, we are looking to identify our most loyal and passionate customers, and giving them tools to share their passion for Chipotle. It's much more about building evangelism than it is about rewarding frequency."[34]

32   In August 2011, CMG released an online commercial titled "Back to the Start," which featured Willie Nelson singing a reworded version of Coldplay's "The Scientist." The commercial told the story (in animated form) of a farmer who moved from inhumane industrial farming that used confined spaces to a more humane sustainable farming method. The popularity of this commercial led to CMG releasing it first in 5,700 movie theatres in September 2011 and running it once on television during the 2012 Grammy Awards show.[35]

33   A one-day festival called "Cultivate" held in Chicago in October 2011 brought together farmers, chefs, and music bands. The goal of the festival was to promote sustainable family farms. Other promotional items included iPhone games and local print advertising to accompany store openings.[36] A marketing expert assessed CMG's nontraditional marketing strategy:

> Chipotle has found a "sweet spot" with millennials by solidifying its reputation for freshness and offering a healthier fare than its competitors. The brand also gains reputation by shying away from traditional media, because younger audiences feel like it's more authentic, down-to-earth and easy to connect with. Millenials view the lack of TV as more authentic. Millenials are likely to dismiss a lot of claims. They are responding to everything the brand does and says.[37]

Finances

34   Exhibit 2 gives a cost comparison of key expenses for CMG and its competitors, Exhibit 3 presents CMG's financial statements, while Exhibit 4 gives a list of the company's stock on specific dates. Third quarter 2012 results showed a revenue increase of 18.4 percent over the same period in 2011 and a net income increase of 19.6 percent. Same-store sales increased by 4.8 percent in the quarter compared to 11.3 percent in third quarter 2011. Revenue growth was attributed to both new restaurant openings and menu price increases. The company launched a system-wide menu price increase in 2011 whose implementation was completed in third quarter 2012.[38]

---

[33]Edwards, "How Chipotle's Business Model Depends on Never Running TV Ads."
[34]"Building Evangelism: Chipotle's Farm Team," www.reasonedpr.com/blog/building-evangelism-chipotles-farm-team/, accessed October 20, 2012.
[35]Chipotle Press Release, February 10, 2012.
[36]"Chipotle's Bold New Marketing Plan," www.monkeydish.com/ideas/articles/chipotle%E2%80%99s-bold-new-marketing-plan, accessed October 20, 2012.
[37]Edwards, "How Chipotle's Business Model Depends on Never Running TV Ads."
[38]Chipotle Press Release, October 18, 2012.

EXHIBIT 2   Selected Cost Comparison—Key Competitors (Costs as Percentage of Revenues)

	2011	2010	2009
YUM BRANDS[a]			
Food & packaging	30.57	29.09	28.62
Labor	30.40	29.63	29.99
Occupancy & other restaurant operating costs	26.97	27.06	27.50
Qdoba			
Food & packaging	29.00	28.30	29.80
Labor	28.00	27.70	28.30
Occupancy & other restaurant operating costs	29.40	30.00	28.90
CMG			
Food & packaging	32.55	30.56	30.69
Labor	23.93	24.71	25.36
Occupancy & other restaurant operating costs	17.56	18.10	19.20

[a] YUM Brands does not break down data for each of its three chains (KFC, Pizza Hut, and Taco Bell).
Source: Company 10-K's.

EXHIBIT 3   CMG Consolidated Statement of Income (For Year Ending December 31 in $ Thousands)

	2011	2010	2009
Revenue	2,269,548	1,835,922	1,518,417
Restaurant operating costs			
Food, beverage, and packaging	738,720	561,107	466,027
Labor	543,119	453,573	385,072
Occupancy	147,274	128,933	114,218
Other operating costs (marketing, credit card, etc.)	251,208	202,904	174,581
General and administrative expenses	149,426	118,590	99,149
Depreciation and amortization	74,938	68,921	61,308
Pre-opening costs	8,495	7,767	8,401
Loss on disposal of assets	5,806	6,296	5,956
Income from operations	**350,562**	**287,831**	**203,705**
Net income (after interest and taxes)	**214, 945**	**178,981**	**126,845**

(Continued)

EXHIBIT 3   *(Continued)*

Consolidated Balance Sheet (condensed for December 31 in $ thousands)

	2011	2010
Assets:		
Current assets:		
Cash and cash equivalents	401,243	224,838
Accounts receivable (net)	8,389	5,658
Inventory	8,913	7,098
Current deferred tax asset	6,238	4,317
Prepaid expenses and other current assets	21,404	16,016
Income tax receivable		23,528
Investments	55,005	124,766
Leasehold improvements, property and equipment, net	751,951	676,881
Long-term investments	128,241	
Other assets	21,985	16,564
Goodwill	21,939	21,939
Total assets	**1,425,308**	**1,121,605**
Liabilities and shareholders' equity		
Current liabilities:		
Accounts payable	46,382	33,705
Accrued payroll and benefits	60,241	50,336
Accrued liabilities	46,456	38,892
Current portion of deemed landlord financing	133	121
Income tax payable	4,241	
Deferred rent	143,284	123,667
Deemed landlord financing	3,529	3,661
Deferred income tax liability	64,381	50,525
Other liabilities	12,435	9,825
Total liabilities	**381,082**	**310,732**
Total shareholders' equity	**1,044,226**	**810,873**
Total liabilities and shareholders' equity	**1,425,308**	**1,121,605**

Summary Consolidated Statement of Cash Flows[a] (for year ended December 31, in $ thousands)

	2011	2010	2009
Net cash provided by operating activities	411,096	289,191	260,673
Net cash used in investing activities	(210,208)	(189,881)	(67,208)
Net cash used in financing activities	(24,268)	(94,522)	(61,943)

[a] The company made an adjustment for exchange rates to reconcile opening and closing cash balances.
Source: Chipotle Mexican Grill, Inc. 2011 10-K.

EXHIBIT 4 CMG Selected Stock Price Data (In $ at Close of Day)

Date	Stock Price
January 26, 2006 *(IPO)*	45.00
January 3, 2007	59.42
January 2, 2008	120.38
January 2, 2009	47.76
January 4, 2010	96.46
January 3, 2011	218.92
January 3, 2012	367.29
April 2, 2012	414.15
April 13, 2012	442.40
May 1, 2012	413.07
June 1, 2012	379.95
July 2, 2012	292.33
August 1, 2012	288.64
October 1, 2012	316.33
October 2, 2012 *(Einhorn)*	302.96

Source: Compiled from Yahoo Finance,
http://finance.yahoo.com/echarts?s=CMG+Interactive#symbol=cmg;range=5y;c
ompare=;indicator=volume;charttype=area;crosshair=on;ohlcvalues=0;
logscale=off;source=undefined;, accessed October 19, 2012.

THE "EINHORN EFFECT"

35 On October 2, 2012, Jeff Einhorn, who headed a hedge fund, made a presentation at the Value Investors Conference in New York City. In his presentation, Einhorn said that CMG was an attractive stock for short sellers because the company faced significant competition, principally from Taco Bell's Cantina Bell menu, and increased food costs, both due to its sustainable sourcing practices and a global increase in food commodity prices. He said that a survey conducted by his firm found that 75 percent of self-identified Chipotle customers also frequented Taco Bell and that Taco Bell came out on top on both price and convenience. Einhorn stated:

> 23 percent of Chipotle customers had already tried Taco Bell's Cantina Bell menu—which features burritos and burrito bowls made with fresh ingredients—and two-thirds of those customers indicated they would return. What's more, the customers most likely to return to Taco Bell were also those most likely to eat at Chipotle, a dynamic that indicates to me that Chipotle is most at risk of losing its frequent customers.[39]

36 Within hours of Einhorn's presentation, CMG's stock began to fall. It fell by more than 4 percent by the end of the day, and stock analysts stated that CMG had been "Einhorned."[40]

[39]Chris Barth, "Hold the Guacamole, Einhorn's Shorting Chipotle," Forbes, http://www.forbes.com/sites/chrisbarth/2012/10/02/hold-the-guacamole-einhorns-shorting-chipotle/?partner=yahootix, accessed October 19, 2012.
[40]Kate Kelly, "GM, Chipotle Get 'Einhorned' by Comments," http://finance.yahoo.com/news/gm-chipotle-einhorned-comments-201207168.html, accessed October 19, 2012.

CMG'S CHALLENGES

37 In his conference call with analysts on October 18, 2012, Ells indirectly compared Cantina Bell with CMG (without actually naming his competitor):

> The way Chipotle does its business is not an easy thing to copy, and though a competitor could offer a similar item, it's probably only on the surface. Take a company that sells grilled chicken, for instance. Yet that company does not have a grill, nor do they have knives or cutting boards. So how do they make real chicken and cut it up? And in the end the customers realize the difference. Be careful of those who have a lower cost opportunity. The customer's not easily fooled. Our interactive format—the burrito assembly line that every customer runs through—is an important part of what Chipotle does.[41]

38 He also indicated that CMG would consider raising its menu prices in 2013 to make up for expected higher food costs. As he conferred with co-CEO Moran following the call, both men listened in on Chief Financial Officer Jack Hartung talking to a reporter:

> The company will be patient with its pricing decisions, so as not to deter customers. We could move quickly, but we're going to choose not to be in too much of a hurry. We don't want to be the first ones out of the box with price increases. We'd rather see what happens with the economy, see what happens with consumer spending, see what other competitors do and how consumers respond.[42]

39 CMG faced a host of challenges. While the depressed economy favored quick service and fast casual restaurants over full service restaurants because of lower check prices, consumer sentiment indicated that the majority of them would either curtail their spending on eating or at best maintain it at current levels. In addition, Taco Bell was proving to be a formidable competitor with its 5,670 U.S. restaurants pushing the higher margin Cantina Bell menu through aggressive and large-scale advertising. Finally, the expected increase in food costs was bound to affect CMG both in its margins and in its quest to increase its usage of sustainable inputs. Both men recalled a statement made by Arnold to an interviewer a few years ago:

> Chipotle is a good example of what can happen when you buck conventional wisdom. We've built a chain of fast-food restaurants shirking many of the things the industry was built on—we spend more on food, not less; we own our restaurants rather than franchising; and we don't market using lots of price promotions and other gimmicks. Going that route, we've built one of the most successful restaurant companies in years.[43]

40 Were sustainability and the "Food with Integrity" campaign luxuries that CMG could ill afford in these difficult economic times? Could CMG continue to use quality and sustainably sourced inputs as differentiators to justify a higher priced menu?

---

[41]Kim Bhasin, "Chipotle CEO Shreds Unnamed Competitor for Not Having Grills, Knives, or Cutting Boards," *Business Insider*, www.businessinsider.com/chipotle-ceo-taco-bell-2012-10, accessed October 20, 2012.
[42]Annie Gasparro, "Chipotle Shares Sink on Outlook," http://online.wsj.com/article/SB10000872396390443684 104578066484037301320.html, accessed October 21, 2012.
[43]"Chipotle's Unique Take on Sustainable Sourcing," www.cokesolutions.com/BusinessSolutions/ Pages/Site%20Pages/DetailedPage.aspx?ArticleURL=/BusinessSolutions/Pages/Articles/ ChipotlesUniqueTakeonSustainableSourcing.aspx&smallImage=yes&LeftNav=Customer+Spotlight+, accessed October 21, 2012.

Case 19

Delta Airlines and the Trainer Refinery

Andrew Inkpen

Michael H. Moffett

As creative as Delta might try to be with Trainer, it is hard to escape the feeling that a capital-intensive, highly cyclical commoditized business with a history of poor returns on capital would be buying. . . more of the same.

"Delta Chases Fuel's Gold," by Liam Denning, *The Wall Street Journal,*
April 5, 2012.

Reduction in refining activity in the Northeast, as reflected in recently announced plans to idle over 50 percent of the regional refining capacity, is likely to impact supplies of petroleum products. The transition period as supply sources shift could be problematic for Ultra-Low Sulfur Diesel (ULSD), gasoline, and jet fuel supplies. Prolonged uncertainty over the coming months with regard to the disposition and operation of important logistical assets such as pipelines, ports, and storage would compound adjustment challenges. Reduced short-term product supply flexibility due to longer delivery times and potential transportation bottlenecks for sources outside the region could also increase price volatility.

"Reductions in Northeast Refining Activity: Potential Implications for Petroleum Product Markets," Energy Information Administration, December 2011.

1   In late April 2012, Richard Anderson, chief executive officer of Delta Airlines (NYSE: DAL), and his acquisition team were evaluating one last time the proposed acquisition of the Trainer Refinery in Philadelphia. Delta had been seriously negotiating and pursuing the purchase of Trainer, owned by Phillips 66 (NYSE: PSX-WI), for nearly a year. Although the team believed that owning Trainer would allow Delta to manage its rising jet fuel costs—particularly in the Northeast Corridor—the analysts, markets, and press had categorically labeled it *Delta's folly.* The time to decide was now (Appendix 1 identifies the limited history of vertical integration into energy by other large non-energy companies).

DELTA'S DILEMMA

2   Delta's problem, the same problem suffered by all airlines, was fuel cost. Fuel costs aver- aged anywhere from 30 percent to 50 percent of total operating costs in the airline industry, and crude oil and jet fuel costs had been on the rise. Delta had been hit hard in 2011, as illustrated in Exhibit 1, as jet fuel prices had risen. Delta's total fuel expenses had risen by nearly $3 billion in 2011 (34 percent) over those of 2010, and 2012 was looking even grimmer.

3   Delta was an airline on the rebound. It had closed 2011 with $35 billion in revenue, up 10 percent from 2010, with profits up 40 percent to $854 million. It was driving profitability by flying fewer planes fewer miles with fuller seats. It had 80,000 employees worldwide and $3.6 billion in cash. It was the world's largest airline in terms of both fleet size and scheduled passenger traffic. And jet fuel costs were killing it.

THUNDERBIRD

SCHOOL OF GLOBAL MANAGEMENT

Source: Copyright © 2013, Helen Grassbaugh, Thunderbird School of Global Management, caseseries@thunderbird.edu. All rights reserved. This case was prepared by Professors Andrew Inkpen and Michael H. Moffett for the purpose of classroom discussion only, and not to indicate either effective or ineffective management.

APPENDIX 1   Previous History: Companies Which Have Vertically Integrated into Energy

There are only a few instances historically in which companies have acquired working interest in energy providers for the firm and the industry.

- DuPont's purchase of Conoco, 1981. This was actually the result of a strategic defense against a hostile takeover by Seagram's, but was close to a true vertical integration acquisition, as Conoco would provide crude oil and natural gas feedstocks for much of DuPont's chemical businesses. The two parted ways in 1998.
- U.S. Steel's acquisition of Marathon refining, 1982. This was an effort to diversify U.S. Steel's business lines. The company holding company, USX, eventually divested the steel businesses in 2001, renaming the remaining company Marathon Oil in 2002.
- The Kansas farm cooperative, Cooperative Refinery Association, purchased a refinery owned by the National Refinery Association in 1944 to provide diesel for its own consumption needs. The refinery, originally built in 1906, continues to operate today. The refinery was purchased by Coffeyville Resources LLC in 2000.
- Private equity and investment banking interests have accumulated larger and larger interests in crude oil production, storage, and transportation over the past decade. These financial firms are quickly becoming a significant owner of oil and gas assets in the United States.

EXHIBIT 1   Delta Airlines, Fuel Cost Summary

Year	Gallons (Millions)	Cost (Millions)	Avg Price (US$/gallon)	Percentage of Total Operating Expense
2009	3,853	$ 8,291	$ 2.15	29%
2010	3,823	$ 8,901	$ 2.33	30%
2011	3,856	$11,783	$ 3.06	36%

Source: Delta Airlines, *2011 Annual Report*, p. 9.

THE STRUCTURE AND PROFITABILITY OF U.S. REFINING

4   The refining industry in the United States is defined regionally by Petroleum Administration for Defense Districts (PADD), a system put in place during the Second World War. The five districts, described in Exhibit 2, differ significantly over the three major drivers of refining profitability: (1) source and cost of the crude oil input; (2) the scale, vintage, and

EXHIBIT 2   U.S. Refining Capacity and Operations by District

PADD District	Fuel Refineries	Capacity (bbl/day)	Percent of Total	Primary Source of Crude Oil
1: East Coast	12	2,153,000	12%	North Africa, West Africa
2: Midwest	25	3,579,000	19%	Canada, U.S.
3: Gulf Coast	44	8,802,100	48%	Southern U.S., Gulf of Mexico
4: Rocky Mountains	15	614,750	3%	Canada, U.S.
5: West Coast	27	3,251,200	18%	Alaska, California, imports
	123	18,400,050	100%	

Source: "The U.S. Oil Refining Industry: Background in Changing Markets and Fuel Policies," Anthony Andrews, Robert Pirog, and Molly F. Sherlock, Congressional Research Service, November 22, 2010, and author analysis. PADD—Petroleum Administration for Defense District.

APPENDIX 2   The Five U.S. Refining Districts

PADD—Petroleum Administration for Defense District.

complexity of the refinery facilities themselves; and (3) the product markets the refineries served. As a result, the different refineries across the districts experienced very different profitability over time. A map of the five districts can be found in Appendix 2.

CRUDE SOURCING

5   The five different refining districts had distinctly different sources of crude oil. The East Coast relied heavily on imported crude oil, much of it from West Africa and North Africa. The Midwest and Rocky Mountain districts historically relied on crude oil via pipeline from Canada, but the recent boom in shale oil in the northern Rocky Mountain states had provided the district with a new, larger, cheaper, and closer source of crude oil. The Gulf Coast district, the core of U.S. refining today with nearly half of the nation's refining capacity, sourced crude oil from the southern part of the U.S. (largely Texas, Oklahoma, and Louisiana), as well as the U.S. Continental Shelf in the Gulf of Mexico. The West Coast district purchased oil domestically (Alaska and California) and internationally (Asia).

6   The cost of crude oil acquisition was the cost driver in refining economics. Although there were a number of different benchmark crudes, the two most prevalent in the Western Hemisphere were Brent Blend (an index of North Sea crude oils) and West Texas Intermediate (WTI, an index of oil traded via Cushing, Oklahoma). Brent Blend had grown to be a dominant price benchmark in recent years as the global crude oil market became more and more liquid, and was often characterized as *water-borne* as opposed to WTI's *land-based pricing*. Brent Blend and WTI had historically served different refining markets, but given competition and the growth in refining demands over time, their prices rarely differed significantly. As illustrated by Exhibit 3, however, this had changed. Beginning in the summer of 2010, Brent Blend prices had traded at varying premiums over WTI. By March of 2012, Brent was trading at $125/bbl to WTI's $99, a spread of $26/bbl.

EXHIBIT 3   Diverging Brent Blend and WTI Prices (US$/bbl)

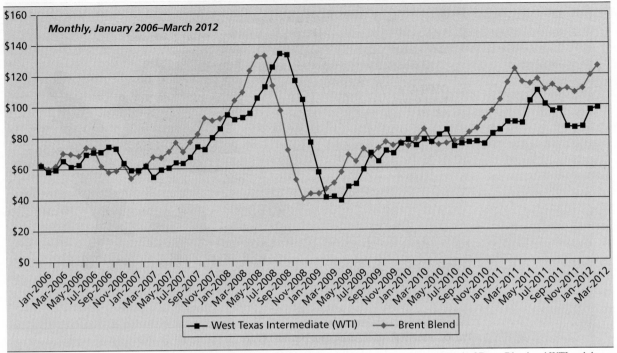

Source: Calculated by authors. Spreads shown are the differences between the monthly average price per barrel of Brent Blend and WTI and the Gulf Coast Kerosene-Type Jet Fuel prices (FOB) as collected by the Energy Information Administration.

7   The spread between prices was driven by growing supplies of domestic oil in the United States and its inability to gain access to major refining centers like the U.S. East Coast and Gulf Coast districts. The rapid development and production of shale oil from domestic sources like that of the Bakken Field in the Dakotas was landlocked. Pipelines were at capacity, and oil was stockpiling at crossroads like that of Cushing. Transportation alternatives like railroad were more costly. The result was a discounting of domestic—WTI—crude oil.

8   This flowed directly through to sourcing costs. As illustrated in Exhibit 4, as recently as January of 2010 the cost of crude oil acquisition across refining districts was largely the same. But by the latter half of 2011, and decisively by the spring of 2012, the costs of crude were diverging dramatically. Crude acquisition costs in the Midwest, where relatively cheap inland crude from the mid-continent and Canada had steadily replaced the more expensive crude oil piped from imports and coastal sources, now enjoyed a $16/bbl discount to the Gulf Coast. This was a dramatic change from the $1/bbl premium it had paid as recently as the spring of 2010.

9   The Gulf Coast refinery district, the largest and most highly developed district in the U.S. complex, had traditionally enjoyed a number of crude oil acquisition cost advantages, including a mixture of inland, offshore, and imported crude oil sourcing options. The Gulf Coast had been using greater and greater volumes of imported oil, primarily West African, which was priced on the basis of Brent Blend. As a result, crude acquisition costs were rising relative to the other refining districts.

10   But it was the East Coast district which was now suffering the highest crude acquisition costs. Although East Coast refineries had purchased crude oil at the same prices as the U.S.

EXHIBIT 4   **Average Refiner Acquisition Cost of Crude**

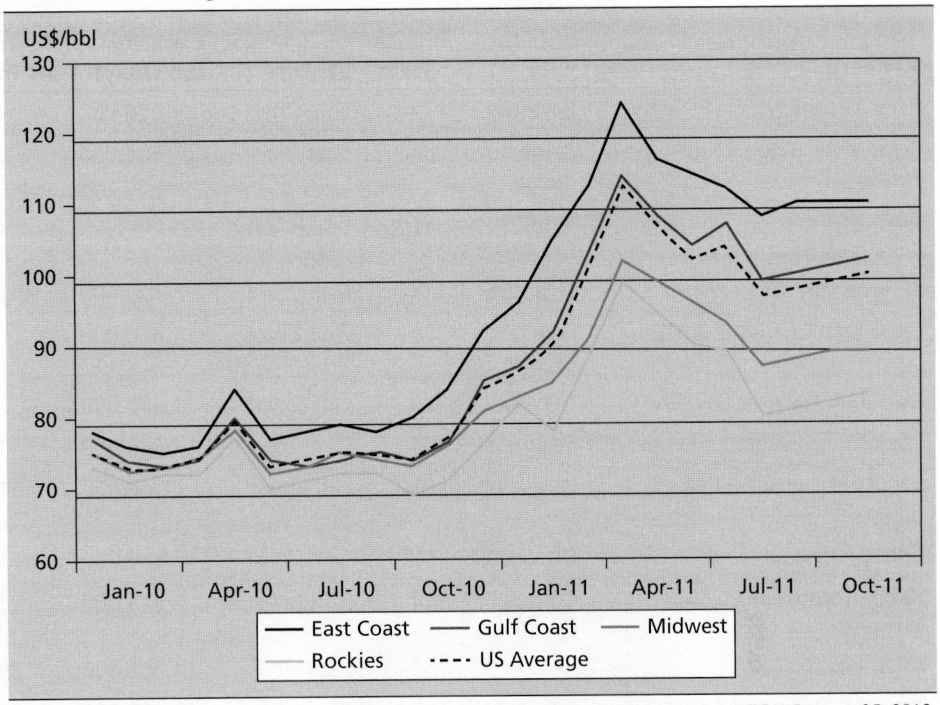

Source: "Diverging Trends in Regional Crude Acquisition Costs," *This Week in Petroleum,* EIA, January 25, 2012.

average and Midwest refineries as recently as the spring of 2010, by late 2011 they were paying a premium of more than $10/bbl over the U.S. average, and more than $16/bbl over the Midwest, as noted previously. By the spring of 2012, the East Coast refinery complex was suffering the highest crude oil acquisition costs in the nation—by far.

Refining Complexity and Vintage

11   The second driver of refining economics and performance was the scale, vintage, and complexity of the refineries themselves. Refining technology had made major advancements over time, with newer refineries typically being of greater size and efficiency.

12   One of the primary methods of categorizing refineries is *complexity,* the characterization of the plant and equipment it is operating.[1] The three categories—*simple, complex, very complex*—distinguish the capabilities a refinery possesses to both utilize a greater range of crude oil qualities and to produce a greater range of refined products from those crudes. Older refineries, or refineries possessing older technology, may be capable of processing only a specific type of crude, and may have little flexibility in the products they may produce from that crude. Newer technology, which of course would also imply higher initial capital costs and potentially higher operating costs, were more flexible in both crude oil inputs and refined product outputs.

[1]One measure of refinery complexity is the Nelson Index. The Nelson Index assigns numerical values to the multitude of refining technologies and equipment. A simple refinery would possess crude distillation, cat reforming, and hydrotreating distillates, for a value between 2 and 5 in the index. A complex refinery would have simple refinery capability plus a vacuum flasher, cat cracker, alky plant, and gas processing capability, a Nelson Index of between 5 and 12. A very complex refinery would be a complex refinery plus a coker, and a Nelson score of 13 and above (See Appendix 5 on page 19-9).

APPENDIX 3   The 10 Largest U.S. Refineries

Refinery	City	State	District	Capacity (bbls/day)	Percent of Total	Status
ExxonMobil Baytown Refinery	Baytown	TX	Gulf Coast	576,000	3.1%	Operating
ExxonMobil Baton Rouge Refinery	Baton Rouge	LA	Gulf Coast	504,000	2.7%	Operating
Hovic Refinery	Kingshill, St. Croix	VI	East Coast	500,000	2.7%	Closed Feb. 2012
BP Texas City Refinery	Texas City	TX	Gulf Coast	475,000	2.6%	Operating
Citgo Lake Charles Refinery	Lake Charles	LA	Gulf Coast	440,000	2.4%	Operating
Marathon Garyville Refinery	Garyville	LA	Gulf Coast	436,000	2.4%	Operating
ExxonMobil Beaumont Refinery	Beaumont	TX	Gulf Coast	345,000	1.9%	Operating
Sunoco Philadelphia Refinery	Philadelphia	PA	East Coast	340,000	1.8%	To be closed July 2012
Chevron Pascagoula Refinery	Pascagoula	MS	Gulf Coast	330,000	1.8%	Operating
Valero Corpus Christi E&W Complex	Corpus Christi	TX	Gulf Coast	315,000	1.7%	Operating
Total, Top 10				4,261,000	23.2%	
Total U.S. Refining				18,400,050	100.0%	

Source: "The U.S. Oil Refining Industry: Background in Changing Markets and Fuel Policies," Anthony Andrews, Robert Pirog, and Molly F. Sherlock, Congressional Research Service, November 22, 2010; updated by authors.

13   The Gulf Coast district dominated the U.S. refining industry, with relatively higher complexity and scale. It was home to 48 percent of the total capacity of the U.S. industry, and eight of the ten largest refineries. Only two of the largest refineries in the nation were outside the Gulf Coast, and one of those, the St. Croix refinery, had closed in 2011 (see Appendix 3). The top ten facilities alone made up more than 23 percent of total capacity. These larger and generally *newer* facilities enjoyed a number of operating benefits, including lower production costs and greater product mix flexibility (see Appendix 3.)[2]

Refined Products

14   The third and final driver of profitability in refining is the nexus of the products generated by any individual refinery and the market for those products. *The more valuable the products a refinery could make, the more it could pay for its crude oil.*

15   Different crude oils generate different relative proportions of derivative products—the gasoline, kerosene (jet fuel), diesel, gas oil, lube oil, and other residuals. But the differing product yields are also a function of the refinery's individual technology and complexity, and the setup of the refinery by operating management (see Appendix 3 for a numerical example). Jet fuel was one of the many derivative products resulting from the refining of crude oil, and was considered something of a

[2]Although there have been no new refineries built in the U.S. in more than 40 years, this often-noted observation is somewhat misleading. The major oil refining companies have undertaken a multitude of massive reinvestment efforts in the old facilities over time, making a definition of age in refining a near impossible task.

APPENDIX 4   Refinery Yield Differences by Crude Oil

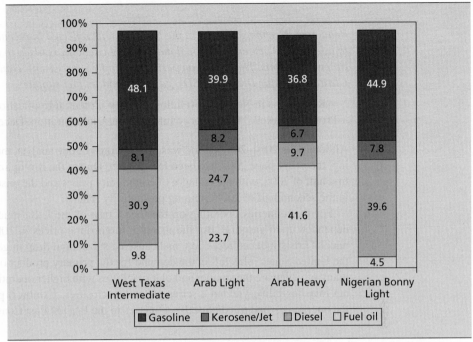

Source: Based on average Gulf Coast winter yields. Data drawn from *The International Crude Oil Refining Handbook,* 2007, Energy Intelligence, www.energyintel.com.

premium product.[3] A barrel of crude oil, depending on what kind of crude and which refinery, may produce only 10 percent or 20 percent of its output as jet fuel (see Appendix 4).

16   These products are themselves considered *commodities,* which are sold into local, regional, and international markets.[4] But the actual buyers are still confronted with costs, complexity, and reliability of suppliers. That is where Delta Airlines and other derivative product buyers come in. As seen in Exhibit 5, refining margins differed dramatically across the five refining districts in the spring of 2012. The margins per barrel were clearly the worst in the Northeast, and had led to the refinery closures. It was these same East Coast refineries which were at the center of Delta's problem.

EXHIBIT 5   U.S. Refining Margins, 2012 (US$/bbl)

Week	Northeast	Midwest	Gulf Coast	Rockies	West Coast
March 16	8.51	29.43	28.98	31.79	21.31
March 23	10.91	29.57	29.70	33.82	20.00

Source: "U.S. Refinery Margins Gain 6 pct-Credit Suisse," *Reuters,* March 26, 2012.

[3]Technically, jet fuel is generically considered a kerosene, and then classified as an unleaded kerosene (A or A-1), or naptha-kerosene (B). Jet A is available and used only in the United States, while A-1 is the standard used and consumed internationally. Jet-B is a mixture used only in very cold climates.

[4]A commodity is in theory a good whose price is set on an open market, possessing no characteristics in the eyes of the market which differentiate it from the same product produced anywhere else by anyone else. By this definition, a metal like copper, which is 99% pure copper by definition and specification, is indeed a commodity, but crude oil, with its multitude of different organic components and obviously different market prices, is not.

EAST COAST REFINERIES

Reduction in refining activity in the Northeast, as reflected in recently announced plans to idle over 50 percent of the regional refining capacity, is likely to impact supplies of petroleum products. The transition period as supply sources shift could be problematic for Ultra-Low Sulfur Diesel (ULSD), gasoline, and jet fuel supplies.

"Reductions in Northeast Refining Activity: Potential Implications for Petroleum Product Markets," U.S. Energy Information Administration, December 2011, p. 1.

17   Although the 2004–2007 period was, in the words of one analyst, the "golden era" of refining, the years since 2007 had been less golden. Due to the run-up in crude oil prices in the first half of 2008, with the collapse of commodity prices and the onset of the financial crisis in the second half of 2008, refining profitability fell.

18   For the refineries operating on the East Coast of the U.S., much of their profitability depended upon gasoline. But the increase in gasoline prices in 2008, followed by the financial crisis-induced recession, had caused a substantial drop in gasoline consumption in the United States. This fall in the demand for the primary product of East Coast refineries, many of which are the smaller and older facilities with higher operating costs and less product mix flexibility, yielded a series of facility closures. Exhibit 6 provides a summary of the operating—and idled/closed—refineries in the PAD01 East Coast district of the United

EXHIBIT 6   U.S. East Coast PADD District 1 Refineries

PADD	East Coast Facilities	City	State	Capacity (bbls/day)	Percent of Total	Status
1-01	Hovic Refinery	Kingshill, St. Croix	VI	500,000	23%	Closed Feb 2012
1-02	Sunoco Philadelphia Refinery	Philadelphia	PA	340,000	16%	To close July 2012/For sale
1-03	ConocoPhillips Bayway Refinery	Linden	NJ	238,000	11%	Operating
1-04	Petroplus Delaware City Refinery	Delaware City	DE	210,000	10%	Idled 2010
1-05	Valero Paulsboro Refinery	Paulsboro	NJ	185,000	9%	Operating
1-06	ConocoPhillips Trainer Refinery	Trainer	PA	185,000	9%	Idled Sept 2011/For sale
1-07	Sunoco Marcus Hook Refinery	Marcus Hook	PA	175,000	8%	Idled Dec 2011
1-08	Chevron Perth Amboy Refinery/Terminal	Perth Amboy	NJ	80,000	4%	Operating
1-09	Amerada Hess Port Reading Refinery	Port Reading	NJ	70,000	3%	Operating
1-10	United Refinery	Warren	PA	70,000	3%	Operating
1-11	Western Yorktown Refinery	Yorktown	VA	70,000	3%	Operating
1-12	Ergon Newell Refinery	Newell	WV	20,000	1%	Operating
1-13	Bradford Refinery	Bradford	PA	10,000	0%	Operating
				2,153,000	100%	

Source: "The U.S. Oil Refining Industry: Background in Changing Markets and Fuel Policies," Anthony Andrews, Robert Pirog, and Molly F. Sherlock, Congressional Research Service, November 22, 2010; updated by authors.

APPENDIX 5   Jet Fuel Crack Spread (US$/bbl, monthly, April 1990–March 2012)

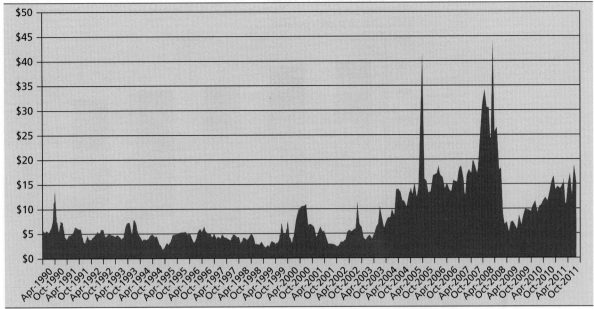

Source: Calculated by authors. Spread shown is the difference between the monthly average price per barrel of Brent Blend and the Gulf Coast Kerosene-Type Jet Fuel prices (FOB) as collected by the Energy Information Administration.

States. The combination of closure and idling (planning for closure if not resold) was radically changing the East Coast product markets.

- In September 2011, Phillips idled the 185,000 bpd Trainer Refinery in Philadelphia. The primary explanation was the facility's lack of profitability.
- In December 2011, Sunoco shuttered its 178,000 bpd Marcus Hook refinery in Pennsylvania. Again, the official explanation by Sunoco was lack of profitability.
- The Hovic Refinery on St. Croix in the U.S. Virgin Islands, a 500,000 bpd joint venture between Hess Corporation and Petroleos de Venezuela (PDVSA), technically also serving the PADD 1 East Coast district, was shut down in February 2012. It will be converted to use as a crude oil storage terminal only.
- Sunoco's 340,000 bpd Philadelphia refinery, the largest operating refinery in the East Coast district after the closure of the Hovic St. Croix facility in February 2012, would be shut down in July 2012 if not sold. A number of private equity firms, including the Carlyle Group, were rumored to be interested. Again, the reason for closure was lack of profitability.

19   Three of the four closures were refineries operating in the Philadelphia area, and the three were also the major providers of gasoline and jet fuel in the Northeast, specifically the Philadelphia and New York areas. The four closures totaled a full 50 percent of the refining capacity within the East Coast district. The closures had been the subject of much debate within the region, cutting hundreds of jobs, reducing state tax revenue bases, and ultimately requiring businesses across the region to search out new sources of the three crude oil derivatives produced at the plants—Ultra-Low Sulfur Diesel (ULSD), gasoline, and jet fuel. Gasoline imports as a result of refinery closures in the East Coast district are shown in Appendix 6.

APPENDIX 6 Gasoline Import Composition as a Result of Refinery Closures in the Eastern Corridor

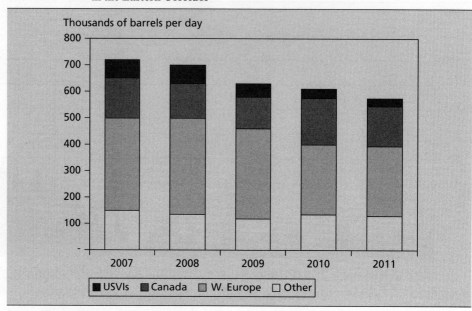

Source: "Potential Impacts of Reductions in Refinery Activity on Northeast Petroleum Product Markets," Energy Information Administration, February 27, 2012.

DELTA, JET FUEL, AND THE TRAINER REFINERY

20 Delta's issues were typical of the airline industry. More than 80 percent of airline operating costs were fixed or semivariable. The only costs that varied per passenger were reservation system commissions, food costs, and ticketing fees. The operating costs of an airline flight depended primarily on the distance traveled, not the number of passengers on board. For example, the crew and ground staff sizes were determined by the type of aircraft, not the passenger load. Therefore, once an airline established its route structure, most of its operating costs were fixed.

21 The industry had one of the lowest profit margins when measured against other industries. Airlines were far outpaced in profitability by industries such as banks, health care, consumer products, and energy. In recent years, *a la carte* revenues such as baggage fees and change fees had become increasingly important for most of the airlines.

22 Although reducing operating costs was a high priority for the airlines, the nature of the cost structure limited cost reduction opportunities. The large airlines' restrictive union agreements usually limited labor flexibility. The airports controlled gates and landing rights and had local monopoly power. Maintenance was largely determined by the equipment providers, such as Boeing and Airbus. Finally, jet fuel, the largest single cost, averaged about 30 percent of total operating costs across the major airlines.

23 Delta had struggled with profitability for a decade. As shown by Exhibit 7, Delta had suffered losses continuously from 2002 to 2009, finally turning a profit in 2010 and 2011. Although total operating revenues had risen from $14 billion in 2002 to over $35 billion in 2011, operating and financing costs had prevented profitability until 2010.[5] The airline's

[5]Delta acquired Northwest Airlines in October 2008; financial results are combined for all years beginning 2007.

EXHIBIT 7   **Delta's Profitability and Fuel Expenses**

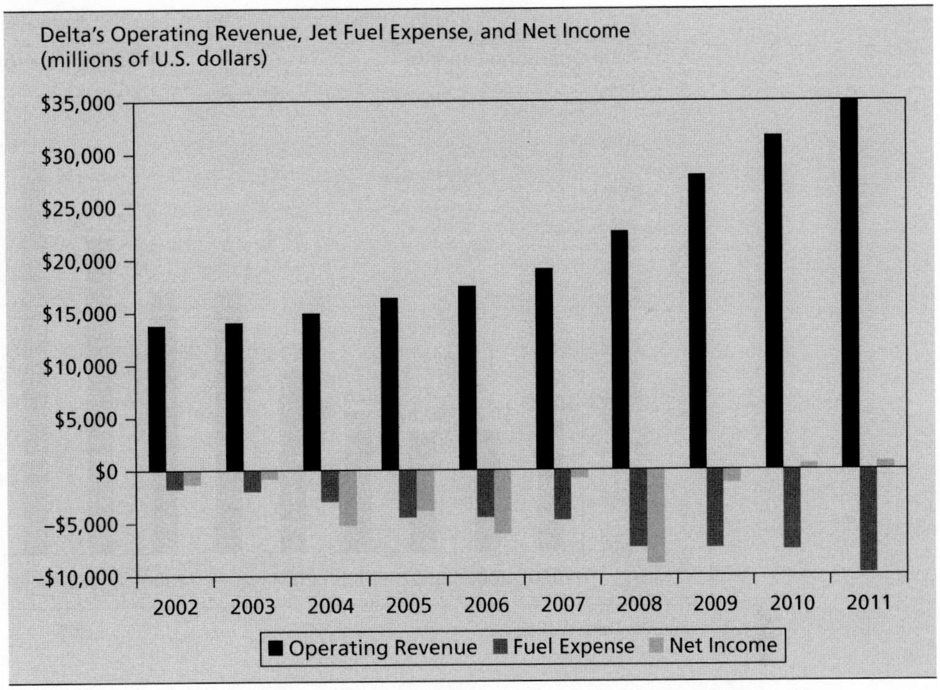

Source: Delta Airlines. Financial results include Northwest Airlines acquisition beginning in 2008.

largest operating expense was salary and related costs every year leading up to 2005, when for the first time fuel expenses surpassed salary costs. Exhibit 8 shows how fuel expense had grown in size and significance since that time.

24   Hedging jet fuel costs had long been a subject of considerable debate in the airline industry. Southwest Airlines had long been famous for reaping regular benefits with its fuel hedging program, and Delta and others had periodically hedged their fuel cost exposures with varying level of success.

25   In recent years, particularly the oil and jet fuel price run-up in 2007 and 2008, many airlines had instituted fuel surcharges on ticket sales, passing on the higher costs directly to the customer. Historically, this had been considered a non-starter strategy, but the rapid rise in prices of the time had made it a common practice across much of the airline industry. It was still an option open to Delta, but given the relatively quieter times in crude oil prices (although at $100/bbl, crude oil was still not back to historical levels), leadership was afraid that customers would not react positively to a return to cost pass-through.

26   Not all airlines had been equally successful at passing along those higher fuel prices in 2008. The 2008 jet fuel price peak had also seen the failure of five different major U.S. airlines.[6] In addition to the higher fuel prices, all five airlines were carrying very large debt service burdens, and with a decline in air travel and an increase in fuel costs, they failed quickly.

Hedging Jet Fuel Expense

27   Much of the debate over fuel hedging had been an inability to agree upon the objective of hedging. There were two streams of thought on the objective: (1) to lock in jet fuel costs

[6]Four of the five airlines filed for Chapter 11 bankruptcy within three weeks of the price of crude oil reaching $100/ bbl: Aloha Airlines, March 20, 2008; ATA, April 2, 2008; Skybus, April 5, 2008; Frontier Airlines, April 11, 2008; and Champion Air, May 31, 2008.

EXHIBIT 8   Rising Jet Fuel Costs at Delta Airlines

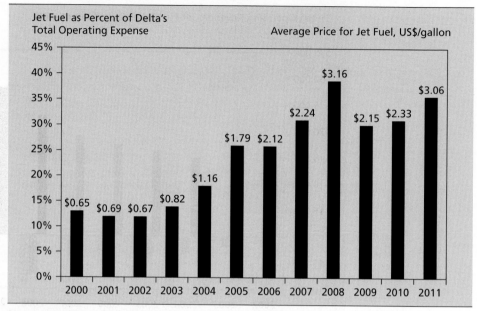

Source: Delta Airlines.

over time which were *cheaper* than the costs of buying the fuel regularly on the spot market; or (2) to lock in a known cost of fuel 12, 18, or even 24 months into the future in order to gain increasing predictability and control over corporate cash flows.

28   Jet fuel hedging instruments (derivatives) were only available on the over-the-counter (OTC) market, where an individual counterparty would write the contract and act as counterparty to the airline. Although these contracts and derivatives could be custom-designed to the buyer's need, they were more expensive and less liquid than exchange-traded financial derivatives. Exchange-traded derivatives, like those traded on the New York Mercantile Exchange (NYMEX), were highly liquid, but unavailable for jet fuel. They were available, however, for crude oil (WTI) and heating oil. In some ways, jet fuel hedgers therefore had to trade off hedging effectiveness for hedge liquidity.[7] As illustrated by Exhibit 9, although jet fuel and crude oil prices were highly correlated, they were not the same.

29   The primary derivatives available were *swaps* and *options*. *Fuel swaps* were contracts which may extend over a one- or two-year period in which the two counterparties would exchange payments, one fixed and one floating (spot). Under the most basic of these contracts, the *plain vanilla swap*, the airline would typically be the fixed-price paying party, allowing it to pay a fixed price for fuel monthly or quarterly for the duration of the agreement. In return, it would receive a floating or spot price payment in return, therefore swapping payments. The obvious benefit to the airline was that it had known payments for fuel expenses for the duration of the agreement. The risk, however, was that it was locked into this payment rate regardless of whether jet fuel spot prices were higher, the same, or even lower than the fixed price. The typical swap agreement required no up-front payment, and was settled on a real-time basis over the life of the contract.

[7]This differential between a jet fuel exposure and a crude oil hedge is the risk that the exposure's value will not change exactly in correlation with the value of the hedge. Termed *basis risk*, it may be small or large depending on the degree of correlation between jet fuel price and crude oil price changes.

EXHIBIT 9   Jet Fuel, Brent Blend, and WTI Prices (US$/bbl)

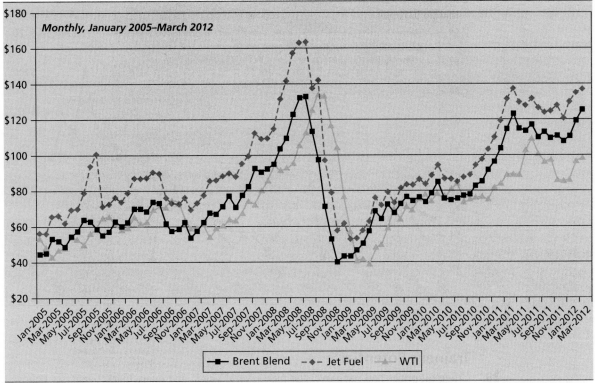

Source: Calculated by authors. Spreads shown are the differences between the monthly average price per barrel of Brent Blend and WTI and the Gulf Coast Kerosene-Type Jet Fuel prices (FOB) as collected by the Energy Information Administration.

30   Options are derivative agreements which allow the holder to either buy an asset at a set price over a period of time (a *call option*), or sell an asset at a set price over the term (a *put option*). As opposed to a swap agreement, an option is just that—the right but not the obligation to exercise the rights provided by the option contract. Delta could purchase a call option or series of call options on jet fuel which would effectively assure it of the price it would have to pay over the contract term. This would assure Delta of a cap on fuel purchase costs. If, however, fuel prices were to fall precipitously, Delta could purchase its fuel on the cheaper spot market and allow its call option derivatives to expire.

31   Options, however, have an up-front purchase price, the *option premium*, which the swap agreement does not. Option premium values are directly impacted by market volatility. Therefore, during periods of perceived crude oil and jet fuel price volatility, option premiums can become quite expensive. One method for financing these call option purchases is the simultaneous sale of put options on the same fuel amounts, but at a somewhat higher price than that of the call option. This combined position, an *option collar*, can be self-funding (a net zero premium payment up front, as the call option premium expense is equaled by the put option premium earned). The final hedge position effectively bounds fuel price costs between a maximum cost set by the call option strike rate, the *cap*, and a minimum set by the put option strike rate, the *floor*.

32   Another strategy which had periodically been employed by airlines was a form of *market-timing*. This was a selective hedging strategy, requiring the company to time its hedging activities in regard to the current spot price of crude oil/jet fuel relative to what it believed was the long-term average—a fundamental mean.

EXHIBIT 10 U.S. Gulf Coast Refining Margins and WTI

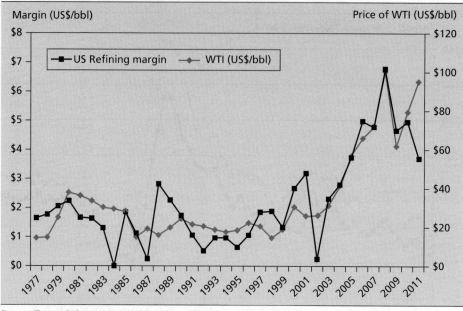

Source: Energy Information Administration and BP Statistical Review.

Trainer's Potential

33 Crude oil prices had risen over the past several years, and many market analysts believed higher prices were here to stay. The spread between jet fuel prices and crude oil prices was rising. Hedging the differential was difficult. If Delta owned its own jet fuel supplier, whatever it lost in higher global jet fuel prices it gained from the increasing profitability of that same jet fuel sold by its own fuel subsidiary. Many analysts, however, argued that the margins potentially earned in the refining segment were driven by a multitude of factors—as seen in the earlier sections, many of which are different from simply the price of the specific crude oil inputs. As illustrated by Exhibit 10, U.S. refining margins were not consistently correlated with WTI price movements.

34 How critical was Trainer itself? The Trainer Refinery could produce more than 23,000 bpd of kerosene/jet fuel, roughly 20 percent of all the jet fuel production on the East Coast. If Trainer was allowed to close (permanently), the East Coast market would become that much more isolated, and Delta's jet fuel costs were likely to suffer as a result. More and more of their fuel sourcing would have to be done from either the United Kingdom or the U.S. Gulf Coast—both of which would be more expensive.

35 And it isn't clear yet how those deliveries would take place. Pipeline capacity is scarce between the Gulf Coast and Northeast (the primary pipeline, the Colonial, is currently operating at near capacity), as well as the availability of intercoastal shipping required under the Jones Act.[8] Even if those barriers could be overcome, and after a period of possible disruption in supply, these sources would still likely suffer higher transportation and delivery charges, as well as a less-secure ongoing supply of the critically important fuel.

[8]The Jones Act, the Merchant Marine Act of 1920, requires that all shipments occurring between U.S. ports, termed cabotage, be performed by U.S. flagships, using ships constructed in the U.S., owned by U.S. citizens, and crewed by U.S. citizens and permanent residents. The result was a costly industrial service sector for intercoastal shipping.

36   Yet Trainer's crude oil was growing ever more expensive. In 2010, the last full year of production, 75 percent of all of Trainer's crude had been acquired from African producers in Algeria, Angola, and Nigeria by tanker.[9] Most of the balance was purchased from cheaper sources like Canada, but lack of pipeline connectivity limited those suppliers. If the Trainer facility could source its crude oil (or a greater proportion) from lower-cost alternatives, those crude oils priced on the basis of West Texas Intermediate like the Bakken Crude from North Dakota, Trainer's cost competitiveness would increase dramatically.

37   Phillips 66's asking price was $180 million, little more than the price of a single new Boeing 777 widebody. The state of Pennsylvania had offered an additional incentive of $30 million to reopen the refinery and put hundreds of workers back to work. But Trainer was an old refinery and would require new investment, maybe $100 million, to gain more efficient production as well as increase the yield on jet fuel—which was definitely desired. Delta's refinery consultants estimated that the investment in retooling the refinery could increase the jet fuel yield from 14 percent to about 32 percent of total output; others argued that a high of 26 percent or 28 percent was more likely. The consultants had also recommended that Delta arrange to exchange or swap the other refinery outputs from Trainer for jet fuel at other key locations in the Delta grid, reducing Delta's need to also market the refinery's products. That assumed, of course, that Delta could put together its owner management team for the refinery and rehire most of the workers who had been laid off the previous fall.

DECISION TIME

38   Richard Anderson decided what was needed was a full-blown final debate before making the final decision. He divided the analysis team into two groups, the *For's* and the *Against's*. Each team would have 20 minutes to make their case.

---

[9]African crude oil had become significantly more expensive relative to U.S. crude oil production in 2011 and 2012 as a result of African prices being based on Brent Blend, the North Sea oil benchmark, which saw rapid price increases as a result of rising tensions with Iran.

Case 20

The Global Oil and Gas Industry

Andrew Inkpen

Michael Moffett

1   The oil and gas industry is one of the largest, most complex, and most important global industries. The industry touches everyone's lives with products such as transportation, heating and electricity fuels, asphalt, lubricants, propane, and thousands of petrochemical products from carpets to eyeglasses to clothing. The industry impacts national security, elections, geopolitics, and international conflicts. The prices of crude oil and natural gas are probably the two most closely watched commodity prices in the global economy. In recent years, the industry has seen many tumultuous events, including the continuing efforts from oil-producing countries like Kazakhstan, Russia, and Venezuela to exert greater control over their resources; major technological advances in deepwater drilling and shale oil and gas; Chinese oil and gas firms and international acquisitions; ongoing strife in Sudan, Nigeria, Chad, and other oil-exporting nations; continued heated discussion about climate change and non-hydrocarbon sources of energy; and huge movements up and down in crude prices. All of this comes amid predictions that the global demand for energy will increase by 30–40 percent by 2040.

OIL AND GAS INDUSTRY BACKGROUND

2   When Colonel Edwin Drake struck oil in northwestern Pennsylvania in 1859, the first phase of the oil industry began. John D. Rockefeller emerged in those early days as a pioneer in industrial organization. When Rockefeller combined Standard Oil and 39 affiliated companies to create Standard Oil Trust in 1882, his goal was not to form a monopoly, because these companies already controlled 90 percent of the kerosene market. His real goal was to achieve economies of scale, which he did by combining all the refining operations under a single management structure. In doing so, Rockefeller set the stage for what historian Alfred Chandler called the "dynamic logic of growth and competition that drives modern capitalism."[1]

3   With the Spindletop discovery of oil in East Texas in 1901, a new phase of the industry began. Before Spindletop, oil was used mainly for lamps and lubrication. After Spindletop, petroleum would be used as a major fuel for new inventions, such as the airplane and automobile. Ships and trains that had previously run on coal began to switch to oil. For the next century, oil, and then natural gas, would be the world's most important sources of energy.

4   Since the beginning of the oil industry, there have been fears from petroleum producers and consumers that eventually the oil would run out. In 1950, the U.S. Geological Survey estimated that the world's conventional recoverable resource base was about one trillion barrels. Fifty years later, that estimate had tripled to three trillion barrels. In recent years, the concept of *peak oil* has been much debated. The peak oil theory is based on the fact that the amount of oil is finite.

THUNDERBIRD
SCHOOL OF GLOBAL MANAGEMENT

Source: Copyright © 2013 Helen Grassbaugh Thunderbird School of Global Management caseseries@thunderbird.edu. All rights reserved. This case was prepared by Professor Andrew Inkpen with assistance from Professor Michael Moffett for the purpose of classroom discussion only, and not to indicate either effective or ineffective management.

[1]Alfred D. Chandler, "The Enduring Logic of Industrial Success," *Harvard Business Review*, March-April 1990, 68 Issue 2, pp. 130–140.

5   After peak oil, according to the *Hubbert Peak Theory,* the rate of oil production on Earth will enter a terminal decline. In the U.S., oil production peaked in 1971, and some analysts argue that on a global basis, the peak has also occurred. Others argue that peak oil is a myth. An article in *Science* stated:

> Although hydrocarbon resources are irrefutably finite, no one knows just how finite. Oil is trapped in porous subsurface rocks, which makes it difficult to estimate how much oil there is and how much can be effectively extracted. Some areas are still relatively unexplored or have been poorly analyzed. Moreover, knowledge of in-ground oil resources increases dramatically as an oil reservoir is exploited.

> To "cry wolf" over the availability of oil has the sole effect of perpetuating a misguided obsession with oil security and control that is already rooted in Western public opinion—an obsession that historically has invariably led to bad political decisions.[2]

6   Regardless of whether the peak has or has not been reached, oil and natural gas are an indispensable source of the world's energy and petrochemical feedstocks, and will be for many years to come. The difficulty in determining oil and gas reserves is that true reserves are a complex combination of technology, price, and politics. While technical change continues to reveal new sources of oil and gas, prices have demonstrated more volatility than ever, and governments have sought more control over resource information and access than ever. As prices rise, reserves once considered non-economic to develop may become feasible.

7   As illustrated by Exhibit 1, crude oil prices ranged between $2.50 and $3.00 from 1948 through the end of the 1960s. The Arab oil embargo of 1974 resulted in a large price

EXHIBIT 1   **The Price of Oil, 1860–2012 (U.S.$ per barrel)**

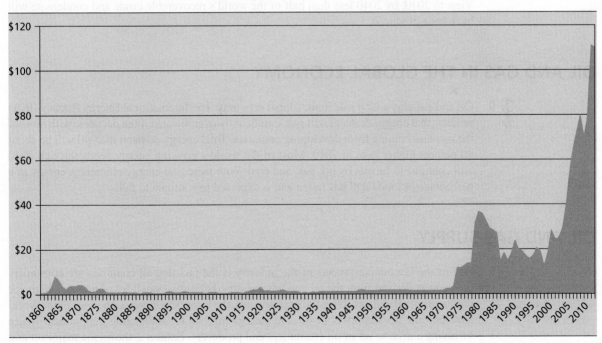

Source: Annual average prices in U.S.$ per barrel. Based on BP Statistical Review of World Energy, June 2012, updated by authors. 1984–2012 is Brent crude.

[2]Leonardo Maugeri, "Oil: Never Cry Wolf—Why the Petroleum Age Is Far from Over," *Science*, 2004, 304, pp. 1114–1115.

increase. Events in Iran and Iraq led to another round of crude oil price increases in 1979 and 1980. The 1990s saw another spike in prices that ended with the 1997 Asian financial crisis. Prices then started back up, only to fall after September 11, 2001. After 9/11, prices rose until the recession at the end of the decade, fell dramatically, and then began rising again.

OIL AND GAS RESERVES

8   Discovering new oil and gas reserves is the lifeblood of the industry. Without new reserves to replace oil and gas production, the industry would die. However, measuring and valuing reserves is a scientific and business challenge because reserves can only be measured if they have value in the marketplace. The oil sands of Alberta, Canada, are a good illustration of how difficult it is to accurately measure oil and gas reserves. Oil sands are deposits of bitumen, a molasses-like viscous oil that will not flow unless heated or diluted with lighter hydrocarbons. Although the oil sands in Alberta are now considered second only to the Saudi Arabia reserves in the potential amount of recoverable oil, for many years these were not viewed as real reserves because they were non-economical to develop. In 2013, the main town in the oil sands region, Fort McMurray, was in the midst of a boom not unlike the gold rush booms of the 1800s. Housing and labor were scarce and the infrastructure was struggling to keep pace with the influx of people, companies, and capital. The development of the oil sands occurred because of a combination of rising oil prices and technological innovation. Oil sands production was predicted to rise to three million barrels per day (b/d) by 2020 and 4.5 million b/d by 2040. According to ExxonMobil's Outlook for Energy: A View to 2040, by 2040 less than half of the world's recoverable crude and condensate will have been produced.

OIL AND GAS IN THE GLOBAL ECONOMY

9   Oil and gas play a vital role in the global economy. The International Energy Agency (IEA) predicts that energy demand will rise significantly over the next three decades, with most of the increase coming from developing countries. Total energy demand in 2040 will be about 40 percent higher than in 2010. Most of the world's growing energy needs through 2040 will continue to be met by oil, gas, and coal. With increased energy efficiency, energy as a percentage of total GDP has fallen and is expected to continue to fall.

OIL AND GAS SUPPLY

10   One of the fascinating aspects of the industry is the fact that all countries are consumers of products derived from the oil and gas industry, but only a small set of nations are major producers of oil and gas. Over the past decades, the large developed economies of the world have become net importers of oil and gas, giving rise to challenging geopolitical issues involving a diverse set of oil consumers and producers. Exhibit 2 shows the major oil and gas-producing nations and their change in output over a decade. Countries like Angola and Brazil have made their way into the top tier of oil producers, whereas the U.S. and Mexico, for different reasons, are on their way down. In natural gas, newcomers like Qatar and Turkmenistan have become major players.

EXHIBIT 2 Major Oil and Gas-Producing Nations

	Oil-Producing Nations			Natural Gas-Producing Nations	
Country	Production Million bpd 2011	Change Since 2001		Production Billion Cubic Meters, 2011	Change Since 2001
Saudi Arabia	11.2	22%	United States	651	17%
Russia	10.3	47%	Russia	607	15%
United States	7.8	2%	Canada	160	−14%
Iran	4.3	13%	Iran	152	130%
China	4.1	24%	Qatar	146	444%
Canada	4.0	32%	China	102	238%
United Arab Emirates	3.3	30%	Norway	101	88%
Mexico	2.9	−18%	Saudi Arabia	99	85%
Kuwait	2.9	31%	Algeria	78	0%
Iraq	2.8	11%	Indonesia	76	19%
Venezuela	2.7	−13%	Netherlands	64	3%
Nigeria	2.5	8%	Malaysia	62	32%
Brazil	2.23	64%	Egypt	61	143%
Norway	2.0	−40%	Turkmenistan	60	28%
Angola	1.7	135%	Uzbekistan	57	10%
Algeria	1.7	11%	United Arab Emirates	51	15%
Kazakhstan	1.8	112%	India	46	74%
Qatar	1.7	129%	United Kingdom	45	−57%
United Kingdom	1.1	−56%	Nigeria	40	168%
Indonesia	.9	−32%	Pakistan	39	73%
World Total	83.6		World Total	3276	

Source: "BP Statistical Review of World Energy," 2012.

INDUSTRY FINANCIAL PERFORMANCE

11   The oil and gas industry has been widely criticized by politicians and the media for its high profits in recent years. In the U.S., at various times there has been talk of an excess profits tax prompting Lee Raymond, former ExxonMobil CEO, to comment in 2005, "I can't remember any of these people seven years ago, when the price was $10 a barrel, coming forward and saying, 'Are you guys going to have enough money to be able to continue to invest in this business?' I don't recall my phone ringing and anybody asking me that question."[3]

12   The oil and gas industry is highly cyclical, and the cycles can last many years. In the 1990s, crude oil prices fell steadily, and in the new millennium the first few years saw steadily rising prices. The Great Recession of 2007–2008 put a damper on some experts' prediction of $200 per barrel prices. Although the oil industry is highly profitable in some years, its long-term profitability is not much higher than average profitability across many industries. In the U.S., the oil and gas industry has earned return on sales (net income divided by revenue) of about 8 percent, compared to an average of about 6 percent for all U.S. manufacturing, mining, and wholesale trade corporations.

[3]*Fox News*, Transcript: ExxonMobil's Lee Raymond, Monday, October 17, 2005, http://www.foxnews.com.

13   As evidence of the cyclical nature of the industry, some years ago *Fortune* reported that the oil industry ranked 30th out of 36 industries in return to investors over the 1985–95 period, 34th out of 36 U.S. industries in return on equity in 1995, and 32nd in return on sales.[4]

THE ROLE OF OPEC

14   The oil and gas industry has seen a remarkable bevy of government regulations and interventions over the past century, from heavy taxation of petrol in Europe to U.S. price controls on domestic production in the 1970s. The creation of the Organization of the Petroleum Exporting Countries (OPEC) represents government intervention on a global scale. OPEC was founded in 1960 with the objective of shifting bargaining power to the producing countries and away from the large oil companies. In 2006, Angola became the 12th member of OPEC.

15   OPEC's mission is "to coordinate and unify the petroleum policies of Member Countries and ensure the stabilization of oil prices in order to secure an efficient, economic, and regular supply of petroleum to consumers, a steady income to producers, and a fair return on capital to those investing in the petroleum industry."[5] Despite being a cartel, OPEC's ability to control prices is questionable. Surging oil prices in the 1980s resulted in energy conservation and increased exploration outside OPEC. Maintaining discipline among OPEC members has been a major problem (as is typical in all cartels). Massive cheating was blamed for the oil price crash of 1986, and in the 1990s Venezuela was considered one of the bigger OPEC cheats in regularly producing more than its quota.

16   Exhibit 3 shows OPEC production and crude oil prices. Although it is difficult to identify any clear continuing relationship between OPEC's production over time and the movement

EXHIBIT 3   OPEC Production and Crude Oil Prices

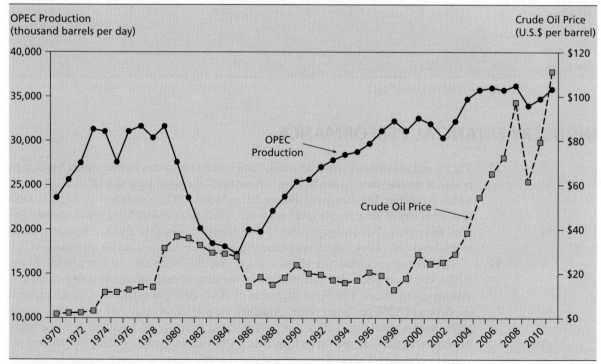

Source: WTRG Economics.

[4]"The Fortune 500 Medians," *Fortune*, April 29, 1996, pp. 23–25.
[5]www.opec.org.

of crude oil prices, the organization has clearly been instrumental in periodic shocks to the system, as characterized by one analyst.

THE RESOURCE CURSE

17   The resource curse is a paradox of the oil and gas industry. Despite high resource prices, the living standards in many oil-producing countries are low because of the inability of countries rich in natural resources to use that wealth to strengthen their economies. Counterintuitively, many of these countries also have lower economic growth than countries lacking an abundance of natural resources.[6] When times are good and oil prices are high, oil-rich countries may prosper. When oil prices fall, as they inevitably do, an overreliance on the oil sector can leave a country in a perilous situation. Moreover, the oil industries of the petroleum-nationalistic countries often suffer from a lack of investment and heavily subsidized domestic petroleum products. For example, although Iran has huge oil reserves, the country's oil industry is in a shambles. Iran's 2012 oil production, although up from a decade ago, was only about two-thirds of the level reached under the government of the former Shah of Iran in 1979. Iran imported about 40 percent of its gasoline and is unable to produce sufficient crude to meet its OPEC quota. In June 2007, Iran introduced gasoline rationing, which reduced imports and resulted in widespread black marketeering. Some experts predicted that without huge foreign direct investment in the industry, Iran's oil production could decline precipitously over the next few decades. According to one analyst:

> Iran burns its candle at both ends, producing less and less [oil] while consuming more and more. Absent some change in Iranian policy, a rapid decline in exports seems likely. Policy gridlock and a Soviet-style command economy make practical problem-solving almost impossible.[7]

18   Mexico has declining production and significant imports of refined products. The Mexican constitution does not allow foreign direct investment in the oil and gas industry. After many years of underinvestment and of Mexican governments using the oil industry as their primary source of revenue, the industry is in dire straits. Without major investment and new technology, Mexico's oil production is poised to fall. For example, production at the Cantarell oil field, one of the largest fields in the world, fell from more than 2 million b/d in 2004 to about 500,000 b/d in 2011.

MAJOR INDUSTRY PLAYERS AND COMPETITORS

19   The organizations that dominate the global oil and gas industry have changed dramatically over time in who they are, what they do, and, of critical significance for the future of the industry, how they compete.

INTEGRATED OIL COMPANIES

20   The term integrated oil companies (IOCs) refers to companies that operate in many industry segments from exploration to refining, marketing, and retail. In the early days of the industry, there was true vertical integration in which producers refined most of their

[6]Richard Auty, *Sustaining Development in Mineral Economies: The Resource Curse Thesis*, 1993, London: Routledge.
[7]Roger Stern, "Iran Actually Is Short of Oil: Muddled Mullahs," *International Herald Tribune*, January 8, 2007, www.iht.com.

production and then marketed refined products through their company-owned retail outlets. In the modern industry, the IOCs operate in many segments, but also buy and sell oil and gas to and from other firms. Somewhat confusingly, the term IOC can also refer to international oil company.

21   For many years, the largest IOCs (also known as oil majors) were the *Seven Sisters,* and included:

1. Standard Oil of New Jersey (Esso), which later became Exxon and then merged with Mobil to create ExxonMobil.
2. Royal Dutch Shell.
3. Anglo-Persian Oil Company, which became British Petroleum, then BP Amoco following a merger with Amoco (which was formerly Standard Oil of Indiana). The company is now known as BP.
4. Standard Oil of New York (Socony) became Mobil, which merged with Exxon.
5. Standard Oil of California (Socal) became Chevron.
6. Gulf Oil, most of which became part of Chevron.
7. Texaco, which merged with Chevron in 2001.

22   Exhibit 4's list of the largest oil and gas companies by stock market capitalization is evidence that the industry is dominated by a mix of global IOCs and national oil companies (NOCs). Based on market capitalization, the largest publicly traded (and in some cases, government-controlled) companies are a diverse and global set of firms such as Petrochina (China), Gazprom (Russia), Sinopec (China), Petrobras (Brazil), Total (France), and Eni (Italy).

EXHIBIT 4   Top 20 Oil & Gas Companies by Market Capitalization

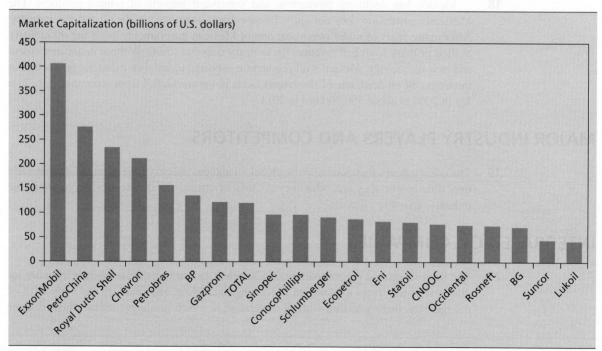

Source: PFC Energy. CNOOC, Ecopetrol, Gazprom, Petrochina, Petrobras, Sinopec, Rosneft, and StatoilHydro are National Oil Companies (NOCs) with both publicly traded shares and government owned shares. ENI is partially owned by the Italian government. All companies on the list are involved in oil and/or natural gas production except for Schlumberger which is an oil field services firm. Market cap as of eoy 2011.

23   The urge to get larger and more integrated can be seen in comments from the Oil and Natural Gas Corporation (ONGC) chairman. ONGC, an Indian state-controlled firm and primarily an upstream company, had made public its commitment to participate in the entire hydrocarbon value-chain. According to the former chairman of ONGC:

> We have to be an integrated oil company. Every major global oil company is an integrated player. I'm not being arrogant, but oil and gas is big business where the big boys play. You can survive in this business only if you are integrated; otherwise, you will be out.[8]

24   Given the long product life cycles and the huge capital investment required in the oil industry, the large IOCs were often described as stodgy and conservative. Before bankruptcy, Enron executives regularly derided the oil majors as dinosaurs that were too slow moving and that would eventually become extinct. The reality, of course, is very different. Oil majors like BP, ExxonMobil, and Shell and their predecessor companies have been around for more than a century. Through experience that is occasionally painful, the IOCs have learned how to deal with the enormous financial and political risks of the oil and gas industry. The IOCs take a long-term view and recognized that cycles and uncertainty are an inherent part of the industry. Lee Raymond, former ExxonMobil CEO, said:

> We're in a commodity [business]. We go through peaks and valleys, but our business is to level out the peaks and valleys, so that, over the cycle, our shareholders see an adequate return on their investment.[9]

25   On the surface, the IOCs looked similar in terms of the activities they performed. All appeared to be vertically integrated from exploration to retail distribution. However, there are fundamental cultural, organizational, and financial differences among the firms. The IOCs used various organizational designs to deal with vertical integration. The IOCs had different portfolios of projects around the world and over the years developed different relationships with various governments and national oil companies.

26   Exhibit 5 provides one perspective on the origins and distinctive capabilities of a few major companies.

EXHIBIT 5   **Distinctive Capabilities as a Consequence of Childhood Experiences: The Oil Majors**

Company	Distinctive Capability	Historical Origin
Exxon	Financial management	Exxon's predecessor, Standard Oil (NJ), was the holding company for Rockefeller's Standard Oil Trust
Royal Dutch/Shell Group	Coordinating a decentralized global network of 200+ operating companies	Shell Transport & Trading headquartered in London and founded to sell Russian oil in China and the Far East
BP	"Elephant hunting"	Discovered huge Persian reserves; went on to find the Forties field (North Sea) and Prudhoe Bay (Alaska)
Eni	Deal-making in politicized environments	The Enrico Mattei legacy; the challenge of managing government relations in postwar Italy
Mobil	Lubricants	Vacuum Oil Co. founded in 1866 to supply patented petroleum lubricants

Source: Robert M. Grant, *Contemporary Strategy Analysis*, Oxford: Blackwell Publishing, 2005, p. 166.

[8]"We Have to Be an Integrated Oil Company," *Hindu Business Line*, August 10, 2003, www.thehindubusinessline.com.
[9]Fox News, Transcript.

NATIONAL OIL COMPANIES

27   One of the most important trends of the past few decades has been the growing importance of NOCs. Although BP, ExxonMobil, and Shell are among the largest publicly traded companies in the world, they do not rank in the top ten of the world's largest oil and gas firms measured by reserves. The largest oil and gas firms based on reserves are, by a large margin, national oil companies (NOCs) partially or wholly state-owned. The NOCs control about 90 percent of the world's oil and gas, and most new oil is expected to be found in their territories.

28   Viewed from a business perspective, the NOCs have a mixed reputation. The national oil company of Indonesia, Pertamina, was described a few years ago as a bloated and inefficient bureaucracy:

> . . . [Pertamina] operated almost as sovereignty unto itself, ignoring transparent business practices, often acting independently of any ministry, and increasingly taking on the role of a cash cow for then-President Suharto and his cronies. During the 32-year tenure of President Suharto, Pertamina awarded 159 contracts to companies linked to his family and cronies. These contracts were awarded without formal bidding or negotiation processes . . . Indonesian petroleum law dictated that every aspect of operation in the country was subject to approval by Pertamina's foreign contractor management body, Bppka. Dealing with the incomprehensible Bppka bureaucracy on simple matters, such as acquiring work permits for expatriate personnel, can take hours of filling in applications and months of waiting.[10]

29   Venezuela nationalized its oil industry in the 1970s and created Petróleos de Venezuela (PDVSA). PDVSA developed a reputation for professionalism and competence and was relatively free from the corruption and cronyism that pervaded, and continues to pervade, so many of the NOCs.[11] By 1998, 36 foreign oil firms were operating in Venezuela, and PDVSA had ambitious expansion plans. In 1999, Hugo Chávez became president and almost immediately began to question the management and autonomy of PDVSA. After a bitter strike in 2002, PDVSA lost about two-thirds of its managerial and technical staff. From a peak of 2.9 million b/d in 1998, output was estimated by OPEC to be about 2.3 million b/d in 2010, and the company imported a significant amount of gasoline. As a company, PDVSA is indistinguishable from the government. Its top officials are appointed from the government. The company is required to spend a tenth of its investment budget on social programs, which included sending low-cost heating oil to poor Americans. Company hiring policy is based on social and political goals; e.g., candidates from larger families are given priority. In 2006, the Venezuelan Congress approved new guidelines to turn 32 privately run oil fields over to state-controlled joint ventures. ExxonMobil, alone among the foreign oil companies, rejected the new joint venture agreements, and sold its stake in the 15,000 b/d Quiamare-La Ceiba field to its partner, Repsol YPF. ExxonMobil subsequently filed an arbitration claim.

30   According to many analysts, nationalization has failed to live up to expectations almost everywhere. NOCs often suffer from excessive and misguided government intervention. Many NOCs operated as the de facto treasury for the country. In Nigeria, for example, oil

---

[10]"Indonesia Considers Legislation That Would End Pertamina's 30-year Petroleum Monopoly," *Oil & Gas Journal*, July 26, 1999, pp. 27–32.
[11]"Special Report, National Oil Companies," *The Economist*, August 12, 2006, pp. 55–57.

revenues represented more than 90 percent of hard currency earnings and about 60 percent of GDP. Nigeria's economic and financial crimes commission estimated that more than $380 billion of government revenues had been stolen or misused since 1960.[12] Some of the Middle Eastern NOCs are required to hire large numbers of locals, leaving them heavily overstaffed. Others, for example in India and Russia, must sell their products at subsidized prices. Underinvestment in the downstream is a chronic problem for many NOCs, resulting in countries like Indonesia and Iran, with huge reserves, having to import petroleum products. Monopoly positions held by many NOCs contribute to underinvestment. In Russia, Gazprom controls the pipeline network, making it difficult for other Russian gas producers to expand their production. Russia also uses its NOCs as agents of foreign policy. A dispute between Belarus and Russia in early 2007 resulted in disruption of oil shipments to Western Europe. This prompted discussions in Western Europe about how to diversify gas supply away from Russian gas.

31   Some NOCs are well-run and profitable enterprises. StatoilHydro of Norway is considered to be among the best of the NOCs. In 2007, Statoil acquired NorskHydro in a $30 billion deal. According to analysts, the motivation for the deal was that a larger company would make it easier for expansion outside Norway. The NOCs of Brazil and Malaysia are also viewed as reasonably well-run companies. Petrobras has developed leading technology in deepwater drilling and has a market capitalization rivaling that of the IOCs.

32   The role that NOCs will play in the future is not clear. Some analysts see NOCs as inefficient and corrupt arms of government that will never compete in a true economic sense. Other analysts raise different issues, suggesting that the NOCs are in a period of transition and will become competitive forces to be reckoned with. Regardless of what happens, the NOCs and their sovereign owners control most of the world's oil and gas reserves. As Paolo Scaroni, the chairman of ENI, the Italian IOC, commented a few years ago:

> Big Western oil firms are like addicts in denial. The oil giants are trying to do business as usual as if nothing was wrong. Yet they are, in fact, having trouble laying their hands on their own basic product. State-owned national or state-controlled oil companies are sitting on as much as 90 percent of the world's oil and gas and are restricting outsiders' access to it. Worse, the best NOCs are beginning to expand beyond their own frontiers and to compete with the oil majors for control over the remaining 10 percent of resources. The first step in overcoming this predicament is admitting that it is a problem.[13]

INDEPENDENTS

33   *Independents* are the non-government-owned companies that focus on either the upstream or the downstream. Many of these companies are sizable players and rank in the top 50 of all non-government-owned oil and gas companies. Exhibit 6 shows the large independents in the upstream.

34   In the downstream refining and marketing area, the largest independents are scattered around the world's largest energy-consuming countries (see Exhibit 7). The downstream independents tend to have lower market capitalizations than the upstream independents.

---

[12]Dino Mahtani, "Nigeria Struggles to Eliminate Corruption from Its Oil Industry," *Financial Times*, January 11, 2007, p. 8.
[13]"Face Value: Thinking Small," *The Economist*, July 22, 2006, p. 64.

EXHIBIT 6   Top 15 Independent E&P Firms

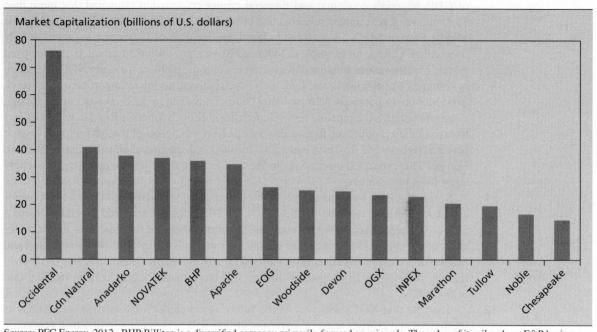

Source: PFC Energy, 2012. BHP Billiton is a diversified company primarily focused on minerals. The value of its oil and gas E&P business was estimated by PFC to be $25–28 billion.

EXHIBIT 7   Top 15 Independent Refining & Marketing Firms

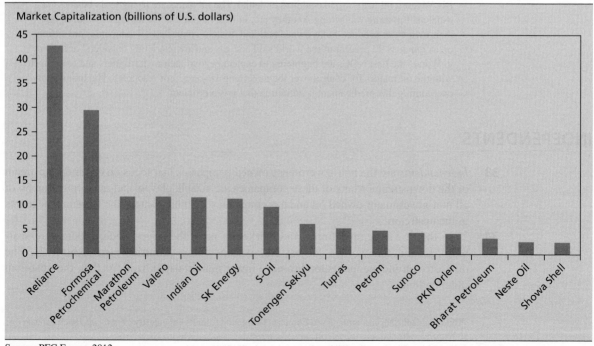

Source: PFC Energy 2012.

OTHER FIRMS

35 In addition to the IOCs, NOCs, and independents, the oil and gas industry includes a huge number of other firms that perform important functions. The oilfield services firms—the three largest of which are Schlumberger (115,000 employees), Halliburton (70,000 employees), and Baker Hughes (58,000 employees)—play a critical role throughout the exploration, development, and production phases. These firms provide both products and services that, according to Baker Hughes' Web site, help oil and gas producers "find, develop, produce, and manage oil and gas reservoirs." Because the oil field service firms do not seek ownership rights to oil and gas reserves, many analysts predict that their role will become increasingly important in the future as partners to the NOCs.

36 Thousands of other firms provide a vast array of services and products for the industry. For example, gas utilities such as Gaz de France and Tokyo Gas are major customers for gas producers. Pipeline companies distribute gas, crude oil, and petroleum products. The firms involved in drilling and seismic services provide drilling rigs and expertise for onshore and offshore wells.

THE OIL AND GAS INDUSTRY VALUE CHAIN

37 In every industry, there are various activities that transform inputs of raw materials, knowledge, labor, and capital into end products purchased by customers. A value chain is a device that helps identify the independent, economically viable segments of an industry.[14] The oil and gas industry value chain is shown in Exhibit 8. Value refers to what customers are willing to pay for, so the value chain helps identify specific activities that create value throughout the chain. Companies can use value chains to determine where they are strong and where they have limited competitive strength. All industries have upstream (close to raw materials and basic inputs) and downstream (close to the customer) segments. In the oil and gas industry, the terms upstream, downstream, and midstream are important descriptors of the industry activities.

UPSTREAM: EXPLORATION, DEVELOPMENT, AND PRODUCTION

38 Upstream activities include exploration, development, and production. In simple terms, after a lease is obtained, oil and gas are discovered during exploration; the discovery requires development; and production is the long-term process of drilling and extracting oil and gas. Since exploration and development must take place where resources are located, and most oil ownership regimes are based on state sovereignty, companies have to deal with complex government policies and regulations. Most countries grant oil and gas development rights to private companies through a process of either negotiation or bidding. The main aim of the private company is profit maximization, whereas the host country government is interested in maximizing revenue. Not surprisingly, these two aims often conflict. Most agreements between oil companies and governments come under the term production sharing agreements.

---

[14]The value chain concept was developed by Harvard Professor Michael Porter, and is the main theme of the book *Competitive Advantage: Creating and Sustaining Superior Performance* (Free Press, 1985). The concept was used by Porter to explain how firms created competitive advantage. Porter's generic value chain included primary and support activities. Primary activities included: inbound logistics, operations (production), outbound logistics, marketing and sales (demand), and services (maintenance). Support activities included: administrative infrastructure management, human resource management, technology (R&D), and procurement. The extension of the firm value chain to the industry is logically consistent, especially in the oil and gas industry where the IOCs compete across most of the major industry segments.

EXHIBIT 8   Global Oil and Gas Value Chain

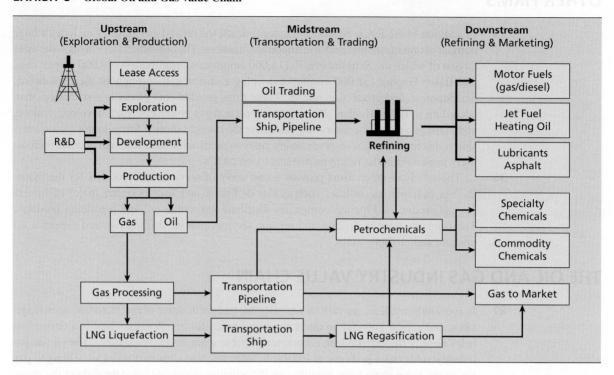

39   The method used to bid for, grant, and then renew or extend oil and gas rights varies from country to country. Once the rights to explore are acquired, a well is drilled. A financial analysis is a determining factor in the classification of a well as an oil well, natural gas well, or dry hole. If the well can produce enough oil or gas to cover the cost of completion and production, it will be put into production. Otherwise, it is classified as a dry hole, even if oil or gas is found. The percentage of wells completed is used as a measure of success. Immediately after World War II, 65 percent of the wells drilled were completed as oil or gas wells. This percentage declined to about 57 percent by the end of the 1960s. It then rose steadily during the 1970s to reach 70 percent at the end of that decade, primarily because of the rise in oil prices. This was followed by a plateau or modest decline through most of the 1980s. Beginning in 1990, completion rates increased dramatically to 77 percent. The increases of recent years have more to do with new technology than higher prices.[15]

40   Most upstream projects are done in some type of partnership structure. For example, a production sharing agreement for the Azeri, Chirag, and Gunashli development in Azerbaijan was signed in September 1994. BP was the operator with a 34.1 percent stake; the partners were Chevron with 10.3 percent, Socar 10 percent, Inpex 10 percent, Statoil-Hydro 8.56 percent, ExxonMobil 8 percent, TPAO 6.8 percent, Devon 5.6 percent, Itochu 3.9 percent, and Hess 2.7 percent.

RESERVOIR MANAGEMENT

41   For companies involved in the upstream, reservoir management is an essential skill. Reservoir management involves ensuring that reserves are replaced and that existing oil and gas

[15]"Oil Price History and Analysis," *WTRG Economics*, http://www.wtrg.com/prices.htm.

fields are efficiently managed. Asset acquisition, divestiture, and partnering are key aspects of reservoir management. Upstream companies try to replace more than 100 percent of the oil and gas produced. Determining the level of proved reserves (the amount of oil and gas the firm is reasonably certain to recover under existing economic and operating conditions) is a complex process. Consider the following comment on the auditing of reserves:

> Though the word "audit" is customarily used for these evaluations, oil and gas reserves cannot be "audited" in the conventional sense of a warehouse inventory or a company's cash balances. Rather, "proved reserves" are an approximation about formations thousands and even tens of thousands of feet below ground. Their size, shape, content, and production potential are estimated in a complex combination of direct evidence and expert interpretation from a variety of scientific disciplines and methodologies. Added to the science is economics; if it costs more to produce oil from a reservoir than one can sell it for profitably, then one cannot "book it" as a reserve. Reserves are "proved" if there is a 90 percent chance that ultimate recovery will exceed that level. As perverse as it may sound, under the "production sharing agreements" that are common in many oil-producing countries, when the price goes up, proved reserves go down.[16]

42   Matthew Simmons, founder of the energy-focused investment bank Simmons and Company, commented that "95 percent of world's 'proven reserves' are in-house guesses," "most reserve appreciation is exaggerated," and "95 percent of the world's 'proven reserves' are unaudited."[17] The pressure to replace reserves has on occasion resulted in some unintended behaviors. In 2004, Shell's CEO left earlier than anticipated after revelations that the company had overstated its reserves by nearly 25 percent.

UPSTREAM PROFITABILITY

43   Profitability is a function of costs and commodity prices. One way to consider profitability is with the breakeven price for crude oil, which is the price that equals the cost of producing the oil. In Saudi Arabia and Kuwait, the breakeven price in 2013 was between $10 and $20/barrel. New oil sands projects in Alberta had a breakeven price of about $80/barrel. For U.S. shale oil projects, estimates of breakeven prices ranged from $50–80/barrel. In the Gulf of Mexico, the breakeven price was about $55–70/barrel.

44   The term breakeven price was also used to understand the relationship between oil-exporting nations and their fiscal management. In other words, what is the oil price that a country requires in order to match oil revenues to planned government expenditures—its fiscal breakeven price. Many oil-exporting nations have seen their fiscal breakeven prices rise significantly over the past few years. For example, the IEA estimated that Iraq's fiscal breakeven price in 2012 was getting close to crude market prices, which created a vulnerability to a decline in oil prices.[18]

MIDSTREAM: TRADING AND TRANSPORTATION

45   The midstream in the value chain comprises the activities of storing, trading, and transporting crude oil and natural gas. As shown in Exhibit 8, once oil and gas are in production, there is a divergence in the value chain. Crude oil that is produced must be sold and transported from the wellhead to a refinery. Natural gas must be moved to markets via pipeline or ship; we provide an overview of the gas business in a later section.

[16]Daniel Yergin, "How Much Oil Is Really Down There?" *Wall Street Journal*, April 27, 2006, p. A.18.
[17]http://www.simmonsco-intl.com/files/HBS%20Energyv20Forum.pdf.
[18]"Iraq Energy Outlook," International Energy Agency, November 2012.

46   Crude oil has little or no value until it is refined into products such as gasoline and diesel. Thus, producers of crude oil must sell and transport their product to refineries. The market for crude oil involves many players, including refiners, speculators, commodities exchanges, shipping companies, IOCs, NOCs, independents, and OPEC. Market-making activities in the oil business have become front page news, and the daily price of crude oil is as frequently reported in the news as is the weather.

47   The ease by which liquids can be transported is a key reason why crude oil has become such an important source of energy. Although pipelines, ships, and barges are the most common transportation platforms for crude oil, railroads and tank trucks are also used in some parts of the world. In recent years, railroads have made a resurgence in the United States and Canada because of the rapid growth in production of oil in North Dakota and Alberta and a shortage of pipeline capacity. The shipping industry is very fragmented and, because oil tankers travel for the most part in international waters, largely unregulated. New technologies in shipbuilding in recent decades have allowed ships to become larger and safer.

48   Pipelines in Alaska, Chad, Russia, and other countries have allowed oil to be transported from very remote locations to markets. The construction and management of pipelines is fraught with geopolitical challenges, which means the pipeline development process takes many years or even decades. Pipelines that cross national borders are enormously complex to negotiate and build. Countries with pipelines that cross their territory have been known to use them as bargaining chips. Terrorists often sabotage pipelines and, in some countries, such as Nigeria and Iraq, oil theft from pipelines and the associated environmental and safety issues are daily occurrences.

DOWNSTREAM: OIL REFINING AND MARKETING

49   The refining of crude oil produces a variety of products, including gasoline, diesel fuel, jet fuel, home heating oil, and chemical feedstock. In the U.S., about 60 percent of refinery product volume is gasoline. Derivative products are sold directly to end users through retail locations, directly to large users such as utilities and commercial customers, and through wholesale networks.

50   The financial performance of the refining sector has always been volatile. The primary measure of industry profitability is the refining margin, which is the difference between the price of crude oil and that of the refined products. Crude prices can fluctuate for many reasons. Weather in the Gulf Coast states, political instability in oil-producing countries, or OPEC actions can all impact the price of crude oil. These fluctuations are not always accompanied by matching changes in the price of finished products, leading to large expansions or contractions in the refining margin.

51   Refiners also get squeezed between the commodity markets for crude oil (crude is the largest cost to a refiner) and commodity markets for refined products like gasoline. According to the New York Mercantile Exchange:

> A petroleum refiner, like most manufacturers, is caught between two markets: the raw materials he needs to purchase, and the finished products he offers for sale. The prices of crude oil and its principal refined products, heating oil and unleaded gasoline, are often independently subject to variables of supply, demand, production economics, environmental regulations, and other factors. As such, refiners and non-integrated marketers can be at enormous risk when the prices of crude oil rise while the prices of the finished products remain static, or even decline. Such a situation can severely narrow the crack spread, the margin a refiner realizes when he procures crude oil while simultaneously selling the

EXHIBIT 9 **ROI on Domestic Refining and Marketing versus Other Lines of Business**

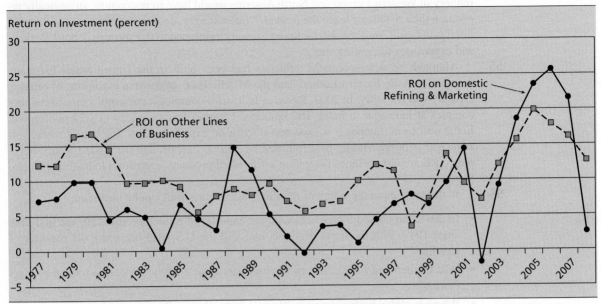

Source: "Return on Investment in U.S. and Foreign Refining and Marketing and All Other Lines of Business for U.S. Major Oil and Gas Companies 1981–2008," United States Energy Information Agency (EIA), December 2009.

products into an increasingly competitive market. Because refiners are on both sides of the market at once, their exposure to market risk can be greater than that incurred by companies who simply sell crude oil at the wellhead, or sell products to the wholesale and retail markets.[19]

52 Exhibit 9 shows that profits on refining are usually lower than profits in other lines of business for oil and gas companies. To put the downstream business in perspective, Lee Raymond, former ExxonMobil CEO, said in 1997, "I've been pessimistic on refining for 30 years, and I've run the damn places."[20] Shell's head of down-stream operations described the business as, "Grubbing [i.e., begging] for pennies in a street . . . If this industry, and especially the downstream, were to let its cost base slip, then we're going to have difficulty getting through those down-low cycles."[21]

53 The profitability of refining is driven primarily by the following factors:

1. The costs of crude oil and energy to run the refinery.
2. The supply and demand for refinery products (i.e., if refining capacity is tight, refining margins usually rise).
3. Refinery product prices, which are set by a combination of the supply and demand of refinery products and crude oil prices.
4. Refinery location and operational skills.

54 After a so-called golden age of refining from 2002 to about 2006, refining entered a new and more uncertain age. By 2013, many U.S. and European refineries were either shut

[19]New York Mercantile Exchange, Crack Spread Handbook, 2000, p. 4.
[20]Richard Teitelbaum, "Exxon: Pumping Up Profits," *Fortune*, April 28, 1997.
[21]Ed Crooks, "Interview: Rob Routs: You Have to Keep Changing," *Financial Times*, October 20, 2006, Special Report Energy, p. 10.

down or on the verge of closure. A report by ATKearney concluded that by 2021, every refinery in Western Europe and North America would have to restructure, strategically reposition their assets, or leave the market.[22] Interestingly, despite the closure of various refineries in North America, total refining capacity continued to rise through debottlenecking and expansions to existing sites.

55   Although no new greenfield refineries had been built in the United States for many decades, in Asia, Eastern Europe, and the Middle East, aggressive expansion of refining capacity was the story. In 2009, Reliance Industries completed the world's largest refinery complex at Jamnagar in India. The Jamnagar complex has a capacity of 1.24 million b/d. In the near term, Jamnagar is expected to focus on export markets. The largest market for Jamnagar is in the Middle East followed by Africa, Europe, and the United States. Shipping costs are only pennies per gallon for finished products, even from India to the United States.

56   In thinking about the future of refining, various questions can be identified:

- In 2011, the United States became a net exporter of refined products for the first time since 1949. Will the trend continue, and will the U.S. also become a net exporter of gasoline?
- Will the demand for electric and hybrid cars have a major impact on refined product demand?
- Where is global biofuel (mainly ethanol) demand going?
- How much refining capacity will close in Europe, Japan, and the United States?
- Will natural gas, as a transportation fuel, gain traction?
- Will there be more integration between refining and petrochemicals assets for the large NOCs?

57   Finally, it was clear that there was no clear "best" competitive model in refining. In North America and Western Europe, the oil majors were divesting or closing refineries. ConocoPhillips and Marathon were splitting into upstream and downstream companies. In contrast, Petrobras, one of the largest NOCs, was expanding refining capacity. Middle East NOCs were also increasing refining capacity. Russian upstream firms were looking to acquire downstream assets.

GASOLINE RETAILING

58   In the gasoline retail sector, competition is intense and margins have eroded over the past 15–20 years. For the oil majors, returns on capital employed are generally lower in retail than in other business areas. The entry of hypermarkets and supermarkets into retail gasoline sales in Western Europe and other markets displaced small dealer networks, and national players found they could make good money from convenience store sales. That said, Shell's head of downstream dismissed the notion that convenience store sales should be the focus for the fuels marketing business:

> The industry thought it could save itself with Coke. We found out that maybe the fuels game is more our game than the convenience store game. It's not a saviour for our industry. The important thing in retail is that you need to keep on changing things: that you keep different customer value propositions and you keep changing them all the time.[23]

[22]*Refining 2021: Who Will Be in the Game?* ATKearney, 2012.
[23]Ed Crooks, *Financial Times.*

59   In the U.S., supermarket and *petropreneur* entry into gasoline sales was also occurring, although not with the same speed as in Europe. In most countries, transportation fuel was seen as a commodity product, which meant spending money on brand development had questionable results. The weakness of brands favored the entry of supermarkets because they compete on price and proximity and can sell fuel as a loss leader. With traditional retail barriers to competition gone, the majors were selling most of their company-owned stores in countries around the world. The buyers were a mix of convenience store specialists, such as Couche-Tard of Canada (more than 4,000 fuel stores in Canada and the United States), franchisers, distributors, and independent dealers.

NATURAL GAS

60   In recent years, natural gas has played a much more important role in the global energy mix. Two factors help explain the increased importance of gas. The first is the continued growth in liquefied natural gas (LNG) supply. For many years, natural gas was a niche product because, unlike crude oil, natural gas is not easily transported. Without a pipeline infrastructure, natural gas in its gas form cannot be transported far from its source. In some parts of the world, such as Western and Central Europe and North America, a network of pipelines allows gas to be produced and distributed efficiently. In the U.S., gas pipeline companies operated more than 285,000 miles of pipe. In other parts of the world, such as offshore Africa or Qatar, pipelines to customers are not feasible. To transport stranded gas, it must be converted to LNG. To liquefy natural gas, impurities such as water, carbon dioxide, sulfur, and some of the heavier hydrocarbons are removed. The gas is then cooled to about -259 degrees F (-162 degrees C) at atmospheric pressure to condense the gas to liquid form. LNG is transported by specially designed cryogenic sea vessels and road tankers.

61   Historically, the costs of LNG treatment and transportation were so huge that development of gas reserves was slow. In recent years, LNG has moved from being a niche product to a vital part of the global energy business. As more players take part in investment, both in upstream and downstream, and as new technologies are adopted, the prices for construction of LNG plants, receiving terminals, and ships have fallen, making LNG a more competitive energy source. LNG ships are also getting much larger and more efficient. In addition, natural gas to liquid technology (GTL) provides an alternative to LNG and converts gas to liquid products, such as fuels and lubricants, which can be easily transported. Questions remained about the economic viability of GTL technology and only a few major projects had been completed, including the largest one, Shell's approximately $20 billion Pearl project in Qatar.

62   Major technological and structural changes continue to occur in the LNG business. The floating liquefied natural gas (FLNG) vessel is a technology that allows producers to commercialize offshore gas deposits without pipelines and onshore infrastructure. FLNGs create opportunities to commercialize gas fields that would otherwise be untouched. Another innovation is the floating natural gas liquefaction, regasification, and storage (FLRSU) vessel which moves the various industrial processes offshore and makes the equipment available for redeployment at the end of the resource life.

63   Changes in the LNG market and in LNG shipping increased flexibility for producers and consumers and shorter contracts were being negotiated. The agreement to develop the huge Qatargas 2 project, jointly owned by ExxonMobil and Qatar Petroleum, was finalized without contracts for gas sales in place. An LNG ship can deliver its gas anywhere there is an LNG terminal, making LNG almost as flexible in delivery as crude oil. There is also speculation that the rapid growth in Middle East LNG supply could lead to a global

convergence in gas pricing and markets, with LNG becoming a traded commodity. As well, buyers and sellers have been taking on new roles. Buyers have been investing in the upstream, including liquefaction plants (e.g., Tokyo Gas and the Tokyo Electric Power Company invested in the Darwin liquefaction plant in Australia). Producers such as BP and Shell have leased capacity at terminals and are extending their role into trading. New buyers have been emerging, including independent power producers.

64   The second factor that helps to explain the increased importance of gas is shale gas. The impact of shale gas on U.S. and global gas markets has resulted in what has been referred to as a game changer for U.S. energy supply. As recently as 2003, the consensus was that the United States would have to import large quantities of LNG to satisfy gas demand. Less than a decade later, U.S. production could easily meet domestic gas demand and several dormant LNG import terminals were being considered for conversion to LNG exports facilities. Although the rest of the world has lagged behind the U.S. shale gas experience, many other countries have the potential to develop shale gas resources. According to the U.S. Energy Information Administration, a number of countries such as France, Poland, Turkey, Ukraine, South Africa, Morocco, and Chile could significantly reduce gas imports if they develop their shale gas resources.

PETROCHEMICALS

65   Petrochemicals are the farthest downstream activity in the value chain. Although all of the major IOCs were involved in chemicals to some degree, they have different strategic approaches. ExxonMobil Chemical, one of the world's largest chemical businesses, produced both cyclical commodity type products, such as olefins and polyethylene, as well as a range of less cyclical specialty businesses. Many of ExxonMobil's refineries and chemical plants were co-located, providing opportunities for shared knowledge and support services and the creation of product-based synergies. In the past, BP and Shell had chemical businesses that were among the largest in the world.[24] In 2005, BP decided that its chemical business was non-core and divested the majority of the business. BP's remaining chemicals businesses became part of the refining and marketing division and were no longer considered a separate corporate division. Shell also downsized its chemicals business. The rising players in chemicals are in the Middle East and Asia, and include NOCs, such as Sabic (Saudi Arabia) and Sinopec (China), and non-state-owned companies, such as Reliance (India).

66   The commodity side of the petrochemical sector is capital-intensive and deeply cyclical. Margins and profitability for commodity chemicals depend on scale, capacity utilization, operating cost discipline, and access to low-cost feedstocks. The specialty market is at the other end of the spectrum. Specialty chemicals are sold on the basis of their performance in customer applications, not chemical composition. Patented products or technologies can enhance the value of specialty chemicals. Product differentiation may be the result of proprietary technologies such as unique catalysts or chemical processes, and it can also be the result of brand names, marketing, customer service, and delivery.

EVOLUTION OF THE INDUSTRY

Innovation and Technology

67   Innovation plays a key role across the oil and gas value chain. Innovations in areas such as deepwater drilling and LNG shipping were discussed earlier. In the upstream, many

---

[24]Peter Partheymuller, "Chemicals," Hoover's, http://premium.hoovers.com.

important technologies have been developed in the past few decades, including increased use of 3-D seismic data to reduce drilling risk, and directional and horizontal drilling to improve production in reservoirs.[25] Innovations in financial instruments were used to limit exposure to resource price movements. In oilfield management, wireless technologies allowed for faster and cheaper communication than the traditional wired underground infrastructure. In refining, nanotechnology has enabled refiners to tailor refining catalysts to accelerate reactions, increase product volumes, and remove impurities, which has led to increased refining capacity. In retailing, innovations such as unmanned stations have reduced retail costs.

Mergers and Acquisitions

68 Mergers and acquisitions have been an important element in the oil and gas industry since its inception. Although the megamergers, such as BP-Amoco, Total-PetroFina, Chevron-Texaco, and Exxon-Mobil, receive much of the press, there are also many smaller deals. In recent years, NOCs have been doing many acquisitions to gain access to resources and to new technology. Private equity-backed acquisitions have also become more prevalent.

69 In looking at the megamergers done over the past few decades, one might conclude that eventually there will only be a handful of oil companies in the world. The reality is different. Research shows that the oil industry is much less concentrated today than it was 50 years ago.[26] There are opportunities for new entrants despite the huge size of the largest IOCs and NOCs. In the downstream, new entrants have had a significant impact on industry structure. In chemicals, Ineos, the privately held British company, grew through a series of related acquisitions to become one of the world's largest chemical companies. In the upstream, the huge financial scale of projects such as Gorgon, Kashagan, Sakhalin I and II, or Qatargas 2 make it unlikely that a new entrant could challenge the majors in the largest and most technological projects. However, if NOCs in China and India continue to acquire and grow, they may develop the technological and financial skills to compete for large complex upstream projects.

China and India

70 In 1998, China became a net importer of oil for the first time. In 2006, China overtook Japan to become the world's second largest importer. By 2030, China will likely be importing about 80 percent of its oil. Clearly, China and Chinese companies are going to be major players in the oil and gas industry. Thousands of gas stations are being built and Chinese companies are aggressively investing in upstream projects around the world. Unlike the U.S. and Europe, China has no qualms about allowing its oil companies to invest in countries like Sudan and Iran. Chinese companies have also been actively buying assets outside China, including the $15 billion purchase of the Canadian company, Nexen.

71 India is also a force to be reckoned with in the global oil and gas industry. India, the fifth largest oil consumer, needs energy to feed its rapidly growing and industrializing economy. Companies such as Reliance are moving aggressively into the upstream, and stodgy state-owned companies such as ONGC, Oil India Limited, and Gas Authority of India are slowly becoming more productive. Like China, India is far from self-sufficient in energy and must find new energy sources.

---

[25]WTRG Economics, http://www.wtrg.com/prices.htm.
[26]Pankaj Ghemawat and Fariborz Ghadar, "The Dubious Logic of Global Megamergers," *Harvard Business Review*, July–August 2000, 78 Issue 4, pp. 65–72.

Unconventional Oil and Gas

72   Growth in unconventional oil and gas production will have a profound impact on the world's energy supply over the next few decades. In fact, what we currently call unconventional will likely lose that label in the coming years. Unconventional gas, mainly shale gas, coal bed methane, and tight gas (gas locked in impermeable hard rock), will constitute the majority of the growth in natural gas production over the next few decades. The production of unconventional oil, which refers primarily to the crude produced from deepwater, oil sands, and shale, will also grow substantially. The exploitation of unconventional resources is the result of technologies such as hydraulic fracturing and horizontal drilling, as well as the entrepreneurial initiatives of industry participants doing what has been done for more than a hundred years—searching for innovative ways to economically create value from scarce resources.

Industry Substitutes and Alternative Fuels

73   Various factors have contributed to a large investment flow into alternative fuel projects, including the rapid rise in oil and gas prices in recent years, concerns about global climate change, perceived competitive opportunities by energy companies (new entrants and entrenched players), and government subsidies. Despite these investments and the often strong public support for them, hydrocarbons will continue to be the world's primary energy source for years to come. By 2040, wind-powered energy is predicted to grow by seven times but will account for only about 7 percent of global electricity supply. Solar power is also expected to increase significantly but will only account for about 2 percent of global electricity supply in 2040.[27]

WHAT'S NEXT FOR THE GLOBAL OIL INDUSTRY?

74   A few predictions seem fairly safe: the global demand for oil and gas will continue to rise over the next few decades; NOCs will continue to expand beyond their home markets; finding new conventional sources of oil and gas will get harder and require innovative new technologies; unconventional oil and gas production will grow substantially; investment in non-hydrocarbon energy sources will continue; the oil and gas industry will remain one of the most vital for the global economy; and, despite the high prices of recent years, the industry will continue to go through up-and-down cycles. Finally, oil and gas firms, and especially the majors, will continue to do what they have done for more than a century: take a long-term view, invest for the future, push the boundaries of technology, and seek new resources and markets in every corner of the world.

[27]ExxonMobil, *The Outlook for Energy: A View to 2040*, 2013.

Case 21

Good Hotel: *Doing Good, Doing Well?*

Armand Gilinsky, Jr.
Sonoma State University

S. Noorein Inamdar
San José State University

Employees who feel transformed by what they are doing are far more likely to be enthusiastic about their jobs. The hotel industry has become far more expert in retaining its hangers than its employees. The turnover in the hotel business is 70–100 percent; ours is closer to 30 percent. Shouldn't a company want to offer its employees the same opportunities for self-actualization? I call this "karmic capitalism."

—Chip Conley, founder and CEO,
*Joie de Vivre Hotels, speech to Association of Fundraising Professionals,
Commonwealth Club, San Francisco, January 22, 2010*

All of our hotels are nonconventional and have a philanthropic community vision. This is one of the main reasons why I plan to stay with Joie de Vivre for a very long time.

—Pam Janusz, *General Manager, Joie de Vivre SOMA Hotels,
personal interview, March 5, 2010*

1   When Pam Janusz, general manager of Good Hotel, arrived at work on Thursday, April 15, 2010, she found some very disquieting news in her e-mail inbox. Pam worked for Joie de Vivre (JdV), a San Francisco-based hotel management company. Earlier that morning, Ingrid Summerfield, JdV's President, had sent an e-mail message marked "urgent." The message confirmed rumors that the owners of Good Hotel and the two other properties that Pam managed, Best Western Americania and Best Western Carriage Inn, had foreclosed on their holdings and sold all three properties to a new ownership group.

2   JdV had renovated Best Western Hotel Britton and Best Western Flamingo and relaunched the two as one new hotel, Good Hotel, in November 2008. Good Hotel was known in the industry as the first to be branded as a "hotel with a conscience"—encompassing a positive attitude, environmental sensitivity, and philanthropy. Exhibit 1 presents marketing information about Good Hotel. Pam had managed Good Hotel, Best Western Americania, and Best Western Carriage Inn, three of JdV's 16 San Francisco properties, since November 2009. A new ownership group planned to run all three hotels in JdV's SOMA ("South of Market Street") group themselves and terminate JdV's management contract at the end of May 2010, barring any unforeseen issues related to the sale. Meanwhile, Pam would be reassigned to another, as yet unknown position at JdV. The remainder of the e-mail message was a request to evaluate the performance of Good Hotel to prepare for its transition to new ownership.

Source: Professor Armand Gilinsky, Jr. of Sonoma State University and S. Noorein Inamdar of San José State University developed this case for class discussion rather than to illustrate either effective or ineffective handling of the situation. The host organization has provided written permission to disseminate this case for academic purposes. The host organization has signed a release letter for this case. Draft dated June 14, 2010.

EXHIBIT 1 The Good Hotel

Philosophy and Customer Experience

The Good Hotel is intended to be the first hotel with a conscience. Our philanthropic and positive approach is designed to inspire the "good in us all."

The Good Hotel is a hip San Francisco hotel that practices philanthropy and believes in doing good for the planet. The eco-friendly hotel décor features reclaimed and recycled construction materials.

Vending machines in the lobby are stocked with wallets made from FedEx envelopes and are one example of our inventive ideas to promote a good lifestyle.

We are also as fun as we are inventive. You'll find humorous touches like "Be Good" written on walls of your room.

What does "good" mean to you? For some, the word may inspire visions of helping a homeless person find shelter for a night. Others may think of global warming and chant the mantra, "reduce, re-use, recycle." Or, maybe your mission isn't to save the world, and it simply connotes a positive fun attitude.

Joie de Vivre Hotels' identity as a socially conscious company inspired us to design this SOMA hotel with all these good intentions. From beds and headboards made from locally reclaimed wood to glow in the dark messages, our guests will discover that we are good with a lighthearted twist.

Hotel Services

- Parking available at $20 per night (plus tax). Hybrid cars receive complimentary parking
- *Good Pizza* serving artisan-style pizzas using only fresh and local ingredients is located adjacent to the hotel lobby
- Business stations located in the lobby
- High-speed Internet access
- Pet friendly hotel offering complimentary treats and water/food bowls upon check-in (additional $25/pet fee applies)
- Access to outdoor, heated pool located across the street
- Bicycles available on loan when you stay with us

Guestroom Amenities

- "Good" Amenities: bed frame made of 100 percent reclaimed wood, light fixture made of glass water bottles and toilet top sink
- 26-inch flat screen TV
- iPod docking station
- Hairdryer
- Iron & ironing board
- Coffee/tea maker
- High-speed wireless Internet access
- Fold-down writing desk
- Curved shower rod

Source: The Good Hotel, guest brochure.

3   "Wow!" Pam exclaimed,

I've been trying to get to know our staff, guests, and neighborhood over the last six months. We have a great staff in place. We were able to beat our financial forecasts for the first quarter of 2010. Our guest service has been steadily rising over the last few months. There have not been any major surprises until today.

4   Pam thought about her and Good Hotel's accomplishments during the past six months and her priorities for the remaining six weeks. She wondered what she would say about

the change in ownership and possible future direction of Good Hotel to her 130 part- and full-time staff that serviced 308 rooms among the three properties, including 117 rooms at Good Hotel. Hotel staff was to remain with the three properties under new ownership.

5 Pam had spent a good deal of her time training the management team in an effort to increase the standards of service at the hotel and in turn guest loyalty. Employee satisfaction was on the rise. Online reviews of the hotel were increasingly frequent and positive. While she anticipated the new owners would maintain Good Hotel as a theme-based property, she needed to prepare her evaluation and recommendation as to whether to continue, expand, or discontinue the Good Hotel concept to the new ownership group, in the next six weeks.

THE U.S. LODGING INDUSTRY

6 Large, branded hotel chains dominated the U.S. lodging industry. Twelve leading hotel chains and their brands are profiled in Exhibit 2. The lodging business was cyclical: hoteliers tended to begin building capacity during the upturns, which came on line just in time for the downturns, according to Standard & Poor's. As a result, the industry suffered from

EXHIBIT 2 Operating Statistics of Twelve Major Hotel Chains, 2007–2009

Company Name	Ticker symbol	# Properties (boutique hotels)	# Rooms	# Emp.	Key brands
Accor SA	ACRF:Y	4,000	500,000	158,162	Sofitel, Novotel, Mercure, Suitehotel, Motel 6
Best Western	[private]	4,000	303,827	1,059	Best Western
Choice Hotels International	CHH	6,021	487,410	1,560	Comfort Inn, Quality Inn, Econo Lodge, Clarion, Rodeway Inn, Sleep Inn
Four Seasons Hotels	[private]	80		33,185	Four Seasons, Regent
Hilton Worldwide*	[private]	3,500	545,000	130,000	Hilton, Conrad, Doubletree, Embassy Suites, Hampton
Hyatt Hotels Corp	H	431	119,857	45,000	Hyatt Regency, Grand Hyatt, Park Hyatt, Hyatt Place, Hyatt Summerfield Suites, Hyatt Resorts, Andaz
InterContinental Hotel Group	IHG	4,438	646,679	7,556	InterContinental, Holiday Inn Express, Crowne Plaza, Indigo, Staybridge Suites, Candlewood Suites
Kimpton Hotel Group	[private]	40 (all)	9,322	6,000	Monaco, Palomar
Marriott International	MAR	3,420	595,461	137,000	Marriott, Courtyard, Fairfield Inn, Ritz-Carlton
Red Lions Hotels	RLH	47	8,910	2,860	Red Lion
Starwood Hotels & Resorts Worldwide	HOT	979 (30)	292,000	145,000	Four Points, Sheraton, Westin, St. Regis, Luxury Collection, W Hotels, Le Méridien, Aloft, Element
Wyndham Worldwide	WYN	7,000	588,000	24,600	Days Inn, Howard Johnson, Ramada, Super 8

(Continued)

EXHIBIT 2   *(Continued)*

FYE 12/31, U.S. $ million	2009		2008		2007	
Company Name	Total Revenue	Net Income	Total Revenue	Net Income	Total Revenue	Net Income
Accor SA	$10,726.3	$864.0	$11,812.0	$1,342.4	$9,938.3	$567.3
Best Western						
Choice Hotels International	4,140.0	98.3	4,936.0	100.2	4,692.0	111.3
Four Seasons Hotels	21.0					
Hilton Worldwide*			7,770.0		8,162.0	572.0
Hyatt Hotels Corp	3,332.0	(43.6)	3,837.0	168.0	3,738.0	270.0
InterContinental Hotel Group	1,538.0	214.0	1,854.0	262.0	883.0	231.0
Kimpton Hotel Group	600.0					
Marriott International	10,908.0	(346.0)	12,879.0	362.0	12,990.0	696.0
Red Lions Hotels Corp	165.4	(6.6)	187.6	(1.7)	186.9	6.1
Starwood Hotels & Resorts Worldwide	4,712.0	71.0	5,907.0	329.0	6,153.0	542.0
Wyndham Worldwide Corp	3,750.0	293.0	4,281.0	(1,074.0)	4,360.0	403.0

*Acquired by the Blackstone Group in September 2007.

Sources: Mergent OnLine and Hoovers/Dun & Bradstreet (ProQuest), and individual company Web sites, accessed April 24 and 25, 2010.

chronic overcapacity: as of October 2009, the U.S. lodging industry comprised approximately 4.8 million rooms at more than 50,000 properties—about one hotel room for every 64 US residents.

7   *Recent performance.* Beginning in the second half of 2008 and continuing through the first quarter of 2010, the lodging industry experienced one of its longest downturns since industry data first became available in the late 1960s. Headline unemployment, declining business and conference travel, relatively unchanged real GDP, and rampant foreclosures were lead contributors to low occupancy rates of 2008 and 2009. Standard & Poor's projected that 2010 would represent a further decline in hotel industry performance. The prolonged industry downturn was expected to drop occupancy levels between 55 percent and 56 percent, representing the worst rate since the Great Depression, according to Standard & Poor's. In December 2009, Smith Travel Research estimated that U.S. hotel rates for the year had declined 8.9 percent, and would fall another 3.4 percent in 2010. Hotel occupancy had declined 8.8 percent in 2009, and was forecasted to drop a further 0.2 percent in 2010. After ending 2009 down 6 percent, demand was forecasted to grow 1.6 percent in 2010, mostly driven by recovering demand in the second half of the year.

8   A key industry statistic, Revenue Per Available Room or RevPAR, declined 17 percent in 2009, and was forecasted to drop a further 3.6 percent in 2010, according to Smith Travel Research. RevPAR was a ratio commonly used to measure financial performance in the hospitality industry. The metric, which was a function of both room rates and occupancy, was one of the most important gauges of health among hotel operators. There were two ways to calculate RevPAR. The first formula was: Total Room Revenue in a Given Period, Net of Discounts, Sales Tax, and Meals divided by number of Available Rooms in the Same Period. Alternatively, RevPAR could be calculated as: Average Daily Room Rate

times Occupancy Rate. RevPAR was arguably the most important of all ratios used in the hotel industry. Because the measure incorporated both room rates and occupancy, it provided a convenient snapshot of a how well a company was filling its rooms, as well as how much it was able to charge. RevPAR, by definition, was calculated on a per-room basis. Therefore, one company might have a higher RevPAR than another, but still have lower total revenues if the second firm managed more rooms.

9   In a lodging industry review of 2009 and preview for 2010, Jeri Clausing of *Travel Weekly,* a popular trade publication, noted:

> Meetings and business travel will be a big factor in the recovery. Already stung by the
> slowdown in travel that accompanies any recession, hoteliers were hit with a double whammy
> in 2009 when luxury and meetings became dirty words. Toward the end of 2009, hotel
> executives said they were starting to see signs of life again in these markets. The bad news for
> hoteliers is that most of the corporate rates have already been negotiated, so even if travel picks
> up more than expected next year, it probably won't show in rates and RevPAR until 2011.

10   *Greening of the hotel industry.* The growing interest in and investments made to support sustainability in the hospitality industry had, by late 2009, moved beyond hotel recycling programs and energy-efficient lighting. According to an 2009 article appearing in *Hotels* magazine, hotels seeking new customers and growth in these difficult economic times could benefit over the long term with investments in sustainability initiatives, including retrofitting existing properties to achieve Leadership in Energy and Environmental Design (LEED) certification and building new properties to LEED standards. A late 2008 Travel Industry Association Study reported that nearly half of U.S. leisure travelers expressed a willingness to pay higher rates for services provided by environmentally friendly travel providers, and of those willing to pay more for "green" lodging, 60 percent said they would pay up to a 9 percent premium. A Deloitte survey from 2008 reported that 28 percent of U.S. business travelers were willing to pay a 10 percent premium to stay in a green lodging facility.

11   *Emerging demographic segment.* A major driver of the growing demand for green lodging came from an emerging demographic segment that consisted of consumers identified as "Cultural Creatives" by American sociologist Paul Ray, and also known as LOHAS (Lifestyles of Health and Sustainability). This segment sought a better world for themselves and their children. They were savvy, sophisticated, ecologically and economically aware customers who believed that society had reached a watershed moment in history owing to increasing public scrutiny of corporations' environmental and ethical practices. The LOHAS consumer focused on health and fitness, the environment, personal development, sustainable living and social justice. This segment was estimated by the Natural Marketing Institute (NMI) to consist of about 38 million people, or 17 percent of the U.S. adult population, with spending power of $209 billion annually. Among all ages of consumers, younger consumers, aged 14–24, were reported to be most concerned about issues such as climate change and environmental protection, and were the major drivers of growth in the LOHAS segment. See Exhibit 3 for a profile of the LOHAS demographic.

12   Of that segment, the NMI identified a sub-segment of tourists comprising five percent of the overall U.S. travel and tourism market and representing a $77-billion market. Major hotel companies like Ritz Carlton and Starwood were known to be creating eco-branded properties. Hospitality designers and architects increasingly were being asked to "green" facilities across the board, from budget properties to high-end resorts.

13   *San Francisco tourism and lodging patterns.* Of the estimated 15.4 million visitors to San Francisco city and county in 2009, more than 4.5 million overnight visitors stayed in commercial accommodations, comprising 32,976 hotel rooms and 215 hotels. Visitors paid a 14 percent occupancy tax that generated about $210 million for San Francisco city and

EXHIBIT 3   The Green Consumer

	All consumers	"Green" consumers
Average age	44	40
Gender		
Female	51%	54%
Male	49%	46%
Ethnicity		
Caucasian/other	75%	62%
Hispanic	13%	21%
African-American	11%	16%
College educated	25%	31%
Median household income	$58,700	$65,700

Source: Brooks, S. (2009). The green consumer, *Restaurant Business,* September, pp. 20–21.

county services, including schools, police, affordable housing, and arts programs. Most tourists in San Francisco took day trips beyond city limits or extended their visit throughout Northern California by taking side trips to other area locales and attractions, such as the Napa/Sonoma wine country (23 percent), Sausalito (14 percent), and the Monterey peninsula (about 10 percent). Exhibit 4 presents San Francisco tourism data and Exhibit 5 shows comparative statistics on the San Francisco hospitality industry for the periods ending March 31, 2008, 2009, and 2010.

14   The San Francisco Convention and Visitors Bureau forecasted that room supply would remain relatively unchanged out to 2015, while demand for rooms would remain flat, in stark contrast to 2004–2008, which represented five consecutive years of growth in both room supply and tourism demand. The Bureau also projected that hotel occupancy rates, average daily rates (ADR) and RevPAR would not begin to recover until 2011–12. One major factor was that the Moscone Convention Center, San Francisco's largest convention and meetings site, was expected to have a weak convention year in 2010 compared to five of the prior six years. Convention center bookings—at places such as the Moscone Center—greatly influenced hotel projections. Nearly 20,000 hotel rooms were in walking distance of the Moscone Center (including Good Hotel, which was five blocks away), and convention travel represented 35 percent of the annual demand for hotel rooms, according to the Convention and Visitor's Bureau. Although eight new hotels were on the drawing board, those new properties were unlikely to alter local room supply in the near-term.

JOIE DE VIVRE

15   Since JdV's founding in 1987, the company had grown to manage 36 boutique hotel properties in California. By 2010, JdV was the second largest U.S. boutique hotel operator after the Kimpton Hotel & Restaurant Group, which had pioneered the boutique concept in San Francisco in 1981.

16   *Boutique hotels.* Boutique hotels differentiated themselves from larger chain branded hotels and motels by providing personalized accommodation and services and facilities. Sometimes known as "design hotels" or "lifestyle hotels," boutique hotels began appearing in the 1980s in major cities like London, New York, and San Francisco. Boutique hotels

EXHIBIT 4 San Francisco Hotel Guest Profile in 2009

Average annual household income:	$93,900
Average spending in SF (per-person, per-day):	$244.33
First-time San Francisco visitors:	17.5%
Traveling with children:	8.7%
Gender:	Male = 53.5% Female = 46.5%
Average age:	46 years old
Average nights in SF hotels:	3.6 nights
Average total length of current trip:	4.6 nights
People per room:	1.77
Used Internet in planning trip:	53.9%
Rental car in San Francisco:	25.8%
Arrived by air:	80.2%
Top five feeder markets of hotel guests [by Designated Market Areas (DMAs)]	Los Angeles – v12.7% San Francisco-Oakland-San Jose – 7.7% Sacramento-Stockton-Modesto – 7% New York City – 5.7% Washington, DC – 3.5%
Primary reason for visit (% of all hotel guests):	39.7% Leisure 35.3% Convention 22.1% Transient business 2.9% Other

Source: http://www.sfcvb.org/research/, accessed April 28, 2010.

EXHIBIT 5 San Francisco Hospitality Statistics, 2008–2010

Avg. Daily Room Rate ($)			
	March 2008	**March 2009**	**March 2010**
Civic Center/Van Ness	$114.16	$ 92.45	$ 90.67
Financial District	230.21	189.47	181.93
Fisherman's Wharf	155.52	116.61	111.48
Union Square/Nob Hill/Moscone Center	200.00	176.57	161.99

Occupancy Rate (%)			
	March 2008	**March 2009**	**March 2010**
Civic Center/Van Ness	79.6%	69.4%	74.3%
Financial District	76.7	69.0	77.0
Fisherman's Wharf	84.0	74.5	86.0
Union Square/Nob Hill/Moscone Center	73.6	66.8	75.2

Sources: http://www.sfcvb.org/research/, accessed April 28, 2010. Hospitality statistics from PKF Consulting.

were furnished in a themed, stylish and/or aspirational manner. Boutique hotels typically were unique properties operated by individuals or companies with a small collection. Their successes in time prompted several multi-national hotel companies to try to establish their own brands in order to capture a market share. The most notable example was Starwood's W Hotels, ranging from large boutique hotels, such as the W Times Square in New York City, to the W "boutique resorts" in the Maldives, to true luxury boutique hotel collections, such as the Bulgari collection, SLS Hotels, Thompson Hotels, The Keating Hotel, and the O Hotel, among others.

17   *Strategy.* According to Chip Conley, JdV's founder and CEO,

> I went into hospitality because I enjoyed commercial real estate but hated the transactional part. If you get it right and your customer sees the product as an extension of themselves, you're refreshed the identity of the customers because they feel that by using the product they're becoming more of that aspirational self, according to Abraham Maslow's "Hierarchy of Needs."[1]

18   In 2007, Conley related JdV's branding strategy to *Travel Weekly*:

> We know California better than anybody else. We are the largest hotelier in the state. About 40 percent of our customers come from within the state. We went through a whole branding process, and what we heard from our customers was that they loved the fact that we create original hotels. We come up with a personality for the hotel by thinking of magazines. It is sort of like a good touchstone for personality. Each [hotel] is its own unique product. You can be geographically diverse, but that means you have to be product-line focused. Or you can be geographically focused and the product line diverse. Holiday Inn is geographically diverse and product-line focused. We are the opposite of Holiday Inn.[2]

19   Among JdV's most recently opened San Francisco Bay Area properties, the Tomo in Japantown was based on two Japanese pop culture magazines, *Lucky* (a popular women's magazine in Japan) and *Giant Robot* (a Japanese magazine devoted to anime and manga and technology-based art). Other properties included the Vitale (*Dwell + Real Simple*), Galleria Park (*Vanity Fair + BusinessWeek*), Kabuki (*Travel & Leisure*), and downtown Berkeley's Durant (*Sports Illustrated + Economist*). The Good Hotel concept was based on two magazines *Ode + Readymade,* and according to Pam, embodied five key words: "Hip, Happy, Humble, Conscious, and Inventive."

20   *Marketing.* JdV spent very little on marketing, preferring to rely mostly on word-of-mouth and social media promotion on the Internet to attract guests to its hotels. According to industry analysts, social media use among travelers continued to grow faster than the travel industry itself.

21   Unique monthly visitors to social travel Web sites such as TripAdvisor.com and Yelp!.com rose 34 percent between the first half of 2008 and the last half of 2009, to 15.9 million, representing year-over-year growth of more than 30 percent in the first half of 2009 and 45 percent in the second half of 2009. By comparison, U.S. travel gross bookings had declined 16 percent in 2009.[3]

---

[1]Speech to Association of Fundraising Professionals, Commonwealth Club, San Francisco, January 22, 2010. See also Chip Conley's 2007 book on the subject of applying Maslow's Hierarchy of Needs to business, *Peak: How Great Companies Get Their Mojo from Maslow*. San Francisco: Jossey-Bass.
[2]Milligan, M. (2007). Joie de Vivre finds inspiration for properties in pop culture. *Travel Weekly*, May 1, http://www.travelweekly.com/article3_ektid92480.aspx?terms=*joie+de+vivre*, accessed May 1, 2010
[3]PhoCusWright (2010) *Social Media in Travel: Traffic & Activity*, April.

EXHIBIT 6   LEED Certified Hotels in Northern California

LEED was an acronym for Leadership in Energy and Environmental Design. Buildings attained LEED certification from the U.S. Green Business Council by earning points in six categories: sustainable sites, water efficiency, energy and atmosphere, materials and resources, indoor environmental air quality, and innovation/design process. Based on the total number of points, a business would then receive a silver, gold, or platinum designation. Lower operation costs were typically associated with a LEED building: approximately 30 to 40 percent less energy use and 40 percent less water. Application for LEED certification of an existing property could cost upwards of $10,000, depending upon the size of the property, the number of rooms, and the level of certification sought. Most hotels tried for certification of new construction, which was much easier and potentially less costly to earn than from retrofitting an existing building.

As of March 2010, there were 12 LEED-certified hotels in America, of which four were in San Francisco [Hotel Carlton (Gold), Orchard, Orchard Garden, and W Hotel (Silver)], with more than 100 proposals in the works. See table below. Other reputable certifications by Green Seal and the Green Tourism Business Scheme in the United Kingdom have led to confusion, with no universal stamp of approval available.

Hotel Name and Location	LEED Rating System and Certification Level*	Building Type
SAN FRANCISCO		
Hotel Carlton	LEED EBOM **Gold**	Commercial
Orchard Garden Hotel	LEED NC Certified (v2.1)	Commercial
Orchard Hotel	LEED EB Certified (v2.0)	Commercial
W Hotel	LEED EBOM Silver	Commercial
OUTSIDE SAN FRANCISCO		
Gaia Napa Valley Hotel, American Canyon	LEED NC **Gold** (v2.1)	Commercial
Gaia Shasta Hotel, Anderson	LEED NC Silver (v2.1)	Commercial

*Rating Systems
LEED CI = LEED for Commercial Interiors
LEED CS = LEED for Core & Shell
LEED EB = LEED for Existing Buildings
LEED EBOM = LEED for Existing Buildings: Operations & Maintenance
LEED H = LEED for Homes
LEED NC = LEED for New Construction (and Major Renovations)
LEED ND = LEED for Neighborhood Development

LEED Certification Levels:
Certified, Silver, Gold, Platinum

Sources: http://www.mlandman.com/gbuildinginfo/leedbuildings.shtml (updated every 8 weeks, accessed 4/25/2010), and http://www.executivetravelmagazine.com/page/What+is+an+LEED+hotel+--+and+where+are+they%3F, accessed 4/25/2010.

22   *JdV's green programs.* In 2009, JdV's senior vice president of operations and green committee chair, Karlene Holloman, launched the company's Green Dreams portal, a dedicated page on its Web site (http://www.jdvhotels.com/greendreams/), where consumers could track the company's ongoing efforts to preserve the environment. Holloman said at the time:

> We want to be transparent and share the progress we've made and the efforts that continue as we strive to have all our hotels green-certified in the near term. In essence, our guests can be green cheerleaders, watching from the sidelines as more of our hotels reach their goals. We hope Joie de Vivre Green Dreams will become a useful tool and resource for our guests and any consumer evaluating green travel programs.[4]

[4]In Gale, D. (2009). The green guests are coming. *Hotels*, 43, January, p. 33.

23   To demonstrate its ongoing commitment to the environment, JdV's hotels had a goal of becoming certified green by their local city or county while using the San Francisco Green Business Certification standards, as these were the most stringent in the state. Some hotels, like Hotel Carlton, went beyond this goal by investing in solar power and achieving LEED certification, making it San Francisco's first hotel to be awarded a Leadership in Energy and Environmental Design (LEED) Gold certification. Exhibit 6 presents a definition of LEED and a listing of Northern California hotel properties carrying this certification as of April 2010.

24   *Financial performance.* In 2009, JdV's hotels, restaurants and spas generated an esti-mated $250 million in revenues, at properties ranging from the high-end Ventana Inn in Big Sur, California, with rooms at $700 per night, to Good Hotel, at $70 per night. JdV's room revenues dropped 18–20 percent in 2008–09, but appeared to be rising at about the same rate in the first quarter of 2010, according to Conley. JdV was privately held and did not release information regarding individual hotel revenues or profits. Nevertheless, Conley publicly stated that JdV had remained profitable throughout the downturn. According to an April 9, 2010 report in the *San Francisco Business Times,* Conley was actively seeking a strategic capital partner for JdV, a partner that could provide an investment of $150 million or more to expand the number of properties under JdV's management.

GOOD HOTEL

25   *Operations.* Formerly managed by JdV as a Best Western motel and an adjacent property, the Hotel Britton, the Good Hotel was refurbished in 2008 and reopened in November of that year. It was located at the corner of Mission and Seventh Streets—a gritty but slowly revitalizing corner of SoMa, as the area south of Market Street in San Francisco was known. In the immediate vicinity were single-room-occupancy housing, the futuristic-looking San Francisco Federal Building and a sleek plaza lined with cafés. Mass transit, including bus, light rail, cable car, and subway, was all within walking distance.

26   Good Hotel's lobby showcased many environmentally and socially conscious features including a bench made of recycled felt blankets, a vending machine branded by *Ready-Made* magazine that dispensed wallets fashioned out of FedEx envelopes ($15) and other goodies; wall art by developmentally disabled artists; and an orange phone that connected to a "philanthropy concierge" who arranged volunteer stints through One Brick, a local nonprofit. There was also a photo booth in the lobby ($3 for two prints); the hotel encour-aged visitors to add to the photo collage of guests prominently displayed in the lobby. The hotel's 38 motel-style rooms opened onto a courtyard parking lot, and the remaining 79 rooms were located in a five-story brick building.

27   In the rooms, which had the feel of a slightly upscale youth hostel, platform beds made of reclaimed pine were draped with fleece blankets made of recycled soda bottles. The pillows were made from old bedspreads salvaged from the previous hotel, a Best Western. Each room had a chandelier made of empty Voss water bottles, a recycling bin, a fold-down metal desk just big enough for a laptop and, overhead, a secret message from the hotel that glowed in the dark. Bathrooms featured a Japanese-style toilet-top sink: the gray water from the sink was collected in the toilet tank, saving water. Rooms provided free Wi-Fi, an iPod docking station and 26-inch flat-screen televisions. A spacious fitness center and outdoor heated pool were available across the street, at the recently renovated Best Western Americania. At checkout, guests donated $1.50 per day to One Brick (donations were auto-matically added to each room night stay), offset their carbon footprint through Carbonfund. org, or went on-line on one of the iMacs in the small business center with an option to give a $200 computer through One Laptop per Child.

28   Writing in the *San Francisco Chronicle* in December 2008, just after the hotel opened, John Flinn described his experience: "San Francisco's new Good Hotel doesn't miss many

tricks in its bid to be the greenest, do-goodingest, most politically correct hotel in America. But even Hummer drivers and spotted owl stranglers will appreciate the gratifyingly low room rates, which start at $67 a night."

29   *Leadership.* Pam received an MBA from the University of Texas at Austin in 2004. She initially was responsible for management of three of JdV's smallest boutique hotels. In 2006, she served as the General Manager of Special Projects relating to transitional hotels, a role in which she was responsible for assisting new JdV hotels and restaurants in acclimating to the culture, processes, and operational standards of the company.

30   In 2007 Pam was promoted to the General Manager role at Hotel Carlton, a certified green business by the city of San Francisco. In this role she became involved in many JdV-wide initiatives including the Safety Task Force, Green Committee and Advisory Panel. Pam led the process at Hotel Carlton to install solar panels that provided 9 percent of the energy used on property, and spearheaded the hotel's application process to become certified by the U.S. Green Building Council at the Gold Level for LEED-EB (existing building). As a member of the JdV Green Committee, Pam also contributed greatly to the new JdV Green Dreams Web site, which outlined and rated the company's environmental initiatives in four main focus areas: recycling and waste reduction, energy conservation, water conservation and pollution prevention.

31   While conducting a tour of Good Hotel in March 2010, Pam remarked that part of her job entailed educating staff members to ensure they were aware of JdV's safety and green programs and could explain them to guests and answer guests' questions. Nearly all guests at Good Hotel were leisure travelers or tourists on a budget. She said,

> Recently, we find travelers are more last minute when reserving their hotel accommodations. We see a lot of walk-in and Internet 'on the day of' reservations which drive occupancy. There is a fine line when setting room rates so we are competitively priced but not too low so we attract clientele that we do not want at our hotels. We've also had to focus a lot on service and safety training due to the fact that this neighborhood is still transitional. Our Green Dreams Web site and personal contact together provide the most effective means of attracting and keeping guests who are concerned about the environment. I was hoping that we could convince the owners of the Good Hotel to apply for LEED certification, like we did at the Hotel Carlton, but they were not in a position to immediately move forward on new investments when I arrived at the hotel.

32   *Financial performance.* Smith Travel Research collected monthly operating statistics for hotels. Statistics for the Hotel Britton (the previous property) and the Good Hotel from March 2008 to the end of March 2010 are shown in Exhibit 7, providing comparisons of occupancy rates, average daily rate, and RevPAR with five selected peer group competitors in its neighborhood, size, and class. Exhibit 8 provides monthly operating data for The Good Hotel from its opening in November 2008 to the end of March 2010.

EXHIBIT 7   Operating Statistics: Good Hotel vs. San Francisco Peer Group, March 2008–March 2010

March 31, 2008						
	Occupancy (%)		ADR ($)		RevPAR ($)	
	Hotel Britton*	Comp Set**	Hotel Britton*	Comp Set**	Hotel Britton*	Comp Set**
Current Month	45.4	67.9	79.38	83.68	36.07	56.79
Year-to-Date	39.3	59.2	73.61	76.76	28.92	45.46
Running 3 Month	39.3	59.2	73.61	76.76	28.92	45.46
Running 12 Month	63.3	69.0	80.23	86.02	50.82	59.38

(Continued)

EXHIBIT 7 *(Continued)*

March 2008 vs. 2007 Percent Change (%)

	Occupancy		ADR		RevPAR	
	Hotel Britton*	Comp Set**	Hotel Britton*	Comp Set**	Hotel Britton*	Comp Set**
Current Month	−18.5	−1.1	28.2	26.9	2.8	25.6
Year-to-Date	0.3	2.9	9.4	14.7	9.7	18.0
Running 3 Month	0.3	2.9	9.4	14.7	9.7	18.0
Running 12 Month	1.1	8.4	6.8	7.8	8.0	16.9

March 31, 2009*

	Occupancy (%)		ADR ($)		RevPAR ($)	
	Good Hotel	Comp Set**	Good Hotel	Comp Set**	Good Hotel	Comp Set**
Current Month	70.3	59.3	65.82	66.51	46.85	39.90
Year-to-Date	55.3	53.4	62.95	63.88	34.36	34.25
Running 3 Month	55.3	53.4	62.95	63.88	34.36	34.25
Running 12 Month	29.7	67.9	85.23	90.22	31.49	60.10

March 2009 vs. 2008 Percent Change (%)*

	Occupancy		ADR		RevPAR	
	Good Hotel	Comp Set**	Good Hotel	Comp Set**	Good Hotel	Comp Set**
Current Month	54.9	−12.7	−17.1	−20.5	29.9	−29.7
Year-to-Date	40.6	−9.8	−14.5	−16.8	18.8	−24.7
Running 3 Month	40.6	−9.8	−14.5	−16.8	18.8	−24.7
Running 12 Month	−53.1	−1.6	6.2	4.9	−38.0	1.2

March 31, 2010

	Occupancy (%)		ADR ($)		RevPAR ($)	
	Good Hotel	Comp Set**	Good Hotel	Comp Set**	Good Hotel	Comp Set**
Current Month	66.2	56.1	73.30	73.66	48.50	41.30
Year-to-Date	57.8	51.7	71.94	67.74	41.60	35.02
Running 3 Month	57.8	51.7	71.94	67.74	41.60	35.02
Running 12 Month	76.7	61.8	78.55	80.27	60.21	49.63

March 2010 vs. 2009 Percent Change (%)

	Occupancy		ADR		RevPAR	
	Good Hotel	Comp Set**	Good Hotel	Comp Set**	Good Hotel	Comp Set**
Current Month	−6.2	−5.7	10.2	9.7	3.4	3.4
Year-to-Date	4.4	−3.3	12.5	5.7	17.4	2.2
Running 3 Month	4.4	−3.3	12.5	5.7	17.4	2.2
Running 12 Month	61.3	−9.9	−8.5	−12.4	47.7	−21.1

Notes

*JdV's Hotel Britton was refurbished and reopened as the Good Hotel in November 2008.

**Comp set was defined as a peer group of competitive hotels selected by hotel management to benchmark the subject property's performance. The competitive set consisted of five San Francisco hotels near Market Street, with a total of 602 rooms, and included: Knights Inn Downtown San Francisco (68 rooms), The Opal Hotel (164 rooms), Hotel Metropolis (105 rooms), Renoir Hotel (130 rooms), and The Powell Hotel (135 rooms).

***Good Hotel was closed for a few months in 2008 during renovation. This closure affects the running 12 month averages from the 2009 reports.

Source: Smith Travel Research, March 2008 and March 2010.

EXHIBIT 8 Monthly Operating Statistics: Good Hotel, November 2008–March 2010

	2008	
	Nov	**Dec**
Number of Rooms	117	117
Occupancy (%)	26.87	55.53
RevPAR ($)	20.53	48.93
TOTAL REVENUE	$2,402	$5,725

	2009											
	Jan	**Feb**	**Mar**	**Apr**	**May**	**Jun**	**Jul**	**Aug**	**Sep**	**Oct**	**Nov**	**Dec**
Number of Rooms	117	117	117	117	117	117	117	117	117	117	117	117
Occupancy (%)	40.14	55.49	70.53	77.35	78.22	87.46	91.98	95.01	92.25	90.65	62.28	69.78
RevPAR ($)	26.57	32.50	46.91	56.29	68.65	68.72	77.01	79.63	80.02	83.33	43.48	39.06
TOTAL REVENUE	$3,109	$3,802	$5,488	$6,586	$8,033	$8,040	$9,011	$9,317	$9,362	$9,750	$5,087	$4,570

	2010		
	Jan	**Feb**	**Mar**
Number of Rooms	117	117	117
Occupancy (%)	56.96	49.54	66.17
RevPAR ($)	40.31	35.39	48.50
TOTAL REVENUE	$4,716	$4,141	$5,675

Source: Smith Travel Research, March 2010.

MAKING THE TRANSITION

33 As Pam went through her in-box, another message, marked "urgent," had been sent by the organizer of a Norwegian tour group requesting immediate cancellation of 100 rooms booked at The Good Hotel for the week of April 18th. Disruption of all air travel and indefinite closure of nearly all airports in Europe had forced cancellation of the tour, due to the huge plume of ash generated by the unexpected eruption of the Eyjafjallajökull volcano in Iceland. Loss of the Norwegian tour group's business meant that many of the 117 rooms would be empty unless last-minute or walk-in bookings showed up. This came at a time when the hotel industry in general was counting on a recovery from the long economic recession in 2008 and 2009, not to mention the normally soft travel bookings during the winter months.

34 In addition to the cancelled bookings, Pam wondered about how to inform and transition the current Good Hotel staff to the new ownership group. She pondered how her recommendation would impact their commitment to the original intent of Good Hotel.

35 Pam's number one task was how best to prepare Good Hotel and its current staff for the transition to new ownership in six weeks' time. She had several weeks remaining to work with her staff to complete a review of Good Hotel, containing her evaluation of the Good Hotel concept.

BIBLIOGRAPHY

———— (2010). Perspectives: green. *Hospitality Design, 32*(2), March, p. 44.

———— (2005). Joie de Vivre looks to grow by growing up. *Hotels, 39*(3), March, p. 18.

———— (2009). Chip Conley, *Marketing News, 43*(3), p. 62.

———— (2010). San Francisco Convention and Visitor's Bureau Web site, http://www.sfcvb.org/research/

Barrett, S. (2008). Operations key in green effort. *Hotel and Motel Management, 223*(5), p. 1.

Brooks, S. (2009). The green consumer, *Restaurant Business,* September, pp. 20–21.

Chan, W.W. (2009). Environmental measures for hotels' environmental management systems. *International Journal for Contemporary Hospitality Management, 21*(5), pp. 542–560.

Clark, R.A., Hartline, M.D., & Jones, K.C. (2009). Effects of leadership style on hotel employees' commitment to service quality. *Cornell Hospitality Quarterly, 50*(2), March, pp. 209–231.

Clausing, J. (2009). Preview 2010: The supply side: hotels. *Travel Weekly,* December 29, http://www.travelweekly.com/article3_ektid208196.aspx?terms=*clausing*&page=6, accessed May 1, 2010.

Clausing, J. (2010). Hotels struggle to harness the power of social media. *Travel Weekly,* April 21, http://www.travelweekly.com/article3_ektid213392.aspx?terms=*clausing*, accessed May 1, 2010.

Conley, C. (2007). *Peak: How Great Companies Get Their Mojo from Maslow.* San Francisco: Jossey-Bass.

Dahle, C. (2004). Weathering the perfect storm. *Fast Company,* 84, p. 29.

Duxbury, S. (2010, April 9). Joie de Vivre Hospitality seeking $150M, new investor. *San Francisco Business Times,* http://www.bizjournals.com/sanfrancisco/stories/2010/04/05/story4.html?b=1270440000%5E3130821&s=industry&i=travel, accessed May 1, 2010.

Flinn, J. (2008, December 18). The Good Hotel. *San Francisco Chronicle,* G-33. http://www.sfgate.com/cgi-bin/article.cgi?f=/c/a/2008/12/18/NS1R14IARP.DTL#ixzz0mmgSnBY8, accessed May 1, 2010.

Gale, D. (2009). The green guests are coming. *Hotels,* 43, January, p. 33.

Henning, M. (2008, March 11). Success comes from developed leadership. *Hotel & Motel Management, 223*(2), p. 12.

Milligan, M. (2007). Joie de Vivre finds inspiration for properties in pop culture. *Travel Weekly,* May 1, http://www.travelweekly.com/article3_ektid92480.aspx?terms=*joie+de+vivre*, accessed May 1, 2010

Mount, I. (2005). Open-book survival. *Fortune Small Business, 15*(5), June, p. 29.

PhoCusWright (2010). *Social Media in Travel: Traffic & Activity,* April.

Speer, J. (2009, June). Reaching the top of the pyramid. *Apparel Magazine,* p. 2.

Standard & Poor's, (2009). Current environment: lodging & gaming. *Standard & Poor's Industry Surveys,* November 19, pp. 1–23.

Weinstein, J. (2006). Brands vs. independents. *Hotels,* 40, July, p. 7.

Woodward, M. (2010). Average growth rate leads cities out of recession. *Hotel & Motel Management, 225*(2), February 1, p. 14.

Woodworth, R.M., and Walls, A. (2009). Thoughts while waiting for RevPar to grow. *Cornell Hospitality Quarterly, 50*(3), August, pp. 289–291.

Case 22

Google's Acquisition of Motorola Mobility: *Will the "Gamble" Pay Off?*

"With mobility continuing to take center stage, the combination with Motorola Mobility is an extremely important event in Google's evolution."[1]

—Larry Page, CEO, Google Inc.

"Google will likely promote the Google brand beyond search and maps on these mobile devices. Google will become the digital hub for consumers vying with Apple and even Amazon and Facebook for consumers' attention online."[2]

—Michael Gartenberg, Analyst, Gartner[3]

"Mergers of this size rarely work well (or smoothly), even when managed by companies that are very experienced at making huge acquisitions (which Google isn't). . . . And, eventually, it's not inconceivable that it will end up the same way the disastrous AOL Time Warner merger did: With a quiet spin-off after years' worth of value destruction."[4]

—Henry Boldget, Former Wall-Street Analyst, Editor-in-Chief, *Business Insider*

GOOGLE'S BIGGEST ACQUISITION EVER

1   On August 15, 2011, U.S.-based Internet search major Google Inc. (Google) announced that it had entered into a definitive agreement to acquire Motorola Mobility Holdings Inc.[5] (Motorola Mobility) for $12.5 billion[6] at $40 per share in cash. Motorola Mobility had been a dedicated partner[7] of Google's smartphone operating system, Android.

2   Analysts said that the acquisition, which heralded Google's entry into the hardware segment, would help Google become more competitive in the mobile computing market, and pave the way for it to become a major player in the market for Internet access through mobile devices. The Google–Motorola Mobility deal, according to Reuters, marked the assimilation of mobile hardware with the underlying software.

This case was written by Indu Perepu, IBS Hyderabad. It was compiled from published sources, and is intended to be used as a basis for class discussion rather than to illustrate either effective or ineffective handling of a management situation.

© 2013, IBS Center for Management Research. All rights reserved. ICMRindiainfo@icmrindia.org

[1]Matt Jarzemsky, Melodie Warner, Yun-Hee Kim, "2nd Update: Google Agrees to Buy Motorola Mobility for $12.5 Billion," http://online.wsj.com, August 15, 2011.

[2]Marguerite Reardon, "Google-Motorola Marriage Good for Consumers," http://news.cnet.com, August 15, 2011.

[3]Gartner is a U.S.-based information technology research and advisory company.

[4]Henry Boldget, "The Verdict: Google-Motorola Will Be a Colossal Disaster," www.businessinsider.com. August 16, 2011.

[5]Motorola Mobility, which was split from Motorola Inc. in January 2011, dealt with smartphones, mobile devices, digital entertainment devices, and video distribution systems, among others.

[6]The price of $40 per share was a premium of 63% to the closing price of Motorola Mobility on August 12, 2011. All $ figures are in US dollars throughout this case.

[7]Google provided Android free of cost and it was an open source operating system for smartphones and tablets. Several companies across the world used Android.

3   Forming a part of the acquisition was a cache of Motorola Mobility's patents in mobile communications and technologies. The patents were likely to help Google defend Android, which had been the target of several patent lawsuits. Google's competitors like Apple Inc. (Apple),[8] Microsoft Corporation (Microsoft),[9] and Oracle Corporation (Oracle)[10] filed several patent suits, not only against Android but also against Android partners like the Samsung Group (Samsung)[11] and HTC Corporation (HTC).[12]

4   Google announced that Motorola Mobility would operate as a separate entity and Android would remain open source software. On the acquisition, Larry Page (Page), Google CEO, said, "Motorola Mobility's total commitment to Android has created a natural fit for our two companies. Together, we will create amazing user experiences that supercharge the entire Android ecosystem for the benefit of consumers, partners, and developers."[13]

5   Though Page reaffirmed Google's stance on Android, analysts said that the acquisition could alienate Google's Android partners who might suspect Google of giving preferential treatment to Motorola Mobility. According to Nick Dillon, analyst from Ovum,[14] "Google will move from the position of partner to that of competitor to Android handset manufacturers, potentially placing significant strain on the Android ecosystem."[15]

6   The acquisition received a mixed response. While a few analysts said it would prove beneficial to Google in many ways, others were not so sure. "The best way to fight a big portfolio of patents is to have your own big portfolio of patents. That appears to be what Google is doing here, arming itself with patents to be able to defend itself in this fast-growing market,"[16] said Herbert Hovenkamp, a law professor at the University of Iowa. On the other hand, Standard & Poor's (S&P)[17] downgraded Google, saying the acquisition posed a risk to the company. Equity analyst Scott Kessler from S&P said that even after acquiring Motorola Mobility, patent challenges remained. He added, "We also believe the purchase would negatively impact Google's growth, margins and balance sheet."[18]

ABOUT GOOGLE

7   Google was founded by Page and Sergey Brin (Brin), students at Stanford University, California, U.S. Its first version was released on the Web site of Stanford University in August 1996. Google opened its first office in Menlo Park, California, in September 1998. The beta version of Google.com handled around 10,000 queries a day. In December 1998, Google was named "One of the top 100 Web sites and search engines for 1998" by *PC Magazine*.

---

[8]U.S.-based Apple is involved in designing and marketing consumer electronics, computer software, and personal computers. Some of its products are the Macintosh computers, the iPod digital music player, the iPhone mobile phone, and the iPad tablet computer.

[9]U.S.-based Microsoft manufactures and licenses products and services related to computing. It is known for its computer operating systems MS-DOS and Windows.

[10]Oracle is a computer technology company that develops hardware systems and enterprise software products.

[11]Samsung is a South Korea–based multinational group. It is involved in engineering, electronics, retail, insurance, entertainment, etc.

[12]Taiwan-based HTC is a manufacturer of smartphones and tablets.

[13]"Google to Acquire Motorola Mobility," Press release from Google.

[14]Ovum provides advice to technology, telecom, and other businesses.

[15]"Google's Boldest Move Yet—Buying Motorola," *The New Zealand Herald*, August 16, 2011.

[16]Michael J. De La Merced, "In the World of Wireless, It's All About Patents," http://dealbook.nytimes.com, August 15, 2011.

[17]S&P, a division of McGraw-Hill companies, is a financial services company based in the U.S.

[18]"S&P Downgrades Google over Its Bid for Motorola," *Toronto Star*, August 17, 2011.

8   By 2000, Google had 60 employees and by June 2000, the company had an index of one billion pages, which made it the largest search engine in the world. Google continued generating revenues through clients who were using the company's search technology and through a keyword targeted advertising program. It also introduced a self-service advertisement program called AdWords.[19] By the end of the year, Google was handling more than 100 million search queries per day.

9   In 2001, Google made its first acquisition, a usenet discussion service. This was later launched as Google Groups. In the same year, Eric Schmidt[20] became the CEO of Google. In 2002, Google News was launched. AdSense[21] was launched in 2003. In 2004, the search index included 6 billion items. Google went public in 2004.

10   Over the years, Google introduced several products that included Orkut, desktop search Google Scholar (2004); iGoogle, Mobile websearch, Google Earth, Google Talk (2005); Google calendar, Google Trends, Picasa web albums, (2006); AdSense for mobiles, (2007); a new version of Google Earth, Google Suggest, the Chrome browser (2008), Google Latitude, (2009), Google Buzz, Google TV, Place Search, (2010), Google Art Project, Google+, Google One Pass, and Google Wallet (2011). Over the years, Google acquired several companies. (Refer to Table 1 for the number of Google's acquisitions per year. Refer to Exhibit 1 for some of the prominent acquisitions.)

11   One of the companies that Google acquired was Android Inc. in 2005. Android Inc. was founded in 2003 and was involved in making software for mobile phones. Andy Rubin[22] (Rubin) and other founders of Android Inc. joined Google, along with several talented engineers from the company. For the next two years, the team developed a mobile device platform, which was named Android.

12   In November 2007, Google announced the Open Handset Alliance with Android, an operating system for smartphones, as its flagship software. (Refer to Table 2 for more about Open Handset Alliance.)

TABLE 1   **Google—No. of Acquisitions per Year**

Year	Number of Acquisitions
2001	2
2003	6
2004	5
2005	11
2006	10
2007	16
2008	2
2009	6
2010	26
2011	18

Compiled from various sources

[19]Adwords placed ads on the right side of the search screen of Google according to the users' search terms.
[20]Google in order to regain the "soul and passion of a startup" revamped its leadership structure and abandoned triumvirate leadership and Page became the CEO in January 2011.
[21]AdSense delivers Google AdWords to individuals' Web sites.
[22]Rubin was the co-founder of Danger Inc., which was acquired by Microsoft in 2008.

EXHIBIT 1 Google—Major Acquisitions

Date	Company	Acquired for US($)	Business
April 2003	Applied Semantics	102 million	Online advertising
June 2004	Picasa	Undisclosed	Image organizer
August 2005	Android	Undisclosed	Mobile software
October 2006	YouTube	1.65 billion	Video sharing
April 2007	DoubleClick	3.1 billion	Online advertising
June 2007	Postini	625 million	Communications security
June 2007	FeedBurner	100 million	Web feed
July 2007	GrandCentral	45 million	VoIP
November 2009	AdMob	750 million	Mobile advertising
February 2010	On2 Video Compression	113.9 million	Video compression tech
June 2010	ITA	700 million	Flight information software
August 2010	Like.com	100 million	Visual search engine
August 2010	Slide	Undisclosed	Social apps
June 2010	AdMeld	400 million	Advertising optimization

Compiled from various sources

TABLE 2 Open Handset Alliance

The Open Handset Alliance, an industry alliance, had more than 84 companies as members. The purpose of this alliance was to share and mold ideas in the open, creating and maintaining standards together. The alliance was established in 2007.

Some of the prominent members in the alliance: handset manufacturers like Motorola, Samsung, HTC, LG; operators like NTT DoCoMo, T- Mobile, Telefonica, Sprint Nextel, China Mobile, KDDI, Telecom Italia; chip suppliers like Intel, TI, Broadcom, Marvell, Qualcomm; and content and software providers including Google, eBay, PacketVideo, and Nuance Communications.

Android was the flagship software of this alliance. The first commercially available phone from this alliance was the T-Mobile G1 also known as HTC Dream.

Compiled from various sources

13   The launch of Android as an open source system brought to the fore mobile software that was customizable. It meant that any program could be removed and replaced with a better program or software from another user. The aim of Google was to make Web-browsing using the mobile phone easy and fast, through Android. (Refer to Exhibit 2 for more about Android.)

14   After the release of the iPhone in mid-2007, the demand for software for mobile phones grew rapidly, and handset makers turned to Android. One of the factors that attracted handset makers to Android was that they could concentrate on designing their phones without bothering too much about the software code. Using Android also reduced the cost of the handsets, as software accounted for 20 percent of the cost. By the end of 2007, negotiations for the first Android phone began. The first Android phone was launched in 2008 by HTC.

EXHIBIT 2 **About Android**

At the time Google launched Android, Symbian was the leading mobile operating system. Symbian was owned by a group of telecom companies and was headed by Nokia. But the market for the software was limited as there were very few phones that supported this operating system and only 10 percent of the mobile phones in 2008 were smartphones.

Android was built on Linux kernel 2.6. Google offered this software free, helping the handset makers reduce the time to market new devices. Google also made Android fully open and customizable. Through this feature, mobile phone makers could make the changes and additions they deemed necessary to bring out different and distinct products. Android also supported third-party apps.

After the formation of the Open Handset Alliance on November 5, 2007, the Android Beta Software Developer's Kit (SDK) was launched on November 12, 2007.

The first Android device, the HTC Dream (G1), was released on September 23, 2008. The smartphone used Version 1.0 of Android, which had features like integration with Google's services, Web browser, HTML and XHTML pages, multiple page show, app downloads and updates, multitasking, instant messaging, Wi-Fi, and Bluetooth. The first update was released in February 2009 for the G1 phone.

Android 1.5 was based on Linux kernel 2.6.27 and was released in April 2009. The additional features of this version included faster camera start-up and image capture, faster acquisition of the GPS location, on-screen keyboard, and the ability to directly upload videos to YouTube and Picasa.

Version 1.6 was released in September 2009. Some of its prominent features were the quick search box, voice search, integrated camera, camcorder, toggle between still and video capture, battery usage indicator, CDMA support, and multilingual text-to-speech.

Android 2.0 was released in October 2009. The most prominent features in this version were multiple e-mail accounts, contact syncronization, Bluetooth 2.1, browser user interface for HTML5, and new calendar features. By then, Android's market share in the smartphone operating system market was 3.90 percent.

Version 2.2 based on kernel 2.6.32 was released in May 2010. It had features like new tips widget for homescreen, improved exchange support, multiple keyboard languages, Adobe Flash, etc. After this, Android's market share increased to 17.70 percent.

Version 2.3 was released in December 2010, with features like User interface refinements, a new keyboard for faster text input, one touch word selection, near field communications, and internet calling.

Version 3.0 for tablets was based on Linux kernel 2.6.36 and was released in February 2011. The Software Developmment Kit of this version was released in May 2011. This version was specifically optimized for tablets and devices with a large screen size. It had refined multitasking capabilities along with rich notifications, home screen customization, Bluetooth tethering, and built-in support for media / picture transfer protocol.

(Continued)

EXHIBIT 2 *(Continued)*

Distribution of Android Versions (July 2011)	
Android 1.5	1.40%
Android 1.6	2.20 %
Android 2.1	17.5 %
Android 2.2	59.4 %
Android 2.3	1.0%
Android 2.3.3	17.6 %
Android 2.3.4	0.5%
Android 3.0	0.4%

Each of the versions of Android was named after desserts. Version 1.5 was called Cupcake, 1.6 was Donut, Version 2.0 was Éclair, 2.2 was Froyo, 2.3 Gingerbread, and Version 3.0 was called Honeycomb. The next version of the software was called Ice Cream Sandwich.

Some of the prominent Android phones were Motorola Droid, T-Mobile MyTouch 3G, HTC Hero, Samsung Moment, Motorola Cliq, HTC Nexus I, Motorola Devour, Motorola Backflip, LG Ally, HTC EVO 4G, HTC Aria, Motorola i1, Samsung Vibrant, Sanyo Zip, Dell Aero, Huawei Ascend, LG Optimus, HTC Thunderbolt, Kyocera Echo, Casio G'zOne Commando, and Pantech Crossover.

Compiled from various sources

ABOUT MOTOROLA MOBILITY

15   Motorola Mobility was formed when the erstwhile Motorola Inc. (Motorola) was split into two companies in January 2011. The other company was Motorola Solutions Inc.

16   Motorola began as Galvin Manufacturing Corporation in 1928. The company introduced an automobile radio in 1930, which was named Motorola. Subsequently the company adopted the name. Motorola went on to introduce products like car radios; portable two-way radios, which were used extensively during the Second World War; televisions; vehicular two-way radios; pocket radios; pagers; DynaTAC, the world's first commercial handheld cellular phone; and the MicroTAC personal cellular phone, among others.

17   Though Motorola was a leading player in the global cellular market during the early 1990s, it could not maintain its position, as it continued to use analog technology while its competitors had moved on to digital technology. Motorola also failed to introduce phones in the developing countries where there was a high demand for low-cost cellular phones. In 1999, Nokia became the top mobile phone manufacturer in the world and Motorola's downward slide continued in the early 2000s.

18   Motorola's fortunes took a turn for the better in 2004 after the introduction of the Razr V3 clamshell phone under the leadership of Edward Zander (Zander). The phone was sleek, attractive, and had several advanced features like a camera, MP3 player, etc. The product was highly successful, and Motorola sold one million phones within a span of six months. The company soon followed this up with the Razr in several colors and a better version of the Razr called the V3i.

19   While the competitors caught up with Motorola and introduced phones with advanced features, most of the phones that Motorola launched after the Razr failed to emulate its success. In the first quarter of 2007, Motorola issued a profit warning.

20   Meanwhile, Carl Icahn (Icahn), a private equity investor and corporate raider, acquired several shares of Motorola. By early 2007, he had 1.39 percent of the shares. Icahn was vocal in his criticism of Zander's leadership. Motorola's fortunes continued to plunge and in November 2007, Zander left the company and Greg Brown (Brown) became CEO.

21   In March 2008, Brown announced that the board had decided to split Motorola into two publicly traded companies. Before the announcement, in a period of 18 months, the market value of Motorola had dropped by more than $37 billion. Analysts were of the view that the split was due to a demand from Icahn who by then held 6.4 percent of the company's shares and had two representatives on the company's board. On several occasions, Icahn said that that abysmal performance of the mobile handset business was having an adverse impact on Motorola's other businesses and stock price.

22   In the first quarter of 2010, Motorola announced that it was planning to finalize the split by early 2011. The company decided to merge its mobile devices and cable-oriented home business into one unit, while the other part would consist of wireless networking and enterprise units. In July 2010, the company filed an initial Form 10 Registration statement with the U.S. Securities and Exchange Commission. By August 2010, Icahn's share in the company was more than 10 percent.

23   Finally, on January 04, 2011, Motorola was split into two companies—Motorola Solutions that produced barcode scanners, RFID products, and professional and commercial two-way radios and was involved in providing communication solutions for government and corporate customers, and Motorola Mobility, which provided mobile devices, smartphones, tablets, and mobile computing devices. It was also an OEM manufacturer for cable TV boxes, set-top boxes, and Internet-connected devices. Motorola Mobility was headed by Sanjay Jha (Jha), who was co-CEO of Motorola.

24   Shareholders of Motorola were given shares in both Motorola Mobility and Motorola Solutions, in a 1-for-7 reverse stock split for Motorola Solutions and 1-for-8 reverse stock split for Motorola Mobility.[23] On January 4, 2011, Motorola Mobility started trading on the New York Stock Exchange with the ticker symbol MMI.

25   Even after the company was split, Motorola Mobility faced several problems. Motorola's Android smartphone, Droid, released in 2009, was successful initially, but failed to maintain the momentum. Motorola's share in the smartphone market, which had been at 15 percent in the second quarter of 2010, dipped to 12 percent by the second quarter of 2011. During the same period, its share in the Android market slipped to 22 percent from 44 percent, showing that Motorola was unable to capitalize on the growth of Android, which was the operating system for 52 percent of the smartphones sold in the U.S. in the second quarter of 2011.

26   This was attributed to product delays of the 4G LTE phone and overpricing of the Xoom tablet and the Atrix 4G smartphone. The Atrix 4G[24] for AT&T was priced very high due to its laptop dock accessory.[25] Similarly, the Xoom tablet was also priced at $799.[26] Though the Droid Bionic was launched with fanfare, Motorola Mobility could not deliver the product on time to Verizon Wireless. This provided competitors the leeway to launch 4G

---

[23]For example, if a person had 700 shares of Motorola, he got 100 shares of Motorola Solutions and 87 shares of Motorola Mobility.

[24]The 4G LTE phone, the Xoom tablet, the Atrix 4G Smartphone, the Atrix 4G, and the Droid Bionic are all products from Motorola Mobility.

[25]$599 for phone and dock bundled together.

[26]In the quarter ending June 2011, Xoom sold 440,000 tablets against 9.25 million iPads.

products. All these factors had an adverse impact on the company, which reported a loss of $56 million for the quarter ending June 2011.

THE BATTLE FOR SUPREMACY

27   After the launch of Android, Google released its new versions rapidly, adding several new features. As Google licensed the Android operating system free of cost, it found widespread adoption by handset manufacturers like Motorola, LG Electronics (LG),[27] and Samsung, apart from HTC. Google's flagship smartphone, the Nexus One, was released in January 2010. The Nexus S[28] was developed in association with Samsung and launched in December 2010.

28   Android phones helped the handset manufacturers secure a formidable position in the smartphone market, and they also announced plans to increase the output of Android-based devices. As of 2011, Android phones were available at various price points and with different features, which helped in their proliferation. While the companies benefited from open source software, Google benefited from revenue through mobile advertising and sale of mobile applications.

29   By mid-2011, there were more than 150 million Android devices. Every day around 550,000 of these devices were sold across the world. Forming a part of the Android family were 39 manufacturers and 231 carriers from 123 countries. By the second quarter of 2011, Android was the leading mobile-phone operating system with a global market share of 43 percent, according to Gartner. Over 46.8 million Android handsets were sold during the quarter, as against 19.6 million handsets with Apple's iOS.[29] Though the Android operating system was found in millions of mobile phones, it held very few patents. (Refer to Exhibit 3 for different smartphone operating systems.)

30   The growing popularity of Android attracted several lawsuits from competitors, whose intention appeared to be to impede its growth. Oracle filed a patent infringement suit against Google in 2010 alleging the use of Java-based technologies in Android. Apple targeted Android partners like Samsung and HTC for violating patents of the iOS. (Refer to Exhibit 4 for more about patent lawsuits in the mobile communications arena.)

31   Similarly, Microsoft filed a patent infringement lawsuit against Barnes & Noble Nook,[30] which used Android, and also filed a suit against Motorola's use of Android. Microsoft collected a fee of $5 for every Android phone manufactured by HTC, due to patent settlement, and was planning to obtain royalties of $15 on every Android phone sold by Samsung. Such royalties were likely to force the manufacturers to opt for alternative operating systems like Windows Phone.

32   In order to equip itself with more patents, in early 2011, Google intended to acquire around 6,000 patents and patent applications in areas like 4G, wireless, data networking, etc. that belonged to Nortel Network Corp. (Nortel),[31] which had filed for bankruptcy. For these patents, Google offered $900 million in April 2011. Later, in July 2011, its bid was increased to $3.14 billion. However, the patents were acquired by a consortium led by Apple[32] for $4.5 billion in July 2011.

---

[27]LG is a South Korea–based consumer electronics company.

[28]Nexus S used the Gingerbread version of Android.

[29]The iOS is Apple's operating system for smartphones.

[30]Barnes & Noble Nook is an electronic book reader developed by the largest book retailer in the U.S., Barnes & Noble.

[31]Nortel was a Canada-based telecom equipment manufacturer. It filed for protection from creditors in 2009.

[32]Other members in the consortium were EMC, Ericsson, Research in Motion, Microsoft, and Sony.

EXHIBIT 3   Mobile Operating Systems

The mobile operating system is the software platform like Windows or Linux on which other programs run. The mobile operating system determines the features of the smartphone like touchpad, e-mail, WAP, text messaging, etc. The apps used in the phone need to be compatible with the operating system. The mobile operating system is either proprietary or open. A proprietary system is owned by the company and its details are not divulged.

Some of the leading mobile operating systems apart from Android are:

Bada
Bada is a mobile operating system from Samsung Electronics that is closed source and proprietary. It was launched in June 2010. Samsung Wave was the first phone to use this operating system. Some of its features are multipoint-touch, 3D graphics, and application downloads and installation.

BlackBerry OS
The BlackBerry OS owned by RIM is a proprietary closed source software and is used in BlackBerry devices. It provides synchronization with Microsoft Exchange, Lotus Domino, Novell GroupWise e-mail, and other business software.

iOS
The iOS developed for the iPhone by Apple is a closed source proprietary software. This is used in a wide range of Apple's products like the iPod Touch, the iPad, and Apple TV. The software is available only on devices manufactured by Apple.

Symbian
Symbian is a public license software from Symbian Foundation, maintained by Nokia. In many countries where Nokia is the market leader Symbian is highly popular. The software is available under an alternative, open, and direct model and works with selected handset makers and development collaborators. Handset makers like BenQ, Fujitsu, LG, Mitsubishi, Motorola, Nokia, Samsung, and Sony Ericsson use this operating system.

webOS
This operating system was developed by Palm. The software is free and open source except for a few closed source modules. It was acquired by HP, which uses it in HP devices like smartphones and touchpads. In August 2011, HP announced that it was planning to discontinue webOS devices but would continue with the webOS software.

Windows Phone 7
This mobile operating system from Microsoft is a closed source proprietary software. The software integrates with Microsoft devices like Zune music player, Xbox, Bing, etc, and also with Facebook and Google accounts.

Compiled from various sources

33   After Google lost the bid, it complained that the companies that had acquired the patents were planning to block the users of the Android platform from launching new products. According to David Drummond, chief legal officer, Google, "A smartphone might involve as many as 250,000 (largely questionable) patent claims, and our competitors want to impose a 'tax' for these dubious patents that makes Android devices more expensive for consumers. They want to make it harder for manufacturers to sell Android devices. Instead of competing by building new features or devices, they are fighting through litigation."[33]

[33]Marguerite Reardon, "Google Just Bought Itself Patent Protection," http://news.cnet.in, August 15, 2011.

EXHIBIT 4   Patent Lawsuits

With smartphones growing increasingly more complex, they tend to depend on a large number of patented technologies. For example, 3G wireless communication capabilities need around 8,000 patents held by 41 companies. Device makers incur almost 10 percent of their costs on patents. Companies that own these patents also benefit immensely. For example, Qualcomm collects $1 billion per quarter in patents. Other patent holders are also trudging a similar path to get benefits from the patents that they hold. Patent holders are also using the patents to restrain competition.

In the mobile industry, major players hold several patents. Apple's patents are in the areas of computing, applications, and touch technologies. Nokia has several patents in communication capabilities. Micorosoft's patents are in the area of mobile device software.

From 2007, the number of patent infringement disputes among handset manufacturers and application developers increased manifold. With the market for smartphones and tablets growing exponentially, the patent-related disputes also witnessed an upsurge. Apple was one of the first companies to start patent lawsuits. It sued companies like HTC, Samsung, Nokia, and Motorola, among others, on IP related issues, product designs, etc. In 2009, Nokia demanded royalties for ten patents that Apple had infringed. In 2010, Nokia launched another patent infringement suit against Apple, alleging that the iPhone and the iPad had violated five patents of Nokia. In June 2011, Nokia and Apple entered into a patent licensing agreement. Through the agreement, Apple agreed to pay Nokia royalties along with a one-time payment. After the agreement, all patent litigation between the companies was put to an end.

Not only major companies, but also small companies which held groundbreaking patents are suing large companies demanding their share in the pie. These include MobileMedia ideas, which acquired patents from different companies and filed lawsuits against Apple, RIM and HTC. Another such company is Spansion, which makes flash memory chips. The company filed a suit against Apple.

Persistent patent battles could lead to higher costs of handsets, as manufacturers have to pay patent holders higher royalties.

Compiled from various sources

34   Meanwhile, Motorola Mobility faced different problems. Most of the Droid phones in the U.S. were sold through Verizon. iPhones were sold exclusively through AT&T due to which Verizon banked on Motorola to have a presence in the smartphone arena. With Verizon launching the iPhone in February 2011, Motorola Mobility's market in the U.S. was adversely affected. The company also faced pressure from irate shareholders. In July 2011, Icahn, after noting the amount Nortel's patents fetched, wanted Motorola Mobility to explore opportunities to put its portfolio of patents to the best use. Motorola Mobility had 17,000 patents and over 7,500 patent applications pending. The patents covered technologies in the areas of 2G, 3G, 4G, H.264, MPEG-4, 802.11, open mobile alliance, and near field communications.

35   Initial discussions with different companies only concentrated on licensing the patents held by Motorola Mobility. Google entered the picture with the intention of licensing or buying Motorola's patents. Later, however, it made a bid to take over the company. Finally, the board of Motorola Mobility decided to sell the company to Google.

GOOGLE ACQUIRES MOTOROLA MOBILITY

36　On August 15, 2011, Google announced its acquisition of Motorola Mobility. After the acquisition, the shares of Motorola Mobility soared by over 60 percent to $39.24, while Google's shares were down 3.2 percent to $546.50.

37　Through the acquisition, Google got hold of a number of patents. This was four times the patents owned by Nortel. Analysts said that there was a huge demand for intellectual property, especially in mobile devices, and Google would benefit immensely from the acquisition. According to Alkesh Shah, analyst, Evercore Partners,[34] "The big thing it plugs for Google is: Google's patent portfolio is only a few thousand, and they have been the target of a significant amount of patent litigation. Motorola's patent portfolio provides a very strong defense against all this litigation."[35]

38　The deal was expected to help Android maintain its lead in the mobile software market, irrespective of patent lawsuits. According to Jim Tierney, chief investment officer, W.P. stewart Advisors,[36] "No matter how you think about this, you have to look at it through the spectrum of the Android ecosystem under incredible attack from an IP (intellectual property) perspective. And this is Google going out and trying to fix that. The biggest implication here is that Google wants Android to be one of the dominant phone operating systems for years to come."[37]

39　Industry experts observed that the acquisition marked Google's entry into hardware. Apart from patents, Motorola also had a strong manufacturing platform, which provided Google with the expertise to manufacture technologically superior Android devices by integrating its software capabilities with Motorola's hardware competence. This would give Google control over the platform and the software that was used for search. A Google phone with the Android system would bring forth a vertically integrated end-to-end system, through which the success of the iPhone[38] and the iPad[39] could be emulated, opined the observers.

40　Motorola Mobility was the second largest supplier of cable boxes in the world. Through the acquisition, Google got access to set-top boxes, using which it could penetrate the market for Internet-enabled television.[40] Also forming part of the acquisition was attractive Televation, which was used to stream live broadcast TV content to a wide range of devices.

41　According to observers, Google's foray into hardware would help the company dominate the mobile advertising market too. More online advertising was expected to shift to mobile platforms, as computing was going mobile through smartphones and tablets. According to Roger Entner, founder of Recon Analytics,[41] "Advertising works better as the advertising engine knows more about you. If that device is always with you, it knows where you go, it knows what pictures you take. It can combine the search you do with the location you are. That makes advertising so much more powerful." [42]

---

[34]Evercore Partners is a U.S.-based investment bank.
[35]Matt Jarzemsky, Melodie Warner, Yun-Hee Kim, "Google to Acquire Motorola Mobility for $12.5 Billion," http://online.wsh.com, August 15, 2011.
[36]W.P. Stewart is a global investment advisor that provides equity portfolio management services.
[37]"How Google's Bold Bet on Motorola Affects Other Android Partners," *International Business Times*, August 16, 2011.
[38]The iPhone is an Internet and multimedia-enabled smartphone from Apple.
[39]The iPad is a line of tablet computers from Apple.
[40]The market for Internet-enabled televisions and set-top boxes was expected to grow to 295.9 million units by 2015 from 86.9 million units in 2011.
[41]U.S.-based Recon Analytics offers independent research and insights for the U.S. telecom market.
[42]Brent Land, Lucas Shaw, "Google-Motorola Deal Points to Future Going Mobile," www.reuters.com, August 16, 2001.

EXHIBIT 5 Motorola Mobility Financial Statements

In US$ Millions	(Year Ending December 31)		
	2010	2009	2008
Net Revenues	11,460	11,050	17,099
Cost of Sales	8,495	8,897	14,280
Gross Margin	2,965	2,153	2,819
Selling, general, and administrative expenses	1,592	1,486	2,218
Research and development expenditure	1,479	1,591	2,358
Other charges (income)	(182)	287	283
Operating earnings (loss)	76	(1,211)	(2,040)
Other income (expense)			
Interest income (expense), net	(52)	(41)	28
Gains (losses) on sales of investments and Business, net Other, net	(28)	(49)	64
Total other income (expense)	(80)	(124)	103
Loss before income taxes	(4)	(1,335)	(1,937)
Income tax expense	75		1,035
Net loss	(79)	(1,335)	(2,972)
Less: Earnings (loss) attributable to Non-controlling interests	7	7	(3)
Net loss attributable to Motorola Moblity	(86)	(1,342)	(2,969)

Source: Motorola, Annual Report, 2010.

42   The acquisition was expected to give Google legal, accounting, and tax benefits, mainly due to the losses Motorola Mobility had recorded for a few years prior to the acquisition. The tax deductions would be to the tune of $700 million a year up to 2019, according to tax experts. Due to the net operating loss reported by Motorola Mobility in the U.S., Google was able to reduce its taxes by $1 billion immediately after the acquisition. The overseas component in the losses posted by Motorola Mobility would benefit Google to the tune of $700 million. (Refer to Exhibit 5 for Motorola Mobility's financials; refer to Exhibit 6 for Google's financials.)

43   While Google was expected to benefit in several ways through the acquisition, the future of Motorola Mobility remained unclear. Though Google promised to run Motorola Mobility as a separate organization, analysts were not so sure this would happen. According to Roger Entner, "While Google says, 'Oh we'll operate this as a stand-alone operation,' it didn't buy Motorola to leave it completely alone."[43]

44   As Motorola Mobility was to be run as a separate company, it needed to meet the demands of a young company like Google. Zander, who had been chairman and CEO of Motorola between 2004 and 2007, said that Motorola needed to perform better in the company of Google. He said, "They are going to have to stand alone and win in the marketplace, or Google will shut them down and just focus on the patents."[44]

[43]Brent Land, Lucas Shaw, "Google-Motorola Deal Points to Future Going Mobile," www.reuters.com, August 16, 2001.
[44]Shayndi Raise, Jack Nicas, Amir Efrati, Don Clark, "When Google Met Moto," http://online.wsj.com, August 17, 2011.

EXHIBIT 6   Google Statement of Income

In US$ Millions	(Year Ending December 31)		
	2010	2009	2008
Revenues	29,321	23,651	21,796
Cost of revenues	10,417	8,844	8,622
Research & development	3,762	2,843	2,793
Sales and marketing	2,799	1,984	1,946
General and administrative	1,962	1,668	1,803
Total costs and expenses	**18,940**	**15,339**	**15,164**
Income from operations	10,381	8,312	6,632
Impairment of equity investments	0	0	(1,095)
Interest and other income	415	69	316
Income before income taxes	10,796	8,381	5,853
Provision for income taxes	2,291	1,861	1,626
Net Income	**8,505**	**6,520**	**4,227**

Source: Annual Report, Google, 2010

THE FUTURE OF ANDROID PARTNERS

45   Google's announcement that it planned to run Motorola Mobility as a separate business, which would continue to be a licensee of Android, was welcomed by the Android partners. JK Shin, president of Samsung Mobile's global operations, said, "We welcome today's news, which demonstrates Google's deep commitment to defending Android, its partners, and the ecosystem."[45] Similar views were echoed by LG and HTC.

46   Android partners like Samsung and HTC were expected to benefit from the deal as Motorola Mobility's patents would help them fight lawsuits. Analysts were of the view that the acquisition would prove beneficial to other Android partners as well, as the patents that came through the acquisition would protect these companies from litigation in the future.

47   But some analysts were of the view that Google would turn from collaborator to competitor for the Android partners. However, Rubin said, "Our vision for Android is unchanged, and Google remains firmly committed to Android as an open platform and a vibrant open source community. We will continue to work with all of our valued Android partners to develop and distribute innovative Android-powered devices."[46] He also reiterated that he had interacted with the top five Android licensees and they had extended their support to the deal.

48   The partners might not buy Google's assurances, opined industry observers. They alleged that the Android partners could view the Google-Motorola relationship with suspicion, wondering if Motorola was getting any special treatment. According to Steve Kovach from Business Insider,[47] "It's very likely Google is going to be working directly with

[45]Jake Smith, "Samsung, Nokia, HTC, and More Reactions over the Motorola Acquisition," http://www.9to5google.com, August 15, 2011.

[46]Matt Jarzemsky, Melodie Warner, Yun-Hee Kim, "Google to Acquire Motorola Mobility for $12.5 Billion," http://online.wsj.com, August 15, 2011.

[47]Business Insider is a U.S.-based business and entertainment website.

Motorola. Motorola is now likely to get the Nexus devices first, the Nexus tablet, whenever a new Google software update comes out, they'll get it first . . . Why would they [Google] give it to any other company? They own Motorola now. It hurts their bottom line."[48]

49   Industry and competitors, however, saw the acquisition in a different light. Nokia said that the acquisition would act as a catalyst for the Windows Phone ecosystem. Nokia's chief executive, Stephen Elop, sounded a warning to the Android partners. He said, "If I happened to be someone who was an Android manufacturer or an operator, or anyone with a stake in that environment, I would be picking up my phone and calling certain executives at Google and say 'I see signs of danger ahead.'"[49]

IS THE ACQUISITION A GAMBLE?

50   The acquisition did not give Google the much needed hold in the tablet market, as all the Android partners put together could not surpass the iPad's share. In the second quarter of 2011, the iPad's market share was 68.3 percent as against 65.7 percent during the previous quarter. The share of Android tablets fell to 26.8 percent from 34 percent during the same period. Google needed a presence in the arena as the market for tablets was projected to grow to 63.19 million units for 2011 from 19.7 million units in 2010.

51   In spite of assurances Google was providing, analysts opined that it was gambling with its Android partners, who had helped it become the largest mobile devices operating system. Though it was a fact that Motorola's patents could shield the partners from lawsuits, analysts warned that if Google gave Motorola Mobility preferential access to the latest Android developments, the other partners could lose their enthusiasm for continuing with their partnership with Google. According to Stephen Patel, analyst at Gleacher & Co.,[50] "The risk to Google of upsetting other device makers far outweighs what benefits they would see if they kept it proprietary to Motorola. You just lose a tremendous amount of distribution and developer support if it's somehow better or exclusive on Motorola."[51]

52   It was important for Google to address the concerns of its Android partners, as any unsettlement on their part could provide competitors' platforms with an opportunity to break Google's bastion and march into its territory. Samsung had already developed its own smartphone operating system, Bada, and other companies might follow suit or opt for Windows Phone 7.

53   As far as the patents were concerned, observers who had studied the patents that Motorola Mobility held said the acquisition would not help in fighting the lawsuit that Oracle had filed. However, other companies, which were on the verge of suing Google, could backtrack after the acquisition.

54   Google was of the view that the regulatory approval for the deal would be through by early 2012. While some analysts opined that the deal would not have any antitrust probe as Google was not involved in manufacturing mobile phones, others were not so sure as the deal needed to go through the Justice Department's Antitrust division. Google needed to prove that its patents would not be leveraged to discourage competition in the smartphone market. According to Jamie Court from Consumer Watchdog: "Should an information monopolist like Google have the power to dominate cellphone manufacturing and control

[48]"How Google's Acquisition of Motorola Mobility Could Affect You," http://www.huffingtonpost.com/2011/08/15/google-acquisition-motorola-mobility_n_927043.html# August 15, 2011.

[49]"Nokia CEO says 'Watch Out' to Android Phone Makers," Reuters, August 17, 2011.

[50]Gleacher & Co is a private investment firm providing services like asset management and investment banking.

[51]Greg Bensinger, "Deal May Turn Android Partners into Rivals," http://online.wsj.com, August 15, 2011.

patents that could require mobile phones to use its information-tracking Android operations and applications? The debate has just begun."[52]

55   Analysts opined that both the companies had very different cultures, as both belonged to different eras and Google was involved in software while Motorola was mostly a hardware company. Over the years, Motorola had faced several problems due to a bureaucratic culture and lack of innovation. After the acquisition, around 19,000 employees from Motorola and 29,000 employees of Google needed to work together. Zander admitted that the hardest thing he had faced in his working career was to change the culture of Motorola. According to Henry Boldget, from Business Insider, "Successfully integrating Motorola—and making the merger work—would require a world-class integration team, along the lines of the ones GE's Jack Welch used to run. This type of integration for Motorola would involve firing *thousands* of people, shutting down factories, re-organizing global supply chains, killing products, parachuting in trusted Googlers, and so forth. Who at Google is going to do that?[53]

56   The deal took Google into a new territory of low-margin hardware businesses like broadband routers, networking equipment, digital security hardware, etc. Google was required to take care of manufacturing, logistics, suppliers, counterfeit products, distribution, retailing, and marketing. Analysts were of the view that the manufacturing business was highly competitive and needed capabilities different from those Google possessed.

57   Observing Google's ambitious acquisition of Motorola Mobility, Ben Parr, editor-at-large at Mashable,[54] opined, "For Google, the Motorola acquisition is a series of gambles. Google is gambling that regulators will approve the deal. It's gambling that Motorola's patents will be enough to force a stalemate in the Google-Apple-Microsoft patent wars. And finally, it's gambling that it has the capability to create the software and hardware for a phone that can truly rival the iPhone."[55]

---

[52]"Google's Motorola Gamble," *Los Angeles Times,* August 18, 2011.

[53]Henry Boldget, "The Verdict: Google-Motorola Will Be a Colossal Disaster," www.businessinsider.com. August 16, 2011.

[54]Mashable is an independent news source covering digital culture, social media, and technology.

[55]Ben Parr, "On Google, Motorola and Rolling the Dice," http://mashable.com, August 17, 2011.

Case 23

Lagunitas Brewing Company, Inc., 2013

I'd been digging getting drunk at the also famous Marin Brewing Co. pub and thought the "gear" of brewing was pretty sexy looking. For me, cool and functional "stuff" has always been sexy. Like a nice reverb unit, or a great speaker, or a vintage guitar—and brewing "stuff" fit right in. I went down to the local homebrew supply shop and got the standard 5-gallon plastic pail, a strainer, the hop packets, and the malt syrup, everything you needed.

—Tony Magee, Founder and CEO, Lagunitas Brewing Company

1   On August 1, 2013, Tony Magee, the founder and CEO of Lagunitas Brewing Company (LBC), stood in Chicago, IL, 2,100 miles away from the current brewery in Petaluma, CA. He had chosen to build his second brewery, providing him the capacity to meet current and expected future demand of his LBC brand. The new brewery, which would immediately allow LBC to increase its production of beer and quadruple capacity, was scheduled to open in early 2014. However, as Magee visualized his future in Chicago, he couldn't help but wonder what the future held and if expansion was the right move. How was LBC to manage and maintain control of its expansion? If demand projections were off, did LBC have enough capacity or too much? Did LBC have the financial resources to withstand more competition or another recession?

2   Nevertheless, LBC's chief marketing officer, Ron Lindenbusch, showed high levels of confidence and held lofty expectations for the Chicago operation:

> We are building an identical brewery to the one that we have built in Petaluma; the equipment is exactly the same. One way we are controlling costs is by not having the typical frills and thrills of other breweries: We don't install fancy copper pipes or stone on the platforms around the tanks, it's not necessary. The Chicago brewery will be all enclosed with a tasting room suspended above the brewery floor, so that visitors can take in all the wonder that is beer making. We want our customers to feel connected to our products and felt that by putting them in the front row, to really see the production process, we could start to build deep-rooted connections for the Lagunitas brand.

U.S. BREWING INDUSTRY

3   The United States and brewing have been inexorably linked since the founding of the American colonies. In 1607, the first shipment of English ales arrived and by 1612 the first New World brewery was established in New Amsterdam. By the mid-1800s, German immigrants founded many of the breweries that built the foundation of the U.S. brewing industry, including Anheuser-Busch, Coors, Miller, and Schlitz. In 1865, American breweries produced 3.66 million barrels (bbls, 1 barrel = 31 U.S. gallons) of alcoholic beverages.

Source: Professors Armand Gilinsky, Jr. of Sonoma State University and Steve Bowden of the University of Waikato and Jack Eldredge, Shawn Purcell, and Clark Rupp III, MBA students at Sonoma State, prepared this case as a basis for class discussion rather than to illustrate effective or ineffective handling of an administrative situation. Distribution of these case materials has been authorized in writing for academic purposes only. Not for reproduction or dissemination without written consent of the authors. Draft dated September 19, 2013.

EXHIBIT 1 Growth in the Number of U.S. Breweries, 1885– 2010

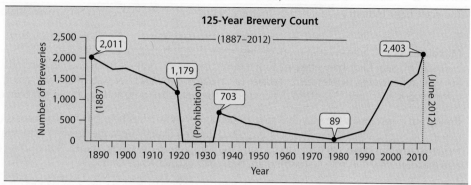

Source: Brewers Association (www.brewersassociation.org)

The Prohibition movements started within the states during 1880–1919 and sought to ban the sale of alcohol. Local Prohibition laws prompted consolidation within the industry. With the passage of the Webb-Kenyon Act in 1914, the U.S. Congress put 1,568 businesses out of brewing operations. After Prohibition was repealed in 1933 by the ratification of the Twenty-First Amendment, the number of domestic breweries climbed to approximately 700 in just five years (Exhibit 1).

4   The latter half of the 20th century saw large-scale breweries exiting the market, as they could not produce sufficient volumes at low enough costs amid growing competition. There was a need to produce and market beers on a national scale, which increased capital requirements, forcing the more inefficient producers out of the market. The brewers that survived did so mainly by remaining small and regional, like Anchor Brewing located in San Francisco, CA. Federal legislation changed again in 1976 allowing smaller, independent brewers to sell their creations on-site. Coupled with changes in consumer tastes, these new brewers began producing darker and fuller flavored beverages like ales, porters, stouts, and dark lagers.

5   U.S. beer market conditions were challenging from 1981 to 1994, with a growth rate of only 1 percent. In contrast the 1980s produced a decade of pioneering in the craft brewing segment (Exhibit 2) and was followed by high growth during the 1990s. Annual volume growth was 35 percent in 1991 and continued to grow every year until reaching a high of 58 percent in 1995. From 1997 to 2003, the craft-brewing segment growth declined to under 5 percent annually. Independent breweries and local brewers saw the beer-drinking clientele gravitate toward their styles of production and as a result, from 2004 to 2008, annual volume growth rates held steady ranging from 6 to 12 percent. Craft brewers represented 6.5 percent of the U.S. beer sales in 2012 and grew 15 percent in volume in that year. In 1980, there were 8 craft breweries, a number that grew to 2,360 breweries by 2012, according to the Brewers Association (Exhibit 3).

COMPANY HISTORY

Founding (1992–1997)

6   In the early 1990s, Magee began home brewing in his Lagunitas, CA kitchen as a hobby. During the first five years of brewing, Magee worked as a printing salesman to earn his living. He confessed that, "[I] wanted out of printing very badly."

7   By early 1993, Magee's wife "evicted him from the kitchen." He then rented a small space in the back of Richard's Grocery Store in the small town of Forest Knolls, CA. He

EXHIBIT 2   Market Segments

The **craft beer industry** is defined by four distinct markets: brewpubs, microbreweries, regional craft breweries, and contract brewing companies.

Microbrewery: A brewery that produces less than 15,000 barrels of beer per year with 75 percent or more of its beer sold off-site. Microbreweries sell to the public by one or more of the following methods: the traditional three-tier system (brewer to wholesaler to retailer to consumer); the two-tier system (brewer acting as wholesaler to retailer to consumer); and directly to the consumer through carry-outs and/or on-site taproom or restaurant sales.

Brewpub: A restaurant-brewery that sells 25 percent or more of its beer on site. The beer is brewed primarily for sale in the restaurant and bar. The beer is often dispensed directly from the brewery's storage tanks. Where allowed by law, brewpubs often sell beer "to go" and /or distribute to off-site accounts. Note: BA recategorizes a company as a microbrewery if its off-site (distributed) beer sales exceed 75 percent.

Contract Brewing Company: A business that hires another brewery to produce its beer. It can also be a brewery that hires another brewery to produce additional beer. The contract brewing company handles marketing, sales, and distribution of its beer, while generally leaving the brewing and packaging to its producer-brewery (which, confusingly, is also sometimes referred to as a contract brewery).

Regional Brewery: A brewery with an annual beer production of between 15,000 and 6,000,000 barrels.

Regional Craft Brewery: An independent regional brewery who has either an all-malt flagship or has at least 50 percent of its volume in either all-malt beers or in beers that use adjuncts to enhance rather than lighten flavor.

Large Brewery: A brewery with an annual beer production of over 6,000,000 barrels.

Source: Brewers Association (www.brewersassociation.org)

EXHIBIT 3   Number of U.S. Breweries and Volume Produced, 2012–2013

U.S. Breweries in Operation	2013 Quantity	2012 Volume (bbls)
Brewpubs	1,124	870,371
Microbreweries	1,139	1,905,212
Regional Craft Breweries	97	10,237,632
Total U.S. Craft Breweries	**2,360**	
Large Non-Craft Breweries	23	
Other Non-Craft Breweries	33	227,702
Total U.S. Breweries	**2,416**	

Source: Brewers Association (www.brewersassociation.org)

expanded the operation by installing a three-tier brewing system and purchasing an all-electric plug-n-play cargo container. Despite no longer brewing in the town of Lagunitas, all the permits and legal documents were under the "Lagunitas" name and Magee thought the name was cool and catchy, so he kept it.

8   From the beginning, Magee had a clear idea of how he would make money in the beer business:

> I would do it the way another great San Francisco brewery did it: wholesale. The margins would be thin, but I would do all the work myself and whatever crumbs were left over, I'd feast on them. I was only planning on producing unfiltered draught beer and to market it as a "private label" product to the 20 or so bars and restaurants in San Francisco and in the tourism-heavy West Marin coastal area where I lived. I would brew, filter, keg, sell, deliver, and service it all solo.

9   By 1994, the brewing operation of Lagunitas overwhelmed the capacity of the small grocery store's septic system. Magee was forced to quickly relocate to Petaluma, California. Once LBC moved into an 8,500-sq.-ft. location in Petaluma, Magee purchased a 14-bbl brew system and the company's first bottling line. With production of six-packs of beer starting in 1995, the bottling line was easy to justify to Magee: "The current 20-oz bottles were easy to hand-fill. But a $2,500 bottling line for 12-oz bottles would allow $1M in product."

10   Over the next three years, LBC grew production from 600 bbls to near 10,000 bbls annually by adding tanks and fermenters, one at a time. As Magee recalled:

> At some point—in June of 1994—it all got to be too much, and while the little brewery was just beginning to carry its own weight financially, selling only the private-label draft beer, I needed to hire some help. This single decision to increase the brewery's daily "burn-rate," and the resultant need for increased sales volume to support the first payroll position, was the beginning of what I can only describe as 12 crazy years of being chased down the street by a rabid pack of wild dogs.

11   Even with incredible growth, financing remained an issue, as no bank believed in the craft beer movement or in Magee:

> There is too much work and too many good customers for you to do a good job by yourself, so you hire one guy, and your daily cost of operation goes up. Now you need to sell more beer to pay for this change, which you can, so you do. To make this extra tasty brew you need to buy more ingredients, which you can, so you do. Unless you sell the beer COD, you will probably need to pay for these ingredients before you get to collect for the beer the ingredients will become, which means you need a little more cash. It's all about the "time of arrival" of the money to your checking account. Your little brewery is a little profitable, but you are growing quickly and the "time of arrival" of money thing is getting harder to manage because you seem to need more than the little bit of money that you are generating in profits if you are going to pay your bills on time—so you need a little more money to put into the bank account to cover the checks that are clearing the account faster and faster. But you have a day job and you just put your paychecks in the brewery because things seem to be going so well.
>
> So you grow a little bit more, you pay for materials—and now salary—before you collect for the brew you're delivering, and you are a little profitable, but actual cash somehow remains scarce. Suddenly, you realize that you need another fermenter and a few more kegs because you are growing and you are starting to short customers' orders, so you buy another fermenter, which also takes more money than you are making. Maybe you have a bank that will lend you money, but in 1996, I didn't.

Bootstrapping (1997–2007)

12   In 1997, the craft beer industry hit hard times. Financing dried up and many breweries folded. Magee remembered those difficult years:

> I counted 23 serious brands that had recently been important brewers and were now gone from the market. There was beer running in the streets. Distributors started getting tired of all the brands, retailers were just numb, beer fans were more than a little bowled over. But it was also a good time to be buying used equipment for the same reasons.

13   As many breweries were closing or stagnating, LBC was thriving and growing fast (Exhibit 4). In 1998, Magee leased a 17,000-sq.-ft. facility across the street from the original 14-bbl brew house in Petaluma. The new facility was built with growth in mind. A 30-bbl brew house was composed of cheaply procured used equipment from casualties of

EXHIBIT 4 Lagunitas Brewing Company: Capacity, Revenues, and Profits, 1992–2012

Period	Year	Petaluma Maximum Annual Capacity (in BBLs)	Sales Revenue (in 1,000's US$)	Net Profit (in 1,000's US$)
Founding	1992	n/a	n/a	n/a
	1993	n/a	n/a	n/a
	1994	n/a	n/a	n/a
	1995	3,420	513	n/a
	1996	5,420	813	n/a
Bootstrapping	1997	8,420	1,263	n/a
	1998	10,420	1,615	n/a
	1999	14,420	2,278	n/a
	2000	17,420	2,787	n/a
	2001	19,420	3,165	n/a
	2002	23,420	3,888	n/a
	2003	24,420	4,151	n/a
	2004	26,420	4,544	270
	2005	32,420	5,674	400
	2006	37,420	6,600	503
	2007	43,420	9,500	804
Evolution	2008	57,420	12,900	595
	2009	72,420	17,100	563
	2010	101,420	24,600	1,500
Expansion	2011	165,420	39,700	1,737
	2012	235,420	59,000	3,107
	2013	400,420	105,000	8,500

Source: Lagunitas Brewing Company, private communication.

the industry downturn, specifically Wisconsin Brewing Co. and Napa Ale Works. While the old plant was slowly phased out, the new one was similarly phased in. Magee fondly remembered moving day:

> When we had the new place mostly ready, we had a big moving party of 1,200 or so of our best friends, and after a 10-beer tasting and some live music while getting loaded at the old plant, a loud horn blew and everybody grabbed anything they could carry that was not nailed down and we all literally marched over to the new McDowell plant in a massive parade led by a mime, a guy on stilts, a purple bear, and a tragic little Civil War–style marching band.

14   The new facility required large amounts of new capital, and Magee sought private equity to provide the financing:

> Eventually, when I had to move the brewery into a larger space, buy bigger brewing stuff, and do a bunch of building renovations, I needed to raise money. I got it from some old friends, and from some new friends, and in 1998, I traded about half ownership of the brewery for $650,000. At that time, I couldn't borrow it from anywhere, so I had to raise it by selling stock.

15   In 2000, increased debt and overhead expenses pushed LBC to pursue faster growth. The next several years were used to "clean up" production with efficiency purchases, such as a new bottling line that did not waste as much beer and a new high-speed centrifuge separator. Both strategies paid for themselves by getting more beer to the consumer without additional inputs. By the end of 2007, production was reaching maximum capacity again.

Exceeding Capacity (2008–2010)

16   In 2008, Magee purchased an automated 80-bbl brew house manufactured in Germany by Rolec, a company renowned for quality brewing products. The new equipment allowed for significant growth. With the installation complete, Magee told local newspapers it would take ten years to reach maximum production and then after that level he would be "happy to stop growing for a while."

17   At that time, LBC's beer was distributed in 35 states. Four trucks a week shipped beer to Manhattan, and five trucks a week to Chicago. According to Magee, "If you look at Highway 80 going across the country, it's literally a pipeline of Lagunitas [beer] being transported all the time."

18   Two years later, LBC was quickly approaching the brew house's maximum production level, running the plant "flat out to keep up with orders." The expansion that was supposed to last ten years only lasted two. In March 2010, amidst an annual growth rate of 46 percent, Magee announced an additional new 250-bbl automated brew house that would allow for annual capacity of over 150,000 bbls, at a cost of $9.2 million. Magee recalled:

> It was like making decisions on the back of a galloping horse, without quite enough information to know exactly what your next step has to be. . . . [There was] tremendous growth, from day to day, there was no such thing as standard operating procedure, it was scary, you look around, there was something new every day.

National Expansion (2011–2013)

19   After an unprecedented 60 percent growth in the first two quarters of 2011, Magee revised his initial demand estimates and increased annual capacity to just under 200,000 bbls in Petaluma. With a total cost just over $14 million, Magee revised his expansion predictions and said, "I can see us growing three to four times in size in the next five to ten years." In 2012 and 2013, LBC expanded again to nearly 230,000 and 400,000 bbls annual capacity, respectively.

20   While the Petaluma brewery continued its expansion with a new building and bottling line (now at 130,000 square feet), LBC began planning a second brewery. The planning included brewery designs, capacity requirements, brewing processes, and how to finance the expansion.

21   The location choice of Chicago was a natural one: Chicago, home to some 8 million people, represented the largest LBC market outside of Northern California. A Chicago brewery gave LBC easier access to its Midwest and East Coast customers and suppliers by taking advantage of Chicago's distribution lines. For example, Magee claimed $1.5M per year was spent to truck beer bottles from a glassmaker in Oklahoma to Petaluma, and after filling them up, back across the United States to the Midwest and East Coast.

22   Additionally, Lindenbusch was optimistic LBC would be considered a hometown beer by Chicagoans: "Lagunitas has deep connections to Chicago. Tony is originally from Chicago and still has family living there. Tony loves Chicago and Chicago loves Tony."

23   Securing financing for the new 300,000-square-foot brewery and initial operating costs of the Chicago brewery was a top priority for Magee. He knew he couldn't finance this expansion phase the same way he had in Petaluma, that is, borrowing from friends, family, and taking second mortgages. In the early days, LBC was paying 1.5 percent on receivables and 10 to 14 percent on equipment. This made it difficult for LBC to acquire bank loans or further investors. Before 1995, LBC had been bleeding cash and showed little profits. Once the debts were all paid, LBC was flush with cash. This made its Chicago endeavor an attractive opportunity for banks and investors, as the investors saw the brewery was growing.

24 LBC secured $17.5 million in funding in 2011 and purchased a plot of land inside the city limits of Chicago. While the cost to do business was much higher inside the city limits, LBC felt it was more valuable to be officially located within the historic city. While other well-known breweries had sought tax advantages for placing their new breweries inside certain states, Magee had been adamant about profitable beer companies not taking advantage of these types of tax deals.

25 Setting up the Chicago brewery identically to Petaluma was crucial to Magee. Everything from the water and physical brewery to the culture inside, all of it had to be the same. LBC set and reset the Chicago annual capacity from 150,000 bbls to 250,000 bbls, as the planning continued. Eventually the 300,000-square-foot Chicago facility would support a 500,000-bbls annual operation. A brewery's capacity (i.e., bottleneck) was determined by the number of fermenters on site. In Chicago, each fermenter produced 750 bbls per batch, with a turnover rate of about 20 times per year.

26 Jeremy Marshall, the head brewer, was to be stationed in Chicago during the early days of operation, because, according to Lindenbusch, "the beer recipes are so solid, the first batch is usually good, and just needs a bit of tweaking from Jeremy." The plan was for Marshall to travel back and forth between Petaluma and Chicago, being responsible for both. The beers in production would be the same at both locations and according to Magee, "a customer should not be able to distinguish between batches brewed in Chicago versus Petaluma."

27 Lindenbusch commented in July 2013:

> One of the reasons we chose Chicago was the water supply. Chicago has very similar water to that in Petaluma. Water is the lifeblood of beer making and really affects the flavor profile. So choosing the right water was important in our decision to select Chicago. We don't want the customer to have a different tasting beer depending on where it was brewed. Both Petaluma and Chicago have no minerals in their water so all we have to do in order to get the correct pH balance is to add in some gypsum. This really helps in guaranteeing continuity in our beers.

28 During that growth period, LBC added key people from major corporations and placed them in upper management roles to help guide the expansion. Much like a traditional corporation, LBC employed a CEO, CFO, COO, VP of marketing, VP of sales, and VP of packaging. Most of the executive team had been with LBC for over ten years and expressed little interest in early retirement. Most of the executive team was in their 50s and empathized with Magee when he said, "I'll die while still on payroll."

29 By 2012, LBC had grown from 13 salespeople to 56 and had added six regional sales managers. As LBC began to increase its national exposure, the need to support its sales team on the ground became paramount. Leon Sharyon, LBC's chief financial officer, explained:

> We realized that we needed a CRM [customer relationship management software] to specifically deal with our needs, so we went out and hired an IT director. Then I called up the dean of the computer science program at Sonoma State [University] and asked him to send me his best three students to work on a project for me. They did so well we offered the students jobs and they have built us a great tool that our sales team uses every day. The impact of arming our sales team with the proper tools as they go into bars, restaurants, and events has really helped.

MISSION AND VALUES

30 In July 2013, Lindenbusch explained how LBC wanted to be viewed:

> We want to be known as an American brewery with American owners and American employees. Our vision is to be known more as an American beer like Bud. We don't want the label of craft or microbrew placed upon us. The craft definition is becoming blurred by various tax and trade association guideline changes. We don't feel we fit the craft mold. Lagunitas is more about getting our beer to as many people as possible.

31 LBC believed with profitability came responsibility to not only maintain high brewing standards, but also support the communities that supported them. This "pay it forward" attitude typically involved helping charities raise money through LBC donations. But rather than extol its virtuous side, LBC preferred to focus its PR efforts on highlighting the fundraising group's mission. As Lindenbusch saw it, Lagunitas and music went hand-in-hand:

> Our marketing efforts primarily revolve around music, in some way or another, whether it's a festival or concert. Sponsoring bands that are hitting the road is one of our next ventures. It will be called "Fueled by Lagunitas," and we basically donate beer and gas. Often we deal with LiveNation for concerts and intend to participate more in various capacities with college radio, PBS, and music festivals. Recently we added our mini amp (amphitheater) at our Petaluma brewery and host concerts and benefits of all types. And we have live music that goes on in our tasting room four nights a week. Our motivation is to help the music and the arts.

32 However, as LBC became a larger player in the craft beer segment, it encountered considerable competition from other craft brewers. Lindenbusch insisted that LBC was now blocked from participating in certain music festivals. Other brewers had already secured exclusive distribution rights to certain events, which stifled the organic expansion and word-of-mouth strategy that LBC had been following since its inception.

COMPETITION

33 As LBC left its small startup roots, it set its eyes on the big domestic competitors, like Miller-Coors and Anheuser-Busch. As the craft brewing segment matured, major American brewers had started to offer similar craft brew–like products such as Blue Moon (MillerCoors) and Shock Top (Anheuser-Busch). Additionally, some craft brewers, such as Sam Adams (Boston Brewing Co.), chose to be contract brewed by the big American brewers.

34 In 2013 LBC occupied the sixth spot in the rankings of domestic craft brewers (Exhibit 5), and the 13th spot for overall U.S. brewers (Exhibit 6). There were over 100

EXHIBIT 5   Top U.S. Craft Brewing Companies (based on 2012 beer sales volume)

Rank	U.S. Craft Brewing Company	City	State	Barrels Sold
1	Boston Beer Co.	Boston	MA	2,100,000
2	Sierra Nevada Brewing Co.	Chico	CA	966,000
3	New Belgium Brewing Co.	Fort Collins	CO	765,000
4	The Gambrinus Co.*	San Antonio	TX	n/a
5	Deschutes Brewery	Bend	OR	255,000
6	**Lagunitas Brewing Co.**	**Petaluma**	**CA**	**244,000**

*Includes BridgePort, Shiner, Trumer, Tappeto Volant, and Pete's Wicked brands

Source: Brewers Association (www.brewersassociation.org)

EXHIBIT 6   Top Overall U.S. Brewing Companies (based on 2012 beer sales volume)

Rank	U.S. Overall Brewing Company	City	State
1	Anheuser-Busch Inc.[a]	St. Louis	MO
2	MillerCoors[b]	Chicago	IL
3	Pabst Brewing Co.[c]	Los Angeles	CA
4	D. G. Yuengling and Son Inc.	Pottsville	PA
5	Boston Beer Co.[d]	Boston	MA
6	North American Breweries[e]	Rochester	NY
7	Sierra Nevada Brewing Co.	Chico	CA
8	New Belgium Brewing Co.	Fort Collins	CO
9	Craft Brew Alliance, Inc.[f]	Portland	OR
10	The Gambrinus Co.[g]	San Antonio	TX
11	Minhas Craft Brewery[h]	Monroe	WI
12	Deschutes Brewery	Bend	OR
13	**Lagunitas Brewing Co.**	**Petaluma**	**CA**

[a]Includes Bass, Beck's, Bud Light, Budweiser, Busch, Goose Island, Landshark, Michelob, Rolling Rock, Shock Top, and Wild Blue brands. Does not include partially owned Coastal, Craft Brew Alliance, Fordham, Kona, Old Dominion, Omission, Red Hook, and Widmer brands; [b]includes A.C. Golden, Batch 19, Blue Moon, Colorado Native, Coors, Keystone, Killian's, Leinenkugel's, Miller, and Tenth & Blake brands; [c]includes Pabst, Schlitz, and 28 other brand families; [d]includes Alchemy & Science and Sam Adams brands; [e]includes Dundee, Genesee, Labatt Lime, Magic Hat, and Pyramid brands; [f]includes Kona, Omission, Red Hook, and Widmer Brothers brands; [g]BridgePort, Shiner, Trumer, Tappeto Volant, and Pete's Wicked brands; [h] includes Mountain Crest and 10 other brand families.

Source: Brewers Association (www.brewersassociation.org)

EXHIBIT 7   Capita per Craft Brewery by State (selected states) in 2012

Capita/Craft Brewery Rank	State	Total Craft Breweries	Capita/Craft Brewery
1	Vermont	25	25,030
2	Oregon	140	27,365
3	Montana	36	27,484
4	Alaska	22	32,283
5	Colorado	151	33,306
6	Maine	37	35,902
7	Wyoming	15	37,575
8	Washington	158	42,560
9	Idaho	29	54,055
10	Wisconsin	83	68,518
20	**California**	**316**	**117,892**
35	Illinois	67	191,502
39	New York	88	220,206
42	Texas	84	299,352
44	Florida	57	329,848
51	Mississippi	3	989,099

Source: Brewers Association (www.brewersassociation.org)

distributors that sold LBC nationwide, and in a few foreign countries. LBC expected further expansion internationally in the next few years.

35   Besides the big American brewers, LBC continued to compete with existing and new craft brewers that entered the market. In addition to the more than 2,400 breweries that existed in the United States, estimates were that 1,500 new breweries were under construction in 2013, according to the Breweries Association. California had the greatest number of craft breweries with 312 but was only mid-range in breweries per capita (Exhibit 7). According to Lindenbusch, LBC considered itself "the low end of the high-end beers [in terms of popularity], such as Corona, Heineken, Sierra Nevada, and a tier above Anchor and Stone."

36   While flavorful beer was one aspect of a successful company, capacity and distribution were other keys. Similar to LBC, many of the craft brewers were expanding operations to fulfill the growing craft beer demand. Sierra Nevada and New Belgium Brewing Co., both major craft brewers, planned to open second breweries in North Carolina.

MARKETING AND DISTRIBUTION

37   Lagunitas had built a successful and identifiable brand with little traditional articulation or consistent messaging. The brand was developed predominately from Magee's personality through catchy and quirky labels with simple typeface and interesting copy. LBC found an industry niche and continued to lead the craft industry by producing strong-flavored and high-alcohol-content beers that failed to be categorized in traditional categories.

38   Lagunitas' marketing methodology lacked traditional media promotions, minimal pricing incentives, and general lack of push marketing techniques. Magee described his hesitation to categorize his brand:

> This is a delicate thing to talk about because I don't want to limit the possible interpretations of what Lagunitas is in your minds or in our own. Having started this ball rolling down the alley, I have never been certain where it would land and there have been more than enough interesting and unforeseeable inputs over the years. If I said we are irreverent does that preclude our being traditional? Is saying that we are funny ruling out our displaying gravitas? If you say we're extreme should people infer that we're challenging to have in the fridge? If I said that our labels are literate, could you infer that we're pretentious . . . ? Like Joseph Campbell's *Hero with a Thousand Faces,* I've always liked the idea of a brand that is equal parts legend, material, and myth, and always a mirror—a chimerical presence, where everyone that apprehends it sees something in it that is unique to their own point of view.

39   LBC had found a promotional niche for itself by "giving away beer and making friends," according to Lindenbusch. For example, in 2012, LBC donated 11,212 cases of beer to festivals and events, and it had already donated 10,045 cases through July 2013. Magee was telling a story through the label artwork and the taste and quality of the beer. The artwork on the bottle matched the art that went into brewing any batch of Lagunitas. LBC realized its "secret" was still in the quality of its beers; as Lindenbusch noted:

> Our labels have personality, humor, intelligence, and art. They are similar to a J. Peterman catalogue, describing a lifestyle rather than a product. However, a consumer may buy our beer for the artwork or story on the bottle, but it is what inside that keeps them coming back.

40   Word of mouth and quality products had been the backbone of LBC's marketing. As the craft brew market expanded, LBC had witnessed revenue growth of 46 percent in 2010 and 60 percent in the first two quarters of 2011. Its major markets at that time were California, Colorado,

Texas, Florida, New York, and Illinois. LBC's marketing strategy was quite simple . . . continue to be Lagunitas. Magee talked about what he called "the personality of Lagunitas":

> We kept the name "Lagunitas" after moving away from that town for a few reasons: it's a beautiful little word, it's hard to say, once you said it you're in, and it looks lovely in type. I work very hard to get personality into the recipes. Not to emulate styles that have gone before us, but I like to think that none of our beers are today's version of yesterday's anything. We are always trying to find new material within those four ingredients: malt, hops, yeast, and water that make up beer. I think that independence of thought and independence of spirit show up in the brand.

41   Pricing strategy played an important role in the formation of the brand. From the beginning, LBC realized that how it priced its product would make huge differences in sales and brand image. When the company first started to produce six-packs in 1998, Magee needed to select a price segment:

> I had a lot of decisions to make about the new bottled brand, but the heaviest one was what we would charge for it. I looked at some market-info (IRI) reports and saw that the average selling price of most every six-pack brand in the top twenty was $5.99 and some even less. This seemed really, really cheap, but it was the world around us. They all had frontline six-pack prices of $6.99, but they all did every other month promotional prices of $4.99, and so the average fell in the middle.
>
> I wanted to make sure that at every opportunity I would aim Lagunitas at participating in the market with only the best brands. That didn't just mean other craft brewers (although we all fished in the same pond), but also it meant imports. I needed to price similarly and participate in the market similarly. These were huge breweries, but I wanted them to be my peers. We weren't sophisticated enough to do effective promotional pricing yet, but I felt that if we wanted to play with the big boys, I'd have to ante up. So, we set our everyday price at $5.99 for a six-pack.

ECONOMIC DEVELOPMENT ISSUES

42   LBC had always had problems in regards to wastewater. Excessive wastewater was a major reason in moving brewery operations often during the early days. The city of Petaluma explored whether additional industrial wastewater treatment capacity was needed. This wastewater issue directly affected Lagunitas. If LBC continued to grow, its wastewater requirements would proportionately increase.

43   High levels of organic matter in the brewing process caused problems for municipal treatment systems. Breweries commonly pretreated their wastewater to meet municipal standards of biological oxygen demand (BOD) and total suspended solids (TSS). Even though LBC pretreated its wastewater, they still incurred thousands of dollars in fines from the city of Petaluma. LBC also had costs associated with the excess wastewater that they couldn't release into the sewers. By 2013, LBC was paying $250,000 every month to truck its wastewater 60 miles away into a neighboring municipal district. LBC purchased a nearby plot of land, two lots south of the brewery in Petaluma, to build its own wastewater treatment plant. Petaluma had to date shown a willingness to work with Lagunitas when to it came to permits and fees.

FUTURE CHALLENGES

44   With 2,400 craft breweries and another 1,500 in various stages of development and completion in mid-2013, the U.S. craft beer market appeared to be in the midst of explosive growth in production. The galloping horse that was LBC had been at the forefront of the

growth in capacity. But LBC had also evolved beyond those craft origins with a clear focus on national distribution and an increasing orientation toward taking on the big boys. The Petaluma brewery was in a good location from a West Coast distribution standpoint, and the Chicago brewery would be in an excellent location for East Coast distribution. Chicago, one of the major distribution centers in the United States, would allow LBC to harness that distribution network to get the product out to consumers more efficiently.

45   LBC expected continued growth for the immediate future, but Magee was all too conscious of the cyclical nature in the craft industry. He admitted that he feared the next "unknowable step." The fast-paced nature and increased competition in the craft industry segment of the beer industry seemed to all but guarantee difficult times ahead. But looking at LBC's history, they were in a good position to weather anything. The Chicago expansion was a key step to being able to break out of the craft beer label and compete on the larger national—and perhaps eventually global—stage. Magee and Lindenbusch expressed hope that the personality of LBC would not get lost in the process.

REFERENCES

http://www.northbaybusinessjournal.com/48262/petaluma-considers/

http://www.youtube.com/watch?v=_sY2nTFY4c0

http://www.northbaybusinessjournal.com/30826/lagunitas-plans-9-million-expansion/

http://www.northbaybusinessjournal.com/36562/video-tony-magee-tells-the-story-of-lagunitas-brewing-co/

Private commuication with LBC CFO Tony Magee, CMO Ron Lindenbusch, and CFO Leon Sharyon

http://www.brewersassociation.org

http://mybeerbuzz.blogspot.com/2013/07/lagunitas-names-chicago-head-brewer.html

http://www.chicagobusiness.com/article/20130727/ISSUE01/307279977/this-man-soon-will-be-chicagos-biggest-brewer

Case 24

Leica Camera: *A "Boutique" Firm Faces A World of Change*

Leica must be kept from becoming a boutique firm for the nostalgically minded.

—Leica Chairman, Dr. Josef Spichtig, 2005 annual report

1   Leica Camera AG CEO and principal owner Andreas Kaufmann was melancholy while strolling the floor of Photokina—the world's largest photography industry trade fair. The biannual event took place in Cologne, Germany, less than 100 miles from Leica's head-quarters in the small town of Solms. Being so close to home made Kaufmann feel more like a host than an attendee, and after having had another tough year in 2008, he did not relish the spotlight. Kaufmann had fired the previous CEO, American Steven K. Lee, a few months earlier after Lee's efforts to turn around the struggling company had rubbed long-time German employees the wrong way.

2   Leica's big announcement at photokina was the launch of the M8.2 digital system camera—an update to the M8 model that had been unveiled two years earlier at the same trade show. The M8 had had problems processing infrared light, which caused some black colors to appear purple. To resolve the problem, Leica had provided free filters to M8 owners and sent 4,000 letters of apology hand-signed by Lee.[1] The M8.2 fixed all that and featured some new exterior finishes, but Leica's most devoted followers were looking for signs of something else: what lay ahead for the company's famed R system cameras and lenses?

3   Kaufmann was preparing to make a decision on the company's well-loved but anachro-nistic R series. The line included expensive analogue SLR cameras and an array of high-end, expensive R lenses that Leica's die-hard fans had amassed since its introduction in 1976. The choices were simple with varying complications—Leica was a small company, and investing resources would be a trade-off. Should Leica invest capital in a product-line extension for the R-series lenses? Would innovation focused on a new digital Leica camera line aimed at professionals be a better choice? Or would investing more capital in a digital product by expanding the M-series line of cameras and lenses make the most sense?

COMPANY HISTORY

4   Photography was all about capturing a moment in time, either to document it, convey a message, or elicit an emotion. The camera and lens were the tools that made that pos-sible, but as photographer Erwin Puts noted, "Leica owners have a special relation to the

Source: This case was prepared using public sources by Case Writer Bill Chapman, Senior Researcher Gerry Yemen, and MasterCard Professor of Business Administration S. Venkataraman. Kaufmann's thoughts are fictionalized for pedagogical reasons. It was written as a basis for class discussion rather than to illustrate effective or ineffective handling of an administrative situation. Copyright ©2012 by the University of Virginia's Darden Business Publishing. All rights reserved. *To order copies, send an e-mail to* sales@dardenbusinesspublishing.com. *No part of this publication may be reproduced, stored in a retrieval system, used in a spreadsheet, or transmitted in any form or by any means—electronic, mechanical, photocopying, recording, or otherwise—without the permission of the Darden School Foundation.*

DARDEN
BUSINESS PUBLISHING
UNIVERSITY*of*VIRGINIA

[1]Mike Esteral, "Late to Digital, Leica Slow to Refocus; German Camera Pioneer Fired American CEO Who Pressed for Filmless Future," *Wall Street Journal,* September 16, 2008, B1.

camera . . . " or as one enthusiast claimed, he "adore[d] his Leica with heart and soul."[2] For many professionals, the brand was more than a wind mechanism for film or a container of image files and a light meter; it was, well, Leica!

5   Leica traced its origin to a mid-nineteenth century German microscope manufacturer Ernst Leitz GmbH. In the 1920s, Oskar Barnack and Ernst Leitz II (a son of a company partner who rose into the management ranks) developed and produced the first small-format camera to enter mass production. Prior to this, cameras had been large and fairly immobile, typically requiring tripod mounting to support their weight. The image captured by the camera was recorded on a glass plate negative, and the resulting photographic print was the same size as the plate. Their innovation was to have a compact camera that created a small negative (35 mm was the standard they eventually settled on) and then later used an enlarger to magnify the image, resulting in a larger print. This process revolutionized photography and led to the creation of consumer cameras. The company name was eventually changed to Leica, a combination of Leitz and the German word for camera.[3]

6   The well-known French street photographer, journalist, and artist, Henri Cartier-Bresson, had been an early adopter of the 35 mm format and took many iconic images including those of Mahatma Gandhi's funeral in 1948 and of the Chinese Civil War. The portability of his Leica, which he had famously wrapped with black tape to cover the shiny parts, helped him blend into the streets to capture people and scenes in a different way than had been possible up to then given the limitations of studio portraiture. In a sense, the Leica was the first point-and-shoot camera.

7   War photographer Robert Capa took "Death of a Loyalist," his iconic image of the Spanish Civil War, with a Leica 35 mm, and Nick Ut famously captured the shot of a naked Vietcong girl fleeing the horror of a napalm attack with a Leica M2. Queen Elizabeth was a Leica fan and was pictured in 1986 on a 60th birthday postage stamp holding a Leica M.

8   The company went through a number of ownership transitions through the latter part of the twentieth century. In 1986, Leica GmbH was formed to manage the camera division of Leitz; a year later, it became an independent division of Wild Leitz AG, a manufacturer of microscopes and surveying instruments. A new headquarters and production facility were built in Solms.

9   In 1990, Wild Leitz merged with the British optical group Cambridge Instrument Company to create the Leica Holding B.V. group. In 1994, former CFO Klaus-Dieter Hofmann was successful in leading a management buyout of the camera division, which was then named Leica Camera AG. The company went public on the Frankfurt stock exchange in 1996. In 2004, the Kaufmann family investment firm—ACM—bought 27 percent of the company and eventually acquired most of the thinly traded shares after further acquiring a 36 percent stake that had been owned by luxury goods manufacturer Hermès International SCA. In 2006, Steven K. Lee, a former VP for Emerging Business and Strategic Development from electronics retailer Best Buy, was hired as CEO to lead the company toward a more digital future.

RISE OF THE SLR

10   In 1959, the Japanese company Nikon introduced the Nikon F, an SLR camera that was adopted by many professional photographers who were recording news events of the 1960s,

[2]Erwin Puts, "Are Leica Owners Photographers or Technophiles?," Tao of Leica, See http://photo.net/leica-rangefinders-forum/00LEb2 (accessed October 2, 2012).

[3]"History: From a Flash of History to the Birth of the Leica Legend," Leica, See http://us.leica-camera.com/culture/history/ (accessed October 11, 2012).

including the Vietnam War. SLR stood for "single lens reflex." "Reflex" referred to a mirror ("reflection") inside the camera, and "single lens" meant that one looked through the main lens of the camera as one framed the shot. Earlier cameras typically used a rangefinder—a secondary opening mounted above or beside the lens. Depending on the distance from the camera to the subject, the rangefinder might not have been framing the exact shot one saw through it; therefore, SLR was seen as an advance by serious photographers. SLR cameras also had very little shutter lag, and when combined with a motorized film loader on the back, the camera could produce rapid-succession shots of high-drama events such as rocket launches.

11   Under pressure to compete with Nikon, Leica introduced its own SLR—the "Leicaflex"—in 1964. This led to a line of SLR cameras that was eventually dubbed the R series; cameras in this series carried names such as R4 and R6 and typically sold in small numbers. Even as the industry moved toward digital cameras in the mid-1990s, a subset of traditionalists resisted the move for aesthetic and philosophical reasons, and Leica was there to serve them with R-series SLRs that retailed for (U.S. dollars) USD2,495 before the purchase of any lenses. *New Yorker* magazine film critic Anthony Lane paid a visit to Solms and wrote that the Leica factory was "the place to go if you want to find the most beautiful mechanical objects in the world," and Leica users reminded themselves via an online discussion board of Cartier-Bresson's metaphor of his Leica as "a big warm kiss, like a shot from a revolver, and like the psychoanalyst's couch."[4] The Leica R series had a very strong penetration among European photographers (especially in German-speaking countries), and its world-class quality and precision made it *the* camera for professionals, enthusiasts, and hobby photographers.[5]

12   Throughout its SLR camera development, Leica designed an array of R-series lenses that many photographers favored. The eye of the camera, or the lens, was thought by some to be the most important part of the image-taking chain, and camera companies invested considerable resources into the design and manufacture of high-quality SLR lenses. Most camera manufacturers made sure their lenses were forward- and backward-compatible within a series and kept that technology proprietary by ensuring their lens mounts were unique to that series. The first reflex lens in the R series was introduced in 1964 with the original Leicaflex camera. Over the years, the company had had numerous optical break-throughs and developed a series of lenses that could be divided into four categories:[6] one-cam lenses (Leicaflex); two-cam lenses (Leicaflex and Leicaflex SL and SL2 models); three-cam lenses (R3 and later Leicaflex models); and ROM lenses (R3 and later models). Cams were used in camera mount technology. Each Leica camera body series had a dedicated lens mount; lenses that were incompatible with that body could not be mounted to it (i.e., lenses that were developed to go on the one-cam technology could not be mounted onto bodies with two-cam technology). Sometimes lens mounts were incompatible even within a manufacturer's series. With the use of camera-specific adapters, R lenses could feasibly be used on almost any SLR camera.[7]

13   Given Leica's experience in the field of microscopy, the company had a strong edge in glass expertise. Essentially there were two choices for lens makers—develop lenses for mass production and less cost or develop lenses for maximum image quality with little cost

[4]Anthony Lane, "Candid Camera," *New Yorker*, September 24, 2007.

[5]Olaf Stefanus, "S, M, X,—And R?" *Leica Fotografie International*, January 1, 2011, 31.

[6]A cam was located on the rear of the lens mount; it communicated aperture opening information to the coupled external light meter of the camera.

[7]Third-party companies came into the picture and started developing adapters that involved this expensive technology.

limitation. Leica was the developer of the best lenses money could buy. With the option of using a combination of over 100 different types of optical glass, the standard Leica lens was composed of around 100 individual parts. A mixture of machine- and man-made, lenses were checked by technicians more than 60 times throughout the manufacturing process (which differed depending on the glass type); roughly 30 production processes were done by hand. The precision adjustment of optical elements within each objective lens required skilled craftsmanship. Each Leica lens had a unique serial number, and the "lens made in Germany" inscription was guaranteed to be visible for decades. Before any lens was delivered, it was completely hand-inspected, and each function was tested. As the company liked to note: "Leica Lenses: A Synonym for Quality, Made in Germany."[8] The cost was almost beside the point—for example, a fast standard Leica lens fetched around (euros) EUR8,000 (USD11,600)—the brand was of utmost importance, and there were waiting lists for expensive Leica lenses.[9] Indeed, demand for Leica lenses had exceeded the firm's manufacturing capacity by the end of fiscal year 2008 and caused an order backlog.[10] Anything associated with Leica had become a collector's item.

20th-CENTURY CAMERA INDUSTRY

14   Other than the development of portable, affordable cameras such as the 35 mm, the major transformation of the camera industry's modern era was the move to digital imaging. A digital camera used a traditional lens to transfer an image into the camera body, but once there, it was captured on digital image sensors rather than on film. This was noteworthy because a digital image could immediately be viewed on the camera itself or a computer screen and could quickly be shared with others by e-mail. In contrast, film images typically needed to be printed later, which was a comparatively slow and expensive process.

15   By 2008, most consumers had switched from film to digital cameras. Nikon had made headlines in 2006 when it announced it would stop making film cameras (in fact, it would continue to produce a film SLR, but most consumers did not know or care). Professional magazine photographer Mark Greenberg told the *Washington Post*: "To use a car industry analogy, it would be the same as Ford saying it is no longer producing an internal-combustion engine. It's really that revolutionary . . . film is done. Digital rules the world now."[11]

16   The invention of digital photography also led to a rise in camera ownership. Essentially there were three categories of people who bought cameras: high-end purchasers who worked in commercial photography (e.g., magazine advertising), middle-segment professional photographers (e.g., photojournalists), and low-end buyers seeking cameras for consumer applications. The onset of *affordable* top-end digital SLRs sat poorly with many professional photographers who showed up to snap photos of events to discover amateurs taking professional-quality pictures. Commercial and professional photographers often remained loyal to perfectly engineered cameras. "Our customers buy for different reasons," one Leica managing director said. "They appreciate precise mechanical and optical engineering."[12] Indeed, there were stories of professional photographers driving around in cars worth USD5,000 with USD70,000 worth of camera equipment in the back seat.

[8]"Leica Lenses: A Synonym for Quality, Made in Germany," video of Leica's lens-making process, 2:33, http://en.leica-camera.com/photography/m_system/lenses/ (accessed October 11, 2012).

[9]Stefanus, 28.

[10]Leica Camera AG annual report, 2007/08, 11.

[11]Mike Musgrove, "Nikon Says It's Leaving Film-Camera Business," *Washington Post*, January 12, 2006.

[12]Alan Cane, "A Blurred Picture: Digital Photography Is Soaring, But Don't Write an Obituary for Film Just Yet," *Financial Times*, March 9, 2004, 11.

TABLE 1   Global Unit Camera Sales in 2007

Total units sold	138,000,000
Digital units sold	126,000,000
Digital SLRs sold	7,000,000

Data source: *2008 Market Share Reporter* (Detroit, Michigan: Gale Group, 2008).

17   By the end of 2002, approximately 23 million U.S. households—nearly 20 percent—owned a digital camera.[13] The next year, 40 percent of U.S. households were expected to own at least one digital camera by year-end. And in a sign that the market was maturing, from 2005 to 2007, the number of households that owned more than one camera increased from 31 percent to 40 percent. The year 2008 was the first one since 1999 for which the *North American Consumer Digital Camera Forecast* predicted only single-digit growth.[14]

18   SLR cameras did not disappear; they went digital. By now, SLRs represented a mere fraction of the overall photography market. In Japan, for instance, there were 10.9 million units shipped in 2007, but only 9.7 percent of those units were DSLR. The balance comprised cheaper and simpler digital cameras. Global trends were similar (Table 1).

19   While profits may have contracted with the shrinking SLR sales, there was a distinction to be made between developed and developing markets. With the instability of the global stock markets and significant drop in market value during late summer 2008, camera sales were expected to be moderate in developed markets. Yet in developing countries, especially in Eastern Europe and China, market size was expected to grow, particularly for entry-level DSLRs.[15]

LEICA CONFRONTS CHANGE

20   Andreas Kaufmann's ACM investment firm found itself at the helm of a company that faced an "existence-threatening" crisis by the end of 2005. While the global camera market grew by approximately 14 percent in 2003, 47 percent of the units sold were digital cameras, and 53 percent were analogue. Leica's legend and reputation for film cameras left it particularly exposed to this trend. Although Leica had launched its first digital camera (the S1) in 1996 at USD30,000 per unit, only 146 were sold.[16] Sales of system cameras (R series as well as the rangefinder M series) fell 25.8 percent for FY 2003–04, and compact (digital) camera sales fell by 23.3 percent. For the first time, in 2004, Leica told investors of the "considerably reduced margins" in digital cameras as well as "shortened product life cycles" and a "shift in sales channels to large distributor formats."[17]

21   Under economic pressure themselves, specialized camera dealers that had handled the bulk of Leica's retail sales were ordering fewer system cameras. In response, Leica management reduced the size of its dealer group but moved to using in-store "shop-in-shop" installations to emphasize the brand and offer "very good service to the sensitive Leica customers."[18] Serving the customer included filling custom orders. For example, at the

[13]"Digital Camera Ownership Almost Mass Market," *Digital Photography Review*, April 22, 2003 http://www.dpreview.com/news/2003/04/22/pmadcreport (accessed October 11, 2012).

[14]Infotrends, "Maturity Changing Dynamics of U.S. Digital Camera Market," http://www.infotrends.com/public/Content/INFOSTATS/Articles/2008/10.28.2008.html (accessed October 11, 2012).

[15]Canon Inc. Form 20-F, 2008.

[16]Laura Stevens and Eyk Hennings, "Blackstone to Buy Minority Stake in Leica," *Wall Street Journal*, October 20, 2011.

[17]Leica Camera AG annual report, 2003/04.

[18]Leica Camera AG annual report, 2003/04.

request of one of its customers (the Sultan of Brunei), Leica revived a discontinued model and produced 20 cameras in Persian Pink to be used as party favors.[19] And it made history when it crafted a Leica lens costing USD2,064,500 for Sheikh Saud Bin Mohammed Al-Thani of Qatar.[20]

22   Despite its superior customer service and custom orders, Leica's situation became even more dire the following year. Sales fell to EUR92 million from EUR157 million four years earlier, a period during which nearly 400 employees had been shed. Operating losses for the fiscal year increased to EUR14.6 million from an operating income of EUR2.9 million the previous year. The global move toward less profitable digital cameras increased (only 36 percent of sales were analogue now), and Leica claimed that the "high development costs" and "rapid succession of product generations" had caused "all market players" to suffer "considerable losses."[21]

23   Management called an ad hoc meeting in March 2005 to announce a loss of "half of the company's registered share capital" and its plans for a capital raise and turnaround attempt. Banks terminated the bulk of Leica's credit lines, and bridge loans were extended by major shareholders. Despite the opposition of some institutional shareholders, the firm did raise EUR22.95 million in additional capital and survived the crisis.

RISE OF JAPAN: CANON AND NIKON

24   The rise of digital photography went hand in hand with the success of a group of Japanese companies. Market leader Canon was launched in 1933 in an apartment in Japan at a time when most high-quality cameras came from Europe. Canon introduced its first 35 mm camera in 1935 to compete with the German Leica model. Following World War II, Canon's slogan became "catch-up with and surpass the Leica," and its less-expensive rangefinder camera became popular with the U.S. occupation forces.[22] By 1967, Canon was a global diversified company that made photocopiers and calculators; it operated under this motto: "Cameras in the right hand, business machines in the left."[23] In 1976, the Canon AE-1 was introduced, an SLR with a built-in microcomputer to help with light metering and other functions.

25   By 2002, Canon was reveling in the rise of digital cameras, crediting them (along with digital video cameras) for the greatly improved profitability of the company's camera division.[24] Canon had launched a new DSLR, the EOS-1D, to take advantage of what it said was a doubling of the market for DSLRs; it even pledged to maintain its lead in the film camera segment by bolstering sales efforts in Asia, Eastern Europe, and South America—markets where it foresaw "lasting expansion." Even at this late date, Canon hoped to "revitalize the global market" for film cameras by launching new products.[25]

26   Canon continued to thrive in the new environment, growing sales and controlling the top spot in both digital cameras and DSLRs; it stopped developing new film cameras in 2006.

---

[19]Ken Rockwell, "Leica Lens Serial Numbers," http://www.kenrockwell.com/leica/lens-serial-numbers.htm (accessed September 28, 2012).

[20]Ryan Whitwam, "The $2 Million Leica Lens You'll Never Get to See," August 25, 2012, http://www.geek.com/articles/gadgets/the-2-million-leica-lens-youll-never-get-to-see-20120825/ (accessed October 2, 2012).

[21]Leica Camera AG annual report, 2004/05.

[22]"Canon Camera Story: 1937–1945," Canon Camera Museum, http://www.canon.com/camera-museum/history/canon_story/1937_1945/1937_1945.html (accessed October 3, 2012).

[23]"Canon up to Now," Canon, http://www.canon.com/about/history/outline.html (accessed August 24, 2012).

[24]Canon Inc. annual report 2002, 31.

[25]Canon Inc. annual report 2002, 2.

Camera sales more than doubled from 2002 to 2006. In addition, Canon was competitive in the interchangeable SLR camera lens segment. With its own high-quality optical glass production and lens machining and assembly processes, Canon offered more than 60 lenses and unveiled four new interchangeable lens models in 2008.

27   The company was well suited for the continual product development that was required due to its in-house production of image sensors and its successful move away from creating physical prototypes toward designing all products using 3-D CAD technology. The strategy was to integrate advanced technology with cameras to develop "innovative, high value-added" products. For example, the technology developed for the professional photography market, such as the EOS-D1, was incorporated into consumer camera products.[26] Canon's target was to appeal to a broad range of photographers, from professionals to entry-level users. And the pairing of technology and innovation helped keep production costs lower.

28   Although it led in the midrange SLR camera segment, Canon intended to achieve further innovations through "aggressive investment in developing new models" and introducing more SLR interchangeable lenses.[27] For photographers looking for high quality and a technical edge, Canon was gaining popularity. The mass-produced SLRs and lenses were popular with enthusiasts, and by 2008, Canon was on its way to owning a 41.3 percent market share for DSLRs (the EOS 50D retailed for USD1,250 for camera body only).[28] Indeed, as the Canon tagline claimed, "image is everything."

29   Close on Canon's heels was another Japanese firm, Nikon. Started in 1917 as an optical instruments company that made, among other things, lenses for Canon cameras, Nikon began producing its own camera bodies in 1948. In 1959, it released the legendary Nikon "F" SLR. An innovation at Nikon was the development of the F system of lenses and accessories, which appealed to professional photographers.[29] "Nikon is the leader when it comes to compatibility among cameras and lenses of different decades," photojournalist Ken Rockwell said. "Most of today's lenses are compatible with ancient cameras, and most ancient lenses can be made to work fine on today's digital cameras."[30]

30   By 2003, Nikon was a diversified firm with 57 percent of its sales in the Imaging Products division, which comprised mostly digital cameras. Though the company was operating at a loss and even suspended its dividend that year, it blamed the weakness on a slowdown in the Precision Equipment (digital steppers) division and spoke of "excellent business conditions" for digital cameras. A major manufacturing plant was established in Wuxi, China, so that more components could be built in-house, reducing the risk of depending on third-party suppliers. Nikon strengthened its position in the "high-end consumer digital" niche with its D100 SLR (USD1,999 for camera body only) and planned on venturing further into the "middle class" and "popular class" camera markets. Nikon credited its sales increases and gain in operating income to the high-margin DSLR cameras and cost-reduction efforts; sales in the Imaging Products division rose 23 percent to (Japanese yen) JPY272 billion, with operating margins of 10 percent.[31]

31   By 2005, Imaging Products sales had grown to JPY354 billion, but operating margins fell 4.7 percent (JPY16.8 billion).[32] Management spoke of an "urgent focus on raising

[26]Canon Inc. Form 20-F, 2008.

[27]Canon Inc. Form 20-F, 2008.

[28]*Technology Outlook 2009*, J.P. Morgan, December 11, 2008, 87.

[29]"Corporate History," Nikon, http://www.nikon.com/about/info/history/chronology/index.htm (accessed August 24, 2012).

[30]Ken Rockwell, "Nikon Lens Technology," http://www.kenrockwell.com/nikon/nikortek.htm (accessed October 11, 2012).

[31]Nikon Corporation annual report 2003, 17.

[32]Nikon Corporation annual report 2005, 22.

profits in the digital compact camera sector" and an "urgent need" to "compress development and production lead times to cope with shrinking product cycles." It intended to increase profits in the SLR segment by focusing on interchangeable lenses and related services.[33] Nikon also acknowledged its film loyalists by launching a USD2,500 F6, which it hoped to make "long-selling and popular."[34]

32   By 2008, net sales in the Imaging Products division had risen to JPY586 billion (with an operating income of JPY84 billion or 14 percent) seemingly in sync with the Nikon tagline "at the heart of the image." The company launched three new DSLR models and reported a "considerable" rise in the sales of existing models (D3 professional flagship for USD4,999). In addition to increased camera sales, lens sales also rose.[35]

33   Management revealed an important change in its approach to design that demonstrated its customer focus: "Products were formerly created under the direction of the design department, but now the marketing department presents ideas to the designer based on market needs."[36] Nikon was accelerating its product development and was driven by the belief that a "full lineup" of products—from high-end to entry-level models—would be key to its success at capturing a larger share of the SLR camera market. The less-expensive and easier-to-use SLR cameras expanded Nikon's market to reach more amateur enthusiasts, and its top models continued to roll out for those who purchased them based on features, not price—the traditional SLR camera market of serious photographers such as Galen Rowell. Nikon controlled 39.9 percent of the global market for DLSRs in 2008, and over 40 million of its interchangeable SLR lenses had sold by the end of the fiscal year (March).

34   After Canon and Nikon, market share was split among smaller players such as Pentax (6.5 percent), Sony (5.2 percent), and Olympus (4.5 percent).[37]

EUROPEAN COMPETITOR: HASSELBLAD

35   Leica was not the only storied European company making high-end cameras and lenses for professionals and collectors. Started as an import firm in Gothenburg, Sweden, in 1841, Hasselblad had discovered that photographic equipment was a growing line of business. Viktor Hasselblad, son of the company founder, was honeymooning in Europe when he happened to meet George Eastman. Eastman was about to found Kodak, the American company that would play a major role in making photography available to the masses. Hasselblad became an important distributor of Kodak products in Europe.

36   Viktor's son Victor Hasselblad, by then a self-styled photography expert, took over the company in the early twentieth century. By that time, Hasselblad had become the blue-blood global camera brand of many a professional photographer. After a stint making cameras and clocks for the military during World War II, the company introduced its first consumer camera in 1948. Called the 1600F, it was an SLR designed to work with Kodak lenses. Over the next 60 years, Hasselblad became known as a maker of "medium-format" cameras featuring film that was larger than the industry-standard 35 mm. Medium-format cameras were most often used by professionals who required higher-resolution images that they could significantly enlarge for fine art displays or billboards. With its integrated system, each camera was weather-sealed and featured a lifetime warranty and dedicated help if replacement parts were needed.

---

[33]Nikon Corporation annual report 2005, 6.
[34]Nikon Corporation annual report 2005, 13.
[35]Nikon Corporation annual report 2008, 12.
[36]Nikon Corporation annual report 2008, 13.
[37]*Technology Outlook 2009*, 87.

37   Hasselblad manufactured its lenses through partnerships with highly skilled optical makers—Carl Zeiss, for example, engineered some of the lenses and the shutters. More typically though, the lens would start as collaboration between Hasselblad and Fujinon, Kodak, Rodenstock, or Schneider and was designed and manufactured to Hasselblad's specifications.[38] Hasselblad would build and assemble the central shutter and iris diaphragm, and its partner would grind the lenses and assemble the rest of the parts.

38   Hasselblad was a relatively small firm, with about 500 employees, that produced cameras for professionals throughout the 1970s and 1980s; it supplied the camera that took the first photos of Neil Armstrong walking on the moon in 1969. In 1981, CEO Jerry Öster saw the first digital camera (the Sony Mavica) but was unimpressed by its image quality. Increasingly, though, Hasselblad became concerned that it did not offer such modern functionality as autofocus. Management eventually concluded that the firm was too small to afford the R&D necessary to develop a modern camera.

39   By the 1990s, a new CEO with an electrical engineering background was installed to develop a digital camera. Company officials realized early on that, while digital image quality was lower than that of analogue, the business utility was potentially higher, so they targeted professional studio photographers who could benefit from digital technology's ease of sharing and ability to make multiple prints quickly and cheaply. Hasselblad used its strong brand reputation to forge a partnership with Philips to provide digital sensors.

40   In 1996, the Swedish Bank UBS bought Hasselblad and realized that, while the company had focused on digital development, it had lost its leadership position in film cameras ("we only had one budget . . . and money had to go to either the digital camera system or the mechanical camera system," one product manager recalled).[39] UBS cut off all digital development, concluding that the Japanese were the only ones equipped to address the image-quality problems that plagued digital and threatened to harm the Hasselblad brand. Internal resources were turned back to developing analogue cameras; digital was pursued via a "digital back" joint venture with Fuji and a product dubbed the H1.[40]

41   For four years, the H1 was plagued by delays and budget overruns; it finally launched in 2002. By that time, digital technology had improved, and the H1 was a cumbersome, expensive combination. Wedding photographers once loyal to Hasselblad had switched to Canon.

42   The Shriro Group, a Hong-Kong-based distributor, acquired Hasselblad in 2003 and downsized quickly to avoid bankruptcy. Knowing that it could not produce a new digital system camera in its weakened state, Shriro acquired Imacon, a Danish maker of digital camera backs, the following year.[41] This had the effect of depriving long-time rival Leica of a key digital partner and allowed Hasselblad to compete in the digital race.

43   At photokina 2008, Hasselblad's longtime partnership with Kodak was still on display as it announced the H3DII-50 medium-format digital camera with a Kodak 50-megapixel sensor. "If you're into cameras, be prepared to faint as you feast your eyes on Hasselblad's high-end H3DII-50 Pro DSLR," said Andrew Tingle, photographer and Web site designer, "offering a staggering 50-megapixel 36 × 48 mm Kodak sensor and a price tag of equally colossal proportions."[42]

[38]Michael J. Hussmann, "The Evolution of Lenses," Hasselblad USA, March 2009, http://www.hasselbladusa.com/media/1663143/the_evolution_of_lenses.pdf (accessed October 11, 2012).

[39]Christian Sandström, Mats Magnusson, and Jan Jörnmark, "Exploring Factors Influencing Incumbents' Response to Disruptive Innovation," *Creativity and Innovation Management* 18, no. 1 (2009), 11.

[40]Sandström, Magnusson, and Jörnmark, 11–12.

[41]Digital backs were electronic image sensors that fit analogue camera backs thus facilitating the transition from analogue to digital imaging.

[42]Andrew Tingle, "Hasselblad Unveils High End H3DII-50 Pro DSLR Featuring Kodak 50 Megapixel Sensor," July 8, 2008, http://nexus404.com/2008/07/08/hasselblad-unveils-high-end-h3dii-50-pro-dslr-featuring-kodak-50-megapixel-sensor/ (accessed October 2, 2012).

The price announced was USD27,995. Acknowledging that "the only reason not to have a Hasselblad was that you couldn't afford one," the company also announced lower pricing for its entry-level H3DII-31 model: USD17,995.[43] The Stradivarius of cameras was now available to consumers. Yet the longtime company creed—"to put the best cameras possible into the hands of the people who use them"—remained.

44   Hasselblad would forever be associated with the best of the best in the world of photography. Its relationship with NASA spanned 40 years and produced photographs from space that scientists depended upon to expand their knowledge. Victor Hasselblad's foundation, formed after his death, was committed to promoting research and academia in photography. Each year it awarded its most prestigious honor to deserving photographers. The Hasselblad was the serious professional's tool, particularly in the fashion industry and among commercial photographers, and its mission statement—"to be the preferred choice among professionally minded photographers"—supported that notion.

OUTSOURCING AT LEICA

45   Perhaps taking a cue from its Swedish neighbor, Leica had also ventured into outsourcing and manufacturing partnerships over the years. In 1998, Leica introduced the Digilux, a USD500 entry in the point-and-shoot digital camera market. It was manufactured by Fujifilm and was dismissed by loyalists as a simple "rebadging" of the Fuji MX-700. By 2004, Leica was partnering with Panasonic to make additional Digilux models with Leica-designed lenses and Panasonic bodies and electronics. Sold by Panasonic under the name "Lumix," the Leica version (dubbed the D-Lux and V-Lux or *PanaLeicas*) sold for up to 45 percent more with the red Leica logo and special packaging but was essentially the same camera.

46   In 2004, Leica used the photokina show to announce a partnership with Danish manufacturer Imacon and Kodak to produce a digital camera back for Leica's R8 and R9 SLRs. It was called the DIGITAL MODUL-R. A digital back was designed to mount to the back of analogue R-series cameras to give them digital functionality but still allow the user to choose between digital and film. Though the cost was over USD5,000, the device got good reviews from users; but it was discontinued following Hasselblad's acquisition of Imacon later that year. The R9 (USD3,473), with its manual wind, remained Leica's "masterpiece" SLR camera according to one reviewer who noted, "it is the last high-end film-based SLR camera ever made."[44]

47   As Leica seemingly searched for the correct exposure on a DSLR, many camera makers were putting out new DSLR models so quickly that one prominent magazine picked a camera that was no longer being made as its "camera of the year." To that, Leica responded, "We could be the shelter for people who react to the changes of model every six months."[45] Yet the launch in 2006 of its first digitized camera in the rangefinder series—the M8 (USD5,000)—provided some SLR users the nod they were hoping for. Leica had maintained the structural characteristics of the M-series body and

---

[43]Hasselblad, "Hasselblad Announces New Products, New Technology and New Directions," press release, September 24, 2008, http://www.hasselblad.com/news/hasselblad-announces-new-products-new-technology-and-new-directions.aspx (accessed October 17, 2012).

[44]"The LEICA DIGITAL-MODUL-R," http://www.leicapages.com/novelties.html (accessed October 17, 2012).

[45]Ian Chapman, "A Camera Focused on Luxury," *Financial Times*, March 31, 2003.

EXHIBIT 1   Leica Camera: A "Boutique" Firm Faces A World of Change

	Camera and Lens Sales, 2006–08 (currency amounts in millions)					
	Net Sales '06		Net Sales '07		Net Sales '08	
Reporting currency	JPY*	USD	JPY*	USD	JPY*	USD
Leica	106	127	145	197	156	245
Canon	1,041,865	8,960	1,152,663	9,798	1,041,947	10,419
Nikon	415,686	3,575	448,825	3,815	586,147	5,861
Hasselblad		NA		NA		NA

*Leica figures are expressed in millions of euros rather than in millions of yen.

	Camera and Lens Operating Income, 2006–08 (currency amounts in millions)					
	Operating Income '06		Operating Income '07		Operating Income '08	
Reporting currency	JPY*	USD	JPY*	USD	JPY*	USD
Leica	(6.1)	(7.3)	4.9	6.7	7.7	12
Canon	268,738	2,311	307,426	2,613	187,787	1,878
Nikon	34,369	296	45,678	388	83,974	840
Hasselblad		NA		NA		NA

*Leica figures are expressed in millions of euros rather than in millions of yen.
Data sources: Canon Inc., Leica Camera AG, and Nikon Corporation annual reports, 2006–08, and historical currency data from Oanda.com.

constructed powerful lenses to go along with it (despite limitations the camera design placed on the lens).[46]

48   The firm credited the enthusiastic reception of the M8 (in spite of the infrared glitch) for its increase in sales volumes and for setting Leica back on track toward sound financials (see Exhibit 1 for sales and operating result comparisons). Demand exceeded M8 production capacity leaving orders backlogged by March 2007.[47] The company that had long been associated with street photography may have found its stride again. Yet the M8 left Leica's small upmarket niche of SLR users asking, "Would the R series be next?"

49   It was clear to Andreas Kaufmann that the future of Leica was not just in digital cameras, but in selling more units to more people. So what would that look like? What products would secure Leica's future? Did it mean continuing to manufacture the R lenses and convincing enough new customers to buy it to make it worthy of investment? Would offering a lower-end range of Leica products attract enthusiasts who might later upgrade? Would expanding capacity and producing larger quantities of the digitized M series be wise? What about a new line—was there development potential for a new universal system? All of this weighed heavily on Kaufmann's mind as he wandered through the 2008 Photokina show.

THE END OF THE R?

50   A mere six months later, Leica quietly posted this statement on its Web site: "New camera developments have significantly affected the sales of Leica R cameras and lenses resulting in a dramatic decrease in the number sold. Sadly, therefore, there is no longer an economic

[46]Stefanus, 24.
[47]Leica Camera AG annual report, 2006/07, 11.

EXHIBIT 2   Leica Camera: A "Boutique" Firm Faces A World of Change

Comments in Response to Leica's R-Series Termination Announcement

"Leica R lenses are actually very marketable and if they can put their ego aside a little they could have done what CZ has done—and much better—by releasing the Leica R lenses for the Nikon and Canon mount. That would have saved the lens line up for sure. They are all FF high end and MF lenses. I don't see how they could have a conflict with the Panasonic AF 4/3 and m4/3 line. Even Panasonic released an R to m4/3 adapter to encourage lens owners to use them on the m4/3 bodies. The R got some very nice ultra wide, macro, and tele longer than 135. All these were probably not going to be done on the M line. It's a shame, really."[1]

"Has anyone noticed that Leica Camera has totally removed the link on their Web site to the R Series? (http://en.leica-camera.com/photography/) Anyone know more about what's going to happen? Will Photokina reveal a new series? Is it the end of the R series? Darn!!!"[2]

"The R10 with a 35 mm full-frame sensor and focus confirmation, at a reasonable price (take the M8 as a reference) is all that is needed now, and it is not so difficult to do. I am sure Leica is working (at the design stage) on it from a long time ago, and they know very well what to do and how to do it. The only problem is where to find the resources for that project. They need to make profits this year. I hope they can present the R10 this year, even if it effectively ships next year. 20 additional months of development is too much for the R line at this moment if no information is provided to actual and potential owners of R lenses."[3]

"If Leica shows a DSLR R camera, I'll be a 'monkey's uncle.' Having used the SL/SL2/R series for eons, many waited on Leica's (Kaufmann's) words for it, and waiting, and waiting, and waiting, and all we got was a really lame answer about swimming with sharks of C and N."[4]

"Leica has been kept alive not necessarily because it makes hardnosed business sense, but because it DESERVES to be kept alive. One hopes that the eventual model will mimic Harley-Davidson . . . an important historical marque that nearly went bankrupt and eventually came back strong based on lifestyle- and brand-marketing as well as good products. There is no other Leica, and there never can be."[5]

"The one thing that none of this has ever been able to quite eclipse is that the R line of lenses is the all-time highest quality lens line ever made for 35 mm photography. Not all the lenses are equally good, not all of them are affordable, not all of them are terribly practical, and isolated lenses by other makers are as good as, or in rare cases slightly better than, their R counterparts; but considering the line as a whole you can't do better purely for optical quality."[6]

"That the Leica R8 and R9 does not have the sales figures in the top of the range Canons and Nikon is near comical in its tragedy especially when considering that the cameraman who did the Canon commercials did them on a Leica R9."[7]

[1]love_them_all, August 12, 2010, comment on Kausthub Desikachar, "Leica R Series: Is It the End?," DPreview Forum, July 31, 2010, http://forums.dpreview.com/forums/post/36024423 (accessed October 17, 2012).
[2]Kausthub Desikachar, "Leica R Series: Is It the End?," DPreview Forum, July 31, 2010.
[3]Neimo, February 10, 2007 (4:27 a.m.) comment on Mike Johnston "Leica Module R Discontinued," The Online Photographer blog, February 10, 2007, http://theonlinephotographer.blogspot.com/2007/02/leica-module-r-discontinued.html#c117114177713766057 (accessed October 17, 2012).
[4]Nobody Special, March 21, 2012 (11:01 p.m.), comment on LR Admin, "What to Expect from Leica on May 10th, 2012, Leica News & Rumors blog, March 21, 2012, http://leicarumors.com/2012/03/21/what-to-expect-from-leica-on-may-10th-2012.aspx/ (accessed October 17, 2012).
[5]bayareafilmguy, February 10, 2007 (6:17 p.m.), comment on Johnston, "Leica Module R Discontinued."
[6]Mike Johnston, February 10, 2007 (3:09 p.m.), comment on Johnston, "Leica Module R Discontinued."
[7]Karl Ivan Froestad Nes, February 10, 2007 (7:01 a.m.), comment on Johnston, "Leica Module R Discontinued."

basis on which to keep the Leica R System in the Leica production programme."[48] That announcement started a firestorm from R camera users who had demand for it (Exhibit 2). Should Leica reconsider or hold steady with its discontinuation?

[48]Leica, "Leica Ceases Production of R9 and R Lenses," press release, March 25, 2009, http://en.leica-camera.com/news/news/3/6378.html (accessed October 17, 2012).

Case 25

Louis Vuitton[1]

SYNOPSIS

1   Moët Hennessy Louis Vuitton (LVMH) enjoyed double-digit growth and healthy profitability in 2010 and 2011. A large part of this growth had been driven by its flagship group Louis Vuitton (LV). In 2011, LVMH announced that long-time LV CEO Yves Carcelle would be replaced at the end of 2012 by Jordi Constans, an executive from the French food product multinational Danone SA. However, after serving less than a month, Constans was replaced in December 2012 by Michael Burke, an LVMH insider who had been with the company for nearly 30 years. While LV had enjoyed rapid growth over the last two years, the question was whether such a growth rate was sustainable. What were the challenges facing LV, and how should these challenges be addressed?

HISTORY

2   Louis Vuitton Malletier was born in 1821 in Anchay, France. At age 16 he moved to Paris and took up a job as an apprentice trunk maker, over time becoming a respected trunk maker in his own right. In 1854, he opened his own company and over the next four years went about redesigning the trunk. In those early days, trunks were oval shaped and therefore not stackable; as such, they were not conducive to the emerging and rapidly growing forms of travel on steamers and trains. Vuitton came up with a flat-top trunk with flat hinges that was stackable and suitable for long journeys. A few years later, and in response to competitors copying his original design, Vuitton invented his famous trunk made of blue and red striped canvas.[2] The canvas protected the contents of the trunk from rain and dust, and customers loved the unique design. This innovation in material and design also made it difficult for competitors to copy. Vuitton's business thrived. He was able to cement his position among aristocracy in Europe and beyond, in places such as Egypt and India, when he was appointed the official packer and trunk maker for Eugenie de Montijo, Napoleon III's wife and a Spanish countess. As a result, the business strengthened further. Vuitton's success is said to have been built on three rules: to master his *savoir faire*, to provide excellent

Source: Manu Mahbubani wrote this case under the supervision of Professor Mary Crossan solely to provide material for class discussion. The authors do not intend to illustrate either effective or ineffective handling of a managerial situation. The authors may have disguised certain names and other identifying information to protect confidentiality.

Richard Ivey School of Business Foundation prohibits any form of reproduction, storage or transmission without its written permission. Reproduction of this material is not covered under authorization by any reproduction rights organization. To order copies or request permission to reproduce materials, contact Ivey Publishing cases@ivey.ca, Richard Ivey School of Business Foundation, The University of Western Ontario, London, Ontario, Canada, N6A 3K7; phone (519) 661-3208; fax (519) 661-3882; e-mail cases@ivey.uwo.ca.

Richard Ivey School of Business
The University of Western Ontario   **IVEY**

Copyright © 2013, Richard Ivey School of Business Foundation   Version: 2013-04-04

[1]This case has been written on the basis of published sources only. Consequently, the interpretation and perspectives presented in this case are not necessarily those of Louis Vuitton or any of its employees.
[2]Dana Thomas, *Deluxe, How Luxury Lost its Lustre*, Penguin, London, 2007.

service to his customers, and to innovate continuously.[3] The newspaper *Le Figaro* in an article in 1889 wrote of Vuitton's fame:

> The Louis Vuitton firm, whose exclusive models are causing a sensation and must always be cited first, appears to have solved the problem of irreproachable manufacturing, of a ruggedness that withstands every test; it offers without a doubt the most beautiful specimens of French manufacturing.[4]

3 Georges Vuitton, Louis Vuitton's son, inherited the company after his father's death in 1892. Georges continued the company's focus on innovation. He invented the five-number combination lock found on the trunks even today. He also designed the famous monogram pattern and the more complex pattern used on the canvas of LV products. Part of the motivation for these latter innovations was to counter the increased counterfeiting facing the company at that time.[5] Georges is also credited with designing hundreds of purses and moving the company into the handbag business. It was also during his tenure that LV started its global expansion. In 1893, LV displayed its products at the Chicago World Fair. In the years following, stores were opened internationally in New York, London, Alexandria, and Buenos Aires.

4 The Second World War brought an end to this expansion. The period was marked by efforts of the Nazi occupiers to move the couture houses and luxury businesses from Paris to Berlin. Factories were closed and LV's international distribution contracts were terminated. After the war, the luxury business revived, but LV was not able to recapture its former position. By 1977, its revenues were only US$20 million and profitability low. It was under these circumstances that Renée Vuitton, the family's matriarch, brought in her son-in-law Henri Racamier to lead the business. Racamier had no background in luxury but was an astute businessman.

5 Racamier discovered that the majority of profits in the value chain were being retained by merchants. To bring these profits in-house, he started bypassing the merchants and opening company-owned stores. He also pushed for rapid global expansion, opening 95 stores by the mid-1980s. The LV brand was pushed aggressively, products were diversified, manufacturing expanded, and new technologies introduced. Racamier also started acquiring companies that produced high-quality products, such as Givenchy and the champagne house Veuve Clicquot. Revenues grew to nearly US$1 billion by 1987.[6] Racamier also took LV public and listed it on the French Bourse and the New York Stock Exchange. Going public allowed him access to capital, which was required to fund ongoing growth.

6 In 1987, as part of this strategy, Racamier agreed to a merger with Moët Hennessy, a company that was much larger than LV, to form the Moët Hennessy Louis Vuitton (LVMH) group. The companies had an agreement that each division would be run independently with its own management and philosophy, with Racamier maintaining his leadership position at LV. However, relationships between the two divisions deteriorated rapidly with disputes and legal battles over how to run the company. Finally, in 1987, Racamier brought in a property developer, Bernard Arnault, to bolster his position against Moët Hennessy and try to reverse the merger. It was a move that Racamier would come to regret. Arnault had different plans, and those plans did not include Racamier.

[3]Ibid.
[4]Pamela Golbin, *Louis Vuitton/ Marc Jacobs*, Rizzoli; Enfield: Publishers Group UK (distributor), New York, 2012, p. 27.
[5]http://voices.yahoo.com/louis-vuitton-history-behind-purse-53285.html, accessed September 11, 2011.
[6]http://www.fundinguniverse.com/company-histories/lvmh-mo%C3%ABt-hennessy-louis-vuitton-sa-history/, accessed September 11, 2011.

BERNARD ARNAULT

7   Bernard Arnault was ranked as the fourth richest man in the world by Forbes[7] in 2011 with much of his wealth being built on LVMH. Arnault was originally a property developer with no background in the tradition and heritage of the luxury industry. He entered the industry with the purchase of the then-bankrupt French textile conglomerate Boussac Saint-Frères for US$80 million; its holdings included the couture house Dior.[8] It was this latter holding, which provided him with a base to establish a luxury goods powerhouse, that Arnault was interested in. He brought his reputation for laser-like focus on profitability and efficiency to the acquisition. The French press dubbed him "the terminator." Fired executives would complain about learning of their dismissal from the press. Over the next few years, Arnault laid off over 8,000 employees and sold off large parts of the conglomerate for US$500 million.[9] He grew Dior into a profitable business using methods of vertical integration similar to those employed by Racamier.

8   When Arnault was approached by Racamier to help the latter bolster his position against the Moët and Hennessy families, rather than backing him Arnault quickly acquired a 45 percent controlling stake in LVMH and garnered support from the Moët and Hennessy families. An 18-month legal battle for control of LVMH commenced between Arnault and Racamier, resulting in a victory for Arnault and the resignation of Racamier. Arnault became the CEO of the company, and control of LV slipped away from the Vuitton family. The stealth by which Arnault was able to acquire a controlling stake in LVMH and the level of bitterness and Machiavellian behavior for control ultimately contributed to the rewriting of French laws around takeovers.[10]

THE PERSONAL LUXURY GOODS INDUSTRY

9   LVMH competed in the global personal luxury goods industry. This industry was projected to have revenues of €212 billion in 2012[11] and included products such as apparel, perfumes, cosmetics, shoes, leather goods, and hard luxury goods. Leather goods included products such as handbags and accessories, while hard luxury goods included watches and jewelry. The global personal luxury goods industry was a subset of the larger €1.1 trillion global luxury industry that included a wide range of products and services from shoes and clothes to yachts and travel experiences.[12]

10   The growth rate for the personal luxury good industry for 2012 was projected to be 10 percent in euro terms. However, since most of the major players in the industry were based in Europe, the euro exchange rate had a significant impact on nominal growth rates. For example, in 2012, the growth rate in constant exchange rate terms was expected to be 5 percent. In 2011, the market had grown by 11 percent in euro terms and 13 percent at constant exchange rates, while in 2010, it had grown by 13 percent in euro terms and 8 percent at constant exchange rates. By 2015, the luxury goods market was expected to grow,

---

[7]http://www.forbes.com/profile/bernard-arnault/, accessed September 11, 2011.
[8]http://www.britannica.com/EBchecked/topic/35681/Bernard-Arnault, accessed September 11, 2011.
[9]Thomas, *Deluxe*.
[10]Ibid.
[11]http://www.bain.com/about/press/press-releases/bain-projects-global-luxury-goods-market-will-grow-ten-percent-in-2012.aspx, accessed February 3, 2013.
[12]http://www.ft.com/intl/cms/s/0/2cd3653e-ac0e-11e1-a8a0-00144feabdc0.html#axzz2JwtMxJt3, accessed September 17, 2012.

EXHIBIT 1 World Luxury Goods Market

Global Luxury Goods Market by Region and Estimated Growth Rates			
	Share of total market in 2011	Estimated Growth 2012 (Euro)	Estimated Growth 2012 (Constant K)
Americas	30%	13%	5%
Europe	37%	5%	3%
Japan	9%	8%	0%
Asia-Pacific	19%	18%	10%
Rest of the World	5%	8%	5%

Source: Claudia D'Arpizio, *2012 Luxury Goods Worldwide Market Study,* 11th Edition, Bain and Company, Milan, October 2012.

at constant exchange rates, to €250 billion with a compound annual growth rate (CAGR) of between 4 percent and 6 percent. Of the various product lines, leather goods and shoes were growing the fastest, and by 2011 these formed the largest product segments. They had grown by an average of 15 percent over the previous decade, and this growth was expected to continue into 2012. Growth, at constant exchange rates, was expected to be 16 percent for leather goods and 13 percent for shoes.[13]

11   The largest markets for luxury goods were in Europe and the United States, though the highest growth rate was in China, which had recently overtaken Japan in market size. Exhibit 1 breaks down revenues by region and shows the 2012 and 2013 growth rates that were projected for each region. Each of the regions, however, had different growth dynamics.

12   A fast-growing and important region was the Greater China market, which included mainland China, Hong Kong and Macau, and had a total market size of €23 billion, 65 percent of which was in mainland China. In 2011, the sales in mainland China had grown by 30 percent, in euro and constant exchange rate terms. For 2012, growth was expected to decelerate to around 20 percent in euro terms and 8 percent in local currency terms.[14] However, these numbers underestimated the size of the Chinese market. By 2011, one in four worldwide luxury goods customers were Chinese. Wealthy customers from mainland China tended to travel widely. They therefore not only bought luxury goods at home but also did so during their travels. Such tourist shopping was fueled by the differences across regions in prices of luxury goods and the risk of getting counterfeit products. For example, in 2011, prices in Europe were over 40 percent cheaper than in mainland China, and these goods were perceived as less likely to be counterfeit when purchased in Europe. Indeed, over one-third of sales in Europe were made to Chinese tourists. In 2011, 60 percent of sales in France were to tourists.[15] LV did make efforts to reduce such price disparity. For instance, in October 2012, the company increased European prices by 8 percent.

13   Growth in Europe on the surface had been steady in 2011. But this masked an underlying weakening in demand as a result of the financial turmoil and austerity measures put in place by governments in southern Europe. There had, for example, been a significant drop in consumption of luxury goods in Italy. However, much of this decline had been offset

[13]Claudia D'Arpizio, *2012 Luxury Goods Worldwide Market Study*, 11th Edition, Bain and Company, Milan, October 2012.
[14]Ibid.
[15]Ibid.

by increased tourism and increased purchases by these tourists of luxury items. Growth in Europe, which had been 9 percent in 2011, was expected to moderate to 5 percent in 2012.[16]

14   In the Americas, growth was expected to remain strong as the United States continued its slow but gradual recovery from the 2008 recession. Growth rates were expected to rise to 13 percent in 2012 compared to 10 percent in 2011.[17] In Japan, while growth in euro terms was expected to be 8 percent due to the rising yen, in constant exchange rate terms, the market was expected to be stagnant with either very low or no growth.

Customer Segments

15   The industry was split between three customer segments: absolute, aspirational, and accessible.[18] At the top of the pyramid was the absolute segment that consisted of individuals of high and ultra-high net worth. These customers looked for true luxury, which was, in the words of Françoise Montenay, the president of Chanel Europe:

> At a minimum, it must be impeccable. Maximum, unique. It's the way you are spoken to, the way the product is presented, the way you are treated. Like the tea ceremony in Japan: the ritual, the respect, the transmission from generation to generation.[19]

16   These customers desired exclusive products backed by brands that were based on heritage and tradition. They generally bought the highest end of the product line in ready-to-wear products or bought made-to-measure products. These customers looked for excellent craftsmanship, the use of high-end materials and an excellent buying experience. They valued their privacy. Vendors set up private fitting areas, which could be salons or private apartments, for these customers to select their designs and to get measured and fitted. In some cases, vendors would fly a salesperson along with a collection to a buyer who might, for example, reside in China. The low-key nature of these purchases extended to the desire for the products not to carry logos that communicated ostentatious consumption. Price was an important factor, with true luxury expected to be priced at levels that most could not afford. In the words of a customer at Daslu, a high-end fashion store in Säu Paulo, Brazil:

> Luxury is not how much you can buy. Luxury is the knowledge about how to do it right, how to take the time to understand and choose well. Luxury is buying the *right thing*.[20] (emphasis in the original)

17   The second segment was the aspirational customer. These included the top 10 percent of income earners such as celebrities, professionals, and business men and women with high disposable incomes. High quality, an exclusive buying experience, and brands based on tradition, heritage and that communicated the high quality of their purchases were important attributes for this group.

18   The final segment was the accessible customer who through the purchase of a luxury product experienced the feeling of having membership in an elite group. They got a taste of the world of the rich and famous. While these customers were more price conscious, the product they bought needed to convey a high level of quality and be backed by a brand that conveyed exclusivity.

19   In all three segments, customers valued products that were made in France or in other parts of Europe, more than those made in Asia or even the United States. The highest growth between 2012 and 2014 was expected to come from the top two segments of the

[16]Ibid.
[17]Ibid.
[18]http://affaritaliani.libero.it/static/upload/bain/bain.pdf, accessed December 7, 2012.
[19]Thomas, *Deluxe*, p. 324.
[20]Ibid., p. 345.

market. By 2011, the absolute luxury segment made up 21 percent of the overall market with growth rates expected to be above the market average with CAGR of 8 to 10 percent between 2012 and 2014. The aspirational segment was expected to grow close to overall market rates with CAGR of 6 to 8 percent during this period, while the accessible segment was expected to grow below the market rate.[21]

20   The behavior of customer segments differed across markets. For example, in China as logo brands became more common, the absolute segment moved away from these brands since they were viewed as becoming less exclusive. Focus of this segment moved toward absolute luxury, which included high-end experience and service, and away from logo products. On the other hand, this issue was less prevalent in Japan where high-luxury brands were heavily indulged in by all customer segments without undermining the attractiveness of the brand in any one segment.

21   Changing demographics and global economic challenges had led to some changes in consumer buying behavior. For example, customers, especially at the higher end of the market, had moved toward placing more value on luxury experiences, such as luxury travel and spas, than luxury purchases.[22]

Pricing and Distribution

22   The major companies in the industry tended to cater to all three segments. For example, PPR offered products through its Puma brand to the accessible customer segment, through the Gucci brand to the accessible and aspirational customer segments, and through brands such as Bottega Veneta to the aspirational and absolute customer segments. Smaller competitors tended to focus on specific customer segments. For example, Hermès focused more on the higher end of the market by offering bespoke, higher quality, and more expensive products. Prices charged by the companies varied according to the segment at which the product was targeted. Generally, lower prices for products targeted the accessible customer segment. Prices for a handbag would start at around US$3,000 for the absolute customer segment and could exceed US$100,000. They would start at around US$1,000 for the aspirational segment and around $300 for the accessible segment.[23]

23   The highest prices were reserved for limited edition products or bespoke, made-to-measure offerings. However, especially at the high end of the market, players tended to compete more through product design, the buying experience, and brand image rather than through price. In general, companies had been able to command a high price for their products. In keeping with these dynamics, companies had tended to invest heavily in advertising to build their brands and in product design and development to deliver unique products. Distribution models also varied considerably with some players selling through resellers while others, such as LV and Hermès, relying on company-owned stores. Many of the more successful companies controlled most aspects of their production and distribution in order to ensure a level product quality and experience that justified high prices for their goods. In many cases, companies used multiple channels, including directly owned stores (DOS), department stores (termed wholesale), and licensing of their brands to third parties. Growth rates varied between the various channels. For example, in 2011, DOS sales had increased by 15 percent in euro terms, and 9 percent at constant exchange rates versus 10 percent in euro terms for the wholesale channel. This trend was expected to continue in 2012.

---

[21] http://www.altagamma.it/img/sezione3/files/397_975_file.pdf, accessed December 7, 2012.
[22] *https://www.bcgperspectives.com/content/articles/consumer_products_automotive_luxe_redux/?chapter=3*, accessed September 24, 2012.
[23] http://www.pwc.com/it/it/publications/assets/docs/marketvision-luxury-2012.pdf, accessed December 7, 2012.

EXHIBIT 2   Financials for LVMH, PPR, and Richemont

	LVMH		PPR		Richemont	
	2010	2011	2010	2012	2010	2011
Revenues	20,320	23,659	11,008	12,227	6,892	8,867
Gross Profit	13,136	15,567	5,369	6,224	4,394	5,651
Operating Profit	4,169	5,154	1,229	1,544	1,355	2,040
Net Profit	3,032	3,065	709	999	1,090	1,540
Shares Outstanding (mm)	478	492	126	126	566	560
Current Assets	11,199	13,267	6,940	5,277	7,024	8,595
Non Current Assets	25,965	33,802	17,754	17,508	2,659	3,158
Current Liabilities	7,060	9,594	6,495	5,472	2,213	2,722
Non Current Liabilities	11,900	13,963	6,549	6,133	488	413
Total Debt	5,266	7,266	5,219	4,678	222	88
Shareholder Equity	18,204	23,512	10,599	10,925	6,992	8,618

Source: LVMH Annual Reports, 2006 to 2011.

Similarly, sales in outlet stores that sold discounted merchandise had risen by 19 percent at constant exchange rates in 2011 and were expected to rise by 20 percent in 2012.[24]

Suppliers

24   Many of the companies, especially at the higher end of the market, designed and manufactured their products in-house. As such, they generally sourced only component parts, such as leather, zippers, and clasps, from external suppliers. Companies were selective in their purchasing and had dedicated functions to ensure the supplies being purchased met the required quality standards. While the industry was dominated by a few large buyers, there was no such concentration on the side of the suppliers.

THE LVMH GROUP

25   LVMH, Moët Hennessy Louis Vuitton, operated five businesses: wines and spirits, perfumes and cosmetics, fashion and leather goods, watches and jewelry, and selective retailing. The group owned over 60 luxury brands.[25] In 2011, sales were €23.6 billion and profits were €3 billion. Exhibit 2 gives the financial details of LVMH group and three of its competitors for 2009 to 2011. The group had enjoyed substantial growth in revenue and profitability over this time period.

Acquisitions

26   While it had grown over the last two decades both through acquisitions and organically, acquisitions had played a major role. The majority of acquisitions had been in companies that produced high-quality luxury products. Some of the major acquisitions included Givenchy

[24]Claudia D'Arpizio, *2012 Luxury Goods Worldwide Market Study*, 11th Edition, Bain and Company, Milan, October 2012.
[25]*http://www.lvmh.com/the-group/lvmh-group, accessed February 3, 2013.*

(1998), Céline fashions (1996), the winery Château d'Yquem (1996), the retail distributor DFS (1996), the perfume chains Sephora (1997) and Marie-Jeanne Godard (1998), Miami Cruise Line Service (2000), which owned duty-free shops, and the designer clothing company Donna Karan International (2000). It also had stakes in multiple luxury goods companies including Fendi, numerous wine makers and brands such as Ole Henriksen and Nude Brands.[26] In 2011, LVMH closed a deal to acquire the jewelry and watch maker Bulgari. Bulgari was a large player in the industry with 2010 revenues of €1 billion, and its integration into LVMH was expected to require substantial attention from the LVMH executive team. Other than Bulgari, LVMH made one other acquisition and invested in two companies in 2011. In general, the rate of acquisitions made by LVMH had fallen over the last few years with greater emphasis placed on buying partial stakes in companies.

27   In 2010, LVMH quietly acquired 17 percent of the outstanding shares of its competitor Hermès. Arnault purchased the shares through derivatives to circumvent the French law that requires a company to report more than a 5 percent ownership interest. This ensured that he did not have to make his position public until a larger share had been acquired. Hermès was surprised by the move and did not accept Arnault's assurance that LVMH had no intention to acquire Hermès or seek a board seat. By 2011, LVMH's stake in Hermès had increased to over 22 percent. To prevent a possible takeover, members of the Hermès family formed a holding company that controlled over 50 percent of the company's shares. In 2012, Hermès filed a lawsuit against LVMH, claiming irregularities in the way LVMH had acquired its stake.

FASHION AND LEATHER GOODS GROUP

28   The Fashion and Leather Group had a number of brands under its umbrella that sold handbags and leather goods. These brands included Louis Vuitton, Loewe, Fendi, Marc Jacobs, and Donna Karan New York. These brands had operated in different customer segments. Louis Vuitton had positioned its products in the absolute and aspirational customer segments. Loewe had been situated at the absolute customer segments and at the higher end of the aspirational customer segments. Prices for its handbags had started at $1,500, though most had been priced at between $2,000 and $4,000. Loewe's high-end handbags had been priced over $5,000 and they had emphasized their made-to-order offering, which had tended to be more expensive. Fendi and Marc Jacobs had offered products primarily to the aspirational customer segments. Handbags prices at Fendi had started at $600 though most handbags had been priced between $800 and $2,500. The high-end handbags had been priced around $4,000. At Marc Jacobs prices had started at $800, most of the handbags had been priced between $1,000 and $2,500, and high-end handbags had been priced between $10,000 and $25,000, though the selection at this range had been limited. Donna Karan New York in contrast had served the accessible customer segment and had priced its handbags between $150 and $500. Details about Louis Vuitton's products and prices are provided in the next section.

29   The Fashion and Leather group's financials are given in Exhibit 3. Revenues for 2011 had grown in euro terms by 15 percent and organic growth, in constant exchange rate, was 16 percent. Revenues in 2010 had grown by 20 percent in euro terms and 13 percent in organic terms.[27] Revenues by region are provided in Exhibit 4.

---

[26]*http://www.hoovers.com/company/LVMH_Mo%EBt_Hennessy_Louis_Vuitton_SA/crxfci-1-1njhxk.html, accessed September 12, 2012.*
[27]LVMH Annual Report, 2011.

EXHIBIT 3 LVMH Revenue and Recurring Operating Profit by Business Group

LVMH Revenue by Business Group			
	2009	2010	2011
Wines and Spirits	2,740	3,261	3,524
Fashion and Leather Goods	6,302	7,581	8,715
Perfumes and Cosmetics	2,741	3,076	3,195
Watches and Jewelry	764	985	1,949
Selective Retailing	4,533	5,378	6,436
Other activities/eliminations	−27	39	−27
	17,053	20,320	23,792

Profit from Recurring Operations by Business Group			
	2009	2010	2011
Wines and Spirits	760	930	1,101
Fashion and Leather Goods	1,986	2,555	3,075
Perfumes and Cosmetics	291	332	348
Watches and Jewelry	63	128	265
Selective Retailing	388	536	716
Other activities/eliminations	−136	−160	−242
	3,352	4,321	5,263

Source: LVMH Annual Reports, 2009 to 2011.

EXHIBIT 4 Fashion and Leather Goods Revenue by Region

EUR Million	2006	2007	2008	2009	2010	2011
Revenue	5,222	5,628	6,010	6,302	7,581	8,712
Asia	20%	23%	25%	28%	30%	32%
France	9%	9%	8%	8%	8%	8%
Europe	19%	20%	21%	21%	21%	20%
U.S.	21%	20%	19%	18%	18%	18%
Japan	26%	22%	20%	18%	16%	14%
Rest of the World (ROW)	5%	6%	7%	7%	7%	8%

Source: LVMH Annual Reports, 2006 to 2011.

30 Even though the group had multiple brands, the largest brand, the one that drove the financial performance of the group, had been Louis Vuitton. As such the financial performance of the Fashion and Leather group had been expected to largely mirror the performance of Louis Vuitton. In addition, decisions made by Louis Vuitton had a direct and substantial influence on the performance of the group.

LOUIS VUITTON

31 After taking control of LVMH, Arnault weeded out the old executives from LV and in 1990 brought in Yves Carcelle as CEO. Under the new leadership and in partnership with Marc Jacobs as head designer, LV flourished. Arnault and Carcelle brought attention to bear on the profitability and efficiency of the business. They continued the practice of selling only through company-owned stores, but they also made other changes. Unlike Racamier, under whose leadership 70 percent of production was outsourced, the two brought production in-house, soon expanding the number of factories in France from five to 10. In 2004, they bought out distributors and took direct control of the distribution channel. According to Arnault, "If you control your factories, you control your quality" and "If you control your distribution, you control your image."[28] In addition, in partnership with Marc Jacobs, an increased focus was put on new product designs and innovations that resulted in a slew of creative and successful products.

32 LV products included a wide range of luxury fashion goods for women and men including handbags, wallets, luggage, accessories, ready-to-wear clothes, shoes, watches, and jewelry, though the company's mainstay, and what it was known for, was its collection of leather products. One area in which LV did not, in 2011, offer products was perfumes. This was an area into which the company was considering expanding. The perfume market stood at €19 billion in 2011[29] and was expected to grow by 5 percent in 2012. The absolute and aspirational segment made up about 25 percent of the market. Of note was that the parent organization, LVMH, had significant experience in the perfume products in its perfumes and cosmetics division. This division had industry-leading brands such as Christian Dior, Guerlain, and Givenchy under its umbrella.

Pricing and Customer Segments

33 LV's product portfolio included offerings for all three segments but had primarily focused on the Absolute and Aspirational customer segments. Prices for handbags had varied from a low of US$300 for clutches to a range of mid-priced products priced between US$750 and US$3,500. At the high end, handbags had been priced anywhere from US$3,500 to US$35,000 with some handbags selling for US$100,000 or more. The higher end handbags had included custom designed bags that took five months to deliver. In many of its stores, an area used to be reserved for the best customer to shop in privacy. In some cities, LV had owned private apartments and yachts, which included amenities such as butler service, where customers would be given design consultations and could be fitted.

34 Prices had been tightly controlled. Products were never discounted or sold in value packs. LV, like many others in the industry, had considerable power to increase prices. While price increases had slowed after the 2008 recession, they started picking up in the second half of 2010. In 2010, prices in the euro zone were increased between 2 and 3 percent. In 2011, prices were increased by 16 percent in the United States, 5 percent in Europe and 11 percent in China.[30] Some of these price increases were made in response to currency fluctuations. Between the second quarters of 2011 and 2012, overall prices were increased by 7 percent.[31] These price increases made up for the smaller price increases that

[28]Thomas, Deluxe, p. 52.
[29]Claudia D'Arpizio, *2012 Luxury Goods Worldwide Market Study,* 11th Edition, Bain and Company, Milan, October 2012.
[30]Transcript from investor conference call on October 18, 2011.
[31]Transcript from investor conference call on July 26, 2012.

had followed the 2008 recession. In the words of a senior executive interviewed for the magazine *The Economist*:

> There are four main elements to our business model—product, distribution, communication and price. Our job is to do such a fantastic job on the first three that people forget all about the fourth.[32]

35   However, while prices had increased in 2011, customers, especially those in the accessible and aspirational segments, were becoming value conscious. It was therefore expected that future price rises would be more moderate.

Distribution

36   As previously mentioned, LV sold most of its merchandise through its own stores. The number of stores had increased from 368 at the end of 2006 to 425 at the end of 2008. By the first quarter of 2010, the store network had increased to 451.[33] Fewer than 10 stores had been inaugurated in 2010, with the retail network totaling 458[34] stores by the end of the first quarter of 2011. These stores were located at prime venues in major cities. Stores in many of the cities were anchored by flagship stores; all stores were designed centrally at LV's main operations in France to communicate the company's French tradition and heritage as well as to provide a unique experience of opulence and luxury. Centralized control of the store designs allowed for a common brand image across them. Some had areas that were available to members only. Membership required recommendation by a current member, a one-time initiation fee, and an annual membership fee. Per store, revenues were €12.7 million, more than double the per store revenue figures for Gucci and Prada.[35]

37   During the opening of the Bond Street store in London, Jacobs commented: "I think it [Louis Vuitton] is one of the few companies … who have made that leap to create an alternative universe . . . another universe that co-exists with the classic universe that it is built on."[36]

38   Products were only sold through LV stores. Brands were not licensed to third parties. Excess stock was destroyed rather than discounted. Products were not sold through outlet stores or in value packs.

39   Tight control of distribution also ensured that LV products did not get "lost" during distribution to show up in the gray market. Another strategy used to counteract gray markets was to ensure that price differentials between markets were not high enough to encourage the creation of gray markets. For example, LV entered Japan when it discovered that third parties were bringing products that had been purchased in stores in Europe into the country and selling them at very high prices. The company set a formula whereby Japanese prices were set at 1.4 times the prices in France, a price point that was significantly lower than what third parties were selling at. More recently, despite difficult local economic conditions, the company increased prices in Europe because Chinese shoppers were buying in Europe rather than in China to take advantage of the high price differential partly caused by high import duties in China.

40   LV had also sold its products online. While it had been difficult to sustain an aura of exclusivity in the online marketplace, this channel had provided access to a larger customer base. Online products had been offered in markets such as the United States, Europe, and

---

[32]*The Economist*, "The Substance of Style." September 17, 2009.
[33]Transcript from investor conference call on July 27, 2010.
[34]Transcript from investor conference call on July 26, 2011.
[35]http://www.businessweek.com/news/2011-11-16/vuitton-sees-growth-tied-to-invitation-only-luxury-salon-retail.html, accessed September 24, 2012.
[36]http://www.youtube.com/watch?v=jyp9QVQvPL4, accessed September 20, 2012.

Japan. They had, however, not been offered in China and other markets in Asia. Further, many of the higher end products, including the made-to-measure products, had not been sold through the online channel.

Manufacturing

41   LV manufactured all its products and did not buy products from third parties for resale. So, when it expanded its product portfolio to include shoes, it set up a shoe production facility in Italy. It operated 17 factories, of which 12 were located in France, three in Spain, and two in the United States. Most of its production was done in-house, with only parts, such as zippers, being sourced externally. In 2011, it opened its newest factory in Marsaz, France. The factory expanded production by 70 people.[37] The new factory, which took over three years to bring into production, helped ease some of the product shortages that in 2010 had forced the company to reduce store hours in France. New employees at the factory were trained by experienced workers. Given the size of the company, the new factory could be considered a small increase in capacity. LV tried its hand at expanding manufacturing internationally. In 2007, it announced the setting up of a shoe factory in Pondicherry, India. However, in 2011, the plant closed due to labor trouble.

Improving Efficiency

42   LV had also focused on improving the efficiency of its production system through the introduction of manufacturing practices inspired by the lean production techniques used by Toyota Motors. The program, implementation of which was started in 2005, reduced the level of specialization of an employee and trained employees in multiple activities, thereby improving productivity. The manufacturing line was reorganized. Originally goods in production would be put on carts and wheeled to workers, resulting in goods staying a long time on carts. The new system organized workers in groups of six to 12, with the complete manufacturing of a product staying within the group. These changes not only increased production efficiency but also, since the workers were less specialized now, allowed the company to shift groups to manufacture different products in response to changes in demand. Increased automation, such as the use of robots, also helped improve efficiency. At its peak, efficiency was increased by 5 percent per year, though a more sustainable rate was expected to be 3 percent per year.

43   However, improved efficiency in manufacturing had some consequences. The LV brand projected its products as being handmade by artisans. Customers, especially those in the top two segments, expected their products to be unique and designed and crafted by artisans. Too much reliance on automated manufacturing processes could undermine the appeal of the brand to these customer segments. For example, in 2010, two of LV's ads were banned in the United Kingdom for implying that its bags were handcrafted while in reality they were machine stitched. As Yves Carcelle said in an interview with the *Wall Street Journal*: "Our paradox is how to grow without diluting our image."[38]

44   The focus on improving efficiency was also true for all other departments. For example, rather than a sales person going to the back room to pick up products and leaving the customer alone, an assistant would bring the products to the sales person. At checkout time, products would be packaged in the back room and brought to the customer. Experienced sales persons therefore could concentrate on selling without interruption.

---

[37]http://online.wsj.com/article/SB100014240527023033627104576409813842858304.html, accessed September 20, 2012.
[38]Ibid.

Product Design and Innovation

45 LV was known in the industry for having some of the top design and creative talent. Creative design and innovation in raw material and manufacturing processes were an important component in keeping ahead of the competition and providing customers with products that were viewed as unique. In an interview, some of LV's employees talked about what this involved:

> There is a connection between sophistication and expertise. . . . For example, with the basket bag this season, it looks very simple, but actually it wasn't simple because it was two layers bonded together—a technique that was embossed and cut out and perforated at the same time. Before that we'd only done perforations, so we were challenging the production team to do [multiple techniques] at the same time. So there's always some way in which we are pushing new and innovative ways of working.[39]

> The words they use at the factory are "We'll try!" . . . It's very rare. I don't think there was anything for the show they couldn't do. . . . We sit down and we work out how we can achieve what we need. I think that's the magic of being here.[40]

46 And specifically on leather goods:

> It's the heart of the business, it's the image of the business—leather goods are the core of the company. Working on the fashion leather goods was amazing training and experience. . . . How do you convey the message of Marc throughout the store network—how is that creativity communicated? I'm not just talking about an advert at the end of the line. It's about how to release things, how things are evolving creatively and implementing that within the business. If the bags are getting more sophisticated how do you speak about that? How do you treat the bags? So there's lots going on there.[41]

Quality

47 Part of making top-quality products involved sourcing high-quality materials. For example, for top-end products, leather was sourced from northern Europe since leather from cattle there had fewer blemishes from insect bites. Products were also put through rigorous testing to ensure quality. Some of the techniques used included a robot that repeatedly dropped a bag containing a three-and-a-half kilogram weight, a machine that opened and closed a zipper 5,000 times, and another that shot ultraviolet rays at the bag to test for fading.[42] All products had a lifetime repair guarantee.

Competition

48 LVMH, the parent company of LV, was the largest player in the industry with 2011 sales of over €23 billion. Other large players included the conglomerates PPR and Richemont. PPR, headquartered in France, marketed a wide range of products from fashions and beauty care to home appliances. It owned brands such as Gucci and Puma. Sales in 2011 were over €12 billion with Gucci accounting for €3 billion of those sales. PPR also sold leather handbags and luggage. Its total sales of luxury goods in 2011 were nearly €5 billion. The other large player, Richemont, was based in Switzerland and also operated a wide range of businesses including jewelry, luxury watches, leather goods, and apparel. Some of its

[39]Golbin, *Louis Vuitton/Marc Jacobs,* p. 143.
[40]Ibid.
[41]Ibid., p. 139.
[42]http://www.businessweek.com/stories/2004-03-21/the-vuitton-money-machine, accessed September 20, 2012.

brands included Cartier, Baume and Mercier, Montblanc, and Piaget. Its sales in 2011 were nearly €9 billion.

49   Many of the companies, especially in Europe, were controlled by founding families who owned either a majority or a sizable minority position in the firm. This was true of larger players such as PPR, where the founding family controlled over 40 percent of the outstanding shares, and of smaller companies such as Hermès, where the founding family controlled over 50 percent of the outstanding shares. The companies were fiercely protective of their brands that in many cases were over 100 years old.

50   Brands that LV competed against were either owned by conglomerates, such as PPR, or by smaller companies such as Hermès or Prada. Exhibits 5 and 6 provide an overview of the main competitors and their sales distribution by region.

51   Details on each of the competitors are provided below.

Hermès

52   Competition from Hermès came in the absolute and aspirational segments. Hermès prided itself on producing exclusive highquality goods that were produced by experienced craftsmen using the best material available. The company promoted itself as innovative and creative with the capability to design and produce unique products. Some of these products, such as Birkin handbags, had a waiting list that was months long. Prices for the Birkin bag started around US$5,000 and went up to five and six digits. Most of the handbags were priced between US$2,000 and US$10,000, though many were priced higher.[43] The company produced some of the most expensive handbags in the world. In 2012, for example, Hermès released a handbag priced at US$2 million. In addition to this ready-made line of handbags, Hermès was also known for designing and manufacturing high-end handbags to customer specifications.

53   Hermès's range of products included leather goods, apparel, saddlery, silk products, shoes, accessories, and fragrances, though 47 percent of its sales came from leather goods.[44] Its products were sold worldwide through company-owned stores and through select retailers. In all cases, Hermès kept tight control of distribution and prices. Revenue breakdown by region, including growth rates, are given in Exhibit 6. Given its rapid growth, Hermès was expected to focus in 2012 on continuing to improve manufacturing capacity. Most of this manufacturing was located in France and emphasized traditional manufacturing practices rather than assembly-line or mechanistic manufacturing processes.

Gucci

54   Gucci was part of the PPR group. It designed, manufactured, distributed, and sold leather goods, ready-to-wear apparel, silks, timepieces, jewelry, and fragrances. Its mission was to provide excellent products and experience for its customers based on heritage, craftsmanship, high quality, and innovation backed by a "Made in Italy" label. In 2012, its handbag prices started in the US$850 range with most priced between US$1,000 and US$3,000. Some bags were priced as high as US$4,700.[45] Most of its products were manufactured in Italy and were largely sold through 376 DOS and some through department stores. The brand was making significant efforts to reduce distribution through resellers and also making efforts to limit merchandise offered at discount prices.

55   In 2011, Gucci achieved revenues of €3.14 billion and a recurring operating profit of €946 million. Revenues had grown by 18 percent in euro terms and 19 percent in constant exchange rate terms from the previous year.[46]

---

[43]http://www.hermes.com/index-ca-en.html, accessed December 3, 2012.
[44]Hermes Annual Report, 2011.
[45]http://www.gucci.com/ca-en/home, accessed February 3, 2013.
[46]PPR Annual Report, 2011.

EXHIBIT 5 Louis Vuitton Competitor Overview

	Gucci		Bottega Veneta		Prada		Hermes		Chanel S.A.[1]		Coach		LV	
	2010	2011	2010	2011	2010	2011	2010	2011	2010	2011	2010	2011	2010	2011
Ownership	Part of PPR PPR:		Part of PPR PPR:		Publicly Traded		Publicly traded.		Privately Held		Publicly Traded		Part of LVMH	
status	Publicly Traded with 40% controlled by insiders		Publicly Traded with 40% controlled by insiders		80% controlled by insiders		Hermes family controlled 50.2%						LVMH: Publicly Traded with over 40% owned by Arnault Family	
Customer Segment Served	Aspirational Accessible		Absolute Aspirational		Aspirational Accessible		Absolute Aspirational		Absolute Aspirational		Accessible		Absolute Aspirational Accessible	
Distribution Channels	Direct owned stores Online		Direct Owned Stores Franchises Select Retail Stores Online		Direct Owned Stores Franchises (33 in 2010, 26 in 2011) Select Retail Stores Online		Direct Owned Stores (193 in 2010, 205 in 2011) Select Retailers (124 in 2010, 123 in 2011) Online		Direct Owned Stores Select Retailers		Direct Owned Stores Franchises Outlet Stores Select Retail Stores Licensing Online		Direct owned stores Online	
EUR Millions														
Revenues	2666	3148	511	683	2047	2556	2401	2841	NA	3000	3127	3581	7581	8712
Recurring Operating Income	757	946	130	205	418	629	668	885	NA	NA	981	1137	2555	3075
Stores	317	376	148	170	309	388	317	328	NA	NA			451	458

Prada revenues excludes royalties of 32m
NA = Not Available
Coach financials converted from US$ to euro at €1 = US$1.33

Source: PPR, Prada, Hermes, Coach Annual Reports. 2010 to 2011.

EXHIBIT 6   Competitor Sales by Region—2011

	Gucci		Bottega Veneta		Prada		Hermes		Coach	
	Revenue	Growth	Revenue	Growth	Revenue	Growth	Revenue	Growth	Revenue	Growth
Europe	881	13%	184	42%	986	17%	1055	17%		
Asia-Pacific (incl China)	1165	23%	239	46%	873	42%	808	17%	508	34%
China	708	29%	155	75%	525	40%	NA	NA		
Japan	378	4%	137	4%	257	16%	472	−1%	635	12%
Americas	567	19%	96	28%	393	20%	464	26%	2439	12%
ROW	157	NA	27	NA	15	29%	43	36%	NA	NA

Prada revenues excludes royalties of 32m
Coach financials converted from US$ to euro at €1 = US$1.33
NA = Not Available

Source: PPR, Prada, Hermes, Coach Annual Reports, 2011.

Bottega Veneta

56   Bottega Veneta was also part of the PPR group. Its revenues in 2011 were €683 million and recurring operating income was €205 million, up 33 percent from the previous year in both euro and constant exchange rate terms. The majority of its products were leather goods, though it also sold shoes, ready-to-wear apparel, and fragrances. Its brand was based on exclusivity, craftsmanship, the highest quality, and innovation, also backed by a "Made in Italy" label. Products were sold through 170 DOS and through other retail channels such as select department stores and franchises. For 2011, sales from DOS had increased by 32 percent and through the wholesale channel by 41 percent.[47]

57   Prices for handbags started at US$1,400, with the upper end of the ready-to-wear collection priced at over US$28,000.[48]

Prada

58   The Prada Group was headquartered in Italy though its shares were listed on the Hong Kong Stock Exchange. In all, 19 percent of Prada Group shares were publicly traded. The group owned a number of well-known brands anchored by its famous Prada and Miu Miu brands that covered mainly leather goods and shoes but also included accessories, jewelry, and fragrances. The company's brands were based on heritage and craftsmanship, high quality, and innovation. DOS accounted for 78 percent of its sales while the rest came from wholesale channels that sold to select department stores across the world. Its goods were manufactured in-house with factories located in Italy and the United Kingdom.

59   Revenues in 2011 were €2.6 billion and net income was €436 million. Revenues had grown by 25 percent over the previous year in euro terms and by 26 percent in terms of constant exchange rates. Sales in the retail channel had increased by 37 percent in 2011, while sales through the wholesale channel had declined approximately 5 percent.[49]

60   Prada priced its bags starting at US$1,000, with most bags priced between US$1,500 and US$4,000. Bags at the high end went for between US$6,000 and US$10,000.

[47]PPR Annual Report, 2011.
[48]http://www.bottegaveneta.com/, accessed February 3, 2013.
[49]Prada Annual Report, 2011.

Chanel

61 Chanel S.A., established in the early 1900s, was a privately held fashion house headquartered in France. The company's products were wide-ranging including sunglasses, perfumes, skin-care products, ready-to-wear collections, handbags, shoes, and accessories. It sold its products through company-owned stores and select department stores. In 2012, its accessories, including handbags and other leather products and apparel, were not sold online.

62 Since it was a privately held company, financial information was not publicly available. However, industry sources pegged Chanel's 2012 revenues at around €3 billion.[50] Other indicators provided a clue to Chanel's position in the marketplace *vis-à-vis* LV. An analysis of Web searches indicated that the four most searched handbag brands online were LV, Chanel, Gucci, and Hermès accounting for 30 percent, 23 percent, 13 percent, and 10 percent respectively.[51] Chanel was also ranked higher than its competitors in terms of brand quality, customer experiences, and social status by high-income earners.[52]

63 Chanel priced its handbags starting at US$1,650, with most handbags priced between US$2,500 and US$5,000. High-end handbags were priced between US$6,000 and US$10,000.

Coach[53]

64 Coach was firmly entrenched in the accessible customer segment. Most of its handbags were priced between US$200 and US$600, with the most expensive ones priced around US$1,000. While Coach was not a direct competitor, it was an example of a company whose product price range overlapped with that of LV. It was the type of company with which LV would have to compete if it decided to enter the accessible customer segment.

65 Coach's products were sold directly through company-owned stores, which included factory outlets, and indirectly through the wholesale channel via department stores. In North America, for example, Coach's products were sold through 354 company-owned retail stores, 180 factory stores, and 990 third-party department stores. However, 81 percent of its revenue came from the direct channel.

66 Coach outsourced its manufacturing with sourcing and product development offices located in Hong Kong, China, Vietnam, South Korea, and India. Its manufacturing was sourced out of China, Philippines, Taiwan, Vietnam, Thailand, India, Peru, Italy, and the United States. There was significant emphasis on product development with 71 percent of 2011 revenue generated from products that did not exist a year earlier.

67 For the 12 months ending June 30, 2012, Coach had annual net sales of US$4.8 billion, with net income of US$1.04 billion. Revenues over the last 12 months had increased by 14 percent and net income by 18 percent.

THE DILEMMA

68 Reviewing the history of LV and its current performance, a number of concerns came to mind. While it was obvious that the company's performance in 2010 and 2011 had been good, were there early signs of trouble? Could the recent performance be sustained? What were the options available to Michael Burke?

---

[50]http://www.businessoffashion.com/2012/10/ceo-talk-bruno-pavlovsky-president-of-fashion-chanel.html, accessed January 14, 2013.
[51]http://blogs.ft.com/material-world/2012/11/20/handbags-at-the-ready/?, accessed January 14, 2013.
[52]http://luxuryinstitute.com/blog/?tag=chanel, accessed January 14, 2013.
[53]Coach Annual Report, 2011.

69   Michael Burke was a veteran of LVMH who had been working with Bernard Arnault since 1986.[54] He had been widely credited for the turnaround of Fendi from a money-losing family business to a highly profitable brand.[55] In December 2011 he had been appointed as the CEO of Bulgari, a large and important acquisition made by LVMH. A year later, as he took over the helm of Louis Vuitton, some of the issues facing him were how should he balance the values and the heritage of Louis Vuitton, the seeds of which had been laid over 150 years ago by its founder, with the pressures to grow the business. How far could he push the Louis Vuitton machine without undermining those values?

[54]http://blogs.ft.com/material-world/2012/12/18/michael-burke-at-vuitton-old-hand-new-house-big-surprise/, accessed February 3, 2013.
[55]http://www.ft.com/intl/cms/s/0/699106c0-24eb-11e1-bfb3-00144feabdc0.html#axzz2JnN4m5oM, accessed February 3, 2013.

Case 26

The Movie Exhibition Industry 2013

Brett P. Matherne, Georgia State University

Steve Gove, Virginia Tech

David Thornblad, Virginia Tech

1 It is apt that 2012's top-grossing film was *The Avengers* for movie studios and exhibitors sought to avenge a dismal prior year at the box office. Domestic box office receipts climbed 6 percent from 2011 to a record-setting $10.8 billion.[1] Three films, *The Avengers*, *The Dark Knight Rises*, and *Skyfall* grossed more than $1 billion *each* in global ticket sales (Exhibit 1). Behind the scenes, the success, even the fundamental health of the exhibition industry, is far less clear. Consider these contradictions:

- Domestic ticket revenues grew 6 percent in 2012, but that volume ranks just 13th since 1980. The 1.364 billion tickets sold is down 13 percent from the most recent high in 2002 of 1.575. The compound annual growth in tickets from 1980–2012 is just 0.91 percent (Exhibit 2).

- 2012's record revenues resulted from ticket price increases, not more attendees. At $7.94, the average ticket price has risen 24 percent since 2005. But over the long-term, prices keep lagging inflation, raising questions about the creation of differentiated value (Exhibit 3).

- The long-term per-capita trend is negative. In 2012 the average number of films seen per capita was 3.9.[2] In 1946, the peak of moviegoing in America, the industry sold 4 billion tickets and the typical American went to 28 films per year at the theater.

- Movies are more widely available than ever, creating new substitutes for where, when, and how to view movies.

2 Exhibitors are especially anxious for moviegoers to return to the theater as the industry has invested an estimated $1.6 billion to convert theaters from film to digital projection since 2005 (Exhibit 4). The main promises of digital projection are decreased distribution costs, 3D capability, and the potential to show alternative content. Despite the sizable investment, financial benefits have yet to materialize for exhibitors. Attendance decreased in 5 of the 8 years since conversion began.

3 Which represents the current and future state of the movie exhibition industry: The bright lights of a red carpet Hollywood premiere or a dimly lit marquee?

---

[1] All ticket sales and box office data in this section is from www.boxofficemojo.com
[2] MPAA 2011 Theatrical Statistics.

EXHIBIT 1 Top 25 Releases of 2012

Movie	3D	3D %	Studio	Genre	MPAA Rating	Prod. Budget (mil.)	Domestic Gross (mil.)	%	Rank	International Gross (mil.)	%	Rank	Total Gross (mil.)	Rank
The Avengers	Yes	52%	Buena Vista	Act Adv.	PG-13	$220.0	$623.4	41%	1	$888.4	59%	1	$1,511.8	1
The Dark Knight			Warner Bros.	ActThrl	PG-13	250.0	448.1	41%	2	632.9	59%	4	1,081.0	2
The Hunger Games			LGF	Act Adv.	PG-13	78.0	408.0	59%	3	278.5	41%	12	686.5	9
Skyfall			Sony	Act	PG-13	200.0	300.9	29%	4	737.6	71%	2	1,038.5	3
Twilight: Brk Dawn 2			Summit	Rom	PG-13	120.0	290.8	35%	5	532.5	65%	6	823.3	6
The Hobbit	Yes	49%	Warner Bros.	Fant	PG-13	175.0	288.7	31%	6	632.2	69%	5	920.9	4
Amazing Spider-Man	Yes	44%	Sony	Act Adv.	PG-13	230.0	262.0	35%	7	490.2	65%	8	752.2	7
Brave	Yes	32%	Buena Vista	Anim	PG	185.0	237.3	44%	8	298.1	56%	10	535.4	11
Ted			Universal	Comedy	R	50.0	218.8	43%	9	289.4	57%	11	508.2	12
Madagascar 3	Yes	45%	Para./DrmWrks	Anim	PG	145.0	216.4	29%	10	525.7	71%	7	742.1	8
Dr. Seuss—Lorax	Yes	50%	Universal	Anim	PG	70.0	214.0	61%	11	134.8	39%	19	348.8	17
Wreck-It Ralph	Yes	38%	Buena Vista	Anim	PG	165.0	181.4	51%	12	173.4	49%	17	354.8	16
Men in Black 3	Yes		Sony	Sci-F Com	PG-13	225.0	179.0	29%	13	445.0	71%	9	624.0	10
Lincoln			Buena Vista	Hist. Drama	PG-13	65.0	161.9	98%	14	3.3	2%	25	165.2	25
Ice Age: Cont. Drift	Yes	35%	Fox	Anim	PG	95.0	161.2	18%	15	714.0	82%	3	875.3	5
Snow White & Huntsman			Universal	Adv	PG-13	170.0	155.3	39%	16	241.3	61%	14	396.6	14
Hotel Transylvania	Yes	?	Sony	Anim	PG	85.0	146.6	46%	17	173.8	54%	16	320.4	18
Taken 2			Fox	Act	PG-13	45.0	139.5	38%	18	232.0	62%	15	371.6	15
Django Unchained			Weinstein	West	R	100.0	139.4	74%	19	48.4	26%	24	187.8	23
21 Jump Street			Sony	ActCom.	R	42.0	138.4	69%	20	63.1	31%	23	201.6	21
Les Miserables			Universal	Musc	PG-13	61.0	131.8	47%	21	150.5	53%	18	282.3	19
Prometheus	Yes	25%	Fox	Sci-Fi Act	R	130.0	126.5	31%	22	276.9	69%	13	403.4	13
Safe House			Universal	Act Thrl	R	85.0	126.4	61%	23	81.7	39%	20	208.1	20
The Vow			Sony/Sc. Gems	Drama	PG-13	30.0	125.0	64%	24	71.1	36%	21	196.1	22
Argo			Warner Bros.	Drama Thrl	R	45.0	115.3	62%	25	69.3	38%	22	184.5	24
Total for Top 25						$2,891.0	$5,536.3			$8,184.1			$13,720.4	
Average for Top 25		41%				$115.6	$221.5	47%		$327.4	53%		$548.8	

Notes: Data from Boxofficemojo.com, MPAA, NATO, and author estimates. 3D revenues is based on opening weekend. Genres as follows: Act = Action; Adv. = Adventure, Anim = Animation; Com = Comedy; Drama = Drama; Fant = Fantasy; Hist = Historical; Musc = Musical; Rom = Romance; Sci-F = Sci-Fi; Thrl = Thriller; West = Western. Some production budgets estimated.

EXHIBIT 2 Domestic Box Office Receipts and Ticket Sales, 1980–2012

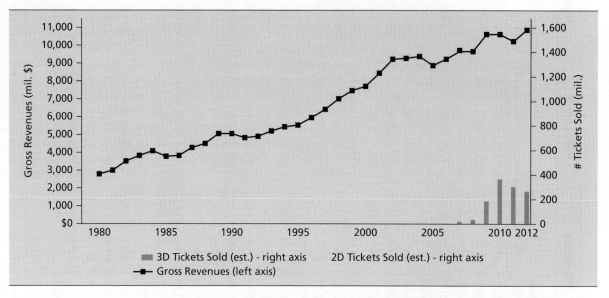

3D Tickets Sold (est.) - right axis   2D Tickets Sold (est.) - right axis
Gross Revenues (left axis)

	Compound Annual Growth Rates			
	Gross	**Overall**		
Period	**Revenues**	**Tickets Sold**	**2-D Tickets**	**3-D Tickets**
1980-2012	4.38%	0.91%	0.23%	
1980s	6.95%	2.38%	2.38%	
1990s	4.48%	2.35%	2.35%	
2000s	3.67%	−0.06%	−1.60%	217.14%
2010s	1.27%	0.95%	6.23%	−14.68%

Source: Boxofficemojo.com and author estimates. 3D ticket volume estimated based on reported 3D revenues with ticket prices estimated as 30% premium over 2D. Portion of 2012 3D revenue and ticket volume is estimated. 3-D CAGR calculated for periods 2007–2009 and 2010–2012.

THE MOTION PICTURE VALUE CHAIN

4   The motion picture industry value chain consists of three stages: studio production, distribution, and exhibition—the theaters that show the films. All stages are undergoing consolidation and technological changes, but the basic three-phase structure is largely unchanged since the 1920s.

Studio Production

5   The studios produce the lifeblood of the industry; they create motion picture content. Content drives attendance and studios are highly concentrated. The top six studios in 2012 created 17 percent of the films for the year, but these films accounted for 76 percent of the box office gross (Exhibit 5). The top 10 studios constitute over 90 percent of box office receipts. This concentration coupled with highly differentiated content gives the studios considerable negotiating and pricing power.

EXHIBIT 3   Ticket Prices 1980–2012

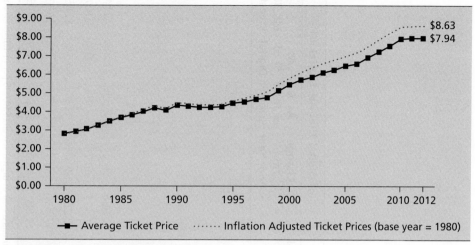

Based on Boxofficemojo.com, MPAA reports and author estimates.

Compound Annual Growth Rates	
Period	**Average Ticket Prices**
1980–2012	3.44%
1980s	4.63%
1990s	3.00%
2000s	3.88%
2010s	0.32%

6   Studios are increasingly managed as profit centers in large corporations. Management is risk adverse as investments are large and a formula for success elusive. Consider the fate of two comic book–inspired films in 2011. Warner Bros.'s *Green Lantern* was considered a flop, grossing $219 million ($116 million domestic, $103 internationally) and ending plans for a series. That same year Paramount's *Thor* grossed $449 million ($181 domestically, $268 internationally), giving the green light to a sequel.

7   Studios focus on 14–24-year-olds, consistently the largest audience for movies. At just 15 percent of the U.S. population, this group purchases 21 percent of all tickets. More narrowly, 10 percent of the population is "frequent" moviegoers who attend more than one movie per month and are responsible for half of all ticket sales.[3] Studios target this audience with PG and PG-13 fare including 19 of 2012's top 25 releases. However, domestic demographic trends are unfavorable. While the U.S. population will increase 42 percent by 2050, this core audience will increase just 35 percent (19 million) or 475 per existing screen (Exhibit 6).

8   The risks for studios are significant as production costs are considerable (Exhibit 1). Studios invested $1.6 billion for the 10 films that ranked among 2012's highest grossing ($165 million per film). Costs have increased faster than inflation. In 1980, the production

[3]MPAA 2011 Theatrical Statistics.

EXHIBIT 4 U.S. Theater Screens 2000–2011

Year	Total Screens		Analog Screens			Digital Screens				of Digital That Are Digital 3D				
	Change from Prior Year	#	#	Change from Prior Year	As % of Total Screens	#	Change from Prior Year	As % of Total Screen	Est. Digital Invest. (mil.)	#	Change from Prior Year	As % of Total Screens	As % of Digital	Est. 3D Invest.
2000		37,396	37,396		100.0%									
2001	-1.7%	36,764	36,764	-1.7%	100.0%									
2002	-4.0%	35,280	35,280	-4.0%	100.0%									
2003	2.5%	36,146	36,146	2.5%	100.0%									
2004	1.2%	36,594	36,594	1.2%	100.0%									
2005	6.2%	38,852	38,862	6.2%	100.0%	200		0.5%	$10					
2006	-1.1%	38,415	36,412	-6.3%	94.8%	2,003	901.5%	5.2%	$100					
2007	1.5%	38,974	34,342	-5.7%	88.1%	4,632	131.3%	11.9%	$256	986		2.5%	21.3%	$74
2008	-0.3%	38,843	33,319	-3.0%	85.8%	5,515	19.1%	14.2%	$311	1,427	44.7%	3.7%	25.9%	$107
2009	1.0%	39,233	31,815	-4.5%	81.1%	7,418	34.5%	18.9%	$453	3,269	129.1%	8.3%	44.1%	$245
2010	0.8%	39,547	23,773	-25.3%	60.1%	15,774	112.6%	39.9%	$985	7,837	139.7%	19.8%	49.7%	$588
2011	0.2%	39,641	14,020	-41.0%	35.4%	25,621	62.4%	64.6%	$1,606	13,001	65.9%	32.8%	50.7%	$975

Notes: Based on author estimates and MPAA reports on number of screens. Estimated investments (cumulative) based on estimated cost of digital screen ($50,000 per installation) and digital 3D ($75,000 per installation). Digital screen counts include digital 3D.

EXHIBIT 5   Top 6 Studios/Distributors 2012

Studio/ Distributor	2012				2000				% Change 2000–2012	
	Rank	$ Share	Total Gross	# Films	Rank	$ Share	Total Gross	# Films	Total Gross	# Films
Sony/Columbia	1	16.6%	$1,792	25	7	9.0%	$682	29	163%	–14%
Warner Bros.	2	15.4%	$1,665	36	3	11.9%	$905	22	84%	64%
Buena Vista	3	14.3%	$1,551	18	1	15.5%	$1,176	21	32%	–14%
Universal	4	12.2%	$1,324	17	2	14.1%	$1,069	13	24%	31%
20th Century Fox	5	9.5%	$1,025	19	6	9.5%	$723	13	42%	46%
Paramount/Dream Works	6	8.5%	$914	21	4	10.4%	$791	12	16%	75%
Total for top 6			$8,273	136			$4,664	81	77%	68%
Industry Total			$10,835	795			$7,661	478	41.4%	66.3%
Top 6 as % of Industry			76.3%	17.1%			61.4%	16.9%	24.3%	1.0%

Source: Author calculations based on data from Boxofficemojo.com.

EXHIBIT 6   U.S. Demographic Trends

Segment	% of Movie Tickets Purchased (2011)	# In 2010 (mil.)	% of Population (2010)	# in 2050 (mil.)	% of Population (2050)	# Increase	% Change
Under 5 years		21.1	7%	28.1	6%	7.0	33%
5 to 13 yrs	15%	37.1	12%	50.7	12%	13.6	37%
14 to 17 yrs	9%	17.0	5%	22.7	5%	5.7	34%
18 to 24 yrs	12%	30.7	10%	39.5	9%	8.8	29%
25 to 44 yrs	28%	83.1	27%	110.9	25%	27.8	33%
45 to 64 yrs	24%	81.0	26%	98.5	22%	17.5	22%
65 yrs+	11%	40.2	13%	88.5	20%	48.3	120%
Total (mil.)		310.2		439.0		128.8	42%

Source: Data: U.S. Census (2008), Table 2. Projections of the Population by Selected Age Groups and Sex for the United States: 2010 to 2050 (NP2008-T2), MPAA Theatrical Statistics, and author estimates.

budget for the highest grossing films averaged just $11 million. In the 1990s films turned to special effects and costs reached $102 million (up 827 percent). Today, special effects alone can top $100 million for a major production. These investments are considerable, yet no guarantee for success: *Green Lantern*, the flop, was made for $200 million while the successful *Thor* cost $150 million.

9   Domestic exhibitors were once the sole distribution channel for films. This has changed dramatically. Films must increasingly cross cultural and language boundaries and appeal to the global market. Over 70 percent of U.S. studio revenues are now international

EXHIBIT 7 Domestic and International Box Office Receipts ($ bil.)

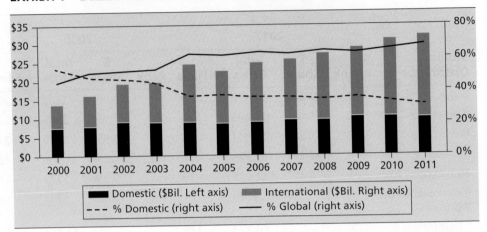

(Exhibit 7). Studios see this as the primary opportunity for growth. While domestic receipts increase on flat ticket sales, both ticket sales and dollar volume are rising rapidly internationally. From 2000 to 2012, domestic receipts grew at an average of just 3 percent while international growth averaged 13 percent annually. The studios are also changing their perspective on ticket prices in large population markets. In India, for example, attendees paid an average of just $0.50.[4] However, Indian exhibitors sold 3.3 billion tickets in 2008. At current growth rates, the attendance volume increase each year in India alone equals total current U.S. annual admissions.[5]

10   This trend of content internationalization shows no signs of abating. While the drama of *Argo* and the humor of *Ted* cost less to produce, they are risky in international markets. Franchise films with known characters, made in 3D and laden with special effects, present the least content risk internationally. Yet these films carry their own risk due to large budgets. The special effects alone for a major film may exceed $100 million. *The Avengers*, *The Dark Knight Rises*, and *Skyfall* all rank in the top 10 for worldwide gross. Combined they constitute an investment of $670 million in production costs.

11   As studios shift their focus to the international market they are less dependent on domestic exhibitors. This increases the threat of disintermediation through alternative distribution channels. Studios increase revenues through product licensing, DVD sales, and international expansion, at the same time the exhibitors—movie theaters—have seen their business decline.

Distribution

12   Distributors are the intermediaries between the studios and exhibitors. Distribution entails all steps following a film's artistic completion including marketing, logistics, and administration. Distributors either negotiate a percentage of the gross from the studio for distribution services or purchase rights to films, profiting directly the box office. Distributors select and market films to exhibitors' booking agents. They handle collections, audits of attendees, and other administrative tasks. There are over 300 active distributors, but most is done

[4]Thakur, A. (2009, July 29, 2009). India dominates world of films. *The Times of India*. Retrieved from Factiva.
[5]Thakur, A. (2009, July 29, 2009). India dominates world of films. *The Times of India*. Retrieved from Factiva.

by a few majors, commonly a division of a studio. Disney Pixar, for example, produced *Brave* while distribution was done by Disney's Buena Vista.

13   Until 2005, the distribution of all motion pictures in the United States entailed the physical shipment of reels of 35mm film, a process little changed from the 1940s. Each theater would receive a shipment of physical canisters containing a "release print" of a film. These prints cost $20,000–$30,000 in up-front costs and $1,000–$1,500 for each print. Print costs for a modern major picture opening on 3,500 screens costs $3.50–$5.25 million. This is borne by the studios and exhibitors, but paid for by movie attendees.

14   Beginning in 2006, distributors and studios encouraged exhibitors to transition to digital projection technology. The technology works by using high-powered LCD projectors to cast the movie onto a specialized screen. In lieu of film, the movies are delivered on reusable hard drives or via satellite or high-speed Internet. The threat of piracy is a major concern for the industry so all files are encrypted. The cost savings of digital distribution over film are considerable: The cost of each hard drive is $150, just 10 percent of the cost of physical film. Additionally, digital projection allows for consistently high-quality images as there is no physical wear to the film, and enables the exhibition of "alternative content"— images other than motion pictures that are obtained outside of the studio system.

15   The transition to digital projection involves considerable capital investment. Each digital projection system can serve a single screen and costs $50,000 to $75,000 including the projector, computers and hardware, and a specialized screen. To encourage the transition, distributors offered rebates in the form of virtual print fees (VPSs) for each film received digitally. These fees, as much as 17 percent of rental costs, expired in 2013.

Exhibition

16   Exhibitors offer a location where audiences can view a motion picture. The basic business model of exhibitors (using movies as the draw and selling concessions to make a profit) has changed little since the time of touring motion picture shows that would set up in town halls and churches. As the popularity of motion pictures expanded, permanent local theaters were established. Studios soon recognized the potential profit in exhibition and vertically integrated, allowing control over audiences and captured these downstream profits. This practice ended in 1948 with the Supreme Court's ruling against the studios in *United States v. Paramount Pictures*.

17   Theaters were divested by studios, leaving the two to negotiate film access and rental fees. Single theater and single screen firms exhibitors fared poorly as studios retained the upper hand in setting rental rates. Exhibitors sought to increase bargaining power and economies by consolidating, multiplying the bargaining power of individual theaters by the number of screens managed.

18   This reached its zenith in the 1980s with the mass rollout of the multiplex concept. Maximizing both bargaining power based on multiple screens while minimizing labor and facility costs, exhibitors constructed large entertainment complexes, sometimes with two dozen or more screens. Most of the original local single screen theaters that had survived were doomed as they were unable to compete on cost or viewing experience and unable to gain access to the capital needed to construct multiscreen locations. Today, the typical exhibitor location has 7–12 screens and is likely to be operated by Regal, AMC, Cinemark, or Carmike. These four operate 1,061 theaters in the United States (just 19 percent), but control 45 percent of the screens (Exhibit 8). This market concentration provides exhibitors with negotiating power for access to films, prices for films, prices for concessions, and greater access to revenues from national advertisers. However, the real power continues to remain with the studios due to differentiated content, the ability to play rival exhibitors against each other, and the increasing potential for disintermediation.

EXHIBIT 8   Leading U.S. Circuits 2012

Circuit	Total Screens	Total Theaters	Screens/ Theater	Analog (% Screens)	Digital (% of Screens)	Digital 3D (%Screens)
AMC (AMC, Loews)	5,128	346	14.5	55.1%	44.9%	31.3%
Carmike (Carmike)	2,254	237	9.5	5.6%	94.4%	33.0%
Cinemark (Cinemark, Century)	3,878	297	13.1	0.0%	100.0%	48.0%
Regal (Regal, United Artists, Edwards)	6,614	527	12.6	28.6%	71.4%	42.1%
Total for 4 Largest Circuits	17,874	1,061	12.4	27.1%	72.9%	39.1%
4 Largest Circuits as % of Industry Total	45.1%	18.6%				
Industry Total	39,641	5,697	6.9	35.4%	64.6%	32.8%

Source: Data from SEC filings, MPAA, NATO, and author estimates. Based on screens entering fiscal year 2012.

THE BUSINESS OF EXHIBITION

19   Exhibitors have three main revenue sources: box office receipts, concessions, and advertising (Exhibit 9). Managers have low discretion; their ability to influence revenues and expenses is limited. Operating margins average a slim 15 percent; net income may fluctuate

EXHIBIT 9   Typical Revenue and Expenses Per Screen at an 8-Screen Theater

REVENUES		
Box office ($285,650/$7.94 = 35,975 admissions; 691/week/screen)	$ 285,650	65%
Concessions (135,250/35,975 admissions = $3.75/admission)	$ 135,250	31%
Advertising ($21,500/35,975 admissions = $0.60/admission)	$ 21,500	5%
Total Revenues ($12.29/admission)	$ 442,400	100%
EXPENSES		
Fixed		
Facility	$ 50,000	11%
Labor	$ 40,000	9%
Utilities	$ 50,000	11%
Other SG&A	$ 60,000	14%
Total Fixed Costs	$ 200,000	45%
Variable		
Film Rental	$ 155,000	54%
Concession Supplies	$ 21,650	16%
Total Variable Costs	$ 176,650	40%
Total Expenses	$ 376,650	85%
OPERATING INCOME	$ 65,750	15%

Source: Based on author estimates.

wildly based on the tax benefits of prior losses. Overall, the business of exhibitors is best described as loss leadership on movies: the firms make money selling concessions and showing ads to patrons who are drawn by the movie.

Box Office Revenues

20 Ticket sales constitute two-thirds of exhibition business revenues. The return, however, is quite small due to the power of the studios. For large exhibitors, film costs average 53 percent of box office receipts. For smaller circuits, average costs are higher. Rental fees are based on the size of the circuit and the time and seat commitment made to a film. The revenues retained by the theater increases with each week following an opening. On opening weekend an exhibitor may pay the distributor 80–90 percent of the box office gross, retaining only 10–20 percent. In subsequent weeks the exhibitor's portion increases. The record-setting revenues at the box office have been the result of increases in ticket prices, the majority of which has flowed back to the studios.

21 The complexity of booking is increasing. The majority of revenues historically come from opening weekend. In industry terminology the "multiple" (the percentage coming after opening weekend) has been declining steadily, falling 25 percent since 2002,[6] putting exhibitors at increasing risk. While exhibition used to be a question of which movie to show, it now also involves decisions as to how many theaters to allocate to analog versus digital and 2D versus 3D. All these factors plus the "make or break" nature of opening weekend complicate the exhibitor's operations.

Concessions

22 Moviegoers frequently lament the high prices for concessions. Concessions average near 30 percent of revenues. Direct costs of just 15 percent make concessions the largest and sometimes sole source of exhibitor profit. These profits are influenced by three factors: attendance, pricing, and material costs. The most important is attendance: more attendees = more concession sales. Per patron sales are influenced by prices—a common moviegoer complaint is high concession prices. The $4.50 and $8.00 price points for the large soda and popcorn are not accidental, but the result of market research and profit maximization calculation. Costs are influenced by purchase volume with larger chains able to negotiate better prices on everything from popcorn and soda pop to cups and napkins.

Advertising

23 The low margins derived from ticket sales cause exhibitors to focus on other sources of revenue. The highest margin, therefore the most attractive, is advertising. Since 2002, advertising revenues, and the time devoted to them at the start of every feature, have increased dramatically, climbing from $186 to $644 million.[7] Exhibitors also generate revenue through preshow and lobby advertising. Though this constitutes just 5 percent of exhibitor revenues, it is highly profitable (i.e., revenue with no direct monetary costs) and growing. Advertising revenues for exhibitors averaged $16,245 per screen.[8] Audiences, however, express dislike for advertising at the theater. Balancing the revenues from ads with audience tolerance is an ongoing struggle for exhibitors (Exhibit 10).

[6]Fritz, B., & Kaufman, A. (2011, December 30, 2011). Solid start, fast fade for movies, *LA Times*. Retrieved from latimes.com/entertainment/news/movies/la-fi-ct-box-office-wrap-20111230,0,2205189.story
[7]NATO press releases, Cinema Advertising, 2005–2012.
[8]NATO press releases, 2005–2012.

EXHIBIT 10   Exhibitor Advertising Revenue ($ mil.)

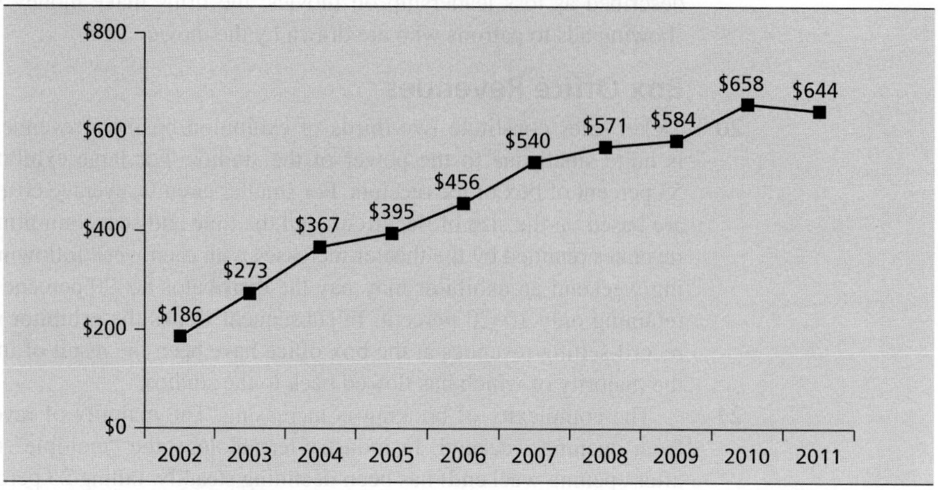

Source: NATO press releases 2005–2012.

THE MAJOR EXHIBITOR CIRCUITS

24   Four "circuits" dominate the domestic exhibition market, serving different geographic markets in different ways.[9] Regal, which operates its namesake Regal Theaters as well as United Artists and Edwards theaters, is the largest with 6,614 screens in 527 domestic theaters. Regal focuses on mid-size markets using multiplexes and megaplexes that average 12 screens per location, with an average ticket price of $8.90. AMC, operating under AMC and Loews chains, is the second largest domestic exhibitor with 5,128 screens in 346 theaters. Averaging nearly 15 screens per location, AMC leads the industry in the operation of large multiplexes. They do so by concentrating on urban areas near large population centers such as those in California, Florida, and Texas. By focusing on 3-D, IMAX, and other premium viewing experiences, AMC achieves the highest ticket prices, averaging $9.04. Cinemark is the third largest player with 3,878 screens in nearly 300 domestic locations under the Cinemark and Century brands. Cinemark serves smaller markets, operating as the sole theater in over 80 percent of its markets. Their average ticket price of $6.72 in 2012 was the lowest of the major chains. Carmike concentrates on small to midsized markets, targeting populations of less than 100,000 that have few alternative entertainment options. They do so with fewer screens at each location. With 237 theaters, they have just 2,254 screens, an average of 9.5 per location. Carmike's ticket price averaged just $6.85 (Exhibit 11).

25   While ticket prices vary considerably, differences in net profit margins are due mostly to differences in utilization and the costs of facilities, labor, and utilities. Despite considerably size differences, the actual cost of content for these circuits varies little among the majors circuits. Regal's is lowest at 52 percent of admission revenues, followed by AMC (53 percent), Carmike (54 percent), and Cinemark (56 percent). While the rentals costs for these circuits are similar, they are lower than for smaller circuits.

26   The circuits' ability to efficiently utilize their facilities varies considerably. Cinemark's average of 41,787 attendees per screen is nearly double Carmike's 22,032 per screen. The differences in utilization combined with differences in the underlying costs of facilities, wages, and

[9]Data on the firms, theaters and screens, location, etc. from Web sites and SEC filings.

EXHIBIT 11   Select 2012 Carmike, Cinemark, and Regal Financials

	Carmike	Cinemark**	Regal
Theater and Attendance Information			
Screens (U.S. only)	2,502	3,916	6,880
Theaters (U.S. only)	249	298	540
Screens per Theater (U.S. only)	10	13	13
Total U.S. Attendance (in thousands)	50,357	163,639	216,400
Avg Ticket Price	$ 6.85	$ 6.72	$ 8.90
Avg Concessions	$ 3.10	$ 3.34	$ 3.46
Avg Attendance per Screen	20,127	41,787	31,453
Avg Admission Revenue per Screen	$137,130	$ 280,797	$ 279,811
Income Statement ($ mil.)			
Revenues			
Admissions	$ 343.10	$ 1,099.60	$ 1,925.10
Concessions*	$ 172.58	$ 546.20	$ 748.40
Other Income*	$ 23.62	$ 50.10	$ 150.70
Total Revenues	$ 539.30	$ 1,695.90	$ 2,824.20
Admissions as % of Revenues	64%	65%	68%
Concessions as % of Revenues	32%	32%	26%
Other as % of Revenues	4%	3%	5%
Expenses			
Exhibition	$ 186.00	$ 610.50	$ 1,000.50
Concessions	$ 23.20	$ 71.10	$ 101.10
Building, Wages, Utilities, & Other Operating Costs	$ 211.70	$ 548.20	$ 1,120.30
Total Cost of Operation	$ 484.60	$ 1,229.80	$ 2,490.00
Operating Income	$ 54.70	$ 466.10	$ 334.20
Operating per admission	$ 1.08	$ 2.85	1.54
Operating Income as % total revenue	10%	27%	12%
Exhibition Costs as % of Admission Revenues	54%	56%	52%
Concessions Costs as % of Concession Revenues	13%	13%	14%
Buildings, wages, utilities, & other costs as % of Total Revenues	39%	32%	40%
Buildings, wages, utilities, & other costs per attendee	$ 4.20	$ 3.35	$ 5.18
Net Income	$ 96.30	$ 171.42	$ 144.80
Net Profit Margin	18%	10%	5%
Balance Sheet (dollars in millions)			
Total Assets	$ 712.70	$ 3,862.41	$ 2,209.50
Total Debt	$ 434.70	$ 1,914.18	$ 1,995.20
Debt: Assets Ratio	0.61	0.50	0.90

Source: Based on SEC filings and author estimates.
*Carmike reports aggregated concession and advertising revenues. Amounts are estimated.
**Theater, screen, and revenue expense data for Carmike's U.S. operations. Net income, assets, and debt figures are consolidated (domestic and international).

other expenses results in high variability in their costs on a per ticket basis. At $5.18, Regal's cost per attendee is the highest, followed by Carmike ($4.20) and Cinemark ($3.35).

27   Despite the trend toward internationalization by studios, exhibitors until recently have been exclusively domestic firms. Cinemark has had the largest international presence with 167 theaters (1,324 screens) in Mexico and seven Central and South American countries. In 2012, AMC was acquired by the Chinese conglomerate Dalian Wanda Group Corp. for a reported $2.6 billion.[10] Wanda, with interests in property, entertainment, and tourism, owns and operates 730 screens in China responsible for 15 percent of the Chinese box office with plans to expand to 2,000 screens. The deal will make AMC the largest global exhibition company.

28   Overall, while the major circuits focus on different geographic locations, there is little differentiation in the offerings of exhibitors within individual markets. Prices differ little, the same movies are shown at the same times, and the food and services choices are nearly identical. Competition between theaters within markets often comes down to distance from home, convenience of parking, and proximity to restaurants.

CHALLENGES FOR EXHIBITORS

29   Exhibitors are faced with an increasing number of challenges in their operating environment.

Benefiting from Digital Investments

30   Exhibitors have made considerable investments in digital projection technology. At the start of 2012, two-thirds of the 39,641 screens in the United States had been converted to digital with the remainder expected to be converted by 2014. The total investment by exhibitors is $1.6 billion. The benefits of this conversion should manifest themselves in lower exhibitor costs and increased revenues. To date, these do not appear to have accrued to exhibitors.

31   On the cost side, digital distribution dramatically reduces distribution costs when compared to physical film. Digital distribution is expected to save $1 billion annually on print costs and distribution. Yet there is little evidence to date these savings will accrue to the exhibitors. Film rental fees, which include distribution costs, have held steady despite the transition to digital. On the revenue side, exhibitors have seen significant additional per ticket revenues from surcharges for enhanced viewing experiences, primarily 3D. 3D content requires the cooperation of studios and exhibitors. For studios, 3D adds 15–20 percent to the cost of production. For exhibitors, 3D requires conversion to digital projection and the added costs for 3D-capable equipment. Among domestic digital projection systems about half are 3D capable. The planned 2009 release of *Avatar* was used to spur digital installations. The film grossed $750 million domestically, with an estimated 82 percent from 3D viewings. The film was a critical and box office success, introducing audiences to a new age of 3D movies and projection. *Avatar*'s success led to an increase, perhaps excess, of 3D releases.

32   Opening weekend revenues attributable to 3D grew at an impressive CAGR of 42 percent from 2005–2012. The portion of opening weekend receipts from 3D movies averaged 63 percent from 2009 to 2011 (Exhibit 12). Today the 3D portion of major releases shows a worrisome trend. In 2011, only 45 percent of *Kung Fu Panda 2*'s box office gross came from 3D and Disney's *Pirates of the Caribbean* had just 47 percent.[11] In 2012, the average

---

[10]Kung, M., & Back, A. (2012). Chinese conglomerate buys AMC movie chain in U.S. *Wall Street Journal*, p. 2.
[11]Boorstin, J. (2011, May 31, 2011). Huge Upside and Ominous Underbelly from a Big Weekend Box Office. Retrieved from http://www.cnbc.com/id/43228469/.

EXHIBIT 12   **3D as % of a Film's Opening Weekend Receipts**

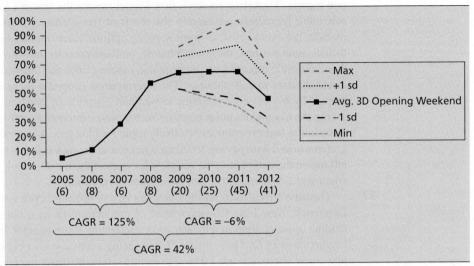

Source: Based on news reports and author estimates. Numbers in parentheses are the number of 3D releases in a year. CAGR calculations based on average opening weekend.

across all 3D films released declined to 45 percent. 3D may be an aspect of the theater experience that audiences are only occasionally willing to pay for. Some industry observers caution that the future opportunity to capitalize on 3D-driven revenues may be limited. "Certain movies are doing well in 3-D and others failing terribly," Bob Greenfield said. "People are getting a lot choosier. I would be surprised if in 2013 and 2014 we didn't see a more reduced slate that focuses on the films that deserve it."

33   Declining 3D attendance is a serious concern for exhibitors. With an average investment of $75,000, the payback period for 3D may be more than 3 years. The extent to which the conversion to digital will benefit exhibitors through cost reductions and revenue enhancement will be determined in the coming years as rental costs and 3D viewership rates are better established.

Countering the Declining Allure of the Theater

34   Traditionally, the draw of the theater may have been far more important than what film was showing. Moviegoers describe attending the theater as an experience, with the appeal based on:[12]

- the giant theater screen
- the opportunity to be out of the house
- not having to wait to see a particular movie on home video
- the experience of watching the movies with a theatrical sound system
- the theater as a location option for a date

35   The ability of theaters to provide these above what audiences can achieve at home appears to be diminishing. Of the reasons why people go to the movies, only the place aspects, the theater as a place to be out of house and as a place for dating seem immune from substitution. Few teenagers want movie and popcorn with their date at home with mom and dad.

[12]Mintel Report, Movie Theaters—U.S.—February 2008—Reasons to Go to Movies over Watching a DVD.

36   The overall "experience" currently offered by theaters is considered inadequate by many moviegoers. Marketing research firm Mintel reports the reasons for not attending the theater more frequently are largely the result of the declining experience. Specific factors include: the overall cost, at-home viewing options, interruptions such as cell phones in the theater, rude patrons, the overall hassle, and ads prior to the show.[13] A recent *Wall Street Journal* article reported on interruptions ranging from the intrusion of soundtracks in adjacent theaters to cell phones. "The interruptions capped a night of movie going already marred by out-of-order ticketing kiosks and a parade of preshow ads so long that, upon seeing the Coca-Cola polar bears on screen, one customer grumbled: 'This is obscene.'"[14] Recounting bad experiences is a lively topic for bloggers. A typical comment: "I say it has gotten worse. I hate paying $9.00 for a ticket and the movie is 90–100 minutes long, people talking on the cell phone, the people who work at the theaters look like they are bored, and when you ask them a question, the answer is very rude."[15]

37   The time allocated to preshow ads can be eye opening, even for industry insiders. Toby Emmerich, New Line Cinema's head of production, faced a not-so-common choice: attending opening night in a theater or in a screening room at actor Jim Carrey's house. Said Emmerich in an *LA Times* article "I love seeing a movie with a big crowd, but I had no idea how many obnoxious ads I'd have to endure—it really drove me crazy. After sitting through about 15 minutes of ads, I turned to my wife and said, 'Maybe we should've gone to Jim Carrey's house after all.'"[16]

The Home Viewing Substitution

38   For many, home viewing is growing as a viable substitute to theater attendance due to rapid improvements and cost reductions in home viewing technology and the widespread availability of timely and inexpensive content. The unique value proposition offered by movie theaters' large screens, the long wait for DVD release, and advantages of theatrical sound systems are also fading.

Home Viewing Technology

39   The average home television set is increasingly a large, high-definition set coupled with an inexpensive yet impressive audio system. Compared to home equipment options of the past, at-home technology increasingly represents a significant substitute for moviegoing. Prior to 2009, television transmissions were formatted as 480 interlaced vertical lines (480i) of resolution, the standard since the 1950s. FCC-ordered changes resulted in all broadcasters converting to digital broadcasts by February 2009, setting the stage for high-definition (HD) digital broadcasts providing up to 1,080 vertical lines of resolution (1080p).[17] This transition started a consumer movement to upgrade televisions. The transition also reduced the difference between home technology and the giant theater screen and sound system offered by theaters.

---

[13]Mintel Report, Movie Theaters—U.S.—February 2008—Reasons Why Attendance Is Not Higher.
[14]Kate Kelly, Bruce Orwall, and Peter Sanders, 2005, The Multiplex Under Siege, *Wall Street Journal*, December 24, 2005. P. P1.
[15]Based on comments found by the authors intermittantly on: http://cinematreasures.org/blog. Accessed 12/11/2008.
[16]Incident reported in Patrick Goldstein, 2005, Now playing: A glut of ads. *Los Angeles Times,* July 12, 2005 in print edition E-1; URL: http://articles.latimes.com/2005/jul/12/entertainment/et-goldstein12; accessed December 5, 2008.
[17]DuBravac, 2007.

40   The average size of TVs has increased dramatically: from 23 inches in 1997 to 36.8 inches in 2012. As LCD technology became the standard for both computer and television screens, manufacturing costs declined. Wholesale prices for televisions fell 65 percent from the late 1990s to 2007.[18] Between 2011 and 2012 alone the average retail price of a 32-inch TV declined from $546 to $435.[19] Consumers, however, spend more on every television, consistently electing to purchase larger and more advanced sets. In 2012 the average TV sold for $1,200.[20] Features such as 3D, Internet connectivity, and applications for Netflix, Hulu, and others are becoming common and add little to retail prices. Sharp, a leading TV manufacturer, predicts that by 2015 the *average* screen will reach 60 inches.[21] Home viewing technology may be reaching its apex. While technologically image size and quality can continue to increase, they are limited by practical realities. The ideal distance for viewing a 42" TV is 5'3". A 70" should be viewed from 8'9". The adoption and benefit of 80"+ sets will require a viewing distance that exceeds the size of most living rooms they would be installed in.

41   Large-screen televisions, low-cost high-definition DVD players, and audio and speaker components are commonly packaged as low-cost home theaters. The average Blu-ray DVD player now costs under $125 and 3D players under $150. Bundled home theater systems offer a movie experience that rivals many theaters, all for under $1,500. Mike Gabriel, Sharp's head of marketing and communications, stated, "People can now expect a home cinema experience from their TV. Technology that was once associated with the rich and famous is now accessible to homes across the country."[22]

Content Availability and Timing

42   The best hardware offers little value without content. Channels for renting or purchasing movies are increasing. "We're seeing a cultural shift occurring where people are consuming their entertainment from Netflix, the iPad, Hulu," said Paul Dergarabedian, president of Hollywood.com's box-office division. "There's more competition for the eyeballs of consumers."[23]

43   Since the 1980s, studios have relied on VHS, then DVD sales to fuel profits. DVD sales peaked at $13.7 billion in 2006.[24] This revenue stream fueled studio profits, but is in decline. In 2011, studio revenues from physical and digital sales totaled $9.5 billion.[25] Physical DVDs are widely available, but are now exceeded by digital purchases (e.g., Apple's iTunes and Amazon). To spur sales, studios have been consistently reducing the time period between theatrical and the DVD release. This "release window" declined from 166 days in 2000 to 120 days in 2012. Exhibitors express concern that these declines cannibalize theater sales. Studios, meanwhile, continue to seek ways to stem declining DVD sales and increase their return on each films. Decreased sales also results in lower prices for content. DVDs average $25 with upgrades to Blu-ray HD adding $5, and 3D and a digital copy for tablet or PC viewing adding another $3 each. Each sale nets the studio $12 to $15.[26]

[18]DuBravac, 2007.

[19]Tuttle, B. (2012). TV prices shrink—Yet average TV purchase costs more. *Time Magazine.*

[20]Tuttle, B. (2012). TV prices shrink—Yet average TV purchase costs more. *Time Magazine.*

[21]Source: Average TV size up to 60-inch by 2015 says Sharp. *TechDigest,* URL: http://www.techdigest.tv/2008/01/average_tv_size.html; accessed 2008/12/11.

[22]Source: Average TV size up to 60-inch by 2015 says Sharp. *TechDigest,* URL: http://www.techdigest.tv/2008/01/average_tv_size.html; accessed 2008/12/11.

[23]Verrier, R. (2012, December 30, 2011). U.S. theater owners get lump of coal at box office. *LA Times.* Retrieved from latimes.com/entertainment/news/movies/la-fi-ct-theaters-20111230,0,7228622.story

[24]Kung, M. (2012, May 10, 2012). Movie Magic to Leave Home For? *Wall Street Journal,* pp. D1–D2.

[25]Snider, M. (2012, 1/9/2012). Blu-ray grows, but DVD slide nips home video sales. *USA Today.*

[26]Jannarone, J. (2012, February 6, 2012). As Studios Fight Back, Will Coinstar Box Itself into a Corner? *Wall Street Journal,* p. C6.

44   Both studios and exhibitors are facing pressure from streaming and rental services. Once dominated by physical stores, movie rentals expanded into physical DVD channels with subscription (e.g., Netflix and Blockbuster) and one-up (e.g., Redbox and Blockbuster) options as well as subscription streaming (e.g., Netflix and Hulu). These offer very attractive prices for consumers, but have been identified by studios as a contributing factor for declining DVD sales. Studios net about $1.25 per DVD sold to a rental company.[27] This allows Netflix to offer a physical DVD subscription service of two DVDs out at any time for under $15 per month. RedBox's kiosk-based rentals are attractive to occasional viewers, costing as little at $1.25 per night.

45   Content streaming services grew from $992 million in 2011 to $2 billion in 2012.[28] Streaming is among the most cost effective for viewers and providers. Estimates put Netflix's average streaming cost at $0.51 per viewing. This is offset by fewer content options. Apple's iTunes provides perhaps the greatest selection, but with rentals at $4 to $6 per viewing, emphasizes selection and HD quality over Netflix's low cost. Streaming sufficiently cannibalized DVD sales to the point that studios imposed a 28-day delay from DVD sales to the availability of streaming. Exhibitors expressed strong encouragement when several studios expressed a desire for a 56-day delay to increase DVD sales.

46   Studios are seeking to increase their share of the rental market, putting them increasingly in direct competition with exhibitors. For the studios, each current video on demand (VOD) showing contributes $3.50 in revenue, far less revenue than DVD sales.[29] Studios continue to develop premium VOD as an alternative. The main feature of Premium VOD (P-VOD) is a decreased release window, including simultaneous release on films in theaters and through P-VOD. Exhibitors threatened a boycott due to Universal's plan for a P-VOD release of *Tower Heist* just three weeks after it opened in theaters. The plan was scrapped due to the threats. While exhibitors won the battle, the potential revenues from the planned $59.99 premium VOD will remain attractive to the studios.

47   Premium cable networks (e.g., HBO, Starz, etc.) offer a programmed lineup of movies, albeit at scheduled times and with monthly subscriptions, but at low per-viewing rates. All major cable and satellite providers offer VOD services and carry multiple channels focusing on films. Overall, the availability of content and the visual and audio experience available in the home is rapidly converging with the offerings available at a movie theater. As a blogger on the movie fan site Big Picture posted:

> I used to go to the movies all the time—Even my blog is called the Big Picture. Then I started going less—and then less still and now—hardly at all. My screen at home is better, the sound system is better, the picture is in focus, the floors aren't sticky and the movies start on time. My seat is clean. And there's no idiot chattering away 2 rows behind me, and (this is my favorite) THERE'S NO CELL PHONES RINGING. EVER.[30]

[27]Jannarone, J. (2012, February 6, 2012). As Studios Fight Back, Will Coinstar Box Itself into a Corner?, *Wall Street Journal*, p. C6.
[28]Zeitchik, S., & Horn, J. (2013). Sundance darlings eye alternative distribution platforms. *LA Times*. Retrieved from http://touch.latimes.com/#section/641/article/p2p-74047654/
[29]Jannarone, J. (2012, February 6, 2012). As Studios Fight Back, Will Coinstar Box Itself into a Corner?, *Wall Street Journal*, p. C6.
[30]The Big Picture | Why Is Movie Theatre Revenue Attendance Declining? URL: http://bigpicture.typepad.com/comments/2005/07/declining_movie.htm. Accessed 12/11/2008.

RECENT EXHIBITOR INITIATIVES

48   Exhibitors are well aware of the increasing number of ways in which to view motion pictures. They have a long tradition of adopting innovations that increase attendance or reduce costs. Exhibitors were among the first commercial adopters of air conditioning, which perhaps drew in as many customers as a refuge from summer heat as for entertainment. Advanced projection systems, screens, and sound systems have been continuously adopted to improve the viewing experience. Other innovations increase experience quality while also lowering costs. Stadium-style seating, now ubiquitous, was originally viewed as an experience differentiator, but equally beneficial is a reduction in the square footage needed per seat. This reduces the size and cost of facilities. Exhibitors continue to pursue a number of strategic initiatives aimed at increasing attendance, increasing the viewer's willingness to pay, and lowering costs.

TECHNOLOGICAL INNOVATIONS

49   The conversion to digital projection and rollout of 3D are not the only projection innovations being pursued. Some directors are opting to increase image quality by doubling the number of frames per second (fps) of film from the long-established standard of 24 to 48. Peter Jackson's 2012 *The Hobbit* was shown in the 48 fps format to a limited number of screens with the required projection technology. The increased frame rate results in an especially crisp image with no blurring that, while jarring to some, is said to create a sense of being part of live action.

50   Several circuits offer extra-large-scale screens as a feature.[31] Traditionally located only in specially constructed dome-shaped theaters in science museums, the original IMAX format utilized film that was 10 times the size of that used in standard 35mm projectors. IMAX now operates more than 600 screens. These circuit-based IMAX digital screens are far smaller than the original IMAX screens, but can be much larger than the typical theater screen. Located within Regal or AMC theater complexes, the screens are often booked and operated by IMAX. Action films, usually in 3D, are a staple. To capture more of this differentiated revenue, several circuits have begun creating their own super-size screens.

51   Sound systems are also being upgraded. In the 1980s, theaters impressed viewers with 7.1 sound systems—two rear channels (left and right), two channels mid-screen, two near the screen, one under the screen, and a subwoofer channel for bass. Such systems have long been available for homes. To keep theater sound as a differentiator, Dolby® Laboratories has created Atmos™[32], a full surround system with up to 64 individual channels for speakers in a theater, including multiple ceiling speakers that can truly immerse the audience in sound. Given the number of speakers involved, this may be a technology that is viable in very few homes. For those seeking still more there is motion seat technology.[33] The heavy footsteps of a dinosaur, for example, are simultaneously seen on the screen, heard through the sound system, and felt through a motion seat that rumbles as if being shaken by the footsteps. Both IMAX and motion seats are offered as upgrades, commonly at premiums of $3 to $7 per ticket.

[31]Dodes, R. (2012, April 19, 2012). IMAX Strikes Back. *Wall Street Journal*. Retrieved from http://online.wsj.com/article/SB10001424052702304299304577347940832511540.html?KEYWORDS=IMAX+strikes+back.
[32]Dolby Laboratories. (2013) Dolby Atmos: Hear the Whole Picture. URL: "See http://vimeo.com/79942809". Accessed 1/5/2013.
[33]Kung, M. (2012, May 10, 2012). Movie Magic to Leave Home For?, *Wall Street Journal*, pp. D1–D2.

ALTERNATIVE CONTENT

52 Exhibitors' transition to digital projection is an enabling technology for alternative content, which consists of virtually any content that is not a motion picture. Revenues for this totaled $112 million in 2010.[34] Some estimate this will reach $1 billion annually—10 percent of current box office.

53 Events have included concerts, live concerts and theater, sporting events, television series premiers and finales, even virtual art gallery tours such 2012's *Leonardo Live*[35] that was broadcast one night only in 500 U.S. movie theaters.[36] The *Metropolitan Opera* is the most successful alterative content. Now in its seventh season, the series features 12 live events on Saturday afternoons broadcast to nearly 700 domestic theaters. A distribution network for alternative content has emerged with companies such as National Cinemedia providing a single contract point for a variety of music, sports, television, and other alternative content. Having a large-scale intermediary for distributor is essential for exhibitors as the cost of pursuing and licensing content is cost prohibitive for all but the largest exhibitor circuits.

54 Most exhibitors seek to incorporated alternative content in ways that attract new attendees during off-peak times, particularly Monday through Thursday when only 5 percent of theater seats are occupied.[37] Bud Mayo, CEO of Digiplex Digital Cinema Destinations, describes the approach: "What happens with those [alternative content] performances is that single event will outgross certainly the lowest-grossing movie playing that theater that day. The relationship has averaged more than 10 times the lowest-grossing movie for the entire day."[38] In marginal dollar terms, alternative content can be a boon on otherwise slow nights. A recent Wednesday showing of Broadway's *West Side Story* at a Digitech theater had an average ticket price of $12.50 and grossed $2,425. In comparison, screens showing films that night grossed just $56 to $73. The alternative content also brought in nearly 200 additional potential customers for concessions.[39]

DYNAMIC PRICING

55 Movie theaters are among the minority of entertainment outlets that have not incorporated differentials based on content, schedule, and seating options. Most events have multiple pricing levels based on seating, night versus day, and weekday versus weekend. Movie theaters, partly due to existing exhibition contracts, commonly have limited flexibility. Matinee and youth and senior discounts are the primary pricing tiers. Ticketmaster, a leader in event ticket sales, is developing a "dynamic pricing" system which incorporates demand into pricing models.[40] This could mean radical changes with lower ticket prices for off-time and poorly attended movies and increased prices for prime seats at peak times on opening weekend. Thus far, no studio or exhibitor will acknowledge investigating the technology.[41]

[34]Sony. (2011). Alternative Content for Theatres. *Sony Digital Cinema 4K*, 1.
[35]Shubin, M. (Writer). (2012). Alternative content at a theater near you. YouTube: ShubinCafe.
[36]Smith, R. (2012, February 15, 2012). Leonardo's London Blockbuster: The Movie. *NY Times*. Accessed via Factiva.
[37]Cinedigm. (2012). Investor Presentation: Jefferies 2012 Global Technology, Media & Telecom Conference. Cinedigm. Retrieved from http://files.shareholder.com/downloads/AIXD/2302444840x0x567367/4a213e2c-11ae-4cdc-8dd1-970919ac80ac/CIDM%20IR%20deck%20050712%20Short.pdf
[38]Ellingson, A. (2012, Oct. 15, 2012). Who's stressed about digital cinema? Not Digiplex's Bud Mayo. *The Business Journal—LA*.
[39]Ellingson, A. (2012, Oct. 15, 2012). Who's stressed about digital cinema? Not Digiplex's Bud Mayo. *The Business Journal—LA*.
[40]Lazarus, D. (2012, April 26, 2012). Movie tickets: Now how much would you pay?, *LA Times*.
[41]Lazarus, D. (2012, April 26, 2012). Movie tickets: Now how much would you pay?, *LA Times*.

CONCESSION INITIATIVES

56   Expanding beyond the standard concession stand offers exhibitors opportunities to capture new revenue streams. Three main formats for concessions have emerged.

Expanded In-Lobby

57   Many theaters have expanded the concession counter beyond candy, popcorn, and soda. This expanded in-lobby dining causes many theater lobbies to resemble mall food courts. In- and off-lobby restaurants operated or licensed by the exhibitor allow for pretheater dining. Taking a page from restaurants where a primary profit center is often the bar, some theaters now configure the lobby around a bar, with expanded and upscale fare, beer, and alcohol service.

In-Theater Dining

58   Many theaters have adopted an in-theater dining format where orders are placed from the seat in the theater by a wait staff. Chunky's Cinema Pub, with three New England locations, locates theaters in lower cost underutilized former retail locations. The format combines burger, salad, and sandwich options with beverages, including beer. The format is flat theater with banquet-style tables. The seating is unique: Old car seats on castors that allow for easy cleaning. Alamo Drafthouse Cinemas takes a similar approach using a stadium seating configuration. A single bar-style table in front of each row of seats serves as a table for customers' orders. In comparison to traditional theaters, these formats see significant increases in food and beverage sales.

Upscale Within-Theater Dining

59   Several circuits are targeting the high end of the theater market, focusing on the experience of the theater with luxurious settings and upscale food. In addition to their standard theaters, AMC has developed Dine-In Theaters with two theater configurations. Their Fork & Screen theaters are much like the Alamo Drafthouse Cinema with enhanced stadium theater seats and in-theater wait service on an expanded menu. Their Cinema Suite theaters make the experience more intimate. Customers, only 21 and older, purchase tickets for specific seats in smaller theaters with reclining lounge chairs with foot rests and in-theater wait service.

60   Theater chain iPic offers perhaps the most luxurious theater experience available outside of a private screening room, complete with reclining leather chairs, pillows, and blankets. Lobbies resemble stylish high-end hotels and feature a cocktail lounge and full restaurants. Complete with a membership program, the theaters operate more like social clubs than traditional theaters. Tickets, $16–$27 per seat, are purchased not from a ticket booth but from a concierge.

ADVERTISING INITIATIVES

61   Exhibitors are keen to expand advertising revenues, but must do so in ways that does not diminish the theater experience. Revenues are generated from advertisements both on- and off-screen. Off-screen advertising such as promotional videos, lobby events, and sponsored concession promotions are 9 percent of revenues. The majority, 91 percent, comes from on-screen ads for upcoming releases, companies, and products that play before the feature presentation. Both exhibitors and advertisers seek ways to make on-screen ads more palatable to audiences. Many ads are produced in 3D with production quality rivaling a studio

release. Theaters are also incorporating innovative technologies such as crowd gaming into ads where the movement or sound of the audience controls on-screen actions. In October 2008, audiences in the UK attending Disney's *Ratatouille* "drove" an on-screen Volvo XC70 through an obstacle-laden course waving their arms while scoring points for avoiding obstacles. Results were ranked in real-time to audiences in other theaters.[42] The equipment required? A wireless video camera placed above the screen, a Web-enabled laptop containing the game linked to the developer's Web site, and specialized motion-sensing technology. These were linked to the theater's digital projector.

62 More interactive approaches are on their way: Fans at a Formula One race in Singapore played the video game Angry Birds, controlling in-game slingshots used to fling birds at the rival pigs based on voice volume. The louder the crowd, the further the birds were launched.[43] Making ads enjoyable, rather than loathed, may create an opportunity to increase this small but high-margin component of exhibitor revenues.

BRIGHT LIGHTS AND RED CARPET OR DIMLY LIT MARQUEE?

63 Are these initiatives enough to return people to the local movie house? Is the future of the movie exhibition industry a return to red carpet glamour? Or will the lights on the marquee dim?

[42]Audience Entertain. (2009, 01/2013/21). AE Case: Volvo XC70 Launch. Retrieved from http://www.youtube.com/watch?v=HYVuLGLnyAM

[43]Reuters. (2011, Sept. 22, 2011). Angry Birds to Swoop on Formula One Track. *CNBC*. Retrieved from http://www.reuters.com/article/2011/09/22/us-angrybirds-idUSTRE78L1IY20110922

Case 27

Netflix, Inc. (A): *The 2011 Rebranding/Price Increase Debacle*

Alan N. Hoffman *Bentley University*

1   In 2011 Netflix was the world's largest online movie rental service. Its subscribers paid to have DVDs delivered to their homes through the U.S. mail, or to access and watch unlimited TV shows and movies streamed over the Internet to their TVs, mobile devices, or computers. The company was founded by Marc Randolph and Reed Hastings in August 1997 in Scotts Valley, California, after they had left Pure Software. Hastings was inspired to start Netflix after being charged $40 for an overdue video.[1] Initially, Netflix provided movies at $6 per rental, but moved to a monthly subscription rate in 1999, dropping the single-rental model soon after. From then on, the company built its reputation on the business model of flat fee unlimited rentals per month without any late fees or shipping and handling fees.

2   In May 2002 Netflix went public with a successful IPO, selling 5.5 million shares of common stock at the IPO price of $15 per share to raise $82.5 million. After incurring substantial losses during its first few years of operations, Netflix turned a profit of $6.5 million during the fiscal year 2003.[2] The company's subscriber base grew strongly and steadily from 1 million in the fourth quarter of 2002 to over 27 million in July 2012.[3]

3   By 2012, Netflix had over 100,000 titles distributed via more than 50 shipment centers, ensuring customers received their DVDs in 1–2 business days, which made Netflix one of the most successful dot-com ventures in the past two decades.[4] The company employed almost 4,100 people, 2,200 of whom were part-time employees.[5] In September 2010, Netflix began international operations by offering an unlimited streaming plan without DVDs in Canada. In September 2011, Netflix expanded its international operations to customers in the Caribbean, Mexico, and Central and South America.

4   Key to Netflix's success was its no late fee policy. Netflix's profits were directly proportional to the number of days the customer kept a DVD. Most customers wanted to view a new DVD release as soon as possible. If Netflix imposed a late fee, it would have to have multiple copies of the new releases and find a way to remain profitable. However, because of the no late fee rule, the demand for the newer movies was spread over a period of time, ensuring an efficient circulation of movies.[6]

5   On September 18, 2011 Netflix CEO and co-founder Reed Hastings announced on the Netflix blog that the company was splitting its DVD delivery service from its online streaming service, rebranding its DVD delivery service Qwikster as a way to differentiate it from its online streaming service, and creating a new Web site for it. Three weeks

The authors would like to thank Barbara Gottfried, Ashna Dhawan, Emira Ajeti, Neel Bhalaria, Tarun Chugh, and Will Hoffman for their research and contributions to this case. Please address all correspondence to: Dr. Alan N. Hoffman, Dept. of Management, Bentley University, 175 Forest Street, Waltham, MA 02452-4705, voice (781) 891-2287, ahoffman@bentley.edu. Printed by permission of Alan N. Hoffman.

[1] http://www.fundinguniverse.com/company-histories/Netflix-Inc-company-History.html
[2] 10-K Netflix Annual Report—2010.
[3] Hoovers company profile—Netflix Inc.
[4] Datamonitor, Netflix Inc. Company Profile. 23 Jun. 2010.
[5] Datamonitor, Netflix Inc. Company Profile. 23 Jun. 2010.
[6] See http://insight.kellogg.northwestern.edu/article/a_surprising_secret_to_netflixs_runaway_success

later, in response to customer outrage and confusion, Hastings rescinded the decision to rebrand the DVD delivery service Qwikster and reintegrated it into Netflix. Nevertheless, by October 24, 2011, only five weeks after the initial split, Netflix acknowledged that it had lost 800,000 U.S. subscribers and expected to lose yet more, thanks both to the Qwikster debacle and the price hike the company had decided was necessary to cover increasing content costs.[7]

6   Despite this setback, Netflix continued to believe that by providing the cheapest and best subscription-paid, commercial-free streaming of movies and TV shows, it could still rapidly and profitably fulfill its envisioned goal to become the world's best entertainment distribution platform.

ONLINE STREAMING

7   By the end of 2011, Netflix had 24.4 million subscribers, making it the largest provider of online streaming content in the world.[8] Subscription numbers had grown exponentially, increasing 250 percent from 9.3 million in 2008. At the same time, Netflix proactively recognized that the demand for DVDs by mail had peaked, and the future growth would be in online streaming. With 245 million Internet users in the United States and 2.2 billion[9] worldwide, Netflix saw the opportunity to expand its online streaming base both domestically and internationally to become a dominant world player. In 2011 Netflix expanded into Canada and Central America, and in 2012 into Ireland and the United Kingdom.[10]

8   The scarce resource for the online video industry was bandwidth, the amount of data that can be carried from one point to another in a given time period.[11] With the introduction of Blu-ray discs, the demand for higher and better quality picture and sound streaming increased, which in turn increased the demand for higher bandwidths. At the same time, cheaper Internet connections and faster download speeds made it easier and more affordable for customers to take advantage of the services Netflix and its competitors offered. If the cost of Internet access were to increase, it would directly affect sales in the industry's streaming segment.

9   Netflix was a leader in developing streaming technologies, increasing its spending on technology and development from $114 million (2009) to $258 million in 2011[12] (8 percent of its revenue),[13] and initiating a $1 million five-year prize to improve the existing algorithm of Netflix's recommendation service by at least 10 percent. Because Netflix had already developed proprietary streaming software and an extensive content library, it had a head start in the online streaming market, and with continued investments in technological enhancements, hoped to maintain its lead.[14] However, increased competition in streaming, ISP fair use charges, and piracy were some of the major challenges it faced.

10   In March 2011, Netflix made its services readily available to consumers through smartphones, tablets, and video game consoles when only 35 percent of the total U.S. market were using Internet-enabled smartphones.[15] Thus, the expansion potential for Netflix in this market

[7]http://money.cnn.com/2011/10/24/technology/netflix_earnings/index.htm
[8]S&P Advantage.
[9]IDC Technology Research Firm Source: S&P Industry Survey.
[10]10-Q Netflix Quarterly Filings—Q3-2011.
[11]http://searchenterprisewan.techtarget.com/definition/bandwidth
[12]Consolidated Financial Statement 10-K.
[13]10-K Netflix Annual Report—2010.
[14]10-K Netflix Annual Report—2010.
[15]http://www.cnn.com/2011/08/31/tech/mobile/smartphone-market-share-gahran/index.html

was substantial. The Great Recession of 2008–2010 was a boon for Netflix as people cut down on high-value discretionary spending, choosing "value for money" Internet offerings instead.[16] However, in its annual letter to shareholders Netflix acknowledged that many of its customers were among the highest users of data on an ISPs network and in the near future it expected that such users might be forced to pay extra for their data usage, which could be a major deterrent for the growth of Netflix as most of its customers are highly price sensitive.

DEMOGRAPHICS

11   The number of Internet users in the United States had increased from about 205 million in 2005 to 245 million in 2012.[17] According to a research report by the Mintel investment research database, the percentage of people using the Internet to stream video has jumped from 5 percent (2005) to 17 percent (2011), significantly growing the market for online streaming services such as Netflix. At the same time, the recession of 2008–2010, with its high unemployment and slow economic growth, had a significant impact on the spending habits of U.S. consumers. More and more people chose to forego an evening at the movie theater in favor of home movie rentals to save on costs.[18] By 2011 the crucial 18–34-year-old demographic saw the Internet as its prime source of access to entertainment. However, this demographic was particularly sensitive to price fluctuations. When Netflix changed its pricing structure in the third quarter of 2011, subscriptions immediately dropped off 3 percent. Mintel Research reported that only 15 percent of the under-18–25 age bracket of the customers were ready to pay $16 per month for premium content via Netflix. In addition, the proliferation of free content over the Internet—Mega video, for example, with 81 million unique visitors and maximum exposure in the 18–33 demographic—became a strong competitor for Netflix, further limiting the pricing power Netflix could exercise.[19]

12   The Mintel report also found that American households with two or more children and a household income of $50,000 or more had a very favorable attitude toward Netflix;[20] Netflix fostered this trend by cutting a deal with Disney[21] that gave it access to content exclusively targeting young children.

13   At the same time that Netflix was increasing its customer base among the 18–34-year-olds and households with young children, both of whom preferred streaming, it lost ground with affluent Baby Boomers who still preferred to rent DVDs over the Internet. Thus Netflix needed to fine-tune its strategy to include this older demographic as people over 60 had $1 trillion in discretionary income per year and fewer familial responsibilities, making them a prime target demographic for expanding Netflix's customer base.[22]

14   The availability of high-speed Internet at home and the shift to online TVs created many opportunities for Netflix. The company recognized that to fully leverage the current world of technological convergence, it needed to compete on as many platforms as possible, and created applications for the Xbox, Wii, PS3, iPads, Apple TV, Windows phones, and Android. The company also collaborated with TV manufacturers to integrate Netflix directly into the latest televisions.[23]

[16]S&P Industry Survey.

[17]Euromonitor, Bentley University Library Database.

[18]S&P Industry Survey.

[19]Noted at the time on the now discontinued adplanner site: https://www.google.com/adplanner/planning/site_profile#siteDetails?identifier=megaupload.com

[20]Media Usage & Online Behavior—Mintel Report, Oct. 2011.

[21]http://www.reuters.com/article/2011/10/31/us-netflixdisney-idUSTRE79U0O420111031

[22]http://www.businessweek.com/magazine/content/05_43/b3956201.htm

[23]Annual Shareholder Letter—Netflix, 2011.

NETFLIX'S COMPETITORS

15   Netflix's great operational advantage in the DVD rental market was its nationwide distribution network, which prevented the entry of many of its potential competitors. While only Netflix provided both mail delivery and online rentals, with the growth of online streaming, Netflix's advantage shrank and it faced increasing competition from Blockbuster, Walmart, Amazon, Hulu, and RedBox.

16   Netflix's one-time strongest competitor, Blockbuster LLC, founded in 1985 and headquartered in McKinney, Texas provided in-home movie and game entertainment, originally through over 5,000 video rental stores throughout the Americas, Europe, Asia, and Australia, later adding DVD-by-mail, streaming video on demand, and kiosks. Its business model emphasized providing convenient access to media entertainment across multiple channels, recognizing that the same customer might choose different ways to access media entertainment on different nights. Competition from Netflix and other video rental companies forced Blockbuster to file for bankruptcy on September 23, 2010, and on April 6, 2011, satellite television provider Dish Network bought it at auction for $233 million.[24]

17   Redbox Automated Retail, LLC, a wholly-owned subsidiary of Coinstar, Inc., specialized in DVD, Blu-Ray, and rentals via automated retail kiosks. By June 2011, Redbox had over 33,000 kiosks in over 27,800 locations worldwide,[25] and was considering launching an online streaming service, perhaps as cheaply as $3.95 per month.

18   Vudu, Inc., formerly known as Marquee, Inc., founded in 2004, a content delivery media technology company acquired by Walmart in March 2010, worked by allowing users to stream movies and TV shows to Sony PlayStation3, Blu-ray players, HDTVs, computers, or home theaters. VUDU Box and VUDU XL provided access to movies and television shows; users also needed a VUDU Wireless Kit to connect VUDU Box/VUDU XL to the Internet. Based in Santa Clara, California, the company was the third most popular online movie service, with a market share of 5.3 percent.[26] Vudu had no monthly subscription fee; instead users deposited funds into an online account, which was reduced depending on how many movies the user rented. In other words, you paid for only what you watched.

19   In February 2011 Amazon.com, a multinational electronic commerce company, announced the launch for Amazon Prime members of unlimited, commercial-free instant streaming of all movies and TV shows to members' computers or HDTVs. In addition, Amazon Prime members were given access to the Kindle Owners' Lending Library, allowing them to borrow selected popular titles for free with no due date. For non-Amazon Prime members, 48-hour on-demand rentals were available for $3.99, or the title could be bought outright.[27]

20   Hulu Plus was the first ad-supported subscription service for TV shows and films that could be accessed by computers, television sets, mobile phone, or other digital devices. Like Netflix, the streaming service cost $8 per month; but unlike Netflix, Hulu offered more recent TV episodes and seasons. However, subscribers had to put up with ads, and Hulu's movie selection was much more limited than Netflix's selection.

21   Marc Schuh, an early financial backer of Netflix, observed that copying software was relatively simple.[28] Anyone could buy the best servers, processors, operating systems, and

---

[24]Datamonitor, Blockbluster Inc. Company Profile. 30 Dec. 2010.
[25]http://www.redbox.com/release_20110811
[26]http://www.theatlantixwire.com/business/2011/08/walmarts-facebook-powered-future/41843/
[27]http://www.csmonitor.com/Innovation/2011/0713/Five-alternative-to-Netflix/Amazon-Prime-instant-video
[28]http://facstaff.uww.edu/mohanp/netflix.html

databases—but timing was crucial.[29] Barnes and Nobles waited 17 months to enter the fray against Amazon, so that by 2012 Amazon had 8 times the profit and 30 times the market capitalization of Barnes and Noble.[30] Similarly, in the same year that Netflix's profits increased sevenfold, Blockbuster lost over 1 billion dollars.[31] Technology with correct timings can help a company gain competitive advantage over rivals. Other barriers to entry include investments in infrastructure aiding supply chain and delays from major production houses for gaining permission to stream their titles.

RISING CONTENT COSTS

22 In the DVD rental business the rental company had the first sale doctrine, in which the company was permitted to rent a single disc many times to recover the cost of the content. But this doctrine did not apply to digital content and the technological shift away from the DVD rental business was in part responsible for the excessive increase in content cost for Netflix.[32]

23 In addition, Netflix's dependence on outside content suppliers such as the six major movie studios and the top television networks contributed significantly to rising costs for the company. As an example, Liberty Media Corporation's Starz LLC had been an early Netflix supplier. In 2011, Starz demanded $300 million to renew its deal with Netflix, testament to the power of suppliers in relation to market demand from an increasing number of competitors. On September 1, 2011, Netflix customers learned they would lose access to newer films from the Walt Disney Company and the Sony Corporation after talks to obtain those movies from Starz broke down. The loss created the impression of a major setback, even though the films were making up a smaller share of viewing than previously.

24 However, Netflix did sign new deals with the CW Network, Dreamworks Animation, and Discovery Communications in 2011.

GLOBAL EXPANSION

25 Beginning in 2007, Netflix shifted its focus to its streaming business in response to customers' move to streaming in preference to DVD rentals and the rising cost of mailing DVDs. Conveniently, expanding its streaming business did not require expanding its physical infrastructure. This strategy has proven to be a major differentiator as it expands internationally in the Americas and Europe.

26 By the end of 2011 the company had started operations in Canada and 43 countries in Latin America and planned to start European operations in early 2012. At the end of the third quarter of 2011, Netflix had 1.48 million international subscribers with predictions of 2 million by the end of the year.[33] The UK was considered a huge potential market. Twenty million UK households had broadband Internet, and 60 percent of those households subscribed to a paid movie service. In Latin America, four times that number had Internet access,[34] making international expansion there especially attractive to subscriber-hungry Netflix.

[29]Information System: A manager's guide to harnessing—John Gallaugher.
[30]FY 2008 and June 2009 market cap figures for both firms: http://www.barnesandnoblesinc.com/newsroom/financial_only.html and http://phx.corporate-ir.net/phoenix.zhtml?c=97664&p=irol-reportsOther
[31]"Movies to Go," *Economist*, July 9, 2005.
[32]Morningstar Investment Report.
[33]Quarterly Letter to the shareholders, 3Q 2011.
[34]Quarterly Letter to the shareholders, 3Q 2011.

27   However, international expansion was potentially risky, as Netflix faced rising content costs from higher studio charges. In addition, international expansion required both broadening its content offerings and tailoring those offerings to meet the specific needs of each of its international markets, which Netflix feared would further increase content costs. It was clear that the correct content mix was crucial, yet a huge challenge for Netflix.

28   In addition, as Canada and the UK were already developed markets, Netflix faced local competition from a proliferation of DVD rental/streaming services. In the UK, for instance, Virgin and Sky already had strong brand recognition and balance sheets, and the Sky network had already contracted exclusive first pay window rights to movies from all six major American studios, tough competition that could easily delay profitability from international operations.

29   Lower per capita income and slower Internet speeds, especially in Latin America, were further potential problems for Netflix's international expansion. In Canada low data usage limits per subscriber were a concern for a data-hungry service such as Netflix.

FINANCIAL RESULTS

30   In 2011, Netflix surpassed $3.2 billion in sales, an annual revenue growth of 50 percent over 2010 ($2.1 billion, see Exhibits 1–3). Subscriber growth was the most important metric for Netflix as its revenue growth was directly correlated to subscriber growth. Netflix grew from 12 million subscribers in 2009 to 20 million in 2010, and then to 27 million in 2012. International operations were set to expand, to become a major source of sales growth for the company in the coming years.

31   However, by 2012, Netflix faced challenges from its pricing changes in the United States and its expansion into international markets, even stating that it expected revenue per subscriber to drop from its 2011 level of $11.56[35] as subscribers choose the streaming-only option of $7.99 over the more expensive streaming and DVD delivery option. For future revenue growth Netflix needed to increase its subscribers numbers both domestically and internationally.

32   In terms of net income, Netflix had steadily improved its bottom line in conjunction with strong top line growth. The company had a net income of $226 million in 2011 for a growth rate of 40 percent over the previous year's $160 million net income. Over the five years from 2006–2011, the company saw an average net income growth of 31 percent per year that, coupled with high revenue growth, was instrumental to Netflix's high stock valuation. However, recently, its operating margin slid from 15 percent in 2010 to 2.9 percent in 2012, a drop directly attributable to the higher cost of content acquisition.

33   Until the end of 2007, Netflix had no long-term debt on its books, but it began to acquire long-term debt in 2008 as a result of its decision to invest in building a strong content library and expand overseas. At the end of 2011, Netflix had $508 million in cash and $200 million in long-term debt.

NETFLIX'S SUCCESS

34   Netflix went from being a company that exclusively mailed DVDs to the largest media delivery company in the world by making some smart strategic decisions. For instance, Netflix jumped on the streaming bandwagon even though it was not really ready. At the time,

[35]Company Filings—8K 3Q.

EXHIBIT 1 Netflix, Inc. Consolidated Statements of Operations (in thousands, except per share data)

	Year ended December 31,		
	2011	**2010**	**2009**
Revenues	$3,204,577	$2,162,625	$1,670,269
Cost of revenues:			
Subscription	1,789,596	1,154,109	909,461
Fulfillment expenses	250,305	203,246	169,810
Total cost of revenues	2,039,901	1,357,355	1,079,271
Gross profit	1,164,676	805,270	590,998
Operating expenses:			
Marketing	402,638	293,839	237,744
Technology and development	259,033	163,329	114,542
General and administrative	117,937	64,461	46,773
Legal settlement	9,000	-	-
Total operating expenses	788,608	521,629	399,059
Operating income	376,068	283,641	191,939
Other income (expense):			
Interest expense	(20,025)	(19,629)	(6,475)
Interest and other income	3,479	3,684	6,728
Income before income taxes	359,522	267,696	192,192
Provision for income taxes	133,396	106,843	76,332
Net income	$226,126	$160,853	$115,860
Net income per share:			
Basic	$4.28	$3.06	$2.05
Diluted	$4.16	$2.96	$1.98
Weighted-average common shares outstanding:			
Basic	52,847	52,529	56,560
Diluted	54,369	54,304	58,416

the online content available for streaming was extremely limited—less than 10 percent of the content that was available from Netflix's DVDs holdings.

35   At that time, Netflix's mail order DVD business was very popular, and customers did not seem to mind waiting a day or two for their DVDs. Netflix then went ahead and offered streaming content, a bold decision that anticipated an as yet unexpressed need for the immediate gratification of streaming, and made Netflix the first entrant into the market for streamed video. It was clear to Netflix that the use of DVDs would gradually decline, and Netflix's aggressive adoption of streaming videos was a sharp marketing move that gave it an edge in the global economy.

36   After its initial launch of online streaming, Netflix kept up-to-date with new trends and customer preferences, especially the quickly changing preferences of Generation Y,

EXHIBIT 2   Netflix, Inc. Consolidated Balance Sheets (in thousands, except share and per share data)

	As of December 31,	
	2011	**2010**
Assets		
Current assets:		
Cash and cash equivalents	$508,053	$194,499
Short-term investments	289,758	155,888
Current content library, net	919,709	181,006
Prepaid content	56,007	62,217
Other current assets	57,330	43,621
Total current assets	1,830,857	637,231
Non-current content library, net	1,046,934	180,973
Property and equipment, net	136,353	128,570
Other non-current assets	55,052	35,293
Total assets	$3,069,196	$982,067
Liabilities and Stockholders' Equity		
Current liabilities:		
Content accounts payable	$924,706	$168,695
Other accounts payable	87,860	54,129
Accrued expenses	63,693	38,572
Deferred revenue	148,796	127,183
Total current liabilities	1,225,055	388,579
Long-term debt	200,000	200,000
Long-term debt due to related party	200,000	-
Non-current content liabilities	739,628	48,179
Other non-current liabilities	61,703	55,145
Total liabilities	2,426,386	691,903
Commitments and contingencies (Note 5)		
Stockholders' equity:		
Preferred stock, $0.001 par value; 10,000,000 shares authorized at December 31, 2011 and 2010; no shares issued and outstanding at December 31, 2011 and 2010	-	-
Common stock, $0.001 par value; 160,000,000 shares authorized at December 31, 2011 and 2010; 55,398,615 and 52,781,949 issued and outstanding at December 31, 2011 and 2010, respectively	55	53
Additional paid-in capital	219,119	51,622
Accumulated other comprehensive income	706	750
Retained earnings	422,930	237,739
Total stockholders' equity	642,810	290,164
Total liabilities and stockholders' equity	$3,069,196	$982,067

EXHIBIT 3 Netflix, Inc. Consolidated Statements of Cash Flows (in thousands)

	Year Ended December 31,		
	2011	**2010**	**2009**
Cash flows from operating activities:			
Net income	$226,126	$160,853	$115,860
Adjustments to reconcile net income to net cash provided by operating activities:			
Additions to streaming content library	(2,320,732)	(406,210)	(64,217)
Change in streaming content liabilities	1,460,400	167,836	(4,014)
Amortization of streaming content library	699,128	158,100	48,192
Amortization of DVD content library	96,744	142,496	171,298
Depreciation and amortization of property, equipment and intangibles	43,747	38,099	38,044
Stock-based compensation expense	61,582	27,996	12,618
Excess tax benefits from stock-based compensation	(45,784)	(62,214)	(12,683)
Other non-cash items	(4,050)	(9,128)	(7,161)
Deferred taxes	(18,597)	(962)	6,328
Gain on sale of business	—	—	(1,783)
Changes in operating assets and liabilities:			
Prepaid content	6,211	(35,476)	(5,643)
Other current assets	(4,775)	(18,027)	(5,358)
Other accounts payable	24,314	18,098	1,537
Accrued expenses	68,902	67,209	13,169
Deferred revenue	21,613	27,086	16,970
Other non- current assets and liabilities	2,883	645	1,906
Net cash provided by operating activities	317,712	276,401	325,063
Cash flows from investing activities:			
Acquisition of DVD content library	(85,154)	(123,901)	(193,044)
Purchases of short-term investments	(223,750)	(107,362)	(228,000)
Proceeds from sale of short-term investments	50,993	120,857	166,706
Proceeds from maturities of short-term investments	38,105	15,818	35,673
Purchases of property and equipment	(49,682)	(33,837)	(45,932)
Proceeds from sale of business	—	—	7,483
Other assets	3,674	12,344	11,035
Net cash used in investing activities	(265,814)	(116,081)	(246,079)

(Continued)

EXHIBIT 3 (*Continued*)

	Year Ended December 31,		
	2011	**2010**	**2009**
Cash flows from financing activities:			
Principal payments of lease financing obligations	(2,083)	(1,776)	(1,158)
Proceeds from issuance of common stock upon exercise of options	19,614	49,776	35,274
Proceeds from public offering of common stock, net of issuance costs	199,947	—	—
Excess tax benefits from stock-based compensation	45,784	62,214	12,683
Borrowings on line of credit, net of issuance costs	—	—	18,978
Payments on line of credit	—	—	(20,000)
Proceeds from issuance of debt, net of issuance costs	198,060	—	193,917
Repurchases of common stock	(199,666)	(210,259)	(324,335)
Net cash provided by (used in) financing activities	261,656	(100,045)	(84,641)
Net increase (decrease) in cash and cash equivalents	313,554	60,275	(5,657)
Cash and cash equivalents, beginning of year	194,499	134,224	139,881
Cash and cash equivalents, end of year	$508,053	$194,499	$134,224
Supplemental disclosure:			
Income taxes paid	$79,069	$56,218	$58,770
Interest paid	19,395	20,101	3,878

which were influenced by branding, social media, and media saturation. Netflix utilized all the platforms that Generation Y would find appealing, from computers and TVs to smartphones and tablets.

37   Continually bearing in mind that the two most important things for Netflix's customers were price per content and quality of content, Netflix kept its priorities straight and never stopped improving the quality of its content or the platforms for delivering that content.

38   Netflix also focused on increasing customer engagement. It allowed customers to rate movies they viewed, thereby enhancing the customer experience and creating a community of viewers. And, by tracking the movies a customer viewed, Netflix was able to track customer preferences, and offer targeted recommendations for viewing. Netflix also exploited customer loyalty to attract new customers, for instance through its "refer-a-friend" offer of one free month of service for both the new customer and the referrer to attract new users who wanted to try the service risk-free.

THE 2011 PRICE INCREASE/REBRANDING DEBACLE

39 Netflix continued to grow robustly by offering a combined DVD mail and unlimited streaming service at a flat rate of $9.99 a month, a rate that was key to Netflix's ability to offer a great value for money service. But with increased competition and expensive new content deals, the company found it increasingly difficult to maintain its operating margin levels. In the third quarter of 2011, Netflix implemented a 60 percent price increase, from $10 to $16 a month for unlimited streaming and DVDs by mail, which immediately resulted in the loss of 800,000 subscribers, pointing to the company's very limited latitude with regard to pricing.[36]

40 In response, Netflix took action that very shortly proved disastrous. In addition to raising its prices and shifting its business model to focus on online streaming. Netflix also attempted to restructure its operations by spinning off its DVD delivery service and rebranding it Qwikster. Rebranding a well-known product or service such as Netflix usually only works if a company is trying to simplify its brand, almost never the other way around, which was, unfortunately, what Netflix tried to do. Netflix attempted to introduce a new entity, Qwikster, by splitting the old entity into two: with two separate Web site, two separate queues, two separate sets of recommendations, two separate customer bases, two separate billing avenues, two new sets of rules customer had to learn about. While Netflix had banked on the competitive advantage of offering "affordability, instant access and usability," the introduction of a separate Web site undercut instant access and usability. Customers, critics, and Wall Street responded harshly.

41 Apart from losing over 800,000 subscribers after its price increase and losing half of its market capitalization, Netflix's rebranding strategy did not seem justifiable to its customers.

42 Netflix botched the rebranding because it neglected due diligence prior to launching it and its price increases. Market research would surely have indicated customer resistance to both. Heavily focused on increasing profits, Netflix did not effectively strategize the rebranding/repricing plan, nor did it anticipate resistance or prepare strategy implementation scenarios. A new strategy should not only increase revenues and profits, it should consider relationship and brand image gains and losses. In springing the rebranding on customers, Netflix undercut the quality of the experience it had previously offered, and the negative reaction was not mitigated by the company's public apology or its rescinding of its decision to split its services. The botched rebranding led to a dilution of Netflix's brand and loss of customer trust. Re-establishing its brand image became a priority for Netflix, though it was not very easy to do. The company needed to offer something genuinely useful to its customers at just the right cost, while increasing the quality of the content offered and enhancing customer experience.

43 Finally, in order for Netflix to expand internationally it needs to invest in the technological infrastructure in the international markets that it lacked but which it desperately needs due to heavy competition, and other legal concerns that appear there.

STRATEGIC CHALLENGES AHEAD FOR NETFLIX

44 Netflix's top management (see Exhibit 4 for a desription of the key members of Netflix's top management team) needed to address many issues to maintain the company's leading position in the home video market. A strategic plan was needed to:

1. Repair the PR damage from the rebranding and price increases of 2011.
2. Focus on growing its subscriber base both at home and abroad.

[36]10-Q Netflix Quarterly Filings—Q3-2011.

EXHIBIT 4   Netflix Management Team

Reed Hastings
Founder and CEO

Reed Hastings has served as the Chief Executive Officer since September 1998 and the Chairman of the Board since inception. Mr. Hastings served as Chief Executive Officer of Pure Atria Software, a maker of software development tools, from its inception in October 1991 until it was acquired by Rational Software Corporation, in August 1997. Mr. Hastings currently serves as a member of the board of directors of Microsoft. Mr. Hastings holds an M.S.C.S. degree from Stanford University and a B.A. from Bowdoin College.

Kelly Bennett
Chief Marketing Officer

Kelly Bennett became Netflix Chief Marketing Officer in July 2012 after nearly a decade at Warner Bros. where he was most recently Vice President Interactive, World Wide Marketing with the pictures group, leading international online campaigns for Warner Bros. movies. Before that Kelly ran digital marketing for Warner Bros. Pictures in Europe, the Middle East and Africa and worked in promotion and business development at the company. He previously held executive positions at Dow Jones International and Ignition Media as well as being a partner in online marketing agency Cimex Media. The Canada-born Bennett is a graduate of Simon Fraser University.

Jonathan Friedland
Chief Communications Officer

Mr. Friedland joined Netflix in February 2011 from The Walt Disney Company, where he was SVP, Corporate Communications. Before that, he spent over 20 years as a foreign correspondent and editor, mainly with *The Wall Street Journal,* in the U.S., Asia and Latin America and co-founded the Diarios Rumbo chain of Spanish-language newspapers in Texas. Mr. Friedland, who has a MSc. Economics from the London School of Economics and a BA from Hampshire College, was a member of the WSJ team that won the Pulitzer Prize for its coverage of the 9/11 attacks.

Bill Holmes
Chief Business Development Officer

Bill Holmes joined Netflix in 2008 and has most recently served as Vice President, Business Development, in charge of the company's global partnerships across the consumer electronics, gaming, operator, service provider and retail markets. Prior to joining Netflix, Mr. Holmes served as Vice President Business Development & Strategy at DivX, Inc. where he oversaw the launch and global adoption of the DivX Certified program into hundreds of millions of consumer electronics devices. Mr. Holmes holds a B.A. degree from Trinity University.

Neil Hunt
Chief Product Officer

Neil Hunt has served as the Company's Chief Product Officer since 2002 and as its Vice President of Internet Engineering from 1999 to 2002. From 1997 to 1999, Mr. Hunt was Director of Engineering for Rational Software. Mr. Hunt holds a doctorate in computer science from the University of Aberdeen, U.K. and a bachelor's degree from the University of Durham, U.K.

David Hyman
General Counsel

David Hyman has served as the Company's General Counsel since 2002. Mr. Hyman also serves as the Company's secretary. Prior to joining Netflix, Mr. Hyman served as General Counsel of Webvan, Inc., an Internet-based grocery delivery service. Mr. Hyman holds a J.D. and a B.A. degree from the University of Virginia.

Patty McCord
Chief Talent Officer

Patty McCord has served as the Company's Chief Talent Officer since 1998. Prior to joining Netflix, from 1994 to 1997, Ms. McCord served as Director of Human Resources at Pure Atria, which was acquired by Rational Software, where she managed all human resources functions and directed all management development programs.

EXHIBIT 4 *(Continued)*

Ted Sarandos
Chief Content Officer

Ted Sarandos has served as the Company's Chief Content Officer and Vice President of Content since 2000. Prior to joining Netflix, Mr. Sarandos was Vice President of Product and Merchandising for Video City.

David Wells
Chief Financial Officer

David Wells has served as the Company's Chief Financial Officer since December 2010 and its Vice President of Financial Planning & Analysis from August 2008 to December 2010. He held the position of Director of Operations Planning & Analysis from March 2004 to August 2008. Prior to joining Netflix, Mr. Wells served in progressive roles at Deloitte Consulting from August 1998 to August 2004. Mr. Wells holds an M.B.A and M.P.P. from The University of Chicago and an undergraduate degree in both Accounting and English from the University of Virginia.

3. Maintain a healthy cash position to meet the growing content cost obligations.

4. Invest in innovative user interface and streaming technologies to create a solid platform for the shift from DVD delivery to streaming.

NETFLIX BOARD OF DIRECTORS

Richard Barton
Chief Executive Officer and Chairman of the Board, Zillow, Inc.

Richard Barton has served as one of the Company's directors since May 2002. In late 2004, Mr. Barton co-founded Zillow, Inc. where he is now Executive Chairman of the Board. Additionally, Mr. Barton is a Venture Partner with Benchmark Capital. Previously, Mr. Barton founded Expedia, Inc. in 1994 and was its President, Chief Executive Officer and director from November 1999 to March 2003. Mr. Barton was a director of InterActiveCorp from February 2003 until January 2005. Mr. Barton also serves as a director for Avvo, Inc. and Glassdoor.com. Mr. Barton holds a B.S. in industrial engineering from Stanford University.

A. George (Skip) Battle
Investor

A. George (Skip) Battle has served as one of the Company's directors since June 2005. Mr. Battle was previously Executive Chairman of the Board of Ask Jeeves, Inc. which was acquired by IAC/InterActiveCorp in July 2005. He was Chief Executive Officer of Ask Jeeves from 2000 to 2003. From 1968 until his retirement in 1995, Mr. Battle served in management roles at Arthur Andersen LLP and then Andersen Consulting LLP (now Accenture), where he became worldwide managing partner of market development and a member of the firm's executive committee. Educated at Dartmouth College and the Stanford Graduate School of Business, Mr. Battle currently serves as Chairman of the Board of Fair Isaac Corporation, a director of Advent Software, Inc. OpenTable, Inc. and Expedia, Inc., and a member of the board of the Masters Select family of mutual funds. He was previously a director of PeopleSoft, Inc.

Timothy Haley,

Managing Director, Redpoint Ventures

Timothy M. Haley has served as one of the Company's directors since June 1998. Mr. Haley is a co-founder of Redpoint Ventures, a venture capital firm, and has been a Managing Director of the firm since October 1999. Mr. Haley has been a Managing Director of Institutional Venture Partners, a venture capital firm, since February 1998. From June 1986 to February 1998, Mr. Haley was the President of Haley Associates, an executive recruiting firm in the high technology industry. Mr. Haley currently serves on the board of directors of several private companies. Mr. Haley holds a B.A. from Santa Clara University.

Reed Hastings,

Chief Executive Officer, President, Chairman of the Board

Reed Hastings has served as the Chief Executive Officer since September 1998 and the Chairman of the Board since inception. Mr. Hastings served as Chief Executive Officer of Pure Atria Software, a maker of software development tools, from its inception in October 1991 until it was acquired by Rational Software Corporation, in August 1997. Mr. Hastings currently serves as a member of the board of directors of Microsoft. Mr. Hastings holds an M.S.C.S. degree from Stanford University and a B.A. from Bowdoin College.

Jay Hoag

General Partner, Technology Crossover Ventures

Jay Hoag has served as one of the Company's directors since June 1999. Since June 1995, Mr. Hoag has served as a founding General Partner at Technology Crossover Ventures, a private equity and venture capital firm. Mr. Hoag serves on the board of directors of Tech Target and several private companies. Previously Mr. Hoag served on the boards of directors of TheStreet.com, Altiris, Inc. and eLoyalty Corporation. Mr. Hoag holds an M.B.A. from the University of Michigan and a B.A. from Northwestern University.

Leslie Kilgore

Leslie Kilgore served as the Company's Chief Marketing Officer from 2000 till 2012. From February 1999 to March 2000, Ms. Kilgore served as Director of Marketing for Amazon.com, Inc., an Internet retailer. Ms. Kilgore served as a brand manager for The Procter & Gamble Company, a manufacturer and marketer of consumer products, from August 1992 to February 1999. Ms. Kilgore holds an M.B.A. from the Stanford University Graduate School of Business and a B.S. from The Wharton School of Business at the University of Pennsylvania.

Ann Mather

Ann Mather has served as a member of the board of directors since July 2010. Since September 2005, Ms. Mather has been a director of Glu Mobile Inc., a publisher of mobile games. Since November 2005, Ms. Mather has been a director of Google, Inc. and serves as chair of its audit committee. Since May 2010, Ms. Mather has been a director of MoneyGram International, a global payment services company, and serves as chair of its audit committee. Ms. Mather is also a director of Ariat International, Inc, a privately held manufacturer of footwear for equestrian athletes. Ms. Mather was previously a director of Central European Media Enterprises Group, a developer and operator of national commercial television channels and stations in Central and Eastern Europe, Zappos.com,

Inc., a privately held, online retailer, until it was acquired by Amazon.com, Inc. in 2009, and Shopping.com, Inc., a price comparison Web site, until it was acquired by eBay Inc. in 2005. Ms. Mather was chair of Shopping.com's audit committee, and a member of its corporate governance and nominating committee. From 1999 to 2004, Ms. Mather was Executive Vice President and Chief Financial Officer of Pixar, a computer animation studio. Prior to her service at Pixar, Ms. Mather was Executive Vice President and Chief Financial Officer at Village Roadshow Pictures, the film production division of Village Roadshow Limited. From 1993 to 1999, she held various executive positions at The Walt Disney Company, including Senior Vice President of Finance and Administration for its Buena Vista International Theatrical Division.

Ms. Mather holds a Master of Arts degree from Cambridge University.

Case 28

Netflix (B): *A Strategic Pivot of Mythic Proportion*[1]

Adapted by Richard Robinson, John Pearce, and Ram Subramanian

1   As we saw in the Netflix (A) case, by the end of 2011, Reed Hastings and the Netflix executive team were trying desparately to stop the fallout caused by their plan to raise prices and separate Netflix into two companies—a DVD mailer called Qwikster and a streaming entity still under the Netflix name. In no time, they had lost millions of customers and saw Netflix's share price fall from $298 to $52.81. The team faced extraordinarily trying times. Eighteen months later, in May 2013, *BloombergBusinessWeek* correspondent Ashlee Vance visited that same team and filed this report on their amazing, uprecedentedly successful turnaround that is reshaping the entertainment, online entertainment, and Internet industry structure:[2]

> On a normal weeknight, Netflix accounts for almost a third of all Internet traffic entering North American homes. That's more than YouTube, Hulu, Amazon.com, HBO Go, iTunes, and BitTorrent combined. Traffic to Netflix usually peaks at around 10 p.m. in each time zone, at which point a chart of Internet consumption looks like a python that swallowed a cow. By midnight Pacific time, streaming volume falls off dramatically.

> As prime time wound down on Jan. 31, 2013, though, there was an unusual amount of tension at Netflix. That was the night the company premièred *House of Cards*, its political thriller set in Washington. Before midnight about 40 engineers gathered in a conference room at Netflix's headquarters. They sat before a collection of wall-mounted monitors that displayed the status of Netflix's computing systems. On the conference table, a few dozen laptops, tablets, smartphones, and other devices had the Netflix app loaded and ready to stream.

> When the clocks hit 12 a.m., the entire season of *House of Cards* started appearing on the devices, as well as in the recommendation lists of millions of customers chosen by an algorithm. The opening scene, a dog getting run over by an SUV, came and went. At 12:15 a.m., around the time Kevin Spacey's character says "I'm livid," everything was working fine. "That's when the champagne comes," says Yury Izrailevsky, the vice president in charge of cloud computing at Netflix, which has a history of self-inflicted catastrophes. Izrailevsky stayed until the wee hours of the morning—just in case—as thousands of customers binge-watched the show. The midnight ritual repeated itself on April 19, when Netflix premièred its werewolf horror series *Hemlock Grove*, and again on May 26, when its revival of *Arrested Development* went live.

2   Netflix has more than 36 million subscribers. They watch about 4 billion hours of programs every quarter on more than 1,000 different devices. To meet this demand, the company uses specialized video servers scattered around the world. When a subscriber clicks on a movie to stream, Netflix determines within a split second which server containing that

---

[1]This Netflix (B) case is based on the article by Ashlee Vance, "Netflix, Reed Hastings Survive Missteps to Join Silicon Valley's Elite," *BloombergBusinessWeek*, May 9, 2013. ©2013, BloombergBusinessweek. All Rights Reserved. May not be reprinted or used without written permission from BloombergBusinessweek.

[2]Ashlee Vance, "Netflix, Reed Hastings Survive Missteps to Join Silicon Valley's Elite," *BloombergBusinessWeek*, May 9, 2013. ©2013, *BloombergBusinessweek.* AII Rights Reserved.

movie is closest to the user, then picks from dozens of versions of the video file, depending on the device the viewer is using. At company headquarters in Los Gatos, Calif., teams of mathematicians and designers study what people watch and build algorithms and interfaces to present them with the collection of videos that will keep them watching.

3   Netflix is one of the world's biggest users of cloud computing, which means running a data center on someone else's equipment. The company rents server and storage systems by the hour, and it rents all this computing power from Amazon Web Services, the cloud division of Amazon.com, which runs its own video-streaming service that competes with Netflix.

4   It's a mutually beneficial frenemy relationship. Over the years, Netflix has built an array of sophisticated tools to make its software perform well on Amazon's cloud. Amazon has mimicked the advances and offered them to other business customers. President Barack Obama's data fueled reelection campaign, for example, was run almost entirely on Amazon with the help of code built by Netflix engineers.

5   While Netflix started out as a DVD-by-mail rental service, it's now striving to become something far more complex: an entertainment power on par with HBO, if not HBO's parent company, Time Warner. Netflix plans to lead the shift to delivering television-style programming over the Internet and has developed sophisticated technology to support that transition. The company has invested hundreds of millions of dollars in original series—*House of Cards, Hemlock Grove, Arrested Development, Orange Is the New Black,* a Ricky Gervais show called *Derek,* and *Turbo: F.A.S.T.,* a kids' show co-produced with Dream-Works Animation—to become a major player in Hollywood. "We think of the technology as a vehicle for creating a better, more modem experience for the content we have," says Chief Executive Officer Reed Hastings. "What we're really competing for quite broadly is people's time."

6   About 18 months ago, Netflix and Hastings were spending much of their time trying to save face. Netflix had awkwardly unveiled plans to raise prices and separate into two companies—a DVD mailer called Qwikster and a streaming entity still under the Netflix name—and lost millions of customers in the process. The share price fell from $298 to $52.81.

7   After issuing a flurry of apologies, Netflix has mounted one of the all-time great come-backs. *House of Cards* arrived to mostly spectacular reviews, while investors were equally enthusiastic about the company's first-quarter results. Revenue rose 18 percent from the same period last year to $1.02 billion, while the company added 2 million subscribers in the U.S. alone, dispelling widespread fears that its growth had slowed. Shares of Netflix are back above $200. It's one of the best-performing stocks of the year.

8   Hastings doesn't have an office. He moves around headquarters meeting with people and plopping down at spare tables to deal with e-mail. When he needs a quiet place, he heads to his watchtower, a room-size glass square built on the roof of Netflix's main building. To get there, you climb a staircase to the roof and walk along a narrow walkway past air conditioning units and other machinery. Usually someone turns on the A/C in advance. The room can get hot since it's basically a greenhouse with a round conference table and spectacular views of the Santa Cruz Mountains.

9   As the watchtower's A/C blasts on a late afternoon, Hastings, 52, sits in one of the suede chairs, exuding calm. He's goateed, skinny, and sounds extremely Californian when he talks about Netflix's prospects. "We are trying to set this up as a continuously learning organization," he says between mouthfuls of granola. "My role is creating that learning atmosphere."

10   There was much learning in 2011, during the Qwikster episode. In a *Saturday Night Live* skit, Jason Sudeikis played Hastings apologizing to consumers while at the same time

Photograph provided through Wikipedia Commons, http://commons.wikimedia.org/wiki/ File:Netflix headquarters.jpg Hastings says he never looked at the building design.

unveiling increasingly complex businesses, culminating with Nutqwakflikster—a nut, insurance, and movie seller. "We know you hate us," the faux Hastings concludes.

11   Qwikster was a fiasco, but far less threatening than a debacle that preceded it. In August 2008, Netflix's technology infrastructure melted down. This was when the company was still known for DVDs-by-mail, and for three days it could not send discs because a crucial Oracle database kept malfunctioning. Reporters and customers took notice. Netflix traced the problem to an expensive, third-party storage system that went haywire after a software update. The incident still annoys Hastings. When the subject comes up in the watchtower, Chief Product Officer Neil Hunt, who's also gathered at the table, suggests they not mention the storage-system vendor by name. Hastings responds, "Let IBM have it, baby." (An IBM spokesman declined to comment.)

12   Hastings and Hunt have worked together on and off for 25 years, meeting when they were both in the research division of Schlumberger, the oil field-services contractor. According to Hastings, Hunt is responsible for Netflix's technology. "It's mostly listening to Neil," he says. "He's on a first principles basis with this stuff. It's not like I saw some golden tablets and then went forward." Still, engineers at Netflix recall Hastings presiding over a number of meetings following the 2008 shipping disaster. He warned that a similar technical issue on the streaming side of the business would be even more devastating. And Hastings began to see that as the streaming business grew, Netflix would need ever more computing horsepower. It could hire an elite team of data-center engineers and build its own computing centers—à la Google, Microsoft, and Amazon.com—or it could move everything to the cloud.

TEAM NETFLIX

THE ENGINEER	THE DATA WHIZ	THE BUYER	THE CREATIVE
Neil Hunt	**Adrian Cockcroft**	**Ted Sarandos**	**Beau Willimon**
Chief product officer	Cloud director	Chief content officer	Independent screenwriter
Has worked with	Runs the systems Netflix	Hastings's point man	*House of Cards*
Hastings for 25 years	rents from Amazon	in Hollywood	show runner

FROM LEFT: GARETH CATTERMOLE/GETTY IMAGES; STEFAN REIMSCHUESSEL/NETFLIX; JIMI CELESTE/PATRICKMCMULLAN/SIPA USA; A DE VOS/PATRICKMCMULLAN/SIPA USA

13 Netflix began to experiment with cloud services from Amazon and Microsoft, where Hastings served as a board member. In 2009 he bet his company's future on Amazon. Up to that point, nothing the size of Netflix had placed so much of its crucial technology on Amazon's systems. Hastings sent an e-mail to Amazon CEO Jeff Bezos, announcing his plans. "I asked him if he was comfortable with that idea," Hastings says. "If not, there was no point going forward." Bezos gave the go-ahead.

14 At any moment, Netflix draws upon 10,000 to 20,000 servers running in Amazon data centers somewhere. The computers handle customer information, video recommendations, digital rights management, encoding of video files into different formats, and monitoring the performance of the systems. When a new device like an upgraded Xbox or a Samsung smartphone comes along, Netflix uses thousands of extra servers to reformat movie files and deal with the new users. By day, some servers handle the grunt work tied to streaming video; by night, they're repurposed to analyze data. The company has been pushing Amazon Web Services to its limits. "We're using Amazon more efficiently than the retail arm of Amazon is," says Adrian Cockcroft, Netflix's cloud architect. "We're pretty sure about that."

15 Few relationships in the technology industry are as complex as Netflix and Amazon's. Netflix's status as Amazon's biggest customer has earned it favorable pricing and direct lines of communication to Amazon's top engineers. When Netflix wants a new software feature, Amazon is quick to deliver it, and other customers eventually benefit from that work. "There's no question in my mind that our platform is stronger from a performance and functional standpoint because of the collaboration we have with Netflix," says Andy Jassy, who heads Amazon's cloud business.

16 Netflix has been forced to build from scratch much of the software it needs to survive. Since it relies on Amazon for data centers, its 700 engineers focus on coming up with tools for, say, automating the ways in which thousands of cloud servers get started and configured. In Silicon Valley, Netflix has become best known for its so-called Simian Army, a facetiously named set of applications that test the resilience of its systems. Chaos Monkey, for instance, simulates small outages by randomly turning services off, while Chaos Kong takes down an entire data center.

17   Companies such as eBay and Intel have started using these products with their own cloud computing systems, as did the Obama campaign during the last election. Scott VanDenPlas, who managed much of the campaign's infrastructure, points to a Netflix software tool called Asgard. It's a system management application that finds groups of servers and outfits them with all the software needed to do a specific job, performing work in seconds that would require a programmer hours or days. "It let us do things quicker and make decisions faster because you know you have this tool in your pocket," says VanDenPlas. When Hurricane Sandy hit two weeks before the election, VanDenPlas shifted much of the Obama infrastructure from Amazon's East Coast data center to its West Coast systems. "I don't think we would have been able to do it without Asgard," he says. "Our operational efficiency became this enormous strategic advantage."

18   Hastings tends to exist in one of two emotional states: relaxed and attentive, or relaxed and dismissive. The things he cares about he'll discuss animatedly; with everything else, he disengages. Architecture? He claims he never looked at the designs for Netflix headquarters, preferring to just walk in and get to work when someone said the facility was ready. "It was the symbolism of not having me focus on the building," he says. But if you want to chat about contemporary computer science techniques such as distributed hashtag databases and the merits of key value stores, then, yes, Hastings does have an opinion.

19   His geeky side became fully apparent in December 2005. He was convinced that the star rating system provided all the information Netflix needed to predict accurately what people want to watch. Others at the company argued that more indicators—whether people started playing something and then stopped, or searched for a particular actor, etc.—were needed as well. Hastings spent two weeks over his Christmas vacation pounding away on an Excel spreadsheet with millions of customer ratings to build an algorithm that could beat the prediction system designed by his engineers.

20   He failed. Still, the attempt sparked the creation of the Netflix Prize, a $1 million bounty to the person or group that could improve its ratings-based algorithm the most. It was the rare meaningful publicity stunt: The winning team, a collection of independent engineers from around the world, built Netflix a better prediction engine. And a company that was famous for red DVD mailers and outmaneuvering Blockbuster started gaining attention as a place for creativity.

21   Netflix can now hire just about any engineer it wants. That's a function of the computer science the company does and its reputation as the highest payer in Silicon Valley. Managers routinely survey salary trends in Silicon Valley and pay their employees 10 percent to 20 percent more than the going rate for a given skill. Fired employees also get ultragenerous severance packages; the idea is to remove guilt as an obstacle to management parting ways with subpar performers.

22   Netflix also tends to employ older people than its peers. "We hire fully formed adults," says Cockcroft. "We let them do five years at Google before taking them on." A walk around the company's offices bears this out. Engineers work in proper cubicles with high walls that are very out of fashion in the Valley, which has embraced open floor plans. The only real flair: Bathroom doors are decorated to look like entertainment legends (Homer and Marge Simpson, for example), and the meeting rooms are named after TV shows and movies, with famous lines written on the glass walls.

23   One regular engineering meeting takes place in the *Office Space* room. (Quotation: "I wouldn't say I've been missing it, Bob.") To kick things off, everyone talks about what they've been watching. One guy says he saw *The Hunger Games* and started getting recommendations for *Bachelorette* and *The Longshots.* "I'm not sure how these have anything to do with *Hunger Games*," he says. "They're all cast as post-apocalyptic movies."

24   The lead engineer brings up a Google Doc with meeting notes on a central screen. Netflix has moved all of its e-mail and collaboration tools to the cloud as well, and some of the limitations of that approach become apparent. No one can figure out how to enlarge the document and put it in presentation mode, so the roomful of engineers squints at barely legible text displayed via projector. No matter. The conversation moves on to a new feature built into the company's Obiwan customer service system. The software interface has been changed to look something like Facebook's News Feed, where every customer complaint has a trail of "stories" about the issue and what people have done to resolve it. The new system doesn't seem to be working as well as the old one, so the engineers propose a battery of tests.

25   Netflix is always testing things. It will select a group of customers, typically by the tens of thousands, and use them as guinea pigs. One group has been given the ability to create avatars for each member of their families, who in turn get individualized recommendations. Others who watch Netflix via the Sony PlayStation have been greeted by a voice that asks what people in the room want to watch.

26   The most rigorous testing concerns recommendations. Netflix has a vast catalog of movies and shows, but much of its content is old and of limited appeal. To make its service feel valuable, Netflix tries to maximize the likability of the titles that get displayed on someone's home page.

27   One of Netflix's mathematicians is known as 10-Foot User Interface Guy because the average person watching the service via TV sits 10 feet away. His job is to arrange the box art of videos in the most appealing way on a big screen. There's also Two-Foot Guy, who deals with laptops, and 18-Inch Guy for tablets.

28   The master copies of all the shows and movies available to Netflix take up 3.14 petabytes of storage space. (In comparison, Facebook uses about 1.5 petabytes to store about 10 billion photos.) Hollywood studios used to send individual films and shows to Netflix on a disc or thumb drive; now they use a Netflix system called Backlot to send encrypted files via the Internet. Netflix then compresses the files and creates more than 100 different versions, each tuned for the varying bandwidth, device, and language needs of its customers. (An hour of video for the iPhone would be about 150 megabytes.) This compressed catalog comes to about 2.75 petabytes.

29   Each night, Netflix performs an analysis to see which shows were the most popular where. From 2 a.m. to 5 a.m. local time, it fills its servers with the appropriate programs. If *Battlestar Galactica* is popular in Houston on Tuesday, then servers in Texas will be loaded up with more episodes in time for Wednesday night. The most popular videos go on high-speed flash storage drives; everything else gets stored on cheaper, slower hard disks. "We use this predictive model to make sure the content is there before the user asks for it," says Ken Florance, vice president for content delivery at Netflix.

30   The biggest bets Netflix is making now are on its original shows. The company won't disclose how much it paid for two seasons of *House of Cards,* though the Hollywood blog Deadline.com says it was about $100 million. Rather than make it a weekly show, Netflix released all 13 episodes at once. That meant viewers could watch the whole season in one marathon sitting. It also meant the producers didn't have to alter the plot to give every episode a cliffhanger ending. "If you give people a more creative format, then they can tell their stories better," says Ted Sarandos, the company's Beverly Hills-based content chief. He adds that Netflix's goal is, in part, to become HBO before HBO can become Netflix. "They do great content that people love. What are the things we do well? It's the delivery technology, the user interface stuff, the integration into computing devices, and the seamless streaming."

31   While it got less hype, *Hemlock Grove* has attracted a bigger audience than *House of Cards,* and *Arrested Development* may well top both. Jenji Kohan, the creator of Showtime's *Weeds,* plans to première her latest dark comedy *Orange Is the New Black* on Netflix this July. Kohan describes Netflix as supremely easy to work with and very hands off. She has yet to even meet Hastings. "I just hear his name, which, by the way, is a great character name," she says. "It's a romance novel name."

32   Amazon is introducing its own series, too, and Hollywood is abuzz with hope that Netflix and Amazon will spend wild sums of money on even more shows. Sarandos, though, says Netflix is very calculating in its buys. The company puts actors' names and the show type through its algorithms to determine the likely size of an audience. "I can justify the spend with our data and do so with a far greater degree of confidence than the television networks," he says. Viewers have given *House of Cards* a rating of 4.5 stars out of five, which Sarandos says suggests the company is on the right track. "It's definitely art and science mixing," he says. Sarandos goes on to say that Netflix will use its data to help pick which actors should be in future shows and who should direct them.

33   Beau Willimon, the show runner for *House of Cards,* says the story and actors were all decided before Netflix bought the series. "Every single casting and story choice was made from the creative side," he says. Even though Netflix has a rich trove of data about the *House of Cards* audience, Willimon has tried to avoid hearing about any viewership statistics. "That sort of data is a dangerous thing," he says. "If you put too much thought into that stuff, you run the risk of trying to pander to people."

34   Despite its stash of data, Netflix refuses to release any viewership numbers. Unlike the networks, it doesn't have to prove the size of its audience to advertisers. "The networks have to spend tens of millions of dollars to promote must-see events and create an audience," says Sarandos. "When we buy ads, it's just to let people in the industry know that something different is happening." Kohan says Netflix has gotten under the networks' skin. "They've pissed a lot of people off," she says. "There is rage because they won't reveal their data. But I think they're being brilliant because everyone is talking about them."

35   Netflix's critics argue that the company has sacrificed too much control over its technology in its effort to get ahead of rivals. "The problem with Netflix is that they are inextricably bound into Amazon for all eternity," says Paul Maritz, a computing infrastructure veteran and CEO of the cloud computing startup Pivotal. "If they want to go somewhere else, it will be hard." Hastings and his staff characterize such criticism as sour grapes.

36   Another concern is that the studios will stop licensing content now that Netflix is in the originals business. Hollywood is right to remain wary of letting any single entity get too powerful. As Netflix expands overseas, it intends to strike worldwide licensing deals instead of hammering them out country-by-country. From a studio perspective, that could give Netflix the ability to come up with lucrative terms that no regional competitor could match.

37   Over the past five years a chart of Netflix's share price has shifted from a smooth, upward curve to more of a scribble. Hastings seems unperturbed. The experimentation is a goal in itself, whether it's big things like corporate missions or little things like the personal technology he uses. For one month, he'll only use products made by Apple, and the next he's on to phones, tablets, and laptops running Windows. May is Google month, and Hastings has one of the company's touchscreen Chromebook Pixel laptops. "I just keep it rotating," he says.

38   The stock, which has been trading in the low 200s at a price-earnings ratio of 300, is just another side effect of learning, and Hastings doesn't consider the ride all that rocky. "There was the Blockbuster battle and there were our own mistakes on Qwikster," he says, ticking off a greatly abbreviated list of his company's melodramas and near-death experiences. "Other than that, it's not that volatile."

Bit Torrent

On a typical weeknight, the millions of people watching Netflix movies online account for up to a third of all downstream Internet traffic in North America.

Share of downstream North American Web traffic by time of day

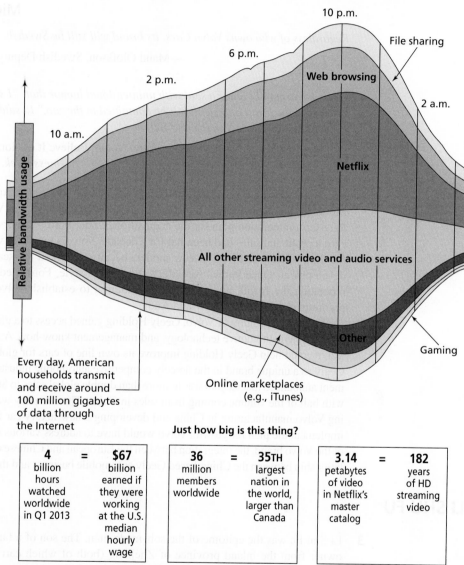

Every day, American households transmit and receive around 100 million gigabytes of data through the Internet

Just how big is this thing?

4 billion hours watched worldwide in Q1 2013	=	$67 billion earned if they were working at the U.S. median hourly wage	36 million members worldwide	=	35TH largest nation in the world, larger than Canada	3.14 petabytes of video in Netflix's master catalog	=	182 years of HD streaming video

GRAPHIC BY BLOOMBERG BUSINESSWEEK. DATA: SANDVINE NETWORKS, BUREAU OF LABOR STATISTICS

Case 29

Volvo and Geely

Andrew Inkpen

Michael H. Moffett

Regardless of who owns Volvo Cars, its brand will still be Swedish.

—Maud Olofsson, Swedish Deputy Prime Minister.

Geely Chairman Li Shu Fu said with unintentional humor that, "I see Volvo as a tiger. It belongs to the forest and shouldn't be contained in the zoo," Li said in Mandarin. "The heart of the tiger is in Sweden and Belgium."

—"Geely Buys Volvo; Believe It or Not, It Could Work,"
Business Week, March 29, 2010.

1   In 2010, Zhejiang Geely Holding Group Co. (Geely Holding) acquired Volvo from Ford Motor Company. In early 2011, various questions remained about Volvo's strategy and the long-term integration plan for the acquisition. Under Ford's ownership, Volvo struggled to earn a profit and sales had been flat for a decade. Volvo's low sales volume made it difficult for the company to invest in new models because it lacked the scale necessary for major development. Once known for safety and Nordic style, Ford tried various approaches to reposition the brand, including a failed attempt to establish Volvo as a rival to German premium marques like BMW and Audi.

2   With the acquisition of Volvo, Geely Holding gained access to a global dealership network, sophisticated automotive technology, and management know-how. A successful integration of Volvo could help Geely Holding improve its own line of cars for global markets and position Geely as a unique brand in the fiercely competitive automobile industry. Volvo's new management announced that its goal was to more than double global sales to 800,000 vehicles by 2020, with half of the volume coming from sales in China. The company was also intent on expanding Volvo manufacturing in China and developing a new luxury car for the China market. To implement the plan for growth, Volvo would have to address various issues, such as the future of the Volvo brand, the integration between the European and Chinese organizations, and the relationship between the China-based Geely automobile business and the global Volvo company.

LI SHU FU

3   Li Shu Fu was the epitome of the self-made man. The son of a farmer and small business owner from the inland province of Zhejiang (both of which carried their own stigma in terms of Chinese class structure), Li had shown industriousness and ambition from the beginning. His first business was photo services for tourists at tourist sites, for which he

Source: Copyright © 2013, Helen Grassbaugh, Thunderbird School of Global Management, caseseries@thunderbird.edu. All rights reserved. This case was prepared by Professors Andrew Inkpen and Michael H. Moffett for the purpose of classroom discussion only, and not to indicate either effective or ineffective management.

used a camera and bicycle purchased with an Rmb100 school graduation gift. He generated a tenfold return in the first six months. That capital in turn provided the seed money for a photo studio and then another business selling silver extract from film processing. In Li's mind, nothing was impossible; one only needed to dream big.

4   Li was the controlling shareholder, founder, and chairman of the board of Zhejiang Geely Holding Group, a company incorporated in the PRC. Geely Holding controlled a company called Proper Glory Holding Inc. (Proper Glory). Proper Glory, a private company incorporated in the British Virgin Islands, was wholly owned by Li and an unidentified associate. Proper Glory owned 50.3 percent of Geely Automobile Holdings Ltd. (Geely Automotive) which began trading publicly on the Hong Kong Stock Exchange in 2004. In 2011, Forbes magazine estimated Li's net worth at $1.9 billion, ranking him 35th among Chinese billionaires. In addition to stories of his wealth and business acumen, Li had been the subject of much characterization over the years. Often referred to as an entrepreneur (he compared himself to John D. Rockefeller) and a car maniac, he was highly charismatic, emotional, and quick witted. Although a persistent and relentless negotiator, he also wrote poetry. According to one observer:

> Mr. Li likes to play up his peasant roots, but it would be a mistake to underestimate this man in his nondescript blue suit, grey socks, and slightly scuffed slip-ons. Business partners use words such as "wily," "crafty," and "brilliant" to describe Mr. Li, and admit that they expect to be outwitted by him in any negotiation.[1]

THE CHINESE AUTOMOBILE MARKET

5   The Chinese government has labeled the automobile industry a *pillar industry*. Pillar industries are those specific industries seen as critical for China's development, and targeted as sources of potential global competitive advantage and job growth.

> By definition, pillar industries involve a preponderance of state control. Some, such as military and national security-related industries (armaments, aircraft, telecommunications), are intended to have complete state ownership, or, at a minimum, state control. Natural resources and shipping also fall into this category.
>
> Other industries, such as autos, steel, and machinery, can have some privately owned firms, but the state intends to remain the dominant investor in these industries as well. The private firms can compete, but the playing field is tilted in the advantage of state-owned firms.[2]

6   The three main players in the industry—the central government, the local governments, the automakers—had very specific interests.

Central Government. The central government's number one priority was to manage the growth of the industry to perpetuate employment. This aided economic stability and regime survival. Over the past 30 years, the central government had also pursued a three-pronged strategy in the automobile industry: consolidation, technology transfer and acquisition, and Chinese brand development.

Local Governments. Outside of Beijing and Shanghai, provincial and municipal governments held enormous authority and influence. Their interests were clear: regime survival through jobs, income generation, and local economic development. The Central

---

[1] "Man in the News: Li Shufu," Patti Waldmeir and John Reed, *Financial Times*, March 26, 2010.
[2] Greg Anderson, "What criteria does the Chinese government use to judge an industry in order to make it a 'pillar industry?'" www.quora.com/.

Government would rarely impose its will upon local governments if those actions would undermine local jobs and income generation.

Automakers. The automakers themselves then fell into three groups by ownership: (1) state-owned enterprises (SOEs), (2) privately owned enterprises, and (3) foreign firms. Because it is a *pillar industry*, foreign firms still may only enter the Chinese market through approved joint ventures with Chinese firms or SOEs; in addition, foreign firms cannot hold majority control of those JVs. The fight for market opportunities and shares now appears to be between the SOE joint ventures and the fledgling privately owned enterprises.

7   The dominance of the SOE cannot be overemphasized when studying China. In the West, "private" means a firm which is not publicly traded. In China, "private" means a company which is not state-controlled. Yet simply because the Chinese firm is not government-owned does not mean that governments—both central and local—do not hold significant sway over its prospects.

Industry Evolution

Make use of exports to get foreign exchange, … make use of imports to get technology.

—*China Automotive Industry Yearbook, 1986*, p. 21.

8   The original state-owned automakers, First Auto Works (FAW) and Second Auto Works (SAW, later renamed DongFeng), were founded in the 1950s to build commercial vehicles for economic and commercial development. At this time, passenger vehicle assembly was limited to very low volumes of taxis and limousines.[3] The industry suffered a significant deconstruction during the Mao Zedung Cultural Revolution (1966–1976), shrinking dramatically. This was followed by Deng Xiaopeng and his philosophy of "learning from the West." For the auto industry, this meant the launch of two key joint ventures, Shanghai-Volkswagen (SAIC, Shanghai Automotive Industry Corporation and Volkswagen of Germany) and Beijing Jeep (American Motors Corporation and Beijing Auto Works) in 1984.

9   The primary objective of these early joint ventures promoted by the Central Government was technology transfer, which in the end proved largely a failure. Foreign joint venture partners were reluctant to put state-of-the-art technology at risk in China, choosing to use relatively basic and sometimes out-of-date platforms for Chinese production. The industry continued to import most of its components, as Chinese parts suppliers continued to struggle with quality and developing skilled workers.

10   The Chinese government's mindset regarding technology transfer and innovation were also part of the problem. *Innovation* was seen as incremental adaptation and change to existing Western technology. The result was a failure to develop core technical knowledge and commercialization skills needed for true innovative development. It was not until late in the 1990s that serious steps were taken to promote local production, restricting imports, facilitating industry consolidation, and requiring increasing quality of product.

11   China's entry into the World Trade Organization (WTO) in 2002 proved to be a turning point for the Chinese automobile industry. Import duties on imported automobiles fell from 100 percent in 2000 to 25 percent by 2006, with automobile component tariffs falling to 10 percent. The result was rapid development of foreign brand-SOE joint ventures as required by law. Joint venture development was expedited by the elimination of local content provisions as well as a key technology transfer provision: China would no longer be allowed to require technology transfer as a condition for establishing a business in China.

[3]Private ownership of an automobile did not become legal in China until 1984.

12   As the Chinese companies developed their skills, the foreign companies were faced with intellectual property issues unique to the Chinese market. The foreign companies often shared their joint venture partners with their global competitors. For example, both General Motors and Volkswagen partnered with SAIC. Reverse engineering of completed cars was common in China and allowed small Chinese companies to design new vehicles at a low cost. Compounding these two issues, the Chinese government had made it clear that it wanted the indigenous Chinese companies to learn as much as they could from their international partners.

Indigenous Brands

The hope of China's auto industry still lies with the private sector. This is a competitive process: First, SOEs compete with foreign capital, and the SOEs lose. Then, foreign capital competes with private [Chinese] enterprises, and the private enterprises win.

—Geely Chairman, Li Shu Fu, March 2009.

13   One way of characterizing the Chinese automobile market today is by nameplate or brand, from the outside-in: (1) imported foreign-made automobiles, usually European luxury cars; (2) cars produced by joint ventures between foreign firms and Chinese firms, sold under brands such as Chevrolet, VW, or Nissan; (3) Chinese products of joint ventures that are developed and produced in China, such as the Baojun 630 sedan produced by the SAIC-GM-Wuling joint venture; (4) cars produced by indigenous Chinese-branded companies. This fourth segment, indigenous brands, was—despite Chinese government interest—extremely small.

14   The reduction of import duties following WTO entry did not result in a major increase in imported automobiles. In response to the WTO changes, many Chinese indigenous firms moved quickly to cut costs and, even more significantly, cut price. The SOE JVs focused on delivering products at the right price for the rapidly growing passenger car market. These JVs proved to be the true benefactors of the market opening, quickly moving to garner market share.

15   Indigenous brand development in the Chinese automobile industry was an opportunity for privately owned Chinese enterprises if Chinese brands could obtain the quality, reliability, and desirability which so far had been the exclusive domain of foreign brands. Private enterprises would also need the access to capital from state-owned banks usually reserved for SOEs. Entrepreneurs like Li Shu Fu had seen a gradual change in their treatment by central and local governments, but only from antagonism to tolerance.

Market Growth

16   Most analyses of the Chinese car market use production data. Official sales data for China are not available. China is the only major auto market in the world where official retail figures are not available. Vehicle-registration data is considered a state secret.

17   In 1996, less than 400,000 vehicles were produced in China. By 2010, China was the world's largest automobile producer with 18 million vehicles produced. The previous five years had an annual growth rate in production of about 25 percent, and expectations were that high growth rates would continue. Exhibit 1 shows production growth for the 2005–2010 period.

18   The Chinese market was also an unusual hybrid of major global companies and domestic firms. Major developed-country markets like the U.S., Japan, and Germany had a small set of global companies (General Motors, Volkswagen, Ford, Toyota, Nissan, for example) dominating sales, a few of which were domestic. Other large-country mass markets, such as the United Kingdom, Brazil, and Indonesia, had no domestic competitors, being completely covered by the global companies. The Chinese market had both, a multitude

EXHIBIT 1 China's Automotive Production Growth (millions)

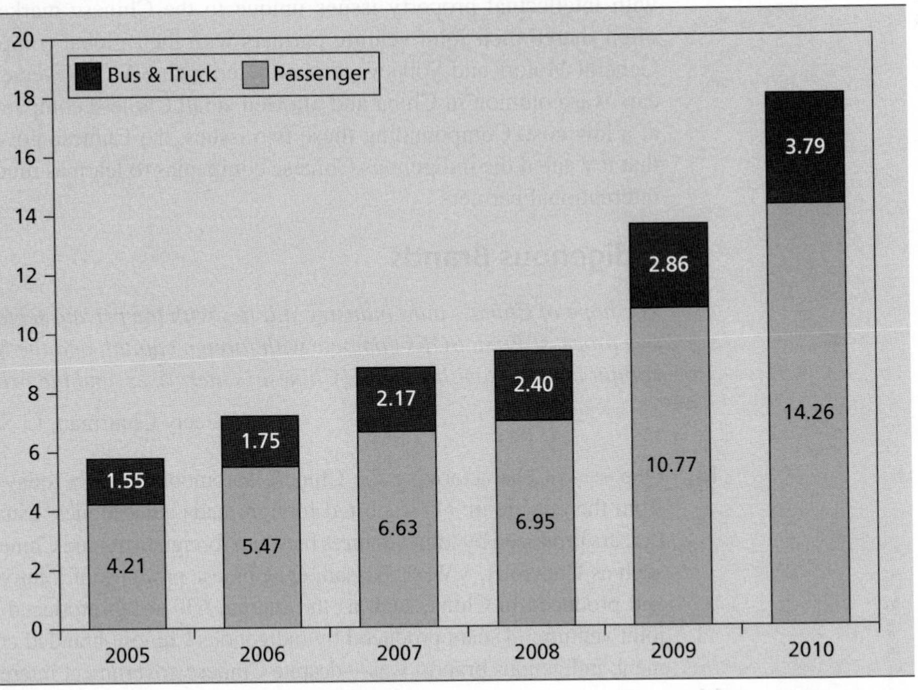

Source: Chinese Association of Automobile Manufacturers.

(somewhere between 70 and 80) of small domestic car companies, and market share dominance by a few major global companies (via JVs).

19   The dominance of a few major JVs with Western automakers in total production in China was clear. As illustrated in Exhibit 2, the top three joint ventures produced 47 percent of new passenger autos in 2010, with the top 12 producing OEMs comprising 90 percent of the total market. But production by JV was not the same thing as brand. As also shown in Exhibit 2, the global brands—once combined across different OEM manufacturers—were clearly dominating the market. The global brands, which could only reach Chinese consumers either through imports or international JVs, were the preferred product. This distinction between manufacturer and brand made the Chinese market uniquely complex.

Chinese Automotive Consumers

Another concern is Volvo's ability to compete against more-established foreign luxury brands such as BMW, Mercedes-Benz, and Audi. These premium cars have a large following among China's rich—many of whom are first-generation drivers and may regard Volvo as a family car lacking sex appeal. "In the last several years, Chinese buyers of luxury cars have been ostentatious," independent auto analyst Michael Dunne said. "They want cars that say, 'Do you know who I am?' Maybe the second round of buyers will want a more subtle image."[4]

20   The Chinese automotive market was dynamic, unpredictable, subject to bursts of government intervention, rife with regional differences in consumer tastes, one of the world's most profitable, and fueled by first-time car buyers who saw automobile ownership as a mark of status and success. In other words, complicated.

[4]"China Carmaker Takes a Big Step with Volvo Deal," David Pierson, Los *Angeles Times*, March 29, 2010.

EXHIBIT 2   **Chinese OEM versus Global Brand Market Shares**

OEM	Partner	2010	Global Brand	2010 Chinese Market Share
SAIC	General Motors, Volkswagen	17%	Volkswagen	16%
DFM Dongfeng	PSA, Nissan, Honda	15%	General Motors	9%
FAW	Volkswagen, Toyota, Mazda	15%	Hyundai	8%
BAIC Beijing	Hyundai, Daimler	9%	Toyota	7%
Changfan	Ford, Mazda, Suzuki	9%	Chery	6%
Guangzhou	Honda, Toyota, Isuzu, Fiat	5%	Renault/Nissan	6%
Chery	------------------	5%	German Luxury*	4%
BYD Auto	------------------	4%	Subtotal	56%
JAC Jianghuai	------------------	3%		
Geely	------------------	3%		
Brilliance	BMW, Toyota	3%		
Great Wall		2%		
Subtotal		90%		
Import		4%		
Others		6%		
Total		100%		

Sources: "Global Auto & Truck Markets," Robert W. Baird & Co., J. D. Power and Associates.

*BMW, Mercedes-Benz, Audi

21   Imported cars constituted fewer than a million units in 2010. Most of the imports were luxury cars, with Mercedes-Benz, BMW, and Lexus having the largest market shares. China's luxury car market was the fastest growing in the world, leading the international car companies to ramp up domestic production of their high-end products. The production of the major international JVs had traditionally targeted the upper income segments of the population, and it was only in the most recent years that products were coming to market for the upper middle class. The Tier 2 and Tier 3 cities, mostly inland cities of large populations but with lower average incomes, had been largely ignored by the international JVs and served mostly by the multitude of small domestic producers. Unlike the case in developed markets, the used car market was embryonic because most car buyers did not have a used car to trade in.

22   Unlike any other major automobile market in the world, *status* was the single most important concern when purchasing a car. And status was also a function of brand name and location of production.

> Victor Sun, a lawyer in China, recently upgraded his Volkswagen Passat to a Volvo for just under 400,000 yuan. "I wanted my car to be classy, understated, and of good value," he said. "Once it becomes a more locally sourced vehicle, it might take some exclusiveness away. I'd also need to reassess its quality."[5]

[5]"Geely's Next Challenge: Selling a Made-in-China Volvo," George Chen and Don Durfee, *Reuters*, January 8, 2010.

EXHIBIT 3   **Chinese Initial Quality Survey Results**

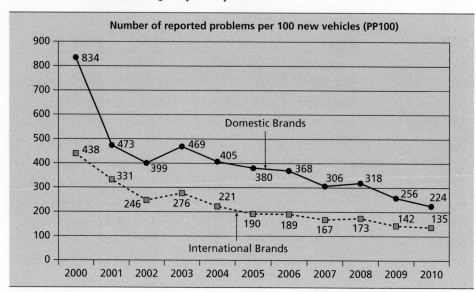

Source: J. D. Power, Asia Pacific, Press Release, October 29, 2010. Number of reported problems, both design and quality of production (defects and malfunctions), in the first two to six months following purchase. A lower value is better.

Changing Tastes

23   Quality concerns were backed by quality statistics. Surveys of initial quality of new vehicles in China indicated a significant difference between international brands and domestic brands, as described in Exhibit 3. Although both categories had improved dramatically over the past decade, international brands were still consistently of higher quality, though the gap between the two brand categories was shrinking. Even with the improvement, however, international brands suffered 135 PP100 in 2010, when similar values for new cars in the United States averaged 108.

24   The role of quality in Chinese consumer purchases was changing. Exhibit 4 shows that price was not near the consideration it was a decade before. A low purchase price was noted by only 12 percent of surveyed buyers in 2010, down from 28 percent a decade before. What was increasingly important was vehicle style, interior roominess, and vehicle quality. The Chinese automotive consumer was becoming increasingly sophisticated.

GEELY AUTOMOTIVE

25   Li Shu Fu created Geely Holding (Geely roughly translates to *lucky* or *auspicious* in Chinese) with borrowed capital in 1986 to build refrigerators. In the following years, Li led Geely Holding's entry into motorcycle parts, then whole motorcycles and scooters in 1994. Although Li's real ambition was to build automobiles, there was little chance of him being awarded a license. First, he was a private entrepreneur, well down the Chinese priority list in the mid-1990s. Second, China's 1994 auto industry policy had explicitly stated that no new passenger car manufacturing permits would be approved. Consolidation was the order of the day.

26   But in what was to become somewhat typical of Li, he found a way around the obstacle. In 1997, Li discovered a prison-owned auto factory in Deyang, Sichuan, on the edge of

EXHIBIT 4   **Changing Chinese Purchasing Priorities**

Reason to Buy (% response)	2000	2010	Change
Low purchase price	28%	12%	−16%
Good vehicle quality	5%	9%	4%
Good vehicle styling	3%	19%	16%
Roominess/interior space	2%	10%	8%

Average Transaction Price (RMB)	2000	2010	% Chg
Premium midsize	341,534	209,802	−39%
Midsize	175,793	120,234	−32%
Entry midsize	134,964	90,737	−33%
Compact	63,980	42,988	−33%
Average exchange rate (RMB/USD)	8.28	6.77	

Average Transaction Price (USD)	2000	2010	% Chg
Premium midsize	$41,248	$30,990	−25%
Midsize	$21,231	$17,760	−16%
Entry midsize	$16,300	$13,403	−18%.
Compact	$7,727	$6,350	−18%

Source: J. D. Power Asia Pacific China Initial Quality Study, April 2011.

bankruptcy. By acquiring the company, he also acquired the factory's official vehicle production certificate. Although the certificate was not for passenger cars, but for trucks and buses, he took the opportunity. In the following year, with the support of the provincial governments—both Sichuan and Zhejiang—he gained permission to produce passenger cars and to build a second factory in his home province of Zhejiang. The Geely was born.

27   As a Chinese car company *not* controlled by the state, Geely was an anomaly. With a market share in China of about 3 percent, the company was not considered one of the top domestic car companies. Geely Automotive exported cars to about 20 countries, mostly emerging markets. In 2010, the company produced 415,000 vehicles, far below its capacity of about 680,000 units (by way of comparison, GM global sales in 2010 were 8.5 million units and BMW, a company focused exclusively on luxury cars, sold 1.2 million cars).

28   Geely cars were priced to sell at the lowest rung of the income ladder and often were characterized as low in quality, reliability, and safety. Geely cars also had interesting names. One was called *King Kong* and an early model was named *You Li Ou*, a play on words that means "better than the Tianjin Xiali or the Buick Sail," two of its competitors.[6] At the 2011 Shanghai Car Show, Geely Automotive showed a concept car named the *Mc-Car*. Geely Automotive seemed to have made good on Li's famous quote that a car is nothing more than "four wheels, one body, an engine, plus a sofa."

29   Despite its small size, Geely Automotive produced a diverse lineup. New cars launched in 2011 included the GLEagle GC6, a sedan designed to compete against cars like the Nissan Sunny/Sentra and Toyota Corolla; the GX6, a crossover vehicle; the GS-CC, a hard-top

[6]"The Little Car Company That Can?" *BloombergBusinessweek*. June 16, 2002.

convertible; the EC6-RV, a small hatchback that the company called a "high-quality, compact European style car"; and the SC7-RV, a "classic family car inheriting British style and fusing Chinese elements." The SC7-RV was developed in a joint venture with British company Manganese Bronze, producer of the London black cab in the U.K., and a company in which Geely Automotive held a minority interest.

30   As shown by the diverse product line and unusual concept cars, Li had grand plans for Geely Automotive. He was known to show up at auto shows and public presentations with PowerPoint slides showing 30 or 40 forthcoming new automobile models, many of which looked very similar to established foreign brands. Li once referred to a prospective new model as a "baby-Rolls Royce," upsetting Rolls Royce. The Rolls Royce knockoff, the GE, had a single rear seat which was a massage chair. Geely Automotive and Li were regularly criticized for copying existing automotive platforms.

31   Li wanted to go big fast, and was not shy about his desire to buy technology. Li dreamed of rising above Geely Automotive's common roots and gaining the prestige and price premiums in the Chinese market enjoyed by some of the global players like Mercedes, Audi, and BMW.

VOLVO

Cars are driven by people. The guiding principle behind everything we make at Volvo, therefore, is, and must remain, safety.

—Assar Gabrielsson and Gustav Larson, Founders of Volvo, 1927.

32   Volvo Car Corporation, or Volvo Personvagnar AB, was founded in Gothenburg, Sweden, in 1927. The name means "I roll" in Latin, and the Volvo logo is based on the chemical symbol for iron. The original vision of the founders was to build a car, nicknamed the *Jakob*, which could withstand the rigors of Sweden's rough roads and cold winters. Over the next 70 years, Volvo cars became known for quality, safety, and somewhat quirky Swedish style. By the 1990s, Volvo had added concern for the environment as a core brand value.

> Swedish steel was good but Swedish roads were bad, particularly when compared to American roads. Most of the cars sold in Sweden were built for straight concrete roads. They had soft springing and were built for high-speed driving. Neither of these qualities were particularly suited for the twisting, pot-holed, dirt roads of Sweden. What [was] needed was an automobile with harder suspension—an automobile that would hold the road. All Swedish people remember the "washboard" roads. Only a really rugged automobile would escape being shaken to bits on such roads. There were certainly enough essential requirements for a Swedish automobile industry.

—Assar Gabrielsson, Founder and Volvo President, 1927–1956, *The Thirty-Year History of Volvo*, by Assar Gabrielsson, Wezata, Goteborg, 1959, p. 3.

33   Assar Gabrielsson founded Volvo in an attempt to fill a perceived gap in the market— the need for an automobile that could survive demanding Swedish roads. U.S. automobile manufacturers dominated many national markets even in the 1920s, including Sweden, but Gabrielsson believed that Sweden could build a car, competitively, that would serve Swedes better.

34   The Volvo organization of 1927 looked very similar to that of the world's largest automotive companies of 2010—it designed and assembled, but it performed little of the

original manufacturing of parts, components, and systems. Automobiles required thousands of components, and the Volvo company Gabrielsson founded did not have the capital or competency to manufacture them. Gabrielsson thought the answer was to involve and integrate Swedish manufacturers nationwide to partner in the process:[7]

> Even the American factories bought certain units for their cars from firms which specialised in certain branches. Volvo took things even further and ordered all parts, all material, and all units from various industries in Sweden. Design and assembly work was done by us. We used the expression "Building the Volvo way" to cover this type of working.

The Volvo Way

It might be because the car is a little square and sluggish, just like the Swedes themselves.

—Jan Wilsgaard, Chief Designer, Volvo Cars, 1950–1990.

35   The "Volvo way" meant that for many years Volvo was a Swedish automotive company selling cars internationally using Swedish design, Swedish manufacturing, Swedish assembly, and Swedish leadership. The leadership team learned quickly that it had to source selective components, particularly electronics and complex carburetor systems, from abroad. Foreign sourcing also had the added advantage of helping Swedish suppliers to reach competitiveness with European suppliers.

36   Volvo struggled from the beginning with lack of scale. Volume growth was never on the same level as major European automobile companies like Renault, Fiat, or Opel, and nothing close to the U.S. firms. The smaller volumes meant that Volvo could make only minor, incremental model changes from year to year. This constancy of design became part of the company's image and acted as feedstock for the Volvo reputation for simplicity, safety, and Swedish cultural conservatism. Jan Wilsgaard, Volvo's chief designer for nearly 50 years and the man credited with defining Volvo's style, had a three-word credo: *simple is beautiful.*

37   Volvo's product line was defined over time by a few models. The Amazon (*Amason* in the Swedish market), launched in 1956, grew its international reputation. The introduction of the Volvo 140 in 1966 (Exhibit 5), defined Volvo's look for roughly the next 30 years. The 140 was followed by the 144, the first of many following models which used a tri-digit numbering system, indicating a series, number of cylinders, and number of doors. The 144 was a first series, 4-cylinder, 4-door sedan.

EXHIBIT 5   **The Volvo 140 Sedan**

[7]*The Thirty-Year History of Volvo*, by Assar Gabrielsson, Wezata, Goteborg, 1959, p. 3.

38   Volvo was largely credited with turning a sedan into a station wagon, part of a growing emphasis on adopting the innovations arising from the American market. Styling was characterized as boxy and often described as a European running shoe. Volvo became the automobile of the *yuppie* (young upwardly mobile professional) urbanite segment, which was young, well educated, and affluent. The cars competed with BMW and Volvo's Swedish counterpart, SAAB.

39   But it was Volvo's continued innovation in diesel engines and safety which defined the company and led much of the global automobile industry for many years. The company's development of highly reliable and efficient diesel engines proved to be a core competitive advantage for its commercial truck and bus product lines, providing the basis of what quickly became greater volume sales than its passenger automobile lines.

40   Volvo's innovations in safety included the introduction of laminated glass (1944), the 3-point safety belt (1959), the rear-facing child seat (1964), the side impact protection system (SIPS, 1991), side safety airbags (1995), head-protecting airbags (1998), and blind-spot detection system with side-view-mirror-mounted sensors (BLIS, 2004). In recent years, the company led the industry in developing adaptive cruise control and collision warning and brake support systems. Every market survey of passenger vehicles said the same thing: Volvo meant safe, reliable, and mundane. A Volvo promotional brochure in 2010 carried the message:

> For decades, we've created cars that encourage people to enjoy life and help protect it in the event of an accident. Many of the most important car safety innovations are the hallmark of Volvo, and hundreds of thousands of people all over the world can say they're still alive thanks to Volvo ingenuity. This is not by coincidence. Our founders stated that safety is, and shall always be, at the heart of what we do. As a result, Volvo is recognized the world over for our passion and dedication to provide the safest cars on the road. The protective character of Volvo also encompasses the world we share. Already in 1972, Volvo was the first car manufacturer to acknowledge and actively respond to the environmental impact of cars. In fact, we invented the three-way catalytic converter, and are constantly innovating to reduce the environmental impact of the cars we make and how we make them. Of course, choosing a Volvo will always be something you do for both yourself and the people around you—because our cars will always consider the well-being of everyone. Even if those people happen to be outside your car or are part of future generations.

The Ford Era

41   Ford purchased Volvo Car from the Volvo Group in 1999 for $6.45 billion. Volvo trucks and commercial vehicles were not part of the deal. (The Volvo name is today used by both business entities, Volvo Car and the publicly traded Volvo Group, which includes commercial trucks, construction equipment, and buses.) Ford's acquisition of Volvo Car was part of its formation of its Premier Auto Group (PAG), a division focused on high-end products. Besides Volvo, PAG included Lincoln, Jaguar, Range Rover, and Aston Martin. While part of the PAG, Volvo expanded its range of vehicles as it was expected to be the primary profit center within the PAG. At that same time, GM purchased Saab, another Swedish automaker, which it eventually shut down after its bankruptcy in 2009.

42   Two events in 2006 changed Volvo's future: Volvo suffered losses for the first time under Ford, and a new CEO, Alan Mulally, took office at Ford. As the global automotive market declined during the 2008–2009 recession, companies like Ford and GM began to downsize, shedding many product lines and business groups. Mulally believed the company should focus solely on its core brand (One Ford Plan), and began to disassemble the Premier Auto Group. Aston Martin was sold to British investors in 2007 and Jaguar and Land Rover to the Tata Group of India in 2009. Ford delayed putting Volvo up for sale as it considered

EXHIBIT 6   Volvo's Global Sales Volumes, 2000–2010

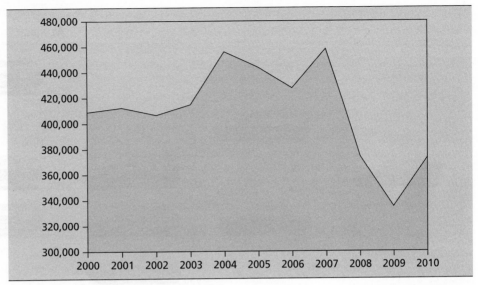

Source: *Volvo Financial Report*, 2010, 2011.

retaining the company for its unique safety culture and technology, but as losses mounted, it began to look for a way out. A number of options were considered including spinning Volvo out on its own, selling it to the Swedish government, or selling it to another car company.

Volvo's Performance

43   Volvo had been for many years a quality automobile, a safe automobile, but not a growth automobile. Sales volumes, as illustrated by Exhibit 6, were flat for most of the last decade, somewhere between 400,000 and 450,000 units annually. Although dropping 27 percent from 458,000 units in 2007 to 334,000 units in 2009, that was much less than that suffered by some of the world's largest companies like GM and Toyota.

44   Under Ford, Volvo last turned a profit in 2006, albeit a small one. But in 2007 and 2008, losses mounted, as illustrated in Exhibit 7. In 2008, Ford announced a $2.4 billion write-down on Volvo and, as the global financial crisis wreaked havoc on automobile markets, Ford decided to sell. In 2010, Volvo sales began to rebound and profit returned.

EXHIBIT 7   Volvo Car's Performance, 2006–2010

Performance	2006	2007	2008	2009	2010
Revenue (SEK million)	122,076	121,620	95,120	95,700	113,100
EBIT (SEK million)	(296)	(1,117)	(9,493)	(5,185)	2,340
Sales (number of cars)	427,747	458,323	374,297	334,808	373,525
Employees	25,553	24,384	22,732	19,650	19,494
Fleet avg CO2 g/km	193	190	182	173	157

EXHIBIT 8 Volvo's Model Line 2010

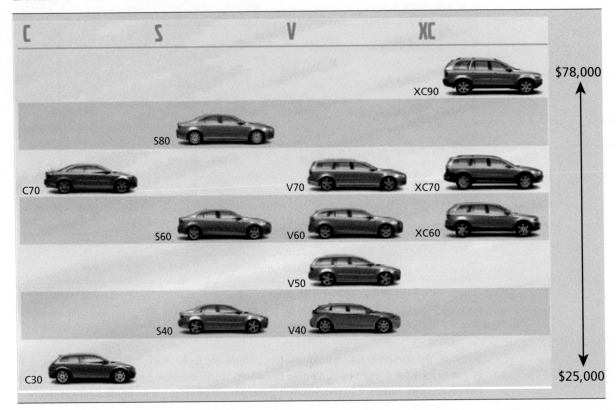

Volvo's Offerings—2011

45   The company had four major lines of vehicles: Coupes/Convertibles (C), Sedans (S), Versatile Estates or Wagons (V), and Crossovers (XC). Although produced on four different platforms, prices varied between $25,000 (£16,000 in the United Kingdom) for the C30 coupe to as high as $78,000 (£50,000) for the V8 AWD XC90 crossover. As shown in Exhibit 8, the recovery of sales volumes in the post-2009 period was spread across three of the four model groups, with the Coupes segment showing declining sales. Also, the introduction of the V60 wagon had been a significant source of growth.

46   In 2010, there were more than 2,000 Volvo dealers in all continents and major markets of the world and Volvo had assembly plants in Sweden and Belgium. Volume sales were spread relatively equally across the four product categories (see Appendix 1).

47   Volvo's largest country markets had not changed in recent years, as illustrated in Appendix 2. Most of Volvo's sales were in Western Europe and North America; the top 10 markets made up 75 percent of total sales volume. The European markets had showed slow growth in the post-2009 recession, including Sweden, although the largest single market, the United States, had fallen from 18.3 percent of total sales in 2009 to 14.4 percent in 2010. The single most encouraging market was China, growing from 6.7 percent of sales in 2009 to more than 8.2 percent in 2010.

Volvo in China

48   Volvo cars were first sold in China in 1984 and, in 1994, Volvo established an office in Beijing. The next year, Volvo began sponsoring the Volvo China Open golf tournament. In 2006, Volvo production began at the Chang'an Ford Mazda Automotive JV plant. Sales in

APPENDIX 1   Volvo's Product Line, Sales and Production

	2009		2010	
Coupes	**Sales**	**Percent**	**2010**	**Percent**
C30	32,409	9.7%	35,981	9.6%
C70	10,792	3.2%	10,158	2.7%
	43,201	12.9%	46,139	12.4%
Sedans				
S40 Compact Sedan	36,954	11.0%	31,688	8.5%
S60 Sedan	14,131	4.2%	14,786	4.0%
S80 Sedan	21,065	6.3%	19,162	5.1%
S80L Sedan (long)	7,106	2.1%	11,778	3.2%
	79,256	23.7%	77,414	20.7%
Versatile Wagons				
V50	54,062	16.1%	56,098	15.0%
V60	–	0.0%	4,609	1.2%
V70	45,836	13.7%	48,877	13.1%
	99,898	29.8%	109,584	29.3%
Crossovers				
XC60 Crossover	61,667	18.4%	80,723	21.6%
XC70 Crossover	18,032	5.4%	22,068	5.9%
XC90 Crossover	32,754	9.8%	37,597	10.1%
	112,453	33.6%	140,388	37.6%
Total	334,808	100.0%	373,525	100.0%

Source: Volvo Car.

APPENDIX 2   Volvo's Production by Plant, 2010

Coupes	**Gothenburg**	**Uddevalla**	**Gent**	**Chongqing**	**Thailand**	**Malaysia**	**Totals**
C30	–	–	35,248	–	–	–	35,248
C70	–	9,532	–	–		–	9,532
Sedans							
S40 Compact Sedan			22,779	5,509		378	28,666
S60 Sedan	–	–	27,579	–		–	27,579
S80 Sedan	16,803	–	–	–	531	120	17,454
S80L Sedan (long)	–	–	–	11,495		–	11,495
Versatile Wagons							
V40	–	–	–	–		–	–
V50	–	–	53,982	–		320	54,302
V60	13,404	–	–	–		–	13,404
V70	48,585	–	–	–		–	48,585
Crossovers							
XC60 Crossover	–	–	83,529	–		141	83,670
XC70 Crossover	21,156	–	–	–		–	21,156
XC90 Crossover	36,375	–	–	–	240	96	36,711
Total	136,323	9,532	223,117	17,004	771	1,055	387,802

Source: Volvo Car.

APPENDIX 3 Volvo's Ten Major Markets, 2009–2011

2011 Rank	Country	2009 Units	2009 Percent	2010 Units	2010 Percent
1	USA	61,426	18.3%	53,952	14.4%
2	Sweden	41,826	12.5%	52,894	14.2%
3	United Kingdom	34,371	10.3%	37,940	10.2%
4	China	22,405	6.7%	30,522	8.2%
5	Germany	25,221	7.5%	25,207	6.7%
6	Belgium	13,223	3.9%	17,969	4.8%
7	Italy	15,896	4.7%	17,509	4.7%
8	Netherlands	14,035	4.2%	14,308	3.8%
9	France	11,596	3.5%	12,211	3.3%
10	Russia	6,894	2.1%	10,650	2.9%
---	Others	87,915	26.3%	100,363	26.9%
	Total	334,808	100.0%	373,525	100.0%

Source: Volvo.

China were about 30,000 cars in 2010 and sales in 2011 looked to be substantially higher. To cater to the Chinese market's taste for larger vehicles, a lengthened version of the S80 sedan (the S80L) was developed for and sold exclusively in China. See Appendix 3.

LI SHU FU'S INTEREST IN VOLVO

49   Li Shu Fu's interest in Volvo began in 2002, but early attempts to talk to Ford were ignored. In 2007, the Rothschild investment bank approached Li about a possible Volvo acquisition. In Li words, "It was like a poor country boy chasing a famous international actress." At first, Ford ignored Li's interest. He remained persistent and philosophical, at one point telling the *Wall Street Journal* that "Volvo is like a mysterious, beautiful woman. We just look at her from far away, amazed. We don't dare get close." But after the severity of the 2008–2009 financial crisis hit home, Ford entertained Li's advances.

> It is not surprising for 12-year-old Geely to bid for 82-year-old car maker Volvo. In China, Geely is a low-market vehicle; for 30,000 yuan you can pick up a new one. Many Geely buyers like to replace the hood emblem with one from a Mercedes-Benz or BMW. Li Shu Fu, Geely's founder, has cherished the dream of making the world's best cars and luxury cars.[8]

50   Initial valuations of Volvo were thought to be somewhere between $2.3 and $2.9 billion. Although Geely Automotive and Volvo had roughly the same unit sales, revenue per car for Volvo was substantially higher than that of Geely Automotive. To do the deal, financing would be critical and would probably require both additional investors and creative structures. Because Geely Holding and Geely Automotive were privately owned, there was no specific Chinese province or government supporting its bid financially.

[8]"Geely's Volvo Deal: Join Hands with an SOE Giant to Resolve Financing Problem," ChinaStakes.com, September 17, 2009.

Geely Holding and Ford Negotiations

51   In April 2009, a delegation of four different automobile companies toured the European operations of Volvo. The four were Dongfeng and Chang'an, both state-owned and publicly listed car companies; Chery, a state-owned car company but not publicly listed; and Geely Holding. Of the four, probably only Dongfeng was capable of utilizing Volvo's sophisticated technology without major new investment. Ford already had a JV with Chang'an in China.

52   It was clear from the start that if Volvo became the target of a Chinese acquisition, the Chinese central government would not allow competitive bidding among Chinese companies. From the group of four Chinese companies, Geely Holding was given approval to be sole bidder. In negotiations, Li allowed advisers to do most of the negotiating, though he did meet with Ford's CFO several times to discuss difficult details.

53   Ford wanted to retain rights over a number of the technology investments made in Volvo. The rights, or safeguards, would protect Ford's technology given that Geely Automotive and other Chinese auto companies might become serious competitors. Most auto analysts believed that any company operating in China would lose significant intellectual property regardless of contractual protections.

54   The buyer would be Geely Holding, not publicly traded Geely Automotive (see Appendix 4). In order to quell stockholder concern, Geely Automotive made it clear that it would not be taking on the financial burden of the Volvo purchase. Geely Automotive was already heavily indebted as a result of its recent expansion efforts in China. The Geely Holding acquisition structure was also thought to quell Swedish concerns that Volvo as a separate entity would be absorbed by Geely Automotive. The deal allowed Geely Holding to license some technology from Volvo for development. Geely Holding also received assurances of continued Ford supplies of engines, stamped steel and pressed body parts, and other custom components.

APPENDIX 4   Geely Holdings & Geely Auto

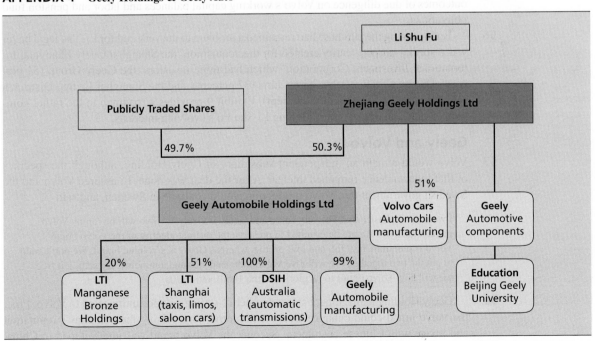

EXHIBIT 9 Li Shu Fu and Geely Holdings

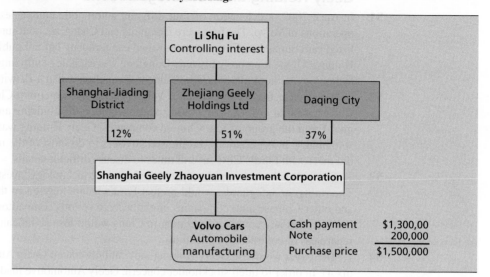

55 A tentative agreement was reached in December 2009. Ford agreed to sell Volvo for $1.8 billion, $1.6 billion in cash and a $200 million note. The sale would not make much of a financial difference for Ford, though it would free the company from further investment in Volvo. Ford would also earn margins on continuing supplier arrangements with Volvo. The late spring and summer of 2010 saw further negotiations, and on August 1, 2010, the final contract was signed. The sale price was adjusted downward to $1.5 billion, $1.3 billion in cash plus a $200 million note carried by Ford. The price adjustment reflected the outcomes of due diligence on Volvo's working capital balances and labor and pension fund obligations.

56 But financing the purchase had remained a problem to the very end for Li. The legal buyer was a special-purpose entity created for the acquisition, the Shanghai Geely Zhaoyuan International Investment Corporation, which had three investors: the Geely Group (51 percent), Daqing City in northeastern China (37 percent), and the Shanghai Jiading District, a suburban area of Shanghai (12 percent). Exhibit 9 provides a roadmap to the rather complex owners and interests surrounding Li Shu Fu's evolving interests.

Geely and Volvo

57 Volvo would remain an independent subsidiary of Geely Holding, although the specifics of that independence remained unclear. After the deal was done, Li assured Volvo and the Swedish government that Volvo production would continue in Sweden, and said:

> I want to emphasize that Volvo is Volvo and Geely is Geely—Volvo will be run by Volvo management . . . We are determined to preserve the distinct identity of the Volvo brand . . . Volvo is premium, tasteful, and low-profile, whereas Geely is a volume brand. We don't want to put the two together. We will give Volvo independence and autonomy. By setting it free, we will help Volvo return to its glories in the 1960s and 1970s.

58 Geely Holding management saw a number of strategic opportunities tied to Volvo. First, the Volvo brand could enhance Geely Automotive cars, raising the company's reputation and image with Chinese customers. Second, the Volvo brand was undeveloped in China.

An expansion of Volvo's product line to support demand in China would allow Geely Holding to move Volvo into competition with the other major European brands in China. Third, Volvo's global product development and sales could benefit from cost reductions tied to Chinese operations.

59 Questions about Geely and Volvo were raised by many analysts. For example:

> Li Shu Fu is a paranoid car maker from a farmer family dreaming of building a luxury brand. He got his understanding of car making from his "four wheels and two sofas" statement, but his car business in China has grown weed-like from nowhere, driven by his determination to sell the world's "cheapest car." Geely's series of cars sell well to the emerging middle class in second-and third-tier inland cities, for bottom prices but poor quality. To Li Shu Fu, making and selling high-quality cars so far has been a pipe dream. Volvo's headquarters, its R&D team, and its overseas factory workers cannot be looking with optimism at their new owners. It may take a long journey for Li Shu Fu to understand brand premium.[9]

New Leadership and Next Steps

> From now on, you can expect us to do things faster, better, and smarter. We will bring new ideas to the market quicker than before. We are focusing on a driver-centric approach and we will stand out from the crowd by delivering a distinct, individualist car experience. Not by copying our main competitors. Instead, we will do it by carving out our own, unique Scandinavian profile.

> Stefan Jacoby, President and CEO—Volvo, LA Auto Show, November 2010.

60 A new President and CEO of Volvo, Stefan Jacoby, was appointed in June of 2010. Jacoby, who had spent most of his professional career with Volkswagen, was known as a strategist. German-born, he had worked closely with VW's Ferdinand Piëch for years before taking over as President and CEO, Volkswagen Group of America. In August, immediately following the finalization of the acquisition, a new Board was formed (Exhibit 10).

EXHIBIT 10 **Volvo Cars New Board of Directors**

Member	Role
Li Shu Fu	Chairman of Volvo Cars, Founder and Chairman of Zhejiang Geely Holding Group
Hans-Olov Olsson	Vice-Chairman of Volvo Cars, formerly Senior Vice President Global Marketing Ford Motor, currently Senior Industrial Advisor to Rothschild
Stefan Jacoby	President and CEO of Volvo Cars
Håkan Samuelsson	Member of the Board of Volvo Cars, formerly MAN AG, Chairman & CEO
Dr. Herbert H. Demel	Executive Vice President, Magna Group
Lone Fønss Schrøder	Wallenius Lines, President & CEO
Winnie Kin Wah Fok	Investor AB, Senior Advisor
Freeman H. Shen	Vice President, Zhejiang Geely Holding Group; Senior Vice President and Chairman Volvo China

[9]Scott Zhou, "Advice to Li Shu Fu: Don't Try to Free Ride Geely on Volvo Too Soon," ChinaStakes.com, March 29, 2010.

61   A new Volvo China organization was set up with Freeman Shen as Senior Vice President and Chairman. Shen joined Geely Holding in 2009 and prior to that was Fiat Group China vice president. Shen was also a Volvo Cars director. Volvo Cars China headquarters was set up in Shanghai and would include a technology center as well as purchasing, design, sales and marketing, manufacturing and finance.

62   To facilitate cooperation between Geely Automotive and Volvo, the Volvo-Geely Dialogue and Cooperation Committee (DCC) was set up in November 2010. Geely Automotive described the DCC as follows:

> The DCC is a forum between both parties to exchange ideas and information relating to the manufacturing and supply of automotive products, the development of new products and related technologies, marketing and distribution of these products to potential customers, and talent training and cultivation. The DCC should facilitate discussion between both parties, with an aim to make the best use of Volvo's cutting-edge technology in safety and environmental care, and Geely's insights for Chinese market and customers, to develop automotive products, technologies and markets.[10]

63   At a press conference held on February 25, 2011, in Beijing, Volvo Cars announced its plan for growth in China. Exhibit 11 contains the official press release. The main question was, would this new strategy work?

EXHIBIT 11   **Volvo Car Corporation Manufacturing Plant to Be Built in Chengdu—Investigations for a Plant Also in Daqing (February 25, 2011)**

Volvo Car Corporation announces its China strategy: At a press conference held today, February 25 in Beijing, Volvo Car Corporation announced its strategy for growth in China. The Board of Directors at Volvo Car Corporation has decided, pending approval of Chinese authorities, to invest in a new plant in the city of Chengdu and continue investigations for a plant also in Daqing.

"We regard the Chinese market as the second home market for Volvo Car Corporation and a very important part of the plan to build a successful future for the company," says Stefan Jacoby, President and CEO of Volvo Car Corporation.

Stefan Jacoby, CEO and President Volvo Car Corporation, presenting Volvo Cars' China Strategy. Chairman of the Board of Directors Volvo Car Corporation Li Shufu and Freeman Shen, Vice President, Volvo Cars China Operations, also on stage.

Li Shufu, Chairman of the Board, continues: "Together with my colleagues on the Board of Volvo Car Corporation, I am very happy with the achievements made by Stefan Jacoby and his leadership team over the past few months. We have developed a solid plan for future growth in the strategically important Chinese market. I am also happy to see that Volvo sales show a strong start in 2011 both in Europe and on the U.S. market."

---

[10]Geely Automobile Holdings Limited 2010 *Annual Report.*

EXHIBIT 11 *(Continued)*

For Volvo Car Corporation and its employees, 2010 was a year characterized by change and transformation. On August 2, the company got a new owner in Zhejiang Geely Holding Group. Since then, Volvo Car Corporation has recorded a number of achievements:

- A new Board of Directors with a high degree of international business experience was appointed on August 2, 2010.
- Stefan Jacoby was appointed President and CEO on August 16, 2010.
- The all-new S60 sports sedan and the V60 sports wagon were successfully launched.
- Global retail sales during 2010 reached 373,525, an increase of 11.2 percent compared to 2009.
- Every quarter of 2010 showed a positive financial result, which gave a full-year result that was better than expected.

Revised Corporate Structure

The company's leadership under Stefan Jacoby worked intensively during autumn 2010 and early 2011 on a revised product plan for the next 10 years in order to deliver on the brand objectives, which in turn also have been undergoing major analysis and development. As a result of the new strategic direction of Volvo Car Corporation, several organizational changes at Headquarters in Gothenburg, Sweden, have also been implemented.

An entirely new Volvo organization led by Freeman Shen, Senior Vice President and Chairman of Volvo Cars China Operations has been created in China. A new Volvo Car China headquarters has been established in Shanghai, including a Technology Centre and all functions for purchasing, design, sales and marketing, manufacturing, finance, etc.

"We are increasing our business presence in China from a national sales company to an organisation with all functions necessary to manage our operation in China," said Stefan Jacoby. "Our aim is to reach a sales volume of about 200,000 cars in the Chinese market by 2015." To achieve the next five-year growth plan in China, the Board and the Executive Management Team have made the following decisions:

- Volvo Car Corporation will, pending the approval of the Chinese authorities, build a manufacturing plant in Chengdu, 1,600 km west of Shanghai. The plant will produce only Volvo cars. The plant is based upon a business case of approximately 100,000 produced cars annually and production is estimated to start during 2013.
- The expansion in China will not affect operations and employment in Europe.
- The board also approved a decision to continue investigating the opportunities for establishing a plant in Daqing in northeastern China.
- Shanghai will serve as Volvo Car China headquarters and centre for product development, design, and sourcing. Among other priorities, Volvo Car China will also support Volvo Corporation R&D in Sweden regarding the development of electric vehicles and hybrids.
- Volvo Car Corporation puts full focus on increasing sales in China and strengthens sales and marketing activities, including expanding dealer shops from 106 to 220 by 2015, train sales consultants, and improve customer experience and satisfaction.
- Volvo Car Corporation will optimize its sourcing network in China for the global market.
- Volvo Car China will start to employ new staff to work with product development for the Chinese market and support local production and purchasing.

"We will build an entirely new plant in Chengdu and further investigate the opportunities for establishing an additional factory in Daqing. Our production in China will, however, not have any impact on decisions affecting capacity utilization of our plants in Sweden and Belgium," says Stefan Jacoby.

(Continued)

EXHIBIT 11 *(Continued)*

Lars Danielson, previously General Manager of the Volvo Torslanda Plant, has been appointed Vice President of Industrial Systems including manufacturing and quality. Lars Danielson is based in Chengdu and is currently planning the complex work involved in constructing a new Volvo plant in the region.

Secure Volvo Quality

Volvo Car Corporation SVP and China Operations Chairman Freeman Shen says, "At our plants in China we will ensure that Volvo's global manufacturing and quality system can be thoroughly implemented."

"The Volvo Car China Technology Centre in Shanghai will develop into a complete product development organization on an international level. It will have the competence and capacity to work together with the HQ in Sweden, participating in Volvo Car Corporation's work process for developing entirely new models," says Freeman Shen.

Stefan Jacoby emphasizes that Volvo will continue to be a contemporary luxury brand, with products built around people. The key strategy for Volvo Car Corporation is to continue to strengthen its business presence in mature markets like Europe and America while proactively exploring new emerging markets.

Li Shufu says, "We continue to uphold our principle that Geely is Geely and Volvo is Volvo. A more globalized, more focused luxury brand will turn our vision of a growing and profitable Volvo Car Corporation into reality. The company will continue to contribute to the development of the global automotive industry by introducing world-first innovations that make an outstanding brand win in the marketplace."

Source: http://www.volvocars.com/intl/top/corporate/Pages/default.aspx?itemid=251.

Case 30

Yahoo! Inc.: *Marissa Mayer's Challenge*[1]

1   At 12:45 a.m. on August 25, 2012, Marissa Mayer, the recently appointed chief executive officer (CEO) of Yahoo! Inc. (Yahoo), sent an e-mail to all employees of the company. The e-mail exhorted them to continue to work hard and keep up their spirits, given the many challenges the company faced.[2] The e-mail indicated to the employees that their CEO, pregnant and due to deliver her first child in early October, was hard at work at that late hour. Mayer was due to meet Yahoo's board in mid-September at Yahoo's headquarters in Sunnyvale, California, in order to present her strategy to turn the company around. The board meeting, originally scheduled for New York City, had been moved to its current location given Mayer's advanced stage of pregnancy. In recent months, Yahoo had reconstituted its board to admit three members who represented an activist shareholder, seen the departure of its previous CEO amid embarrassing circumstances, suffered the loss of key senior executives, and faced the phasing out of its investment in Alibaba, a Chinese Internet company. After a highly secretive search, Yahoo's board had convinced Mayer to move from Google (where she was the company's twentieth hire) to take over the leadership position at Yahoo.[3] The Yahoo board, the investment community, and Yahoo's employees were all eagerly waiting for Mayer's vision for confronting the company's challenges.

THE INTERNET CONSUMER SERVICES INDUSTRY[4]

2   The Internet was a vast network of interconnected smaller networks of computers, supported by both tangible infrastructure (physical hardware) and intangible infrastructure. In 2012, the Internet was the essential medium for communication and content and its importance to everyday life was regarded as higher than that of the telephone, television, and computer. Companies that provided the intangible infrastructural support to

Source: Ram Subramanian wrote this case solely to provide material for class discussion. The author does not intend to illustrate either effective or ineffective handling of a managerial situation. The author may have disguised certain names and other identifying information to protect confidentiality.

Richard Ivey School of Business Foundation prohibits any form of reproduction, storage or transmission without its written permission. Reproduction of this material is not covered under authorization by any reproduction rights organization. To order copies or request permission to reproduce materials, contact Ivey Publishing, Richard Ivey School of Business Foundation, The University of Western Ontario, London, Ontario, Canada, N6A 3K7; phone (519) 661-3208; fax (519) 661-3882; e-mail cases@ivey.uwo.ca.

Copyright © 2013, Richard Ivey School of Business Foundation   Version: 2013-05-24

[1]This case has been written on the basis of published sources only. Consequently, the interpretation and perspectives presented in this case are not necessarily those of Yahoo! Inc, or any of its employees.

[2]Nicholas Carlson, "Marissa Mayer Sent a Late Night E-mail Promising to Make Yahoo 'The Absolute Best Place to Work,'" August 27, 2012, www.businessinsider.com/marissa-mayer-sent-a-late-night-email-promising-to-make-yahoo-the-absolute-best-place-to-work-2012-8, accessed September 22, 2012.

Richard Ivey School of Business
The University of Western Ontario   **IVEY**

[3]Yahoo! Press Release, July 16, 2012, http://files.shareholder.com/downloads/YHOO/2435053555x0x583265/6948e13b-7b6c-49d8-9011-a7220229460e/YHOO_News_2012_7_16_General.pdf, accessed May September 22, 2012.

[4]Standard & Poor's Industry Surveys: Computers: Consumer Services & The Internet, April 5, 2012.

the Internet were clustered into segments whose boundaries were rapidly changing and dissolving. Of these clusters, companies such as Google and Yahoo comprised the content and electronic commerce segment. This segment consisted of players who offered search engines and portals to enter and navigate the Internet, as well as a wide gamut of destinations for information and shopping. These players sought to monetize the traffic that passed through their offerings via advertising and transaction fees. Players in this segment often expanded to other Internet segments in order to consolidate their competitive position.

3   Search sites allowed users to find relevant information on the Internet. The quest for companies in this sub-segment was to use technology to offer accuracy and speed to users as a way of differentiating themselves from others. In March 2012, the top three players in terms of market share were Google (66.4 percent), Microsoft (15.3 percent), and Yahoo (13.8 percent). While Google had held onto its leadership position, Microsoft's Bing (launched in 2009) had taken market share away from Yahoo and a host of smaller players. As per an agreement reached between Microsoft and Yahoo, Bing was to power all of Yahoo's search offerings by mid-2012. Search sites monetized traffic through banner (display) and keyword advertising.

4   Portals were sites that aggregated content (some of which was their own, while the vast majority belonged to others) in a unified way and were often the starting point for users' Internet activity. Microsoft, Yahoo, and AOL were the leading portals. However, Google, which was essentially a search site because of its simple interface, offered iGoogle, a customizable portal. Like search sites, portals obtained revenue through advertising, although many of them received transaction fees from several fee- or subscription-based sites that were accessed through the portal.

5   Players in the portal segment attempted to offer an array of destination sites for information, entertainment, and electronic commerce. The goal of these players was to drive traffic to the myriad sites and monetize the traffic via display and click-through advertising, as well as by selling several fee- or subscription-based services. In this sub-segment, competition was intense between pure portal sites and search sites that offered various destination options. The key metric to measure traffic to these sites was the number of unique visitors for a specific period (see Exhibit 1). In recent times, however, advertisers looked at the average time spent by users at a site as a key measure of advertising rates. In this area, social networking sites such

EXHIBIT 1   **U.S. Internet Traffic Data for January 2012 (Top Five)**

Site[a]	Unique Visitors (Millions)[b]	Reach Percentage[c]
Google	187.368	85.1
Microsoft	179.220	81.4
Yahoo!	177.249	80.5
Facebook	163.505	74.3
Amazon	109.997	50.0

Source: Standard & Poor's Industry Surveys: Computers: Consumer Services & The Internet, April 5, 2012.

[a]Includes various sites owned by the specific company.

[b]This represents the number of times a site was opened; page views indicates the number of pages opened by a visitor in a site and is also used as a traffic metric. For example, Yahoo reported over 700 million page views in January 2012.

[c]The percentage of Internet-active individuals who visit the site (one of all the sites owned by a company) at least once during the month.

as Facebook and Twitter had a distinct advantage over portals and search sites. A 2012 study reported that the average time spent by a user on Facebook was 405 minutes a month and that Facebook alone accounted for nearly 15 percent of the time users spent online, compared to 10.6 percent for all of Google's sites, and 8.6 percent for Yahoo's sites.

6   Internet advertising revenues in the United States were $31.7 billion in 2011[5] (compared to $38.5 billion for broadcast television and $30 billion for cable television), representing an increase of 22 per cent over 2010. An industry expert explained the significance of crossing the $30 billion mark:

> This historic moment, with an especially impressive achievement in mobile, is indicative of an increased awareness from advertisers that they need to reach consumers where they are spending their time—in digital media. Pushing past the $30 billion barrier, the interactive advertising industry confirms its central space in media. Across search, display, and digital video, digital provides a wealth of opportunity for brands and consumers. With the proliferation of smartphones and tablets, it is likely that the tremendous growth in mobile will continue as these screens become even more crucial to the marketing mix.[6]

7   The fastest-growing segment of Internet advertising was mobile advertising, which totaled $1.6 billion in 2011, an increase of 149 percent over 2010. An industry expert commented on mobile advertising:

> The year 2011 saw mobile advertising become a meaningful category. By combining some of the best features of the Internet, along with portability and location-based technology, mobile advertising is enabling marketers to deliver timely, targeted, relevant, and local advertisements in a manner that was not previously possible. It is for these reasons that we see strong growth to continue with mobile advertising.[7]

8   In 2011, the 10 leading search and portal companies accounted for 71 percent of total online advertising revenues, while the next 15 accounted for 11 percent. Search revenues of $14.8 billion (up from $11.7 billion in 2010) made up 46.5 percent of total revenues (up from 44.8 percent in 2010), while display-related advertising was $11.1 billion (versus $9.6 billion in 2010) or 34.8 percent. Of the two prevalent pricing models, performance-based pricing (cost per click-through) had been the dominant model since 2006 and accounted for 65 percent of all advertising in 2011.[8]

9   As reported in *Standard & Poor's Industry Surveys*, there were around 613 million Web sites worldwide in February 2012, a significant increase from 285 million in 2011. Several factors were responsible for the growth of the Internet. Chief among them were the increasing affordability of computers and increasing Internet penetration rates. In a virtuous cycle, as component prices fell rapidly, PC manufacturers passed on the price decreases to customers, who in turn increased the demand for PCs, leading to lower prices due to manufacturers' economies of scale and purchasing power savings. For example, nearly 80 percent of U.S. households owned a PC in 2012, up from 63 percent in 2000, and the vast majority of users had bought a PC or a similar device for Internet connectivity. In 2011, North America had the largest Internet penetration rate of 78.6 percent, followed by Oceania/Australia with 67.5 percent, and Europe with 61.3 percent. However, the fastest-growing market in percentage terms was Africa, and the fastest-growing market in absolute

[5]IAB Internet Advertising Report, April 2012, www.iab.net, accessed September 24, 2012.
[6]Ibid.
[7]Ibid.
[8]Ibid.

EXHIBIT 2   Worldwide Internet Usage as of December 21, 2011

Region	Internet Users	Percentage of Total Worldwide Internet Users	Internet Growth Rate Percentage (2000–2011)	Penetration (Percentage of Total Population)
Africa	139,875,242	6.2	2,988.4	13.5
Asia	1,016,799,076	44.8	789.6	26.2
Europe	500,723,686	22.1	376.4	61.3
Middle East	77,020,995	3.4	2,244.8	35.6
North America	273,067,546	12.0	152.6	78.6
Latin America/Caribbean	235,819,740	10.4	1,205.1	39.5
Oceania/Australia	23,927,457	1.1	214.0	67.5

Source: Internet World Stats, www.internetworldstats.com/stats.htm, accessed August 28, 2012.

terms was Asia, which had over a billion Internet users in 2011 versus 114,300 in 2000. While the average worldwide Internet penetration rate was 32.7 percent, Asia's was only 26.2 percent (only higher than Africa's 13.5 percent),[9] indicating the growth potential of this region (Exhibit 2 provides a profile of worldwide Internet usage).

YAHOO'S COMPANY BACKGROUND[10]

10   In February 1994, two graduate students at Stanford University in California, David Filo and Jerry Yang, wanted to find a way to keep track of their favorite Web sites on the Internet. As the list of Web sites became larger each day, they began categorizing them into groups and subgroups. They developed a Web site to capture their categorization method and called it Yahoo!, naming it after the dictionary definition of the word: "rude, unsophisticated, uncouth." Housed in their two computers in a campus trailer, their search engine began to attract the attention of their friends and soon others who needed a way to find Web sites of interest on the Internet. By the fall of 1994, Yahoo recorded its millionth user hit and Filo and Yang realized that they had chanced upon a business opportunity. They obtained venture capital funding and appointed Tim Koogle (a Motorola veteran and Stanford graduate) as the company's first CEO. Yahoo went public through an initial public offering (IPO) in April 1996. The company offered the first online navigational guide to the World Wide Web and monetized this opportunity by selling advertising space on its site. Soon after its IPO, Yahoo formed Yahoo! Japan and Yahoo! Europe to offer search services to Internet users worldwide. The company grew organically and via acquisitions, to both broaden its reach and generate additional revenue streams.

11   When Terry Semel replaced Tim Koogle as CEO in 2001, Yahoo had 3,000 employees, 24 global properties, and annual revenues of over $717 million. During this time, it had dropped Inktomi as its search engine provider and moved to using the then-startup Google. Semel continued Yahoo's push to seek new revenue sources by getting into music, blogging, and photo sharing and posting.

[9]Internet World Stats, www.internetworldstats.com/stats.htm, accessed September 24, 2012.

[10]"Yahoo! Inc. Company Information," www.hoovers.com/company-information/cs/company-profile.Yahoo!_Inc.7fdc8a9aba94345b.html, accessed May 2, 2012; "The History of Yahoo!—How It All Started . . ." Yahoo! Media Relations, http://docs.yahoo.com/info/misc/history.html, accessed September 18, 2012.

12   Jerry Yang, one of Yahoo's co-founders, replaced Terry Semel as CEO in 2007. Yahoo faced intense competition from Google in the Internet advertising space and the two companies competed with each other to acquire complementary businesses. A combination of intensifying competition and the global economic slowdown resulted in Yahoo's first employee layoffs in early 2008 and a second round at the end of the same year. In 2008, Microsoft made a second bid to acquire Yahoo, after its 2006 bid had been rejected. Jerry Yang and Roy Bostock (Yahoo's board chairman) convinced the company's board to reject Microsoft's offer, considering it as undervaluing Yahoo.

13   Carol Bartz replaced Jerry Yang as CEO in 2009. She was charged with turning around the company and toward that goal she announced a search engine partnership with Microsoft, sold several underperforming acquisitions, and discontinued certain services. In addition, Bartz expanded Yahoo's global presence by making key acquisitions in regions such as the Middle East. However, Yahoo's revenues declined for the third consecutive year in fiscal 2010 and the company announced further employee layoffs to cut costs. Bartz was fired by Yahoo's board in late 2011 after failing to turn around the company. She was replaced on an interim basis by Tim Morse, the company's chief financial officer.

14   In January 2012, the board announced that Scott Thompson, then the president of PayPal, would become the company's new CEO. Thompson's tenure was short as he was forced to step down on May 13, 2012, after it was revealed that he had falsified his educational background on his resumé. During Thompson's tenure, Daniel Loeb, who controlled the hedge fund Third Point LLC, became an activist investor at Yahoo and demanded sweeping changes at the board and top management levels.

15   After Thompson's departure, Roy Bostock and two other board members stepped down and Fred Amoroso became board chairman. Yahoo appointed Ross Levinsohn (who headed the company's media business) as interim CEO and began an intense search for a permanent leader. At the July 12, 2012, annual stockholders' meeting, Daniel Loeb and two of his nominees were elected to Yahoo's board. On July 16, 2012, the board announced that Marissa Mayer, a senior executive at rival Google, was to be Yahoo's new CEO. Ross Levinsohn, who had fully expected to be named Yahoo's permanent CEO, resigned from the company after Mayer's appointment.[11]

CORPORATE GOVERNANCE AT YAHOO

The Microsoft Bid

16   On February 1, 2008, Microsoft made an unsolicited bid to acquire Yahoo by offering (in cash and stock) $31 per share, valuing the company at $44.6 billion. Yahoo's stock price had closed at $19.18 the previous day. When Yahoo's board rejected the offer, Microsoft increased its bid price to $33 per share.[12] Once again, Yahoo rejected the bid, demanding $37 per share (valuing Yahoo at $47.5 billion). In a letter to Steve Ballmer, Microsoft's CEO, offering the rationale for rejecting the bid, Yahoo stated:

> Our Board . . . unanimously concluded that it (the bid) was not in the best interests of Yahoo! and its stockholders. Our Board cited Yahoo!'s global brand, large worldwide audience, significant recent investments in advertising platforms and future growth prospects, free cash flow and earnings potential, as well as its substantial unconsolidated investments, as factors

[11]Kara Swisher, "Exclusive—Ross Levinsohn Departs Yahoo," http://allthingsd.com/20120730/as-expected-ross-levinsohn-departs-yahoo/, accessed May 2, 2012.

[12]"Microsoft Makes Unsolicited Bid for Yahoo," *NBCNEWS.com*, www.msnbc.msn.com/id/22947626/ns/business-us_business/t/microsoft-makes-unsolicited-bid-yahoo, accessed September 18, 2012.

in its decision. . . . We are not opposed to a transaction with Microsoft if it is in the best interests of our stockholders. Our position is simply that any transaction must be at a value that fully reflects the value of Yahoo!, including any strategic benefits to Microsoft, and on terms that provide certainty to our stockholders.[13]

Carl Icahn's Proxy Fight

17 After Microsoft withdrew its offer on May 3, 2008, activist investor Carl Icahn (who had invested in Yahoo earlier and owned 4.98 per cent of Yahoo's common stock) launched a proxy fight to replace all 10 board members with his own nominees at the upcoming annual stockholders' meeting. Icahn's intention was to force the sale of Yahoo to Microsoft upon gaining control of the board.[14] On July 21, 2008, Yahoo announced that it had settled with Icahn by appointing him to the board and giving board seats to two of his nominees. In return, Icahn agreed to withdraw his proxy fight. He eventually resigned from Yahoo's board in October 2009 and in 2010 began to rapidly decrease his investment in the company.

Third Point LLC's Activism[15]

18 Daniel S. Loeb, who headed the hedge fund Third Point LLC, began accumulating Yahoo shares in 2011 and by March 2012 held 5.8 percent of the company's outstanding shares. He began to actively campaign for changes after several unfruitful meetings with CEO Scott Thompson. Loeb was firm in demanding that Yahoo's strategic direction should be to find ways to monetize the millions of site visitors per month. Rather than focus on pushing Yahoo into new businesses, which was Scott Thompson's vision, Loeb wanted Yahoo to focus on its media business. He argued that in hiring two executives to the board with a technology background (which Yahoo had done in February 2012), Yahoo was moving away from the media business. In addition, Loeb demanded that the company sell its Alibaba stake as well as its 35 percent stake in Yahoo Japan and use the capital to strengthen its core advertising business. Loeb filed a proxy statement to gather support for his four nominees (three of whom had advertising backgrounds, the fourth was himself) to replace the more technology-oriented Yahoo board members.

"Resumégate"

19 On May 3, 2012, a Silicon Valley Web site reported that Daniel Loeb had written to Yahoo's board about a possible discrepancy in CEO Scott Thompson's educational background. Loeb had alleged that Thompson had inaccurately indicated that he had graduated with dual degrees in accounting and computer science, whereas in reality he had graduated with just an accounting degree. Since Yahoo had reported Thompson's educational background in regulatory filings, this error amounted to a misrepresentation of facts.[16] Yahoo's board admitted that Loeb was correct in his accusations and after an internal investigation, Thompson resigned from the company. Patti S. Hart, a member of Yahoo's board who

[13]Yahoo! Press Release, April 7, 2008, http://files.shareholder.com/downloads/YHOO/2435053555x0x185760/ab576752-f008-457a-b678-186098240468/YHOO_News_2008_4_7_General.pdf, accessed May 2, 2012.

[14]David Litterick, "Yahoo! Rejects Microsoft and Carl Icahn Bid," *The Telegraph*, July 14, 2008, www.telegraph.co.uk/finance/newsbysector/mediatechnologyandtelecoms/2793196/Yahoo-rejects-Microsoft-and-Carl-Icahn-bid.html, accessed September 18, 2012.

[15]Evelyn M. Rusli, "Activist Investor Charts Plan to Revitalize Yahoo," *The New York Times*, March 9, 2012, pp. B1, B5; and proxy statements filed by Third Point LLC, http://files.shareholder.com/downloads/YHOO/2435053555x0xS899140-12-176/1011006/filing.pdf, accessed May 2, 2013 and http://files.shareholder.com/downloads/YHOO/2435053555x0xS899140-12-204/1011006/filing.pdf, accessed May 2, 2012.

[16]Poornima Gupta, "Yahoo CEO Scott Thompson's Resume Is Faked, Third Point Alleges," *The Huffington Post*, www.huffingtonpost.com/2012/05/03/scott-thompson-resume-yahoo_n_1475700.html, accessed September 18, 2012.

EXHIBIT 3 Yahoo's Board Members

Name	Member Since
Alfred Amoroso (Board Chairman)	February 2012
John Hayes	April 2012
Sue James	January 2010
David Kenny	April 2011
Peter Liguori	March 2012
Daniel Loeb	May 2012
Marissa Mayer (CEO and President)	July 2012
Thomas McInerney	April 2012
Brad Smith	June 2010
Maynard Webb	February 2012
Harry Wilson	May 2012
Michael Wolf	May 2012

Source: "Board of Directors," Yahoo!, Inc., http://investor.yahoo.net/directors.cfm, accessed May 2, 2012.

took the lead role in vetting Thompson at the time of his appointment, resigned following Thompson's departure.

20   At the July 12, 2012, annual stockholders' meeting, Daniel Loeb and two of his nominees were elected to the company's board. His fourth nominee voluntarily took himself out of the running after Third Point and Yahoo reached an agreement. Exhibit 3 lists Yahoo's board members.

Yahoo's Business Operations[17]

Products and Organization

21   In 2012, Yahoo was a global digital media company that attracted visitors to its Web site by offering personalized content and experiences and monetized the visits via advertising (81 percent of total revenues in 2011) and transaction fees. The company's online properties and services (called Yahoo! Properties) were classified into three categories: Communications and Communities, Search and Marketplaces, and Media.

22   Products in the Communications and Communities category included Yahoo! Mail, Yahoo! Messenger, Yahoo! Groups, Yahoo! Answers, Flickr, and Connected TV, and were aimed at enabling users to "organize into groups and share knowledge, common interests, and photos."[18] While some of these services were free of charge and supported by advertising revenue, other services were fee- or subscription-based.

23   Offerings such as Yahoo! Search, Yahoo! Local, Yahoo! Shopping, and Yahoo! Travel in the Search and Marketplaces category were "designed to quickly answer users' information

[17]This section was based on the following sources: Yahoo! Inc. 2011 10-K; "Yahoo! Inc. Company Information," www.hoovers.com/company-information/cs/company-profile.Yahoo!_Inc.7fdc8a9aba94345b.html, accessed May 2, 2013; Nicole Perlroth, "Revamping at Yahoo to Focus on Its Media Properties and Customer Data," *The New York Times*, April 11, 2012, p. B4.

[18]http://investor.yahoo.net/secfiling.cfm?filingID=1193125-12-86972&CIK=1011006, accessed May 2, 2012.

EXHIBIT 4   **Yahoo! Inc. Revenue Breakdown**

Ex. 4a Revenue Sources ($) in thousands			
	2009	**2010**	**2011**
Display	1,866,984	2,154,886	2,160,309
Search	3,396,396	3,161,589	1,853,110
Other[a]	1,196,935	1,008,176	970,780
Total	**6,460,315**	**6,324,651**	**4,984,199**

[a]Listings-based services revenue, transaction revenue, and fees revenue.

Ex. 4b Revenues by Geographic Segment ($) in thousands			
	2009	**2010**	**2011**
Americas	4,852,331	4,425,457	3,302,989
EMEA[a]	598,300	579,145	629,383
Asia Pacific	1,009,684	1,320,049	1,051,827
Total	**6,460,315**	**6,324,651**	**4,984,199**

[a]Europe, Middle East, and Africa.

Source: Yahoo! Form 10-K, Annual Report, http://investor.yahoo.net/secfiling.cfm?filingID=1193125-12
-86972&CIK=1011006, accessed May 2, 2012.

needs by delivering innovative and meaningful search, local, and listings experiences on the search results pages and across Yahoo!"[19] In December 2009, Yahoo entered into a ten-year agreement with Microsoft whereby Microsoft would get a 12 percent share of search revenues and would provide Yahoo with the technology that ran its search engine. The agreement discontinued Yahoo's existing relationship for this purpose with Google. Yahoo generated revenues from this category via listing fees and transaction fees in addition to advertising.

24   Products such as Yahoo! Homepage, Yahoo! News, and Yahoo! Finance formed the cornerstone of the Media category, whose goal was to engage users with "compelling content."[20] While the majority of revenues for this category came from advertising, Yahoo! Sports services such as Yahoo! Fantasy Football were fee-based. Exhibit 4a provides a breakdown of Yahoo's revenues.

25   Yahoo managed its global business geographically, reporting financial results by three segments—Americas, EMEA (Europe, Middle East, and Africa), and Asia Pacific (Exhibit 4b reports financial results per geographic segment). Yahoo sites were in 45 languages in 60 countries.

Sales, Marketing, and Product Development

26   Since advertising was the primary revenue driver, Yahoo organized its sales team into three categories based on the type of customer served. The field advertising sales channel sold display and search advertising to leading advertisers and agencies. The mid-market channel sold advertising to medium-sized businesses, and the reseller/small business channel sold it to regional and small business advertisers. While Yahoo employed its own sales teams in the United States, it used a combination of internal salespeople and external sales

[19]Ibid.
[20]Ibid.

agencies in international markets. The marketing team ensured that the Yahoo! brand name continued to be widely recognized and drew traffic to the company's various properties. Yahoo used a combination of organic and acquisition-driven paths to product innovation. It spent $1 billion in internal product development in 2011 (versus $1.1 billion in 2010 and $1.2 billion in 2009), employing a team of software engineers and forming alliances with universities to improve existing products and create new ones.

Human Resources

27 When Yahoo announced cuts to its workforce of 2,000 employees in April 2012, it was the sixth major round of layoffs in the last four years. The company's employee headcount in September 2012 was around 12,000 spread out in 25 countries. Depending on their tenure and position in the organization, employees were compensated by salary, bonuses, commission, and stock options. The vast majority of the employees worked in the product development area, followed by sales and marketing, administration, and operations. Yahoo used a matrix structure where products such as Messenger, Mail, and Yahoo! Finance were the "verticals," and support functions such as public relations and legal were the "horizontals." The structure was created during former CEO Terry Semel's tenure (2001–2007).

Finances

28 Exhibit 5 provides Yahoo's financial statements for a three-year period, while Exhibit 6 contains summary stock prices for the company. Yahoo had not declared a dividend in its history. A $100 investment in Yahoo stock on December 29, 2006, would have resulted in an investment value of $59 on December 30, 2011, in comparison to $140 for the NASDAQ 100 Index, $99.50 for the S&P 500, and $137 for the S&P North American Technology-Internet Index.

EXHIBIT 5   Yahoo! Inc. Financial Statements Consolidated Statements of Income (Condensed for year ending December 31 in $ thousands)

	2009	2010	2011
Revenue	6,460,315	6,324,651	4,984,199
Cost of Revenue	2,871,746	2,627,545	1,502,650
Gross Profit	**3,588,569**	**3,697,106**	**3,481,549**
Operating Expenses:			
Sales and Marketing	1,245,350	1,264,491	1,122,302
Product Development	1,210,168	1,082,176	1,005,090
General and Administrative	580,352	488,332	495,804
Amortization of Intangibles	39,106	31,626	33,592
Restructuring Charges, net	126,901	57,957	24,420
Total Operating Expenses	**3,201,877**	**2,924,582**	**2,681,208**
Income From Operations	386,692	772,524	800,341
Other Income, net	187,528	297,869	27,175
Earnings in Equity Interests	250,390	395,758	476,920
Net Income (after provision for taxes and income attributable to non-controlling interests)	**597,992**	**1,231,663**	**1,048,827**

(Continued)

EXHIBIT 5   *(Continued)*

Assets		
	2010	**2011**
Current Assets:		
Cash and Cash Equivalents	1,526,427	1,562,390
Short-term Marketable Debt Securities	1,357,661	493,189
Accounts Receivable, net	1,028,900	1,037,474
Prepaid Expenses and Other Current Assets	432,560	359,483
Total Current Assets	**4,345,548**	**3,452,536**
Long-term Marketable Securities	744,594	474,338
Property and Equipment, net	1,653,422	1,730,888
Goodwill	3,681,645	3,900,752
Intangible Assets, net	255,870	254,600
Other Long-term Assets	235,136	220,628
Investments in Equity Interests	4,011,889	4,749,044
Total Assets	**14,928,104**	**14,782,786**

Liabilities & Equity		
Current Liabilities:		
Accounts Payable	162,424	166,595
Accrued Expenses & Other Current Liab.	1,208,792	846,044
Deferred Revenue	254,656	194,722
Total Current Liabilities	**1,625,872**	**1,207,361**
Long-term Deferred Revenue	56,365	43,639
Capital Leases & Other Long-term Liab.	142,799	134,905
Deferred & Other Long-term Liabilities	506,658	815,534
Total Liabilities	**2,331,694**	**2,201,439**
Stockholders' Equity	12,596,410	12,581,347
Total Liabilities and Equity	**14,928,104**	**14,782,786**

Yahoo! Inc. Summary Statements of Cash Flow (in $ thousands for year ended December 31)			
	2009	**2010**	**2011**
Net Cash Flow Provided by Operating Activities	1,310,346	1,240,190	1,323,806
Net Cash (Used in) Provided by Investing Activities	(2,419,238)	509,915	202,362
Net Cash (Used in) Provided by Financing Activities	34,597	(1,501,706)	(1,455,958)
Effect of Exchange Rate Changes on Cash & Cash Equivalents	57,429	2,598	(34,247)
Net Change in Cash & Cash Equivalents	(1,016,866)	250,997	35,963
Cash & Cash Equivalents at Beginning of Year	2,292,296	1,275,430	1,526,427
Cash & Cash Equivalents at End of Year	**1,275,430**	**1,526,427**	**1,562,390**

Source: Adapted from Yahoo! Inc. 2011 10-K. Yahoo! Form 10-K, Annual Report, http://investor.yahoo.net/secfiling.cfm?filingID=1193125
-12-86972&CIK=1011006, accessed May 2, 2012.

EXHIBIT 6   **Yahoo! Inc. Selected Stock Price Data ($ at close of market)**

Date	Price
Jan. 2, 2008	19.18
Jan. 2, 2009	11.73
Jan. 4, 2010	15.01
Jan. 3, 2011	16.12
Jan. 3, 2012	15.47
Sept. 4, 2012	15.74

Source: Yahoo! Finance, http://finance.yahoo.com/, accessed May 2, 2012.

Enter Marissa Mayer

Early Actions

29   Prior to joining Yahoo, Marissa Mayer had a 13-year career at Google, where she held a variety of positions. She was responsible for launching more than 100 products at Google and was a key player in developing Google's home page. Her last position at the company was vice-president of Local, Maps, and Location Services, where she led the product management, engineering, design, and overall strategy for the Google Maps suite of products.[21]

30   One of the first things that Mayer did at Yahoo was to announce that she would review every hire that the company made, a practice similar to that done at Google by the company's two co-founders. While this slowed down hiring at Yahoo, one anonymous company employee was quoted as saying:

> It's gotten a little frustrating. But I can't say that I blame her. The problem at Yahoo in the past couple of years has been "B-players" hiring "C-players" who were not fired up to come to work and were tolerated too long. I mean nobody good wanted to come to Yahoo. If I am inheriting a mess like that, I'd want to review all the talent that comes in the doors, too.[22]

31   She quickly instituted a number of changes at the company. Principal among them were a weekly all-employee meeting every Friday afternoon, free food in the company cafeteria, replacement of employees' BlackBerry phones with a choice of iPhones or Android-based phones, and the launch of a program termed "PB&J," an acronym for Process, Bureaucracy, and Jams. The PB&J program was to solicit employee input on a variety of things including improving the work culture and increasing productivity. One employee reacted to Mayer's actions:

> While the free food and iPhones are nice, it was the midnight email that finally won my heart. Redundant processes and policy, and bureaucracy, are the worst enemies to innovation and efficiency. Of course, change will not happen overnight. There are so many things that need to improve in order to get us back in the same league as Google and Apple. But I have faith in the company and Marissa. And I truly hope the company will be great again.[23]

[21]"Board of Directors," Yahoo!, http://investor.yahoo.net/directors.cfm, accessed September 19, 2012.

[22]Nicholas Carlson, "Marissa Mayer Reviews Every New Hire at Yahoo," *Business Insider,* September 4, 2012, www.businessinsider.com/marissa-mayer-is-reviewing-every-single-new-hire-at-yahoo-2012-9, accessed September 19, 2012.

[23]Nicholas Carlson, "Marissa Mayer Sent a Late Night E-mail Promising to Make Yahoo 'The Absolute Best Place to Work,'" *Business Insider,* August 27, 2012, www.businessinsider.com/marissa-mayer-sent-a-late-night-email-promising-to-make-yahoo-the-absolute-best-place-to-work-2012-8, accessed September 19, 2012.

Challenges

32   The privately owned Alibaba Group was one of China's biggest Internet companies specializing in electronic commerce. In 2005, Yahoo invested $1 billion in Alibaba for a 40 percent equity share. It also handed over the responsibility of operating its Yahoo! China Web site to Alibaba. The two companies began negotiations in 2010 on the future of Yahoo's investment. Softbank, a Japanese Internet and telecommunications company, had also invested in Alibaba. In addition, Softbank had a 65 percent stake in Yahoo! Japan, with Yahoo owning the rest. Alibaba and Softbank wanted to buy out Yahoo's stake in Alibaba as well as its stake in Yahoo! Japan. While Yahoo agreed to the Alibaba divestment (it had made no decision on the Yahoo! Japan issue), the bone of contention was in structuring the deal to minimize Yahoo's tax bill on the capital gains. In late August 2012, Yahoo announced that it would sell half its Alibaba investment immediately for $7.6 billion (resulting in after-tax cash of $4.3 billion) and the rest when Alibaba was expected to go public in 2015.[24] The key challenge to Mayer in this area was how to use the proceeds of the Alibaba investment. Early on, she had indicated that she would use the proceeds to make critical acquisitions, but pressure from shareholders had caused her to back off from this position.

33   In addition to the Alibaba issue, Mayer faced the main strategic challenge of establishing Yahoo's identity as a company. While it had started out as a technology firm, its principal revenue source was currently advertising. However, many Yahoo insiders still regarded themselves as working for a technology company that had a presence in media. Daniel Loeb's insistence that Yahoo's best bet was to find a way to monetize its visitor traffic indicated that he wanted Yahoo to morph into a media company. Given Mayer's technology background and experience at Google, would this morphing play to her strengths? The growing markets were Asia and Africa, regions where Yahoo had only a weak presence. Should Yahoo acquire companies to benefit from growth in these markets? In addition, the Internet was moving to a mobile platform where Yahoo had only a marginal presence. While the mobile platform was showing tremendous growth (albeit from a small base), it was not clear whether it would support traditional revenue sources. Management faced these issues prior to meeting with the company's board in September.

---

[24]Charles Arthur, "Yahoo Sells Chunk of Alibaba Stake," *The Guardian,* September 19, 2012, www.guardian.co.uk/technology/2012/sep/19/yahoo-efinance, accessed September 24, 2012.

Glossary

A

adaptive mode The strategic formality associated with medium-sized firms that emphasize the incremental modification of existing competitive approaches.

adverse selection An agency problem caused by the limited ability of stockholders to precisely determine the competencies and priorities of executives at the time they are hired.

agency costs The cost of agency problems and the cost of actions taken to minimize them.

agency theory A set of ideas on organizational control based on the belief that the separation of the ownership from management creates the potential for the wishes of owners to be ignored.

agile organization A firm that identifies a set of business capabilities central to high-profitability operations and then builds a virtual organization around those capabilities, allowing the agile firm to build its business around the core, high-profitability information, services, and products. Creating an agile, virtual organization structure involves outsourcing, strategic alliances, a boundaryless learning approach, and Web-based organization.

ambidextrous organization Organization structure most notable for its lack of structure wherein knowledge and getting it to the right place quickly is the key reason for organization. Managers become knowledge "nodes" through which intricate networks of personal relationships—inside and outside the formal organization—are constantly, and often informally, coordinated to bring together relevant know-how and successful action.

B

balanced scorecard A management control system that enables companies to clarify their strategies, translate them into action, and provide quantitative feedback as to whether the strategy is creating value, leveraging core competencies, satisfying the company's customers, and generating a financial reward to its shareholders. A set of four measures directly linked to a company's strategy: financial performance, customer knowledge, internal business processes, and learning and growth.

bankruptcy When a company is unable to pay its debts as they become due, or has more debts than assets.

barriers to entry The conditions that a firm must satisfy to enter an industry.

benchmarking Evaluating the sustainability of advantages against key competitors. Comparing the way a company performs a specific activity with a competitor or other company doing the same thing.

board of directors The group of stockholder representatives and strategic managers responsible for overseeing the creation and accomplishment of the company mission.

boundaryless organization Organizational structure that allows people to interface with others throughout the organization without need to wait for a hierarchy to regulate that interface across functional, business, and geographic boundaries.

breakthrough innovation An innovation in a product, process, technology, or the cost associated with it that represents a quantum leap forward in one or more of these ways.

business model A clear understanding of how the firm will generate profits and the strategic actions it must take to succeed over the long term.

business process outsourcing Having an outside company manage numerous routine business management activities usually done by employees of the company such as HR, supply procurement, finance and accounting, customer care, supply-chain logistics, engineering, R&D, sales and marketing, facilities management, and management/development.

business process reengineering A popular method by which organizations worldwide undergo restructuring efforts to remain competitive. It involves fundamental rethinking and radical redesigning of a business process so that a company can best create value for the customer by eliminating barriers that create distance between employees and customers.

C

cash cows Businesses with a high market share in low-growth markets or industries.

CCC21 A world-famous, cost-oriented continuous improvement program at Toyota (Construction of Cost Competitiveness for the Twenty-first Century).

chaebol A Korean consortia financed through government banking groups to gain a strategic advantage.

company creed A company's statement of its philosophy.

company mission The unique purpose that sets a company apart from others of its type and identifies the scope of its operations in product, market, and technology terms.

concentrated growth A grand strategy in which a firm directs its resources to the profitable growth of a single product, in a single market, with a single dominant technology.

concentric diversification A grand strategy that involves the operation of a second business that benefits from access to the first firm's core competencies. A strategy that involves the acquisition of businesses that are related to the acquiring firm in terms of technology, markets, or products.

conglomerate diversification A grand strategy that involves the acquisition of a business because it presents the most promising investment opportunity available. A strategy that involves acquiring or entering businesses unrelated to a firm's current technologies, markets, or products.

consortia Large interlocking relationships between businesses of an industry.

continuous improvement A form of strategic control in which managers are encouraged to be proactive in improving all operations of the firm. The process of relentlessly trying to find ways to improve and enhance a company's products and processes from design through assembly, sales, and service. It is called *kaizen* in Japanese. It is usually associated with incremental innovation.

core competence A capability or skill that a firm emphasizes and excels in doing while in pursuit of its overall mission.

corporate lattice A concept based on research by Cathleen Benko and Molly Anderson suggesting that the working structure of an organization today is like a lattice—a three-dimensional structure extending infinitely vertically, horizontally, and diagonally. The work of a lattice-functioning organization is done in a virtual, dynamic, project-based manner resembling nodes on a network, each with the possibility of connecting anywhere and anytime to others to provide answers and ideas and to form teams or communities.

corporate social responsibility The idea that business has a duty to serve society in general as well as the financial interest of stockholders.

D

dashboard A user interface that organizes and presents information from multiple digital sources simultaneously in a user-designed format on the computer screen.

debt financing Money "loaned" to an entrepreneur or business venture that must be repaid at some point in time.

declining industry An industry in which the trend of total sales as an indicator of total demand for an industry's products or services among all the participants in the industry has started to drop from the last several years with the likelihood being that such a trend will continue indefinitely.

differentiation A business strategy that seeks to build competitive advantage with its product or service by having it be "different" from other available competitive products based on features, performance, or other factors not directly related to cost and price. The difference would be one that would be hard to create and/or difficult to copy or imitate.

discretionary responsibilities Responsibilities voluntarily assumed by a business, such as public relations, good citizenship, and full corporate responsibility.

disruptive innovation A term to characterize breakthrough innovation popularized by Harvard Professor Clayton Christensen; usually shakes up or revolutionizes industries with which they are associated even though they often come from totally different origins or industry settings than the industry they "disrupt."

divestiture A strategy that involves the sales of a firm or a major component of a firm.

divestiture strategy A grand strategy that involves the sales of a firm or a major component of a firm.

divisional organizational structure Structure in which a set of relatively autonomous units, or divisions, is governed by a central corporate office but where each operating division has its own functional specialists who provide products or services different from those of other divisions.

dogs Low market share and low market growth businesses.

downsizing Eliminating the number of employees, particularly middle management, in a company.

dynamic The term that characterizes the constantly changing conditions that affect interrelated and interdependent strategic activities.

E

eco-efficiency Company actions that produce more useful goods and services while continuously reducing resource consumption and pollution.

ecology The relationships among human beings and other living things and the air, soil, and water that supports them.

economic responsibilities The duty of managers, as agents of the company owners, to maximize stockholder wealth.

economies of scale The savings that companies achieve because of increased volume.

emerging industry An industry that has growing sales across all the companies in the industry based on growing demand for the relatively new products, technologies, and/or services made available by the firms participating in this industry.

empowerment The act of allowing an individual or team the right and flexibility to make decisions and initiate action.

entrepreneurial mode The informal, intuitive, and limited approach to strategic management associated with owner-managers of smaller firms.

entrepreneurship The process of bringing together the creative and innovative ideas and actions with the management and organizational skills necessary to mobilize the appropriate people, money, and operating resources to meet an identifiable need and create wealth in the process.

equity financing Money provided to a business venture that entitles the provider to rights or ownership in the venture and that is not expected to be repaid.

ethical responsibilities The strategic managers' notion of right and proper business behavior.

ethical standards A person's basis for differentiating right from wrong.

ethics The moral principles that reflect society's beliefs about the actions of an individual or group that are right and wrong.

ethnocentric orientation When the values and priorities of the parent organization guide the strategic decision making of all its international operations.

expert influence The ability to direct and influence others because they defer to you based on your expertise or specialized knowledge that is related to the task, undertaking, or assignment in which they are involved.

external environment The factors beyond the control of the firm that influence its choice of direction and action, organizational structure, and internal processes.

external interface boundaries Formal and informal rules, locations, and protocol that separate and/or dictate the interaction between members of an organization and those outside the organization—customers, suppliers, partners, regulators, associations, and even competitors.

F

feedback The analysis of postimplementation results that can be used to enhance future decision making.

formality The degree to which participation, responsibility, authority, and discretion in decision making are specified in strategic management.

fragmented businesses   Businesses with many sources of advantage, but they are all small. They typically involve differentiated products with low brand loyalty, easily replicated technology, and minimal scale economies.

fragmented industry   An industry in which there are numerous competitors (providers of the same or similar products or services the industry involves) such that no single firm or small group of firms controls any significant share of the overall industry sales.

functional organizational structure   Structure in which the tasks, people, and technologies necessary to do the work of the business are divided into separate "functional" groups (e.g., marketing, operations, finance) with increasingly formal procedures for coordinating and integrating their activities to provide the business's products and services.

functional tactics   Detailed statements of the "means" or activities that will be used by a company to achieve short-term objectives and establish competitive advantage. Short-term, narrow-scoped plans of functional areas that detail the "means" or activities that a company will use to achieve short-term objectives.

G

generic strategy   A core idea about how a firm can best compete in the marketplace. Fundamental philosophical option for the design of strategies.

geocentric orientation   When an international firm adopts a systems approach to strategic decision making that emphasizes global integration.

geographic boundaries   Limitations on interaction and contact between people in a company based on being at different physical locations domestically and globally.

global industry   An industry in which competition crosses national borders on a worldwide basis.

globalization   The strategy of pursuing opportunities anywhere in the world that enable a firm to optimize its business functions in the countries in which it operates.

golden handcuffs   A form of executive compensation where compensation is deferred (either a restricted stock plan or bonus income deferred in a series of annual installments).

golden parachute   A form of bonus compensation designed to retain talented executives that calls for a substantial cash payment if the executive quits, is fired, or simply retires.

grand strategy   A master long-term plan that provides basic direction for major actions directed toward achieving long-term business objectives. The means by which objectives are achieved.

grand strategy clusters   Sets of grand strategies that may be more advantageous for firms to choose under one of four sets of conditions defined by market growth rate and the strength of the firm's competitive position.

grand strategy selection matrix   A four-cell matrix that helps managers choose among different and grand strategies based upon (1) whether the business is operating from a position of strength or weakness and (2) whether it must rely solely on its own internal resources versus having the option to acquire resources externally via merger or acquisition.

growth industry strategies   Business strategies that may be more advantageous for firms participating in rapidly growing industries and markets.

H

holding company structure   Structure in which the corporate entity is a broad collection of often unrelated businesses and divisions such that it (the corporate entity) acts as financial overseer "holding" the ownership interest in the various parts of the company, but has little direct managerial involvement.

horizontal boundaries   Rules of communication, access, and protocol for dealing with different departments or functions or processes within an organization.

horizontal acquisition   A grand strategy based on growth through the acquisition of one or more similar firms operating at the same stage of the production-marketing chain.

I

ideagora   A Web-enabled, virtual marketplace that connects people with unique ideas, talents, resources, or capabilities with companies seeking to address problems or potential innovations in a quick, competent manner.

implementation control   Management efforts designed to assess whether the overall strategy should be changed in light of results associated with the incremental actions that implement the overall strategy. These are usually associated with specific strategic thrusts or projects and with predetermined milestone reviews.

incremental innovation   Simple changes or adjustments in existing products, services, or processes.

industry   A group of companies that provide similar products and services.

industry environment   The general conditions for competition that influence all businesses that provide similar products and services.

information power   The ability to influence others based on your access to information and your control of dissemination of information that is important to subordinates and others yet not otherwise easily obtained.

innovation   A grand strategy that seeks to reap the premium margins associated with creation and customer acceptance of a new product or service. The initial commercialization of invention by producing and selling a new product, service, or process.

Innovation Time Out policy   A policy implemented at Google and other firms allowing many employees to set aside a portion of their workweek, often one day per week, to examine and develop their ideas for new products or services the company might pursue. This concept is believed to help companies in two key ways—accelerating the creation of new product/service offerings or improvements in those that exist; and keeping employees challenged and engaged in ways that aid retention and keep staff learning and growing.

intangible assets   A firm's assets that you cannot touch or see but that are very often critical in creating competitive advantage: brand names, company reputation, organizational morale, technical knowledge, patents and a unique "bundle of resources"—tangible and intangible assets and organizational capabilities to make use of those assets.

intrapreneurship   A term associated with entrepreneurship in large established companies; the process of attempting to identify, encourage, enable, and assist entrepreneurship within a large, established company so as to create new products, processes, services, or improvements that become major new revenue streams and/or sources of cost savings for the company.

intrapreneurship freedom factors Ten characteristics identified by Dr. Gordon Pinchot and elaborated upon by others that need to be present in large companies seeking to encourage and increase the level of intrapreneurship within their company.

invention The creation of new products or processes through the development of new knowledge or from new combinations of knowledge.

isolating mechanisms Characteristics that make resources difficult to imitate. In the resource-based view context these are physically unique resources, path-dependent resources, causal ambiguity, and economic deterrence.

J

joint venture A grand strategy in which companies create a co-owned business that operates for their mutual benefit. Commercial companies created and operated for the benefit of the co-owners; usually two or more separate companies that come together to form the venture.

K

keiretsu A Japanese consortia of businesses that is coordinated by a large trading company to gain a strategic advantage.

L

lattice A metaphor used to describe the reality of the nature and structure of work in organizations today—a three-dimensional structure extending vertically, horizontally, and diagonally whereby people communicate and work with others anywhere, anytime, to provide answers and ideas, form teams, and solve problems.

leadership development The effort to familiarize future leaders with the skills important to the company and to develop exceptional leaders among the managers employed.

leader's vision An articulation of a simple criterion or characterization of what a leader sees the company must become in order to establish and sustain global leadership. IBM's former CEO, Lou Gerstner, described IBM as needing to become the leader in "network-centric computing," an example of such a characterization.

learning organization Organization structured around the idea that it should be set up to enable learning, to share knowledge, to seek knowledge, and to create opportunities to create new knowledge. It would move into new markets to learn about those markets rather than simply to bring a brand to it, or find resources to exploit in it.

legal responsibilities The firm's obligations to comply with the laws that regulate business activities.

liquidation A strategy that involves closing down the operations of a business and selling its assets and operations to pay its debts and distribute any gains to stockholders.

long-term objectives The results that an organization seeks to achieve over a multiyear period.

low-cost strategies Business strategies that seek to establish long-term competitive advantages by emphasizing and perfecting value chain activities that can be achieved at costs substantially below what competitors are able to match on a sustained basis. This allows the firm, in turn, to compete primarily by charging a price lower than competitors can match and still stay in business.

M

market development A grand strategy of marketing present products, often with only cosmetic modification, to customers in related marketing areas by adding channels of distribution or by changing the content of advertising or promotion.

market focus A generic strategy that applies a differentiation strategy approach, or a low-cost strategy approach, or a combination—and does so solely in a narrow (or "focused") market niche rather than trying to do so across the broader market. The narrow focus may be geographically defined, or defined by product type features, or target customer type, or some combination of these.

market growth rate The projected rate of sales growth for the market being served by a particular business.

matrix organizational structure Structure in which functional and staff personnel are assigned to both a basic functional area and to a project or product manager. It provides dual channels of authority, performance responsibility, evaluation, and control.

mature industry strategies Strategies used by firms competing in markets where the growth rate of that market from year to year has reached or is close to zero.

milestone reviews Points in time, or at the completion of major parts of a bigger strategy, where managers have predetermined they will undertake a go–no go type of review regarding the underlying strategy associated with the bigger strategy.

modular organization An organization structured via outsourcing where different parts of the tasks needed to provide the organization's product or service are done by a wide array of other organizations brought together to create a final product or service based on the combination of their separate, independent, self-contained skills and business capabilities.

moral hazard problem An agency problem that occurs because owners have limited access to company information, making executives free to pursue their own interests.

moral rights approach Judging the appropriateness of a particular action based on a goal to maintain the fundamental rights and privileges of individuals and groups.

multidomestic industry An industry in which competition is segmented from country to country.

O

operating environment Factors in the immediate competitive situation that affect a firm's success in acquiring needed resources.

opportunity A major favorable situation in a firm's environment.

organizational capabilities Skills (the ability and ways of combining assets, people, and processes) that a company uses to transform inputs into outputs.

organizational culture The set of important assumptions and beliefs (often unstated) that members of an organization share in common.

organizational leadership   The process and practice by key executives of guiding and shepherding people in an organization toward a vision over time and developing that organization's future leadership and organization culture.

organizational structure   Refers to the formalized arrangements of interaction between and responsibility for the tasks, people, and resources in an organization.

outsourcing   Obtaining work previously done by employees inside the companies from sources outside the company.

P

parenting opportunities framework   The perspective that the role of corporate headquarters (the "parent") in multibusiness (the "children") companies is that of a parent sharing wisdom, insight, and guidance to help develop its various businesses to excel.

passion (of a leader)   A highly motivated sense of commitment to what you do and want to do.

patching   The process by which corporate executives routinely "remap" their businesses to match rapidly changing market opportunities—adding, splitting, transferring, exiting, or combining chunks of businesses.

peer influence   The ability to influence individual behavior among members of a group based on group norms, a group sense of what is the right thing or right way to do things, and the need to be valued and accepted by the group.

perseverance (of a leader)   The capacity to see a commitment through to completion long after most people would have stopped trying.

planning mode   The strategic formality associated with large firms that operate under a comprehensive, formal planning system.

policies   Broad, precedent-setting decisions that guide or substitute for repetitive or time-sensitive managerial decision making. Predetermined decisions that substitute for managerial discretion in repetitive decision making.

pollution   Threats to life-supporting ecology caused principally by human activities in an industrial society.

polycentric orientation   When the culture of the country in which the strategy is to be implemented is allowed to dominate a company's international decision-making process.

portfolio techniques   An approach pioneered by the Boston Consulting Group that attempted to help managers "balance" the flow of cash resources among their various businesses while also identifying their basic strategic purpose within the overall portfolio.

position power   The ability and right to influence and direct others based on the power associated with your formal position in the organization.

power curves   A power curve is a depiction of a fundamental structural trend that underlies an industry.

premise control   The systematic recognition and analysis of assumptions upon which a strategic plan is based, to determine if those assumptions remain valid in changing circumstances and in light of new information.

primary activities   The activities in a firm of those involved in the physical creation of the product, marketing and transfer to the buyer, and after-sale support.

principles (of a leader)   A leader's fundamental personal standards that guide her sense of honesty, integrity, and ethical behavior.

process   The flow of information through interrelated stages of analysis toward the achievement of an aim.

product development   A grand strategy that involves the substantial modification of existing products or the creation of new but related products that can be marketed to current customers through established channels.

product differentiation   The extent to which customers perceive differences among products and services.

product life cycle   A concept that describes a product's sales, profitability, and competencies that are key drivers of the success of that product as it moves through a sequence of stages from development and introduction to growth, maturity, decline, and eventual removal from a market.

product-team structure   Assigns functional managers and specialists (e.g., engineering, marketing, financial, R&D, operations) to a new product, project, or process team that is empowered to make major decisions about their performance responsibility, evaluation, and control.

punitive power   Ability to direct and influence others based on an ability to coerce and deliver punishment for mistakes or undesired actions by others, particularly subordinates.

Q

question marks   Businesses whose high growth rate gives them considerable appeal but whose low market share makes their profit potential uncertain.

R

referent influence   The ability to influence others derived from their strong desire to be associated with you, usually because they admire you, gain prestige or a sense of purpose by that association, or believe in your motivations.

regiocentric orientation   When a parent company blends its own predisposition with those of its international units to develop region-sensitive strategies.

relative competitive position   The market share of a business divided by the market share of its largest competitor.

remote environment   Economic, social, political, technological, and ecological factors that originate beyond, and usually irrespective of, any single firm's operating situation.

resource-based view   A new perspective on understanding a firm's success based on how well the firm uses its internal resources. The underlying premise is that firms differ in fundamental ways because each firm possesses a unique "bundle of resources"—tangible and intangible assets and organizational capabilities to make use of those assets.

restricted stock   Stock given to an employee who is prohibited or "restricted" from selling the stock for a certain time period and not at all if the employee leaves the company before that time period.

restructuring   Redesigning an organizational structure with the intent of emphasizing and enabling activities most critical to a firm's strategy to function at maximum effectiveness.

retrenchment A business strategy that involves cutting back on products, markets, operations, or other strategic commitments of the firm because its overall competitive position, or its financial situation, or both are not able to support the level of commitments to various markets or the resources needed to sustain or build its operations in some, usually declining or increasingly competitive, markets. Unlike liquidation, retrenchment would have the firm sell some assets, or ongoing operations, to rechannel proceeds to reduce overall debt and to support the firm's efforts to rebuild its future competitive posture.

reward power The ability to influence and direct others that comes from being able to confer rewards in return for desired actions or outcomes.

S

Sarbanes-Oxley Act of 2002 Law that revised and strengthened auditing and accounting standards.

self-management Allowing work groups or work teams to supervise and administer their work as a group or team without a direct supervisor exercising the supervisory role. These teams set parameters of their work, make decisions about work-related matters, and perform most of the managerial functions previously done by their direct supervisor.

short-term objective Measurable outcomes achievable or intended to be achieved in one year or less. Desired results that provide specific guidance for action during a period of one year or less.

simple organizational structure Structure in which there is an owner and a few employees and where the arrangement of tasks, responsibilities, and communication is highly informal and accomplished through direct supervision.

Six Sigma A continuous improvement program adopted by many companies in the last two decades that takes a very rigorous and analytical approach to quality and continuous improvement with an objective to improve profits through defect reduction, yield improvement, improved customer satisfaction, and best-in-class performance.

social audit An attempt to measure a company's actual social performance against its social objectives.

social computing The area of computer science focused on the intersection of social behavior and computational systems using blogs, e-mails, instant messaging, wikis, sharing information, and so on; creating or recreating social conventions and contexts via software and hardware as well as more computational-oriented offerings that leverage to collective opinion like online auctions, prediction markets, social choice, tagging, and social sentiment. Facebook, Groupon, Google+, Twitter, LinkedIn, and Farmville are a few examples of social computing.

social computing guidelines These policies, rules, or suggested guidelines are rapidly being put into place at most companies to guide employees' job-related involvement on social networking and computing sites for both personal and business reasons. IBM has pioneered formal social computing guidelines since it has a strategic priority of encouraging IBMers to engage in online social computing as a key way to keep IBM innovative and technology savvy.

social justice approach Judging the appropriateness of a particular action based on equity, fairness, and impartiality in the distribution of rewards and costs among individuals and groups.

special alert control Management actions undertaken to thoroughly, and often very rapidly, reconsider a firm's strategy because of a sudden, unexpected event.

specialization businesses Businesses with many sources of advantage. Skills in achieving differentiation (product design, branding expertise, innovation, and perhaps scale) characterize winning specialization businesses.

speed-based strategies Business strategies built around functional capabilities and activities that allow the company to meet customer needs directly or indirectly more rapidly than its main competitors.

stakeholder activism Demands placed on a global firm by the stakeholders in the environments in which it operates.

stakeholders Influential people who are vitally interested in the actions of the business.

stalemate businesses Businesses with few sources of advantage, most of them small. Skills in operational efficiency, low overhead, and cost management are critical to profitability.

stars Businesses in rapidly growing markets with large market shares.

stock options The right, or "option," to purchase company stock at a fixed price at some future date.

strategic alliances Alliances with suppliers, partners, contractors, and other providers that allow partners in the alliance to focus on what they do best, farm out everything else, and quickly provide value to the customer. Partnerships that are distinguished from joint ventures because the companies involved do not take an equity position in one another.

strategic business unit An adaptation of the divisional structure in which various divisions or parts of divisions are grouped together based on some common strategic elements, usually linked to distinct product/market differences.

strategic control Management efforts to track a strategy as it is being implemented, detect problems or changes in its underlying premises, and make necessary adjustments.

strategic intent A leader's clear sense of where she wants to lead the company and what results she expects to achieve.

strategic management The set of decisions and actions that result in the formulation and implementation of plans designed to achieve a company's objectives.

strategic positioning The way a business is designed and positioned to serve target markets.

strategic processes Decision making, operational activities, and sales activities that are critical business processes.

strategic surveillance Management efforts to monitor a broad range of events inside and more often outside the firm that are likely to affect the course of its strategy over time.

strategic thrusts or projects Special efforts that are early steps in executing a broader strategy, usually involving significant resource commitments, yet where predetermined feedback will help management determine whether continuing to pursue the strategy is appropriate or whether it needs adjustment or major change.

strategy Large-scale, future-oriented plans for interacting with the competitive environment to achieve company objectives.

strength   A resource advantage relative to competitors and the needs of the markets a firm serves or expects to serve.

structural attributes   The enduring characteristics that give an industry its distinctive character.

support activities   The activities in a firm that assist the firm as a whole by providing infrastructure or inputs that allow the primary activities to take place on an ongoing basis.

SWOT analysis   SWOT is an acronym for the internal Strengths and Weaknesses of a firm, and the environmental Opportunities and Threats facing that firm. SWOT analysis is a technique through which managers create a quick overview of a company's strategic situation.

T

tangible assets   The most easily identified assets, often found on a firm's balance sheet. They include production facilities, raw materials, financial resources, real estate, and computers.

technological forecasting   The quasi-science of anticipating environmental and competitive changes and estimating their importance to an organization's operations.

threat   A major unfavorable situation in a firm's environment.

three circles analysis   An internal analysis technique wherein strategists examine customers' needs, company offerings, and competitor's offerings to more clearly articulate what their company's competitive advantage is and how it differs from those of competitors while the strategists are in the midst of strategic analysis activities.

turnaround   A grand strategy of cost reduction and asset reduction by a company to survive and recover from declining profits.

U

utilitarian approach   Judging the appropriateness of a particular action based on a goal to provide the greatest good for the greatest number of people.

V

value chain   A perspective in which business is seen as a chain of activities that transforms inputs into outputs that customers value. Customer value derives from three basic sources: activities that differentiate the product, activities that lower its cost, and activities that meet the customer's need quickly.

value chain analysis   An analysis that attempts to understand how a business creates customer value by examining the contributions of different activities within the business to that value.

vertical boundaries   Limitations on interaction, contact, and access between operations and management personnel; between different levels of management; and between different organizational parts like corporate vs. divisional units.

vertical acquisition   A grand strategy based on the acquisition of firms that supply the acquiring firm with inputs such as raw materials or new customers for its outputs, such as warehouses for finished products.

virtual organization   Corporations whose structure has become an elaborate network of external and internal relationships. In effect, a temporary network of independent companies—suppliers, customers, subcontractors, and businesses around the core, high-profitability information, services, and products. Creating an agile, virtual organization structure involves outsourcing, strategic alliances, a boundaryless learning approach, and Web-based organization.

vision statement   A statement that presents a firm's strategic intent designed to focus the energies and resources of the company on achieving a desirable future.

volume businesses   Businesses that have few sources of advantage, but the size is large—typically the result of scale economies.

W

weakness   A limitation or deficiency in one or more resources or competencies relative to competitors that impedes a firm's effective performance.

Photo Credits

Chapter 3

p. 58: © AP Photo/Gene J. Puskar

Chapter 6

p. 154: © Julie Cordeiro/Boston Red Sox

Chapter 8

p. 253: © Eric Millette/The Forbes Collection

Chapter 9

p. 289: © Norm Betts/Bloomberg via Getty

Chapter 10

p. 301: Courtesy of Dirk Brown

p. 308: © Monica M. Davey/epa/Corbis

Chapter 11

p. 353: © The McGraw-Hill Companies, Inc. All Rights Reserved.

Chapter 12

p. 372: © AP Photo/Reed Saxon

p. 375: © AP Photo/Mark Lennihan

Chapter 13

p. 402: © Mike Simons/Getty

p. 411 (top left): © AP Photo/Paul Sakuma

p. 411 (bottom left): UpperCut Images/Getty Images

p. 411 (right): © AP Photo/Nati Harnik

Chapter 14

p. 416: Book cover of *Taiichi Ohno's Workplace Management*, © Gamba Press, 2007. Photo cover courtesy of Wilson Publishing Services.

p. 429: © InnoCentive, Inc.

Name Index

Page numbers followed by n refer to notes.

Subject Index

Case Index